GREEK THOUGHT

HARVARD
UNIVERSITY
PRESS
REFERENCE
LIBRARY

GREEK THOUGHT

A Guide to Classical Knowledge

Edited by Jacques Brunschwig and Geoffrey E. R. Lloyd
with the collaboration of Pierre Pellegrin

Translated under the direction of
Catherine Porter

THE BELKNAP PRESS OF
HARVARD UNIVERSITY PRESS
CAMBRIDGE, MASSACHUSETTS
LONDON, ENGLAND
2000

First published as *Le Savoir Grec: Dictionnaire Critique,*
copyright © 1996 by Flammarion

Published with the assistance of the French Ministry of Culture National Book Center

Library of Congress Cataloging-in-Publication Data
Savoir grec. English.
Greek thought : a guide to classical knowledge / edited by Jacques Brunschwig
and Geoffrey E. R. Lloyd, with the collaboration of Pierre Pellegrin.
p. cm. — (Harvard University Press reference library)
Includes bibliographical references and index.
ISBN 0-674-00261-X (alk. paper)
1. Greece—Intellectual life—To 146 B.C.
2. Greece—Politics and government—To 146 B.C.
3. Intellectuals—Greece—Biography.
4. Thought and thinking.   I. Brunschwig, Jacques.
II. Lloyd, G. E. R. (Geoffrey Ernest Richard), 1933–.
III. Pellegrin, Pierre.   IV. Title.   V. Series.
DF78.S2813 2000
938—dc21   00-036032

CONTENTS

3/01

CURRENTS OF THOUGHT

Illustrations follow pages 174, 318, 510, and 654

TRANSLATORS' NOTE

An informal group of translators based in Ithaca, New York, we agreed in the fall of 1996 to translate the portions of *Greek Thought* originally written in French and Italian. Working largely in bilingual pairs, we met regularly to share problems and search for solutions. A broad group of willing collaborators made our task much easier. We wish to express our gratitude first and foremost to Jacques Brunschwig and Geoffrey Lloyd, coeditors of the original French edition, for their generous assistance and support. We also offer thanks to all the authors who graciously read our drafts, answered questions, and made invaluable corrections and suggestions as needed. Other specialists and consultants helped us at many points along the way: thanks in particular to Charles Brittain, Terence Irwin, Mark Landon, Philip Lewis, Culver Mowers, Pietro Pucci, Hunter Rawlings, Geoffrey Rusten, and Daniel Turkeltaub for their collaboration. The unfailingly helpful staff allowed us to use the excellent collection housed in Cornell's Olin Library with maximum efficiency, and the Department of Classics at Cornell University kindly shared its own well-stocked library. Finally, we are indebted to Jennifer Snodgrass and the editorial staff at Harvard University Press for overseeing this complex project with exceptional patience and professional acumen.

RITA GUERLAC
DOMINIQUE JOUHAUD
CATHERINE PORTER
JEANNINE PUCCI
ELIZABETH RAWLINGS
ANNE SLACK
SELINA STEWART
EMORETTA YANG

INTRODUCTION: ON HOME GROUND IN A DISTANT LAND

ALPHA, BETA, AND THE REST, all the way to omega: most of us, on first acquaintance with the Greek alphabet, have toyed with writing our own names with its characters, so close and yet so remote from our own. Their attraction for us is unequaled. Roman inscriptions are lofty and admirable: their letters decorate the pediments of our civic buildings as well as commercial signs. At the extremes of the graphic spectrum, Egyptian hieroglyphics look down upon us from the pinnacle of their forty centuries; Chinese ideograms fascinate us by their symbolism and by the complicated enigma of their design. The Greek alphabet, halfway between the strange and the familiar, is at the perfect distance from our own—of which it is a remote ancestor. It is unfamiliar enough to let us know we have left home. Yet it welcomes us with signals clear enough to avoid complete illegibility. Better than a new dissertation on the eternal modernity of ancient Greece, or one more warning against the myths that nourish such dissertations, the paradoxical kinship of the alphabets offers a limited but illuminating metaphor for the complex relation that ties our present to a past that is also ours, and that continues to inhabit our present, visibly or invisibly.

What we have just said about the Greek alphabet could be repeated, even more justifiably, about everything that has been written with those letters. Despite severe losses, the Greek alphabet has transmitted to us countless texts: poems, myths, histories, tragedies, comedies, political and legal discourses, formal speeches, dialogues, treatises on philosophy, cosmology, medicine, mathematics, zoology, and botany; through direct action, indirect influence, polemical reaction, rereading, and reinterpretation, these texts inaugurated and have nourished the whole tradition of Western thought. Here again, the feelings of familiarity and distance are interwoven. We are on home ground in a distant land; we are traveling without leaving our own room. All our thinking, in one way or another, passes through reflection on the Greeks.

The key to the unparalleled originality of the Greeks may be that their culture, by definition, did not have the Greeks behind it. Of course it did not spring up out of nothing, any more than their alphabet did (its basic elements were borrowed from the Phoenicians); we need not regret that today's historians and scholars, with increasing conviction, are replacing the celebrated "Greek miracle" with unmiraculous Greeks. But however important the

Greeks' debt to preceding civilizations, they quickly made their borrowings their own and turned them against their creditors, who represented in their eyes either a civilization turned upside down (the prestigious and astonishing Egypt) or the opposite of civilization (the despotic and barbaric Mesopotamia). Like all those who have followed, the Greeks reflected on the Greeks; but their reflections were like no one else's, simply because they themselves were the Greeks. Their thinking, like God's thinking according to Aristotle, was thinking about thinking.

The Greeks' culture of self-awareness predated the Socratic "Know thyself." Very early, their mythology, newly codified by Homer and Hesiod, gave rise to its own critics (Xenophanes, Heraclitus) and its own interpreters, allegorists or not. The Milesian cosmologies carried on a dialogue; each was intended to resolve a difficulty posed by its predecessor. The intimidating Parmenidean challenge, which threatened to smother physics, elicited almost immediate responses by Empedocles, Anaxagoras, and the Atomists. Socrates, disappointed by the physics of his forerunners, kept his distance from things and turned toward discourse. Plato transposed the ancient myths; he interpreted Socrates, constructing the conditions that made Socrates possible and that would have made his condemnation impossible. Aristotle criticized Plato, as he criticized most of his predecessors, even while he strove to retain what deserved preservation. Epicureans and Stoics, from their own moment in history, mustered enough distance to seek their own masters in a remote past before Plato and Aristotle, in Democritus and Heraclitus. Plato's heritage was diffused and dispersed in a gamut that ranged from skepticism to Neoplatonic metaphysics. Commentary, the critique of texts and the accumulation of glosses, which began astonishingly early, flourished at the beginning of the common era.

But even more striking than the critical turns taken by Greek culture in its successive stages is the work that each of its artisans performed on himself. It would have seemed impossible for Greek scientists, historians, or philosophers to do their work without knowing, or at least without wondering, under what conditions (intellectual as well as moral and political) it was possible to do science, history, or philosophy. To judge by their works, it is clear that the same thing was true for sculptors, architects, musicians, and dramatic poets: their style is manifestly not the result of rote practice or of an empirical tradition based on natural ability. Even shoemaking was taught; even cooks claimed to be conscious auxiliaries of philosophy. Every activity, every perception, every direct relation to an object raised seemingly simple questions that are as disconcerting as those addressed by Socrates to his interlocutors—questions that interpose distance and require the mind to adjust its relation to everything it encounters: "What is it all about?" "What are you really looking for?" "What exactly do you mean?" "How do you know what you have just said?"

If the work we are presenting under the title *Greek Thought* has one central ambition, it is to call attention to this fundamental reflexivity that seems to us characteristic of Greek thought, and which gives it even today a formative value and a capacity to challenge. In this book we do not address "Greek science," or "Greek philosophy," or "Greek civilization." Excellent works, both introductory and comprehensive, exist on these subjects, works with which we do not propose to compete. We have not sought to explicate, or even to summarize, the whole of what the Greeks knew, or thought they knew; nor do we tally up what they did not know, the gaps in their knowledge. Similarly, we have not wanted either to repeat or to summarize histories of Greek philosophy; and nothing will be found here that touches directly on Greek art, Greek literature, or Greek religion. Instead we have sought to step back from the products to the processes that gave rise to them, from works to actions, from objects to methods. Of foremost interest to us is the typically Hellenic aptitude for raising questions that are at once "second order"—since they occupy a secondary position in relation to questions that bear immediately on the world, the beings that populate it, the events that take place in it, the activities that transform it—and "first order" or "primary," because they must logically be raised first, and solved in one way or another. The term "Socratic fallacy" has sometimes been used to designate the idea that one could not say whether a given individual was courageous or not, so long as one was unable to say universally what courage is. Fallacy or not, Greek thought finds in this quest for lucidity its most radical task. Classical knowledge, in the sense in which we are using the term, is not the knowledge indicated by expressions like "knowing that Socrates was condemned to death" or "knowing that the diagonal of a square is incommensurable with its side." It represents, rather, the knowledge denoted in expressions such as "knowing what one is saying," "knowing what one is doing," "knowing what one wants."

This dimension of Greek thought, which takes as its objects not only first-order knowledge, but also life, language, production, and action, strikes us as essential and characteristic, and it is to this dimension that we draw the reader's attention. We look at the Greeks looking at themselves. We evoke not history as they made it and experienced it, but the stories they told themselves about it; not their poetry, but their poetics; not their music, but their harmonics; not their speeches, but their rhetoric. We present their theories about the origin, meaning, and functions of religion. We say nothing about their language itself, but we do offer some of their reflections on the origin, elements, and forms of language. Their political institutions are mentioned, of course, but in the framework of the ideas and theories used to conceptualize and justify those institutions. We recall the principal doctrines of individual philosophers and scientists, or of philosophic and scientific schools, to show what philosophical activity, the development of a theory, the public presentation of a doctrine, meant to those individuals and groups.

This book is subdivided into five parts. The first might seem to grant too important a place to philosophy, to the detriment of science: in accordance with contemporary parlance, people we call scientists know things, whereas one must no doubt be a philosopher, and even a sort of philosopher that may be on the verge of extinction, to think that philosophy is a form of knowing. But this division between science and philosophy does not correspond at all to the conceptual frameworks of antiquity; at most it puts in an appearance, with many qualifications, in the Hellenistic era, when specialized knowledge begins to acquire a certain autonomy, though philosophy still claims the right to provide the specialists with their principles and to pass judgment on their methods. Plato clearly subordinates mathematics to dialectics; but the vocabulary in which he expresses that subordination, far from leaving mathematics in its customary category as a science, instead contests that categorization. As for Aristotle, although he was more inclined to see the individual sciences as models according to which the criteria of scientific thought could be elaborated, he grants physics only the status of a "second philosophy." The emergence of philosophy as we have described it is also the emergence of knowledge, and of thought in general. Several articles in this first group ("Images of the World," "Myth and Knowledge") describe the popular and mythic background against which the figure of the philosopher stands out, different in so many ways from his modern counterparts. Other articles ("The Question of Being," "Epistemology," "Ethics") offer a first broad staking out of the principal fields in which philosophy emerged. Thus right at the start, the critical approach of the work as a whole is sketched out: trying to avoid both the traps of historicism and those of *philosophia perennis*, we seek to put our object in a perspective that inevitably refers to a modern point of observation. In this enterprise we are concerned with measuring the legacy that Greek thought has bequeathed to its posterity, the use that posterity has made of it, and the continuities and discontinuities that this complex relation has engendered between inheritance and heirs—and it is not the least of the paradoxes that, in the inheritance itself, the heirs have found, among other things, the possibility of becoming themselves untrammeled producers of knowledge.

The second part is devoted in particular to politics: does not the "invention" of politics, along with that of philosophy and mathematics, belong most indisputably to ancient Greece? Here again, invention is not parthenogenesis. Although the Egyptians and the Babylonians had mathematics, Greek mathematics is characterized by a specific way of proceeding by articulated definitions and proofs. Similarly, institutions and practices of power, as well as reflections on forms of government, on the relations between governors and the governed, and on the nature of the political order, existed outside Greece; but Greece is distinguished by the formation and organization of the city-state, the practice of public debate, the procedures of collective decision-making, the writing and publication of laws, and, in political analysis, a style of justification and argument that resembles (whatever causal sequence we might wish to privilege) the discourse that emerged in the fields of philosophy and science. From this invention of politics, we examine not so much the historical birth of the city-states and the development of their institutions as rather the reflection on those events and the theoretical and practical justification of those institutions; the definition of the various roles among which political action and thought were distributed; the confrontation, sometimes quite openly conflictual (Simone Weil said that the Greeks did not possess the self-satisfied hypocrisy of the Romans) but sometimes harmonious, between the practices of civic life and the ideology in which they are cloaked ("Inventing Politics," "Utopia and the Critique of Politics"); and the debates between reflection and participation in public affairs, which pose the perennial question of the sage's commitment to or detachment from his own city-state ("The Sage and Politics").

The third part, "The Pursuit of Knowledge," starts out by offering overviews of the institutional and conceptual frameworks for the extraordinary explosion of desire for knowledge, a desire that Aristotle views as naturally implanted in the heart of all people. Then follows a series of articles on the various branches of knowledge (including some that look to us like pseudoscience today). We have organized them alphabetically rather than adopting the classification—or rather one of the various classifications—that prevailed among Greek thinkers themselves: the theoreticians' agenda, that is to say the ordered set of questions to which any respectable doctrine was obliged to offer answers, from the formation of the world to the origin of humanity, human culture, and institutions, was fixed in its broad outlines at a very early date, and for several centuries manifested an astonishing degree of stability. Yet that agenda was enriched, diversified, and modified in multiple ways, and the classifications proposed rarely failed to become controversial. Certain disciplines, such as logic, did not come into their own until well after the early period of Greek thought; others, like medicine or harmonics, were quickly pervaded by debates on the extent to which they should be attached to or cut off from the common trunk of general philosophical and scientific theories. All things considered, we judged it preferable to fall back on the naïve security of alphabetical order.

In the final parts readers will find a series of articles on the major Greek philosophers and scholars, as well as on the principal schools and lasting currents of thought. Among so many glorious and singular individuals, the choice was necessarily a difficult one. Our selection is certainly more restrained than that of Diogenes Laertius in his *Lives and Opinions of Illustrious Philosophers*; but it goes further forward in time, and it makes room for scientists and historians as well as for philosophers. Anticipating our own second thoughts, some may find that we have been unjust toward certain figures such as Xenophanes, Sophists other than Protagoras, the Cyrenaics or the

Megarians, Eudoxus of Cnidus, Theophrastus, or Philo of Alexandria. Still, we had to make choices, and any selection reflects judgments that can always be contested. Most of the thinkers or scholars to whom it was not possible to devote a separate section are mentioned, along with their works, within one article or another, and can be traced through the index. The bibliographies and cross-references also help make up for the inevitable disadvantages of choice and dispersal.

Finally, a word about the choice of contributors. As general editors responsible for the overall project and its implementation, the two of us who sign this Introduction are pleased and proud that our association can modestly symbolize the alliance between two major centers of research on the history of ancient thought, Cambridge and Paris; we are even more pleased and proud to have worked all our professional lives, each in our own way, in the conviction that the differences between the Anglo-Saxon and Latin worlds in traditions, methods, and instruments of analysis and research in no way prevent contact, exchange, productive discussion, and the production of a common work. This book bears witness to that shared conviction.

The authors to whom we turned, British or American, Italian or French, have all contributed to the considerable progress that has been made, over the last several decades, in the knowledge and understanding of the intellectual world of ancient Greece. They all have their own personalities, which we have not asked them to suppress; their freedom of opinion and judgment has been intentionally respected. As we have said, the gaze of the moderns looking upon the Greeks looking upon themselves remains obviously, and deliberately, our own gaze, and it measures distances, proximities, gaps, and debts from this standpoint. But this gaze of ours can never be entirely unified: contemporary scholars, sometimes because of the particular fields in which they work, sometimes because of the diversity of their overall approaches, do not all necessarily interpret or appreciate our relation to Greek thought in the same way. No one is in a position to dictate that all these scholars subscribe to the latest trend, or conform to the next-to-latest fashion; if we somehow had such power, we would surely have refrained from using it.

We thank our collaborators for agreeing to write their articles in a style that is not always the one they are accustomed to. We know how wrenching it is, for academics conscious of their scholarly responsibilities, to give up footnotes and erudite references. But we deliberately chose to call upon authors for whom that renunciation would be painful, rather than those whose habits would not have been particularly disturbed.

Finally, we want to thank all those without whom the long and difficult enterprise represented by this volume would have run aground on one or another of the countless reefs that threatened it. Louis Audibert, the literary director at Flammarion, had the initial idea; he followed its realization from beginning to end with incomparable vigilance and care. Pierre Pellegrin played a very effective role in the revision process; he provided the liaison and the coordination that our geographic distance from each other, and from many of our authors, made particularly necessary. And we do not want to fail to thank the technical team at Flammarion, which supported us as much by its high expectations as by the help it offered us toward meeting them.

JACQUES BRUNSCHWIG, GEOFFREY E. R. LLOYD
Translated by Catherine Porter and Dominique Jouhaud

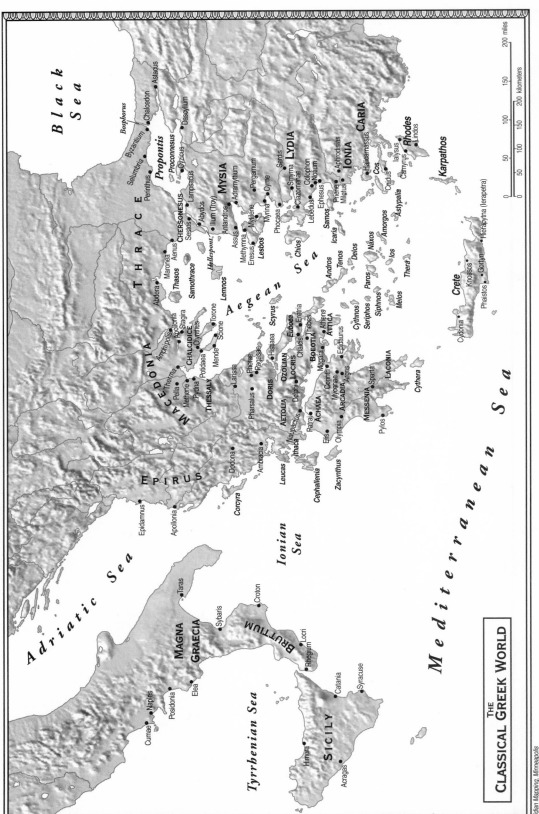

THE CLASSICAL GREEK WORLD

Meridian Mapping, Minneapolis

Black Sea

Astacus
Chalcedon
Bosphorus
Byzantium
Selymbria
Perinthus
Dascylium
Propontis
Proconnesus
Cyzicus
Lampsacus
Abydos
Sestos
CHERSONESUS
Illum (Troy)
Hellespont
Assus
Antandros
Methymna
Eresus
Lesbos
Mytilene
Myrina
Phocaea
Chios
Pergamum
Adramyttium
Cyme
MYSIA
Sardis
LYDIA
Smyrna
Clazomenae
Colophon
Notium
Ephesus
Lebedos
Samos
Priene
Miletus
Aphrodisias
CARIA
Halicarnassus
IONIA
Cnidus
Cos.
Rhodes
Lindos
Ialysus
Camyrus
Karpathos
Astypalia
Icaria
Amorgos
Tenos
Delos
Naxos
Ios
Thera
Paros
Siphnos
Melos
Seriphos
Cythnos
Andros

THRACE
Aenus
Maronea
Abdera
Thasos
Samothrace
Lemnos

Aegean Sea

MACEDONIA
Amphipolis
Apollonia
Stagira
CHALCIDICE
Olynthus
Torone
Mende
Scione
Potidaea
Therma
Pella
Methone
Pydna
THESSALY
Larissa
Pherae
Pharsalus
Pagasae
Scyrus
Histiaea
Euboea
Eretria
Chalcis
Thebes
BOEOTIA
Athens
ATTICA
Megara
Epidaurus
Corinth
Mycenae
Argos
ARCADIA
Sparta
LACONIA
MESSENIA
Pylos
Cythera
DORIS
OZOLIAN LOCRIS
Delphi
AETOLIA
Naupactus
ACHAEA
Patrai
Elis
Olympia

EPIRUS
Dodona
Ambracia
Leucas
Ithaca
Cephallenia
Zacynthus
Corcyra
Epidamnus
Apollonia

Adriatic Sea

Ionian Sea

Taras
Croton
Sybaris
Locri
MAGNA GRAECIA
BRUTTIUM
Rhegium
Elea
Posidonia
Naples
Cumae

Tyrrhenian Sea

Catania
Syracuse
SICILY
Himera
Acragas

Mediterranean Sea

Crete
Cydonia
Knossos
Gortyn
Phaistos
Hierapytna (Ierapetra)

200 miles
200 kilometers

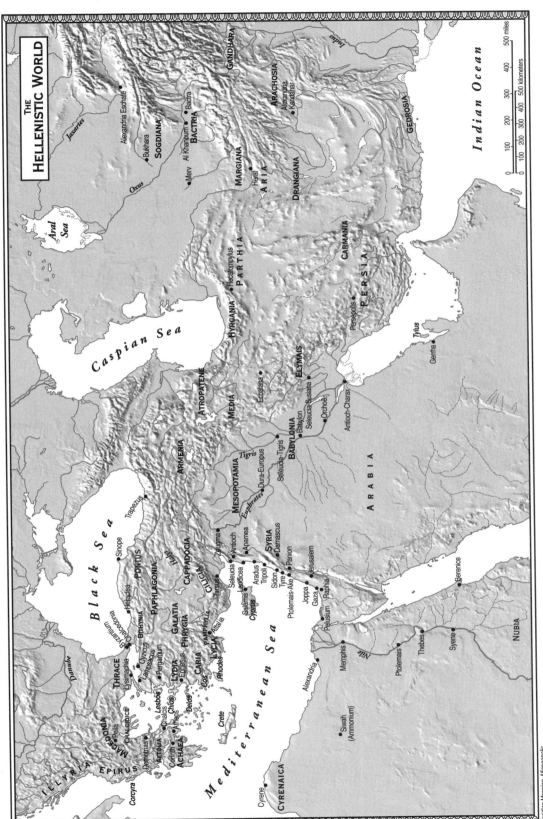

THE
HELLENISTIC WORLD

Indian Ocean

0   100   200   300   400   500 miles
0 100 200 300 400 500 kilometers

GANDHARA

Jaxartes

Alexandria Eschate

Aral Sea

Oxus

Bukhara
SOGDIANA
Al Khanoum • Bactra
Merv • BACTRIA

MARGIANA
Herat • ARIA

Hecatompylus
PARTHIA
DRANGANA

Alexandria
• Kandahar
ARACHOSIA

GEDROSIA

Caspian Sea

HYRCANIA

ATROPATENE

MEDIA
Ecbatana •

ELYMAIS
Babylon •
BABYLONIA
Seleucia-Susiana •
Orchoë •
Antioch-Charax •

CARMANIA
PERSIA
Persepolis •

Tylus

Gerrha •

ARMENIA

MESOPOTAMIA
Tigris
Dura-Europus •
Seleucia-Tigris •

Euphrates

Black Sea

Trapezus •

Sinope •
PONTUS
PAPHLAGONIA
Heraclea •
BITHYNIA
Halys
CAPPADOCIA
Zeugma •
Antioch •
Apamea •
SYRIA
Damascus •
Panion •
Tarsus •
CILICIA
Seleucia •
Laodicea •
Selinus •
CYPRUS
Aradus •
Tripoli •
Sidon •
Tyre •
Ptolemais-Ake •
Joppa •
Jerusalem •
Gaza •
Raphia •
Pelusium •

ARABIA

Danube
THRACE
Byzantium •
Chalcedon •
Lysimachia •
Cyzicus •
Lampsacus •
Pergamum •
PHRYGIA
GALATIA
LYDIA
Ephesus •
CARIA
Aegean
Lesbos
Chalcis •
Chios
LYCIA
PAMPHILIA
Attalia •
Rhodes •

MACEDONIA
Pella •
CHALCIDICE
AETOLIA
Demetrias •
ACHAEA
Corinth •
Athens •
Delos

ILLYRIA
EPIRUS

Corcyra

Crete

Mediterranean Sea

Alexandria •
Siwah •
(Ammonium)

Memphis •
Nile
Ptolemais •
Thebes •
Syene •
NUBIA

Berenice •

Cyrene •
CYRENAICA

Meridian Mapping, Minneapolis

PHILOSOPHY

THE PHILOSOPHER

PHILOSOPHY IS A HISTORICAL PHENOMENON. It emerges out of a need to have a certain kind of answer to certain questions, for instance questions as to the origin of the world as we know it. It obviously would be very frightening to live in a world in which the behavior of things, especially where it affected one's life, seemed completely unintelligible. There were traditional answers available to such questions; in fact, various traditions provided answers. But these answers were in conflict with one another. Thus, as people became aware of the different traditions and their conflict, the traditional answers began to fail to satisfy people's need to feel they have a secure understanding of the world in which they live, of nature, of social and political organizations, of what makes communities and individuals behave the way they do. What were needed were answers of a new kind, answers that one could defend, that one could show to be superior to competing answers, that one could use to persuade others, so as to reestablish some kind of consensus.

It was a long time before attempts to provide such answers led to an established practice and a general enterprise or discipline. But once a discipline of philosophy was established, it naturally came to respond to two different sets of needs or demands: the external ones, which originally gave rise to the practice of philosophy, and also internal demands as to what counted as acceptable or good practice in terms of the discipline. Both demands or needs would ensure that the discipline would change over time. As the culture evolved, the external needs would change, and with it the discipline, to the extent that it continued to be responsive to them. And the internal demands would also force change. New answers would raise new questions, and the answers to those questions could force a revision of the answers to the original ones. Thus the practice of philosophy changed and will continue to change over time, and all the more so as the two sets of demands or needs may come apart or even come into conflict with each other. Indeed, once the discipline develops a momentum or life of its own—achieves a degree of autonomy—its practitioners may become more or less oblivious to the external needs that gave rise to it.

For the reasons given, then, philosophy has changed considerably over time. It is not just the questions and answers that have changed, so have the demands made on acceptable answers. Indeed, the whole conception of the enterprise subtly changes as philosophers try to respond to changing external

3

needs and changing internal demands, and this, of course, affects their philosophical practice.

When we study ancient philosophy, we are guided by our contemporary conception of the philosophical enterprise. This makes it easy for us to overlook the fact that the ancient philosophers had a very different conception of their philosophical activity. As a result, we get a very distorted picture of what ancient philosophers were doing and saying. If, for instance, we consult modern accounts to inform ourselves about Euphrates, Apollonius of Tyana, and Dion of Prusa, their existence is barely acknowledged, perhaps only to question whether they were really philosophers. One does not get any sense that they arguably were the most renowned and respected philosophers of their time, the turn from the 1st to the 2nd century. The aim of the following remarks is to provide at least a rough sketch of how the ancients themselves thought of philosophy and its practitioners.

This is a vast topic. A complete treatment would require a discussion of how the conception of a philosopher found its expression in the statues and busts of philosophers set up by philosophers and nonphilosophers, in private and in public, from the 4th century B.C.E. onward, or how this conception was reflected in literature from the late 5th century B.C.E. onward, or in imperial legislation in late antiquity. Much of this evidence also reflects the extent to which the need that the philosophers tried to satisfy by their practice was recognized as a social need. But I will here restrict myself to a sketch in rather abstract terms of the conception the philosophers themselves had of their enterprise and how it evolved.

It is perhaps best to begin with the very term *philosophos* and its cognates. The term is one of a large family of adjectives, then also used as nouns, formed from *philo-* and some noun, a formation particularly common at the turn from the 5th to the 4th century B.C.E. These terms are used to characterize a person in whose life the item designated by the noun plays a remarkably large role as an object of positive concern. Thus a *philotimos* is a person who to a remarkable and quite unusual degree is motivated by a concern for honor. Correspondingly, a philosopher would be somebody who, in what he does and how he lives, to an unusual degree is influenced by a concern for wisdom. But obviously one can show a particular concern for wisdom without being a philosopher, without being a member of a distinct, identifiable group of people called "philosophers" engaged in a distinct enterprise called "philosophy." Indeed, in their earliest extant uses, the word *philosophos* and its cognates do not seem to refer to a distinct group of persons and a distinct enterprise. If Clement (*Strom.* V.141) quotes Heraclitus correctly, Heraclitus said that men who aspire to wisdom *(philosophoi andres)* need to be inquirers *(histores)* into a good many things. It is clear from fragments B40 and B129 that Heraclitus does not think that knowing a lot of things *(polymathie)* will in itself make one wise, but he does think that one will not become wise if one does not take the trouble, which people ordinarily do not bother to do, to try to find out about a good many things. Nor does Herodotus (I.30) have philosophy in mind when he has Croesus say to Solon that he must be traveling to distant lands "philosopheōn," out of love for wisdom. Solon does not travel around on business or as a political ambassador; he is engaged in *historia* of the kind Heraclitus recommends to those who aspire to be wise, trying to find out about other parts of the world, other nations, their customs and institutions, and their way of understanding things. Nor does Thucydides want Pericles to say in his Funeral Oration that the Athenians are philosophers when he has him say that the Athenians distinguish themselves among the Greeks in their concern for wisdom *(philosophoumen)*.

The first time we encounter the word *philosopher* in its later, familiar use is in Plato's dialogues. There it and its cognates occur with such frequency that we are tempted to think that term must have come into use in the late 5th century and perhaps was already used by Socrates. In any case, from Socrates onward the term *philosopher* takes on a precise meaning that goes far beyond the vague idea of a person who shows a remarkable concern for wisdom, and philosophers have a definite conception of philosophy, which involves the following assumptions.

First, wisdom is a certain kind of knowledge that is at least the decisive necessary, if not sufficient, condition for having a good life. Thus, to be a philosopher is not just to show an unusual concern for wisdom; wisdom, for a philosopher, becomes a concern that does, and should, override any other concern. Socrates is going to be a paradigmatic philosopher in this, as in other regards. Notoriously, Socrates lets his concern for wisdom override his concern for his craft, for his family, and ultimately for his life. Given how difficult it is to be wise, an overriding concern for wisdom does leave little space for competing concerns. It ideally transforms one's whole life. Philosophy is not something that, as a philosopher, one could pursue as a career, or as one of many interests.

Second, it is not just that wisdom for a philosopher is an overriding concern. A philosopher will also think (until far into late antiquity, when this claim will be challenged by Christians and others) that the only way to concern oneself with wisdom so as to become wise is the philosopher's way.

These two assumptions together amount to the implicit claim that to attain the good life, to become a good person, to be saved, one has to be a philosopher. In this, philosophers from Socrates onward agreed. They differed in how they identified wisdom, in whether they assumed that wisdom was a necessary or also a sufficient condition for the good life, and as to how, as a philosopher, one would strive to attain wisdom. In this way, they differed in their conception of the philosophical enterprise. To be more precise, from Socrates onward we can trace in great detail the evolution of the conception of philosophy, as philosophers came to develop different views as to the nature of the wisdom in question and the way to attain it. But before we can turn to this, we have to return, at least briefly, to the Presocratics.

We tend, with some hesitation, to let philosophy begin with Thales and the Milesians. So did Aristotle and the ancient doxography dependent on Aristotle. But it goes without saying that this way of looking at things is very much the product of retrospective history; it is very much in hindsight that we can see that Thales started a tradition that contributed to the formation of the discipline that came to be known as philosophy. In fact, it is only Aristotle's rather biased, one-sided, and unrepresentative view, expressed, for instance, in *Metaphysics*, that lets Thales appear as such a plausible candidate for the title of the first philosopher. According to this view, wisdom *(sophia)* is theoretical wisdom, which primarily is a matter of grasping the ultimate principles of reality, and Thales and his successors, as if driven by the truth itself, were slowly moving in the direction of Aristotle's position on the principles of reality. But obviously it would be naive to think that Thales set out to found a new discipline, or that he set out to identify the ultimate principles of reality, thereby starting a new discipline. He, among many other things, also tried to develop a new account, and to some extent a new kind of account, of the origin of the world as we know it.

In fact, we have to ask ourselves quite generally to what extent those whom we have come to call Presocratic philosophers did see themselves, and were seen by their contemporaries, as forming a distinct group pursuing a distinct enterprise that would become known as philosophy. What should give us pause is that down to the later part of the 5th century B.C.E. there was not even a word for "philosopher." We have already seen that the term *philosopher,* to refer to philosophers, only came into use just before Plato. It is true that the ancients, when they talked at all about the origin of the terms *philosopher* and *philosophy,* attributed them to Pythagoras (Diogenes Laertius, praef. 12; Cicero, *Tusc.* V.8–9). But for this they clearly relied on a passage in a lost work by Heraclides Ponticus, a follower of Aristotle. And Heraclides, for his claim, had no more to rely on than a story about Pythagoras, obviously part of the already proliferating legend of Pythagoras. Nor was there any other term that could have been used to refer to philosophers. Diogenes Laertius (praef. 12) shows some awareness of the problem that poses itself, even if we, wrongly, assume that Pythagoras introduced the term *philosopher.* He says that philosophers were called "wise" *(sophoi)* or "sophists." It is true that some of the Presocratics, for instance Thales, were called wise or were even canonized as one of the Seven Sages. But not all of them were called this, and those who were shared the honorific epithet with others— poets, rhapsodes, lawgivers, and statesmen. Moreover, philosophers would hardly have thought of themselves as wise. There also was the term *sophist,* used to refer to somebody who, through his own efforts, had acquired some claim to some kind of wisdom. Given that wisdom tended to be regarded as a matter of long, often painful experience, as something that grew on one, if one was able to learn and observe, the very term could invite negative associations, as implying that there was a shortcut to wisdom, perhaps even that wisdom was a matter that one could readily attain through the appropriate instruction. But the term originally had a positive connotation and continued often to have a positive sense even in Plato and later. Herodotus calls Pythagoras a "sophist" (I.29.1; IV.95.2). Diogenes of Apollonia refers to his predecessors as "sophists" (A4 D.K.). And the author of *On Ancient Medicine* (cap. 20) twice seems to be referring to natural philosophers as "sophists." But it is also true, as Diogenes Laertius pointed out (praef. 12), that the term *sophist* was not restricted to those we call philosophers. It was used equally for poets (Pindar, *Isth.* V.28) and for statesmen such as Solon (*Isocr.* XV.313). That before the latter part of the 5th century there was no special word for philosophers very much suggests that up to that time philosophers did not regard themselves, or were not regarded by others, as a distinct group. This impression is strengthened if we look at the fragments of the Presocratics to see whom they regarded as the proper group of persons they wanted to be compared to and against whom they in some way competed. In particular Xenophanes and Heraclitus repeatedly refer to others by name. Thus Xenophanes refers to Homer, Hesiod, Simonides, Epimenides, Thales, and Pythagoras. Heraclitus refers to Homer and Hesiod, but also to Archilochus, Hecataeus of Miletus, Bias of Priene, Thales, Pythagoras, and Xenophanes. Here the reference class is made up of persons who have a reputation for being wise, or who at least have or make a claim to be heard or listened to, but again it includes, without distinction, poets, statesmen, and those whom we call philosophers.

What these references suggest is that those we call philosophers thought of themselves, and were thought of by others, as being concerned with wisdom in a fairly vague and broad sense, in such a way as to be comparable to or even in competition with poets and politicians and lawgivers. We get some idea of the wisdom they aspired to or came to be renowned for if we look at Thales. Thales came to be regarded as one of the Seven Sages. Indeed, according to Demetrius of Phaleron, it was Thales who was the first to be called "wise" (Diogenes Laertius I.22). Herodotus has three stories to tell about Thales that give us some idea of how Thales' wisdom was perceived: supposedly Thales managed to predict the solar eclipse of May 585, which happened precisely as the Medes and the Lydians were joining battle, and which hence one would be tempted to regard as ominous (Herodotus I.74); Thales advised the Ionians to form one political community with its boule in Teos, given Teos's central location—advice which, if heeded, might have prevented the return to Persian rule (I.170); when Croesus had difficulties crossing the River Halys with his troops, Thales ingeniously solved the problem by diverting the river (I.75).

Wisdom here seems to be seen as something that proves itself in a practical way. There is some emphasis on Thales' political insight. There is little or no emphasis on the theoretical achievement the prediction of an eclipse would involve. If Thales had not supposedly been able to predict the eclipse, and if it had not ominously coincided with the battle, Herodotus hardly would have seen a reason to refer at least indirectly to Thales' attempts to theoretically understand the world. And there is no reason to suppose that Thales himself would have wanted to deny that wisdom has to prove itself in practical ways. There certainly is no reason to suppose that Thales conceived of the wisdom he aspired to as entirely a matter of theoretical insight. And, though Thales' successors may have had a more articulate conception of this wisdom and their concern for it (as, for instance, Heraclitus clearly did), it does seem that they all continued to think of this wisdom as being something of considerable practical relevance, as we see in Empedocles' or Democritus's case. As late a figure as Democritus still thought that it was part of his chosen role to produce not only an atomistic theory but also a very large number of gnomic, "ethical" sayings. It also is telling that Democritus clearly does not yet have a definite conception as to how the theoretical and the practical aspects of wisdom are related, or a conception of the philosophical enterprise in the pursuit of which one would try to develop both a theory of reality and an ethical theory. Indeed Democritus does not produce an ethical theory; he produces wise, moral reflections.

At the same time, we also have to acknowledge that the Presocratics from Thales to Democritus, as part of their general concern for wisdom, tried to provide an account of reality or a theory of nature. And this in the end would solidify into a generally recognized enterprise of which they saw themselves as forming a part. It is in this way that they slowly came to be seen as a separate group. The first extant use of the word *philosophia* seems to be in *On Ancient Medicine* (chap. 20), where it refers to the kind of enterprise in which Empedocles and other inquirers into nature were engaged. But at an early point it would not be so clear that the philosophers for this reason formed a distinct group. After all, Hesiod and Pherecydes of Syros were also offering an account of the world and its origin. Philosophers like Parmenides or Empedocles presented themselves as being poetically inspired. We also have to remember that the clarity with which this tradition comes to stand out as a distinct tradition is in good part a matter of retrospective history and the selective transmission of the evidence. But however clearly the tradition emerges in the 5th century, it also seems clear that it is not a tradition of the pursuit of theoretical wisdom but a tradition of the pursuit of a much more broadly conceived wisdom, of which the attempt to come to a certain kind of theoretical understanding of the world forms just a part, albeit a crucial one.

If, because of our focus on the pursuit of a theoretical understanding of the world, we do not see that those engaged in this pursuit felt committed to a much more broadly understood wisdom with at least a strong practical component, we will find it difficult to understand how Socrates could see himself, and be seen by others, as part of a tradition going back to the Milesians. In fact, it will seem to be a historical accident that philosophy emerged as one discipline with a theoretical and a practical part, rather than as two independent disciplines, one in the tradition of Thales, in pursuit of a theoretical understanding of the world, and the other a discipline, first suggested by Socrates, in pursuit of a practical understanding of how one lives well.

It is notoriously difficult to determine the historical truth about Socrates' position. But to go by the evidence provided by Plato and Xenophon, Socrates identified wisdom with the knowledge of those things that we need to know if we are to live well, namely the good, the bad, and related matters. To be more precise, Socrates seems to have thought that these related matters formed, precisely because they were related, the subject of a systematic body of truths and hence the object of a discipline or art later called ethics or "the art of life." What is novel about this is that, instead of isolated moral reflections of the kind we find earlier among the Presocratics or in poets, or the kind of art attributed, for instance, by Plato to Protagoras (*Protagoras* 318.E5–319.A5), Socrates suggests a systematic discipline based on an insight into the good, the beautiful, the pious, and the courageous, and their interrelations. It is the knowledge and understanding of these matters that constitutes wisdom, precisely because it is the understanding of these matters that is relevant to the kind of life we have. By contrast, if we follow the evidence of, for instance, Plato's *Phaedo* and *Apology*, Socrates turns his back on the tradition of trying to give a theoretical account of reality as it does not contribute to wisdom, because this sort of account is either beyond us or, in any case, does not contribute to wisdom as Socrates conceives of it, to our understanding of the good and related matters.

So at this crucial point in the history of philosophy, when philosophers finally have come to see themselves clearly as a distinct group engaged in a distinct enterprise, when Socrates advances a certain conception of the enterprise that will constitute the historical starting point from which later conceptions of philosophy derive, philosophy is conceived of as a practical enterprise—and this in a twofold sense. First, Socrates' interest in the knowledge that constitutes wisdom is not a theoretical interest but an interest born of the idea that one should put one's mind, if to anything, then to one's life—that there is a whole body of truths to be known about how one should live, if one wants to live well. To the extent that Socrates can assume that the Presocratic interest in wisdom always also had been practical, he can see himself as continuing a long tradition, though in a very refocused form. Second, in spite of his extreme intellectualism—that is to say, his view that the way we act is completely determined by our beliefs, in particular our beliefs concerning the good and related matters—Socrates' life seems to have been characterized by a remarkable degree of asceticism. This strongly suggests that Socrates thought that it is not a matter of pure rational argument which beliefs we espouse and which we fail to espouse, but that, precisely because some of our beliefs are so deeply embedded in the way we feel and behave, our openness to their rational rejection or their rational acceptance, our openness to rational argument, also is a matter of our pattern of behavior and the control we have over our behavior.

From Socrates onward all philosophers in antiquity thought of philosophy as being practical in the sense of being motivated by a concern for the good life and as involving a practical concern for how one actually lives and how one actually feels about things. But they greatly differed in the way they understood this. Most important, few philosophers, like the Stoic Aristo and many Cynics, accepted Socrates' narrow conception of wisdom as a matter of a certain ethical knowledge.

Plato rejected this narrow conception of wisdom and, correspondingly, of philosophy as moral philosophy. And one can easily see why:

I. Socrates, it seems, relied on a substantial notion of the soul as what guides our behavior and whose health and well-being should thus be a primary concern of ours. His extreme intellectualism seems to have been based on a conception of the soul as a mind or a reason, such that our desires turn out to be beliefs of a certain kind.

II. Socrates relied on the assumption that there are, objectively, such things as the just and the pious.

III. Socrates also relied on the assumption that there is, objectively, such a thing as the good, which we can identify by reflecting on how people behave and how they fare.

The first two assumptions, to be sustained, presuppose an account of reality in terms of which we can explain human beings, their constitution, and the role the soul plays in the explanation of their behavior, and which also allows us to explain what kinds of things the just and the pious are supposed to be. As to the third assumption, we may question whether the good is not a global or universal feature in the sense that things quite generally have to be understood in terms of the good, and that the use of the term *good* in the sphere of human affairs has to be understood as just a special case of a much wider use of the term. It is for reasons of this sort that Plato comes to think that ethics has to be embedded in, and supported by, a theoretical account of reality. Correspondingly we get a broader, but still precise, conception of wisdom as involving both a theoretical understanding of reality and a practical knowledge of what matters in life. And with this move philosophy, as Plato conceives of it, looks like a clarification and focusing of the enterprise of the Presocratics, allowing us to distinguish clearly between philosophers, poets, and statesmen.

Just on the basis of what I have said so far, the need for a theoretical understanding of the world might be thought to be entirely due to the fact that our practical knowledge of how to live needs the support of such a theory. This is how Epicureans and Stoics will understand the matter. But the relative priority of the theoretical and the practical parts of wisdom get reversed in Plato and his later followers because of a certain conception of the soul. The soul is conceived of as preexisting and as just temporarily joined to a body. It thus has two lives and two sets of concerns. Its own concern is to live a life of contemplation of the truth. But, joined to the body, it also has to concern itself with the needs of the body. In doing this it easily forgets itself and its own needs, it easily gets confused so as to make the needs of the body its own. To know how to live well is to know how to live in such a way that the soul is free again to clearly see and mind its own business, namely to contemplate the truth. Thus we have an extremely complex inversion of the relative weight of one's theoretical understanding of reality and one's practical knowledge of how to live. It is one's understanding of reality, and the position of the soul in it, that saves the soul by restoring it—to the extent that this is possible in this life—to its natural state, in which it contemplates the truth. Hence a good life will crucially involve, as part of the way one lives, contemplation of the truth. Practicing the right way to live will also be a means to enable the soul to free itself from the body, to see the truth, and to engage in the contemplation of the truth.

Aristotle does not share Plato's dualist view of the soul. Nevertheless he has a view of human beings according to which a distinctly human life is a rational life, and hence a perfect human life involves the perfection of reason. But the perfection of reason involves not just the acquisition of the practical wisdom as to how we live but also the acquisition of the theoretical understanding of the world, both because practical wisdom requires such an understanding and because the mere contemplation of the truth is an end in itself and hence a crucial part of a good life. In fact, Aristotle sometimes talks as if contemplation were the part of a good life that accounted for its goodness. Nevertheless, even in Aristotle the philosopher's concern for theoretical wisdom is practical in the sense that it is a concern for a certain kind of life, namely a life that is perfected and fulfilled because it is dominated by a theoretical understanding of the world. Moreover, even Aristotle recognizes that there is no wisdom without practical wisdom, and that the acquisition of practical wisdom requires a highly practical effort on the part of the philosopher to learn to act and feel about things in a certain way. Our talk of Aristotle's "ethical theory" obscures the fact that, on Aristotle's view, the point of moral knowledge precisely is knowledge and understanding not of facts of a certain kind but of behavior of a certain kind, and that this moral knowledge and understanding cannot be acquired without involving oneself in acquiring the disposition to respond reliably to situations in a way appropriate to them, emotionally and in what one does.

When we turn to Hellenistic times, the priority between theory and practice changes again, decisively in favor of practice. Skeptics question whether any theory is available, and whether, even if it were available, it would help in living wisely. Epicureans and Stoics do assume that both ethical knowledge and an account of the world are attainable. But they are very clear about the fact that the philosopher's concern for ethical knowledge is a concern for the good life, and they both insist that a true account of the world is purely instrumental toward grounding and securing one's ethical knowledge. In the case of the Epicureans, the interest in a theory of nature is a purely negative one. The Epicureans assume that human beings living in a world that they do not understand are prone to be overcome by irrational fears they cannot control and which will not just put a truly good life out of their reach but will ruin the life they have. In particular they are prone to be overcome by the fear that the gods will punish them for their failures, if not in this life, then in an afterlife. They tend to understand natural phenomena as indications of divine anger, threats, or punishments. A moral life is impossible for a person given to such fears. The point of Epicurean physics is to free us from such terrors in order to create the psychological space for Epicurean ethics and a life in accordance with it. The Stoics have a far more positive attitude toward physics, and in particular the part of physics called theology, even if they regard this knowledge as purely subservient to the end of being practically wise. We learn from Stoic physics that the world is governed by an immanent divine rational principle that arranges the world down to the smallest detail so as to be a perfect world. We also know from Stoic physics that we are constructed in such a way as to be naturally guided by reason toward the good, and that, hence, as part of our development, we have to acquire the appropriate beliefs as to what is good, bad, or neither. It is in the light of this understanding of the world, then, that Stoic ethics will tell us what is good, bad, or neither; what it is appropriate for us to do, if we are guided by a concern for the good; and how good action consists precisely in this, doing what is appropriate out of concern for the good.

Now, what is characteristic of Epicureanism and Stoicism is not just the emphasis on ethics but, within ethics, the concern to provide practical guidance and the emphasis on the need to involve oneself practically. I will try to indicate, at least briefly, the nature of this concern in the case of Stoicism. The Stoics revert to Socrates' extreme intellectualism. They deny an irrational part of the soul. The soul is a mind or a reason. Its contents are impressions or thoughts, to which the mind gives assent or prefers to give assent. In giving assent to an impression, we espouse a belief. Desires are just beliefs of a certain kind, the product of our assent to a so-called impulsive impression. Since all that we do depends on our beliefs and, more especially, our desires, all we do ultimately depends on which impressions we give assent to. There are impressions one is justified in giving assent to, and there are impressions one is not justified in giving assent to. Hence, in the ultimate analysis, there is just one way in which we can err or sin, namely in giving assent to an impression that we are not justified in giving assent to. In this sense all sins are equal.

What is so disastrous about them is always the same: they involve assent to an impression that might be false or even is false. But given the logical connection between all beliefs, any false belief, however insignificant it may seem, threatens to destroy the true beliefs incompatible with it that we already have, and thus our chance to become wise. Now, among the impulsive impressions people are prone to give unjustified assent to are those that evoke the so-called passions or affections of the soul, like anger or fear or lust. They all involve the false belief that something is a good or an evil that in fact is neither. On the Stoic view only wisdom or virtue is a good. Thus any passion involves a false belief that is incompatible with a fundamental truth of ethics the mastery of which constitutes a crucial part of wisdom. Therefore a philosophical concern for wisdom involves the eradication of all passion, and this obviously is not just a matter of rational argument. Philosophical wisdom involves an indifference to all things but wisdom and virtue. A corollary of this and of the thesis of the equality of all sins is that all we do requires the same kind of careful attention as to what is appropriate: our eating and drinking, our waking and sleeping, the way we dress, the way we talk. All that we do has to be done wisely. There is thus a vast field of practice for a philosopher who is concerned to acquire a firm and solid knowledge of what matters. For reasons I will return to, this emphasis on the practical side of being a philosopher will become even stronger in later Stoicism. We tend to understand these concerns as reflecting an unphilosophical attitude, because they are untheoretical or even antitheoretical. It is crucial to understand that these concerns, given the Stoic understanding of philosophy, are eminently philosophical; they are, after all, concerns for the cognitive state of the philosopher.

Both Epicureans and Stoics proceed on the assumption that our life crucially depends on our having the right philosophical beliefs, the correct dogmata, concerning certain issues: the existence of God, divine providence, the nature of the soul, the good, the affections of the soul. In this sense orthodoxy comes to be a concern, a matter of anxiety, in a way it had not been before. By contrast, it should be pointed out at least briefly, the Academic Skepticism of Arcesilaus, Carneades, or Clitomachus suggests a life that is wise precisely in being undogmatic, in making do without dogmata. Like Socrates, Arcesilaus and Carneades do not write anything, they do not develop any theories, they do not commit themselves to any philosophical theses they are then going to defend or argue for. They, too, do not fit our ordinary notion of a philosopher, but they were thought of by their contemporaries as philosophers second to none, and, it seems, quite rightly so, even by our standards of philosophical sophistication and resourcefulness, not to mention their argumentative skill and cleverness.

Skepticism seriously dented the optimism with which many philosophers had set out in the hope of attaining the wisdom necessary for a good life. But even independent of Skeptical doubts about the attainability of wisdom, by the turn from the 2nd to the 1st century B.C.E. there were enough reasons to be disillusioned with the course philosophy had taken and what it had achieved. It had not produced any consensus on the questions that seemed crucial. Philosophers, for all their efforts, did not give the impression that they were any nearer to the good life than nonphilosophers. To the contrary, they could easily be seen as quibbling, as wasting their time on pointless subtleties, as being vain and ambitious. Horace writes to Lollius (*Ep.* 1.1.1–4) that he is reading Homer, who is so much better and clearer in telling us what is good and what is bad, what is beneficial and what is not, than Chrysippus or Crantor. Hero of Alexandria pours scorn on the efforts of the philosophers to tell us how to attain tranquillity.

Various diagnoses of the crisis suggested correspondingly different remedies. There was the suggestion that the crisis was due to the personal inadequacy of philosophers, and that personal reform was needed. There was the suggestion that Hellenistic philosophy was inadequate, for instance in its refusal to acknowledge an intelligible realm transcending the physical world, and that one had to return to the ancient philosophers. There was the suggestion that the philosophy of the time just reflected the corrupt culture and society of the time, and that one had to turn to an earlier, less corrupt age for guidance in one's view of the world and for a sounder notion as to how one should behave, perhaps to an age as far back as Homer and Hesiod.

These diagnoses gave rise to different trends. One very conspicuous development, which greatly affected the conception of philosophy and its practice,was the return to the ancient philosophers Pythagoras, Empedocles, Democritus, and in particular Plato and Aristotle, and more specifically to the texts of Plato and Aristotle. These were newly edited, and they began to be commented upon. The study of philosophy increasingly became a study of canonical philosophical texts. New philosophical ideas were developed and expounded in the context of commenting on canonical texts and the problems they raised. This, as we can see in the case of Alexander of Aphrodisias, Porphyry, or Simplicius, often involved a great deal of erudition, which easily became a substitute for genuine philosophical thought. Seneca complained that what was once philosophy had been turned into "philologia" (*Ep.* 108.23).

Another important trend was personal reform. This trend was extremely complex and was motivated by rather different considerations, which we can here distinguish only in the roughest way. Epictetus complained that most so-called philosophers were philosophers only up to the point of saying the sorts of things one expects philosophers to say, without being serious about it in practice (Gellius, *N.A.* 17.19.1). Surely part of what Epictetus meant was that whether one really believed and understood what one said as a philosopher had to show itself in one's life, that there had to be a congruence between doctrine (and preaching) and life, a point insisted on repeatedly at the time. There were two ways this was interpreted in practice. Cynics, it seems, tended to assume that philosophy theoretically amounted to a few simple tenets, for instance the tenet that everything but virtue is completely indifferent. These are easy to grasp but extremely difficult to hold on to in actual life, and it is a Herculean task to actually live in accordance with them. As opposed to what is often said, Stoics in later times did not think that philosophical theory could be reduced to a few theorems, nor did they discourage theory; they did discourage getting lost in theoretical subtleties instead of trying to live up to a highly complex theory in actual life. This was what, for instance, Epictetus insisted on and what Euphrates was praised for (*Epict.* IV.8.17–20). We see how even Stoic ethics was divided into a theoretical part and practical parts (Seneca, *Ep.* 89.14), especially if we take the testimony concerning Eudorus (*Stob. Ecl.* II.42, 13ff W.) to reflect Stoic doctrine. But what is at issue here is not just making one's life consistent with one's views, which is an enormous task, but also arranging one's life and one's disposition in such a way that one is open to the truth and can come to have the right view of things. We find ascetic tendencies even in the Stoics of the 1st century C.E., for instance in Attalus or in Chaeremon.

Most naturally, though, asceticism fitted the different forms of Platonism. Given that the soul can see the truth unimpeded only if it manages to disentangle itself from the body and its concerns, and given that it will free itself from its confusions only if it no longer focuses on the body and its needs but instead looks upward and focuses on the intelligible realm, asceticism seems to be precisely the way to put one's soul in a position to see the truth.

The philosophers of late antiquity considered earlier philosophers like Pythagoras, Plato, and Aristotle as authorities and their writings as authoritative. This is in particular true of Plato, especially since from the late 3rd century C.E. onward philosophers, almost without exception, claimed to follow Plato. But what did it mean to follow Plato as an authority, and what did one regard as the source of this authority? To follow Plato as an authority meant that one believed oneself to somehow be barred from direct access to the truth, to wisdom, for instance because one lived in an age in which earlier insights, an earlier wisdom, had been lost through disregard and corruption; it meant that one believed that Plato had known the truth and thus that one had at least indirect access to the truth through reconstructing what Plato had thought. As to the source of this authority, one did not primarily think that Plato had been such an excellent philosopher that he must have known the truth; one thought, rather—as we can see, for instance, from Numenius— that there was an ancient wisdom that Plato, being the person he was and the excellent philosopher he was, had access to, an ancient wisdom also to be ascribed, for instance, to Pythagoras, and reflected in Homer. In the light of this, Plato's writings came to have a status rather like Scripture (cf. Origen, *C.C.* VI.17), and all the more so as they are written in such a way as to only hint at the truth and to require complex exegesis. Thus, reconstructing Plato's thought was not seen as the historiographical task of reconstructing what the historical Plato had thought, but as reconstructing the true philosophy— held, among others, by Plato—by means of Plato's writings.

Now it is important to see that if one relied on the authority of Plato in reconstructing the true philosophy, one believed that Plato's writings were merely a means toward attaining the truth that, once attained, would make reference to Plato redundant. One could even believe this if, in reconstructing the true philosophy, one also relied, for instance, on the Chaldean Oracles, which one took to be divinely inspired. So the philosophical enterprise was still thought to crucially involve the development of an appropriate rational theoretical understanding of reality, and a practical attitude toward it based on this understanding, though the means by which one gained this understanding do not correspond to our conception of philosophical method. But the very view Platonists develop concerning reality, following Plato's remarks in *The Republic* about the Good as being beyond being and the intellect (*Rep.* 509 B), put the enterprise of a rational theoretical understanding of reality into question. For the first principle, in terms of which everything else is supposed to be understood and explained, now seems to be beyond intelligibility. This not only affects the conception of philosophy but also raises the question, to what extent can the wisdom philosophers try to attain be achieved without divine cooperation, grace, or intervention, if the grasp of the first principle is beyond our intellect?

This question perhaps was raised first toward the end of the 1st century C.E. by Apollonius of Tyana, a follower of Pythagoras, who aspired to be a divine or holy man. Philostratus in the *Life of Apollonius* (V.37) presents Euphrates as being engaged in a discussion with Apollonius concerning the very nature of philosophy. Euphrates argues for a conception of philosophy "in accordance with nature," that is to say, a philosophy relying on the means nature has provided us with to attain the wisdom that nature ideally means us to attain. And he warns against a conception of philosophy that involves the invocation of God *(theoklytein),* based on a mistaken conception of the divine that provokes such philosophers to great follies. Apollonius, just like his follower Alexander (cf. Lucian's *Alexander*), does indeed seem to have encouraged the belief in his miraculous powers and the growth of a religious cult (Origen, *C.C.* VI.41). In any case he seems to be the first philosopher we can identify who introduced theurgy into philosophy, that is to say, the idea that certain invocations, perhaps combined with the appropriate ritual practice, could bring God to reveal himself, or bring subordinate divine beings, or even daemons, to reveal themselves and their knowledge. Theurgy, at least a certain conception of it, plays a crucial positive role in Iamblichus's conception of philosophy and that of his followers. One important point, though, is that even if, as a philosopher, one refused to resort to theurgy, one might still believe that it offered a nonphilosophical way to attain the very same wisdom, the very same knowledge, that frees and saves the soul and provides us with the good life. This further undermines the claim philosophers had made that there was no way to become a wise and good person, to have a good life, except the philosopher's way of becoming wise. But then this claim had already long been undermined by the assumption of an original, perhaps inspired, wisdom that philosophers only strove to recover.

Against this background it is easy to see why many early Christians could think of Christian doctrine, in general, as the new true philosophy and of Christian theology, in particular, as the new true theology, replacing the theology of the Stoics, the Peripatetics, and the Platonists. Justin, for instance, is just a particularly striking example among many who regarded Christianity as a philosophy (cf. *Dialogue with Trypho*, II.1). Justin, a philosopher, a Platonist, converted to Christianity but continued to think of himself as practicing philosophy in explaining and expounding Christian doctrine and converting others to Christianity. We should not regard this as a claim to be taken lightly. It is, of course, true that Christians relied on authority for their beliefs, even on the authority of revealed or inspired truth. But this did not distinguish them from pagan philosophers. We also should keep in mind that, though Christian theologians relied on authority, at least originally they seem to have assumed that the understanding they were led to by authority was a philosophical understanding that in the end made reliance on revealed truth superfluous. Origen's dependence on Scripture is striking, but in the case of both Origen and Augustine, at least the earlier Augustine, the theological view we arrive at and the way it is supported looks very much like a philosophical position held on philosophical grounds, and I do not see any reason not to regard Origen as a philosopher in the way this was understood in antiquity.

Christians also came to use the word *philosopher* to refer to monks, and to think of the monastic life as the truly philosophical life (cf. Basil, *De const.* 5; Gregory of Nyssa, *V. Macr.* p. 411, l. 12). Again I think that it would be a great mistake not to take this seriously. If, for instance, we think of Philo's description of the Essenes or Chaeremon's description of the Egyptian priests, both based on a conception of the sage, both misunderstood as referring to historical precursors of monasticism, we realize how indebted early monasticism was to Cynicism, the Stoic focus on the inner life and the attachment to the Good, and often a Platonist worldview in which salvation involved withdrawing from the world, turning inside into the soul, and ascending through the soul, as on a ladder, to its source. In ancient times even pagans would have readily understood that the monk's life is a philosophical life. It rather looked like one form of being serious about being a philosopher.

Now it seems that early Christian authors, like Clement of Alexandria, were tempted by the idea that it was a philosophical understanding of the world, in the light of revelation, that would save the soul and lead to the promised life. But Origen, for instance, in spite of his enormous theological efforts, very clearly rejected this elitist idea. It was the ability, available to everybody, to hold on to the belief in Christ as revealed in his Incarnation and, through him, the belief in God, that saved. Indeed, the invocation of Christ was seen not as an alternative to philosophy but as the only way to the good life.

But once this view became dominant, the philosophical enterprise lost the motivation that had been its main motor: the thought that a good life was a wise life, and that wisdom had to be obtained by philosophical theory and practice. What one now was guided by in one's life was religious belief rather than philosophical belief, and what was now required was religious and religiously motivated moral practice rather than philosophical practice. This meant that philosophers could go on producing theories about the world, or even about how one should act, but these theories no longer were seen as having decisive relevance in life. Their place had been taken by something else. This is not the occasion to discuss the enormous shift involved, but it is reflected in the fact that even today in our ordinary moral thinking and in our philosophical ethics there seems to be little or no place for the exercise of theoretical wisdom in the good life, and in the fact that virtue seems to be identified, with an amazing ease, with moral virtue, as if theoretical wisdom were morally irrelevant.

In this way philosophy was reduced to a theoretical exercise, an exercise one can do well without, without having to fear for one's life or one's soul, an exercise of, at best, marginal relevance to our life. But it is a mistake to think that just because history took this turn, good philosophy has to be something that ultimately is irrelevant to our life, to the life of those we live with and our life with them, and to the life of our communities and societies. And it certainly would be a mistake to project our conception of philosophy as a rather academic enterprise of developing philosophical theories back on the ancients.

MICHAEL FREDE

Bibliography

Burkert, Walter. "Platon oder Pythagoras? Zum Ursprung des Wortes 'Philosophie.'" *Hermes* 88 (1960): 159–177.

Cassin, Barbara, ed. *Nos Grecs et leurs modernes.* Paris: Le Seuil, 1992.

Detienne, Marcel. *Les maîtres de vérité dans la Grèce archaïque.* Paris: Maspero, 1967.

Dixsaut, Monique. *Le naturel philosophe: Essai sur les Dialogues de Platon.* Paris: Les Belles Lettres/Vrin, 1985.

Dumont, Jean-Paul. *Eléments d'histoire de la philosophie antique.* Paris: Nathan, 1993.

Goulet, Richard, ed. *Dictionnaire des philosophes antiques,* vols. 1 and 2. Paris: CNRS, 1989, 1994.

Hadot, Ilsetraut. *Seneca und die griechisch-römische Tradition der Seelenleitung.* Berlin: De Gruyter, 1969.

Hadot, Pierre. *Qu'est-ce que la philosophie antique?* Paris: Gallimard, 1995.

Irwin, Terence. *Plato's Moral Theory: The Early and Middle Dialogues.* Oxford: Clarendon Press, 1977.

Jordan, William. *Ancient Concepts of Philosophy.* London: Routledge, 1990.

Malingrey, Anne-Marie. *Philosophia.* Paris: Klincksieck, 1961.

Nussbaum, Martha. *The Therapy of Desire: Theory and Practice in Hellenistic Ethics.* Princeton: Princeton University Press, 1994.

Ritter, Joachim, and Karlfried Gründer, eds. *Historisches Wörterbuch der Philosophie,* 8: "Philosophie" (contributions by M. Kranz, G. Bien, and Pierre Hadot). Basel/Stuttgart: Schwabe, 1989.

Schofield, Malcolm, and Gisela Striker, eds. *The Norms of Nature: Studies in Hellenistic Ethics.* Cambridge: Cambridge University Press, 1986.

Voelke, André-Jean. *La philosophie comme thérapie de l'âme.* Fribourg: Editions universitaires, 1993.

Related Articles

Schools and Sites of Learning; Epicurus; Cynicism; Aristotle; Socrates; Sophists

IMAGES OF THE WORLD

WHAT DID ANCIENT GREEK MEN AND WOMEN believe about the world they lived in and their own place in it? Before we begin to attempt an answer to that question, two prior problems must be faced, the first to do with the nature of the evidence available to us, the second concerning the possible goal of our inquiry.

We have no direct access, of course, to the opinions of ordinary men and women at any period in antiquity. We cannot use the methods of modern sociology—interviews, questionnaires, polls—to find out what the ancient Greeks believed. With the exception of some archaeological and epigraphic evidence, we rely entirely on literary texts. Some of these report, to be sure, what was generally believed. But that just tells us what view the authors in question held about that subject. That is to say, the evidence is still indirect and has been mediated by the ancient authors themselves. Moreover the texts that have come down to us are in no sense a random or unbiased sample of what was written. The processes by which certain texts have survived and others not, some authors are well represented by their own works and others not at all, at every point involve selection and value judgments, whether these were made by the ancients themselves or by those who stand between them and us—especially the anonymous scribes of late antiquity and the Middle Ages.

The second difficulty follows from the first. Although we speak loosely of the "worldview" of the great literary figures of antiquity, Homer, Hesiod, Aeschylus, Sophocles, and so on, we must always remember that most of the authors in question were not presenting cosmological theories at all. The problems of extracting something that can be called a worldview from works of high literature are easily underestimated, and indeed the very ambition to carry out that enterprise is questionable. The recurrent temptation that has, at all costs, to be resisted, is to make the authors we study more coherent than the evidence justifies—to ascribe to them carefully worked-out positions on the nature of the earth, the heavens, the place of humans in the scheme of things, and so on, as if their aim was to provide answers to those questions.

So not only do we have no direct access to the beliefs of ordinary men and women, but the texts we do have are mostly literary artifacts of considerable complexity that are innocent of any intention to theorize about the world order.

None of that is to deny, of course, that there are cosmologists who did, precisely, set themselves the task of presenting a view about the world as a whole. The sequence of cosmological doctrines proposed by Greek philosophers from Thales and the other early Presocratic thinkers down to late antiquity is the subject of detailed analysis in a later chapter. Those doctrines often owe something, sometimes a good deal, to popular beliefs and assumptions. Nevertheless it must be emphasized that there is a fundamental distinction between pretheoretical notions and explicit theories.

Thus, before the first philosophical cosmologies in the 6th century B.C.E., it is doubtful whether we would be correct in speaking of any *unified* conception of the world as such at all. The idea that the cosmos, or world order, is such a unity only becomes explicit for the first time with the philosophers. They use a variety of images, models, and analogies to express diverging notions of the nature and type of unity in question. Some pictured the cosmos as a living creature, others as an artifact— the work of a divine and benevolent Craftsman—and yet others as a political state, though again the type of state varied. Some saw the cosmos as ruled by a single kinglike authority, while others represented cosmic order as a matter of the balanced relationship between equal forces. We even have Heraclitus describing war as what rules everything and strife as justice.

Several philosophers combine more than one conception of the cosmos as a unified whole, and their cosmological notions often interact with their ideas about other things. If the world is viewed as a living organism, or a political state, so too, conversely, the body and the state can be considered microcosms. Moreover, as noted, these philosophical models can certainly be said to draw on prephilosophical ideas. Long before the notion that the world is under the control of a single cosmic principle had been proposed in cosmological theory, Zeus had been imagined as a supreme ruler. However, the fundamental difference remains. Zeus may be king among gods and humans, but he is certainly no abstract cosmological principle.

The aim of this study is to explore some of the prephilosophical and popular beliefs and assumptions that form the background to the systematic inquiries eventually undertaken by the Greeks in the various areas of learning they cultivated. Subsequent chapters will discuss astronomy, cosmology, physics, biology and medicine, and so on. But what, in general, did Greeks of the classical and Hellenistic periods assume or believe about the world they lived in and their own place in it? The first step must be to evaluate the cultural inheritance of the two supreme masters of archaic poetry, Homer and Hesiod.

However much Homer may have been represented as the teacher of the Greeks, it is, as noted, only in a loose sense that we can talk of a worldview in the Homeric poems. Expectations that we should be able to find a coherent, unified, comprehensive set of ideas on the subject are misplaced. What we have to review are ideas introduced in passing, at particular junctures in the narratives of the *Iliad* and *Odyssey*. We can certainly not assume that the ideas expressed at different points and by different characters in the epics necessarily correspond to the beliefs of either the poet (or poets) or their contemporary audiences. The dramatic function of the introduction of some general idea always takes precedence over any theoretical or speculative concern.

But having expressed those warnings, we may remark that the heavens, or sky—*ouranos*—are frequently described as "brazen" or "iron," as if the sky could be thought of as a bright, solid object. Round the earth runs the "river" of Ocean "from whom all rivers flow and the entire sea, and all the springs and deep wells" (*Iliad* 21.195ff). Below the earth there is Hades, the abode of the dead, and below that again is Tartaros, "as far beneath Hades as heaven is above earth" (*Iliad* 8.16). The seasons are distinguished, and day and night are each divided into three parts. In the night sky the movements of the stars are noticed and several constellations are named: Pleiades, Hyades, Orion, the Bear also called the Plough, the last said to be the only group that never sets, that "has no part in the baths of Ocean" (*Iliad* 18.489).

There are vivid descriptions of storms, winds, waves, fire, of animals and of animal behavior. There are famous similes, in the *Iliad* and *Odyssey*, that refer to the migrations of birds (for example, cranes, *Iliad* 3.3ff), to eagles that prey on snakes (*Iliad* 12.200ff), to the skulking of an octopus in its lair (*Odyssey* 5.432ff). All of this may suggest close observation of what *we* would call "nature": but we must be careful. Although the term later used for nature, *phusis*, is found in one text in the *Odyssey* referring to the form of a particular plant, or maybe more precisely to the way it grows (*Odyssey* 10.302ff), there is, in Homer, no overarching concept or category that picks out the *domain* of nature as such—as opposed either to "culture" or to the "supernatural." The plant in question in that text in the *Odyssey* is a magic one, *moly*, which will enable Odysseus to resist the charms of Circe. Many of the descriptions of birds occur in passages where their behavior is considered to provide omens for the future, as is the case, for instance, at *Iliad* 12.200ff, mentioned above.

The vivid accounts of phenomena of different kinds in the *Iliad* and *Odyssey* provide the backdrop for the development of the narrative. But at the center of the drama, in both epics, lies the relationship not between humans and nature but between humans and gods. The *Odyssey* relates not just Odysseus's own efforts to secure a safe homecoming but also the efforts of gods and goddesses, Athena, Poseidon, and the rest, to help or impede him. The account of the siege of Troy is a matter not just of the battles between Trojans and Achaeans but also of the interventions of the gods on either side.

So if we attempt to reconstruct the image of the "world" conveyed in the Homeric poems, the central preoccupation that both *Iliad* and *Odyssey* exhibit is with the relations between humans and gods. How far that feature just reflects the dramatic demands of the narrative we are in no position to answer in any determinate way. We cannot say how far Homer and his audience *believed* in the representations of the gods that the epics contain. But that those representations are at the center of both works is beyond question. The characters in the poems live in a world where indeed the sequence of the rising and setting of constellations is orderly, and so too is the usual behavior of animals, their acting true to type—the lion always courageous, the deer fearful. But within the dramatic conventions of the epics, the possibility that the gods may be at work is always present, the possibility that they may use "natural" phenomena as portents, appearing themselves, even, in the shape of birds (as when Athena flies off as a lammergeier, *phēnē*, *Odyssey* 3.372, or like a swallow, ibid. 22.239f) or in the guise of humans (as in the famous last fight of Hector before Troy, where Athena adopts the appearance of his brother Deiphobos to persuade him to stay outside the walls and fight Achilles, *Iliad* 22.226ff).

Appearances, evidently, are often not what they seem. The world is far from chaotic, far from incoherent: indeed it manifests abundant signs of regularity and order. Yet the ways of the gods are mysterious, their whims dangerous, their power undeniable. Even Zeus, who rules over gods and humans (*Iliad* 2.669), finds it hard to control the other gods and is disobeyed and deceived by them. He has to exert himself to maintain his own rule, but his intentions are obscure, his interventions unpredictable. *How* his will is to be fulfilled is never a foregone conclusion, even if it is certain that it will be fulfilled.

When we turn to Hesiod, some of the difficulties that arise in the interpretation of the *Iliad* and the *Odyssey* are mitigated. Unlike Homer, who never speaks in the first person, Hesiod introduces himself in his poems. Moreover, both *Theogony* and *Works and Days* are essentially didactic works in which he strives to persuade his audience of a point of view, his point of view. While *Works* deals primarily with the regulation of human affairs and *Theogony* gives an account of the genealogies of the gods, in both the supreme god, Zeus, underpins order and justice. In both it is legitimate to speak not just of a divine rule ordering things but of a moral order.

Works and Days offers a mass of specific injunctions, notably in the last section of the poem detailing what activities should or should not be performed on particular days of the month. "Some days are a great benefit for those who live on the earth, others are changeable, neutral, bringing no advantage. One man praises one, another another, but few know . . . But the person who knows all these things and is blameless in front of the immortals, judging the bird omens and avoiding excess, he is blessed and fortunate" (824ff). The misdemeanors of the "bribe-devouring kings" are a recurrent theme. Not only are they at fault for spreading dissension among men, but the city ruled unjustly will never flourish. "Those who give straight verdicts to strangers and to locals alike, and who do not deviate in any respect from what is just, for them the city flourishes and the people bloom in it" (225ff). They are never affected by hunger, the earth bears a plentiful livelihood, in the mountains the oak trees bear acorns and harbor bees, the sheep are weighed down by their fleeces, the women bear children like their fathers. But conversely where there is injustice and excess, there the entire city suffers (238ff). There Zeus brings hunger and pestilence, the people perish, the women do not bear children.

The just behavior of humans, especially of their kings, is thus represented as being rewarded with prosperity, and injustice with calamities. Zeus oversees the order of things. Indeed the present race of mortals—the age of iron—is represented as the end of a sequence where one race is superseded by another: the gold, in turn, by silver, by bronze, by the race of heroes, before the present age of iron. And the eventual downfall and destruction of this race, too, is predicted and associated, again, with the neglect of justice and shame (180ff, 192f).

While *Works and Days* focuses especially on human behavior, *Theogony* takes as its chief topic the origins of the gods. This has often been represented as a prephilosophical cosmology. Yet that description is misleading in three principal respects. First, this is no account of how things are in the world in which we live, but rather one of origins. Second, the story of origins focuses principally on the gods and the divine, not on the physical features of the world as we know it. Third, the story is evidently a mythical account, not one that purports to proceed by way of an analysis of cosmic principles that still govern physical phenomena. There can be no doubt that one of the primary concerns in the tale, as set out, is to describe the foundation of the moral order that is instituted by the supreme god, Zeus. The steps by which he came to be supreme ruler are set out, namely the sequence of his victories over his rivals and his enemies, first the Titans and then Typhoeus. While it would clearly be wrong to see this as mere allegory, Hesiod leaves us in no doubt that the supreme rule achieved by Zeus is the institution of the reign of justice.

Theogony is, then, precisely what its title implies, a story of the births of the gods, and so no cosmogony, let alone cosmology. It is not unified in the way in which philosophical cosmologies invoking a determinate set of principles were to be. At the same time it is a remarkably comprehensive account, and it is one that uses the theme of genealogies to link the origins of very diverse figures. Most of the gods in question are conceived anthropomorphically. In many cases their uniting is described in terms that directly imply sexual intercourse. Yet there are some exceptions. At the very beginning of the story (*Theogony* 126ff), Earth produces a number of offspring, including Heaven himself, *ouranos*, "without delightful love" (132), and again (at 211ff), Night produces Death, Sleep, and other children "without having slept with anyone." Yet these are still *births*. The offspring are still said to be born, even though not as the result of sexual intercourse but rather, as it were, by parthenogenesis. Moreover not all the divine figures in the story are imagined in personal, let alone human, anthropomorphic, terms. When the high mountains are born (129), these are said to be "the pleasant haunts of the gods."

Vitalist terms and images, the language of conceiving, bearing, intercourse, provide the main unifying link running through the account, but it is not, of course, that Hesiod set out to elaborate a *theory* of the cosmos as a living creature. The contrast between *Theogony* and some later philosophical cosmologies that did just that should not be underestimated. For Plato, for instance, the visible cosmos is itself a living creature, and the Stoics, in turn, thought of the cosmos as a whole as instinct with life. But the very term *cosmos* (*kosmos,* world order) implies a *unified* conception of the world as such, for which there is no equivalent in Hesiod.

It would also be a gross mistake to represent Hesiod's interests as limited to or circumscribed by what we can recognize as the physical features of the world. There are, to be sure, references to mountains and stars, but the account focuses principally on gods and goddesses, most of whom are construed as strong willed, not to say willful, individuals, in many cases resistant to the wishes of Zeus though still ultimately ruled by him. Moreover, the divine creatures described include not just the familiar anthropomorphic Olympians but also theriomorphic beings, hybrids, monsters. The account of births and battles encompasses the Cyclopes with one eye; Cottus; Briareus and Gyes, with fifty heads and a hundred arms; the Erinyes produced from Ouranous's genitals; the Harpies; Cerberus, the fifty-headed hound; the Hydra, the Chimera with lion, goat, and snake heads; Pegasus; the Sphinx; and many, many more.

The crucial point is the one already noted in relation to Homer. Hesiod has no concept that corresponds to that of *nature as such*, either as opposed to culture or as opposed to the supernatural. The account in *Theogony* takes in not just what might be described as regular (and so in that sense natural) phenomena, but also the strange, the unique, the monstrous. All find their place in the overall story of the gods, their offspring, and their relations with the supreme ruler, Zeus. While in both *Theogony* and *Works and Days* we can analyze Hesiod's knowledge of what *we* call the natural world—the seasons, the constellations, the behavior of animals, and so on—in neither poem is the original focus of interest on nature as such at all. Evidently if the farmer or the fisherman is to have any success, he would be well advised to learn as much as he can about such matters as the signs of changing weather. However, it is, in Hesiod's view, just as important that he should regulate his behavior correctly in relation to the gods. Mortals are the beneficiaries of Prometheus's gift of fire, the origin of all the arts and crafts. Yet that gift was a theft from Zeus—for which he duly exacted vengeance. Womankind itself, the offspring of the first woman, Pandora, was the form that vengeance took. Thanks to Pandora, mortals are condemned to a life of toil, pain, and disease. Though justice will be rewarded, the prospects for humankind are ultimately bleak. We live in an age of iron, but, as noted, its days are numbered. Meanwhile, Hesiod warns, it is essential to honor the gods and to behave justly toward humans. Morality and religion are the kernel of his message, and such knowledge as he retails concerning physical and biological phenomena is subordinated to those ends.

Homer and Hesiod are literary craftsmen of great genius, and their subsequent influence on Greek thought is incalculable. For this reason any study of later beliefs about the world, in the classical and even in the Hellenistic period, has to begin with them. This does not mean, of course, that their ideas were taken over straightforwardly into popular belief, nor that all of their complex notions about the world and the place of humans in it were accepted or passed without challenge. Moreover, new ideas, new knowledge, new beliefs and assumptions come to the fore that have no Homeric nor Hesiodic antecedents.

We may now broaden the scope of our discussion by focusing on three features of this question in particular. First, we may consider the way in which criticisms of Homer, Hesiod, or beliefs represented as traditional and associated with them were expressed by writers of different types—poets, philosophers, historians, "sophists"—in their endeavors to make their reputation and to gain prestige. Second, there are aspects of Greek popular belief, beginning in the classical if not in the archaic period, that diverge at points quite fundamentally from the ideas that are presented in either Homer or Hesiod. Third, there is the question of the extent to which the expansion of knowledge associated with the development of philosophy and science especially penetrated and affected beliefs about the world more generally.

Direct attacks on the Homeric and Hesiodic conceptions of the gods figure prominently in the poems of Xenophanes (born in the early 6th century B.C.E.). Both Homer and Hesiod are named when he condemns them for representing the gods as immoral, as "thieving, committing adultery and deceiving one another" (frg. 11, cf. frg. 12). Far more basically, the whole notion of anthropomorphic deities is satirized. "But mortals think that gods are born and that they have clothes and voices and shapes like their own" (frg. 14). "The Ethiopians say their own gods are snub-nosed and black, the Thracians say theirs are blue-eyed and red-haired" (frg. 16). The idea of the subjectivity of notions of the divine is extended then to animals: "If oxen and horses and lions had hands and could draw with their hands and produce works of art like men, horses would draw the forms of the gods like horses, and oxen like oxen, and they would make their bodies such as each of them had themselves" (frg. 15). It is noticeable, however, that Xenophanes replaces this crude anthropomorphism with an idea of the supreme god as Mind—an idea still based, in part, on a human model.

Xenophanes thus inaugurated an attack on one fundamental feature of the traditional Olympian religion, and other criticisms of the foundations of religious belief were voiced in the 5th century, notably by two of the sophists. Thus according to Prodicus of Ceos the true origin of the ideas that people have about the divine lies in their own experience and needs: "The ancients considered as gods the sun and moon and rivers and springs and in general everything that aids our life because of the benefit from them, just as the Egyptians consider the Nile a god . . . For this reason bread was worshipped as Demeter, wine as Dionysus, water as Poseidon, fire as Hephaestus, and so on with each of the things that are good for use." Again, more cynically, the idea that the gods were invented by humans for the purposes of moral and social control is found in a passage from the *Sisyphus* of Critias, even though we do not have the context for this quotation and cannot be certain how far it represents Critias's own views: "A man of clever and cunning wit first invented for men fear of the gods, so that there might be something to frighten the wicked, even if they do or say or think something in secret."

While any such view would be classified as "atheism" by Plato, he rejected the idea of gods in the shape of humans as firmly as Xenophanes had done. More important, the ideas that the gods bring misfortunes to humankind and that they can be bought off with sacrifices are both directly associated with Homer and both roundly condemned in *The Republic* (364c ff, 379a ff). Plato returns to those themes, among others, in his last work, *Laws,* where in book X he attacks three brands of impiety: the denial of the existence of gods, the notion that they exist but pay no attention to human affairs, and the idea that they can easily be bought off with prayers and sacrifices.

As in other spheres of thought, so too in relation to ideas about divinity, the philosophers often advanced their own speculative and abstract theories in explicit or implicit contradistinction to popular beliefs. We shall be returning in due course to other areas of belief about the world where this is the case. For now we should remark, first, that there is a good deal more to common Greek beliefs about the gods than is suggested by Homer and Hesiod, and second, that those philosophical criticisms and attacks are only of very limited impact.

I will take the second point first. The anthropomorphic representations of the Olympian gods were and remained a central feature of the established city cults. The notion that sacrifices pleased and propitiated the gods continued to be as firmly rooted in popular belief in the 4th century as before—despite Plato's attacks. Even though Socrates had been charged with impiety (among other things), it is remarkable that Plato's onslaught, in *Laws,* might be thought completely to undermine the city-state religious cults, and yet there was no suggestion that he ran into trouble because of his views. This illustrates, to be sure, the pluralism of Greek religion—a point amply endorsed by the rich and complex theological debates that continued to be a feature of philosophical speculation down to late antiquity. But the other side to that coin is that the philosophers' debates, even on the nature of the gods, made little difference to the beliefs and practices of ordinary men and women.

Important further aspects of those beliefs and practices should now be mentioned to underscore the point that they extend far beyond the limits suggested by Homer and Hesiod. From their poems one could hardly have inferred a great deal concerning the worship of Dionysus, for instance. Yet as Euripides' play *Bacchae* vividly illustrates, that came to be at the center of a markedly different type of religious experience, *enthusiasm*, or the possession by the god, for its devotees. Again the fact that those devotees were (mostly) women is a reminder that their cults existed in parallel to those associated with the city's official celebrations of its divine patrons.

A second important element in classical Greek religion is represented by the mystery religions associated with such centers as Eleusis. Though most of the details both of the beliefs and of the rites performed are obscure, it is clear at least that the mysteries were essentially concerned with a notion of the afterlife that differs markedly from that described in Homer. In *Odyssey* 11 Odysseus descends to the underworld to encounter ghosts in the form of insubstantial wraiths, with whom communication is possible only after they have drunk from a sacrifice of blood. Achilles famously proclaims that any existence on earth is preferable to ruling among the dead. The mysteries, by contrast, evidently held out the hope of salvation for the initiates. The balance of attention between this world and the next is reversed. Though associated originally with notions of purification and, precisely, initiation, the idea that the fate of your immortal soul is crucially dependent on how you have behaved in this life was, of course, to be given a fundamental *moral* point by Plato.

Third, at the local level, the cult of the heroes and the worship of local manifestations of the Olympians and other gods were clearly an important part of lived religious experience for many Greeks. Hesiod had already referred to the golden race becoming "guardians," to the silver race as blessed "chthonians" to whom honor is due, and to heroes who live a carefree life in the Islands of the Blessed (*Works*, 122ff, 141f, 170ff). But again this gives no inkling of the many local hero cults important in the Greek countryside, heroes often worshipped as the protectors and guarantors of health, fertility, and prosperity.

The contrast between human and divine takes many different forms, and much early Greek thought and belief concerning the world and the place of humans in it is articulated around one or another of those various forms, humans and Olympians, humans and chthonians, humans and heroes. Yet of course not all those thoughts and beliefs were linked directly or indirectly with those contrasts. We may now turn to consider what was known or believed about the physical world, though, to be sure, we should not assume that even in the 5th century B.C.E. the Greeks necessarily had any explicit category that corresponds precisely to what we mean by the expression "physical world."

Once again reactions to Homer provide one starting point. The Homeric epics, I have said, offered certain ideas concerning such matters as the stars and the seasons and the passing of time. Ocean is represented as running around the world. Odysseus's wanderings take him to many places, although what we might term the geography of these is, at points, indeterminate. The interest shown in the *Odyssey* in faraway places sometimes concentrates on the behavior of the inhabitants—the way in which such folk as the Laestrygonians, the Lotus-Eaters, the Cyclopes suggest just so many contrasts to the societies of Ithaca, Sparta, Mycenae.

But just as Homer and Hesiod were criticized by later writers for their ideas about the gods, so are there explicit criticisms of their views on other matters, whether or not an explicit concept of nature, *phusis,* was invoked in the process. Herodotus offers a particularly interesting and complex case study. The Greeks in general, he says (IV.8), affirm in their speech that Ocean, beginning from the risings of the sun, flows around the whole earth; but in practice they do not show this. And again he writes: "I know of no river of Ocean: but I suppose that Homer or some earlier poet invented the name and brought it into their poetry (II.23)." We may, however, remark that Herodotus himself is often unsure how to treat the possibly fabulous stories that he nevertheless recounts concerning the remoter regions of the earth. He is as learned as anyone in his day on the topic of geography. Yet there are obvious limits to his knowledge, some that he glosses over, others that he recognizes, points that he could not verify firsthand and where he could not satisfy himself that the accounts he had been given were reliable. Moreover, as we shall see later, his notion of the natural world is still one that leaves room for the divine at work.

The story of the development of early Greek philosophy, science, and medicine is, to a very considerable extent, the story of the increasing deployment of the notion of nature. Our information about the earliest Greek philosophers ascribes to them a wide variety of theories and explanations concerning phenomena of different types. Admittedly this evidence is hard to evaluate, since often the context in which those theories were introduced is not given, nor indeed is their justification. However, it is noticeable that a large number of the phenomena for which such theories are offered are ones that had often (even if not exclusively) been associated with divine interventions, as, for example, the theories relating to earthquakes, thunder and lightning, the rainbow, and so on. It is not as if every time thunder is mentioned in the *Iliad*

Zeus or some other god is implicated: the similes in Homer often describe what we would call natural phenomena without any invocation of deities. However, the association with gods is frequently made. The rainbow is seen as a portent or personified as Iris, a messenger of the gods; earthquakes are the work of Poseidon or Zeus; and so on.

One feature that the theories ascribed to the early philosophers have in common is that they exclude personal deities. Xenophanes even explicitly asserts that the rainbow is no more than a cloud. These are indeed *naturalistic* explanations, even though the causes invoked are often merely speculative. Nor are such theories just confined to those whom we normally classify as philosophers. Herodotus, too, discusses various possible causes of the Nile's flooding in summer (II.20ff). However, he also leaves room for the intervention of gods. This is particularly true when he discusses whether some affliction, such as a disease or madness, may be the result of divine displeasure. Although he sometimes expresses his doubts, he also on occasion goes along with such an idea. After describing the death of Pheretime following a disease in which her body became infested with worms, he comments: "Thus, it would seem, over-violent human vengeance is hated by the gods" (IV.205). Again recording a Thessalian story that the Vale of Tempe was created by Poseidon, he offers a rationalizing endorsement, remarking that this is reasonable since Poseidon is the earthshaker, and it was an earthquake that caused the rift in the mountains.

Among our fullest sources for such attempts to give naturalistic accounts of strange or frightening phenomena are the medical writers of the 5th and 4th centuries collected in the so-called Hippocratic Corpus. The treatise *On the Sacred Disease* especially is principally devoted to showing that the disease in question (identifiable from the vivid and detailed description as epilepsy) is a natural one like any other. It has, the author claims, a natural cause, which he identifies as stemming from the blocking of the veins in the body especially by phlegmatic discharges. It is not that no disease is "divine": rather, all are. But the reason for this is that all are natural, and nature itself is divine. The key point is that naturalistic explanations can be given for every type of disease and supernatural interventions ruled out.

The arguments that this medical writer develops reveal the polemical background to his thesis. The people he chiefly attacks are those he calls "purifiers," the sellers of charms and incantations, who offer fanciful accounts of how different types of epilepsy are caused by different deities (the Mother of the Gods, Poseidon, Enodia, Apollo Nomius, Ares, Hecate) and who further claim to be able to cure the disease by means of their charms and incantations. He is emphatic not just that the disease has a natural cause but also that it, like every other disease, can be cured by natural means—especially the control of diet and regimen.

Evidently the Hippocratic writer's own theories are put forward as direct alternatives to the accounts and therapies of his rivals. The practice of medicine was an intensely competitive business. The invocation of the categories of the natural, and of cause and explanation, forms an essential part of the battery of arguments by which the Hippocratic writers sought to refute the views of those who represented a rival tradition of medical practice.

We can view this whole development as the "naturalizing of the world." But we should be wary of speaking of the wholesale replacement of "myth" by "science," and this for three principal reasons. First and foremost, it is not as if the scientists themselves necessarily had a very clear idea of what the true causes of the phenomena in question were. Nor, where diseases were concerned, were they usually in a very good position to effect cures. Moreover, the disagreements on both causes and cures were extensive among all those who shared the *ambition* to give naturalistic explanations. Some held that earthquakes are caused by the earth shifting on the water on which it floats; others held that it was subterranean air that caused the movement. Some pictured the stars as ignited clouds, or coals, but Anaximander represents them as appearing at apertures in invisible fiery wheels. Some theories of diseases invoked elemental ingredients in the body (though there was disagreement about what they were); others, primary opposites such as hot, cold, wet, dry, sweet, bitter; while yet others referred to the humors. But there, too, there was no agreement as to which the important ones were and how many of them there were. Were they pathogens, the causes of diseases, or their effects? Or were they, rather, natural ingredients in the body, even the elementary constituents of which the body is composed? Other theories of disease referred to imbalances not between opposed elements but between opposed states, such as those of "repletion" and "depletion."

Second, it is not as if the new wise men were all advancing their ideas in a spirit of dispassionate and disinterested inquiry. We should not underestimate the extent to which the rival theories proposed were put forward by their authors in a bid at self-advertisement, to gain prestige. The early philosophers and medical writers did, to be sure, engage in some empirical investigations. But the idiosyncrasies and the extravagance of some of their theories in part reflect the need to impress their audience. The egotism with which many of these writers proclaim their own new and superior theories betrays the rivalry for prestige that existed between them. One striking case is the author of the treatise *On Regimen* (written probably in the early 4th century B.C.E.). His theory is that health depends on a balance between food and exercise, to be analyzed in terms of the interaction between two primary elements in the body, fire and water. But the way he commends this view is as a brand-new discovery, *exeurēma*. This is "a fine thing for me the discoverer and useful too for those who have learnt it. For none of my predecessors attempted to understand it, though I judge it to be in every respect of great importance."

The third reason relates to the degree of penetration of scientific ideas into popular beliefs. How far, we may now ask, did the work of the scientists change the beliefs and attitudes of other men and women? The philosophers and medical writers often deploy a concept of nature that implies that explanations are, in principle, available for every kind of phenomena. There may be events that are "against nature" in the sense that they are exceptions to the general rule: they will then need explanations in terms of other, natural factors. But nothing is "against nature" in the sense of standing outside nature, for that is a domain that, by definition, encompasses *every* kind of phenomena. If some members of the literate elite thereby expressed their conviction that the natural is explicable, how far were their beliefs shared by others who were not themselves engaged in attempting naturalistic explanations?

As already observed, the question can hardly be given a determinate answer, but certain indications point to the limitations of the influence of the naturalizing of the world among Greeks in general, whether in the classical or the Hellenistic period. We may take three examples to explore the question: eclipses, dreams, and diseases.

Two references to eclipses of the sun in early lyric poetry suggest the astonishment and wonder that they occasioned. In the 7th century B.C.E. Archilochus wrote (74): "There is nothing in the world that is unexpected, nothing to be sworn impossible, nothing marvellous, now that Zeus the father of the Olympians has made night from noon and hidden the light of the shining sun so that bitter fear came on humans." Whether or not Archilochus would have endorsed the idea that Zeus himself was directly responsible, there is no reason to doubt his reference to the consternation caused among ordinary people. Similarly in the mid-5th century Pindar addresses the sun in *Paean* X: "Star supreme, hidden in daytime: why have you made helpless the power of men and the way of wisdom, rushing forth on a dark track? Do you bring some new and strange disaster?"

By the time Pindar, at least, was writing, it is likely that the main elements of a correct explanation of solar eclipses were available from natural philosophy. It is true that the story of the prediction of a solar eclipse by Thales as early as 585 B.C.E. was much embroidered in late sources. Our earliest information comes from Herodotus (I.74), and he merely states that Thales predicted this to within a year and gives no indication of how he did so. Certainly in the sequence of Presocratic natural philosophers that runs through Anaximander, Anaximenes, Xenophanes, Alcmaeon, and Heraclitus, the ambition to provide some causal account is evident. Heraclitus, for instance, is reported to have held that eclipses of the sun and moon occur when "their bowls are turned inwards" (Diogenes Laertius IX.10).

But the first step toward a correct appreciation of the causes of lunar eclipses comes with the recognition that the moon derives its light from the sun, mentioned perhaps by Parmenides and explicitly attributed to Anaxagoras by Plato. Later reports have it that Anaxagoras appreciated both that the cause of a lunar eclipse is the intervention of the earth's shadow and that the cause of a solar eclipse is the intervention of the moon. By Aristotle's time he was so far convinced that the earth is the cause of lunar eclipses that he appealed to the shape of the shadow it casts as supporting his argument that the earth itself is spherical.

But just how far any such explanations were accepted is another matter. Thucydides (II.28) notes that a solar eclipse can occur only at the new moon, and he uses a word in this connection, *dokei,* that can either imply that this is just an opinion or (more probably in this context) that it is generally agreed. However, the famous story of the consternation caused by an eclipse of the moon during the retreat of the Athenian army from Syracuse indicates that not everyone accepted that such an event had straightforward natural causes—whatever the scientists might say. Nicias orders the army to stay in place (VII.50), and this evokes the following comments from Plutarch *(Life of Nicias* 23): "the obscuring of the sun towards the end of the month was already understood by common folk as being caused somehow by the moon. But what it was that the moon encountered and how, at the full, it should suddenly lose its light . . . this was not easy to comprehend." Noting that Anaxagoras had already provided the explanation, Plutarch comments that he was no ancient authority, nor was his account well regarded. Whatever the general Nicias himself believed and whether or not he deserved the label "superstitious" attached to him, it is clear that he thought it necessary to respond to the event. Whether or not all the soldiers under his command would have taken an eclipse as an unnatural and inexplicable event, we cannot, of course, tell. But Nicias evidently thought the chances that their confidence would be seriously undermined were sufficiently great to dictate the adoption of a policy which, on military grounds alone, was quite unwarranted.

Far more clearly, the widespread assumption about dreams was that they may foretell the future. Homer had already distinguished dreams that come through the Gate of Horn—that give true signs—from those through the Gate of Ivory—that do not (*Odyssey* 19.560ff), and later writers who specialized in dream interpretation generally recognized that not all dreams provide useful indications of the future. Here the bid to attempt naturalistic explanations of the phenomena was far less effective than it was in such a case as that of eclipses. Some of the doctors treated dreams as indications of physical disturbances in the body, and many thought it possible to use them in the diagnosis of particular diseases. *On Regimen* IV, for instance, associates dreams in which a star behaves anomalously with excessive excretions of moisture and phlegm in the body. But if the star appears pure and bright and moves eastward, that is a good sign. Aristotle, too, thought of dreams as *daimonia* (divine) but only because nature herself is. Yet he, too, is prepared to maintain that dreams provide indications of the movements in the body transmitted to the soul.

Some of the naturalistic explanations of the causes of dreams thus preserved the idea of their predictive character. But for many, no doubt, the basis of the assumption that dreams are predictive was more straightforwardly the belief that they were sent by the gods, even though the message they conveyed often needed careful decoding.

This becomes apparent if we turn to the third topic mentioned above, namely diseases. As has been noted, there were some doctors who insisted that all diseases are natural, all have natural causes, even that all can, in principle, be cured by natural remedies. Yet from the classical period to late antiquity there were plenty of Greeks who believed that there was much more to health, disease, and cure than just straightforward physical causes and effects. The cults of healing gods and heroes, preeminently that of Asclepius, grew rapidly from some time around the middle of the fifth century B.C.E. Their success can be judged from the imposing shrines devoted to such cults, at Epidaurus, Cos, Pergamum, and many other centers.

What is particularly remarkable is that these cults grew in popularity at the very time that rationalistic Hippocratic medicine too was developing, that is, for the one hundred fifty years or so from the mid-5th century onward. Whatever other doctors or philosophers may have thought of the claim in such works as *On the Sacred Disease,* that all diseases are natural, that claim, so far as we can tell, made little or no difference to the popularity of the notion that divine intervention could produce a cure. The practitioners of temple medicine, far from being abashed by Hippocratic naturalism, ignored it and indeed went from strength to strength. Nor was it just humble or ill-educated folk who hoped that Asclepius would help them but also some members of the literate elite. In the 2nd century C.E. the distinguished orator Aelius Aristides records in great detail his own ailments and the cures he ascribes to Asclepius.

Much of the detail of the procedures used by the practitioners of temple medicine is obscure. But we have the evidence from inscriptions found at Epidaurus that suggests that Asclepius was asked for help over a wide variety of cases, ranging from injuries from wounds to acute diseases and including nonmedical misfortunes such as losing a child or a treasure. It is striking that in marked contrast to the records of case histories in the Hippocratic *Epidemics,* where failures are often acknowledged, the inscriptions at the shrines of Asclepius claim 100 percent success. Often patients were instructed to spend the night in the shrine—a practice known as incubation. They would there be expected to have a dream in which the god appeared to them and either gave them advice on therapy or actually cured them while they slept. If the former, the dream would be interpreted by the temple staff and, if the advice was followed and the god duly recompensed with payment, cure would follow. The god is often represented as proceeding in ways very similar to those used by other Greek healers, applying salves, prescribing drugs, even intervening surgically. But the great difference—for the faithful—was of course that merely human practitioners are fallible, the god infallible.

It is clear from the parody of temple medicine in Aristophanes' *Ploutos* that some Greeks were well aware that some who practiced in the shrines of Asclepius were charlatans exploiting the gullibility of the faithful. Yet the fact that the shrines continued to flourish down to the 2nd century C.E. and beyond is testimony enough to their ongoing popularity.

The naturalization of the world, as it may be called, was, then, in no sense a matter of a total victory over traditional beliefs and assumptions. On the one hand, there were plenty of learned writers, philosophers, "sophists," and doctors who insisted, on general grounds, that the domain of nature encompassed *all* physical phenomena. Yet their chief point of weakness consisted in the obvious difficulty they encountered, over a wide variety of topics to do with common as well as rare events, to give anything like a convincing causal explanation. They might well insist that in principle one could be given, but that was easy to represent as just a pious hope until such time as they could deliver a convincing account. In some cases, to be sure, that was possible, and achieved. Eclipses are one such topic. Again the doctrine that the earth is spherical is one that Aristotle was able to prove with a battery of arguments, some based on good observational evidence (the shape of the earth's shadow in a lunar eclipse, the differences in the configurations of the constellations at differing latitudes). At the same time, over many problematic phenomena Greek science was and remained at a loss to offer convincing theories, and this is a matter not just of their not seeming convincing to us but also of their not achieving a consensus among the learned themselves.

On the other hand, there were many ordinary people whose notion of "nature" was a good deal looser than the concept invoked by the philosophers. To be sure, characterizing the domain of the natural as the domain of what is regular, familiar, predictable, became familiar enough. Yet there was a good deal of uncertainty about what precisely that comprised and a fair degree of readiness to accept that there were *exceptions*—not just exceptions to the general rule that were nevertheless explicable in terms of other natural chains of causes and effects, but exceptions that fell completely outside the domain of nature as such. On this looser view of nature, the ordinary was contrasted with the extraordinary: the gods could do what they liked, and the fates of humans were in the hands of divine forces beyond mere mortal comprehension.

The mismatch between what some of the learned claimed and what most people accepted is an ongoing feature of the Hellenistic, as of the classical, period. Of course more knowledge of the natural world and of particular features of it came to be available, some readily accessible to large numbers of people, some still the province of specialists. The advances in such areas as geography, technology, physics, biology, and medicine are rehearsed in subsequent chapters. Geographical knowledge certainly expanded in the Hellenistic period, in part as a result of the conquests of Alexander. Those conquests also gave a greater sense of the unity of the inhabited world, even though contrasts between Greeks and barbarians were still vividly apprehended. With the development of cartography came the idea of producing not just an impressionistic map of the world but one framed by determinate coordinates. Although technological progress was slow, technical control in some areas, at least, increased—in agriculture, in shipbuilding and navigation, in military technology.

Developments in astronomy, especially, led to a greater appreciation of the tiny dimensions of the earth by comparison with the sphere of the fixed stars as a whole—a point to which Aristotle had already drawn attention. For the astronomers, although no single model to explain the movements of the sun, moon, and planets was *entirely* satisfactory, such theories were accepted as providing an adequate general framework for the understanding of those movements, for example of their main periodicities, and they often gave good approximate results for the movements of the heavenly bodies both in longitude and latitude. In the 2nd century B.C.E. Hipparchus was led to discover the precession of the equinoxes, the slow retrograde motion of the equinoctial points in relation to the fixed stars. Yet as has been remarked, that idea was rejected by most of the learned, let alone by any ordinary people. Nor should we underestimate the extent to which the motivations of the scientists, the astronomers especially, were not just to give good scientific explanations but to demonstrate the beauty of the cosmos, its order, the evidence it yields of a divine benevolent design. Moreover the study of the stars involved not just their own movements but also their possible influences on events on earth, a discipline that could be as learned and elaborate as astronomical model building itself.

Greek science eventually opened up a vision of the world that was in sharp contrast with what had passed as common sense in the archaic and early classical periods. The earth was spherical, not flat, and tiny in relation to the universe. While most continued to believe that it was at the center, some denied that, and Aristarchus suggested that the sun was. The inhabited world could be charted using the methods of cartography the mathematicians developed. Causal explanations of many strange phenomena were in principle possible, even earthquakes, thunder, and lightning. The kinds of animals and plants could be classified and analyzed; the anatomy of the human body came to be well understood and so, too, many of its physiological processes. The courses of many diseases were studied even if no effective cures for most of the acute conditions were available.

What we are accustomed to think of, with the benefits of hindsight, as the achievements of Greek science were considerable, and their impact on the attitudes of those engaged in the investigation of nature was profound. Although the difficulties of the task were often stressed, the possibility of understanding was held out as a splendid goal, and the investigation of nature was even considered to be one of the supreme activities that a human could engage in. Those who maintained that the cosmos manifests design and providentiality especially spoke of its study sometimes as an act of piety, the way to a true appreciation of the divine, even though that notion of the divine stood in sharp contrast to most traditional ideas.

Yet the number of people who had even a smattering of knowledge of these intellectual developments was always, in every generation, tiny. There was no educational nor institutional framework ensuring the widespread diffusion of the findings of the scientists, nor even guaranteeing their transmission. The opportunities for study offered at Plato's Academy, at Aristotle's Lyceum, at the Museum and Library in Ptolemaic Alexandria, were always limited to a privileged few. For most, the key feature of their attitude toward the world they lived in was not the sense of humans as part of an investigable nature, but rather the more traditional image of humans defined by contrast with personal, and often willful, gods.

GEOFFREY E. R. LLOYD

Bibliography

Cornford, Francis M. *Principium Sapientiae*. Cambridge: Cambridge University Press, 1952.

Furley, David J. *Cosmic Problems*. Cambridge: Cambridge University Press, 1989.

————. *The Greek Cosmologists*, vol. 1. Cambridge: Cambridge University Press, 1987.

Guthrie, W. K. C. *A History of Greek Philosophy*. 6 vols. Cambridge: Cambridge University Press, 1962–1981.

Jaeger, Werner. *The Theology of the Early Greek Philosophers*. Trans. Edward S. Robinson. Oxford: Clarendon Press, 1947.

Kirk, G. S., J. E. Raven, and Malcolm Schofield. *The Presocratic Philosophers*, 2nd ed. Cambridge: Cambridge University Press, 1983.

Koyré, Alexandre. *From the Closed World to the Infinite Universe*. Baltimore: Johns Hopkins University Press, 1968.

Lloyd, Geoffrey E. R. *Methods and Problems in Greek Science*. Cambridge: Cambridge University Press, 1991.

Sambursky, S. *The Physical World of the Greeks*. Trans. Merton Dagut. London: Routledge & Kegan Paul, 1956.

———. *The Physical World of Late Antiquity*. London: Routledge & Kegan Paul, 1962.

Vernant, Jean-Pierre. *Myth and Thought among the Greeks*. London: Routledge & Kegan Paul, 1983.

Vidal-Naquet, Pierre. *The Black Hunter: Forms of Thought and Forms of Society in the Greek World*. Trans. Andrew Szegedy-Maszak. Baltimore: Johns Hopkins University Press, 1986.

Vlastos, Gregory. *Plato's Universe*. Oxford: Clarendon Press, 1975.

Related Articles

Astronomy; Geography; Cosmology; Theories of Religion

MYTH AND KNOWLEDGE

Going as far back as we can in ancient Greece, we find that human knowledge, both practical and theoretical, originated with the gods. All the efforts made over the centuries to ground knowledge firmly in observation and to confirm it by experimentation never severed that link; indeed, by the end of antiquity it had grown stronger.

MYTH

In ancient Greece, up to Plato's time, the word *sophia* could be assigned any meaning at all, since it was not tied to any particular content in the physical world. To be *sophos* meant to be master of one's own actions, to have control over oneself and others; hence, carpenters, ship captains, doctors, political leaders, seers, and poets, in particular, could all be called *sophoi*. Those who possessed this sort of knowledge traced it back to the god who had inspired it or revealed its secret. Thus all knowledge came, in one way or another, from a god, whether it was the common knowledge shared by all members of a community or the particular knowledge of a given technical skill.

Since Plato viewed poets as imitators, judging that in their compositions they represented all sorts of activities as if they themselves were the instigators, he called Homer the "teacher" of Greece, the supreme authority in the area of virtue, law, and even technology (*Republic* X.606e–607a). In granting such importance to Homer, however, Plato's intention was to denounce his harmful influence on education. Nevertheless, for most Greeks of the classical period, Homer and all other poets were considered agents for transmitting the knowledge that Greeks shared about what they viewed as their past or what they recognized as their values.

Besides giving the poets inspiration, and granting them continued poetic skill, the Muses occasionally provided help with particular performances. The description of Demodocus in the *Odyssey* shows that the poet was constantly guided by divine inspiration: "'And summon the divine minstrel, Demodocus; for to him above all others has the god granted skill in song, to give delight in whatever way his spirit prompts him to sing'" (*Odyssey* VIII.42–45). The Muse also inspires Demodocus directly at certain moments: "But when they had put from them the desire for food and drink, then to Demodocus said resourceful Odysseus: 'Demodocus, truly above all mortal men do I praise you, whether it was the Muse, daughter of Zeus, that taught you, or Apollo' . . .

and the minstrel, moved by the god, began, and let his song be heard" (*Odyssey* VIII.487–489, 499–500). Whether constant or exceptional, the assistance the poets sought could be represented as dependence on a source outside of human consciousness. It operates on two levels, cognitive and pragmatic: the Muse grants the bard both knowledge related to what he is going to say and authority over the audience he is to address.

In his invocations to the Muses, the daughters of Zeus and Mnemosyne (Memory), Homer sought the revelation of information. Thus, in the invocation that opens the catalogue of ships, he asks: "Tell me now, you Muses who have dwellings on Olympus—for you are goddesses and are present and know all things, but we hear only a rumor and know nothing—who were the leaders and lords of the Danaans" (*Iliad*, II.485–490). The urgency of his plea is clear. In the 266 verses that follow, the poet describes twenty-nine fleets, giving the geographic origin of each and the name of its commander.

While Homer asks the Muses to grant him knowledge of the past, knowledge that he contrasts with ignorance, Hesiod, in *Theogony*, regards the Muses as authorities in matters of truth and falsehood, for they allow access to true knowledge and avoidance of false knowledge. Pindar, too, claims that the Muses have granted him special knowledge, as they did Ibycus and Bacchylides. Even more than Hesiod, Pindar insists on the truth of this knowledge, for he is deeply aware that poetry (*Olympian Odes, Nemean Odes*) can also convey falsehood.

Whatever its connection with truth, the knowledge the Muses dispensed to poets derives from Memory (*Theogony*). This explains why Mnemosyne is often considered the mother of the Muses. Even in the *Iliad*, the Muses are connected with memory; thus we know the belief is an ancient one. What is the nature of the memory involved in poetry? Some see it as a gift of prophecy. This is true for Plato, but not for Hesiod or Homer; for them, it is not the bard who sees the events of the past but the Muses, who transmit their knowledge to him and thus do not grant him the gift of seeing directly what he relates. What do the Muses see? In an oral culture like the one the *Iliad* and the *Odyssey* describe, and to which the ancient poets remain faithful, memory serves above all to immortalize the glory of the most distinguished members of a group of people. The poet's task is to transmit those aspects of its past that a group of people has decided to commemorate; in other words, it is in a work of poetry that a society reveals itself to itself.

From a technical standpoint, memory is also the instrument the poet uses to compose the poem he sings. In the framework of the epic, the poet has to keep in mind a vast system of formulas and word groups that he uses to construct large sections of his work. In this light, inspiration is no longer incompatible with the techniques used by poets, as it was for Plato; in fact, it provides the raw material for the poet's technical skill. Viewed narrowly as a method of communication that requires perfect mastery, the poet's knowledge appears to be a specialized skill, just as knowledge is specialized for seers, legislators, political leaders, and *demiourgoi* (craftsmen) in general.

For Greeks generally, the three Moirai (personifications of *moira*, the amount of life accorded to every human being), the daughters of Zeus and Themis (Cosmic Justice), rule the life of every mortal from birth to death. The sisters, Clotho, Lachesis, and Atropos, divide this responsibility among themselves, spinning, winding, and cutting the fragile thread of an individual life. Although the supreme god, Zeus, possesses comprehensive knowledge of the future, he cannot change the course of destiny. The fact that the past, the present, and the future are inexorably fixed by fate makes it possible for the seer to practice his art, but he depends on the goodwill of the gods.

Seers, prophets, sibyls, and oracles constantly intervene in Greek religious life; this explains the exalted position the oracle at Delphi held in the ancient world. Moreover, the terms that distinguished an omen from an observation were numerous and instructive, since they eventually served to constitute the vocabulary of diverse realms of knowledge. Any divinatory sign could be called *semeion*, literally the "sign"; its interpretation required that the seer or his assistants, exegetes or prophets, possess both knowledge and skill.

Whether Apollonian oracles were involved or not, consultation of the gods followed rules developed in an earlier age that gave the practice of divination a certain overall uniformity and efficacy. Originally Apollo produced his oracles at Delphi only once a year, but over time he adopted a monthly schedule, though some believe that his consultations were suspended during the winter months, when the god abandoned his people. Questions could be asked by a community, a city, or an individual. Strict rules of purification were required as a precondition: no one could appear before the god without first being cleansed of all faults. Often the responses of the Pythia had to be explained by interpreters.

This divinatory knowledge, bearing on the future, the present, and the past of a group or an individual, was quite naturally linked with the knowledge possessed by both legislators and politicians. The organization of the life of a society through the establishment of a code of law, its ongoing management through decisions affecting the future in one way or another, and knowledge of the past, which could account for particular disasters, were regarded as so important and so delicate that they were always seen in ancient Greece as requiring the guarantee of divine intervention.

One entire mythic tradition holds that the exercise of justice is consistent with certain forms of divination, especially with incubation. King Minos, who consulted with Zeus every nine years in a cavern on Mount Ida, where the god had raised him, is a perfect example: considered the first to have civilized Crete, he is thought to have reigned with justice and goodness and to have passed excellent laws. Moreover, similarities between political power and the various forms of divination are numerous: at Thebes (Pausanias IX.26, 3) and at Sparta (Herodotus VI.57), the royal houses carefully guarded the oracles, for they played an important role in the affairs of state. Even after the king had yielded his position and relinquished power to bureaucratic officials, it remained customary to turn to the divinatory process on occasion. According to one tradition, various forms of political power and certain judicial customs are based largely on knowledge that is mantic in nature.

The lives of individuals and groups are punctuated by crises that challenge the normal order of things. In times of crisis, it becomes necessary to call on "specialists" who are able, if not to solve the problem, at least to identify and understand it. In the area of religion, the role of private initiative is clearly linked to the state of the society that developed around the 6th and 5th centuries B.C.E. The Mysteries were voluntary, personal, and secret initiation rites aimed at reforming the spirit through a religious experience.

The Mysteries are a form of personal religion that depends on an individual decision and aims at obtaining spiritual well-being through intimacy with the divine. Nevertheless, this deeper quest for the hereafter must not make us neglect the seemingly more humble aspects of religious life. A different form of personal religion, an elementary, widespread, and down-to-earth practice, must have constituted the background for the Mysteries: the making of vows. People who are sick, in danger, or in need, and, conversely, people who achieve a certain wealth, make promises to the gods and honor them by offering gifts. This phenomenon is so common that it is rarely discussed in depth. The practice of making vows can be seen as a major strategy for human beings confronted with an uncertain or hostile future.

There seem to have been at least three major forms of organization in the practice of the Mysteries: a clergy attached to the sanctuaries (Eleusis, Samothrace); an association of initiates belonging to a cult; and itinerant individuals, practitioners or charismatic figures. The latter category takes shape in myth with Melampus, Calchas, and Mopsus; in classical antiquity it is represented by Empedocles, and in late antiquity, by Apollonius of Tyana or Alexander of Abonuteichos.

In ancient Greece, even artisanal knowledge is viewed as a divine gift and is always linked in some way to a god. This connection, which is not of a didactic nature, works on several levels. First, the origin of a particular skill is located in a god who becomes a prototype, the originator of a certain technique—metallurgy or pottery, for example. Then this god comes to be regarded as the guardian of the secrets of a group of specialists who wish to maintain the exclusivity of the processes they use, such as the metallurgists who worship the Telchines at Rhodes, or the Cabiri at Lemnos. Finally, the effectiveness of the techniques has to be assured. During the firing, the potter invokes Athena. He asks her to "raise her hand over the kiln." The goddess indicates the precise moment when the contents are fired to perfection, when the glaze is most brilliant. She intervenes by chasing away from the kiln a host of demons with descriptive names: the Breaker, the Cracker, the Burster.

Hephaestus and Athena remain the most typical divinities of this sort. In the *Iliad*, Hephaestus appears first as a cupbearer of the gods, as a master of metals and talismans, and especially as a master of fire, the element with which he is most closely identified.

Hephaestus definitely has mastery of fire, but only of one particular type. His is the technical fire used by artisans, not hearth fire, which belongs to Hestia, or celestial fire, Zeus's lightning. In fact, Hephaestus is master only of the fire used by metalsmiths. Fire for baking clay is reserved to Prometheus, probably by virtue of the fact that he is a "Titan," a name derived from *titanos*, quicklime, a mixture of earth and fire (Aristotle, *Meteorology* IV.11.389a28). Moreover, Hephaestus worked only in noble metals, such as gold, silver, bronze, and brass. The fire used to make everyday tools belongs to the Dactyls (the Fingers), also called Akmon (the Anvil), Damnameneus (the Hammer), and Kelmis (Cast Iron). In fact, the Dactyls of Mount Ida in Phrygia, where the use of iron is very ancient, are credited with inventing metallurgy. For the Dactyls, as for Hephaestus, metallurgy and magic are inseparable. Hephaestus is also associated with other figures who combine metallurgy and magic: the Telchines, the demons of Rhodes (associated with seals), and the Cabiri, originally from Lemnos (identified with crabs).

Hence, Hephaestus appears as the god of the alloy par excellence. As a metallurgist, he can make chains and break them. But his action is above all magical, and he usually binds his victims with intangible chains: notably Hera, whom he immobilizes on a throne (Plato, *Republic* II.378d), and Ares and Aphrodite, whom he traps in an invisible net after surprising them in an act of adultery (*Odyssey* VIII). If he has the ability to tie them up, he can also untie them. He frees his own mother, a deed that allows her to return to Olympus. But Hephaestus is most celebrated for giving movement, and thus a certain freedom, to beings who are in principle immobile. Hephaestus has at his disposition two servants of gold who work in his shop like living beings: he has bellows in his forge that blow without his help, and he also makes self-moving tripods (*Iliad* XVIII).

Associated with Hephaestus or on her own, Athena occupies a central place among the gods of technology. She has numerous aspects: she is a warrior goddess armed with a sword and Zeus's shield, a protectress of carpenters, a mistress of harness and yoke, and a ship's pilot; she is the patroness of weavers and potters and the inventor of the plough. Wherever Athena intervenes, she demonstrates qualities of manual dexterity and practical intelligence that she inherited from her mother, Metis, the wife whom Zeus devoured in order to absorb her substance. Athena, mistress and protector of craftsmen, is usually seen as a serene and familiar divinity, though she does not tolerate competition. Thus the imprudent Arachne sees her too-perfect work torn up by the goddess, and she herself is transformed into a spider (Ovid, *Metamorphoses* VI).

Besides these two great gods of technology, the pantheon of Greek mythology includes a series of heroes known for their remarkable dexterity, like Odysseus, and those who are granted the title of "first inventor," such as Epeius, Palamedes, or Daedalus. Each of these mortals distinguishes himself at least as much by his intellectual qualities as by his practical skill. In the case of Daedalus, for example, prototype of the artist and the artisan, his genealogy clearly shows the dual aspect of the perfect craftsman.

DETOUR THROUGH REASON

The 6th century B.C.E. saw a number of attacks directed against religious beliefs and the practice of magic in the name of speculative thought, which was based principally on concepts of "nature" and "causality," and which tended to emphasize observation.

For doctors and certain other specialists, "nature" *(physis)* implied an inherently consistent relationship between cause and effect. Therefore they denied any more or less transcendent intervention of divine or "supernatural" forces that would disrupt the regularity of that connection. Invocation of the gods was replaced by observation, which led to the discovery of the connection between cause and effect, and by rudimentary experiments that were able to confirm the reliability of that connection.

In Ionia, people speculated about "nature" in an effort to account for the way things were and to describe the entire process by which the world, humankind, and society were constituted, without reference to the traditional gods.

With the exception of Gorgias, who ironically attacked Zeno and thus Parmenides in *On Nature (Peri physeos)*, the Sophists did not leave complete written texts, and their thought seems to concentrate on language and human institutions. However, using a new technique they called rhetoric, they vied with the poets for the honor of transmitting universal knowledge: the word "sophist" is derived from *sophos*, clever or wise. Traveling from town to town, often charging a high price for their teaching, which was closely tied to their technique, these new masters of discourse sometimes enjoyed a considerable success that can be explained by the political ambitions motivating some of their students. Among these masters were Protagoras, Gorgias, Prodicus of Ceos, and Hippias: Plato describes the latter (in *Lesser Hippias*) as representing the highest ideal of encyclopedic knowledge, knowledge that is the equivalent of art and has nothing to do with the gods. In ancient Greece, the term *tekhne* (art) designated a level of skill distinguished from that of the nonspecialist by a consistency that depended on the codification of rules based on cause and effect, a skill whose product could be evaluated rationally.

Paralleling these attempts at universal understanding, a few specific areas of knowledge developed and vaunted their autonomy. They relied on elaborate reasoning oriented toward observation, and they occasionally introduced techniques of verification.

The position of the author of *On the Sacred Disease* (late 5th century) is a good illustration of the change in attitude that was occurring at the time in ancient Greece. On the one hand, he uses an argumentative method that would be codified later, first by Aristotle and then by the Stoics. On the other hand, he is convinced that "nature" implies a certain consistency between cause and effect that can be discerned by observation and "confirmed" by verification, and he denies any divine intervention that might upset the relationship. Like everything natural, illnesses have causes that the physician must discover if he wants to cure them. This attitude came to be shared by most of the authors of the *Hippocratic Corpus*.

Dissection seems to have been practiced as early as the 5th century, perhaps starting with Alcmaeon. Some of the authors of the *Hippocratic Corpus*, and, later, Aristotle, attest to its use. However, it did not become widespread, or provide interesting results, until Herophilus and Erasistratus (3rd century B.C.E.) set out to establish fundamental distinctions between the nerves and other tissues and among different types of nerves. The history of dissection shows how an empirical technique came to be applied successfully to anatomical and physiological problems. Two obstacles slowed this evolution: repugnance (Aristotle, *Parts of Animals* 645a.28ff) and the fact that a successful dissection required not only patience, meticulous care, and manual dexterity, but also and above all a clear notion of what to look for.

We should not forget that Greek science and philosophy developed in a world where the vestiges of traditional thinking had not entirely disappeared. For example, long after the 5th century, temple medicine and the influence of healers and purifiers prospered and actually expanded. Moreover, two aspects helped to reconcile "rational" medicine and temple medicine. The priests used medications, dietary prescriptions, and phlebotomy. Certain "rationalist" doctors, for their part, used some of the same terms that also appeared in religious contexts, for example, "purification."

The gathering and recording of information about the known parts of the inhabited world constituted a research field that was explored from a very early date. Anaximander is credited with making the first map in ancient Greece. However, it was Hecataeus of Miletus who really began the tradition that continued with Herodotus and Thucydides, and ended with Hipparchus, Posidonius, Strabo, and Ptolemy. Many of these writers describe the origin of everything, including the gods, as beginning in chaos.

Herodotus goes so far as to formulate grounds for differentiating his accounts from those of the poets. He bases the validity of his own discourse on two criteria: what he observes personally, in which case he speaks of *opsis* (sight) and *gnome* (thought, intelligence) (II.99l), and what he has learned from selected informers, which he calls *historia*. He uses this term, which suggests the questioning of eyewitnesses, even when his informants are relying entirely on an oral tradition. Thucydides is more demanding when it comes to choosing his sources, but he still does not completely separate *opsis* and *akoe* (hearing) (I.20–22). He considers undoubted only those events that he has seen for himself and those his contemporaries have witnessed, provided that their reports withstand his close scrutiny; he regards facts he has learned by hearsay as unreliable if, lacking a qualified informant, he has been unable to question the source directly. However, this does not stop him from viewing Minos as a historical figure (I.4).

Before Plato, Greek mathematics remained a heterogeneous field, according to the sparse information found in Euclid's *Elements,* a text compiled two centuries later. There are four broad areas of primary interest: (1) the theory of numbers: the division of numbers into odd and even, the study of some elementary propositions related to this division, the classification of "figured" numbers, and the generation of these numbers with the help of *gnomon*; (2) metric geometry, chiefly concerned with the resolution of problems of measurement, such as calculating the area of flat surfaces; (3) nonmetric geometry, represented mainly by several works on three major problems: squaring the circle, trisecting the angle, and duplicating the cube; (4) the application of mathematics to music theory.

The practice of mathematics seems to have had a decisive influence on methods of argumentation, by allowing the development of notions of hypothesis and proof, on the one hand, and by stimulating interest about the problem of fundamental principles, on the other. We may go even further, and suggest that the use of mathematics in the areas of music and astronomy raises the following question: how can the physical world be understood and even changed with the help of mathematics that are not at all physical? In addition, astronomy presented a surprising feature: the possibility of transforming apparent irregularities, smaller in scale than sublunary ones, into perfect regularities with the aid of mathematics, the pinnacle of science; this possibility could be considered the manifestation of the divine in the physical world.

Astronomy is of particular interest as the intersection between theory, implying the use of mathematics (geometry in particular), and observation. This type of research was just beginning in the 5th century with Meton and Euctemon. However, it was not until the appearance of Eudoxus, who attended Plato's Academy, that a general solution was found to the problem of the movement of the planets. This solution, involving the theory of concentric spheres, was later picked up and modified by Callippus and by Aristotle.

The epicyclic model used by Hipparchus to explain the movement of the sun and the moon, a model later adapted by Ptolemy, represents the best example of a theory combining mathematical rigor with serious empirical observation. In any case, Ptolemy shows more confidence in the mathematical aspect of his theory than in its empirical basis. The difficulty of making exact observations, the unreliability of instruments, the lack of universal units of measurement, and the absence of a practical numerical system are not enough to account for such an attitude. In both astronomy and dissection, observations served to illustrate and support theories rather than to test them.

Moreover, the author of the *Epinomis* (Philip of Opus, probably), who takes the origins of astronomy back to the observation of the sky by the Egyptians, Babylonians, and Syrians, attests to the fact that the motivations of scholars were complex when astrology and astronomy converged. For most researchers, studying the stars allowed them not only to forecast the movements of celestial bodies but also to predict events on earth.

RETURN TO MYTH

The strength of Greek science resides basically in its formal techniques, both dialectic and demonstrative; the Greeks put tremendous energy into developing an axiomatic system and using mathematics as a privileged tool to understand natural phenomena. They also made important contributions to the empirical method, both in research and in practical application; history and geography were the first fields for which the collection of data was careful and thorough, although this practice soon extended to include medicine.

However, the method was not without weaknesses. The search for certainty within an axiomatic system using mathematical language sometimes entailed an absence of empirical content. Further, "witnesses" and "experiments" were more often used to corroborate a theory than to test it. In short, it seems likely that it was competitive debate, agon, that finally provided the framework in which natural science would develop in ancient Greece.

This competitive debate on the intellectual level made the appearance and development of new areas of knowledge possible in ancient Greece, and in turn had the effect of encouraging a radical rethinking of poetic discourse. Up to that point, only the positive aspect of poetry had been considered. But as soon as a poet ceased to meet the expectations of the public, which was passionate about proof, critics concentrated on the negative side of his work, which became grounds for censure. The poet was no longer perceived as an unreliable teacher but as a deceitful and immoral trickster.

In most of the developing areas of knowledge, scholars felt no need to rely on mythology, unlike the historians and especially the philosophers, whose attitudes regarding myths were marked by a pronounced ambivalence: to appropriate mythology for their own use they invented new myths or reinterpreted the old ones.

No philosopher was as radical as Plato, who flatly condemned traditional myths, refusing any type of allegorical interpretation. Paradoxically, however, the roots of Plato's philosophical thought grew out of myths, although not always the traditional ones. For example, the doctrine of Forms is based on recollection, which, in *Meno*, is explicitly related to religious belief. And whenever Plato speaks of the soul, he must make use of myth and create new eschatological myths, those at the end of *Gorgias* and *The Republic*, and those in *Phaedrus* and *Laws*. Finally, Plato goes back to myth when he seeks to evoke the origin of the universe, humankind, and society, as he does in *Timaeus* and *Critias*.

Unlike Plato, most philosophers and historians tried to "save" traditional myths, hoping to discover beneath their literal meaning, which they found morally shocking and scientifically ridiculous, a deeper meaning conforming to the latest doctrines of morality, psychology, and even physics. Overall, it was a matter of translating into philosophical terms the most important or unusual elements of mythology. This type of exegesis was called by many names over the course of centuries, including "allegory"; we still use the names today for purely practical reasons whenever greater precision is not called for.

After flourishing in the 6th century B.C.E., the interpretation of myth, though widely practiced during Plato and Aristotle's time, reached its fullest flowering with the Stoics. They practiced not only moral interpretation (relating divinities to virtues), psychological interpretation (relating divinities to mental faculties), and physical interpretation (relating divinities to elements or to natural phenomena), but also historical interpretation. The latter was inspired by Euhemerus, for whom gods and heroes were human beings deified because of their important services to humankind.

The attitude of the Stoics with regard to mythology was challenged by the Epicureans and those who belonged to the New Academy. These groups mocked the Stoics' habit of reducing the gods to common and trivial material objects, or to mere mortals, and they denounced the tendency to turn the ancient poets into pseudo-historians or pseudo-philosophers.

But, starting around the 1st century B.C.E., a new exegetic movement developed that would respond to this objection by combining myths and Mysteries, according to one line of reasoning. The myths and Mysteries are complementary means used by a god to reveal truth to religious souls. Mythology envelops divine revelation in written legends, while the Mysteries present it in the form of living tableaux. Henceforth, in this context, wherever religion, philosophy, and poetry are found together, the poet is seen as an initiate to whom truth has been revealed, and he passes it on in a way that makes it accessible only to the few who are worthy to receive it. This is why he uses coded and ambiguous discourse, and why he introduces a realm of secrecy where everything is explained by enigmas and symbols, as in the Mysteries. The poet is no longer an unwitting philosopher but a theologian who does his best to convey, cautiously, the truth he has attained directly through philosophy.

This conviction would be shared by the Neoplatonists of the 5th and 6th centuries C.E., who went to great lengths to establish a link between Platonic doctrine, which they considered a "theology," and all other theologies, Greek and barbarian alike. With them, the circle was closed. Mythology, like philosophy in general and Plato's in particular, conveyed a single truth that had to be sought in Plato, Homer, Orpheus, and the Chaldean Oracles, a truth that was inseparable from the supernatural and the practice of certain forms of magic.

The swing of the pendulum described above illustrates the power and limits of reason. Reason is a marvelous instrument for deducing a great number of propositions from a limited number of axioms. But since these axioms are arbitrary and not based on reason, reason remains dependent on premises and values that are foreign to it. Hence the constant tendency, in the Greek world, to attribute the origin of all human knowledge, both theoretical and practical, to the gods.

Luc Brisson
Translated by Elizabeth Rawlings and Jeannine Pucci

Bibliography

Texts and Translations

Homer. *The Iliad.* Trans. A. T. Murray, rev. William F. Wyatt. Loeb Classical Library.
———. *The Odyssey.* Trans. A. T. Murray, rev. George E. Dimock. Loeb Classical Library.

Studies

Brisson, Luc. *Introduction à la philosophie du mythe, I: Sauver les mythes.* Paris: Vrin, 1996.
———. "Mythes, écriture, philosophie." In *La naissance de la raison en Grèce.* Ed. Jean-François Mattéi. Paris: Presses Universitaires de France, 1990. Pp. 49–58.
———. *Plato the Myth Maker.* Trans. and ed. Gerard Naddaf. Chicago: University of Chicago Press, 1999.
Brisson, Luc, and F. Walter Meyerstein. *Puissance et limites de la raison.* Paris: Les Belles Lettres, 1995.

Detienne, Marcel. *The Masters of Truth in Archaic Greece.* Trans. Janet Lloyd. New York: Zone Books, 1996.

Lloyd, Geoffrey E. R. *Magic, Reason, and Experience: Studies in the Origin and Development of Greek Science.* Cambridge: Cambridge University Press, 1979.

Related Articles

Images of the World; Physics; History

THE QUESTION OF BEING

THE GREAT INTELLECTUAL ADVENTURE that is Greek philosophy may be regarded, on a somewhat simplistic view, as structured around three basic questions, occurring historically in the following order: What is the world made of? or What *is* there?; What should we do?; How can we know? These may be seen as lying behind what were later distinguished (perhaps first, in a formal way, by Plato's pupil Xenocrates) as the three main divisions of Greek philosophy, physics, ethics, and logic.

I am here concerned only with the first and most basic question, since that constitutes the inquiry about being. Before beginning a historical survey, it would be well to attempt a definition of the concept with which we are concerned. In the context of Greek thought, then, "being" (often characterized by the additional qualification "real" or "true") denotes some single, permanent, unchanging, fundamental reality, to which is habitually opposed the inconstant flux and variety of visible things. This reality is initially seen simply as a sort of substratum out of which the multiplicity of appearances may evolve, but progressively there come to be added to it other features, such as absolute unity (or, conversely, infinite multiplicity), eternity (ultimately timelessness), incorporeality (or, conversely, basic corporeality), and rationality (or, conversely, blind necessity). In short, "being" (*on*, or *orousia*) becomes in Greek philosophy the repository of all the concepts that can be thought up to characterize the idealized opposite of what we see around us—its counterpart, which comprises all aspects of the everyday physical world, being termed "becoming" *(genesis)*.

PREHISTORY OF THE CONCEPT

As was natural, the question of being was first posed in its most simple form. The first impulse that led, in early 6th-century Miletus, toward what we in retrospect regard as distinctively philosophical (as well as scientific) inquiry was the question raised by Thales: "What is the one single constituent of all that we see about us?" The two salient features of this first philosophical question were (1) that it was assumed that things were not as they *seemed* (that is to say, a conscious wedge is driven between appearance and reality); and (2) that it was assumed that there was *one* and *only one* thing that things really were (or came from).

It has been pointed out often enough now to be more or less universally agreed that to a large extent Thales' thinking was conditioned by previous Greek mythological thinking, such as that of Hesiod in particular (specifically his concept of Chaos, and of the separation of entities out of it), and perhaps also by his (albeit superficial) acquaintance with Egyptian mythology (and specifically its notion of all things arising out of a kind of primeval Nile), and this gives a distinctive slant to his speculations that conditioned the direction of Greek thought ever afterward. But it can also be argued that, once one has set oneself to think about the basic constituent of things, the idea of one single original substance seems more or less to impose itself logically.

One might well object, admittedly, that there seems no absolute reason in logic why the original substances should not be two, or four, or indeed any number, but the Milesian answer would have to be that, if you postulate more than one, you also have to explain on what principle they enter into combination to produce the world, and then that agent of combination becomes the real first principle. It remains true that, not long afterward, the Pythagoreans appear to have postulated an opposed pair of principles, and then, with Empedocles, we find the concept of a quartet of "root" substances, along with a pair of opposed structuring forces, but in either case, as we shall see, there are complications. In the case of the Pythagoreans, the One or Monad, as active principle, could be seen as the true first principle, the Indefinite Dyad, or Multiplicity, being taken as a kind of matter; and even with Empedocles, Love and Strife could be taken as two poles of single cosmogonic process.

But to return to Thales: he, too, after he has fastened on a candidate for his original substance (the fact that he chose water for this—a plausible enough choice—is not of great importance for our present discussion), is left with some considerable problems, which we have no idea how he faced (though we do get some idea how they were faced by his immediate successors, Anaximander and Anaximenes). First of all, it is by no means clear whether Thales meant to claim simply that all things, by one means or another, derived once upon a time from water, or (more radically, and more interestingly for our purposes) whether in some way all things are now basically composed of water, and can be viewed as water *in a certain mode or state*. In either case, his problem is to explain the mechanism or agency by which this development took place—or is constantly taking place. That is the problem with a single first principle. One avoids the problem facing dualists, or advocates of a multiplicity of principles, of explaining what brings their two (or more) principles together, but one is left with the problem of explaining why any development should take place at all.

This is what Aristotle is getting at when he condemns the early physicists for concerning themselves only with, in his terms, the *material cause,* and neglecting the efficient cause, or beginning of motion. He discerns the lack of an explanation of the process of change, either from what once was to what now is, or from what *really is* (true being) to what appears. His complaint may be somewhat anachronistic, but he draws attention to a serious problem that faced Thales and his immediate successors, and which Thales himself seems hardly to have addressed at all.

It does seem to have been addressed, however, by his successor Anaximander, if we can deduce that from the conclusions to which he came. Anaximander first of all rejected water (and presumably all other existing elements—though we do not know that a canon of four had yet been established) as a suitable first principle, and chose instead something he termed the Indefinite or Unlimited *(apeiron)*. The problem was, presumably, to explain why, if one chose to privilege a substance like water, one should arrive at a situation where some of the original water has changed into other things, and some of it has remained water—unless the original water was somehow different from what we know as water, and in that case one might as well call it something else—which is essentially what Anaximander does.

The other advance that may be credited to Anaximander is the recognition and naming of the *process* whereby the original substance differentiates itself, and transforms itself into the variety of visible things. He envisaged this as a sort of eddy, or "whirl" *(dinē)*, as in the water of a river, which causes a process of sorting out to take place.

This in turn, however, produces a difficulty, which may well have led his successor Anaximenes to retreat from the bold concept of "the Unlimited," and to propose air as his candidate for the original substance. Anaximander, after all, does not make clear what there is in the Unlimited that is available to be sorted out. Is the Unlimited to be thought of as a truly distinct original substance, or as a sort of cosmic soup in which the elements or "seeds" of all existent things, or at least of the main cosmic substances, are held in solution? If the latter, then there is no great problem about postulating a suitable motion that will tend to sort them out, but then the original substance becomes no more than an amalgam of all existing substances, and the "whirl" becomes the true first principle (as indeed it does later, as Mind, in the more sophisticated system of Anaxagoras, in the mid-5th century). If one chooses the former alternative, however, one is left at a loss to explain just what it is that is going to sort itself out, since the concept of sorting involves some inherent basis for differentiation (e.g., of lighter and heavier particles).

But we should not dwell too long on the Milesian physicists. We are here, after all, only in the prehistory of the concept of Being. It is not clear, that is to say, that the Milesians were concerned to postulate a contrast between appearance and reality, or that they were in search of anything like a permanent substratum beneath the illusory flux of everyday things. They seem to have been concerned simply with *origins*, and with the mechanism of change. This was, of course, not an insignificant intellectual achievement, but it would require a "paradigm shift" (to use the term of the philosopher of science Thomas Kuhn) before we get to the more philosophically productive question of what the real substance of the world *now* is, or what is the true mechanism or process that holds it together as a world.

APPROACHES TO BEING

This significant advance is made toward the end of the 6th century by the philosopher Heraclitus of Ephesus, another town in Asia Minor not far from Miletus. First, however, let us dwell a moment on that interesting figure Xenophanes of Colophon, an older contemporary of Heraclitus, since he seems to be the first to make a reasonably clear distinction between the mode of cognition necessary to comprehend (true) being, and the mode that is normal among men for acquainting themselves with the physical universe. A famous utterance of his runs: "Certain truth has no man seen, nor will there ever be a man who knows about the gods and about everything of which I speak; for even if he should fully succeed in saying what is true, even so he himself does not know it, but over all things there is wrought opinion [doxa]."

Admittedly, Xenophanes is profoundly pessimistic as to the capacity of the human mind ever to attain knowledge of reality (and as such his utterance became in later times a charter document for skepticism), but the important thing for our present purpose is that he presents the opposition between two levels of cognition, the first of which he does not name—using only parts of the verb *know (oida)*—but the second of which he terms *doxa*, opinion, a term that was taken up later by Plato. This serves to remind us that with the question of being there is intimately bound up the question of knowledge.

Heraclitus expresses contempt for Xenophanes, as he does for all of his predecessors and contemporaries, but he is perhaps to some extent indebted to him for the distinction just mentioned. It is with Heraclitus that the issue of true reality and our cognition of it first present themselves clearly in Greek thought. Later doxographers, most misleadingly, linked Heraclitus to the Milesians as a thinker who tried to fix on a single original substance for the world—in his case, fire—but it is just in this postulation of fire and its role in Heraclitus's system that the great difference with his predecessors becomes apparent. For Heraclitus is not interested in the derivation of the world from an original substance; he is concerned with the real organizing principle of the world as it is now (and as it always has been).

Like Xenophanes, Heraclitus has a poor opinion of the capacity of humanity in general for grasping the truth ("The knowledge of the most famous of men is but opinion," frg. 28; "Human nature has no insight, but divine nature has it," frg. 78), but unlike him, he feels that he himself has grasped it. For Heraclitus attained a vision of how the world works, of what it is that makes it a world *(kosmos)*, in the sense of an ordered whole. The secret, the key factor, is what he terms *logos*. The precise meaning of this, its relation to the element of fire, and the role it plays in his philosophy, has been the subject of much debate. Here I am simply concerned to emphasize the way in which Heraclitus presents us with a deeper layer of reality underlying the flux of appearances. The real being of the world is manifested in what he terms "the turnings of fire," a cosmic tension of opposites that keeps the totality of things in existence. It is both a substance and a process, but it constitutes the reality with which the illusory appearances believed in by the ordinary man are contrasted.

Apart from Heraclitus, the other important contributors to the creation of a concept of true being, in the sense of a structure that holds the world together, are the Pythagoreans (I use the collective term, instead of speaking of Pythagoras as an individual, as it is by no means certain to whom the various features of early Pythagoreanism are to be credited). I mentioned the Pythagoreans earlier as having proposed a pair of opposite principles, "unity" and "indefinite duality," as the operative elements in the universe. What I want to emphasize now is that, like Heraclitus but much more emphatically, they proposed a mathematical model of the universe according to which it is by the action of unity, or the principle of odd number, on duality, or even number, that everything else in the world comes to be, and that the true structure of all existents may be expressed as a series of mathematical formulas. Number thus constitutes a sort of skeletal reality underlying, and holding together, the disparate flux of appearances. Admittedly, the Pythagoreans seem to have pursued this insight in a rather simpleminded way, but we are rather poorly informed on their true doctrine by reason of their habit of secrecy. At any rate, they bequeathed to Plato, as we shall see, the stimulus to a very sophisticated view of the nature of reality.

THE ESTABLISHMENT OF THE CONCEPT: PARMENIDES AND ANAXAGORAS

Heraclitus had identified the true structure of the world as a creative tension of opposites, controlled by rationality and mathematical proportion (both meanings of *logos*). The next step was to be taken by a remarkable figure from the west of the Greek world, Parmenides of Elea (in southern Italy), and it is with him that the concept of being comes fully to fruition. Indeed, on the question of being Parmenides set guidelines to which all later philosophy had to react in one way or another. In the process of defining being, and of devising logical arguments to establish its necessity, it is arguable that he, and not Thales, becomes the father of philosophy as we understand it.

Parmenides declares, famously, in fragment 8 of what survives of his poem, that Being is one, motionless, uniform, and eternal. Not-Being is utterly unthinkable—an incoherent concept. And the belief of the general mass of mortals that things come to be and change and move and perish is condemned as illusory (frgs. 2, 6). The vexed question, however, ever since he made these rather Delphic pronouncements, is what exactly was he talking about?

His position seems to make the best sense if the subject of his notorious *esti* (is) is taken to be "everything that exists" — or, rather, if his existential verb is given no subject at all, just because its subject is so general. In fact, Parmenides seems to have been struck, in a way in which no one before him had been, by the remarkable fact that *there is something rather than nothing*. It is the contradictory of this that he declares, quite reasonably, to be "a track utterly impenetrable" (frg. 2). If one takes the true subject of his inquiry as being the sum total of existence, then, I think, his whole argument becomes entirely rational and persuasive, instead of being the collection of perverse paradoxes that Aristotle, and later philosophers in general, would have us believe it to be. What Parmenides condemns as the error of popular belief is the notion that something can come to be out of nothing, or perish into nothing, and that existence *as a whole* can experience motion or change, or be more existent in one place and less in another. He is not, in the first part of his great poem, concerned to deny that individuals can move from place to place, or grow old and die, or that myriad changes take place in the physical world. He is simply concerned with the totality of what exists, and as such his analysis of the characteristics logically appertaining to it is entirely sound.

That said, there are two aspects of his doctrine of Being over which controversy persists; they should be mentioned here because they become essential features of Being in the tradition stemming from Plato. These are eternity and incorporeality. As regards the former, it is certain that Parmenides at least endowed his Being with what was only much later recognized as "sempiternity," that is, unending temporal succession (he declares that it "always is," and never was nor will be, frg. 8), but it is not quite clear whether he arrived at the concept of a truly atemporal eternity. Similarly, it is by no means clear that he ever arrived at a distinction between the corporeal and the incorporeal (even though his follower Melissus certainly declared that Being had no body, frg. 9). A key statement in frg. 8 (ll. 42–44) is worth quoting, since it illustrates the complexities of his position: "And since there is a last limit, it is completed on all sides, like the bulk of a well-rounded ball, equal in every way from the middle."

Here we find Being apparently described both as having limits and possibly also as being in some sense corporeal (much controversy surrounds the precise sense of its being "like the bulk of a well-rounded ball"). As regards the former characteristic, it must be pointed out that being "completed on all sides" does not imply, for Parmenides, that there is anything outside Being that would bound it; he simply wants to assert that it is not infinite (another question on which Melissus differed from him), since this was essential in his mind to its being an ordered whole. The assertion that it is at least analogous to a sphere may most charitably be interpreted in the same sense, to indicate that there is no beginning or end to it, nor any variation in its density; it can be seen, perhaps, as a primitive forerunner of the theory of the curvature of space. But neither of these assertions encourages one to believe that Parmenides had developed a clear notion of either infinity or incorporeality. It is certainly interesting, as noted above, that his follower Melissus of Samos makes both these assertions about his version of Parmenidean reality, but it is not quite certain, on the evidence presented to us (Aristotle is particularly contemptuous of Melissus), that he appreciated the full significance of his own assertions. At least, however, he may be said to have adumbrated certain further developments in the concept of Being.

The second part of Parmenides' poem (of which much less, unfortunately, is preserved than the first) concerned the physical world of birth, change, movement, and decay that mortals believe in, and the relation of this account to the "truth" uttered by the Goddess in the poem's first part has given rise to much speculation, and much misunderstanding. Parmenides, speaking through the Goddess, gives no account of how the appearances of this world relate to the realm of true Being. If anything, the implication is that they do not. The Goddess, at the end of frg. 8, simply says: "Here I cease for you my trustworthy account and thought about the truth. Henceforward learn mortal opinions, listening to the deceitful arrangement of my words." She then goes on to set out quite a comprehensive Milesian-style cosmogony, though with two opposite principles, in the Pythagorean manner, Fire and Night. This leaves it quite unclear what the status of this world is and what relation Being may have to it—a problem that Plato later set himself to working out.

The explanation for this seems to be that Parmenides was not in fact interested in cosmogony. Being, for him, is no sort of creative principle. It is something of quite another sort, and it is that that in modern times Martin Heidegger has seen more clearly, perhaps, than anyone else. What Parmenides is concerned with is rather the *ground* of all existence: why there is something rather than nothing, to borrow the later formulation of Leibniz, and, given that there is, what must be its essential characteristics. When he shifts from a discussion of that to a description of the physical world, the transition is like the shifting of a camera's focus, switching from the general background to the details of the foreground. In the foreground are the mass of existents *(Seiende)*; in the background is Being itself *(Sein)*. There is no question of *deriving* the former from the latter; that is not Parmenides' concern. He did, however, as I say, leave it as a puzzle to later thinkers (who, indeed, seem largely to have misunderstood what he was about) what the relation of the two could be.

This was by no means the only problem that he bequeathed to his successors. On the question of the infinity of real being there continued to be the difficulty that, to the Greek mind, what is infinite cannot be knowable, in the sense of being able to give an account *(logos)* of something; knowledge seemed to be possible only in the case of what is finite and thus is possessed of a structure that is at least notionally comprehensible. On the one hand, both for Parmenides and for later thinkers, Being must be comprehensive, in that there can be nothing external to it, but on the other hand it must be comprehensible by the mind, so that it cannot be devoid of limit. This is very probably the consideration that led Parmenides to characterize it, rather oddly, as "a well-rounded sphere."

This requirement becomes more acute still when, as a consequence of the speculations of Anaxagoras (who is himself reacting to the challenges laid down by Parmenides), the supreme principle of reality is declared to be itself a mind, since this mind must first of all comprehend itself, and this it cannot properly do if it is infinite. Anaxagoras himself does not seem, however, to have drawn this conclusion, as he is attested (frg. 12) to have declared Mind (nous), which is for him the first principle of all creation, to be apeiron, and he plainly means that in all of its possible senses: it is infinite or indefinite in extent (frg. 14), since it extends as far as matter does, and that is composed of an infinite amount of particles; it is infinite in time, since it exists forever (frg. 14); and it is internally indefinite (the other meaning of apeiron), since it is declared to be homogeneous, "all alike" (frg. 12). He also offended against both Parmenidean and the later concept of true Being by presenting it as beginning its work of creation at a point in time (frg. 12), though it then continues forever.

Anaxagoras, however, despite the importance of his contribution to later thought on this subject, was primarily interested not in the nature of his first principle in itself, as was Parmenides, but rather in what Parmenides was not interested in, which is the way in which the first principle generates everything else. This leads him, perhaps, to commit certain incoherences that he might not otherwise have committed. His assertion of the infinity of Mind is motivated by his concern that there should be nowhere where the particles of matter are to be found from which it should be absent, and it seemed to him necessary that the particles should be infinite in number, and therefore in extent. Mind, however, is entirely unlike the particles of matter, "mixed with no other thing" (frg. 12), and it is this that enables it, in Anaxagoras's view, to initiate and control the whole cosmogonic process.

Mind, therefore, becomes in effect the antithesis of body, though Anaxagoras does not explicitly declare it to be incorporeal (he speaks of it only as being "the finest and purest of all things," and as being unmixed with any other thing). The conclusion is almost inevitable, however, that that is what it is, even though he may not have developed the terminology with which to express this. Mind is also conscious and intelligent, though it is not quite clear that it is self-conscious; its primary activity and raison d'être is to initiate and supervise the circular motion that creates the cosmos, not to think about itself. That, perhaps, makes it easier for Anaxagoras to permit it to be infinite.

Anaxagoras deserves great credit (and indeed received it from later ancient thinkers) for clearly separating the moving cause of the universe from the material one, and for identifying that cause as a mind, but he was also criticized by Plato (in *Phaedo* 97bff), and after him by Aristotle (*Met.* 985a18), for not, in their view, making proper use of Mind once he had postulated it. Plato makes Socrates complain of his disappointment, after coming upon the book of Anaxagoras and becoming excited by the discovery of the concept of a mind as the initiatory element in the universe, then to find that Anaxagoras seemed to make no further use of this Mind for the rational direction of the universe toward some good end.

This seems at first sight somewhat unfair, since Anaxagoras (in frg. 12) does speak of Mind as not only setting everything in motion but also keeping it in motion, but what Plato really feels the lack of is a teleological explanation of the world, and here he seems to be justified. Aristotle speaks equally strongly. Anaxagoras, he says, "uses Mind as a mechanical device for world-making. When he is at a loss for the reason why something necessarily is, then he drags it in, but elsewhere he explains events by everything rather than Mind."

Anaxagoras, then, does bequeath to later Greek thought the immensely important concept of intellectuality as a component of true Being, and explicitly connects this first principle with the production of the phenomenal world, as Parmenides was not concerned to do; but he still leaves a good deal of unfinished business for Plato and his successors. Apart from the issue of teleology, the fact that Anaxagoras's concern seems not to have been primarily with the nature of the first principle in itself meant that issues such as infinity (and thus self-knowledge) and immutability (he sees no difficulty in declaring that Mind began to set all things in motion after an indefinite period of inactivity) do not occur to him as problems.

There is one other philosophical tradition that concerned itself with the nature of true Being during this period, and that is that of the Atomists, Leucippus and Democritus. They too responded in their way to the challenge of Parmenides, but they did so by fragmenting reality into an infinite quantity of individual, irreducible realities, which they termed *atoma*, "unsplittables," circulating randomly in the void (the existence of which they also postulated) and forming themselves into combinations of ever greater complexity.

Thus just before the time of Plato, we have a radical challenge laid down to the teleological view of the world, but also to most of the characteristics of Being established by Parmenides. Instead of an absolute unity, we are presented with a Being that is infinitely many; instead of absolute motionlessness, incessant, random motion; and instead of absolute uniformity, a large (though not infinite) variety of shapes and sizes. At the same time, though, Being (that is, each individual atom) is ungenerated and imperishable, unchangeable, incapable of being added to or subtracted from, homogeneous, finite, and a plenum, continuous and indivisible.

For Democritus, only atoms and the void are "real"; all else, everything appearing to the senses, is mere "appearance" (frg. 9). He does not, however, present this contrast in the same spirit in which Parmenides presented it. The physical world is only "appearance" in that it is *really* made up of atoms, and combinations of atoms, and void; it is not to be dismissed for that reason as beneath contempt. In fact, Democritus took a good deal of trouble to explain how physical objects, and the world as a whole, might have arisen. From our perspective, however, what is important about the Atomist worldview is that it presents us, very starkly, with the concept of an ultimate reality that possesses all the characteristics that had come to be seen as proper to such a reality *except* the element of purposiveness or rationality. The world develops quite at random, though according to a sort of necessity (viz. that of the survival of combinations of atoms that "work," and of the dissolution of those that fail to do so); mind, in the Atomist universe, as in the contemporary scientific one, is an "emergent" phenomenon (arising first at the level of man), not an originating and directive one. This was the feature of atomism that Plato took as a fundamental challenge, making Democritus the éminence grise behind the teleology of *Timaeus,* for example, and of Book X of *Laws.*

The Atomist view of reality was to be revived after an interval, in the ancient world, by Epicurus, and was to have an enormous influence on the modern worldview, but in the short term it met with the determined opposition of both Plato and Aristotle and their followers.

THE FULL FLOWERING: PLATO, ARISTOTLE, AND THE OLD ACADEMY

A concept of Being, then, has by the last quarter of the 5th century B.C.E., by virtue of a series of progressive or contrasted (but always logically connected) steps, become pretty firmly established in Greek thought. It remained for Plato, and then Aristotle, to bring it to fruition.

The chief philosophical influences on Plato, apart from his reverence for the personality and ethical teaching of Socrates, were Parmenides, Anaxagoras, and, above all, the Pythagorean tradition. We have already seen that, in contrast to the Milesian tradition, the Pythagoreans postulated the interaction of two opposite principles in the generation of the universe. For Plato, however, their most important insight was the mathematicization of reality.

The initial stimulus, so far as we can see, that drove Plato to the formulation of his distinctive philosophy was a desire to provide a metaphysical underpinning for the intuition of Socrates that there were objective realities underlying the basic terms of ethics and aesthetics, in such a way that these terms did not simply represent subjective impressions or arbitrary conventions. It seems, however, that although Socrates argued for an objective reality corresponding to such terms as *justice, courage,* or *beauty,* he had not arrived at any very definite notion as to what status these entities might have, or whether they constituted a system or "world" quite separate from our physical one. Plato therefore seems to have set out on an intellectual quest, after Socrates' death, for a metaphysical framework that would enable him to give a satisfactory account of these entities, and such others, as the objects of mathematical reasoning.

A first source of inspiration was undoubtedly Parmenides, but the uncompromising unity and uniformity of his concept of Being, as well as the lack of any explicit connection between it and the world of illusion in which we operate as human beings, and indeed the lack of any degree of reality accorded to this world, constituted a discouragement. In the course of his travels in the 390s, however, Plato came into contact in southern Italy with the Pythagorean tradition in the person of Archytas of Tarentum, and this gave a new and productive turn to his thought.

We do not have a clear idea of what the most advanced state of Pythagorean thinking may have been about the formal composition of bodies (relying as we do on the rather dismissive reports of Aristotle and others dependent on him), but it seems that, while they thought of physical objects, and even concepts such as justice or equality, as essentially mathematical formulas, they regarded the formulas as being inherent in the objects, and not as transcendent.

This interested Plato, but it did not satisfy him. In thinking over the Pythagorean system, it occurred to him to combine it with that of Parmenides (who was himself, after all, according to tradition, a pupil of the Pythagorean Ameinias) and postulate an articulated world of Forms, possessing all the features of Parmenidean Being (except, necessarily, absolute unity, since the Forms are many), but which also act as paradigms, and in some way causes, of the ever-changing multiplicity of physical individuals.

The realm of true Being is given by Plato not only an internal structure but also an essential role in the creation and ordering of the physical world. Here Anaxagoras, too, comes into the picture, because it is an essential feature of Plato's world of true Being that it is governed by Intellect, and that it is indeed itself an intellect. The true state of affairs in this connection is rendered somewhat obscure by Plato's devious methods of exposition (though these caused much less trouble to his own followers than they do to modern scholars). In his dialogue *Timaeus,* he appears to present us with a scenario involving a creator-god modeling a physical world (at a point in time) on the basis of his contemplation of an independently existent world of Forms. This world of Forms is described as an "eternal living being" and as an object of intellection *(noēton),* but not as an intellect *(nous).* Plato's own immediate followers in the Academy, Speusippus and Xenocrates, maintained (in response to the criticisms of Aristotle, who persisted in taking the account presented in the dialogue in a literal sense) that Plato presented this creationist scenario only "for educational purposes," even as one would present the construction of a geometrical figure step by step, and that in reality we are dealing with a supreme intellect, whose contents are the Forms and which causes these Forms to be projected, in the form of geometrical figures made up of combinations of basic triangles, onto what Plato calls "the Receptacle" *(hupodochē)* or "spatial extension" *(chōra),* a sort of "field of force," consisting of empty three-dimensionality, which nonetheless has a distorting and disruptive effect on the geometrical emanations of the Forms as they are projected into it.

This is the interpretation that remained traditional in the Platonist tradition from the period of the Old Academy on (with the exception of the 1st-century C.E. Platonist Plutarch, who, however, presents a dualist interpretation of the dialogue that no one would accept today), and on which later Platonist theology and metaphysics are based. Modern scholars have been confused by the fact that Plato's dissident pupil Aristotle criticizes his master on the basis of a literal interpretation, but the best explanation of this is that Aristotle is taking a polemical stance and behaving disingenuously, as he was quite capable of doing. Indeed, at one point *(Met. I.6),* he seems to give the game away by accusing Plato of neglecting the *efficient* cause of things (in terms of Aristotle's own system of causes) and recognizing only the formal and the material causes, which he could not possibly have accused him of had he taken the creator-god of *Timaeus* seriously.

Even, however, if we accept the consequences of a nonliteral interpretation of *Timaeus,* we are still left with problems regarding the coordination of the metaphysical scheme presented there with that appearing in other notable passages of Plato, particularly in Book VI of *The Republic* (which is earlier than *Timaeus*) and in the early pages (16–30) of *Philebus,* which may have been composed slightly later but is best regarded as more or less contemporary. In *The Republic* (VI.508–509), we find Plato expounding the concept of a supreme principle, which he terms "the Good" and which he presents as having the same relation to the other contents of the realm of true Being (that is, the Forms) as the sun has to the contents of the physical universe, in the sense that it is the ultimate basis of all value, by virtue of which all other things acquire their "goodness" and even their existence—even as the sun is seen to be the cause not only of the growth and flourishing of natural objects but even of their very existence. This supreme entity, the Good, is described in a famous phrase, the meaning of which is much disputed, as "not being Being, but passing even beyond Being *[epekeina tēs ousias]* in dignity and power," on the ground that it is postulated as the cause of being to all other things, and thus must itself be in some way "above" or "beyond" this.

In later times, certainly, this was seen as an utterance of great importance, as introducing for the first time the concept of an entity or force superior even to Being, which in some way or other fulfills the role of its cause, or ultimate ground. Whatever Plato may have meant to convey by it (and it seems to me inevitable that he meant something like this), this statement becomes the foundation for a whole metaphysics of "hyper-reality" in later Platonism. Our immediate problem, however, is to decide how it is to be related to such other Platonic entities as the creator-god of *Timaeus* and the Intellect that is the "cause of the mixture" of Limit and Unlimitedness in *Philebus*. This latter deserves some discussion in the present context, because it seems to introduce into the realm of Being for the first time a degree of articulation that is new and unfamiliar. Admittedly, in a famous passage of *Sophist* (248Eff), which is a somewhat earlier dialogue, Plato makes the Eleatic Stranger declare that he cannot conceive of true Being as devoid of intellect, life, and movement; and elsewhere in the dialogue he sets out a system of five "greatest kinds," Being itself, Sameness, Otherness, Motion, and Rest, which between them structure the realm of Being and manage the relationships between the individual Forms, which are, indeed, stated to have degrees of participation in one another; but in *Philebus* we find included as part of the realm of true reality the element of Unlimitedness *(apeiria)*, constituting a "negative," but also productive, element in reality, which turns out to be necessary for the generation of anything at all. In *Timaeus* this element is also present, as the so-called Receptacle of what comes to be, but it is not so clearly included as an element of true Being, being set over against the Creator-God and his Paradigm as a sort of refractory substratum that he cannot fully bring to order. Even there, however, it is included among the basic and permanent realities that make up the universe, but in *Philebus* Limit and Unlimitedness are coordinate principles that require proper and harmonious blending by what Plato calls "the cause of their mixture." This entity, later characterized as Intellect, is presented as distinct from, and superior to, the pair of Limit and Unlimitedness, but I think it is better seen as bearing more or less the same relationship to Limit, in particular, as the Creator-God of *Timaeus* has to the world of Forms, being no more than its "executive" aspect, so to speak.

The next question, though, even if one accepts that both *Timaeus* and *Philebus* have to do with a supreme cosmic Intellect, is what relation this entity may have to the Good of *The Republic*. There is no suggestion, after all, that the Good is an intellect, and it is declared to be "above" Being, whereas at least the supreme principle of *Timaeus* is declared unequivocally to be "being" *(on)*. There is no reason, it must be said, that there should be absolute coherence between the two concepts, but one would like to think that they could be accommodated within one broad metaphysical framework. For later Platonists the relationship was not problematic: the Good was the highest god, while the Creator-God of *Timaeus*, despite his demythologization, was seen as a secondary divinity, concerned more immediately with the creation of the physical world than was the Good. This is not a solution, however, that can satisfy us. All these principles must be considered as supreme in their way, and if the Good is described as being "beyond Being," that is perhaps because its transcendence and causal function are being stressed, rather than its permanent existence and rationality. At any rate, this short passage of *The Republic* VI introduced a new element into the Greek concept of the supreme reality, and one that was to have a long history.

Another aspect of the realm of true Being must be noted at this point, and that is the concept of a world-soul, or of soul in general as a force in the universe. The Greek concept of soul denoted originally no more than a life force, and as such it could be claimed that the original substances postulated by the Milesian philosophers, Water, Air, or the Unlimited, were in a sense possessed of soul, since they were initiators of movement in the cosmos. This was never made explicit, however, probably because Thales and his successors assumed the presence of a life force in a way too naive for a later philosopher such as Aristotle to comprehend. The fully developed concept of a world-soul has to wait for Plato, and even with him it does not appear as such before *Timaeus*. In *Phaedo*, however, we are presented with a concept of soul in general as a substance that is immortal and indestructible, and of a nature to be akin to the unchanging world of Forms (78–79). This, then, becomes a further distinct element in the Greek concept of true Being, possessing a set of characteristics making it the opposite of physical body and of a nature to rule over it. This close involvement with body, in distinction from Intellect and the Forms, remains a feature of soul throughout the history of Greek thought from Plato onward. The concept is developed further in a famous passage of *Phaedrus* (245), where soul is characterized as self-motive, and the cause of all motion in the universe, and this is presented as an argument for its immortality. In *Timaeus*, the soul is presented as being fashioned by the Creator-God on the basis of an elaborate formula that enables it, in turn, to cognize every level of the universe and administer the physical part of it. Even if we deconstruct this account of its creation, we are still left with the concept of logical dependence of the soul on Intellect and the world of Forms. This introduces the concept of *levels of reality* into the realm of being in a way that was not there before. Indeed, when one adds on the Good at the top, so to speak, one finds oneself with no less than three levels of reality, such as were fully formalized only much later in the history of Platonism, in the system of Plotinus in the 3rd century C.E.

Last, we have the problem of the status of the physical world, apparently, at least, denied all real existence by Parmenides. Plato is much concerned to define a level of existence for physical objects, inferior, certainly, to the realm of true Being but superior to that of total nonexistence, and also to define a level of cognition appropriate to this. In a remarkable passage in Book V of *The Republic*, he defines the status of the physical world as being intermediate between true Being and absolute nonbeing, and identifies the mode of cognition proper to it as "opinion" (*doxa*—adopting the term first used in a technical sense by Xenophanes). Later, in *Sophist,* with apologies to Parmenides, he isolates a sense of "not-being" that implies not complete nonbeing but only "otherness" from Being, and later again, in *Timaeus,* he presents the physical world as an "image" *(eikon)* of the world of true Being (the articulated sum total of the Forms), existing in time, which he presents as a "moving image" of eternity, the mode of existence of true Being.

Most shadowy and dim of all, but still existent in a sense, is the substratum of the physical world, which he presents in *Timaeus* as, on the one hand, empty space, and thus nonexistent, but also, on the other hand, as having the effect of a distorting mirror, causing an irreducible degree of imperfection and randomness in the projections of the forms that are imposed on it. This is not quite the later (Aristotelian and post-Aristotelian) concept of "matter"—though later thinkers, from Aristotle himself on, had no hesitation in identifying it as such!—since it is not a raw material *out of which* things come to be but only a receptacle *in which* they do.

We should note, in conclusion, an aspect of Plato's doctrine of Being that makes at best a veiled appearance in his dialogues (it can be discerned, for example, behind the Limit and Unlimitedness of *Philebus*), but of which we have fairly reliable information from Aristotle and other, later sources: his postulation of two ultimate principles of reality (borrowed from the Pythagoreans), Unity and Indefinite Duality, and his derivation of all things, beginning with the primary numbers, arranged as a decad, and then the Forms (now viewed as mathematical formulas), from the action of the former on the latter. As I have said, in connection with the Unlimitedness of *Philebus,* the introduction of a quasi-material principle (which comes to be thought of as somehow "female") at the highest level of reality, where it serves as the origin of all differentiation and individuation, is a most significant development in the concept of true Being, recognizing as it does that from a single, unitary first principle nothing else can logically arise without the postulation of some further element, even a passive and subordinate one, that can serve as an instrument, or "conduit," of diversification, and thus of the generation of other entities. Why Plato never chose to set out the details of this doctrine in writing is not entirely clear. He may never have felt entirely comfortable about the level of insight that he had reached regarding the mechanics of the process, even though he was convinced that something like it must be the case. At any rate, he bequeathed this doctrine to his immediate successors, who developed it in various ways.

The full dimensions of the Greek concept of Being are present, then, at least in solution, in the dialogues of Plato. In the works of his immediate successors, however, a good deal of formalization and clarification takes place that had considerable influence on later stages of Greek thought. His nephew Speusippus, first of all, who succeeded Plato as head of the Academy, seems to have pushed the mathematization of reality to new lengths, utilizing as first principles unity and multiplicity—a variant of the indefinite duality postulated by his master—and postulating an elaborate series of levels of reality, first numbers, then geometrical entities, then soul, with the product of the union of unity and multiplicity in each case constituting the first principle of the next level down (a process that attracts the satirical attention of Aristotle, but that has a logic of its own).

Another important contribution of Speusippus was to declare that his first principle, unity, was beyond being, and could not properly even be described as a "good" (an implicit criticism of Plato's characterization of his first principle as such). On the whole, Speusippus, rather than Plato himself, may be seen as the father of later Platonist negative theology.

His successor, Xenocrates, however, conceded to Aristotle that the supreme principle must be an intellect *(nous)*, and thus truly existent (rather than superior to being), but he also described it as a monad, or unity, and recognized opposite to it a dyad, or duality, from the union of which all else derived. Both Speusippus and Xenocrates mathematized the system of Forms, but the details of their innovations are obscure, since Aristotle's reports of them are oversimplified and tendentious. They bear witness, however, to a continued tradition of lively speculation on the nature of being within the Old Academy, the results of which were transmitted to later generations of Platonists.

If we turn next to Aristotle, we find a thinker who is in many respects in revolt against his master, Plato. Nevertheless, in one essential respect, he can be seen to follow his lead. In a famous passage of Plato's *Sophist* (employed by Heidegger, we may note, as a keynote quotation at the beginning of *Being and Time*), the Stranger from Elea addresses himself in these terms to previous theoreticians of Being (244A): "It is clear that you have long been aware of what you mean when you use the expression 'being'; we, however, who used to think we understood it, have now become perplexed." Just before that (243DE), he had posed this question to his imaginary interlocutors: "All you for whom all things *are* the hot and the cold, or some pair of that sort, what is this term that you apply to each of these, when you say that both of them 'are,' and that either of them 'is'?" This decisive question, that of the meaning of being, cannot be posed unless one ceases for a moment to ask "What is *x*?" in order to raise the more basic question "What is it to *be* at all?" The problem is, in a word, to try to determine by virtue of what characteristics one can recognize that something is a being. In a way, Plato is here reversing the procedure of Parmenides, who had sought to fill in what was lacking in the utterance, "If something is a being, then it is . . ."; he is trying to fill in what is lacking in "If something is . . . , then it is a being." A little later (247E), the Stranger proposes, at least on a provisional basis, to take as a mark of being the power to act and be acted on: "I suggest that for anything to have real being, it should be so constituted as to possess some sort of power either to affect something else or to be affected, in however small a degree, by the most insignificant agent, though it be only once." This characteristic mark of being allows him, to a certain degree, to arbitrate the dispute that springs up between the materialists (the "Sons of Earth"), for whom only those things exist that offer some resistance to touch—that is, bodies—and the idealists (the "Friends of the Forms"), for whom the only existent things are immobile and unchanging realities, that is to say, intelligible and incorporeal entities. The former must agree to enlarge the scope of their ontology, to find a place in it for invisible and intangible entities that are nonetheless active, such as the soul and the virtues; while the latter must in turn modify their position, to accommodate the sort of possibility that intelligible realities may experience, which consists in being known by the soul.

This return to the question of the meaning of "being" that Plato had thus provoked was perhaps never pursued with more seriousness, and indeed obstinacy, than by Aristotle (notably in the so-called central books of *Metaphysics*). But one of his fundamental doctrines consists precisely in rejecting the principal presupposition of the question: there is no sense in inquiring into the meaning of "being," because being "is said in many ways"—and even in many times many ways. The principal Aristotelian distinctions are (1) the distinction of "categories" (of any entity, one can state separately that it *is*, that it is *of a certain quality*, that it is *of a certain quantity*, and so on, with the consequence that essences, qualities, quantities, and so on, emerge as separate types of being, irreducible to one another) and (2) the distinction between being in potency and being in act. These become, in the hands of Aristotle, powerful instruments for resolving long-standing problems, and for dissolving the paradoxes in which previous thinkers had become entangled and of which the Sophists had made good use in order to cause further confusion. For example, the distinction between potency and act permits us an intelligible resolution, *pace* Parmenides, of the puzzle of change and generation: what makes a new appearance in the world is no longer condemned to be either an illusion (that which seemed to come into being but was in fact already there) or a miracle (that of a creation ex nihilo); it is, rather, the actualization of that which was already there, but only in potentiality. To take another example, the distinguishing of the categories allows us to understand how a being may change its quality while remaining essentially what it is.

However, the metaphysical tools put in place by Aristotle do give rise to considerable problems for him, such as would exercise a constant influence on all subsequent philosophic speculation. If being is to have a multiplicity of mutually irreducible senses—or, in other words, if being is not a single genus, embracing all types of being as its species—what becomes of the traditional ambition of philosophy to constitute itself as the comprehensive science of being in its totality? Must one not renounce this ambition, and limit oneself to the various departments of science, each confined to the study of a particular class of subject matter, governed by its own principles? Aristotle did nevertheless seek to salvage the legitimacy of a "science of being qua being" by introducing a relationship between the various senses of "being" that respected their irreducibility, while at the same time mitigating their divergence: they all relate to that meaning that is primary among them, the category of *ousia* ("essence" or "substance"—or should one say "being-ness"?) in this sense, for example, that every quality is the quality of an *ousia*, and similarly for all the others. Thus the old question, "What *is* there?" which Aristotle describes as "a subject of investigation and of difficulty for a long time past, and even now—in fact, forever," can be posed in a new form ("What is *ousia*?"), and the reference of the old question back to that of the various senses of being may be reformulated as a referral of the new question to that of the various senses of *ousia* (*Met.* VII.1–2).

One of the most celebrated aspects of Aristotle's response to this question is a negative one: the realities conventionally designated by the terms *universal* and *general* do not fulfill the necessary conditions for being admitted to the rank of *ousia*. In this regard Aristotle stands Platonism on its head: he refuses to posit a world of transcendent Forms, superior to that of physical individuals and more real than it. For him, the primary, and most real, type of substance is that of the physical individual, or rather, on the basis of a deeper level of analysis, the "form" inherent in a particular piece of matter. All other levels of being, such as genera and species, he declared to be "secondary," and less real. At the same time, however, he did not abandon the idea of a supreme, unchanging reality guiding the universe. All he wished to do was to purge the cosmos of the system of transcendent forms and ideal numbers that seemed to him to have been postulated superfluously by Plato and his followers Speusippus and Xenocrates. He himself was quite prepared to recognize what he termed an "Unmoved Mover," a cosmic divine intellect that "thinks itself," being totally absorbed in the contents of its own mind, and that constitutes itself as the prime mover of all creation simply by being an ultimate pole of attraction—an end toward which all things strive after their fashion (beginning with the heavenly bodies, whose eternal revolutions are their attempt to imitate its motionlessness), a ceaseless impulse that keeps everything in being. This intellect is thus a more sophisticated successor of Anaxagoras's Nous, and also, in all probability, of the Good of *The Republic* (significantly, Aristotle uses the comparison with the sun in one important passage, *On the Soul* III.5, where he alludes to his supreme being), and as such it formed the basis for all later speculation as to the nature of the supreme deity down to the time of Plotinus.

Otherwise, though, Aristotle can be seen as reestablishing the *immanence* of Being in the physical world, in stark opposition to the impulse to transcendentalism observable in Plato and his more faithful followers. The contrast can also be seen as one between a mathematical model of the universe and a biological one (Aristotle was an enthusiastic biologist). For him, the world is a complex of individual, primary substances *(ousiai)*, all working toward their own perfect state by reason of natural capacities inherent in them, and together forming a coherent world, held together by a common striving toward a first principle, which he saw as an intellect, motionless and engaged in self-contemplation, but which is a source of movement for all other things, and indeed a source of enlightenment for individual human intellects, which are of the same substance as it.

LATER DEVELOPMENTS OF THE CONCEPT

Aristotle, then, despite his opposition to his master, Plato, and to his former colleagues in the Academy, does not reject teleology, nor is he, properly speaking, a materialist. It is characteristic of Stoicism and Epicureanism, the main philosophical schools of the Hellenistic era (3rd and 2nd centuries B.C.E.), to maintain the principle of the immanence of Being in the world, though they differed radically on the question of teleology. Broadly speaking, the Stoics looked back to Heraclitus and his concept of the *logos*, or principle of vital tension in the universe, though they developed it into a much more comprehensive principle of ineluctable fate (almost like a cosmic computer program working itself out throughout history), while the Epicureans saw themselves as the heirs of the Atomist tradition and rejected any principle of purposiveness or divine guidance in the universe: like the Atomists, their reality was atoms and the void. Both schools, however, united in their opposition to the Platonist concept of a transcendent, immaterial reality—though the Stoic Logos, viewed as "creative fire," emerges as something interestingly akin to the modern concept of energy, as opposed to matter, and does, periodically, exist on its own, in times of cosmic conflagration (when all else dissolves into primordial fire).

The Hellenistic concept of Being (to which Aristotle's own successors in the Peripatos seem to have thoroughly subscribed) was thus uncompromisingly materialistic and this-worldly. Only in the 1st century B.C.E., with the return of the Platonist school from skepticism (which it had adopted from the mid-3rd century on) to dogmatism, and the contemporaneous revival of interest in Pythagoreanism, do we find a reestablishment of the concepts of a transcendent, immaterial order of reality, and of a hierarchy of being. In various Platonists of the first two centuries C.E., such as Plutarch and Numenius (and in the Platonizing Jewish philosopher Philo of Alexandria), we find systems comprising a first principle who is an intellect but also a monad; a "female," dyadic principle serving as the "mother" of all creation; a system of more or less mathematized forms, and a Stoic-style Logos acting as an organizing principle for these; and, last, a world-soul—itself an offshoot of the primordial dyadic principle—that acts as a conduit for the projection of the forms on matter to produce the physical world. This was the prevailing system of reality in the era when Christianity was beginning to take notice of Hellenic philosophy, and it had a profound effect on the development of early Christian metaphysics.

During the 2nd and 3rd centuries, however, a contradiction became apparent in the concept of the first principle of reality as both an intellect and a radical unity—these being, broadly, the bequests of Anaxagoras and of the Pythagorean tradition to Greek thought. Both aspects were held in the highest honor by Greek thinkers, and they wished to surrender neither of them as characteristics of the first principle. However, under the relentless dialectical analysis of the last great original mind of the Greek philosophical tradition, Plotinus, it was intellect that came to be abandoned. Intellection, after all, even self-intellection, could be seen as inevitably involving *two* elements, a thinking subject and an object of thought; even if these were substantially identical, they were nevertheless conceptually distinct. Such a degree of duality came to seem to Plotinus no longer compatible with the role of the first principle as a ground of all unity in the universe, and he took the significant step, which inaugurated the period of Platonism known as Neoplatonism, of declaring the first principle, the One, to be *above Intellect and Being*, these being characteristics of a secondary principle, which he identified as Intellect (Soul, as a separate principle, constituting a third). He saw these two higher principles being distinguished by Plato in the first two hypotheses of the second part of his dialogue *Parmenides*—a work on the true purport of which even to this day no agreement can be reached.

With this radical step of Plotinus's (though one, it must be said, to some extent anticipated by Speusippus) we may end this survey of the Greek concept of Being. From Thales to Plotinus (and beyond) it is characterized by the search for a single adequate ground of all that we see around us, and as such it is one of the most important of Greek contributions to human thought. In all its ramifications and variations, it has played an absolutely fundamental role in the metaphysics of the Western world, no less than in its theological speculation. The question that has consistently underpinned our discussion—that of the relationship, in Greek reflection on Being, between the inquiry into what "really" exists and the question of what it is for any given being to "be" at all—already pervades the composite work that tradition has bequeathed us under the name of the *Metaphysics* of Aristotle: in it are juxtaposed, in a manner that is complex and not without inconsistencies, two conceptions of philosophy, the one of philosophy as the science of superior and primary Being, the other as the science of "being qua being"—that is to say, as the universal science of all being. In later times, the oscillation between these two conceptions will be obscured in some cases by the identification of being qua being with divine Being, while in other cases being is hardened into a scholastic opposition between "general metaphysics," as the science of being in general, and "special metaphysics," as the science of the supreme Being. What may be termed "the modern age" may be seen, in large measure, as being encapsulated by the deconstruction of what Heidegger termed "the onto-theological constitution of metaphysics," stimulated by Nietzsche's denunciation of traditional metaphysics as an "aberrancy of grammar"; "being," in Lacan's words, is no more than an *effet de dire.*" What we seem to have here, in a strange way, is a triumph of the sophistic tradition: even in the process of abandoning the Greeks, we are not leaving them behind.

JOHN DILLON

Bibliography

Aubenque, Pierre. *Le problème de l'être chez Aristotle: Essai sur la problématique aristotélicienne.* Paris: Presses Universitaires de France, 1962.

Aubenque, Pierre, ed. *Concepts et catégories dans la pensée antique.* Paris: Vrin, 1980.

Burkhardt, Hans, and Barry Smith, eds. *Handbook of Metaphysics and Ontology.* 2 vols. Munich: Philosophia Verlag, 1991.

Gilson, Étienne. *L'être et l'essence.* Paris: Vrin, 1948.

Guthrie, W. K. C. *A History of Greek Philosophy.* 6 vols. Cambridge: Cambridge University Press, 1962–1981.

Heidegger, Martin. *Parmenides.* Frankfurt: Klostermann, 1982. Eng. trans. A. Schuwer and R. Rojcewicz. Bloomington: Indiana University Press, 1992.

———. *Sein und Zeit.* Halle, 1927. Eng. trans. J. Macquarrie and E. Robinson, *Being and Time.* Oxford: Blackwell, 1962.

Kahn, Charles. "The Greek Verb 'To Be' and the Concept of Being." In *Foundations of Language.* 1966. Pp. 245–265.

———. *The Verb "Be" in Ancient Greek.* Dordrecht and Boston: Reidel, 1973.

MacIntyre, Alisdair. "Being." In *The Encyclopedia of Philosophy,* vol. 1. Ed. Paul Edwards. New York: Macmillan, 1967. Pp. 272–277.

Owen, G. E. L. "Aristotle on the Snares of Ontology." In *New Essays on Plato and Aristotle.* Ed. Renford Bambrough. London: Routledge, 1965. Pp. 69–95 (repr. in Owen, *Logic, Science and Dialectic: Collected Papers in Greek Philosophy.* London: Duckworth, 1986).

Owens, Joseph. *The Doctrine of Being in the Aristotelian Metaphysics.* Toronto: Pontifical Institute of Mediaeval Studies, 1951.

Reinhardt, Karl. *Parmenides und die Geschichte der griechischen Philosophie.* Bonn: Cohen, 1916.

Robin, Léon. *La pensée grecque et les origines de l'esprit scientifique.* Paris: Albin Michel, 1948.

Related Articles

Cosmology; Physics; Aristotle; Plato; The Academy; Sophists; Logic; Anaxagoras; Parmenides; Plotinus; Platonism

EPISTEMOLOGY

THE INTELLECTUAL ADVENTURE of Greek thought, considered not simply in terms of the extent of the knowledge acquired but also as a reflection on the nature of knowledge—its origin, objects, methods, and limits—gives the impression of a great profusion of ideas, and also of great disorder and countless theoretical rivalries. The Greeks knew a lot of things, some of which they learned from others and some of which they discovered themselves. They opened up what Kant called "the sure path of science" to certain fundamental scientific disciplines, most notably mathematics. They loved the search for truth and the acquisition of truth with a passion, indeed so exuberantly that they sometimes believed, as Aristotle did, that human beings by nature desire knowledge for itself, seeking no benefit beyond the pleasure it brings. They also believed they knew many things—more, to tell the truth, than they actually did know. They were sometimes cruelly mistaken, and they did not always have valid excuses. They often had—or displayed—too much confidence in their own powers: in spite of their dazzling intuitions, their theories of physical change and matter, their cosmogonies and their cosmologies, what they believed about nature and the origin of animal and human life belongs only quite indirectly to the history of scientific truth. Some among them took as science, and even as models for certain types of science, disciplines that we do not hesitate to categorize as pseudo-sciences. They may have succeeded in creating authentic sciences, but they did not reach agreement on the criteria by which authentic knowledge is recognized (indeed, this is still a problem today).

Did they give insufficient thought to the conditions that must be met if one is to be able to say that one knows something? Quite the contrary. The supreme originality of the Greek philosophers and scholars may well lie in the fact that they raised questions of a sort that would be classified today under the heading of epistemology. They succeeded in asking questions that might be called reflexive (What does it actually mean to know?), critical (Can we really know something? And if so, what sort of thing?), methodological (What means are available to us for answering a question?), or transcendental (How must the world be constituted, and how must we ourselves be constituted if we are to know something about the world?).

But here too, the various responses, and even the questions, offer powerful contrasts. The conquering thrust of Greek knowledge stands out against an initial store of a sort of epistemological wistfulness: from the standpoint of divine knowledge, human faculties are severely limited, not to say worthless. In seeking to transgress these limits, in discovering the invisible enveloped in the folds of space and time, humans run the risk of arousing the anger of the gods, who are protective of their own privileges and quick to chastise hubris, proud excess. Does not the most famous of the Greek philosophers, Socrates, owe the essence of his celebrity to the story of the oracle that designated him the wisest of men, a superiority that he himself interpreted as signifying that he was the only one who did not believe he knew what he did not know? But alongside this pessimism, which moreover will never disappear, we note a large number of expressions indicating real epistemological enthusiasm, derived from and reinforced by the fact that reason is increasingly aware of its own powers. This attitude draws confidence from its own successes, and perhaps too, more fundamentally, from the tacitly and almost universally accepted idea that we humans are not in the world (to quote Spinoza) as an empire within an empire, as an island enclosed in representations that constitute a screen between ourselves and the real: quite to the contrary, we are at home in the world, we are an integral part of it, we are made of the same ingredients as everything else in it, so much so that the immediate problem is not one of knowing how we can attain truth in our words and our thought, but rather how we can miss it. The question of the possibility of error will occupy great minds at least up to the time of Plato, who grapples with it repeatedly and laboriously before he finally answers it in *Sophist*.

The contrast between epistemological pessimism and optimism may be seen as the initial matrix of the great debate between skepticism and dogmatism that traverses Greek philosophy—as it does perhaps, subsequently, all philosophy, if it is true that in some sense skepticism, which is originally a spirit of research and critical examination, is identified with philosophy itself, and if it is true that dogmatism, in the ancient sense of the term, is not to be confused with the use of arguments based on authority but signifies, on the contrary, that after a process of reflection, effort, and inquiry, one has succeeded in developing a well-argued and rationally teachable doctrine.

To come to grips with the mass of Greek texts and documents that incorporate reflection on knowing, it is tempting to sort thinkers and even periods into categories, according to a division that would reproduce those of dogmatism and skepticism. Certain philosophers have been particularly sensitive to the successes of knowing, in its various forms: not particularly vulnerable to the assaults and suspicions of skepticism, they are principally interested in the nature of knowledge. They ask questions like the following: What does it mean to know? Are there different types of knowledge, and if so, what are they, and how do they differ? From what other intellectual states is knowledge distinct, and how is it differentiated? What are the structures of scientific thought? Other philosophers, attracted by skepticism or spurred on by the challenge it poses, have wondered instead whether human beings are capable of acquiring knowledge. If the answer is negative, what arguments allow us or compel us to doubt or reject the proposition that humans have such a capacity? What is the nature of the obstacles that oppose it? If the response is affirmative, what means do we have at our disposal to gain access to knowledge, and to assure ourselves that we have achieved it? These two types of problems are not entirely independent of one another. If it is true that knowledge cannot be defined in a completely arbitrary way (a statement such as "He knows that Socrates is a horse, but Socrates is not a horse," for example, would be unacceptable under any circumstances), one can nevertheless develop a more or less restrictive or generous notion of knowledge; moreover, such flexibility is nourished by the richness and suppleness of the Greek terms pertaining to knowing. What one says about the nature of knowledge is obviously linked to what one says about its possibility and its limits. The higher one places the bar of knowledge, the harder it is to cross: one can even place it high enough for it to become impossible to cross, or for it to appear impossible, and often it takes next to nothing for the loftiest of ambitions to tip over into total pessimism. This reversal from pro to con can be avoided, however, either by showing that, at least in certain cases, the bar of knowledge can be crossed, or by challenging the description of knowledge that creates such obstacles and replacing the bar with a different one.

The great questions addressed by the theory of knowledge are thus interrelated, and the theory itself is not autonomous within Greek thought. Only little by little do we encounter works that focus exclusively on providing an epistemological justification of their authors' positive doctrines (the lost *Confirmations* of Democritus may have been the first work of this type), on analyzing the nature of knowledge in general (Plato's *Theaetetus*, which moreover does not achieve an explicit "solution" of the problem) or the structures of scientific knowledge (Aristotle's *Posterior Analytics*). In the Hellenistic period, priority is finally granted, within the general ordering of a system, to works and theories explicitly devoted to the "criterion of truth," such as Epicurus's *Canon* and the Stoic doctrine of impressions *(phantasia)*. One of the factors that worked against the autonomy of the theory of knowledge was unquestionably the idea that there has to be a correspondence between the characteristics of a body of knowledge worthy of the name and the properties that can be required of the real or possible object of that knowledge: a determinate description of knowledge determines a distinction between the types of entities that can be known and those that cannot. Everybody acknowledged in principle that one can know only what is true, and that whoever knows truth, as Plato put it, "touches upon being" (cf. *Theaetetus* 186d–e); there were constant exchanges between the theory of knowledge and what can be called ontology (a word that first appeared in the 17th century). The zones of being were divided up as a function of epistemological cleavages (perceptible versus intelligible); conversely, certain ontological divisions entailed important epistemological implications (being versus becoming, necessary versus contingent, supralunar versus sublunar).

The theory of knowledge was thus in constant relations of action and reaction with the theory of being, as a known or knowable object; it was also in relation with the theory of the soul, as a subject knowing or capable of knowing. If knowledge institutes a relation between the soul and being, it attests first of all, in general, to the affinity or kinship that unites them and that makes possible the institution of this relation, and thus, more particularly, the institution of the resemblance that must exist between the elements and structures of each. The idea that "like knows like" made its appearance very early, and—with a few interesting exceptions—was quite commonly accepted, in various forms. This means not only that the resemblance between the elements of being and the elements of the soul is the objective cause of the possibility of knowledge, but also, conversely, that that very possibility is for us the sign of the resemblance. In other words, the theory of knowledge is a privileged instrument of self-knowledge. Greek thought constantly stressed the importance of such knowledge, but also its difficulty, for the knowledge of the self by the self was not viewed as having the transparent immediacy of a cogito: to know oneself, one must know oneself knowing something, and one must reflect on the conditions of that cognitive experience. The set of relations between levels of being, knowledge, and the soul that have just been outlined could be illustrated by the method Aristotle adopts in his treatise *On the Soul*. His study focuses initially on the objects of the soul's cognitive activities and operations (for example, what is felt and thought); from these objects, it turns toward the activities and operations themselves (the act of feeling, the act of thinking); finally, returning from actuality to potentiality, Aristotle is prepared to define the essence of the faculties of feeling and thinking.

I shall not attempt to offer a systematic historical picture here of the various conceptions of knowledge that were presented and supported by the philosophers and the philosophic schools of Greece: the subject is too rich and too complex to be summed up in a brief panorama. Instead, I shall propose a series of gnoseological sketches, in the form of comparative variations intended to show relationships among a certain number of operations belonging to the domain of knowledge and related areas. I shall not dwell on the quite real differences that distinguish the theories; rather, I should like to stress a few fundamental constants that manifest, from one end of the immense historical arc that we call Greek antiquity to the other, a continuity that is often astonishing.

KNOWING AND SEEING

We have to start from the conventional view according to which, in the beginning, the Greeks more or less identified knowledge with sense perception, and especially with visual perception. Their cognitive vocabulary bears unmistakable traces of this: one of the most common verbs for saying "I know," for example, is *oida,* which comes from the same Indo-European root as the Latin *videre,* to see. However, we must note that, grammatically, *oida* is a perfect form that means not "I see" but precisely "I am currently in the situation of someone who has seen." What I know is thus not what I am seeing now but what I have seen, that at which I have been perceptually present, what I remember after ceasing to see it, what I can imagine when I am no longer seeing it, what I can recognize if I happen to see it again, what I can recount or describe because I have been an "eyewitness" to it.

In contrast to knowledge that is based on direct personal perceptual experience but exceeds experience within a temporal framework and grafts onto its own passivity the possibility of various active performances, what is the status of the information possessed by someone who has not seen, but to whom I have narrated or described what I have seen? If knowledge acquired through direct experience is identified with knowledge as such, what we would call "hearsay knowledge" has to be viewed quite simply as nonknowledge. This is the case in a famous passage in Homer, where the poet solicits the aid of the Muses to be able to list the leaders of the Greek army: "for you are goddesses and are present and know all things, but we hear only a rumor and know nothing" (*Iliad* II.484–487). Homer's text contrasts the amplitude of divine knowledge with the insignificance of human knowledge, but at the same time it shows what accounts for them both: the knowledge granted to goddesses and denied to human beings is based on divine presence and human absence in the face of what is to be known, and on the direct experience of this presence (available to goddesses) and this absence (the lot of humans).

Such a conception implies a rigorous, twofold limitation on accessible knowledge. What knowing subjects are apt to know is determined by their capacity to see. Human sight is exercised only within narrow limits of place and time; it is invariably linked to a single point of view that excludes others. In addition, the realm of knowable objects is limited to that of visible objects. That is why the philosophical legacy of this conception is to be sought in particular in sensualist or empiricist doctrines. Plato himself, however, in a paradoxical and controversial passage of *Theaetetus,* declares that when a past phenomenon is in question, for example a crime, only an eyewitness can know what happened, and if the judge, persuaded by the discourse of the orators, reaches a correct verdict in spite of everything, this will come about "without knowledge" (*Theaetetus* 201c).

The influence of the visual model on ancient theories of knowledge has sometimes been overestimated; still, this is not a reason to underestimate it. Moreover, the model itself encompassed various possibilities for expansion. If we start from the idea that I know that with which I have the same relation as I have with the people I know because I have met them, people I am capable of identifying and recognizing (this has been called "knowledge by acquaintance"), according to this model of knowledge it is not impossible to conceive of certain objects that are not currently visible for me, in the space and time that I occupy and from the point of view that is mine. Certain exceptional individuals may have the privilege of "seeing" something that, although visible in theory, escapes ordinary sight, something that is hidden away in the subterranean or celestial regions, in the shadows of the past or in the obscurity of the future: the soothsayer is a "seer," the pythoness a "clairvoyant." The visual model may even be transposed to objects that are inherently invisible— abstract and purely intelligible entities, for example; it is tempting to picture the intellectual faculty that grasps them as a sort of "eye of the soul," which exercises its specific form of "vision" on them. This visual metaphor is present in particular in illustrious Greek terms such as *theoria* or *theorein*, which refer first to sight and to spectacles and then, metaphorically, to speculation and intellectual contemplation. In a famous image, attributed to Pythagoras, someone who is going to the Olympic Games not to do business there or to compete, but only as a spectator, is compared to the philosopher, who is a spectator on the world; and it is the latter who is said to enjoy the best sort of life. In the supremely illustrious and influential central books of *The Republic*, Plato bases his theory of knowledge, in its most classic form, on a detailed analogy between vision and knowledge, along with their respective conditions and objects. The analogy must no doubt be understood only as an identity of relations: what vision is to visible things, for example, intellection is to intelligible things, and the truth that illuminates the intelligible is to the light that illuminates the visible. Still, it is easy to move from this idea to that of a resemblance (an analogy in the broad sense) between the terms of these relationships, for example between intellectual knowledge and vision. Such an extension is not necessary, however; Aristotle, in his treatise *On the Soul*, does not hide the fact that he bases his theory of thought on an identity of relations between thinking and feeling, on the one hand, and the object that is thought and the object that is felt, on the other; but he has no intention of claiming that thought and feeling are the same thing—a thesis that he attributes to most of his predecessors and that for his own part he rejects.

KNOWING AND TOUCHING

The visual model of knowledge is sometimes rivaled, on its own ground, by a tactile model. Sight is exercised at a distance, which accounts for its strength (its scope is not limited to the immediate environment) but also for its weakness (at too great a distance it loses its precision, and in the intervening space factors of confusion may arise). Touch has less scope for action, but it makes up for this inferiority with the infallible immediacy of the contact it supposes between the feeling body and the felt body; through touch, the world knocks directly at our door. The tactile world will thus be, par excellence, that of the materialists, who "maintain stoutly," according to Plato, that "that alone exists which can be touched and handled" (*Sophist* 246a). The Democritan theory of simulacra associates sight, which appears to be a sense that operates at a distance, with a particular sort of contact, since it results from the action of tenuous envelopes that are emitted by the felt body and that travel through the intervening space to touch the feeling body.

Touch, which Lucretius exalts as "the sense of the body," has even succeeded in supplying nonmaterialist philosophers with a cognitive model that ignores the corporeality of the entities in contact in favor of the immediacy of the contact itself. Aristotle resorts to tactile images when he defines the type of knowledge that is appropriate for "simple" entities. Since by definition they are "uncomposed," there can be no question of grasping one part of them and missing another part: according to a binary logic, the intellectual grasp of simple entities is accomplished completely or not at all. Touch thus provides a model for a form of knowledge that owes its singular value to the fact that it has as its alternative only ignorance, and not error.

SAVOIR AND CONNAÎTRE

Let us open up a discussion here for which visual and tactile models pave the way. The French language, envied by others on this point, distinguishes syntactically between *savoir*, to know as one can know that something is the case (e.g., that 2 + 2 = 4), and *connaître*, to know as one can know a person (to "be familiar with"). One says *connaître quelqu'un* or *quelque chose*, "to know someone" or "something"; the verb *connaître* is not used with *que* to say "to know that something is this or that." The verb *savoir* is not used with *quelqu'un* or, usually, with *quelque chose*; it is used with *que* to say "to know that something is this or that." Ordinary expressions thus distinguish knowledge of the objectal type from knowledge of the propositional type. In Greek, cognitive verbs are not specialized in this manner: most allow both an objectal and a propositional construction. Certain common syntactic possibilities in Greek blur the distinction even further: a participle may be substituted for a propositional construction (instead of saying "I know that you are telling the truth," one will say, for example, literally, "I know you telling the truth"); and the subject of the completive proposition may appear by anticipation as object of the main verb (instead of saying "I know that Socrates is dead," one will say, for example, literally, "I know Socrates that he is dead").

This absence of a watertight separation between knowledge of things and knowledge of states of affairs has doubtless encouraged the idea that to know that a thing is this or that is to know the thing itself, to know it well enough and in the manner that is required to know that it is this or that; in other words, it is to find in the very nature of the thing, the ultimate object of objectal knowledge, the reasons why it is this or that. This reasoning has led to significant restrictions on the legitimacy of the use of the verb "to know" (savoir) in a propositional context: if a given thing is this or that, but without being so by virtue of its nature (for example, if it is so only accidentally, through a temporary encounter, or else relatively, in a certain light, whereas in another light it is not so), one will refuse to say that one knows (or that one "really" knows) that it is so. Strictly speaking, one cannot know that Socrates is seated, since when he stands up he does not cease to be Socrates, nor that he is small, since he is so in comparison to a taller man, but not in comparison to a shorter man.

KNOWLEDGE AND HEARSAY

The visual model leads to denying the status of knowledge to information obtained from an eyewitness by someone who has not himself been a witness to the phenomenon. Such rigorism is not unprecedented, but it would be a mistake to believe that it is a legacy of the "Homeric conception" of knowledge. It has been noted with good reason that Homer's heroes are perfectly prepared to say that they know things that they have not witnessed directly, but that they have learned through an uninterrupted chain of oral and public testimony, the validity of which can be controlled by observing that no counter-testimony, solicited or not, is put forward to contest it. This is the case, for example, in genealogy (Iliad XX.203ff).

This example allows us to look at the theoretical inferiority of hearsay knowledge in a more nuanced way: everything depends on the quality of those who have been heard to speak, and on the method available for evaluating their truthfulness. At the lowest level we find vague and unverifiable rumors; at the highest level, we find the transmission of information by one or more witnesses who, one has good reasons to think, have seen the thing themselves, who have no reason to recount it in some way other than the way it happened, and who are in general good enough observers to be worthy of being believed. The model of hearsay knowledge also entails—especially among historians but also among orators—a reflection on the tools available for assessing the testimony. This reflection is extended among the philosophers, who often use the image of a messenger to illustrate various epistemological situations: we still commonly speak, in their wake, of the "testimony of the senses." But this model can be inflected in either a dogmatic or a skeptical direction. How can we be sure, if we view the senses as witnesses, that the messenger delivers his message accurately, since it is clear from the experience of "sensory illusions" that the senses are not always reliable? The Greek philosophers sometimes ambitiously pursued the ideal or the dream of a sensory message that would contain the guarantee of its own authenticity, in the form of a sort of unmistakable and unfalsifiable mark of fabrication; sometimes, too, they settled for a method of verification that entailed evaluating the degree of plausibility of the sense impression, cross-checking it against other sensory evidence, or optimizing the conditions of the experience.

KNOWING AND INFERRING

Oral transmission is not the only way the scope of perceptual knowledge can be extended. In human beings, feeling is sedimented in memory, and this process itself gives rise to experience (in the sense in which one speaks of a "person of experience," someone who has seen and retained a great deal). When experience is reflected, when it is formulated in a universal way, when it grasps the causes of its own successes, it serves as a basis for practical knowledge *(techne)* and for theoretical science *(episteme)*. This natural process, observed even before Plato and described several times by Aristotle as well as by philosophers of the Hellenistic period, comes into play again, methodologically, in the inferential process of induction *(epagōge)*. Aristotle attributes the discovery of induction to Socrates; it consists in passing from a number of particular cases that have something in common to a general law that sums them up and encompasses them all (not without risk of error, in instances where the review of particular cases is incomplete).

Another possibility for extending perceptual knowledge consists in reflecting on what one is seeing, and in using it as a sign or index on the basis of which one can attain indirect but authentic knowledge of what is not immediately present before one's eyes: the inhabitants of Ithaca see Ulysses returning to his homeland in the form of an old beggar, but (except for his old dog) they do not identify him; knowing is not seeing, since one can see without knowing who it is that one is seeing. To reach the point of knowing that the beggar is none other than Ulysses, those close to him infer it by relying on signs *(semata):* the scar whose existence is known to the nurse Eurycleia, the possession of secrets that Ulysses alone shared with Penelope, who is questioning him. It is not logically out of the question that a beggar might have the same scar as Ulysses, or that Ulysses might have confided to a traveler something that only Ulysses was thought to know; but by refining the model for identifying and interpreting signs, one can reduce the probability of a coincidence or a hoax to practically zero. The beggar is Ulysses: such is, in sum, the best explanation that can be inferred on the basis of the collected facts.

Philosophical reflection on the conditions and powers of inference through signs occupied an important place in ancient epistemology; it should not be overshadowed by a tendency to focus on observations drawn from the deductive model of mathematics. The Hellenistic schools in particular gave it considerable space in their debates. Their interest is easy to understand if we consider the number, quality, and intellectual and social prestige of the disciplines in which the real or presumed acquisition of knowledge was rooted in observation of phenomena considered as signs from which nonobservable phenomena could be inferred. The science of nature, in all its dimensions, is a prime example. A very early set of questions came to constitute—and remained, almost unchanged—the agenda for all self-respecting philosophical doctrines; these questions were essentially ones that could be answered only via the method summed up in the dictum proffered by Anaxagoras and strongly endorsed by Democritus: "Sight of the unclear: Phenomena" (*opsis tōn adelōn ta phainomena* [Anaxagoras, frg. 21a]); in other words, appearances offer a glimpse of the imperceptible. Rational reflection on appearances broadens the scope of vision (in another way entirely from the exceptional powers of the "seer"), to the point of constituting a quasi-vision of what eludes sight. In addition to the natural philosophers, the use of signs is of course quite important to other groups as well: to historians, who reconstitute a buried past on the basis of present indexes; to orators, who do the same thing in tribunals, seeking a more recent past, and also in political assemblies, to predict what is going to happen on the basis of the current situation, or what would happen if a given measure were adopted; to soothsayers, whose purported business it is to interpret signs—and their task is taken very seriously by the Stoics, among others; and, finally, to doctors, who enumerate and define the symptoms of various illnesses in relation to the external conditions of their appearance, and who can establish a prognosis with a certainty that makes people mistake them occasionally for soothsayers.

However, just as there are witnesses and witnesses, there are signs and signs; the same value is not attributed to all types of semiotic inference, and the terms used sometimes distinguish the simple index *(semeion)* from the definitive sign *(tekmerion)*. The characterization of one phenomenon as the sign of another, the unicity and determination of that other, the necessity of the bond that makes it possible to conclude that the latter exists on the basis of the former—all this can be subject to argument. This is why the theory of knowledge acquired through signs takes a very different tack among the rationalists and the empiricists, as the Hellenistic debates attest. One classification, of uncertain origin, distinguishes the so-called commemorative signs from the so-called indicative signs. Commemorative signs allow us to conclude on the basis of an observable phenomenon that another phenomenon is present, one that is also observable in principle but temporarily hidden. The second phenomenon has often been observed concomitantly with the first; for example, smoke is the commemorative sign of fire. Indicative signs are presumed to allow us to conclude on the basis of an observable phenomenon that another phenomenon is present, one that is nonobservable by nature. The latter is presumed to be of such a nature that in its absence the observable phenomenon with which it is associated cannot be produced: for example, perspiration is the indicative sign of the existence of invisible pores in the skin. A rationalist obviously has to believe that indicative signs exist in order to produce doctrines concerning the intimate nature of things and the hidden causes of phenomena; in a sense, this is precisely what being a rationalist means, for only reasoning can assure us that the visible effect could not take place without the hidden cause. The empiricist, on the contrary, will reject this possibility and will simply note, in an almost Pavlovian reflex, that if fire and smoke have often been manifested together, the spectacle of smoke in isolation leads us to think that there is fire somewhere, and that one could verify this by changing the conditions of the observation.

The chief sources of knowledge discussed up to this point, vision and its two extensions, the oral transmission of testimony and semiotic inference, correspond to the three master words of the empiricist doctors: *autopsia,* or direct and personal vision; *historia,* or recollection of the testimony of past or present experts; and *metabasis,* or inferential transfer, passing from knowledge acquired by one of the preceding means to additional knowledge of something that is provisionally out of reach.

KNOWING AND UNDERSTANDING

Having explored some of the extensions of the visual model of knowledge, let us return to the model itself to identify the limits that it was ill-suited to transcend. We may see, hear, or touch many things; we may accumulate impressions and information; we may explore the world on all sides; we may become very "knowing," in a weak sense of the word. Still, all this will not lead us to be "knowing" in the literal sense, if we do not understand what we have seen and heard. Not only does sense experience in general not procure, or not suffice to procure, authentic knowledge but, in addition, particular sense experiences can scarcely lay claim to the status of knowledge if they are not taken up again, one way or another, by the intervention of the intellect. One such intervention is already needed, at minimum, if we are to express such experiences in speech, to tell others what we are seeing and say it to ourselves, categorizing the experience conceptually in a propositional structure ("this is white"); a different sort of intervention is required for more complex elaborations that are necessary to the interpretation of a particular experience ("this is snow") or a general experience ("snow is white"). Thus it is not surprising that one of the first thinkers in whose work we encounter the idea that seeing does not yet amount to knowing, and that piling up information *(polumathie)* does not yet amount to having an intellectual grasp *(noos)* of that information, is Heraclitus, the philosopher of the untranslatable *logos*—both discourse and reason. The eyes and the ears, for example, are poor witnesses for those who have barbarian souls, he says; since a barbarian is someone who does not know Greek, we may take this to mean that sense experience brings no knowledge to someone who is incapable of interpreting the message it conveys because he or she does not know the language in which the message is couched. The underlying metaphor has had a long career: the world is a book that is readable only by those who know the rules for reading it. To know is to understand, that is, to bring back together (the prefix of the Greek word for "understand," *sunienai,* has the same meaning as that of the Latin *comprehendere*), to organize experience according to the structures that belong to reality, to bring to speech the reason that governs things. To know a single thing is not to know it; taken to the extreme, there is no knowledge but total knowledge, and no knowledge but knowledge of everything.

The earliest Greek thinkers, armed only with their naked reason, plunged headlong into an assault on knowledge of the whole, of the principles on which everything is based and of all the ensuing consequences. Perhaps their extraordinary audacity derives from the fact that their conception of knowledge left them no other choice: they had to know everything or know nothing at all. Not until Aristotle does the principle of a total science begin to give way to the idea that a science is a structured set of utterances bearing on entities that belong to a specific class and to that class alone (numbers, figures, natural beings), and even Aristotle does not give up the attempt to preserve the idea of a universal science. He goes about it from various angles, moreover, sometimes proposing the idea of a "science of being as being," a study of the properties that belong to every being by virtue of the simple fact that it is a being (and not by virtue of the particular type of being it is), and at other times advancing the presumably different idea of a "primary" science having as objects the principles of all things, and that would thus be "universal because primary."

KNOWING AND BELIEVING

These extraordinarily ambitious programs are very probably rooted in an idea that, quite early, even before Heraclitus, carved out a path for itself in Greek thought, a path that is perhaps the crucial idea behind all of ancient epistemology. This idea is that opinion (or belief, for both words can translate *doxa*) is not science: believing is not knowing, even if what one believes is true. In one famous fragment, Xenophanes sketches a formidable argument: in certain areas at least, "the clear and certain truth no man has seen nor will there be anyone who knows about the gods and what I say about all things. For even if, in the best case, one happened to speak aptly of what has been brought to pass, still he himself would not know it. But opinion *[dokos]* is allotted to all" (frg. 34).

The argument has often been interpreted in a radically skeptical sense: we may stumble across a true opinion by chance, but we have no way to recognize it as such, just as, in a dark room containing an array of vases, only one of which is made of gold, we have no way of being sure that we have picked out the golden vase. In this view, Xenophanes prefigured a celebrated paradox, presented by Plato in *Meno*, that played a stimulating role in epistemological reflection over a long period of time: how can we look for a thing when we have absolutely no knowledge of what it is? How can we identify the thing we have set out to look for, among all those things we do not know? And, supposing we stumble across the thing by chance, how can we know it is the very thing we were seeking, since we did not know it? If we do not want to settle for believing we have found the thing we were seeking, without any good reason for our belief, the wisest course, it seems, is to give up seeking entirely.

The foregoing paradox is the reverse of the idea that we know nothing if we do not know everything. It rules out the acquisition of new knowledge; it blocks the movement that, from a commonsense perspective, seems to be able to lead from ignorance to knowledge on a particular point (on this basis, it represents the application, in the epistemological field, of the difficult problem that continually confronted Greek thought, the problem of the intellectual understanding of movement, of becoming, of the appearance of something new). In response to this paradox, Plato attempts precisely to rescue the idea of total knowledge, by advancing his theory of recollection: the soul, immortal and reborn time after time, has seen all things, has already learned all things; what it does not know it has merely forgotten; it will recover its latent knowledge as soon as a dialectic "midwife" helps it to remember by asking the appropriate questions. To know *(connaître)* is to recognize *(reconnaître)*, to recognize what one already knew, what one had forgotten. There is a posteriori knowledge only in appearance; in reality there is only a priori knowledge.

Let us return to Xenophanes' argument. He does not necessarily militate in favor of radical skepticism: it is no doubt possible to acquire an objectively true opinion by rummaging around at random in the basket of opinions; but it is not impossible that one may be able to help "chance" by reflecting on one's experience, "by seeking for a long time," as Xenophanes says, and by using one's reason to reach opinions that are not arbitrary in the least, or necessarily illusory, but at least plausible. Xenophanes seems to be convinced of this when he presents, in his own name, a strikingly new theology and a prudent cosmology. However, the unbridgeable gap between opinion—even true opinion—and science remains: one can say what turns out to be objectively true without being certain that what one is saying is true. What does opinion lack, then, in order to be knowledge? Xenophanes does not answer this question with any precision; perhaps he is saying, in a purely negative way, that a man who has a true opinion does not have knowledge about that about which he has a true opinion; in that case, he is marking a difference without trying to say in what that difference consists. The attempts that have been made since Xenophanes to answer this question have perhaps contributed to naming the difficulty rather than resolving it: thus when one says, in the classic fashion, that knowledge is justified true belief, one would have to be able to say under what conditions a true belief is justified. In *Theaetetus,* a grandiose attempt to answer the question "What is science *[episteme]*?", Plato rejects the identification of science first with sensation, and second with true belief. He then suggests identifying it with "true belief accompanied by an account *[logos],*" but with remarkable honesty he has the dialogue end in failure, or so it seems at first. Despite several attempts, the interlocutors do not succeed in providing the notion of *logos* with a satisfactory content.

KNOWING AND PROVING

We may believe that we can justify an opinion the way we verify a hypothesis: by testing it, by subjecting it to the test of its consequences. But we are then at risk of committing a classic error, an error that was identified as such by the Greeks but that is nevertheless still a threat, the so-called error of "the assertion of the consequent" (if *p*, then *q*; now, *q*; therefore *p*). For example: if there are invisible pores in the skin, then sweat can appear on the surface; now, sweat appears; thus there are pores. But nothing says that a different explanation might not be the correct one: moisture on a carafe is not evidence that the glass is porous. We may perhaps reinforce the plausibility of the pore hypothesis by multiplying the consequences to be examined, by determining that all of these confirm the hypothesis, and that none invalidates it; but refuting the competing hypotheses does not suffice to establish the one that we believe—perhaps owing to a lack of imagination—to be the only one that remains conceivable. The multiplication of tests will never procure the only type of premise that would be appropriate, namely, that sweat can appear not simply *if* but also *only if* there are pores.

To get around the obstacle, we have to reverse our perspective. To justify an opinion, we have to orient the investigation not toward its consequences but toward the principles of which it is itself the consequence. We must seek to put to work the *modus ponens* (or positing mode), which is perfectly valid: if *p*, then *q*; now, *p*; therefore *q*. To know that *q* (that something is this or that) is to know why it is thus (because *p*).

In one passage in *Meno,* Plato gives a cursory presentation of the idea that true opinions are "unstable" and easily escape our soul's grasp (probably because they risk being abandoned as soon as experience seems to invalidate them or skillful discourse seems to refute them); what transforms them into knowledge is "an account of the cause" or "an explanation of the cause" (the word *aitia,* which appears in this formula, designates, as it were, that which is "responsible" for the state of things on which true opinion bears; thus *aitia* is the objective cause of that state of things, and it allows us to explain that things are thus rather than otherwise; it is the "reason for being" of the state of things). This reasoning "binds" true opinions, and transforms them into knowledge by rendering them "stable" (Greek theories of knowledge owe a lot to the fact that the word *episteme*, through its root, evokes the ideas of cessation, rest, stability). Aristotle only extends the indication in *Meno* when he says that "we consider that we have unqualified knowledge [*episteme*] of anything . . . when we believe that we know (i) that the cause from which the fact results is the cause of that fact, and (ii) that the fact cannot be otherwise than it is" (*Posterior Analytics* I.271b9–12). To know something in the sense thus defined, it is necessary and sufficient to prove it, that is, to deduce it from its principles—the clearest and most impressive example of this being mathematical knowledge.

To know that the thing cannot be otherwise than it is, is to know that it is necessary: thus we are touching on an essential ingredient of the Greek notion of knowledge. Essential, but also ambiguous: for if I know that a thing is necessary, what is it that I know, exactly? One distinction, which will become classic, opposes the "necessity of the consequence" to the "necessity of the consequent." It is conceivable, for example, that if a certain number of conditions are met at the same time (a barrel of gunpowder, a naked flame that touches it), a certain effect will necessarily follow (here we are dealing with the necessity of the consequence, a hypothetical or relative necessity). But this does not imply that the explosion itself is necessary (here we would be dealing with the necessity of the consequent, an intrinsic or absolute necessity); for that to be the case, each of the conditions, and their simultaneous fulfillment, would have had to be (intrinsically) necessary.

One of the limitations of Greek thought seems to have been the absence of a clear grasp of this distinction (despite certain attempts and approximations): from the reasonable idea that one can know only what is hypothetically necessary, it had a tendency to move on to the less reasonable idea that one can know only what is absolutely necessary. Can we say that we know that an explosion took place on a certain day at a certain hour? No, in contradiction with the customary use of the verb "to know," if we accept the commonsense view that the convergence of factors necessary and conjointly sufficient to set it off was not in itself necessary. Yes, in conformity with the customary use of the verb "to know," if we admit, this time in contradiction with common sense, that the convergence of these factors was itself necessary, and that it derived, for example, from a universal network of linked causes that can be called destiny. In each case, we lose on one side what we gain on the other. The mathematical model, here, is both seductive and dangerous, for it seems to allow us a way out of the dilemma. If the premises of a demonstration are either held to be axiomatically necessary, because they are "evident," or else themselves demonstrated on the basis of the axioms, the truth demonstrated is endowed with the two sorts of necessity at once—which makes it difficult to tell them apart. Factual truths will henceforth be reserved to the domain of true opinions; truths of reason will fall in the domain of knowledge.

By a natural extension, once again, only eternal truths will belong to knowledge. It is not necessary, but it is tempting, to think that what is always true is so if and only if it is necessary; that what is sometimes true is so if and only if it is possible; and that what is never true is so if and only if it is impossible. These reciprocal shifts between time and modality are favored, as Jaakko Hintikka has shown, by a particular feature of ordinary language that obtains in English as well as in Greek. Ordinary statements are "temporally indefinite": they are dated only according to the moment of their enunciation. "It is daylight" is true if it is daylight at the moment one says, "It is daylight." But one can pronounce the same sentence, "It is daylight," at midnight as well as at noon; hence the temptation to say that this same sentence, which was true at noon, has become false twelve hours later. By the same token, we shall refuse to call "knowledge" the cognitive situation in which we find ourselves with respect to the truth of "It is daylight" (at the moment when it is true), for it does not have the requisite "stability." If the identity of the sentence is taken as the marker of the identity of the opinion it expresses, nothing in the concept of opinion is opposed to a case in which an opinion becomes alternately true and false, according to changes in the situation; but knowledge, for its part, as Aristotle says, "cannot be sometimes knowledge and sometimes ignorance." We cannot then, strictly speaking, say that we know that it is daylight: we sometimes have a true opinion about this, sometimes a false one.

To escape from the incalculable consequences of this set of conceptions, we would have to reintegrate into the meaning of the utterance, in an absolute form, the "date stamping" that it receives from the moment of its enunciation. We shall say, for example, that the sentence "It is daylight," pronounced on August 16, 1995, at noon, expresses a certain proposition: "It is daylight on August 16, 1995, at noon," and that it is this proposition, not the sentence, that is true. A different sentence, pronounced after that date, will express the same proposition in a different form: "It was daylight on August 16, 1995, at noon," and the truth value of the single proposition expressed by these two different sentences will remain the same. Conversely, the sentence "It is daylight," uttered on August 16, 1995, at midnight, expresses a different proposition, "It is daylight on August 16, 1995, at midnight," which is false and which will remain the same false proposition in the various expressions that it can be given by different sentences, such as "It was daylight on August 16, 1995, at midnight." This reintegration of the date of enunciation in the signification of the utterance was missed by the Greek philosophers, even by the Stoics, who however did distinguish between sentences and the propositions that sentences signify. For them, in fact, a temporally indefinite sentence, such as "It is daylight," is the expression of a "complete signified," lacking in none of the determinations that make it possible to assign it a truth value; thus this truth value was itself variable in time.

The distinction between opinion and science, or unqualified knowledge, combined with the ancient principle of knowing like through like, led to the conclusion not only that true opinion lacked something it would need to have if it were to be knowledge, but also that that lack was essential to it, and irremediable. To be sure, Plato had acknowledged in *Meno* that "an account of the cause" made it possible to transform true opinion into knowledge, but in *The Republic* he seems, on the contrary (at least on a first reading), to think that such a metamorphosis is impossible, because opinion and knowledge have to do with two entirely separate domains of objects: opinion, midway between knowledge and ignorance, has to do with becoming, which is itself midway between being and nonbeing; science has to do with immutable being. About particular perceptible things, and, by contamination, about the principles that govern them, if there are any, there can be only opinion (as was the lesson of the splitting of Parmenides' poem into two parts), at best, a plausible opinion (and this will be the lesson of *Timaeus*). Aristotle will have his work cut out for him in his effort to preserve the possibility of a scientific status for physics; even as he continues to acknowledge in principle that there is no science but that of the necessary, he weakens the link between knowledge and necessity by making a place, between the immutable and the unpredictable, for a possible object for a science of nature: that which is produced ordinarily and regularly, most of the time and in most cases *(hōs epi to polu)*.

KNOWLEDGE AND INTUITION

The movement of demonstration or proof, which goes back from the propositions to be demonstrated to the premises on the basis of which they can be proved, raises a problem that Aristotle identified clearly. If there were no form of knowledge other than demonstrative knowledge, we would find ourselves caught up in an infinite regression: if, in order to know something, we have to be able to prove it on the basis of something else, which we also have to know, and so on, then to know something, we would have to know an indefinite number of things. This regression ad infinitum is ruinous, for the finite mind cannot traverse an indefinite series; thus if one can know nothing except by proving it, one can know nothing at all. There is one way out, which certain mathematicians known to Aristotle had accepted: this consists in turning the demonstrative series back on itself, in a circle, instead of allowing it to extend in a limitless linear fashion. But Aristotle rejects this solution, because it comes down finally to proving a thing by itself. His solution is to admit that "one has to stop," and that it is possible to do so, in the movement back from theorems to their premises: demonstrative knowledge is possible only if it is anchored, at the end of a finite number of stages, in principles that it is neither possible nor necessary to prove. There is proof only if there is some unprovable element; there is demonstrative knowledge only if there is a nondemonstrative mode of knowledge.

The whole question, then, is whether one can posit principles in a manner that is not arbitrary—that is, with some reason to posit one set of principles rather than another set, yet without proving them. The modern idea according to which one can construct axiomatic-deductive systems by arbitrarily designating certain propositions as axioms and certain others as theorems— so long as one can also construct other systems in which the status of these propositions is reversed—is wholly foreign, it seems, to ancient thought: between the principles endowed with explanatory power and the consequences explained by these principles, asymmetry is held to be essential and irreversible. If the ancients had to admit that the position of the principles is arbitrary, the dogmatics would have had to convert to skepticism. The skeptic Agrippa, in order to turn Aristotle's analysis against dogmatism, condemns infinite regression and circular reasoning as Aristotle had, and settles for blocking the ultimate escape route that Aristotle had reserved for himself by arguing that if there is no reason to adopt a given principle rather than some other one, then the so-called principles are only unfounded hypotheses. This is why the remedy against the peril of skepticism has always been sought in a frantic quest for what Plato was the first to call an "anhypothetic principle" (i.e., one not posited by hypothesis).

But how can one determine the mode of knowing, by definition nondemonstrative, that is appropriate to knowledge of such a principle? On this point, the lesson provided by the mathematical model, the consummate example of demonstrative knowledge, is ambiguous, as a rapid comparison between Plato and Aristotle will show.

To assess the limits of the influence exercised by mathematics on the Platonic theory of knowledge, it suffices to reread the well-known pages of *The Republic* (Books VI and VII) where Plato describes the place he assigns to mathematics in the education of philosophers. In his eyes mathematics has the immense pedagogical advantage of "conducing to the awakening of thought" (*Republic* VII.523a), of "drawing the soul away from the world of becoming to the world of being" (VII.521d). But mathematics can play only an instrumental and propaedeutic role, for it suffers from two essential limitations: on the one hand, it uses (and necessarily so, according to Plato) perceptible objects, figures and diagrams, which it treats as images of purely intelligible realities about which it reasons; on the other hand, it is based on hypotheses that it takes to be known and that it deems to need no justification. Moreover, these two limitations are related to one another: the truth of the propositions that mathematicians take as primordial seems to them capable of being declared "self-evident to all," because this truth is visible, so to speak, on the very figure that they draw. Thus the title of science, which is given to mathematics by common usage, cannot be accepted without some impropriety; the hypothetical character of its principles allows it to claim consistency, but not truth. Only dialectics is truly a form of knowledge, because it calls into question everything that may be called into question, because it does not settle for any evidence procured by some perceptible figure of the intelligible, and because it goes back to the "anhypothetic principle" that will allow it to establish the pseudofoundations of mathematics itself.

This is doubtless not the place to discuss the Platonic identification of the anhypothetic principle with the form of the Good, the enigmatic "greatest thing to learn" (*Republic* VI.505a.2−3). But we can observe that Plato remains rather evasive on the mode of knowing that is appropriate to such an object: it seems that it is a matter sometimes of "seeing" it, "contemplating" it, as a sort of intelligible thing, and sometimes of "rendering an account [of it] to oneself and others," "defining it in one's discourse" by "exacting an account of the essence" and by "distinguishing and abstracting it from all other things" (cf. *Republic* VII.517−520, 532, 534). Plato specifies, however, that "the one who is unable to do this, in so far as he is incapable of rendering an account to himself and to others, does not possess full reason and intelligence [*nous*] about the matter" (VII.534b.4−6), and that this holds true for the good as well as for any other form. We shall thus resist the idea that here *nous* represents a mode of knowing that is intuitive in nature, the only one capable of apprehending, in a mute and quasi-mystical vision, an ineffable and absolutely transcendent object. Moreover, *nous* had been introduced, at the end of Book VI, as the name of that cognitive attitude of the soul that has as objects not the form of the Good alone but all the intelligible forms and their various dialectical relations; and the term *dianoia*, which is explicitly distinguished from *nous*, and which is appropriate to mathematical thought, does not mean "discursive knowledge," as it does in other contexts, but something like "intermediate" or "transitional intellectual grasp" *(dia-noia)* between opinion and intellectual understanding, strictly speaking.

In a sense, Aristotle is Plato's heir when he evokes "the most certain [*bebaiotate*] principle of all" (*Metaphysics* IV.iii.1005b11−12, 17−18, 22−23; 1006a4−5), the principle of noncontradiction. Returning to Plato's term *anhupothetos*, "not based on hypothesis," he specifies that "[it is] the principle which the student of any form of Being must grasp" (*Metaphysics*, IV.iii.1005b14−15). To know it, there is obviously no question of proving it: "If . . . there are some things of which no proof need be sought, they cannot say what principle they think to be more self-evident" (IV.iv.1006a10−11). Against those who, more or less seriously, have spoken in such a way that they seem to reject it, the only way to justify it is to proceed "refutatively," that is, to show by a dialectical path that, starting from the moment when the interlocutor agrees to enter into the sphere of meaningful dialogue, he cannot fail to respect the principle.

However, the principle of noncontradiction (leaving aside exceptions that can always be created for the sake of argument) does not normally enter into a proof as a premise; it functions rather as a fundamental rule of meaningful discourse. Contrary to Plato (and the difference is a significant one), Aristotle grants full-fledged scientific status to the particular disciplines that, like arithmetic or geometry, involve a specific realm of entities belonging to the same class, like numbers and figures. Each of these sciences, which are demonstrative, has its own principles; they have some principles in common only in the sense that such principles can be applied analogically to more than one science. Dialectics, whose nature is precisely not to bear on any one class in particular, thus seems less apt to justify proper principles than common principles, and the question of how one reaches the point of knowing the unprovable principles of the particular sciences, and what type of knowledge is implied in knowing them, is raised anew in pointed fashion.

Aristotle tries to answer this question in the last chapter of *Posterior Analytics*, a chapter that is as difficult as it is well known. I shall focus here only on the fact that Aristotle designates *nous* as being the cognitive state *(hexis)* that apprehends principles, and that is, on that basis, more exact and more true than demonstrative knowledge itself. It has often been thought (indeed, since ancient times) that in this context the word *nous* designates a true intellectual intuition, a sort of vision of the mind grasping its objects with the same self-evidence and the same immediacy as ocular vision grasping its objects; it would be a question of a faculty specifically adapted to the acquisition of knowledge of unprovable principles. Against this interpretation, it has been pointed out (by Jonathan Barnes) that the chapter at issue raises two separate questions: How do principles become known to us? What is the cognitive state of the person apprehending them? To the first question, Aristotle gives an undeniably empiricist reply: principles become known to us at the end of an inductive process that moves through the classic stages of perception, memory, experience, and science; about intellection, nothing is said. *Nous* comes into play only in the reply to the second question: in the available vocabulary, this is a noun that is appropriate to designate knowledge whose object is a principle, once this knowledge *has been acquired* by way of induction, as described above, just as the noun *science* (demonstrative science) is appropriate to designate knowledge whose object is a proven theorem, once that knowledge has been acquired by way of deduction. If intellectual intuition is conceived as a means for *acquiring* knowledge, we then have to say that *nous* is not an intellectual intuition.

Thus twice in succession, in Plato and again in Aristotle, we have come close to the idea that the supreme instrument of knowing, the one that is capable of making principles known to us and that governs all other knowledge, can be assimilated to a sort of vision of the mind; but then, twice in succession, we have also (it seems) watched Plato and then Aristotle ultimately sidestep that idea. Not until the sort of synthesis of Platonism and Aristotelianism that we find in Neoplatonism, a creative synthesis that is not overly hampered by concern for textual exegesis, do we see the return in force, in the vocabulary of intellectual knowledge and beatific union, of the ancient metaphors of vision and contact. In a certain way, the circuit that we have been trying to trace thus turns out to close.

JACQUES BRUNSCHWIG
Translated by Catherine Porter and Dominique Jouhaud

Bibliography

Texts and Translations

Anaxagoras. *The Fragments of Anaxagoras.* Ed. David Sider. *Beiträge zur Klassichen Philologie,* vol. 118. Meiseheim am Glan: Verlag Anton Hain, 1981.

Aristotle. *Metaphysics.* 2 vols. Trans. Hugh Tredennick. Loeb Classical Library.

————. *On the Soul.* In *On the Soul; Parva Naturali; On Breath.* Trans. W. S. Hett. Loeb Classical Library.

————. *Posterior Analytics.* In *Posterior Analytics; Topica.* Trans. Hugh Tredennick. Loeb Classical Library.

Long, Anthony A., and David N. Sedley, eds. *The Hellenistic Philosophers.* Cambridge: Cambridge University Press, 1987.

Plato. *Meno.* In *Laches; Protagoras; Meno; Euthydemus.* Trans. W. R. M. Lamb. Loeb Classical Library.

————. *Phaedo.* In *Euthyphro; Apology; Crito; Phaedo; Phaedrus.* Trans. W. R. M. Lamb. Loeb Classical Library.

————. *The Republic.* 2 vols. Trans. Paul Shorey. Loeb Classical Library.

————. *Sophist.* In *Theaetetus; Sophist.* Trans. Paul Shorey. Loeb Classical Library.

————. *Theaetetus.* In *Theaetetus; Sophist.* Trans. Paul Shorey. Loeb Classical Library.

Xenophanes. *Fragments/Xenophanes of Colophon.* Trans. J. H. Lesher. Toronto and Buffalo: University of Toronto Press, 1992.

Studies

Asmis, Elizabeth. *Epicurus' Scientific Method.* Ithaca, N.Y.: Cornell University Press, 1984.

Barnes, Jonathan, Jacques Brunschwig, Myles Burnyeat, and Malcolm Schofield, eds. *Science and Speculation: Studies in Hellenistic Theory and Practice.* Cambridge: Cambridge University Press, 1982.

Berti, Enrico, ed. *Aristotle on Science: The Posterior Analytics.* Padua: Antenore, 1980.

Canto-Sperber, Monique, ed. *Les paradoxes de la connaissance.* Paris: Odile Jacob, 1991.

Denyer, Nicholas. *Language, Thought and Falsehood in Ancient Greek Philosophy.* London: Routledge, 1991.

Everson, Stephen, ed. *Epistemology.* (Companions to Ancient Thought, vol. 1). Cambridge: Cambridge University Press, 1990.

Granger, Gilles-Gaston. *La théorie aristotélicienne de la science.* Paris: Aubier, 1976.

Hintikka, Jaakko. *Time and Necessity.* Oxford: Clarendon Press, 1973.

Ioppolo, Anna-Maria. *Opinione e scienza: Il dibattito tra Stoici e Accademici nel III e nel II secolo a. C.* Naples: Bibliopolis, 1986.

Lesher, James H. "The Emergence of Philosophical Interest in Cognition." *Oxford Studies in Ancient Philosophy* 12 (1994): 1–34.

Lyons, John. *Structural Semantics: An Analysis of Part of the Vocabulary of Plato.* Oxford: Blackwell, 1966.

McKirahan, Richard D. *Principles and Proofs: Aristotle's Theory of Demonstrative Science.* Princeton: Princeton University Press, 1992.

Robin, Léon. *Les rapports de l'être et de la connaissance d'après Platon.* Paris: Presses Universitaires de France, 1957.

Schofield, Malcolm, Myles Burnyeat, and Jonathan Barnes, eds. *Doubt and Dogmatism: Studies in Hellenistic Epistemology.* Oxford: Clarendon Press, 1980.

Striker, Gisela. "Kriterion tes aletheias." In *Essays on Hellenistic Epistemology and Ethics.* Cambridge: Cambridge University Press, 1966. Pp. 22–76.

Vlastos, Gregory, ed. *Plato: A Collection of Critical Essays, I: Metaphysics and Epistemology.* Garden City and New York: Doubleday, 1971.

Related Articles

Myth and Knowledge; Demonstration and the Idea of Science; Epicurus; Pyrrhon; Skepticism; Observation and Research; Aristotle; Plato; The Academy; Stoicism

ETHICS

THE PHILOSOPHICAL LEGACY of ancient Greece is philosophy itself. This statement is particularly true of moral philosophy and ethical thought. While the first Greek philosophers—the Presocratics beginning in the 6th century B.C.E., and, most important, Socrates, Plato, and Aristotle in the 5th and 4th centuries—managed to break away from the poetic, mythical, edifying forms traditional in moral discourse, their primary contribution was to formulate rational and reflective approaches to the study of human behavior. By making reflection on behavior a quest for principles related to the understanding of human nature and well-being, the Greek philosophers laid out a model for the philosophical approach to ethics.

But that is not all. For twenty-five centuries writers, moralists, and thinkers have kept coming back to ethical issues first articulated in ancient Greece. Even today, the categories we use to interpret moral experience (for example, virtue, or weakness of will) come directly from Greek philosophy, in a way that is no longer true of our ideas about physics or biology. The current state of moral philosophy is even more revealing. The numerous authors who deplore the difficulties the major trends in contemporary moral thought (especially Kantianism and Utilitarianism) encounter in responding to the complexity and ambiguity of moral problems are turning to ancient philosophy to find a richer understanding of the way morality relates to life.

How can this be so? How do we explain the fact that part of our moral experience links us so directly to a world that ended two thousand years ago, a world whose material, economic, social, and political conditions have nothing in common with our own? Greek thinkers lived in a world in which slavery, inequality, and the inferiority of certain people were universally accepted realities. Moreover, moral philosophy in antiquity was often associated with a physical and cosmological interpretation of the universe that is completely unacceptable today. Furthermore, the world of the Greek thinkers predated, and was in some respects wholly foreign to, Christianity, which has given us concepts essential to our ethical comprehension of the world, ideas such as the inherent moral value of every human being and the existence of universal obligations.

The issue would be clearer had the appropriation of Greece by the Western tradition not been so strong: it is difficult to know what Greek thought really was, independent of what it has come to mean for us. This appropriation has certainly contributed to our idealizing Greece, but in a somewhat perverse manner. Often, the attempt to establish seamless continuity with Greek thought has led us to see it as representing a "dawn" that culminated in daylight only after a period of progress driven by modern philosophy. This kind of "progressivism" is often related to the conviction that Greek moral thought is in some way comparable to our own, and rather inclines us to see ourselves as much more moral than the Greeks: we have expanded on their discoveries, and above all we have discarded the rigidity, the inequality, and the lack of universality of the Greek world. Western countries have indeed put an end to slavery; but the spectacle of the modern world would hardly convince a Greek of our moral superiority. Moreover, our familiarity with the Greeks, nourished by the implicit conviction that Greek ethics remained at an inferior stage, leads to something worse, to an idea that the Greeks had an imperfect notion of what is for us the very essence of morality, that they had no idea of free will, and no conception of moral autonomy, of moral obligation, or of individual responsibility for one's actions. Even if there were grounds for such a charge (and a close reading of the texts raises doubts on this score), the fact remains that the Greek theory of action and responsibility is fully as complex and multifaceted as our own, and it is an essential ingredient in the Greek concept of morality. So unless we resolve the issue by begging the question, and claiming that morality can be defined only as we have defined it, there is no reason to believe that the Greeks' conceptualization of morality was incomplete simply because it was different from our own.

The subject of this essay is not so much immediate ethical experiences or convictions themselves as the reflection on them, the modes of understanding and systematizing that have been applied to ethical experience. Such a distinction between the immediate and the reflective, between popular morality and philosophical ethics, partially alleviates the difficulty created by the fact that the Greek world is both so foreign and so familiar to us. The social practices, institutions, and popular morality of ancient Greece were far removed from our own. But when we read the philosophers—Plato, Aristotle, the Stoics—we are in familiar territory; their thoughts are in part our own. The dissociation between ethical practices and moral reflection remains somewhat enigmatic. How can we know where rational and theoretical reflection in ethics begins? Moreover, can moral philosophy really be separated from human behavior and from literature, and is it not illusory to try to separate the common definition of morality from its philosophical elaboration? In the case of ancient Greece, the influence of Socratic moral thought provides a partial answer, for that thought is presented explicitly as breaking with conventional, popular morality. The truth of the break is complex and subtle, but it invites us, in a work devoted to Greek thought, to deal only in passing with the morality that emerged from the great Greek literary works, Homeric epics and the tragedies, and to explore in greater detail those works in which the aim of explaining and systematizing is more explicit. This way of dividing up the corpus follows a chronological pattern. The great Greek literary works that were the foundation for moral education in Greece either predated Socrates or were produced during his lifetime. In contrast, most of the important works of Greek moral philosophy came after Socrates. From the end of the 5th century B.C.E. to the beginning of the Christian era, Greek literature itself seems to have incorporated the methods of analysis and systematization that were spread first by the sophists and later by the Socratics.

The sequence of philosophical thought that brings together Socrates, Plato, Aristotle, Pyrrhon, and the Hellenistic philosophers (Epicureans, Stoics, and Skeptics) is the principal object of the present study, which is organized around three questions. The first concerns the meaning of the Socratic question: "How should I live?" The second deals with the connections between nature and virtue. The third deals with the philosophy of action. Some introductory remarks will make it easier to appreciate the impact of Socrates' break with tradition.

MORAL REFLECTION BEFORE THE TIME OF SOCRATES

At the end of the 1st century B.C.E. Cicero wrote, in a now famous phrase from his *Tusculan Disputations,* that Socrates invented philosophical thinking in ethics. Three hundred years earlier, Aristotle had already acknowledged Socrates as the first philosopher to have sought universals and definitions in the field of morality. This view, widespread in ancient times, remains the prevailing one today. It is probably true that it was Socrates, especially as represented by Plato, who made ethics the subject of autonomous reflection, requiring a reflective and critical attitude as well as specific arguments and concepts. But moral reflection was obviously not invented by Socrates, even though, prior to his time, it was expressed and transmitted through the literary tradition. The tragedies of Sophocles and Euripides and Thucydides' *Peloponnesian War* attest to the importance of the debates over normative issues. At the same time, a full discussion about the foundations of moral standards and political laws was developing around the sophists. To appreciate the import of Socrates' break with the past, we need to review the major developments in ethics that preceded it.

Discussions about ethics in Socrates' time arose against the background of an immense cultural heritage, based largely on Homeric culture, that was to be consigned to a secondary position by the post-Socratic development of philosophical ethics. Homer's work, composed in the 8th century B.C.E., had a profound influence on Greek culture. The major ethical model that emerged from the Homeric epics was the heroic ideal of self-affirmation. Socrates criticized the sophists and other elements of contemporary culture for reaffirming this ideal. According to the *Iliad,* "old Peleus charged his son Achilles always to be bravest and preeminent above all" (XI.783–784). The same ideal is reflected in Achilles' aggressiveness, in the intensity with which he asserts his desires, and in Odysseus's cleverness and endurance. In Homeric morality, virtue depends as much on the hero's exploits and accomplishments as on events that affect him; virtue must be recognized by a few peers who compete in the accomplishment of virtuous deeds. However, virtue, like the favor of the gods, is unpredictable. When Ajax, tricked by Athena, fights with a herd of cattle, he loses his reputation and his moral standing. Homeric ethics thus associates a morality of shame or honor, relating to shameful acts and events that can deprive a person of virtue, with a competitive and assertive ideal of excellence.

Some decades later, in the 6th century, Hesiod's *Works and Days* revealed a very different conception, in which a morality of constraint and self-discipline is contrasted with a morality of self-affirmation. The judgment of Zeus was more favorable to those who adhered to the difficult course of justice *(dike)* than to those who indulged in excess and arrogance *(hubris)*. Popular wisdom, as expressed in the aphorisms of the Seven Sages and the Delphic oracle's precept "nothing in excess" *(meden agan)*, are indicative of this latter trend. The influence of this traditional wisdom was long lasting, and to some extent it outlived Socrates' criticism. It inspired not only the sophists but also some Hellenistic thinkers two centuries later to offer advice, models for leading a good life, and examples of virtue and good behavior.

Another important element was the gradual appearance, during the 6th century, of the idea of a spiritual principle, the *psukhe*, or soul, no longer viewed as simply the breath departing the body at the moment of death but as a true mark of independent being, of a substantive existence that persists after death. Until that time, immortality had been regarded as a privilege of the gods, not as the property of a noncorporeal quality of human beings. The development of this belief was linked to the existence of religious circles (probably Orphic and Pythagorean, but their identity is uncertain) and associated with notions of metempsychosis and the memory of former lives lived through the soul's various incarnations. While Plato's concepts of recollection and of the soul's immortality provided a considerably modified formulation of the notion of the prior existence of the soul, these Platonic concepts nevertheless drew comparable ethical consequences from that notion: the possibility of conceiving of man as a center of intentional actions for which he is accountable, and of conceiving of punishment or retribution after death, a reparation that could extend over a whole cycle of reincarnated lives.

Among the Presocratics, ethical reflection centered on notions of wrongdoing and reparation. Justice *(dike)* meant the implacable nature of a correction or punishment for transgressing order or measure, or for disturbing the balance among the world's elements. The natural order designated by the word *kosmos* is a well-ordered construct, and injustice and excess were measured as a function of the political, aesthetic, and moral significance that it possessed:

"Sun will not overstep his measures; otherwise the Erinyes, ministers of justice, will find him out," wrote Heraclitus (frg. 226, in Kirk et al.). A fragment from Anaximander suggests that "the source of coming-to-be for existing things is that into which destruction, too, happens 'according to necessity; for they pay penalty and retribution to each other for their injustice according to the assessment of Time'" (frg. 101, ibid.), thus according *dike* the status of a natural element of the *kosmos* or of nature *(phusis)*. However, Anaximander does not seem to have conceived of the human world as capable of being ordered in the same way as the *kosmos,* whereas Heraclitus made cosmic law the model for human law, as well as its source and authority: "For all the laws of men are nourished by one law, the divine law: for it has as much power as it wishes and is sufficient for all" (frg. 250, ibid.). By conceiving of the human world as a world of laws, Heraclitus was perhaps seeking to oppose the early manifestations of relativism that grounded human laws in conventions.

Democritus's contribution to the development of rationalism in ethics was remarkable. A contemporary of Socrates and the founder of atomism, this philosopher produced works of moral philosophy compiled in two ample collections of maxims and short texts (more than two hundred quotations or excerpts published long after his death). Democritus seems to have conceived of laws as indispensable to harmony and to human survival and as embodying moral requirements necessary for the protection of mutual interests. Such a conception of law *(nomos)* in contrast to nature *(phusis)* is probably in part a reworking of an epistemological contradiction between reality—the true being of things, made up of atoms and nothingness—and the beliefs of mortals, which are either fallacious or illusory. But the most interesting aspect of Democritus's thoughts about ethics is his treatment of the good life as developing from a fundamental goodness, and especially from an internalized goodness that consists in a state of mind. Democritus calls this condition *euthumia* ("good humor," sometimes translated as "tranquillity"). Even in antiquity, there were disagreements about whether *euthumia* was the condition in which the greatest and purest pleasure was felt, or whether such a state could be attained by limiting desires and therefore eliminating frustrations. The essential points are that this internal goodness is located in the soul, that reason is the faculty best suited to preserving it, and that attaining it is the principle underlying good actions: those who possess *euthumia* act in fairness and loyalty. This position seems to anticipate the most characteristic theses of Socratic thought, those that treat justice as the characteristic property of the soul, a property wholly dependent on the exercise of reason. Thus in Democritus we find an approach that is close to the conventionalism of the sophists, linked with an internalized conception of moral good that left its mark on all post-Socratic ethics.

It is impossible to understand the importance sophistic thought took on at the end of the 5th century B.C.E. without recalling the principal cultural and historic facts that shaped the preceding decades. First, there was the experience of a certain degree of cultural diversity. Beginning in the 7th century, Greeks had numerous contacts with other civilizations. Two writers in particular contributed to this familiarity: Hecataeus of Miletus, a historian and geographer of the 6th century, and Herodotus, a contemporary of the early sophists and author of the *Histories*, a collection of travel narratives. Herodotus himself seems to have offered a conservative and positivist interpretation of what we would call "cultural relativity" today: "For if it were proposed to all nations to choose which seemed best of all customs [*nomos*], each, after examination made, would place its own first" (III.xxxviii.1.4). An equally positivist interpretation of laws was held by the sophist Protagoras, whom Plato described in *Theaetetus* as believing that "and likewise in affairs of state, the honourable and disgraceful, the just and injust, the pious and its opposite, are in truth to each state such as it thinks they are and as it enacts into law for itself, and in these matters no citizen and no state is wiser than another" (172a).

The political events of the 5th century were also of considerable importance. Thirty years of uninterrupted war (culminating in the defeat of Athens in 404), of violent class conflicts, incessant political battles, and the radicalization of Athenian democracy, helped undermine the foundations of traditional morality and helped introduce the idea of irreversible decadence in Athens. There are numerous accounts of this crisis in the tragedies and also in Thucydides' *History of the Peloponnesian War*; for example, he describes the moral effect of the plague in Athens, the cruelty of the Athenians during the rebellion in Corcyra, and the cynicism of the Melian dialogue, in which Athenians justified their violent repression, declaring that "by a necessity of their nature wherever they have power they always rule" (V.cv.2). The fear of a state of growing immorality in which only the appearance of morality persists can be detected in Thucydides' remark: "The ordinary acceptation of words in their relation to things was changed as men thought fit . . . and if in any case oaths of reconcilement were exchanged, for the moment only were they binding" (III.lxxxii.4–7).

The sophists were generally held responsible for this alteration of traditional values. It is true that the most famous among them, Protagoras, Prodicus, and Hippias, claimed to teach virtue and were paid for doing so, a fact that must have been shocking in a culture in which moral training was still widely considered to be shaped by heroic example, or through a personal relationship with an elder. But Protagoras defined the object of his teaching as "good judgment [*euboulia*] in [his] affairs, showing how best to order his own home, and in the affairs of his city, showing how he may have most influence on public affairs both in speech and in action" (Plato, *Protagoras* 319a). This definition reveals that, contrary to popular opinion, the purpose of the sophists' moral teaching was to promote conformity, albeit with a somewhat critical attitude, rather than to encourage immorality or create dissension. To portray the sophists as advocates of immorality is to give a false impression of their work, an impression that shores up the charge brought against them as "corrupters of the young." Socrates was reproached for the same thing; indeed, this was the principal grievance mentioned in the charges brought against him. Yet there is no reason to believe that the charge was any more justified in the case of the sophists than it was for Socrates. In the middle of the 19th century, the English historian George Grote showed very convincingly that the accusation of immorality brought against the sophists (of which there is absolutely no hint in Plato's dialogues) was unfounded and expressed more than anything else the Athenians' prejudices against this new intellectual attitude. Nevertheless, the sophists' ability to play with arguments, and to use all the resources of logic to sustain paradoxical or inadmissible arguments, along with their ability to use persuasion to ridicule objective standards of justice, supported the belief that their sole ambition was to dissolve all prevailing forms of moral consensus.

The sophists' moral system was basically a kind of conventionalism according to which moral and legal standards were grounded in the *nomos* and in human institutions. As conditions of communal life, these standards derived their authority from the consensus or convention that produced them. Moreover, they varied from one community to another. When Protagoras recounted the myth about the origins of human history in the Platonic dialogue that bears his name, he emphasized that Zeus had sought to impart to everyone, without exception, two moral qualities that make community life possible: reverence *(aidōs)* and justice *(dike)* "to bring respect and right among men to the end that there should be regulation of cities and friendly ties to draw them together" (*Protagoras*, 322c). The presence of these two sentiments explains why citizens are willing to submit to social standards. This view of morality accords with the idea that an understanding of rational self-interest justifies obedience to laws; people obey laws not because morality demands that they do so or because laws are the result of a contract that includes the concept of inherent obligation, but because they serve the interests of the individual and the community. These interests include the love of one's friends, and the recognition and respect of the community. According to this type of conventionalism, the principal moral qualities essential to communal life are acquired by practice, use, and instruction, as well as by the "public and private effort of citizens to behave ethically," reinforced by the threat of punishment. Protagoras apparently foresaw the difficulty, inherent in any system of convention, of accounting for the stability and the imperative nature of moral standards. Consequently, he tried to show that one could give up the idea that moral standards are objective while fully appreciating their rationale, and one could seek to justify those standards in terms of the material, social, and moral benefits they afford.

Around the end of the 5th century the epistemological importance of the opposition between *nomos* and *phusis* that lay at the heart of sophistic conventionalism appears to have subsided. Thenceforth, reference to *phusis* was meant to enhance in nature the power of self-affirmation and the overbearing quality of the passions, whereas *nomos* stood for a set of restraints resulting from the reciprocal checks on ambitions intended to protect the interests of the weak. As the sophist Antiphon (perhaps the oligarch who was executed in 411) said, "The demands of the laws are the result not of natural disposition but of agreement, but the demands of nature are exactly the opposite," or "Many of the things which are just according to the law are at variance with nature" (in *The Older Sophists*, p. 219), for laws are in effect chains designed to control natural urges. This statement, in conjunction with others, seems to suggest the existence of a naturalist approach quite distinct from the "conventionalist" approach, inasmuch as it rejects any notion of morality as allegiance to laws. There are very few sources that provide direct information about the views of the main proponents of this radical "naturalist" approach. The reconstructions we find in Plato—expressed by figures such as Callicles in *Gorgias* and Thrasymachus in *The Republic*, for example—remain our primary source. This naturalism was endorsed mainly by ambitious men, those eager to profit from the moral decay of the time and to rid themselves of the restraints imposed by laws. For the naturalists, law was stigmatized as a mere product of convention, and also as an artifice that guaranteed power to the weak, whereas true moral principle, based in nature, dictated that the strongest would be the richest and most powerful. This affirmation of the ideal of man's true nature recalled the heroic conception of virtue. However, it differed from the Homeric tradition in a number of ways. First, it lacked any notion of honor, so essential to heroic virtue; second, it used the behavior of wild animals rather than the exploits of warriors to demonstrate the legitimate power of nature; third, it was characterized by resentment of the power that the weak had acquired by force of numbers.

These naturalist attitudes shared the conventionalist idea that moral standards are instituted by and have meaning for a given society. But they reflect a belief that justice based in law is merely justice of the weak. In fact, there were two different axiological systems, two methods of defining the just and the unjust, depending on their relationship to laws or to nature. So long as there was no conflict of interest, the legal standards stood, but when a stronger interest emerged and refused to comply with the law, the advocates of radical moral naturalism emphasized that no moral pretext could force such an interest to obey, and that the laws of nature had to prevail. These conventionalist and naturalist schools of thought are the objects of repeated criticism throughout antiquity. The best example is found in Plato, who tries to show that conventionalism leads directly to naturalism. Faced with an interest that refuses to cooperate, conventionalism is powerless to the extent that it has no other counterargument than the need to protect the interest of the weakest. But how can the interest of the weakest have an intrinsic moral value greater than that of the strongest? Morally, there is no difference. The only way to resolve the dilemma, according to Plato, is to refrain from establishing a morality based on interest in favor of one established on objective standards. One of the greatest inspirations of Socratic and Platonic moral philosophy was the critique of popular, consensual morality.

Socrates broke with ethical rhetoric based on models of good behavior; he preferred rational analysis of behavior and character. According to Socrates, rationality is the best means of attaining virtue. Rational examination of one's own life and that of others, criticism of false beliefs, and a relentless quest for greater coherence between thoughts and actions are the way to self-improvement; these convictions define the very essence of the hidden nature of morality. Socrates' influence is found again in the philosophical schools that developed after his death (Cynics, Cyrenaics, Megarians) and in the moral philosophies of the Hellenistic period. It influenced Plato as well; he was probably in his late twenties when Socrates died, and he devoted the next fifteen years to writing the so-called Socratic dialogues, which reflected Socrates' thinking in large part. However, Socrates' influence was uneven: strong in the case of Cynicism and Stoicism, it was very limited in the case of Epicureanism. Furthermore, the dialogues Plato wrote during his mature years and old age (*The Republic* and *Philebus*) reflect ideas that are not at all Socratic (such as the conviction that there are irresolvable psychological conflicts and the idea that the good life is a mixed life). Lastly, Aristotle's moral philosophy is quite far from the Socratic approach both in its method (starting from the standard definition of virtues) and in its refusal to equate virtue with wisdom. Still, no essay devoted to Greek ethical thought can fail to encounter constant questions about the degree to which post-Socratic ethics (in Plato, Aristotle, and the Hellenists) reexamined and integrated themes inherited from Socrates, and in particular about the effect of Socrates' distinction between philosophical reflection and conventional, popular morality.

"HOW SHOULD I LIVE?"

The Socratic question "How should I live?" is at the origin of moral philosophy. The very wording of the question is important, particularly the pronoun *I*. This *I* does not refer to a particular subject, but to a moral character that remains to be shaped. Thus the question is one of knowing what kind of life one should lead, what activities and attitudes one should cultivate in order to construct a psychological reality that has intrinsic coherence. Moreover, the *I* is the agent at the origin of intentional acts and the source of reasons to act, reasons that express and reinforce the agent's well-being. As for *should*, it does not refer to an abstract moral obligation, to a rule, or even to a set of empirical or natural constraints. Rather, it suggests a rational requirement rooted in human nature. One of the most striking characteristics of Greek ethics is its understanding of the moral development of man on the basis of his very nature. But it would be incorrect to see this appeal to human nature as an attempt to "naturalize" comparable to the effort underlying parts of the moral and social sciences today. Among the ancient authors, recourse to nature was not an attempt to interpret all reality as being simply a set of physical or physiological states. On the contrary, the study of human nature has a moral aspect inasmuch as it sheds light on the normative system present in man himself—to know what man ought to be is to know the purpose of life.

The pervasiveness of the question of purpose is another characteristic of Greek ethics. In taking up Socrates' definition of human nature as rationality, Plato linked it to a conception of the soul that also included desires and emotions; for the best-disposed soul strives for a life of moderation and order, and for a form of union with the divine. In Aristotle, the highest state a human being can attain is defined as one of contemplation of the divine, but this definition developed out of a very different understanding of human nature as a natural substance and the view that man's greatest faculty, reason, reaches the perfection of its exercise through contemplation.

All Hellenistic ethics ascribed great importance to identifying the one ultimate end that all actions endeavored ultimately to attain. Cicero's treatise *De Finibus* (1st century B.C.E.) was intended principally to list and discuss the various definitions of the final purpose of life, or the ultimate end. The best way to appreciate the diversity of Hellenistic ethics is to examine their definition of the final end *(telos)*. For the Stoics, the aim of life is defined as the perfection of human reason in conformity with the rational order manifest in nature. *Telos* means "living in harmony" or "living in harmony with nature." Cleanthes may have understood the formula as one that urged harmony not only with rational human nature but also with the common nature of the universe. As for the Epicureans, they saw pleasure as the ultimate goal, the only good sought for itself, whereas other goods are desired as a means to that end.

In any case, despite the diversity of these definitions of human nature and human goals, ancient philosophers shared an understanding of human life as the very locus of morality. The attitudes and values embedded in human nature are realized and expanded within the dimension of human life. A morally excellent goal cannot exist apart from the agent, since it consists not in accomplishing a particular action but rather in the fact of becoming a particular person, one who has ordered his soul in the way that is right for him. Moreover, human life is seen as a practice, a way of acting in which man is the author. Man's goal is thus good practice *(eupragia)*; accomplishment, a form of success. It can be conceived of as the exercise of an art based on skill or knowledge that allows one to take advantage of life's circumstances. Of course, human life is not without its frailties, and it is at the mercy of many variables, but seeing life as a deliberate exercise highlights the agent as the principle of action, in other words, the human being who deliberates, desires, acts, and justifies his actions. As we have seen, the individual's moral culmination is attained when that individual has established himself as the origin of his own choices. Indeed, one of the characteristics of a successful life is that it is the life of an agent who has chosen his very life and who recognizes that he has done so.

In addition, a life imbued with morality is also the most rational life. In *Apology*, Plato indicates that Socrates saw himself as entrusted with a god-given mission to spend his life in philosophy examining himself and others, to persuade every man to concern himself not with his body or wealth but with his soul alone. Such a mission bears directly on morality. First of all, it points to a way of ordering goods. Physical pleasure, wealth, private interests, and political success are of little value compared to the true good that human beings can attain in this life. The exercise of critical reason is the best means of reaching this virtuous state of the soul, because it allows one to shed false beliefs about good and evil. Examination and conversation with others can bring to light the implicit moral beliefs of the interlocutor, expose the contradictions in his beliefs, and, once they have been refuted, convince him to give up a false belief. It means "laying bare the soul," as Plato says in *Charmides*, by exposing its beliefs, its rationalizations, its intentions. This surprising conviction that moral goodness results from rational inquiry corresponds to Socrates' insistence that he himself did not have any substantive knowledge of morality, that he did not know, for example, what was socially acceptable behavior or what qualities properly characterized men and citizens. But he said that he did have, besides the knowledge that he did not know such things, a particularly human form of knowledge that was capable of distinguishing between what is truly good for the soul and what is neither evil nor good.

Another characteristic feature of post-Socratic thought is that it regarded reason and knowledge as the fundamental components of the ego. The desire for a rational understanding of the self, which Socrates was the first to express, is fully developed in Plato's work. But whereas Socratic reflection applied to the practical, to know-how and to contextualized moral knowledge (since the pursuit of ethics involved other people and considered human existence as it was being lived), Plato sought to bring the philosophical foundation of this rationalist approach to light by relating it to knowledge of the intelligible reality that is Good incarnate. Knowledge of the Good and the process of internalizing it are Plato's response to the question: "How should I live?"

In contrast, nothing could be farther from Aristotle's thought than the Platonic desire to make ethics the work of knowledge. For Aristotle, the objective of morality is not knowledge of the essence of the good, or virtue, but the fact of becoming virtuous. Ethical reflection is not a theoretical pursuit but a form of practice meant to improve the soul by explaining why one should strive to be virtuous. Unlike Plato, Aristotle refused to seek the sort of rigor and accuracy in morality that he saw as valid only in the sciences. Finally, whereas Plato dismissed arguments and majority opinion, Aristotle advised starting from common beliefs and proceeding in a dialectical manner to identify difficulties and problems, showing things in rough outline and using only the appropriate degree of rigor. By rejecting the Platonic idea that one's grasp of human good must be based on abstract and universal knowledge of the good in general, Aristotle, alone among philosophers, tied the meaning of the question "How should I live?" directly to the question of the nature of the *I*. For human beings, as for all living species, the good depends on developing and exercising one's natural abilities under favorable circumstances.

The Cynics attempted to understand moral philosophy as a form of exercise or practice, as an asceticism, rather than as a system of reasoning and knowledge. This tension between the practical and theoretical purposes of philosophy appears throughout the history of Hellenistic thought. One philosophical tendency, primarily concerned with practice and with the correct way to live, is illustrated by Skepticism, and some aspects of Epicureanism: the Stoics called this approach "the shortcut to virtue." Another tendency, though concerned with ethical practice, sought to base that practice on knowledge of the natural world and logic, renewing Plato's theoretical ambition. Stoicism is the best example of this latter approach; ethics remains at the heart of philosophy but it draws on philosophy's other components as well: logic (the analysis of ideas) and physics (the study of physical realities and the cosmos).

No matter which of these paths was chosen, moral philosophy in the Hellenistic period was chiefly aimed at giving individuals reason to believe that they could attain complete control of their own happiness in the world, in the here and now. Whereas Plato maintained that the highest form of human happiness is always subject to the indeterminacy that affects the physical world, and Aristotle saw happiness as inseparable from fortune, the ideal of life and happiness that characterized the Hellenistic philosophers was presented as attainable by all people in all circumstances. This model of autonomy based on rational understanding of what human beings need to be happy and to act morally—in other words, the free exercise of reason—was first taken up by the Cynics and the Cyrenaics. Cynics scorned everything except reason. Guided by reason, they could endeavor to live free of all constraint and tradition, indifferent to external goods, fortune, and public opinion. Even among Cyrenaic sages, who recognized moral value only in immediate pleasure, we find the same idealization of a life of total self-control at all times, attained through mastery over pleasures.

The moral example offered by the wise man's life was to become the hallmark of Hellenistic philosophy. Each school of philosophy had a different conception of the sage, but each one embodied a combination of reason, self-control, the cult of virtue, and autonomy. These qualities, and the internalization of the morally good, were aspects of moral excellence. The sage answered for no one but himself. He was armed, equipped in the military sense of the word, with wisdom that prepared him to face any hardship, because he had reduced his needs to the bare minimum, to those basics that nature provides in the ordinary way. He could live either, according to the Epicurean ideal, a life free of any form of trouble, or, according to the Stoic ideal, a life that passed quietly, without turmoil, completely independent of chance and circumstance.

VIRTUE AND NATURE

Socrates defined virtue as an ideal of moral autonomy and reason that afforded protection against any threat from other people and against the vicissitudes of fate. This viewpoint characterized all post-Socratic thought, and it influenced European culture at least until the 17th century. It broke with the Homeric idea of morality as the affirmation of the self; it also contrasted with the sophistic model of human accomplishment, or skill in conducting affairs in both the public and private spheres. Still, there is ample evidence that the Socratic definition of virtue never completely replaced the aristocratic view, or the conventional and instrumental definition that persisted in popular morality. Sufficient evidence of this point is found in the obstinacy of some of Plato's interlocutors, including the young Meno, who spontaneously defines virtue as "to desire what is honourable and be able to procure it" (*Meno* 77b).

It is important to stress the widespread usage of the term *arete* (virtue or excellence) during Socrates' time and in Plato's dialogues. Eyes, ears, horses may all have *arete*. In all these uses, the term describes a function (sight for eyes, speed for horses) and it also designates the perfection and excellence of that function. Similarly, as it was commonly used for human beings, *arete* designated the action that was most characteristic of man, and the perfection of that action. Socrates and Plato added several new dimensions to this word that was already rich in meaning. As man is capable of voluntary action, *arete* embodies the specific quality, the excellence of the originating agent at work, in other words, the human soul. Moreover, Plato, like Socrates before him, insisted that *arete* should apply only to the human soul and should be defined primarily in terms of reflection and knowledge, as the faculty that affords a clear grasp of the purpose of action and of the means to attain it. *Arete* in the Socratic-Platonic sense is defined both by this connection to the good, conceived as the well-ordered soul, and by the presence of knowledge.

A conception of this sort presupposes a radical critique of the common understanding of virtue. This is undertaken in Book I of *The Republic*, where Plato addresses the virtue of justice. As Socrates is quick to point out, one of the traditional answers to the question "What is justice?" (justice means re-paying what one owes) leads to many inconsistencies. Another definition, proposed by Thrasymachus, identifies justice with the promotion of self-interest. This self-centered conception of practical rationality would allow any government in power to pass laws that are in its own interest and to claim that they are just. To refute this view, Socrates takes pains to show how illogical it is to conceive of justice as "the interest of the strongest." The interest of the agent, which is the sole moral aim of rational self-interest, has to be based on knowledge of what is good for each agent. But the good of the agent, or rather the proper disposition of his soul, can never be achieved by injustice. Moreover, Socrates stresses that a conception of morality exclusively devoted to self-interest is probably not compatible with any social organization. To achieve his ends, the immoralist needs to be surrounded by individuals who respect the common moral code. A third view, finally, is proposed by Glaucon: the motivation and rationale for a just life derive solely from the fact that the power to act is limited. Justice means "a compromise between the best, which is to do wrong with impunity, and the worst, which is to be wronged and be impotent to get one's revenge" (*The Republic* II.359a). Situated between these two extremes, justice is not loved as a good but respected, owing to man's powerlessness to commit injustice.

Here we have three ways of defining virtue: as tradition, as self-interest, as the reconciliation of conflicting interests. Socrates criticizes them all by un-covering their common feature: they all treat justice as a "foreign" good, use-ful not to the one who practices it but to the one in whose favor it is practiced. But in Socrates' view, justice, the most precious good a man can ever attain, benefits not the person who profits from it, but only the one who practices it. Virtuous action is expected to be its own justification, and there is never any benefit to acting without justice, because such action objectively harms one's soul, even if the unjust deed remains concealed and goes unpunished. Con-versely, a just person cannot be harmed by unjust treatment insofar as no in-justice can harm the one good that is his own, the order of his soul. This argu-ment, which Socrates develops with Polus in *Gorgias*, leads to the conclusion that it is preferable to be treated unjustly rather than to commit injustice, and when guilty of an injustice, it is best to submit to the punishment that will heal the soul. One has to choose virtue, not because it is rational not to oppose justice, given the advantages and well-being that it brings, but because it is ra-tional to act justly.

Virtue is also defined as closely related to knowledge. Socrates declares that man's wickedness originates solely in his ignorance: ignorance of the princi-ples of action or of the distinctive features of the circumstances in which one acts. The connection established here between virtue and knowledge is open to criticism. Knowledge of the good alone does not provide an incentive for virtue, and it is always possible to act irrationally. But the close relationship between knowledge of the good and virtuous action does assist our under-standing of the import of Socrates' analogy between virtue and a craft such as shoe making, navigation, or medicine. It is true that whereas a craftsman is free not to practice his craft, or to do it badly, a virtuous man has no reason not to use the sort of knowledge that equates with virtue, in that the knowl-edge in question is knowledge of what fosters his own happiness. The defini-tion of virtue as knowledge leads to the idea of knowledge as a mental activity that helps to maintain the order of the soul. Moral virtues are conditions of mind related to the perception of right and wrong. But virtue, the object of this knowledge, is difficult to determine, and several Socratic dialogues con-clude with the impossibility of stating what it is.

The problems associated with the intellectualism of Socrates' approach led Plato to develop a more complex notion of virtue. In place of the simplicity of the Socratic theory, in which the soul is construed as composed of rational and irrational parts, Plato offered a moral psychology of great subtlety. The soul, according to Plato, comprises three parts: the rational component, the *thumos* (heart, or emotion), and most desires. Each of these parts has a source of motivation. Moral virtue is not simply conceived as a cognitive state, re-lated to the validity of a proposition describing what is to be done; rather, vir-tue is defined in terms of the entire soul, which it shapes and organizes. As the psychological basis for our behavior, virtue grasps the logic of right and wrong, but insofar as virtue corresponds to the establishment of an order re-lating the rational and the irrational in a specific way in each instance, it in-cludes the emotions and the appetites, for these too are sources of voluntary physical action and must remain subject to rational judgment regarding the good. In the process of deepening the definition of virtue by recognizing the role of emotion and desire in motivation, Plato was careful to reject any in-strumental justification of morality. The choice of virtue should not result from the calculation of pleasures and pains that Socrates appears to suggest in *Protagoras,* for choosing on that basis would be to confuse true virtue with the inferior virtue described in *Phaedo.* It is by exercising virtue that the soul can recover its true nature and move closer to union with the divine. Accord-ing to *Theaetetus,* "to become like God is to become righteous and holy and wise" (176b). Virtue consists in imitating within one's own soul the harmoni-ous movement of the soul of the universe, but it also involves a form of knowledge that is accessible only at the end of a process of recollection. Only the rulers of the city-state in *The Republic* have access to knowledge of virtue; other citizens possess only valid opinions. It is important to remember that there is a certain tension in the Platonic conception of virtue, which is defined either as the pure exercise of thought (according to *Phaedo* and *Theaetetus*) or as a complex blend of reflection, desire, and emotion (in *The Republic*). This tension may account for the fact that one of the greatest differences be-tween Aristotle and Plato lies in the definition of virtue.

Aristotle defines virtue as the optimal state of the rational potential of human nature. But he is careful to make a distinction between two forms of virtue, or excellence: intellectual virtue (in other words, the virtues of abstract intellect, knowledge and intelligence, or of the practical intellect, practical wisdom) and moral virtue, which is "a settled disposition of the mind determining the choice of actions and emotions, consisting essentially in the observance of the mean relative to us, this being determined by principle, that is, as the prudent man would determine it" (Aristotle, *Nicomachean Ethics* II.vi.15). Moral virtues, or virtues of character, are made up of both present desire and rational disposition. In fact, practical wisdom, *phronesis*, plays an essential role in deliberation, in understanding the purpose of life, and in practical judgment in a given situation; however, knowledge of what is good is never enough to make someone virtuous. For while virtue is the essential element of a full and self-sufficient life, it also requires a plurality of goods as the very condition of its practice.

The moral virtues, to which pains, pleasures, and emotions are rightfully related, are defined both as medieties and as attributes of perfection. The criterion of mediety, or perfect mean (by which is meant not a moderating principle but an element of appropriateness and suitability), is a formal criterion that enables us to appreciate the rightness of the feelings, emotions, and pleasures associated with virtuous action. Hence courage is the mediety between two corresponding vices, excess and omission, or cowardice and recklessness. Moderation is the mediety between a form of unrestrained indulgence and indifference to pleasure. In addition, the formal criterion of mediety leads to the notion that the forms of virtue may have some variability. One text in *Politics* explicitly defends Gorgias's definition of multiple virtues against Plato's criticism: a man's virtue is different from a woman's or a slave's; a systematic enumeration of virtues is thus more accurate, and a better guide for action, than a so-called universal definition.

The Epicureans and the Stoics construed virtue as the essential condition for achieving life's purpose, which they defined as the moral perfection of humankind. Another significant aspect of Hellenistic morality is related to the connection between morality and nature and the recommended balance between moral reasons and natural reasons. The idea of a "natural tendency" *(horme)* is fundamental in this regard. The Epicureans were its most prominent defenders. Epicurus advises man to return to those first truths from which education has led him away, for it then becomes clear that natural tendencies lead to pleasure. Feelings of pleasure and grief are immediate and irrefutable indicators that what is pleasing is good. This is what human nature reveals: this nature becomes apparent not at the moment of its fulfillment, as Aristotle thought, but in the young child whose nature has not yet been corrupted. The Stoics accepted the same premise, but in their view, natural tendencies led not to pleasure but to self-directed concern, to the instinct for survival and self-fulfillment. Through their capacity for appropriation to themselves, or familiarity *(oikeiosis)*, human beings seek natural benefits that are the very ends ordained by nature. The process of selecting what is beneficial gradually takes on a kind of practical self-awareness and develops in conformity with nature's intent; actions aim at increasingly higher goals, chosen objects and principles of just action. The pattern of motivation that leads one first to find what benefits the individual and then to do what is morally right remains more or less the same, but the reasons and objectives have changed. Virtue based on rationality is the perfection of reason (not an exercise of rationality, as Aristotle saw it).

The first and most unusual of the post-Socratic philosophers, Pyrrhon, attempted to eliminate human desire; thus he seems to have placed himself, in advance, outside the mainstream of Hellenistic ethics. Yet even in Pyrrhon's work we can see traces of the recognition of a vital impulse *(horme)*, a tendency shared by all, that leads an individual to choose whatever appears to be in his own best interest. Arcesilaus, a representative of a later probabilism, is thought to have claimed that this "tendency" naturally leads men to what is appropriate. Even the Neopyrrhonians of the 1st century B.C.E. held that ethical conduct depended on passive submission to appearance and on a minimal impulse. Still, in making serenity and happiness contingent on suspension of judgment, the Neopyrrhonian school probably represented the most thoroughgoing attempt in Hellenistic philosophy to avoid relying on the continuity between the initial impulse and morality.

The Neopyrrhonian approach was, however, the exception. Generally speaking, natural inclination is the best indicator of human good, the pursuit of which leads naturally to the pursuit of moral good or perfection attributable to virtue. At the beginning of Book II of his treatise *On Duties,* Cicero emphasized that the useful *(agathon,* in Greek, meaning both the good for the individual and the good per se) cannot be separated from moral beauty *(honestum,* which translates the Greek *kalon).* This bond was so strongly proclaimed by the Stoics that their Skeptic critics accused them of holding two distinct notions of the good. The association between naturalism and rationalism, fairly typical of Hellenistic ethics, was the focus of Skeptic criticism.

HAPPINESS AND THE PHILOSOPHY OF ACTION

The intrinsic connection between morality and human life is not foreign to our own experience of morality, but what may appear problematic to us is that the goal of the moral life was happiness. Greek ethics seems to be eudemonist, an ethics of happiness that closely relates the pursuit of morality to the pursuit of happiness. How can we define this reality made up of happiness, felicity, prosperity, which the Greeks called *eudaimonia*? It is clearly not just a subjective feeling of happiness (as the 19th-century English Utilitarians described it); even the Epicureans, who equated pleasure with the good, avoided any subjective definition, and the Cyrenaics (constituting one of the Socratic schools) may have been the only ones who defined happiness as the maximization of excellent subjective states of being. *Eudaimonia* really meant a way of being, determined both by the proper order of the soul and by just actions.

Happiness is most commonly defined as pleasure. One of the first and most ardent defenders of this definition is Callicles, in *Gorgias,* who says that a happy life is a "life of luxury and licentiousness and liberty" (492c). Socrates argues against this view, emphasizing the insatiable nature of the strongest physical desires (and the frustration that always results from the attempt to satisfy them). The most convincing intellectual refutation of hedonism, however, is found in *Philebus.* Pleasure, as a whole, belongs to the limitless. It is only a catalyst and does not have a nature of its own; hence it cannot be confused with the good that is the basis of a happy life. Moreover, any perception of pleasure presupposes that thought accompanies pleasure. A life of pure pleasure would thus be stigmatized by its incompleteness and doomed to a continuous quest for objects that might satisfy its inherent desires.

However, hedonism is not simply the defense of a conception in which pleasure is characterized by its immediacy, its immediate intensity, with no room for any distinction between good and bad pleasures. There is also a rationalist conception of hedonism (set forth, for example, in *Protagoras*) that identifies happiness with the maximization of pleasure over a lifetime. In this view, the individual has the ability to step back from immediate gratification in order to weigh it against future pains that could ensue or against possible greater pleasures to come. From a eudemonist viewpoint, the only way to refute this argument is to show that the concept of pleasure is ontologically inconsistent or that pleasure cannot be counted as an independent and neutral criterion for judging the ideal human condition.

It was Epicurus who carried this holistic view of pleasure to its highest philosophic level. According to Epicurus, the life of pleasure, as the entirety of satisfactions one has experienced, is the only happy life, because it is the only life that can be regulated and that can bring about a state of tranquillity and independence from external conditions. The individual attains a kind of autonomy by changing and adapting his desires, for these are the products of beliefs that man can control through reason. Happiness is characterized by the absence of bodily pain and the absence of disorder in the soul. Although pleasure is the only intrinsic good, happiness also requires prudence and other ethical virtues, because "the virtues have grown into one with a pleasant life, and a pleasant life is inseparable from them" (in Diogenes Laertius, *Lives of Eminent Philosophers* II.x.132). The ultimate source of pleasure lies in reflecting on the minimal conditions for bodily satisfaction: a wise man can thus be happy under torture. The Cyrenaic philosophers, a century before Epicurus, seem to have criticized this conception. They stressed that pleasure is the aim of all action, but for this reason they refused to identify happiness with pleasure, because the satisfactions of pleasure have a rhapsodic and detached quality that happiness cannot have. Happiness, therefore, cannot be defined as pleasure or the sum of pleasures.

In Socratic thought, alongside the definition of happiness as pleasure, which was adopted by the Epicureans in particular, we find the origin of two other ideas that have had widespread influence on later thought. In *Gorgias*, Socrates evokes the life of the wise man who limits his desires to those that can be satisfied and who therefore experiences a tranquillity that guarantees his happiness by immunizing him against dissatisfaction and loss. This view reappears among the Cynics. Happiness seems to be defined as the fact of living, after a kind of physical or mental asceticism, in harmony with nature or in conformance with reason. The essence of happiness is self-mastery, manifested by the ability to live well in all imaginable circumstances.

A final conception of happiness that seems also to be Socratic in origin defines human life as the life that is best able to maximize the natural talents of the individual. The Platonic conception of happiness as the fulfillment of the rational desires that express and confirm the order of the soul is similar to this view, but in fact the Aristotelian and Stoic definitions correspond to it most closely, though from two different perspectives. For the Stoics, happiness, or the possession of moral good, is the fulfillment of natural tendencies oriented above all toward human good. For Aristotle, happiness corresponds to the state of perfect fulfillment of the best human capacities. However, this definition of happiness is in stark contrast to hedonism. Aristotle shows in this way that the most properly human quality that a happy life must manifest is not the capacity to experience pleasure but the exercise of reason. He also stressed the fact that, since pleasure combined with intelligence is better than pleasure alone, pleasure cannot be the good. A century later the Stoics tried to show, in opposition to the Epicureans, that man's most natural tendency is not the pursuit of pleasure but knowledge of himself and his own condition.

Thus the most general definition of *eudaimonia* involves performing certain acts, being a certain kind of person, leading a particular type of life. The well-being of the soul leads to happiness, and virtue is the sole reward. This is the deepest meaning of Greek eudemonism. It adds to the conceptual link between virtue and happiness the certainty that the two are always compatible in practice. One can be both happy and virtuous, since no suffering can deprive the individual of his virtue, which is the objective source of happiness. This interdependence of virtue and happiness may take on different meanings. Virtue alone may suffice for happiness, with no need for anything else whatsoever (this is the strictly Socratic position that was adopted by the

Stoics). More generally, happiness as a state conditional on virtue requires other forms of the good. Thus, *eudaimonia* is defined in terms of the pursuit of true goods, possessing an objective value. For Plato, these goods, in addition to knowledge, include order, moderation, and limits, and as these goods are present in all human reality, they help to make that reality good. To an intellectual good Aristotle adds certain external goods, such as health and reputation; these are necessary for the exercise of moral spontaneity. But *eudaimonia* also refers to the perfected state of the soul. The eudemonism of Greek ethics is a form of perfectionism, to the extent that the moral achievement of an agent depends on the intrinsic value or perfection of the activities and states responsible for happiness. But happiness cannot result from the mere possession of these goods, not even a single instant of happiness. Except for the Stoics, all Greek philosophers made happiness a quality of human existence in its entirety.

Happiness is thus an ultimate goal that allows us to explain our actions and desires. It is only in regard to happiness that we cannot legitimately ask: "Why have you done this?" Socrates held that reason was the only source of moral action. Consequently, weakness of will *(akrasia)*, or acting against one's better judgment out of pleasure, pain, or fear, does not exist. Moreover, no one can act voluntarily against virtue, for that would mean disregarding what is most important to one's own soul.

In contrast to the Socratic position, Plato's philosophy of action, and the moral psychology associated with it, offers a complex and differentiated theory of the origins of motivation. The rational part of the soul is able to act "in consideration of the best." At the other extreme, irrational desires, stemming from the appetitive part of the soul, lack any regard for the good. As for the desires that stem from the third part of the soul, the emotional part, these all have to do with an affirmation of individual self-worth; in this sense they arise from a truncated conception of the good, but they can be put to use by reason. When Plato sought to account for an irrational action, or for someone's acting against his better judgment, or for the existence of psychic conflicts, he did not contrast desire, or will, with reason; he contrasted one (rational) desire with another (irrational) desire. Reason always opposes appetite through resistance of the will and desire. Moreover, unlike Socrates, Plato accepted the reality of the psychic phenomenon of *akrasia*, or the possibility that someone would act against his better judgment. However, Plato was emphatic about the nonintentional nature of this type of act, since an act's intentionality is always connected with the fact that it proceeds from a judgment about the good. Hence only rational action is voluntary in the fullest sense, and actions motivated by anger or violent emotion are voluntary only to the degree that they can involve rational consideration.

Plato's view, according to which a source of motivation is linked to each part of the soul, does not appear in Aristotle. In *De Anima*, Aristotle suggests that desire *(orexis)*, stemming from the part of the soul that desires, is the sole motivation for all actions, whether they are rational (in which case we are dealing with a rational desire, or wish) or they originate in emotions and appetites. In this approach the philosophy of action gains coherence, since there is only a single source of motivation, inherent in a specific part of the soul, but even this leads to problems. Beliefs about the good or about judgment are incapable of motivating action by themselves, unless desire is involved. The inability of reason to motivate action corresponds, moreover, to its inability to determine the aims of human action. Indeed, several of Aristotle's texts seem to show that reason can ponder only the means of action, not its aims (defined by desire). Finally, like Plato, Aristotle did not accept the possibility of acting against one's better judgment, but he did acknowledge that an individual can do wrong intentionally and with a certain rational justification, based on some belief that is only partially adequate to the situation and that runs counter, if only by accident, to the best judgment.

The contrast between Plato and Aristotle sheds light on a debate that runs throughout the history of moral philosophy. Plato was the first to maintain that there is a source of motivation specific to reason, and that belief about the good is an "active" force, capable of motivating and defining ends. Aristotle, by contrast, has often been seen as inaugurating a tradition, shared by Hobbes, Hume, and all anti-intellectualist schools, according to which reason is passive and only desire determines ends.

In this sense, Plato and Aristotle stand in clear contrast to the Stoics, who are more faithful to the Socratic conception in their desire to identify moral life with rational life. The Stoic sage, if there was such a person, always knew what the right action was in all circumstances and had to be able to act accordingly. The Stoics showed that there is a direct association between beliefs about action and the good. Only reason can motivate action: therefore it is enough to accept the rational impression that indicates what action to take or avoid. An action is just if the assumption behind it is valid. There is no weakness of will, but there are errors of judgment when one submits to assumptions that present as good anything other than virtue or reason. Passions can cloud rational thought, which is why they must be not controlled or disciplined, but eradicated. Compared to the moral psychology of Plato or Aristotle, that of the Hellenistic philosophers seems shockingly simplistic. Notions of psychic conflict and the belief that there are disruptive forces that keep principle or logical conviction from governing action are foreign to Hellenistic ethics.

Moreover, Hellenistic ethics introduced the question of human freedom from both a physical and a moral perspective, an approach that has very little counterpart in the work of Plato or Aristotle. Epicurus was very mindful of the possibility of removing his atomistic physics from the necessitarianism that seemed inseparable from it in the work of Democritus, and that threatened to deprive the moral responsibility of the agent of any reality. The theory of *clinamen* (or the minimal deviation of atoms: the term was used by Lucretius in his poem *De Natura*) makes it possible to conceptualize not only bodies and a stable physical world but also the possibility of the formation of moral character, an autonomous source of actions that cannot be reduced to a mechanistic sum of all the atoms that form an individual. The Stoics were interested, finally, in the problem of destiny, a physical problem in which the universal principle of causality was at stake, and a moral problem, since it was linked to the potential for human freedom. A complex physical theory suggests that moral action, although necessarily stimulated by an impression from outside the individual, is also shaped by the character of the individual who expresses his moral disposition through his assent.

THE GOOD, AND THE GOOD LIFE

The keystone of moral philosophy in antiquity was the idea of the good, and it played an essential role in Plato's moral philosophy. Knowledge of the good allowed the philosopher to judge what is good in human beings and in the universe as a whole. It is only after philosophical training that the future ruler of *The Republic* is able to see the "most brilliant aspect of being," possessing the formal characteristics of beauty, order, and harmony. His soul then seeks to reproduce in itself the ordered movements of the soul of the world and to achieve an equivalent good in human affairs. However, as was frequently the case in Plato's work, this initial approach, which presupposes asceticism and detachment, has to be viewed in tandem with another that supports the notion of the good as the highest ideal of human beings, a perfect and self-sufficient reality. This specifically human good is defined in *Philebus* as a diverse and harmonious life that combines all knowledge with the purest pleasures. The best life, the choice of which is the choice most accessible to man, is defined in the myth of Er at the end of Book X of *The Republic* as not mediocre but a life of moderation, "the life that is seated in the mean" (619b).

This is where Aristotle differs most from Plato. The Platonic idea of the good, according to Aristotle, is incoherent, without internal consistency, and, more important, useless. Plato erred in thinking that the concept could be applied in a univocal way. In fact, the good is expressed according to different categories of being: in substance it is God or intellect; in quality, virtue; in quantity, moderation; and so forth. The good cannot be a single and universal notion, and the Platonic thesis holding that the good is moderation results from an error of category. In addition, since the good is a homonymous designation, endowed with multiple meanings, it cannot be the object of a single science. Finally, even if there were a good in and of itself, it would be an unattainable model; human beings could neither know it nor use it. The moral individual does not need it to direct his thought or deeds.

Plato regarded the good as an objective, intelligible, knowable reality, and as a guide for human action. The good is fundamentally one, independent of the human mind and an impartial criterion of the merit of one's actions and behavior. A similar definition of the good can be found throughout the Intuitionist tradition beginning in the 17th century, in the work of the English philosopher G. E. Moore at the beginning of the 20th century, and among adherents of moral realism closer to our own time. For Aristotle, on the other hand, the good is a way of qualifying states of things, persons, and actions. Goodness as applied to reality depends on the nature of the particular element of reality in question; the goodness of that element cannot be defined independently of its specificity; hence there is an irreducible plurality of goods. Thomas Aquinas, Hume, and contemporary defenders of a return to virtue such as Alasdair MacIntyre and Charles Taylor have much in common with this view.

The answers of the Hellenistic philosophers to the question "What is the good?" seem simpler and more substantial: for example, the good can be pleasure or living according to nature. But these thinkers were also very concerned with the accessibility of the good. All Hellenistic philosophers emphasized the difficulty of perfecting moral good in oneself. They agreed that the wise man is a model, an ideal of attainable human perfection. The Stoics stressed that even if virtue is the only good, the sage can show in everything he does (significant as well as trivial actions, successes as well as failures) the rational disposition that is the mark of virtue. Under the Roman empire, the Stoics developed spiritual exercises that led to detachment from the body and from external goods as the means of attaining a level of equanimity (an "inner citadel," according to Marcus Aurelius).

Once again Pyrrhon and the Skeptical tradition represented a break with the core of Greek ethical thought. Whereas Pyrrhon defined the supreme good as a state of internal perfection, conceived as an *aphasia* (the inability to speak, or meaningless speech: for Pyrrhon things were without essence and were inexpressible), in other words as an absence of stress and ultimately an absence of feeling, the Skepticism that arose in the Academy starting in the 3rd century held that the only perfection possible for humankind was found in refraining from making any erroneous commitment. By discarding the view of the moral good as a set of affective and mental states (internal serenity, calm, or even the elimination of feelings) in favor of the notion of a suspension of judgment *(epokhe)*, in other words as an attitude toward the world of representations, the Skeptics set themselves distinctly apart from the rest of Hellenistic thought.

The distinctive feature of Greek ethical thought was that it centered morality around the agent, and the moral development of the individual began within himself and ended with the shaping of his moral character. Kant criticized Plato's moral philosophy for defending a self-centered form of morality, but the criticism holds true for all Greek moral thought, which was indeed formally self-centered in the sense that if every individual has a good reason to act morally, this reason is essentially related to his moral character. The principle of morality that is inscribed in the moral agent never consists in a set of preferences to be satisfied apart from any moral viewpoint. To the contrary, as Bernard Williams says, the ultimate aim "is not, given an account of the self and its satisfactions, to show how the ethical life (luckily) fits them. It is to give an account of the self into which that life fits" (*Ethics and the Limits of Philosophy*, p. 32).

A modern reader may be surprised by this. Although we understand virtues and morality in an essentially altruistic sense, how are we to understand an ethical perspective that does not give priority to concern for others? When Socrates stressed that the main concern of man must be the quality of his soul, he never alluded to the fact that serving others was in itself a moral end. The happiness that is sought, however objectivist its definition might be, is obviously that of the agent and not of others. But the formulation of this exclusive concern for one's own soul should be qualified, for the Platonic theory of love, which is aimed at the moral improvement of others; the Aristotelian concept of justice; the Stoic idea of familiarity; and the Epicurean notion of friendship all evidence a concern for taking others into account in the definition of morality. Insofar as the objectives of morality and justice are rational, it is possible to convince other moral agents to adopt them. More generally, the validity of moral reasoning applies equally to all. Lastly, the exercise of altruistic virtues contributes to the happiness of the agent himself. Aristotle said that the man who dies for his country or his friends is a man who loves himself, for he earns for himself a larger share of the good.

THE INFLUENCE AND THE LEGACY OF GREEK ETHICAL THOUGHT

The unbroken line of ancient philosophers that we have established here—from the Presocratics to Socrates, Plato, Aristotle, the Stoics, the Epicureans, and the Skeptics—has been recognized only in the past two hundred years. Previously, knowledge of Greek thought was selective and spotty. During the Middle Ages, the principal available texts were those of Aristotle and the Stoics, primarily; the only work by Plato that was known was *Timaeus*. By the end of the medieval period, Aristotelianism seemed to hold out the possibility of a stable and ordered understanding of the world in relation to God, whereas Platonism was seen either as rational and humanistic, or as poetic or magical speculation. Raphael's famous painting *The School of Athens* presents two central figures, Plato and Aristotle, the former with his eyes turned toward heaven, the latter with his hands facing the earth. But the rediscovery of Platonism during the Renaissance also inspired a wave of humanism, while Aristotle was seen (at least by Descartes) as the defender of essences and of mysterious analogies. Even today, how can we be sure that our way of viewing Greek philosophy is accurate? The Hellenists' immediate successors did not really perceive the conflicts and polemics among schools that seem so clear-cut today. Cicero does not seem to have seen much difference between Plato and Aristotle: he emphasized instead their common opposition to Epicurus's thought, and to some extent to the Stoics.

Nevertheless, ancient moral philosophy exerted considerable influence on the history of philosophy, and even today Aristotle's theory of virtues, Plato's and Aristotle's conception of human motivation, the Cyrenaics' and Stoics' definition of pleasure are at the heart of numerous debates. The persistent reference to the Greeks may lead one to doubt the historicist view of philosophy (in which moral problems are defined by historical circumstance). In fact, some of our own moral issues are the same as those raised by the Greeks, and our tentative answers borrow certain elements from Greek thought. This should cause us to question the notion of moral progress from antiquity to today, for the primary effect of such progress would have been to consign Greek notions to the distant past.

At last we can try to answer our initial question about the meaning of morality for the Greeks. It was a morality without abstract laws or categorical imperatives. The essential moral question involved knowing what kind of life to live and how to shape one's character. In this sense, Greek ethical thought represents the most complete form of a concept of morality based on the strength of the appeal of the good, where the agent's moral achievement is in direct proportion to the pursuit of happiness (as opposed to a conception based on an imperative, where morality depends on obligations and the agent disappears). By the same token, altruism is based on a concept of the good for individuals, even if we can find in classical thought, among the Stoics, indicators pointing to a moral theory based on duties and obligations.

In Greek ethics there is no strict distinction or clear separation between the moral and the nonmoral, or between general obligations and private moral ideals. It is a godless morality, without abstract rules, for its standards always involve determining what kind of life one should lead. Moreover, there is no concept of universal obligations or of humanity as a whole, nor do we find any reckoning with specifically historical considerations. The Greeks did not attempt to explain reality in terms of historical process, nor did they believe that categories of human thought were dependent on man's material, social, or historical circumstances.

Greek ethical thought is, finally, integrated into human life to a remarkable extent. The Greek concept of morality embraced fate, chance, and the vicissitudes that characterize human life. In that context, it defended a view of man as moral, rationally self-sufficient, free, and protected against contingencies. The quest for moral autonomy, so strong in Hellenistic philosophy, is the response of Greek ethics to the conviction that moral perfection is uncertain at best, as Greek tragedy keeps reminding us.

MONIQUE CANTO-SPERBER
Translated by Elizabeth Rawlings and Jeannine Pucci

Bibliography

Texts and Translations

Anaximander. In *The Presocratic Philosophers*. Ed. G. S. Kirk, J. E. Raven, and M. Schofield.

Antiphon. Trans. J. S. Morrison. In *The Older Sophists*. Ed. Rosamond Kent Sprague. Columbia: University of South Carolina Press, 1972. Pp. 106–240.

Aristotle. *Nicomachean Ethics*. Trans. H. Rackham. Loeb Classical Library.

Arnim, Hans von. *Stoicorum Veterum Fragmenta*, 2nd ed. Stuttgart: Teubner, 1964.

Bréhier, Emile, and Pierre-Maxime Schuhl. *Les Stoïciens*. Paris: Gallimard, 1988. Coll. Bibliothèque de la Pléiade.

Cicero. *De Officiis*. Trans. Walter Miller. Loeb Classical Library.

Démocrite et l'atomisme ancien: Fragments et témoignages. Ed. and trans. Maurice Solovine, rev. Pierre-Marie Morel. Paris: Pocket, 1993.

Dumont, Jean-Paul. *Les Présocratiques*. Paris: Gallimard, 1991. Coll. Folio/Essais.

"Epicurus." In Diogenes Laertius. *Lives of Eminent Philosophers*, vol. 2. Trans. R. D. Hicks. Loeb Classical Library.

Giannantoni, Gianni. *Socratis et Socraticorum reliquiae*. 2nd ed. Naples: Bibliopolis, 1986, 1990.

Heraclitus. In *The Presocratic Philosophers*. Ed. G. S. Kirk, J. E. Raven, and M. Schofield.

Herodotus. *The Histories*. Trans. A. D. Godley. Loeb Classical Library.

Homer. *Iliad*. Trans. A. T. Murray, rev. William F. Wyatt. Loeb Classical Library.

Kirk, G. S., J. E. Raven, and M. Schofield, eds. *The Presocratic Philosophers*, 2nd ed. Cambridge: Cambridge University Press, 1983.

Long, Anthony, and David Sedley. *The Hellenistic Philosophers*. Cambridge: Cambridge University Press, 1987.

Pyrrhon. *Testimonianze*. Ed. Fernanda Decleva Caizzi. Naples: Bibliopolis, 1981.

Plato. *Gorgias*. Ed. and trans. W. R. M. Lamb. Loeb Classical Library.

———. *Meno*. Ed. and trans. W. R. M. Lamb. Loeb Classical Library.

———. *Protagoras*. Ed. and trans. W. R. M. Lamb. Loeb Classical Library.

―――. *The Republic.* Ed. T. E. Page. Trans. Paul Shorey. Loeb Classical Library.

―――. *Theaetetus.* Ed. and trans. Harold North Fowler. Loeb Classical Library.

Thucydides. *History of the Peloponnesian War.* Trans. Charles Forster Smith. 4 vols. Loeb Classical Library.

Studies

Adkins, Arthur W. H. *From the Many to the One: A Study of Personality and Views of Human Nature in the Context of Ancient Greek Society, Values and Beliefs.* Ithaca, N.Y.: Cornell University Press, 1970.

―――. *Merit and Responsibility.* Oxford: Clarendon Press, 1960; Chicago: University of Chicago Press, 1975.

―――. *Moral Values and Political Behavior in Ancient Greece from Homer to the End of the Fifth Century.* New York: Norton, 1972.

Annas, Julia. *The Morality of Happiness.* Oxford: Oxford University Press, 1993.

―――. *Platonic Ethics, Old and New.* Ithaca, N.Y.: Cornell University Press, 1999.

Aubenque, Pierre. *La Prudence chez Aristote.* Paris: Presses Universitaires de France, 1963.

Burnyeat, Myles, ed. *The Sceptical Tradition.* Oxford: Oxford University Press, 1990.

Cooper, John. *Reason and Emotion: Essays on Ancient Moral Psychology and Ethical Theory.* Princeton: Princeton University Press, 1999.

Dover, Kenneth J. *Greek Popular Morality in the Time of Plato and Aristotle.* Oxford: Basil Blackwell, 1974.

Goldschmidt, Victor. *Platonisme et pensée contemporaine.* Paris: Aubier Montaigne, 1970.

Goulet-Cazé, Marie-Odile. *L'Ascèse cynique: Un commentaire de Diogène Laërce VI 70–71.* Paris: Vrin, 1986.

―――. *Le Cynisme dans l'Antiquité.* Paris: PUF, 1993.

Hadot, Pierre. *The Inner Citadel: The Meditations of Marcus Aurelius.* Trans. Michael Chase. Cambridge, Mass.: Harvard University Press, 1998.

―――. *Qu'est-ce que la philosophie antique?* Paris: Gallimard, 1995. Coll. Folio.

Irwin, Terence. *Plato's Ethics.* Oxford: Oxford University Press, 1995.

―――. *Plato's Moral Theory: The Early and Middle Dialogues.* Oxford: Oxford University Press, 1986.

Kenny, Anthony. *Aristotle on the Perfect Life.* Oxford: Oxford University Press, 1992.

Kerferd, G. B. *The Sophistic Movement.* Cambridge: Cambridge University Press, 1981.

Nussbaum, Martha. *The Fragility of Goodness.* Cambridge: Cambridge University Press, 1986.

―――. *The Therapy of Desire: Theory and Practice in Hellenistic Ethics.* Princeton: Princeton University Press, 1994.

Pearson, Lionel. *Popular Ethics in Ancient Greece.* Stanford, Calif.: Stanford University Press, 1962.

Snell, Bruno. *The Discovery of the Mind: The Greek Origins of European Thought.* New York: Harper, 1960.

Vegetti, Mario. *L'Etica degli antichi.* Rome-Bari: Laterza, 1989.

Vlastos, Gregory. *Socrates: Ironist and Moral Philosopher.* Ithaca, N.Y.: Cornell University Press, 1991.

Williams, Bernard. *Ethics and the Limits of Philosophy.* Cambridge, Mass.: Harvard University Press, 1985.

———. "Philosophy." In *The Legacy of Greece: A New Appraisal.* Ed. Moses Finley. Oxford and New York: Oxford University Press, 1981. Pp. 202–255.

Related Articles

The Statesman as Political Actor; Antisthenes; Epicurus; Plutarch; Sophists; The Sage and Politics; Aristotle; Plato; Socrates; Stoicism

POLITICS

THE STATESMAN AS
POLITICAL ACTOR

AMONG THE POPULATION of the small Greek city-states to which we compare our modern nation-states, only a very small fraction were citizens. The overwhelming majority consisted of foreigners or, more often, slaves. Women, who represented more than half of the free, native-born minority, had no political rights; men gained the use of those rights only when they came of age and served in the army. In the heart of the city-state, the small number who enjoyed the rights of citizenship formed an elite. Of this group, those who were actively involved in affairs of state typically represented an even smaller elite, in practice if not by law. For it was the statesmen who governed. Even in a direct, popular democracy, where law conferred on all citizens equal access to all functions of government, not all were able to avail themselves of the privilege, either from lack of financial means and therefore lack of freedom to undertake unpaid duties, or from lack of an elementary education. That in effect left the statesmen, in the best of cases, as the elite of the elite, for only a few of the small number of citizens possessed both fortune and education. But "the best of cases" were exceptions in the history of Greek city-states. Most of the time, the city-states reserved the right to govern to a minority of citizens who attained this status by virtue of their wealth or education. The elite occasionally included a prominent individual, or one who was at least backed by a distinguished or powerful family.

Thus what was meant by "statesman" varied widely according to circumstances, since each regime brought a particular type of citizen to power. Historians and other early thinkers between the 5th and 4th centuries B.C.E. (from Herodotus to Aristotle) attempted to catalogue and classify these regimes by type; their nomenclature is still in use today.

Three large groups were identified, according to the number of citizens exercising power: under a monarchy, power was concentrated in a single individual, while under the other two regimes it was held either by a minority or by a majority of citizens. Within each group, a more qualitative criterion made it possible to distinguish between two types of regimes and contrasted two universal principles of legitimacy: strength, or power, versus excellence, or virtue. Thus monarchy sustained by military force was known as tyranny, while monarchy supported by virtue was known as royalty. If power procured by wealth gave legitimacy to a government of the few, the regime was called an oligarchy or, in the city-state context, a plutocracy. If its legitimacy derived from virtue, the result of education or family lineage, it was called an aristocracy. If the majority governed simply on the strength of numbers, then the regime was known as a democracy. And if that majority was characterized by some degree of excellence, then the regime was called a republic *(politeia)*; often, to describe this very theoretical type of regime, the Greeks simply used the same word they used to designate any political regime.

This kind of classification offers a rather limited means of distinguishing among all the forms that political order can take in reality. More refined political analyses, such as those Aristotle attempted in some of his works, show that we cannot be content with such simplifications. But we can learn a surprising amount from them by looking at the idea of the statesman they suggest.

In fact, a theoretical classification of constitutional regimes reveals that legitimacy in politics is always based on some form of superiority. A wide range of political types can be sketched in from this outline: certain features would be borrowed from aspects of strength, power, or even violence, and others from varying degrees of virtue. The Greeks were less concerned about combining these characteristics in order to reconstruct an accurate historical picture than about distinguishing among them in order to measure, in philosophical terms, the distance between one type of statesman and another. In their view, the superiority of a monarch over his subjects, whatever its nature, power or virtue, must necessarily be greater than the superiority of the few over many, whereas superiority in a democracy or a republic does not imply the superiority of the governor over the governed but rather a greater number of those governing over the number governed.

The combination of quantitative and qualitative criteria used to distinguish among political regimes reveals two extremes between which all political types fall. The extremes correspond to exceptional if not mythical figures in whom we recognize, on the one hand, a monster of brutality, and on the other, what might be called a monster of virtue. The former, the despot, creates between himself and his subjects the inhuman distance that separates a master from his slaves; the latter, a quasi-divine king, creates instead a benevolent distance like that separating a father from his sons. Together they represent the two poles between which all other representations of statesmen oscillate. In contrast, at the center, equally divided between the two tendencies, despotic and paternalistic, we see the familiar figure of the statesman who can claim no apparent distance between himself and those he governs. The equality among all citizens keeps such a leader from being a king, and ought to keep him from being a despot; he is asked, in a sense, to imitate the benevolence of the former and to avoid the brutality of the latter. But the principle of equality threatens to deny him the distance between himself and his subjects that the king enjoys naturally and that the despot imposes. In other words, he must face the risk of anarchy that the egalitarian principle presents and that, in the name of liberty, exempts the citizens from having any master at all, revealing the democratic majority for what—in the absence of a certain virtue—it really is: a brute force. To the Greek mind, it is the republic that cultivates virtue in theory. This is what permits the Greeks to agree freely to obey those who, once educated, have acquired the qualities of leadership.

This theoretical perspective is less idealistic than it seems. Since citizens of the small Greek city-states were, as we have said, a very small fraction of the population, the training process that sought to prepare each of them to become, in adulthood, an educated "republican" statesman, is less utopian than it would be in our modern states. The ancient Greek process sought to extend to the families of all citizens the virtues cultivated by only a few of them. However, the virtue that education was supposed to produce in a few honorable families was, in Greece as elsewhere, a rare commodity, often replaced by an appetite for wealth or power, and the legitimacy sought by the rich or powerful, in the name of aristocracy, was often deceptive. In fact the political model of the oligarch, born into a powerful family, extended to popular regimes that were just as despotic in two ways: like the oligarch, the democrat limited the exercise of his authority to the pursuit of wealth and power, and in that same pursuit he oppressed those he governed instead of seeking the common good.

The Greek world is thus of interest in two ways. On the one hand, the statesman as described by the philosophers suggests the high standard that a statesman ought to uphold in any regime. On the other hand, the figures that allow us glimpses of reality show at what a low level political leaders usually operate, in comparison to the ideal assigned to them.

This gap, which the Greeks were the first to measure, inclined them to show politics generally as the art of the possible, rich in expectations and poor in results. Moreover, it signifies for us an important difference between two things we can learn from Greek history. On the one hand, we learn that Greek thought tends to identify the good statesman with qualities that basically have nothing to do with whether or not he shares power, or whether he shares it with a few or with many. On the other hand, we learn that the question of this sharing of power, which distinguishes among monarchies, oligarchies, and democracies, was the touchstone of political quarrels; seen in this way, a good statesman is someone who defends the interests of one party, however broad or narrow. Ideology, in this context, is scarcely distinguishable from philosophy. This becomes apparent when we consider the way the Greeks judged political leaders in specific instances.

As we know, the Greek world and its emblematic figures, memorable champions of democracy as well as evil tyrants, have fascinated Western culture ever since the 18th century. This fascination is the result of numerous illusions that the historian is at pains to dispel. Patience and perseverance are in order, for these illusions have been in place for a long time. They were created by antiquity itself, from which we cannot expect an impartial judgment on these great statesmen but rather an often impassioned trial, with witnesses on both sides. Looking for signs of truth in the fabrication of ancient ideologies, modern historians have become increasingly interested in these inventions themselves. Today we are beginning to measure how much the old legends, fed by bias, have slipped into the apparently faithful accounts that the ancients gave of their own history, and also how much the distortion of truth betrays the influence not of naive beliefs, as we used to think, but of insidious political or philosophical ideas that should not deceive anyone today.

The "Great Men" honored by Greek memory were not selected impartially. Plutarch, for example, Platonist that he was, includes portraits of the Athenian Phocion, and Dion of Syracuse, largely because they were viewed as disciples of Plato. Alcibiades, whom Plato quotes so freely and whose name is given to two of the dialogues, is featured by Plutarch for similar reasons. Moreover, in antiquity the practice of history and especially of biography was basically meant to provide edifying examples, if not pure propaganda. Both hero and antihero were bearers of thinly veiled messages, one of the most obvious of which was the warning against tyranny, forever masking what the autocratic rulers of earliest times really were like. According to Plutarch, again, Dion and Timoleon of Syracuse and Aratus of Sicyon all fought against tyrants; the Lacedaemonian Lysander installed others (the Thirty) in Athens. Pelopidas of Thebes rid his fatherland of the Lacedaemonian oppression and fought the tyrant of Pherae, whereas Philopoemen, "the last of the Greeks," had set an example of resistance to the same Lacedaemonians, and later to the Romans. The message is clear, but conventional. Other accounts convey just the opposite message. The extraordinary achievement of Alexander the Great and of the Diadochi has been retold in numerous accounts that respond in large part to the wish to justify and legitimize a new kind of monarchy, one that might otherwise appear barbarian in every sense of the word, and that is clearly despotic. Creating a halo effect, the eulogists reveal an ideology with populist overtones. However, Lacedaemonia is not simply emblematic of oppression: it also evokes, for example, the heroism of Philopoemen, Pelopidas, and Epaminondas. Indeed, the greatest names in its history, starting with Lycurgus, are the subject of highly flattering myths. In the 3rd century B.C.E., the kings Aegis and Cleomenes, famous for their shared desire to restore a lost discipline, owe their glory to the idea of Spartan virtue, an idea that had been widely honored since the preceding century and particularly, owing to a certain degree of infighting, in vanquished Athens following the Peloponnesian Wars. At about the same time, Athens, worn down by demagogues, also found orators in the reactionary party who would glorify the great men who had been ostracized during the preceding century: Themistocles, Aristides, Cimon. Anyone, sooner or later, can become a hero;

someone will recognize in him some virtue worth defending. As for the invented statesmen-heroes, they had already invented others in their day: Cimon claimed to have brought the ashes of the legendary Theseus back to Athens from Scyros!

With distance, the truth behind these legends of infamy or glory fades away. But what obscures the truth also uncovers something about the thinking of both the glorifiers and the critics. Who was Theseus, so-called king of Athens, who vanquished the Minotaur and was the author of Attic "synoecism"? Or Cadmos of Thebes and the founding rulers of the city-states? We do not know, but we can at least guess the feelings of those who sang of the great deeds attributed to them during that time. Just who were Aristides, called "the Just," and, later, Pericles, who gave his name to Athens's golden age? Even with sources like Thucydides and the historians, scholars disagree; but no one contests the nostalgia these figures have engendered and the idealized pictures to which they gave rise after the fall of their city-state in the 4th century, when popular unrest and a general loss of vigor exposed Athens to attacks from neighboring powers. We know very little about the famous Spartan king Agesilaus at the beginning of the 4th century, and even less about the tyrant Hieron who ruled Syracuse in the 5th, but in the works the Athenian aristocrat Xenophon dedicated to each of them, we get a fairly good sense of a terseness typical of the Athenian oligarchy of that time, and an ambivalence toward the most famous tyrants, enlightened princes as well as despots, that also disturbed Plato.

Such images easily fall into groups: mythic heroes, protagonists of the illusory Athenian democracy, leaders of the Spartan mirage, a horde of dreadful tyrants, the remarkable lineage of Alexander the Great and his successors. All of these examples conceal many mysteries, but they inform us about a great many more or less explicit convictions that came into conflict over time in antiquity and that constitute its ideological heritage. A summary of all the research on the emblematic figures of Greek politics can be no more than a rough sketch.

The limits of time and space within which the most important types appeared are significant and well known. With the exception of the mythic heroes, known chiefly through the epic cycles and tragedies, they are concentrated between the 6th and the 4th centuries B.C.E., in other words, between the time when absolute monarchies were on the decline in the city-states and when the new Hellenistic monarchies, a legacy of Alexander the Great, came to replace the regimes of the factions, sometimes called the "Equals." This was a short period, overall, just a parenthesis in a long history of kings or despots, against a background of resistance to the "barbarians" of the Levant (Persians), victory over the invader (the Persian Wars), and finally the elimination of Persia's power by invasion (Macedonian conquests). The heroes of the victorious resistance to the Persians, Athenians in particular, such as Miltiades at

Marathon (490 B.C.E.) and Themistocles at Salamis (480), embody the freedom of the Greek people, a freedom maintained against external despotic domination after it had been established internally by the abolition of autocratic and monarchic authority. The image of such heroes combines the ideal of independence from foreigners with the ideal of a republican regime, and it unites the memory of absolute monarchs of a not entirely civilized past with the image of the Persian dynasties of a barbarian world, condemning both. Alexander, on the contrary, the Macedonian hero who brought about the elimination of Achaemenid dominance, later failed to unify in himself the archaic image of a patriarchal and semibarbarian monarchy with the image of the leader of the Greeks in their revenge against the Persians and the image of an absolute sovereign who was himself successor to the Achaemenids. He was a hero from another world, Hellenized rather than truly Greek.

In an area of numerous small city-states, colonies, and large cities—sometimes allies, sometimes rivals—most of the major political figures that emerged, before Alexander and the Diadochi, came out of one of the two hegemonic powers, Sparta and Athens, which, while temporarily united in the victorious fight against the Persians, later confronted each other during the Peloponnesian Wars and beyond. Thus the images of statesmen appeared under one of the two characteristic constitutional regimes of the period between the absolute monarchies of the past and those to come, the former appearing more oligarchic and the latter more populist, but each at odds with the other, mainly because of the war, and each with defenders who worked hard to demonstrate their favorite's merits. However, in addition to the great Athenians whom we tend to situate in memory before the defeat by Sparta, and in addition to the great Spartans who were the crafters of a tradition of victories, there are other notable dynastic figures, the "tyrants" who built short-lived but powerful empires: the Cypselides of Corinth, the Orthagorids of Sicyon, the Gelonids and the two Dionysiuses of Syracuse, Polycrates of Samos. In their own way these figures represent the Greek model of princely autocracy, as opposed to republican egalitarianism. This model is ambiguous in several respects: a patron of the arts and literature, the "tyrant" sometimes redresses the anarchic excesses of liberty, sometimes indulges in the greatest abuses of bellicose despotism. Pisistratus and the Pisistratides, in Athens itself, followed this pattern. But the great city-states Sparta and Athens also took on the appearance of tyranny in their relations with their allies, who were ruled with brutality. In particular, the occupation of Thebes by the Spartans (beginning in 383 B.C.E.) and, earlier, the cruel atrocities of Athens in Eubea (445) and in Samos (439) have gone down in history as expressions of an imperialism that challenges the ideal of civic law and virtue. In Thucydides' account, Pericles, who was responsible for these acts, cynically acknowledged his tyranny. In the same way, outrageous alliances between the Athenian Conon (394) and later the Spartan Antalcidas (387), and Achaemenid Persia, against their

Greek enemies contradict the Panhellenic ideal that the publicist Isocrates sought to revive and for which he courted Philip of Macedonia. In Greek history there is no single figure that can be considered a truly universal emblem and that is not, instead, the expression, however dubious, of a particular party, even though a series of clearly contrasted images can be found.

Owing to the nature of our sources, Athenian history comes to mind first and provides the best-known profiles. After its restoration under Euclid's archonship (403 B.C.E.), the so-called Athenian democracy became, during the 4th century, a republic of wheeler-dealers, demagogues, and mercenaries whom the great orator Demosthenes depicted and tried in vain to stir up during his quarrels with Aeschines. Powerless to oppose the expansionist moves of Philip of Macedonia after Chaeronea (338), Athens was ready to fall to the level of a municipality controlled from the outside by a regent. It was a popular republic without heroes.

Before that, in the 5th century, it had been a republic of generals (strategoi) elected and overseen by the most powerful faction of citizens in the Assembly. After Marathon (490 B.C.E.), the polemarchos archon no longer presided over the military affairs of the city-state and a line of brilliant strategoi, emerging from the Persian Wars, dominated the political scene. Pericles, who died of the plague in 429, was one of them. Frequently reappointed to his position, despite the rules, and with the vast resources of the League of Delos (which he exploited) behind him, he inspired and secured financing for some very popular measures in the city-state, most notably the institution of salaries for judges. At the end of the Peloponnesian War, Alcibiades, Cleon, Demosthenes, and Nicias, the last great strategoi, had in fact brought Athens to the point of disaster. Compounded by pressure from the Spartans, the situation led the city-state to experiment during an eight-month period (404–403) with the oligarchy of the Thirty (including Theramenes and Plato's uncle Critias), which was the period of the tyranny.

But Thrasybules overturned the Thirty and restored democracy. The defeat by Sparta and the collapse of the empire had naturally raised other hopes. Many aristocrats, like Xenophon, did not conceal their admiration for the Spartan regime and system of education. Some disciples of Socrates, who was condemned to death by a popular tribunal at this time (399), also mistrusted democracy. In addition, during this period the general Dionysius I was ruling Syracuse with brilliance. He became known as the "archon of Sicily": he was viewed as representative of Plato's ideal of the philosopher-king. But the tribune Lysias, an opponent of the Thirty, had spoken of Dionysius as a tyrant, and Athens was committed once more to the principles of the "isonomy," bequeathed by Pericles and Ephiales, who themselves had inherited it from the reforms instituted during the preceding century by Cleisthenes (508) and, even before him, by Solon (592).

The long "democratic" tradition and the memory of the Thirty made it impossible for the reign of Pisistratus and his sons, who ruled in the interim between the two great reformers, from 561 to 510, to be judged as anything other than a parenthetical episode of tyranny. In short, for the century without significant heroes that began in 403, the great Athenian statesmen belonged entirely to the past, and often the distant past. The little-known Atthidographers, who reconstructed this past with the aid of dubious and scarce pre–Persian War sources, were obviously divided in their judgment. In fact, these writers are actually the principal source for later ancient historians and for scholarly works devoted to institutions, such as Aristotle's *Athenian Constitution*. (Indeed Xenophon, Thucydides, and Herodotus omit institutional politics entirely from their war chronicles.)

Whether they are well preserved or fragmentary, these documents—along with speeches by Attic orators and ideas spread by 4th-century thinkers—attest to a view of the statesman within the framework of Athenian democracy (adult male, nonslave) as a free citizen. But the statesman thus defined had low standing, and was easily denounced; he had the same status as the individuals who made up the mass of people, out of work and poor, at the mercy of the demagogues, ready to do or destroy anything depending on their own immediate interests, and at times willing to defy the laws. These men of the majority were, in principle, in control of the legal system and, through election, most of the magistrates in charge of enforcing the laws (archons, judges, generals, and the like). In practice, though, the majority yielded to the small number who were masters of rhetoric, those who led the Assembly and the popular tribunals, manipulated opinion, and usually took public office—the source of reputation and fortune—for themselves. With few exceptions, these were the real governors: their word prevailed in politics. Sophistic eloquence, which came to prominence in the 4th century, took root in the democratic ground of Athens beginning with the era of Pericles, whose ties to the first specialists in rhetoric are well known. Such statesmen were quick to elude the vigilance of even the most rational and enlightened thinkers, and the only limit to their sovereign authority was the weight of tradition, ordained by constitutional decrees and laws regarded as inviolable.

Before it was destroyed, this tradition had been strong in Athens, and Athenians had proven themselves rigorous in their adherence to it, with the aid of professional informers (sycophants). The tradition put down deep roots in the wake of the Persian Wars, when ostracism could strike anyone who stood out and threatened the egalitarianism of the democracy. No one was exempt, not even the victor at Salamis. Aristides, called "the Just," embodied Athenians' respect for institutional order by writing, for an illiterate member of the Assembly, his own name, Aristides, on the ostracism list. Ultimately the greatest Athenian statesmen, those who symbolized the man of politics in the highest degree, were those who contributed to the creation of the democratic tradition itself: in other words, the ancient lawmakers like Solon and Cleisthenes.

LEGISLATORS

The prestige of the great lawmakers was no accident. It was consistent with a particular hierarchy of political functions of which the Greeks were fully conscious. In this respect, popular sovereignty, firmly established in the Athenian democracy and in all the city-states like Athens, complicates the picture somewhat, with the principle of equality. In fact, ancient democracy, which was not representative, granted all citizens the same political rights, which they exercised in the Assembly. But it maintained strict distinctions among the powers that each person exercised by right under the sovereign authority of the laws. As for the resolutions taken by the Assembly itself, they had the force of law and had to conform strictly to constitutional law, which Athenians called "ancestral rules." All political functions, whether invested in subordinates or their superiors, were ultimately subject to the power of the legislator, and he himself was subject to the fundamental decrees of venerated ancestors.

The Athenian democracy thus offers us one of the best illustrations of the idea that the true statesman is one who knows how to make laws for his people. In this notion lies a conviction that to some extent went beyond ideology. For it was not really linked to a particular political regime but was shared, except during crises, by all the regimes of law that the city-states created. Moreover, it was a conviction that grew out of philosophical reflection and questioned the validity of regimes of law themselves. If a degree of political maturity can be claimed by classical Greece, it lies in the recognition that political authority is absolutely sovereign, that it subordinates all other authorities in the city-state, that such sovereignty must be based on law and that law must be sanctified by ancestral tradition.

The idea that early lawmakers exercised an ancient wisdom that was threatened with destruction by every untimely innovation appears conservative to us today. It seems to run counter to our idea of progress. It did not prevent the Greeks, and particularly the Athenians, from desiring political change, but it meant that the boldest innovations were proposed, quite openly in most cases, as a return to some major political rule that had been neglected. The Athenian Plato went so far as to maintain that his revolutionary plan for the ideal city corresponded to the actual situation in Athens at the memorable time of its victorious battle against the princes of Atlantis! His readers, who did not make such clear distinctions as we do between ordinary law and fundamental law, knew that the introduction into the city-state of the slightest legal modification, though it might appear meaningless, could ultimately threaten the regime in power. The Athenian statesmen were thus careful to pass only laws that would be in accordance with tradition, or at least to give the impression of doing so.

Among the greatest legislators responsible for the most significant democratic reforms and who thus gave roots to the tradition, some were able to operate only by skillfully breaking with certain traditions and restoring others. Cleisthenes provides a particularly noteworthy case in point. He belonged to the ancient and illustrious family of the Alcmeonides, who claimed to have exemplified resistance to tyranny at the time of the expulsion of the last Pisistratid. Against the defenders of the regime installed by Pisistratus, he embraced the people's side and triumphed over the opposition with the support, apparently, of the council of the city-state. His triumph sanctioned a return to the older regime inherited from Solon. But the restoration that he favored was accompanied in 509–508 by a celebrated reform that broke with the heritage of Solon. This reform replaced the four traditional, familial "tribes" from which statesmen were previously drawn, with ten territorial tribes responsible for sending fifty representatives each to the Council, thus increasing membership from 400 to 500. Cleisthenes has been acclaimed ever since for having brilliantly succeeded with that reform in "uniting the people," who until that time had been divided along family and tribal lines. The new territorial tribe was not a real division of the people, for in establishing each of his tribes, Cleisthenes had actually joined communal districts (demes) from three separate regions of Attica, each region supplying the tribe with ten demes. The move completely overturned tradition: now that he belonged to a deme whose name he used rather than his father's name, each citizen came under the jurisdiction not of his district, a distinct region, but of a federation that united ten such districts from each region, mirroring the organization of the city-state as a whole. Cleisthenes' plan exploited space to overcome the political distance that space produces. This plan ended the aristocratic power of families once and for all, to the benefit of democracy. Yet it came about as part of a movement to restore traditions that the tyranny had interrupted. And it was accomplished in such a way as to leave conspicuously in place all the institutions handed down from Solon. The restoration of tradition was more visible than the break with the past. When the break with the past and the progress democracy had made became apparent some time later, tradition appeared to have suffered very little; in hindsight, even Solon's legacy seemed democratic.

At the beginning of the 6th century, Solon was not in favor of popular power. Aristocratic, very wealthy himself, and with well-to-do supporters, during his archoncy (592–591) he proposed and passed a series of laws, many of which were constitutional in scope and favored a political regime explicitly based on taxation. Solon's well-known law abolishing slavery for debts—an act benefiting the poor who were on the point of losing their freedom and whose situation threatened to destroy the city-state—gave him the reputation, centuries later, of demagogue and anarchist. He was neither. Little is known today about the details of his work, and it was poorly understood even by the ancients, who interpreted it in a variety of ways. Solon softened the old, very strict, penal code associated with the name of Draco; he established the power to appeal judicial rulings before the people; he was the first to post laws in public view. All of these actions combined to produce a major redirection of tradition toward democracy. But Solon's fiscal and monetary policies favored a division of society into rigid economic classes. Eligibility for the highest offices was a function of the tax rolls, and the old superior judges formed the Areopagus, responsible for overseeing the legality of the political administration, like a Supreme Court, above the Council. The legislation enacted under Solon constituted a sizable counterweight to democratic tendencies.

Solon's greatness may have resided, in fact, in his seeming ambiguity. And that is probably the basis for his reputation among the Greeks as a wise and exemplary legislator. Quite wisely, indeed, he did not openly espouse the cause of any party but rather worked to balance opposing forces to deal appropriately with the crisis of the moment. To do this, he employed the instrument of law. His restraint and diplomacy gave Solon a significant edge over many others in the reputation for wisdom. His skillful use of law led him to be ranked above the greatest dynasts as one of the founders of true political order and justice. The prevailing consensus of posterity attests to an appreciation of Solon that goes beyond partisan ideology on this point.

These judgments converge with a body of complex beliefs in which notions such as progress play a different role and have a different meaning from the ones they have for us. For the Greeks, the legislator was essentially a civilizing agent, and in the progression of civilizations the earliest legislators represented a decisive stage, taking over from those to whom we owe the invention of the earliest techniques of art and craftsmanship. That was how Aristocles of Messina saw them, carrying on a long philosophical tradition, at the beginning of the Christian era. According to Aristocles, the legislators' creative genius was originally hailed as a new kind of wisdom: "Turning their eyes then to the affairs of the city-state, men invented laws and all the ways of building city-states; and they called this faculty of intelligence wisdom" (cited in Philoponus, *Nikomachou Arithmetikes eisagoges*). We know, and Aristocles knew, that later, during the time of the philosophers, wisdom must have represented a more profound and universal intelligence, speculative in nature. But this latter type had been described as the model of supreme knowledge that Aristotle himself required of the legislator, in defining the highest form of wisdom as "that science [that] is supreme, . . . which knows for what end each action is to be done; *i.e.* the Good in each particular case, and in general the highest Good in the whole of nature" (*Metaphysics* I.ii982b4–7). The

legislator provided a preview of such wisdom, for in principle he ruled supreme and knew the reasons for the rules that he set down for everyone to
follow.

Protagoras of Abdera claimed that the first of these "master builders," who
knew how to dispense justice and make laws, must have received a sense of
right and wrong from Zeus (according to Plato, *Protagoras*). The lack of historical information about the earliest legislators meant that their initiatives
were represented according to the most common practices of the classical period. These legislative practices, projected onto the most distant past, consisted of learning about comparable customs and rules in use in various
places, evaluating their relative merits, and then adopting the best or most appropriate ones. Comparative studies of statute law in the service of political
reform did not exist, however, before the second half of the 5th century. The
Greek city-states were unusually unified during that period, owing to the
Persian Wars. They had acquired a sense of community and the conviction
that each one of them had to face up to the same long-standing problems — in
particular, the need to correct the unequal distribution of wealth that had already been a concern for the venerable legislator Pheidon of Corinth and
would later preoccupy Phaleas of Chalcedon. So they began to compare the
various political regimes and to imagine a perfect constitution. Drawn to the
powerful city-state of Athens, the leader of a maritime league, philosophers
began to work on this dream. Hippodamus of Miletus, who was responsible
for planning Pireaus, was one of the first to provide some ideas for such a regime. Protagoras of Abdera, known for his teaching of politics, took up the
same project and played a major role in the writing of laws for the colony of
Thurioi (443).

The compilation of basic laws continued after the Peloponnesian War that
divided the Greeks and led them to look nostalgically on the period when
they had been united against the Persians. The victory of Sparta and its allies
naturally led to greater attention to the laws of the conquerors. The Athenians Xenophon and Critias distinguished themselves with such a compilation, which Aristotle later systematized. The quest for a model regime, one
that an autocratic prince, a revolution, or favorable circumstances in a colony
could establish (as at Thurioi), conflicted with the more modest and realistic
quest for good laws that could be adopted by regimes in power in the interest
of reform. This comparative and selective critique of laws in use was fashionable in the 4th century, when influential leaders inspired orators and governed assemblies, obtaining endorsement of political policies that they had
found worthy elsewhere. "They thought that it was easy to make laws by
gathering together those that are well thought of," said Aristotle, who did not
share the view that it was easy to find laws that would suit a given situation
perfectly *(Nicomachean Ethics)*.

The claim to be resurrecting the work of the most celebrated legislators in history—a task undertaken quite often by pseudo-archaeologists—attests to specific convictions that are more interesting than the dubious factual information their authors eagerly set forth. The most important and widespread of these beliefs is that the best legal institutions are validated by their longevity and their universality. Some of the political institutions considered enviable by classical Greek authors were ones they had observed in their neighbors and attributed to some prestigious leader. In Italy people recalled an old king of the Oenotri, named Italos, and in Egypt an ancient pharaoh of the 13th century, Sesostris (Ramses II). Each of these legendary rulers had bequeathed to his country well-known and oddly similar institutions. Comparable institutions were found in Crete, where they were attributed to the famous king Minos, a contemporary of Theseus. These were vague memories buried in legend, from a prehistoric time when the Achaeans, of whom Homer sang, were compared to earlier civilizations of the Mediterranean world. According to another tradition in Crete, Onomacritus of Locris learned of some discoveries that were passed down by his disciple Thales and are thought to have inspired the laws of the Spartan regime attributed to the great Lycurgus. These rules apparently also inspired legislation given to the Locrians of Cape Zephyrion by Zaleucas, who is also said to have taught the legislator Charondas of Catana in the Chalcidian colonies of Sicily and Italy. These lines of transmission were imaginary, according to Aristotle (*Politics* II); still, they indicate that for many, the work of the great legislators was not to be admired for its originality but for its universality, its validation by virtue of its permanence or at least its significant longevity. The work attributed to Lycurgus (9th to 8th century?) that was still being invoked at the end of the Peloponnesian War impressed everyone, not least of all the conquered peoples. The Athenian Plato, seduced by the "sister" constitutions from the Doric city-states of Crete and Sparta, was among them; he shows us the "Seven Sages" of Greece, united in a common admiration of "laconism" *(Protagoras).*

We could find many more examples. All of them allow us to glimpse a past constructed to answer to the same order of beliefs. In this regard, the idea of justifying the label Sages for seven figures of their own history did not necessarily imply at the outset a desire on the Greeks' part to recognize the greatest legislators of their past. However, Solon was included in the list, as was the Lacedaemonian ephor Chilon (perhaps because he was credited with great militaristic reforms); also Bias, the judge-arbiter of Priene, and the powerful Pittacus of Mytilene, both of whom had enacted rigorous laws designed to stifle factions in their city-states. Another figure, Periander of Corinth, known for his severity, also took his place in the ranks of the Sages. However, Plato excluded Periander and replaced him with the obscure Myson, for a reason that is less obscure. Periander belonged to the group of autocratic princes, along with Thrasybulus of Miletus, Polycrates of Samos, Lygdamis of Naxos, Orthagoras in Sicyon, and Pisistratus in Athens; branded a tyrant, Periander has suffered the disgrace attached to the word ever since. Thus, over time, the identification of those who were to be held up as the most illustrious figures of the past was revised and the reasons for the greatness of the heroes viewed as above criticism were elaborated with real effort. One school of thought, reflected by Dicaearchus, claimed to include in the latter category only "shrewd men with a turn for legislation" (according to Diogenes Laertius, I.40), excluding even those who were considered in their own day to be "sages" for showing supreme philosophical wisdom of the speculative kind. This opinion remained prevalent and was shared much later by Aristocles, who attributed to the great lawmakers of the past a kind of wisdom that had foreshadowed the wisdom of the first philosophers: "Such were the Seven Sages who invented political virtues."

The line that runs from Dicaearchus to Aristocles (both of Messina) belongs to a tradition going back to Aristotle. Aristotelian thought gives us the best insights into the way the Greeks understood the connection between legislative knowledge and wisdom, between political competence carried to its highest degree and the pure and simple wisdom that the first philosophers sought. The good legislator, credited with work of quality *(eunomia)*, lacks the superior knowledge that the philosopher is after in his search for first principles of the universe, but he does possess knowledge, or something comparable, know-how, in his ability to provide the city-state and its inhabitants with fundamental principles that govern their actions in the form of necessary laws and that show them the source of the good and of happiness.

The Athenian Solon, a distant ancestor of Plato, was unanimously included among the Sages and was also the first to be recognized as a "philosopher." His legislation owed some of the many honors it received in classical literature to this concept of the good legislator. Wishing to establish some balance between the small number of wealthy people, who were bound by public responsibility, and the vast majority of the poor, who were freed from obligations and protected by laws, Solon, like the legendary Lycurgus, to whom Aristotle compared him on this point (*Politics* 1296b18–21), was destined to go down in history as the champion of a middle class that embodied a felicitous mix of popular, aristocratic, and oligarchic forces within the city-state. A similar balance was seen in the institutions of Lacedaemonia, between the aristocratic and royal gerousia (the council of elders) and the popular ephors (overseers) representing the Equals (the small number who were citizens). In Lacedaemonia, not only did this balance, however precarious and imperfect, last two centuries after Solon, up to the high point of classical thought, but it was also the small city-state of the Peloponnesus that brought Solon's powerful city-state to its knees. The lesson was learned not only by classical thinkers but also by historians: the balance of rival political forces in the state is described by Polybius as a characteristic of the Roman state, grounded in law, that accounts for its immense vitality.

POLITICAL THINKERS

Continental Greece became a Roman province in 146 B.C.E., by which time almost all of the Greek city-states had lost their independence. Most had been living for nearly two hundred years under the control of one or another of the great new monarchies founded by the officers of Alexander the Great. These monarchies, like Roman rule later on, had novel features, not just because of their size but because of their origins. The leagues (amphictyonies) and other confederations that had once united some of the Greek city-states under an authoritarian ruler were usually based on contractual laws. The new monarchies had been established instead by conquest, and their rulers' only claim to legitimacy was the sword.

One contemporary philosophical school, tending toward cynicism, held that force could be made legitimate by law. Among the philosophers of a Hellenistic period that was poorly endowed with political thinkers, there were also some less radical individuals associated with Stoicism; these latter endorsed certain prestigious monarchies whose princes they compared to all-powerful Zeus, regulator of the natural world. They favored myths that ascribed divine lineage to those princes, rare leaders of men like Alexander himself. The same attitude toward the new kings harks back to even earlier thinkers who, imagining the foundation of the earliest monarchies in the city-states, or that of dynasties above the law, suggested that these were inconceivable without the clear superiority of enlightened princes, gods among men. The cynical view is reminiscent of another opinion, also much older, favoring the rights of the strongest and opposing the tyranny of the weak that had been imposed by law. These debates, rekindled by the new conditions that characterized the Hellenistic period, lead us back to the heart of the classical period when they began, when philosophy sought for the first time to define the characteristics of the true statesman.

The complexity and importance of the affairs of the city-state had soon produced agreement among all thinkers on one important point: one cannot enter politics unprepared without doing harm to oneself and to fellow citizens. But it is probably Plato who placed the greatest stress on the need for an apprenticeship in politics. In sum, he sought in the statesman a firm universal knowledge, nourished by the source of all intelligibility, that is, by the absolute Good, which is situated beyond being. Plato's *Republic* describes the numerous and lengthy stages of political apprenticeship, including the acquisition of the physical and moral qualities necessary to the proper exercise of one's intelligence and the gradual acquisition of the intellectual qualities and the erudition necessary for understanding the absolute Good, beyond all contingencies of time and place. In this, and it is his most significant thesis, Plato clearly equates the philosopher's course with the path that leads to the science of politics.

For Plato the well-being of the city-state depends on the philosopher's becoming king or the king's becoming a philosopher. This is not an argument that favors or opposes monarchy. For the philosopher who would govern with the objective of always doing what is right, Plato demands only a kinglike power. He wants to see either the alliance of an absolute ruler with philosophy, or the alliance of philosophy with kingly power. Either case would allow knowledge, inspired by the immutable Good, to reflect that Good in the city-state without the constraint of existing laws.

For this reason, defining the true "statesman" in a dialogue of that name, Plato argues initially in favor of an ideal illegality. In other words, he is in favor of government that disdains rigid written statutes, products of mere tradition or convention, a government in which sovereign authority is exercised by a ruler inspired by knowledge of the transcendental Good, a sort of "god among mortals" (Plato, *Statesman* 303b). Such a statesman would not be subject to any law but would himself embody the law.

Nevertheless, Plato later enjoins this philosopher-king, whom he places above the law, to be a legislator and codifier of fundamental rules reflecting the Good, so as to protect from the whims of future rulers the perfect order that is to replace all existing legal and constitutional laws, which are by nature partial and imperfect. Plato goes even further. In his last great work, *Laws,* he attempts just such a codification, which is made necessary by the impossibility of finding in the world of politics a man who, endowed with divine grace, could ensure an ideal government or a code of ethics in his own image. Thus the philosopher himself provides the outline of the most urgent laws, dictated by the absolute Good, laws according to which the statesmen are invited to govern: "We have to empower intelligence and the laws that it inspires," says an interlocutor in the dialogue (713c). From this perspective, the statesman no longer has the job of making laws. He becomes the servant of an intangible legislation established by the philosopher.

The Platonic project originates in a conviction that politics can never be totally entrusted to the arbitrary power of the common people without leading to chaos, but also in a belief, born a century earlier in Socratic circles, and in all enlightened circles, that politics must in fact rest on a certain type of knowledge. The idea of using knowledge to establish and legitimize sovereign power is a revolutionary one that was launched by a group traditionally called the Sophists, whose movement has been rehabilitated today. The Sophists shared Socrates' concerns. He had established once and for all the need to base law on reason and hence the impossibility of ever again accepting a law that was not supported by convincing argument.

Two implications underscore the importance of this principle. First, it triggered official criticism not only of several fundamental laws in effect but also of laws in general and of the very concept of laws. Certain theses defended by some of the speakers in Plato's dialogues must have been exploited to this end: Thrasimachus, for example, argues (in *The Republic* I) that all laws promote only the interests of the most powerful; this seems to be contradicted by Callicles (in *Gorgias*), who argues that legislation always defends, unjustly, the interests of the weak, whom it protects from the power of the strong. This type of criticism, not without a certain rationality, has an extraordinary influence. It tends, in effect, to make reason itself an authority superior to established laws, in assessing what is right. Moreover, for Protagoras of Abdera, the need to justify, or the advantage of justifying, every political act leads to the idea that politics, like any other science, can be taught, by teaching language and the rhetorical art of persuasion. This type of claim, too, endorsed by future generations, has important consequences. It tends to posit technically sophisticated eloquence as the founding instrument of law. Criticism did away with some prejudices, while rhetoric rebuilt them afresh.

But Plato clearly foresaw that, in a sense, no one could undertake this dual task without self-destructing and without undermining justice itself: one could not, without contradiction, question law in general, on the one hand, and offer rhetoric as a universal instrument for establishing rights, on the other. In short, a claim of absolute skepticism about the legitimacy of existing laws could not be reconciled with absolute relativism, when it came to promoting the rules that take the place of law. For Plato, on the contrary, to reject a sure foundation implied a quest for an unshakable certainty, which the partial and ephemeral consensus obtained from rhetorical argument could not provide. It was therefore necessary to rely on knowledge that reached the hypothetical foundation of justice: in other words, science attaining the knowledge of absolute Good. As for rhetoric, Plato reduced it to the level of the subordinate powers in the city-state that the legislator (the "royal weaver") had to harmonize; its role was to defend only those rules that the science of the Good inspires in the legislator.

The science to which Plato attached all political action, beginning with the acts of legislators, is therefore a truly philosophical form of wisdom. It relates to the first and universal source of all that is good. This principle, in relation to which all human goods are measured, is thus not itself human, or subjective, as is the principle on which citizens can agree through discussion. Immutable, eternal, always the same, it is objectively what human order and all the realities of the varied and ever-changing world can only approximate. The criterion of political excellence eludes the statesman who models his action on another political institution that is considered good, but it is self-evident to the philosopher who, on the contrary, looks away from the institution in order to see in thought only the indisputable Good-in-Itself, of which it is a part. Platonic idealism exempts the just principle of law from the consideration of all that is already considered just in human terms, and it thereby subordinates politics to a wisdom alien to political order itself.

The idealist quest for absolute objectivity is sharply criticized by Aristotle for two principal philosophical reasons. First, the good is not reducible to a single principle, a universal source of all that is good; and only the strictly human good, within human reach, concerns the political order. Second, this strictly human good cannot be considered in the form of an absolute, independent of human institutions, that could be known even if one were ignorant of the institutions; on the contrary, objective knowledge of it includes the consideration of what is generally thought of as good by the very best thinkers.

However, the kind of knowledge that allows the philosopher to judge particular political systems in comparison to a perfect system is not the science that Aristotle intends to require of statesmen or legislators themselves. This is where Aristotle's originality lies. For Aristotle, the best system that can be described, not in the abstract but within the human order, is not even a regime that absolutely must come into being in the end. Here the philosopher clearly means to do justice to a certain relativity of the good in human terms. The basic laws that would establish the best possible political regime depend on the best possible circumstances, and these circumstances are contingent: the legislator can hope for them, but he is powerless to create them. So the true good that is the goal of the law is not and should not be what is good in an absolute sense, but always what is the best for the men for whom the laws are written. The absolute, even the human absolute, is thus seen, in most circumstances, to be apparent rather than real (see *Politics* VII).

This point of view has one immediate consequence. It prohibits the philosopher from dictating, as Plato did, laws that the statesman ought to receive and according to which he ought always to govern. In other words, the statesman finds himself exempted by Aristotle from some inescapable authority of philosophical wisdom, and by right he regains his autonomy and the responsibility to decide what laws really are the most appropriate for his own time and situation.

Despite appearances, however, Aristotle does not return to the subjectivity of the Sophists. The statesman's decisions must always result from virtue and deep knowledge that is analogous, in its own domain, to philosophical wisdom. This virtue is not simply ability, like the proficiency of rhetorical masters who are indifferent to an objective quality, good or bad, of the measures they propose and on which they seek consensus. It is a true wisdom *(phronesis)* that takes into account only what is best for the city-state, regardless of any contradictory opinions others might have. This wisdom enables the statesman to see the true good for his city-state, infallibly and beyond argument, rather than what merely appears to be good. According to Aristotle, this capability comes directly from the education the statesman has received, from moral values acquired in childhood, inasmuch as these values conform to those shared with the best citizens and thus lead toward the highest standard of good that can be conceived under the circumstances.

Once the statesman is properly oriented toward acting for the ultimate good, the rest is simply a matter of skill and technique. The wisdom of the statesman, within these limits, consists in finding the means of attaining the objectives determined by an understanding of the good of his own city-state.

But this general knowledge, for Aristotle, is not the source of politics per se. It may benefit from theoretical knowledge, drawn for example from history, and even from very speculative philosophical views; however, the wisdom that characterizes the statesman is specifically knowledge of leadership. Leadership is not simply the knowledge of what is generally the right decision, nor even of what is the right decision under the particular circumstances that require reflection; it extends to the ability to judge in practice what is the right thing to do at the right time.

Aristotle is aware of this fundamental demand of the art of politics when he argues, as Plato did, for a regime of laws. The disadvantages of written laws had led Plato to assert the advantage of a royal art that is exercised without law, but he ultimately acknowledges the need for laws on account of the caprices to which statesmen are subject. Although more realistic than Plato, and aware that most monarchies are also governed by laws, Aristotle does not exclude the exceptional cases in which some absolute monarch might legitimately exercise authority beyond the law, himself embodying the law as "a kind of god among mortals" (*Politics* III.128.12). But, like Plato, he tends to recommend that the best statesmen should always legislate and thus establish a state based on law. To legislate does not mean ordering citizens to do one thing or another; it means furnishing a general rule that directs them to do a certain type of thing. The law that is addressed without discrimination to all is a form of intelligence that governs without passion. The law's compelling power, for the statesman who must enforce it, is precisely what bends the passions of the ruler to the intelligent rule that it expresses.

The states based on law advocated by Aristotle, outside of which there is no political order, strictly speaking, are just collectives subjected to a dynastic power. In this context, statesmen themselves are (as they are for Plato) mere enforcers of the law, workers in the service of the legislator-overseer. The latter, the architect on whom the political order depends, is no longer, as he was for Plato, the wise man inspired by the transcendent principle behind all regulations but a supremely wise man, guided by the good of his own citizens, which he can identify thanks to his good training.

During Plato's time and probably even before, thinkers tended to rank the life of the philosopher above all others because it was dedicated to the study of sublime questions, even though most people considered those questions useless. Plato himself ranked cultivation of the mind above all else, because it responded to a natural curiosity; he denigrated the statesman's interest in financial issues, which he thought was usually motivated by a desire for fame and fortune. In describing the ideal of the philosopher-king or the king-philosopher, he offered a way to reconcile politics with the higher values of the mind. He knew that philosophical wisdom, oriented toward the intelligible world, turns its possessor away from the physical world and human affairs as it deepens and is absorbed by its object. Thus the wise man ran the inevitable risk not only of being rejected and misunderstood by the city-state, but also of having to force himself, against his will, to stoop to the worldly level. Rather than dreaming about compelling the wise man to serve, and at bottom persuaded that he would not be accepted by his fellow citizens, in the end Plato preferred to supply his own example of a philosopher who prompts the city-state to accept his laws. By the same token, political life for him was condemned to remain the devalued, almost servile existence of those who bow before a law they hardly understand and force themselves to obey its precepts.

Aristotle corrects the picture. The speculative life of the philosopher, comparable to that of the gods, remains, in his eyes, without equal. But active political life regains its worth. The one who embraces it is liberated from the authority of any other wisdom. He depends on no one, apart from other statesmen, to tell him what to do. Autonomous and free, he finds the principles of his wisdom in political action itself. At this level, the political life is that of a mature man. Moreover, it demonstrates the height of human maturity: knowing how to lead, rather than how to obey.

Furthermore, the political life borrows from the peaceful life of the philosopher the model of action that it embodies and that the statesman aims to instill in those he governs. The political life does not imitate the life of businessmen nor does it make laws that favor the ridiculous cult of wealth; it does not imitate the powerful, or harbor a bellicose soul in an imperialistic city-state. The statesman, on the contrary, is obliged to want the city-state to display the same interest in itself that the philosopher displays: he must want all of its citizens, when they act, to demonstrate the same concern for perfection that the philosopher endeavors to cultivate when he is thinking. The statesman rules each individual just as each one rules himself, with the wise man's ambition of perfecting himself. His action, his legislative action in particular, seeks to orient the actions of every individual, but, like the actions of every individual, the legislator's action finds its reward in itself; to this it adds only the supplementary benefit of working for the benefit of others. The true statesman is courageous and demands courage of all, seeking not the doubtful advantages that one may hope to get from victory and its consequences but rather the certain increase in virtue that acts of courage procure, even in defeat. Thus Aristotle portrays the political life as the very image of a life actively devoted to perfecting others and oneself, in which intelligence, unfettered by all philosophical wisdom, serves human beings in their essential humanity.

The Stoics, who, in contrast to the classical philosophers, were much more concerned about morality than speculation, later developed an ideal of wisdom that represented human perfection from every point of view, but for which political life was not important. A citizen of the world, the wise Stoic could adapt well to all conditions, even servitude. But a certain number of Stoics, cultivating self-perfection, became advisers to princes during Roman times, as Seneca was to Nero, or were princes themselves, like the illustrious emperor Marcus Aurelius, who left us his *Thoughts,* set down in Greek. When Marcus Aurelius became emperor, "Plato's ideal was realized," said Renan. Renan was wrong, of course, for the wisdom of Marcus Aurelius, to the extent that we consider him wise, had nothing in common with the virtue Plato envisioned. Philosophy for Marcus Aurelius was only a way to find life a little less intolerable. And the fatalistic rigidity of the morality that sums up his philosophy had nothing to do with Aristotle's ethical principles. The exercise of power was, for Marcus Aurelius, a burden borne out of duty, rather than the highest expression to which human perfection aspired, as it was for Aristotle. The example of Marcus Aurelius actually serves as a reminder that the image of the statesman, even the philosopher-statesman, is never precisely what the philosophers seek to make it.

RICHARD BODÉÜS
Translated by Elizabeth Rawlings and Jeannine Pucci

Bibliography

Texts and Translations

Aristotle. *Metaphysics,* vol. 1. Books I–IX. Ed. T. E. Page. Trans. Hugh Tredennick. Loeb Classical Library.
———. *Nicomachean Ethics.* Trans. H. Rackham. Loeb Classical Library.
———. *Politics.* Trans. H. Rackham. Loeb Classical Library.
Diogenes Laertius. *Lives of Eminent Philosophers.* Trans. R. D. Hicks. Loeb Classical Library.
Philoponus. *Nikomachou Arithmetikes eisagoges.* Leipzig: Teubner, 1864.
Plato. *Laws.* Trans. Harold North Fowler. Loeb Classical Library.

Studies

Bodéüs, Richard. *Le philosophe et la cité: Recherches sur les rapports entre morale et politique dans la pensée d'Aristote.* Paris: Les Belles Lettres, 1982.
———. *Politique et philosophie chez Aristote.* Namur: Société des études classiques, 1991.
Bordes, Jacqueline. *La notion de "politeia" dans la pensée grecque avant Aristote.* Paris: Les Belles Lettres, 1982.
Carlier, Pierre. *La royauté en Grèce avant Alexandre.* Strasbourg: Association pour l'Étude de la Civilisation Romaine, 1984.
Citati, Pietro. *Alexandro Magno.* Paris: Gallimard, 1990.

Finley, Moses I. *Democracy Ancient and Modern*. New Brunswick, N.J.: Rutgers University Press, 1973.

Hansen, Morgens H. *The Athenian Democracy in the Age of Demosthenes* (1978). Blackwell Classical Series. Oxford: Blackwell Publishing, 1991.

Levêque, Pierre, and Pierre Vidal-Naquet. *Cleisthenes the Athenian: An Essay on the Representation of Space and Time in Greek Political Thought from the End of the Sixth Century to the Death of Plato*. Atlantic Highlands, N.J.: Humanities Press, 1996.

Mossé, Claude. *Histoire des doctrines politiques en Grèce*. Paris: Presses Universitaires de France, 1969.

———. *La tyrannie dans la Grèce antique*, 2nd ed. Paris: Presses Universitaires de France, 1989.

Nicolet, Claude, ed. *Du pouvoir dans l'antiquité: Mots et réalités*. Paris and Geneva: Droz, 1990.

Piérart, Marcel. *Platon et la cité grecque*. Brussels: Académie royale de Belgique, 1974.

Romilly, Jacqueline de. *La Grèce antique à la découverte de la liberté*. Paris: Editions de Fallois, 1989.

———. *La loi dans la pensée grecque des origines à Aristote*. Paris: Les Belles Lettres, 1971.

Strauss, Leo. *The Argument and the Action of Plato's Laws*. Chicago: University of Chicago Press, 1975.

———. *The City and Man*. Chicago: University of Chicago Press, 1977.

Vidal-Naquet, Pierre. *Politics Ancient and Modern*. Trans. Janet Lloyd. Cambridge, Eng.: Polity, 1995.

Related Articles

Inventing Politics; Aristotle; Plutarch; Xenophon; The Sage and Politics; Plato; Polybius

INVENTING POLITICS

THE GREEKS INVENTED POLITICS. But what do we mean by that? The word itself comes from Greek. *Politike* is knowledge relating to the polis, the city-state, just as *oikonomike* is knowledge about the *oikos*, the house, in the sense both of property and of family. This knowledge, according to a myth recounted by the Sophist Protagoras in Plato's dialogue of the same name, is said to have been granted by Zeus to everyone, allowing all to participate in the affairs of the city-state. Protagoras concluded: "Hence it comes about, Socrates, that people in cities and especially in Athens, consider it the concern of a few to advise on cases of artistic excellence or good craftsmanship, and if anyone outside the few gives advice they disallow it, as you say, and not without reason, as I think: but when they meet on a consultation on civic art, where they should be guided throughout by justice and good sense, they naturally allow advice from everybody, since it is held that everybody should partake of this excellence, or else that states cannot be" (*Protagoras* 322d–323a).

This is how Protagoras explained the political regime that existed in Athens starting at the end of the 6th century B.C.E. and that was known from the 5th century on as democracy. But at the same time he was accounting for the nature of the Greek city-state: a community of men who held in their hands the power to make decisions following debate, precisely what was known as politics.

Thus the invention of politics is inseparable from the birth of the original form of the state, namely, the city-state. For the ancients, and notably for the philosophers of the 4th century B.C.E., the birth of the city-state was related to the necessity for people to help one another and to meet their own needs: to procure food, clothing, and shelter from cold and heat. For this reason, as Aristotle says, man is a *politikon zōon*, an animal created to live in cities. But because he possesses *logos*, unlike other animals, he alone is able to distinguish between good and evil, justice and injustice, and that is what constitutes *arete politike*, civic virtue.

Historical reality was quite different. Beyond the Greek world there existed "despotic" states, where the priceless possession of the Greek citizen, freedom, was unknown. The Greek world itself had known political forms that predated the city-state: the "Mycenaean" states, revealed by a reading of the tablets discovered in the ruins of the palaces that were at their center, can be compared in their organization to the countries of the ancient Far East. These palaces disappeared abruptly toward the end of the 13th century B.C.E. Their disappearance, which is not easy to explain, was followed by the "dark ages" from the 12th to the 9th century, when numerous sites were abandoned, material civilization declined, and the use of writing was lost. We begin to see a renaissance toward the end of the 9th century with the reappearance of human settlements on long-abandoned sites. However, there is no agreement on criteria that would allow us to determine whether or not to call these settlements city-states: the presence of an urban agglomeration surrounded by walls, of a sanctuary where offerings are collected, of an open space that may have served as an agora, or a necropolis. As valuable as it is, archaeology is silent on these questions, and we must look to literary sources for answers, sources that for the most part follow the birth of city-states by two or three centuries—with the exception, of course, of the two great epic poems that have come down to us under Homer's name and that probably date from the 8th century.

Writing had by that time reappeared, but in a very different form from that of the Mycenaean syllabary. Borrowed from the Phoenicians, the source of our own alphabet, the new writing was to become an exceptional tool; it made it possible to transcribe not only epics that had been passed down orally for centuries but also the laws governing the first city-states. Through Homer's poems we can make out the features foreshadowing what the Greek city-state would be, not only in Ithaca, where Ulysses was king, but also in the island of the Phaeacians, those "ferrymen" who enabled him to return to the world of men. Each city-state consisted of an urban core and surrounding land. In the center of the town, which at Scheria is surrounded by a wall, there was an agora where meetings of the demos were held. Around the agora, there were public buildings: a temple "in stone" at Scheria, a fountain at Ithaca. That these were city-states is beyond question, even if they were headed by kings and the demos played only a consultative role. Civic space was clearly delineated, the community had a real existence, and in the case of Ithaca, whose king was absent for twenty years, those who formed the majority *(hoi polloi)* were ready to side with Telemachus, Ulysses' son, the victim of Penelope's suitors. Even Scheria, though it belongs to the realm of imagination, evokes in many ways the "colonial" city-states that the Greeks established starting in the middle of the 8th century, first along the southern coasts of Italy and Sicily, then along the entire perimeter of the Mediterranean and as far away as the shores of the Black Sea.

Some of these colonial cities have been thoroughly excavated, bringing to light a topography that confirms what the poets' descriptions suggested: the city-state has to be viewed, from the beginning, as a constructed space where a self-governing human community was established. True, neither the poems nor the traces left in the ground allow us to describe the community itself. Some inequalities existed at its heart, as we learn from material found in tombs, and from the vocabulary found in contemporary or subsequent literary sources opposing the *kakoi* to the *aristoi*, the "bad ones" to the "good ones." There is no doubt that the period called archaic, which lasted from the 8th to the 6th century, was a troubled era symbolized by the emergence of tyrannies in numerous cities, but it also saw the creation of institutions and laws attributed by Greek tradition to legislators who were models of wisdom and civic virtue. One of our main sources of knowledge about this period is the historian Herodotus, who lived in the 5th century B.C.E. Thanks to him, too, we can glimpse the types of political regimes that were to emerge at the end of the archaic age.

Paradoxically, it is through the conversation of three noble Persians that Herodotus develops what appears to be the first expression of a theory of political regimes. The first, Otanes, after denouncing the abuses of power in the hands of a single person—that is, a tyrant—extols the merits of the *isonomia,* a system based on equality among all members of a civic community: "All offices are assigned by lot, and the holders are accountable for what they do therein: and the general assembly arbitrates on all counsels" (Herodotus, III.80). The second, Megabyzes, was equally opposed to tyranny but refused to confer sovereignty *(to kratos)* on an ignorant mass and preferred that the city-state be placed in the hands of the best people *(aristoi),* necessarily few in number *(oligoi):* this type of regime is thus known as an oligarchy. The third Persian, Darius, opposed both isonomy and oligarchy; he advocated monarchy, in which power was in the hands of a single person *(monos),* but the monarch was to protect the people's interests. Herodotus was obliged to end his account with a tribute to monarchy, as he was in Persia at the time and Darius had been called to power. In Greece, where monarchy evoked either a distant past or abhorrent tyranny, the only choice was between oligarchy and democracy. At least this is what we are led to believe by the evolution of the two city-states whose history during the archaic period can be reconstructed with some accuracy, Sparta and Athens.

We should note at the outset that each presents a different problem. Sparta is in fact an atypical city-state about which the Greeks fantasized to the point that we can speak of a "Spartan mirage." At the origin of this mirage is the name of a legislator, Lycurgus, who is thought to have established *eunomia* at Sparta. A large part of what is known about him actually comes from Plutarch, who lived at the end of the 1st century C.E. In his biography of Lycurgus, Plutarch put together the pieces of a tradition that seems to have developed first in the Socratic world, then in Plato's Academy, and finally in the entourage of the 3rd-century reformer kings who set out to "reestablish the laws of Lycurgus." These laws are thought to have dealt partly with setting up political institutions, partly with the equitable distribution of civic land among the Spartans, and finally with establishing rules concerning education, which was to be strictly supervised by the city-state. In political terms, Sparta might pass in the eyes of Athenians for an oligarchy, since authority was shared by two kings, a council of elders (the *gerousia*) whose members were elected for life, and an assembly, whose power was limited to approving the measures proposed by the kings and elders. However, in the 4th century, in philosophical circles where Lycurgus's city-state was admired, there was a tendency to consider the Spartan Constitution a "mixed" constitution, since it had a democratic element represented by a college of five ephors elected each year by all Spartans. In fact the writings of Xenophon, who was very knowledgeable about Spartan society, and even more Aristotle's vigorous critique in *Politics,* suggest that the reality in Sparta was far from being as perfect as the admirers of the Laconian city-state would have us believe. The serious crisis that broke out there in the 3rd century is the most obvious confirmation of this inference. But once again, we know Sparta only as outsiders saw it, and we have nothing comparable to the rich documentation that is available about Athens.

We know a great deal more about Athens, indeed, first of all owing to its Constitution, the only one of the 158 collected by Aristotle and his students that has survived. The Constitution of Athens includes a historical first section that recalls the *metabolai,* the changes that Athenian institutions underwent between the earliest times and the establishment of democracy in 403 B.C.E. Some of the material in this account consists of reconstitutions; these tell us more about 4th-century preoccupations than about the reality of a past that is difficult to ascertain. Nevertheless, the material does offer a glimpse of the main stages in an evolution that would lead up to the highest expression of Greek political life: democracy.

Three moments in this evolution appear to be essential: Solon's archonship in 594–593, the tyranny of Pisistratus and his sons from 561 to 510, and Cleisthenes' reforms in 508–507. About the period before the 6th century B.C.E. we know little except what comes from mythical accounts, such as the one that depicts Theseus, the victor over the Minotaur, as the author of synoecism, the combining of several villages into one that was thought to have been the origin of Athens—a view that archaeological digs are beginning to confirm. The Constitution of Athens clearly evokes a Constitution of Draco that would in fact be an early body of laws against murder destined to end private wars between aristocratic families and to block the attempt of a certain Cylon to take the tyranny into his own hands. But all of this remains quite vague. One fact alone stands out, emphasized by all our sources: there was a climate of tension at the dawn of the 6th century, and the crisis was resolved by the legislator Solon, who was elected archon in 594.

According to Solon's own testimony (he was a poet as well as a legislator), the crisis was linked to the system of land tenure and to the tragic situation of a subjugated peasantry, the *hectemoroi* named in the Constitution of Athens, who were obligated to pay one-sixth (or was it five-sixths?) of their harvest to the landowners. Solon abolished the servitude of the peasantry by removing the posts *(horoi)* in the ground that marked their dependency, but he did not go ahead with the egalitarian redistribution of public land, as the poorest peasants were demanding. Nevertheless, he drafted laws that applied to everyone, a practice that became the foundation of civic community. Later on, tradition—echoed in the Constitution of Athens and Plutarch's Life of Solon—credited him with other measures, including a census-based classification of all Athenians, and the figure of Solon was glorified to such an extent that he appeared to be the founder of democracy. However, as far as we can ascertain from Herodotus's account and from the Constitution of Athens, discontent persisted and a new crisis gave rise to the tyranny of Pisistratus.

Pisistratus had to make three attempts before he was able to solidify his power. Claiming to be the defender of the demos, the common people, both rural and urban, he asserted the unity of the city-state around its gods: Athena, the protective goddess for whom he initiated the feast of Panathenians, and Dionysus, the popular god of the countryside to whom he consecrated the feast of Dionysians, the essential element of which were theatrical contests that would become illustrious in the following century with the productions of the great tragic poets. Faithful to the tradition of tyrants as builders, Pisistratus also contributed significantly to the development of the city of Athens, thereby increasing the influence of the urban demos in the life of the city-state. However, tyranny could be only a transitory regime. When Pisistratus's son, Hippias, was defeated by a coalition of Athenian aristocrats, with the support of the Spartan king Cleomenes, the strength of the demos was such that simply returning to the status quo ante was out of the question.

This was understood by one of the aristocrats, Cleisthenes the Alcmeonide, who decided, according to Herodotus, to "bring the demos into his own camp" in order to get rid of his enemies, but in so doing he overturned the organization of the city-state. For the four "tribes," based on a more or less imaginary kinship, into which all Athenians were divided, Cleisthenes substituted ten territorial tribes, each encompassing three *trittys*, groups of demes situated in each of the three great regions of Attica: the city, the coast, and the interior. According to Aristotle, his intent was that "every device must be employed to make all the people as much as possible intermingled with one another and to break up the previously existing groups of associates" (*Politics* 1319b26–28). In other words, Cleisthenes' goal was to break up the relationships of patronage on which the power and authority of the large aristocratic families were based. The institution of a Council of 500, the members of which were recruited annually by lottery among Athenians over the age of thirty, fifty per tribe, was meant to achieve this "mixing" and to contribute even more to removing the demos from the influence of those whom the great historian Moses Finley called the "local bosses."

Cleisthenes did not found democracy, but he created the conditions that would allow its development in the course of the following century. It will suffice to recall a few essential stages. Replacing election of the archons by random selection (487–486) effectively limited the power and influence of aristocrats over their dependents. The growth of the judicial power of the Council of 500 (Boule) and of the popular tribunal of the Heliaia, whose members also were chosen by random drawing among all Athenians, was the work of Ephialtes in 462–461 and removed almost all authority from the aristocratic council of the Areopagus, made up of former archons. Broadening the base for recruitment of the archons—a position that until 457–456 was reserved for the very rich, members of the first two census classes—to include the third class, small landowners, resulted in "democratizing" the archon function. Finally, and most important, Pericles' introduction of the *misthophoria*, the practice of paying judges and, later, council members, would complete the evolution toward democracy.

In an oration that Thucydides, the great historian of the end of the 5th century, attributes to Pericles, this pay for public service is implicitly justified: "Nor, again, on the grounds of poverty is a man barred from a public career by obscurity of rank if he has it in him to do the state service" (Thucydides, 2.37.1). The author of the Constitution of Athens echoes another tradition: Pericles is said to have introduced *misthophoria* to outdo his rival, Cimon. The latter, an extremely rich man, opened up his domains so that all might benefit from its fruits to their satisfaction: "For as Cimon has an estate large enough for a tyrant, in the first place he discharged the general public services in a brilliant manner, and moreover he supplied maintenance to a number of the members of his deme" (*Athenian Constitution* XXVII.3). Pericles, lacking the means for such generosity, was advised by one of his friends "to give the multitude what was their own, and he instituted payment for the jury-courts" (ibid. XXVII.3–4). Although this anecdote is discounted by most historians, one cannot fail to observe that in such actions Pericles showed the same concern as his great-uncle Cleisthenes had for ending the patronage system. Other reforms contributed to the democratization of the regime as well, such as the establishment of regular sessions of the people's assembly and the introduction of judicial procedures that reinforced the control of the demos over magistrates.

These procedures led to the disappearance of the practice of ostracism, a practice traditionally attributed to Cleisthenes. His goal had been to avoid any possibility of a return of tyranny. Ostracism required the removal from the city of anyone who seemed to pose a danger to democracy. A person who was deemed dangerous was ostracized by the action of an assembly made up of at least 6,000 citizens; each was to write on a shard (*ostrakon*) the name of the individual who was to be exiled for ten years. In fact, most of those ostracized—including some of the principal leaders of the city-state—were removed from public life for little more than two years. This curious practice has come to light through the discovery of a number of shards on the hills of the Acropolis and in the Agora. The variety of handwriting styles, sometimes very crude, attests to the number of Athenians who were capable of copying a few letters. But some 192 shards have also been found bearing the name of Themistocles and showing only a small number of different styles, thus indicating that votes of ostracism could have been prepared in advance.

The quorum of 6,000 participants poses another problem. If we estimate the number of citizens at around thirty thousand, as Plato and Aristophanes imply, are we to assume that this quorum was rarely attained for ordinary assemblies—in other words, that barely one-fifth of all citizens actively participated in the affairs of the city-state?

Historians' answers to this question are contradictory. For some, this limited participation proves that political activity concerned only a minority, and that the term *democracy* does not really apply. Others, taking a different view, have seen this "apathy" of the demos as a sign of the harmonious functioning of the institutions in question. However, Finley has firmly rejected the latter interpretation as harmful and dangerous when applied to modern democracy. He rightly emphasizes the fact that the composition of the assemblies varied, depending on circumstances and the time of year. We are immediately reminded of the peasant in one of Aristophanes' comedies who explains that he does not really like going to town to attend assemblies: "So here I am waiting, thoroughly prepared to riot, wrangle, interrupt the speaker whenever they speak of anything but Peace" (*Acharnians* 37–39). As Finley also notes, the presence of important issues on the agenda—such as, in this case, peace—might attract people to the assembly who felt directly implicated (farmers concerned about an enemy encroaching on their land, candidates for the draft worried about being sent to the fleet, and so on) but who, in other circumstances, would have neither the time nor the inclination to become involved.

Thucydides indirectly provides proof that on the basis of the proportion of the total number of citizens represented by the quorum one cannot infer that participation of the demos in decision making was more formal than real. In 411, taking advantage of the defeats suffered by the Athenians in the war against Sparta and its allies, the enemies of democracy seized power, designated 400 councilors to direct the affairs of the city-state, and decided that thenceforth full citizenship would be limited to 5,000 Athenians, the rest being excluded from assemblies. The army and the Athenian fleet were then stationed at Samos, where they could watch the movements of the enemy and also the Athenian allies preparing to defect to escape an increasingly powerful authority. The oligarchs, masters of the city, sent commissioners to Samos charged with defending the revolution and the restriction of full citizenship to the 5,000: "although because of their military expeditions and their activities abroad, the Athenians had never yet come to consult upon any matter so important that five thousand had assembled" (Thucydides, VIII.72.1). The response was immediate. Soldiers and sailors met in the assembly, discharged strategists suspected of sympathy for the oligarchy, and appointed others known to be faithful to democracy. Thucydides adds: "Moreover they rose in their place and made various recommendations for their own guidance, in particular urging that there was no need to be discouraged because the city had revolted from them; for it was the minority who had abandoned them, who were the majority, and also were in every way better provided with resources" (Thucydides, VIII.76.3).

There could be no better affirmation of the very real attachment of the citizens to democracy and to their participation in the affairs of the city than this. The false argument of the oligarchs collapsed before the feeling of the sailors and soldiers that they were the majority. This is at the very heart of the Athenian political system. Isonomy, established by Cleisthenes, meaning equality of all without regard to birth or fortune, was the very foundation of democracy. This was the basis for the principle of majority rule, which implies that once a decision is made, even by a small majority, as was the case in 427–426 when the Athenians decided to spare the people of Mytilene who had left the alliance, the minority accepts the decision. Though considered normal today, this attitude was not taken for granted at the time, all the less so in that no divine intervention was invoked. The important thing was respect for the laws and, also—we must have no illusions on this point—power relations at the time of the vote. The decision concerning the people of Mytilene was taken at the end of a debate in which one of the speakers had demonstrated the inanity of the first vote calling for the killing of rebel Mytilenians. The speaker's talent had changed enough votes to amend the decision taken the day before.

We should not believe, however, that the demos often overturned a decision of the majority from one day to the next. Thucydides chose to discuss the Mytilenean affair at length in his account of the Peloponnesian War, because it allowed him to present two contrasting speeches about the history of the relations between Athens and its allies, and about the evolution of the Delian League, which, from its beginning right after the Persian Wars, had been gradually transformed into the Athenian empire. In fact, the numerous decrees carved in stone that have come down to us demonstrate that Athenian democracy functioned much better than its critics claimed. The publication of these decrees (issued in the name of the Boule, which prepared them, and in the name of the demos), along with the mention of the name of the person who had made the proposal and of all those who brought amendments, show that no vote of the assembly could be ignored and that anyone could find out what decisions had been made.

These decisions dealt with an infinite number of areas, since the assembly had sovereign power. War, peace, embassies, finances, public buildings, the organization of religious festivals, everything fell within its sphere and was subject to its legislation. At the end of the 5th century, right after two oligarchic revolutions that had failed when confronted by the determined demos, a commission of *nomothetes* (legislators) had been set up to verify that there were no contradictory laws and to restore order to a body of laws that the long Peloponnesian War had somewhat disrupted. This commission had outlived its initial task, and the proposed text of every new law had to be submitted to it before being presented to the assembly.

Some have believed, on this evidence, that the sovereignty of law had replaced popular sovereignty in the 4th century, thus countering the usual criticisms of the excesses of democracy. But in fact this view ignores everything that escaped the control of the commission—in other words, all decisions having to do with the overall politics of the city-state. The *nomothetes* are rarely mentioned in these decrees, and so we must not look at the commission as some sort of constitutional council.

It is probably also an exaggeration to say that in the 4th century the popular tribunals growing out of the Heliaia had supplanted the assembly in controlling political life. True, the political processes played an important part in the life of the Athenian democracy, as attested by the numerous defenses that have come down to us, in particular those that Demosthenes and his adversary Aeschines composed. The former espoused a policy of active resistance to the plotting of the Macedonian king, while the latter advocated reaching an understanding with him. But the proceedings in which both found themselves implicated grew out of previous alternatives that had been proposed to the assembled demos. Nevertheless, it was also through their own efforts that these choices were brought before the popular tribunal. This has posed a problem that has been the object of recent debate, the problem of the "political class," of "the elite," and of relations between that elite and the citizenry in general.

The question had already been raised by the ancients themselves. The orators who spoke before the people and shaped their decisions were considered useless, dangerous demagogues who sought only to flatter the populace and grow rich at their expense. The same grievances were found in the plays of Aristophanes, in the dialogues of Plato, in the fictional speeches of the rhetorician Isocrates, and in the real speeches of the orators themselves, in charges brought against their adversaries. The term *demagogue* originally meant someone who leads the demos as the pedagogue leads the child *(pais)*, but it quickly took on the same negative meaning that it continues to have today. Moses Finley, in an article published in 1962, showed, contrary to the common view, that the demagogues in the literal sense of the word constituted "a structural element of the Athenian political system" (p. 69), of that direct democracy in which sovereign assemblies convened several thousand people.

Clearly, anyone who desired to speak was free to do so. But he had to be able to make himself heard. This is what the young Charmides explains to Socrates in Xenophon's *Memorabilia*. To the philosopher who objects that those whom he addresses, artisans, peasants, and merchants, are ignorant, Charmides answers that he dreads exposing himself to their mockery. However, in another passage of the *Memorabilia*, Xenophon has Socrates making remarks that prove that it was not simply a matter of possessing the art of persuasion, the *peitho* essential for being heard by the demos: one also had to be able to make concrete arguments; know the condition of the city-state's military forces if the vote concerned an expedition; know how much money could be raised for it, what would have to be imported to meet the needs of the population, and how much to budget for expenses. Xenophon compared the knowledge demanded of an orator, a statesman, to that of the master of the *oikos*, with the difference that the statesman was concerned with not just one but ten thousand "homes." Obviously this is rather far from what Plato's Socrates required of the leaders of the city-state. But Xenophon's Socrates does a good job of expressing the concerns of the author of *Economics* and *Ways and Means*, a man more familiar with the concrete realities of the city than was the master of the Academy. In addition, he defined quite well, during those first decades of the 4th century, the terms of access to the "political class": the art of persuasion combined with concrete and factual knowledge.

Which men, among all the citizenry, were most likely to satisfy all these requirements? To answer this question, we have to turn to literary sources, historical accounts, and allusions made by the comic poets and in orators' speeches, rather than to epigraphic documents that mention names, most of which are unknown. In the 5th century the political class came mostly from old aristocratic families. Even Themistocles, whose mother was said to have been born into the servant class, boasted of prestigious ancestors. These "well-born" men enjoyed a status attributable to their pedigree as much as to their fortune, which might be large, as Cimon's was, or more modest, like that of Aristides, who died so poor that the city had to assume the care of his children. As *strategoi* they directed the politics of the city-state. Even though they might be effective leaders of military campaigns, they were not professional soldiers, at least not before the 4th century, when they became leaders of the armies that were themselves composed of professional mercenaries. Of the ten generals elected each year, some found themselves among the ranks of ordinary soldiers a year later. Elected by the *demos*, they were accountable at the end of their year's service. And it is also because they were elected by the demos that, even during a military campaign, they could be called to account before an assembly of citizen soldiers. This explains the Samos affair mentioned above. And one can find in Thucydides' account, as in that of his successor Xenophon, numerous examples of speeches given by a general before his soldiers to explain the conduct of the war. Thus we can see why the function of the *strategoi* was essentially a political one, and why most of the leaders of the city, up to the time of the Peloponnesian War and beyond, took on this function, to which they could be reelected indefinitely. Miltiades, Themistocles, Aristides, and Cimon were generals several times, and Pericles was reelected for fifteen consecutive years. It is in this capacity that he was "the first citizen" and that he exercised a quasi-monarchical power in the city. True, he had to share the responsibility with nine colleagues, and he was held accountable every year. But because he was a gifted speaker he had great influence over the demos, as Thucydides made clear.

Starting with the Peloponnesian War, however, if we are to believe the contemporary commentators, things began to change. While someone like Alcibiades still represented the ruling aristocratic class and combined in his own person the skills of an orator and those of a military leader, war itself, by virtue of the length of the campaigns and the remoteness of the various battle sites, tended more and more to transform *strategoi* into generals. From then on, the tribune fell into the hands of men whose backgrounds were more modest and who did not necessarily bear any public responsibility. It is with this group that the term *demagogue* takes on a negative connotation. Were they really—as the enemies of democracy claimed—irresponsible, and all the more confident of their impunity since they were not magistrates and therefore not accountable? We should keep in mind, first of all, that a number of them had held public office at one time or another in their careers. Cleon, the demagogue par excellence, was elected *strategos* on several occasions, and Demosthenes, Athens's most famous orator in the 4th century, had held several financial posts.

But even those without public positions were not free to act with impunity: there were in fact judicial procedures for bringing charges against them. The *graphe para nomōn*, used to charge someone with an illegal action, and especially the *eisangelia*, prosecution for an action against the state, represented both a constant risk for orators and a powerful weapon in the hands of the demos. If we can believe the orator Hyperides, one provision of the law of *eisangelia* made it possible to prosecute an orator who proposed any measure that ultimately proved harmful to the people. The numerous legal actions brought against politicians in the 4th century attest to the efficacy of these provisions in Athenian law: orators and *strategoi* remained under the constant control of the demos. From that time on, both groups came from the same milieu: they were wealthy men whose income came from artisans' studios, mining concessions, or maritime loans. Such origins no longer left them open to reproach, nor did the lack of glorious ancestors in the family. Moreover, it is possible that the ties linking them to what one might prudently call the "business world" had allowed them to gain a better understanding of the concrete problems that faced the city, the most important ones being the problem of increasing revenues and that of supplying grain. The best-known orators had advisers on hand capable of providing them with the exact infor-

mation they needed to impose their policy decisions on the assembly. This
"entourage" of *philoi,* friends, had another function as well: its members
could propose unpopular measures for which the politician in power was not
eager to take direct responsibility.

An example illustrates this practice, and it also explains the presence of unfamiliar names in the decrees. In 348, when Demosthenes wanted to allocate
budgetary surpluses reserved for entertainment to a military account in order
to prepare for a war against Philip that he considered imminent, he had one of
his friends, Apollodorus, propose the measure. Apollodorus, whose father was
a rich banker originally from the servant class, had received Athenian citizenship and dreamed of a political career. He abandoned the bank he had inherited and accepted Demosthenes' patronage. His proposal was attacked in a
graphe para nomōn, and he received a harsh penalty. At this time, two policies were in conflict: Eubules and his friends, including Aeschines, advocated
pursuing peace with the king of Macedonia, while Demosthenes was the chief
spokesman for the group advocating a policy of confrontation with the Macedonian leader. Eubules was supported not only by the wealthy, who bore the
burden of military expenses, but also by a large part of the demos, who
wanted to preserve surplus funds allocated for entertainment, and who in addition were not inclined to leave home on a military campaign. Eubules therefore had little trouble getting one of his friends to attack the decree and to
condemn Apollodorus. Several years later, the threat posed by Philip had become more apparent after the provision of fresh supplies to Athens was jeop-
ardized by his actions in the Dardenelles, through which grain from the countries around the Black Sea had to pass. Demosthenes took up his proposal
again, confident that he had the support of the demos, and this time he was
successful.

However, it was also Demosthenes who accused the people in the assembly
of attending oratorical contests simply as spectators and then forgetting the
very next day the decisions they had taken the day before. Were these simply
the words of a speaker outraged because the crowd had failed to listen to him?
Possibly. But such charges cannot be dismissed so quickly, nor can one dismiss
out of hand complaints about corrupt judges, or about the sudden wealth of
certain *strategoi.* These accusations and examples came, for the most part,
from speeches composed for a trial; they are invaluable sources of information about Athenian political life, but their use poses a real problem for the
historian. Does the very nature of the sources explain the negative picture?
Or should we assume that they reflect a new reality: the decline of Athenian
democracy following the Peloponnesian War, which, according to Thucydides,
disrupted not only the material life of the city-states but also the moral behavior and attitudes of the people?

It is not easy to offer a categorical reply to this question. It is true that
Athenian democracy in the 4th century—prey to financial difficulties and

trying vainly to reestablish its hegemony in the Aegean—was no longer what it had been during the time of Pericles. But must we therefore speak of "decline" or "crisis"? The crisis that erupted in the days following Athens's defeat was overcome relatively quickly, and by the middle of the century the city-state saw an economic recovery reflected in the lists of the silver mining concessions in the Laurion mountain region and the increased activity in Piraeus. But this may be precisely where we find a partial response that can only be formulated as a hypothesis.

Wealth had in fact long been sought primarily for the opportunity it offered those who possessed it to secure the goodwill of the demos through private largesse, as Cimon did, or through public generosity, by providing for sumptuous performances of liturgies, rites and festivals sponsored by the city as public service. Every year, indeed, financing various displays of religious life (donating animals for sacrifices, organizing public banquets, training the chorus for musical and dramatic competitions) and outfitting the fleet for war were responsibilities left to the wealthiest Athenians, whose names were no doubt supplied by the archons and the generals. The agonistic, competitive spirit inherited from the earlier aristocratic society prevailed in the performance of these liturgies: everyone hoped to present the most brilliant chorus, to arm most effectively the ship that was entrusted to him, and to hire the best crews. The conferring of a crown by the city-state was the reward for those who were most successful in this competition. Bragging about how much one had spent for the city-state, and about how much one had received, was a powerful argument both with the demos and with judges, and neither accusers nor accused failed to use it. Starting in the 4th century, we see an increase in something called *antidosis,* a process of exchange, in which a citizen, called on to perform one of the liturgies, asked someone he considered wealthier to perform it in his place. Obviously, such exchanges might be accounted for by reversals of fortune. One might also suspect that those who tried to avoid their obligations might be putting self-interest before the interest of the city-state. This would clearly indicate that they were using their fortunes either for the sorts of luxuries Demosthenes denounced in his speech against the rich king Midias (fancy houses, expensive carriages, exotic clothes, and so on), or in a reflection of the tasteless materialism that Aristotle denounced in *Politics,* in which money and the amassing of great fortunes were the only object. Athens's economic development in the second half of the 4th century is perhaps at the origin of this new channeling of private wealth into business, banking, and mining. But it is easy to see what this suggests: by devoting their wealth to the city, the rich gained the gratitude of the demos; by turning it toward other objects, they showed their lack of interest in politics.

During the same period, the arrangements that had enabled the Greeks to resolve the contradiction between a political system based on the equality of all citizens and a social system of inequality broke down. It is clear that the opposition between rich and poor, which had been masked by official discourse in the preceding century and which had in fact been reduced, owing to the advantages that accrued from Athenian hegemony in the Aegean (the author of *The Athenian Constitution* claimed that the empire supported twenty thousand Athenians, since the taxes and tributes raised from the allies provided for the payment of salaries to soldiers, sailors, judges, and so forth), had become a recurrent theme of both political speeches and written theories. However, it should be noted that Athens escaped the internal conflicts that broke out in a number of the city-states in the Greek world. There is no doubt that the explanation for this civil peace lay in Athens's democratic regime.

As a whole, the civic community was still a privileged group. In 451 Pericles had clearly defined the limits of citizenship, the Athenian's double descent on both the mother's and the father's side. The restoration of democracy in 403 had solemnly reaffirmed this position. In this respect Athenian women, though their legal and political status was that of minors, nevertheless belonged to the civic community, and Athenian democracy was no more exclusive on this point than were modern democracies up to fairly recent times. However, it was probably more exclusive with regard to foreigners, whether they were Greeks or were residing permanently as aliens. The awarding of citizenship was actually quite exceptional, and if citizens and foreigners often found themselves doing business together, the difference between them was still great; for example, the foreigner could not acquire a house or property. We can thus better appreciate the influence of politics on economics. Citizens, foreigners, and slaves could work side by side in fields, on public works, and on the quays of Piraeus, but only citizens owned land and took part in decision making.

It is important to specify that this exclusion primarily concerned political life. There were private relationships between citizens and foreigners. Plato's dialogue *The Republic* takes place at the home of the foreigner Kephalos, and we know about the help Kephalos's son, the orator Lysias, gave to the democrats at the time of the second oligarchic revolution. But nevertheless, when Thrasybules, who had led the democratic resistance, wanted to grant Lysias Athenian citizenship, he encountered opposition from the other leaders of the city and his proposal was defeated. While it is true that Athens, unlike Sparta, welcomed foreigners, citizenship remained a privilege rarely awarded to outsiders.

Here we have both the limitations and the greatness of Athenian democracy: because they were born Athenians, a poor peasant and a modest artisan had the same rights as a rich landowner or a mine owner; a slave, whether he was a banker who handled huge sums of money or a laborer working in the Laurion mines, could be sold or tortured at the will of his owner; and a rich foreigner, though he contributed to the prosperity of the city, was not permitted a seat in the Assembly. This should not prevent us, however, from recognizing that the Greek experience, particularly in Athens, had a value unique in the history of human societies.

CLAUDE MOSSÉ

Translated by Elizabeth Rawlings and Jeannine Pucci

Bibliography

Texts and Translations

Aristophanes. *Acharnians,* vol. 1. Trans. Benjamin Bickley Rogers. Loeb Classical Library.

Aristotle. *Athenian Constitution,* vol. 20. Trans. H. Rackham. Loeb Classical Library.

———. *Politics.* Trans. H. Rackham. Loeb Classical Library.

Herodotus. *Histories,* vol. 3. Trans. A. D. Godley. Loeb Classical Library.

Plato. *Protagoras.* Trans. W. R. M. Lamb. Loeb Classical Library.

Thucydides. *History of the Peloponnesian Wars,* vol. 4. Trans. Charles Foster Smith. Loeb Classical Library.

Studies

Cartledge, Paul. *Agesilaos and the Crisis of Sparta.* London: Duckworth, 1987.

Connor, Robert William. *The New Politicians of Fifth Century Athens.* Princeton: Princeton University Press, 1971.

Davies, John K. *Wealth and the Power of Wealth in Classical Athens.* New York: Ayer, 1981.

Finley, Moses I. "Athenian Demagogues." *Past and Present* 21 (1962): 3–24. Repr. in *Democracy, Ancient and Modern,* 2nd ed. London: The Hogarth Press, 1985. Pp. 38–75.

———. *Politics in the Ancient World.* Cambridge: Cambridge University Press, 1983.

Hansen, Mogens H. *The Athenian Democracy in the Age of Demosthenes.* Oxford: Oxford University Press, 1991.

Levêque, Pierre, and Pierre Vidal-Naquet. *Cleisthenes the Athenian.* Trans. David Ames Curtis. Atlantic Highlands, N.J.: Humanities Press, 1996.

Meier, Christian. *Die Entstehung des Politischen bei den Griechen.* Frankfurt: Suhrkamp Verlag, 1980.

Mossé, Claude. *Demosthène ou les ambiguités de la politique.* Paris: A. Colin, 1994.

———. *Politique et société en Grèce ancienne: Le "modèle" athénien.* Paris: Aubier, 1995.

Ober, Joshua. *Mass and Elite in Democratic Athens.* Princeton: Princeton University Press, 1989.

Ostwald, Martin. *From Popular Sovereignty to the Sovereignty of Law.* Berkeley: University of California Press, 1985.

Schmitt-Pantel, Pauline. *La Cité au banquet: Histoire des repas publics dans les cités grecques.* Rome: Ecole française de Rome, 1992.

Sinclair, Robert. *Democracy and Participation in Athens.* Cambridge: Cambridge University Press, 1988.

Vernant, Jean-Pierre, and Pierre Vidal-Naquet. *La Grèce ancienne,* vols. 1–3. Paris: Seuil, 1990–1992.

Related Articles

The Statesman As Political Actor; Socrates; Utopia and the Critique of Politics

UTOPIA AND THE
CRITIQUE OF POLITICS

In early 405 B.C.E. Athens was close to being defeated in the long, debilitating, and destabilizing Peloponnesian War against Sparta (431–404). At that moment of extreme crisis, Aristophanes produced his prize-winning comedy *Frogs* during the Lenaia festival in honor of Dionysus. According to convention, there was a point in the play where the leader of the Chorus (in this instance representing *mustai*, initiates in the Eleusinian Mysteries) stepped forward to speak seriously in the playwright's name. Aristophanes chose to use this moment to launch a savage tirade against the poor, debased quality of Athens's political leaders: "knaves, newcomers, aliens, copper-pated slaves, all rascals—honestly, what men to choose!" (ll. 730–732).

Such complaints against political leaders are familiar enough in our modern democratic societies, especially in times of general crisis. But in 405 democracy in Athens, and indeed in the world, was barely a century old, a tender and precious plant. The freedom with which Aristophanes was able to mock not only individual politicians but even key institutions of the democracy itself (especially the popular jury courts), in the context of a national religious festival, is in the circumstances really quite remarkable.

Athens was not of course the whole of Greece; it was indeed a highly atypical city (polis), both quantitatively and qualitatively. Almost certainly it was not the first Greek community to acquire the form of a polis, and it may even have been a little backward in doing so. However, from the reforms of Solon (ca. 600) onward Athens was never far from the center of Greek theoretical and practical political developments. And it is from this city of words that almost all the surviving literary evidence for the politics, the political, political theory, and political practice in ancient Greece before the death of Alexander (322) is directly or indirectly derived. The "politics" written about in this chapter will therefore be largely—though not exclusively—Athenian politics, and even more precisely Athenian democratic politics. Nevertheless, the temptation to identify Athens with Greece, or at least to write as if they were identical, must and will be firmly resisted here.

THE POLITICAL IN GREECE FROM HOMER TO SOCRATES

There had been polities in Mesopotamia and Egypt, political units of some considerable degree of organized sophistication, since the 4th millennium B.C.E. The late-developing civilizations of Minoan Crete and Mycenaean Greece were, for all their cultural brilliance, only pale imitations, politically, of their Middle Eastern models. Somewhere around 1200 the Mycenaean polities went into terminal decline, and after a dark age of several centuries, what emerged were not merely new polities but polities of a new kind, the polis. It was within the matrix of the polis that the political took a hitherto unprecedented form. Politics in the strong sense of that term was born.

Such politics consists in open debate and decision making among relatively equal power-holders on matters of major public consequence. It includes a high degree of open criticism and self-criticism. There are hints of this form of politics in the Homeric poems (ca. 700), but contemporary proof of the existence of the new type of political community and accompanying politics first appears in the 7th century: in the poems of the Boeotian Hesiod and the Spartan Tyrtaios, for example, or in a decree of the city of Dreros in Crete. That decree was found built into the wall of a temple (of Apollo of Delphi), reminding us that the Greek city was a city of gods as well as men. But it was not a sacred city in the sense of being theocratic—it was left to a bitter critic of Greek politics, Plato, to advocate that utopian "reform." Hesiod notably combined a critical attitude to his local ruling class with a rejection of its claim to enjoy a special relationship with the gods. The divine will, even if it was known for sure what it was, was not allowed to decide by itself any public debate over a Greek community's policies.

Such debate, crucially, took place *es meson* or *en mesoi,* as the Greeks put it, out in the open in the city's "central space." In time, this center was usually formalized architecturally in the shape of an agora, or place of gathering. The Greeks' very idea of the polis was in a general sense egalitarian, in that all those relevantly qualified were deemed to have an equal right to make their public contribution in word *(agoreuein)* as well as deed. But in the early polis the number of those relevantly qualified was both absolutely and relatively small—limited by criteria of both birth and wealth. The great majority of free adult males, and all adult females, lacked or rather were deprived of any political power properly so called.

In Athens the reforms of Solon (594) formally widened the circle of those entitled to a say. If it was he, too, who introduced the practice of counting votes, making the vote of the poor and humble citizen count for exactly the same as that of the richest and noblest, he also enormously expanded the scope of citizen equality. But the implementation of his reforms was interrupted by the usurpation of power by the tyrant Pisistratus and his sons (560–510). No matter how populist a Greek tyrant might be, as Pisistratus was, his rule nevertheless marked the suspension of politics in the strong sense. When politics resumed in Athens following the murder of one of Pisistratus's sons and the expulsion of another, the political result was unprecedented. The reforms of Cleisthenes (508/7) ushered in the world's first democracy.

It may not have been called "democracy" straightaway. One contemporary catchword that certainly was in use was *isonomia*, meaning equality of dignity and political status for all citizens under the laws. In Athens this could have been given a specifically democratic construction, but elsewhere the term could be applied to constitutions in which only a minority of citizens enjoyed political power. Another contemporary catchword, however, was peculiarly democratic: *isēgoria*, the equal right of a public say "in the center," and by extension an equal right to participate in the decision making that followed the public speaking. In Athens, to signal the novelty of this development, the Assembly of all Athenian citizens was convened no longer in the Agora (which retained other political functions) but on a hill nearby, the Pnyx.

It was to *isēgoria* that Herodotus (V.78) attributed the remarkable military successes of post-Cleisthenic Athens against both foreign (Persian) and Greek invaders between 506 and 490, culminating in the Battle of Marathon. The word *dēmokratia* seems to have been a later coinage—and even possibly a coinage of its opponents; it is not in fact attested before about 430, although it is likely to have been invented at least thirty years before then. For those who supported the new kind of self-government, *dēmokratia* was the sovereign power *(kratos)* of the people *(dēmos)* in the sense of all the citizens, the collective citizen-body. For its opponents, however, it was a sectarian and selfish power exercised by the poor mass of the common people in their own exclusive interests over their betters—the elite few, the noble and rich.

Here, then, in this fundamental social divide lay a further great stimulus to reflexive criticism, embracing for the first time properly theoretical reflection as well as a powerful motive for practical oppositional politics. It was, in brief, the conjunction of the Cleisthenic reforms with victory over Persia, against a long-term background of the conduct of politics "in the center," that enabled the birth of critical political theory in Greece by not later than 450. Critical political theory soon gave rise, in its turn, to ever more sophisticated critiques of politics as such.

A POLITICAL THEATER

The comedy of Aristophanes was political theater in a relatively straightforward sense. But Aristophanes shared the democracy's stage with tragic poets, whose theater was no less political, if in different ways. Since about 500 the Theater of Dionysus had been the scene of an annual play festival, the Great, or City, Dionysia, celebrated in March and April. From 486 comedy was added to tragedy at the Dionysia, and in about 450 both tragedy and comedy were incorporated in a second, more parochially Athenian Dionysiac play festival, the Lenaia (the setting of *Frogs*), celebrated annually in January and February.

The Theater of Dionysus was no less a public political space, no less "in the center," than the Agora and the Pnyx. The audience, mainly Athenian citizens, was participating in a democratic political ritual. Whereas the plots of political comedy were drawn from real contemporary life (if fantastically exaggerated or caricatured), those of tragedy were normally derived from the heroic past and only rarely set in Athens. Yet in the hands of Aeschylus, Sophocles, and Euripides, Athenian tragedy, even when it was ostensibly concerned with events of what we would call the Mycenaean Bronze Age, was just as political in a contemporary, democratic sense as the comedy of Cratinus, Eupolis, and Aristophanes. The tragedians' skill was to reinterpret the traditional stories in such a way as to give them contemporary significance, even twisting them to pose a challenge to contemporary thinking on the most basic civic issues, including the proper distribution of political power.

The career of Aeschylus, indeed, coincided precisely with the earliest and most dynamic phase of Athenian democratic political development, from the 480s to the 450s. He could therefore hardly avoid contributing to the fierce debates of his day. In the *Suppliant Women* of 463, for example, although the play is set in Argos in the heroic period, the king of Argos is no Bronze Age absolute monarch but a sort of citizen-king who not merely consults but heeds the verdict of the Argive (read, Athenian) Assembly. In fact, the language in which Aeschylus reports the unanimous vote of the Argives (*dēmou kratousa kheir*, "the sovereign hand of the People") was as near as he dared come to a grossly anachronistic use of the prosaic and newfangled word *dēmokratia*.

Two years after the *Suppliant Women* was staged, a further democratic reform was effected in Athens at the instigation of Ephialtes and his junior assistant Pericles. It is hard to resist the inference that the play and the reform were somehow ideologically connected. Three years later the link between democratic reform and Aeschylus's *Oresteia* trilogy (458) is unmistakable. One central element of the reform concerned the administration of justice, the establishment of the People's Court staffed by mass juries of ordinary citizens as a vehicle of popular democratic power. Another, related element was the political emasculation of the old aristocratic Areopagos Council. Aeschylus could hardly incorporate a direct reference to these measures in the *Oresteia*, but he could and did represent the Areopagos in its remaining function as a homicide court and emphasize the triumph of civic justice over aristocratic blood feud. All the same, Aeschylus was careful not to seem to endorse any partisan interpretation of the reform. Soon after it had been passed, Ephialtes was assassinated; there was a danger of a renewal of the sort of civil strife *(stasis)* that had followed the overthrow of the tyranny fifty years earlier. The message of Aeschylus's Athena to her people was therefore one of measured moderation: no *stasis,* no political extremism, but a middle way between anarchy and despotism.

Some seventeen years later, Sophocles' *Antigone* set a woman—excluded by her gender from formal politics and, moreover, a "bad" woman by reason of her incestuous birth—in fatal opposition to the legitimate authority of Thebes, incarnated by her uncle Creon. Yet Antigone, despite the formal illegality of her action in burying the brother whom Creon has declared a public traitor, nevertheless, confusingly, has the gods on her side, whereas Creon, for all his formal legitimacy of authority, has strayed too far beyond the limits of human political power in exerting his will in contravention of "unwritten" divine law. The context of *Antigone* is Thebes, but this is a dramatic Thebes that functions as an anti-Athens, the sort of city Athens was in danger of becoming if self-awareness did not lead to self-restraint, and if man-made law, no matter how democratically enacted, were privileged above divine ordinance.

Euripides' active career as a tragic playwright, like that of Sophocles, both scaled the heights of Athens's democratic and imperial exuberance and plumbed the most miserable depths of military defeat and political counterrevolution. In the younger playwright's more avant-garde theater, the criticism of politics took a new, pessimistic turn. Not only did Euripides expose on the stage the horrors of relentless imperialism, as in the *Trojan Women* (415), and the wretched delusions of self-serving demagogy, as in the *Orestes* of 408; he even, in the prologue to his lost *Philoctetes,* made Odysseus, the epitome of the wily politician, muse aloud about the possible advantages of political quietism, of withdrawal from the public, civic political arena altogether: "What am I to think? If I were to stay quietly *[apragmonōs]* in the ranks, I would fare no worse than the wisest." A standard Greek expression for "affairs of state" or "public life" was *pragmata* (transactions). The adverb translated "quietly" here means literally "in such a way as to be uninvolved with public, political affairs of state."

THE SOPHISTS AND POLITICS

Euripides himself at the very end of his life withdrew from participation in the affairs of the Athenian democracy in the most obvious way possible. He accepted an invitation to the court of the Macedonian king Archelaus, a monarch who not only could be thought to represent the opposite pole to Athenian democratic self-government but was also considered by many Athenians to be a non-Greek barbarian. Barbarians or "the Barbarian" had been another fruitful source of Greek political reflection and introspection in the seminal decades after the repulse of the Persian invasion of 480–79. Underlying the entire history of Herodotus, for instance, is a discourse on the absolute power embodied in the Persian monarchy as constituting the opposite of the Greek "republican" way of doing politics. After Herodotus, however, and especially after the Peloponnesian War, barbarian monarchs began to be seen as models to imitate rather than avoid.

The quietist musings of Euripides' Odysseus symbolized another, no less antidemocratic kind of withdrawal, as can be seen when they are set side by side with the democratic ideology expressed in the Funeral Speech of Pericles (originally delivered in 430), as written up by Thucydides. One of the most unambiguously democratic tenets of this ideologically complex oration was Pericles' claim that participation in public affairs was not just an option but a duty for all Athenians, regardless of their economic or social standing. Otherwise, though, the speech as Thucydides represents it contains remarkably little that can be called explicitly democratic in either ideology or theory, and this is one reason it has sometimes been claimed that the Athenians did not actually develop a coherent, objective democratic theory but rather lived their democracy concretely and pragmatically.

Recent work, however, has shown that claim to be false. There is explicit as well as implicit democratic theory to be found, conspicuously in the speeches of the 4th-century orators and politicians Demosthenes and Aeschines. All the same, if we are seeking abstract and explicitly theoretical discussions of the peculiar virtues and vices of democratic government, and rival constructions of the essence of democracy itself, it is indeed necessary to turn to sources who were not actually politicians or indeed Athenian citizens, however strongly they may have been affected by their experience of Athenian democratic practice. In the first instance, that means turning to the thinkers known collectively as the Sophists—a term of convenience only, since they did not form a philosophical school.

One such Greek Sophist or Sophistic circle at some point before 450 had a stunningly simple but limitlessly brilliant intuition. All forms of political rule must necessarily, it was perceived, be species or subspecies of just three genera: rule by one, rule by some, rule by all. That classification is as exhaustive as it is economical. There is a hint in an ode of Pindar that the idea was formed as early as the 470s, but its first extant expression is to be found in the *Histories* of Herodotus, which probably were not composed and certainly were not published in the form we have them before 450. By the time Herodotus came to write up his "Persian Debate" (III.80–82) Greek theoretical discussion had moved beyond the mere discovery of the tripartite classification of political rule to a more minute taxonomy of the three genera's species and subspecies, and to a closer evaluation of their strengths and weaknesses. Put differently, already in Herodotus we have in outline the sixfold schema of constitutional development, or rather degeneration, postulated by Plato in *The Republic* (written in the 380s).

The text is known as the "Persian Debate" because Herodotus purports to transcribe an authentic discussion between three noble Persians that allegedly occurred in the late 520s at Susa in southern Iran, the administrative capital of the Persian empire. Actually, it is almost literally unthinkable that any Persians should have conducted themselves in this way, since they embraced neither the institution of the polis nor the Greeks' idea of the political; and it is doubly preposterous that a Persian noble should have been imagined as making an eloquent plea for democracy in the late 520s, some fifteen years before democracy's invention at Athens. Yet this is precisely what the first of the three speakers in Herodotus's debate is represented as doing—in everything but name. The name he in fact uses to describe his ideal regime, which he calls the "fairest" name of all, is *isonomia*.

This choice may be a sign that the debate in its original form was composed before the word *dēmokratia* had been coined. But equally—and more likely—the prodemocracy speaker will have avoided *dēmokratia* deliberately, for tactical reasons. The line of attack that he knew his opponents would take depended on construing *dēmos* in its negative sense of "the masses," the poor, ignorant, stupid, and fickle mob, rather than "the People" as a whole. The speaker's choice of *isonomia* to describe what was clearly meant to be understood as democracy (decision making in common by all, sortition not election for office, accountability of all officeholders) would therefore preempt or at least blunt the force of such an attack.

Who exactly composed the original of Herodotus's debate, and how Herodotus got to know of it, are unknown. Nor can we say for certain what political position Herodotus himself adhered to. The fact that the promonarchy speaker (Darius) "won" the debate is immaterial, since historically Darius did seize the Persian throne in 522 and so had to win. In the rest of Herodotus's work, as noted above, Persian monarchy stands negatively for absolutist despotism. Nevertheless, although Herodotus might praise Athenian *isēgoria* for its practical, military effects, he could also himself savagely criticize the Athenian *dēmos* for precisely the defect charged against all democratic government by his pro-oligarchic and promonarchic debaters—that the masses were ignorant and easily gulled (5.97).

Of the three set speeches in the debate, the prodemocratic one not only comes first but also is the longest and most detailed in argument. It has therefore quite plausibly been connected with the teachings, written or otherwise, of the early Sophist Protagoras of Abdera. He at any rate is the one Sophist of the period in question known to have held either explicitly democratic views (he is reported to have drafted the constitution of democratic Thouria, an Athenian-led colonial foundation of the 440s) or theoretical principles that could be given practical democratic expression, most famously his *homo mensura* ("Man is the measure") doctrine.

Protagoras and his younger fellow countryman from Abdera, Democritus, are indeed among the tiny number of surviving philosophical writers whom there is even the slightest reason for labeling in any sense "democratic" theorists. If Antiphon the Sophist is identical with Antiphon the radically oligarchic politician (intellectual leader of the counterrevolution of 411), his politics were far more typical of the general antidemocratic tendency of Sophistic and other intellectual thinking. This is hardly surprising. All known thinkers belonged to the Greek social and economic elite, the leisure class, and democracy was in principle an antielitist regime.

A HISTORIAN'S VIEW OF POLITICS

Antiphon the politician was a teacher of rhetoric as well as a practical (mainly backroom) politician and speechwriter. Among his pupils may have been the historian Thucydides, if common literary style and a striking encomium (Thucydides, 8.68.2) are anything to judge by. Not that Thucydides was a historian in the modern sense, a "colleague" of ours; he used his history more philosophically, as a vehicle for the subtlest political analysis. Thomas Hobbes, whose first work was a translation of Thucydides directly from the Greek (1628), rightly called him "the most political historiographer that ever writ."

Because Thucydides chose to don a mask of impersonal objectivity, it is hard to identify his own political opinions and outlook from his work. The balance of the internal evidence, however, tips strongly in favor of the view that, whatever else he may have been, Thucydides was probably not an ideological democrat. This is indicated, for example, both by his use of the contemptuous generalization "as the masses habitually do" and by his principled as well as pragmatic preference for the short-lived Athenian regime of the "5,000," probably a temperate oligarchy ("a moderate blending in the interests both of the few and of the many," 8.97.2). At any rate, he certainly was not a supporter of the radical, post-Periclean democracy by which he was exiled—for military failure as an admiral—in 424. This helps to account for his prejudicially negative representation of Cleon (the target also of Aristophanes' comedy *Knights* of 424) as a demagogic misleader of the masses, the living embodiment of a sectarian and capricious regime.

More interesting even than Thucydides' views of democracy in general, or of Athenian democracy in particular, are his explicit and implicit comments on the political, as it was played out in the wider Greek world under the extreme strain and upheaval of the Peloponnesian War. These generalizing comments he imparted in three main ways: explicitly, in his immortal analysis of *stasis,* the Greek word for any civil tension and discord that might and too frequently did culminate in outright civil war, and implicitly, in the "Melian Dialogue," a freely invented debate about the nature and validity of imperial power, and also in the studied dissonance between the speech and action of two of his principal characters, Cleon and Alcibiades. In all three cases, what was preeminently at stake were the relationship between *logos* and *ergon* and the questions whether those two terms constituted a polarized opposition, and if so, how far apart they were.

There was nothing new to Greece about *stasis,* in the sense of outright civil war, when a peculiarly fierce bout convulsed Kerkyra (Corfu) in 427. For Thucydides, however, this marked a significant milestone in the history of *stasis,* since thereafter, thanks to the special circumstances of a war between two ideologically polarized power blocs, it is said to have engulfed the entire Greek world (a pardonable exaggeration). What Thucydides, like Aeschylus, hated about *stasis* was the extremism that caused it and that it in turn exacerbated. But Thucydides' peculiar contribution to its analysis was to lay his finger on the verbal manipulation (*logos* means both "speech" and "reason") and thus moral dishonesty that it necessarily entailed. It was not so much that key value-terms of the Greek moral-political code altered their meaning; rather, partisan ideologues (*stasiōtai*) used these terms in opposite or perverted senses, changing their reference. Hence, to take a fundamental example, what Thucydides the outside observer judged negatively to be "unreasoning rashness" *(tolma alogistos)* was regarded wholly positively by engaged participants as the sort of courageous (literally "manly") behavior expected of one's close comrades *(andreia philetairos).*

A similar point about the use of language in propaganda is put by the historian into the mouths of his Athenian speakers early in the so-called Melian Dialogue, which is artfully set in 416/15, near the turning point of the war. In normal diplomatic intercourse, as happened most spectacularly in the exchanges immediately preceding the outbreak of the war, opponents tend to make claims which, although not necessarily knowingly false, are nevertheless dressed up in the manner thought most favorable to their side's perceived cause. The Athenians on Melos, however, are made by Thucydides to announce in advance that they will not be adopting this traditional negotiating ploy: they will avoid "fair names" *(kala onomata),* and instead call a spade a spade, so to speak.

Whether the real Athenian negotiators did in fact employ such an opening gambit on Melos is quite another matter, and perhaps rather unlikely. At least it perfectly suited the purposes of Thucydides, the "politic historiographer," to have them behave this way, for he could thereby tear off the veil of self-serving propaganda that the Athenians, like any other imperial power, habitually used to cloak their true designs, and so reveal in all their awful nakedness the eternal verities of imperial power. Imperialism, as Thucydides made abundantly plain, is ultimately and essentially a matter of superior force, the rule of the strong over the weak. Politics, by contrast, especially democratic politics, is in principle (not necessarily in practice) the antithesis of that. Our phrase "power politics" is really an oxymoron.

Most subtle of all, however, was Thucydides' deconstruction of the ostensibly political professions of his antiheroes Cleon and Alcibiades. In 427 a vital debate took place in the Athenian Assembly concerning the fate of Athens's revolted but now subdued ally Mytilene. As the centerpiece of his account of that debate Thucydides placed in Cleon's mouth a memorable tirade. Its chief point was that the Athenians had debased what was designed as a time and a place for exchanging and acting on wise political counsel into a forum for competitive rhetoric. Yet Cleon's own speech, as Thucydides composed it, comes adorned with precisely the rhetorical tropes and ornamental flourishes that Cleon affects to despise and reject, and the counsel he offers the Athenians is the reverse of what Thucydides considered to be wise.

As for Thucydides' Alcibiades, he too is convicted out of his own mouth in an Assembly speech, the one he is given to deliver in 415 in favor of the (calamitous, as it turned out) Sicilian expedition. He is shown up as practicing a twofold deception on the Athenian people: in his claim that he aimed more for the good of the city, when actually it was solely his own good that he had in view, and in his pretense that his past advice and actions had brought Athens substantive political gains, when at most he had achieved some temporarily advantageous diplomatic readjustments. In opposition to Cleon and Alcibiades, Thucydides set up his hero, Pericles, as an implicit and explicit paradigm of political leadership. Not only did his Pericles genuinely place the city's good ahead of his own, and really advance the city's material interests by both his words and his deeds, but he also throughout his whole career kept *logos* and *ergon* in balance and harmony.

Thucydides, despite the disillusionments of his own failed political career and the catastrophe of Athens's defeat, seems never to have abandoned his governing notion that politics was capable of being practiced according to defensible canons of human rationality. For him, "chance" was simply that, an unforeseeable occurrence that confused the neat trajectories of predictable lines of causation, while "the divine" was a factor of negligible historical consequence. In his discourse the peculiarly human attribute of *logos*—speech, a speech, argument, reason—remained something sacrosanct. For those who misused or abused *logos*—civil war partisans, international diplomats, and deceitful politicians like Cleon and Alcibiades—Thucydides reserved his greatest contempt.

SOCRATES AND THE SOCRATICS

The vast bulk of the formal political theory of the Greeks that is extant is to some degree hostile to democratic politics, if not to all politics. The founder of this antidemocratic and antipolitical tradition, apparently, was Socrates, a flamboyantly idiosyncratic and controversial figure who with characteristic eccentricity committed not one word of his philosophy to writing. No doubt Aristophanes' caricature of him in *Clouds* (423) was savagely unfair, but it does seem to have contributed to his negative popular image and thus helped to influence the sentence of death for impiety and immoralism that was passed on him in the People's Court in 399. Perhaps Socrates really was a good democratic citizen, in the sense that he duly observed the rituals of the democracy and—unlike his most famous pupil, Plato—undertook his share of public political activity (for instance, by sitting on the Council of 500 as well as fighting for his country). However, there is no unambiguously sound evidence that he was a good democrat in an ideological or theoretical sense. "The majority is always wrong" is not a congenial political slogan or philosophical tenet to an egalitarian society that on principle made major decisions of public policy by majority vote of all citizens present, regardless of birth, wealth, or intellect.

The Socrates of Plato differs significantly and sometimes irreconcilably from the Socrates of Xenophon, but the two rival pictures of their common mentor agree closely in representing Socrates as an invincible foe to the technical incompetence of democratic procedure. As he and his pupils saw it, the masses lacked the necessary intelligence, education, and specialized skills to be able to judge what was the best course of action for Athens to pursue, or even the best means to implement their ill-founded decisions. The condemnation of Socrates to death by a popular jury of 501 largely "ordinary" Athenian citizens was for these upper-class Athenian disciples simply confirmation of their general assumption of democratic ineptitude. Yet they did also seek to give their critiques of democratic politics—and, in Plato's case, of all mundane politics—a gloss of impartial principle. Their criticisms fall under four main headings.

First, freedom and equality, the chief rallying cries of ancient, as of modern (if in very different terms), democracy. What a Greek democrat valued as the freedom from arbitrary domination by the rich and well-born and the freedom to make a measurable contribution to the running of his community, the Socratics dismissed as mere license and anarchy, if not a case of the world turned upside down. Equality was something that all Greeks except a handful of hereditary monarchs and actual or would-be tyrants regarded positively, which was why value-terms prefixed by *iso-* (such as *isonomia*, *isokratia*) could be appealed to by both oligarchs and democrats. Democratic egalitarianism, however, the Socratics found unacceptable, because it treated as equals people who, to their superior eyes, manifestly were not equals in fact.

Second, it was thus contrary to natural justice, as they saw it, that by the use of the lot for appointment to office, all citizens should be treated as both functionally and symbolically equivalent. It was, they thought, literally pre-posterous that the poor, ignorant, stupid, uneducated, and fickle majority of citizens should be able, merely because of their superior numbers, to outvote and exert a collective tyranny over the wealthy, informed, intelligent, edu-cated, and reasonable elite minority.

This latter objection gave rise to a third. Since the law was what the major-ity willed, and the majority's will might change from one mass meeting to the next, it was not the law that ruled in a democracy but the majority of the citi-zens—the poor, ignorant, and so on, majority—that ruled, in defiance of the law.

Fourth and, for our purposes, finally, it was objected that democracy, so far from being government of all the people by the people for the people, was a none too subtly disguised class rule of the poor over the rich in the interests of the poor. Those members of the elite who viewed democracy in this way were therefore acting perfectly logically by their own lights in withdrawing from democratic politics.

This may have been Plato's rationale for withdrawal. No doubt, too, he was genuinely disgusted with the behavior of some members of his immediate family, not least Critias, during the overthrow of democracy in 411 and again in 404. The coups, countercoups, lies, and bloodletting that the *stasis* at Ath-ens inevitably entailed will not have recommended everyday politics to an intellectual like him. However, no less important, both for the history of Socratic-Platonic political philosophy and the history of Greek political cul-ture generally, is the entirely new political orientation introduced by Socratic and Platonic ethics and metaphysics.

A passage of Plutarch, which may or may not be literally historical, cap-tures this change rather well: "Of the inscriptions at Delphi that which was thought to be the most divine was 'Know Thyself'; it was this, as Aristotle said in his Platonic works, that started Socrates off puzzling and inquiring." Socratic introspection gave ethical enquiry an individualistic and esoteric turn. Virtue, it was argued by Plato above all, should be sought in the individ-ual soul, and the good of the soul was prior to the good of the community of souls that constituted the polis. Socrates was said to have wished to be thought of as a citizen of the whole world. A contemporary of his went fur-ther and desired not to be thought of as a member of any particular human political community. For those who seriously entertained such notions, utopia was but a short step away.

Helios on his chariot, drawn by four horses. Vase from Canossa, Greek colony in southern Italy, 330 B.C.E. (Munich, Antikensammlung.) Illustration of the mythological view of the cosmos. "The wise horses bore me, straining at the chariot, and maidens led the way . . . the daughters of the Sun made haste to escort me, having left the halls of Night for the light" (Parmenides, "Proem" 288).

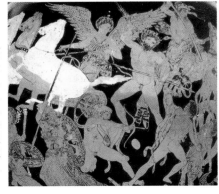

Gigantomachy scene (battle of the gods and the giants), with Zeus surrounded by Heracles, Athena, and Dionysus. Amphora, late 5th century B.C.E. (Paris, Louvre.) In the Greeks' view, the gods were the masters of all knowledge, technical and theoretical.

The four cosmic elements. Fresco from the crypt of the cathedral in Anagni (Latium), 1250.
From top to bottom: Fire, Air, Water, Earth. The lines represent the possible transformation
of these elements into one another according to the principles established by Aristotle.

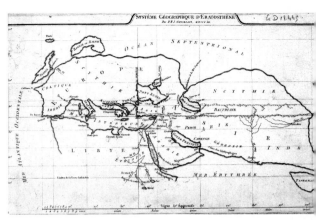

Map by Eratosthenes (ca. 275–195 B.C.E.). *Eratosthenes systema geographicum*, 1790. (Paris, Bibliothèque Nationale.) Characteristic of Hellenistic geography, this map incorporates new information acquired during Alexander's expedition into Asia.

Gnomon. Egypt, 1st century C.E. (Munich, Deutsches Museum.) Forerunner of the sundial, it was used mostly by astronomers and geographers to construct a geometric representation of the universe. Eratosthenes used it to measure the earth's meridian.

Eudoxus (406–355 B.C.E.), *On Spheres*. Egyptian papyrus, 2nd century C.E. (Paris, Louvre.)

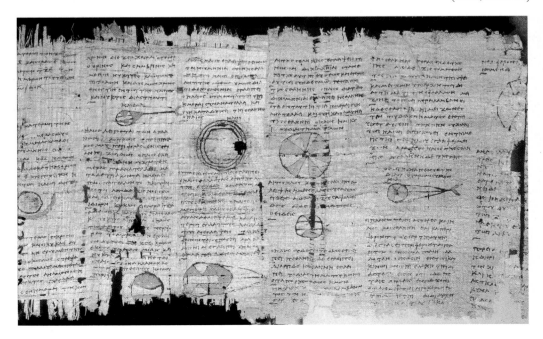

Claudius Ptolemy (100–170 C.E.) in the Alexandrian Library. *Claudius Ptolemeus geographicorum libri,* 15th century. (Venice, Biblioteca Marciana.) The figures of Claudius Ptolemy and Ptolemy I Soter, ruler of Egypt and founder of the Library, are amalgamated.

Claudius Ptolemy, map. 15th century. (Venice, Biblioteca Marciana.) Remarkable for its precision, this map offers a faithful representation of the entire inhabited world.

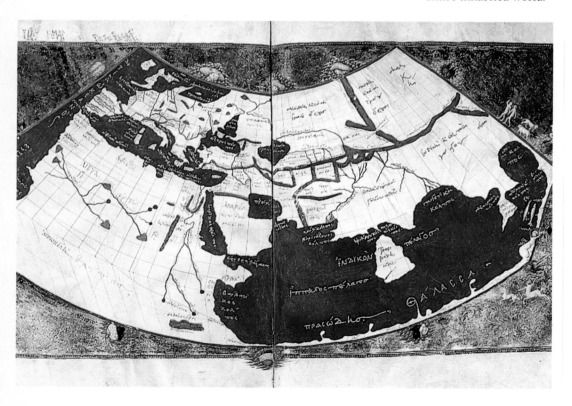

Nicole Oresme at his desk, with an armillary sphere. *Le livre du ciel et du monde*, commentary on Aristotle's *De caelo* by Nicole Oresme, 15th century. (Paris, Bibliothèque Nationale.)

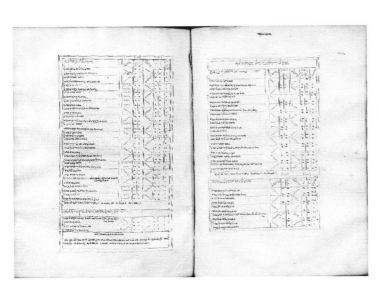

Claudius Ptolemy, *Almagest*. Hebrew manuscript, 15th century. (Paris, Bibliothèque Nationale.) A copy in Arabic, written in Hebrew characters, of the astronomical tables and lists of fixed stars used to calculate planetary movement.

Euclid, *Elements* (ca. 300 B.C.E.). Manuscript, 12th century. (Paris, Bibliothèque Nationale.) Demonstration of the "Pythagorean theorem" (Proposition 47, Book I).

Bust of Pythagoras (570–480 B.C.E.). (Rome, Museo Capitolino.) Pythagoras's theory of numbers inspired many reflections on music and harmonics.

Archimedes, *On the Sphere and Cylinder*, Book II. Copied in 1544 by Christoph Auer. (Paris, Bibliothèque Nationale.) Approximation to the circumference of the circle by inscribed and circumscribed polygons.

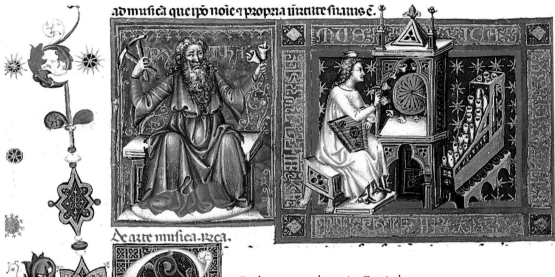

Pythagoras and music. Cassiodorus, *Institutiones*. Manuscript, ca. 1340. (Paris, Bibliothèque Nationale.)

Aristides Quintilianus, treatise. From edition of Marc Meibom, 1652. Tables of musical signs.

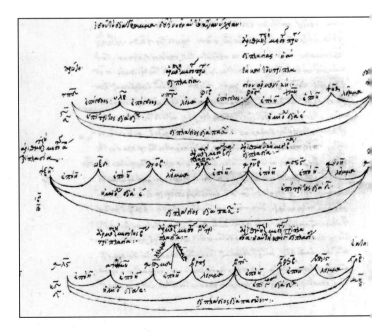

Theon of Smyrna, treatise. Manuscript, 16th century. (Paris, Bibliothèque Nationale.) Division of the harmonic canon.

Apollo and his *kithara*. Detail from a vase attributed to the
"Berlin Painter," ca. 480 B.C.E. (Basel, Antikenmuseum.)

THE POLITICS OF EUTOPIA

The pseudo-Greek word *utopia*, which was cobbled together by Thomas More in 1516, was consciously ambiguous: the *u*- prefix could stand for ancient Greek *ou* (not) or *eu* (well), or both. More himself left no doubt that his Utopia was a "No-place" (like Samuel Butler's reversed world Erewhon), but in common modern parlance the term has been used chiefly to refer to imaginary literary confections where (in the phrase of Voltaire's Doctor Pangloss) all is for the best in the best of all possible worlds. In the sense of *eu*topia, the genre to which More's *Utopia* belongs was as ancient as Western literature itself. Homer's list of desirably blessed residences—all the more desirable in the impoverished Dark Age during which the oral epic tradition took shape—includes Syrie, the island of the Lotus-Eaters, and Phaeacia, among others.

The utopian impulse or propensity is always rooted in dissatisfaction with the perceived status quo, but it has given rise to very different concrete proposals. All utopiographers have tended to criticize existing forms of society indirectly by inviting readers to contemplate a hypothetically superior society founded, artificially, by a supremely wise legislator on universalist lines. But their inventors' perceptions of their societies' present evils have differed sharply, as have their historical understandings and their moral, political, and social ideals. The solutions offered to the basic problems of constructing utopia have therefore varied widely. For instance, although Karl Mannheim's distinction between "ideology," the worldview of a dominant class that emphasizes the enduring stability of existing social arrangements, and "utopia," which represents the beliefs of a subordinated class or classes, may adequately accommodate some 20th-century utopiography, it cannot do justice to ancient Greek utopianism.

Three common features, however, have typically united all utopiographers across the ages. The first is a unity of form. Utopia constructors tend to opt for the more dramatic, fictional, even fantastic approach to social amelioration exemplified in, say, Plato's *Republic* or *Laws*. Non-utopian social and political reformers, such as Aristotle, do not avoid the notion of the ideal state altogether, as we shall see, but prefer to evaluate the status quo by the standards of general principles of moral and political philosophy and then to devise means of bringing defective practice and ameliorative theory into closer alignment. Second, utopiographers tend to be at one in the totality of their vision, omitting piecemeal criticisms and disdaining partial programs of reform. Third, in their projected ideal societies they have usually judged order to be more important than freedom.

In its specifically political form, Greek utopianism, or at any rate written utopiography, was a development of the 5th century. Its earliest recorded practitioner was Hippodamus of Miletus, better known as a gridiron town planner, whose inclinations were egalitarian and democratic. But in its Athenian manifestation it was born from an unholy union between philosophic antidemocratism and personal disgust with or failure in contemporary practical politics. Just as Aeschylus and Sophocles found Argos and Thebes good to think with dramatically, so Athenian political utopians of a Sophistic or Socratic tendency found Sparta a suitably different and distant place on which to project their longings for radical political change at home.

Plato's older relative Critias has been enshrined in history's hall of infamy as leader of the "Thirty Tyrants," a bloodstained junta that ruled Athens briefly in the Spartan interest from 404 to 403. It is not clear how far Critias intended to, or thought he really could, turn Athens into another Sparta, though there are tantalizing hints—his introduction of ephors, for example. But his general philolaconism of outlook is blatant enough. Indeed, he wrote works of encomium on Sparta in both prose and verse, thereby founding the literary tradition of the so-called *mirage spartiate.* By this is meant the partly distorted, partly invented image of Sparta as an ideal society, good not only to think with but also to imitate.

It was left to Xenophon and, above all, Plato to move beyond encomium to Spartan-inspired utopianism. Xenophon's utopia (in the sense of *ou*-topia) was the *Cyropaedia* ("Education of Cyrus"). This took the novel form of a historical romance set in the Persian empire under its founder Cyrus the Great (559–530). Xenophon's Cyrus, however, was not the real Achaemenid King of Kings but a lightly disguised Greek leader, a composite figure representing an ideal combination of Xenophon himself and his Greek political patron and exemplar King Agesilaos of Sparta (of whom he also wrote a biographical encomium). Cyrus's *Homotimoi* (Honoured Equals) consciously recall in name as well as function the title *Homoioi* (Peers) by which the Spartan citizens of full status were known.

Xenophon's Agesilaos was the living embodiment of the "Lycurgan" Sparta he praised in his essay on Spartan society, the *Lakedaimoniōn Politeia;* here is to be found Xenophon's *eu*-topia, a supposedly real Greek city founded at a stroke long ago, in all its ideal perfection, through the enactments of a wondrously provident lawgiver, Lycurgus. It is striking how both the *Cyropaedia* and the *Lakedaimoniōn Politeia* end with an extended lament over the present decline of Persia and Sparta from the lofty and utterly admirable ideals of their respective founders. This was the signature, as it were, of the quintessentially conservative political thinker that Xenophon, the passionate advocate of order and hierarchy, consistently showed himself to be.

Plato's debt to Sparta was less immediate and predictably much more complex. So too was his utopianism. The nature of the relationship between the massive but dull work of his old age, *Laws,* and the literary masterpiece of his middle years, *The Republic,* is controversial. *Laws,* which purports to be the constitutional code of a new, ideal settlement called Magnesia that is to be founded on Crete, looks as though it ought to be the working out in detail of the blueprint sketched in *The Republic*. Yet so many and so large are the differences between them that *Laws* may better be thought to represent Plato's "second best" state. This could have been necessitated by his realization that Platonic philosopher-kings, the governing ideal and ideal governors of *The Republic*, were not exactly available on demand.

Common to both treatises, however, are Spartan-looking features such as state regulation or restriction of private property, industry, commerce, use of money, and foreign contacts; common meals; and equality between the sexes, involving the direction of sex and marriage toward service of the community. The latter in particular seems to be the sort of proposal Aristophanes delighted in satirizing in his extant *Ecclesiazusae* ("Women Attending the Assembly") comedy of ca. 392, in which the citizen women of Athens establish an anti-utopian feminocracy. However, *The Republic* at least is also underpinned by a peculiarly Platonic metaphysics, which makes its relationship to any political actuality fundamentally problematic. *Laws* comes without such an explicit philosophical apparatus, but that does not make it any more realistic and practical. Plato's moral objectives consistently remained fundamentally at odds with the customs, beliefs, and perceived interests of almost all Greeks. Moreover, his passionate advocacy of Magnesia as an ideal theocracy was a startling novelty, quite alien to Greek political and religious tradition.

TOWARD A PRACTICAL UTOPIA

What non-utopian political thinkers of the 4th century yearned for no less than their utopian contemporaries were, above all, stability and harmony: a stability of political institutions and a harmony of political outlook and aspiration. Of actually existing states, Sparta, again, seemed to offer the closest thing to their practical realization in combination. Yet commentators were notoriously unable to agree on how to classify the Spartan *politeia*, since it could not be fitted neatly into any of the three recognized genera of rule (by one, some, or all). They therefore either opted for one of these three, and attempted to explain away the remaining anomalies, or cut the Gordian knot by classifying Sparta as a mixture of all three. Historically, the former were surely correct. But ideologically, the mixed-constitution theorists were the more interesting, since they were seeking a novel solution to the polarization of rich and poor citizens that in the real world, from the late 5th century on, regularly generated *stasis* and an unstable alternation between oligarchy and democracy.

Thucydides gives a hint in his characterization of the regime of the 5,000 ("a moderate blending," 8.97.2) that he may have espoused an early version of mixed-constitution theory, but its best attested and most distinguished exponent was Aristotle. Most Greek states in Aristotle's day governed themselves by either a form of democracy or a version of oligarchy, but none was wholly acceptable to him. Both oligarchy and democracy were sectarian, class-based forms of political rule, the former being the rule of the rich in their class interest, the latter the rule of the poor in theirs. Of actually existing constitutions, therefore, only one, which he rather confusingly called *politeia* (polity), did he consider tolerable, though not ideal. This was because the balance of power in a polity was held by those citizens who were neither very rich nor very poor but, being moderately well off, occupied an economic situation "in the middle" between the rich and the poor. Aristotle's was thus a "checks and balances" version of mixed-constitution theory, very different from the usual "blending" version and owing nothing to Sparta, whose "lawgiver," in his view, had done a bad job.

Yet not even the relatively pragmatic Aristotle was able to slough off completely his Socratic-Platonic inheritance. Committed as he was to the view that man was a *politikon zōon*, designed by his nature to fulfill his innate end *(telos)* within the peculiarly Greek framework of the polis, Aristotle found himself sketching his version of the ideal *polis* for his Lyceum pupils just when his former pupil Alexander of Macedon was putting an end to the real Greek polis as a model of truly political self-government. If we were to classify this Aristotelian ideal, we would have to call it a suspiciously Platonic species of aristocracy, and one that, despite his profound reflection on the Greek world as it was, would have had almost as little chance of practical realization as his teacher's utopian schemes. Perhaps there was more to be said in favor of the mundane, normal politics of the real Greek world than the critics, especially the utopians, were prepared to allow.

PAUL CARTLEDGE

Bibliography

Baldry, Harold C. *Ancient Utopias.* University of Southampton Inaugural Lecture, 1956.

Bertelli, Lucio. "L'Utopia greca." In *Storia delle idee politiche, economiche, e sociali,* vol. 1: *L'antichità classica.* Ed. Luigi Firpo. Turin: Unione Tipografico-Editrice Torinese, 1982. Pp. 463–581.

Carey, John, ed. *The Faber Book of Utopias.* London: Faber, 1999.

Carter, Laurence B. *The Quiet Athenian.* Oxford: Clarendon Press, 1986.

Cartledge, Paul A. *Agesilaos and the Crisis of Sparta.* London: Duckworth, 1987.

Dawson, Doyne. *Cities of the Gods: Communist Utopias in Greek Thought.* New York: Oxford University Press, 1992.

Dillery, John. *Xenophon and the History of His Times.* London and New York: Routledge, 1995.

Dodds, Eric R. *The Ancient Concept of Progress and Other Essays.* Oxford: Clarendon Press, 1973.

Finley, Moses I. "Utopianism Ancient and Modern." In *The Use and Abuse of History,* 2nd ed. London: Hogarth Press, 1986.

Govtorov, Vladimir A. *Antichnaya Sotsial'naya Utopia: Voprosy Istorii i Teorii* (Ancient Social Utopia: Questions of History and Theory). St. Petersburg: Leningrad University Press, 1989.

Humphreys, Sally C. *The Family, Women and Death: Comparative Studies,* 2nd ed. Ann Arbor: University of Michigan Press, 1993.

Logan, George M. *The Meaning of More's "Utopia."* Princeton: Princeton University Press, 1983.

Lovejoy, Arthur O., and George Boas. *Primitivism and Related Ideas in Antiquity.* Baltimore: Johns Hopkins University Press, 1935.

Manuel, Frank E., and Fritzie P. Manuel. *Utopian Thought in the Western World.* Oxford: Blackwell, 1979.

Moore, Barrington Jr. *Privacy: Studies in Social and Cultural History.* New York and London: M. E. Sharpe, 1984.

Neville-Sington, Pamela, and David Sington. *Paradise Dreamed: How Utopian Thinkers Have Changed the Modern World.* London: Bloomsbury, 1993.

Pöhlmann, Robert von. *Geschichte der Sozialen Frage und des Sozialismus in der antiken Welt.* Ed. F. Oertel. Munich: Beck, 1925.

Roberts, Jennifer T. *Athens on Trial: The Antidemocratic Tradition in Western Thought.* Princeton: Princeton University Press, 1994.

Schofield, Malcolm. *Saving the City: Philosopher-Kings and Other Classical Paradigms.* London and New York: Routledge, 1999.

Terray, Emmanuel. *La politique dans la caverne.* Paris: Seuil, 1990.

Vogt, Joseph. *Ancient Slavery and the Ideal of Man.* Oxford: Blackwell, 1974.

Related Articles

The Statesman As Political Actor; The Sage and Politics; Epicurus; Socrates; Cynicism; Inventing Politics; Rhetoric; Plato; Xenophon

THE SAGE AND POLITICS

Should the sage—that is, the wise man or perfectly rational person—engage in politics? The Epicureans said no, unless some emergency forces him into it. The Stoics said yes, unless something prevents it.

The question was by no means the only issue relating to politics that was discussed by these thinkers. The Epicureans developed a sophisticated account of the origins of society and of law in terms of the optimalization of a mutual interest in security, and they were insistent on the need for government. There still survive among the *Key Doctrines* of Epicurus (341–271 B.C.E.) maxims on justice conceived as a contract for mutual nonaggression, and deriving the validity of laws from their efficacy in securing common advantages. In a few tantalizing fragments we can glimpse the Epicurean conception of what an ideal community of friends would be like. As for the Stoics, Plutarch tells us that "Zeno happens to have written a lot (given his conciseness), Cleanthes too a lot, and Chrysippus a very great deal on the political order, ruling and being ruled, judicial decisions, and oratory" (*Stoic Contradictions* 1033b). Although we have only a few extracts and scraps of other testimony about most of these writings, rather more information is available about the ideal community of the wise described by Zeno (334–262), founder of Stoicism, in his work *Politeia*, conventionally translated *Republic* but less misleadingly as *Political Order*. Like Diogenes the Cynic (mid–4th century B.C.E.) in his *Politeia*, Zeno described a community of the virtuous and free in which all the political and religious institutions of the city-state were swept away, and women and children were possessed in common. Love and friendship were to be the bonds generating the common purpose that holds the city together.

For evaluating the theoretical stance of Epicureanism and Stoicism toward politics and the life of the polis as they actually were, however, the crucial evidence is supplied by their answers to the question whether the wise man is engagé. The two leading treatments of the question—by Epicurus and by Chrysippus (ca. 280–206), third head of the Stoa—were offered in each case in works entitled *On Modes of Life*, in which the authors evidently debated alternative views of the right choice of life for the wise person. These treatises stood within a long tradition. Plato in the *Gorgias* makes the issue between Socrates and his interlocutors Gorgias, Polus, and Callicles turn in the end on an existential choice: between the life of the orator, practicing on the public stage and pandering to the whims of the masses, or the philosophical life, directed to making men better. Plato's *Republic* works with a notion of *three* principal modes of life, reflecting the dominance of one or another of the three parts of the soul: the life devoted to the pursuit of money, the life focused on honor and ambition, and the life of the philosopher. This same trichotomy is taken up by Aristotle at the beginning of the *Nicomachean Ethics*, although pleasure is what he makes the actual goal of the lowest mode of life. His pupils Theophrastus and Dicaearchus, writing at the beginning of the Hellenistic period, appear to have disagreed over the relative weight of the claims of the political and the philosophical life.

Epicurus's work *On Modes of Life* ran to four books and was clearly one of his most important ethical writings. No actual quotations from it survive, but we know some of the main theses it propounded. Book 1 condemned participation in politics, Book 2 the Cynic way of life. Although the sources attribute no major positive prescription to the treatise, there can be little doubt that it will have recommended the quiet life of "withdrawal from the many" (*Key Doctrines* 14) in company with friends (ibid. 27–28). "Live unknown" *(lathe biōsas)* was one of the Epicureans' most notorious slogans, summing up in two words the way the key decision should go. For the Epicureans' advice on more specific practical choices, we have to rely on a hodgepodge of evidence, and notably on a disorganized scissors-and-paste compilation reproduced by Diogenes Laertius (*Lives of the Philosophers* 10.117–121). This includes the barest summaries of their stances inter alia on sexual relations and marriage (negative), treatment of slaves (humane), behavior at a symposium (restrained), music and poetry (the wise man will discuss it but not write it), and making money (he will do so only from imparting his wisdom, when hard up).

What was the rationale of the thesis that the wise man will keep out of politics? This has to be reconstructed from various things the Epicureans say about security *(asphaleia)*. The basic framework within which their views were worked out is constituted by a theory about law and society. Our information here is rather fuller than for some of the other positions that have been mentioned, thanks to a long discussion of the subject extracted by Porphyry (3rd century C.E.) from a work by Hermarchus, Epicurus's successor as head of the school. In briefest outline, the theory holds that the function of a law-governed community is to provide its individual members with protection against some fundamental threats to life and happiness, whether these originate from outside the city (e.g., wild animals or hostile neighboring communities) or from within (notably from persons intent on their own advantage at the expense of the community's). But law is not our only security against the hostile behavior of our fellow citizens. Epicurus proposes further social strategies designed to reinforce the sense of confidence members of a law-governed community may expect to enjoy. First, we need friends: for the benefits friends perform, but much more for the "assurance of their help"

(*Vatican Sayings* 34). Whereas life would otherwise be "full of dangers and fear," the formation of friendships "strengthens the mind"; without them we are unable to "hold on to a joy in life which is steady and lasting" (Cicero, *De Finibus* 1.66–67). In sum, friendship—and the knowledge it brings that there are those who will lend aid when needed—enhances security. Second, Epicurus advises that "the purest form of security comes about from the quiet life and withdrawal from the many" (*Key Doctrines* 14). Given that security is what a wise person wants from society above all else, the optimal strategy for individual members of the community is to have nothing to do with political activity. The reason is, presumably, that politics is full of faction, treachery, and mishap, and that anyone who thinks otherwise is badly mistaken—as *Key Doctrines* 7 points out sarcastically: "Some have wanted to become famous and respected, thinking that this way they would achieve security from men. If, then, the life of such persons is secure, they attain nature's good. But if it is not secure, they do not possess the thing which (in line with what is natural) they desired in the first place."

So Epicurean rejection of political activity was conceived as according with the fundamental premises of their general theory of society and the relation of the individual to the community. The overriding value they attached to security explains why, as Plutarch complained, "they write about political order in order to prevent us from engaging in political life, about rhetoric to stop us practising oratory, and about kingship to make us avoid the courts of Kings" (*Against Colotes* 1127a). Epicureanism did allow exceptions to the general rule, when "the time and necessity" force participation. The deficiencies of the evidence at this point leave us having to guess what might count as a sufficient emergency. Since on Epicurean theory we have no security at all without society, one might conceive that when the very existence of the community is in danger, the wise person will join in political or military action designed to defend it, whether the danger be of a collapse of law and order or of some external threat. Cassius and a number of other opponents (and indeed supporters) of Julius Caesar were Epicureans. It is conceivable that Cassius would have justified his choice of the political life, as well as his participation in the conspiracy of the Ides of March, as something required by the threat Caesar posed to the liberties that the Roman constitution was designed to ensure. At the same time, when Diogenes Laertius tells us that the wise person will pay court to a king "if the occasion demands," the tactic being recommended sounds more like the prudent behavior of someone concerned not to endanger his personal safety by giving offense in high quarters.

The main objection to the general Epicurean position is put succinctly by Plutarch: the Epicurean wise man shares in the advantages of a life in a city-state but makes no contribution to them (*Against Colotes* 1127a). The Epicureans claim to attach high value to the security that law, political order, magistracies, and kingships promote, but they put them in jeopardy "by withdrawing themselves and their associates from the political order, by saying that great commands bear no comparison with the crown of an undisturbed mind, and by declaring that to be a king is just a mistake" (ibid. 1125c). Against the charge of parasitism, the best defense of their advocacy of the quiet life is perhaps to stress the realism about politics that it presupposes. There will always be plenty of people who want fame and power at whatever the cost, as Epicurus seems to have conceded. So unless there is a general collapse of public order or a threat to the body politic, there is, as a matter of fact, no *need* for the rational person, intent on his own security, to enter the political arena.

It is less easy to understand the way the Stoics' very different views on the political life fitted into a more comprehensive theoretical structure. Chrysippus's *On Modes of Life* (like Epicurus's treatise, also in four books) evidently identified three choices of life as appropriate for the wise person: kingship or, failing that, life at court; the political life, broadly construed; and teaching philosophy. We know quite a bit about the way the Stoics elaborated the first two approved choices in particular. But there is no evidence of a ranking order among them, nor of how it may have been argued that they and only they satisfied more general requirements of the Stoic conception of the good life.

Only the wise are kings, according to a famous Stoic paradox probably first propounded by Zeno of Citium. Chrysippus explained that by kingship here was meant supreme rule by someone not required under the law to give an account of his conduct as ruler. The paradox was defended by the argument that a ruler must know what is good and evil: on Stoic premises only the wise person can command that knowledge, so only he is *qualified* for rule in general and kingship in particular. Next best to being king oneself is acting as an adviser to a king at court or on campaign. This was particularly recommended where the king in question showed a disposition to virtue and an eagerness to learn, but Chrysippus is quoted as allowing it even in cases where there was no evidence on his part of progress in moral education. In line with this doctrine, leading members of the school did indeed take up positions at court. Zeno's favorite pupil, Persaeus, became adviser to Antigonus Gonatas of Macedon, and eventually one of his generals. And we hear tell of Sphaerus (mid- to late 3rd century B.C.E.) at the court of Ptolemy Philadelphus in Alexandria, as well as by the side of Cleomenes III of Sparta, where he is said to have assisted the king in the reintroduction and reform of the traditional Spartan educational system. It has sometimes been suggested that the early Stoics had a theoretical commitment to democracy that Zeno at Athens and Sphaerus in Sparta will have endeavored to promote in practice, but the evidence does not sustain this hypothesis. In the mid- to late 2nd century the leading Stoic Panaetius became a friend of the great Roman senator Scipio Africanus, but what influence he exerted over him is a matter for conjecture.

The Stoics held that man is by nature a political animal, designed for an active, practical life, not for a solitary existence. From this thesis they derived a number of consequences for the conduct of the perfectly rational person. First, as is natural for a creature capable of mutual affection, he will marry and have children (contrary to Epicurus's general rule), both for his own sake and for that of his country. Second, provided his country has a moderate government, he will be prepared to endure hardships and death on its behalf. Third, he will engage in politics, especially when the political order shows signs of progress toward the perfect forms of constitution—e.g., (presumably) aristocracy or the mixed constitution advocated by Dicaearchus, as well as the republic of the wise sketched in Zeno's *Republic*. There will be circumstances when something prevents him from political activity: usually corruption in society, making it difficult or impossible for him to benefit his country or (to put it in terms also used in the sources) to encourage virtue and restrain vice—which is said to be the point of politics. Finally, education, the drafting of legislation, and the writing of books capable of benefiting those who encounter them are held to be activities that are the special province of the good (identified by the Stoics, on Socratic principles, with the wise). Are kingship and life at court seen as special variants of the political life? They can hardly be regarded as constituting an outright alternative to it, given that the political mode of living is represented by the Stoic account as the expression of social impulses that are *natural* to us all, and given too that the political is here being construed as encompassing a wide variety of public-spirited activities. But the sources indicate no trace of any attempt to explain the relationship between the first two modes of life open to the sage.

The third mode of life endorsed by Chrysippus is the one devoted to philosophy. On his view this is not to be equated with the quiet life of leisured retirement, which—in a thinly veiled reference to the Peripatetics and Epicureans, respectively—he criticized as nothing but a thinly veiled or frankly acknowledged hedonism. He seems to have preferred to describe the third way of life as "being a sophist": i.e., setting up and practicing as a professional teacher of philosophy. The reason for this provocative and apparently bizarre choice of nomenclature is not hard to find. Plato had insisted in *The Republic* that government and making money were two utterly different and indeed, properly speaking, incompatible practices. Again, one of his principal indictments of the sophists who throng the pages of his dialogues is that their fundamental motivation is mercenary, despite their professed concerns for virtue and knowledge. He implies that a true philosopher will not seek or accept payment from a pupil. Chrysippus seems to have thought these attitudes unrealistic, and at odds with the proper valuation of money as something "preferred," even if ultimately indifferent from the point of view of achieving happiness. For him, a mode of life implies (as it evidently need not for Epicurus) making a living, which in turn implies making money. So not only does he stress in what he says about the third mode of life he identifies that the wise person *makes money* from teaching philosophy, even going so far as to discuss the details of the etiquette governing the charging procedures, he also insists that the sage will make money from a life at court, if he chooses that mode of life, or from politics and his friends in high places, if he goes into politics. Indeed Chrysippus instructs him to "practice oratory and engage in politics as though wealth were a real good, and reputation and health too" (Plutarch, *Stoic Contradictions* 1034b).

Stoicism and Epicureanism have often been perceived as the deracinated philosophies of life one might expect in an age when political power was ebbing away from the city-state to the courts of the Hellenistic kings. On this view the individual and his happiness are represented as the new exclusive focus of moral philosophy, displacing obsolescent questions about the best political order for the city. It is an assessment called into question by the discussion above.

Epicureanism undoubtedly advocates quietism, and out of a fundamental preoccupation with what is in the best interests of the individual. But the conceptual framework within which it works out its argument for quietism is the one by now traditional in Greek political thought: Epicurus is thinking of a largely self-sufficient community restricted in size; and he and Hermarchus conceive it in terms of the contractualist versions of how society originates and functions that had been advocated particularly in the sophistic literature of the second half of the 5th century. The Epicurean analysis operates throughout at a level of high abstraction. There is no indication whatever that Epicurus and his circle had begun to reflect seriously on new Hellenistic forms of political organization, or on their effects on the powers of city-states and their citizens. If *all* the Hellenistic philosophies had advocated abstention from political life, it might nonetheless have been plausible to postulate a new zeitgeist, not yet captured in philosophical formulas but dictating philosophical positions all the same. In fact the most radical critique of the city-state— by Diogenes the Cynic—predates the Hellenistic age; and although later Cynics, the dissident Stoic Aristo, and some Cyrenaic philosophers are found repeating it in one form or another around the beginning of the period, and urging men to follow nature and consider themselves citizens only of the world, voices like theirs fall largely silent on this theme as time goes on. Indeed the Cynic poet Cercidas (late 3rd century) was to become heavily involved in the politics of his own city, Megalopolis. As was noted above, Epicurus, for his part, dissociated himself from Cynicism. The earliest trace of Cynic cosmopolitanism in Epicurean texts comes in a fragment of Diogenes of Oenoanda (LS 22P; 2nd century C.E.).

For the most part the major philosophical schools appear to have been as committed in the Hellenistic period as they ever were to endorsing political activity of a conventional kind. The neatest and most celebrated illustration of their recognition of such political responsibilities is supplied by the choice of the heads of the Academy (Carneades), the Stoa (Diogenes of Babylon), and the Peripatos (Critolaus) to represent the Athenians as their ambassadors on a visit to Rome in 155 B.C.E. (Carneades caused a sensation by giving lectures on successive days first for and then against justice.) So far from exhibiting signs of deracination, Chrysippus goes out of his way to emphasize the depths of the immersion of the wise man in the world immediately around him: whether he opts for the court or politics or sophistry, he will be making money. As was suggested above, this sounds like a reproof to Plato for promoting too idealistic a conception of political and indeed philosophical activity. Moreover, Stoic political philosophy still looks to be heavily oriented toward the city-state and the idea of the city, defined as "an organization of people living in the same place who are administered by law." Chrysippus seems to have said a good deal more about politics than about life at court, and the range of commitments he associates with it remains just as wide as those that (for example) Aristotle assigns to the man of practical wisdom who exercises rule in the sort of city-state discussed in *Politics*. Indeed, perhaps what is most striking about the Stoic account of the political life is just how thoroughly traditional it is.

What was novel and ultimately revolutionary in Stoicism was its conception of the ideal community of perfectly rational persons, all subject to the same law: not the positive law of any existing society, but an internalized natural law of reason, prescribing to everyone what they should or should not do. The natural moral law is the only law that can command our ultimate obedience; other key political concepts that were defined in terms of law, such as city and civilization, have in the end to be understood in this light. Hence the *only* true city is the cosmic community of wise men and gods living in accordance with the moral law. Chrysippus's allegiance to this theory did not prevent him taking the view described above about the political involvement of the sage in the imperfect world around him: i.e., as practicing politics (if he does) as though wealth and honor were real goods. But in the writings of the leading Stoics of the early Roman empire—Seneca, Epictetus, Marcus Aurelius—the claims of citizenship of the universe come to dwarf those of the existing societies in which we find ourselves: the cosmic perspective progressively displaces the vantage point of ordinary life. It is important for understanding the political thought of the Hellenistic age that this *is* a later development. Chrysippus's sage is engagé.

Malcolm Schofield

Bibliography

Aalders, G. J. D. *Political Thought in Hellenistic Times.* Amsterdam, 1975.
Branham, R. Bracht, and Marie-Odile Goulet-Cazé, eds. *The Cynics: The Cynic Movement in Antiquity and Its Legacy.* Berkeley, 1996.

Erskine, A. *The Hellenistic Stoa*. Ithaca, N.Y., and London, 1990.

Goldschmidt, V. *La doctrine d'Epicure et le droit*. Paris, 1977.

Griffin, Miriam T. *Seneca: Philosopher in Politics*. Rev. ed. Oxford, 1992.

Grilli, A. *Il problema della vita contemplativa nel mondo Greco-Romano*. Milan, 1953.

Joly, R. *Le thème philosophique des genres de vie dans l'antiquité classique*. Brussels, 1956.

Long, A. A., and D. N. Sedley. *The Hellenistic Philosophers*. 2 vols. Cambridge, Eng., 1987.

Schofield, M. *The Stoic Idea of the City*. Cambridge, Eng., 1991. Rept. Chicago, 1999.

Related Articles

Epicurus; Socrates; Plato; Stoicism

THE PURSUIT OF
KNOWLEDGE

SCHOOLS AND SITES
OF LEARNING

PHILOSOPHY, THE PURSUIT OF WISDOM, has had a two-fold origin," Diogenes Laertius writes at the beginning of *Lives of Eminent Philosophers.* "The
one school was called Ionian, because Thales, a Milesian and therefore an
Ionian, instructed Anaximander; the other school was called Italian from
Pythagoras, who worked for the most part in Italy" (I.13). Diogenes further
divides philosophers into ten sects *(haireseis);* the term designates a coherent positive doctrine, or at least a criterion with respect to the phenomenal
world (I.20).

Diogenes thus classifies philosophers according to the very parameters we
are considering here: schools and sites of learning. Concerning the sites, Diogenes and his sources tell us that philosophy was originally divided among
diverse tendencies that ran from one end of the Greek world to the other,
from Asia Minor to Greater Greece. In fact, philosophy originated in the farthest reaches of the Hellenic universe, and it did not reach Athens until fairly
late. Still, according to Diogenes, whether or not a philosopher belonged to a
particular school depended on the content of his thought; it did not necessarily imply membership in a given institution.

The philologists of the 19th and early 20th centuries saw the origin of the
idea of the university in the philosophical schools of antiquity. Thus they depicted these schools in modern terms, especially the Academy and the Lyceum: as scientific institutions with tenured full, associate, and assistant professors; beginning students and doctoral candidates; classrooms and courses.
These images are often only innocent metaphors, but they have sometimes
introduced distortions into the way we represent the ancient philosophers'
activities.

This phenomenon is limited to the arena of classical studies; medievalists
and historians of education have stressed the differences between the ancient
philosophic schools and modern universities. The latter have an official status
recognized by the state; some form of public approval is required for position-
holders within these institutions; and the course of study leads to a certificate
attesting to the degree obtained. It has been said that if a modern student had
sat long enough at Socrates' feet he would have demanded a diploma, something to show for his efforts. But great teachers such as Socrates did not issue
diplomas. Moreover, in modern universities, membership in an institution

does not mean that one has to subscribe to a particular line of thought; in contrast, in the ancient world, there would have been widespread astonishment if a faithful follower of the Academy had defended, sword in hand, the superiority of Epicurean ethics. The ancient philosophic schools, even the most highly organized, were in principle free institutions, and adhering to them implied, as Diogenes says, the adoption of a firm theoretical position. We may conclude, following the *Oxford English Dictionary*, that the philosophic schools of Antiquity consisted of groups of "persons who . . . are disciples of the same master, or who are united by a general similarity of principles and methods." The word *school* refers only rarely to a specific institution.

It is difficult to generalize about the way the various schools were organized. Sources are often lacking, and the ancient authors rarely bothered to describe the organizational aspects of their activity. Furthermore, a school's organization was directly linked to the doctrine it professed. Today, all departments of philosophy look alike; in ancient times, philosophers had a great deal of freedom to choose the forms through which knowledge would be organized and transmitted. I shall merely indicate a few models, which the individual schools resembled in varying degrees. The simplest distinction we can make is between two types: (1) elementary, atomic structures constituted by a master and one or more disciples, which dissolved when the master died; (2) more complex and hierarchical organizations, with different levels of teachers and disciples, which existed over a considerable span of time. In the history of ancient thought, which lasted more than one thousand years, we find these same two structures over and over, with intermediate nuances.

THE PRESOCRATICS

Greek speculation, in its earliest period, was characterized by an immense diversity of horizons; philosophers lived in different milieux, from Asia Minor to Sicily, and they engaged in controversies across lands and seas. Subsequently, with the growing importance of Athens as the principal city of Greece, philosophic debate was confined to the Athenian city-state alone.

In Greece, philosophy was almost always an urban phenomenon, and it was often linked to important, wealthy city-states. The first "philosophers," Thales, Anaximander, and Anaximenes, flourished in Miletus, a wealthy city-state and very active commercial center in the 7th and 6th centuries, up to its destruction in 494 B.C.E. Anaximander is said to have been Thales' disciple, and a relative. We do not know this for certain, but if we take it as a fact, we have the first instance of family ties between master and disciple, a phenomenon we shall come across frequently in all periods. In those early days, however, the philosophic organization was limited to the master-disciple bond. It seems certain that this was the case with Parmenides and Zeno of Elea; Plato describes them as master and disciple and also as lovers. Diogenes Laertius, for his part, claims that Zeno was adopted by Parmenides; if this is true, here is another example of master-disciple family ties. The Eleatic circle must have been fairly broad if, as Plato tells us, the Stranger of Elea belonged to the group associated with Parmenides and Zeno. Let us note that Plato is not yet using precise terminology to indicate relationships to particular schools.

A philosopher's thinking could also be communicated in written form. Heraclitus seems to have had no direct disciples, but "so great fame did his book win that a sect was founded and called the Heracliteans, after him" (Diogenes Laertius, *Lives* IX.6). Aristotle, too, refers to "those who claim to be following Heraclitus," without thereby designating true disciples. Cratylus must have figured among those to whom Aristotle was alluding, for Plato, in his youth, was one of Cratylus's intimate friends. Cratylus does not seem to have lived in Ephesus or in Ionia, and yet he followed the theories of Heraclitus, and criticized them to a certain extent (*Metaphysics* 987a.32, 1010a.11).

Pythagoras is the only philosopher in connection with whom we can speak of a school. But Pythagoras is a semimythical figure, halfway between archaic religiosity and true philosophy. His sect presents a quite complex set of features, but it may be that the Pythagoreans constituted a political *hetairia* as well as a religious and philosophic association.

A whole series of ritual prescriptions having to do with every aspect of the disciples' daily lives are linked with Pythagoras's name. It was forbidden to eat at least certain parts of the flesh of certain animals. Some behaviors were prescribed, such as setting out on the right foot rather than the left, wearing particular clothing, having certain attitudes toward one's fellow citizens, and so on. These prescriptions recall the mystery cults, and reveal a strong inclination toward the other-worldly and the divine. This set of rules constituted a *bios*, a specific way of life on which the identity of the Pythagorean group was based in large part. Their community was characterized by a series of doctrines on number, on the ordered harmony of the cosmos, and on mathematical sciences such as astronomy and music. It is not clear when this more "scientific" aspect began to be part of the sect's cultural identity, but Pythagoreanism did not exist in written form before Philolaus's era.

The Pythagorean sect was highly cohesive. Pythagorean friendship committed its members to helping one another, even if they were not personally acquainted. Disciples who had been expelled were regarded as dead, for they had been marked as unworthy or as heretics. Still, some sources emphasize a distinction among disciples according to whether they were acusmaticians or mathematicians: this distinction points either to two successive stages in the deepest understanding of Pythagoras's doctrine, or else to an opposition between two groups that had split over the interpretation of his message. The acusmaticians took the sect's prescriptions for living and its taboos as their fundamental tenets; the mathematicians did not reject these injunctions, but for them the doctrine of number lay at the heart of Pythagorism. It seems, too, that the mathematicians considered the acusmaticians, like themselves, to be authentic Pythagoreans, whereas the latter group did not recognize the former.

We know little about how the sect was organized. Its teaching seems to have called for a long period of silence before one was admitted to argue in Pythagoras's presence and with the master himself, but this is not certain. The Pythagorean school cannot be defined as a true philosophic school, even though it may have been taken as a model influencing the birth of the Athenian schools of the 4th century.

SOPHISTS, RHETORS, DOCTORS

From the outset, the Greek world was studded with specialists who went from one city-state to another to proffer their services. The main groups are mentioned by Homer: soothsayers, healers, carpenters, and singers (*Odyssey* XVII.383–384). Many of these groups were organized as hereditary guilds in which fathers transmitted their art to sons.

The Sophists were itinerant teachers; we know that they sojourned frequently in all the Greek city-states, where they taught young men for wages. Gorgias went to Argos and Thessaly, Protagoras to Sicily, Hippias to Sparta and Sicily; each achieved a certain degree of success. Athens drew a large number of learned men, including many philosophers, such as Parmenides, Zeno (if Plato's account is accurate), Anaxagoras of Clazomenae, and a number of Sophists. Like all itinerant craftsmen, the Sophists were paid for their lessons: from three or four to a hundred *mines* for a complete course (one *mine* was worth one hundred drachmas, and one drachma represented the average daily salary of an artisan).

Sophistic teaching covered a very broad range of topics: astronomy, geometry, linguistics and grammar, theology, and literature. The Sophists provided an education of a high level, to increase their disciple's general culture and to make him better able to convince his fellow citizens. Isocrates, for example, recounts a public debate about literature held by the Sophists in the Lyceum before an enthusiastic audience (*Panathenaicus* 18–19); we know that a number of Sophists were concerned with the problem of squaring the circle; many Presocratic themes, Eleatic in particular, were taken up again by Protagoras and Gorgias. Sophistic teaching varied according to its audience. In Sparta, Hippias recited the genealogy of gods and men, and described the occupations worthy of a young Spartan, thus adapting his message to his hearers' tastes; in Athens, on the contrary, a democratic city-state ruled by an Assembly, he focused on rhetoric and dialectics (or eristics). The course must not have been very long, for it was intended as preparation for public life.

The Sophists' activity in Athens came dangerously close to the political sphere: their connections with the leading families—the source of most of their disciples—and the innovative content of their teaching aroused public hostility, especially in democratic circles. Around 433, Diopeithes decreed that anyone who did not believe in the gods or who presented arguments *(logoi)* about celestial spaces should be taken to court. Plutarch, who relates this episode, sees it as an attempt to discredit Pericles by bringing charges against his master Anaxagoras *(Life of Pericles* 32). In the years that followed, Protagoras, Diagoras, Theodorus "the Atheist," Socrates, and others faced— or were at least threatened with—similar charges. The Athenian people's distrust slowly faded, but it resurfaced periodically, generally in connection with important political events, such as Alexander's death.

When they arrived in a city, the Sophists sought to win clients by demonstrating their abilities in public. In a world where official degrees and diplomas were unknown, such exhibitions of personal competence were necessary. They took place in sites where the biggest crowds gathered, such as the sanctuary in Olympia or the theater in Athens. The Sophists would read a prepared speech or would improvise at the public's request. Sometimes, however, a Sophist already well-known to the public did not need to establish his talents (Plato, *Protagoras* 310b). Sure of his audience, he would withdraw to some private place, usually the home of a wealthy citizen, where he would have enough room to bring together his own disciples; there he would give his lessons, for a fee, to his host and others. We know that the Sophists were welcomed in the greatest houses of Athens, for example those of Callias, Euripides, and Megacleides. But they could also hold their meetings in gymnasiums or public squares, and from ancient comedies we learn that Sophists held forth in the Lyceum, in the Academy, and at the entrance to the Odeon.

In *Protagoras* (314e–316a), Plato describes the behavior of the Sophists in action. One walks about, surrounded by his most important disciples, who are followed by their juniors; another, seated on a chair, speaks to listeners seated on stools arranged in a half-circle; a third receives his disciples from a reclining position and engages in dialogue with them while stretched out on his bed. These same scenes reappear virtually unchanged in descriptions of many other, later groups. Teaching does not presuppose the use of particular instruments; oral teaching and debate were the rule, and the Sophists were proud of being able to produce lengthy speeches and to answer specific questions and engage in dialogue with their interlocutors. The rhetorical part of their teaching must have consisted in learning entire texts by heart, or in mastering rhetorical schemas for later use.

Isocrates recounts an incident that allows us to glimpse life in one school of rhetoric. The master writes an argument *(logos),* then corrects it while rereading it with three or four disciples; he then asks one of his former students to do the same thing, summoning him from home (apparently the latter had left the school and was leading the life of an ordinary citizen [*Panathenaicus* 200]). Theophrastus followed similar practices in his school, and maintained that his public readings were useful in helping him correct his own work.

Thus the institutional characteristics that typified the activity of philosophers began to crystallize. Sites devoted to teaching began to appear: the homes of the wealthy, city squares, public gymnasiums. The latter, according to Vitruvius (*De architectura* V.xi.2), had arcades where philosophers could stroll about with their disciples, and exedras furnished with benches, to facilitate discussion. The choice of a teaching site was often related to the type of philosophy being taught: Socrates chose public streets and squares so as to demonstrate his availability to all his fellow citizens and to show his lack of interest in remuneration, for speakers could only be sure of collecting money from the public in an enclosed teaching space. The Cynics did the same thing, in every era, and they always tended to prefer the public display of "natural" behaviors to the transmission of complex doctrines. In contrast, the Academicians, the Peripatetics, the Stoics, and other groups taught in enclosed spaces well-equipped with scientific instruments and libraries, and in the homes of wealthy and powerful individuals.

It may be useful to compare the teaching of philosophy with that of medicine. In Greece, medical training was concentrated in a few city-states, such as Cos and Chios; it had no official status, and no diplomas were awarded. In the beginning, the trade was passed on from father to son. We know the names of various members of Hippocrates' family: they were all doctors at the Macedonian court, and the family tradition was maintained up to the Hellenistic period. But there came a time when disciples from outside the family were accepted; Hippocrates' famous *Oath* includes the terms of a sort of contract according to which the disciple agrees to consider the master's relatives and friends as his own, and to provide them with help and assistance.

Medical schools consisting of a master and his disciples were organized in a fairly straightforward way. The teaching involved lessons and exercises; the disciples observed the master at work, helped him, and became accustomed to using instruments. All our sources take pains to make accurate lists of disciples of famous masters, whether they are talking about doctors, philosophers, or rhetors; such lists attest to the worth of the people selected. The master's lessons were eventually written down, and they constituted the doctrinal patrimony of the school, as was the case later on for schools of philosophy. Thus the teachings of the Cnidus school were compiled in a text called *Cnidian Sentences,* which has been lost; the Cos school produced the *Hippocratic Corpus.* An analysis of the latter text shows that complete doctrinal orthodoxy was not required; the various authors represented in the *Corpus* often put forward divergent theses simultaneously. These writings also include manuals of medical rhetoric and dialectics, to be used in meetings among colleagues in order to assure oneself of employment; they propose rhetorical and eristic schemas along with basic medical notions to be used in debates.

PLATO'S SCHOOL

Socrates' disciples did not create true schools. Even the Megarians, the best organized, did not have real schools; instead, they had independent masters who brought groups of disciples together, sometimes for long periods.

Plato, in contrast, established a school. According to Diogenes Laertius, whose account of Plato's life is not entirely clear, Plato taught at the Academy when he returned from his first trip to Sicily; later he lectured "in the garden at Colonus," adjacent to the Academy (*Lives* III.5–7). Thus we have two sites for the school, either in the Academy or in a garden on Plato's property. Since the school had no institutional organization, and since it consisted only of a spontaneous group of friends, its location might well have varied for practical reasons. The type of teaching and the research carried out in the school did not actually require much equipment.

Plato's school marked the history of philosophic thought for centuries to come, from both theoretical and institutional standpoints. But the school was constituted from elements that came out of earlier traditions. A passage from Philodemus provides a good description of Plato's role: "He functioned as an architect, and set problems" (*Academicorum Index*, Plato Y.4–5). However, unlike the Pythagoreans, Plato did not impose any doctrinal orthodoxy. He may have gotten the idea of setting up a community devoted to philosophy during his stay in Sicily, from his contacts with the Pythagoreans, but the Academy was organized very differently, owing in particular to the absence of dogmatism. Olympiodorus writes in his *Life of Plato* (61) that Plato succeeded in freeing himself from the Pythagorean practice of doctrinal secrecy and from an unquestioning acceptance of the master's word as well as from Socratic irony; indeed, he maintained courteous relations with his own students. The school's lack of orthodoxy meant that Plato's chief disciples could criticize fundamental points of his metaphysics. The unity of the school was based on the fact that the disciples set themselves common problems to discuss: Being, the Good, the One, Science; these were quite different problems from those addressed elsewhere—in Isocrates' school, for instance.

The establishment of a philosophic school by an Athenian was the pretext for countless jokes on the part of comic writers; Plato was ridiculed, represented with a furrowed brow (Amphis) or depicted as strolling about and talking to himself (Alexis). In *The Shipwrecked*, Ephippus parodies the "lively little fellows" who were Plato's disciples, and Epicrates tells how the master and his pupils were defining nature and carving it up into genres, when a Sicilian doctor was heard making clamorous objections. Rather than allowing the discussion to be disrupted, Plato politely asked his disciples to start over. Plato's role, even in this description, is precisely that of the master who sets problems and directs the disciples' investigation.

The Platonic school had no internal literature at first, for Plato insisted that the doctrinal core of his thinking could not be written down (Epistle VII 344c); the absence of a doctrinal corpus created problems for the life of the school. At the same time, there was a literature addressed to those outside the school, intended to spread knowledge of Plato's philosophy beyond the circle of his disciples. Philodemus asserts that "his writings brought countless people to philosophy" (*Academicorum Index* I.12–14). Aristoxenus, for his part, tells how Plato gave a talk one day on the Good before an uninitiated public, without much success (*Elementa harmonica* II.1). This event is echoed by an amusing line from a comedy: "I have more trouble understanding these things, O Master, than Plato's notion of the Good" (Amphis, *Amphicrates* frg. 6K).

The complete training of a Platonic philosopher, compared to that of a Sophist, took a long time; Aristotle, for example, spent twenty years at the Academy. Life in the school gradually became an end in itself.

The value of the teaching offered by a Sophist, a rhetor, or a philosopher was measured above all in the number and quality of his pupils. Isocrates was proud to have had famous Athenians, noted statesmen, generals, and even foreigners as students. Philodemus of Gadara and Diogenes Laertius preserved the list of Plato's disciples, including Xenocrates, Crantor, Archesilaus, Telecles, Cacydes, Carneades, Antiochus of Ascalon, Zeno the Stoic, Chrysippus, Diogenes of Babylon, Antipater, and Panaetius.

Plato's will makes no allusion either to the garden or to the school. According to Diogenes, Plato chose to be buried near the Academy. Pausanias describes his tomb, and points out that it is located beyond the Academy proper. The custom of burying a master on the grounds of his school was characteristic of the chief philosophic schools of Athens. The hypothesis according to which the school was a religious guild dedicated to the cult of the Muses has been ruled out. We do not know whether Plato thought that his community would survive after his death. It did so, however, thereby distinguishing itself from earlier groups, which had disintegrated when the master left or died.

FROM PLATO'S DEATH TO THE FIRST CENTURY B.C.E.

At the end of the 4th century, the four great schools that would forever link the name of Athens to that of philosophy were established within the city-state. But Athens was not the only home of philosophers: many of the minor Socratics set up schools elsewhere, for example at Megara, Elis, Olympia, and Eretria. The Platonics traveled widely—to Atarnea, in the Pontus region, and to the court of Macedonia; Epicurus did the same thing. But it is telling that both Aristotle and Epicurus, after beginning their activity elsewhere, decided to go back to Athens to establish their own schools in a city-state whose importance guaranteed a huge audience for their doctrines. Zeno of Citium opened his school in the same city for the same reasons. Thus the four principal Hellenistic philosophic schools were created in Athens, two by Athenian citizens and the other two by foreigners.

The schools now took on their ultimate form. A special vocabulary was instituted in the philosophic community: in addition to the venerable term *diatribē*, the term *schole* was used to designate the course of study, lessons, and seminars. This meaning of the word was unknown in the time of Plato and Aristotle; then, it designated "free time." According to Philodemus, the school was called *hairesis*, "choice," in the sense of the selection of a philosophic doctrine; sometimes the analogous term *agoge* was used instead. The terms *kepos* (garden), *peripatos* (stroll—here in the sense of the place where people walked), and *exedra* were also common. One could thus designate a school by alluding to the activities that took place there, the doctrines espoused, or its physical structure.

Dicaearchus (frg. 29) spoke out against the tendency of philosophy in his day to become institutionalized; he argued that one could do philosophy anywhere—in public squares, in fields, or on the battlefield—without any need for a chair, textual commentary, or set hours for lessons or for strolling about with one's disciples. Menedemus of Eretria is criticized in some sources for his indifference to the conditions under which he taught. He required no special order or seating arrangement; his disciples could choose to sit or walk about while listening, and their master had the same options (Diogenes Laertius, *Lives* II.130).

On Plato's death, his community did not fold; his nephew Speusippus succeeded him as head of the school (Philodemus, *Academicorum Index* VI.28–29). This succession can probably be attributed to the fact that, as a family member, Speusippus could inherit the garden where most of the common activity took place. There is no contradiction here, since family ties were often intertwined with school ties. Speusippus himself seems to have held most of his meetings in the garden. The ancient sources are quite specific about the sites where the various scholarchs directed common activities. Speusippus had statues of the Muses erected in the garden, with a dedication crediting them as the sources of the school's philosophic doctrines. As the head of a school, Speusippus became the most prominent figure of the community, but we do not know whether that gave him the authority to influence the thinking of other, older members. The fact remains that when Speusippus took over, Aristotle went off to establish a school outside of Athens; Xenocrates may have done the same thing. Speusippus defied his uncle's taboo on writing down the fundamental doctrines. The titles of his dialogues and notes taken during his lessons have been preserved.

When Speusippus died, the youngest disciples chose his successor by vote. In the selection process, voting alternated with designation by the previous scholarch. Xenocrates won by a small margin over the other candidates, it seems; he had seventy votes, which suggests that the community must have been fairly large. Xenocrates' primary residence was the school (Diogenes Laertius, *Lives* IV.6). Polemon, too, spent most of his time in the garden of the Academy, so much so that the disciples built huts so they could live near him, near the place of the Muses *(mouseion)* and the exedra where he gave his courses. Polemon, Crates, and Crantor seem to have lived in the same house, the first two as lovers; all three were buried in the garden, following the school's custom. After the death of Polemon, the third head of the Academy, we hear no more about Plato's garden.

With the establishment of other philosophic schools, problems of membership and orthodoxy began to arise. Who could legitimately claim to be "Platonic" or "Epicurean"? In the case of the Academy, membership did not depend on strict obedience to the founder's doctrine. Indeed, Plato's dialogues were conceived so as to allow various interpretations; as for Speusippus and the other directors, their works never had a canonic role. To be an Academician, at this stage of the school's history, meant rather that one belonged to a group that had historical continuity and an identity maintained throughout its various theoretical evolutions. Compared with that of the Pythagoreans or the Epicureans, this identity appeared fairly weak. The very fact that the ancient authors could distinguish among several phases in the Academy's history shows clearly that it was not conceived as having a rock-solid unity; however, it was not diversified, either, to the point where it would split into opposing factions.

Aristotle did not establish a school. As a metic, he could not own property in Attica; however, he may have taught in a rented private house. The surviving Aristotelian texts make it clear that his courses could not have been held in a gymnasium; he needed a site specifically devoted to teaching, because he used instruments and books.

The Peripatetic school typically focused on collecting and cataloguing empirical data, as Aristotle's *History of Animals* and Theophrastus's *History of Plants* attest. The Peripatetic school also collected 158 city-state constitutions, classified by political regime, as well as the names of the winners of the Pythian Games, as attested by an inscription from Delphi where both Aristotle and Callisthenes are mentioned. The school used lists, anatomical tables, geographical maps, models of the heavenly sphere, and star charts. Its goal was not to prepare anyone for political life; rather, it offered a choice of lifestyle and a path to happiness—a *bios*. The corpus of Aristotle's lessons formed the school's conceptual patrimony, just as the *Hippocratic Corpus* did for the Cos school. Aristotle also wrote a series of works for the public, to incite people to take an interest in philosophy, but these have been lost.

Aristotle did not go hunting for disciples; neither he nor Plato showed evidence of the embarrassing tendency toward self-celebration that characterized both the Sophists and the doctors. The subsistence of the philosopher and his school, in both cases, depended not on salaries paid by the disciples but solely on the personal patrimony of the group members, or of the school. In fact, Aristotle's will reveals that he was a rich man, and the fortune of the Peripatetics was legendary in ancient times.

There is no mention of Aristotle's school in the text of his will. On Alexander's death, Aristotle had been subject to attacks by the popular party and was forced to emigrate; it is probable that he gave no thought to the survival of his school after his own disappearance. The birth of the Lyceum *(peripatos)* as an institution dates from the time of Theophrastus, Aristotle's principal disciple (321–287); Demetrius of Phaleron, Peripatetic and Athenian statesman, who governed Athens at the time, granted Theophrastus, whose student he had been, the right to own real estate in Athens. Theophrastus bought a garden where he organized the Aristotelian school, modeled on Plato's. The school did not bear its founder's name, since Theophrastus was seeking to carry on the community Aristotle had started.

Theophrastus's will provides a good deal of information about this community. His goal, in founding it, was to make theoretic life *(bios theoretikos)* a reality: "The garden and the walk and the houses adjoining the garden, all and sundry, I give and bequeath to such of my friends hereinafter named as may wish to study literature and philosophy there in common" (Diogenes Laertius, *Lives* V.52–53). It was forbidden to sell the property or to make private use of it; the group was to use the garden as if it were a temple (which means that it was not one), in a spirit of familial concord. The possessions included a sanctuary devoted to the Muses with several statues, a small portico, a larger one with geographical maps in stone, a garden, a *peripatos*, and some houses. Theophrastus, too, had himself buried in a corner of the school and had a funerary monument erected, as the Academicians had done. The ten disciples who benefited from the property were guaranteed a certain material comfort. Here, too, there were close family ties: the beneficiaries included direct heirs, testamentary executors, some of Aristotle's nephews, and friends of long standing. We find the same interweaving of school and family ties as in the medical schools.

The fall of Demetrius of Phaleron led to the final persecution of the philosophers by the popular party. A certain Sophocles of Sunium proposed a law forbidding any philosopher from directing a school without the Assembly's permission, on pain of death. All the philosophers had to flee Athens, but they came back the following year, when a Peripatetic, Philon, charged Sophocles' law with illegality, and won. From then on, Theophrastus lived peacefully, surrounded by large numbers of disciples.

The wills of the other Peripatetic scholarchs have also survived. Strato succeeded Theophrastus, and he left the school to Lyco, along with his library and some furniture (but excluding, for unknown reasons, the manuscripts of Strato's own lessons). He asked the other disciples to cooperate with Lyco, and, like Theophrastus, provided for his own funerary monument, probably to be erected on the school's grounds. Lyco in turn left the school to a group of disciples, charging them with electing a scholarch capable of governing the community and making it grow. His library was left to one disciple, while another was given the task of producing a faithful edition of Lyco's own lessons; this too, as we shall see, was the customary practice. Like his predecessors, Lyco arranged for his own funerary monument and statue.

These wills show that the Peripatetic scholarchs were men of means; the texts were handed down, in all probability, because they were kept in the school as evidence of the tradition of the institution. Athenaeus (547d–e) preserved a fragment from Antigonus of Carystus in which the latter described the situation of the school in Lyco's day. Antigonus criticizes the practice of common monthly banquets in which even former members of the school participated; we are told that there was an official position on the "good behavior" of the members, who were concerned with collecting funds for their shared expenses, and, in case of necessity, with providing from their own personal funds, according to the custom of the Athenian "liturgies"; in addition, he cites the office of "curator of the cult of the Muses." The poorer disciples were exempt from these liturgies. The school met either in the *kepos* or in a rented house in Athens.

After Theophrastus and Strato, the school underwent a rapid decline. The ideal of the theoretic life was insufficient to establish an orthodoxy; in addition, the Aristotelian method encouraged the fragmentation of philosophy into erudite studies and detailed investigations focused on specific topics. In time, a legend grew up attributing the school's decline to the loss of Aristotle's works over the centuries; however, the legend has no basis in fact.

Epicurus came back to Athens to found his school in another garden, following Theophrastus's example, the same year that the law of Sophocles of Sunium was brought to trial. Epicurus established his garden outside the city walls, not far from the Academy. As an Athenian citizen, he had more legal rights in the area of real estate than Theophrastus had, and his community was established on a firm footing: Epicurus left his garden to his natural heirs, on condition that they make it available to Hermarchus and his disciples, and, after them, to their chosen successors. The goal of his school was to give all philosophers the means to carry on their philosophic activity, provided that they followed Epicurus's doctrines; the subsistence of its oldest members was ensured. Philodemus recorded excerpts from Epicurus's letters in which he required that, out of a spirit of friendship, the richest members had to pay an annual quota and had to give financial aid to members in difficulty (frgs. 74, 76, 92, 97, 99, 120, 121, 123).

Epicurus named a director and defined a philosophic orthodoxy. Hermarchus was assigned to take care of Epicurus's library, which included the teachings of Epicurus himself, collected in a series of books *peri physeos,* "on nature." Here, too, family and philosophic bonds were interwoven: the sons of prominent members were given jobs in the school, and their daughters were married to the best disciples. Monthly meetings were held, and a funerary cult of Epicurus and his family was also instituted. Unlike the other schools, Epicurus's seems to have been open to all social groups, including courtesans and slaves.

Unlike the Aristotelians, the Epicurean community was infused with a practical ideal: in the place of scientific research and erudition, Epicurus proposed a particular way of living and philosophizing, the only way that could enable man to free himself from pain and find happiness. Epicurus placed great stress on the need to learn the principal doctrines by heart and meditate on them. In *Letter to Herodotus,* he declared that he had written a brief summary of his thought so that readers could memorize it and use it at any point in life.

Internal relations within the school were maintained in an atmosphere of collaboration and emulation. Certain members were obviously more advanced than others, but there was no hierarchy, and a spirit of friendship permeated all relationships. Seneca informs us (*Letter* 52.3−4) that Epicurus identified several ways of leading his disciples to the truth, according to their various temperaments: one advanced on his own, another needed help, a third had to be pushed. In his treatise *Peri parresias,* Philodemus stressed the intensity of the group relations: to be sure, the leader was the best of all, but each one felt responsible for the progress of the others. This led to the practice of public self-criticism of one's own errors, and to public denunciations of others' mistakes. One day, according to Plutarch, Colotes was so excited by Epicurus's speech that he kneeled down before him; the master, judging the act contrary to his doctrine, knelt down in turn, in order to reestablish equality and friendship *(philia)* between them (frg. 65, Arrianus). The Epicureans customarily wore rings bearing the master's likeness, and had pictures of the school's founders in their homes.

On the institutional level, the importance of the Stoic school is not comparable to the enormous influence it had on Greek philosophic life. Zeno and his successors Cleanthes and Chrysippus had no private garden in which to create a community. Zeno gave his lectures in a public place, the Stoa Poecile (or painted portico) on the Agora, one of the most heavily frequented spots in Athens; thus his site contrasts with the more secluded locations of the other schools. His teaching met with success, and the Athenians awarded him great honors. Diogenes Laertius (*Lives* VII.10−12) reports a decree of the Prytaneis in honor of Zeno, after his death: he was offered a crown of gold and a tomb in the Ceramicus at state expense, as a reward for practicing philosophy, exhorting young people to virtue, and living in conformity with his own doctrines. The earlier hostility toward philosophers seems to have died out.

Zeno's group survived its founder's death, and Cleanthes took over as head of the school. The functions of a Stoic scholarch are not very clear; the position may have merely entailed a certain cultural preeminence among Zeno's fellow disciples. The school's somewhat loose organization led in time to several schisms: Ariston founded his own school in the Cynosarges gymnasium, outside the city to the south; two of his disciples are known to us. Cleanthes' successor, Chrysippus, completely reorganized Stoic doctrine (hence the saying "but for Chrysippus, there had been no Porch" [Diogenes Laertius, *Lives* VII.183]); he wrote more than seven hundred works. Whereas Zeno and Cleanthes were metics in Athens, Chrysippus was a naturalized citizen, but this did not lead him to establish a philosophic community in an independent garden (Plutarch, *De Stoicorum repugnantiis* 1034a). He continued to teach at the Stoa at regular hours, and perhaps also at the Odeon, near the theater of Dionysus. The Stoics were not rich, and they lived mainly by teaching their own disciples, for pay (Quintilian, *Institutio oratoria* XII.7.9). This does not seem to have shocked the Athenians, who were accustomed to such practices.

A few details about these practices have been passed down. Cleanthes was paid in advance, after some discussions with his students. Chrysippus recognized that selling wisdom was a way of life suited to the philosopher, and he pointed out ways of requesting one's pay gracefully, avoiding arguments. Stobaeus recounts a debate among the Stoics that took place because some of them were concerned that the practice of teaching for pay reduced them to the level of the Sophists (II.7.11m).

The problem of the unity of the Stoic school is particularly vexed. Even the ancients had noted that Stoicism allowed for a certain autonomy of thought. However, the various Stoic positions were expressed in a common vocabulary, which attested to membership in the same school (the case of Herophilus's medical school was analogous), and the need to respond to adversaries' objections led to a continual reformulation of basic definitions. The dynamic unity of Stoicism sufficed to allow the identification of a Stoic philosophy.

It is impossible to follow the vicissitudes of all the schools and groups of philosophers of this period: they were loosely organized and often short-lived communities, dependent on the presence of a master in a certain place. Still, we can trace the evolution of the principal schools after their founding.

Original philosophic production did not constitute, as we might be inclined to think today, the only important aspect of Greek philosophers' activity. Like the neo-Thomists or the Marxists of the 20th century, these philosophers carried on their work in three directions. They expanded on the theoretical inspiration of the school's founder in areas the latter had neglected; they looked after the critical edition of the master's work and the interpretation of his writings; they entered into polemics with the other schools. Even more than with theoretical development, they were concerned with the training of disciples and with the practice of their own particular philosophy as a way of life.

Once accepted as an integral part of ordinary cultural life, philosophy began to split off into sects, under the somewhat skeptical eye of the public. In the 1st century B.C.E., Diodorus of Sicily wrote a highly polemical text claiming that the Greeks practiced philosophy to earn money; in his view, this accounted for the perpetual innovations, the new schools, and the polemics that produced confusion and uncertainty among the disciples. In fact, the best-known schools seemed to make it a point of honor to contradict one another (Diodorus, II.29.5–6). In compensation, in the imperial era, wealthy young people got into the habit of frequenting the major philosophic schools in turn, thus showing a certain impartiality; they were implicitly rejecting each school's claim to be the only good one.

As we have seen, the Peripatetics never had a philosophic orthodoxy. After Lycon, the Lyceum seems to have undergone a rapid decline. Several sources (Cicero, *De finibus bonorum et malorum* V.13–14; Plutarch, *De exilio* 14; Clement of Alexandria, *Stromateis* I.14.63) allow us to reestablish the list of his successors (Ariston, Critolaus, Diodorus of Tyre, and so on), though in most cases we know nothing of their philosophical orientations. Only for Critolaus is there evidence of an intention to remain faithful to Aristotle's teachings (Wehrli, frgs. 12–15). Athens had entered into an alliance with Mithridates, owing to a decision by the tyrant of the period, the Epicurean Aristion; the city was attacked by Sulla, and the Academy and the Lyceum were destroyed during the siege. A certain Apellicon is mentioned among other Peripatetics involved in Athens's alliance with Mithridates. Apellicon seems to have been in possession of Aristotle's writings at the time, but the fate of the latter's works is not clear. There is evidence, however, that in the first or second half of the 1st century B.C.E., Andronicus of Rhodes, working either in Rome or in Athens, produced an edition of Aristotle's courses, dividing them into treatises. Starting from the time of their publication, these texts played a major role in the history of European thought.

The evolution of the Academy after Polemon was quite complex. As we have seen, the problem of orthodoxy in the Platonic school was complicated by the fact that the dialogues presented quite diverse philosophical positions. Arcesilaus inaugurated the Academy's "skeptical" period, which was marked by a radical theoretical shift. However, the school did not change its name. Arcesilaus is said to have admired Plato and to have owned his library (Diogenes Laertius, *Lives* IV.32; Philodemus, *Academicorum Index* XIX.14–16). This probably means that he intended to be faithful to Plato's writings. What we know about the way the school functioned shows that it followed the practices of its time. We have lists of disciples and precise indications about where the various masters taught. We know that Lacydes (late 3rd century) taught at the Academy, in the Lacydeus garden, and that Carneades, Carneades the Younger, and Cratetes of Tarsus taught in the gymnasium or in the exedra. What we know about the succession of scholarchs in the period is rather complicated and unclear; there were numerous schisms and regroupings. Such shifts occurred in particular around the time of a new scholarch's election, when it was customary for disgruntled members to leave the group (a practice begun by the Academicians in Speusippus's day).

In the Academy, the masters entrusted their favorite disciples with the task of pulling together their notes and ensuring the publication of their courses, as was done in the Peripatus. This was the origin of some malicious anecdotes of a type also attested in the medical schools: for example, Arcesilaus was accused of altering, inventing, or burning Crantor's courses. Pythodorus transcribed Arcesilaus's lessons; Zeno of Sidon and Diogenes of Tarsus transcribed those of Carneades. The latter's notes were reread in public (as was the case for those of Isocrates and Theophrastus), and we know that Carneades severely reproached Zeno for his editorial work, while he praised Diogenes for his.

At the time Athens was reconquered by Sulla, the current scholarch, Philon, left for Rome, where his teaching met with success. His disciple Antiochus of Ascalon left Athens for Alexandria during that period, then returned to Athens to teach at the Ptolemaion (a gymnasium with its own library). It is not clear whether he succeeded Philon or whether he started a new school called the Ancient Academy in reaction against the Skeptics' Academy; the sources are ambiguous (Philodemus, *Academicorum Index* XXXIV.33; Cicero, *Brutus* 307; Plutarch, *Lucullus* 42). In any case, Antiochus did have a school, and he was succeeded by his brother and disciple Ariston, Cicero's master and a friend of Brutus.

The school had been in a process of disintegration for some time. The abandonment of its initial site, the countless modifications of its doctrines, the quarrels over the appointment of scholarchs, and the establishment of autonomous schools were all factors in the Academy's gradual disappearance from view. Ariston's disciples Cratippus of Pergamum and Ariston of Alexandria became Peripatetics. The former taught Horace, Brutus, and Cicero's son, also named Cicero, who obtained Roman citizenship for his master, while a decree of the Areopagus urged Cratippus to remain in Athens to teach. In Philon's day, a certain Aenesidemus, who may have been a former Academician, criticized the philosophy taught in the Academy, charging that it was nothing but Stoicism in disguise; he gave renewed impetus to Skeptic philosophy.

Epicureanism and Stoicism seem to have survived longer. When St. Paul arrived in the Areopagus in Athens, around 52 C.E., he found only Stoic and Epicurean philosophers (Acts 18:18). Hermarchus and Polystratus were Epicurus's first successors, and in Cicero's day Zeno of Sidon and Phaedrus were scholarchs. Diogenes Laertius points out that, unlike the other schools, which had vanished, the Epicurean school had had an uninterrupted line of scholarchs up to his own day (*Lives* X.11). Two epigraphs by the emperor Hadrian make it clear that the school in fact still had its original site in Epicurus's garden, on the road leading to the Academy. Hadrian granted money for the construction of a gymnasium as well as funds to meet the philosophers' material needs; however, confronted with their pressing demands for subsidies, on several occasions he urged the Epicureans to return to the ideal of a modest life that their master had advocated. The imperial decree was to be preserved in the school, along with Epicurus's writings and works.

Compared with the intellectual atmosphere of the other schools, especially the Academy, with its complex doctrinal evolution, Epicurus's garden seems somewhat monotonous. Numenius of Apamea (2nd century C.E.) praised the school's unshakeable faithfulness to its master's thought. Not that there were no internal debates; however, to judge by notes written by Philodemus of Gadara, they focused chiefly on the interpretation and development of Epicurus's seminal ideas and those of his intimate friends. Some critics challenged the school's traditions and claimed to be referring directly back to Epicurus; such moves were characteristic of all schools in all periods. The importance of Epicurus's writings for the school's identity led his disciples to study the master's works philologically, as doctors studied Hippocrates' writings.

After Chrysippus, the importance of the Stoic school seems to have declined in Athens. We know the names of his successors, Zeno of Tarsus, Diogenes of Babylon, and Antipater of Tarsus, and we have a few fragments of their work. We know that Antipater went against tradition in his old age and taught in his own home rather than in the Stoa. Later, Panaetius took over the school, having first been *proexagein* (the term is unclear; it may designate someone who gave preparatory courses) under Antipater; a certain Paranomus played the same role under Panaetius. The latter appears to have gone back to teach at the main Stoa. In this school, too, theoretical innovations were presented as interpretations of Zeno's thought, but opposing arguments were probably quite common as well. Successors to Zeno continued to be named until the end of the 2nd century C.E. (*Inscriptiones atticae* II.1155). We find no references to property belonging to the school.

Alexandria was one of the greatest scientific centers of the Hellenistic period. The Ptolemaic sovereigns encouraged study and research, under the influence of the Aristotelians Theophrastus, Straton of Lampsacus, and Demetrius of Phaleron (Diogenes Laertius, *Lives* V.37, 58, 77). The influence of the Peripatetic philosophy was present in a general way, but conceptual links between Peripatetic philosophy and Alexandrian science are hard to find. The term *Peripatetic* was applied at that time to any educated person and to all biographers—even those with anti-Aristotelian leanings—who came from Alexandria (Hermippus, Satyrus, Sotion, and others). In contrast, Stoic philosophy had little influence on Alexandrian cultural life.

The great Library founded by the Ptolemaics contained more than four hundred thousand volumes, including the works of Plato and Aristotle. Galen tells us that the kings had ordered the confiscation of all books transported by ships docking in Alexandria; the books were to be returned only after they had been copied (*Galeni in Hippocratis epidemiarum librum iii commentaria iii*, p. 606). The Museum was located next to the royal palace. Like the Athenian schools, it included a *peripatos*, an amphitheater, and a great room for banquets attended by all its members. It was common property, and someone named by the king was in charge of maintaining a cult to the Muses (Strabo, XVII.I.8). Members of the group were exempt from paying taxes (*Orientis Graeci Inscriptione Selectae* 714), and they were supported by revenues from the Museum's own property. Their activity was more philologic and scientific than philosophic; according to Philon of Byzantium, even technological research was encouraged.

This community of scholars kept strictly to itself, not mixing with local culture, despite the great tributes to the ancient wisdom of the Egyptians paid by Herodotus, Plato, and Aristotle. Alexandria always remained a Greek city situated outside the confines of Egypt proper.

The Ptolemaics welcomed various philosophers to their court, such as the Stoic Sphaerus, the Cyrenaics Theodorus and Hegesias, and the Epicurean Colotes, who dedicated his treatise *On the Point That It Is Not Possible Even to Live According to the Doctrines of Other Philosophers* to Philadelphus. But there were no real philosophic schools until the 1st century B.C.E., when the schools in Athens were destroyed by Sulla. Antiochus of Ascalon, as we have seen, spent some time in Alexandria, but the Platonics Eudorus, Ariston, Cratippus, and Aenesidemus also taught there regularly, along with a certain Potamon, the founder of eclecticism, who chose from each sect the maxims that he liked best. His school did not last very long (Diogenes Laertius, *Lives* I.21).

In this period, Alexandria was also a very important center for teaching medicine. The school of Herophilus, a disciple of Praxagoras of Cos, had prospered there for centuries. This was a private institution, probably located in Herophilus's own house. Alexandria's kings supported the school's practice of dissecting cadavers and of vivisection, contrary to Greek tradition. Herophilus in fact used criminals released from the royal prisons (von Staden, Testimonia 63a). He trained paying disciples in his own home, as was done in the Hippocratic school: his teaching included practical exercises and readings from the master's texts. Herophilus wrote his own manuals, which constituted the conceptual and practical basis for his school throughout its long and complex history.

After Herophilus, the school took particular philological interest in the works of Hippocrates, producing glossaries, commentaries (some written by order of the Ptolemaic kings), critical editions, doxographic works, and polemics against the other schools. The rival Empirical school, and later Galen, produced the same sorts of works. The Empirical school was founded in the 3rd century B.C.E. by Philinos of Cos; it challenged Herophilus's precepts. In the 1st century B.C.E., Herophilus's school gave rise to other schools, such as the one that was established in Laodicea, near the temple of the god Men Karou.

GREECE AND ROME FROM THE FIRST CENTURY B.C.E. TO THE THIRD CENTURY C.E.

Rome's attitude toward philosophy was at first reminiscent of that of Athens, but with more rigor. In the 2nd century B.C.E. a series of decrees led to the expulsion of the Greek philosophers from Rome, and the Roman world opened up only slowly to philosophy. The most famous episode has to do with three philosophers sent by Athens as ambassadors to the Roman Senate in 155 B.C.E.: the Academician Carneades, the Stoic Diogenes, and the Peripatetic Critolaus (no Epicureans among them). The three of them alarmed Cato to such an extent that he promptly had them expelled (Plutarch, *Lives*, "Cato," m22).

But the ruling classes began to protect philosophers. Panaetius stayed in the home of Scipio Aemilianus in Rome and accompanied him to the eastern Mediterranean (Cicero, *Academica* 2.ii.5). This first example typifies the situation of philosophers in Rome: generally speaking, noble Romans went to hear the Greek philosophers in their own homeland, or took them as spiritual counselors or teachers for their children. Many other examples can be cited: Tiberius Gracchus took the Stoic Blossius of Cumae as his adviser; Philodemus of Gadara lived in Calpurnius Piso's villa in Herculaneum. The noble Romans of the day, like noble 5th-century Athenians, often opened their homes to philosophers. In "On the Virtues and the Opposing Vices," Philodemus justified accepting benefits in exchange for teaching as the best way of life for a sage (XXIII.22–30). We have seen that Philon of Larissa went to Rome, and Lucullus turned his home into a "Greek foyer," even while showing a decided preference for Antiochus of Ascalon (Plutarch, *Lucullus* 42). The quality of life of a philosopher established in the home of a noble Roman depended on the latter's goodwill, and the philosopher's existence could easily become parasitic, as is evident from caricatures penned by Petronius, Lucian, and Aulus Gellius. Philosophers would flock to the doors of rich young citizens and wait all morning for the men (who had been up all night) to wake up and receive them.

There were no authentic philosophic schools in Rome. The greatest authors of the 1st century B.C.E. and the 1st century C.E., such as Cicero, Seneca, and

Musonius Rufus, were men involved in politics who devoted only their leisure hours to writing philosophical texts in Latin. Lucretius himself, about whom we know very little, belonged to the highest class. Certain authors, such as Brutus, Caesar's assassin, and the emperor Marcus Aurelius, continued to write in Greek.

The custom of having philosophers as friends and clients persisted under the empire; the Cynics and the Stoics were the first to develop such a practice. Augustus protected the philosopher and doxographer Arius Didymus, who was an invaluable imperial adviser. Thrasyllus, the editor of Plato's dialogues, lived uneasily in Tiberius's court (Tacitus, *Annals* VI.20–21). Philosophers continued to be expelled, for instance Epictetus under Domitian, at the end of the 1st century C.E.: Epictetus took refuge in Nicopolis, where he opened a school with full legal standing. His lessons were transcribed and published by his disciple Arrian.

During that period, schools of philosophy proliferated throughout the Greek world, especially in Athens, Alexandria, Tarsus, Aegae, and Pergamum; in the West there were schools only in city-states of Greek origin, such as Naples and Marseilles. The teaching of philosophy in schools remained a predominantly Greek affair, although among the Roman nobility there were philosophic circles like that of Quintus Sextius, often evoked by Seneca; Quintus Sextius gave up his political career to establish a brotherhood, a blend of Stoicism and Neopythagoreanism (Seneca, *Epistulae* 98.13; *Naturales quaestiones* VII.32.13).

The end of the Academy and of the Peripatetic school did not spell the end of the associated schools of thought. Independent masters surrounded by disciples, some of whom became masters in their turn, carried on the spirit of those communities. M. Annius Ammonius, Plutarch's master, is one example. Born in Egypt, then a resident and magistrate in Athens in the 1st century C.E., he lived on into Domitian's era, teaching Platonic philosophy. The renaissance of Platonic thought, connected with Middle Platonism, probably originated in groups of this sort.

As an example of the activity of one of these teachers, we can recall what Aulus Gellius said about Calvenus Taurus, his teacher of Platonic philosophy in Athens. Taurus taught in his own home, where his visitors included important people. His teaching was largely based on readings of the Platonic texts (Aulus Gellius, XVII.20); his disciples often took credit for deciding what to read (I.9.9–10). The more intimate disciples were invited to closed meetings, philosophical suppers where food was scarce but talk was plentiful. They discussed *problemata*, questions of physics and dialectics: for instance, "At what moment does a dying person die?" "What·does it mean to get up?" "Why does oil congeal easily, while wine does not?" (VII.13; XVII.8). We have an abundant literature concerning *problemata* of this type, passed on in the names of Aristotle, Alexander of Afrodisias, Plutarch, and others. The philosophy of this period is above all exegesis, and even the authors who protested vigorously against this tendency, such as Epictetus (*Diatribai* II.21.6e, 23, 27) were in the habit of constantly interpreting the texts of past authors in their own pedagogical practice.

The first to follow this path, as we have seen, were the Epicureans, but they were soon followed by the other schools. The purpose of the commentaries was the clarification and systematization of the masters' doctrines; this was particularly necessary in the case of Aristotle and Plato, but there are even hostile commentaries written against works by masters of the other schools. Even the history of the previous interpretations was taken into account in this period. Manuals and introductions to the founders' works began to be written, such as those Albinus and Alcinous produced about Plato.

Athens's prestige as the seat of the chief philosophic schools of the Hellenistic period and as the place of residence of private teachers associated with the various schools led Marcus Aurelius, in 176 C.E., to establish teaching chairs in Athens for all branches of knowledge, at the expense of the empire, as a gift to humanity as a whole. Chairs of Stoic, Platonic, Epicurean, and Peripatetic philosophy were created: positions were awarded for life, pay was very high, and candidates were selected by a vote of the best citizens (Lucian Eunuchus, V.3). The initial selection of philosophy professors was made by Herodes Atticus (Philostratus, *Lives of the Sophists* 2). The object was to teach the various types of philosophy to the young, who tended, as we have seen, to frequent the major philosophic schools in turn.

We know very little about these schools, although we have the names of some of the Peripatetic philosophers, such as Alexander of Damascus, who had met Galen in Rome and consulted with him before going to Athens. The most important name associated with these schools is that of Alexander of Aphrodisias, who alludes to being named master of philosophy by the emperor (*De fato* 1). He declares that he is head of Aristotelian philosophy by virtue of this charge, which gives him special preeminence; his first product was a polemical text against the Stoics. What characterized the "chair" was the cultural preeminence the master enjoyed among his disciples, and the polemical role the master played vis-à-vis other schools. The few minor works we have by Alexander include instructional texts; there may also be some texts by his disciples. We do not know how the school ended; the last mention of it indicates that Eubulus, a teacher of Platonism, had contacts with Plotinus.

There were chairs of philosophy in other cities as well: Galen completed his studies in the four schools in Pergamum, while Apollonius of Tyana did the same thing near Aegae. Both undertook their philosophical studies in their youth, at about age fourteen, and pursued them for only a few years.

In the Greco-Roman age, medical teaching continued as before to be conducted privately, in the school of a master. There were centers in which the teaching was carried out by many instructors, as in Ephesus, Pergamum, and Alexandria, but these were never official schools, nor did they specialize in the various branches of medicine. Teaching continued to involve both lessons and clinical practice. There were forms of common life, such as dining together (Galen, *De tremore, palpitatione, convusione et rigore* 7). The masters often compiled their lessons in written form, or else the disciples transcribed them. But there were some masters who limited themselves to oral teaching. The disciple who went off after the training period to practice medicine in a city often took with him a written compilation of his master's lessons. Sometimes the schools were possessive about the masters' writings and refused to show them to anyone outside the group.

Reading the Hippocratic texts was part of a doctor's education, and thus there were many written commentaries, corresponding to the oral commentary on the texts produced inside the school. We have a number of written commentaries by Galen: these are works with a practical aim, directed at disciples who already had acquired a basic knowledge of medicine. Galen sought to establish the authenticity of the Hippocratic texts, and the correct reading of difficult passages, in a conservative spirit; he shunned erudition and philology as ends in themselves (he referred to them as "Sophistics"), and for this reason he did not concern himself with the history of interpretations of the text. In this respect the medical commentaries differ from those produced in the philosophical schools, though they are otherwise very similar.

THE NEOPLATONIC ERA

In the middle of the 3rd century, Plotinus carried on and renewed the tradition of the philosophical schools. According to Porphyry *(Life of Plotinus)*, the master lived in a patrician residence, where he founded a genuine school made up of a somewhat complex group, including faithful disciples and less diligent dignitaries. One of the latter, Amelius, seems to have collaborated with his master in teaching; he was assigned to write a commentary on *Timaeus* (Proclus, *In Platonis Timaeum commentaria* II.300.25), polemical texts against rival schools, and refutations of the objections of unpersuaded disciples. Plotinus also tutored quite young disciples, aiming to turn them into accomplished philosophers. His teaching was based on exegeses of the texts of Plato and Aristotle, which were read and discussed during meetings of the school, along with the principal commentaries. Plotinus encouraged his disciples to raise objections, but one can detect the beginnings of a certain intolerance toward the dialogic method.

In his teaching, Plotinus treated his pupils with cordiality. On four occasions during his lifetime he experienced a mystical union with divinity. His books were written in a single draft, without even being recopied, as if they were already present in his mind. Polemics against the other schools were generally left to his disciples, though Plotinus himself wrote refutations. His group gave banquets and lectures to celebrate the birthdays of Socrates and Plato.

Plotinus's school was the only true philosophic school that Rome ever knew. Other philosophers established quite similar schools elsewhere, such as the school of Aedesius at Pergamum (Eunapius, *Vitae sophistarum* VII.1–2). Except for these schools, Neoplatonic philosophy was concentrated in Athens and Alexandria.

The school that Plato had founded in Athens did not survive past the 1st century B.C.E. However, its prestige lasted for centuries, and in the 4th century C.E. it was reestablished as an institution. Athens remained an extremely important center of literary and philosophical studies in this period, and virtually all of its cultural life remained in the hands of pagans; Christian students made up only a small though combative minority (Gregory of Nazianzus, *Orationes* XLIII.14–24). This was the climate in which Plutarch of Athens, descendant of an aristocratic family connected with the Mystery tradition, undertook to reestablish Plato's school in his own home, located south of the Acropolis in an affluent residential neighborhood. As in Alexandria, Neoplatonic philosophy was the privilege of the well-to-do. Damascius's *Life of Isodorus* provides many details.

Plutarch once again gave rise to a foundation, a quite wealthy institution that grew over time, thanks to numerous bequests: in Proclus's time, its income amounted to 1,000 *nomismata* per year. The foundation, like those of the 4th century B.C.E., sought to ensure financial independence for philosophers. In an outburst of enthusiastic archaism, Damascius declared that Plato's garden was still part of the school's property; according to him, this property had been maintained without interruption for ten centuries. While this is not credible, it may be that the Platonists had acquired a garden that was, or was thought to be, on the grounds where Plato had taught.

The school's goal was to read Plato's dialogues, comment on them, and spread Platonism among its disciples. The master played the role of guide in reading and studying. His best disciples lived with him and were treated as his sons, according to ancient custom. The characteristic vocabulary of the schools reappeared: disciples *(mathetai)*, meetings *(sunousia)*. There may have been a second, subordinate master, as Amelius was for Plotinus, but we cannot be certain. Teaching was provided strictly in the form of lectures, and Plutarch of Athens rarely allowed a student to ask questions and interrupt his explanations. Still, a certain tradition of discussion and dissension persisted within the school, such as the disagreement that pitted Domninos against Proclos. A mystical, theurgic tendency linked to the mystery cults paralleled the philosophic teaching and sometimes overtook it; this was the case for Aegae, in contrast to Damascius. Owing to its real estate holdings, the school was able to subsist until the beginning of the 6th century, whereas the schools founded by Plotinus in Rome, Iamblichus in Syria (early 4th century), and Aedesius in Pergamum did not outlive their founders. We have a fairly reliable list of the successive heads of Plutarch's school up to Damascius.

The rebirth of the Athens school came about in a hostile environment, at a time when Christianity was showing its most sectarian face. Philosophers had to stay indoors or find a deserted place to sacrifice to their gods (Marinus, *Life of Proclus* 11.e.29). Proclus could still cherish the illusion that the domination of Christianity and the persecution of pagans would come to an end, but Damascius appears more pessimistic, despite all his efforts to strengthen the Athenian school, and Simplicius speaks of the complete destruction of culture and philosophy. Damascius's intransigent anti-Christian stance led to the prohibition of his teaching.

In 529 a decree of the emperor Justinian banned, among other things, the teaching of philosophy (Malagas, *Chronographia* XVIII). The closing of the school was definitive: Plato was no longer taught in Athens. A few years later, we are told (Agathias, *Histories* II.28–32), several philosophers, including Damascius and Simplicius, decided to emigrate to Persia, to the court of Chosroes (king of Armenia) or to the city-state of Carrhae. The following year, a treaty between the two empires allowed the philosophers to return to their homeland and live there in peace; we do not know if they had permission to teach. Philosophers must have been viewed as important figures if they were singled out for special attention in a treatise between two great emperors of the time. Damascius may not have returned to Athens, however; he seems to have died in Syria. As for Simplicius, the author of important commentaries on Aristotelian physics, we know relatively little. He participated in the expedition to Persia, and after the 532 treatise was able to devote himself to writing commentaries, as a private citizen, either in Athens or in Carrhae. After his death, there is no further evidence of pagan philosophers in Athens.

In Alexandria, a long line of professors taught Platonic philosophy, for example Ammonius Saccas (who was Plotinus's master), Origen, and many others. Philosophy teachers in Alexandria are thought to have been paid on occasion from the public treasure, though the evidence for this is scanty and uncertain; they may simply have been paid by their own disciples. A certain Anatolius, senator and philosopher, is said to have been chosen by his fellow citizens to reestablish the school in Athens. A Christian who later became bishop of Laodicea, he may have been Iamblichus's teacher. In the 3rd century, relations between the pagan and Christian communities were somewhat tense, since philosophic teaching remained the privilege of the pagans and the upper classes, while the Christianized masses looked on the practice of philosophy with suspicion. These relations grew worse in the following century. The mathematician and philosopher Hypatia, a disciple of Plotinus at a century's remove, conducted her teaching in public; she fell victim to the hostility of a violent Christian crowd, stirred up by the patriarch Cyril, and was massacred in front of the door to her house. Supported by imperial power, the Christians made the pagans' lives increasingly difficult; physical conflicts between the two groups were not uncommon (Damascius, *Life of Isodorus* pp. 77.1–17; 255. 2–3; Zacharias Scholasticus, *Life of Severus* p. 23.26).

The last pagan philosopher of the Alexandrian school was Olympiodorus, who defended pagan doctrines quite courageously. After him, there were only Christian masters in Alexandria, foremost among them Philoponus, who defined himself as a grammarian *(grammatikos)* rather than as a philosopher. In addition to publishing treatises by Ammonius (435–526), adapting them as he saw fit, Philoponus wrote a polemical treatise against the pagans, *Against Proclus on the Eternity of the World,* in the same year that the Athens school was closed. Elias, apparently a disciple of Olympiodorus, and David were also Christians. So was Stephanus, who was named professor of philosophy at the imperial court of Byzantium after Heraclius acceded to the throne. Stephanus appears to have been the last of the Neoplatonic Alexandrian philosophers.

Carlo Natali
Translated by Catherine Porter and Jeannine Pucci

Bibliography

Texts and Translations

Antigonus of Carystus. *Fragments.* Ed. and trans. Tiziano Dorandi. Paris: Les Belles Lettres, 1999.

Diogenes Laertius. *Lives of Eminent Philosophers.* Trans. R. D. Hicks. 2 vols. Loeb Classical Library.

Galeni in Hippocratis epidemiarum. Ed. G. C. Kühn. Leipzig: B. G. Teubner, 1821–1833.

Hadrian. In Simone Follet, "Lettres d'Hadrien aux Epicuriens d'Athènes." *Revue des études grecques* 107 (1994): 158–171.

Inscriptiones atticae aetatis quae est inter Euclidis annum et Augusti tempora. Ed. U. Koehler. 5 vols. Berlin: G. Reimer, 1877–1895.

Philodemus. *Agli amici di scuola* (PHerc. 1005). Ed. and trans. A. Angeli. Naples: Bibliopolis, 1988.

———. *Storia dei filosofi: Platone e l'Academia* (PHerc. 1021 and 164). Ed. and trans. Tiziano Dorandi. Naples: Bibliopolis, 1991. (See also the selections in Konrad Gaiser, *Philodems academica.*)

———. *Storia dei filosofi: La Stoa da Zenone a Panezio* (PHerc. 1018). Ed. Tiziano Dorandi. Leiden and New York: E. J. Brill, 1994.

Plato. *Epistles.* In *Timaeus; Critias; Cleitophon; Menexenus; Epistles.* Trans. R. G. Bury. Loeb Classical Library.

Porphyry. *Plotinus.* Trans. A. H. Armstrong. Loeb Classical Library.

Studies

Burkert, Walter. *Weisheit und Wissenschaft: Studien zu Pythagoras, Philolaos und Platon*. Nuremberg: H. Carl, 1962.

Cambiano, Giuseppe. *La filosofia in Grecia e a Roma*. Rome and Bari: Laterza, 1983.

Clay, Diskin. "Individual and Community in the First Generation of the Epicurean School." In *Syzetesis: Studi sull' epicureismo greco e romano offerti a Marcello Gigante*. 2 vols. Naples: G. Macchiaroli, 1983. Pp. 255–279.

De Witt, Norman Wentworth. "Organization and Procedure in Epicurean Groups." *Classical Philology* 31 (1936): 205–211.

Donini, P. L. *Le Scuole, l'anima, l'impero: La filosofia antica da Antioco a Plotino*. Turin: Rosenberg and Sellier, 1982.

Evrard, Etienne. "A quel titre Hypatie enseigna-t-elle la philosophie?" *Revue des études grecques* 90 (1977): 69–74.

Fowden, Garth. "The Platonist Philosopher and His Circle in Late Antiquity." *Philosophia* (Athens) 7 (1977): 359–383.

Fraser, Peter Marshall. *Ptolemaic Alexandria*. Oxford: Clarendon Press, 1972.

Gaiser, Konrad. *Philodems Academica: Die Berichte über Platon und die alte Akademie in zwei herkulanensischen Papyri*. Stuttgart-Bad Canstatt: Fromman-Holzboog, 1988.

Garbarino, Giovanna, ed. *Roma e la filosofia greca dalle origini alla fine del II secolo a.C.: Raccolta di testi con introduzione e commento*. Turin: G. B. Paravia, 1973.

Glucker, John. *Antiochus and the Late Academy*. Göttingen: Vandenhoeck and Ruprecht, 1978.

Goulet, Richard, ed. *Dictionnaire des philosophes anciens*. Vols. I–II (A–D). Paris: CNRS, 1989–1994.

Griffin, Miriam T., and Jonathan Barnes, eds. *Philosophia togata: Essays on Philosophy and Roman Society*. Oxford: Clarendon Press; New York: Oxford University Press, 1989.

Haase, Wolfgang, and I. Temporini. *Aufstieg und Niedergang der Römischen Welt*. Vol. 36 ("Philosophie"), vol. 37 ("Wissenschaft"). Berlin and New York: Walter de Gruyter, 1987–1994.

Hadot, Ilsetraut. *Le problème du néoplatonisme alexandrin: Hiéroclès et Simplicius*. Paris: Institut d'études augustiniennes, 1978.

Hadot, Pierre. *Qu'est-ce que la philosophie antique?* Paris: Gallimard, 1995.

Jouanna, Jacques. *Hippocrates*. Baltimore: Johns Hopkins University Press, 1998.

Lynch, John Patrick. *Aristotle's School: A Study of a Greek Educational Institution*. Berkeley: University of California Press, 1972.

Marrou, Henri-Irenée. *A History of Education in Antiquity*. Trans. George Lamb. New York: Sheed and Ward, 1956; New American Library, 1964.

Meyer, Ben F., and E. P. Sanders, eds. *Jewish and Christian Self-Definition*. Vol. 3: *Self-Definition in the Graeco-Roman World*. London: SCM Press, 1982; Philadelphia: Fortress Press, 1983.

Müller, Reimar. *Die Epikureische Gesellschaftstheorie*. Berlin: Akademie-Verlag, 1972.

Natali, Carlo. *Bios theoretikos: La vita di Aristotele e l'organizzazione della sua scuola*. Bologna: Il Mulino, 1991.

Staden, Heinrich von. *Herophilus: The Art of Medicine in Early Alexandria.* Cambridge and New York: Cambridge University Press, 1989.

Taormina, Daniela Patrizia. *Plutarco di Atene: L'uno, l'anima, le forme.* Rome: University of Catania, 1988.

Trabattoni, Franco. "Per una biografia di Damascio." *Rivista di Storia della Filosofia* 40 (1985): 170–201.

Related Articles

Medicine; Ptolemy; Aristotelianism; Milesians; Pythagoras and Pythagoreanism; Epicurus; The Academy; Cynicism; Platonism; Stoicism

OBSERVATION AND
RESEARCH

To what extent did ancient Greek philosophers and scientists engage in systematic empirical research? How far, in particular, did they attempt controlled experimentation? In what circumstances, and for what reasons, did they undertake programs of detailed observation? At what point, and again for what reasons, were the value and importance of such programs explicitly recognized in self-conscious methodologies?

To begin to answer these questions we need, first, to make certain conceptual distinctions. First, we should distinguish between observation and deliberate research, although the one no doubt shades into the other. It is not our task here to attempt to analyze everything that any Greek philosopher or scientist can be said to have observed, in the sense of carefully perceived. Rather, what we are concerned with is the practice of observation: it is deliberate and systematic observation that entitles us to use the term *research*.

The behavior of animals, the habitats of plants, and the configurations of constellations have always been possible subjects of interest, and in the first two cases, especially, the ethnographic literature demonstrates that many modern societies, including many without any advanced technology whatsoever, possess detailed and often quite recondite knowledge, acquired through careful observation. We should guard against two assumptions here: first, that such observations are always carried out with practical interests mainly, if not solely, in mind, and second, that the knowledge, once acquired, is never subject to revision. Of course the uses of plants as foods and medicines are of interest to every society. Often, however, their symbolic associations, values, and significance are an added focus of attention. The stars may be studied to help determine the seasons or the weather, but their groupings may also carry powerful symbolic associations. Again, although the stock of knowledge may be represented as stable, that may be misleading. What is known or believed about plants or animals may, in the process of transmission from one generation to the next, be subject to modification. How far any such modification is recognized *as such* will vary. But just as an understanding of the uses of plants as medicines is slowly built up from observation and experiment in the loose sense of trial-and-error procedures, so continued experience may serve as a source of critical reflection on even well-entrenched beliefs.

Similar factors are at work in early scientific research, but the extra factors that scientific research involves are that the scientist is engaged in the acquisition of systematic understanding and in the resolution of theoretical issues. These issues may take the form of specific problems, such as whether the earth is flat or round, whether plants exhibit gender difference, whether the seat of cognitive activity is the brain, the heart, or some other organ. However, some detailed scientific programs of research do not serve to resolve clearly formulated problems but present themselves as more purely descriptive in aim. They may, for example, be directed to establishing a classification. Yet even when the research is said to be carried out with a view merely to establishing the data, theory enters in, in determining what counts as the significant data. Every classification presupposes a conceptual framework of some kind. Clearly in some actual classifications, symbolic considerations or practical human interests may be the dominant factor.

Aristotle correctly points to a distinction between the observations carried out by fishermen in the course of their work and those that are undertaken specifically for the purposes of establishing data about fish. That is a valid distinction between possible motives in the conduct of observation. However, when Aristotle proclaims his own interest to be in the investigation of animals for its own sake, he too has, of course, *theoretical* concerns, for instance in determining the genera and species of fish. Moreover, we should recognize that the quality of the observations conducted is not determined solely by the expressed intentions of the observer. The fishermen whom Aristotle consulted sometimes appear to have known more than he did about the facts of the matter—about the actual behavior of fish—although their observations were not undertaken for the purposes of scientific research.

The distinction between observation and theory is a relative, not an absolute one. No observation, no research, is undertaken *without* some theoretical interest, without some theoretical framework, and the interaction between theory and observation will be of particular concern to us in this study. The theoretical framework often provides the key both to the domains of phenomena explored and to the way in which they were investigated, and this in two distinct ways. First, there is the question just mentioned, of the motivations of research: how far is there a clear intention to investigate the phenomena for the purposes of understanding? But then second, and more specifically, theoretical frameworks will be crucially relevant to the way in which the problems addressed are formulated. As we shall see time and again, in Greek science a program of research is directed to the resolution of quite specific problems. Part of our task here, then, will be to identify those problems, to consider why they were the specific focus of attention, and to explore the ways in which the conduct of observations was affected by the particular theoretical issues being investigated.

These references to the theoretical framework of observation lead me to my final preliminary conceptual point, namely the distinction between the *practice* of observation and research, and the *explicit recognition* of their importance. It is one thing for a scientist or philosopher to engage in detailed investigations of animals, plants, minerals, stars, musical concords, or diseases. It is another to have an explicit methodology that allots a determinate role to empirical data in scientific study. A further part of our task will be to consider at what point, and for what reasons, Greek philosophers and scientists developed such methodologies. In other words, when was the importance of observation and research self-consciously recognized?

I have spoken so far of Greek philosophers and scientists in general terms. I am concerned, here, not just with whose primary interests lay in metaphysics, let alone in moral philosophy, but also with those who engaged in any of the different domains of what the Greeks called *phusikē*, the study of nature. This includes, at one end of the spectrum, what we should call the exact sciences, notably astronomy, acoustics or harmonics, and optics. These are called the "more physical of the mathematical studies" by Aristotle in *Physics*, 194a7ff. At the other end of the spectrum we must also include not just what we call the life sciences (biology, botany, and so on) but also medicine. Naturally, we must pay due attention to the fact that the primary concerns of different types of investigators—doctors, astronomers, writers on music, philosophers, and so on—differ in important ways. Nevertheless all have a contribution to make in answering the principal questions we have posed.

Special difficulties are presented by the unevenness of the source material. We have comparatively rich sources for medicine in the 5th and 4th centuries B.C.E. Aristotle, Galen, and Ptolemy are represented by considerable bodies of extant work. However, our sources for the early Pythagoreans, for the 5th-century atomists, and for some of the major Hellenistic biologists are very thin, and we have to depend on the often tendentious reports and interpretations of other writers. We have to make the best use of the evidence we have but acknowledge the tentative nature of our conclusions, given the biases and lacunae in our sources.

In what must be a highly selective survey, I shall divide the discussion into three main sections on broadly chronological lines: the evidence for observation and research in the period before Aristotle, the theory and the practice of observation and research by Aristotle himself, and the role of observation and research in philosophy and science in the post-Aristotelian period.

PRESOCRATIC NATURAL PHILOSOPHERS

At first sight it might appear that there is little positive, but a good deal that is negative, to say about either the theory or the practice of observation and research, so far as the Presocratic natural philosophers are concerned. The first point would relate to their practice. Neither in their general cosmological theories nor in their reported specific explanations of detailed natural phenomena does much attention seem to be paid to the collection and evaluation of empirical data. Second, in certain prominent epistemological doctrines, reason is privileged, and perception downgraded, in such a way that one might speak not just of an indifference to empirical research but of an attitude of positive hostility toward it.

Both points are certainly valid to some extent. However, both stand in need of qualification. First, so far as epistemological theory goes, it is true that in the tradition represented by the Eleatic philosophers, Parmenides, Zeno, and Melissus, the evidence of the senses is condemned as misleading. Parmenides warns, in frg. 7, against being deceived by the senses and ordinary belief: "Do not let habit, born of experience, force you to let wander your heedless eye and echoing ear or tongue along this road" (that is, the Way of Seeming). Again Melissus, in his frg. 8, develops a reductio argument that starts from the common assumption that the evidence of sight and hearing is acceptable, but ends with their rejection. They tell us that things change, whereas it is clear, Melissus believes, that change is impossible. This is on the usual Eleatic grounds, that nothing can come to be from what is not.

These anti-empirical views are echoed, though in modified form, by several later philosophers, and the downgrading of perception was to be a well-developed theme, with many variations, in Plato. However, there is another side to the picture. Several of the Presocratic philosophers produce dicta that show that they explicitly set at least some store by what we may call research. Thus Xenophanes at one point insisted that "the gods have not revealed all things to men from the beginning: but by seeking men find out better in time" (frg. 18). Both Empedocles and Anaxagoras are critical of the deliveries of perception, but accord them a role nevertheless. Anaxagoras is reported to have said that "through the weakness [of the senses] we are unable to judge the truth" (frg. 21). Yet in a further famous dictum (frg. 21a) he advocated using the "things that appear" as a "vision" of things that are obscure. We are told that that principle was approved by Democritus, who elsewhere (frg. 125) insisted that the mind derives its data from the senses, even if he also categorized the senses as yielding only "bastard" knowledge by contrast to the "legitimate" knowledge we have of such principles as atoms and the void (frg. 11).

But what may we say about the actual performance of the early natural philosophers in observation and research? Their general cosmological doctrines are usually based on certain recurrent models or analogies, representing the cosmos as a whole as a political state, as a living creature, or as an artifact. Neither those doctrines nor the overall theories concerning the basic constituents of physical objects that go with them make much use of direct empirical observation. In the case of Presocratic element theories, the same familiar examples are cited over and over again—interpreted differently according to the theory concerned. These same "data" were indeed treated as evidence *for* those theories, despite the fact that it must have been well known to the theorists who cited the data that their interpretation was contested.

Thus it was commonly supposed that air changes to cloud, then to water, then to earth and indeed to stones. This sequence is referred to in connection with the theories of both Anaximenes and Anaxagoras, and it even reappears in Melissus's refutation of change. Yet Anaximenes interpreted the sequence in terms of his principles of rarefaction and condensation: each of the changes is an instance of condensation, while air also "rarefies" to become fire. However, Anaxagoras cited the same "data" in connection with his theory that "in everything there is a portion of everything." His view of the changes would be that air already contains cloud, water, earth, stones, and indeed every other kind of thing, and that all that happens in change is that the proportion of the different kinds of things change in the objects we see. Even Melissus, when he argues from the position of his opponents in order to refute their ideas about change, puts it that "earth and stones seem to come to be from water."

This example indicates that the criteria by which Presocratic physical theories were judged relate to their simplicity or economy or to the force of the abstract arguments used to justify them, rather than to the richness of the empirical data they encompassed. In the main, the Presocratic philosophers made few attempts to *extend* the data available to them by empirical research; nor did they, as a general rule, try to *decide between* rival interpretations of the same known or assumed data by experiment.

There are, however, exceptions to what remains the general rule. Thus Xenophanes (one of the philosophers cited above whose epistemological doctrines incorporate a recommendation to engage in research) is one such exception. According to an admittedly late source, Hippolytus, Xenophanes cited the evidence of what we should call fossils to support his view that the relations between land and sea are subject to fluctuation and that what is now dry land was once covered by sea. Not only are shells found inland and on mountains, but also the impressions of certain living organisms turn up in the quarries of Syracuse, on Paros, and on Malta. Whether or not Xenophanes himself engaged in his own research in this connection, he was evidently at some pains to marshal what are no mere common-or-garden observations in support of his theory.

But the best example of more sustained empirical research in pre-Platonic philosophy relates to certain investigations in the field of harmonics attributable to some of the Pythagoreans. Admittedly the stories that purport to record Pythagoras's own experiments, leading to the discovery of the intervals corresponding to the concords of octave, fifth, and fourth, are late fabrications. Indeed many of the stories relate to tests that would not, in fact, have yielded the results claimed. However, the tradition of empirical investigation of the musical harmonies certainly antedates Plato, since in *The Republic* he criticizes this approach to the problems. At *Republic* 530d Socrates first agrees with the view, which he ascribes to the Pythagoreans, that harmonics and astronomy are "sister sciences." But he then goes on to criticize as "useless labor" the attempt to measure audible sounds and concords against one another. Evidently others besides the Pythagoreans are involved. But he objects to the Pythagoreans too, for "looking for numbers in [the] heard harmonies, and not ascending to problems." For Plato himself, the chief aim of the proper study of harmonics that he has in mind in *The Republic* is to train the young potential philosopher-kings in abstract thought: for that purpose empirical research is otiose, even a distraction. The Pythagoreans themselves, however, on this testimony, appear to have engaged in some detailed investigations of an empirical nature in connection with their examination of the underlying relationships of musical scales and harmonies.

Here, then, we have evidence of a more deliberate program involving observation and research. But we must be clear that the reasons for undertaking it are quite distinctive. We hear from a variety of sources, Aristotle especially, that the Pythagoreans maintained that "all things are numbers," though the interpretation of that dictim is far from clear and indeed disputed. Aristotle represents some of them, at least, as committed to the belief that numbers *constitute* things: they are (as Aristotle would have put it) the matter of which other things are composed. It may, however, be more likely that the Pythagoreans, or most of them, were committed only to the much weaker doctrine that the underlying relationships of things are *expressible numerically:* on that view the concord of an octave is expressible by the ratio 1 : 2, but not constituted by that ratio as its matter. However, whichever interpretation of the dictum itself is to be adopted, it is clear that the doctrine that "all things are numbers" provided the chief stimulus to investigate the musical scales and harmonies. The aim of those investigations was undoubtedly to illustrate and support that general doctrine. So we may be clear that the first sustained empirical research in Greek philosophy had distinct theoretical aims.

The term often used for natural philosophy in early Greek texts is *peri phuseōs historia,* the inquiry concerning nature, but the kind of *historia* involved often relied heavily on abstract argument. That term, *historia,* itself was, however, often used in other contexts where research is the key characteristic of the inquiry. Two fields, especially, exemplify this in the period before Plato, namely the domain *we* call history, and medicine. Clearly the writings of Herodotus and Thucydides in each case represent the results of a very considerable effort of research. Whether the subject is past events, as in Herodotus, or contemporary ones, as in Thucydides, different accounts had to be collected and evaluated. Herodotus often intrudes in his text in the first person singular, reporting the results of his own personal observations or recording his personal opinion as to the veracity or verisimilitude of the stories he relates (although he does not always state the *basis* on which he formed his judgments). Thucydides, in turn, constantly exercises his critical skills in the assessment of the evidence both of human witnesses and of material remains, drawing, from time to time, on what we should describe as archaeological data in his reconstruction of the period leading up to the Peloponnesian War.

But while the practice of research in the domain of history provides an important part of the intellectual background of philosophy and science, it is the second field, medicine, that is more directly relevant to the development of positive attitudes toward empirical research in science. There can be no doubt that a prominent tradition in clinical medicine, as exemplified in some of the Hippocratic treatises from the 5th and 4th centuries B.C.E., both stressed the need, in principle, for careful observation and put that principle into practice. This is true, in particular, in the context of the assessment of individual case histories, though the chief preoccupation of Greek doctors was not so much diagnosis as prognosis, the foretelling of the outcome of the disease. We have, however, to investigate the contexts and motives for the efforts at observation and research we find, and assess their strengths and limitations.

We may begin with the evidence for an explicit recognition of the need for careful observation in relation to individual clinical cases. A chapter of the first book of *Epidemics* sets out an impressive list of the points to be attended to (chap. 10, Littré): "Then we must consider the patient, what food is given and who gives it . . . the conditions of climate and locality both in general and in particular, the patient's customs, mode of life, pursuits and age. Then we must consider his speech, mannerisms, silence, thoughts, habits of sleep and wakefulness, and dreams, their nature and time. Next we must note whether he plucks his hair, scratches or weeps. We must observe his paroxysms, stools, urine, sputum and vomit . . . Observe, too, sweating, shivering, chill, cough, sneezing, hiccough, the kind of breathing, belching, wind whether silent or noisy, haemorrhages and haemorrhoids. We must determine the significance of all these signs."

More famously still, the opening chapter of the treatise on *Prognostic* describes what to look for in examining a patient's face (the Hippocratic facies). The doctor should observe the color and texture of the skin, and especially the eyes, where he should study whether "they avoid the flare of light and weep involuntarily," whether "the whites are livid," whether the eyes "wander, or project, or are deeply sunken," and so on. Moreover this treatise not only tells the doctor what to look out for, but sets out some of the inferences to be drawn from particular signs. Thus this on urine (chap. 12): "Urine is best when there is a white, smooth, even deposit in it the whole time up to the crisis of the disease . . . Sediment like barley-meal in the urine is bad . . . Thin white sediment is a very bad sign, and it is even worse if it resembles bran . . . So long as the urine is thin and yellowish-red, the disease is not ripened . . . When a patient continues to pass thin raw urine for a long time and the other signs indicate recovery, the formation of an abscess should be expected in the parts below the diaphragm. When grease forms patterns like cobwebs on the surface of the urine, this constitutes a warning, for it is a sign of wasting."

Such accounts as these about how to conduct a clinical examination display a remarkable appreciation of the variety of points to be considered, and an acute sense of the need for thoroughness and attention to detail. Moreover the principles they set out were not just idealized recommendations, but were—sometimes at least—closely followed in practice. Several books of *Epidemics,* notably the first and the third, contain detailed reports of individual case histories, recording the progress of a particular patient's disease, generally day by day, over quite long periods. In some cases there are occasional observations up to the 120th day from the onset of the disease. The entries under each day vary from a single remark to an elaborate description running to some nine or ten lines. Thus in case three of the first series set out in *Epidemics* III we find this entry for the fourth day: "Fourth day; vomited small quantities of yellow bilious matter and, after a while, a small quantity of rust-coloured material. There was a small haemorrhage of pure blood from the left side of the nose: stools and urine as before: sweating about the head and shoulders; spleen enlarged; pain in the region of the thigh; a rather flabby distension of the right hypochondrium: did not sleep at night; slight delirium." In this case observations continue daily until the twenty-first day and further occasional entries are made up to the fortieth, when—exceptionally—this patient reached a crisis and recovered. I say exceptionally, for it is one of the striking features of the case histories in *Epidemics* that their authors had no compunction in setting down the details of the diseases of patients whom they failed to save. In books one and three, indeed, the majority of those recorded end in death.

Evidently the authors of these case histories successfully practice the principles recommended in the theoretical texts we considered earlier. The observations of the progress of individual cases are certainly carried out with great care and thoroughness. The reports contain few explicitly interpretative comments, and no overall theory of disease is presented. The terms used in the descriptions are, to be sure, to a greater or lesser degree "theory laden": although these treatises do not propose, nor even presuppose, any schematic doctrine of humors, references are nevertheless made, on occasion, to the "bilious" or "phlegmatic" material in the patients' discharges.

The principal aim of these case histories is clearly to provide as exact a record as possible of the cases investigated. But we can and should be more precise than this about the writers' aims. In particular we may remark that they have a distinct motive for carrying out and recording their observations *daily*—over and above a laudable desire to be thorough—in that they adhere to the common Greek medical doctrine that the courses of acute diseases are determined by what were called "critical days." These were the days on which marked changes took place in the patient's condition—whether for better or worse. Establishing the periodicity of the disease was crucial for diagnosing it, as the terminology of "quartan," "tertian," "semitertian," and so on indicates.

Moreover, particular attention is sometimes paid, in the case histories, to whether pains or exacerbations occurred on the *odd* or the *even* days from the onset of the complaint. Elsewhere in *Epidemics* (for example, I.12, Littré) we find detailed tables setting out the supposed critical periods for diseases that had crises on even days, and for those on odd days. In the Pythagorean Table of Opposites, reported by Aristotle in *Metaphysics* (986a22ff), odd is correlated with right, male, and good, and even with left, female, and evil. So the expectation that exacerbations may occur on even days may be said to correspond to Pythagorean assumptions. However, it is not necessary to see the medical writers represented in *Epidemics* as themselves all Pythagoreans, nor do they straightforwardly endorse a correlation between even days and evil. We have to bear in mind that the fundamental distinction between odd and even is common to all Greek arithmetic. Moreover, as noted, even days are sometimes associated with crisis and recovery, not with exacerbation and death. It is rather the case that the classification of numbers into odd and even provides part of the general background to the investigation of periodicities in the medical case histories: the doctors believed that they *might* be significant and they accordingly paid them particular attention in recording the changes to their patients' conditions.

The doctrine of critical days, and an interest in determining the periodicities of diseases, form the general theoretical framework guiding these detailed observations. Some of the conclusions presented in these treatises take the form of sweeping generalizations, as for instance when general theories of critical periods are put forward. But many of the conclusions stated are explicitly qualified. The writers state what happened "for the most part" or "in the majority of cases," and exceptions are often noted. It is not the case that these writers conducted their observations merely to confirm general rules that they had already formulated in detail. Rather, those detailed rules are, in the main, generalizations arrived at on the basis of their particular observations, including, no doubt, many others besides those recorded in the case histories as we have them.

The undertaking and recording of careful observations in the context of clinical medicine provide our best early examples of sustained observation and research. But as we have seen, there are particular reasons for this, for the observations were, in part, stimulated by the theory of critical days. Elsewhere the performance of the writers represented in the extant Hippocratic treatises presents a different picture. The medical writers were evidently often just as speculative as the natural philosophers. As in Presocratic philosophy, so too in many Hippocratic works, theories of the constituent elements of the human body or of material objects in general are proposed with little direct empirical support. The physiological processes inside the body are inferred on the basis of what are assumed to be analogous processes outside it. The anatomical structure of the body, similarly, was rarely investigated directly. Although very occasional references are to be found in 5th- and early 4th-century medical texts to the practice of animal dissection, that technique was not systematically deployed before Aristotle. Anatomical structures were inferred from external observation of the body, from what became visible during wounds or lesions, from what was known of animal bodies from sacrifices and butchery, or from analogues with non-living objects. None of this detracts from the claims that may be made for the ability of many Greek doctors as observers, but we must recognize that there were considerable variations in the extent to which those skills were exhibited in different contexts.

ARISTOTLE

Before Aristotle we have seen that the evidence for the practice of empirical observation and research is limited to particular fields and to particular theoretical concerns. It is Aristotle who provides the first general methodology that secures a distinct and important role for the collection and evaluation of what he calls the *phainomena*—though, as we shall see, his use of that term cannot be held to correspond to what we would describe as empirical phenomena. Aristotle's methodological principles were worked out, in part, in opposition to the views of Plato, and it will be convenient for us to begin this section by examining the similarities and differences between these two major philosophers.

Aristotle agrees with Plato that the particular, qua particular, is not a proper object of scientific knowledge or understanding. Proper understanding relates to universal truths. However, where Plato often represents particulars as merely imitating forms, or participating in them, Aristotle's ontology proposes a very different account of the relationship between forms and particulars. In the doctrine he sets out in *Categories*, primary substances, such as this or that individual human being, are what basically exists. Qualities, quantities, and so on depend, for their existence, on there being substances that exhibit the qualities and quantities in question. But the primary substances of *Categories* are analyzed, in *Physics* and elsewhere, in terms of a combination of form and matter. An individual human being is a *sunholon*, a composite whole, consisting of form and matter. But form and matter are not the components in the sense of constituents of the composite whole. Rather they are better described as aspects of the individual substance. We may ask, concerning an individual substance, what it is made of—its material cause—and what makes it the substance it is—its formal cause, and two further types of question will take us to what brought it about (the efficient cause) and the good it serves, its goal or end (the final cause).

But whereas, for Plato, the particulars are often imagined as falling short of the forms, for Aristotle they exemplify the forms, for his forms are seen as answering to the question of what makes the individual substance the substance it is—what makes the individual human being, say, the human being it is. In the doctrine of recollection set out in *Phaedo* Plato certainly allowed that this process may be initially stimulated by *perception,* for example of the ways in which particulars resemble or are unlike the qualities they represent. Thus a pair of equal objects may initiate the process of recollection leading to the apprehension of the form, equality, itself. But for Aristotle the particular substances are what primarily exists, and although the scientist is concerned with forms and with the other types of causes, it is not as if these can be recollected.

The important conclusion that immediately follows from this is that the attention paid to empirical data is not directed at individuals qua the *individuals* they are. The scientist's interest, for Aristotle, lies in the universal, not in particulars as such. The starting point of inquiry is often described as the *phainomena.* But this term covers not only what appears directly to the senses but also what is commonly thought or believed—what appears in the sense of what appears to be the case. When Aristotle wishes to specify perceptible phenomena, he does so by adding the phrase "according to perception" to the term *phainomena.*

Moreover, the collection and evaluation of "what appears" are important not just to establish the data and to set out what is commonly believed, but more particularly to identify the problems that require solution. Aristotle frequently prefaces his own discussion of a subject area with a survey of earlier views. This is done not so much to gain a historical perspective on an issue, let alone for the sake of a historical account itself, as to set out the chief difficulties, *aporiai,* that require resolution and elucidation.

Aristotle has, then, an ontology that takes particulars as basic, and an epistemology that insists that the proper objects of scientific understanding are the forms those particulars possess. He has, too, a general methodology that advocates the review of the common opinions on a subject, as well as the empirical data, before turning to the chief theoretical problems that occupy him. That methodology is put into practice with remarkable consistency throughout his work, including not just his treatises on physical subjects but also those, for example, on politics. Naturally the degree to which the *phaenomena* in question correspond to what we should call observational data varies. Thus in the work called *Physics* Aristotle is largely concerned with problems in what we should call the philosophy of science, such as the nature of time, place, and infinity and the question of the kinds of causes that should be admitted. Here he proceeds by way of abstract argument more often than by way of direct appeal to the results of observations. He pays due attention, to be sure, to the same familiar, real or supposed, data of experience that had figured in earlier, Presocratic deliberations, and he certainly subjects those earlier discussions themselves, and the common opinions, to an extensive, acute, and often damning critique. But as a whole the empirical data marshalled in *Physics* mostly amount to little more than some well-known facts or what were taken to be such.

The situation is quite different in the zoological treatises, where the *phaenomena* reviewed are often observed data, and where Aristotle has often been at pains to extend those data with the findings of his own original research. In a manner that recalls the work of the historians, he and his collaborators collected and evaluated the view of a wide variety of people who could be expected to have special knowledge concerning one or another aspect of animal life or behavior. He repeatedly refers to what he has been told by hunters, fishermen, horse rearers, pig breeders, eel breeders, doctors, veterinary surgeons, and midwives, among others. He draws, too—more surprisingly from our point of view, but quite consistently from his—on literary sources, including, for instance, Herodotus, whom, however, he sometimes treats with disdain as a mere "mythologist."

To this secondhand evidence are added the results of his own and his collaborators' independent research, though he often remarks that the facts are difficult to ascertain, that observation is difficult, that further research is necessary. He does this, for example, in his famous discussion of the generation of bees. Here he first puts forward a set of theories that largely reflect his own a priori preconceptions. Thus one of the factors that leads him to conclude that the worker bees are male is his belief that there is a greater probability of males' being better equipped with offensive and defensive weapons than females. Yet at the end of his discussion he writes (*On the Generation of Animals*, 760b27ff): "This then seems to be what happens with regard to the generation of bees, judging from theory [*logos*] and from what are thought to be the facts about them. But the facts have not been sufficiently ascertained, and if they ever are ascertained, then we must trust perception rather than theories, and theories too so long as what they show agrees with what appears to be the case [*phaenomena*]."

In one domain, in particular, Aristotle can be considered a major pioneer. I have noted that dissection was very rarely used before him, and Aristotle himself implies that his fellow Greeks felt a certain squeamishness on the question. Thus he remarks in *On the Parts of Animals* (645a28ff) that "it is not possible to look at the constituent parts of human beings, such as blood, flesh, bones, blood vessels and the like, without considerable distaste." Human postmortem dissection, in fact, was still not on the agenda. Yet so far as animals were concerned, Aristotle was successful in overcoming his own expressed inhibitions, for he provides clear evidence that he and his associates undertook extensive and careful dissections of some scores of different animal species.

The motives for this were not research for its own sake. On the contrary, Aristotle explains with the greatest care and emphasis that the investigation of the parts of animals is not directed primarily at an inquiry into the material constituents but into their forms and final causes. As always, there are clear *theoretical* issues at stake: the understanding of the structures and functions of the parts of animals. The research is guided throughout by his notion of the different causes to be investigated, and within the four causes, the essence (or formal cause) and the good (final cause) are of greatest importance. The method of dissection was, then, used primarily to reveal the operations of those two causes, though, to be sure, his use of the technique brought to light much that he was in no position to have anticipated. While animals are said to be inferior objects of study when compared with the divine heavenly bodies, he remarks that the latter are remote and difficult to observe. So animals have the advantage that "we have much better means of obtaining information" about them, and "anyone who is willing to take sufficient trouble can learn a great deal concerning each of their kinds [viz. both animals and plants]" (*On the Parts of Animals,* 644b28ff). Once he appreciated how he could proceed to that investigation, and given that he had the motive to do so—to reveal the essences and the good—the possibility of an altogether more systematic program of research opened up, and Aristotle himself progressed far in its implementation even while much work, of course, remained for his successors.

The impressive observations Aristotle carried out, in zoology especially, are guided, as I said, by the conceptual framework provided by his doctrine of the four causes. But I must add that his particular theoretical preconceptions influence both his program of research and many of his reported findings, and there are certainly limitations, in places severe ones, to the observational work he conducted. We can see the role of his theoretical preconceptions in such an example as his analysis of the internal parts of animals. His work here is guided by his doctrine of the different vital faculties, or faculties of soul, such as reproduction, digestion, perception, locomotion, and so on. Thus in his inquiry into the internal parts of the main groups of bloodless animals he appears especially concerned to answer such questions as how and where food is taken in, how and where residues are discharged, where the controlling principle of the animal is located, what modes of perception it enjoys (does it smell? does it hear?), and how it moves. His work on the digestive tract of many species is thorough. But without any idea of the role of what we call the nervous system, either the sensory or the motor nerves, he has only superficial remarks to make about the way in which perception and locomotion occur. In the latter case, while he discusses the arrangement of the organs of locomotion with some care, he pays little attention to the internal musculature of the animals concerned.

Not dissecting human subjects, he mistakes certain basic features of human anatomy. Thus he holds that the heart has three chambers and that the brain is largely empty. The former idea corresponds to his belief that there should, ideally, be a single control center (the middle chamber) and the latter to his conviction of the paramount importance of the heart, an idea that left the brain with a very subordinate role. However, so far as his views of the importance of the heart go, he appealed to empirical investigations of the development of the eggs of hens to support the conclusion that the heart is the first organ in the body to become distinct in the growing embryo.

Again he represents males as essentially stronger and longer lived than females; when he finds species of animals that are exceptions, he does not modify his general belief but treats the animals in question as inferior. What is *natural,* in many cases, corresponds not to what is the case in a majority of instances but to the norm or ideal set by the higher animals, especially by the species deemed to be supreme among animals—namely, humans. Thus, believing that right is inherently stronger than and superior to left, and yet recognizing that right-left distinctions are not always strongly marked in animals, he claims nevertheless that in humans the right is especially right-sided. Again he defines upper as the direction from which food is taken in, and accepts the consequence that plants, fed from their roots, are functionally upside down. In humans alone, indeed, the upper parts are directed toward the upper part of the universe. In humans alone, he is prepared to say (*On the Parts of Animals,* 656a1off), the natural parts are *according to nature.*

Aristotle's work thus exemplifies, in striking fashion, the *inter*dependence of theory and observation. The observations are conducted not for their own sake but for the help they give in the resolution of theoretical issues. Aristotle was not the only researcher, in ancient or in modern times, whose observations are often marshalled directly to support his preconceived theories. He accuses others of not being patient in the conduct of their research, and of assuming the conclusions they wish to reach before they have verified whether the data support them. Yet the same is sometimes true of his own work. At the same time, we cannot fail to be impressed by the range of the empirical studies he undertook. While theoretical preconceptions override observational exceptions on many occasions, the latter are sometimes allowed to contradict and so to modify the former. Above all, as I noted, he often stresses that not all the relevant evidence has been collected, and he is prepared to suspend judgment on detailed issues until further research has been undertaken. His is the first *generalized* program of empirical inquiry into natural science, undertaken for the sake of the causal explanations that such an inquiry can yield.

RESEARCH IN PHILOSOPHY AND SCIENCE AFTER ARISTOTLE

In the period after Aristotle, the separation of many of the branches of science from general philosophy becomes more marked. The main dogmatic philosophical schools of the Hellenistic period, the Epicureans and the Stoics, based primarily in Athens, both emphasized the importance of the study of nature—but only within limits. "Physics" included, especially, element theory, but also detailed explanations of natural phenomena, particularly those that continued to be considered strange or frightening, such as eclipses, earthquakes, thunder and lightning. But for both these schools, "physics" was undertaken as a means to an end, not as an end in itself. Some knowledge of physics was necessary to secure peace of mind, *ataraxia*, without which happiness is impossible. But the end of philosophy, its goal, was essentially moral, to secure that happiness, and once satisfactory explanations on the primary physical problems had been reached, it was pointless, indeed distracting, to continue inquiry.

The Epicureans, especially, rejected much of the work of the natural philosophers as useless, even as no better than mythology. Epicurus insisted that when several explanations of a single phenomenon (such as eclipses) seem possible, then *all* should be accepted and kept in play. As a principle that has a laudable undogmatic, indeed antidogmatic, ring. But the Epicureans' own actual proposed explanations were often fanciful and not only insufficiently critical but also ill-informed. Epicurus itemized some four or five different theories of eclipses, all of which were to be entertained as possible; yet these do not include the real explanation, which had not been in any doubt to practicing astronomers since the middle of the 5th century. With rare exceptions, such as the independent-minded middle Stoic Posidonius, in the 1st century B.C.E., the major Hellenistic philosophers undertook no detailed empirical research themselves.

In the specialized sciences the situation is very different. The development of these inquiries in the Hellenistic period is in part a history of the development of demonstration. At the same time there are also important developments in the range of empirical work conducted. In what has to be a drastically selective survey, we will concentrate here on four fields especially: astronomy and optics among the exact sciences, and anatomy and physiology among the life sciences. A more extensive account would have to include far more, notably the empirical investigations in harmonics in the work of Aristoxenus, Ptolemy, and Porphyry; those in geography in Eratosthenes, Hipparchus, Posidonius, Strabo, and Ptolemy; those in botany in Theophrastus; those in pharmacology in Dioscorides; as well as many developments in clinical medicine in a long list of distinguished medical writers.

One by-product of the conquests of Alexander was that the Greeks gained greater access to Babylonian astronomy. Some knowledge of Babylonian observational work in that domain is attestable in the 4th century, possibly also in the late 5th century, but this related largely to such basic data as the values of the fundamental periods of the planets, sun, and moon. But the two major astronomical theorists, Hipparchus (2nd century B.C.E.) and Ptolemy (2nd century C.E.), drew extensively on Babylonian records. Ptolemy, for instance, chose the first year of the reign of Nabonassar (845 B.C.E.) as the beginning of his system of dating and cited several specific lunar eclipses observed by Babylonian astronomers in the 8th, 7th, and 6th centuries.

But if Greek astronomy in the Hellenistic period exploited the results of Babylonian work to good effect, the Greeks also engaged in careful astronomical observation on their own account. Some of the contexts in which they did so are largely unconnected with the chief issue in astronomical theory, the construction of models to account for the movements of the planets, sun, and moon. Thus first Hipparchus and then Ptolemy produced detailed star catalogues. That of Hipparchus is not extant, and its contents have to be inferred, largely from the evidence that Ptolemy provides. However, it appears to have contained some 850 stars. The coordinate system that Hipparchus used was a mixed one. Some of our data relate to equatorial coordinates (the right ascension or declination of the star) or to mixed equatorial and ecliptic ones (the so-called polar longitude). There was as yet, it seems, no single definite system of spherical coordinates for stellar positions.

By the time we get to Ptolemy himself, however, each star is located by ecliptic coordinates (celestial longitude, measured east or west along the ecliptic, and celestial latitude, north or south of the ecliptic). The extent to which Ptolemy merely copied out Hipparchus's catalogue, with adjustments for the variations of the positions of the stars in his own day, is disputed. But it is clear, first, that he drew heavily on Hipparchus (it would have been foolish not to have done so) and, second, that he added to the earlier catalogue, including some 1,020 stars. Whoever takes the credit for the data on which the extant catalogue in the *Syntaxis* (VII and VIII) is based, we may say it provides clear evidence of sustained observation. It has been estimated that the mean error in longitude is about 51' and that in latitude about 26'. Ptolemy further describes the instruments he uses for these and other observations—the dioptra, the meridional armillary, the plinth or quadrant, the parallactic ruler, and the armillary astrolabe, all of them, with the exception of the last, quite simple—and more important, he remarks on the difficulties of their accurate construction and use.

The motivation for the construction of a star catalogue is more descriptive than theoretical. However, it provides, of course, a clear map of stellar positions, an essential prerequisite for the determination of planetary positions, the chief issue in astronomical theory and the key also to the practice of astrology. Moreover, the careful observation of the positions of stars in the band of the ecliptic led Hipparchus to a momentous consequence—the discovery of the phenomenon known as the precession of the equinoxes, the slow retrograde motion of the equinoctial points with respect to the fixed stars. Comparing his own results for the position of the star Spica in Virgo with those recorded by his predecessors, Hipparchus was led to investigate whether there was a systematic shift either just in the stars close to the ecliptic, or in all stars. He was aware, of course, of the inaccuracy of much of the observational work done before him, and, like Ptolemy after him, suspected systematic errors in some of his instruments. Yet he concluded that there is indeed such a shift and that the whole of the outermost celestial sphere rotates at a rate of around one degree in 100 years (that was the figure Ptolemy himself adopted, though it may have been the lower limit for precession in Hipparchus's calculation).

This ranks as one of the most striking ancient examples in which an observational program undertaken with no specific theoretical issue in mind yielded a result that was utterly unexpected—and in which that result was accepted despite the radical revision it implied in the previously held view of the absolute fixity of the sphere of the outermost stars. Indeed, so strong did that conviction remain, in common belief, that Hipparchus's discovery was often ignored or dismissed. Ptolemy, to be sure, accepted precession and devoted a detailed discussion to its verification. But many later commentators, including otherwise well-informed scholars, such as Proclus and Philoponus, expressed their frank disbelief that precession occurs—despite the fact that with the passing centuries the comparison between earlier and later stellar positions should have suggested, more and more forcefully, that it does.

The other main context for detailed observational research in astronomy was, of course, in relation to the main theoretical issue that had preoccupied Greek astronomers from the 5th century B.C.E. onward, the construction of geometrical models to account for the apparently irregular motions of the moon, sun, and planets. By Ptolemy's day, the preferred models employed eccentric circles and epicycles, or combinations of them, and Ptolemy himself introduced certain theoretical elaborations, notably the equant, the point other than the earth or the center of the eccentric with relation to which uniform motion is to be measured. That assumption came to be criticized as, in effect, breaching the fundamental principle that the motions *are* uniform.

Ptolemy's ambition was not just to provide general, qualitative solutions to the problems of planetary motion—that is, to resolve the geometrical problems in general terms. He aimed to give an exact quantitative account, determining, for each planet, the degree of eccentricity, the size of the epicycle or epicycles in relation to the deferent, and the planet's apsidal line, as well as the speeds of revolution—the periodicities—of the epicycle and deferent. If Ptolemy's own report is to be believed, Hipparchus himself had been unable to give a satisfactory detailed account of the planets, though his models for both moon and sun were fully quantitative. It would appear, then, that Ptolemy was himself responsible for the first complete theory of planetary motion, providing detailed solutions from which the exact position of the planet at any time in the past, present, or future can be determined.

For this purpose he cited a number of specific observations in his exposition of each individual planet. Yet in part, no doubt, to keep that exposition as simple and as clear as possible, he cited close to the *minimum* number of observations needed to extract the specific parameters of the motion of each planet. Evidently these are chosen with a view to getting the eventual results he proposes—and the general quality of his observational work has again in this context (as in relation to his star catalogue) been impugned. There can be little doubt that he allows himself adjustments to specific observed positions, just as he does in the roundings he repeatedly makes in the purely mathematical part of his calculations. By the standards of accuracy applicable to later astronomical theory, his procedures are slapdash. Yet his overall success in arriving, in most cases, at results that give good approximations to the observed planetary movements is considerable. The very fact that he saw himself as forced to introduce certain complexities into his theoretical models (especially for Mercury and the Moon) in order to obtain an adequate fit between theory and observation may be taken as testimony to the attention he paid to the latter. Although within the *Syntaxis* itself he does not present all the data he uses or feels he needs to take into account, it is only because of that need that he was induced to modify and elaborate the models he proposed.

In optics, the second field I have chosen for consideration, there are theoretical disputes both about the nature of light and the directionality of vision. In the former case, one school of thought held that light should be interpreted as the transport of particles through the void, while another held, rather, that it corresponded to the transmission of a certain tension in a continuous medium. In the latter, there were those who argued that the light ray proceeds outward from the eye to the object, others who held that it goes from the object to the eye. None of these physical debates directly affects the empirical investigations of such questions as the laws of reflection and refraction. Once again it is Ptolemy who provides the fullest evidence for those investigations, though we may be sure that both reflection and refraction, as such, were known before him.

The treatise he devoted to the subject, *Optics,* is extant only in a Latin translation of an Arabic version, and at points we have reason to question the accuracy of the text as we have it. It is clear, however, that the original contained detailed accounts both of the experimental verification of the laws of reflection and analyses of refraction, including attempts to determine the variation in the extent of refraction, for different angles of incidence, for different pairs of media, namely from air to water, from air to glass, and from water to glass.

This provides the occasion for some general remarks about the role of experimentation in Greek natural science, where it has often been argued that one of the greatest shortcomings of the Greeks lies in a failure to appreciate the value of experimental methods. It is clear, first of all, that in many fields in which Greek scientists were interested, experiment is impossible. This is the case in astronomy, for instance, where there can be no question of intervening directly to test hypotheses via specially contrived situations. The same is broadly true also of meteorology and geology. The Greeks were in no position to investigate thunder and lightning, or earthquakes, by creating such phenomena artificially, even in miniature. Rather, their usual procedure was to appeal to some real or supposed analogue, as Anaximanes is reported to have done in the case of lightning, which he compared to the flash of an oar in water. But any such procedure begged the question of whether the phenomena compared are indeed similar in the relevant characteristics.

In the investigation of the physical elements, some limited experimental procedures are occasionally invoked. Aristotle, for instance, claims that sea water, on evaporation, turns into fresh. He also suggests that wine does so, a result that may prompt reflection not so much on Aristotle's ability as an observer as on the procedures he employed, and on the conceptual framework within which the results were evaluated. The main drawback to the effective deployment of the experimental method in relation to his physical theory lies in the vagueness of the definitions of the simple bodies, earth, water, air, and fire themselves. They are identified with combinations of the primary qualities, hot, cold, wet, and dry, but what we encounter as earth or water or air or fire is never the *pure* simple body, always to a greater or lesser extent a mixture. Thus the "water" that Aristotle claims came from wine on evaporation might well be what he took the vapor from heated wine to produce on recondensing: if he conducted any such test, the condensate would no doubt have been a colorless, more or less tasteless fluid that would pass as easily as "water" as naturally occurring samples.

Yet in some cases, as the evidence in Ptolemy's *Optics* shows, detailed experimental investigations, using apparatuses devised for the purpose, were carried out. Ptolemy measures the actual refraction he says he has observed between his pairs of media and sets out his results for angles of incidence at 10-degree intervals from 10 to 80 degrees. In all three cases the first result is introduced with the qualification "nearly," and they are all stated in terms of degrees and half degrees. He thus appears to make some allowance for approximation. Yet the more surprising feature is that *all* the results tally exactly with a general law that takes the form of the equation $r = ai - bi^2$, where r is the angle of refraction, i the angle of incidence, and a and b are constants for the media concerned.

Evidently *Optics* presents results that have already been adjusted to match the underlying general theory. I shall cite cases of experimental procedures where no such adjustments have been made when we come to anatomy and physiology in the next section. But we may remark at this stage that a common, even though far from universal, feature of such testing procedures as the Greek scientists used is that they are appealed to not so much as neutral ways of *deciding between* alternatives antecedently deemed to be more or less equally plausible, but rather as an extension of the use of evidence to *corroborate* a particular theory or set of results. In this regard, experiment is used not so much as an—ideally—neutral testing procedure but as testimony to support a distinct point of view.

The two remaining fields we should consider are closely related and may be taken together, namely anatomy and physiology. I have already discussed the development and use of dissection in Aristotle, where it was limited to animal subjects but was the chief factor enabling Aristotle to reach a far clearer picture of many internal structures than his predecessors had had. Two scientists working chiefly at Alexandria at the turn of the 4th and 3rd centuries B.C.E., Herophilus and Erasistratus, took the next step of dissecting human subjects. Indeed reports suggest that they also carried out vivisections on humans—on "criminals obtained out of prison from the kings," as Celsus puts it. Clearly this research depended heavily on the support of those kings, notably the first two Ptolemies. It appears, however, that after Herophilus and Erasistratus the use of human subjects for postmortem anatomical research declined, even though in the 2nd century C.E. Galen suggests that osteology was still taught at Alexandria using humans.

The extension of the technique of dissection to human subjects was one factor that contributed to the very rapid development of anatomical knowledge in the immediate post-Aristotelian period. Herophilus and Erasistratus, between them, were responsible for a large number of important discoveries, the most significant of which was that of the nervous system. The term used for nerve, *neuron*, had originally been used indiscriminately of a wide variety of structures, including tendons and ligaments. The role of what we call sensory and motor nerves in the transmission of sensation and the control of the muscles was, accordingly, totally ignored. Aristotle, as we saw, believed that the heart is the seat of the controlling principle in the body, but his account of the connections between it and the organs of sensation is desperately vague and unclear.

Whether or not Herophilus and Erasistratus were stimulated by a sense of the inadequacy of Aristotle's work in this area is not clear. We have, in any case, to reconstruct their work from the quotations and comments in later sources such as Galen. But the *general* problem of where the controlling principle is to be placed, whether in the heart or the brain, was one of the most commonly debated issues in the work of both medical writers and philosophers. The problem goes back at least as far as the mid-5th-century philosopher Alcmaeon, who, like Plato after him, opted for the brain as control center. Alcmaeon may even have investigated the back of the eye with a probe in order precisely to establish its connection with the brain, but the idea that he dissected the brain or any other part of the body has to be discounted as going well beyond what our evidence suggests. While he may have described a channel, *poros,* at the back of the eye, it was certainly not yet identified as what came to be called the optic nerve.

It was the step of identifying certain structures as sensory nerves and others as motor nerves that marks the discovery of the nervous system as such. It was here that Herophilus and Erasistratus achieved the breakthrough. Although Galen criticizes Herophilus's work as incomplete and explains that Erasistratus carried out detailed investigations only in certain areas toward the end of his life, that should not be taken to diminish the importance of their fundamental realization of the role of the two main types of nerves.

Nor were their anatomical investigations confined to the single problem of the transmission of sensation and movement. Herophilus, for instance, was responsible for, among other things, the first clear description of the four membranes of the eye, and for the identification of the ovaries as female testicles. Erasistratus is credited with the discovery of the four main valves of the heart, controlling the flow of materials into the right and the left side. Galen reports that he identified the various ventricles of the brain, and two of the specific structures in the brain, the torcular Herophili and the calamus scriptorius, were described and named for the first time by Herophilus.

Much of this work was, no doubt, done on animals, and the extent of the use of human subjects was not necessarily very great. Yet their inclusion enabled comparisons to be made directly between humans and other animals, as opposed to merely inferring human structures on the basis of real or supposed analogies with other species. Herophilus's comparison between human and animal livers is reported by Galen, as is Erasistratus's between human and animal brains. And Herophilus would not have arrived at his name for the duodenum had he not measured the length of that structure in humans (for the name he coined implies its twelve-fingers' breadth).

This effort in research was not just descriptive in character. Apart from the issue of the control center in the body, there were theoretical debates on such physiological processes as respiration and digestion. Thus Erasistratus may have used vivisection to support his account of digestion, which he interpreted in purely mechanical terms: the stomach and digestive tract do not "concoct" the food but transform it into usable nourishment by grinding it down. He was, too, convinced that the arteries normally contain air and that the blood that flows from them in a lesion comes from neighboring veins through invisible capillaries. But whatever theoretical issues were at stake, it is clear that he had a highly developed sense of the need, importance, and difficulty of empirical research. Thus Galen quotes him as follows: "Those who are completely unused to inquiry are, in the first exercise of their mind, blinded and dazed and straightforwardly leave off the inquiry from mental fatigue and an incapacity that is no less than that of those who enter races without being used to them. But the man who is used to inquiry tries every possible loophole as he conducts his mental search and turns in every direction and so far from giving up the inquiry in the space of a day, does not cease his search throughout his whole life. Directing his attention to one idea after another that is germane to what is being investigated, he presses on until he arrives at his goal."

Despite what may seem to us the brilliant successes of Herophilus and Erasistratus, the method of dissection remained controversial, for a variety of reasons. Animal, and especially human, vivisection was condemned, almost universally, as cruel and immoral. But postmortem dissection was also rejected by two of the main Hellenistic medical sects (the so-called Empiricists and Methodists), on the grounds that the evidence it yields is not relevant to the understanding of the living creature, only of the dead one. Similarly, animal vivisection was of no use for determining vital processes, since it depended on a violent intervention on the living creature. In addition many doctors argued that medicine was a matter of curing the sick, and the doctor should not be concerned with explaining the how and why of the workings of the body, only with how to remedy malfunctions. No doubt, too, a respect for the dead was a general inhibiting factor militating against the use of human subjects (though we may reflect that in other contexts the ancients sometimes showed little compunction for desecrating the dead, when the dead were their defeated enemies). However, for whatever combination of reasons, human dissection certainly declined (as I noted) after Herophilus and Erasistratus themselves.

Yet Galen in the 2nd century c.e. certainly carried on the tradition of anatomical research even while he worked almost exclusively on animals. We must also point out that dissection and vivisection, in his hands, were not just tools of research. Sometimes their role was rather as *publicity*, as support for the claims to having knowledge that was superior to that of rivals. Medicine was always highly competitive, and one way a doctor could make a name for himself was with his ability as an anatomist. Galen reports occasions when dissections were carried out in public, with rival experts claiming to predict the results and even taking bets as to who had got it right. Thus he describes how he discomfited some Erasistratean opponents by challenging them to establish their claims that the arteries naturally contain air. On a further famous occasion an elephant was dissected in public in Rome, with Galen (on his own account) again outdoing all his rivals with his predictions of what the dissection would reveal. In such contexts it is clear that dissection was used neither for teaching, nor for research, but rather for display.

Yet we must also acknowledge that Galen's own anatomical descriptions show clear signs of careful observation and well-directed research. Building on the work of his predecessors he was able to take the investigation of the nervous system a good deal further than they. He undertook systematic experiments to determine the effects of severing the spinal column at different points, either by cutting right through it or by making a half section. He sets out the results in the treatise *On Anatomical Procedures,* where he identifies the precise role of the nerves entering the spinal column between each of the pairs of vertebrae from the sacral to the cervical. Here we have experimental vivisections used to determine functions, with no interference from theoretical preconceptions.

The history of dissection in antiquity illustrates very clearly the complex interaction of observation and theory. In some cases the idea of investigating animal bodies using such a technique was stimulated by a particular theoretical dispute, as when the issue was the control center—the heart or the brain? In others, dissections were carried out not so much to confirm or refute a particular theory as to enable the formal and final causes of the parts of animals to be clarified. In that case, in Aristotle especially, dissection becomes a more general method, and its findings might include new discoveries that corresponded to no particular theoretical preoccupation. Those findings might, indeed, lead to the reformulation of the problems themselves—as later happened with the discovery of the nervous system. Dissection was always guided by theories and assumptions of some sort, but once one of those assumptions was a realization that the problems themselves might be more complex than had generally been believed, the investigation was more open to the unexpected. Thus the use of the method could and did generate what were effectively new problems, leading in turn to new programs of research. We cannot say precisely what Herophilus and Erasistratus were *looking for* when they identified the valves of the heart as valves, but once their role in controlling the flow into and out of the two sides of the heart was established, the question of the relations between the arterial and venous systems and the possibility of communication between them produced major new issues for physiological debate—issues that were, indeed, to remain unresolved throughout antiquity.

We may now, in conclusion, briefly take stock of the findings of our survey. The need to conduct observations and carry out research may seem an obvious feature of the work of anyone seriously engaged in natural scientific inquiry. Yet the history of the idea and the practice of observation and research in Greek antiquity indicates that both took time to develop, posed conceptual and practical difficulties, and remained controversial. First among the difficulties were the doubts expressed about the reliability of perception and the strong preference, expressed by prominent philosophers from Parmenides onward, for taking reason and argument alone as trustworthy guides to the truth. But even among those who did not adopt an ultrarationalist position, the mere recognition that perception is of some value was not, by itself, enough to stimulate deliberate research. That had always to be motivated either by some particular theoretical problem to be resolved or by a general framework of explanation dictating the detailed examination of a variety of phenomena—for example (as in Aristotle's case), to identify the problems and to discover the formal and final causes underlying the appearances.

Often we find observation used merely to confirm or refute a particular thesis: once that goal was achieved, further investigation ceased. Often, too, observations, including those conducted in relation to experimental situations, were cited directly to support a particular preconceived opinion. Antiquity provides many instances of hasty or superficial observations, where the researcher has concluded, all too swiftly, that the data confirm his theory, interpreting those data in the light of the theory or even adjusting the results to provide such confirmation. (Of course, such jumping to conclusions is far from confined to *ancient* science.)

However, when a particular theoretical or conceptual interest existed, sustained observations were carried out in such fields as clinical medicine, zoology, astronomy, and optics, and these observations included some that not only did not confirm but even tended to conflict with the preconceived opinions of the researchers. Hippocratic clinical observations often did not fit *any* neat schema of critical days. Aristotle, too, had to admit exceptions to many of his generalizations in zoology, even though he sometimes resorts to secondary elaborations to explain away the apparent counterevidence. Hipparchus's discovery of precession went against the grain of his own assumptions as well as those of all his contemporaries. While observations were always carried out in the light of *some* theory, there are cases where, once the data had been collected, the nature of the problems was transformed—as with the discoveries of the nervous system and the valves of the heart. Thus while theory guides research, there was also important feedback, when the observations themselves led to the formulation of new problems and the generation, in turn, of further programs of research.

The value and importance of empirical research never became universally accepted principles of natural science, neither before Aristotle nor after him; neither by the philosophers nor by the medical writers nor by those engaged in particular inquiries in the exact or the life sciences. But that did not prevent particular investigators, in particular contexts and in particular periods, from advocating such research in principle—often in the face of hostile attitudes and criticisms from rationalists, pragmatists, and skeptics—nor from implementing those principles in practice. The ancient world provides many examples where an excellent methodological principle is advocated but the advocates themselves hardly live up to the claims they make for the methods. While some recommendations of the value of empirical investigations were no more than the wishful statement of high-sounding ideals untranslated into practice, that was not always the case. The sustained programs of research actually carried through, with great determination, by some of the Hippocratic doctors, by Aristotle, by Herophilus, Erasistratus, Hipparchus,

Ptolemy, and Galen, indicate that high-sounding principles were not just idealized recommendations but indeed, in their case, implemented in full measure in practice.

GEOFFREY E. R. LLOYD

Bibliography

Bourgey, Louis. *Observation et expérience chez Aristote*. Paris: Vrin, 1955.

―――. *Observation et expérience chez les médecins de la collection hippocratique*. Paris: Vrin, 1953.

Burkert, Walter. *Lore and Science in Ancient Pythagoreanism* (revised translation by E. L. Minar of *Weisheit und Wissenschaft*, Nuremberg: Hans Carl Verlag, 1962). Cambridge, Mass.: Harvard University Press, 1972.

Kudlien, Fridolf. *Der Beginn des medizinischen Denkens bei den Griechen*. Zurich: Artemis Verlag, 1967.

Le Blond, Jean-Marie. *Logique et méthode chez Aristote*. Paris: Vrin, 1939.

Lloyd, Geoffrey E. R. *Magic, Reason, and Experience: Studies in the Origin and Development of Greek Science*. Cambridge: Cambridge University Press, 1979.

―――. *Methods and Problems in Greek Science*. Cambridge: Cambridge University Press, 1991.

Neugebauer, Otto. *The Exact Sciences in Antiquity*, 2nd ed. Providence, R.I.: Brown University Press, 1957.

―――. *A History of Ancient Mathematical Astronomy*. 3 vols. Berlin: Springer Verlag, 1975.

Van der Waerden, B. L. *Science Awakening*, 2nd ed. Oxford: Oxford University Press, 1961.

Related Articles

Epistemology; History; Aristotle; Skepticism; Astronomy; Medicine; Epicurus

DEMONSTRATION AND THE IDEA OF SCIENCE

THE NOTION OF DEMONSTRATION is closely linked to one, and in many respects the most important, concept of science in Greco-Roman antiquity. It will, accordingly, be convenient to deal with these together. However, it must be stressed at the outset that the idea that scientific knowledge should be based, ideally, on demonstration is far from being the *only* concept of science proposed in antiquity. Moreover the notion of demonstration itself took different forms in the work of different writers and in different contexts. The definition we find in Aristotle's *Posterior Analytics,* that demonstration proceeds by strict deductive argument from premises that are themselves indemonstrable, was, as we shall see, worked out in part in direct contradistinction to other, less formal and less rigorous, ideas.

So far as our extant evidence goes, attempts to give strict demonstrations antedate the formulation of the explicit concept by several decades. The first sustained deductive argument in philosophy (the first such in European literature) comes in *The Way of Truth,* the philosophical poem written by Parmenides and thought to date from around 480 B.C.E. Where this resembles and where it differs from later styles of demonstration are alike suggestive.

Parmenides' main substantive conclusions about the nature of reality are set out in frg. 8, and they take the form of a series of tightly knit deductive arguments. Several of these are in the form of a reductio, and most appeal, directly or implicitly, to an exclusive choice between alternatives assumed to be exhaustive; we shall consider some examples in due course. However, the whole deductive chain depends on a starting point that Parmenides evidently takes to be undeniable. In frg. 2, where he distinguishes between two possible ways of inquiry, he states that "it is and it cannot not be." This itself is supported by arguing that the opposite, the other "way," namely that "it is not and it needs must not be," must be rejected. That has to be rejected on the grounds that "you could not know what is not, at least, nor could you declare it" (that is, assert it as true). As frg. 3 goes on to say: "It is the same thing that can be thought and can be."

The sense of the verb *to be,* the subject we must understand, and the precise nature of the alternatives presented are all disputed issues. But that does not affect the main point, which is that, at the outset, Parmenides was evidently attempting to establish a starting point that all would have to accept.

One way to understand this is to take it that he is claiming that for any *inquiry* to get anywhere it must be an inquiry into something. It must have a subject matter. One cannot conduct an investigation into the totally nonexistent. If an inquiry is to take place at all, it must be into "what is." But as for our rejection of "it is not," we must remark first on the complete indeterminacy in the statement of the two ways, and second that it appears that Parmenides forces a choice not between strict contradictories but between contrary propositions. The contradictory to "it cannot not be" (i.e., it is necessarily the case that it is) is not "it needs must not be" (it is necessarily the case that it is not) but rather "it is not necessarily the case that it is."

More important still, the basis of the subsequent deductive chain of argument is not a set of clearly identified *axioms*. Even if Parmenides no doubt would have insisted that his statement that "it is and it cannot not be" must be accepted as true, his starting point evidently does not take the form of anything like an axiom set or set of indemonstrables.

However, once the starting point is taken as secure, Parmenides gives an articulated argument, in frg. 8, recommending a whole series of highly counterintuitive conclusions, for example that it is ungenerated and indestructible, not subject to movement nor change, and both spatially and temporally invariant. Again, many points of detail, some of them important ones, are obscure or controversial. But the main structure of the argument is generally agreed, and that it has a rigorous deductive form is not in question. Parmenides sets out what he is going to establish at frg. 8.2ff and then proceeds to demonstrate each point in turn in a carefully constructed sequence of arguments. Thus the first conclusion, namely that it does not come to be, is shown by a reductio (frg. 8.20ff): "If it came to be, it is not." But—as had been shown—"it is not" must be denied. And so we must reject coming-to-be. Similarly, movement and change in turn are rejected, since they presuppose a coming-to-be, namely that of the new situation created by the supposed movement or change. But coming-to-be had just been ruled out by the earlier argument. And so movement and change have also to be rejected.

To these reductio arguments we can add others that take other forms. Thus as an extra consideration telling for the conclusion that "it is ungenerated," Parmenides produces an argument that appeals to what we might call the principle of sufficient reason. At frgs. 8–9f the demand is: "What need would have raised it to grow later, or earlier, starting from nothing?" If no cause can be adduced, no explanation given, as to why the universe came to be at one time rather than at any other, then we may consider this an argument for rejecting the notion that it came to be at all. The relevance of this argument is not confined, of course, to such earlier Greek cosmogonical theories as Parmenides himself may have had in mind.

The *aims* of *The Way of Truth* are clear: Parmenides sets out to establish a set of inescapable conclusions by strict deductive arguments from a starting point that itself has to be accepted. Those are features it shares with later demonstrations. However, the terminology in which he describes what he is doing is a very limited one. This is not just a matter of his not having any terms to describe the various argument schemata, such as reductio, that he uses. He has no word for deduction, nor for premise, let alone axiom. True, he offers what he calls a "much-contested *elenchos*" (frg. 7.5ff) and that has sometimes been taken to be translatable as "proof." However, it seems more likely that the primary sense here is that of "refutation"—as in later Socratic *elenchos*, where, in Plato's dialogues, Socrates exposes the inconsistencies of his interlocutors' beliefs. As for the sequence of conclusions set out in the body of *The Way of Truth*, they are simply introduced with the remark that there are many signposts, or marks, *sēmata*, on this way, indications, that is, that it is ungenerated, indestructible, and so on.

The immense impact that Parmenides had on subsequent Greek philosophy derives as much from his methods as from his conclusions. Certainly so far as the latter are concerned, the later Presocratic cosmologists responded directly to the challenge posed by Parmenides' denial of change and coming-to-be. They accepted his principle that nothing can come to be from the totally nonexistent, but postulated that what is is itself a plurality. Change and coming-to-be can then be interpreted in terms of the interactions of already existing things. But the pluralists, too, use indirect proofs, or reductio, even if not all their deductive arguments were directly modeled on those of Parmenides.

In Parmenides' own Eleatic followers, Zeno and Melissus, however, the range of dilemmatic arguments deployed increases. Zeno, especially, attempts to establish a monistic ontology by the systematic rejection of all rival pluralist positions. He appears to have proceeded by considering, and refuting, all possible ways of construing "the many." Whatever notion of *division* is invoked to distinguish the various items that constitute the plurality, the idea will turn out to be incoherent, undermined by its own self-contradictions. For example, the "many" will turn out to be both "limited" and "unlimited," both "large" and "small." As in Parmenides himself, we have arguments that appeal to terms that are themselves left highly indeterminate—as indeed is also the case with the terms *one* and *many*, where Zeno evidently takes it that to refute the latter is to establish the former.

Deductive argument used for constructive or destructive purposes is thus commonly deployed in Greek philosophy from the middle of the 5th century B.C.E. onward. From about 430 we have further explicit evidence for sustained deductive argument in mathematics. Our first extant set of mathematical proofs is the work of Hippocrates of Chios. His work on the quadratures of lunes is reported at some length by Simplicius, who tells us that he drew on the account of the 4th-century historian of mathematics, Eudemus. Though, as so often, some of the details are obscure, and the extent of the reworking of

Hippocrates' arguments in the process of transmission is unclear, there is no reason to doubt that the substance of the four main proofs given represents the work of Hippocrates himself. These proofs establish the quadratures of lunes with an outer circumference equal to, greater than, and less than, a semicircle and that of a lune together with a circle. In each case Hippocrates identified a lune that *can* be shown to be equal to a rectilinear area and proved the equality.

These proofs are impressive not just for the extent of the mathematical knowledge displayed but also for the general rigor of the demonstrations. For instance, Hippocrates does not just *construct* lunes with outer circumferences greater and less than a semicircle, but in both cases he provides proofs of these inequalities. However, if the quality of the proofs is high, the lack of technical vocabulary to describe the procedures used is as remarkable in Hippocrates as it had been in Parmenides. Later Greek mathematicians were generally careful to specify the nature of the indemonstrable primary premises on which their demonstrations were based, for example, definitions, postulates, and axioms or common opinions. However, in the quadrature proofs Simplicius reports that Hippocrates took as his "starting point" *(archē)* the proposition that similar segments of circles are to one another as the squares on their bases, and this was evidently in no sense an axiom or indemonstrable. It was indeed a proposition that (we are told) Hippocrates *showed* by *showing* that circles are to one another as the squares on their diameters (though *how* he showed that is, unfortunately, not recorded).

In this context, then, it looks as if Hippocrates worked with a concept of starting point or principle that is relative to, and serves as the foundation of, a particular sequence of mathematical arguments. The question of whether he also had the notion of the *ultimate* starting points for the *whole* of geometry revolves around the evaluation of the evidence for his work on the elements. Our chief source here is Proclus's sketch of the early history of mathematics in his commentary on book I of Euclid's *Elements*. Here we are told that the first person to have composed a book of elements was Hippocrates, and Proclus identifies several other mathematicians between Hippocrates and Euclid (including, for example, Archytas and Theaetetus in the 4th century) who "increased the number of theorems and progressed toward a more systematic arrangement of them."

So far as Euclid's own *Elements* goes, there can be no doubt that *its* aim was the systematic deductive presentation of the whole of mathematics, starting from three types of primary indemonstrable premises, which he calls definitions, postulates, and common opinions. Moreover the term *elements* itself was undoubtedly used in mathematics, as well as in philosophy, before Euclid himself (whose work is traditionally dated around 300 B.C.E.). Thus Aristotle reports in *Metaphysics* (988a25ff) that "we give the name 'elements' to those geometrical propositions, the proofs of which are implied in the proofs of all or most of the others."

The questions then arise of how systematic and comprehensive Hippocrates' work was, and whether it was clearly based on ultimate starting points identified as elements, and in both cases we are unfortunately reduced to conjecture. Proclus takes Hippocrates as the originator of the tradition that culminates in Euclid, but how far was he justified in doing so? The proofs used in the quadratures of lunes reported by Simplicius certainly presuppose, as I noted, an extensive knowledge of elementary geometry, corresponding to much of the content of Euclid, books I–IV and VI. We should certainly not rule out the possibility that Hippocrates attempted an overall deductive presentation of a substantial body of theorems. However, caution is indicated so far as the development of explicit concepts corresponding to the notion of axioms is concerned.

There is good reason for hesitation on that score in the evidence we have of the hesitant development of the vocabulary of axiomatization in the period between Hippocrates and Aristotle. The testimony of Plato is particularly significant in this respect. Plato several times refers to the use that geometers make of what he calls "hypotheses." In *Meno* (86e ff) this is a matter of investigating a complex problem by "hypothesizing" that it is equivalent to some other problem and exploring that. There, while much of the detail of the interpretation of the passage is disputed, it is clear that the "hypothesis" is in no sense an ultimate starting point or assumption. In *The Republic* (510c ff), however, Plato again cites mathematical examples to illustrate what is here a different notion of "hypothesis." Mathematicians, we are told, "hypothesize" "the odd and the even, the figures and the three kinds of angles and other things like these in each inquiry. They do not give an account of these either to themselves or to others, as if they were clear to all, but beginning with them they go through the rest consistently and end with what they set out to investigate."

It is not clear whether either of these texts in Plato reflects an *actual* use of the term *hypothesis* in earlier mathematics. But whatever the original terminology, Plato indicates that certain basic assumptions, taken as clear, were employed as the starting points for mathematical deductions. Plato himself complains that the mathematicians do not give an account of those starting points. *His* ideal is that hypotheses should be related to the supreme Form of the Good, the "unhypothesized beginning," from which (he claims) the whole of the intelligible world—including the geometers' hypotheses themselves—can be in some sense derived. But while his account of *their* procedures points to the role of certain principles in mathematics, the precise character of these principles is still left, in certain respects, unclear. He mentions "odd and even," "the figures," and "the three kinds of angles." But it is an open question whether, for example, these are to be construed as—or to in-clude—definitions (like the definitions of odd and even in Euclid VII, Definitions 6 and 7) or existence assumptions (corresponding to Aristotle's hypotheses) or—as seems possible in the case of the figures—as assumptions concerning the possibility of carrying out certain constructions (like the first three of Euclid's postulates). Plato thus provides confirmation that mathematics used starting points of some kind, on which deductions could be based, but his work is also evidence of a certain indeterminacy in the conception of those foundations. A fortiori, then, we should be cautious about ascribing a clear concept of the axioms, let alone clear ideas concerning the different kinds of possible indemonstrable starting points, to Hippocrates of Chios in the latter part of the 5th century.

Our conclusions concerning Hippocrates may, then, be summarized as follows. The evidence of the work on quadratures established his mastery of an impressive body of elementary geometry and his skill in the practice of rigorous deductive argument. There is some evidence that the systematization of geometry that culminates in Euclid's *Elements* begins with him. But it is very doubtful that he had a clear, explicit concept of the axioms or of other kinds of indemonstrables as such.

The further question then arises of whether the notion of deductive argument was developed independently in mathematics and in philosophy, or whether it appeared first in one of these two fields and was then taken over by the others. To answer this we have to tackle the much more difficult problem of the status of the ascriptions of certain mathematical proofs to Thales and to Pythagoras and the dating of the discovery of such famous mathematical theorems as that of the incommensurability of the side and the diagonal of the square.

Several of our late antique sources, among the commentators on Euclid and the Neopythagorean writers, ascribe a number of important theorems to both Thales and Pythagoras. Proclus, for instance, uses terminology that suggests that he is confident that Thales not only discovered certain theorems but also found their proofs. Yet the reliability of this evidence is very much in doubt. Aristotle is always hesitant in his remarks about Thales, who seems to have left no writings. Thus Aristotle conjectures the reasons for Thales' choice of water as his principle (of "Images of the world"), presumably because no definite evidence on the point was available in Aristotle's own day. Again Aristotle does not attempt to reconstruct Pythagoras's own contributions to philosophy of mathematics in his history of early thinkers in *Metaphysics* and elsewhere, contenting himself with an account of what the "so-called Pythagoreans" believed, where he probably has in mind thinkers of the mid-5th century at the earliest.

In these circumstances it does not seem very likely that even Eudemus, in the late 4th century, let alone any much later writer, had access to reliable, specific evidence concerning Thales. As regards Pythagoras, the further complicating factor is the general tendency, in many late writers, to ascribe important discoveries and inventions to the heroic founders of Greek philosophy. The fulsome accounts of Pythagoras's mathematical research that we find in some who considered themselves his followers owe more to their pious desire to revere the founders of their group than to the available historical data.

Yet certain theorems, and their proofs, may well antedate Hippocrates of Chios. I have already remarked on the extent of the geometrical knowledge implied by his work on quadratures. It is extremely unlikely that *all* the theorems he knew were his own discovery. In the case of the theorem that states the incommensurability of the side and diagonal of the square, we can be sure that that was known to mathematicians of Theodorus's generation (around 410). We know this from Plato's *Theaetetus* (147d ff), where Theodorus and his associates are represented as studying incommensurables from that which corresponds to the square root of 3 onward—presupposing the case corresponding to the square root of 2 as already familiar. The question is how long before Theodorus that incommensurability was known—and to know the proposition is, in this case, to know its proof, for we are not talking of having a rough idea that the side and the diagonal have no common measure, but of being in a position to show that they do not. While we have no means of settling the issue decisively, any more than we can be confident about *which* of several possible proof methods was the one first used to establish the theorem, the most likely conjecture is that this was a discovery dating from around the middle of the 5th century.

It may be noted in parenthesis that although some have seen this discovery as leading to a "foundation crisis" in mathematics, the reverse is rather the case. The fact that this provides such a fine example of a mathematical proposition that is demonstrable, and indeed was demonstrated, must have encouraged mathematicians in their bid to secure such proofs. As we see from *Theaetetus*, mathematicians of Theodorus's period, building on that first discovery, set to work to investigate more complicated cases. Incommensurabilities, so far from inhibiting mathematical inquiry, became the basis for what may even be called a research program. While the original discovery of the incommensurability of the side and diagonal of the square would have posed a problem for ontology—that is, for the view that physical objects are constituted by numbers as their matter—that is a separate issue. Besides, although Aristotle sometimes ascribes such a view to Pythagoreans, this is not so much a direct statement of their position as an inference concerning what Aristotle himself believed their position entailed. So far as mathematical study itself goes, the discovery of incommensurability may well have encouraged, rather than discouraged, the search for demonstrations.

Our review of the available evidence leaves *open* the possibility that the first strictly deductive arguments aiming at demonstrations were indeed those in Parmenides' *Way of Truth*. At the same time, we cannot rule out the further possibility that in mathematics, too, in approximately the same period, similar arguments had also begun to be developed. In general terms, the style of argument in both domains is, not surprisingly, similar. Thus we find that reductio, or indirect proof, is as important in early mathematics as it is in philosophy from Parmenides onward. At the same time, we cannot represent mathematics as entirely dependent on proof forms that can also be exemplified in philosophy. Mathematics certainly comes to develop its own, specifically mathematical, modes of demonstration, especially that based on the method of exhaustion, generally ascribed to Eudoxus in the late 4th century. This was a mathematical procedure that exploited the assumption of the infinite divisibility of the geometrical continuum. It enabled the areas of curvilinear figures (such as a circle) to be determined by successively closer rectilinear approximations, and was of general applicability and, from the 4th century onward, the geometrical proof procedure par excellence. While the *ambition* to provide demonstrations was common to both mathematics and philosophy, the demonstrative techniques employed in either domain were, to some extent at least, independent of one another.

Demonstration provides the basis for claims to certainty, and as such it had a fundamental role in both philosophy and mathematics from the mid-5th century onward. But the ambition to prove theories and conclusions came to be a dominant preoccupation in many areas of natural science as well. It is now time to consider the range of competing models of scientific understanding that were made explicit in the period before Aristotle. While one such model took it that knowledge depends on demonstration, others adopted laxer requirements for science. The evidence from the extant Hippocratic treatises of the late 5th and early 4th centuries is particularly interesting in this regard, since it shows both how some medical theorists sought to adopt or adapt the models provided by mathematics and philosophy, and how others resisted those tendencies and offered an alternative analysis of the status and proper methods of medicine.

The treatise known as *On Ancient Medicine* is a work that dates from the late 5th or, more likely, the early 4th century. The author attacks those who practiced medicine on the basis of what he calls a "hypothesis," a term he uses in the sense of "postulate" or "assumption." To be sure, it is not just *any* use of any kind of assumption that he has in mind. Certainly he himself uses a variety of concepts that we might characterize as assumptions. Rather, the use the writer particularly objects to is when a small number of such assumptions are taken as the basis for an entire theory of medicine. He criticizes his opponents especially for "narrowing down the causal principle of diseases," treating all diseases as if they were the outcome of just one or two factors such as "the hot," "the cold," "the wet," and "the dry." He compares the medical use of such assumptions to the methods used by some of the natural philosophers—those who investigate "things in the heavens or under the earth." While he does not mention mathematics, mathematical deductive arguments based on a limited number of starting points might be a further analogue to the methods he criticizes in medicine, and the evidence we have noted before from Plato suggests that the term *hypothesis* may have been used in mathematics at least before Plato himself.

Reconstructing the precise method attacked in *On Ancient Medicine* is difficult, and we are not in a position to name particular theorists whom this author may be taken to have definitely had in mind. Yet it seems that his principal objection is to treating medicine as if the whole subject could be deduced from a small number of starting points or principles. We have seen before that a well-defined notion of axioms may not antedate Aristotle himself. At the same time, both mathematics and philosophy provide examples of systems of deductive arguments based on a small number of starting points of some kind. It is some such ambition, to systematize the whole of medicine and treat it as a deductive structure derivable from a limited number of principles, that the author of *On Ancient Medicine* resists. He does so in the name of a rival view that insists that certainty and exactness are not possible in medicine, which is a matter, rather, of experience, of practice, of a trained eye. In the author's own view medicine is certainly a skill, a *technē*—where there are recognizable distinctions between good and bad practitioners—but it is a skill for which a better analogy would be seamanship than speculative philosophy.

This is not the only treatise that throws light on the growing dispute, within medicine, between two main competing conceptions of the subject. On the one hand, there are those whose ambition it was to assimilate medicine, as far as possible, to an exact science, who claim that it can achieve, even has achieved, certainty. One such is the author of the work *On the Art* who, recognizing that medical practice is fallible, explains this not in terms of the shortcomings of medicine itself, nor of its capacity to achieve cures, but rather in terms of the inability of patients to follow orders. Again there are several writers who claim that they can show, indeed have shown, the necessity of their conclusions, even on such problematic topics as the fundamental constituents of human bodies or of physical objects in general, or on the causes, and cures, of diseases. Thus we find dogmatic theories on those subjects presented in such works as *On the Nature of Man, On Regimen,* and *On Breaths.* True, some of these authors appeal to what we may call empirical evidence, as *On the Nature of Man* refers to the effects of drugs in inferring the presence of certain humors in the body. But while, in refutation, the combination of evidence and deductive argument in that work provides an impressive basis for the demolition of rival, monistic views, the attempts to show the necessity of the alternative pluralist theory are, naturally, quite inconclusive.

Yet the ambition to secure fundamental principles from which the whole of physiology and pathology can be derived is widespread.

On the other hand, resistance to the view that medicine can possibly be held to be deducible from a small number of postulates is represented not just by the author of *On Ancient Medicine* but by the undogmatic and anti-dogmatic tendencies to be found in many of the more purely empirical works. Many medical writers emphasize the conjectural nature of the art of medicine, not just in relation to the application of general principles to particular cases, but in the matter of the nature of the general principles themselves. One such treatise is *On the Places in Man*, which observes that there is a good deal of variability in medicine and remarks on the difficulties, in practice, of determining the right moment for intervention. The work *On Diseases* goes further. Exactness is not attainable either on the question of the differences between one physique and another, one illness and another, or on the issue of the timing of the doctor's own interventions. Medicine as a whole, this author states, has no demonstrated beginning or principle that is correct for the whole of the art of healing.

We thus find already in the period before Aristotle the main battle lines drawn up for what was to be the major ongoing epistemological and methodological dispute throughout ancient Greek medicine and even science as a whole. Against those who were for treating medicine as a deductive, exact science, there were those who insisted on its inexactness. Against those who sought necessity, there were those who considered that probability is the most that can be attained. Against those who thought that for understanding to be scientific it had to be certain, there were those who argued that medicine, for instance, is based on experience and must, to some extent, employ guesswork or conjecture, and yet it can still be claimed to be a rational inquiry, a *technē*, with its proper principles and methods.

We shall follow the fortunes of this debate in Aristotle and beyond, but for some of the background to the demand that science be demonstrative Plato provides crucial further evidence. His analysis of the concept of proof is a good deal more sophisticated than that of any earlier writer. In several of the dialogues, notably *Gorgias, Phaedo, The Republic,* and *Phaedrus*, the notion of proof, *apodeixis*, is elaborated in contradistinction to that of mere persuasion (where the key Greek term is *peithō* and its cognates). The latter is often associated with rhetoric, and it is the need to contrast true philosophy, and dialectic, with mere rhetoric that provides some of the stimulus to elaborate a strict concept of proof.

Certain contexts in which persuasion is used attract Plato's special attention. In the law courts and assemblies, what the judges or the people as a whole may be persuaded of may or may not be true, may or may not be the best policy. Sophists, and those who taught the art of public speaking, often aimed at, and were content with, achieving persuasion alone, whether or not that went with the truth—or so, at least, Plato claims. Like Aristophanes and others, Plato condemns those who made the worse, or weaker, argument seem the better or stronger, and more especially those who taught others how to manipulate arguments thus. If rhetoric and sophism are, at best, amoral, and often positively immoral, dialectic is the sincere search for the truth for its own sake. This might take the form of question and answer—as in the Socratic *elenchus*—but if so, it was not a question of refuting a thesis for refutation's sake but of doing so to discover the truth. Here it is not a matter of persuading a mass of jurors, or a lay audience, but of gaining the agreement of the person whose ideas are under examination. Moreover the procedure is not directed at the person himself but at the subject under discussion. If there is a competitive element in the correct method, it is a rivalry to get to the truth.

Plato does not offer a formal definition of *apodeixis*, but he explains his views on dialectic and on the accounts that philosophers should be expected to be able to give in justification of what they claim to know. In *The Republic*, especially, "dialectic" is contrasted with the procedures of the mathematicians and is rated higher than theirs on two counts in particular. First, the mathematicians make use of visible diagrams, while dialectic is a totally abstract study. More fundamentally, the mathematicians (as already noted) are said to give no account of their hypotheses but to take them "as evident to all." The dialecticians, by contrast, can and should do so, proceeding upward from their starting points to higher and higher hypotheses until they arrive at what Plato calls an unhypothetical first principle, to be identified with the Form of the Good, the Form in virtue of which all the other Forms acquire both their being and their knowability.

Much in this description is obscure, but it is obvious that with the unhypothetical first principle we are dealing with no mere axiom of the kind that came to be used in mathematics—in Euclid, for example. This is no mere proposition accepted as self-evidently true. It is rather, one supposes, a principle deemed to be essential to the correct conduct of any inquiry. Presumably Plato's point is, or includes, the idea that the order and regularity of the intelligible world exhibit *goodness*. As we can see from *Timaeus*, the account that Plato requires in cosmology is teleological, in terms of the beneficent interventions of the divine Craftsman who brings order into chaos. Moreover, in more general terms, for something to be revealed as ordered is, for Plato, for it to be revealed also to be good. Thus the Forms, as principles of order, may be said to depend (in a sense) on this supreme Form, the Form of the Good, since without it they would not be the principles of order that they are.

Difficult as it is to interpret this notion, we can understand the *claims* made on behalf of a dialectic thus founded on the principle of Goodness. The dialectician who *has* grasped the Form of the Good will be in a position to give an account of his recommendations and explanations in every field of study.

Once the whole complex, articulated structure of the Forms is apprehended as the structure it is, certainty will be attainable—even if Plato is careful not to imply that Socrates *has* attained it, let alone that he himself had. The *ambition* to attain it is, however, clear. The method based on a principle that is itself unhypothetical is a method that can *secure* its results, not just in relation to the Good itself, but with regard to all the Forms seen to depend on it.

Moreover, this account of the highest form of study inevitably has repercussions on Plato's evaluation of other inquiries. We have remarked that mathematics is ranked below dialectic in *The Republic*. In *Philebus* (55ff) we have a more complex stratification of the various branches of knowledge. At the top comes dialectic, of course. But below that mathematics is subdivided into a higher, purer study—the philosophical study of numbers in themselves, for instance—and a lower, applied one—the arithmetic used in practical calculation. Lower still, there are arts such as architecture, music making, navigation, and medicine, but these are distinguished and graded according to the extent to which they make use of numbering, weighing, and measuring. Thus architecture, which does so to a considerable degree, is rated higher on this score than music making, said to be based not on measurement so much as on guesswork. It is notable that while Plato is prepared here to accommodate medicine as *a* branch of knowledge, it is one of the lowliest, as being an essentially conjectural discipline.

Aristotle is at once clearer and more systematic than Plato, and it is Aristotle who may be said to provide the first *explicit* definition and explanation of an axiomatic deductive method of reasoning. In *Posterior Analytics* (71b11ff) he defines demonstration, *apodeixis*, as deductive, specifically syllogistic, in form, and he insists that it should proceed from premises that must be true, primary, immediate, and explanatory of the conclusions. They must be explanatory, since the knowledge or understanding that demonstration yields is, strictly, not of mere facts but of their explanations or causes.

Thus Aristotle is clear on three fundamental points. First, deductive argument is wider than demonstration, for deductive arguments may be valid or invalid, and valid deductions can be drawn from premises irrespective of whether those premises are true or false. For demonstrations, the deductions must be valid *and* the premise true as well as primary and explanatory. Second, not all true propositions can be demonstrated. The primary propositions from which demonstrated conclusions follow must themselves be indemonstrable—to avoid an infinite regress. For what premises could they be demonstrated from? Third, the primary indemonstrable premises needed for demonstrations will take different forms. Aristotle specifies definitions, hypotheses, and axioms. By definitions he has in mind not nominal definitions of terms but real definitions—that is, accounts that correspond to the realities of the subject matter investigated. He explains his notion of hypothesis in terms of the assumptions, such as that of the existence of objects defined.

Thus in his mathematical example, the definition of a point tells us what "point" signifies, but the corresponding hypothesis is the assumption that there are such. Finally there are the axioms, both general laws setting out the principles on which all communication is based (the laws of noncontradiction and of excluded middle) and axioms specific to particular inquiries. Again Aristotle's example is a mathematical one, the equality axiom that states that if equals are taken from equals, equals remain. Aristotle takes it that any attempt to *prove* this would itself have to presuppose the principle in question.

If we bear in mind the indeterminate nature of the "starting points" assumed in extant mathematics or in philosophy before Aristotle, including even in Plato himself, we can see that the distinctions that Aristotle introduces between the different types of indemonstrable, and his analysis of their role in demonstration, achieve a remarkable clarification of the issues. At the end of the *De Sophisticis Elenchis* (183a37ff, 183b34ff) he writes of his own originality in having given the first formal analysis of deductive argument, and we may agree that there is no reason seriously to dispute his claim.

Here, then, is a powerful procedure by which not just truth but certainty can be attained, secured by valid deductive arguments proceeding from self-evident primary premises. Many of Aristotle's examples in *Posterior Analytics* are mathematical, and although Greek mathematical reasoning is not syllogistic in form, it was, of course, in that domain that the practice of axiomatic deductive reasoning could and did have its main area of application. Yet Aristotle's own scientific activity was rather in the field of natural philosophy, especially zoology, and questions arise as to whether such an ideal of demonstration is applicable there and, further, whether Aristotle thought it was.

Certainly there are examples drawn from physics, from meteorology, from astronomy, from zoology and botany, along with mathematical examples, in *Posterior Analytics,* and these clearly indicate that at the time that work was composed, at least, Aristotle was hopeful of applying some of its ideas in those fields too. There is, to be sure, no problem in seeing Aristotle as endeavoring to implement some of the ideals *for explanation* that are set out in *Analytics,* in practice, throughout his work, even if he rarely, if ever, presents his results in clear syllogistic form, that is, in a fashion that exhibits transparently their syllogistic structure. But there is a fundamental difficulty concerning the indemonstrables that are appropriate to, and possible in, physics.

The general axioms of reasoning are, of course, applicable in physics as in all communication. But nothing *follows from* them. They will not figure in demonstrations except in the rare case where the demonstrator wishes to show some logical principle directly linked to them. But Aristotle never gives a clear zoological or botanical example of an axiom *specific* to those domains (on a par with the equality axiom in mathematics), and indeed it is hard to supply any plausible example of one. Definitions, to be sure, are an important topic of investigation in the physical treatises. Yet these are not then used as the indemonstrable primary premises from which are deduced demonstrated conclusions corresponding to the ideal requirements of *Posterior Analytics*. Moreover many of the key terms used in his physical works are explicated in ways that acknowledge that no simple univocal definition can be given of them. They are "said in many ways." Such is the case not just with the abstractions discussed in *Physics,* such as the notions of time, space, continuity, and the like, but also with some of the fundamental concepts on which his physical theories are based. This applies, for instance, to element theory. The primary opposites, hot, cold, wet, and dry, are explicated roughly in the work *On Coming-To-Be and Passing-Away* but are recognized, in *Parts of Animals,* to be "said in many ways."

The mismatch between the practice of the physical treatises and the ideal model of demonstration set out in *Posterior Analytics* poses a problem that remains at the center of scholarly controversy. On one line of interpretation, *Posterior Analytics* should be seen not as recommending that proper science be formal, but simply as showing how a formal description of proper science can be given. Yet this still leaves plenty of problems concerning the securing of indemonstrables that are appropriate to the concerns of proper science. On another view, the object of this treatise is to explain how a science can be *taught,* and Aristotle is accordingly not exercised with how the scientific investigator goes about his own researches. The actual procedures of the physical treatises might more often be better described as dialectical than demonstrative. On a third view, Aristotle may have modified his ideas as his own scientific activities developed, including his views on the *ideals* that are suitable to such investigations, as well as his views on their actual practice.

This is not the place to enter into the details of these disputes. But one fundamental point may be made that goes to the heart of the question. This is that there is, in any case, no question of *Posterior Analytics* presenting the *only* theory or concept of demonstration, *apodeixis,* in Aristotle. When we turn to the rest of his work we find him using and developing a variety of different notions of demonstrations, in different contexts. He sets out a second carefully worked-out theory of demonstration in *Rhetoric,* where he uses the term *enthymeme* for what are, precisely, rhetorical demonstrations. Not only does their form differ from the demonstrations analyzed in *Posterior Analytics*—they do not, for instance, proceed from indemonstrable primary premises and indeed do not conform to the rules for the valid modes of the syllogism—but, furthermore, Aristotle explains that they will be useful not to establish incontrovertible conclusions but rather for the purposes of securing conviction in relation to what is unclear or disputed.

There should be nothing surprising in this further theoretical analysis of a rhetorical mode of demonstration in Aristotle's *Rhetoric.* We should bear in mind that from its very beginning, Greek forensic and deliberative oratory had repeatedly presented what the orators themselves call demonstrations, of the facts of the case, of the guilt or innocence of the parties concerned, of the rights and wrongs of the policies under discussion. While, as we saw, the chief effort of Plato was to *deny* that rhetoric as usually practiced achieved more than mere persuasion, the terminology both he and Aristotle used for the highest kind of demonstration in philosophy is the *same* as that which the orators themselves used of *their* claims to have proved points beyond reasonable doubt. Aristotle indeed duly acknowledged that there is *rhetorical* demonstration, even though in his account of it he is far from just describing the usual procedures of the orators, which he would fault on a number of grounds.

It is not that the physical treatises of Aristotle exemplify rhetorical demonstration as he defines it. Yet in the scattered methodological remarks we find in *Metaphysics* as well as in the zoology and elsewhere, there is a clear recognition that demonstration may be more or less strict, indeed more or less necessary, depending on the subject matter in hand. Whether or not we say that Aristotle's position on the topic of demonstration in physics changed, we must agree that we find a variety of views expressed on the styles of demonstration possible and appropriate on different problems and in different areas. The actual practice of his scientific investigations is, then, a good deal more flexible, and looser, than the requirements of *Posterior Analytics* might lead one to expect. Finally it must be added that if he had attempted to set out demonstrations in the *Posterior Analytics* style in the physical and zoological works, on the vast majority of occasions this would hardly have improved the investigation. To have insisted on indemonstrable primary premises that are true, immediate, and necessary, on many of the problems he was concerned with, would have bought surface clarity only at the cost of artificiality and arbitrariness.

The theory of rigorous demonstration that was set out in *Posterior Analytics* came closest to implementation in practice not in Aristotle's own physical works, but in the mathematical work of Euclid. As noted, Greek mathematics was never cast in syllogistic form—nor indeed can most mathematical reasoning be so cast without great strain. But the work that above all exhibited what the comprehensive presentation of a systematic body of knowledge set out in strict deductive form looked like in practice was Euclid's *Elements*. Just how far Euclid may have been directly influenced by Aristotle, and how far he was following and elaborating the models provided by earlier mathematics, is uncertain. Like Aristotle he adopts a triadic classification of indemonstrables, though his triad does not match Aristotle's exactly. His definitions and common opinions correspond to the definitions and axioms in Aristotle well enough, and one of his common opinions is the equality axiom cited also by Aristotle. However his third kind of indemonstrable is the postulate, and these clearly differ from Aristotle's hypotheses. The first three of his postulates in *Elements*, book I, relate to the possibility of carrying out certain constructions (for example, to draw a straight line from any point to any point), and the other two assume certain truths concerning geometrical constructions that form the basis of what *we* call Euclidean geometry, namely that all right angles are equal, and that nonparallel straight lines meet at a point.

But the question of indebtedness is a subsidiary issue. What is both uncontroversial and of first-rate importance is that *Elements* thereafter provides *the* model for the systematic demonstration of a body of knowledge, a model influential (as we shall see) not just in mathematics but far beyond it. Of course by modern standards of axiomatization, that in Euclid's mathematics is far from perfect. Among minor points of criticism are that he includes certain redundant definitions (for example, that of rhomboid). Among more important ones are that several of his key terms remain undefined and unexplicated, as, for instance, his notion of measure, where, as with the notion of proportion, *Elements* seems to draw on a variety of traditions and has not resolved all the problems of consistency that they pose. Moreover the very notion of attempting explicit definitions of all the fundamental terms in geometrical discourse itself appears odd to a modern view, at least insofar as it seems supererogatory to provide such in the case of *primitive* terms. *Their* sense is precisely what the geometry developed on their basis explicates—in a manner more appropriate than any formal definition could achieve.

At this point, interestingly, the thrust of possible modern criticisms contrasts with that of some ancient objections to *Elements*. Some ancient commentators complained not that Euclid had done too much, but that he had not done enough—not that he tried to be too explicit, but rather that he had taken as axioms propositions that should have figured as theorems to be proved. A sequence of later writers, including Ptolemy and Proclus, complained that the parallel postulate should have been demonstrated. They sometimes themselves attempted proofs, though their offerings all suffer from circularity. With the benefit of hindsight we can now see the wisdom of treating this as a postulate in the context of the geometry Euclid constructed on its basis. Whether this was Euclid's own contribution is unclear, but since Aristotle reports that attempts to prove assumptions concerning parallels are open to the charge of circularity, the notion of adopting the postulate concerned as a postulate can hardly have antedated Euclid by many years.

Neither Euclid nor anyone else in antiquity seriously envisaged the possibility of non-Euclidean geometries. Euclid almost certainly assumed that *Elements* presents not just a consistent set of mathematical truths but a set that corresponds to the reality of spatial relationships in the world. Most Greek mathematics, indeed, adopts a confidently realist position about the relationship between mathematics and physics, even when some theorists allowed that certain physical phenomena are capable of different mathematical accounts. But that did not stop Euclid taking as a postulate a proposition that he may well have known others would have attempted to prove. However, if the adoption of the parallel postulate was controversial, no one was in any doubt concerning the impressive strengths that the argumentative structure of *Elements* as a whole exhibits. First there is the economy and clarity with which individual theorems are established, using direct or indirect proofs, especially reductio and the method of exhaustion. Second there is the careful articulation of the whole into a single comprehensive system.

After Euclid, proof in the style of *Elements*, proof *more geometrico*, as it was later to be called, became a potent ideal imitated in a wide variety of disciplines. Thus Euclid's own optics, parts of music theory, parts of theoretical astronomy, and statics and hydrostatics were presented in this style, with first the setting out of the postulates, common opinions, axioms, definitions needed, then the deductive demonstration of a body of theorems. There can be no doubt that much of the work so produced ranks among the most remarkable achievements of Greek science. This may certainly be said of Archimedes' statics and hydrostatics, for instance, where, in the first case, he explores the consequences of a set of postulates concerning balances and proceeds to the proof of the law of the lever, and, in the second, demonstrates, again on the basis of appropriate postulates, the principle named after him: that solids heavier than a fluid will, if placed in the fluid, be carried down to the bottom of the fluid, and they will be lighter in the fluid by the weight of the mount of fluid that has the same volume as the solid.

However, certain constraints on scientific work must also be acknowledged to have come from the concentration on the Euclidean ideal. In mathematics itself, the preoccupation with the strict demonstration of results may well have had an inhibiting effect, if not on mathematical inquiry itself, at least on what mathematicians chose to publish as their results. The exception here that proves the rule is Archimedes' *Method*. Quite exceptionally for a Greek mathematical text, this work discusses discovery as well as demonstration and presents a method that, Archimedes says, is heuristic without being demonstrative. The method is called a mechanical one, and it depends on two interrelated assumptions, first that a plane figure can be thought of as composed of the parallel lines that it contains, and second that it can be thought of as balanced against some other area or set of lines at a certain distance (the distance being imagined as a balance from which the figures are suspended). Now it is not clear from what Archimedes himself says, and it is disputed in modern scholarship, whether his reason for refusing to think this method a demonstrative one was the use of the mechanical assumption (which breached the categorical distinction between physics and mathematics) or that of indivisibles (which breached the assumption of the geometrical continuum), or indeed of both. But that point need not concern us here; the point that does is that Archimedes allows informal methods no more than a heuristic role and insists that the results thereby obtained must thereafter all be proved strictly using reductio and the method of exhaustion.

The inhibition that Greek mathematicians generally, and not just Archimedes, felt about presenting results other than in strict demonstrative form must have acted as a break on investigation. Archimedes' heuristic method remained unexploited by later Greek mathematicians (indeed all but ignored), and if that was partly because the treatise that described it was not generally known, that is not the whole story, since some of the theorems in his *On the Quadrature of the Parabola* implicitly depend on a similar method. The problem was the more general one of the reluctance to rely on informal methods.

I remarked that it was not just in mathematics and the exact sciences that proof in the Euclidean manner became the ideal. Our next topic should be the imitation of these methods in the natural sciences, such as physiology, psychology, and even medicine. By far the most outstanding example of this comes in the work of the 2nd-century C.E. medical writer Galen, and it will be convenient to concentrate our discussion on him.

Galen's reputation, in antiquity, did not depend just on his preeminence as a physician, since he was also considered a notable philosopher and he certainly made impressive original contributions to logic in particular. Unfortunately his masterpiece in that field, the fifteen-book work *On Demonstration*, is not extant, but it is clear from his own and other references to it that it contained a comprehensive analysis of the subject. In the short treatise *That the Best Doctor Is Also a Philosopher*, Galen gives three types of reasons to support the thesis that gives the work its title. First, the doctor should be morally upright and in particular free from avarice. Second, the doctor will need to study natural philosophy in order to base his medical theories on the correct physical principles, for example the theory of the elements. But third, the doctor should also be trained in scientific method, especially in demonstration. It is not just that doctors should, in his view, have a clear grasp of elementary logic and be able to distinguish valid and invalid inferences. Galen wants far more, namely that the doctor should be able to present scientific demonstrations on theoretical points throughout his work.

This is not just an abstract, theoretical claim, for Galen evidently puts it into practice on many occasions in his own biological treatises. Negatively and destructively he often criticizes his opponents' arguments as invalid, inconsistent, based on ambiguous terms, and so on. For this purpose and for his own constructive demonstrations he draws not just on Aristotelian, but also on Stoic, logic, using in particular Stoic formalizations where the variables expressed as numbers stand not for terms but for propositions. Thus both the Stoic elementary propositions later known as Modus Ponens and Modus Tollens are referred to: "if p, then q; but p; so q," and "if p, then q; but not q; so not p."

In many cases the points he claims to demonstrate are fairly straightforward consequences of hypotheses that state generally accepted principles. But he also attempts demonstration of some of his fundamental physiological and psychological doctrines. Thus in the work *On the Doctrines of Plato and Hippocrates* he sets out to prove his modified version of Plato's tripartite psychology (a theory maintained also, he would claim, by Hippocrates). According to Galen there are three main faculties of the soul (or life force), namely the appetitive, the spirited, and the rational. The first is to be located in the liver, the source of the veins; the second is placed in the heart, the source of the arteries; and the third in the brain, the source of the nervous system.

These are positions that he claims are demonstrable, and he himself proceeds to demonstrate them. Interestingly enough he distinguishes between the ease and certainty of the demonstrations of the locations of the higher two faculties of the soul, and the relative complexity of the arguments that establish that the appetitive function is to be placed in the liver. In the case of the rational faculty he proposes the simplest of syllogisms: "where the beginning of the nerves is, there is the governing part. The beginning of the nerves is in the brain. Therefore the governing part is there." Here the key step is, of course, that which establishes the origin of the nerves in the brain, and for this he refers to his own and earlier anatomical investigations. Thus if the carotid nerves leading up to the brain are ligated, the animal immediately loses consciousness. This provides the connection Galen needs, and with this secure he moves to state the whole proof as outlined above. His method is similar in the case of the role and function of the heart, but he concedes that no direct procedure, using ligation, is possible in the case of the liver. However, he believes he can establish well enough that the veins originate there, and that the nutritive and appetitive functions have their origin there too.

Galen thus frequently uses his knowledge of argument schemata to help in the construction of the proofs of physical, physiological, and psychological theories. Many of his arguments can readily be presented in rigorous formal terms: he presents some of them in that form himself. But the chief question that arises relates to the problem that I have already mentioned in connection with Aristotle. Valid deductive arguments lead to true conclusions if and only if the premises are themselves true. If the premises are accepted by an opponent, then he has to accept the conclusions as well; if the premises are agreed to provisionally as working hypotheses, we can say that we have dialectical arguments recommending the conclusions. However, the fundamental problem is that for strict demonstration we need ultimate primary premises that are themselves indemonstrable, and the question is, what will count as such in such domains as physiology or pathology?

We can agree that definitions will play some such role, but they will hardly be adequate for the task on their own. To supplement them, Galen appears to hold that some very general physical and pathological principles have the status of axioms. One such is the doctrine that nature does nothing in vain, which he treats as a regulative principle of physiological explanation. If that is denied, no proper explanations of the functions of the parts of the body can be given. The principle itself cannot be proved, but it provides the foundation for the investigation of nature. Similarly in pathology Galen frequently cites the principle he ascribes to Hippocrates, that opposites are cures for opposites, and indeed some such doctrine will certainly be needed for the purposes of his medical demonstrative arguments.

Yet in both cases these principles have serious shortcomings *as axioms.* The view that nature does nothing in vain was rejected by many philosophers and scientists, notably by both the pre- and the post-Aristotelian atomists. Moreover the particular version of the doctrine that Galen adopts is especially controversial, since in his view (at least as he sometimes expresses it) the doctrine states not just what is generally true but what is true without exception. Unlike Aristotle, who allows that some of the parts of the body do not directly serve a good purpose but are the residues or by-products of physiological processes, Galen sometimes writes as if there were no such exceptions—difficult as that doctrine is to sustain in practice, in the face of such evident problems as that of the presence of pathogenic substances in the body.

Again the trouble with the doctrine that opposites are cures for opposites is that it leaves quite unclear what will count as "opposites." As Aristotle pointed out, hot, cold, wet, and dry, for instance, were "said in many ways" and their application to foods, drugs, processes was in fact highly disputed. A substance might appear hot to the touch but not *be* hot, depending on the theory invoked in its analysis. What counted as "repletion" and "evacuation" was equally massively indeterminate. So while most Greek medical theorists may indeed be said to have accepted, in one form or another, the idea of attempting to counteract opposites to achieve a cure, the *content* of that doctrine varied considerably from one theorist to another.

Neither medical science nor physiology had, in Galen's day, the remotest chance of actually securing primary premises that are both indemonstrable and true, from which to derive *incontrovertible* conclusions. Galen's concern with the validity of arguments, his own and those of his opponents, is entirely admirable. Yet his further ambition to construct medicine and physics as far as possible on the model of mathematics and the exact sciences seems, in the state of the sciences at the time, extravagant. His obsession with logically rigorous formalized demonstrations is all the more paradoxical in that, if we consider the ways and means that might be thought appropriate to establishing the types of anatomical and physiological conclusions with which he is concerned, the best method would often rely on the very kind of empirical procedure, namely dissection, that Galen himself used so skillfully. What we still call *anatomical demonstrations,* for example to exhibit the structures and functions of particular nerves or the processes of digestion, are amply represented in such works as *On Anatomical Procedures.* Yet Galen still rates these empirical procedures as inferior to the strictly logical demonstrations he yearns for in physiology and pathology.

A long line of prominent philosophers and scientists stretching from Parmenides down to Galen and beyond exemplify the recurrent Greek concern with rigorous demonstration. In large part this concern reflects the desire for certainty, and in some cases it is clearly a negative reaction to the perceived weaknesses of merely persuasive argument. This was associated by Plato with the practices of orators in the law courts and assemblies, where indeed persuasive argument was commonly and most effectively deployed and sometimes even represented by the orators themselves as demonstrative.

Here then was one ideal for philosophy and science. Yet it was not the only conception of their goal, even if it was the dominant one in the work of several prominent theorists. I mentioned an alternative, empirical conception of the proper methods of scientific inquiry in the pre-Aristotelian medical literature. It is now time to review briefly, in conclusion, some of the later evidence for those who adopted a view of science that did not place the emphasis on the types of rigorous demonstration exemplified in the Euclidean tradition.

For this purpose we should first turn back to some points in Aristotle himself. We have seen that he set out, in *Posterior Analytics,* a very strict theory of demonstration but in practice, in the physical treatises, rarely if ever presents arguments that strictly conform to that theory. We noted, too, certain texts that suggest the possibility of looser styles of demonstration appropriate to certain problems in physics and elsewhere. While for the highest form of demonstration necessity and universality are definite requirements, physics deals, as he often stresses, with what is true always *or for the most part.* It is clear from the inclusion of propositions that state truths that hold "for the most part" in *Posterior Analytics* that Aristotle's aim, there, was to present a theory of strict demonstration that would also encompass them, although he encounters difficulties in so doing. But conclusions based on premises that state generally accepted or well-founded but not certain premises are given a recognized place in Aristotle's analysis in that they provide the basis of his account of what he calls dialectical reasoning. In practice, too, and not just in theory, much effort is devoted, in the physical treatises, to the critical evaluation of what was commonly believed, where Aristotle sometimes rejects but sometimes accepts, in modified form, what others also held.

Thus while Aristotle's own preference for demonstration over any merely dialectical procedure is clear, the latter provides the basis not for an alternative model for the highest science, but at least for supplementing the models that insist on demonstration in either its stricter or its laxer modes. After Aristotle, however, there were those who rejected with some vigor the whole concept that scientific inquiry, to be legitimate, had to yield results that could be claimed as incontrovertible.

Once again our main evidence comes from some of the medical writers, even though in the immediate post-Aristotelian period much of the work of important medical theorists is lost and their views have to be reconstructed from later reports. However, the evidence we have in both Celsus and Galen enables us to infer the main lines of a wide-ranging methodological and epistemological dispute about the status, aims, and proper methods of medicine, a dispute that continued from the late 4th century B.C.E. down to Galen's own day. The medical writers labeled "dogmatists" were not a well-knit sect. Rather, that term was used of any theorist who sought causal explanations of hidden phenomena in physiology or pathology. But more important for our purposes here are the views of two other rather more clearly defined groups regularly contrasted with the dogmatists. These are the Empiricists (starting with Philinus of Cos around the mid-3rd century B.C.E.) and the Methodists (who took their origin from the work of Thessalus and Themison around the 1st century B.C.E. and the 1st century C.E.). In both cases these theorists rejected the whole endeavor to give causal explanations of such physiological processes as respiration and digestion, and in both cases the method of dissection was criticized as irrelevant to the study of the living, normally functioning individual.

The alternative aim that the Empiricists and Methodists presented as the true goal of medicine is a pragmatic one. There is no need to inquire into how we breathe, Celsus reports the Empiricists arguing, but only what relieves labored breathing. There is no need to find out what moves the blood vessels, only what the various movements signify. The inquiry into obscure causes and natural actions is superfluous because nature cannot be comprehended. This was a view with which the Methodists, too, generally agreed, even while they reformulated the grounds for it, arguing not that it is impossible to comprehend nature, but rather that it is useless to do so. That is an issue on which judgment should be suspended.

The traditions of rationalist, dogmatic medicine were thus seriously undermined, and reasoning itself was viewed with some suspicion. In theorizing, the Empiricists held, it is always possible to argue on either side of the question, but then it is far from clear that victory in the argument goes to the person who has the better grasp of the subject. Both groups held that the aim of medicine is not theoretical knowledge but achieving cures. What counted was not book learning but practical experience. The Empiricists' method was to try to determine how to treat the particular case in hand on the basis of similarities with past cases. They proceeded on the basis of analogies, or as they put it, they used the "transition to the similar." Some of their opponents criticized them on the grounds that they would be at a complete loss if faced with an entirely new type of disease. But the Empiricist response to that might well have been that it was no good attempting to *deduce* a cure from a would-be universal principle, in such cases, since that would beg the question of *whether* the new disease could indeed be treated as an instance of some such general principle or otherwise brought under an existing general law.

The Methodists shared the pragmatic aims of the Empiricists but went much further than them in rejecting not just research into hidden causes but the basic assumption of most traditional Greek medical theory, namely the possibility of identifying and classifying kinds of diseases. That is, they rejected the fundamental notion of disease entities. What the patient suffers from, and what the doctor has to try to cure, are what they called "common conditions," *koinotētes*, the "lax," the "restricted," and the "mixed." These were not single diseases but rather, as their name suggests, general states. In evaluating a patient's state the doctor would need to take into account the *whole* condition and arrive at a plan for therapy only on the basis of a full assessment of that. Although extant Methodist writings, such as the gynecological work of the 2nd-century C.E. writer Soranus, still use traditional terms for diseases, we should not be misled by this into supposing that their authors endorsed these. Rather, the terms were used for the sake of a lay audience who would have some idea of what they referred to, even if their understanding had to be reeducated to an acceptance of the very different approach to questions of pathology that the Methodists themselves adopted.

A tension between the demand that science should be exact, yield certain results, give demonstrations that proceed from self-evident premises via valid deductions to undeniable conclusions, and a quite different view of science that allowed a place for the probable, for conjecture, for empirical experience, characterizes both the practices and the theories of Greek science from its early beginnings down to the 2nd century C.E. and beyond. We can see this tension in play *within* many of the sciences that I have so far not had occasion to mention. A good example is provided by music. In music theory there were those who took their stand by the experience of practicing musicians: their aim was to describe the perceived phenomena of actual musical performances, where indeed the great variety of modes in Greek music provided plenty of scope for analysis. At the opposite end of the spectrum, there were writers for whom music theory was a branch of mathematics, whether or not they agreed specifically with Plato's recommendation, in *The Republic,* that the study should concern itself solely with which numbers are essentially concordant with which. On one view, reason was not just a better guide to the underlying laws of harmony, it was the sole criterion. Thus when it became evident that the numerical relationship corresponding to the interval of an octave plus a fourth, namely $8:3$, is neither multiplicate (like $2:1$ or $3:1$) nor superparticular (like $3:2$ and $4:3$), the reaction of some theorists was to conclude that whether or not such an interval *sounded* like a concord, it could not *be* one, since it did not meet the requisite arithmetical condition for such. To that Theophrastus commented that what music theory studies is not number but sounds, even if the relationships between concordant sounds are expressible numerically, as ratios between integers.

In astronomy, too, there are, on the one hand, broadly descriptive studies and, on the other, the attempt to create geometrical models to account for the apparently irregular movements of the sun, moon, and planets. In some cases we have extant treatises that limit themselves to the purely geometrical analysis, for example, of interacting spheres in motion. One such is Autolycus of Pitane's work *On Moving Spheres* and another is Theodosius's *Sphaerica*. Neither of these carries the study forward to the point where a direct application is made to observed phenomena. No empirical data as such are brought to bear, and the discussion remains geometrical throughout. Similarly Aristarchus's work *On the Sizes and Distances of the Sun and Moon* is largely a hypothetical discussion of how the proportions of these sizes and distances can be worked out on the basis of certain assumptions.

However, much of Greek astronomical theory is not just geometrical, even while it uses geometry in the development of models to explain the movements of the sun, moon, and planets. The position of Ptolemy is especially revealing and will provide our last concrete example of the recurrent tension in Greek science between the desire for certainty and exactness and the need to accommodate imprecision in the detailed application of theory to empirical data.

In the opening chapters of *Syntaxis* Ptolemy contrasts mathematics (under which heading he includes the astronomical study he is himself about to engage in) with both theology and physics. Those two studies are both conjectural: not much knowledge can be acquired about the gods, and physics deals with unstable phenomena. Mathematics, by contrast—the claim is—yields certain results, based as it is on indisputable geometrical reasoning. Similarly in his astrological treatise, *Tetrabiblos*, the attempt to make predictions concerning events on earth is contrasted with the prediction of the movements of the heavenly bodies themselves, with the latter being far less certain.

Mathematical astronomy itself, these remarks imply, can yield exact conclusions. Yet in practice the application of Ptolemy's models to the particular movements of each of the planets, the sun, and the moon is permeated by approximations of one type or another. True, the geometrical reasoning is exact. So far as the geometry goes, nothing could detract from the claim that these are indeed Euclidean-style demonstrations. However, as soon as empirical data are brought into play—as they must be if the models are to be determinate quantitative models for each of the heavenly bodies, as opposed to merely impressionistic qualitative ones—there are elements of inexactness. These spring both from the acknowledged inexactnesses of particular observations (owing to the errors of instruments or observers or to the difficulties of observation) and from features of the calculations, the frequent adjustments that Ptolemy makes within the purely arithmetical parts of his computations, as, for instance, when he converts chords to arcs or vice versa. The outcome is indeed a set of fully determinate models, with definite parameters enabling the movements of the planets, moon, and sun to be predicted. Yet the elements of appreciation throughout are manifest.

The notion of demonstration thus lies at the heart of a methodological and epistemological dispute that runs through Greek philosophy and science from their very beginnings, a dispute often articulated around the contrast between reason and perception or, more generally, experience. Some Greek scientists opted resolutely for one of these two broad criteria to the exclusion of the other. That pushed the science they did toward either pure mathematics and logic or a pragmatism stripped of general theory. Some demanded strict demonstration in the geometrical manner, while others insisted on a relaxation of the requirement that science be demonstrative, allowing proper science to include—or even to consist in—conjecture. In between the two extreme positions there were those who sought a compromise, allowing both reason and experience a role, though in a variety of combinations. The fundamental dilemma that surfaces in many of the greatest works of ancient science and is, of course, far from being confined to ancient science is that the purer the science, the more it approximates pure mathematics in form, but then the further removed it will be from the very data that the science purports to explain. The tension was between the aim to make science exact and demonstrative and the need for it to be applicable. While some chose the goal of exactness at the cost of applicability (Archimedes) and others (among the medical writers) abandoned demonstrativeness for the sake of practice, the works of Galen in anatomy and physiology, and of Ptolemy in astronomical theory, exhibit the tensions that arise from the uneasy match between the desire for certainty and the actual recognition of the elements of approximation in many of the results obtained.

Geoffrey E. R. Lloyd

Bibliography

Berti, Enrico, ed. *Aristotle on Science: The Posterior Analytics*. Padua: Antenore, 1981.

Burnyeat, Myles, ed. *The Sceptical Tradition*. Berkeley: University of California Press, 1983.

Détienne, Marcel, and Jean-Pierre Vernant. *Cunning Intelligence in Greek Culture and Society*. Trans. Janet Lloyd. Repr. Chicago: University of Chicago Press, 1991.

Gentzler, Jyl, ed. *Method in Ancient Philosophy*. Oxford: Clarendon Press, 1998.

Gotthelf, Allan, and James G. Lennox, eds. *Philosophical Issues in Aristotle's Biology*. Cambridge: Cambridge University Press, 1987.

Irwin, Terence H. *Aristotle's First Principles*. Oxford: Clarendon Press, 1988.

Knorr, Wilbur R. *The Evolution of the Euclidean Elements*. Dordrecht: Reidel, 1975.

Kullmann, Wolfgang. *Wissenschaft und Methode*. Berlin: De Gruyter, 1974.

Lloyd, Geoffrey E. R. *Magic, Reason, and Experience: Studies in the Origin and Development of Greek Science*. Cambridge: Cambridge University Press, 1979.

Mignucci, Marco. *L'argomentazione dimostrativa in Aristotele*. Padua: Antemore, 1975.

Mueller, Ian. *Philosophy of Mathematics and Deductive Structure in Euclid's Elements.* Cambridge, Mass.: MIT Press, 1981.

Netz, Reviel. *The Shaping of Deduction in Greek Mathematics.* Cambridge: Cambridge University Press, 1999.

Schofield, Malcolm, Myles Burnyeat, and Jonathan Barnes. *Doubt and Dogmatism.* Oxford: Clarendon Press, 1980.

Tannery, Paul. *Pour l'histoire de la science hellène,* 2nd ed. Paris: Gauthier-Villars, 1930.

Related Articles

Epistemology; Logic; Medicine; Epicurus; Galen; Stoicism; Observation and Research; Mathematics; Aristotle; Euclid; Parmenides

ASTRONOMY

THE EARLIEST USE of astronomy among the Greeks appears in the poems of Homer and Hesiod (8th century B.C.E.). By that time the Greeks, like many other agricultural societies, had identified and named certain prominent stars and star groups (Arcturus, the Pleiades, and so on). We can see especially from Hesiod's *Works and Days* that the heliacal risings and cosmical settings of these (their first appearance and last disappearance just before dawn) were used to mark important points in the agricultural year, such as the time to begin plowing or harvesting. In the absence of a settled calendar, such an "astronomical calendar" was very necessary, and this traditional Greek astronomy was eventually codified in a kind of almanac (which, like modern almanacs, also contained weather predictions). Even after the development of scientific astronomy, these *parapegmata* continued to be popular, and examples were produced by some of the most eminent Greek astronomers. The early Greeks had also recognized the existence of planets and named some of them, but they had not yet recognized that the morning star and the evening star are the same planet, Venus.

Although a number of astronomical topics (such as the causes of eclipses) were discussed by the philosophers of the 7th and 6th centuries B.C.E. (supposedly beginning with Thales), their speculations should be described as cosmological rather than astronomical. But by the 5th century some astronomical truths had been enunciated, although they were not yet universally accepted even by the educated. Thus in the early 5th century Parmenides of Elea, in his remarkable philosophical poem, stated that the earth is a sphere and that the moon receives its light from the sun. In the next generation Empedocles correctly inferred that the cause of a solar eclipse is the moon passing in front of the sun. But equally important in the development of Greek astronomy during and perhaps even before the 5th century is the transmission of knowledge from Mesopotamia, where observational astronomy had been systematically practiced and recorded since the 8th century, and where astronomical systems were already being developed. This is apparent in the work of Meton, the first Greek who can properly be called an astronomer.

Meton is dated by his observation of the summer solstice at Athens in 432 B.C.E. Although not very accurate (it is a day in error), it marks the beginning of a new stage in Greek astronomy, for Meton made the observation by means of an instrument, simple but large and effective, that he had constructed for the purpose. Meton is also famous for his introduction of the nineteen-year luni-solar cycle, in which the solar year and the (true) lunar month are reconciled by the intercalation, in a fixed pattern, of a thirteenth month in seven years out of the nineteen. This is an obvious example of Mesopotamian influence, for a similar cycle had been in use in Babylon for some time. However, Meton was still operating within the framework of traditional Greek astronomy, since both his observations and his cycle were directed toward the composition of a *parapegma* almanac.

It is not until the next generation that the most original and profound Greek contribution to astronomy appears. This is the idea of using a geometrical model to explain the apparent motions of the heavenly bodies. Perhaps inspired by the success of geometry in revealing "truths" by deductive methods, some Greeks of the early 4th century sought to apply it to the heavens, particularly the often puzzling behavior of the planets. Later sources attribute to Plato the requirement that the apparent movements of the planets should be explained by uniform and orderly motions. Although no such passage appears in his works, it is consistent with views that he does express; but in this he is probably following the lead of others, notably his contemporary Eudoxus, a mathematician of the first rank, who in addition to his profound contributions to geometry also devised the first geometrical model to explain the motions of the heavens.

By the time of Eudoxus the picture of the universe generally accepted among educated Greeks was as follows: the earth is in the center, spherical and motionless; at the outer edge is a sphere on which the fixed stars are located, which rotates about the earth once daily; in between are the sun, the moon, and the planets, which also rotate about the earth, but with different motions and in different directions. The planets were particularly difficult to fathom. In the late 5th century the philosopher Democritus was still unsure as to their number, and their motions were puzzling, since they sometimes reversed direction (becoming "retrograde"). Eudoxus's explanation for this was brilliant in its combination of ingenuity and simplicity. He proposed that each body was carried by one or more spheres rotating uniformly about the earth as their common center (hence it is known as a homocentric system), but with different poles, these spheres all being connected with one another so that the motion of the outer was transmitted to that of the inner. Thus the outermost sphere of the fixed stars revolves round the earth once daily, about the poles of the equator, carrying with it the spheres of the sun, moon, and so on. The sun, for instance, is fixed on a sphere whose poles are those of the celestial ecliptic, and which rotates once annually in the direction opposite to the daily rotation. The moon required additional spheres to account for its deviation in latitude from the ecliptic. For the planets the great problem was accounting for their retrogradations. Eudoxus discovered that if one examines the motion of a point located on the equator of a sphere rotating with uniform velocity, this sphere in turn being fixed on another sphere with different poles, rotating with the same velocity but in the opposite direction, the combined motion of the point will be a figure eight (called by the Greeks a *hippopede,* or horse-fetter, which had that shape), the length and breadth of which is determined solely by the distance between the poles of the two spheres. Accordingly he supposed that each planet had such a combination of two spheres (now visualized as a *hippopede*) superimposed on the equator of the sphere carrying it around the ecliptic. This would in principle produce the variation in speed, and even the retrogradation, observable in the planets, as well as a deviation in latitude. The period of rotation on the *hippopede* was necessarily the "synodic period" of the planet (the time in which it returned to the same position with respect to the sun), while the period of rotation on the sphere carrying it was the "sidereal period" (the time in which it returned to the same fixed star).

As a theoretical construct Eudoxus's system was extraordinary, but when confronted with some easily observable astronomical facts it was clearly defective. First, no homocentric system could account for the variation in brightness of Mars and other planets, the most obvious explanation for which is a variation in their distance from the earth. Another defect was that the system could produce retrogradation for Mars only by the assumption of a grossly wrong synodic period. Although Aristotle adopted it in a modified form (which is the only reason we know anything about it), it was soon superseded by other geometric models. It is nevertheless of great interest as the first attempt by a Greek to apply mathematics to astronomy, in which the principle was established that any explanatory model must employ uniform circular motion. It is also important as an indication of the state of the Greeks' astronomical knowledge in the early 4th century: for instance, the planets enumerated by Eudoxus are the same five, with the same names, that became canonical (and are indeed the only planets known to antiquity), Saturn, Jupiter, Mars, Venus, and Mercury. Since these had all been known in Mesopotamia long before, the question of Babylonian influence arises. This influence is even more certain in another astronomical work by Eudoxus, a description of the heavens, as visible in Greece, in which he grouped all the fixed stars into the constellations that are still in use today. This work is a combination of traditional Greek nomenclature and mythology with Babylonian elements (most obviously in the twelve constellations of the zodiac). It is impossible to separate Eudoxus's own contributions from earlier elements, but the substance became definitive when it was cast into poetic form by Aratus in the early 3rd century: his poem *Phaenomena* was immensely popular both in the Greek and later in several Latin versions, and indeed was the principal source of most educated laymen's knowledge of the heavens.

The surviving astronomical works from the late 4th and the 3rd century, mainly treatises of elementary "spherics," do not do justice to the intense interest in both theoretical and practical astronomy that characterized the period after Alexander's conquests led to the rapid expansion of Greek culture to new areas. However, the two seem to have been kept separate, observational astronomy being directed toward the traditional areas of the *parapegma* (involving determination of the times of equinox and solstice, and observations of the positions of fixed stars relative to the horizon), while theoretical astronomy was concerned only with constructing geometric models to explain the motions of the heavenly bodies. During this period were proposed the two models that came to dominate classical Greek astronomy: the eccentric and epicyclic hypotheses. In the eccentric model the planet or other body is supposed to rotate with uniform motion on the circumference of a circle placed eccentrically to the earth. In the epicyclic model the body rotates uniformly about the center of a small circle ("epicycle") that in turn is carried with uniform motion about a larger circle (the "deferent") whose center is the earth. It is obvious that either of those models will produce a variation in the distance of the body, and it is easy to show that each will also, under suitable assumptions (which include the rotation of the center of the eccentric about the earth), produce retrogradation in a planet. The ingenious Greek geometers must have soon discovered that under such assumptions the eccentric and epicyclic models are fully equivalent in a mathematical sense, and it was no doubt in the context of this kind of mathematical transformation that Aristarchus of Samos (ca. 280 B.C.E.) came to formulate his famous heliocentric hypothesis, according to which the sun is the center of the universe and the earth, like all the other planets, revolves about it, while rotating daily on its own axis (the latter rotation had already been envisaged by Heracleides of Pontos in the 4th century). While this might have been acceptable from a purely mathematical viewpoint, it was at odds with ancient physics, and also entailed that the fixed stars must lie at an unthinkably enormous distance (since their relative positions remained unchanged during the earth's annual orbit). As a result, the heliocentric hypothesis was never taken seriously by ancient astronomers.

For all their versatility, the epicyclic and eccentric models were used only as a tool of astronomical explanation and demonstration. This can be seen in the elegant use of them by the mathematician Apollonius of Perge to show how one could, in theory, derive the "stationary points" of a planet (the points on its orbit where it begins and ends its retrogradation). Neither Apollonius nor anyone else at this period seems to have been interested in actually doing the calculation for a real planet at a real time. That would have involved far more in the way of information about its motions and position, and also in methods of calculation, than any Greek possessed at that time. The great change in this respect, and the evolution of Greek astronomy from an explanatory to a predictive science, came with Hipparchus, whose working life was spent in Nicaea and Rhodes from about 150 to 125 B.C.E.

Although all but one of Hipparchus's numerous monographs are lost, enough can be learned from mentions of his work in Ptolemy's *Almagest* and other treatises to reconstruct the outlines of his revolutionary innovations in Greek astronomy, and to be sure that, besides his own extraordinary contributions, both observational and theoretical, he owed a great debt to Babylonian astronomy. By the time of Hipparchus the Mesopotamian astronomers had not only compiled an archive of systematic observations going back 600 years, but they had also developed elaborate and ingenious mathematical tables for calculating and predicting the positions and resulting phenomena of the moon and the other heavenly bodies. Some of both the observational and computational material, inscribed on clay tablets, has been recovered from the site of Babylon in the past century. The mathematical tables have no underlying geometrical model: instead they are based on very precise period relations (of the type "720 retrogradations of Venus occur in 1,151 years"), combined with simple arithmetical functions (for instance, a body might be supposed to move between a minimum and maximum velocity in steps of equal increments). The calculations were greatly simplified by the use of the sexagesimal place-value system (comparable to our decimal system, but with a base of 60) that had been developed in Mesopotamia many centuries earlier. While stray elements of Babylonian astronomy are found in the Greek world before Hipparchus, he is the first Greek who displays an intimate acquaintance with both the observational and the computational aspects of it. We have no information about how he obtained this knowledge, but it is so wide and deep that we must suppose some kind of personal contact with the astronomer-scribes of Babylon. From his source he derived, for instance, a complete list of all eclipses observed at Babylon going back to the 8th century.

Both Babylonian observations and Babylonian methods can be traced in Hipparchus's work. But he did not simply copy what he found. For example, all the mean motions of the moon that he used are identical with those derivable from the Babylonian lunar ephemerides, but we know that Hipparchus used eclipse observations, both Greek and Babylonian, to confirm them. Moreover, he took from the Babylonians the idea of computing astronomical positions by means of tables, but he adapted it to the Greek idea of representing the phenomena by geometric models. That meant that he had to determine the size of the moon's epicycle, for instance, and then, from that and some observed position, compute tables that would allow the lunar position to be determined at any given time. To this end he developed a method, using three (Babylonian) eclipses, of finding the lunar eccentricity (this can be expressed as an abstract mathematical problem: given three points on the circumference of a circle, and the angles that they make at the center of the circle and some other point within the circle, determine the distance between the center and that other point). No Greek or Babylonian before him had done anything of the kind. In his calculations he was aided by the Babylonian sexagesimal system for fractions, but he had to invent trigonometry by himself (he is the calculator of the first trigonometrical function in history, a "chord table" that is closely related to our sine function).

As a pioneer in the reform of Greek astronomy, to make it the predictive mathematical science it eventually became, Hipparchus made enormous progress but did not complete all that, in his view, needed to be done. He produced working theories, based on eccentric and epicyclic models, for both sun and moon, using Babylonian period relations and both his own and Babylonian observations; thus he was able, for the first time among the Greeks, to compute eclipse phenomena. In the case of solar eclipses this confronted him with the problem of lunar parallax, for which he needed to determine the distance to the moon. Although his predecessors had investigated this (the only surviving treatise of Aristarchus is on the sizes and distances of sun and moon), their work had been largely conjectural or else based on methods that could not lead to a secure result. Hipparchus was the first to calculate an essentially correct lunar distance, of about sixty earth radii (his estimate of the solar distance, like almost all before the invention of the telescope, was far below the true value). He did extensive investigations of the fixed stars; not only did he criticize the descriptions of them by Eudoxus and Aratus (ironically, the work in which he did this is the sole treatise of Hipparchus that has survived, only because it was connected with Aratus's popular poem) but he also determined the positions of a large number of stars in numerical coordinates for the purpose of inscribing all the constellations on a star globe. In the course of his investigations he discovered the phenomenon of the "precession of the equinoxes"—that the fixed stars are not in fact fixed with respect to the celestial equator, but appear to perform a motion in longitude along the ecliptic so slow that it could be detected only by comparing observations hundreds of years apart. Hipparchus confirmed this phenomenon (which in modern times is explained by the very slow rotation of the earth's axis) from a number of different types of observation, but was unable to fix its amount precisely. In planetary theory his work was also left unfinished. The planetary models of his Greek predecessors had all been based on a single "anomaly," or factor causing nonuniform motion, the period of which was the planet's return to the sun—hence it is known as the synodic anomaly. Hipparchus must have known from his study of Babylonian planetary ephemerides that those who compiled them had recognized two anomalies, the synodic and the sidereal (the period of which was the planet's return to the same point in the ecliptic). He was able to demonstrate that the theories of his Greek predecessors could not account for the phenomena resulting from the two anomalies, but did not himself produce any alternative theory for the planets. He did, however, present period relations for the mean motions of all five planets (which we now know were derived from Babylonian sources), and he compiled a list of all the planetary observations he could extract from Babylonian and Greek sources, reduced to a common calendar, for the use of his successors.

No successor capable of properly appreciating and developing Hipparchus's achievements appeared for almost three hundred years, but certain aspects of his work were enthusiastically seized on. In particular, the enormous expansion in the Greco-Roman world of horoscopic astrology (which depends on the computation of the positions of the heavenly bodies at birth or some other critical time) in the century after Hipparchus is intimately connected with the change of direction he had introduced into Greek astronomy. It was mainly for this purpose that planetary tables were constructed, based on epicyclic and eccentric models, and indeed taking account of both the anomalies that Hipparchus had demonstrated, but in a fashion that was neither mathematically consistent nor logically defensible (although they did produce results acceptable to the astrologers). We know of these strange hybrids primarily from Indian astronomy of the *siddhāntas* (which was derived from the Greek astronomy of this post-Hipparchan period), since the original Greek works were lost, except for a few fragments, after Ptolemy's *Almagest* made them obsolete. Indeed, the period between Hipparchus and Ptolemy is one of the most obscure in the history of that science among the Greeks.

Ptolemy, whose great astronomical work, known as the *Almagest*, was completed about 150 C.E., set out to reform what he clearly regarded as the dismal state of the science of astronomy in his time. While he had the highest regard for the achievement of Hipparchus and recognized the value of the Babylonian observations, he disapproved of the Babylonian computational techniques that Hipparchus had continued to employ alongside Greek geometrical methods, and that were still common among the practicing astronomers and astrologers of his own time. He rigidly excluded these arithmetical methods from his treatise, which was designed to present the whole of mathematical astronomy (as the Greeks understood the term) in a logical and comprehensible fashion, starting from first principles. *Almagest* is a masterpiece of clear and orderly exposition that deserved the dominance it rapidly achieved in the field of scientific astronomy. I shall merely summarize here the main points in which it corrects or completes what Hipparchus had done.

For astronomical problems involving the observer's position on the earth's surface (for instance the calculation of the time taken for an arc of the ecliptic to rise at a given terrestrial latitude), which Hipparchus had solved by a combination of approximative and descriptive methods, Ptolemy employed the full rigor of spherical trigonometry (which had been developed only in the generation before Ptolemy, by Menelaus). In lunar theory Ptolemy, using the method developed by Hipparchus for finding the lunar eccentricity from three eclipses, achieved a more accurate result than his predecessor, showing where Hipparchus had made computational errors. But he also demonstrated that while the model proposed by Hipparchus works well for lunar positions near conjunction or opposition with respect to the sun, at intermediate positions great discrepancies with observation could appear. To account for these he introduced a modification, which was in some respects an unhappy one: although it satisfied the requirements of observation with respect to the longitude, it also produced a variation in the distance of the moon from the earth far greater than it really is, and ignored the fact that the visible variation in the size of the moon's disk refutes this feature of his model. In the theory of parallax, although Ptolemy's estimates of the distances of the sun and moon are not very different from those of Hipparchus, his methods of computing the resulting parallaxes are, apparently, much more rigorous, which ought to mean that computations of solar eclipses based on Ptolemy's tables were more reliable.

Ptolemy's catalogue of fixed stars, while relying heavily on data derived from Hipparchus, was organized in a new way, using the coordinates of celestial longitude and latitude (whereas previously most observations of star positions had been based on the declination, the distance of the star from the celestial equator). This organization was designed to take account of the motion of precession, since the catalogue could be reduced to later epochs simply by adding a constant value to the longitudes. Ptolemy determined the value of precession as 1 degree in 100 years (a value that Hipparchus had suggested as a lower limit).

Ptolemy's most original contribution to astronomy was in the theory of the planets. Like some of his predecessors, he represented the two anomalies by a combination of eccentric (to take account of the sidereal anomaly) and epicycle (for the synodic anomaly). But by careful analysis of different types of observations he came to the conclusion that the eccentricity that produced correct longitudes for a given planet also produced variations in the planet's distance from the earth that were about twice too great. He solved this dilemma by introducing the "equant" point: while retaining the same eccentricity, he supposed that the uniform motion of the planet's epicycle was counted not about the center of the epicycle on which it rode, but about another halfway between the center and the eccentric point representing the earth. This innovation was frequently criticized during the Middle Ages and into the Renaissance, since it seemed to violate the principle of uniform circular motion. However, it was undeniably successful in representing the phenomena: it has been shown that the longitudes derived from an equant model with the proper eccentricity differ from those derived from a Kepler ellipse of the same eccentricity by an amount well below 10 minutes of arc, which represents the limit of accuracy of ancient observations. Unfortunately, introduction of the equant greatly complicated the process of deriving the eccentricity from observations, since a problem that had previously been soluble by an adaptation of the method that Hipparchus had devised for the lunar eccentricity had been transformed into one that was no longer soluble by Euclidean methods (it amounts to solution of an equation of the eighth degree). Ptolemy overcame this difficulty by assimilating the insoluble problem to the soluble one, finding a preliminary eccentricity that he then used to find "corrections" to the observational data, from which a new eccentricity was derived, producing new corrections, and so on. This is the most ingenious use of an iterational mathematical procedure from antiquity, and fortunately it does converge on the correct result. Ptolemy's theory of the planets was completed by the construction of geometrical models to represent the planetary latitudes, very complicated because of the constraints of the geocentric imperative, but undoubtedly far superior to anything that had preceded.

Although *Almagest* is the earliest save one of Ptolemy's astronomical works, the structure he built in it is little changed in his later work. His *Ready Tables* introduced some improvements in organization over the tables presented in *Almagest*, but the underlying astronomical constants and models are the same except in the latitude theory, which is improved and simplified. The latitude theory is also improved in his *Planetary Hypotheses,* but the great importance of that work is the influence it had on cosmological views during later antiquity and the Middle Ages. This work, the ostensible purpose of which is to allow the reader to produce a working model of the universe, adopts the Aristotelian principle that nature does nothing in vain: hence there is no space wasted in the universe, which entails that the "spheres" of the planets (actually shells enclosed by spheres in which the mechanism of epicycle and eccentric operate) are contiguous. This enabled Ptolemy to compute the precise distances of all heavenly bodies, starting from the known lunar distance, right out to the sphere of the fixed stars. For good measure he added the sizes of all the bodies (based on estimates of their apparent diameters). The result is a universe that is very small by modern standards (Ptolemy's distance from the earth to the fixed stars is about the same as the modern computation of the distance from the earth to the sun). But the picture it presents is the one that was almost universally accepted right down to the end of the Middle Ages, in both Islamic and Christian lands (with minor modifications to accommodate the account in Genesis). It is recognizable, for instance, in Dante's *Divine Comedy*.

Although Ptolemy intended *Almagest* to be definitive only for his own time and looked forward to improvements on it in the work of his successors, those did not appear at all in later antiquity and appeared only in limited areas in the Middle Ages. Yet there were some serious shortcomings in the work, even by the standards of antiquity. Because of his too great reliance on Hipparchus's solar theory, both the position and the mean motion he attributed to the sun were in error, an error that increased over time. We have already noticed that his lunar model produced far too great a variation in the distance to the moon. Because Ptolemy used lunar eclipses to establish the position and mean motion of the moon, the error in the solar mean motion and position was also transmitted to that body (although fortunately this had very little effect on eclipse computations). Ptolemy's value for precession is also too low by an amount precisely corresponding to the error in the solar mean motion. The parameters embodied in his planetary theory, on the other hand, could hardly have been improved in his time, except in the case of Mercury, where the poor quality of the observations open to him led him to propose an unnecessarily complicated (and very inaccurate) model.

Despite these imperfections, *Almagest* was so superior to anything preceding it that it soon established itself as the standard work on astronomy, a position it occupied for over a thousand years in both Europe and the Middle East. In antiquity no advance was made beyond it, for the works of Pappus and Theon in 4th-century Alexandria are mere commentaries on Ptolemy. *Almagest* was translated into Persian and Syriac in late antiquity, and into Arabic (more than once) in the 8th and 9th centuries, and it contributed to the flowering of astronomical studies in Islamic lands. There, indeed, significant improvements were made to the solar and lunar elements, but the rest was accepted largely unchanged. Star catalogues, such as that of al-Ṣūfī, were essentially copies of the *Almagest* catalogue with the longitudes increased by a constant for precession; and despite criticisms of the equant and proposals of alternative models, almost all planetary tables down to the beginning of the modern era were based on Ptolemy's elements. It was not until the 16th century, with the work of Copernicus, Tycho Brahe, and Kepler, that Greek astronomy, as formulated by Ptolemy, finally became obsolete.

G. J. TOOMER

Bibliography

Delambre, Jean-Baptiste Joseph. *Histoire de l'astronomie ancienne.* 2 vols. Paris, 1817.

Grasshoff, Gerd. *The History of Ptolemy's Star Catalogue.* New York, Berlin, and Heidelberg, 1990.

Heath, Thomas Little. *Aristarchus of Samos.* Oxford, 1913.

Jones, Alexander. "The Adaptation of Babylonian Methods in Greek Numerical Astronomy." *Isis* 82 (1991): 441–453.

———, ed. *Astronomical Papyri from Oxyrhynchus.* Philadelphia, 1999.

Neugebauer, Otto. *A History of Ancient Mathematical Astronomy.* 3 vols. Berlin, Heidelberg, and New York, 1975.

Tannery, Paul. *Recherches sur l'histoire de l'astronomie ancienne.* Paris, 1893.

Toomer, G. J. "Hipparchus and Babylonian Astronomy." In *A Scientific Humanist: Studies in Memory of Abraham Sachs.* Ed. Erle Leichty et al. Occasional Publications of Samuel Noah Kramer Fund, 9. Philadelphia, 1988.

Toomer, G. J., ed. and trans. *Ptolemy's Almagest.* London and New York, 1984. Rev. ed., Princeton, 1998.

Related Articles

Images of the World; Demonstration and the Idea of Science; Geography; Ptolemy; Observation and Research; Cosmology; Mathematics

COSMOLOGY

With very few exceptions, the Greeks who wrote about the natural world took the earth to be stationary, as human intuition suggests: we learn the difference between moving and staying in place by taking our place on the earth as the fixed point of reference. But if the earth is at rest, it follows that the stars, planets, sun, and moon are in motion relative to the earth, and observation coupled with some simple inferences suggest that they move around the earth, probably on circular paths.

It can hardly fail to be observed that the sun and the moon move on different paths, and that by contrast all the stars move without changing their own relative positions, on paths different from those of the sun and the moon. Closer observation shows that there are five other heavenly bodies whose paths vary with respect to the "fixed" stars: they soon got the name *planētai*, "the Wanderers."

A crucial consequence of the decision that the earth is stationary is that the whole system of stars, planets, sun, and moon came to be thought of as a finite whole. At first there was some hesitation about the relative distances of the heavenly bodies from the earth, but by the time of Plato and Aristotle there was general agreement that the stars are farthest from the earth. Since the constellations of stars keep their own relative positions, forming unvarying patterns and never varying perceptibly in size or brightness when the sky is clear of cloud, they were taken to rotate around the earth as a unity, equidistant from the earth, and to form the boundary of the whole system.

Thus there was room for doubt about what, if anything, lies outside the boundary of the fixed stars. There were those who claimed that outside the boundary there is either unlimited empty space or else nothing whatever, not even space. Others claimed that there are unlimited numbers of other worlds, invisible to us, in the space beyond the boundaries of our world, just as there are other cities beyond our own city walls.

Both camps were agreed, however, on certain features of our own world: that it is a system characterized by durability in time (though not necessarily forever), and by regularity. The regular movements of the heavens provided the standard for measuring the seasons, with all their qualitative differences, and they divided night from day. The wonderful regularity of the whole system justified its being called cosmos—a word that signified beauty and good order.

To distinguish those who believed our world to be all that there is from

279

those who believed there is something outside our world, Greek writers distinguished between the concepts of the world *(cosmos)* and the universe *(to pan)*; we shall preserve this distinction in what follows. "Cosmos is a system composed of heaven and earth and the natures contained in them": this definition, quoted from the pseudo-Aristotelian treatise *On the Cosmos* (391b.9), was more or less standard. The universe, on the other hand, consists of our cosmos together with whatever else exists, if anything does.

Later writers, led by Aristotle, recognized that there was a new beginning in thought about the natural world in the Ionian Greek city of Miletus, on the Aegean coast of Asia Minor, in the 6th century B.C.E. Three Milesians were mentioned: in chronological order, Thales, Anaximander, and Anaximenes. Nothing that they wrote survives; we know of them only through quotations in much later authors. What seems clear is that they broke away from the earlier stories about nature that we characterize as myth, in which the leading characters are anthropomorphic gods and goddesses.

According to Aristotle, whose brief words about his earliest predecessors founded the Greek tradition of the historiography of philosophy, the break with "myth" was quite sharp. If we knew more, we might be able to reconstruct a more gradual story of a transition from religious to naturalistic ways of thinking—very probably at the same time as a transition from Near Eastern to Greek conceptions of the world. There are traces of the intermediate stages in the few surviving fragments of Pherecydes of Syros, a contemporary of the earliest philosophers recognized by Aristotle. But although in general Near Eastern mythology may be recognized as the source out of which Greek natural philosophy grew (especially among the Ionian Greeks, who were in constant touch with their Near Eastern neighbors), direct connections are hard to prove. The Greek tradition outlined by Aristotle, prejudiced or not, is clearer.

Hesiod had written, in *Theogony*, a story of the birth of the world, more or less after the pattern of sexual generation: "Out of Chaos, Erebos and black Night came to birth, and from Night again there came forth Aether and Day, whom she bore after lying with Erebos. And Earth first bore the starry Heaven, equal to herself, to cover her about" (123–127). The Milesians, so far as we can judge from the scanty evidence, still spoke of the origin and growth of the world, but in nonanthropomorphic terms. Thales, famously, held that the world originated from water ("because the seed of all things is moist," said Aristotle); Anaximander wrote that from the primitive Boundless came something like "a seed of the hot and the cold"; Anaximenes made air the primitive substance and introduced compression and rarefaction of air as the mode of generation of the different world masses. Other metaphors besides biological growth appear. Anaximander attributed something of the regularity and balance of natural change (summer and winter, perhaps) to "justice"—not the justice of Zeus, but an internal relation between the contending powers themselves. Anaximenes compared the air that generated the differentiated world to "psyche"—the life force of animals. All three produced descriptions of the earth and the heavens, and meteorological phenomena, but the interpretation of the evidence is too controversial to be discussed here.

What is perhaps the most important achievement of the Milesians is that their work started a tradition of criticism: unless the later sources from whom we learn about the Milesians found patterns of development where there were none, each later thinker knew the work of his predecessor, found weaknesses in it, and substituted something he thought better on rational grounds—a more fundamental starting point, a more persuasive analogy, a more plausible explanation.

The next generation of thinkers of this style continued the critical tradition. Xenophanes of Colophon (still in Greek Asia Minor, near Ephesus, although he migrated to the Western Greek world) and Heraclitus of Ephesus are the first two whose work survives in relatively substantial quantities. Both criticized their great forerunners: "Homer and Hesiod attributed to the gods everything that is a shame and a reproach among men: stealing, adultery, deceit of each other" (Xenophanes, frg. 11). "The teacher of most men is Hesiod. This man they take to know most things—who did not know day and night; for they are one" (Heraclitus, frg. 57). Examples could be multiplied. The point is this: if we apply our human understanding to the traditional stories, they fall short; we must seek something more consistent with our best conceptions of what is rational. The powerful gods of tradition should be better, not worse, than men. Day and Night should be personified as self-subsistent individuals: they are conceptually linked, as being inseparable parts of a single unit of time. The critical tradition reached a high point with the 5th-century philosopher Parmenides of Elea (on the west coast of southern Italy), who conclusively changed the course of philosophical speculation. But before attempting to assess his contribution, we must briefly go back in time.

The Greek communities of the Aegean region produced the recognized pioneers of Greek cosmology. But in the 5th century the cities of southern Italy and Sicily also produced philosophical heroes. It seems that migration from East to West brought this about. At some point Xenophanes left the Aegean and moved to Italy. More significant was the move of Pythagoras from Samos in the Aegean to Croton in south Italy, some time in the second half of the 6th century. Although Pythagoras himself wrote nothing, and extraordinarily little is actually known on good authority about his life and teaching, his influence on subsequent philosophy was very great. "Those called Pythagoreans," to use Aristotle's phrase, came to be recognized as a group with certain highly distinctive views both about the physical world and about religion and morality. In cosmology, their importance was very great, in many ways, but especially through the eponymous Pythagorean of Plato's cosmological treatise, *Timaeus*.

Pythagoras, or his followers, introduced mathematics into cosmology. It is true that Thales is said to have predicted an eclipse of the sun and the dates of the solstices (probably learning from Babylonian records), and that Anaximander had given mathematical values to the distances of the sun, moon, and stars from the earth—probably 27, 18, and 9, respectively (he was highly unusual in supposing the stars to be the nearest of the heavenly bodies). But Pythagorean theory elevated mathematical structure to the status of the primary element, instead of the Milesian primitive material (water, the Boundless, or air).

Pythagorean theory is wrapped in mystery, and it is impossible to trace its chronological development. But it is not implausible to guess that one of the earliest bases on which theoretical edifices were built was the discovery that musical consonances were expressible in numerical ratios. The ratio of the octave is 1 : 2; the fifth is 3 : 2; the fourth is 4 : 3. It was a striking discovery that the string of a musical instrument stopped at these intervals produced sounds that were recognizably "in tune." Moreover these four numbers, 1 + 2 + 3 + 4, add up to 10. "The whole cosmos [say the Pythagoreans] is arranged according to attunement [*harmonia*] and the attunement is a system of three concords, the fourth, the fifth, and the octave" (Sextus, *Math.* 7.95). At some stage the components of the cosmos, stars, sun, moon, five planets, and earth, since they total only nine, were supplemented in Pythagorean theory by a tenth, the "counter-earth." Earth and counter-earth circled around the central fire—hence the Pythagoreans were unique among early philosophers in displacing the earth from the center of the cosmos.

At the beginning of the 5th century Parmenides' criticisms of all cosmological theories of growth changed the course of philosophical thought. He challenged the cosmologists to give a rational account of change: previous theories claimed that "what *is*" comes to be out of "what *is not*"—but one cannot think or speak intelligibly about what *is not*. To put it in the simplest terms, the effect of this was to generate theories in which physical change is explained as a rearrangement or restructuring of enduring elements. The first elements to be proposed were materials, such as the earth, water, air, and fire of Empedocles, or the atoms of Democritus. Next came the eternal Forms of Plato, which stood as eternal models while the changing physical world "shared in" or "copied" them. They were succeeded by Aristotle's immanent forms: change in general was the actualization of a form previously present in potentiality.

Parmenides himself, although the argument of the first part of his poem (like Xenophanes and Empedocles, he wrote in epic hexameters) challenged the very idea of change and difference, added a cosmogony of his own, based on a fundamental duality of night and light. Quotations are scarce; they include a line that appears to be the first statement that the moon shines with borrowed light, as well as a complex astronomical theory and an account of the origins of the human race. After Parmenides but before Plato, three different cosmological theories were put forward that clearly attempted, in different ways, to respect Parmenides' ban on "coming to *be* out of what *is not.*" In this period Greek cosmology began to develop in two basically different directions. The first led to the view that our world is unique, and is under the direction of divine forces; this culminated in the work of Plato, Aristotle, and the Stoics. The second was the way of the Atomists, Leucippus, Democritus, and Epicurus, whose universe contained many worlds, put together without the aid of gods by the unguided motions of atoms in the void.

Through the whole of the period when Greeks dominated the philosophical and scientific thought of the Western world, the "one world" theorists had the support of those who applied mathematical reasoning to the cosmos. Plato, Aristotle, and the Stoics made use of the calculations and theorems of geometrical astronomy. The Atomists, on the whole, could make little use of the results of the exact sciences. In the absence, particularly, of knowledge of fundamental laws of motion, they could not easily match their atomic theory of matter with astronomical measurements. As Cicero once put it: "That turbulent hurly-burly of atoms will never be able to produce the orderly beauty of this cosmos" (*De finibus* 1.20).

Empedocles of Acragas in Sicily, and Anaxagoras of Clazomenae were the first to meet Parmenides' challenge—the former in epic verse and in the Italian style, the latter in prose and in the Ionian manner. Anaxagoras began his book with a description of the beginning of the world: "All things were together, infinite in both number and smallness." Instead of the Milesians' single originative substance, Anaxagoras substituted a mixture of all things, so finely and completely mixed that nothing was distinguishable in the overwhelming clouds of air and aether. At some point in time, the primitive mixture was disrupted by a cosmic force of Mind, which began a process of rotation and thus progressively separated out the ingredients from each other. Earthy things went to the middle, lighter things to the boundary of the whirl, where they can still be seen in part as they carry the heavenly bodies around. Mind alone was distinct in kind from all the rest: the heavenly bodies were earthy in substance, nothing but white-hot stones.

Anaxagoras spent many years in Athens, where his ideas became well known. The biographers report that he was prosecuted for the impiety of his materialist theory of the sun and moon. His theory of Mind as the creative agent in the cosmos, however, may have had more real importance for the philosophy of nature. Although Plato expressed disappointment that Anaxagoras made little use of the theory in his cosmology (*Phaedo* 98b), the idea that the cosmos is the product of Mind, rather than a natural growth or an accident, was there to stay: it received the fullest development in Plato's *Timaeus*, it was modified by Aristotle, and it was exaggerated by the Stoics.

Empedocles, like Anaxagoras, held that cosmic growth and change is brought about by the rearrangement of things unchanging and permanent. But he drastically reduced the range of the basic materials, to the quartet that became standard: earth, water, air, and fire. He increased the causes of cosmic change from one to two: a force that attracted unlike constituents to each other, called Love, and an agent of separation, called Strife. Both forces are at work in our world, but on the large scale their dominance eternally alternates, from a period of total unity, under the rule of Love, to a period or a moment of total disruption, through Strife, after which the rule of Love begins again. The surviving fragments contain fascinating images of the formation of the cosmos, including a theory of the first formation of vegetation and of animal species, limited to viable kinds through the survival of the fit.

The atomic theory is associated with the names of Leucippus, about whom very little is known, and Democritus of Abdera. It is another attempt to meet Parmenides' challenge by constructing a changing world out of eternally unchanging elements—*atoma*, "uncuttable" bits of identical matter, too small to be perceived individually, making up compounds whose perceptible properties result from the size, shape, and motion of the atoms and the extent of void space between them. In this theory there are no motive agents like Mind, or Love and Strife; the atoms collide and rebound or get linked up together as chance or "necessity" dictates. As has been mentioned already, a cosmos for the Atomists is just one compound among many in the infinite void: like all compounds, worlds come into being and are dissolved again into their component atoms. The first beginning of a cosmos is a "whirl" *(dinē)* of atoms in some region of space, which sorts the atoms by size and shape ("mechanically," as we might say) so as to form an earth, seas, air, sky, sun, moon, and stars. The end comes when the motions no longer hold things together in due order.

Most, perhaps all, of the theories mentioned so far regard the earth as a flat disk, and correspondingly suppose that the direction of free fall is perpendicular to the surface of the earth, and therefore in parallel lines. It is a problem for the theories to explain why the earth itself does not fall, as a piece of earth falls when released from a height. What supports it? Most answered that it somehow floats on a cushion of air, because of its great area.

Plato's *Phaedo* first makes the important move to a completely spherical cosmology. The earth, says Socrates in the dialogue (108–109), is round, and being in the middle of the heavens it needs no support from air or any other such force to prevent it from falling—the homogeneity of the heavens and the equal balance of the earth are sufficient. The picture is elaborated in *Timaeus*, where we have again a spherical cosmology. The earth is at the center of the sphere of the heavens, and all the earthy material in the universe tends toward this center, all the fiery matter toward the perimeter, with the two intermediate elements, water and air, between them. The four elements stand to each other in continuous geometric proportion—but Plato does not specify the quantities involved (whether volumes, or intensity of quality, or whatever).

The four elements, which themselves consist of particles shaped like four of the five regular solids, make up the body of the world: its soul (for it is a living creature) is the stuff of which the heavenly bodies are made. In a long and elaborate fantasy Plato describes an armillary sphere constructed out of two circular "soul-strips," one representing the equator of the sphere of fixed stars, the other, inclined (as the ecliptic is) at an angle to the first, being split into rings representing the motion of the seven "wandering" bodies. The whole system, including its axis, turns with the motion of the fixed stars, but the rings of the planets, sun, and moon also turn with their own motion around the axis, in the reverse direction, and the earth, at the center, rotates around the spinning axis so as to counteract that motion and thus remain stationary.

The cosmic "animal" thus described is neither eternal nor self-generated: it is made by a divine Craftsman (dēmiurgos), copying an eternal model. Like all good craftsmen, he aims at the highest possible degree of beauty in his work but is limited by the capabilities of the material with which he works. There are thus two explanatory factors to be reckoned with in the detail of the physical world: the perfection aimed at by Mind, and the limitations imposed by the "Necessity" of the material. At once, a controversy arose about Plato's meaning: were the Demiurge and his creation to be taken literally, as Aristotle took them? Or were they a device of literary exposition, as Plato's successors Xenocrates and Speusippus held? The controversy continues. But whether myth or science, *Timaeus* was a dominant influence for many centuries.

In Plato's account of the heavens in *Timaeus*, the movements of the sun, moon, and planets are sketched in symbols that make little claim to astronomical accuracy. Each moves on a circle of the world-soul, itself composed of "Sameness," "Difference," and "Existence." Sameness no doubt symbolizes the regularity of their motions, Difference their independence from the stars and from each other, and Existence their eternity. In his last dialogue, *Laws* (821), Plato rebukes people for attributing wandering motions to some of the heavenly bodies, calling them *planetai*, and indicates that although the planets depart from the uniform rotation of the stars, they nevertheless move with a strict regularity of their own.

It was the aim of contemporary astronomers to compose a model of the heavens that would describe with accuracy the motions of all the visible heavens. Eudoxus of Cnidos, who created a school at Cyzicus known for its mathematical astronomy, spent time at Plato's Academy in Athens. Whether Plato was acquainted with the detail of his astronomical work when he wrote *Timaeus* is controversial, but there may well be a reference to it in *Laws*. In any event, there is no doubt that Plato's greatest pupil, Aristotle, studied the theories of Eudoxus and his pupil Callippus, and made them the basis for his own account of the heavens.

Aristotle's whole system is constructed out of concentric spheres, with the earth, itself spherical, occupying the center of the whole. The essence of the model is as follows. The fixed stars are assumed to be set rigidly in the outermost sphere of the heavens, which turns at a constant speed about its north-south axis once daily. Each of the planetary bodies has its own set of spheres. The innermost sphere of each set carries the planet. The outermost sphere moves on the same axis and with the same speed and direction as the sphere of the stars. This sphere carries with it the poles of a second sphere, concentric with the first, rotating about its own, different axis also at a constant speed. The axis of the second sphere is inclined to that of the first so that its equator, as it rotates, passes through the middle of the signs of the zodiac (i.e., along the ecliptic circle). Each of the planetary bodies has a sphere that shares the position and direction of motion of this second sphere; if the planet were fixed on the equator of this second sphere, it would rotate daily around the earth along with the fixed stars but change its position with relation to the zodiacal signs a little each day.

But the planets are observed to deviate from regular motion on the ecliptic circle. To account for the deviation, Eudoxus posited a third and fourth sphere for each planet, nested inside the first two, with different axes and velocities. The planet is assumed to lie on the equator of the fourth, innermost sphere. The third and fourth spheres are so arranged that the planet follows a path (relative to the ecliptic) known as a *hippopede*, or horse-fetter, roughly equivalent to a figure eight.

Each sphere rotates at a constant velocity, but they differ from each other. For the sun and the moon, Eudoxus postulated only three spheres each, the third being to account for the recession of the nodes. Callippus, a more obscure figure who adopted and modified Eudoxus's model of concentric spheres, added two spheres each to the sun and the moon, to account for their anomalies, and one further sphere to each of Mars, Venus, and Mercury.

All that is visible to the observer, of course, is the light of the heavenly bodies: the spheres are invisible. The heavenly bodies themselves do not move at all; they are carried around by the motion of the sphere in which they are set. The stars are all set in the single, outer sphere of the whole universe; each of the planetary bodies is set in the equator of the innermost sphere of its set of spheres.

The seven sets of spheres are nested inside each other, in the order Saturn, Jupiter, Mars, Venus, Mercury, sun, moon. In Eudoxus's scheme, there are no eccentric spheres and no epicycles, as in later astronomical theories. Consequently it was assumed that all the heavenly bodies remain at a constant distance from the earth; it is a weakness in the system that it has no way of explaining differences in the brightness of the planets at different times. This, then, was the astronomical model taken over by Aristotle. What he undertook to do was to turn it into a *physical* theory, in which the spheres were not geometrical postulates but material bodies.

The astronomical model, as we have seen, used the motion of the sphere of the fixed stars as the base on which the other motions were overlaid. For the construction of a physical theory, this created a difficulty concerning the motions of all the planetary bodies except the outermost one, since the sets of planetary spheres are implanted in each other. Jupiter's set, to take an example, is inside the set of Saturn's spheres. But the motion of the innermost of Saturn's spheres—the sphere that carries Saturn on its equator—is obviously not identical with that of the sphere of fixed stars; its function is precisely to justify Saturn's deviation from that motion. The outermost sphere, however, of the next planet (Jupiter) must move with the motion of the fixed stars. Consequently the physical theory must return to this base, by interpolating a set of spheres whose motions *cancel out* the special motions of Saturn. Let S^1, S^2, S^3, S^4 be the spheres that explain Saturn's motions; S^4 is the one that carries Saturn. Then we postulate, inside S^4, a sphere S^{-4}, which rotates on the same axis and at the same speed as S^4, but in the reverse direction. Its motion is thus identical with that of S^3. We postulate S^{-3} and S^{-2} in similar fashion. Now S^{-2} has the same motion as S^1—i.e., the motion of the fixed stars. The first of Jupiter's spheres, J^1, has its poles fixed inside the sphere S^{-2}.

Aristotle took over Callippus's modifications of the Eudoxan system and held to the thesis of a complete and separate set of spheres for each planetary body. The total amounts to fifty-five, no counteracting spheres being required for the moon, since there are no heavenly bodies beneath it.

We have now described the structure of the concentric spheres. But physical spheres must have physical *body*. So Aristotle is faced with the question: what are the heavenly spheres made of? They can hardly be made of any of the four familiar elements, earth, water, air, or fire, because each of these (he claims) has a characteristic natural motion that is in a straight line: earth and water toward the center of the universe, air and fire toward its circumference. The motion of the heavens, according to Aristotle's view in *De caelo*, requires us to posit a fifth element whose natural motion is not rectilinear but circular, and whose nature is not changeable, like the four sublunary bodies. Since he regards it as superior, in more than one sense, to the other four elements, he names it the first body, but it is generally referred to as aether.

There are indications that Aristotle rather tentatively gave a role to aether in the sublunary world as well as in the heavens. Cicero knew something to this effect, from his acquaintance with some of the works of Aristotle that are now lost: "He [Aristotle] thinks there is a certain fifth nature, of which mind is made; for thinking, foreseeing, learning, teaching, making a discovery, holding so much in the memory—all these and more, loving, hating, feeling pain and joy—such things as these, he believes, do not belong to any one of the four elements" (*Tusculan Disputations* 1.10.22). It is hardly likely that Aristotle *identified* the mind with aether, but it is possible that at some time he wrote of the soul, or some of its faculties, as being based in an element different from the usual four. There is some confirmation of this in his own more cautious words in *De generatione animalium* 2.3 (736b29–737a1). The semen of animals contains a "vital heat" or "breath"—which is analogous to the element of the stars.

The evaluative strain in this passage is significant. The extra element is called "divine" and is associated with the ranking in "honor" of the soul that is based on it—this refers, no doubt, to a *scala naturae* that puts man, the rational animal, at the top and grades the lower animals according to their faculties. Aether is not merely the element endowed with the natural faculty of moving in a circle, which is the main emphasis in *De caelo*. It is also eternal, and therefore divine, and free from the corruption of the earthly elements.

Aristotle was committed to a dualism as sharp as Plato's distinction between the intelligible and unchanging Forms and the perceptible and perishable material world. The heavens are the realm of a matter that moves eternally in circles, is incorruptible, unmixed, divine. With the possible limited exception of the material base of the animal soul, everything in the cosmos inside the sphere of the moon—the sublunary world—is made of different materials, all of them rectilinear and therefore finite in motion, perishable, liable to mixture and interchange among themselves. This was a dualism that lasted, notoriously, until the time of Galileo.

Plato's cosmos was created, according to Aristotle's view of *Timaeus*, at some particular time, but he took the view that there could be no beginning of the heavenly motions without setting up the incoherent concept of a beginning of time. There were no creator gods, therefore, but there were sustaining gods. Aristotle's theology, set out rather elliptically in *Physics* 8 and *Metaphysics* 12, claims that the eternal rotation of the heavenly spheres is the work of god, or gods: in *Metaphysics* 12.8 Aristotle allocates a Mover to every sphere; sometimes he puts all the emphasis on the supreme God, the Unmoved Mover of the outer sphere of the heavens.

He writes (in *Metaphysics* 12.7) with reverence about the life of God—a life of thought, better than the best that humans can enjoy only for a short time. God does nothing directly to cause the motions of the heavens: he moves the spheres "as one being loved." This implies that the spheres themselves are beings with souls, capable of feeling a desire to share the eternal activity of divine thought. Aristotle says remarkably little about this animistic aspect of his cosmology, which was much developed in postclassical times.

It is interesting that Aristotle's pupil and successor as head of the Peripatos, Theophrastus, raises critical questions about his master's theology in the work that survives under the title *Metaphysics*. If the Mover is one, how do the heavenly spheres come to have different motions? If more than one, how are they harmonized? Why does love of an unmoved god impel the spheres to move? What is especially desirable about rotary motion? Perhaps such questions suggest something of the exploratory nature of Aristotle's theology.

Theophrastus continued Aristotle's interest in the philosophy of nature and added much to the already large library of Peripatetic work in this area. A substantial amount survives: small treatises on winds, on stones, and on fire, and two large collections, *The History of Plants* and *The Causes of Plants*. One of his most influential works survives only in fragments, *The View of the Physicists (Physikōn Doxai)*; a good deal of our knowledge of early Greek cosmology comes directly or indirectly from this work. The Peripatetic school continued its interest in some of these fields for at least one more generation, with Theophrastus's successor Strato of Lampsacus. Aristotle's denial of the existence of empty space—indeed the whole structure of his theory of place—was questioned and modified by both Theophrastus and Strato.

In the 4th and later centuries, the character of the Greek cosmologists underwent great change. The most important development was the rapid advance of mathematical astronomy; the key names in this area are Aristarchus, Archimedes, Apollonius of Perga, and Hipparchus. Hipparchus's work, in the 2nd century B.C.E., formed the basis for Ptolemy's *Almagest* (2nd century C.E.), which became the standard textbook on astronomy for many centuries.

In passing, we must note that Aristarchus of Samos was the one serious astronomer in the Greek period who entertained the thesis that the heavens are at rest and the earth moves in a circular orbit around the sun. Unfortunately we are told very little of what Aristarchus made of this thesis, and there are surviving bits of his work that make no use of it at all; it may have been no more than an exploratory hypothesis.

In post-Aristotelian cosmology, Epicurus offered the most radical opposition to Plato and Aristotle. Although he came from an Athenian family, Epicurus lived most of his early life in Samos and the Ionian cities of the mainland. There he became acquainted with the atomic theory of Democritus, adopted it, modified it in some respects, and set up a school in Athens to disseminate it to his followers. The contrast with Plato and Aristotle could hardly have been more complete. In place of a unique, finite, eternal cosmos, Epicurus posited an infinite number of worlds, coming into being and passing away like any other material compounds. Instead of divine creation or maintenance, Epicurus attributed the birth of the worlds to the accidental collisions of atoms whirling about in the infinite void. Instead of a unified material continuum, Epicurus posited atoms and void space. Instead of a spherical earth, Epicurus reverted to the flat earth of earlier cosmologists, and instead of the centrifocal theory of motion of Plato and Aristotle, he claimed that the natural motion of all atoms is downward, parallel fall.

We have two primary sources for Epicurean cosmology: a brief summary in Epicurus's own *Letter to Herodotus (Ep. Hdt.)* and a much fuller account in Lucretius's poem *De rerum natura (DRN)* especially the fifth book. Both begin, almost in the manner of a geometrical textbook, with a set of basic propositions.

First, the universe consists of "body and void." The existence of body can be known through the direct evidence of the senses; the existence of void can be known indirectly, as being necessary to explain the observed fact of motion. Body exists in the form of eternally unchangeable atoms.

Second, the universe is infinite. The argument for this is that anything finite has a limit, and a limit is discerned by contrast with something else (Aristotle had claimed that this is a requirement for *contact*, but not for limit). Since there *is* nothing other than the universe, the universe has no limit and consequently must be infinite (*Ep. Hdt.* 41; *DRN* I.1007).

Third, atoms exist in an inconceivably large, but not an infinitely large, number of shapes. If they were not so many, it would be impossible to account for the observed differences between compounds; if they were infinite, atoms would have to vary infinitely in size also, and some atoms would be so large as to be visible, which is contrary to what is observed to be the case. This last proposition needs an extra premise to support it: namely, that atoms do not vary continuously in shape but differ by finite quanta—*minimae partes*, as Lucretius calls them.

Epicureans asserted that all atoms have a natural tendency to move downward. We can observe that every perceptible object that has weight moves downward when its fall is unimpeded, and there is no reason to deny this same tendency to atoms. Aristotle's theory of the natural upward motion of fire and air is rejected. But what does "downward" mean? Aristotle had argued that it meant toward the center of the universe, but the infinite universe of the Epicureans had no center. Epicurean metaphysics allowed for no forces acting on the atoms except by collision; there was no room for a theory of attraction at a distance. So it was not possible for them to adopt the idea later put forward by the Stoics, that matter was attracted to its own center, so that downward motion could be regarded as the manifestation of this attraction toward the center of the cosmic mass. Epicurus and his followers were left, as it seemed, with no option but to take up the assumptions of the builder who uses a plumb line, that all falling bodies fall in parallel lines at right angles to the earth's surface—therefore that the earth's surface is, generally speaking, flat. The flat earth was a commonplace of the 5th century and earlier, but after Plato and Aristotle it became hard to accept. Lucretius does his best with it by poking fun at the idea of upside-down creatures on the other side of the world, which he took to be a consequence of the geocentric theory of motion.

It is hard to know what degree of obstinacy and obscurantism, if any, was required to maintain this reactionary position at the end of the 4th century B.C.E. Aristotle's argument for the sphericity of the earth had largely depended on his own centrifocal theory of the natural motions of the elements (*De caelo* 2.14.297a8–b23), and we have seen that the Epicureans rejected that theory. But Aristotle already knew of astronomical reasons for believing the earth to be spherical, particularly the observation that as one moves on a north-south line, different stars appear in the zenith (ibid. 2.14.297b23– 298b20). This could be explained by the Epicureans only on the assumption that the stars are rather close to the earth: the effect is like that of walking across a large room under a painted ceiling. Other astronomical problems, such as the shape of the earth's shadow on the moon during an eclipse, could be accounted for by a disk-shaped earth as well as by a sphere.

Given, then, that atoms are endowed with a natural tendency to fall downward through the void, and that "downward" means in parallel straight lines, it appears that some extra assumption is needed to explain how it comes about that atoms form compounds. One might suppose that collisions could occur by virtue of differences of speed among the falling atoms: but that is ruled out a priori. The reason given by Epicurus is that differences of speed are explained by differences of resistance of the medium through which motion takes place. But the void offers no resistance whatever, hence there is no reason why any atom should fall faster or more slowly than any other. All of them move at a speed described in the phrase "as quick as thought."

That is not to say that *compounds* cannot move at different speeds. All variations of speed are possible, between the two limiting cases of the speed of motion of individual atoms, "as quick as thought," on the one hand, and rest, on the other. In a compound, atoms are to be thought of as moving, individually, at standard atomic speed without intermission, but remaining within the boundaries of the compound. A stable compound is one in which the component atoms move backward and forward, up and down, and side to side, colliding with each other within the same space. The compound itself moves when the algebraic sum, so to speak, of the motions of the individual atoms has some positive value in one direction or another. The limit of speed is reached when all the component atoms are moving in the same direction—a state of affairs achieved only by thunderbolts, apparently.

But if differences of speed cannot account for collisions between atoms, what can? To deal with this difficulty, the Epicureans introduced their most famous physical thesis—the swerve of atoms (*parenclisis* in Greek, *clinamen* in Latin). The swerve is fully described by Lucretius (*DRN* 2.216–293), but there is no mention of it in the extant fragments of Epicurus himself. However, ancient writers had no hesitation in attributing it to him.

The swerve served two purposes in the Epicurean system: to explain the possibility of collisions between atoms, and to account, in some way, for the voluntary motions of animals, including humans. Among modern writers there is no agreement even about the basic mechanics of the swerve, so to speak. Do all atoms swerve, or only some of them? Presumably all of them may do so, since otherwise there would be an unaccountable difference in kind between the swervers and the nonswervers. But how often do swerves take place? Opinions differ widely; the answer depends largely on one's interpretation of the swerve's role in voluntary motion. Does an atom, when it swerves from the straight downward path, take up a straight motion at an oblique angle to the vertical? Or does it swerve momentarily, like a car changing lanes on a motorway? Each answer has its advocates. Some things are clear. The swerve of an atom has no cause in events previous to its occurrence; it is in principle unpredictable and random. Moreover in its cosmological role it is not to be thought of as the beginning of the world, or of any world. We are not to think of an uninterrupted downward rain of atoms that is at some moment for the first time disturbed by the occurrence of a swerve: rather, atoms have fallen, swerved, and collided for all eternity.

Epicurus avoids the dualism of Aristotle's theory of motion; rectilinear motion is the rule, and the observed circular motion of the heavenly bodies is explained by a variety of mechanisms, such as the effects of winds—much as the straight flow of water has the effect of causing the waterwheel to rotate. But Epicurean astronomy is not, on the whole, to be taken seriously. Its object is to promote peace of mind: that means, above all, to reassure humankind that the gods are in no way concerned with the operations of nature in this or any other cosmos. To be troubled with such things would be inconsistent, Epicurus claims, with the supreme happiness and tranquillity that are part of what it means to be a god. Sense perception cannot tell us exactly how the heavens move. But by analogy with rotating objects within our earthly experience, we can make suggestions about the behavior of the heavenly bodies. So long as our suggestions are possible and do not conflict either with perception or with our a priori beliefs about the gods, we must accept all of them. Epicurus does not even attend to consistency: he suggests, for example, that the moon's light may be reflected from the sun but also that the sun may be extinguished and rekindled each day.

Like Plato and Aristotle, the Stoics held that the cosmos in which we live is the only one in the universe. It is spherical in shape, with the stars, planets, sun, and moon moving in circular paths once daily around the earth, which is stationary at the center. Their cosmos, like Aristotle's, is a corporeal continuum, with no void space inside it, and matter itself is continuous, not atomic. This much is enough to place the Stoics squarely in the same camp with

Platonists and Aristotelians, against the Atomists. But differences arise at once, and they are of great significance.

One major difference is that whereas Aristotle believed our cosmos to be everlasting, the Stoics held that it has a birth, a death by conflagration (*ekpyrōsis*), a rebirth, and so on forever. Both Aristotle and the Stoics believed that our cosmos is unique, but the Stoics added that it has a limited lifespan that is endlessly repeated. Sometimes the surviving reports of Stoic doctrine distinguish between *kosmos* and *diakosmēsis*—i.e., between the ordered world and its ordering. This marks an important distinction. When the present cosmos perishes, it will not pass out of existence altogether, to be replaced by an entirely new one. The same material persists, but the *order* changes. So although in a sense the Stoics and Epicureans were in agreement that our world will come to an end, the Epicurean theory of the birth and death of quite different worlds was of a different sort altogether from the Stoic theory.

Plato in *Timaeus* had combined the similes of biology and the crafts in describing the origin of the cosmos—leaving posterity to doubt whether either simile was to be taken literally. The Stoics chose the biological model, but used it in a way that was almost mystical. Whereas Plato described a Craftsman God working on a material to make the cosmos, which then took on its own life, Zeno takes God to be identical with the cosmos in its initial state (about which I shall say more shortly). God is the principle of life. At first there is nothing else, then God creates a difference within himself, such that as the principle of life he is "contained" in moisture. This is the living "sperm" that produces the cosmos according to the "formula" of which it is the bearer; God is the *spermatikos logos*. God is at the same time material fire and providential intelligence.

It is as if the Stoics deliberately combined numerous elements from earlier theories. The emphasis on fire recalls Heraclitus; the cosmogonic role of a transcendental divine intelligence recalls Anaxagoras, as well as Plato; and the embryological model of the seed goes back at least that far, if not even to Thales and Anaximander themselves, the founders of the Greek cosmological tradition. The careful analysis of the sperm into a moist vehicle and an active "formula," or *logos*, is found also in Aristotle's *De generatione animalium*.

The decision to view the cosmos as a living creature may be regarded as the foundation of Stoic cosmology. We can guess at the reasons that made it an attractive picture. Like living organisms, the cosmos is a material body endowed with an immanent power of motion. It consists of different parts, which collaborate toward the stable functioning of the whole, each part performing its own work. The relation of the parts to each other and to the whole exhibits a kind of fitness, not always obvious in detail but unmistakable in the large picture. This sense of fitness suggests rationality: it is an easy inference that the cosmos itself is possessed of reason, and since reason is a property confined to living creatures, this again suggests that the cosmos is a living being.

The cosmos is permeated by Reason *(Logos)*—this is the most distinctive claim of the Stoics, with ramifications into every field of their thought. It is far more than the epistemological claim that it is possible to understand the workings of the cosmos rationally. It amounts, in fact, to a very large metaphysical theory. Being thoroughgoing materialists, the Stoics had to give a corporeal form to the Logos. Since nothing less than divine power could move and control something so vast as the cosmos, they identified the Logos with God. And as we have seen in the passage quoted above, they assumed that the Logos was something that can have no origin itself but must be the origin of everything else. Thus far the Stoic notion is preserved rather exactly in the first verse of St. John's Gospel: "In the beginning was the Logos, and the Logos was with God, and the Logos was God."

It may be that the notion of "seed-formula" *(spermatikos logos)* saved or prevented the early Stoics from working out a detailed cosmogony in the manner of book 5 of Lucretius's poem. The surviving reports tell us very little about their cosmogonical ideas, beyond the generation of the four elements. As these reports (inadequate though they are) make clear, it was a crucial thesis of the theory that when the cosmos is periodically consumed by fire and becomes a single fiery mass, the seed-formula is preserved intact. The seed-formula for the cosmos as a whole, and for each one of the natural kinds specifically, is present from the beginning; the formula is eternal, the generative force is immanent. So there is no need, as there is in the Atomic theory, for an account of the gradual emergence of more complex forms from simple elements.

The end of the world—or, more exactly, of the present phase of the world—comes about through conflagration; the technical term is *ekpyrōsis*. This argument follows a long tradition, stretching back into mythology, that told of the periodic destruction of the world either by fire (the myth of Phaethon) or by flood (the myth of Deucalion). The tradition was mentioned in Plato's *Timaeus* (22d–e), and this is enough in itself to account for its being known to the early Stoics.

They had reasons for preferring fire to flood. It was a thesis of Stoic physics that the heavenly bodies, and especially the sun, consumed fuel in the form of "exhalations" from the world below them. If parts of the sublunary cosmos were thus assimilated by the fiery sun, it was reasonable to assume that the same might happen to the whole cosmos in due course. But quite apart from this argument, the Stoics could hardly do other than choose a fiery rather than a watery end for the life of the cosmos. The end of the cosmos was to be the beginning, the seed, of the next phase: the active power in the seed was heat, rather than moisture. In Stoic theory, this heat was identified with God;

living creatures (including the whole cosmos) thus contain an innate providential agency that accounts for their well-adapted structures and capacities.

But why, we may ask, did the Stoics adopt a cyclical theory of destruction and rebirth at all? Why could they not follow the path of Plato, who held that God would not destroy his own creation, or of Aristotle, who held that the cosmos is eternally the same, without beginning or end? We can make some reasonable guesses. It must be observed, first, that Aristotle was the exception in Greek cosmology. From the myths of Hesiod through all the rest of the earlier history of natural philosophy, there was speculation about the origin of the world. It was less universally agreed that the world would come to an end: Lucretius treats this as a surprising thesis. All the same, many previous philosophers did theorize that our world would come to an end. Another reason for the end of the world order in conflagration is also reported. God is a living being, composed of body and soul, and his soul is always growing. Thus there will come a time when he becomes nothing but soul. If one thinks of the conflagration in this way, it can be seen not as the death of the cosmos but as its fullest life.

The cyclical theory is connected with the astronomical idea of the Great Year. The ordinary year is determined by the position of the sun relative to the earth; a year has elapsed when the sun and the earth return to the same relative position. Astronomers speculated about the length of time that elapses between two moments at which the sun, the moon, and the five known planets were all in the same relative position (*Timaeus* 39d). This period, of which different estimates were made, was the Great Year. It appears that the period between one conflagration and the next was supposed to be one Great Year.

This could hardly be otherwise if the Stoics were to claim, as they did, that events in one world were precisely repeated in the next. Socrates will defend himself against Anytus with the same words, and will be condemned by the same jury, every time the cosmic wheel turns full circle. One does not have to accept that the stars exercise a causal influence on the affairs of men: it is enough that the exact description of an event must include all its features, including the position of the sun, moon, and planets when it occurs, so that if it is to be exactly repeated those features of it must be the same. The notion that all events are exactly repeated in each successive cosmic period was thought very striking, particularly by opponents of Stoicism. The reasons for adopting this bizarre theory are not reported by our sources. They must lie in the Stoic theory of causation, coupled with the premise that divine Providence organizes the cosmos for the best. For if this world is the best, succeeding worlds could differ from it only at the cost of being worse, and no reason could be given for the existence of a worse world. So each cosmos must be exactly the same as the last one.

Zeno created the concept of "designing fire" *(pyr technikon)*. The notion of an innate heat in animals was familiar from earlier biology, and Zeno extended it to the heavenly bodies, presumably because of the life-giving heat of the sun. Chrysippus appears to have given the doctrine a new form, with the concept of *pneuma,* or breath. This, too, had an earlier history, especially in Aristotle's biological works, and Zeno had identified it with the psyche in animals. In nonphilosophical contexts, the word can mean either "breath" or "breeze"—the noun is from the verb *to blow.* (Latin *spiritus* and English *spirit* are later translations.) Chrysippus made a cosmic principle out of it, and it became one of the most characteristic Stoic ideas.

Pneuma is a mixture of hot and cold, fire and air, and it pervades the entire universe, down to its smallest parts: the Stoics developed a new concept of "through-and-through mixing" to describe the total union of pneuma with the rest of the substance in the world. All physical body, in Stoic theory, is divisible ad infinitum: the doctrine of total mixture asserted that two bodies may be mixed in such a way that no particle, however small, lacks its portion of either body. By mixing with the whole world, pneuma exercises control over everything. It is the vehicle of (perhaps more strictly, it is identical with) God's providence. It seems to follow from this doctrine that two bodies can occupy the same place, at least in the case where one of the bodies is pneuma. The Stoics differed entirely from Plato and Aristotle in this matter. Plato might say that a physical body "has a share of" or "participates in" a Form, but the Form itself was an immaterial being. Aristotle's secondary categories of being, such as qualities, were dependent on and inherent in bodily substances but were not bodies themselves. Both Plato and Aristotle held that the psyche is not itself a bodily thing. The Stoics held that only a body can act on another body or serve as an efficient cause of a body's actions or passions. Hence such beings as souls or qualities were all to be regarded as bodies—not perhaps capable of existing independently but nevertheless corporeal. All such things consisted of pneuma in its various aspects.

As the active ingredient in all things in the world, pneuma is responsible for the "tension" that holds all the world and everything in it together. The guiding idea in this doctrine is that there is a difference between an identifiable thing and a formless heap of matter. It is most obvious, of course, in a living being, but even a lake or a rock has a principle of unity that differentiates it from a mere quantity of water or mineral. The Stoics said that inanimate things were held together by their "holding power" *(hexis),* plants by their nature *(physis),* and animals by their soul *(psyche),* and each was identical with the pneuma that permeated them and held them in tension. In one graphic description, it is "pneuma that turns back toward itself. It begins to extend itself from the center toward the extremities, and having made contact with the outer surfaces it bends back again until it returns to the same place from which it first set out." This theory has important implications for the theory of natural motion.

The Stoics, like Aristotle, held that there is no void space within the cosmos: matter fills the whole region within the exterior spherical boundary within any interstices. This decision probably arose from the need to preserve the unifying tension imparted to the whole by pneuma. Void intervals would interrupt and endanger the unity. At the same time, the Stoics differed from Aristotle in positing a void space stretching in all directions outside the boundary of the cosmos, and some of their reasoning is preserved in this case. If the substance of the cosmos is periodically consumed by fire, it requires space for expansion; before the *ekpyrōsis* this space must be empty, and it must stretch to infinity, since there is nothing that could limit it.

The thesis that there is infinite void space outside the cosmos carries an extremely important corollary. No sense can now be made of the notion of the center of the *universe*. The center would have to be picked out either by being equidistant from the boundary of the universe everywhere, or by some distinction of quality within it. But if the universe has no boundary, the first cannot apply, and the second is ruled out because there can be no qualitative distinction between any point in the void and any other. Hence Aristotle's dynamic theory, which uses the center of the universe as its focal point, must be rejected: the focal point must be the center of the cosmos itself.

The Stoics applied their theory of *hexis* or "holding power" to the cosmos as a whole. Any identifiable object in the Stoic material continuum was said to be characterized by a holding power that gave it stability and identity. The holding power was provided by the all-pervasive pneuma, whose motions prevented the object from collapsing and dispersing. This must apply to the cosmos as a whole, as well as to its individual contents: the corporeal continuum that composed the cosmos was permeated by a force that drew all of its contents toward *its own* center. This is the closest that classical Greek cosmologists came to a theory of gravity. But centripetal motion in the geocentric cosmos could not by itself explain the motion of the heavenly bodies. If the earth stands still, as they assumed, then the heavens go round in circles, and this circular motion appears to have been explained in purely animistic terms: the heavenly bodies *choose* to move in this way.

The total interpenetration of the divine pneuma through the whole physical world raised in an acute form the problem of freedom of choice in rational beings. There was much debate about it, reflected, for instance, in two surviving works—Cicero's *De fato* and Alexander of Aphrodisias's work of the same title. This divine power is a causal agent, is directed toward maintaining the good order of everything in the cosmos, and is, literally, everywhere. Determinism is total. How, then, can human beings choose freely to act as they do? What sense can be made of moral praise and blame? The Stoics' arguments are too complex to summarize satisfactorily. Briefly, the solution offered by Chrysippus appears to be that it is enough that an action be *our* action—that is, that some essential part of the causing of the action be brought about by us. If our contribution can itself be traced to other causes, that does not affect the issue: the action is still ours, and it is rational that we should be regarded as the agent. Cleanthes summed up the position thus: "Lead me, Zeus and Destiny, wherever you have ordained for me. For I shall follow unflinching. But if I become bad, and am unwilling, I shall follow nonetheless."

DAVID FURLEY

Bibliography

Barnes, Jonathan. *The Presocratic Philosophers*. London: Routledge, 1979.

Brague, Rémi. *Aristote et la question du monde*. Paris: Presses Universitaires de France, 1991.

Cornford, Francis M. *Plato's Cosmology*. London: Routledge, 1937.

Dicks, D. R. *Early Greek Astronomy to Aristotle*. London: Thames and Hudson, 1970.

Duhem, Pierre. *Le système du monde*. Part 1: *La cosmologie Hellénique*. Paris: Hermann, 1913.

Furley, David. *The Greek Cosmologists*, vol. 1. Cambridge: Cambridge University Press, 1987. Vol. 2 forthcoming.

Guthrie, W. K. C. *History of Greek Philosophy*. 6 vols. Cambridge: Cambridge University Press, 1962–1981.

Heath, T. L. *Aristarchus of Samos: The Ancient Copernicus*. Oxford: Clarendon Press, 1913.

Koyré, Alexander. *From the Closed World to the Infinite Universe*. Baltimore: Johns Hopkins University Press, 1957.

Long, A. A., and Sedley, David. *The Hellenistic Philosophers*. Cambridge: Cambridge University Press, 1987.

Solmsen, Friedrich. *Aristotle's System of the Physical World: A Comparison with His Predecessors*. Ithaca, N.Y.: Cornell University Press, 1960.

Sorabji, Richard. *Matter, Space, and Motion*. London: Duckworth, 1988.

——. *Time, Creation, and the Continuum*. London: Duckworth, 1983.

Vernant, Jean-Pierre. *The Origins of Greek Thought*. Ithaca, N.Y.: Cornell University Press, 1982.

Vlastos, Gregory. *Plato's Universe*. Seattle: University of Washington Press, 1975.

Related Articles

The Question of Being; Astronomy; Physics; Epicurus; Stoicism; Images of the World; Geography; Aristotle; Platonism

GEOGRAPHY

To DRAW OR WRITE about the earth": the Greek origin of the word *geography* suggests a potentially misleading familiarity. While the contemporary field of geography readily acknowledges Herodotus, Eratosthenes, Strabo, and Ptolemy as its precursors, suggesting a continuity of thought, objective, and methods, it is important not to confuse the Greeks' knowledge of geography with that of their successors. This is particularly true since geography has been troubled throughout its history by arguments over its identity and boundaries as well as its goals and methods. Is its task to describe the earth, to produce an inventory of places and peoples? Does it constitute, for example, an explanatory principle for the movements of history? Or does it aim to construct models of space, maps, diagrams, and tables of facts?

The recent concern in the history of science with questions of cultural anthropology has led to research into the nature of Greek geography and, in turn, to an expanded understanding of the field and its influence. As a result, geography appears to be less a formal discipline with a separate identity than a field of knowledge and experience, manifesting multiple and parallel approaches to the environment of the earth.

Starting with Eratosthenes of Cyrene, who became librarian at Alexandria around 245 B.C.E., geography—the term first appeared about that time—was organized around the project of mapmaking and developed, a posteriori, a genealogy of authors: Anaximander, Hecataeus, Eudoxus, Dicaearchus. The absence of Herodotus, of Hippocrates' treatise *On Airs, Water and Places*, and of authors of travel narratives and periegeses (descriptions taking the form of real or imagined voyages)—for example, Scylax—is significant. Eratosthenes himself appears to be the founder of Hellenistic geography, and in their polemics Hipparcus of Nicaea, Polybius, and Strabo each claim him as a forebear. In the 2nd century C.E., Marinus of Tyre and Ptolemy perpetuate this tradition. These few names indicate the ambiguous nature of what we view as "Greek geography": a shifting field of knowledge where cosmology, astronomy, geometry, history, ethnography, and medicine come together; a meeting place where travel narratives, abstract descriptions, maps, and commentary on maps converge.

One can give this geography some historical depth by distinguishing its successive phases. The oldest emerged in the cities of Ionia, with Anaximander (mid-6th century B.C.E.), Hecataeus of Miletus, and then Herodotus (around 450 B.C.E.). This phase corresponds to the development of colonization in the Mediterranean and Black Sea areas, and to one of the founding projects of Greek historiography. The second phase is that of Hellenistic geography, which existed in the philosophical schools of Athens: in Plato's Academy, with the works of Eudoxus of Cnidos, and in Aristotle's Lyceum, with the works of Dicaearchus of Messana. The study of geography later moved to Alexandria, the capital of the kingdom of the Lagides and the major intellectual center, thanks to the creation of the Library and the Museum. Eratosthenes' map incorporated a mass of new information gathered during Alexander's expedition to Asia. Similarly, Roman expansion led to new geographical development in the work of the historian Polybius, as well as in Strabo's writings at the beginning of the Christian era.

This sort of historical outline requires a great deal of prudence, however. The links connecting the objective factors involved in the broadening of the spatial horizon with the advance of geography are far from mechanical: the ways facts are integrated, interpreted, and diffused belong to a complex process. Moreover, the genealogy leading from Anaximander to Ptolemy creates an illusion of progress that is both linear and cumulative. This genealogy is the product of one interpretation of the history of Greek geography, going back to Eratosthenes himself. But while the succession and cumulative progress of knowledge may apply to cartography, it cannot be said to constitute a global model of the evolution of geographical knowledge. Paradoxically, in fact, mathematical cartography turns out to have had only very limited influence on the contemporaneous geographical consciousness. Texts, more than maps, were the principal bearers of geographical knowledge: in addition to the practical difficulty of transferring images onto metal or wooden panels or onto papyrus, there was the problem of the esoteric nature of Hellenistic maps, which were more like geometric diagrams than figurative maps of the world. The scientific basis of these maps, like the language they used, was incomprehensible to the overwhelming majority of readers, including cultivated and literate authors such as the 2nd-century geographer and traveler Pausanius, who mentions only once the works of "those who claim to know the dimensions of the earth."

If one of the tasks of the history of geography is to determine what the concurrent visions of the world in Greek society might have been, it should be recognized that the geography of the *Odyssey*, Herodotus's ethnography, the geo-ethnographic view of the tragic poets, and the literary geography of the Alexandrian poets, such as Callimachus and Apollonius of Rhodes, all had much greater influence than the works of either Eratosthenes or Ptolemy. The latter influenced only a small, elite group of scientists in erudite circles. Neither geographer had a school. It was only in the Islamic world, and later during the European Renaissance, that the usefulness of Ptolemy's *Geography* was understood.

It is impossible to separate "scientific" geography from the whole collection of renderings, including literary and anachronistic ones, that constituted the worldview of that time. For "history of geography" we should substitute "history of parallel geographies," subtly woven together through alteration, polemics, and the circulation of information.

MODELING / REPRESENTING

One of the most remarkable aspects of Greek geography lies in the early emergence of cartography. Maps themselves symbolize a powerful intellectual endeavor on the part of human beings to set themselves apart from the terrestrial environment and to construct, through reason and imagination, a point of view from above and beyond the earth.

Greek maps are distinct from the cosmological charts found in Egyptian and Mesopotamian civilizations, which offered a schema for understanding the whole world in a single graphic rendering, integrating earth, sky, and the divine powers that personified them. From the time the first map appeared in Greece with the diagram of Anaximander of Miletus (6th century B.C.E.), maps moved away from mythico-religious thinking and, a fortiori, from the cosmogonical models found, for example, in Hesiod's *Theogony*. From that point on, Ouranos (the Heavens), Ge (the Earth), and Okeanos (the Oceans) are secularized, intellectual objects, subject to the principles of geometry, which constitutes one of the dominant paradigms of Ionian science. In addition, maps deal with the *oikoumene*, "the inhabited world," as opposed to the Earth as a cosmological entity. Miletus, as the departure point for numerous colonial expeditions, particularly around the Black Sea, was undoubtedly one of the places where geographical information converged, and where tales about the experiences of navigators and founders of cities were collected. But so far as we can judge, Anaximander's map was not intended for travelers or for colonial expeditions. It was not an aid to navigation of the Black Sea coast but a sketch of the whole inhabited world, projecting onto the earth's surface a shape and an a priori organization that were thus made available to mathematical calculations and the geometric study of forms and symmetries.

The first map sparked the imagination of later geographers, who stressed the audacious genius of its creator, but we can say nothing about its content without extrapolation. However, with the creation of this map, traditionally designated as the first one, we find certain essential elements of Greek cartography coming together: the link with strong cosmological hypotheses, leading to the projection of lines on the earth's surface (which in Anaximander's map was flat), a structure related to the organization of the heavens conceived as a finite sphere on which the earth occupies the exact geometrical center; an effort to give drawings a geometrical cast, charting a graph of the earth through a process of mental calculations; a close connection between the sketch and a treatise bearing on a number of related ideas. Like Anaximander, who wrote a treatise titled *On Nature* (an intellectual project typical of Ionian science and going beyond the framework of geography), Eratosthenes supplemented his map with a treatise called *Geographika*, in which he explained how the map was constructed, and he also included a history of the discipline, a critique of the map's predecessors and descriptive developments. In Ptolemy, by contrast, we find a perfect concordance between the cartographic project and the treatise. There is nothing to suggest that this geometrized Greek cartography ever took on the appearance of medieval maps of the world, with their rich iconography. The esoteric nature of the early drawings, and the necessity of mastering complex knowledge both to produce them and to read them, meant that they were destined for a small circle of specialists in philosophical schools or in a great center of learning like Alexandria. It must be stressed that these maps of the inhabited world were of a strictly theoretical nature; according to all available sources they were not used by travelers, administrators, planners, or anyone else.

Anaximander was not a geographer but a "physician" in the Greek sense. His intent was not to draw a "geographical map" but to devise a visual model of the earth encompassing both the cosmos and meteorological phenomena. When, in 423 B.C.E., the comic poet Aristophanes presented *The Clouds* in Athens, he satirized intellectuals and Sophistic schools, and the map of the world appeared among instruments of astronomy and geometry: an abstract contrivance, of no use to the city-state, and linked to pure speculation, with no political value. The schools of Plato and Aristotle continued the tradition of scientific study, and the works of Eudoxus of Cnidos and Dicaearchus are similarly important milestones between the Ionians and Alexandria. By the 3rd century B.C.E., the cosmological model has changed. The earth is henceforth conceived as a sphere whose geometric organization mirrors that of the heavenly sphere: meridians, parallels, equator, tropics, poles. The *oukemene* (inhabited world) occupies one portion of the northern half of the sphere. The habitable zone lies between the equator and the Tropic of Cancer. Geometrization still predominates with the drawing of the major lines of reference, like the parallel of Dicaearchus, which crosses the entire inhabited world from the colonies of Heracles all the way to India, passing through the Mediterranean, Attica, Rhodes, the Gulf of Issus, and the Taurus Mountains.

We are acquainted with Eratosthenes' work today largely thanks to Strabo, who often used it in polemics. With Eudoxus and Dicaearchus on the one hand and Eratosthenes on the other, we move from Athens to Alexandria, from the city-state par excellence to a new city, the capital of a Hellenistic kingdom; from private philosophical schools where most activity is oriented toward teaching to a royal foundation where intellectuals work with state subsidies. Alexander's expedition and the flood of new information on Asia it produced constituted another major breakthrough. The fall of the Persian empire opened the doors of the Orient to the Greeks. It also allowed for the expansion, not to say the complete revision, of knowledge that had evolved very little since the time of Herodotus (mid-6th century B.C.E.) and Ctesius, a doctor who had been a hostage at the court of King Artaxerxes II (early 4th century B.C.E.). The new era essentially offered unprecedented resources to research, and the Library at Alexandria played a critical role.

Eratosthenes was the first cartographer to work in a library. He grasped the intellectual implications of the influx of new sources that demonstrated, by their number, their contradictions, and their very novelty, the need to correct the old maps. While his geodesic work, such as the famous measurement of the meridian arc between Alexandria and Syena, is in the tradition of speculative thought on the part of geographer-philosophers, particularly of the Academy, Eratosthenes' map and his geographic work appear to be uniquely Alexandrian creations. This is reflected in the importance of Euclidean geometry (*Elements* was published in Alexandria around 300 B.C.E.), with its heuristic potential for graphing parallel and perpendicular lines following from the orthogonal projection chosen by Eratosthenes (in which meridians do not converge toward the poles), and even more in the new methods of intellectual inquiry based on the accumulation of written documents from different lands and of different genres.

By compiling and critiquing his sources, Eratosthenes was able to determine where regions were located and extrapolate their shapes. However, he was not a traveler himself. Establishing the arc of the earth's rotation represented an experimental procedure, but this was not typical of his work in geography. Unable to determine all the positions in latitude and longitude through astronomical calculations (which would remain problematic until precise clocks were perfected in the 18th century), Eratosthenes had to use voyagers' accounts; in other words, he had to translate estimated distances, which varied widely, into a system of measurable disjunctions, gaps that could then be transferred to points on the map.

Thanks to all these theoretical calculations, it was possible, starting with partial sources collected in the Alexandrian Library, slowly to construct the view of the entire inhabited world, and to build up a body of knowledge about the most remote regions a priori, by taking a critical approach to eyewitness accounts. Maps were part of this development, providing visual and mathematical coherence each step of the way. They provided a consistent means for verifying the effects of a local decision on the overall structure, and for making the necessary responses and adjustments suggested by modifying the placement of a parallel or a base meridian. The map is completely oriented toward geodesic work and the schematization of space in relative and measurable geometric form.

Eratosthenes' work marks the beginning of a tradition of the map as the working tool of the geographer, a device that allows for easy transmission from one geographer to another, and for control over, even correction of, one's predecessors' work. Hence we see Hipparchus of Nicea, in his work *Against Eratosthenes,* criticizing the work of the Alexandrian cartographer, whom he reproaches for a lack of mathematical rigor and for his makeshift fashion of establishing positions based on data from travelers. Later, in the first two books of his *Geography,* Strabo echoes these criticisms in order to defend Eratosthenes against Hipparchus's fierce attacks.

Following Eratosthenes, cartographers built on the work of their predecessors. The earlier work provided the starting point, the framework, and the space in which to apply a variety of critical methods that enabled the mapmaker to bring it up to date, to complete and perfect it. This was Ptolemy's position in the 2nd century C.E. vis-à-vis the work of his predecessor, Marinus of Tyre.

The author of treatises on astronomy, mathematics, and optics, Ptolemy made a number of contributions to geography with his astrological geography *(Tetrabiblos),* his *Canon of Remarkable Cities,* and finally his *Geography.* The last work, in the form in which it has come down to us, consists of eight books. Book I and part of Book II are devoted to a theoretical description of mapmaking methods, in particular the representation on a flat surface of the convergence of longitudinal lines toward the poles. The second part of Book II and Books III and IV are in the form of a catalogue of 8,000 points expressed in degrees of longitude and latitude, making it possible to transfer these points onto regional maps with perpendicular representation.

Ptolemy's importance lies in the dual nature of his work as both theory and inventory. The only text by a cartographer to survive (despite all the problems involved in passing down maps and despite the many stages the writing of the text may have been through), Ptolemy's work gives geography a strong definition, oriented toward defining the purpose of maps: the mimesis, or representation, of the inhabited world in its totality, in contrast to chorography, the mapping or description of a particular region according to its natural configuration. This fundamental distinction will play an essential role in geography during the European Renaissance. A veritable inventory of the places of the world at the height of the Roman empire, Ptolemy's *Geography* also provides, in its tabulations, an impressive body of geographical positions readily transferable to maps. This was the only means of protecting the coordinates from the distortions inherent in the manual reproduction of texts and drawings. These 8,000 positions no doubt result in large measure from the manipulation of fictional data; the role of conjecture and approximation and of completely unverifiable data is masked by the authoritative and persuasive effect of the lists of coordinates that obscure all traces of their source. These tables of positions later played an important role in the geography of ancient Islam, which continued the Ptolemean tradition, and in the European Renaissance, where they made it possible for cartographers to recreate the maps of Alexandrian scholars before modernizing their topographic content.

From Anaximander to Ptolemy, Greek cartography appeared to be a highly specialized process and technique. Other accounts acknowledge the circulation of round maps, derived undoubtedly from Ionian prototypes, and both Plutarch, at the end of the 1st century C.E., and Lucian, in the 2nd century, hint at the existence of archaistic maps, freed of the complex mathematical equipment of the Alexandrian production.

DESCRIPTION / INVENTORY / EXPLANATION

Although mapmaking did have a theoretical objective and dealt with the entire inhabited world, governed by the geodesic order and cosmological hypotheses on the similarity of the heavenly and earthly spheres, it was by no means the only tool available to the field of geography. The difficulties of reproducing and transmitting drawings, like the high degree of specialization needed for making them, limited the influence of maps. Moreover, mapping maintained a series of complex links with verbal discourse, which extended its influence beyond the highly specialized circles in which it was used. The map imposed a new order, implicit or not, on geographical description, introducing a form of spatial organization that shaped the corresponding written text. Between map and treatise there is a complex system of interaction: the former provides for visualization and mnemonic images, while the latter affords the indispensable means for conveying knowledge about countries and peoples—itineraries, descriptions, place names, ethnographic digressions, myths, natural science, and so on. Often, the descriptions give the cartographer the material he needs, while the maps can implicitly shape the written description.

Anaximander's map began a tradition in which geographic description—as we understand it today—is supported by prior evidence of a global form that provides a narrative model: the circular voyage. It is tempting to correlate this first map with the *Periegesis* of Hecataeus of Miletus (late 6th century B.C.E.). This work is presented as a tour of the earth, an intellectual journey around the Mediterranean, describing the three continents of the inhabited world (Europe, Libya, Asia); in a sort of catalogue of countries, it lists all the places and peoples on the route. Each stop offered the possibility of integrating a variety of information (ethnographic, for example). Once a principle of global order was established, it was possible to insert new places, to digress and deal with new developments, without disturbing the structure of the whole. This circular model, which resembles a circumnavigation of the Mediterranean coast, also allowed for inland excursions toward the lands and peoples in the interior of a continent. The circumnavigations and other *periodoi ges* (trips around the earth) thus appear to be an odd compromise between the navigators' accounts—adopting the latter's narrative rules, their metonymic logic, sometimes even their detailed topographic information—and maps, which offered a global structure based on an intellectual and ecumenical itinerary, using material from real voyages without being bound by the limits of those voyages. Maps also provided the opportunity to move from real but limited voyages to intellectual, global journeys, virtual tours of the earth.

The history of *periploi* (circumnavigations) and *periegeses* in Greece is crisscrossed by this dialectical tension between, on one hand, the actual tour, the account of the voyage, and, on the other, its intellectual reconstruction within a descriptive model in which circularity is a measure of completeness and comprehensiveness. It is not just by chance that the ancient sources use the expression "circling the earth" for texts and maps. *Periegeses* and *periploi* are both genres associated with discovery and exploration (as in the voyage attributed to Hanno, involving navigation along the Atlantic coast of Africa, or the journey made by the Alexandrian admiral Naearchus, who directed the Greek fleet from the mouth of the Indus to the mouth of the Euphrates), and also with commercial itineraries (the *Periplus of the Erythraean Sea*), and with the first forms of ecumenical geography (the journey of Scylax of Caryanda, *Stadiasmus Maris magni*, the *Periegesis* of Denys).

Whereas Hecataeus of Miletus sought to present the world's places and peoples in an orderly fashion, using Anaximander's map to organize the accounts of travelers and to integrate parts of the voyage into an ideal circle (an enterprise similar to the one he undertook with Greek mythology and which he rationalized in his *Genealogies*), Herodotus's purpose was quite different. Just as *Histories,* in dealing with the recent past and the causes and course of the conflict between the Greeks and the barbarians, differed from the genealogies of Hecataeus, who went further into the distant past and explored an area of conjectural knowledge, the representation of space Herodotus presented differs from the Hecataean model and also from Anaximander's geometric rationalism. However, both models have left traces in Herodotus's text, despite the historian's ironic tone with reference to the excessive symmetry of the Ionian map.

In his contribution to a major question of meteorologics, the location of the sources of the Nile, Herodotus allows himself a surprising degree of cartographic extrapolation. He interprets north-south symmetry on both sides of a base axis, making the Nile, to the south, the equivalent of the Danube, to the north; thus he can find sources of the first corresponding to those of the second (which are located in the Celtic countries, near the city of Pyrenees). So too, when he sets out to explain the sequence of peoples in Asia Minor, or in Scythia, Herodotus resorts to geometry and to a type of description in terms of shapes and orientation that assumes the existence of geographic maps.

The most important innovation in Herodotus's geography, however, lies in the close connections he makes with historical research. Places, and the people inhabiting them, fall within the same intellectual order as events of the past: they are objects of inquiry, understood through the convergence of observation and hearsay, and through the exercise of a critical mind that defines the field of the plausible without always explaining its criteria. Where Ionian rationalism had drawn a circle around the inhabited world with a compass, Herodotus opened up vague boundary areas, where human knowledge stops short of the ocean's edge. These boundary areas are places of alterity and excess, of natural wonders or happy, almost godlike people: the long-lived Ethiopians, Indians, Arabs living in lands of spices. This landscape of the outer limits of the human world remained rooted in the ancient imagination and probably contributed more to creating a picture of the world than did all the geometry of Alexandria. It continued into the Middle Ages and the Renaissance, thanks largely to the rediscovery of Latin encyclopedias.

In Greece, geography could be said to be limited to the inhabited world, in other words, to the *oekoumene*, a limit that even Eratosthenes respects. In Herodotus's work, this area is the theater for the conflict between the Greeks and the Persians. The Persian Wars played an essential role in developing a conception of cultural identity that set the Greeks apart from the Barbarians. The Persian Wars established a cultural and political opposition between peoples that in turn raised questions for the Greeks about their own identity, by leading them to recognize in themselves certain characteristics that are reversed in the mirror image offered by another people.

The ethnographic framework established in Herodotus's work is one aspect of intelligibility in the conflict, and it is also an object of obvious fascination and curiosity. But despite the overlapping discussions of Egyptians, Persians, Ethiopians, or Scythians, which appear at times as digressions in the text, the link with the Persian Wars is never entirely lost. Herodotus's *Histories* are set in a space that has been schematically charted within the Ionian tradition. The stakes in the conflict might be termed geopolitical, in that they resulted from the dangerous proximity between the Persian empire and the Greek city-states of the coast of Asia Minor; the latter's revolts unleashed the hostilities and brought war to the land and seas of Greece itself. Herodotus describes Aristagoras, the Milesian ambassador at Sparta, equipped with a geographic map that he uses to try to persuade King Cleomenes to fight for the liberation of the subjugated cities and to conquer the Persian empire itself, including the treasures of Susa. In the process, the historian conveys brilliantly the scales of distance and power, the forces in conflict, the role of the sea separating Greece and Persia, and the formidable ethnic coalition arrayed against the Greeks.

We lack the milestones that would allow us to trace the evolution of geographic literature up to the 4th century B.C.E. Ethnography and "barbarian customs" appear frequently in titles of works attributed to the logographer Hellanicus of Lesbos, who seems to have made a specialty of local and regional history. The physician Ctesias, in his works on Persia and India, also dealt with historical, ethnographic, and political data; his work remained without peer until the expedition of Alexander the Great. We can assume that ethnographic preoccupations were manifested in the collection of *Constitu-*

tions attributed to Aristotle. The *Periodos ges* by Eudoxus of Cnidos had a scientific and cartographic orientation, and it probably included descriptive information as well.

Herodotus inaugurated a tradition in which geographic knowledge is closely linked to history: it constitutes a framework for history, helps make history intelligible, and provides an introduction to ethnography, which characterizes foreign peoples. In its ecumenical aspect, geography was naturally associated with the genre of universal history. Ephorus supplemented his *History* with a cartographic diagram that was preserved for us by a Christian writer, Cosmas Indicopleustes. It is a simple rectangle with the four cardinal points marked, as well as the peoples living at the frontiers: Celts, Scythians, Indians, and Ethiopians. With Polybius (2nd century B.C.E.), we rediscover this dimension of ecumenical geography in a monumental *History*, which sets out to cover the genesis of the Roman empire and attempts to make sense of the dramatic events that the author himself has experienced. There is a notable geographic dimension to this work. Book XXXIV takes the form of a treatise on geography that is relatively autonomous within the overall structure. The description it offers incorporates information acquired from Alexandrian mapmaking and on occasion takes up highly polemical debates (Polybius defends the geographic competence of Homer, who anchored Odysseus's navigations firmly in the Mediterranean, against Eratosthenes, who relegated them to the ocean and to the domain of pure fiction).

Polybius's historical work influenced both his conception and his practice of geography. He was keenly aware of how much the world had grown as a result of the Roman conquests, and he recognized the need for a reconfiguration of Eratosthenian geography. Roman expansion was one of the major historical events of the epoch, and geography gave Polybius a tool for ordering history. He adopted a broad, quasi-cartographic view that led him to grasp the simultaneity of events in different theaters of action; the temporal order of his work as a chronicler thus coexists with a geographic order that allows him to present events in Asia Minor, continental Greece, North Africa, Spain, and elsewhere. The descriptions of the different theaters of action—cities or battlefields—constitute an important dimension of his story and fit nicely with the Polybian conception of "pragmatic history," where experience prevails over book learning. Polybius himself was a traveler, indeed an explorer, and he portrays himself as an Odysseus turned historian.

Strabo is close to Polybius in many respects. His historical work (which has been lost) took up where *Histories* left off. But in contrast to his predecessor, he devoted a separate work to geography. In calling his treatise *Geography*, Strabo established himself as a successor to Eratosthenes and set himself apart, as had Polybius, from the genre of "circumnavigations." His text is one of the major surviving accounts of Alexandrian geography. The first two books continue the Eratosthenian model: they present a summary of the history of Greek geography (though Strabo breaks with his predecessors in reinstalling Homer as the founder of the line), a critical examination of these predecessors, and a discussion of Eratosthenes' theses, the general frameworks of the Alexandrian map and the polemics sparked by Hipparchus, and the scientific knowledge required to enter into the debates. But Strabo's *Geography* is not a cartographic treatise. It is not meant for the same public as Eratosthenes' work, since Strabo wanted to be of service to Roman statesmen and provincial administrators who needed information on population, economics, and natural resources. His text was meant as a description of the Roman empire, from the Iberian Peninsula (Book III) to Egypt and Libya (Book XVII).

However, despite its introduction and the intent to serve the empire, in its detailed descriptions this *Geography* resembled a complex and heterogeneous literary construction, reworking sources of information from various periods. The description of Greece itself is taken in large part from the "Catalogue of Ships" in Book II of the *Iliad* and from Homer's Alexandrian commentators. For other regions, Strabo borrows whole segments of *periploi* (Artemidorus), and he lists the places spread along the coastline. In India, Strabo seems to forget the harshly critical cast of his earlier statements; he relies on the testimony of Megasthenes, Daeimachus, and other Hellenistic sources who presented a picture of India and its people that combined aspects of wonder with ethnographic observation. At the same time, for Iberia and for Gaul Strabo relied largely on the Stoic Posidonius, who combined ethnographic observations with a particular interest in natural resources and economics.

A collection of regional descriptions from a variety of genres and sometimes from different epochs, Strabo's work is representative of a field of inquiry that goes beyond what we ordinarily mean by "geography." Literary criticism, mythology, history, *mirabilia* (marvels), ethnography, and cartography are all aspects of the spectrum of geographic knowledge, unified only by a relation to space. Against this dizzying inventory of places and peoples and their characteristics, one can posit a few powerful ideas that introduce a coherent worldview. Strabo was interested only in the territory under Roman authority or along its borders. His was a geography of the inhabited world. For Strabo, topography and climate may determine the degree of civilization of people, but acculturation tempers the deterministic model: Rome plays a clear civilizing role.

Was Strabo a precursor of the 19th-century European universal geographies? He illustrates an encyclopedic tendency in geography, now freed of the mathematical framework of the Alexandrians, a geography that became a means of understanding political reality, the human and civilized world, identified with the Roman empire. The encyclopedic tendency reappears in a minor text of the 2nd century C.E., the *Pariegesis of the Inhabited World*, by Denys of Alexandria, who offered students in the schools, in the brief form of a mnemonic poem, a mental map on which the world of gods, the world of heroes, and the world of men were superimposed.

GEOGRAPHIC KNOWLEDGE

From the Presocratics to Ptolemy, Greek geography offers a combination of distinct intellectual projects. While it is true that this long tradition entailed an accumulation of layers of knowledge about the inhabited world, certain specific aims must be kept in mind.

Some scholars looked to geography for a principle of cause and effect, capable of explaining human phenomena. Climatic determinism, destined to survive in the tradition of modern geography, was the object of the Hippocratic treatise *On Airs, Water, and Places* (second half of the 5th century B.C.E.). This manual for the itinerant physician presented a set of correspondences between the environment (topography, climate, hydrography) and the health of the population. Local observations were recorded in a larger deterministic system, governed by the equilibrium or disequilibrium of the relations between hot and cold, dry and wet; these relations were viewed as one of the causes of human disease, and also as a factor explaining cultural and physical differences among peoples living in neighboring regions. In this model, Greece and Asia Minor occupied the temperate center, where extremes are balanced. The Stoic Posidonius used the distribution of climatic zones on the earth as an explanation for physical variations among people living in different regions. Astral determinism also offered an explanatory grid for physical and cultural variations (Ptolemy's *Tetrabiblos*).

Another tradition is that of meteorology, the science of natural phenomena occurring on earth and in sublunary space. Beginning with the Presocratics, questions arose about earthquakes, the Nile River floods, winds, and rain. This tradition inspired Aristotle's *Meteorologics*, a treatise devoted to the classification of these phenomena and to research into their causes. Members of Aristotle's school, such as Straton of Lampsacus and Posidonius *(On the Oceans)*, followed this line of inquiry. Even Eratosthenes had been interested in geophysical phenomena such as the tides, earthquakes, and volcanoes.

Cartography may well be the tradition whose coherence and objectives were most strongly marked by Greek thinkers, starting with Eratosthenes. Resting on a set of astronomical premises and geometric theorems, the discipline emerged as a theoretical activity practiced by philosophers who sought to model the world, from the celestial sphere to the graphic projection of the inhabited earth. Mathematical order, symmetry, and the isomorphism of the heavenly and earthly spheres were at the heart of their investigations. Contrary to what one finds in ancient China, Greek maps were not used to govern, improve, or manage territory. They were not instruments distributed to all levels of the local administration; rather, they represented the activity of a small number of celebrated thinkers working in private philosophical schools (Athens and Rhodes) or in the cultural institutions of Hellenistic rulers (Alexandria and Pergamum). Maps were, above all, the working instruments of cartographers, scholars committed to collecting results, hypotheses, calculations, and attempts at geometric formalization.

For travel by land or sea, travel accounts always superseded maps. For giving shape to the geographic horizon, Homer, Herodotus, and the tragic and Hellenistic poets played a role beyond that of the scientists and thinkers of Alexandria. Their representations, though often archaic, were at least consistent with the literary culture taught in schools. What we term geography today is the result of the convergence of a number of intellectual domains: philosophy, astronomy and mathematics, historiography, physics, and ethnography. All these disciplines are inextricably linked to the exploration of a world that is defined primarily by its human populations and the political and historical issues at stake in their coexistence.

CHRISTIAN JACOB
Translated by Elizabeth Rawlings and Jeannine Pucci

Bibliography

Aujac, Germaine. *Strabon et la science de son temps.* Paris: Les Belles Lettres, 1966.

Harley, Brian, and David Woodward, eds. *The History of Cartography,* vol. 1: *Cartography in Prehistory: Ancient and Medieval Europe and the Mediterranean.* Chicago: University of Chicago Press, 1987.

Janni, Pietro. *La mappa e il periplo: Cartografia antica e spazio odologico.* Rome: Università di Macerata, 1984.

Nicolet, Claude. *Space, Geography and Politics in the Early Roman Empire.* Ann Arbor: University of Michigan Press, 1991.

Pedech, Paul. *La géographie des grecs.* Paris: Presses Universitaires de France, 1976.

Prontera, Francesco, ed. *Geografia e geografi nel mondo antico: Guida storica e critica.* Bari: Laterza, 1983.

————. *Strabone: Contributi allo studio della personalità e dell'opera.* Perugia: Università degli studi. Vol. 1, 1984; vol. 2, ed. Gianfranco Maddoli, 1986.

Van Paassen, Christian. *The Classical Tradition of Geography.* Groningen: J. B. Wolters, 1957.

Related Articles

Images of the World; Herodotus; Ptolemy; History; Polybius

HARMONICS

EVERYWHERE PRESENT in everyday life as well as religious and political life, music was for the ancient Greeks not only the most beautiful of the arts but also the object of the highest philosophical speculation. A mass of textual, visual, and archaeological documents bears witness to the Greek predilection for musical activity: literary, papyrological, and epigraphical evidence; figural representations on ceramics or in relief sculpture; vestiges of the stringed, wind, and percussion instruments that have survived in significant numbers; and, above all, some fifty scores (on papyrus or in inscriptions) give us a rich and varied picture of the musical life of the ancient Greeks. But as much as music was a fervently practiced art, it was also a skill and a science the nature, object, and method of which are defined in writings that are both technical and theoretical. More broadly, music entered the political realm: in Sparta and, to a lesser degree, in Thebes and Mantinea, music and politics were so tightly linked that laws were established governing musical practice and musical education.

The Athenian citizen, for his part, was expected to know how to sing and play at least the *lyra* (an instrument for amateurs, as opposed to the kithara, which was used only by professional musicians). After spending years learning how to read, write, and do arithmetic, Athenian children went for three years to a *kitharistes,* who served both as a teacher of the *lyra* (despite the title) and as a teacher of music in general. The *kitharistes* taught by example, using memory as his principal tool.

Nothing in that era suggests that musical education went further than rudimentary lessons in vocal and instrumental practice. The ancient sources give no indication that a student was expected to acquire theoretical knowledge of any depth. In Book VII of his *Politics,* Aristotle makes it clear that the goal of musical education was not at all to train accomplished musicians—and still less virtuosi—but only to complete the student's general education with basic skills in music. If it is true that the transmission of music was and remained a fundamental given in Greek civilization, it was limited, in the case of amateurs, to the inculcation of ideas entirely oriented toward the practical performance of music and did not even include written notation: school scenes on Attic ceramics show the teacher face to face with his pupils, *lyras* in hand. The scrolls that are sometimes shown on their laps contain poetic texts but never musical scores. In Athens, Thebes, Sparta, and Mantinea, musical city-states par excellence, citizens could neither read nor write music.

To find traces of more advanced musical instruction that includes instruction in music theory as well as stringed instrument technique, we have to go to Ionia, to Magnesia ad Meandrum, and especially to Teos, site of one of the most powerful professional corporations of artists known to antiquity, the Dionysian *technitai* (artists). An inscription dating from the beginning of the 3rd century C.E. describes the sequence of studies to be carried out in a school founded by a generous donor named Polythrous. A *kitharistes* was hired for an annual salary of 600 drachmas, to teach certain young men the art of playing the kithara, with and without plectrum (a technical specialization not included in the ordinary course of study), but in addition—and this is a crucial innovation—he also taught musical theory, *ta mousika*. The text stipulates that examinations in music were to be given annually.

In Magnesia ad Maeandrum, according to a 2nd-century C.E. inscription, the year-end awards given the best pupils included prizes for *melographia* and *rhythmographia*, as well as prizes for kithara playing, *kitharoedia* (singing to kithara accompaniment), and arithmetic. The references to "melodic writing" and "rhythmic writing," probably in the form of musical dictation, strongly imply a passage from the level of advanced mastery of a technically difficult stringed instrument to a higher level involving musical theory.

The term *ta mousika* warrants some explanation. This plural neuter is not equivalent to *he mousike*, music, a term that very often refers to general musical culture, including not only music as such but also what was later called the quadrivium. *Ta mousika* implies a plurality that is still concrete and applied, that has not quite reached full theoretical knowledge of the subject or of the various disciplines that constitute the subject. According to the great theoretician Aristoxenus of Tarentum, only the second sort of knowledge defines the *mousikos*, the authentic musician. Furthermore, inscriptions tell us that some musicians, having the same education as the young men of Teos, went from one city-state to another giving talks on the topic of *ta mousika*, addressing a public made up not of specialists but of amateurs interested in the subject. Thus we find a decree in the city of Tanagra, dating from 171–146 B.C.E., honoring a certain Hegesimachus of Athens, described by the text as *mousikos hyparkhon*, "a professional musician by trade," and his son, who over a period of several days gave talks during which they used musical instruments and discussed the instruments themselves. In so doing, according to the inscription, they demonstrated the excellence of their *techne*, in other words, their technical skills as musicians. The term *techne*, quite different from *episteme*, is undoubtedly one of praise. It is found in a large number of honorific inscriptions marking free performances or lectures given not only by musicians but also by physicians and orators. Nevertheless, it clearly delineates the boundaries of the knowledge that has been put on display: theoretical knowledge, unquestionably, and to some extent scientific, but no more than that; it is still anchored in musical practice (that of a specific instrument, for example) and not inhospitable, in all likelihood, to considerations involving the history of music, all of which was excluded from the compass of the musical *episteme.*

This distinction between *techne* and *episteme* has direct consequences for the form of the musical treatises that have come down to us—approximately fifty of them, covering a period of about ten centuries (from the end of the 6th century B.C.E. up to the 5th century C.E.). Indeed, there are two distinctly different types of authors: on the one hand, there are musicographers, and on the other, theoreticians. The first wrote fairly short works for the most part, with titles that indicate clearly enough the limits of their ambitions: thus Cleonides and Bacchius the Old produced works called *Eisagōge* (Introduction) or *Encheiridion* (Manual), and the Pythagorean writer Nicomachus of Gerasa wrote a brief work that is only a draft prefiguring a scientific treatise. Theoreticians, for their part, give us works like *Peri mousikes* and *Peri harmonikes* (On Music, On Harmonics), the implicit underlying feminine term being *epistemes,* science.

In the texts, these two types of studies diverge significantly. After a rapid and superficial approach to the subject, the musicographers quickly enter into purely technical considerations, in a language stripped of any literary pretensions. Concepts are studied one by one, in the form of successive definitions, in increasing order of difficulty and complexity as each new element is added and combined with the others. The aim is to impart progressively, through a series of affirmations that belong neither to criticism nor to research, a sort of musical catechism that the student will eventually have to memorize from beginning to end. The *Introduction* by Bacchius the Old even proceeds by way of question sets (as if the teacher were examining the student) and model answers:

> "How many kinds of consonant intervals are there in the perfect system?"
> "Six."
> "What are they?"
> "They are the fourth, the fifth, the octave, the octave plus the fourth, the octave plus the fifth, the double octave."

The theoreticians of music, for their part, were all associated with one or another of the great philosophical schools of antiquity. There was no theoretician who was not a philosopher; conversely, there was no philosophical school that did not construct its own doctrine of musical science. Ancient Pythagoreanism is illustrated by the treatises of Philolaus (only fragments of which survive, unfortunately), then of Archytas of Tarentum; Aristoxenus, author of the oldest work on harmonics that we have, was first a student of the Pythagoreans before he became a follower of Aristotle's teachings; Theon of Smyrna was a Platonist; Philodemus of Gadara identified himself with

Epicureanism, and in his *Peri mousikes* he challenged the musical doctrines of the Stoic Diogenes of Babylon; even the Skeptics, with Sextus Empiricus, had their own ideas about the nature and function of music, essentially aimed at dismissing all the other philosophical schools.

These treatises, which are reasonably lengthy, have some common features. They always integrate into their respective musical systems the fundamental ideas of the school from which they come, principles and methods included. All of them reflect, starting in their very first paragraphs, on the nature of musical science and its place in the system of learning and knowledge: How does it relate to mathematics, physics, or even metaphysics? What are its criteria? How does it operate, and in what form? Unlike the musicographers, the theoreticians are always careful to contest and refute opposing theses with solidly supported arguments, either to challenge particular points or else to undermine an entire doctrine starting with its basic assumptions.

A third group has to be distinguished both from the musicographers and from the theoreticians: those who are broadly categorized, despite their differences, as "Harmonists," and who left no known works. We find their theories only in the form of polemical summaries by their adversaries, chiefly Plato and Aristoxenus. Insofar as one can judge by these indirect and partial accounts, their theoretical teaching did not include any philosophical reflections. Their basic focus was on musical practice, whether in terms of playing an instrument, like the *aulos,* or in terms of musical notation. One of the illustrious representatives of this tendency (since there is no way in this context to speak of a particular school) was the 4th-century Athenian kitharist Stratonicus. He is said to have had students in harmonics, and to have been the first to devise a musical diagram.

It is difficult to assign to Plato a position of his own among the musical currents of antiquity, not only because he did not leave any specialized treatise on music but also because his thinking on harmonics and musical practice does not really constitute a doctrine as such. Largely inspired by the Pythagorean system of calculating intervals, to which he subscribed, ironic in his opposition to the Harmonists who built their theories by "fiddling" with the strings of their instruments, Plato opened the way for those who would later be called Neoplatonists (such as Theon of Smyrna and Aristides Quintilianus) rather than actually constructing his own science of music.

The history of the philosophico-musical literature of Greek and Roman antiquity is also the history of a persistent schism, one that lasted nearly ten centuries. It opposes—irreconcilably, despite the efforts of the great Alexandrian astronomer Ptolemy, among others—the Pythagorean and Neopythagorean schools to Aristoxenus of Tarentum and his successors. The quarrel erupted in the second half of the 4th century, when Aristoxenus wrote his major work, a magisterial treatise on harmonics known under the traditional but probably erroneous title of *Harmonika stoikheia* (Harmonic Elements).

Before Aristoxenus, musical and harmonic science was the province of the Pythagoreans and—with the reservations noted above—the Harmonists. For someone like Philolaus or Archytas, music was "sister" to mathematics and astronomy, as a science of numerical relations governing the musical intervals, of which they are both the essence and the expression. The central idea is that the universe is structured according to a perfect order, an order defined by numbers and by which the human soul must be penetrated if it is to participate in this perfection itself. Music, and especially harmonics, are among the manifestations of this order: starting from the observation (at first experimental, with the earliest observations on a single-stringed instrument called a *monochordon*) that consonant intervals correspond to simple numerical relations in the superpartial form of the ratio $(n + 1) / n$, the Pythagoreans in a sense reversed this proposition: harmonious intervals are consonant *because* they may be expressed as (or because they simply *are*) remarkable numerical relations. In this system of thought, it goes without saying that musical science, reduced here to harmonics and acoustics, stems from "physics," understood as a science of the order governing the entire universe, and that this science used the tools of mathematics to express itself. Consequently, any melody perceptible to the ear can be deemed beautiful only inasmuch as it is the audible expression of an abstract perfection, which transcends it. The disciple's efforts, then, will be to abstain from any musical practice blemished by imperfection, which would be capable of altering the harmony of his soul. Whence the injunction, thought to go back to Pythagoras himself, to play only the *lyra*, whose seven-stringed *accordatura* reflects the order of the seven planets, among other things in order to participate in the order of the world. Starting from such principles, the musical treatises of the first Pythagoreans have titles like Philolaus's *Peri physeos* (On Nature), or *Peri arithmetikes* (On Arithmetic).

With Aristoxenus of Tarentum the era of music in thrall to mathematics quickly came to an end. A close follower of Aristotle, who throughout his work had called into question several aspects of the Pythagorean theses even though he had not formulated a complete doctrine of his own, Aristoxenus established, for the first time in antiquity, a musical science independent of mathematics, an autonomous science ruled by its own principles and endowed with a method suited to its own nature, to the objects it studies, and to its own goals, based on two criteria directly related to its own specific features: the ear, *aisthesis*, and rational thought, *dianoia*. There were to be no more calculations of intervals: the object of harmonic science was now to be musical sound itself and not mathematical entities.

The split between the two doctrines was thus absolute. It bore on the roots and the very foundations of the science of harmonics. In historical terms, the schism was complete around 325 B.C.E. From then on, everything was marked by the irremediable opposition between Pythagoreanism (or, to a lesser degree, Platonism) and Aristoxenism. Thinkers had no choice but to take sides and ally themselves with one of these formidable doctrines or the other; they had to defend its principles and conclusions anew, and to struggle against the opposing school, unless they positioned their arguments on strictly technical grounds, just as the more modest musicographers had done in their didactic writings.

The only significant attempt to reconcile the two doctrines is found in the *Harmonika* in three books by Ptolemy, written in the 2nd century C.E. This voluminous text is of crucial importance in the history of Pythagorean musical thought. Without ever calling into question Pythagorean acoustics and physics, with which he openly identified, and still less the mathematical nature of the science of intervals, which he never tired of calculating, Ptolemy comes across here as a figure both remarkable for his independence and admirable for the critical spirit that he develops toward his subject. In spite of his protestations of obedience, he in fact strives to point out everything in Aristoxenus that, as he sees it, represents an intelligent and authentically musical contribution to harmonics, especially anything that has to do with auditory sensation, which he then uses as a criterion as reliable as *dianoia*.

But there was never any real syncretism. The last theoretical writings in Latin, by St. Augustine and by Boethius (ca. 480–524), who wrote *De institutione musica*, and later the *Harmonics* in Greek by the Byzantine author Manuel Bryenne (around 1320), still remained dependent on one tradition or the other. Boethius, very much in the Pythagorean camp, and Manuel Bryenne, a strictly orthodox Aristoxenean, are the last champions of the two causes.

Around the edges of the purely theoretical treatises, we know of works that are undoubtedly derived from an early source—of which, unhappily, there are almost no surviving fragments—dealing with instruments: *Peri organon, Peri aulon, Perio aulon treseōs* (On Instruments, On Auloi, On Piercing of Auloi), attributed to writers who are notoriously Pythagorean (such as Euphranor) or Aristoxenean (beginning with Aristoxenus himself). In these texts, which one might view at first glance as technical works, since they seem to originate in the *techne* of instrument making, what is at issue goes far beyond the practical realm. The aim is to undermine the opposing doctrines and to shore up one's own theses, starting from instrumental realities, which serve both as the experimental basis and as material proof in support of a doctrine. This is why the set of surviving fragments of these works are included in philosophico-musical treatises.

In spite of the considerable divergences that set theoreticians against one another across ten centuries of musical literature, a sort of consensus arose concerning the place assigned to harmonics within the various disciplines that make up the *mousike episteme*, and (more surprisingly) concerning the various elements included in *harmonikē*. This term must not be understood in the modern sense of the word *harmonics,* which is the science of chords and their sequences. Indeed, even if we have some evidence that the ancients used a sort of polyphony, this was never the object of the slightest attempt at codification, either by musicographers or by theoreticians.

The oldest classification of musical disciplines in which *harmonikē* appears goes back to Lasus of Hermione, who taught in Athens during the 6th century. This classification has not come down to us directly; it is mentioned by the Latin author Martianus Capella in his *Nuptials of Philologia and Mercury,* written between 410 and 439 C.E. Lasus distinguishes three major components of musical knowledge (technical, practical, and performative), themselves subdivided into three branches. *Harmonikē* is the first branch of the technical component, where it precedes rhythmics and metrics.

The second classification that will leave a lasting mark on Greco-Roman musical theory is that of the theoretician Aristoxenus. It is no longer a matter of oral teachings here, since Aristoxenus is the author of the oldest treatise on harmonics that has survived almost intact. For him, harmonics is the first of the musical sciences, by its importance in the order of the acquisition of knowledge: "The science of *melos* is complex; it is divided into several parts. Among them, we have to consider the science called 'harmonic [*harmonikē*],' which comes first in rank and has an elementary value. In fact, it is the first of the theoretical disciplines: from it stems everything relating to the theory of systems and tones; and it is fitting to ask nothing more of anyone who has mastered this science, because that is its goal; all the subjects at a higher level that are studied once the poietic science makes use of systems and tones do not belong to harmonics, but to the science that encompasses both harmonics and all the sciences that study the entire set of musical questions. And it is the possession of this latter science that makes the musician" (*Harmonic Elements* 1.11–2.7).

Aristoxenus's magnum opus, *On Music,* has not survived. In it he must have written at length about his conception of the various elements that constitute a musical knowledge worthy of the status of *episteme.* To attempt to restore it, we are obliged to extrapolate from the introduction and from the remaining portions of his *Elements of Rhythm,* as well as from the indications he left in the treatise on harmonics and in the fragments of works cited by other writers.

There is no doubt that harmonics and rhythmics are theoretical sciences, clearly distinct from the science of instruments *(organikē)* and from musical practice. The writer introduces the notion of "poietic science," which includes both the art of musical composition and that of poetic writing (both governed by strict rules). In any event, the documentation remains so sparse that one cannot seriously envision proposing an Aristoxenean flow chart for musical science.

The problem of the transmission of texts does not arise with the third and

The Tower of the Winds in Athens, built by Andronicus, 1st century B.C.E. The tower housed a hydraulic clock. It is described by Vitruvius in *De architectura.*

"Neither rectilinear without circular motion, nor revolutions without rectilinear motion, can accomplish the raising of loads." Illustration from Vitruvius, *De architectura* X.3.2, 1572 edition. "The very same weight, which one cannot move at all without a lever, one can move quite easily with it, in spite of the additional weight of the lever" (Pseudo-Aristotle, *Mechanics*).

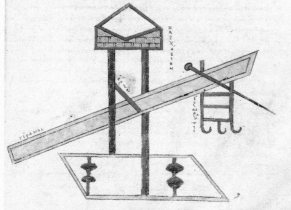

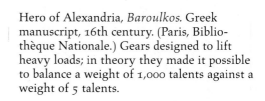

Hero of Alexandria, *Baroulkos.* Greek manuscript, 16th century. (Paris, Bibliothèque Nationale.) Gears designed to lift heavy loads; in theory they made it possible to balance a weight of 1,000 talents against a weight of 5 talents.

Catapult. Athenaeus, *De machinis.* Constantinople, 11th century. (Paris, Bibliothèque Nationale.) A major innovation in the art of war, the catapult was probably invented around 400 B.C.E. by engineers in the service of Dionysius of Syracuse.

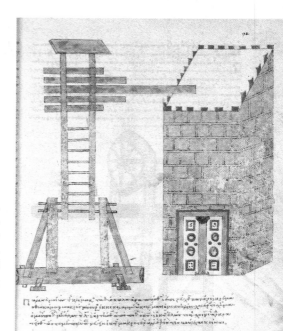

Machine for attacking a tower. Philon of Byzantium, treatise. Constantinople, 11th century. (Paris, Bibliothèque Nationale.) The quest to perfect such war machines was a major driving force behind technological progress in ancient Greece.

Examining a patient. Relief,
1st century B.C.E. (Rome,
Museo della Civiltà Romana.)

Surgical instruments
and cupping instru-
ments. Relief from the
Asclepieion, Athens.
(Rome, Museo della
Civiltà Romana.)

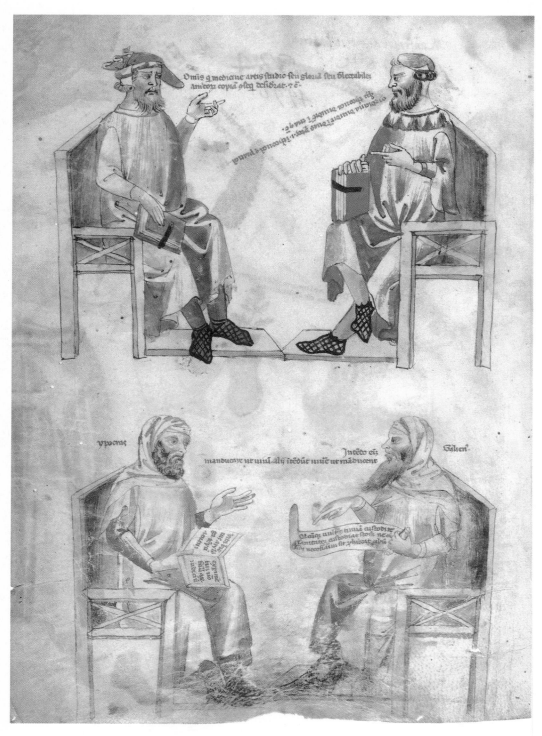

Manfredo dei Monti Imperiali, *Book of Herbs and Plants*. Italy, first half of the 14th century. (Paris, Bibliothèque Nationale.) Above, a man holding Hippocrates' *Prognostics* with Galen's commentary. Below, Hippocrates, holding the book of *Aphorisms*, seated across from Galen.

Apollonius of Citium, commentary on Hippocrates, *Peri arthrōn* ("On Joints"). Late 10th-century manuscript. (Florence, Biblioteca Medicea Laurenziana.) Two assistants stretch the patient's spinal column, while the doctor sits on his back.

The four temperaments. *Guild Book of the Barber-Surgeons of York*, ca. 1500. Clockwise from upper left: melancholic, sanguine, phlegmatic, and choleric.

Dioscorides (1st century C.E.), *De materia medica*. Manuscript, Italy, 9th century. (Paris, Bibliothèque Nationale.)

Asclepius curing a patient. Relief in marble, 5th century B.C.E. (Athens, Archaeological Museum of Piraeus.)

Divination scene.
Amphora, ca. 520 B.C.E.
(Boulogne-sur-Mer,
Château-Musée.) A hoplite
examines a victim's liver,
which is presented by a
young boy.

The Pythia at Delphi. Bowl
by the Kodros painter,
ca. 440 B.C.E. (Berlin,
Staatliche Museen.)

Odysseus consulting Tiresias in Hades' dwelling. Vase, southern Italy, 5th century B.C.E. (Paris, Bibliothèque Nationale.)

Gold strip from a Greek tomb. (Vibo Valentia, Museo Vito Capialbi di Vibo Valentia.) The text presents a new concept of the afterlife, in which the deceased finds himself in the company of heroes, following Empedocles' religious ideas or beliefs.

last classification, that of the *Peri mousikes,* written in the 3rd century C.E. by the theoretician Aristides Quintilianus, who was influenced as much by the Pythagoreans and the Platonists as by Aristoxenus. This is the most complete treatment by far that we have. For the first time, as respect for the Pythagorean tradition required, there is a section on physics in the theoretical part, which deals with arithmetic and physics properly speaking. The phenomenon of sound as such is examined, along with acoustics, before the arithmetic calculation of intervals is formulated. It goes without saying that the Aristoxenean school rejects even the very existence of this physical aspect of the musical sciences. The second, or technical, section takes up the tripartite subdivision that goes back to Lasus, was adopted by Aristoxenus, and was shared by all the schools: harmonics, rhythmics, and metrics. The second major subdivision is "practical," or "educational." It includes, on the one hand, composition (melody, rhythm, poetics), and on the other, execution (reminiscent of Lasus), which regroups the organic (instrumental playing), the odic (chant, or song) and the hypocritic (dramatic action).

What was the object of "harmonics"? If we consider the entire corpus of musical, theoretical, and musicographic literature of antiquity, it seems that all the schools, beyond the basic quarrels that divided them, were more or less in agreement on the various elements encompassed by harmonics, even though there was never any agreement as to its nature and methods. All the writers listed these elements in the opening lines of their works. They numbered six or seven, depending on whether *melopoiia,* musical composition, was included or not. Everyone also agreed that harmonics was the science of *melos,* or musical sounds (in contrast to meters or rhythms), considered as by nature perfect in organization; the role of the science of harmonics is to discover and then to articulate the laws that govern the structured relations among these elements. The seven traditional sections of works on harmonics are presented in the following order: (1) sounds; (2) intervals; (3) systems; (4) genera; (5) tones, or *tropoi;* (6) *metabolai;* (7) musical composition *(melopoiia).* This terminology, except for the first two terms, is unique to Greco-Roman antiquity. It warrants a few words of critical explanation.

(1) Sounds: These are the *phthongoi,* sounds belonging specifically to music, as distinct both from noise (Theon of Smyrna gives thunder as an example) and from spoken sounds. For Pythagorean thinkers, sound should initially be defined as a physical, or acoustic, phenomenon: it is produced by a shock of air, and its pitch depends directly on the speed of its movement. The more rapid the movement propagated through air or fluid (according to Nicomachus), the higher the resulting sound will be. Aristoxenus leaves these questions to the physicists. Harmonic science is concerned with distinguishing musical sound from the sound of the speaking voice; in language, the voice proceeds by continuous movement, without isolating pitch levels, while musical sound is "the stopping of the voice on a single pitch," in a strictly dis-

continuous movement of the voice. Thus for Aristoxenus and his followers, musical sound cannot be identified with any movement whatsoever.

In the Aristoxenean theory of sound, there are a certain number of consequences bearing on the theory of language and, consequently, on the art of oratory. In the 1st century C.E. Quintilian returned to Aristoxenus's theses on the movements of the voice in his *De musica* in order to derive instructions of a practical nature.

(2) Intervals: Although musicographers and theorists unanimously call intervals *diastemata,* they do not agree on much else. They still recognize that an interval is made up of two sounds that are produced successively or simultaneously, whether they are identical or different in pitch. The names and definitions of intervals is another matter altogether. In the ancient terminology of Philolaus the Pythagorean, as reported by Nicomachus, the fourth is called *syllaba,* the fifth *dioxeia* (literally, "climbing toward the sharp"), and the octave, *harmonia.* This vocabulary was quickly abandoned, it seems, even by the Pythagoreans, to be replaced by the generally agreed-upon terms *dia tessarōn, dia pente,* and *dia pasōn,* to indicate the fourth, the fifth, and the octave. These terms derive directly from the playing of stringed instruments. The notions of "string" and "note" are confused by then: *chordōn* (*chorde* is the Greek term for string) is implicit in each of the three terms: "across four [strings]," "across five [strings]," "across all [strings]."

As soon as we come to intervals smaller than the *ditonos* (our major third), the terminologies diverge. The tone is called *epogdoon (diastema)* by the Pythagoreans, but *tonos* by the Aristoxeneans. The fact is that the terminology in this instance is a direct reflection of the way in which each school describes and defines intervals. The Pythagoreans, as we have seen, expressed intervals through numerical relations, while Aristoxenus considered them only in terms of how they were perceived by the ear and how they could be defined by careful reflection.

According to the old Pythagorean school, the octave is the relation 2 to 1; the fifth, the relation 3 to 2; the fourth, the relation 4 to 3; and the tonic (the "difference" between the fifth and the fourth), the relation 9 to 8. How were these numerical relations established? By the so-called experiments on the monochord, mentioned throughout Pythagorean and Neopythagorean literature: if a string stretched between two pegs is pressed, or stopped, at its midpoint, the sound it produces is one octave higher than the sound produced by the string left unstopped. Stopped at three-quarters of its length, the sound produced is the fourth above; at two-thirds, the fifth above, and so on. These observations, which were tried out on a graduated monochord (in more and more complex fashion over time), were verified or extended by arithmetic calculation: by combining a fourth and a fifth: $(4/3) \times (3/2) = 2/1$, we obtain the relation to the octave. To discover the numerical relations of the tonic, one proceeds by "subtraction" (actually by division) of the two same relations: $(3/2) : (4/3) = 9/8$.

The relation 9/8 is *epogdoon,* because it introduces the number 8 *(octo)* and another number that goes beyond it by one unit, or one-eighth. The fourth, 4/3, is for the same reason called *epitrite.* The octave is quite naturally "double," *diplasion.* The common point for all these relationships is that they have the superpartial *(epimore)* form $(n + 1)/n$: their numerator (as one would say today) is one integer larger than their denominator.

As soon as one gets to the subdivision of the tone, the differences between schools become absolute. In fact, while Aristoxenus declared that the human voice and musical instruments were capable of producing an accurate half-tone (identified as such by the ear), the Pythagoreans for their part believed that an accurate half-tone could not exist. Why? Because, as the Pseudo-Euclid said, "There is no middle in the double relation" (for which it would actually be necessary to find the square root). How does one proceed then to "find" a half-tone?

It is necessary to "remove" a *ditonos* from a fourth, since the fourth, as everyone acknowledged, is composed of two tones and a half. This produces the following equation:

$$4/3 : (9/8)^2 = 4/3 : 81/64 = 256/243$$

This half-tone, multiplied by itself, is not equivalent to the *epogdoon* interval of the tone. It is smaller than the true half-tone, as may be seen by a very simple calculation, which consists in looking for the "difference" between the tone 9:8 and the *leimma* expressed by the ratio 256:243:

$$9/8 : (256/243) = 2187/2048$$

This new half-tone is called an *apotome.* To designate the two half-tones obtained in this way with a single word, the term *diesis* is used; it means "division" or "passage," depending on how it is interpreted.

The partisans of the Aristoxenean school rebelled against a method that resulted in using calculations to create intervals that no voice and no instrument could produce and that the ear could not identify. According to Aristoxenus of Tarentum, this was an outrage against nature and against the phenomenon of music itself. Thus when he used the term *diesis,* he was designating the quarter-tone or the third-tone as they are used in vocal and instrumental practice.

(3) *Systemata,* or systems, involve two intervals and at least three sounds in a succession governed by precise rules. The system of reference that informs the logic of harmonics is the tetrachord, or fourth, which remains the

basic unit throughout the ten centuries of Greek and then Latin musical literature. The limits of this system are fixed, with each boundary note separated
from the other by two and half tones, while the two intermediary sounds
may change position according to the genus to which the system belongs.
Two tetrachords can be conjunct or disjunct, depending on whether a disjunctive tone remains between them or the upper note of the lower tetrachord
is also the lower note of the upper tetrachord. In the first case, the system
covers a seventh; in the second, it extends to the octave. The maximum reach
of the system of tetrachords combined among themselves, by conjunction
and disjunction, is two octaves, which thus create the great "perfect system" *(systema teleion)* that was completed during the Hellenistic period. It
is made up, from low to high, of an "added" note, called for this reason
proslambanomene, then of tetrachords, each of which has a particular name.
As is clear from the accompanying figure, the third tetrachord is sometimes
disjunct, if its lower note falls one tone higher than the highest note of the
mesōn (middle tetrachord), and sometimes conjunct, if the two tetrachords
share a common note.

(4) Three genera (singular, genus) were known in antiquity: the enharmonic, the chromatic, and the diatonic. They depend on the place occupied by
the two "mobile" degrees within tetrachords. Their structure assumes three
principal forms (from high to low), according to the ancient theoreticians:

Diatonic: tone−tone−$\frac{1}{2}$ tone
Chromatic: tone $\frac{1}{2}$−$\frac{1}{2}$ tone−$\frac{1}{2}$ tone
Enharmonic: ditone−$\frac{1}{4}$ tone−$\frac{1}{4}$ tone

As is apparent here, the lower intervals of the tetrachords have a tendency
to become "compressed." When the sum of the two lower intervals is equal to
or smaller than the "rest of the fourth" (Aristoxenus), the genus is then

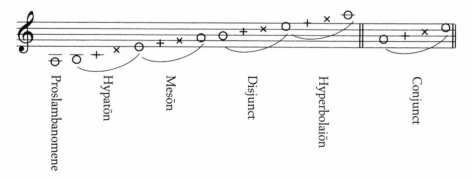

The "perfect" system with five tetrachords

"compressed"; this was particularly appreciated in vocal and instrumental musical practice. In good theory, or at least in Aristoxenean theory, no subdivision of the fourths is allowed in which the median interval is larger than the upper interval.

Beyond the three principal genera, both Greeks and Romans knew and practiced variants that they called *chroai*, a vivid term that may be translated by "shades" or "colorations," recalling its link with *chrōma*, color, as well as the chromatic (genus). On reading the theoretical texts, we understand that the instrumentalists must have made considerable and even abusive use of *chroai*. Aristoxenus is vituperative on the subject of their anarchic misuse, which leads him to try to normalize their use starting from general principles such as the exclusion of a median interval larger than either of the two others. The Neopythagorean treatises did not have this concern, probably because the issue was not closely tied to practice. On the contrary, as if carried away by their vertiginous calculations, they ended up proposing scores of ever more numerous variants, with intervals that were increasingly difficult to link with any musical reality: this is especially the case with Ptolemy in his *Harmonika,* in the 2nd century C.E. However, musicians seem to be in agreement in allowing six "shades" (not counting the enharmonic genus), namely, in addition to the three genera listed above,

Soft diatonic: tone $\frac{1}{2}-\frac{3}{4}$ tone$-\frac{1}{4}$ tone
Hemiolic chromatic: tone $\frac{3}{4}-\frac{3}{8}$ tone$-\frac{3}{8}$ tone
Soft chromatic: tone $\frac{5}{6}-\frac{1}{3}$ tone$-\frac{1}{3}$ tone

(5) Tones or tropes *(tonoi, tropoi):* Contrary to a very widespread misunderstanding (derived, it must be said, from erroneous interpretations of Greek texts by certain late Latin theorists), these have nothing to do with "modes," which would presuppose distinctions that were never made in the Greek and Roman worlds. The *tropoi* (called *harmoniai* up to Plato and Aristotle's time, when they still encompasssed only an octave) are the various ways of spacing the great perfect system, in any genus, starting from a thetic base note that varies from one *tropos* to another. The progression takes place from half-tone to half-tone and is articulated around five principal *tropoi*. From low to high, these are the Dorian, the Iastian, the Phrygian, the Aeolian, and the Lydian, the names explicitly referring to the presumed ethnic origins of the *tropoi*. At a fourth below, the *tropos* is called *hypo-* and, at a fourth above the principal *tropos,* it is called *hyper-*. The spacing of intervals evolved gradually over centuries, with some differences of opinion here and there as to the respective place of one interval or another, or as to the appropriate name for a given tone. The survival of Mixolydian, in the place where one would have expected the Hyperdorian, is evidence of this evolution.

In the classical period, or when a later author takes the ancients as his model (this is true of Plutarch when he looks to pre-Aristoxenean sources as his models), there is no mention of either *tropos* or tone; instead, we simply find adverbs ending in -sti: *dōristi, iasti, phrygisti, lydisti,* and so on. This ancient terminology is still found in Aristophanes as well as in Book VIII of Aristotle's *Politics,* but it ceases to have currency in Aristoxenus's *Harmonic Elements,* in the last quarter of the 4th century. There, for example, Aristoxenus speaks of *lydios tonos* and no longer of *lydisti.*

To close this controversial chapter on Greek *tropoi,* let me add that their tripartite classification coincides with the distinction between the three "regions of the voice" *(topoi tēs phōnes),* low, medium, and high *(hypatoeidēs, mesoidēs, andnetoidēs),* a distinction accepted in all the schools of harmonics.

(6) *Metabolai* correspond more or less to our modern modulations. There is a *metabolē* when we pass from one system, genus, or *tropos* to another, from conjunction to disjunction, and this is true whether the borrowing is temporary or, on the contrary, it entails a complete structural change. Here we are entering into the realm of the laws that regulate what Aristoxenus names, in terminology that recalls that of his master Aristotle, musical alteration *(alloiōsis),* but without really impinging on the use of the elements of harmonics. At this stage of musical science, the phenomenon is described and designated by name, but its practice has not yet been codified; this codification will depend directly on the choice and usage (according to Aristides Quintilianus) of the composer or practitioner. But the analysis of metabolai is actually located at the threshold of the seventh and last part of harmonic science, a part that, for this reason, does not appear in certain treatises: *melopoiia,* or melodic composition.

(7) *Melopoiia* stems in fact as much from musical theory as from its practical application. In the classifications proposed by Lasus or Hermione or Aristides Quintilianus, it enters into the executive or practical element, since it presumes actual usage, a *chresis.* However, in writings on harmonics, *melopoiia* does not consist in defining laws of composition or music writing; quite the contrary. In Aristides Quintilianus, who has the most to say on this subject, the chapter devoted to it is limited to defining the "figures of melody" *(schemata tes melodias)* in analytic and descriptive terms. A given melodic line is deployed in three different ways. In the *agōge,* conduct, it proceeds by ascending or descending movement. When the melody skips steps, alternating movements toward lower notes with movements toward higher ones, there is *ploke,* interweaving, or *melos keklasmenon,* broken melodic line. Finally, *petteia* designates a stationary line, whether the note is held or repeated on different syllables. It is used frequently in all the surviving ancient scores.

These, then, are the constituent parts of harmonic science. The Platonic school and the Pythagoreans do not stop here; they are convinced that music produces specific effects on the soul and body (which is not the case for any of the other arts), effects that warrant description and explanation in an effort to codify musical practice more effectively. This is what they call the *ethos,* a concept that deals not only with *tropoi* but also with instruments and the type of musical work. It is because the Phrygian *tropos,* particularly well adapted to the aulos, is soft, and thus debilitating to the human soul, that Plato and the Pythagoreans banish its use, along with the wind instruments that correspond to it. In contrast, they recommend the Dorian for its virility, suited to stimulating human energies.

Aristoxenus denies that music could have moral effects, but despite the austerity for which he was famous in antiquity, he still acknowledges that certain genera, such as the enharmonic, are more noble and more beautiful than others. For him, the only applicable aesthetic categories are those of the beautiful and the ugly. Those of good and bad remain outside harmonic science as he conceives it.

Our overview of the constitutive parts of harmonics may be perplexing in that it lacks (in our own contemporary terms) anything having to do with musical notation. However, in the most scientific treatises as in the short didactic manuals, there is not the slightest development on this question, which is studied along with the very first rudiments of music in the modern world. Worse still, and even more surprising, is the fact that no theoreticians, no musicographers ever cite any passage borrowed from some work by a great composer, nor do they ever provide musical examples of the sort that are so frequently found in our works of basic music theory, harmony, and orchestration. The break between theoretical reflection and musical practice remains absolute throughout antiquity.

This exclusion of notation has a deep-seated reason, which Aristoxenus explains at length, and not without a certain venom, in the preamble of the second part of his treatise. It is not only true, he says in substance, that the notation of a melody is not, as some would have it, the ultimate end of harmonic knowledge, but it is not even a component of that knowledge. Likewise, the notation of meter is neither the goal nor an integral part of metrics. He invokes two main arguments to defend his view. First, by relying on the acuteness of his ear, a notator is capable of writing the musical signs of a melody that he hears and that turns out to be in the Phrygian mode, even though he has no true, that is to say theoretical, knowledge of the Phrygian, for in order to write down the music he perceives, he has only to identify the spread of the intervals, without attaining a true grasp of the *melos.* Second, this grasp comes about through an intellectual understanding of the *dynamis* of sounds, systems, and genera—that is, of their function within the sonic space.

Aristoxenus's diatribe attests to the existence in Greece of schools of music—or rather of harmonics—where, after a course of study meant to inculcate the necessary musical notions, pupils received instruction in melodic and rhythmic notation. We have proof of this, moreover, in the recently published papyrus of Oxyrhynchus no. 3705: it is the exercise of an apprentice notator, where an iambic line, always the same one, is given several musical renderings. The teacher has deliberately sprinkled errors throughout the notation, either in the signs themselves or else in the choice of notes (in which case there is a violation of the complex laws that govern the relations between the accentuation of Greek words and the pitch level of the musical sounds that can be attributed to them).

As an art, a skill, and a science, music has always occupied a privileged, indeed primordial, place in Greek civilization: the abundance of written testimony, direct and indirect, amply attests to this. The Roman world never produced theoreticians as great as those of ancient Greece: the musicographical works of the Latin authors are very heavily indebted to the Greek thinkers, whom they did not, however, always understand.

In contrast, from the 6th century B.C.E. to the 5th century C.E. Greece saw a constellation of musicians (teachers of music, Harmonists, and musicographical and philosophical specialists) who worked endlessly to advance musical knowledge in all its forms. The manuscript tradition has preserved only a small part of their works. While our knowledge of harmonics and its evolution may be satisfactory, the loss of treatises on *"organikē"* and, above all, manuals of musical composition is only in part compensated for by the survival of scores and of vestiges of musical instruments, thanks to which we have succeeded in grasping only the particular and material expression of the two traditions of musical knowledge from which they arise. However, we can hope to discover new papyri analogous, for example, to papyrus Hibeh 54, which will bring us fragments of these lost treatises.

But, in a phenomenon unique in ancient civilizations, Greece has left us written, figured, and archaeological traces of the kind that give us, if not a complete image, at least a significant glimpse of the science of music and its history; the most precious of these are the roughly fifty scores that have been spared from the ravages of the centuries. If, after two thousand years of silence, we are today in a position to decipher, transcribe, and even play them, let us not forget that we owe this not so much to the musician-philosophers as to a humble musicographer named Alypius, who left us tables of musical signs, in both vocal and instrumental notations, used in the entire set of scores that antiquity has bequeathed to us. Musical notation may not have warranted the status of science; it is nevertheless notation that has enabled Greek music to be reborn, after twenty centuries of silence.

ANNIE BÉLIS
Translated by Emoretta Yang and Catherine Porter

Bibliography

Texts and Translations

Aristides Quintilianus. *De musica.* Ed. R. P. Winnington-Ingram. Leipzig: Teubner, 1963.

———. *On Music in Three Books.* Ed. and trans. Thomas J. Mathiesen. Music Theory Translation Series. Ed. Claude V. Palisca. New Haven: Yale University Press, 1983.

Musici Scriptores Graeci: Aristoteles, Euclides, Nicomachus, Bacchius, Gaudentius, Alypius et melodarium veterum quidquid exstat, recognovit prooemiis et indice instruxit Carolus Janus. Leipzig: Teubner, 1895; repr. Hildesheim: Olms, 1962.

Ptolemy. *Die Harmonielehre des Klaudios Prolemaios.* Ed. Ingemar Düring. Göteborgs Högskolas Arsskrift 36 (1930): 1; repr. Hildesheim: Olms, 1982.

Studies

Barker, Andrew. "Harmonic and Acoustic Theory." In *Greek Musical Writings,* vol. 2. Cambridge: Cambridge University Press, 1989.

Bélis, Annie. *Aristoxène de Tarentum et Aristote: Le "Traité d'harmonique."* Etudes et commentaires, vol. C. Paris: Klincksieck, 1986.

———. "Les Hymnes à Apollon." In *Corpus des inscriptions de Delphes,* vol. 3. Paris: De Boccard, 1992.

———. *Les musiciens dans l'Antiquité.* Paris: Hachette Littératures, 1999.

———. *La musique dans l'Antiquité grecque et romaine.* Paris: La Découverte, forthcoming.

Chailley, Jacques. *La musique grecque antique.* Paris: Les Belles Lettres, 1979.

Gevaert, Fr. Aug. *Histoire et théorie de la musique de l'Antiquité.* 2 vols. Gand, 1875, 1881; repr. Hildesheim: Olms, 1965.

Lohmann, Johannes. *Mousiké et logos: contributions à la philosophie et à la théorie musicale grecques.* Trans. Pascal David. Mauvezin: Trans-Europ-Repress, 1989.

Michaelides, Solon. *The Music of Ancient Greece: An Encyclopedia.* London: Faber and Faber, 1978.

West, M. L. *Ancient Greek Music.* Oxford: Clarendon Press, 1992.

Compact Disc

De la pierre au son: Musique de l'Antiquité grecque. Ensemble Kerylos, dir. Annie Bélis. Reference K617-069.

Related Articles

Demonstration and the Idea of Science; Poetics; Pythagoras and Pythagoreanism; Mathematics; Ptolemy

HISTORY

HISTORY IS THE CRITICAL OR ANALYTICAL STUDY OF THE PAST, not simply the recording of the past or a concern for tradition. Although many societies have shown an interest in their past, the development of a critical historical literature is a rare phenomenon. Only three societies in world history have independently created such an attitude to their past: these are the Jews, the Greeks, and the Chinese. All other traditions of historical writing are dependent on one or more of these.

Each of the three traditions has its own characteristics. The Jewish tradition began with the concept of the covenant of God with His chosen people, and the story of His concern for their destiny, their sufferings as a result of their disregard for His laws, and their triumphs over adversity because of His protection. The priestly authorities who in the 6th and 5th centuries B.C.E. compiled an authoritative account of Jewish history had access to a wide variety of sources, legal, poetic, prophetic, and narrative; they showed great skill in combining these, and paid special attention to documentary evidence. But subsequent Jewish historiography from the age of the Maccabees onward is weak and largely derivative on the dominant Hellenistic Greek tradition, and the true successor to Jewish historical writing is the tradition of church history, developed in the Roman empire, from Eusebius to the Renaissance.

Chinese historical writing began with the Annals, written to record and defend the activities of a government supposedly obedient to the principles of Confucius. The first sign of a critical attitude is found in the work of Sima Qian, hereditary grand historian of the Qin dynasty in the late 2nd century B.C.E.; his work is distinguished by a vivid narrative style and a critical approach to the moral failings of the rulers of China that was in turn based on his sense of betrayal and isolation after he was sentenced to castration for involvement in a court intrigue. Although the organizational method that he evolved had great influence, his critical approach was less often imitated, and most later Chinese historical writing simply sets out to record public events or glorify the emperor.

The Greek tradition is for us the most difficult to understand, since it represents the origin of modern Western attempts to organize and explain the past; there is no clear break between the Greek view and our view of the function of historical writing, and many of our fundamental attitudes are based on reinterpretations of the Greek attitude to the past. The knowledge of the

Greeks is our knowledge, and its investigation involves our own conception of the purpose and methods of history today.

HISTORY AS LITERARY GENRE

The survival of ancient Greek and Roman texts through their use in rhetorical schools and copying by hand in the monasteries of Europe through the Middle Ages has for historical texts resulted in a more or less continuous *catena*, or chain of historical narratives. "Natural selection" resulted in the survival, for the most part, of only one of the available histories of a particular period, and the process of selection was largely determined on stylistic grounds rather than in relation to the authority of the texts. Thus Herodotus and Thucydides survived because they were fundamental literary prose texts; Xenophon's Attic style ensured his survival over more serious narratives. Arrian's account of Alexander the Great, written nearly five hundred years after the events, was preferred to earlier and more authoritative accounts. The *Historical Library* of Diodorus, a superficial compilation of the late 1st century B.C.E. that reproduced in a pleasant and undistinctive style a variety of earlier authors, ensured the disappearance of those texts. Of the great works of the Hellenistic age, only Polybius survives in part. The same process of selection occurred with the historians of Rome, where, for instance, the Greek writer Dionysius of Halicarnassus is responsible for the decimation of much early Roman historical writing.

Therefore, to understand the nature of Greek historical writing, both that which survived to influence the Western tradition and that which did not, it is necessary to recreate as far as possible the entire corpus of Greek historiography as it once was. The 19th century was much concerned with the factual accuracy of surviving historical accounts and the lost narratives on which they were based. This science or art of "source criticism," established by B. G. Niebuhr (1776–1830), focused attention on the need to rebuild the context of our historical narratives from a factual point of view, and the publication in 1891 of the papyrus of the Aristotelian work on the constitutional history of Athens demonstrated how much of the lost genre of local history might be recovered. It was in 1909 that the young Felix Jacoby published his famous article "On the Development of Greek Historiography," in which he laid out both a new theory of the interrelations between the various historical genres of the Greeks, and a program for the publication of all the "Fragments of the Greek Historians" on generic principles. This publication, the basis of all study of Greek history today, was begun in 1923 and was largely completed (except for antiquarian history, biography, and geography) by his death in 1958. Despite occasional attempts to undermine the vision of Jacoby, his program of 1909 still stands as the most successful and complete account of Greek historical writing.

The origins of Greek history lie in the undifferentiated sphere of early Greek prose writing, which was as much myth about the geography of the world and the customs of other peoples as a record of the unfolding of historical events. The earliest prose genres were therefore genealogy and mythography, closely followed by geography: these were exemplified in the two known works of the late 6th-century author Hecataeus of Miletos, and many 5th-century writers can be found practicing a variety of genres. The first true historian was Herodotus, who combined in one work the ethnographic interests of Hecataeus with the epic narrative of a war between East and West. His work incorporated most of the themes of Greek history that were later separated out, and he introduced many of its more distinctive literary conventions, such as the absence of documents, the inclusion of speeches, the complex interplay of digressions from the main theme. After Herodotus, historical writing developed according to two main currents.

The first was local history of individual cities and peoples. Once thought to be earlier than general history of the Herodotean type, this was shown by Jacoby to be a development from the late 5th century, and to be essentially a breaking down of the grand themes of Herodotus to create a history adapted no longer to the conflict between civilizations, but to the interests of individual city-states. It was local history that introduced, or at least privileged, two new elements, the retelling of local myth and the use of archives: "These men made similar choices about the selection of their subjects, and their powers were not so very different from one another, some of them writing histories about the Greeks and some about the barbarians, and not linking all these to one another but dividing them according to peoples and cities, and writing about them separately, all keeping to one and the same aim: whatever oral traditions were preserved locally among peoples or cities, and whatever documents were stored in holy places or archives, to bring these to the common notice of everyone just as they were received, neither adding to them nor subtracting from them" (Dionysius of Halicarnassus, *On Thucydides* 5). Local history was later developed and adapted to the new needs of the Hellenistic world: it could remain as the history of individual communities or city-states, but it could also include religious, ethnographic, and geographic elements in relation to the newly conquered territories, such as Babylon, Egypt, and India. This ethnographic type of history always remained conscious of its debt to Herodotus.

Thucydides was contemporary with the earliest group of these historians and occasionally criticized or used them. But his form and his methodology were essentially based on a critical dialogue with Herodotus. On the one hand, he accepted the theme of a great war; on the other, he rejected absolutely the methods of Herodotus. He denied the possibility of a detailed history of the past, believing that only broad generalizations could be made; instead he asserted the importance of a narrative of contemporary affairs, written by a protagonist as the events were happening. Even under these circumstances he was insistent on the difficulty of discovering the true facts. In a famous and obscure programmatic statement (*History of the Peloponnesian War* 1.22) he claimed to reject invention in speeches in favor of a close adherence to what was said (a claim that he perhaps found impossible to adhere to as his work progressed). He arranged his narrative according to an idiosyncratic chronology of campaigning seasons, which privileged military events, just as his use of the artificial device of paired speeches privileged political decision making.

The power of Thucydides' vision of human affairs established the idea of a history devoted to politics and war, telling the story of a great event or a period that possessed unity as the sphere of action of an individual or group of individuals. The age of Philip, the story of Alexander the Great, the account of the age of the Diadochoi or the rise of Rome, provided later historians with a thematic unity that provided a natural starting point and conclusion. But Thucydides' narrative had in fact been unfinished and was continued by Xenophon and others as contemporary memoirs to whatever point seemed to them significant. From this arose the idea of a universal history, whether of the Greek world or of the "inhabited world" *(oikoumene)* in general. These histories might be essentially narrative accounts of politico-military events, or (the more they included the non-Greek world) they might approximate back again to the Herodotean model. Toward the end of the Hellenistic period such grand historical encyclopedias tended to be more derivative, more superficial, and more complete in their coverage of a narrative, which might include myth as well as history.

In such a way it is possible to understand the development of a complex and varied historical literature determined according to the changing rules of a literary genre. Each element within the picture can be located in the broader spectrum, whether it is chronography, mythography, or the local history of a particular city, such as Athens. From an undifferentiated beginning of works in prose devoted to describing and analyzing the world inhabited by men and their actions, there were gradually separated out a variety of special types responding to particular needs and interests. But this interpretation is essentially a literary one, based on form and theme; it scarcely distinguishes between an almost entirely fictional personal narrative, like the *Persicha* of Ctesias, and serious attempts, like that of Polybius, to understand one's world.

HISTORY AS SCIENCE

It is of course possible to view history from a quite different perspective. The essential characteristic of history according to the canons of 19th-century positivism is that it tells a true story; and the history of the science of history is the story of the development of the importance of truth as an aim for history, and of the methods by which the historian may arrive at the truth. Again we may take as representative of this approach to the ancient historians the name of a contemporary scholar and student of historiography, Arnaldo Momigliano. For him history was an art that aimed at the truth. Its development was the story of successive generations of writers who shared this aim, and who attempted with greater or lesser success to realize it. He was not interested in those who failed this austere test of relevance to the continuing study of history today.

The criterion of truth was proclaimed in the first sentence of the first Greek historical work, Hecataeus's book *Genealogies:* "Hecataeus the Milesian speaks thus: I write these things as they seem true to me; for the stories told by the Greeks are various and in my opinion absurd" (*FGH* 1, frg. 1). But Hecataeus's interest in the truth led to a misguided attempt to recover historical events from mythical narratives by removing the incredible or supernatural elements. This rationalization of myth produced a story that could be believed rather than one that was true, but such was the power of heroic myth that Greek conceptions of truth never escaped from the hope that there was something that was true in their mythic past. Both Herodotus and Thucydides clearly believed in the historical truth of selected elements of mythology, and failed to realize that their selection of facts merely reflected the prejudices of their age. Subsequent historians, too, thought it possible to write a narrative that extended back into the mythic past, or to interpret the religious myths of other peoples as part of a historical narrative. The result was a blurring of the line between myth and history that maintained the principle of historical truth while involving a fatal elision between myth and history.

With the development of oral history and anthropology it has become possible to view Herodotus as providing a methodological model. His attempt to record the oral traditions of a wide variety of Greek and native peoples, however uncritical and selective it may seem, compares favorably with many discussions of non-European peoples in the early modern age. He can rightly be seen as the founder of a form of history that was not bound by concepts of political narrative but attempted to view societies as a whole, through the interrelationship of religious, social, and geographic factors; his apparently naive reproduction of individual stories can also be compared with the recording techniques of modern oral historians, who must exclude interpretation from the basic recording of their data. Already in the 16th century Herodotus was admired for his ability to transcend cultural boundaries and record the customs of foreign peoples, and respect for his abilities increased as European writers attempted to come to terms with alien worlds like those of South America, the Ottoman empire, and Japan. As 19th-century excavations and explorations revealed the material basis of the cultures of ancient Egypt and the Near East, respect for Herodotus's account of these peoples increased:

his narrative, however flawed, remains the basis of Persian history, and his Hellenistic successors, Manetho and Berossus, still provide the narrative framework for Egyptian and Babylonian history. Thus Herodotus's inclusiveness and curiosity created a methodology—based on the natural social forms of human geography, myth, religion, narrative history, and customs—whose flexibility across cultural boundaries has resulted in his becoming a model for modern anthropologists and historians of culture. His very failure to consider any form of causation other than the natural course of events and culturally inherent conflicts, which once seemed to suggest a prescientific attitude to history, can now be seen as an appropriate response to the unimportance of causal models for the understanding of social and cultural history. Modern critics attack Herodotus not for his unscientific attitude to history, but for his contribution to the creation of the concept of the otherness of non-Greek cultures: Herodotus is seen as the inventor of "orientalism," the idea of a conflict between East and West, described in terms of the victory of freedom and courage over despotism and luxury, which is thought to vitiate much of Western historiography in relation to the non-European world. Herodotus the *"philobarbaros"* has become Herodotus the orientalist: however unfair this characterization, it demonstrates the respect of the modern world for Herodotus as the founder of Western historiography.

If Herodotus established the Western canons of "katastematic history," of societies at rest, it has always been easy to see Thucydides as the originator of "kinetic history," of societies in motion and in conflict. His invention of the idea of different levels of causation is exemplified in the account of the origins of the Peloponnesian War, with its immediate and underlying causes. Thomas Hobbes called him "the most politick historiographer that ever writ"; he was obsessed with the decision-making process in fully conscious political societies; he attempted (with less success) to understand the economic basis of imperialism and warfare. He described the collapse of social systems under the impact of plague and revolution. His insistence on the need for contemporary recording of events makes him the founder of all sociology and political science. Finally, his attitude to evidence and his concern for the need for true knowledge of the facts have made him the model for the concept of modern scientific history, as formulated by 19th-century positivist historians. In certain passages he can even be seen to have anticipated the insistence on documentary evidence and archival research that was the contribution of Leopold von Ranke to 19th-century historical research methods.

Thucydides certainly provided the model for the main tradition of Western historiography, with its interests in political and military history, factual accuracy, and causation. Polybius is his worthy successor in these respects, introducing another central concept in Western historical thought, the theme of *grandeur et décadence*, the rise and decline of a great imperial power. If this tradition is now viewed more critically, it is because of the crisis of positivism and the fact that we no longer see power as the crucial factor in the formation of human society.

More controversially, Momigliano tried to see the local historians of antiquity as the forerunners of the antiquarianism that was so dominant a feature of the Western historical tradition from the 16th to the 18th century. But systematic antiquarianism derives from the Roman antiquarian tradition, not local history, whose works did not survive to influence the antiquarians of modern Europe. Although it is true that the Aristotelian *Constitution of Athenians* is the earliest surviving treatise on constitutional antiquities, it was not discovered until after the publication of Mommsen's *Römisches Staatsrecht*, which was the culmination of the fusion of legal and historical studies in the 19th century. The need for a model precedes its discovery, and the historian only finds what he is looking for.

The problem of antiquarianism highlights one of the two weaknesses revealed by the methodological analysis of Greek historiography. Greek historiography is bound by tight literary conventions that encourage the use of (usually invented) speeches and formal descriptions of places and events but discourage and even prohibit the citation of documents. Compared with Jewish historical writing, Greek historians seem little interested in the written evidence for their statements; on the rare occasions when a document is cited in Thucydides, this is usually adduced as an indication that that particular section of his narrative is unfinished. Only in local history and in the Aristotelian tradition is documentary evidence prominent; Greek historical writing is often more literary and more rhetorical than the scientific interpretation would allow.

A second weakness in Greek historiography is the comparative absence of interest in biography and in the study of human personality as a motive force in history. The later development of a biographical literature under Roman influence, with the *Parallel Lives* of Plutarch, has indeed disguised the absence of a true biographical tradition in earlier Greek literature; the evidence analyzed by Momigliano in his controversial book *The Development of Greek Biography* (1971) serves merely to reinforce this conclusion. Personal motivation of course abounds in Greek historians, but the comparative neglect of human biography is an aspect of the insistence on communal decision making in Thucydides and the tendency to consider the individual in terms of social context rather than personality.

HISTORY AS MYTH

New questions about the nature of Greek historiography are raised by modern developments in historical writing. History is now seen as a form of discourse related to an ideology, designed to establish a view of the past that corresponds to present preoccupations; alternatively, modern historians seek to change the present through a reinterpretation of the past. The relativity of all observation and of all theory in the human sciences implies the relativity of all historical narrative. The basic evidence is no longer a fact but the interpretation of an event, in which the human agent is implicated from the start; as Thucydides saw, different protagonists in a battle will experience different battles, but the historian no longer feels able to determine which battle is the true one. The historian is simply the last in a chain of witnesses: he can no longer play God with his adjudication.

This new view of the nature of history implies a new interpretation of Greek historiography. It is not necessary to assert the preeminence of rhetoric in history, for relativity does not imply the dominance of persuasion over truth. Rather we should explore the relationship of history to myth in our own age and in antiquity. Here Greek historical writing provides a model, and its development can be seen in the light of the changing function of ancient myth.

The origins of Greek historical writing lie in the fascination of the Greeks for the heroic age, as described in myth and epic poetry. In the 7th and 6th centuries myth came to be used as a means of structuring the past and validating the present; one of the dominant forms of myth in ancient Greece was the "charter myth," a narrative of past mythic events that offered an explanation for a present situation or justified present activities. The "Return of the Sons of Hercules" was a myth created to explain the Dorian presence in the Peloponnese, and it may well owe its popularity in Spartan tradition to a parallel need to justify the conquest of the Messenians in the 7th century. It is hard to know in such situations where oral tradition ends and free mythic creation begins. But the rationality of such narrative is demonstrated by its function as a means of relating past and present; in a later age it was possible for Greek historians simply to adapt these myths to the purposes of historical narrative by ignoring the folktale motifs and the aspects of divine intervention. In Herodotus, Io ceases to be a cow driven mad by a gadfly through the envy of Hera and becomes simply a girl seduced by a Phoenician trader, whose abduction was the starting point for the hatred between East and West; the eponymous Europa was no maiden transported by Zeus disguised as a bull but a daughter of the king of Tyre, seized in retaliation by Greek pirates. These rationalizations were what Hecataeus meant by his claim to find truth in the stories of the Greeks; Thucydides can similarly transmute the stories of the age of heroes into a historical narrative.

Myth is history, and the earliest historians were myth makers or myth writers. Herodotus moves easily from the mythic prefigurations of the Trojan and Persian Wars to point out "who it was in actual fact who first injured the Greeks" with the equally mythic story of the origins of the Lydian dynasty. Myth and truth are intermingled, and the narrative techniques of the myth maker combine with those of the "enquirer" or historian. Even the end point of his history, the account of the Persian Wars, is the product of a generation of poetic praise and oral tradition, on the basis of which Herodotus sought to create a new prose epic to glorify a new age of heroes, those who had defeated the modern Trojans. Pleasure and truth are equally important to the myth maker, as Thucydides pointed out.

But even Thucydides, with his claim that his work is not a "display piece for instant listening, but a possession for all time," could not escape the mythic origins of Greek historiography. His own story began in the interpretation of myth and was itself a new myth for the age of the polis. His methods and techniques were designed to explain the methods and principles behind the world he inhabited. There decisions were taken in mass assemblies, symbolically represented in narrative by paired speeches, and warfare was a series of set battles fought on specific days and won or lost according to set rules, not a continuing activity involving a whole generation of Greek protagonists and affecting their daily lives in every aspect. Thucydides' conception of the amorality and tragic quality of the events he describes is a mythic interpretation of the world of the polis, and it created a model not for all history but for those aspects of later history that could be related to the political and military concerns of the polis.

Each later historian created his own *mythos* for the events he wished to describe, and his activity was conditioned by the ideology of the world he inhabited. Histories of periods conceived as unities, histories of great expeditions like that of Alexander, histories of the rise and fall of empires, histories of native peoples, can be seen as each involving its own mythic discourse; these discourses interconnect, without establishing rigid generic rules and without offering any progression toward a perfect form of positivist history. The Greek tradition does not offer us a complete set of models of discourse for all possible forms of history; it is imperfectly formed in certain aspects and incomplete in others. But the great variety of these discourses creates for us a series of alternative models, which can free us from the conception of history as a single mode of discourse, and on which we can base our own conceptions of the various *mythoi* of history. History is not separable from myth: like myth, it is a story that aims at the truth rather than one that is true.

OSWYN MURRAY

Bibliography

Jacoby, Felix. *Die Fragmente der griechischen Historiker.* Berlin and Leiden, 1923–1958. Cited as *FGH.*
———. "Über die Entwicklung der griechischen Historiographie und den Plan einer

neuen Sammlung der griechischen Historikerfragmente" (1909), repr. in his *Abhandlung der griechische Geschichtsschreibung.* Leiden, 1956. Pp. 16–64.

Momigliano, Arnaldo. *The Classical Foundations of Modern Historiography.* Berkeley, 1990.

———. *Contributo alla storia degli studi classici e del mondo antico.* 14 vols., Rome, 1955–.

Strasburger, H. "Die Wesensbestimmung der Geschichte durch die antike Geschichtsschreibung" (1966), repr. in *Studien zur Alten Geschichte,* vol. 2. Hildesheim, 1982. Pp. 963–1014.

Related Articles

Epistemology; Geography; Plutarch; Thucydides; Sophists; Utopia and the Critique of Politics; Herodotus; Polybius; Hellenism and Judaism

LANGUAGE

As an explicit field of investigation, language in ancient Greece was a relative latecomer. Its beginnings go back to the second half of the 5th century B.C.E. when, with rhetoric emerging as a profession, Protagoras and Prodicus initiated inquiry into "the correctness of names." In the next century Plato and, especially, Aristotle made significant contributions, but the study of language as distinct from logic began to flourish in systematic ways only during Hellenistic times (ca. 300 B.C.E. onward). Ptolemic Alexandria, with its Museum and Library, provided the patronage to support such notable scholars as the Homerists and librarians Zenodotus and Aristarchus, the poet and encyclopedist Callimachus, the polymath Eratosthenes, and the grammarian Dionysius of Thrace.

Other cultural centers apart from Athens became prominent at this time too, including Pergamum, whose library was second only to that of Alexandria. The literary and linguistic investigation of older literature now deemed "classical" (especially Homer) stimulated closer reflection on the Greek language than had been practiced hitherto. Simultaneously, Stoic philosophers, centered largely in Athens, were making innovative contributions to the study of language as a part of their work in "dialectic." It is to this period and these cultural events that we can attribute the identification of grammar and philology as determinate fields of inquiry.

Hellenistic interests in the study of language are certainly important. Yet it would be misleading to give the impression that language had been previously neglected in Greek perceptions of what we may broadly call anthropology. The truth is, rather, that self-consciousness about language can be traced right back to our earliest literary record of the Greeks, the epic poetry of Homer. The poet of the *Iliad* (II.867) characterizes the inhabitants of Miletus and other Ionian cities by the term *barbarophonoi*, foreign speaking. *Barbarian* in this composite word does not convey the ethnic slur that it would acquire later, but rather refers to people who are distinguished by language from the Greeks. Homeric epic, quite apart from its semantic content, is a linguistic tour de force. It was the product of a centuries-long oral tradition, and much of its vocabulary differs significantly from the dialects of everyday speech. As Hellenic civilization developed, its people, especially in Athens, became acculturated to a subtle recognition of the lexical, rhythmical, and stylistic differences between literary genres. Thus Aristophanic comedy derives much of its effect from parodying the high style of epic and tragedy. It also

338

delights in the invention of absurd words, mockery of intellectual discourse, and sudden shifts between gross colloquialisms and high-sounding phrases.

Such sensitivity to language was scarcely grounded in any formal understanding of grammar and linguistic structure. Just as one does not need knowledge of musical theory to have a keen musical ear, so the great products of Attic literature in the 5th century B.C.E. were appreciated by people whose scientific grasp of language was rudimentary. Yet Sophoclean tragedy and Thucydides' history, to mention but two examples, manifest extraordinary virtuosity in diction and style. Both authors were almost certainly influenced by the Sophists Protagoras and Prodicus, foreigners to Athens but particularly successful as teachers in that community; Aristophanes alludes to their newfangled ideas about grammar in *Clouds*, his comedy attacking intellectuals. Protagoras and Prodicus gave lectures to persons who were eager for instruction in both the interpretation of poetry and the practical skills of persuasive speech. There is then a connection, and clearly not an accidental one, between the beginnings of linguistic study and a culture already attuned to complex literary forms. But Greek sensitivity to language not only predates the work of the Sophists; it also helps to explain why and how that work developed.

PRETHEORETICAL INTERESTS IN LANGUAGE

In spite of their political and dialectical divisions, the Hellenic peoples looked to their common language as the strongest mark of their ethnic identity. Herodotus, an elder contemporary of Thucydides, conjectured that the Greeks were coeval with the age of their language; their ancestors, such as the Pelasgians, will have spoken "a barbarian tongue" (I.57). Herodotus was an indefatigable traveler and inquirer. He carefully noted the names of places and objects, not just Greek names but also the way things were called in other languages. He registered numerous linguistic observations: the hybrid of Egyptian and Ethiopian spoken by the Ammonites (II.42), the affinity between the Carian and Caunian languages (II.172), the negative connotation of the term *Ionian* for the first Greeks (II.143), the conclusion of all Persian names in the same letter (II.139). It is to Herodotus that we owe the lovely story about the Egyptian king Psammetichus (II.2): he deprived two infants of hearing any speech in order to determine, by the first articulate sounds that they uttered, the identity of the oldest language. When they were heard to say "bekos," the Phrygian word for bread, he gained his answer.

Herodotus was highly atypical in his explicit interest in languages other than Greek. We may assume, however, that his educated contemporaries would have shared his realization that languages have histories, that lexical differences between languages are entirely compatible with shared meanings, and, above all, that language is a prime determinant of human and cultural identity. No doubt too they were sharply observant, as he was, about the alphabetic properties of words. All of these points are important as assumptions or tendencies that influenced the earliest theoretical investigations into language.

Still more important, and in evidence as early as Homer, are a number of presuppositions about the linkage between speaking and thinking. I say "speaking" rather than "language" to do justice to the Greek intuition that a speech act is not simply or even primarily the utterance of articulated sounds but the expression of a thought that "says something" or "makes sense" *(legein ti)*. To make the point sharply, though anachronistically, one could say that before theoretical investigation began, *parole,* the semantics and affects of discourse, received more attention than *langue,* the lexical instruments of expression.

For Homer, as for all succeeding Greek authors, speaking is both the primary form of social life and the chief vehicle of thought or internal reflection. Not only are the *Iliad* and *Odyssey* packed with speeches, but Homer also uses direct speech as his way of narrating the most significant moments of both epics: for instance, the quarrel between Achilles and Agamemnon; the failure of the embassy to persuade Achilles to return to the fray; the final meeting of Priam and Achilles; and the encounters between Odysseus and Polyphemus, Eumaeus, Penelope, and her suitors. What is most significant about these episodes, for understanding Greek presuppositions about language, is the poet's capacity to engage his audience with three functions of discourse—true or false storytelling, antithetical argument or mutual attempts at persuasion, and the expression of strongly felt emotions. This is not to say that those who experienced Homer and other poets were inattentive to their language as *langue.* Aristophanes' *Frogs* displays remarkable interest in the lexical and metrical differences between the tragedies of Euripides and those of Aeschylus. Thucydides (III.82) writes a most powerful account of the way words were manipulated in the revolution at Corcyra. But before Hellenistic times *onoma,* "name," is the closest the Greeks came to having a generic term for "word." Inquiry into semantic, epistemic, and rhetorical issues advanced much more rapidly at first than the study of grammar and syntax.

Because language was widely regarded as the vehicle of thought, it was taken to be the principal difference between humans and other animals, and more implicitly as a capacity that humans share with gods. Probably because of their anthropomorphic divinities, Greek mythology makes little use of talking animals. (The horses of Achilles are an exception, but they were immortal!) The standard epithet to distinguish nonhuman from human animals was *alogos,* "lacking speech" and hence also lacking reason or thought. When the chorus of Sophocles' *Antigone* illustrates the "wonders" of man, they celebrate the learning of language along with the development of technology, agriculture, and medicine. (Similarly Plato, *Protagoras* 322a.)

These presuppositions about the cultural significance of language are emphasized by Isocrates in his treatise *Antidosis* (253ff), written in the middle of the 4th century B.C.E. to defend himself as an expert teacher of persuasive discourse. His remarks can be assumed to chime with opinions widely held by his audience: "In our other properties . . . we have no advantage over other animals; in fact we are inferior to many of them in speed, strength and other provisions. Yet because we have been engendered with the capacity for mutual persuasion and for indicating our intentions to ourselves, not only have we escaped from the life of beasts, we have also come together and established communities and made laws and discovered crafts—indeed practically everything we have devised has been secured for us by discourse. For it is this that has legislated concerning right and wrong, and without these prescriptions we would not be able to live together. Through it too we blame those who are bad and praise the good, educate the undiscerning and assess the wise. For we regard appropriate discourse to be the best index of a sound mind."

Although Isocrates has his professional axe to grind, his observations about "discourse" match Greek preconceptions that stretch right back to Homer. It would be possible to translate *logos,* his word for "discourse," as language. My only reason for not doing so is to avoid giving the impression that Isocrates is concerned here with linguistics *as distinct from* the social, psychological, and semantic functions of speech. Taking him as representative of the general Greek interest in language at the time of Plato, we may now consider the technical contribution of early Greek philosophy to the subject.

THE STUDY OF LANGUAGE IN GREEK PHILOSOPHY FROM HERACLITUS TO PLATO

Heraclitus and Parmenides, the two giants of early Greek philosophy, did not investigate language from perspectives we would term grammatical or syntactical. Each of them, however, did a great deal to ensure that topics intimately tied to language (for instance, truth and falsehood, reason in argument, naming and predicating) would be fertile ground for subsequent philosophers.

Heraclitus uses the term *logos* to signify both his "account" of the nature of things, and the "rationale" that governs natural processes. He intends his auditors to regard his *logos* as the objective truth. In a series of aphoristic sentences (such as "The way up and down is one and the same," D-K 22.B.60) he seeks to articulate the union of opposites, which the partial perspectives of everyday life tend to conceal. Although Heraclitus does not say so explicitly, one has the impression that his sentence structure and choice of words are intended to provide a direct reflection of extralinguistic reality. Two examples will make the point: "Immortal mortals, mortal immortals, living their death, dying their life" (D-K 22.B.62). The probable point of this aphorism is to challenge, as powerfully as possible, conventional ideas about the distinction between permanence and temporality. "For the bow, the name is life, but its work is death" (D-K 22.B.48). In this cryptic sentence, Heraclitus exploits his hearers' knowledge that one of the Greek words for a bow has the same alphabetic structure as the word for life *(bios)*; what differentiates the words is their accented syllable. Ignoring the latter point, Heraclitus draws a contrast between the name of the bow and its destructive function. He uses the pun to draw attention to the extralinguistic connection between life and death.

Heraclitus also makes use of the striking expression "barbarian souls" (D-K 22.B.107). The point he wants to make here is that "vision and hearing are misleading witnesses" to persons who are incapable of *interpreting* his words about the true nature of things. He composes his riddling sayings as challenges that are semantic, structural, and ontological: to understand the real pattern of things, you need to be an exegete of Heraclitus's cryptic yet truthful discourse.

Parmenides makes much more sober uses of language. Most striking in his argument is the identity he seeks to establish between what can be spoken and what can be thought. In a remarkable stretch of sustained argument, he undertakes to establish the predicates that are the only true and speakable ways of characterizing "what is"—that it is without origin and ending, complete, motionless, temporally present, one and continuous (D-K 28.B.8). Parmenides does not call these "predicates," but he appears to have an implicit understanding of the distinction between a referring expression ("what is") and a description (the "name" of something attributable to "what is"). In a later part of his argument he underlines the link between thought and language by characterizing erroneous opinions as "the naming of two forms" (in contrast with the one "being" he has laid out for consideration). His manner of stigmatizing error in terms of unwarranted "naming" draws on the assumption that names are normally given to things in the belief that the things so named are real. This assumption predates philosophy in the Greek world, but what is it about a name that makes it correct? This question was explicitly thematized a generation or so later by Protagoras and Prodicus. What is known about their work, much of it reaching us via Plato's ironical pen, is rather sketchy. But the evidence is sufficient to show the main tendencies of linguistic study around the year 400 B.C.E.

"Correctness of names" (*orthotes ton onomaton* or *orthoepeia*) is the closest early Greek thinkers came to identifying language as a determinate field of study. What did it involve? Protagoras is credited with dividing the "classes of names" into "males, females, and things" (Aristotle, *Rhetoric* III.5.1407b6). He is also said to have distinguished different types of sentences (*logos;* variant accounts of the details are given, Diogenes Laertius IX.53–54). In making these observations, Protagoras's purposes seem to have been prescriptive rather than purely descriptive. We have reports that he criticized Homer for committing a fault of gender at the beginning of the *Iliad* by making *menis*, "wrath," feminine (its standard gender in Greek) rather than masculine, and for "commanding" the Muse, instead of invoking the goddess by means of a sentence with the form of a "wish" (D-K 80.A.28–29). In the dialogue Plato named for him, Protagoras charges the poet Simonides with self-contradiction (339c). On the basis of these examples, Protagoras took incorrectness of names to involve a faulty match between language and the designation intended by its user.

Prodicus is also a participant in the discussion of Simonides' poem. Socrates, who undertakes to defend Simonides, appeals to Prodicus as the expert in distinguishing the meaning of apparently synonymous terms. The purpose of his appeal is to remove Protagoras's charge of self-contradiction. Socrates' efforts are a deliberate travesty, but they are broadly in line with Prodicus's principal concern—to avoid ambiguity by drawing fine distinctions between words of closely similar meaning. We are told that "he tried to attach a specific sense to each individual name" (D-K 84.A.19). The function of Prodicus's analysis of language, like the critical comments of Protagoras, was normative. Each of them wanted to legislate for language that would be correct, not by the standards of actual usage but as a better instrument for designating thoughts and their intended reference. This emerges particularly clearly from Protagoras's complaints about the feminine gender of *menis*. What he finds unsatisfactory is the disparity (common enough in Greek) between the gender of the word and the masculine connotations of the thing it names.

Our best evidence for the question concerning "correctness of names" is Plato's dialogue *Cratylus*. The subject for investigation is whether, as Cratylus maintains, the correctness of a name consists in its "natural" connection to the thing named or, alternatively, whether "convention and agreement" are the sole basis of linguistic correctness, as Hermogenes proposes. (Independently of Plato we know that Democritus endorsed the convention option, and that the opposite thesis—names as "natural outgrowths"—was defended by the author of the Hippocratic treatise *De arte* II). Plato's discussion, masterminded by Socrates, proceeds by first canvassing the naturalist option. Numerous words are analyzed with a view to showing that their letters and syllables "imitate" incessant change, which is Cratylus's Heraclitean conception of nature. However, the undertaking fails when Socrates points out that there can be no one-to-one correspondence between linguistic sounds and meaning: thus, the letter *l* (lambda), which has been presumed to signify softness, is an element of the word *sklerotes*, which means hardness (435b ff). Convention, then, is certainly one factor in the way names correctly function, though mimetic correspondence between names and things must not be completely excluded either. On the basis of this compromise, Plato seems to advise his readers to reject the study of names as a proper route to the investigation of reality. So Socrates concludes: "We should seek to learn and investigate things *from themselves* and not from their names" (439b.6).

Cratylus is a complex dialogue. On the one hand, it reflects the principal points of contemporary debate about language with its allusions to Protagoras, Prodicus, and persons who are "expert in dividing up the elements of words" (424c, which may allude to the sophist Hippias; cf. *Hippias major* 285d). On the other hand, in spite of his reservations about everyday language as a reliable sign of the nature of things, Plato clearly makes independent linguistic observations of his own. Rather than attempting to sift these out specifically, it seems best to highlight the dialogue's most significant contributions.

In the sphere of phonetics, historical linguistics, and morphology, *Cratylus* probably gives a fair idea of linguistic study at this date. Syllables are distinguished from individual letters, and the latter are divided into vowels and consonants (393e, 424c). There is a clear recognition that "names" and larger linguistic units are compounded out of simple "elements" (*stoicheia*, 422a). Like Herodotus, Plato is well aware that languages change through time. It is suggested that any "natural" correctness names now have must be derived from "primary names"—an original language, established by the gods or by a superhuman name giver (389d, 425d). Numerous etymologies are advanced. Most of these depend on a mimetic relationship between sound and meaning, but we also find attempts to derive divine names from verbs whose *sound and meaning* suit the name (for instance Apollo from *apolluon*, "one who destroys").

In the field of syntax, Plato makes the first recorded attempt to distinguish between "names" (*onomata*) and other expressions, which he calls "things said" *(rhemata):* "Diphilus" is a (proper) name, but with the addition of a second iota and a change of accentuation, we get *Dii philos,* meaning "beloved of Zeus" (399a), which is what we today would call an adjectival expression. Little is made of this distinction in *Cratylus,* but in the later dialogue *Sophist* (262e) Plato invokes it to argue that a sentence *(logos)*—an expression of truth or falsehood—requires the combination of an *onoma* and a *rhema* (e.g., "Theaetetus is sitting"). His concept of *rhema* is the closest anyone before Aristotle came to distinguishing predicative expressions from names or subject terms.

Noteworthy though they are, these observations of *Cratylus* are overshadowed by the dialogue's contribution to semantics. Before Socrates elaborates his string of etymologies, he outlines a theory of "natural names," which is put forward as valid for all languages (389d). The requirement of a "naturally correct name" is to communicate and discriminate reality. Particular names are correct if (1) they satisfy this general function of naming and (2) they satisfy it in ways that are specific to the thing named. Names are "assigned to" letters and syllables, but they are not reducible to their alphabetic properties.

The same name can be expressed by different combinations of letters. What Plato here calls names the Stoics would later call *lekta*—meanings that transcend the particular languages in which they are expressed. For Plato the correctness of a name has more to do with epistemology and logic than with linguistics. When he talks about the Form that a correct name must instantiate, we are reminded that what primarily interested him was not language but the identification of Forms (extralinguistic and nonphysical entities) as the ultimate referents and foundation of true discourse about the world.

ARISTOTLE AND EPICURUS

Plato and his intellectual contemporaries may have had a more technical understanding of language than our evidence for the first half of the 4th century B.C.E. records. The justification for thinking so is the scope of Aristotle's observations. Although Aristotle was a massive innovator in the sphere of logic, he can scarcely have invented all the terminology and formal distinctions to be found in those of his works that study language most directly—*Categories, On Interpretation, Topics, Rhetoric,* and *Poetics.* What we learn there is not only Aristotle's approach to language but also the probable extent of linguistic knowledge in Greece prior to Alexandria, Stoicism, and the explicit development of grammar.

Like Plato, Aristotle was primarily interested in language as the vehicle of thought. The meaning and the truth or falsehood of "what is said" concerned him much more deeply than grammar, morphology, or syntax. He is often criticized for having conflated logic and linguistics. But although a Roman schoolboy at the time of Cicero would learn more formal grammar than Aristotle knew, his instinctive feel for the structure of language is more advanced than anything attested before his time. He regarded the way people talk about the world as material that a philosopher must include in reviewing the basic data of inquiry. More than any other Greek philosopher before the Stoics, he developed a precise terminology for expressing his methods of analysis; for instance, the distinction between "form" and "material," "potentiality" and "actuality," "essential" and "accidental," "without qualification" and "in some respect." Via his medieval disseminators, these distinctions have colored modern language in such expressions as per se, per accidens, simpliciter, sine qua non, and the like.

So far as technical features of language are concerned, Aristotle takes account of the vocal movements necessary to generate particular vowels or consonants (*Poetics* 20). He distinguishes between "voice" ("a sound that signifies something") and other kinds of uttered sounds (*De anima* II.3). He regularly differentiates between linguistic "signs" and "significates" (though the Stoics were the first to canonize this terminology): vocal utterances "signify" or "symbolize" thoughts and the "things" (states of affairs) that thoughts betoken (cf. *On Interpretation* 1). Language, considered as utterance, is comprehended by the term *lexis* (expression), and is distinguished from thought (*dianoia; Poetics* 19). The parts of *lexis* comprise, at their simplest, letters and syllables, and a *logos* (phrase), at their most complex. Other parts include individual words, which Aristotle enumerates as particles, conjunctions, names, verbs, and the "inflection" *(ptosis)* of the latter pair (*Poetics* 20). In defining the verb *(rhema)*, he emphasizes its function of signifying time (*On Interpretation* 3).

From a Stoic and later grammatical perspective, this classification of *lexis* is confusing and incomplete. It is confusing because it groups together sentences, phrases, individual words, and single letters or syllables. It is incomplete because it omits certain parts of speech. Aristotle's terminology also suffers from vagueness, as when he describes verbs that are not constituents of sentences as "names" (*On Interpretation* 16b19). "Name" (*onoma*) for him is still an imprecisely collective term, although it has become much closer to "noun" than in its earlier Greek usage. Nonetheless, Aristotle's approach to formal properties of language is considerably more systematic than anything of which we have earlier evidence. He makes acute remarks about the gender of names, and about compound and other types of names (*Poetics* 21). His observations about inflection show that he understands the difference between semantics and morphology (*On Interpretation* 16a32).

To his credit perhaps (given earlier practices), he shows little interest in etymology. Previous efforts in this area (as Plato's *Cratylus* indicates) had been premised on a "natural" relation between the elements of language and features of the world. Aristotle opts firmly for convention as the basis for linguistic "symbols" (*On Interpretation* 1): "Letters and vocal sounds are not the same for everyone, but the mental states of which they are primarily the symbols are the same for everyone; and the actual things of which these mental states are likenesses are also the same." On Aristotle's teleological view of mental life, we perceive or think things by having their perceptible or intelligible forms present to consciousness. That apprehension is probably what he means here by characterizing mental states as "likenesses" of actual things. On his view, what underwrites meaning is isomorphism between the structure of reality and the structure of the thoughts to which we give linguistic expression.

He begins *Categories* by distinguishing between homonyms, synonyms, and paronyms. Modern scholars are sometimes disturbed because Aristotle treats these concepts as referring to "things" and not "terms." Aristotle's ancient commentators too, writing against the background of later developments in grammar, were puzzled about his procedure: Is *Categories*, they asked, a treatise about terms, meanings, or things? Their standard response was that it combines all three, and this is surely the most promising way to do justice to Aristotle's very powerful essay. *Categories* is about language, in the sense that its findings cast light on, and are informed by, the distinction between isolated words and sentences, subject terms, and predicates, the difference between names and definitions. But the "categories" themselves are not expressions but "*things* said," i.e. the kinds of "being" that expressions signify. The aim of this work and its companion piece *(On Interpretation)* is not the elucidation of language as such but investigation of reality through reflection on the way we talk about it.

Aristotle's bias toward logic rather than linguistics was continued by his successor Theophrastus, who made important refinements to Aristotle's analysis of syllogisms and also contributed to rhetorical theory. However, the formal study of language as distinct from logic does not appear to have advanced in the post-Aristotelian Lyceum. The chief centers of innovative philosophy at this date (ca. 300 B.C.E.) were elsewhere—the Garden of Epicurus and the Stoa frequented by Zeno of Citium. At face value the Epicureans, in contrast with the Stoics, "reject dialectic [including the formal study of language] as superfluous" (Diogenes Laertius, X.31). But although our focus here will be on Stoicism, Epicurus had views on language that are far too interesting to be passed over without brief comment.

On the question of language's origin, Epicurus developed a theory nicely suited to the empiricism characteristic of his anthropology in general. In place of a primeval name giver, whether human or divine (Lucretius, V.1028–1090), Epicurus proposed that at a certain stage of human development, "people's own natures underwent feelings and received impressions which varied peculiarly from tribe to tribe, and each of the individual feelings and impressions caused them to exhale breath peculiarly, according also to the racial differences from place to place" (*Epistula ad Herodotum* 75–76). In their primary form, then, vocal utterances were an involuntary response to experience. What turned them into "the names of things" was "utility," by which Epicurus refers to the principle he regularly invokes in explaining social developments: early peoples discovered that the sounds they were instinctually uttering could serve their needs for communication. Subsequently, the primitive languages within each group were refined "on a collective basis," with a view to avoiding ambiguity and improving concision. In addition, new terms were deliberately introduced by intellectuals to designate things beyond the immediate data of experience.

This theory is striking in its economy, and also in its subtle recourse to both nature and artifice as explanatory factors. Although Epicurus emphasizes the peculiarity of each linguistic group and the experiences of its members, we should hardly suppose, as some interpreters have done, that he envisaged a primary stage in which each individual had his own private language. The variations to which Epicurus is so sensitive differentiate between linguistic communities and not between the members of one community. What facilitated the development of each language, he seems to presume, is the unity of experience of each group, together with their common environment and physiology.

Earlier theorists had taken the "naturalness" of language to involve a mimetic correspondence between words and things. Epicurus shows no interest in such attempts at etymology. For him language is an anthropological fact, with its differences explicable by the different circumstances of different cultures. As for the naturalness of a given language's means of expression, here too his empiricism stands him in good stead. Since language originates as an uncontrived response to feelings and sensory experiences, basic meanings must be ascertained by identifying "the primary concept corresponding to each word" (*Ep. Hdt.* 37–38). By "primary concept" he almost certainly refers to what Epicureans regularly call *prolepseis*. These "anticipations," mediated by repeated experience and memory, provide Epicurus with his answer to the question of how words can signify things: they symbolize (as Aristotle too had supposed) the thoughts that persons naturally come to have as a result of the way the world impinges on them. Epicurus seems to have supposed that careful attention to the empirical foundations of language would enable persons to discover primary meanings, uncontaminated by convention and metaphor. For him the key to understanding language was neither logic nor grammar but the study of physical reality.

HELLENISTIC SCHOLARSHIP AND STOICISM

Epicurus was born in Samos, but he inherited Athenian citizenship from his father. The leading Stoic philosophers, starting with Zeno, were all immigrants to Athens. They came from cities in Cyprus (Zeno and Chrysippus) or Asia Minor (Cleanthes, Antipater) or even further afield (Diogenes of Babylon). If their first language was Greek, which is possible but not certain, it will hardly have been in the Attic dialect. The beginnings of Stoicism coincide with the rapid diffusion of Hellenic language and culture into Egypt and Asia as a consequence of Alexander the Great's conquests and the division of his spoils into the kingdoms governed by his successors. The Hellenistic world, as this epoch is conventionally called, was most dramatically symbolized by the foundation of new cities, most notably Alexandria, which became the capital of the Ptolemaic kingdom. Athens, though reduced to political insignificance, remained the center of philosophy. But it was Alexandria, thanks to Ptolemaic patronage, that attracted the literary scholars and scientists whose work was facilitated there by the foundation of the great Library and Museum.

Both institutions need to be seen in large part as symbols of cultural ecumenicism. The Ptolemies, to be sure, had the worldly ambitions of every monarch, but the scholarly work they supported was grounded in their desire to preserve, refine, and propagate those works of literature that collectively defined Hellenic identity. Since Homer was indisputably preeminent, Hellenistic scholars devoted particular attention to producing improved texts of the epics and to commenting on their language and content. Starting with Zenodotus, a tradition of scholarship developed that culminated in the 2nd century B.C.E. in the work of Aristarchus of Samothrace, the greatest of all Alexandrian literati. He edited and commented on the texts of Herodotus as well as Homer and other archaic poets.

Aristarchus was complimented with the title "eminent grammarian" (*grammatikotatos*), but he was not primarily a student of language or grammar in a technical sense; rather, as we would say today, he was a philologist and exegete of literature. The chief pioneers of linguistic study in the Hellenistic world were the Stoics. However, it is important to recognize that they, too, were keenly interested in Homer. Their founder, Zeno, wrote a work entitled *Homeric Problems* in five books. Virtually nothing is known about its content, but if we can draw conclusions from the evidence surviving from the later Stoic Chrysippus's work on Homer, the Stoics were primarily interested in precisely the kind of linguistic exegesis being practiced in Alexandria (H. von Arnim, *Stoicorum Veterum Fragmenta* III.769–777). It is this philological focus that will have distinguished their work on Homer from investigations of his poems that earlier philosophers, especially Aristotle, had already made.

In contrast with Epicurus, who professed to despise conventional *paideia*, the Stoics were concerned from the beginning to invoke the Greek poets in support of their own doctrines. In doing so, they not only aligned their school with traditional culture but also did so in ways that suggest a deliberate policy of assimilation. Many factors were doubtless at work here. These include the Stoics' status as arrivistes to Athens, the new fashion for ecumenicism, and, at a deeper level, the rationale of Stoicism itself. As the most systematic of Greek philosophies, Stoicism was grounded in the claim that the world is rationally organized through and through. The rationality of human nature, they taught, manifests itself in our capacity to speak, and especially in our capacity to express patterns of thought whose logical structure mirrors the structure of nature itself.

This faith in the universality of reason, as manifested in language, must be accounted a major factor in the Stoics' practice of proposing etymologies for numerous words, particularly the proper names and epithets of the many divinities in the Greek pantheon. By interpreting the "original meaning" of these terms, they wanted to show that Homer and Hesiod were the transmitters of primeval myths whose authors understood the world correctly, as etymology could reveal. Thus they took the name Hera to signify air (*aer*) and Cronos to signify time (*chronos*; Cicero, *De natura deorum* II.64–66). Most of their etymologies, like these examples, were as fanciful as those presented by Plato in *Cratylus*, but the rationale behind them, as distinct from the linguistics involved, was genuinely scientific: language is an intelligent construction, and analysis of language provides prime evidence of how people think and what they believe. Contrary to what is often said, the Stoics did not claim that Homer and Hesiod were "allegorical" exponents of Stoicism. Their interest in these early poets was "etymological"; they used them as sources for the *original meanings* of those who had told myths about the gods.

Zeno wrote a book titled *On Hellenic Education*. Together with the points just mentioned, the title of this work (which is all that survives of it) helps us to place the Stoics' work on language in its proper intellectual context. Their contributions to this field should be approached from multiple perspectives. For some of their findings they were clearly indebted to Plato and Aristotle. But they were also responding to interests similar to those awakened in Alexandria, while at the same time pursuing a study that reaches to the core of their philosophy.

Although our evidence for the Stoics' work on language is fragmentary and transmitted largely secondhand, it is sufficient to show that they were the primary innovators in most areas that were developed by the Greek and Roman grammarians of later antiquity. Among the most important innovations of the Stoics we may note the following: definition of *five* "parts of speech"—proper name, appellative, verb, conjunction, article—to which a sixth part, adverb, was later added (Diogenes Laertius, VII.57); identification of at least three of the "oblique" cases or types of inflection—accusative, genitive, and dative (ibid. VII.64–65)—and possibly the vocative as well; adumbration of the concept of conjugation, classifying four "times of action" for verbs—present, imperfect, perfect, and pluperfect (Priscian, VII.I.8.39). In addition, the Stoics took account of the differences between transitive, reflexive, and intransitive predicates (Diogenes Laertius, VII.64), foreshadowing the grammatical distinction between active, middle, and passive verbs. These categorizations were extended by those who later wrote on grammar specifically. Yet the Stoics did not think of themselves explicitly as grammarians. They wrote as students of language quite generally or, rather, as students of what they called "logic" or "dialectic." An appreciation of this point is essential if we are to grasp the general thrust of their work in this area.

They were the first Greek theorists to make a formal distinction between the "vocal" and the "semantic" aspects of language, or between "signifiers" and "significations" (Diogenes Laertius, VII.43). Signifiers, consisting of spoken or written symbols, are corporeal (ibid. VII.55). They range from the simplest "elements" (letters and syllables) to complete words, phrases, and, finally, sentences (combinations of at least a noun and a verb). The signification of a sentence is something of a quite different order. It is neither the utterance nor the thing referred to (which must be a body or bodily state, according to Stoicism), nor the individual thought of the speaker or hearer (also a bodily state, for the Stoics), but an "abstract" or "incorporeal" thing called a "sayable" (*lekton*; ibid. VII.63). *Lekta* are "meanings." They are what someone who says or writes, "Socrates is reading a book," means to say, and they are what someone who understands those words understands on hearing or reading them.

Considerable difficulty (partly due to defective evidence) attaches to any modern attempt to give a complete analysis of the Stoic theory of meaning. It appears that they regarded nouns, taken in isolation from sentences, as signifying not *lekta* but "qualities"—"common" ones in the case of appellatives like *man,* and "peculiar" ones in the case of proper names (Diogenes Laertius, VII.58). However, in "complete *lekta,*" which are the semantic correlate of sentences, the function of nouns is to "complete" the "predicate" (signified by a verb), by supplying it with an "inflection" *(ptosis).* Thus in the expression "Socrates is reading a book," the respective functions of the words *Socrates* and *a book* are to provide a "nominative" and "accusative" inflection for the predicate *is reading* (ibid. VII.64). We would call those functions subject and object, but the Stoics instead treated them in terms we are accustomed to call grammatical rather than semantic.

The *lekton* exemplified above is what the Stoics called an *axioma,* conventionally translated "proposition." Its defining characteristic is to be either true or false. In addition, the Stoics distinguished other kinds of *lekta*—questions, commands, imperatives, oaths, exclamations, and vocatives—that do not possess a truth value (Diogenes Laertius, VII.65–68). They also systematically analyzed types of propositions, including "hypothetical ones," which are of cardinal importance in their logic (ibid. VII.71–76). All of these *lekta* are identified in logical or semantic terms, and never by the grammatical form of the words through which they are expressed.

This point again illustrates the fact that the Stoics, notwithstanding their pioneering work in language, did not draw modern boundaries between grammar, semantics, and logic. Although they were interested in inflection, the main focus of their linguistic work was in semantics as distinct from morphology and accidence. Even such syntax as we may attribute to them—for instance, distinguishing between different kinds of predicates—has to do with meaning, or *lekta,* rather than formal grammar. That having been said, there is no question that they enormously advanced the study of complex speech acts, especially the forms of expression by which statements and inferences are made.

One writer of later antiquity (*SVF* II.146) attributes to the Stoics a theory about "primary utterances," pristine terms, as it were, from which subsequent words are derived. The original names, according to this report, will have been "mimetically" related to "things," as in the theory presented by Plato in *Cratylus.* As for later words, they were formed on principles of "resemblance," "affinity," or "contrast" with things (so Augustine, *Contra dialecticos* 6)—the latter being illustrated by the notorious *"lucus a non lucendo"* ("a grove, from the *absence of* illumination"). This material is difficult to control, and impossible to assign to individual Stoic philosophers.

Chrysippus was certainly prepared to invoke etymology to make philosophical points, as in his bizarre claim (*SVF* II.884) that the movements made by the face when one pronounces the first person pronoun *ego* signify that the chest is the center of consciousness. Yet he also insisted that language, at the level of expressions *(lexeis)*, is irreducibly ambiguous (*SVF* II.152). Whatever he may have thought about the "natural" relation of original languages to things, the focus of his semantic theory is not on the phonetic properties of words but on *lekta*. Since *lekta* are not words but meanings, they transcend any particular language, just like tokens of Plato's "Form of name." They explain how language can mediate a speaker's thought to a listener, and, further, how translation between languages is possible.

So far as the philosophy of language goes, the Stoics represent the highpoint of Greco-Roman antiquity. Although there is little contemporary evidence to go on, their findings and methodology concerning diction were certainly influential on Alexandrian philology. As investigators of "classical" texts, Alexandrian scholars were chiefly interested in trying to codify the rules of Hellenism (i.e., the standard of good Greek), to explain rare or obscure terms, to pronounce on questions of authenticity, orthography, and the like. Thus grammar, in something close to its modern sense, was born as the symbiosis between Stoicism and Alexandrian scholarship.

This point can be amplified by reference to the Pyrrhonean philosopher Sextus Empiricus. He provides an excellent conspectus of what Greek grammar signified during the earlier years of the Roman empire. In his treatise *Against the Grammarians*, Sextus cites several definitions of grammar. He also gives detailed accounts of its subject matter in ways that enable us to distinguish between common assumptions and controversies. Particularly controversial, it seems, was the question of whether grammar should be regarded as aiming at the formulation of precise rules, like the study of musical harmony, or whether instead its rationale was more conjectural and empirical. Dionysius the Thracian, an exponent of the latter conception, defined grammar as "experience in what is said *for the most part* by poets and writers of prose" (Sextus, *Against the Grammarians* 57). Other grammarians opted for a stricter conception of grammar as a "diagnostic art" seeking "the greatest possible precision" (ibid. 76).

Modern scholars (following the Roman grammarian Varro in his work *De lingua Latina* VII.I–X) frequently refer to this controversy as one between "analogists" and "anomalists": analogists sought to establish grammatical rules, which could serve as the standard for evaluating deviations from a norm, whereas anomalists were concerned with analyzing language as a phenomenon resistant to such determinate codification. This controversy may well be anachronistic so far as Alexandria and Stoicism are concerned, but it is plausible to suppose that Alexandrian philologists like Aristarchus were more sympathetic to the analogical approach than Stoic philosophers will have been.

Sextus Empiricus divides the study of grammar into three parts—historical, technical, and special (*Against the Grammarians* 91–96). The first and the last of these directly reflect the scholarship initiated in Alexandria, for they deal with commentary on texts and legends (the historical part) and the language of prose and verse (the special part). What we today call grammar is subsumed under the technical part. Its subdivisions, as enumerated by Sextus (97–247), comprise, first, "elements" (individual letters, together with their quantity and accent); second, "syllables" (including their quantity); third, complete words and parts of speech; fourth, orthography; fifth, Hellenism; sixth, etymology. What is glaringly absent from this list, it may seem, is syntax. But an explanation for its absence is not hard to find. The list of topics corresponds very closely to the study of "utterance," as canonized by the Stoics (Diogenes Laertius VII.56–59). And they, too, as we have seen, did not identify syntax as a topic to be studied under this heading. In fact the first grammarian to study syntax systematically was probably Apollonius Dyscolus, whose work may have been unknown to Sextus Empiricus, his near contemporary. Sextus's treatise *Against the Grammarians* confirms the impression that it was the Stoics who primarily stimulated the field of investigation called grammar. As philosophers, they were distinctive in showing so much interest in the phenomenal aspects of diction. Yet in spite of this, they would probably have agreed with Plato and Aristotle that language is primarily worth studying for the light it can shed on the *things* we talk about.

ANTHONY A. LONG

Bibliography

General Works

Baratin, Marc, and Françoise Desbordes. *L'analyse linguistique dans l'antiquité classique.* 2 vols. Paris: Klincksieck, 1981.

Fraser, P. M. *Ptolemaic Alexandria.* Oxford: Clarendon Press, 1972.

Manetti, Giovanni. *Le teorie del segno nell'antichità classica.* Milan: Bompiani, 1987.

Pfeiffer, Rudolf. *History of Classical Scholarship,* vol. 1: *From the Beginnings to the End of the Hellenistic Age.* Oxford: Clarendon Press, 1968.

Pinborg, Jan. "Classical Antiquity: Greece." *Current Trends in Linguistic Theory* 13 (1975): 69–126.

Schmitter, Peter, ed. *Sprachtheorien der abendländischen Antike.* Tübingen: Gunter Narr, 1991.

Steinthal, Heymann. *Geschichte der Sprachwissenschaft bei den Griechen und Römern.* Berlin: Dümmlers Verlag, 1890.

Specialized Works

Atherton, Catherine. *The Stoics on Ambiguity*. Cambridge: Cambridge University Press, 1993.

Ax, Wolfram. *Laut, Stimme, und Sprache: Studien zu drei Grundbegriffen der antiken Sprachtheorie*. Göttingen: Vandenhoeck and Ruprecht, 1986.

Blank, David L. *Ancient Philosophy and Grammar: The Syntax of Apollonius Dyscolus*. Chico, Calif.: Scholars Press, 1982.

————. *Against the Grammarians*. Oxford: Clarendon Press, 1998.

Brunschwig, Jacques. *Papers in Hellenistic Philosophy*. Trans. Janet Lloyd. Cambridge: Cambridge University Press, 1994.

Everson, Stephen, ed., *Companions to Ancient Thought*, vol. 3: *Language*. Cambridge: Cambridge University Press, 1994.

Frede, Michael. *Essays in Ancient Philosophy*. Minneapolis: University of Minnesota Press, 1987.

Kerferd, G. B. *The Sophistic Movement*. Cambridge: Cambridge University Press, 1981.

Lamberton, Robert, and J. J. Keaney, eds. *Homer's Ancient Readers: The Hermeneutics of Greek Epic's Earliest Exegetes*. Princeton: Princeton University Press, 1992.

Long, A. A., ed. *Problems in Stoicism*. London: Athlone Press, 1971; repr. 1996.

Long, A. A., and D. N. Sedley. *The Hellenistic Philosophers*. 2 vols. Cambridge: Cambridge University Press, 1987.

Schenkeveld, D. M. "Language," in Keimpe Algra et al., eds., *The Cambridge History of Hellenistic Philosophy*. Cambridge: Cambridge University Press, 1999.

Schmidt, R. T. *Die Grammatik der Stoiker*. Braunschweig and Wiesbaden: Friedrich Vieweg and Sohn, 1979.

Schofield, Malcolm, and Martha Nussbaum, eds. *Language and Logos: Studies in Ancient Greek Philosophy Presented to G. E. L. Owen*. Cambridge: Cambridge University Press, 1982.

Sluiter, Ineke. *Ancient Grammar in Context*. Amsterdam: VU University Press, 1990.

Related Entries

Logic; Antisthenes; Heraclitus; Sophists; Rhetoric; Epicurus; Hellenism and Christianity

LOGIC

A BASIC PRINCIPLE must be noted before we begin to deal with the origins of logic in Greece: we shall be examining not the way logic is used, but the theory of logic. It is one thing to follow rules, grammatical rules, for instance; it is something else again to theorize the correct use of those rules. Most people apply the rules of their own language correctly; however, they are rarely able to supply the general rules that justify the way they use language. The same thing holds true for logic. Almost all philosophers use it, sometimes well; few of them have developed a theory of logic. In what follows, when I speak of "logic" I shall be referring to the theory of logic; when I ask who were the earliest philosophers who concerned themselves with logic, the question will bear on those who developed a theory of logic.

We shall also have to adopt a viewpoint that implies the adoption of a theoretical stance, one that is decidedly less obvious than the preceding observation. What are we to understand by "logic"? We cannot answer this question through recourse to history, by considering the meaning that the ancient authors gave expressions such as *"he logike (techne)"* or *"he dialektike (techne),"* because of the variety of meanings these expressions have, and especially because authors such as Aristotle, even though they may be universally recognized as logicians, have no word that corresponds to our word *logic*. My own theoretical choice, which may not be accepted by everyone, is to use the word *logic* to refer to a theory of inference that is rationally capable of distinguishing between correct and incorrect types of argumentation.

An important consequence of this choice is that every self-respecting logical theory has to bear on types of inferences, not on isolated arguments; criteria making it possible to group similar inferences together must therefore exist. In other words, any theory of inference must include an understanding of the logical form or structure of inferences, a basis on which they can be organized according to schemas of inference. The notions of logical form and schemas of inference would require a more precise (and more complicated) characterization, but the idea must be familiar to anyone who has dealt with logic at all. Let us consider the two following inferences (where the horizontal line separates the premises, above, from the conclusion, below):

(1)   All men are mortal
       All Athenians are men

       ———————————————

       All Athenians are mortal

(2) All quadrupeds are donkeys
     All whales are quadrupeds
     _____
     All whales are donkeys

We see clearly that the first inference is correct, and it is easy to be convinced that the second is correct as well, even though its premises and its conclusion are false, unlike those of (1). This simple observation shows that if (1) and (2) are correct, this does not depend on the truth or falsity of the propositions at stake but on the fact that the propositions exhibit the same logical form: in the case in point, a series of relationships that are described by the predicative linking verb *are* and specified by the quantifier *all*. *Are* and *all* thus constitute part of the logical form of these inferences, whereas *man*, *Athenian, mortal, quadruped, donkey*, and *whale* are irrelevant to the determination of the validity of (1) and (2). The moral of this story is that logic begins where a theory of inference based on recognition of its logical form comes to light, at least in a rudimentary manner.

When did logic begin? If we take the word in the sense I have just suggested, we cannot say that it began with Plato. In his writings we find neither a conscious distinction between logical form and content nor a theory of inference. The doctrine of division, which represents his major effort to develop a formal analysis of the relationships between concepts, is not a theory of inference, as Aristotle understood quite clearly, and it does not aim to bring to light structural relationships among concepts. It has often been thought that the doctrine of division was the direct antecedent of the Aristotelian theory of syllogisms. But Plato's division is not identical to Aristotle's syllogism, nor is it even similar in logical form. The most charitable interpretation of their relationship is to say that division is the psychological antecedent of the syllogism; reflection on division may have led Aristotle to discover the syllogism, rather as reflection on Ptolemy's system may have led Kepler to construct his theory.

Efforts to discover the Platonic ancestry of the Aristotelian syllogism in the last part of *Phaedo*, where the relationships between individuals and Forms are described, seem more promising, at least at first glance. There Plato maintains, for example, that if A is the contrary of B, what is part of A is not part of B. It is possible to translate this position into a logical thesis that, appropriately manipulated, would exhibit a logical structure similar to the Aristotelian syllogism. Nevertheless, while such observations may be logically impeccable, they can have offered Aristotle only food for thought, on the same basis as the deductions of the mathematicians.

The use of a fully formed logical theory first appears with Aristotle. He perceives clearly that the validity of an inference depends not on its content but on the structure of the propositions it includes. At the beginning of his

Prior Analytics, he distinguishes among three types of arguments: demonstrative or scientific arguments, dialectical arguments, and syllogistic arguments. Truth is necessary in the first type: to make deductions that produce scientific knowledge, one must start with true premises. The same does not hold true for dialectical arguments, in which what counts is that the premises are propositions accepted by the adversary and capable of being generally approved by those who witness the debate. In the case of a simple syllogism, inference pure and simple, the only thing that counts is the logical structure of the premises, independent of their truth or falsity. This view implies a distinction between logic and epistemology: the predicative structure of the propositions included in inference is the only thing that counts for logic; taking their truth or their plausibility into account belongs to the realm of applications of logic to particular sectors of knowledge, in this case science and dialectics.

This, then, is a broad overview of the chronological framework of the birth of logic in Greece. But it would be a distortion of historical truth to limit ourselves, in this connection, to references to Plato and Aristotle. To be sure, Aristotle's logical reflection was born in the context of Platonic philosophy, especially if by this we mean not only the countless debates carried out by the characters in Plato's dialogues but also the discussions to which his writings gave rise within the Academy, where Aristotle, we must not forget, spent twenty years. However, other factors surely contributed to the birth of logic.

Let us recall, first of all, the extraordinary development of Greek mathematics. We know very little about pre-Euclidean geometry, though we know enough to say that it was organized along strictly deductive lines. Inferences played a decisive role and produced startling results, such as the demonstration of the incommensurability of the diagonal with the side of a square. How can one fail to feel the need to verify the steps in such a demonstration systematically, to assure oneself that this powerfully counterintuitive result was not the conclusion of faulty reasoning?

Let us turn next to the Sophistic movement and its sustained interest in language and in the function, sometimes positive and sometimes misleading, that it plays in argumentation. Authors such as Eubulides and Diodorus Cronos were formed in this melting pot of linguistic discussions. Eubulides was a disciple of Euclides, the founder of the so-called Megarian school. We know little about Eubulides, but he deserves to be counted among the logicians: he is credited with inventing some famous paradoxes, including the Liar Paradox and the paradox of the Sorites. Let us suppose that everything I say is false. What would then be the truth value of the proposition: "What I am saying is false"? A little reflection shows that if the proposition is thought to be true, it has to be taken as false, and if it is taken as false, it is true, which is contradictory. Similarly, a grain of wheat is certainly not a heap *(sōros)* of wheat, whereas a billion grains of wheat surely form a heap. But it is difficult to deny that if n grains do not make a heap, $n + 1$ grains do not make one either: no magical grain can transform into a heap what is not yet a heap. Thus, based on experience, a billion grains do not make a heap, contrary to the initial assertion.

We do not know how Eubulides formulated these paradoxes; the versions that survive come from later authors, Stoics in particular. Nor do we know why Eubulides invented the paradoxes. Some scholars have supposed that, following an Eleatic inspiration, he wanted to show the contradictory character of experience; others have thought that he invented the paradoxes to attack Aristotle (and indeed he had criticized him quite impolitely). But his interest was perhaps guided by the taste for discovering disconcerting aspects of language. In fact, contrary to one view that has come down from the ancient tradition, Eubulides' paradoxes are not merely head scratchers or curious playthings: they conceal fundamental difficulties in logic and in some of the basic notions of which they make use, the concept of truth in particular. Aristotle does not seem to have been conscious of their subversive import; only the Stoics tried to study them, with the idea that to neutralize them it was necessary to give up something important in our philosophical conceptions.

Diodorus Cronos is a very complex figure. According to most historians, he belonged to the Megarian school, as did Eubulides. Others think he belonged to the dialectical school, separate from the Megarian school but with connections to it. His disciple Philon may also have belonged to that school; Diodorus engaged in polemics with Philon on the subject of the truth conditions of conditional propositions, as we shall see.

Diodorus's fame rests on the so-called Dominator argument, thanks to which he thought he had proved that only what is already or what will be is possible. Unfortunately, our sources have given us incomplete information about the structure of the argument. According to these sources, Diodorus viewed the following three propositions as incompatible:

(i)   Everything that has happened is necessary;
(ii) From the possible the impossible does not follow;
(iii) That is possible which is not and will not be.

Since, according to Diodorus, one must accept (i) and (ii), one must reject (iii) and thus conclude that possibility cannot involve something that in fact is not at any moment: if tomorrow it does not turn out to be the case that I go to the movies, then it is impossible for me to go to the movies tomorrow. The reason that these three propositions are incompatible is not clear; all the reconstructions intended to explain it end up introducing new premises more or less surreptitiously. What seems certain, however, is that the ancients viewed Diodorus's inference as logically correct; they sought to respond to him by rejecting one or the other of his premises, so as to avoid the paradox of a reduction of the possible to the factual. We know, for example, that Cleanthes denied the necessity or the irrevocability of the past, while Chrysippus rejected the logical thesis according to which from a possible an impossible does not follow. Certain historians also supposed, but without compelling arguments, that the famous ninth chapter of Aristotle's *On Interpretation* (or, more accurately, "On Expression"), where determinism and the logical status of propositions having to do with future contingent events are discussed, was a response to Diodorus's Dominator argument. The existence of these sophisticated debates in Aristotle's day suffices to show that we must not view the Platonic Academy as the only site that nourished a logical culture and a conscious interest in the formal aspects of argumentation.

Aristotle's logic is included in a group of works traditionally designated as the *Organon,* that is, "the instrument"—understood primarily as the instrument for philosophy. *Organon* comprises six treatises: *Categories, On Interpretation, Prior Analytics, Posterior Analytics, Topica,* and *Sophistical Refutations.* These works are unanimously judged to be authentic, except for *Categories,* about which doubts have been raised in the modern era. In contrast, although Andronicus denied the authenticity of *On Interpretation,* that text is accepted as authentic today. It is also agreed that *Sophistical Refutations* does not constitute an autonomous treatise but is, rather, the last book of *Topica.*

Unfortunately, it is very difficult to establish an absolute and relative chronology of Aristotle's texts on logic. Most of them are thought to have been youthful works, written while he was a member of the Academy or shortly thereafter. But some scholars believe that *On Interpretation* is a late work, if it is true that that work contains a polemic against Diodorus Cronus that could only have been written toward the end of Aristotle's life. However, these hypotheses are by no means held unanimously, and it is more prudent to suspend judgment in the absence of compelling evidence. Similarly, the relative chronology of these texts has not been definitively established. Certain parts of *Topica* that contain no reference to the theory of syllogisms must have been composed before *Prior Analytics.* There is thus a nearly unanimous tendency to consider *Topica* to be the first treatise of *Organon,* by virtue of the fact, too, that the work seems to be an immediate reflection of the forms and content of the discussions that must have taken place within the Academy; in contrast, the question of the chronological relationship between *Prior Analytics* and *Posterior Analytics* has been the source of endless argument.

We cannot go into the details of these discussions here. By choosing to identify logic with the theory of inferences, I shall refer in particular to *On Interpretation,* which includes many indications concerning the conception of propositions, and to *Prior Analytics;* I shall occasionally mention *Posterior Analytics,* where the theory of science is presented, and *Topica,* a text chiefly devoted to dialectics, that is, to techniques that allow one to win arguments.

Aristotle proposes at least two complementary characterizations of the notion of proposition. One consists in defining it in terms of predication: a proposition is the attribution, affirmative or negative, of something to something. In this sense, Aristotle is only following the line set forth by Plato, who in *Sophist* distinguished between the act of naming and the act of predicating, the proposition being the result of the latter. But Aristotle also proposes another, more complex characterization of propositions. In *On Interpretation*, he considers the proposition to be a particular type of *logos*, a term generally translated—rather badly—by "discourse." A *logos* is a verbal expression of which certain parts, taken separately, have a meaning, without being affirmations or negations. "Pierre is a man" is a discourse, because its components, *Pierre* and *man* have meaning without being propositions.

Discourses can be *apophantic* or *nonapophantic*. The former are those that can be called true or false; in contrast, in the case of the latter one cannot properly speak of truth or falsity. Aristotle cites the example of prayer; to this others have added discourses such as orders or exhortations, drawing on a typology that, according to Diogenes Laertius, goes back to Protagoras. Some have seen this Aristotelian distinction as an anticipation of the modern distinction between performative and nonperformative speech acts. Without attempting to pass judgment on these sorts of connections (which are always risky), it goes without saying that Aristotle identifies propositions with particular types of apophantic discourses; affirmation and negation—that is, the attribution or the denial of attribution of a predicate to a subject—are viewed as propositions.

At least two observations on this subject are called for. First, it is clear that Aristotle considers the predicative structure to be the basic structure of propositions, and that he interprets this structure in terms of relationships between a predicate and a subject. These two theses have been challenged in modern times. In fact it is not at all self-evident that a proposition such as "It is raining" must be understood according to the model "Dion is running," even though the Greek language, unlike French or English, can understand "It is raining" as the equivalent of "Zeus is raining." Furthermore, since Frege, we have tended to think that the best logical analysis of a proposition such as "Socrates loves Callias" is not to make *Socrates* the subject and *loves Callias* the predicate; we prefer to view the predicate of this proposition as *loves,* and to see this predicate as having two subjects, *Socrates* and *Callias*. It is then much easier to account for inferences containing relational propositions. Aristotle is conscious of the specificity of relational predicates, but he does not succeed in analyzing them in terms different from those used for nonrelational predicates so far as their function in propositions is concerned.

The second observation has to do with the relation between affirmation and negation, the minimal cells of apophantic discourse. Although Aristotle seems, in *On Interpretation,* to subordinate negation to affirmation, he does not seem to have had the idea—one that is widespread among the moderns and fairly self-evident on its own terms—that negation is a compound proposition, achieved starting from an affirmation through the addition of an operation of negation; this idea was put forward by the Stoics. From Aristotle's viewpoint, negation seems to be as primitive and as elementary as affirmation. Not only is predication customarily defined as a liaison or separation of terms, but it also brings into correspondence with this operation two states of affairs, positive and negative, respectively, that make the corresponding propositions true or false.

If we set aside singular propositions concerning contingent future events, everyone agrees that, according to Aristotle, every proposition is true or false—that is, in modern terms, every proposition has a truth value (this is what we call the principle of bivalence). By interpreting a well-known passage of *Metaphysics*, perhaps somewhat audaciously, we may say that this value is the true one if the state of affairs expressed by the proposition is in effect, and that it is false if the opposite state of affairs is in effect.

The details of the Aristotelian doctrine are less banal. For Aristotle, a proposition always has a truth value, but it does not necessarily *always* have *the same* truth value. Let us consider, for example, the proposition:

(3)   Callias is running.

The verb *is running* contains a temporal reference that we can make explicit, from Aristotle's perspective, by adding to (3) a reference to the present, thanks to an expression such as "now." Aristotle analyzes the truth value of (3) as follows: "Now," which is contained implicitly in the proposition, refers to the moment when (3) is uttered; if at this moment Callias is in fact in the process of running, (3) is true; otherwise, (3) is false. But if we refer to two acts of utterance that are separate in time, (3) may be true at one moment and false at another. The truth value of an Aristotelian proposition thus cannot be understood, in Frege's manner, as an extension of the proposition. One must say, rather, that truth value is the value of a function of time, applied to a particular propositional content. This perspective is meaningful only if we acknowledge the existence of authentically temporal propositions such that the reference to temporal indicators such as *now, before,* and *after* cannot be reduced to objective dates. Moreover, we cannot tell whether Aristotle had the idea of propositions that are atemporal in their content. Whereas we would be inclined to say today that the proposition $2 + 2 = 4$ leaves out the temporal dimension, there is some evidence that Aristotle would have preferred to say that $2 + 2 = 4$ is a proposition that is *always* true.

If an elementary proposition is an affirmation or a negation, it is clear that its primary components will be nouns and verbs. Aristotle distinguishes between proper and common nouns, or, in a more appropriately logical formulation, between singular and universal terms. These are not distinguished by the function they fulfill in predication: a universal term can serve as a predicate but also as a subject; a singular term cannot serve as a predicate (except in the case of predications of identity). Aristotle expresses this thesis by saying that every universal term is, by its nature, suited to be the predicate of several distinct individuals. This of course does not mean that at least two individuals have to fall under the extension of a term if we are to be able to call it universal. It means, rather, that only universal terms are capable of fulfilling the role of being true of several individuals. Even a term that is true of nothing, such as *tragelaphos* ("goat-deer"), or even one that cannot be true of anything, such as "different from oneself," is universal, because if it were true of something, it could be true of at least two distinct individuals.

A nontrivial question connected with the distinction between universal and singular terms is that of reference in each case. It is not difficult to imagine that singular terms refer to the individuals to which they apply. But the delicate question, in Aristotle's perspective, is knowing to what universal terms refer. Aristotle's polemic against Plato, with regard to the existence of Forms, allows us to rule out the possibility that he considered ideal individuals as the correlates of universal terms. From his standpoint, no ideal man exists who represents that to which the term *man* refers: there is no individual who is the objective counterpart of man, as Callias is the correlate of the name Callias. However, Aristotle's critique of Plato does not rule out the possibility that the term *man*, if it is not an individual's proper name, can be the proper name of an attribute, the one that consists in being human. If we suppose that this attribute is shared by several individuals, the way a jointly owned apartment is shared, we might offer the hypothesis that "man" represents the attribute that Callias and Socrates share with other human beings, precisely the one that is present in all human beings. In this light, the difference between Plato's position and Aristotle's would be reduced to the fact that the former's Forms are ideal individuals, existing independently of the things of our world, whereas the latter's attributes are entities that are identically present in several individuals, and that cannot exist unless at least one of those individuals exists. But from the semantic viewpoint, the two philosophers would have the same perspective: universals, no less than singular terms, are the proper names of entities that exist in the world.

Although this conception may appear seductive, it is difficult to believe that it is Aristotle's, at least in the most mature phase of his ontology. In book Z of *Metaphysics*, he seems to maintain that the *ousiai* of individuals—that is, their substantial forms—are different for different individuals. Different *ousiai* belong to Socrates and to Callias, even though they are both men, so that the being-human of the one is not the being-human of the other. There is thus not a single reality to which the term *man* corresponds. If this is the case for universals like *man*, that is, for terms that refer to the *ousiai* of individuals, it is perhaps legitimate to extend that conclusion to all universal terms, such as *white, good, three cubits high.*

On this basis, then, we may presume that for Aristotle universal terms are not really referential. Referring to something, capturing it, is a function reserved to singular terms: to put it crudely, "Callias" or "Socrates" may be viewed as labels of objects. In contrast, according to this hypothesis, the defining characteristic of universal terms is that they are (at least in principle) true of a multiplicity; that is, they play the role of predicates. They denote nothing, even though they are true of individuals, and even though they are radically distinct, in this sense, from singular terms. Naturally, they have a meaning. But for a universal term to have a meaning does not imply that it has a denotation, because its task is to be true of an individual, not to indicate one.

The problem that this interpretation raises is the problem of understanding what guarantees the legitimacy of true predications. In fact, if truth consists, according to Aristotle, in stating things as they are, and if there is nothing that corresponds to the term *man*, on what basis can we legitimately maintain that "Callias is a man" is true, and that "Socrates is a lizard" is false? Aristotle does not lean in the direction of a response that might appear natural and that has been adopted quite often in the modern era, namely, the psychological response: universal terms, from this standpoint, refer to concepts that represent the ways in which we classify reality. "Callias is a man" is then a true proposition because we all agree to classify Callias as a man, and not as a lizard.

Aristotle operates instead on the terrain of ontology, unfortunately without ever clearly explaining his point of view. To attempt a clarification on the basis of some rather tortuous texts, let us consider two individuals a and b, of whom it is true to say F—for example, that they are men. If a and b are men, in them are present two distinct and different *ousiai*, respectively the being-man of a and the being-man of b. Let us call these two *ousiai* Fa and Fb. It is legitimate to suppose that Fa and Fb are not distinguished by the fact of being man: Socrates is not human in a different manner from Callias, and the one is not more human than the other. What makes the difference between Socrates' being-man and Callias's being-man is not being-man taken in itself, but simply the fact that one being-man belongs to Callias and the other to Socrates. One may view the two *ousiai* as two absolutely identical spheres that can be distinguished from each other only because they occupy different parts of space.

From this viewpoint, the relation that unites attributes with universal terms becomes clearer (or at least less obscure). The universal terms have as their meaning what might be called the *f*-ness of Fa, of Fb, and so on: they represent the various properties of things, without regard to the relations that these properties have with different individuals. Thus no universal term denotes anything at all, given that the *f*-ness of Fa, of Fb, and so on, does not exist independently of the fact that it is the *f*-ness of F*a*, of F*b*, and so on. Still, the attribution of a universal term to an individual is neither arbitrary nor the simple result of an epistemic operation of classification based on psychological categories.

The distinction between universal terms and singular terms allows Aristotle to classify propositions as singular or universal; to avoid confusion, let us call the latter "general" propositions. Singular propositions are those that have a singular term, such as *Callias,* as their subject; general propositions have a universal term, such as *man,* as their subject.

The introduction of this latter type of proposition allows Aristotle to introduce a supplementary division: general propositions may be universal, particular, or indefinite. Universal propositions are those whose subject is determined by a universal quantifier (such as *all* or *none* in the case of negative propositions); particular propositions are the ones whose subject is specified by a particular quantifier or, as one says today, existential, such as *some.* Probably for the first time in the history of Western thought, we are witnessing here the introduction of quantifiers as relevant components of the logical structure of propositions; this alone would suffice to make Aristotle one of the great logicians.

Since every proposition can be affirmative or negative, we thus obtain four types of general propositions: affirmative universal ("Every man is mortal"), negative universal ("No man is mortal"), affirmative particular ("Some man is mortal"), and negative particular ("Some man is not mortal"). For convenience, I shall adopt the medieval usage here and call affirmative universals *a* propositions, affirmative particulars *i* propositions (from the first two vowels of the Latin *affirmo*), negative universals *e* propositions, and negative particulars *o* propositions (from the two vowels of the Latin *nego*).

Indefinite propositions constitute a separate and much less clearly defined category: they are propositions with a universal subject in which no quantification is specified, such as "Man is white" and "Man is not white." Observing that indefinite propositions imply the corresponding particular propositions, Aristotle seems to reduce the former to the latter. It is clear, moreover, that "Man is not white" is not the logical negation of "Man is white," owing to the fact that the first does not necessarily have a truth value opposed to the second.

Aristotle devotes considerable effort to examining the relationships that come into play between the types of propositions identified by his classification. Thus he states that the negation of an affirmative singular proposition reverses its truth value: of the two propositions "Socrates is white" and "Socrates is not white," one is true and the other false. But one cannot say the same thing about a pair of singular propositions in which two contrary or incompatible predicates are attributed to the same subject, such as "Socrates is healthy" and "Socrates is ill": in such instances, according to Aristotle, it is not always the case that one of the two propositions is true and the other false. But one cannot infer from this argument that, according to Aristotle, every singular proposition must have an existential import—in other words, that the subject term refers to something that exists. In fact, Aristotle maintains that when Socrates does not exist, the proposition "Socrates is not healthy" is true: thus for him there are true singular propositions whose subject does not denote an existing object. It does not seem legitimate, either, to maintain that existential import is for him a necessary condition of the truth of affirmative singular propositions, whereas this would not be the case for negative singulars: in a controversial passage of *On Interpretation*, Aristotle asserts that if "Homer is a poet" is true, one cannot deduce from this that Homer exists. He thus imposes no general condition of existence on the truth of singular propositions: everything depends on the type of predicate considered. Predicates of the type *healthy/ill* are such that to be able to affirm them truthfully of an individual, one must presuppose that that individual exists; this is not the case for the predicate *poet*, which according to Aristotle may be attributed legitimately to an individual, even if that individual does not exist. Singular propositions, whether they are affirmative or negative, thus do not have existential import, generally speaking.

Probably for epistemological reasons, Aristotle's interest is focused chiefly on quantified general propositions and their relationships. His doctrine on this point is traditionally called the theory of the *logical square*. He calls propositions *a* and *o* and propositions *e* and *i* contradictory, and he asserts that they cannot either both be true or both be false. The logical relation between propositions *a* and *e*, called *contraries*, is different: they can both be false, but they cannot both be true. Aristotle does not assign a label to propositions *i* and *o*, which the later tradition will call *subcontraries;* they can both be true, but he does not say explicitly that they cannot both be false, though this thesis is implicitly contained in the one according to which the contradictories of two contraries are precisely the subcontraries. The tradition has also made explicit, under the name of *subalternation*, a supplementary relation that connects propositions *a* and *i*, and *e* and *o*, respectively. Aristotle is perfectly aware of the law that governs this relation: from the truth of the universal proposition that of the corresponding particular proposition follows; in other words, from *a* there follows *i*, and from *e* there follows *o* (the inverse, naturally, is not true).

The doctrine of the logical square, broadly accepted in the Middle Ages and in the modern era, has been severely criticized by contemporary logicians. To understand these criticisms, let us first observe that, once the rule of contradictories is accepted, the other rules follow all together: for example, one cannot accept the rule of contraries and reject that of subalterns; a counterexample invalidating the one would affect all the others. Next, let us note that the doctrine supposes a precise interpretation of the nature of the quantification. In particular, a proposition *i*, such as "Some Athenian is noble," must be understood as affirming that there is at least one individual who is Athenian and noble. Similarly, "Some Athenian is not noble" must mean that there is at least one individual who is Athenian and who is not noble. The contradictory of this last proposition, "Every Athenian is noble," will thus be true if and only if there exists no individual who is Athenian and not noble. The consequence of this is that when no individuals of a certain type exist, everything that one says about their totality is true. For example, let us suppose that no witches exist; in this case, the assertion "Every witch is wicked" is true, since in the hypothesis according to which no witches exist, there are not any witches, either, who are not wicked. For a symmetrical reason, its contrary, "No witch is wicked," is also true. It is thus not logically correct to maintain that two contrary propositions cannot both be true. Moreover, "Some witch is wicked," the subaltern of "Every witch is wicked," is false if no witches exist: it would be true only if there were at least one individual who was a witch and wicked; now, by hypothesis, there is not one. The law of subalternation is thus not always valid, and, consequently, the entire doctrine of the logical square is to be rejected.

This critique is based, clearly enough, on two distinct presuppositions. The first is the recognition of *empty* terms, which are true of nothing at all. The second concerns the analysis of quantification: every true particular proposition affirms the existence of an individual who exemplifies the subject term, and every universal proposition entails the negation of that existential implication.

Defenders of the Aristotelian conception customarily reject the first of these presuppositions. In fact, if one excludes empty terms, if every term has at least one exemplification, the logical square is exempt from counterexamples, and its rules are valid. At first glance, the defense appears to be efficacious. If logic is a serious thing, why worry about witches, elves, or magic mountains? An ideal city-state governed by logicians would banish such entities, which may inhabit the imagination of children but not the reflections of philosophers and wise men. Still, the fact remains that Aristotle grants language the possibility of using empty terms: one of his favorite examples is the *tragelaphos*, the "goat-deer." Furthermore, it cannot be affirmed that empty terms are derived only from fables. To prove that there exists no natural number inferior to zero, that is, to prove that that expression is empty, is an exercise that mathematicians can carry out; to establish that there exists no human being anterior to the Neanderthal is a false scientific conclusion. If we were to limit Aristotle's logic to nonempty terms, we would limit its applicability, and we would render it even more incapable than it is of accounting for scientific inferences.

The effort to avoid the impasses of the logical square has led some to search for a different way out. Through reliance on the texts in which Aristotle maintains that in certain cases, affirmative singular propositions, unlike negative ones, have an existential import, this thesis has been generalized, leading to a conclusion that every affirmative proposition has such an import and no negative proposition does. From this point on, the logical square is safe from modern objections. In fact, from this perspective, "Every witch is wicked" becomes false, and thus no longer constitutes a counterexample to the rule of subalternation. Nevertheless, this solution entails at least two difficulties. First, we cannot see clearly whether for Aristotle all affirmative singular propositions have an existential import or only some of them, as we had understood earlier. The generalization of the thesis of *Categories* runs up against the obstacle of *On Interpretation*. Furthermore, in *Analytics,* Aristotle applies systematically to syllogistic schemas what we know as proof "by exposition," which requires that the terms contained in the premises, whether affirmative or negative, possess an exemplification. Thus it does not appear legitimate to attribute to Aristotle the idea that only affirmative propositions have an existential import, if we suppose, barring proof to the contrary, that his doctrine is coherent.

There may be one last way to save the Aristotelian conception, one that has not been explored until now. It consists in abandoning the second presupposition of the modern critique, that is, the thesis according to which all particular propositions have an existential import. From this standpoint, there is no longer any reason to assert that "Every witch is wicked" is true and that the corresponding particular proposition is false. Naturally this cheap rescue operation has its price, which cannot be spelled out in detail here (in particular, it becomes difficult to determine the truth conditions of particular propositions). Let me suggest this direction for research, emphasizing simply that Aristotle's theory does not allow us to assimilate his idea of quantifiers readily to that of the moderns, even though the attempt has often been made.

The heart of Aristotle's logic is his doctrine of inference. The Aristotelian word for "inference" is *sullogismos,* which we must be careful not to translate as "syllogism," because Aristotle normally uses the term not to designate the particular inferences whose theory he is developing, namely, syllogisms, but to designate the general class of inferences of which syllogisms are a privileged type, for, according to him, every logically correct inference can be reformulated as a syllogism.

The Aristotelian definition of inference is presented with particular care at the beginning of *Prior Analytics;* it calls for two important observations. Aristotle first posits as an essential condition that the conclusion of an inference be different from its premises; this means that he rules out inferences of the type "A, thus B," which are nevertheless legitimate from the modern viewpoint, and even welcome, owing to the very fact that their banality guarantees their correctness. Aristotle seems on the contrary to maintain that an inference must always lead to something new. Furthermore, we must not read the Aristotelian definition with our eyes fixed on the modern conception of the notion of logical consequence—the one that, at least since Tarski, has referred to the notion of truth. There is nothing of the sort in Aristotle: he says neither that the truth of the conclusion necessarily follows that of the premises, nor that if the premises are true, the conclusion is also true. He simply maintains that if the premises *are posited,* a conclusion necessarily follows, which no doubt means that the positing of the premises is a sufficient condition of the positing of the conclusion. "Position" must not of course be understood in a psychological sense: it is not because one asserts the premises that one is compelled to assert the conclusion; Aristotle is well aware that this is not at all the case. It is rather a question of an ideal positing, through which a set of premises finds itself isolated. If this isolation occurs and if the premises are appropriate, one is legitimately authorized to posit the conclusion following the premises. In this sense, the premises are the sufficient conditions, not of the existence of the conclusion, for the latter does not exist when it expresses a false proposition, but of the fact that it comes after the premises in the process that leads from the premises to the conclusion. In this perspective, the Aristotelian notion of inference, unlike the modern notion, makes the notion of cause a reference that cannot be eliminated.

Aristotle formulates the inferences whose theory he is developing by means of letters that take the place of the general terms of their constitutive propositions. There has been much discussion about the meaning of these letters. It is probably not appropriate to speak in this connection of *variables* in the modern sense, as has been done (in the proper sense, a variable x is what is connected by a quantifier, "for every x" or "for some x," which are never these letters). What comes closest to Aristotle's letters is the idea (theorized by Quine, among others) of *dummy letters,* which can be indefinitely substituted for the concrete terms of ordinary language.

One type of Aristotelian inference thus has a form of which the following schema would be an example:

(4)   A belongs to all B
      B belongs to all C
      _____

      A belongs to all C

in which A, B, and C take the place of general terms, and in which the expression "A belongs to all B" translates the characteristic way in which Aristotle expresses an affirmative universal, logically equivalent to "every B is A." This schema always includes two premises, in which a common term, the *middle,* appears twice, whereas the other two terms (the *extremes*) are the ones that appear in the conclusion. More precisely, the *major* extreme is the predicate of the conclusion, and the *minor* is the subject.

According to the type of relation that the mean has with the extremes in the premises, syllogisms are grouped into *figures*. Aristotle considers three of these: in the first, the middle term is the subject of the major term and the predicate of the minor term; in the second, the middle term is the predicate in both premises; in the third, the middle term is the subject in both. Schema (4) is thus an example of the first figure. Here is an example of the second:

(5)   A does not belong to any B
      A belongs to all C
      _____

      B does not belong to any C

Here is an example of the third:

(6)   A belongs to all C
      B belongs to all C
      _____

      A belongs to some B

The figures are not schemas of inference but ways of categorizing such schemas. Aristotle recognizes four types of valid syllogisms as syllogisms of the first figure; they are traditionally called *modes* and given the following names: Barbara, Celarent, Darii, Ferio. The second figure also has four modes: Cesare, Camestres, Festino, Baroco, and the third has six: Darapti, Felapton, Disamis, Datisi, Ferison, Bocardo. (4) is in the Barbara mode, (5) in the Cesare mode, and (6) in Darapti.

These bizarre names have a mnemotechnic function. Their vowels indicate, in order, the types of premises and conclusion that characterize the inference. For example, Barbara, the first mode of the first figure, has propositions of the *a* type as its premises and its conclusion.

Aristotle divides the inferences he is theorizing into two major groups: perfect syllogisms and imperfect syllogisms. The members of both groups are syllogisms and satisfy the definition, but the former, unlike the latter, are self-evident and thus require no justification of their validity. Imperfect syllogisms require justification of their validity: Aristotle calls this process "reduction" and articulates it as a deduction of these syllogisms from perfect syllogisms. Once derived in this way, an imperfect syllogism is perfected; in this sense, it becomes self-evident. The perfect syllogisms fulfill, in a way, the function of axioms in the theory, although they do not satisfy the condition of independence characteristic of axioms.

Aristotle considers syllogisms exemplifying the first figure to be perfect, and those exemplifying the other figure imperfect. His idea is fairly simple: let us isolate a group of inferences that are certain and incontrovertible, and let us show that those that can give rise to doubt depend on those that are incontrovertible, so that denying the latter implies rejecting the former. What is less clear is the identification of perfect syllogisms with those exemplifying the first figure. Aristotle appears to associate the perfection of the latter with the fact that they rely directly on the definition of universal predication. But his thesis is not entirely clear.

To derive the modes of the second and third figures starting from those of the first figure, Aristotle basically uses three methods. The first depends on the use of rules for conversion of propositions, which are discussed in a chapter of *Prior Analytics*. The conversion of a proposition is the substitution of its predicate for its subject and vice versa. The problem lies in establishing under what conditions this substitution preserves truth, and, when it does not, whether one can obtain the same result by weakening the quantification of the proposition. The conclusion of the investigation is that universal negatives can be converted simpliciter, as was said in the Middle Ages—that is, by simple substitution between predicate and subject. "A belongs to no B" is converted into "B belongs to no A," *salva veritate* (truth remaining intact). Similarly, affirmative particular propositions can be converted simpliciter: if "A belongs to some B," it is legitimate to infer that "B belongs to some A." In contrast, universal affirmative propositions can be converted only *secundum quid*, that is, by weakening the quantification: from "A belongs to all B," we can move to "B belongs to some A." Finally, Aristotle rightly notes that negative particular propositions cannot be converted, in the sense that no possible conversion always preserves their truth.

Aristotle is able to prove, by applying the rules of conversion, that most of the second- and third-figure modes depend on the first-figure modes. In the second figure, the conversion of the negative premises of Cesare and Camestres makes it possible to get Celarent, and that of the negative premise of Festino makes it possible to get Ferio. In the third figure, Darapti, Datisi, Felapton, and Ferison are reduced by conversion of the minor premise, the first two being reduced to Darii and the next two to Ferio. Disamis is also reduced to Darii by conversion of the major premise.

Conversion is not applicable to Baroco in the second figure, nor to Bocardo in the third figure: in fact, conversion produces no valid first-figure mode. Aristotle then falls back on the method of reduction to the impossible. Let us suppose that Baroco and Bocardo are invalid. Henceforth, in one case at least the premises will be true and the conclusion false; in other words, the premises and the negation of the conclusion will both be true. But this cannot be, because the negation of the conclusion, together with one of the premises, gives rise in Barbara, the first mode of the first figure, to the negation of the other premise. Since the invalidity of these two modes is impossible, they have to be counted among the valid modes.

Thus all syllogisms of the second and third figure are reduced to syllogisms of the first figure, and in this sense they are justified. However, Aristotle mentions a third type of proof for syllogisms of the second and third figure; he calls this type exposition *(ekthesis)*, and uses it as an auxiliary proof. The interpretation of this type of proof is controversial; we cannot go into the details here. It will suffice to say that if exposition plays a secondary role in syllogistic reductions, it takes on capital importance in proofs of the laws of conversion; the rule of conversion of negative universals, on which the proof of the other rules relies, is proved by exposition.

Aristotle does not stop at proving that all the second- and third-figure modes he is considering are valid, once the validity of the first-figure modes has been recognized. He shows, too, that all the other combinations of premises, in the three figures, do not give syllogistic conclusions. Let us consider for example the following pair of propositions:

(7)   A belongs to all B
       B belongs to no C

The position of the middle term, B, might lead us to believe that we are dealing with the antecedent of a first-figure mode, and that we can establish a connection between A as predicate and C as subject. Aristotle proves that this hypothesis is false, owing to the fact that, whatever predicative relation we establish between A and C, truth is not preserved. In other words, it is always possible to find a case in which the propositions of (7) are true and the presumed conclusion is false. For example, if we substitute "animal" for A, "man" for B, and "horse" for C, we get the following pair:

(8)   Animal belongs to all man
       Man belongs to no horse

This pair of propositions is true. But if we were to suppose that from (7) it follows, for example, that A belongs to no C, the substitutions that gave us (8) would lead to "Animal belongs to no horse," which is false. Thus we cannot affirm that from (7) it follows that "A belongs to no C." Thanks to other substitutions of terms, it is easy to prove in a similar fashion that (7) and "A belongs to all C" are true at the same time. From (7), then, no proposition follows having A as its predicate and C as its subject. We have to conclude that (7) is not a valid syllogistic antecedent.

Aristotle thus proves not only that his system of inferences is valid but also that it is syllogistically complete, given that his schemas constitute the only valid modes in the three figures. In truth, Aristotle is defending a much more ambitious thesis. He judges that every correct inference can be expressed, in the final analysis, thanks to one of the syllogistic modes of his three figures. Actually, this claim is trivially false, as Augustus De Morgan proved more than a century ago: a perfectly legitimate inference such as:

All horses are animals

All horses' heads are animals' heads

is absolutely incapable of being reformulated as an Aristotelian syllogism.

Even though Aristotle explicitly defends the thesis of the strong completeness of his system, we probably should not take his claim too seriously, since in other passages he shows that he is aware of inferential schemas that are correct but irreducible to the syllogistic form. Such is the case, for example, with what is called *Modus Ponens*, which can be formulated as follows:

(9) If A, then B
     A

     B

Quite clearly, an inference of this sort (in which the letters represent propositions, not terms) cannot be transformed into a syllogism; nevertheless, Aristotle recognizes its legitimacy. His idea, which is developed by the ancient commentators, is that an inference such as (9) must be considered not as an inference properly speaking but rather as a rule that governs and constructs inferences. Let us suppose that we want to prove B, but that we have no proof of B. If we know, or at least if we admit, that A implies B, we can consider the proof of A sufficient to be able to affirm B. Schemas such as (9) are thus assigned a role in syllogistic without being granted the status of inferences, properly speaking, that would be placed on the same level as syllogisms.

We cannot conclude this presentation of Aristotle's position without alluding, however briefly, to his modal logic. A proposition such as "Every man is mortal" is a nonmodal or *categorical* proposition. However, the same proposition can be qualified as necessary or as possible, depending on whether one adds to it expressions such as "it is necessary that" or "it is possible that."

Alongside his nonmodal or *categorical* syllogistic, Aristotle devoted a great deal of effort to the parallel development of a modal syllogistic—that is, a theory of inferences including propositions supplied with modal specifications. His problem is the following: given a valid categorical syllogistic schema, what becomes of the conclusion if the premises are specified as necessary or possible? If, for example, the premises are both necessary, Aristotle rightly establishes that the conclusion is also necessary. But what happens if one of the premises is necessary and the other possible, or if one is modalized and the other not? Aristotle analyzes all possible cases very meticulously. But unlike what happens in his categorical syllogistic, here his investigation does not always meet with success: many of his theses appear odd and not very convincing. For example, he maintains that in Barbara, if the major premise is necessary and the minor is categorical, the conclusion is necessary, whereas if the major is categorical and the minor necessary, the conclusion is categorical. To explain this odd point of view, we may suppose that Aristotle interprets "necessarily A belongs to every B" as meaning "every B is necessarily-A"; the modal operator in this case acts only on the predicate of the proposition. Consequently, by virtue of the fact that B belongs to all C, one may legitimately deduce that necessarily-A belongs to all C. Aristotle's viewpoint thus becomes entirely legitimate.

However, this interpretation does not account for other affirmations on Aristotle's part, particularly in his analysis of conversion, which appears to imply, on the contrary, that the modal operator applies to the categorical proposition as a whole. There is from this point on an oscillation in the understanding of the modal operator, and this systematic ambiguity disrupts the foundations of the theory, thus greatly diminishing the interest of the Aristotelian system of modal inferences.

Aristotle does not usually define modal operators. He certainly does not appear to have the idea that modern semantic theories seem to suggest, namely, that a proposition is necessary if it is true in all conceivable situations or, as they say, in all possible worlds, whereas it is possible if it is true in at least one of these worlds. Certain interpreters think that his idea of necessity is connected to time: A is necessary if it is always true. The difficulty of this conception is that, on this basis, a proposition is possible if it is true at one moment at least, which seems to run counter to the intuition, apparently shared by Aristotle, that there are possibilities that are never realized. The perspective that seems most in harmony with the texts is that of a syntactic characterization of modality: a proposition is possible if from the supposition that it is true no contradiction follows. Along the same lines, although Aristotle never says this explicitly, a necessary proposition could be defined as a proposition whose falsity would lead to a contradiction. But Aristotle does not systematically develop this line of interpretation of modalities, the seeds of which are nevertheless present in his work.

Let us consider one more problem related to the logic of modalities, a problem that, although marginal in Aristotle's logic, has been and remains at the heart of a vast historical and theoretical debate: the problem of contingent future propositions and their relation to determinism. Let us consider a contingent proposition concerning the future: "Tomorrow there will be a naval battle," to use Aristotle's example. Tomorrow, this proposition will surely have a truth value: if the event takes place, the proposition is true; if the event does not take place, it is false. Let us suppose that tomorrow there really is a naval battle: then today it is already true to say that tomorrow there will be a naval battle. But if it is true to say this already today, tomorrow there cannot not be a naval battle. The future is therefore in reality not contingent; it is already determined.

The interpreters do not agree on the response Aristotle would have made to this difficulty to maintain the contingency of the future. The most broadly accepted thesis is that he would deny that a contingent future proposition had a truth value before the event to which it referred took place or not: before the battle occurs, it is neither true nor false to affirm that tomorrow there will be a naval battle. Since the event in question is contingent, the truth conditions of the propositions that speak of it ahead of time are not given; these propositions thus have no truth value, and the objection of the determinist is completely disarmed. The disadvantage of this solution is that one must then admit that Aristotle set limits to certain logical principles, in particular to the principle of bivalence, according to which every proposition is true or false: in effect, he is now acknowledging propositions that are neither true nor false. The general definition of the proposition as the site of truth or falsity would have to be reconsidered and corrected.

Moving on to Stoic logic, we shall focus again on the notion of inference, and it is necessary to begin by describing the Stoic notion of proposition (which the Stoics call *axiōma*). According to them, the proposition is a *lekton*, a term that corresponds to a fundamental notion and that is difficult to translate (it is generally translated by "expressible" or "sayable"). Sextus characterizes it fairly clearly: a *lekton* is what we understand when we hear a meaningful verbal expression pronounced. One might say that *lekta* are the contents of our words, and it is no accident that the *lekton* is often identified with the *semainomenon*, the signified. In fact, the Stoics distinguished— much better than Aristotle did—between three levels of reality: the level of things, *tunchanonta* in their language; the level of signifiers or verbal expressions; and finally the level of *lekta*. To highlight the differences, the Stoics stressed that signifiers and things are corporeal entities, whereas *lekta* are incorporeal. Thus it becomes clear that *lekta* cannot be assimilated to concepts, which are themselves material in that they are affects of the soul, which is a corporeal reality. *Lekta* are rather the contents of our concepts, and to illustrate the distinction, despite the risk of anachronism, one could evoke the Fregean distinction between *Vorstellung*, representation, which is something that belongs to the conscious subject and that is proper to that subject, and *Sinn*, which is what the various representations have in common when one is thinking of the same thing. These representative contents recall the Stoics' *lekta*, and it is not without reason that certain authors have related the *lekta* to the Fregean notion of *Sinn*, meaning.

According to the Stoics, *lekta* are either imperfect or perfect. Imperfect *lekta* correspond to the terms that are the constituents of propositions, while perfect ones correspond to the content of propositions; they are what is signified by a proposition. The underlying idea seems to be that propositions have a complete meaning, in contrast to their simple constituents. As for Aristotle, every proposition, for the Stoics, is either true or false; some defend this thesis so rigorously that they accuse Aristotle of not defending it enough, since, as we have seen, he eliminates contingent future propositions from its scope.

For the Stoics, propositions are either simple or complex, depending on the presence or absence of connectors *(sundesmoi)*. Simple propositions (which could be called *atomic* in modern terminology) are either definite, indefinite, or intermediary. Definite propositions are those whose subject is a demonstrative or "deictic," such as "This one is a man." Indefinite propositions, such as "Someone is walking," do not refer to a specific individual. Intermediary propositions, such as "Socrates is a man" or "Man is mortal," are different from the other types in that they do not have a deictic as their subject, unlike definite propositions, but they are not indeterminate like the indefinites. Sextus Empiricus, who presents this doctrine, reports that according to the Stoics the truth of an indefinite proposition implies the truth of a corresponding definite proposition. He also seems to suppose that the truth of an intermediary proposition implies that of a corresponding definite proposition, but this thesis seems to be disproved by the position attributed to Chrysippus, according to which "Dion is dead," pronounced after Dion's death, is true, even though the corresponding deictic, "This one is dead," has no truth value, as we shall see later on.

The theory of complex propositions that has been handed down is better articulated. The Stoics distinguished among several species of complex propositions, or, to use modern jargon again, *molecular* propositions; one of their principal merits is that they elaborated a theory of relations among propositions that logically precedes the Aristotelian theory of relations among terms. They considered first of all disjunctive propositions, in which *or* is the principal connector. Disjunctive propositions are either exclusive (one of the two propositions that constitute them is true and the other false) or inclusive (nothing prevents both propositions from being true); in their theory of inference, as we shall see, the Stoics make greater use of the first type than of the second. But the distinction is blurred by the fact that they seem to characterize exclusive disjunction in stronger terms than the terms, today called verifunctional, in which I have just introduced it: they seem to require, for disjunction to be true, not only that one of its constituents be true and the other false, but also that they be mutually incompatible. If we give this term a modal value, we have a strong definition of disjunction that goes beyond the purely verifunctional conception. The Stoic definition of conjunctive propositions, in contrast, comes closer to a verifunctional presentation: in a conjunctive proposition, the principal connector is *and,* and a conjunctive proposition is true if and only if all its constituents are true.

But the sort of complex proposition that most interested the Stoics is the conditional proposition, of the type "If it is raining, then the earth is wet." There are at least two reasons for this. First, this type had been extensively discussed in the tradition to which the Stoic school was most directly attached. In addition, the truth conditions of conditional propositions were linked, for the Stoics, to the notion of the validity of the arguments. The polemic over conditionals had begun with a discussion between Diodorus Cronus and his disciple Philon. The latter had maintained that a conditional is true either if its antecedent is false or if its consequent is true. According to this criterion, "If the Earth flies, then there is sunshine during the day" is true, and "If there is sunshine during the day, then the Earth flies" is false. This conception comes curiously close to the modern notion of *material implication,* but the analogy cannot be carried too far. In fact, from the viewpoint of material implication, a conditional such as "If I am speaking, then $2 + 2 = 4$" is not only legitimate but also true. Its legitimacy depends on the fact that the connector "if . . . then" is conceived in a verifunctional fashion: in other words, any two propositions may be the constituents of a conditional, on the sole condition that they be true or false. This is not of course what happens in ordinary language, where other conditions are required to construct a meaningful conditional. The ancients probably presupposed these conditions of ordinary language without analyzing them.

Diodorus maintained, against Philon, that a proposition such as "If it is night, then I am speaking," true according to Philon when I am actually speaking, must in reality be judged false, because there is a moment when it is night and when I am not speaking. This observation shows that Diodorus's notion of the conditional is more powerful than Philon's, and that it is qualified in terms of time: for a conditional to be accepted as true, it does not suffice that it not be the case that its antecedent is true and its consequent false; it is also necessary that that situation *never* occur. In other words, a conditional is true, according to Diodorus, if its consequent is true every time the antecedent is true.

In a well-known passage of his *Hypotyposes,* Sextus Empiricus presents two additional types of conditionals, arranged by increasing force. After Philon's conditional and Diodorus's, there is a third type, which Sextus attributes to "those who introduce connection": it is true only if the negation of the consequent is *incompatible* with the antecedent. A fourth conditional has as its distinguishing feature that its consequent is potentially contained in the antecedent. The testimony of Diogenes Laertius suggests that the definition in terms of connection should be attributed to the Stoics. For them, he says, a conditional such as "If it is day, then Dion is walking" is false, because the negation of the consequent, "Dion is not walking," is not incompatible with the antecedent "it is day." Conversely, a conditional such as "If it is day, it is light" is true, because the negation of its consequent is incompatible with its antecedent. The notion of incompatibility must then be understood as a modal notion: a conditional is true if the conjunction of the negation of its consequent and of its antecedent is *impossible*. This interpretation of the Stoic conditional brings to mind the definition of *strict implication*, introduced by Lewis in modern logic. But one must stress the difference that affects the conception of the modal operator of impossibility here. In modern schools of semantics posterior to Lewis, the notion of impossibility is a logical notion connected to that of a possible world: a proposition A is (logically) impossible if it is not true in any possible world, a possible world being a world in which the only invariants are determined by the laws of logic and mathematics. From this point of view, it is difficult to believe that a conditional such as "If it is day, it is light" can be deemed true: there is no logical impossibility in conceiving of days without light. But the Stoic notions of necessity and possibility were linked to physical notions rather than logical ones; furthermore, Stoic metaphysics, which conceives of the development of the world as identical to that of the *logos*, did not support any differentiation between physical and logical. The definition of the modal operators transmitted by our sources confirms this interpretation: the notion of possibility is defined here with reference to the presence of favorable external conditions. Once again in a polemic against Philon, the Stoics maintained, for example, that it is impossible for a piece of wood at the bottom of the sea to burn, because the external circumstances prevent the realization of this possibility that otherwise the wood would have in its own right. Their notion of possibility is thus largely conditioned by physical possibility, and there is no reason to think that it would be otherwise for the other modalities. In any event, it is clear that the Stoic conditional is stronger than Diodorus's: Diodorus merely imposes an invariance of truth with respect to time, whereas the Stoics extend that demand to all possible situations.

Why did the Stoics feel the need to fall back on such a strong conception of the conditional? The question is related to that of the validity of arguments. In general, an argument is characterized in extremely abstract terms: it is simply a matter of a series of propositions, the last one of which is called the *conclusion*, whereas the others, called *premises*, have the function of allowing access to the conclusion. According to Sextus Empiricus, for the Stoics, arguments are either nonconclusive or conclusive. Conclusive arguments may in turn be true or not true, depending on whether the propositions that constitute them are true or not, and true arguments are either demonstrative or nondemonstrative. As was the case with Aristotle, the truth of the constituent propositions is not a necessary condition of the validity of the arguments, which proves that the Stoics, too, had a *logical* theory of arguments.

The crucial point is of course the distinction between conclusive and non-conclusive arguments. The Stoic position, at least starting with Chrysippus, is simple and clear: an argument is conclusive if the conditional that has as its antecedent the conjunction of its premises, and as its consequent its conclusion, is true. Given this, we can understand why the Stoics preferred a type of conditional that was stronger than Philon's or Diodorus's. Naturally, the adequacy of a similar definition of conclusive arguments, or to put it in modern terms, of logical validity, depends heavily on the notion of necessity that specifies the conditional. In all plausibility, it is a question of a physical and not a logical necessity; this obviously compromises the legitimacy of identifying the Stoic position with the modern position insofar as the notion of validity in terms of universal necessity is concerned.

The Stoics divided conclusive arguments into those that were conclusive "but not according to the method" and those that were conclusive "according to the method." We do not have a formal definition of the first group; we can only make conjectures on the basis of the examples preserved. It is reasonable to suppose that an argument that is conclusive but not according to the method is an argument that satisfies the general definition of conclusive arguments, but without exemplifying a logical schema. Let us consider the following argument:

(10) Coriscos is a man

Coriscos is an animal

This argument is valid because, at least in one sense, the negation of its conclusion is incompatible with its premise. But if we were to formalize it, we would get the logical schema "A, thus B," in which "A" and "B" hold the places of any two propositions, a schema that in general is not valid or always conclusive. This means that (10) is correct only in function of the content of the two propositions in question.

According to our conjecture, arguments that are conclusive according to the method must be those that are particular cases of logical schemas. The Stoics divided the latter into *syllogistic* arguments (a term that has a very different meaning for them than it does for Aristotle) and arguments that were *reducible to syllogistic arguments*. It is plausible that the arguments called syllogistic in one branch of the tradition are those that, elsewhere, are called *anapodictic* (unprovable) and that have a role more or less comparable to that of the axioms of a logical theory. But they are not axioms properly speaking (nor are they rules of inference), because it is normally required of the axioms of a theory that they be independent, that is, that they not be derived from other axioms, which is certainly not the case with the Stoics' unprovable arguments. We may believe that these were chosen on the basis of their immediate and incontrovertible character.

The first unprovable argument corresponds to what modern logicians, following the example of their medieval forebears, call the *Modus Ponens* (or more precisely, the *Modus Ponendo Ponens*). The following argument is an example:

> If it is raining, the earth is wet
> It is raining
> _____
> The earth is wet

The Stoics expressed the corresponding schema by means of numbers that took the place of propositions and that had a function analogous to that of the schematic letters of Aristotelian syllogistic, with one difference: the latter, as we have seen, take the place of general terms, not of propositions. Thus the Stoic schema had the following form:

> If the first, the second
> The first
> _____
> The second

It is easy to observe that in this case "the first" and "the second" take the place of the propositions that constitute, respectively, the antecedent and the consequent of a conditional.

The second unprovable argument corresponds to the *Modus (Tollendo) Tollens,* which consists in concluding the negation of the antecedent of a conditional on the basis of the negation of its consequent:

> If the first, the second
> Not the first
> _____
> Not the second

The third unprovable argument is based on a conjunctive proposition. If we posit its negation, and if we affirm one of its components, then our conclusion must be the negation of the other, that is:

Not (the first and the second)
The first

Not the second

The last two unprovable arguments concern disjunction: the first of them at least requires the strong notion of exclusive disjunction to be considered valid. It is the fourth unprovable argument that makes it possible to conclude the negation of one of the members of the disjunction on the basis of the position of the other:

The first or the second
The first

Not the second

Finally, in the last unprovable argument, one infers one of the members of the disjunction on the basis of the negation of the other:

The first or the second
Not the first

The second

The correctness of this last inference does not formally require exclusive disjunction; inclusive disjunction is sufficient. But for the uniformity of the system, it is probably appropriate to think that the *or* of the first premise has, as in the fourth unprovable argument, an exclusive sense.

According to the Stoics, all arguments that are conclusive "according to the method" are reducible to the five unprovable arguments; this reduction constitutes the inverse of a deduction of the former on the basis of the latter. The idea resembles the one we have seen at work, in Aristotle, in the reduction of syllogisms of the first and second figure to syllogisms of the first figure. The difference is that the Stoic undertaking is much more formal, in the sense that the Stoics seem to have formulated a series of rules that govern these deductions. They called these rules *themata*, and we know that there were five of them, but we do not have explicit formulations for all five. Without going into detail here, we can get an idea of the type of rules represented by the *themata*, and of their function, by considering, for example, the following two inferences, which are examples of the first unprovable argument:

(11) If A, then (if A then B)
     A
     _____

     If A then B

and

(12) If A then B
     A
     _____

     B

The third *thema* explicitly authorizes us to replace, in (12), the premise "if A then B" by the premises of which it is the conclusion in (11). In this way we obtain the following inference, which is reduced, by the inverse route, to the first unprovable proposition:

(13) If A, then (if A then B)
     A
     _____

     B

The Stoic attitude toward modal logic is particularly innovative, especially if one considers the contribution of Chrysippus, the school's great logician. On the definition of the modal operators, the Stoics were opposed to Philon and Diodorus, but I prefer to consider here the Stoic response to Diodorus's Dominator argument. This response is not unified. We know that Cleanthus had attacked the most "physical" premise of the argument, the one that concerns the necessity of the past. Chrysippus, on the other hand, denied the validity of the "logical" premise according to which from the possible no impossible follows. He invoked the following counterexample. Let us consider the conditional

(14) If Dion is dead, the latter is dead

and examine its antecedent. When Dion is living, the proposition is false, but it can become true: it becomes true as soon as Dion dies; "Dion is dead" is thus a possible proposition. As for the consequent of (14), "the latter is dead," during Dion's life it is never true. But what happens when Dion dies? Unlike "Dion is dead," "the latter is dead" does not become true, because "the latter" is a deictic that, referring to a person, cannot be the subject of a proposition except in the presence of the person in question. Once Dion is dead, the proposition "the latter is dead" is "destroyed"; it no longer possesses the truth value "true." This proposition can never become true; it is impossible. We thus have a case of a possible from which an impossible follows.

Without going into detail here, let us simply note that Chrysippus's argument requires a distinction between what is never true (impossible) and what is always false (necessary). "The latter is dead" is never true, although without being always false, since at the moment when Dion dies, the proposition is destroyed and has no more truth value. We are perhaps in the presence of a prefiguration of the "lacunary" semantics that arouse so much interest among contemporary logicians. We cannot rule out the possibility that this distinction between impossibility and necessity, in which the first is a feebler notion than the second, allowed Chrysippus to claim that one could accept the possibility of true predictions relative to future events, even while rejecting the determinism that, according to some, this possibility would imply, according to Cicero's testimony in his *De fato*. But the Ciceronian texts are controversial, and no interpretation has won unanimous acceptance.

If Cicero is to be believed, Chrysippus was not the only one to cast doubt on a well-supported logical thesis in order to avoid determinism: Epicurus, denying the validity of the principle of bivalence for future contingent propositions, had done much worse. His idea seems to be that a contingent proposition in the future can be declared true only when its truth conditions are given, that is, the situations that make it possible to attribute to it a truth value. To go back to Aristotle's example, one cannot attribute a truth value to "Tomorrow there will be a naval battle" before one of two situations comes about: either the one that irrevocably determines the event or the one that the event itself constitutes. In this sense, the proposition is at present neither true nor false, and the principle of bivalence does not apply to it. Consequently, one cannot conclude from the truth of propositions concerning the future that the realization of the corresponding events is necessary.

Although plausible, this solution to the problem of determinism, which according to some goes all the way back to Aristotle, gave rise to ridicule and hostility among ancient authors. Cicero speaks of it scornfully, and the ancient Peripatetics carefully avoided attributing it to their master, Aristotle. Boethius reacted violently to the idea, put forward by certain Stoics, that Aristotle would have recognized limitations on the principle of bivalence in the case of future contingent propositions.

I shall conclude this brief presentation of ancient logic by mentioning one other characteristic feature of the Stoic position, found most notably in Chrysippus. As we have seen, the Megarian school was distinguished by its interest in logical parodoxes. Not only was the invention of the most important of these attributed to Eubulides, but in addition, Diodorus committed suicide, it is said, because he could not bear the shame of having been unable to solve a paradox that had been proposed to him in public. This unverifiable anecdote reflects the interest and the tension that the introduction of paradoxes had aroused, as well as the difference in attitude toward them between the Megarian and Stoic traditions, on the one hand, and the Platonic and Aristotelian traditions, on the other. Galen sets forth the latter effectively: logical paradoxes have to be studied to provide the apprentice philosopher with the means to avoid being embarrassed by false experts. To master paradoxes, all one needs is a certain skill and familiarity with the laws of correct logic.

The Stoics, especially the most ancient ones, studied paradoxes very closely. In the catalogue of Chrysippus's works that has been preserved, many treatises are devoted to sophisms; many titles, in particular, have to do with the Liar Paradox. The few allusions found in Cicero do not allow us to understand very well what solution he may have proposed for this paradox. He seems to have suggested that the crucial proposition "I am lying" is a proposition endowed with meaning, and yet that it is not capable of being qualified as true or false. If this was Chrysippus's point of view, it is easy to see that it implied a revision of one of the foundational principles of Stoic logical theory, namely, the thesis according to which every proposition is true or false. In this sense, Chrysippus's attitude is much closer to the modern perspective than the Platonico-Aristotelian tradition is. To escape from paradoxes, it does not suffice to refine one's logical competence and to ferret out linguistic and structural errors; one must resign oneself to revising certain intuitions concerning the fundamental notions of logic, for example, the notion of truth. Chrysippus seems to have embarked on this path because he was aware that at least some paradoxes, far from being captious arguments destined to embarrass the naive, translate the obscurity of certain fundamental notions and thus require, if they are to be resolved, a revision of our way of approaching them.

After the apogee of ancient Stoicism, the creative thrust of Greece in the domain of logic began to decline. On one side, the Peripatetics exhausted themselves in challenging the Stoic innovations, seeking to show that their good aspects were already present in Aristotle and that the rest was false or devoid of interest. On the other side, the Stoics seemed unaware of the rival school, and they undertook to give new foundations to the logic developed by their first masters. Their efforts succeeded in creating a sort of logical *koine*, which was crystallized in manuals and which was used even by the Stoics' critics. But the taste for innovation was fading, even if brilliant intuitions come to light here and there. One of these is certainly the solution of the problem of logical determinism that appeared in the framework of Neoplatonism, with the distinction between what is true in a determinate fashion and what is true in an indeterminate fashion. The proposition "Tomorrow there will be a naval battle" is true or false before the conditions that determine whether or not the event occurs are given. However, before those conditions are realized, the proposition is true only in an indeterminate fashion; the possibility that the contrary event will occur remains open. It is only tomorrow, when the event in question occurs or when the conditions that determine it irrevocably are met, that the proposition receives a determinate truth value: at that moment, the possibility of the contrary no longer exists. Although it is presented by authors such as Ammonius and Boethius as an interpretation of Aristotle's position, this perspective is particularly innovative, and it has important implications for the notion of possibility and the semantics of propositions.

The discussion reported by Ammonius about the possibility of quantifying the predicate of a proposition is equally interesting. Aristotle had denied the legitimacy of such a quantification; Ammonius devotes many pages to challenging its attempt at systematic development. His faithfulness to the master leads him astray here: by accepting this perspective, he would easily have arrived at a conception of relational propositions comparable to the modern conception, with immediate advantages for inferences that include such propositions. But these are only details, and they betray a lack of innovative spirit and logical creativity. A new forward thrust does not come until the high Middle Ages, when scholars gather in the Oriental legacy and develop it in profoundly original ways.

MARIO MIGNUCCI
Translated by Catherine Porter and Jeannine Pucci

Bibliography

Ackrill, John L., ed. *Aristotle: Categories and De Interpretatione, Translated with Notes and Glossary.* Oxford: Clarendon Press, 1963.

Becker, Albrecht. *Die aristotelische Theorie der Möglichkeitsschlüsse: Eine logisch-philologische Untersuchung der Kapitel 13–22 von Aristoteles Analytice Priora I.* Berlin: Jünker and Dünnhaupt, 1933.

Blanché, Robert. *La logique et son histoire, d'Aristote à Russell.* Paris: Armand Colin, 1970.

Bochenski, Innocentius M. *A History of Formal Logic.* Trans. and ed. Ivo Thomas. 2nd ed. New York: Chelsea, 1970.

Brunschwig, Jacques, ed. *Les Stoïciens et leur logique.* Paris: Vrin, 1978.

Döring, Klaus. *Die Megariker: Kommentierte Sammlung der Testimonien.* Amsterdam: Grüner, 1972.

Döring, Klaus, and Theodor Ebert, eds. *Dialektiker und Stoiker: Zur Logik der Stoa und ihrer Vorläufer.* Stuttgart: Steiner, 1993.

Frede, Michaël. *Die stoische Logik.* Göttingen: Vandenhoeck and Ruprecht, 1974.

Hintikka, Jaakko. *Time and Necessity: Studies in Aristotle's Theory of Modality.* Oxford: Clarendon Press, 1973.

Hülser, Karlheinz. *Die Fragmente zur Dialektik der Stoiker.* 4 vols. Stuttgart: Frommann-Holzboog, 1987–1988.

Kneale, William, and Martha Kneale. *The Development of Logic*. Oxford: Clarendon Press, 1962.

Lear, Jonathan. *Aristotle and Logical Theory*. Cambridge: Cambridge University Press, 1980.

Lukasiewicz, Jan. *Aristotle's Syllogistic from the Standpoint of Modern Formal Logic*. 2nd ed. Oxford: Clarendon Press, 1957.

Mates, Benson. *Stoic Logic*. 2nd ed. Berkeley: University of California Press, 1961.

Mignucci, Mario. *Il significato della logical stoica*. 2nd ed. Bologna: Pàtron, 1967.

Mignucci, Mario, ed. *Aristotele: Gli analitici primi. Traduzione, introduzione, commento*. Naples: Loffredo, 1969.

Muller, Robert. *Les Mégariques: Fragments et témoignages*. Paris: Vrin, 1985.

Nortmann, Ulrich. *Modale Syllogismen, mögliche Welten, Essentialismus: Eine Analyse der aristotelischen Modallogik*. Berlin: De Gruyter, 1996.

Patzig, Günther. *Aristotle's Theory of Syllogism*. Trans. Jonathan Barnes. Dordrecht: Reidel, 1968.

Ross, W. D., ed. *Aristotle's Prior and Posterior Analytics: A Revised Text with Introduction and Commentary*. Oxford: Clarendon Press, 1949.

Thom, Paul. *The Logic of Essentialism: An Interpretation of Aristotle's Modal Syllogistic*. Boston: Kluwer, 1996.

Vuillemin, Jules. *Nécessité ou contingence: L'aporie de Diodore et les systèmes philosophiques*. Paris: Editions de Minuit, 1984.

Weidemann, Hermann, ed. *Aristoteles: Peri Hermeneias, übersetz und erläutert*. Berlin: Akademie Verlag, 1994.

Related Articles

Epistemology; Aristotle; Stoicism; Language; Aristotelianism

MATHEMATICS

To THE ANCIENT GREEKS we owe the notion of mathematics as a form of theoretical knowledge, a body of propositions arranged in a deductively ordered sequence. In this conception, the project of geometry is not the manipulation of figures in physical constructions but the understanding of their properties in pure thought. The transition from *praxis* to *theōria*—from mathematics as *technē* (techniques for dealing with practical activities) to mathematics as *epistēmē* and *gnōsis* (a form of pure knowledge)—occurred only once in human history, namely, among the classical Greeks. No earlier mathematical tradition gives evidence of such a theoretical dimension, and where one encounters mathematical theory among later traditions, it is in the context of some manner of borrowing from the ancient Greek precedent, either through translation of texts or through personal contacts. But already at the time of Plato, ca. 370 B.C.E., as we see in mathematical passages such as *Republic* 510c–d, this shift, with the accompanying emphasis on deductive reasoning in mathematics, could be taken as given and cited as a paradigm toward the rigorization of epistemology in general.

In the following account I shall attempt to trace out the developing relation of the two strands, the technical and the philosophical. It is well to bear in mind, however, that our principal documents, the Greek mathematical treatises, patterned on the model of Euclid's *Elements,* are directed toward the exposition of technical subject matter. Although executed with a sophisticated sense of the demands of demonstrative method, they are not formal foundational efforts as such and only rarely and obliquely address issues of an explicitly metamathematical sort. In this regard, their situation is hardly different from that of textbooks in any mathematical field today, but it must condition any project that seeks to reconstruct the character and origins of the theoretical sensibility itself among the ancients.

ORIGINS

In the modern conception of mathematics, practical forms like commercial arithmetic and surveying geometry are taken to be but a prelude to the essential forms of mathematics. The progression from such applied forms to the corresponding abstract fields may be viewed either as pedagogical or as conceptual. But it is reasonable to see a chronological element as well: that the earliest forms of mathematical activity in any given culture would be of this practical sort, only later developing from this into theory.

Remarkably, those Greeks who speak of the origins of mathematics pass over the essential issue of the timing, manner, and intent of the earliest reorientation from practice toward theory. Instead, they are more concerned with the origins of mathematical technique, that is, the first discoveries of specific technical results. One typical account assigns the first geometry to Egyptian surveyors, compelled to reestablish property markers after the Nile floods; Proclus maintains this, and passages from Herodotus and other early authorities indicate the likely tradition Proclus here relied on. In just this way, according to Proclus, the precise knowledge of numbers *(tōn arithmōn akribēs gnōsis)* took its start among the Phoenicians' activities in commerce and exchange. At the same time, Proclus projects certain interpretive conceptions of his own, for he observes: "It is not at all surprising that the discovery both of this (sc. geometry) and the other sciences *(epistēmai)* commenced from need *(chreia)*, since everything in *genesis* proceeds by moving from the incomplete *(ateles)* to the complete *(teleion)*. It is thus reasonable that the transformation *(metabasis)* would occur from perception *(aisthēsis)* to reckoning *(logismos)* and from this to mind *(nous)*."

Despite Proclus's Neoplatonist gloss, his view of theory as developing out of practice seems reasonable, and there is some evidence, albeit quite slender, corroborating it. Presumably, the oldest forms of arithmetic inquiry grew out of practical activities, such as commerce. Still, Proclus's citation of the Phoenicians as the precedent for the Greeks raises questions, since we possess little information on how the early Greeks did arithmetic, and that does not necessarily point to borrowings from the Levant.

Two different numeral systems were already current among the Greeks before the middle of the 5th century B.C.E., as attested in inscriptions. The more primitive system, sometimes called acrophonic, since some of its numerals are formed from the initial letters of the corresponding number words, follows the base-ten additive principle, much like the Egyptian hieroglyphic system and the Roman numeral system. This mode quickly becomes unwieldy for representing large numbers, however, and has little value for the execution of arithmetic operations. It appears that such numerals served their primary function as recording symbols, where the computations could be performed via abacus. More than a dozen specimens of abacus survive from the classical period to support this view.

Alternatively, in what is sometimes called the Herodian system, the Greeks represented numbers via the letters of the alphabet: to represent each of the initial values from 1 to 9, they used in sequence the first nine letters (with the archaic *digamma* inserted in sixth position); for the next range, by tens from 10 to 90 they used the next nine letters (with archaic *qoppa* in ninth position), and for the hundreds, the remaining nine letters (with archaic *sampi* last). This scheme is extended to higher numbers by special marks: for thousands, a stroke is prefixed to the corresponding digit symbol, from 1 to 9, while for multiples of 10,000 the symbol M (for *myrias*) is written with the appropriate numeral as superscript. For still higher values, a variety of schemes were introduced, but, as one would expect, the contexts demanding these were rare and specialized. For instance, Theon of Alexandria (4th century C.E.) requires third-order myriads (signified by the symbol MMM) to work out his computation of the volume of the earth in cubic stades.

Modern critics, familiar with the so-called Hindu-Arabic numerals that utilize a more powerful place system, typically underestimate the computational capacity of the Greeks' alphabetical scheme. But in practice, the arithmetic operations are performed in this system little differently than in a place system. It would be difficult to insist that Greek arithmetic, whether practical or theoretical, was hindered in any way by this alphabetical mode during the span of twelve centuries when it was prevalent. Since the Greek alphabet is certainly derived from the Phoenicians, one might naturally suppose that the alphabetical numeral system traced back to the same source. This is Proclus's view, as we have seen, perhaps for this very reason, and it may be correct. But confirmation from old Phoenician inscriptions is wanting. When the same alphabetical mode (in Semitic characters) is attested in Semitic inscriptions, it is in the Hellenistic period, apparently under the influence of Greek precedents.

In terms of the most elementary forms of arithmetical training, the Greeks appear to have been directly influenced by Egyptian models. Plato cites with approval the Egyptian practice of employing games to teach children the arithmetic procedures (*Laws* 819b). Certain computational methods, attested in Greek papyri from the Hellenistic period onward, are hardly distinguishable from those in the oldest surviving Egyptian papyri from the middle of the second millennium B.C.E. Most striking is the technique of computing with fractions, where values are expressed in terms of sums of unit-fractional parts; for instance, the equivalent of $\frac{2}{7}$ is written as 4'28' (that is, $\frac{1}{4} + \frac{1}{28}$). This same mode persists among the Greeks, even after the introduction of a more flexible general mode of fractions (of form p/q).

A correspondingly early link with Mesopotamian numerical methods is difficult to discern. Already within the Old Babylonian dynasties (early second millennium B.C.E.), a sexagesimal place system was developed for carrying out the arithmetic operations. This powerful innovation, however, seems long to have had no circulation outside Mesopotamia and to have reached the Greeks not before the 2nd century B.C.E. Even then, the Greeks adopted it only within the special field of astronomical computation (see below), which doubtless was the context of its transmission to them. Some special areas of number theory have counterparts in Mesopotamian documents. In particular, a remarkable tablet from the Old Babylonian period (Plimpton 322 at Columbia University) lists numbers related to fifteen cases of so-called rational triples (integers a, b, c such that $a^2 + b^2 = c^2$) in a manner that indicates awareness of a general rule for their formation. Among the Greeks the same numbers, including their formation rules, are found in Euclid, Diophantus, and the Neopythagorean arithmetics, and may well have been known in the classical period, perhaps through transmission from Eastern sources. But the time and manner of this transmission, if such is the case, has not been determined.

A similar ambiguity attends speculation on the origins of geometry. A powerful set of geometric techniques are documented in Mesopotamian sources. And it happens that geometric identities of the same form are set out in Euclid's Book II (e.g., propositions 5 and 6), and they are applied in Euclid's *Data* and Diophantus's *Arithmetica*. Such coincidences suggest a Mesopotamian source for this part of the early Greek geometry, as Solomon Gandz, Otto Neugebauer, and B. L. van der Waerden have argued. Acceptance of this proposal, however, has been far from unanimous.

How is the question of transmission to be resolved? It would seem reasonable that geometric techniques of this kind were transmitted to the Greeks by Egyptian teachers—who in their turn were indebted to an even earlier transmission from the older Mesopotamian tradition. Encountering this tradition in Egypt in the 5th century, Greek scholars would naturally take it to be a native tradition.

PYTHAGOREANS AND ELEATICS

In describing the earliest phases of Greek mathematical theory, both ancient and modern commentators typically turn to Pythagoras and his school. It is maintained, according to the account in Iamblichus, that when the Samian, expelled from his home city for political reasons, completed travels in Babylon and Egypt, he established his base at Croton in Magna Graecia and there founded an ascetic community devoted to studies in philosophy, theology, politics, cosmology, and mathematics. Proclus credits Pythagoras for founding the philosophical curriculum on mathematics and for abstracting geometry from its concrete manifestations. But he is here apparently only glossing a line taken from Iamblichus: "Pythagoras converted the philosophy of geometry into the figure of a liberal education, by examining its principles from above and investigating its theorems both immaterially [*ahylōs*] and conceptually [*noērōs*]" (ed. Friedlein, 65.16–19). However prominent a reputation the Pythagoreans have come to acquire, the most reliable evidence of early Greek mathematics does not easily sustain such a view. In the case of Proclus's testimony, for instance, this commentator, who has no reason at all to underrate the Pythagorean role, assigns to Pythagoras only two geometric findings: "He discovered the subject of the irrationals and the construction of the cosmic figures." But even this is dubious, since it anachronistically assigns to Pythagoras what appear to be later studies of the irrationals and the construction of the regular solids.

The prominence of the Pythagoreans thus appears to be a historical construct fostered by Neoplatonists like Iamblichus and Proclus, who conceived the Pythagoreans as prototypes of their own Neoplatonism. Surveying the testimonia most likely to be based on the oldest accounts, such as Aristotle and Eudemus, one can attribute to the Pythagoreans a relatively modest core of mathematical study: a central core of arithmetic studies, together with a few related studies in geometry and its applications in cosmology and the theory of nature.

In arithmetic the Pythagoreans inquired into the properties of number, such as odd and even numbers, figured numbers (e.g., triangular and square numbers), and the like. Certain results of this sort appear to have been examined via quasi-geometric configurations in which the units of the numbers are figured as points (or marks, such as the letter *alpha*), perhaps inspired by the pebble counters *(psēphoi)* used in the abacus.

The early Pythagorean arithmetic also embraced studies of ratios and their application to the harmonic intervals, for instance, that the interval of the octave *(dia pasōn)* is expressible by the ratio $2 : 1$, the fifth *(dia pente)* by $3 : 2$, the fourth *(dia tessarōn)* by $4 : 3$, and the whole tone by $9 : 8$. These are plainly set out in a fragment from Philolaus (late 5th century B.C.E.), although they are likely to relate to earlier studies, perhaps by Pythagoras himself. In the more elaborate scheme developed by the Pythagorean Archytas of Tarentum early in the 4th century B.C.E., the consonant intervals are associated with epimoric ratios (that is, those of form $n + 1 : n$), and he establishes that subdivision of any such interval (most notably, the whole tone interval $9 : 8$) into equal half intervals is impossible arithmetically.

However modest this body of arithmetic results may seem, one must recognize that they already partake of that important transition we are examining: these are researches into *arithmētikē* in the theoretical sense, the properties of numbers purely as such, rather than of numbers taken to be the measures of bodies or objects of one sort or another.

For the Pythagoreans, arithmetic became a template for inquiring into cosmology and the theory of nature. Their view is encapsulated by Aristotle in the slogan, "All is number." But its meaning, if indeed one may rightly assign it to the Pythagoreans, is ambiguous. On some accounts, it has been interpreted to entail a form of "number atomism" in which pebble configurations of the type illustrated above might be extended into representations of all physical bodies. Some such notion may be intended in an obscure testimonium relating to the Pythagorean Ecphantus. But Aristotle seems to have in mind a more general concept: that the structural relations among things can be expressed in terms of numerical ratios. One might suppose that such an association of mathematics within reasoning about nature might sponsor concerns over the logical coherence of mathematical claims and their validation. But Aristotle's examples of Pythagorean applications of mathematics do not support this view, for much of Pythagorean speculation is mere numerology: the *tetraktys* (the number 10 figured as a triangular array, $1 + 2 + 3 + 4$) symbolizes health and perfection, 4 represents justice, and so on. Aristotle even seems to ridicule certain applications of this scheme, as when he criticizes the Pythagoreans for introducing a hypothetical planet to bring the number of heavenly bodies up to ten.

In the historical sources, a few direct attributions of geometric results are made to Pythagoreans. To them, according to Proclus, Eudemus assigns the theorem that the sum of the angles in a triangle equals two right angles. Proclus and others know of traditions that ascribe to Pythagoras himself the theorem that in any right triangle the square of the hypotenuse equals the sum of the squares of the two sides adjacent to the right angle. But in Plutarch this attribution occurs in the context of a dubious anecdote: that Pythagoras sacrificed an ox in celebration of the discovery of the "famous figure" (*periklees gramma; Moralia* 1094b). Plutarch himself is uncertain whether the anecdote relates to the theorem on the hypotenuse or to the technique of area application. Even worse, Pythagoras would hardly have celebrated any such discovery in this way, given that his reform of Greek cultic practice focused on the abolition of animal sacrifice.

A few testimonia assign to Pythagoreans the construction of regular polygons, in particular the pentagon (a symbol of special significance in the group), as well as the regular dodecahedron. Following the pattern of Euclid's construction of the pentagon, one sees the connection to the "area application" technique which, as we have seen, Eudemus assigns to the "Pythagorean Muse," and through this a possible link to older Mesopotamian methods.

One special field of early geometry deserves further comment. Some time after Pythagoras, researchers in his following became aware of the phenomenon of the "irrational" (*arrhēton*) among geometric magnitudes. According to one later tradition, a certain Pythagorean was penalized by death in shipwreck for making this knowledge public, and some have argued this Pythagorean to be Hippasus of Metapontum, elsewhere reported to have perished by drowning for claiming the discovery of the construction of the dodecahedron as his own. This inference is not assured, however, and even so, the manner and timing of the first discovery of the irrational would remain, as they have, a subject for vigorous debate.

Kurt von Fritz has proposed that the irrational was first recognized by Hippasus through the construction of the regular pentagon (namely, the figure that forms the faces of the regular dodecahedron), for the diagonal d and side s of the pentagon satisfy the extreme and mean ratio, that is, $s + d : d = d : s$, so that $s + d$ and d can be made, respectively, the diagonal and side of a larger pentagon. The construction can be extended in the same proportion either in the upward direction (by successively adding the side and diagonal to form the new diagonal), or alternatively, downward (by subtracting: $d : s = s : d - s$, and so on). In the latter case, one realizes that the possibility of continuing the sequence, to produce ever smaller pentagons, conflicts with any supposition that the initial ratio $d : s$ could equal a ratio of integers; for the successive reduction of integers is necessarily bounded by the unit, and so cannot continue indefinitely. This subtractive procedure, called *anthyphairesis* (or the Euclidean division algorithm, in modern parlance), is the foundation of Euclid's arithmetic theory (Books VII and X), being his means for constructing the greatest common measure of given integers or of given commensurable magnitudes. Prima facie, then, it would not seem unreasonable that this same method underlay the early studies of the ratio of the side and diagonal of the pentagon.

However attractive this reconstruction may seem, it lacks support in the sources. The earliest extant accounts relating to the irrational, in mathematical passages in Plato and Aristotle, never mention the pentagon in this regard but invariably focus on the diagonal and side of the square as the paradigmatic case. For instance, Plato speaks of the "rational and irrational diameters of the pentad" (*Rep.* 546c), meaning 7 and $\sqrt{50}$, respectively, and one may infer in this an oblique reference to a numerical procedure for generating an indefinite sequence of such values—the so-called side and diameter numbers, described by the later Neopythagorean writer Theon of Smyrna (ca. 100 C.E.), that is, (1,1), (2,3), (5,7), . . ., (s,d), $(s + d, 2s + d)$, and so on. As the very terminology reveals, the ancients realized that each pair $s : d$ provides an approximation to the ratio of the side and diameter of the square (i.e., $1 : \sqrt{2}$), although no proof—at best only the ingredients for one—is transmitted in the accounts surviving from Theon, Iamblichus, and Proclus. Associated with this, also indicated in Plato's terminology, is that the limiting value $1 : \sqrt{2}$ is "irrational" *(arrhētos)*.

No explicit proof of this incommensurability survives in early sources. But Aristotle alludes to a proof in which the hypothesis of rationality reduces to an impossibility: that the same numbers will be even and odd. A proof of this form is presented among materials appended to Book X of Euclid's *Elements.*

It seems reasonable that the earliest encounter with the irrational followed a pattern comparable to the proof known to Aristotle. It could not have been *discovered* according to this logical format, however, since reasoning by contradiction begins with the explicit statement of the proposition as already known. A geometric configuration seems possible in which the subdivision of the square, as in Plato's *Meno* 82b–85b, leads to ever smaller squares, always preserving the same ratio as the initial side and diameter. Supposing numerical values for both the initial side and diameter, one finds that both these values are even, as are the sides and diameters of *all* the smaller squares derived from them by successive halving. One would realize, however, that any finite number permits of being bisected only finitely many times. A geometric reasoning of this sort would elicit, as if by accident, an awareness of the paradox entailed by assuming numerical values for the side and diameter, and through this realization one could begin to consolidate the reasoning in light of an explicit concept of the "irrational."

Toward the close of the 5th century the knowledge of irrationals was extended. Archytas's theorem that no epimoric interval can be bisected by a numerical term — that is, that no integer is the mean proportional between two numbers that have the ratio $n + 1 : n$ — entails a geometric corollary: that the line constructed as mean proportional between lines in an epimoric ratio must be incommensurable with those lines. Although we cannot say whether Archytas actually proposed such a geometric corollary, the manner of its construction and proof would generalize immediately to the theorem that the mean proportional between any two lines whose ratio is not a ratio of square numbers is incommensurable with those lines. Some scholia assign this theorem (an equivalent to *Elements* X.9) to Plato's younger contemporary Theaetetus. Indeed Plato (*Theaetetus* 147c–148a) describes how the young Theaetetus inferred a form of the same theorem as he contemplated a more limited result presented by his teacher Theodorus of Cyrene: that the *dynamis* (that is, square) of 3 feet, for instance, and that of 5, and so on, each has a side that is incommensurable with the unit foot; by stopping at 17 (for reasons unstated in the account) Theodorus left open the description of the whole class of incommensurables entailed by this construction, the project completed by Theaetetus.

Reconstructions of Theodorus's procedure abound, for Plato presents no technical details of the proof beyond the enumeration of the cases. However, inferring from a dramatic episode of this sort, the actual history of these researches is problematic, since Plato's dialectical intent (showing how Theaetetus articulates the general definition under the suggestion of Theodorus's recitation of cases) is clear. Since the discovery of incommensurability most likely arose in the context of the special case of the side and diameter of the square, it is not unreasonable that the first extensions of this discovery would likewise have involved special cases. If Plato's passage does not warrant assigning to Theodorus a role within this transitional research, however, then we have no documentation for assigning any name to it at all.

In view of this limited basis of Pythagorean mathematics, some accounts have looked elsewhere for the emergence of a deductive sensibility. One approach, initiated by Paul Tannery (1887) and modified by Helmut Hasse and Heinrich Scholz (1928), supposes that the discovery of irrationality provoked a "foundations crisis" that stimulated research into the logical basis of geometric theory, culminating in the rigorous methods of limits and proportions instituted by Eudoxus. A variant of this view, set out by Árpád Szabó, locates the stimulus toward rigor, as well as the intuition of the "anti-empiri-cal," in the Eleatic paradoxes. To Parmenides, according to this account, one must assign the development, indeed the very invention, of indirect reason-ing. For by inferring the inadmissible, that "what-is-not is," from hypotheses about the reality of change, difference, plurality, inhomogeneity, and the like, Parmenides presumed to establish the invalidity of those hypotheses, that is, that "what-is" must be eternal, immutable, altogether homogeneous, and one. Similarly, Zeno argued that the conventional suppositions about plural-ity and motion lead to contradictions: if there is a plurality, then being is at once infinitely great and infinitely small (frg. B1–2); if there is motion, then the finite stretch would require infinite time to traverse (the "dichotomy" and the "Achilles"), the moving body would be at rest (the "arrow"), and the dou-ble speed would equal the half speed (the "moving rows"). In these paradoxes, not only is the technique of *reductio ad absurdum* forged into an instrument for reasoning, but also the fundamental concepts of mathematics—number, magnitude, infinite divisibility—come under scrutiny. Accordingly, Szabó at-tempts to construct a path from the early Pythagorean arithmetic studies, un-der the pressure of Eleatic criticisms, to the expounding of dialectical method by Plato, ultimately to the theoretical synthesis in Euclid's *Elements*.

Hypotheses of this type must be judged on their intrinsic plausibility, for explicit support from mathematical documentation in the pre-Euclidean pe-riod is lacking. It is remarkable, however, that none of the ancient discussions of early mathematics, including the accounts in Proclus and the Neopythago-reans, assigns to the Eleatics any role in the development of mathematics as such. Moreover, if Szabó finds it most appropriate to focus on early arithmetic for the first systematization of patterns of proof, it is a puzzle that the major development of theory actually occurs in geometry. Indeed, the arithmetic works nearest to the tradition of Pythagorean arithmetic—the introductions by Nicomachus and Iamblichus—display no proof structure at all.

Such accounts all share the notion that the impulse toward formulating, scrutinizing, and tightening proofs must have come from outside the mathe-matical field. It is true that a mathematical tradition might adhere to practical techniques without producing a systematic structure of validation (as witness the Egyptian and Mesopotamian traditions). But this need not always be the case. If we can imagine, for instance, how certain Greek geometers, examining the familiar construction for doubling the square, could suddenly realize the paradox involved in supposing that both the side and diameter had integer values, then the project of working out a proof would follow simply from the impulse to make sense of this discovery. Thus, some form of proof structure, however tentative, could be occasioned as a consequence of the earliest explo-ration of incommensurables.

Organizing the larger domains of geometry did not occur all at once. It was the result of an evolution that spanned at least a century and a half between the Pythagoreans (if we place the beginning of this movement with them) and Euclid, and the interactions with more general philosophical inquiries seem always to have been subtle and bilateral. Moreover, explaining the rise of proof in mathematics via the impetus of Presocratic speculations in philosophy must assume that the emergence of theory and proof in the latter context is well understood. This is far from clear, however. Inquiries into Presocratic modes of reasoning, most notably by G. E. R. Lloyd, have grounded its characteristic emphasis on techniques of validation in the special political circumstances of classical Greece (e.g., the emergence of the polis and the relatively open forms of political interaction entailed by it). Within such an environment the simultaneous emergence of concerns over justification in mathematics and philosophy would seem as plausibly assignable to a parallel response to such political and social stimuli, as to a specific unilateral influence of the one discipline on the other. In any event, it seems that the proper investigation of this question must assimilate the methodological developments in all areas—mathematics, science, medicine, and philosophy—without presupposing a predominant influence by any one of them on the others.

IONIANS

Other than Pythagoras, Proclus names only six figures as being distinguished for geometry in the period before Plato: Thales of Miletus; Ameristus, brother of the poet Stesichorus; Anaxagoras of Clazomenae; Oenopides of Chios; Hippocrates of Chios; and Theodorus of Cyrene. This bare outline can be filled out in a few instances by means of testimony from other commentators.

According to Proclus, Thales was first to recognize that the circle is bisected by its diameter, that the base angles of isosceles triangles are equal, and that the vertical angles formed by the intersection of two lines are equal. But in the case of the theorem that two triangles having two of their angles and the included side equal are congruent (I.26), which, according to Proclus, Eudemus said was necessary for Thales' reported determination of the distance of ships at sea (ed. Friedlein, 352), one sees that the attribution is conjectural even on Eudemus's part. Moreover, in the light of the triangulation techniques employed in Egyptian teachings, which Thales presumably would have known, a more efficient method based on similar triangles was available to him. Proclus (and Eudemus, for that matter) are also misleading in these instances in suggesting that Thales had somehow *proved* forms of the corresponding Euclidean propositions. Thales' understanding probably did not go beyond the awareness of certain geometric properties and measuring techniques.

Proclus assigns to Oenopides the constructions of the line perpendicular to a given line from a given point "as being useful for astronomy" (*Elements*

I.12) and the construction of an angle equal to a given angle (I.23). Oenopides also figured the inclination of the ecliptic via the construction of the fifteen-sided regular polygon (Theon of Smyrna, ed. Hiller, 198). Hippocrates is noted for his reduction of the problem of cube duplication to finding two mean proportionals (cited by Proclus, ed. Friedlein, 213; and by Eratosthenes, as reported by Eutocius, *In Archimedem*, ed. Heiberg, III.88). On Hippocrates' quadratures of the lunes (figures bounded by two circular arcs) we possess a long fragment from Eudemus, as presented by Simplicius in his commentary *Physics* (ed. Heiberg, 60–68).

Hippocrates' quadrature of lunes indicates a fully developed geometric format. Regrettably, the substantial fragment preserved by Simplicius from Eudemus's *History* includes Simplicius's own glosses, contaminating the older text with citations of Euclid. Beyond that, it would be impossible to determine how Eudemus himself (or a prior authority) had modified Hippocrates' treatment. Nevertheless, this fragment reveals a high level of technical expertise as well as a fully articulated scheme of demonstration, with a regularized geometric terminology. In the first and simplest of the four cases examined, a right isosceles triangle is inscribed in a semicircle, and on its base a circular segment is drawn similar to each of the segments formed between the semicircle and the legs of the triangle. Then, since this larger segment equals the sum of both of the smaller segments, adding to each the part of the triangle lying above the larger segment, one finds that the lune (bounded between the two circular arcs) equals the triangle.

The constructions of the next two cases are more complicated, and each includes the proof that the outer bounding arc of the lune is greater or less, respectively, than a semicircle. In the final case, the lune, taken together with a given hexagon, is shown to equal the circle circumscribed about the hexagon.

This fragment thus displays the basic geometric manner fully actualized: figures are constructed and their properties are stated and proved in proper logical sequence. Certain necessary results are explicitly postulated on the basis of prior proved results (e.g., that similar segments of circles are to each other as their bases in square; cf. *Elements* XII.2); many results are assumed in the course of the proofs—e.g., the so-called Pythagorean theorem on right triangles and its extension. One presumes that the exposition of these results could be accepted from Hippocrates' own collection of "Elements," cited by Proclus, which must have embraced much of Euclid's account of rectilinear and circular figures in *Elements* Books I, III, and VI.

As Eudemus observes, Hippocrates' constructions are of interest for their connection to the circle quadrature. Not only are the lunes, as figures bounded by circular arcs, comparable to the circle itself, but also the fourth case of lune, where it is equatable with a given rectilinear figure, would yield a quadrature of the circle, since their difference, the hexagon, is a given rectilinear figure. Hippocrates' position on the circle quadrature is difficult to construe. But in his fourth construction Hippocrates has indeed *reduced* the problem of circle quadrature to that of squaring a particular lune. His handling of the problem of cube duplication is precisely in this manner: not solving it as such, Hippocrates instead reduces it to another problem, that of finding two mean proportionals between given lines. This reductive strategy for dealing with more difficult problems itself may be considered an important methodological development, as a preliminary form of the method of analysis.

In sum, by the close of the 5th century B.C.E. the field of geometry known to Hippocrates already has taken the form of a deductively ordered science. It has matured well beyond the elementary level to include many results and methods more advanced than anything suggested in the contemporaneous nontechnical literature, such as the mathematical passages in the Presocratics or Plato.

Proclus's account of the early group of geometers notably omits any mention of Parmenides or Zeno, Democritus, or any of the Sophists. As discussed above, the Eleatic critiques of the common conceptions of plurality, magnitude, and motion in principle ought to have had implications for the emergence of mathematical theory. Apparently, the mathematical authorities consulted by Proclus did not describe them as influencing the historical development of the field. The doxographers assign several mathematical writings to Democritus, and he is cited for two geometric theorems (that the pyramid and cone equal a third of the corresponding prism and cylinder, respectively). The most significant fragment of mathematical bearing, however, deals with the following paradox. Does the parallel sectioning of a cone yield consecutive sections that are equal or unequal? If unequal, then the surface of the cone would be irregular and jagged, but if equal, then the cone would not differ from the cylinder, in being composed of equal circular sections. Although the conception adumbrated here of sectioning figures into parallel indivisible components becomes a powerful heuristic method for finding their measures, as one encounters it with Archimedes, for instance, and also with Cavalieri, Kepler, and others in the 17th century, this fragment does not indicate that Democritus made any technical use of it.

As for the Sophists, Antiphon and Bryson are criticized by Aristotle for fallacious arguments on the circle quadrature. Antiphon supposed that by inscribing a regular polygon in the circle and then successively doubling the number of sides, eventually the polygon would merge with the circle, as its sides became indistinguishable from the corresponding arcs. Bryson compared the circle with the sequences of inscribed and circumscribed regular polygons, arguing that since each polygon is quadrable, then the quadrable figure that is greater than every inscribed figure and less than every circumscribed figure would equal the circle. These arguments, although defective as solutions of the circle quadrature, turn on conceptions of limiting polygonal sequences that become significant in the work of Eudoxus, Euclid, and Archimedes.

Ultimately, the notion that the Eleatics or Democritus or the Sophists played a central role in the development of early Greek mathematics rests entirely on modern interpretations and reconstructions. The various fragments and testimonia bearing on the issue indicate that mathematical conceptions did occasionally get taken up within the philosophical speculations of these thinkers, as they elaborated their major theories of being, knowledge, and perception. But Proclus, our most extensive source on the early history, makes no claim that such inquiries directly influenced the historical development of mathematics, and nothing in the extant mathematical literature would justify that claim. It is the case, however, that the paradoxes we have mentioned from Democritus, Antiphon, Bryson, and others, as well as the Eleatics, indicate that the subject matter of geometry was drawn into the philosophical discourse for dialectical scrutiny. In effect, geometry becomes susceptible in this period to the same intellectual stresses that affect the development of philosophy more generally. Following proposals by G. E. R. Lloyd, one may look toward the general political environment within the classical Greek poleis, and particularly that of 5th-century Athens, as fostering this trend toward explicit justification strategies in philosophy on one side, and in geometry on the other.

MATHEMATICS AND THE ACADEMY

In the latter half of his survey of Euclid's precursors, Proclus begins with Plato, described as having stimulated mathematical study through his frequent inclusion of mathematical passages in his works and his effort "everywhere to awaken wonder about this subject among students of philosophy." Proclus next names three contemporaries of Plato, Archytas of Tarentum, Theaetetus of Athens, and Leodamas of Thasos, who "increased the theorems and put them into a more systematic arrangement." He then provides notes on ten other geometers, of whom Eudoxus of Cnidus and his followers are most prominent, and concluding with Plato's associate Philip of Mende (presumably the same as Philip of Opus), who "at Plato's instructions took on the project of researching those things that he thought would contribute to Plato's philosophy."

The clear impression of Proclus's account is that the entire development of geometry in the century before Euclid was dominated by Plato's institution, for he remarks that "all these pursued their collaborative researches with each other in the Academy." Modern accounts tend to follow the same line of interpretation. But the fact that this very view is one that we would naturally expect from Proclus's Neoplatonism recommends caution. It can be supported from Plato's friendship with Archytas, whose work seems to underlie a geometrical passage of *The Republic* (528b–d) and the harmonic doctrines of *Timaeus,* and Plato apparently held Theaetetus as an intimate friend, remembered as a central character in *Theaetetus* and *Sophist.* But the situation with Eudoxus is less clear: although the later testimonia describe him as a disciple of Plato's, Eudoxus established in his own right a prominent school of technical studies at Cyzicus that was hardly a mere offshoot of the Academy. But Proclus is surely right in assigning special significance to the work of Theaetetus and Eudoxus, for, as the following summary indicates, their discoveries stimulated researches fundamental for a major part of Euclid's *Elements.*

Theaetetus was most noted for advancing the study of irrational lines. By definition, lines are "commensurable" when they have a common measuring line, that is, when they have a ratio expressible in terms of integers; equivalently, the squares on these lines have a ratio of square integers. Taking any two lines whose squares are commensurable to each other but whose lengths are not (that is, lines whose squares have a ratio in integers that are not both squares), Theaetetus showed that certain combinations of the lines—specifically, their geometric, arithmetic, and harmonic means—are not commensurable with the given lines in square. Theaetetus's work does not survive, but Euclid's Book X transmits a theory of irrational lines that develops from it.

The paradigm case of lines that do not fit into this condition are the diameter and side of the regular pentagon inscribed in a circle of unit radius; these satisfy the conditions of Euclid's fourth class of irrationals, the major and minor, respectively. The actual case of the side of the pentagon, proven to be a minor irrational, is given in XIII.11. This theorem bears directly on the construction of the regular dodecahedron (*Elements* XIII.17). From certain testimonia one infers that Theaetetus wrote on the construction of the five regular solids, a presumptive source for Euclid in Book XIII of the *Elements.*

The theory of irrationals presupposes a general theory of the divisibility of integers, such as that presented in Euclid's Book VII. The basic conception here is that of relatively prime numbers, being those that possess no common measure other than the unit. For determining the greatest common measure of given integers, Euclid employs the procedure of continued subtraction of terms and remainders (termed the Euclidean division algorithm in modern textbooks), whose Euclidean term is *anthyphairesis.* On this basis one can establish the basic theory of numerical proportion and from this, important general theorems on divisibility, such as that relatively prime numbers are the least of those having the same ratio (VII.21); that any number relatively prime to two numbers is relatively prime also to their product (VII.24); that any prime number that measures a product of two numbers measures one or both of those numbers (VII.30).

Bridging the theory of numbers and the theory of irrationals is the procedure of *anthyphairesis*, which in Euclid's Book X becomes the condition for determining the greatest common measure of commensurable magnitudes. From a passage in Aristotle's *Topics* (158b29) one infers that this procedure (here called *antanairesis*) was adopted for defining proportionality among magnitudes and for proving that a line drawn parallel to the sides of a parallelogram divides its area and base proportionately. The appearance of this definition indicates awareness that a theory of proportion established in terms of integers would not be adequate for the purposes of studying ratios of geometric magnitudes, given the existence of incommensurable magnitudes.

Sensitivity for foundational issues especially marks the work of Eudoxus. His primary work is in the measurement of curvilinear figures, like the circle and sphere, to which the basic results obtained for rectilinear figures do not immediately apply. One knows, for instance, that Hippocrates assumed that circles are to each other as their diameters in square. But a valid proof of this theorem would require some form of limiting procedure, such as that implied in the paradoxes of Antiphon and Bryson, in which sequences of regular polygons can be taken in relation to the circle. By a special manner of demonstration (termed misleadingly in modern accounts the method of exhaustion) Eudoxus showed that, by hypothesizing the negation of the property for the given figures, one could construct certain rectilinear figures that, although they are known to have the property in question, by being taken sufficiently close to the given figures, must also satisfy the negation. In this way, one obtains a logically correct proof based strictly on finitistic lines. The Euclidean theorems that circles are as the squares on their diameters (XII.2), that spheres are in the third power of their diameters (XII.16−18), and that pyramids and cones are one-third of the prisms and cylinders, respectively, having the same altitude and base (XII.5−7, 10), appear to represent the basic mode adopted by Eudoxus.

Similarly Euclid's Book V, presenting the general geometric theory of proportions, seems to develop out of a new theory proposed by Eudoxus. On the model of the exhaustion technique, one sees that a theorem on proportions can be established in the indirect manner, by assuming the negation and constructing commensurable magnitudes that, while having the property in question, nevertheless must also satisfy the negation. In the Euclidean version this conception is regularized in a modified form (V.Def. 5): four magnitudes are said to be in proportion, i.e., $A : B = C : D$, when for any integers m, n it is the case that mA and mC are simultaneously greater than nB, nD, or equal to them, or less than them. By this definition, one both finesses the difficulties posed by the existence of incommensurable magnitudes and also excludes the problematic case of indivisible magnitudes. Modern critics invariably praise this definition as an astute forerunner of the modern definition of "real number," as worked out by R. Dedekind and C. Weierstrass in the 19th century. Certainly Eudoxus must receive credit for the underlying conception of the Euclidean definition, possibly formulated in an indirect manner comparable to the proofs by exhaustion in *Elements*, Book XII. But the proofs of the propositions in Book V are sometimes badly managed, so that one would hardly assign this particular form of the theory to Eudoxus. Presumably Euclid's treatment is based on a form of the theory revised by disciples in Eudoxus's circle.

In the more advanced fields, geometry in the 4th century benefited from the introduction of several new methods whose power would become apparent later at the hands of such as Archimedes and Apollonius. One such method was that of "analysis," which was foreshadowed in Hippocrates' method of the reduction of problems, as he reduced the cube duplication to the finding of two mean proportionals; it relates also to a certain geometric method "by hypothesis" that Plato mentions in *Meno* (86e–87b). The earliest extant specimen of geometric analysis as such relates to the problem of the finding of two mean proportionals, as solved by Eudoxus's disciple Menaechmus. If to the given lines A, B one assumes the two mean proportional lines X, Y, as known, then since $A : X = X : Y$ it follows that $X^2 = AY$, and since $A : X = Y : B$, it follows that $AB = XY$. The former condition, viewed as a locus for X, Y, describes a given parabolic curve, while the latter describes a given hyperbola. Thus, since the two curves are given, their intersection is given. In the formal construction of the problem, one would then invert this reasoning into a "synthesis": given A, B, one constructs the parabola and hyperbola articulated in the analysis, and their intersection yields the desired lines X, Y. The fragment does not elucidate in what sense the two curves are "given."

Menaechmus's curves can also be produced as planar sections of the cone (in addition to the parabola and hyperbola, there arises a third case, the ellipse). The first explicit mention of any of these curves as a conic section appears in the pseudo-Aristotelian *Problems* (XV.7), where the shape of the gibbous moon is said to resemble "a section of a cone." The first extensive elaboration of the properties of the conic sections appears to come from Euclid only shortly after this passage.

Other cases of special curves, besides those of Eudoxus and Menaechmus, are attested from this period. Archytas finds the two mean proportionals via the mutual intersection of given solid surfaces (a cone, torus, and cylinder), entailing a certain space curve as the common section of the torus and cylinder. Dinostratus, brother of Menaechmus and fellow disciple of Eudoxus, introduced another form of kinematic curve, generated by the composition of a linear and a circular motion. This curve was employed toward the solution of the circle quadrature, whence it received the name *quadratrix*. Since, however, this application of the curve requires lemmas not introduced before Archimedes, it seems that Dinostratus used it for other purposes, such as the trisection of the angle. Both in its formation and its use, the curve provides a precedent for the Archimedean spiral.

Such technical advances in geometry stimulated efforts, notably with Aristotle, to assimilate them into the general philosophical account of scientific knowledge. The method of analysis, for instance, is cited, if somewhat misleadingly, as a fruitful mode of heuristic reasoning (*Nicomachean Ethics* 1112b11–24), analogous to deliberative procedures seeking stated ends via accessible means. In *Prior Analytics* Aristotle articulates and classifies the modes of syllogistic reasoning, and demonstrates their relations in accordance with a standard geometric expository format. In *Posterior Analytics*, he inquires into the basic structure of scientific knowledge, in effect, extending the established format of geometry to other domains. Noteworthy is his distinction between propositions susceptible of proof and certain kinds of prior premises whose validity must be postulated.

But among modern critics far greater attention has been directed toward another metamathematical issue: the status of the infinite. Aristotle carefully distinguishes two cases, the "actual" or completed infinite versus the "potential" or progressive infinite. In one analysis of Zeno's paradox of the dichotomy, for instance, Aristotle rejects the notion that one can actually have marked off (whether physically or mentally) an infinite number of intervals (sc. the half, the quarter, the eighth, and so on) in finite time, but asserts that one can continually mark off parts only in succession (*Physics* 263a4–b9). As this distinction between "potential" and "actual" infinites corresponds precisely to that between Eudoxus's finitistic proofs via exhaustion and the presumptive infinitist arguments suggested by Antiphon's construction, one accordingly reads in many modern accounts that the ancient Greeks were stricken by a *"horror infiniti"* to abolish any applications of the infinite in their mathematics. But this view seriously misrepresents the Greek tradition. Infinitely small magnitudes, for instance, figure not only in the paradoxes of Zeno but also in the geometric reasonings known to Democritus (and presumably also Hippocrates), and were fruitfully exploited by Archimedes and others later. What the ancients recognize, however, is that infinitist conceptions are restricted to a heuristic role that, however valuable for research, does not extend into the context of formal demonstrations. It is this formal tradition, stemming from Eudoxus to Euclid and the comprehensive treatises following his model, that dominates within the extant literature. If a greater portion of the informal accounts survived, however, our view would be drastically modified.

EUCLID

Beginning with Euclid, active during the first half of the 3rd century B.C.E., we enter what one may call the "golden age" of Greek geometry. According to Proclus, Euclid "collected the *Elements*, by arranging many of the things of Eudoxus, bringing to completion many other things of Theaetetus, and converting still others, proved rather loosely by his predecessors, to irrefutable proofs." This places Euclid squarely in the tradition of technical exposition of the preceding century, honing the prior treatments of the domains inaugurated by Theaetetus, Eudoxus, and their disciples. Set in the context of what we know of these prior efforts, *Elements* appears to fit this description precisely.

(1)   The body of constructions of rectilinear plane figures and the properties of congruent triangles, forming the nucleus of Book I, is already substantially present in the reports about Oenopides and Hippocrates, while constructions and properties dealing with circles (Book III) and similar triangles and quadrilaterals (Book VI) are also associable initially with Hippocrates, whose collection of "elements" may well have set the first precedent for these parts of Euclid's *Elements*.

(2)   From the Pythagoreans come the constructions of the "application of areas" (the end of Book I, Book II, and the end of Book VI) and possibly also the constructions of the regular polygons (Book IV).

(3)   The general theory of proportions of geometric magnitude (Book V) is founded on the researches of Eudoxus.

(4)   The arithmetic books include a masterfully organized account of the divisibility of integers, which is based on the concept of relative primality (Book VII) and may develop from Theaetetus's researches; the more loosely organized parts on geometric progressions, the divisibility of square and cubic numbers, and the like (Book VIII and the opening of Book IX) may derive ultimately from Archytas, while appended results on odd and even numbers and a construction of "perfect" numbers (end of Book IX) may owe to Pythagoreans.

(5)   The imposing theory of irrational lines, constituting the largest book (Book X, about a quarter of the bulk of the entire *Elements*), stems from researches begun by Theaetetus and continued, it appears, by Eudoxus and his followers.

(6)   The general theory of solid geometry, forming the solid analogue of the plane geometry of Books I and VI, was in its infancy in Plato's time (as *Rep.* 527 indicates), but achieved its first major advances through Archytas and Eudoxus.

(7)   To Eudoxus one may also assign the method of "exhaustion" exploited for measuring circles, cones, and related figures (Book XII).

(8)   Finally, the constructions of the five regular solids are assignable to Theaetetus (Book XIII).

In each instance, there must have been considerable distance between the initial researches here indicated and the final versions in *Elements*. Book IV on the regular polygons could hardly, as such, be a Pythagorean treatise, even though a scholium makes that claim. Similarly, Book V is not, as such, by Eudoxus (the defects in several of its proofs would alone suffice to disqualify it), nor are Books X and XIII, as such, by Theaetetus. Indeed, Book X combines with some inconsistency two different accounts of the theory of irrationals. In all cases, one must assign to the figures named by Proclus in the followings of Theaetetus and Eudoxus the editing, revising, and extending of these fields.

What this leaves for Euclid's role is difficult to say. The inconsistency of technical performance—the ostensibly "Theaetetan" Books VII, X, and XIII are generally well executed, but although Book XII is also well done, Book V is notably flawed, despite their both allegedly being from Eudoxus—would suggest Euclid's access to an ensemble of completed expositions. But *Elements* is not likely to be merely a transcript of prior treatises. At the same time, Euclid himself is probably not the actual discoverer of very many of its theorems or constructions. One might suppose that the uniformity of expository style (e.g., in terminology and format of proofs), to the extent there is such uniformity, would be due to the editor. But even here one must be cautious, for the refining and homogenizing effect of later editors must have been considerable; indeed, it is impossible to know for sure how much of the extant text is free of influence from the edition produced by Theon of Alexandria (mid-4th century C.E.).

While Euclid's editing appears to have retained certain defects of his sources, one can discern nuances of logical refinement that could well be Euclid's own. The project of assembling treatises on the different fields of geometry into a corpus covering the whole domain commits the editor to a specific order of exposition. At various points there arises the need to establish results without recourse to technical methods that are being deferred. When one perceives this process in *Elements*, one can surmise Euclid's responsibility for the special form of proof, since we assume he was first to order the treatises in this way. Two examples may be cited.

First, with the theory of proportions deferred to Book V, Euclid is restricted to methods of congruence in his treatment of plane figures in the first four books, where, accordingly, certain propositions receive quite intricate proofs, even though considerably simpler proofs are possible via similarity principles.

Second, in Book I the condition for parallels is formulated as a special postulate (post. 5) in an unusual form: that when two lines are cut by a third line such that the interior angles formed on one side of the line are together less than two right angles, then the two lines will converge on that side of the line.

This principle, being in effect the converse of prop. 28 (that when two lines are cut by a third such that the interior angles on the same side equal two right angles, then the lines are parallel), is invoked for the first time in the proof of prop. 29, establishing that when two parallel lines are cut by a third the interior angles on the same side of that line equal two right angles. This is, in fact, merely the contrapositive formation of the postulate. A body of commentary attempting to prove the postulate is reported by Proclus, who presents arguments of his own and Ptolemy's; one finds traces of such efforts even before Euclid, in passages from the Aristotelian corpus. It emerges, then, that Euclid took the bold move of proving his key proposition on parallels (I.29) by framing its equivalent (in post. 5) as a postulate. Neither Euclid nor any other of the ancients, of course, perceived the depth of this tactic: that it was necessitated by the independence of the postulate from the others, being the criterion for the Euclidean form of plane geometry, as distinct from the non-Euclidean geometries (the so-called elliptical and hyperbolic geometries) based on its negation.

Among the theorems dependent on the parallel postulate is I.32: that the angles of a triangle sum to two right angles. This theorem, as we have seen, figured in the Pythagorean geometry, although the earlier treatment would not have handled the assumptions about parallels in Euclid's manner. Indeed, Aristotelian passages on parallels mention that if the parallel principle is violated, then so also would the angles of the triangle have a sum different from two right angles (e.g., *Prior Anal.* 2.17.66a11–15). Further, the theorem in I.16 (that the exterior angle of a triangle is greater than either of the nonadjacent interior angles), which Euclid proves without recourse to the parallel postulate, would have no place in the older system, since it would be trivial in the light of I.32.

Another Euclidean work, *Data*, is a companion to *Elements*. It covers the same basic domain as the first six books of *Elements*, the properties of rectilinear and circular plane figures, but adopts a special format suiting it specifically for applications within analyses.

Pappus includes Euclid's *Data* among about a dozen works that constituted a standardized corpus of analysis *(topos analyomenos)*. Euclid's lost *Porisms*, as well as his lost *Surface Loci*, were also included in this set. Presumably, his lost treatise *Conics* would also fall within it, for although Pappus does not cite this work in this context, he does cite the treatise that superseded it, Apollonius's *Conics*. These lost works have proved elusive for reconstruction, despite some detailed efforts based on Pappus's rather substantial notes on *Porisms* and *Surface Loci*. The former includes results that inspired the efforts founding projective geometry, as by Desargues and Pascal in the 17th century. Both works may have related to the extension of the field of conics.

Euclid compiled important works in the geometric sciences. In astronomy, *Phaenomena* provides a geometric account of the basic phenomena of risings and settings of segments of the ecliptic. In harmonics, Euclid's *Section of the Canon* explores the limits of the commensurable division of harmonic intervals, thereby codifying the earlier studies by Archytas; indeed, Tannery has suggested that this tract was actually not by Euclid but by a disciple of Archytas. In optics Euclid produced two treatises—*Optics*, on the phenomena of direct vision, and *Catoptrics*, on phenomena pertaining to vision via reflected rays. Here too there may have been precedent studies, as perhaps by Plato's associate Philip of Opus (the ancient testimonia are inconclusive). Any forms of these precedents in writings from the 4th century, however, were effectively superseded by the Euclidean versions, which remained models of exposition in their respective fields for centuries, long after they were overtaken by more advanced research.

ARCHIMEDES

Today often considered the finest mathematical mind from antiquity, and frequently ranked with the likes of Newton, Gauss, and Einstein as among the most gifted of mathematical physicists ever, Archimedes (fl. ca. 250 B.C.E., d. 212), had already become a legend for his scientific achievements, both theoretical and practical, among the ancient commentators.

Archimedes' basic project in geometry was continuous with the work of Eudoxus: to determine the measurements of geometric figures via the "exhaustion" technique. On the model of Eudoxus's theorem on the circle, Archimedes established that any circle equals half the product of its radius and its circumference, and that the ratio of the circumference to the diameter of the circle (sc. the constant we represent by π) is less than $3\frac{1}{7}$ but greater than $3\frac{10}{71}$. Similarly, Archimedes found the area of any parabolic segment to equal $\frac{4}{3}$ the triangle having the same altitude and base as the segment (*Quadrature of the Parabola*, prop. 24). This result is of particular interest, Archimedes himself observes, in that it marks the first case where a curved figure in the class of the circle or the conics has been found equal to a rectilinear figure.

For these proofs Archimedes states a special principle of continuity (now sometimes called the Archimedean axiom), which fills a perceived gap in the Eudoxean proofs, namely their assumption of a "lemma" (that any finite magnitude, on successive bisection, can be reduced to less than any preassigned finite magnitude of the same kind). This Archimedes reformulates in a manner more flexible for application in proofs (that of two finite magnitudes, the lesser, by being added to itself a suitable, finite number of times, can be made to exceed the greater). One infers that Archimedes does not have before him the Euclidean treatment of this material, since Euclid's definition of "having a ratio" (*Elements* V, def. 4), his proposition on the bisection (X.1), and his applications of these in the "Eudoxean" propositions of Book XII would have rendered Archimedes' lemma superfluous.

Determining centers of gravity involves a form of weighing of the figures, as if on a balance. In *Method* Archimedes exploits this notion for the measurement of areas and volumes, in what he terms his mechanical method. Archimedes also first articulated the basic principle of hydrostatics: that floating bodies displace their equal in weight, while submerged bodies displace their equal in volume. The principle underlies his solution of the legendary problem of the crown: to determine whether a given artifact was made of pure gold, or of an alloy of gold mixed with silver. Hitting on the principle of the solution, it is said, Archimedes charged naked from the baths crying, "Eureka!" But his writing *On Floating Bodies* presents these principles in a less impassioned frame. There Archimedes determines the conditions of stability for buoyant spherical segments and paraboloid segments. Although such results might in principle have applications in the design of ships, Archimedes appears to have applied his analysis to those particular solids whose volume and center of gravity, being known, permitted their solution. It emerges as an exercise in pure geometric theory rather than practical application.

ALEXANDRIANS AND APOLLONIUS

Archimedes' work stimulated active research by a group of talented geometers in the decades to follow. It will be possible here to cite only a few areas of research and the geometers specifically engaged in them.

Eratosthenes of Cyrene, noted as director of the Alexandrian Library and a scholar of diverse interests, was a correspondent of Archimedes' and engaged in a variety of mathematical studies, including efforts in number theory and geometry. Among these was his work in mathematical geography, for which he introduced a modified estimate for the measurement of the earth, 250,000 stades (equivalent, approximately, to 25,000 miles) by comparing the elevation of the sun at the time of the summer solstice at Syene and Alexandria.

Just as Archimedes had employed his mechanical method for the measurement of figures, a result of a closely related sort is due to Dionysodorus: the measure of the torus (or anchor-ring, in modern nomenclature), the solid formed by the revolution of a circle about an axis parallel to its plane, is expressed in terms reminiscent of a more general method proposed in Pappus and equivalent to the barycentric rule stated in the 17th century by Paul Guldin. In this case, the volume would equal that of a cylinder whose base equals the figure (the circle) whose revolution gives rise to the solid, and whose height is the distance traversed by that figure's center of gravity.

An interesting study of isoperimetric figures is due to Zenodorus, who showed, inter alia, that the circle is greatest in area of all plane figures having the same perimeter, and that the sphere is greatest in volume of solids having the same surface area. The treatment, while well crafted over all, suffers some major gaps: it does not adequately cover the entire domain of possible figures, for instance, but compares the circle only to the rectilinear plane figures and the sphere only to regular and conical solids; and it omits any proof of the existence of the maximal figures. One finds in Archimedes' work results of a closely related sort.

An Archimedean solution for the angle trisection appears to have inspired an effort by Nicomedes to solve this problem by means of a special curve, called the conchoid. Other applications of this curve, defined via a sliding ruler *(neusis)* construction, correspond to *neusis* constructions in Archimedes' *Spirals.*

To Diocles is due an interesting study on burning mirrors. This writing is lost in Greek, save for fragments excerpted by the commentator Eutocius, but a version survives through its medieval Arabic translation. Among its propositions is a practical construction of the parabola via its focus-directrix property and a proof that the parabolic contour directs solar rays all to a single point, while a spherical contour directs rays not to a point, but to a given segment of its axis. A few ancient authorities assign to Archimedes constructions of burning mirrors, as well as a general study in the theory of catoptrics. But the effort of Diocles, nearly contemporary with Archimedes, by virtue of its omitting any mention at all of related work by him, would relegate the later testimonia to misattribution.

Chronologically, one might include in this group of Archimedes' successors Apollonius of Perga, whose principal field was the study of conic sections and the solution of problems via geometric analysis. However, as these areas are important for, but not central to, Archimedes' work, one might better view Apollonius in the succession of Euclid, also notable for studies in conics and analysis.

In his eight-book treatise *Conics,* Apollonius consolidates the field of the elements of the conics, considerably extending it beyond the prior treatises of Euclid and Aristaeus (now lost). Apollonius generalizes the definition of the curves as sections of an arbitrary cone (not an isosceles cone, as in prior treatments). His account of their basic properties, as developed in Books I and III, in effect provides the analogue of Euclid's account of the circle in *Elements* Book III, including such results as the construction of tangents and the properties of intersecting chords and secants. Apollonius notes how these results are applicable toward the solution of conic problems, e.g., the three- and four-line locus, the finding of conics in accordance with specified incidence conditions (passing through given points, or having given lines as tangents), and so on. The actual solutions of these problems, however, do not appear in *Conics* itself but must have constituted separate treatises. Book IV on intersections of conics provides basic material for diorisms (finding criteria of solvability of problems). The remaining four books are more specialized in aim: Book V on drawing normal lines to conics, Book VI on constructions relating to similar conics, Books VII and VIII on conic problems. Of these, Book VIII is lost, and the other three survive only through their Arabic translation.

In his survey of the analytic corpus, Pappus describes six other works by Apollonius, in addition to *Conics*. Although all are lost in Greek, one of them, *On Cutting of a Ratio*, is extant in its Arabic translation, and scattered fragments of a few others are also preserved in Arabic sources.

Although modern accounts of Greek mathematics typically suppose that the restriction to planar constructions served as a normative principle already in research antedating Euclid, the explicit statement of this principle occurs only once in the extant literature, in a tentative observation by Pappus. One does see such a restriction implicit, however, in these efforts by Apollonius, if not before. Its presence indicates the maturity of the geometric discipline at his time, when the multiplicity of solutions permitted the ordering and ranking of the various methods.

LATE ANTIQUITY

With the work of Apollonius and his contemporaries early in the 2nd century B.C.E., we reach the highpoint of the discipline of geometry, as initially marked off by the pre-Euclidean contributors and consolidated by Euclid. A scattering of interesting results are preserved in the later commentators, such as Pappus (early 4th century C.E.) that may be attributable to research in the intervening period, but by and large the interest directed toward geometry from the 2nd century B.C.E. on would more accurately be called scholasticism than research. Although for this very reason the later period is typically described as one of decline, there were several areas where important work continued to be done.

Mathematical astronomy witnessed a major development involving astute applications of geometric theory as well as advances in observational and computational expertise. The field of "spherics"—in its simplest geometric form, the study of the properties of triangles described on the surface of a sphere—represented by the earlier treatises of Autolycus and Euclid, was further developed, first in the *Sphaerica* of Theodosius (ca. 2nd century B.C.E.) and subsequently in the *Sphaerica* of Menelaus of Alexandria (early 2nd century C.E.). With regard to the geometric description of planetary motions, the provisional models of Eudoxus and Callippus were set aside in favor of schemes involving eccentric and epicyclic motions, far better suited to the phenomena at issue. The geometric properties of the eccentric and epicyclic models were studied by Apollonius, who recognized their equivalence and determined, for instance, the geometric condition for stationary points and retrogrades. In extending these methods, Hipparchus of Rhodes (2nd century B.C.E.) profited from the receipt of observational data and parameters (e.g.,

measures of the periods of planetary motions) from the tradition of arithmetical astronomy then thriving at Babylon. The Hipparchean system, fortified by refinements both in data and theory, was further elaborated by
Ptolemy of Alexandria (mid-2nd century C.E.) in *Mathematical Syntaxis,*
which (under its Arabo-Latin title, *Almagest*) continued as the definitive
treatise in geometric astronomy throughout the Middle Ages and the Renaissance.

To calculate planetary positions from the geometric theory, one requires
the appropriate computational methods, such as arithmetic algorithms and
trigonometric tables. Although precedents for trigonometric calculations are
found in Aristarchus and Archimedes, credit goes to Hipparchus for producing a table of chords suitable for general use. This also marks the introduction
among the Greeks of the sexagesimal arithmetical algorithms, which, like the
basic quantitative parameters, were derived from the Babylonian precedent.
Although the fact of this borrowing seems not to be in question—it is even
remarked on by later Greek authorities—the precise manner of the transfer
has not been clarified.

Arithmetic treatment of geometry carried through in the manual on practical geometry, *Metrica,* by Hero of Alexandria (mid-1st century C.E.). Here
the computational mode is strictly in the alphabetical numeral system, long
conventional among the Greeks, although it is enriched by algorithms for
fractional and root computations. Hero's treatment benefits from the geometric discoveries of Archimedes—he includes Archimedes' estimate for π
(i.e., $3\frac{1}{7}$), his measuring rules for the circle, parabola, ellipse, conical and
spherical surfaces, and the sphere and the cylindrical segments, as well as
Dionysodorus's rule for the torus (indeed, Hero is our unique testimony to
the latter). It is clear, however, that the basic notion of a metrical form of geometry is not new with Hero: we have precedents in pre-Euclidean mathematical passages, as well as in surveying practice among both the Greeks, and
the Egyptians and Mesopotamians before them.

But arithmetic theory receives a major technical advance in the work of
Diophantus of Alexandria (ca. 3rd century C.E.) whose *Arithmetica* is an ambitious treatise in thirteen books expounding methods of solving arithmetical
problems. In his exposition Diophantus presupposes the theory of Euclid and
basic identities (including the solution of quadratic relations) that are established geometrically within the Euclidean tradition. But his own format is exclusively arithmetic, displaying certain features that would inspire the founders of algebraic method (e.g., Viète and Fermat) in the early modern period.
Throughout the hundreds of problems examined in this treatise, Diophantus
applies a consistent format: problems, although stated in general, are solved in
the context of specific numerical values. The solving method is reminiscent of
analysis among the geometers, in that the solving number is assumed and the
conditions it is to satisfy are then formulated as an equation relating the sev-

eral powers of the unknown. A nomenclature and symbolism are introduced extending up through the ninth power of the unknown. For instance, to find two numbers whose sum is given and the sum of whose squares is given (I.28), Diophantus posits the given numbers to be 20 and 208, respectively, and sets the difference of the two numbers sought as twice the unknown ($2x$), whence the greater is $x + 10$, the lesser $10 - x$, and the condition on the sum of their squares leads to the relation $2x^2 + 200 = 208$. One thus finds x to be 2, whence the numbers are 12, 8. Although this is a relatively simple example of Diophantus's art, it reveals his basic procedure as well as his understanding of more general aspects of his problems, and even a flair for nontrivial approaches suited to the special features of given cases.

In 4th-century Alexandria technical study was cultivated within the academic curriculum, as we see in the work of Pappus. His commentaries on Ptolemy and Euclid were much consulted by later commentators, such as Theon and Proclus. His eight-book anthology, *Collection*, reflects an active, competitive environment in more advanced geometric studies. This compilation includes a rich body of material, in many cases preserving unique evidence of important areas of the later development of geometry.

Theon of Alexandria (mid- and late 4th century) followed Pappus as teacher of technical studies at Alexandria. He issued new editions of Euclid's *Elements* and *Data*, which all but superseded the pre-Theonine versions. In Theon's astronomical work he was assisted by his daughter Hypatia (late 4th century, d. 415), who became the leading figure among the Neoplatonists in Alexandria. Her notorious death by lynching at the hands of Christian fanatics left a deep impression not only on later historians of the church, who deplored the incident, but even more on the legendizing about ancient science and religion in the modern age. Among her technical works were commentaries on Diophantus and Apollonius, which unfortunately do not survive.

In the later centuries, technical studies become more an adjunct of the philosophical curriculum than a course pursued for its intrinsic merit. In Athens at the Platonic Academy, Proclus included mathematics in his commentaries on Plato (particularly on *Timaeus* and *The Republic*). His commentary on Euclid's Book I, as we have seen, preserves much historical information, as well as ample philosophical glosses relating Euclid's propositions to Neoplatonist interests.

Ammonius in Alexandria (late 5th to early 6th century), a follower of Proclus, devoted his principal work to lectures and commentaries on Aristotle. But he encouraged technical interests among his disciples, the principal among them being Eutocius, Philoponus, and Simplicius. Eutocius (fl. early 6th century) apparently took over leadership of the school for a relatively brief period after Ammonius's death. But Eutocius is significant more for his commentaries on Archimedes and Apollonius, and his new edition of the first four books of *Conics*, the basis of the extant tradition of that work. While

Eutocius's mathematical expertise is not to be exaggerated, his technical comments are usually sound, and he incorporates invaluable historical material, including the reconstruction of a lost section of Archimedes' *Sphere and Cylinder* (together with related fragments from Diocles and Dionysodorus) and an anthology of accounts of the cube duplication, preserving the substance and, in several instances, the texts of eleven different contributors, including Archytas, Menaechmus, Eratosthenes, Nicomedes, and others.

Philoponus, a contemporary of Eutocius, compiled commentaries on Aristotle, initially based on the lectures of Ammonius. These include some mathematical material of interest, e.g., on cube duplication and circle quadrature, as the particular passage gives occasion. But his major work is in theology and cosmology, as in his polemical attacks against the Aristotelian cosmologists for their doctrine of the eternity of the world.

Simplicius produced an extensive set of commentaries on Aristotle, of which those on *Physics* and *De caelo* preserve several important fragments of early mathematics, most notably, the account of early circle quadratures, including Hippocrates' treatment of the lunules, and the account of Eudoxus's system of concentric spheres.

Anthemius of Tralles (early 6th century) and Isidore of Miletus (early to middle 6th century) bring the focus of technical studies to Constantinople. Anthemius, noted for his designs of mechanisms, was appointed chief architect in the reconstruction of Hagia Sophia (532–537). His expertise in geometry is represented in his extant tract on burning mirrors, and his being the dedicatee of Eutocius's commentaries on Apollonius. Isidore also combined practical activities (e.g., as Anthemius's assistant at Hagia Sophia) and scholarly efforts. In the latter regard, he was esteemed as a lecturer on geometry, composing a commentary on Hero's *Vaults* (not extant), a set of results on regular solids (extant as part of the so-called Book XV of *Elements*), and a revision of Eutocius's commentaries on Archimedes.

It would appear that, by contrast with the philosophically oriented curriculum at Alexandria, the Constantinople school emphasized practical and technical study. This may reflect a growing antagonism toward pagan philosophy within the Christian establishment from the time of Justinian onward. But a few centuries later, when the excesses of the iconoclastic movement gave way to orthodoxy in the late 9th century, a revived commitment to philosophical study carried with it an interest in the mathematical classics. Under humanists like Leon "the Philosopher," new editions of Euclid, Archimedes, Apollonius, and their commentators were compiled, and these ultimately became the basis of what now survives of this tradition. Their effort assured the transmission of the finest specimens of formal exposition, particularly in elementary geometry. Their coverage of more advanced fields and of informal treatments was spotty by comparison, and this has left an unbalanced impression of the primacy of formalist concerns over heuristic methods in ancient mathematical research. But in both these respects the Byzantine humanists fostered the advancement of mathematical studies in Arabic and Latin scholarship in the Middle Ages and the Renaissance. Possessing only the finished architecture, as it were, of ancient mathematics, the later geometers were compelled to recreate the scaffolding, or what they took to be the secret methods perversely withheld by the ancients.

WILBUR KNORR

Bibliography

Bowen, A. C., ed. *Science and Philosophy in Classical Greece.* New York and London, 1991.

Burkert, Walter. *Lore and Science in Ancient Pythagoreanism.* Trans. Edwin L. Minar, Jr. Cambridge, Mass., 1972.

Fowler, D. H. *The Mathematics of Plato's Academy.* Oxford, 1987.

Heath, T. L. *History of Greek Mathematics.* 2 vols. Oxford, 1921.

Jones, Alexander. *Pappus of Alexandria: Book 7 of the Collection.* 2 vols. New York, 1986.

Klein, Jacob. *Greek Mathematical Thought and the Origin of Algebra.* Cambridge, Mass., and London, 1968.

Knorr, W. R. *The Ancient Tradition of Geometric Problems.* Boston, 1986.

———. *The Evolution of the Euclidean Elements.* Dordrecht and Boston, 1975.

———. *Textual Studies in Ancient and Medieval Geometry.* Boston, 1989.

Kretzmann, Norman, ed. *Infinity and Continuity in Ancient and Medieval Thought.* Ithaca, N.Y., 1982.

Lloyd, G. E. R. *Magic, Reason, and Experience.* Cambridge, 1979.

Mueller, Ian. *Philosophy of Mathematics and Deductive Structure in Euclid's Elements.* Cambridge, Mass., 1981.

Neugebauer, Otto. *A History of Ancient Mathematical Astronomy.* 3 vols. Berlin and New York, 1975.

Szabó, Árpád. 1969. *The Beginnings of Greek Mathematics.* Trans. A. M. Ungar. Dordrecht and Boston, 1978.

Tannery, Paul. *Mémoires scientifiques,* vols. 1–3. Paris and Toulouse, 1912.

Van der Waerden, B. L. *Science Awakening.* Groningen, 1954.

Zeuthen, H. G. *Die Lehre von den Kegelschnitten im Altertum.* Copenhagen, 1886; repr. Hildesheim, 1965.

Related Articles

Epistemology; Astronomy; Archimedes; Plato; The Academy; Demonstration and the Idea of Science; Harmonics; Euclid; Zeno; Pythagoras

MEDICINE

AT THE END OF HIS TREATISE *On Youth, Old Age, Life, and Death*, Aristotle wrote: "But as to health and disease, not only the physician but also the natural scientist must, up to a point, give an account of their causes. . . . Facts show that their inquiries are, to a certain extent, at least coterminous. For those physicians who are cultivated and learned make some mention of natural science, and claim to derive their principles from it, while the most accomplished investigators into nature generally push their studies so far as to conclude with an account of medical principles" (480b21). Actually, Presocratic "physicists" exhibited an interest in medicine that has never been contested, so much so that some of them, such as Empedocles, Alcmeon of Croton, and Archelaus, were considered physicians as well as philosophers. Parmenides himself, according to some ancient sources, founded a "school" of medicine. Among the objects of most intense study for the ancient natural philosopher were the various vital phenomena, to the point that "physicists" were sometimes inclined to view these phenomena as models that explain the entire universe. According to Aristotle, if the natural philosopher must concern himself with the principles of health and sickness, it is because neither of the two can be "the properties of things deprived of life" (*On Sense and Sensible Objects* I.436a19). The very meaning of the term *physics* changed, of course, between the time of the Presocratics and Aristotle: for the latter, physics was no longer a comprehensive science claiming to explain the creation of the entire cosmos. Aristotelian physics is the theoretical science of living beings, those that contain in themselves the principle of their own motion. In other words, living beings constitute the paragon of physical reality.

The two passages from Aristotle cited above suggest three historical and epistemological observations. The first concerns the grounding of medicine in physics—in the ancient sense of the word—and points toward what is specific to Greek medicine. As Aristotle noted, medicine has a place only among living creatures and for their benefit. Nevertheless, biology and medicine are not related to physics in the same way. Biology (which is not quite the proper term for describing ancient speculation about living creatures) is just one part of physics, and therefore of philosophy, and has never claimed to be anything else. Among physicians, however, beginning in the 5th century B.C.E., there was disagreement over how much medicine should depend on philosophy, a question Aristotle no doubt had in mind when he wrote the texts quoted above. The Hippocratic treatise *On Ancient Medicine* is critical of medicine's adoption of the methods of Presocratic natural philosophers, while in the preface of his treatise on medicine Celsus, a Latin encyclopedist of the early Christian era, contrasts physician-philosophers such as Pythagoras, Empedocles, and Democritus with Hippocrates, "who separated this branch of learning from the study of philosophy" (*De medicina*, Prooemium 8). The second observation concerns the history of natural philosophy: it was not until Aristotle's day, when physics had dropped its claims of embracing all science, that the connection between the study of vital phenomena and the practice of medicine became meaningful. In addition, we should recall that even for Aristotle, who came closer to it than anyone else, our modern notion of biology had no exact equivalent among the ancients. In Aristotelian physics, the elements (fire, air, water, earth) that constitute matter belong to the same category as the living, inasmuch as they contain the principle of their own movement, and the entire cosmos is considered to be alive. Michel Foucault demonstrated that at the beginning of the 19th century a concept of biology could develop—Lamarck was one of the first to use the term; indeed, he introduced the word in French—only when life itself had been grasped as a specific way of being. A second condition was also necessary: biology, in the modern sense, requires the proper demarcation of the boundaries of the living world. Aristotle satisfied the first of these conditions but not the second. Finally, the relationship between biology and medicine was not understood in the same way by physicians and natural philosophers. While physicians unquestionably looked to physicists for theoretical models, the latter only rarely modified their systems in light of medical discoveries.

Until now, medical historians have emphasized the *unity* of Greek (or Greco-Roman) medicine as compared to medical theory and practice in other cultural spheres, particularly those of Babylon and Egypt. These historians, who have often acknowledged the hegemony of Hippocratic medicine, have, as a result, underestimated the diversity of ancient medicine. Tracing ancient medical science to what might be called its historic and theoretical center should allow us to take into account these two aspects of Greek medicine, its specificity and its fullness.

ALEXANDRIAN MEDICINE: HEROPHILUS

During the first half of the 3rd century B.C.E., Herophilus of Chalcedonia practiced and taught medicine at Alexandria. I might have chosen to focus on someone less brilliant, on a physician more representative of the medicine of his time, but there are advantages in choosing a scholar as exceptional as Herophilus. Although we have only a few fragments and some testimony cited by later authors, we know somewhat more about him than about his less renowned colleagues, particularly owing to the important work of Heinrich von Staden. Moreover, Herophilus's high standing gave him particular importance in one of the key transformations in Greek medicine, the birth of medical schools.

Before practicing medicine himself, Herophilus studied with Praxagoras of Cos, possibly in Alexandria but more likely in Cos, Hippocrates' homeland. However, he eventually settled in Alexandria, where he practiced and taught medicine. While Athens was still the philosophical capital of the Greek world, Alexandria was its scientific center. The famous Library, established and funded by the dynasty of the Ptolemys, brought together veritable research institutes of every known discipline, centered around the Museum. While there is no proof that Herophilus was a court doctor appointed by the king, or even that he was connected to the institution of the Museum, we know that he had political connections, because he was the first to practice, on a large scale, not only human dissection on cadavers but also, according to Celsus, human vivisection on condemned prisoners taken from the king's dungeons. No doubt the exceptional position of Alexandria, a Greek city recently founded in Egypt, permitted a partial lifting of the prohibitions having to do with human cadavers; some scholars have suggested that dissection probably seemed less shocking in a culture where the dead were embalmed. As for vivisection, it was possible only because explicit permission had been granted by the Ptolemaic kings, who had a strong desire to see Alexandria recognized as the intellectual capital of the world. Scholars have proposed numerous hypotheses regarding the possible influence of Egyptian medicine on Herophilus and the other Greek physicians in Alexandria. From earliest antiquity, Egyptian doctors were famous; Persian and Hittite kings had personal physicians who were brought from Egypt. Herophilus and his colleagues may have benefited from certain drugs used by the pharaohs' doctors from time immemorial, but the medicine Herophilus practiced was unmistakably Greek and showed no signs of Hellenic-Egyptian syncretism.

It is often said, incorrectly, that Greek medicine was "rational" whereas Egyptian medicine was "magical." Thanks to some papyri which have come down to us from as far back as the 20th century B.C.E., we have fairly detailed information about pharaonic medicine. These composite texts contain a mix of invocations to the gods and magic formulas, but they also demonstrate frequent recourse to reason and observation. They offer a description of the vascular system and an explanation of diseases based on the flow of morbid humors in the body that closely resemble what is found in the corresponding texts of the *Hippocratic Corpus*, but the Egyptian papyri were written fifteen centuries earlier. Given the well-known competence of Egyptian physicians, pharmacologists, surgeons, and obstetricians, it is clearly unacceptable to classify Egyptian medicine with the magico-charlatanism that has existed everywhere and throughout history.

Nevertheless, the differences between Egyptian and Greek medicine are enormous, and they emerge clearly when we look at the training of future physicians. The Egyptian doctor was trained in the temple, where he learned to observe his patients' symptoms and to use them as the basis for applying certain formulas from manuals, some of which—but only some—were clearly magico-religious. In his *Politics,* Aristotle mentions that Egyptian physicians were not authorized to depart from the treatments prescribed in the manuals until four days after the onset of the disease, and that a doctor transgressed this rule at his own risk, for he would then be held responsible for any negative consequences. In contrast, as a young man, Herophilus studied with a teacher in one of the medical "schools" where, as in our own university hospitals today, both treatment and training took place. He probably had to pay for his training, but he was then entitled to membership in the medical circle, a "brotherhood" in the strictest sense. The text of the well-known Hippocratic oath, which probably dates from the beginning of the 4th century B.C.E., imparts a religious cast to the new doctor's obligation to become a member of his teacher's family: "I swear by Apollo physician, by Asclepius, by Hygeia, by Panacea and by all the gods and goddesses . . . to hold my teacher in this art equal to my own parents; to make him partner in my livelihood; when he is in need of money to share mine with him; to consider his family as my own brothers, and to teach them this art, if they want to learn it, without fee or indenture; to impart precept, oral instruction, and all other instruction to my own sons, the sons of my teacher and to indentured pupils who have taken the physicians' oath" (Hippocrates, *The Oath* 299). Texts such as this one bear crucial traces of a history that requires analysis.

In Greece, alongside the customary medicine of bone setters and charlatans, a form of religious medicine was also practiced, in the sanctuaries of Apollo and later in those of Asclepius, such as the one at Epidaurus. We have a good deal of information about these practices from texts as well as from archaeological material, particularly votive steles. They reveal, for example, that patients sometimes sought "incubation," which involved sleeping in the temple so that the course of action they should adopt might be revealed while they slept. But we also have information going back at least to Homeric times about a form of lay medicine that differed markedly from its magico-religious counterparts; its practitioners were considered technicians. Thus the Greek army, sent to fight Troy, had its own physicians in addition to the necessary carpenters, ships' pilots, and cooks. In its idealization of the harsh virtue of primitive times, Plato's *Republic* tells us that this ancient medicine was almost exclusively devoted to traumatology. Starting in the 6th century B.C.E., medical centers appeared, for example, in Cyrene in what is now Libya, and in Croton, in southern Italy. However, from the 5th century on the center that was best known, owing to the exceptional fame of Hippocrates, was on the island of Cos, where Herophilus was trained a little less than a century after the master's death. In addition, itinerant physicians traveled throughout the Mediterranean world, practicing their art, competing with local physicians and among themselves; in most cases, however, they did not teach.

ANTECEDENTS: THE *HIPPOCRATIC CORPUS*

The conditions Herophilus encountered had developed slowly, as a careful reader of the oath might have guessed. Hippocrates became a doctor because he came from the family of the Asclepiades, in other words, from those who claimed to be descendants of Asclepius, initially a demigod of medicine who was later fully "deified." Asclepius's two sons, Podalirus and Machaon, were physicians in the Greek army during the Trojan War. The two largest medical "schools" of the classical age, in Cos and in Cnidus (a city situated on the continent of Asia opposite the island of Cos), where most of the treatises of the *Hippocratic Corpus* were produced, were family associations; both claimed Podalirus as their ancestor. Although not all of the Asclepiades' male descendants were destined to study medicine, medical science was passed down within families: Hippocrates' grandfather, father, sons, and grandsons were all physicians. It is quite likely that, two hundred years earlier, Herophilus could not have become a doctor. It was during Hippocrates' time, and perhaps even thanks to him, that people outside the family were permitted to come to Cos to study; this probably happened later at the other centers as well. The oath recalls the old tradition by symbolically integrating outsiders into their teachers' families.

Such an important transformation must be viewed in light of a fundamental fact of Greek intellectual history: the birth of physics, or natural philosophy, in the polis. While the social structure of the pharaonic monarchy was able to keep the practice and teaching of medicine under the control of the priests, it must have been increasingly difficult for Greek medical families to retain their privileged position. Beginning in the 6th century B.C.E., within the context of free inquiry and competing hypotheses that prevailed during the composition of a number of treatises on nature, "physiologists" assumed the right to oversee the processes of disease, asserting that they alone were capable of explaining them. As for the city-states, they sought to recruit competent physicians, "competence" now entailing not only the reputation of a famous family but also the rational examination of doctrines and therapeutic methods. Plato and Aristotle tell us that the city-states required candidates to take serious examinations to become public doctors, a position that was specific to the polis. Hence the transmission of knowledge and experience strictly within families was bound to conflict with the public ideals of the city. In this new world, medicine could either become sectarian, in the strictest sense of the word—for the city-states had suppressed, without entirely eliminating, the cultic societies and other more or less secret associations—or it could go public. The *Hippocratic Corpus* bears more than one trace of this debate, which profoundly affected medicine in Hippocrates' day.

Indeed, it is by understanding the way medicine was adapted to a political environment, in which philosophy was the dominant intellectual consequence, that we can better assess one of the great contradictions running through the *Hippocratic Corpus,* embodied in the contrasting treatises of Cos and Cnidus. The contradiction may have been overstated by some interpreters, but it was certainly not invented by them. The author of *On Regimen in Acute Diseases,* a treatise dating from the end of the 5th century B.C.E., probably belonged to the Cos "school"; in other words, the author was probably a follower of Hippocrates or of one of his immediate successors. In that treatise, three distinctive features of the rival "school" of Cnidus are described: the physicians of Cnidus used a rigid and very detailed classification of diseases (for instance, they recognized four sorts of jaundice and three types of tetanus); they used only a very small number of remedies (the treatise mentions milk, whey, and purges); they referred to a work called *Cnidian Sentences,* which the author says had been collectively revised. For modern interpreters of the *Hippocratic Corpus,* the Cnidian school represents the outcast wing of classical Greek medicine, denounced as archaic and empirical, as opposed to the medicine of Cos practiced by Hippocrates himself, which some scholars see as the forerunner of 19th-century experimental medicine inspired by the work of Claude Bernard.

Thus Book II of the treatise known by the title *Diseases* in the *Hippocratic Corpus,* regarded as Cnidian in origin, has two principal characteristics. This treatise is a catalogue of illnesses presented in order, "from head to toe": diseases of the head, nose, neck, chest, and so on. For each of the diseases—many varieties of which are listed in succession—the presentation follows the same order: identification (in other words, the name of the disease: tetanus no. 1, tetanus no. 2), semiology, therapy, and prognosis. This order is most scrupulously adhered to in the second part of the treatise, which appears to be older than the first. Thus the treatise must be viewed as a well-organized work, and not simply as a collection of notes or patients' charts, examples of which can also be found in other parts of the *Corpus.*

Let us take, for example, one of the chapters in the work: "Another jaundice: there are mild fevers and a heaviness of the head . . . in some cases, the fever actually goes away; the person becomes yellow—powerlessness of the body, and he passes thick yellow-green urine. Wash this patient in hot water and give him drinks. When he seems to you to be better, and his color is better, administer a medication to his nostrils; afterwards, have him drink a medication that acts downwards. Let him eat very soft foods and drink diluted sweet white wine. If he does these things, he recovers" (*De morbis* II.39).

On the basis of a collection like this one we can sketch the professional and intellectual portrait of a physician of Cnidus. He does not limit himself to following recipes: he must determine precisely the moment when the different phases of the cure must be initiated ("when he seems to you to be better"), and in this it is clear that *De morbis* II and *Cnidian Sentences* do not function at all like the collections of treatments rooted in magic. Behind such texts as these we detect long experience in treatment and a considerable accumulation of observations. Nevertheless, the doctor in the case described is a practitioner who applies knowledge that he has had no part in generating and the basis of which is never explicitly presented. This empirical and authoritarian medicine is well adapted to transmission through the family line, but its practitioners must have had difficulty "coming to terms" intellectually under questioning by philosophers.

Doctors thus came to follow the example of philosophers and rhetoricians. This is the source of another distinction that runs through the *Hippocratic Corpus*. Until recently, some of the treatises—for example, *On Winds* and *On Art*—were regarded as exercises in rhetorical virtuosity and attributed to some Sophists with a passing knowledge of medicine, for whom the term *iatrosophists* was coined. Jacques Jouanna has shown that there is no reason to think that these treatises were not written by physicians who believed in the theses that they were defending. Thus the author of *On Winds* really believed that all sickness had a single cause, namely, the air. He used rhetorical techniques appropriate to his audience: he was not addressing colleagues, but speaking to lay people whom he sought to convince. Perhaps such a discussion should be put in the context of the institution of public doctors, since *On Winds* and *On Art*, both of which have a clearly apologetic tone in that they defend medicine against its critics, are obviously addressing citizens whose opinion, in the end, will determine the actions taken by the city. These treatises from the *Hippocratic Corpus* contrast with others, of various sorts, written for specialists, physicians, and "natural philosophers." Let us examine three types.

Treatises such as *Fractures,* which explains the steps to take in treating fractures and dislocations, may be called technical. We may call another group of works documentary: the seven books of *Epidemics* are a collection of patients' records, written by different authors in different eras. For example: "Meton was seized with fever and painful heaviness in the loins. *Second day.* After a fairly copious draught of water, had his bowels well moved. *Third day.* Heaviness in the head; stools thin, bilious, rather red. *Fourth day.* General exacerbation; slight epistaxis twice from the right nostril; an uncomfortable night; stools as on the third day . . . Fifth day, violent epistaxis of unmixed blood from the left nostril; sweat; crisis. After the crisis, sleeplessness; wandering; urine thin and rather black. His head was bathed; sleep; reason restored. The patient suffered no relapse, but after the crisis bled several times from the nose" (*Epidemics* I, Case vii.196–208).

In Book II of *Diseases* we are far from the type of description provided by the foregoing example. Here, the physician, probably one of the itinerants mentioned above, supplied examples not of illnesses but of patients. This collection of cases was intended for use by the physician himself and by his colleagues in the school. The *Hippocratic Corpus* also includes "speculative" treatises that specifically address the problem of the connection between medicine and philosophy.

Herophilus was thus associated with the Hippocratic tradition of medicine, a tradition grounded in rationality but claiming both practical and theoretical autonomy vis-à-vis philosophy. Starting with Celsus, if not before, it was standard practice for historians and doxographers to treat certain figures in pairs: Hippocrates was paired with Diocles of Carystus, who wrote the first treatise on anatomy, in the 4th century; Praxagoras of Cos was paired with Chrysippus, of Cnidus, and Herophilus with Erasistratus. The latter, somewhat younger than Herophilus, was the other great figure in Alexandrian medicine and was probably a student of Chrysippus, just as Herophilus was a student of Praxagoras. This suggests that Erasistratus chose to be trained in the Cnidian school, the rival to Cos; by that time, the Cos school seems to have lost the empirical and archaic character that it had in the time of Hippocrates.

The expression "Hippocratic tradition" does not refer to a duly constituted doctrine, for the treatises of the *Hippocratic Corpus*, even when we consider only those texts from Cos written before the middle of the 4th century B.C.E., are highly divergent. But this doctrinal diversity is framed, as it were, by a few "invariables" that appear to be more significant than the actual content of the theories offered in the collection. Hippocratic doctors had a common understanding of illness and of the way the body functions; traces of this shared view first appear in the writings of the Pythagorean doctor Alcmaeon of Croton (6th century B.C.E.). Using a political metaphor, Alcmaeon defined health as the balance between the elemental qualities that make up the body (hot, cold, dry, wet, sweet, bitter . . .), while in sickness a single one of these qualities was believed dominant. Considered for years to be the chief legacy of Hippocratic medicine, the theory of humors originated in the speculations of the Presocratic natural philosophers. Several systems of humors are found in the *Hippocratic Corpus*, but the most famous—and the one that survived, through the work of Galen, right up to the beginning of the 19th century— came from Hippocrates' son-in-law, Polybius, in his treatise *On the Nature of Man*. Polybius describes the body as the site of the interlacing flows of blood, the warm and humid spring humor; yellow bile, the hot and dry summer humor; black bile, the dry and cold autumnal humor; and phlegm, the cold and wet winter humor. Pathology described the deviant behavior of these humors, of which we may have too much or too little; they may overflow, leaving a vacuum to be filled by others, or they may become concentrated in certain organs, causing inflammation or decay.

Medical knowledge was thus primarily directed at prognosis: owing to his experience, the physician could predict the course of the illness and its various phases. Particular attention was given to what were known as the "critical days" and to the cycle of symptoms, particularly of fevers (resulting in certain medical expressions in use right up to the 20th century to designate fevers that recur regularly, for example every three or four days). Yielding to the temptation of arithmetic logic, as some philosophers did, the authors of a few of the treatises in the *Hippocratic Corpus* sought to establish a numerical basis for the rhythms of human life and of the universe: according to the treatise *Flesh,* the number seven, through its multiples and divisions (3 + 4), provided the key to understanding the evolution of diseases as well as the growth of the fetus. Treatment basically consists in helping to provoke a crisis, during which the body's equilibrium is reestablished; for example, the remedy for an excess of a given humor is a discharge of that humor. The most important factor is timing: the doctor's intervention must come at the right moment, neither too soon nor too late.

Despite the often harsh criticism that certain treatises in the *Hippocratic Corpus* level against philosophy and its theoretical imperialism, we can see a deepening commonality between Hippocratic physicians and the philosophers, whom skeptics later call Dogmatists, a label that "rationalist" physicians inherited: the truth of the symptom lies not in what is seen but in *hidden causes* that the doctor has to discover, just as science must try to reveal the hidden network of causes that governs all phenomena. Herophilus falls squarely within this perspective, and several ancient sources tell us that he sought the explanation of disease in humoral pathology. Moreover, he helped strengthen this rational approach to medicine through his contribution to the development of the medical arts.

THE NEW FACE OF MEDICINE

Herophilus was above all a skillful anatomist, owing to his extensive practice of dissection and human vivisection. His contemporary, Erasistratus, also practiced dissection on a wide scale, and possibly human vivisection as well, though this is not confirmed. Their immediate successors, however, abandoned human dissection, and it was almost never practiced again in the West until the end of the Middle Ages. In "linear" histories of medicine that ascribe to each name a set of "discoveries" adding up to everything known to modern medicine, Herophilus is credited with discovering the distinctions between sensory and motor nerves, the hemispheres of the brain, and the ovaries and Fallopian tubes, although he had no awareness of the process of ovulation. In addition he also described, quite precisely for his time, the system of veins and arteries that his teacher, Praxagoras, seems to have been the first to identify clearly—though Herophilus continued to believe that the arteries carried blood mixed with "breath"—and he was responsible for a thorough study of the pulse that made him famous in antiquity. By differentiating between the strength, size, and rate of the pulse, and by resorting to analogies in music, he was one of the first to introduce a concept of rhythm into the life sciences. Herophilus explored other areas as well, in particular physiology—he studied respiration in detail—and psychiatry; his analysis of dreams won him praise from Freud.

One aspect of the search for hidden causes involved opening up cadavers and the bodies of living human beings. A North African doctor of the 4th century B.C.E., who condemned the practice of vivisection on humanitarian grounds, reports that Alexandrian physicians, including Herophilus, dissected cadavers to discover the causes and circumstances of death. It seems likely, therefore, that dissection, far from being practiced by Herophilus in the name of some experimental empiricism, was actually, in his view, a means of uncovering "intermediate" causes, those that lay between "obvious" but nondetermining causes such as, according to Celsus, "heat or cold, hunger or surfeit" (*De medicina*, Prooemium, 11) and fundamental hidden causes that can be discovered only through reasoning. It appears that Herophilus fulfilled the program of the rationalist physicians better than any of his predecessors. When Celsus redefines the objectives of the form of rational medicine that originated with Hippocrates, he seems to include the contributions of the Alexandrian anatomists: "They, then, who profess a reasoned theory of medicine propound as requisites, first, a knowledge of hidden causes involving diseases, next, of evident causes, after these of natural actions also [as he says later, Celsus means physiological functions like respiration and digestion], and lastly of the internal parts" (*De medicina*, Prooemium, 9).

This question of causes is crucial, and it goes beyond medicine. In the Alexandrian world, Aristotle's influence was powerful: Strato of Lampsacus, successor to Theophrastus as head of the Lyceum, was the teacher of King Ptolemy II Philadelphus, and by and large the Alexandrian scientific establishment continued to pursue Aristotle's encyclopedic project. Moreover, the rising influence of the Stoics was reflected in the fact that etiology was one of the central questions of philosophy. In this respect, Herophilus's theoretical stance is more complex than it appears. Its complexity surfaces in the contradictory doxography concerning Herophilus, in which some writers hold that he meant to infer from observable phenomena the hidden causes that govern them (this is the position of the rationalists or Dogmatists), while others report that he meant to describe perceived phenomena and declared the hidden causes inaccessible (the position of the Empiricists). After demonstrating that these extreme interpretations are mistaken, Heinrich von Staden offers what is probably an accurate interpretation of Herophilian epistemology: like Aristotle, Herophilus starts with the observation of perceptible phenomena in order to arrive at their causes; however, recognizing that real causes often elude the doctor in physiology and pathology, he settled for *hypothetical* causes.

Old and new elements are combined in a most striking way in Herophilus's work. The most radical innovation in Herophilus's medicine, compared with that of Hippocrates, resides in the practice of dissection itself. Herophilus and perhaps his teacher Praxagoras before him illustrate the distinction Aristotle made between theoretical physicians—whom he credited with knowledge of physics—and ordinary therapists (*Politics* III.11): they brought into the intellectual arena the theoretical physician—we would say the biologist—who was absent from the *Hippocratic Corpus*. However, when it came to treating patients Herophilus remained faithful to the old Hippocratic tradition of the humors and to traditional pharmacology and surgery.

Erasistratus divided medicine into two principal branches: the first, called scientific, included anatomy, physiology, and the investigation of causes; the second, called stochastic, dealt with diagnosis, prognosis, and treatment. Physicians in Alexandria allowed the two traditions to coexist. They sought to further the development of a life science that saw pathologies simply as deviations from normal conditions, explained by the same causes as normal states. Their project was undoubtedly an ancient one, but Aristotle had given it an especially appealing form. In this theoretical enterprise, Aristotle's influence was so strong that physicians did not hesitate to adopt not only his fundamental principles—for example, finality—but also his errors: Praxagoras endorsed Aristotle's cardiocentrism.

The discoveries of the anatomists of Alexandria and their successors refined and improved the Aristotelian explanations but did not overturn their theoretical framework. However, all this theoretical development seems to have had only minimal influence on treatments: Erasistratus frequently recommended bleeding, and Herophilus relied on the pulse more than the authors of the *Hippocratic Corpus* might have done, but the fundamental aim was to restore the balance among the humors through diet, exercise, or traditional drugs (purges, diuretics, or emollients). Medical practice thus remained Hippocratic. Though surprising at first glance, this coexistence of Aristotelian biology and Hippocratic treatment is easily explained: the anatomo-physiological discoveries of the physicians of Alexandria, as remarkable as they are, were not readily applicable to treatment. The gap between theory and practice in medicine could not be grasped as such by the practitioners themselves. As a result, there was a widespread effort to reevaluate the *Hippocratic Corpus* that amounted almost to a rewriting: not only was Hippocrates represented as a rationalist doctor who closely resembles his followers in Alexandria, but also a tradition was established—perhaps beginning with Herophilus himself, and certainly with his disciple Bacchius—of writing commentaries on the principal treatises of the *Corpus*. This blend of Aristotelianism and

Hippocratism grew in an unprecedented way in the 2nd century C.E. through the work of Galen, who adopted Aristotelian finalism and at the same time ensured the influence of the humoral theory for centuries to come.

MEDICAL SCHOOLS AND NOSOGRAPHIES

Within a short time this new way of conceptualizing medicine, if not of practicing it, introduced a number of theoretical and institutional innovations. Medical schools have been mentioned a number of times in this essay; I have placed the term in quotation marks at the first mention of a school when I refer not to a school per se but to a group that left its mark in the *Hippocratic Corpus*. In fact, scholastic organization was a fundamental aspect of ancient *philosophical* life. The first school worthy of the name, besides the Pythagorean brotherhood that was a mix of philosophy and religion, was Plato's Academy. As a hierarchical and institutional reality, endowed with what we today would call an institutional identity, the school of philosophy was a place of immense affective investment for its students. The relationships among the students and between the students and the head of the school (the scholarch) resembled family ties, and with them the strength and complexity of Oedipal relations. Even if, in some cases, at the Academy in particular, the master did not impose a true *orthodoxy*, his doctrine became an obligatory point of reference. Whenever one speaks of a "school" to designate the physicians gathered at Cos, at Cnidus, and, even though much less is known about them, at Croton or Cyrene, the term is used broadly and, in the last analysis, incorrectly.

Beginning with Herophilus, on the contrary, the students of a given master formed associations called sects—the term we use to translate the Greek term *hairesis*, meaning choice or preference and from which we get the word *heresy*. Their purpose was to defend and spread the master's doctrine and practice, which they sometimes helped to articulate, clarify, or expand. It is difficult to evaluate the influence that the philosophers exercised in this regard over the physicians, but it was certainly of some importance. Thus people spoke of the Herophilians, or "the people around Herophilus." However, it would be an exaggeration to say that Herophilus gave these medical sects their definitive forms, particularly the rigid institutional structure that they assumed in the following century and maintained until the decline of the ancient world. Herophilus's school, which was founded on a coherent doctrinal system but remained relatively informal from an institutional point of view, combined the old and the new.

Herophilus's school lasted more than two centuries in Alexandria, then moved to Asia Minor, occupying a site surrounding an ancient temple near Laodicia. It was probably there that it acquired stronger institutional structures, possibly because of the proximity of the temple, but more probably to conform to the new model that had become dominant. In theory, the Herophilians adhered to the tradition of rational medicine bequeathed by Hippocrates, and thus were categorized among the Dogmatists. They also preserved and expanded the rich pharmacopoeia perfected by their master, and most of them stayed faithful to pulse-taking as the primary basis of diagnosis. However, the practice of dissection appears to have ceased very early. Herophilus's school experienced something common to all schools, of philosophy as well as of medicine: betrayal. One defector, Philinus of Cos, founded the Empiricist sect, and in so doing inaugurated a new era in medicine.

Early medicine, beginning with the end of the Hellenistic period, is ordinarily thought to have been dominated by competition among the three major schools: Dogmatist, Empiricist, and Methodist. To these is sometimes added the Pneumatist school, so-called because it insisted on the importance of breath *(pneuma)* and explained illness as a result of the *pneuma*'s becoming too cold or warm, too fast or slow, too heavy or light; the Pneumatists attempted to cure patients by correcting these problems, substituting heat for cold, and so on. In reality, these sects are not simply different instances of the same model.

There really was no Dogmatist (sometimes called rationalist) school—because no doctor ever called himself a "Dogmatist." The term was used first by their adversaries, and later by historians and doxographers. As we have seen, the historical and the critical traditions both placed Herophilus in the school that traced its roots back to Hippocrates himself. The Empiricists, however, did constitute a school in the strict sense of the word, by virtue of their rivalry with Herophilus's disciples, who constituted a "proto-school," a rivalry all the more bitter since the founder of the empirical sect was a defector from the Herophilian ranks. The Empiricists' argument with the Dogmatists was essentially epistemologic, and Galen, with some malice, claimed that they often agreed on the treatment of a particular patient, disagreeing only on the underlying method; this, in the end, is consistent with what we have already noted about the composite character of Hellenistic medicine. For the Empiricists, hidden causes are unknowable and only experience can reveal the proper treatment of a particular illness. According to this view, medicine is no longer a science. Of course, it is not simply a matter of the experience of a single individual, for the Empiricists recognized the validity of what they called *historia*, the cumulative experience of predecessors as transmitted through oral teaching and in written observations. Similarly, experience gained from one case could be extended, since the Empiricists did not exclude analogies, which allowed them to apply to one organ what they had observed in another, or to apply to a given drug the results of experiments undertaken with a different one. The influence of Skeptic philosophy on Empiricist physicians, whether that of the Pyrrhonians or of the Skepticist Academy of Arcesilas, seemed self-evident to many commentators. The question of influence is actually a very difficult one, and, like many others, it is far from being resolved: the history of the Empiricist school remains to be written, and whoever takes on this difficult task will confront a number of obstacles, not least of which is the tenacious prejudice of modern historians toward Empiricist physicians.

A careful reading of the records, particularly those of Galen, reveals important differences among Empiricist physicians. Philinus took an extreme position by refusing to consider even what tradition calls obvious causes, for example, wounds and overeating. Thus, though all Empiricists officially adhered to the same mandate to reject all rational arguments in medicine, there were vastly different interpretations of this stance. If a physician like Serapion of Alexandria (3rd to 2nd century B.C.E.), whom Celsus cites as a founder of the Empiricist school, condemned all use of reasoning in matters of medicine, certain later Empiricists, like Heraclides of Tarentum (1st century B.C.E.), were not as strict. They advocated a sort of reasoning that they called epilogism, as opposed to the analogism of the Dogmatists. Epilogism, besides its defensive value for Empiricism vis-à-vis its adversaries, might allow for the discovery of hidden phenomena and relationships, but only the kind that, under other circumstances, could be *observed*. Thus they still refused to proceed by inference from observation of perceptible things to something that could be known by reason alone. With Menodotus (1st to 2nd century C.E.), Empiricism ended up employing inductive reasoning in a way that appears very modern.

The Empiricists have to be taken quite seriously. They were neither Sophists seeking to achieve a dialectical tour de force—to build a medical system that did not depend on reason—nor reactionaries longing for the prerational time of archaic medicine. These physicians were responding to contemporary or prior nosological attitudes in tones that were both positivist and rational. It was never a question of encouraging physicians to act in some irrational, animal-like way, but of rejecting what philosophers called demonstration *(apodeixis)*. The Empiricists have been widely criticized for their rejection of anatomy and especially of dissection. Was this not simply a clear indication of the contradiction, already referred to, between the theoretical virtuosity of the new medicine and its inability to apply the benefits of this virtuosity to treatment?

The third of the medical schools of antiquity, the Methodist school, was founded by physicians who were just as anti-Dogmatist as the Empiricists but who were not satisfied with the Empiricist critique of Dogmatism. The ancients themselves disagreed about the identity of the founder of the Methodist school. Some considered it Themison of Laodicia (1st century B.C.E.) and others Thessalus of Tralles (1st century C.E.). Although we have some groundbreaking works, such as *De medicina methodica* by Prosper Alpinus (1611) and *L'histoire de la médecine* by Daniel Leclec (1723), until recently there has been little interest in a system of medicine that has been the object

of sharp attacks since ancient times, particularly by Galen. There is undoubtedly important work waiting to be done: entire texts by Methodist physicians
are available to the historian of Methodism, including works by Soranus of
Ephesus (1st to 2nd century C.E.) and Caelius Aurelianus (ca. 5th century C.E.),
although we have no statement of the doctrine itself by a Methodist doctor.

Like the Empiricists, the Methodists thought that the physician should not
try to explain diseases by inferring hidden causes from what can be observed.
However, they adopted a different attitude toward hidden realities: while the
Empiricists believed that such realities did not exist, the Methodists did not
take a position on this point, saying that hidden realities, whether they existed or not, were of no consequence for the physician. They held certain
Dogmatist notions, but gave them a somewhat different meaning. For example, for the Dogmatists, *endeixis* (indication) was the ability of certain phenomena to *indicate* particular entities or connections that were imperceptible.
As Galen said: "Although they [the Methodists] were especially interested in
phenomena [like the Empiricists], they differed on the use of the indication";
the Methodists' indication is not the same as the Dogmatists' (*On Sects* 14)
"in that it comes from what is apparent" whereas the Dogmatists drew indications from causes that were not manifest. Actually, the use of the term *indication* by the Methodists applied to only one situation, that of a remedy indicated by a pathological condition, whereas in Dogmatist philosophy, at least in
one famous case, the soul could be indicated by movement. The use of the
term *indication* by Dogmatists and Methodists is more a case of homonyms
than of shared concepts.

The principal difference between Methodists and Empiricists lies in the fact
that for the former the treatment of a pathology is not determined experi-
mentally (either by firsthand experience or by induction from what can be
observed). The central idea of Methodism is that symptoms themselves are
indicative of treatment, in the way that thirst indicates its own remedy, drinking. But how are the symptoms to be read? Through a unique and universal
conceptual construct, that of "self-evident communities."

This is a complex doctrine, one that is not well understood and that
changed during the history of the Methodist school. For instance, the number
of communities varied, especially when some Methodists introduced "therapeutic communities." Let us limit ourselves here to the doctrine that seems to
have been the most widely recognized. According to this doctrine, there are
three communities *(koinotetes)*: the strict *(stegnon)*, the loose *(roōdes)*, and
the mixed *(epiploke)*. In the body, every pathological condition comes from a
state of constriction or slackening, or a combination of the two. This suggests
that the body itself can be described in terms of condensation and rarefaction.
The Methodists thought that they could overcome in this way both the practical and the epistemological hurdles posed by phenomenism. Galen explained
this well: symptoms could be similar and yet require different treatment; con-

versely, it could be necessary to employ the same remedy for seemingly different symptoms. There are interesting examples: the same therapy ought not to be used for the same affliction "as in the case of phrenitis, for example the feeling of tightness in the diaphragm, or the feeling of slackening," whereas one would employ the same treatment for pleurisy and phrenitis "if they both result from constriction" (Pseudo-Galen, *De optima secta*, ed. Kühn, I.163). However, for the Methodists it was not only "self-evident communities" that indicated the remedy to be used (a condition of tightness would call for a loosening). They also took into account phases in the evolution of disease, but according to a predetermined "chart" applicable in every case: all sickness has a beginning *(arche)*, a development *(auxesis, epidosis)*, a high point *(acme)*, and a decline *(parakme, anesis)*.

Where do the self-evident communities come from? According to Galen, "They were not 'apparent' in the sense of being obvious to the senses. Not every condition (of tightness, etc.) can be perceived by the senses, but the condition was 'apparent' if it could be grasped in and of itself, even if it was not observable" *(De optima secta*, ed. Kühn, I.175). The author added that for the Methodists, "apparent" *(phainomenon)* is more or less synonymous with "obvious" *(enarges)*. Put another way, apparent communities avoid two charges: that of being perceived by the senses, with all the uncertainty implied by acquiring knowledge through sensory perception, and that of being rationally established on the basis of "indicative signs."

From the descriptions of Methodism, we have the general impression that we are dealing with an absurd, if not grotesque, speculation, an impression attributable largely to the low opinion of it held by Galen, who is our principal source. Adopting the theory of apparent communities led the Methodists to espouse paradoxes that were shocking to their contemporaries. They said, for example, that it was useless to be concerned with symptoms and circumstances—age, sex, environment, and so forth—in determining treatment. In fact, the Methodists attempted to establish a genuine empiricism by rethinking the role of sensory perception in medical theory and practice. They refused to choose between pure empiricism, which proved to be intolerable, and a priori rationalism; they understood that the Dogmatist approach combined heterogeneous realities, and that no real connection was possible between the general causes imagined by theoreticians and medical practice.

One of the principal features of the new medicine that developed after Herophilus can be found in changes that appear in the accounts of pathological conditions. This is particularly noticeable toward the end of the 2nd century B.C.E.—the beginning of the period of nosographies, which continued for several centuries. The new approach involved defining nosological entities and classifying them by types and species, leaving the doctor to decide, on the basis of the combination *(syndrome)* of the patient's symptoms, what illness he was treating. Although it is difficult to identify the steps in a typical account by the authors of these nosographies, some of the same headings often reappear: a description of symptoms, a report of other physicians' opinions on the illness, an account of the treatment applied, and often an explanation of symptoms based on the "medical system" of that particular author. This process is very different from the one found in *Epidemics* in the *Hippocratic Corpus:* medicine has been described as passing from a description of patients—for individual cases are meaningless unless all the specific symptoms manifested under specific circumstances are brought together—to a description of illnesses, as in proceeding from prognosis to diagnosis. To be sure, we need to recall that in the *Hippocratic Corpus* there were treatises describing diseases—I cited an example from *Diseases* II above—and that the Hippocratic prognosis was, in some ways, a diagnosis; but the change was profound nevertheless. In the nosographies, diseases are defined in terms of one major distinction that has survived into our own time: the distinction between acute and chronic illness, which was probably introduced by Themison.

However, ancient physicians themselves did not seem to have grasped how new the medicine they practiced really was. Just as we have seen this "new" medicine claim descent from Hippocrates, as the practitioners' habit of writing commentaries on the *Hippocratic Corpus* plainly shows, the authors of nosographies constantly denied there had been any change. As Galen writes in his minor work *Quod optimus medicus sit quoque philosophus* (That the Good Physician Is Also a Philosopher): "Failure to know how to classify illnesses by species and genus results in mistakes in treatment; this is what Hippocrates taught when he urged us to follow the rational method."

RATIONAL BUT NOT SCIENTIFIC MEDICINE

Rational medicine, first introduced by Herophilus, saw little change until the end of antiquity. It retained many of the features common to prescientific speculations, particularly the expansion of theory, which served to mask its impotence in actual practice.

From a contemporary point of view, early medical theory offered two very different aspects. Beginning in the 3rd century B.C.E., a remarkable amount had been learned about the human body through observation and experience, sometimes by chance, as when a bodily injury revealed hidden functions and structure, and contrived experience, as in the case of anatomy, the practice of human and animal vivisection. The human skeleton was well understood, with only a few minor exceptions that surprise us today, but these probably resulted from animal experiments. Muscles, though unknown to Aristotle (who explained movement by a system of tendons), were also recognized. The major systems were well identified. Distinction was made between veins and arteries in the circulatory system, although the idea of actual circulation of blood had not emerged; the ancients believed that the blood that circulated in blood vessels collected in the body to make flesh, and had to be continually produced by food; this was the gist of Aristotle's theory. At the same time, the description of the nervous system, which distinguished between sensory and motor nerves as revealed by experiments in vivisection, showed a marked advance in Hellenistic medicine. The central nervous system was thoroughly described, but without any idea about how it worked. There were huge advances in the anatomy of the lungs, but again without the slightest idea of the purpose of respiration; most physicians believed that it primarily served to cool off the body. Functions remained obscure, obviously, as we noted in the cases of cerebral and respiratory function: digestion was generally thought of as either steeping or grinding, and the glands were not thought of as organs of secretion but as spongy growths intended to absorb excess liquid in the body.

The therapeutic consequences of these discoveries were relatively small, and while, as we have seen, physicians remained generally committed to the old Hippocratic pharmacopoeia, it was because the positive discoveries that they had made about the human body could not bring about a revolution in treatment. However, it seems that by Galen's time important advances had been made in surgery and in areas as delicate as odontology or ophthalmology, though trepanation and the setting of fractures and dislocations had been practiced since Hippocrates' day. As for medication, although fairly effective antipyretics for reducing fever had been in use for a long time, there was nothing at all like a disinfectant, for the simple reason that there was no concept of infection.

Another aspect of ancient medical theory is found in the relationship between medicine and what we call biology. The obstacles encountered by physicians attempting to translate the new knowledge in anatomy and physiology into remedies did not stop them from basing their treatments on theoretical considerations that were in turn based on certain assumptions about the human body and its functions. Erasistratus explained fever as the partial obstruction of blood vessels owing to some residue that impeded the normal flow of blood.

Galen, synthesizing the Hippocratic humoral theory, Aristotelian finalism, and the physiology in Plato's *Timaeus,* developed a network of correspondences between organs, functions, humors, and the outside world that came to dominate Western and Arabic medicine up to the Renaissance. Consequently, the speculative, theoretical aspect of medicine remained similar to philosophical speculation.

Since early biology remained speculative—a part of physics understood as "natural philosophy"—it was never able to benefit from the many advances over Aristotelian descriptions afforded by the observations and experiments of anatomists. Bachelard and others have shown that an intellectual construct of this type is not open to rectification or refutation resulting from experiments that could always be simplified and integrated. At the very most, an untenable position such as cardiocentrism was abandoned even by Aristotelians like Galen. Physicians continued to construct systems of general explanations—what might be called medical biology—that obviously never found practical application. The critics, first Empiricists and then Methodists, tried to stop this speculative folly. Nevertheless, such folly was characteristic of ancient medicine and gave it a very different conceptual orientation from that of modern science.

PIERRE PELLEGRIN
Translated by Elizabeth Rawlings and Jeannine Pucci

Bibliography

Texts and Translations

Aristotle. *On Sense and Sensible Objects*. In *On the Soul; Parva naturalia; On Breath*. Trans. W. S. Hett. Loeb Classical Library.

Celsus. *De medicina*. Trans. W. G. Spencer. Loeb Classical Library.

Galen. *De optima secta ad Thrasybulum Liber*. In *Opera omnia*. Ed. and Latin trans. C. G. Kühn. 20 vols. Leipzig: 1821–1833; repr. Hildesheim: Olms, 1964–1965.

———. *Three Treatises on the Nature of Science*. Trans. Richard Walzer and Michael Frede. Indianapolis: Hackett, 1985.

Hippocrates. Trans. W. H. S. Jones. Vols. 1 and 2. Loeb Classical Library.

Studies

Bourgey, Louis. *Observation et expérience chez les médecins de la collection hippocratique*. Paris: Vrin, 1953.

Grmek, Mirko D. *Diseases in the Ancient Greek World*. Baltimore: Johns Hopkins University Press, 1989.

Grmek, Mirko D., ed. *Western Medical Thought from Antiquity to the Middle Ages*. Cambridge, Mass.: 1998.

Lloyd, Geoffrey E. R. *Early Greek Science*. New York: Norton, 1971.

———. *Greek Science after Aristotle*. New York: Norton, 1973.

———. *Magic, Reason, and Experience: Studies in the Origin and Development of Greek Science*. Cambridge and New York: Cambridge University Press, 1979.

———. *Science, Folklore, and Ideology: Studies in the Life Sciences in Ancient Greece*. Cambridge and New York: Cambridge University Press, 1983.

Pigeaud, Jacky. *La maladie de l'âme et du corps dans la tradition médico-philosophique antique*. Paris: Les Belles Lettres, 1989.

Staden, Heinrich von. *Herophilus: The Art of Medicine in Early Alexandria*. Cambridge and New York: Cambridge University Press, 1989.

Related Articles

Images of the World; Schools and Sites of Learning; Demonstration and the Idea of Science; Hippocrates; Skepticism; Epistemology; Observation and Research; Galen; Pythagoreanism

PHYSICS

A<small>NY HISTORY OF THE SCIENCES</small> that would extend back to antiquity must encounter what one might call the "homonymic obstacle." Is it possible to include Aristotle's biology and Claude Bernard's in a single history, as linguistic usage suggests, since the names of modern sciences are often either those of ancient disciplines (mathematics, astronomy, medicine) or they have had names of Greek or Latin origin attributed to them (biology, linguistics)? Asking this formidable question forces us, first of all, to distinguish among different types of continuity: the theoretical permanence of mathematics is hardly comparable to the identity, problematic in itself, of the object of the life sciences, or to the common therapeutic aim of doctors ancient and modern. But homonymy is most deceptive in the case of physics, so profound was the Galilean rupture. Homonymy entails ambiguity: when our atomic theory was conceptualized by modern physics, for example, it was, properly speaking, *through wordplay* that it acquired Democritean antecedents. Moreover it was explicitly *against* ancient—or rather, Aristotelian—physics that Galilean physics, the first of the sciences in the modern sense of the term, developed (if we leave aside the uncertain case of mathematics). No other science has required such theoretical parricide in order to come into being. And yet the absence of conceptual continuity between ancient and modern physics does not exclude perhaps more fundamental modes of insinuation. Through their research in physics the ancients were led to formulate epistemological principles without which the modern sciences, particularly physics, could not exist. But these principles—determinism, or sufficient cause, for example—do not belong to ancient physics as such and were quickly adopted, at least from the time of Aristotle, by a specialized discipline known in the Hellenistic period as logic. In contrast, some concepts and schemas operative in ancient speculation in these areas have proven to be of incontestable heuristic value for modern scientists. This is largely due, however, to the intellectual history of the latter, and it is difficult to say how modern physics might be different if the ancients had not forged notions like that of continuum or reversibility.

The noun *physics* derives from the Greek *physike* (literally, natural things), which implies science *(episteme)*, discipline *(methodos)*, art *(techne)*, and so on. In the philosophical schools of the Hellenistic period, physics was a part of philosophy, along with logic (or dialectics) and ethics, according to a tripartite division that apparently goes back to the ancient Academy. This is the product of a reductive movement the principal stages of which we must now examine.

THE INQUIRY INTO NATURE

Philosophy itself actually started out as physics. No one has yet seriously challenged the idea, which comes to us directly from the ancients themselves, that with the so-called Milesian school in the 7th century B.C.E. a new way of considering the universe appeared, namely, philosophy. Properly speaking, then, philosophy has not always existed everywhere and at all times, and it is legitimate to investigate its relationships with earlier, contemporary, and later attempts at explanation, whether competing or complementary.

Philosophers as concerned with the history of philosophy as Aristotle and his immediate successors acknowledged philosophical antecedents outside the sphere of Greek culture. We must remember that we owe to these philosophers not only most of the accounts we possess concerning the Presocratics but also the interpretive framework within which we are compelled to read these accounts. We know from Herodotus that the Greeks were fascinated by the great empires of the Near East, pharaonic Egypt in particular. But what Socrates, in the intellectual autobiography Plato supplies for him in *Phaedo*, termed the "inquiry into nature" *(historia peri physeōs)* comes into being with Thales of Miletus and his successor Anaximander. The expression is neither a Socratic nor a Platonic innovation, since the Hippocratic treatise *On Ancient Medicine* uses it to designate the work of "Empedocles and others who wrote on nature." Moreover, ancient historians and doxographers credited most Presocratic philosophers with works entitled "On Nature" *(Peri physeōs)*. Some wrote nothing else; some, like Empedocles, may have composed other texts. It is by no means certain that the texts actually bore this title, if only because the notion of "title" may be a later one; a work was usually designated in antiquity by its opening words. But this is not critically important, since the fundamental unity of Presocratic philosophy remains.

What is this nature *(physis)*, this object of study of the first philosophers, who were called physicists *(physikoi)* or physiologists *(physiologoi)* by Aristotle for this very reason? It derives from the root *phy-*, whose original meaning seems to have been increase, grow, be born, and, transitively, cause to grow, engender. The word existed in Greek before Thales; it is likely that Anaximander turned it into a philosophical term, or perhaps one should say grounded philosophy in it. The *Odyssey* uses it to designate the nature (in the sense of properties) of a plant that protects Odysseus against the witchcraft of Circe. But it was probably its philosophical use that made it a common Greek expression. Among the earliest Presocratics the word has three main senses, which occur both separately and concurrently in the texts. *Physis* designates first of all the primordial substance from which everything is derived.

It is therefore a principle, or *arkhe,* which is the second key term in the philosophy of the *physiologoi.* But *physis* is also the process of growth and differentiation of things out of their original substance. This is closest to the original meaning of the root *phy-.* Last, *physis* is the result of the process of growth and coming into being. This is the sense that the usual translation of *physis* as nature captures best; the Latin *natura,* from *nasci,* be born, shows the same semantic breadth as *physis.* In this latter sense *physis* denotes the characteristic properties of a thing, of a collection of things, or even of all things. Thus the *physikoi* attempted to construct explanatory models for the production of natural phenomena (including human beings and their societies) from primordial nature, by means of qualities (hot, cold, moist), entities (water, air, fire), and processes (condensation, rarefaction). These secular and rational models derive their persuasive force from reason, and, analogically, from everyday experiences such as evaporation, desiccation, or putrefaction.

To grasp the originality of this *physical* philosophy, historians are (fortunately) in the habit of comparing it with what preceded it. An overview of the plentiful literature devoted to this question is offered in the masterful studies that Jean-Pierre Vernant, Pierre Vidal-Naquet, their colleagues, and their students began to publish in the 1960s. They have definitively shown that the birth of "physical" philosophy must be traced back to the profound alteration, still largely enigmatic and profoundly consequential, that was the advent of the original social formation we know as the Greek city-state (polis). Philosophical—in other words, physical—explanations of the universe are consonant with *political* power, which is exercised within the framework of laws usually established by the citizens or their representatives, through the persuasive power of public speeches. Mythological explanations of the order of things, on the contrary, are based on an *authority* that they both legitimize and reinforce. Myth, divine or heroic tales full of violence, sex, prohibition, and transgression, provided ancient Greek society with a foundation that man tampered with at his peril. Thus mythological accounts of the universe are particularly well suited to ruling dynasties whose sovereigns can claim that their power is divinely sanctioned.

But accepting this analysis does not obviate the need to develop or qualify it further. Scholars comparing mythological and physical explanations of the universe generally rely for the former on Hesiod's *Theogony,* and to a lesser extent on his *Works and Days.* In Hesiod's account, Chaos and Earth, primordial powers along with Love, together engendered Erebos and Night, who gave birth to the Upper Air and Day. But Earth also coupled with Sky, whom she had herself engendered, and one of their offspring, Cronos, brought the rule of his father Sky to an end, castrating him before being himself dethroned by one of his children, Zeus, who established the current order of the universe. Humankind lived in harmony with the gods until Prometheus, who had the job of dividing the food between the two, secretly favored humans. As an act of vengeance Zeus deprived humankind of fire, which the philanthropic Prometheus stole back for them, suffering accordingly. Anaximander's account is completely different. From a primordial substance described as "infinite," pairs of opposites—hot/cold, dry/moist—are "ejected"; a preponderant role seems to have fallen to moist. It is disputed whether this "ejection" results from a "mechanical" interaction of material particles, or manifests the generative power of the infinite, sometimes described as a living being. Living creatures are born from the desiccation of a moist substance that is possibly terrestrial, humankind being the final product of an evolution from aquatic animals.

As the first of the *physiologoi* whose system can be described with some precision, Anaximander is often taken to be paradigmatic of this earliest phase of physics. But echoes of several other systems have come down to us: according to one, everything derives from water through condensation and rarefaction; for another, everything derives from air; for a third, from fire; still others, whose traces are preserved in the *Hippocratic Corpus,* hold that everything is derived from other primordial substances, compound or simple. This diversity, an object of mockery from a fairly early date—at least from the time of Socrates—calls for two remarks. On the one hand, it is emblematic of the new spirit that marked the advent of physics. No longer appealing to authority, physical explanations originated in the imagination, broadly construed, of those who conceived them. They were *hypotheses* put forward for acceptance, and also for criticism, by everyone endowed with reason. This is a characteristic, likewise inherited from the Greek polis, that ancient philosophy upheld to the end, even after authoritarian regimes had put an end to political freedom in the city-states: philosophy was deployed in the free confrontation of diverse systems and opinions, where no single orthodoxy held sway. In contrast, in bringing all these explanations together under the heading of "inquiry into nature," the ancients were certainly aware that what they held in common theoretically—their explanation of the origin of things in terms of transformations of a primordial substance from which all things ultimately derive—was far more characteristic of them than the ways in which their accounts diverged.

The following discussion will depart from Jean-Pierre Vernant's schema on two points: one has to do with myth itself, and the other with the structure of the physical explanation of the universe. The works of Hesiod, written toward the end of the 8th century B.C.E., are perhaps not the ones best suited to illustrating the distinction that Vernant seeks to make. Comparing Hesiod to the Babylonian myth related in the poem *Enuma Elish,* Gérard Naddaf notes several interesting points of contrast between the two texts. In the first place, the Hesiodic myth lacks the essential characteristic of correspondence to a ritual that allows, through symbolic reenactment of the heroic mythos, for both the periodic renewal of world order and the reinforcement of royal prerogative in cyclical—that is, immutable—time. From this viewpoint the function of the Hesiodic account, written after the great dynasties such as that of Mycenae had disappeared, is more literary than social; it reads as a narrative sequence of "reigns": Ouranos, followed by Cronos, followed by Zeus. To be sure, there is the occasional "return of the repressed" in the Hesiodic myth; for example, having defeated the coalition led by Cronos and dispatched its members to Tartarus, Zeus must deal with Typhon, a monster attempting to restore primeval chaos. Typhon's desperate attempt is a reminder that primordial chaos was suppressed but not eliminated. At the same time, the actual "creator" element in Hesiod's cosmogony is remarkably impersonal: the universe arises through the interaction of relatively abstract entities (Chaos, Earth, Eros). This is not the case later on in Hesiod, when the gods' accounts take center stage.

Reading the fragments of the first *physiologoi* with these remarks concerning Hesiod in mind, one notes that the undeniable differences between the poet and the philosophers are accompanied by a remarkable convergence. Scholars disagree as to whether certain Presocratics conceived of the universe as having infinite extension in time and space. Did Anaximander, Heraclitus, and Anaxagoras believe that the cosmogenesis they described was indefinitely repeated in time whenever the cosmos returned to its primordial stage? In any case, all pre-Aristotelian physics remained imprisoned in a *narrative structure* that it shared with the Hesiodic account: the creation of the world took place in linear time and in a necessary order, while the events in this *(hi)story* arose out of the automatic and necessary interaction of the properties of the elementary entities at work in cosmogenesis.

The *physiologoi* do seem at least to have overcome the rupture between primordial and contemporary time created by myth, through a prefiguration of the idea of "laws of nature," just as modern physicists would come to abolish the Aristotelian rupture between supralunary and sublunary worlds. It has even been suggested that in these rules, which are valid for every point in the universe, one should see an intellectual reflection of the law of democracy, which applies equally to all citizens, while the mythological rupture between primordial and present time reflects the insurmountable difference of status between divine rulers and their subjects. In fact this is overly simplistic. Many of the Presocratic cosmogonies articulate different *periods* that can hardly be viewed as governed by the same rules. According to the Milesians, the universe had a period of dawning in which the phenomena we see before us were not yet visible, and it was Empedocles who designated most clearly the difference between cosmic phases governed by different principles (Love and Hate). Nevertheless, even for physicists who distinguished among periods, at any given moment all reality obeyed the same laws.

Perhaps most fascinating of all in these meager vestiges of the earliest physicists—and this may be attributable to some resonance with our own unconscious desires—is this claim of complete apprehension of reality as a whole. Milesian Nature, from which all beings arise and to which all beings return, is indeed that great mother-without-father, inexhaustible and benevolent, the need for which all children have experienced. The physicist makes his first appearance in search of the principle or principles underlying all things, yet this search takes place within the framework of a Nature that is, ultimately, the sole reality. In this sense the Milesians' concept of Nature was the opposite of the modern one, since nature is defined for us by what it is not. Therefore for them there is no phenomenon that is not natural, and the inquiry into nature encompasses all things. For many centuries the treatises that bore this title (or that acquired it later on) were constructed along the same lines: the author begins by examining the formation of the cosmos, starting from a principle or principles that he has chosen; then he describes the genesis of living creatures and explains their characteristics and endowments, with humankind generally coming at the end of this description, and he finally considers the formation and history of human societies. These analyses have in common the fact that they appeal only to the "mechanical" action of factors utilized in the genesis of things. Here perhaps is their principal difference from earlier mythical cosmogonies, including Hesiod's: the cosmos of the earliest physicists is devoid of intentions, of passions, and of choices. The gods themselves are natural entities and are therefore subject to the laws of nature. Theology is thus a part of physics, and Anaximander, for example, transfers traditional attributes of divinity, such as ingenerability, incorruptibility, immortality, and eternity, to *physis*.

THE ELEATIC SCHOOL AND THE ATTEMPTS TO RESTORE PHYSICS

The first radical challenge to ancient physics, at the beginning of the 5th century B.C.E., came from Parmenides of Elea and his school, called Eleatic after the city in which it was founded. Throughout antiquity and even beyond, philosophers have had to respond to Parmenides' critique. Situating oneself in relation to Parmenides was considered almost an obligatory phase of philosophical inquiry very early on, and quotations from his poem *On Nature* are thus sufficiently numerous to give us a fairly accurate idea of some of his views. Parmenides criticizes first of all the philosophical nonchalance of the earliest physicists, who saw nothing problematic in deriving all living things from a single principle. Thus the "infinite," which Anaximander takes as a first principle, is indeterminate—this is also the sense of *apeiron*, translated as infinite—and is therefore not a being, even though at the same time it is an engenderer of all things. It may issue from a woman's mouth, but this is paternal discourse, in other words, discourse that prescribes and forbids in the name of the principle of reality, which Parmenides addresses to the adherents of the ancient physics. "I shall not allow you to say nor to think that being comes from non-being" (frg. 8.7–9), says the goddess who instructs the poet, before demonstrating to him the absurdity of the speech "of mortals." Why is a living being born at one instant rather than another, in one place rather than another?

The Eleatic school profoundly altered the shape of physics. For Parmenides, the all-encompassing science became an impossible science. The manner in which the second part of Parmenides' poem is to be understood will no doubt continue to be debated for a long time to come; it proposes, paradoxically, a cosmology of the same type as those of his predecessors, which the philosopher has just severely criticized. Should we see it as a "physics lesson," similar to Alceste's "poetry lesson" to *les précieux* in Molière's *Le misanthrope*, in which Parmenides proves that in the domain of the "false" he is just as capable as the rest, and perhaps more so? Or as an example of what one should not do? Or of a physics belonging to the sphere of appearance and opinion, and not that of truth? In any case, physics lost its status as a rigorous science. Parmenides' greatest victory is clearly visible in later Greek philosophy: henceforward no one would question that intelligibility belonged to what is eternal and immutable, while what is perishable or mutable belonged at best to the realm of opinion.

After Parmenides, no one dared return to the old inquiry into nature. But philosophers did attempt to make physics once again possible. Aristotle saw that the atomist hypothesis of Leucippus and Democritus reintroduced the possibility of plurality and movement while maintaining the central tenets of Eleatic philosophy: that that which is, in the strictest sense of the term, is complete, homogeneous, ingenerable, and incorruptible, and that being and nonbeing are unable to mix or to derive one from the other. But instead of positing a single entity, the atomists imagined an infinity of particles that are whole, indivisible (this is what "atom" means), eternal, and in constant movement in an infinite void that is "nonexistent." Aggregations of these atoms, spontaneously generated, produce the various entities (cf. Aristotle, *On Coming-To-Be and Passing-Away* I.8.325a23ff).

The same could be said for the systems of Empedocles and Anaxagoras: the Eleatic prohibition against the derivation of being from nonbeing is fundamental. "Of all mortal things none has birth, nor any end in accursed death, but only mingling," Empedocles wrote (frg. 350, in Kirk et al.). Everything is made from new combinations that are eternally unmade, and that arise from four fixed elements: Air, Fire, Water, and Earth. Remarkably, the word that has to be translated here as birth is *physis*, the central term of the ancient physics overthrown by the Eleatic school. Anaxagoras, probably a contemporary of Empedocles, also stated that "nothing comes into being nor perishes, but is rather compounded or dissolved from things that are" (frg. 469, Kirk et al.).

All these "restored"—i.e., post-Parmenidean—physical systems share with the Milesian school a "mechanism" that is strongly criticized by both Plato and Aristotle. It is by virtue of their properties, which we would call physico-chemical, that elementary particles come together to form the compounds we see in the world around us. Thus the sole conditions that must be satisfied for two atoms to join together are that they have forms making them suitable for it and that they encounter each other, which is purely a matter of chance. But in an infinite time and space, *all* combinations must necessarily arise.

"IN SOCRATES' TIME"

In the first book of his treatise *On Parts of Animals,* after he has explained that the Presocratics did not arrive at a correct analysis of natural phenomena, because they had no conception of substance that would allow a finalist explanation, Aristotle adds: "In Socrates' time an advance was made so far as the method was concerned; but at that time philosophers gave up the study of Nature and turned to practical [virtue], and to political science" (I.i.642a29).

When the Athenians accused him of, among other things, looking into what took place in the heavens and beneath the earth—of pursuing an inquiry into nature—Socrates answered that he had no interest in these matters, which "he did not understand." The accusation may have been simply anachronistic, since in the autobiography of Socrates found in Plato's *Phaedo* we see Socrates turning to the speculations of ancient physicists before expressing disappointment and turning away. From this position (and it is unimportant for our purposes whether we are following an actual chronology or one reconstructed after the fact), Socrates is solely concerned with making his fellow citizens better, in the ethical sense of the term. His complaint against the earlier physicists is that their accounts were exclusively based on what the Aristotelian tradition would term material and efficient causalities. Hence the famous example in *Phaedo* (98c), where the cause of Socrates' being seated at that particular moment in prison would have been ascribed by the earlier physicists to his body's being made of bones and sinews articulated in a particular manner. For Socrates, the true cause of his being in prison was that, owing to a certain conception of duty and justice, he preferred to submit to the verdict of Athenian judges rather than evade it. Socrates levels an additional charge at the authors of physical treatises that appears in Plato's *Apology*—notably in the ironic passage where Socrates states that he has no intention of disparaging the man who, wiser and cleverer than he, possesses sure and certain knowledge concerning nature—but that is more fully reported by Xenophon. In the latter's account, Socrates states several times that the science of nature is greater than the powers of the human spirit, or that it is by design that the gods have left us in the dark on this subject.

It is difficult to know exactly to whom Aristotle was referring when he mentioned philosophers "in Socrates' time." He may well have meant both those who counted themselves in some manner disciples of Socrates, that is, the Socratics (but does this include Plato?), and people like the Sophists, whose relations with Socrates were more tenuous, and also, finally, more complex. The role of the Sophists in the history of Greek physics needs to be reexamined, for although it was undoubtedly the conditions surrounding the exercise of power in the polis, and notably in democratic regimes like that of Athens, that principally fostered or even directly provoked the rise of the Sophistic movement, the theoretical foundations as well as the uncertainties of the pre- and post-Parmenidean physicists seem to have decisively influenced the content, as well as the method, of the Sophists' teaching. Certain Sophists, Hippias for example, claimed to teach disciplines, such as astronomy, that were directly related to physics. Texts such as Gorgias's *On Not Being*, as well as the relativistic accounts of the doctrines of Protagoras offered by both Plato and Aristotle, seem to indicate that the Sophists were particularly alert to divergent views among the earlier physicists. Thus they helped to deepen the divide between physics and what would later be called practical philosophy. In the famous Sophistic distinction between that which is by nature and that which is by convention, the intelligent causality that is human free will is seen as operating in the sphere of the conventional. Here Socrates and the Sophists could easily find common ground. From this perspective, Aristotle was right: the Socratics (Cynics, Cyrenaeans, and, to a lesser extent, Megarians) abandoned physics to take up practical philosophy, and also logic.

This second criticism of ancient physics was perhaps even more devastating than that of the Eleatic school. Ancient *physis* was, in effect, dismembered: human beings, who remained part of it at least as living creatures subject to the constraints of all living organisms, claimed exemption from theoretical explanations that applied to all things, on the one hand, and claimed the right to impose their own laws on their environment, on the other. This paved the way for a conception of nature nearer to our own, in which men could proclaim themselves "lords and masters," while the ancient unified view would persist in a solitary and nostalgic existence, flowering now and again among widely diverse authors.

Where is Plato in all this? The position of the most celebrated of Socrates' disciples relative to this sidelining of natural philosophy—which had become of little interest in the world of men, as well as inaccessible to human thought—is not easy to pin down. At first glance it seems hard to imagine that Aristotle would include the author of *Timaeus* among the philosophers "in Socrates' time" who had abandoned natural philosophy. Here, too, Gérard

Naddaf has proposed an appealing hypothesis: Plato was undertaking on his own behalf a project similar to that of authors of inquiries into nature, but for a purpose that was principally ethical and based on new premises.

From *Phaedo* on, Plato's critique of the speculations of ancient physicists manifests an ethical dimension. To say that Socrates was sitting in prison owing to his muscles and sinews is to ignore the ethical reasons that led him to prefer death to flight. This view is presented much more pointedly in *Laws*: because they offer mechanistic explanations of the formation of the universe, inquiries into nature are accused of corrupting youth by turning them away from belief in the gods. For Plato, a morality that was sound, and therefore effective, had to be based on the True, whence the detour in *The Republic* through the changeless world of Forms, dominated by the Form of the Good. In Naddaf's view, Plato's aim, at least from the time of *Timaeus* (written later than *The Republic*), was to demonstrate that a true morality was in accordance with the order of the universe. Acquaintance with this universe became indispensable to any philosopher who sought to introduce the new morality into the city-state. Plato intended to write his own "inquiry into nature" in a trilogy of dialogues: *Timaeus,* which describes the formation of the universe and its inhabitants, including man; *Critias,* which traces the history of civilization up to the sinking of Atlantis and the Athenian army (only the beginning of this dialogue survives, and we do not know whether Plato completed it); and *Hermocrates,* which was never written, but which was intended to tell the story of the renewal of civilization—our own—after the cataclysm. This last enterprise was finally completed, Naddaf suggests, in the third book of *Laws.* In doing so, Plato followed the rules of the inquiry-into-nature genre, which tended to begin with a cosmogony *(kosmogonia)* and proceeded to the creation of animals *(zoogonia),* man *(anthropogonia),* and finally society *(politogonia).*

But the basic conception of this enterprise is completely new: Plato was the first philosopher to propose an inquiry into nature that is creationist rather than evolutionist. The strongest evidence for this radical departure is that some of Plato's immediate successors tried to bring it into line with conventional approaches. Xenocrates, for example, is thought to have declared the creationist theory of *Timaeus* to be a mere pedagogical fiction. This creationism, discernible in the finalism of *Phaedo* when it maintains that the true explanation of things resides in the *intention* of their creator, also has a strong ethical component: morality is sound inasmuch as it is based on an order of the universe that was expressly intended by God. This idea, according to which the order of the world was optimally devised by a divine intelligence, was upheld before Plato, notably by Diogenes of Apollonia, a disciple of Anaxagoras. It is surprising that the Socrates of *Phaedo* does not allude to it; perhaps he would have had to revise his global condemnation of the inquiry into nature, and perhaps that was precisely what he wanted to avoid. But between maintaining that the order of the world derives from an intelligent principle and declaring that this order was established by a divine being also preoccupied with the moral destiny of humankind, there is a step that Plato appears to have been the first to take. This is why the physico-teleological proof of the existence of the divinity in Book X of *Laws* may be considered the culminating point of both Plato's inquiry into nature and his reformulation of ethics.

One may wonder why Plato found it necessary to provide both a cosmological and a theological moral foundation, when in *The Republic* the Idea of the Good was sufficient to engender morality and construct the ideal constitution. The discussion at the beginning of *Timaeus* is explicitly described as continuing from "yesterday's discussion"; the reference (as we know from the summary provided) is to the organization of the ideal city-state in *The Republic*. This sequence has been deemed so bizarre, given the widely divergent perspectives of *The Republic* and *Timaeus,* that some modern scholars have made the unlikely claim that there must have been a second, lost version of *The Republic.* To justify the trilogy being inaugurated, Socrates claims at the beginning of *Timaeus* that the earlier treatment was like a painting whose figures he would like to see become animate; he particularly desires to see how the ideal city would function in war. According to Luc Brisson in the introduction to his translation, "*Timaeus* begins with a summary of the ideal Constitution as described in *The Republic* . . . , followed by the story of Athens' ancient victory against Atlantis, because Plato is trying to establish 'in nature' the ideal Constitution described in *The Republic*" (p. 10). This should no doubt be viewed as one of the events in the "realist conversion" that scholars perceive in Plato's final years.

This Platonic rehabilitation of the inquiry into nature, in the form of a creationist cosmogony and anthropogony, does have its complexities. The principal one is to be found in ten much-discussed passages in *Timaeus* in which Timaeus downplays his own discourse, saying that he can make no claims as to the truth of statements about that which is "firm and discernible by the aid of thought" (29b); he can only hope to produce statements "inferior to none in likelihood," a "likely account" (29d). The discourse of physics, because it has to do with sensible reality, which is fleeting and obscure, cannot take on the rigor of scientific discourse. These statements must have influenced Xenocrates in his reading of *Timaeus* mentioned above. In any event, the passages in question support the hypothesis that Plato's inquiry into nature does not have its end in itself, but that its aim is in the last analysis ethical. The actual study of nature does not suffice, according to Plato, to belie Parmenides' condemnation of natural science. Therefore, strictly speaking, Plato may be included among the philosophers who, "in Socrates' time," turned away from physical inquiry—Aristotle said *theoria physika.* The (second) restoration of physics belongs to Aristotle.

ARISTOTELIAN PHYSICS

Aristotle's natural philosophy marks the high point of the physical thought of the ancients. It was Aristotelian physics that medieval thinkers were at pains to understand and develop; it was also Aristotelian physics that was attacked by 17th-century physicists. In his review of earlier doctrines—as he did in other areas, but perhaps to a greater extent with physics—Aristotle tried to show that each harbors a grain of truth, viewed from the proper perspective. Aristotle was not an eclectic, however; his method of theoretical reappropriation of earlier doctrines is virtually the opposite of eclecticism—which naturally makes the Stagirite suspect as a historian of philosophy. Aristotle devoted a fascinating but little-known treatise, *On Coming-To-Be and Passing-Away*, to putting the great problems of Presocratic philosophy "in perspective."

Neither a complete science nor an impossible one, physics for Aristotle is the science of a domain of existence. Entities that possess the principle of motion in themselves are called "natural," the term *motion* being understood in its global Aristotelian sense of change across all categories affected by movement. A living plant has in itself the principle of its own growth; the element Fire has in itself a tendency to move toward the periphery of the universe. A table, on the other hand, has the principle of its becoming-a-table located in something other than itself, i.e., in the craftsman manipulating his tools. From a certain viewpoint, all entities in this world are natural, including tables, since they are made of wood, which is, or once was, a natural object. But this point of view is not *essential:* being made of wood is not a table's essential characteristic. What defines a table is its use, and this is due more to the carpenter than to the tree from which the table is made. The study of physics is then limited to certain entities that Aristotle enumerated in the first lines of the treatise *Meteorologica:* entities in motion and their elements, including heavenly bodies, living creatures, and "meteorological" phenomena, which encompass objects we ourselves would term meteorological—rain, hail, rainbows—and also tides, the sea, currents, earthquakes, and phenomena such as comets, shooting stars, and the Milky Way (which Aristotle located in the atmosphere.)

This theoretical science of self-moving entities takes Parmenides' criticism into account. First of all, the system of physical beings, the cosmos, is finite, closed, and eternal. To be sure, Aristotle refrains from representing all the transformations that occur in it as simple *alterations* of one or more substances that are always the same, as did, according to Aristotle, those philosophers who held that the universe derived from a single, fundamental reality. Here he is alluding to the Milesians, not without putting them through the Caudine Forks of Aristotelianism. Contrary to what the Stagirite claims, Anaximander's infinity cannot be reduced to a *material* in the Aristotelian sense, since, far from being a passive object, infinity is the generator of all things. Even in Aristotelian physics, then, there is generation and disappearance of natural entities, but in an uninterrupted sequence of transformations that is based on the continuous transmutation of elements one into another. Aristotle took from Empedocles the concept of the four basic constituents of matter: Earth, Water, Air, Fire. But he defined each by a *pair* of fundamental properties: hot and cold, dry and moist. Fire is hot and dry, Air is hot and moist, Water is cold and moist, Earth is cold and dry. Elements may be transformed into one another through the gain or loss of these qualities, and this occurs more readily, though not exclusively, between two elements that possess a common quality: Air results from Fire through dry transforming into moist, and so on. The Aristotelian cosmos is fundamentally cyclical, since, for example, heavenly bodies follow the same orbits throughout eternity. This is a fundamental transformation in ancient physics. With Aristotle, for the first time, the discourse of physics lost the narrative structure that tied it so closely to Hesiodic narrative. The problem of the absolute origin of all things disappeared, and cosmology became independent of any cosmogony. The human world, however, is embedded in history; Aristotle states more than once in *Politics* that the time of monarchies is past. But this linearity, with which physics is not concerned, is inscribed within a more fundamental circularity, since the human race is periodically decimated by various cataclysms that oblige the survivors to reinvent civilization. Conversely, the first physicists, being interested in the genesis of all things, had included the study of the development of human civilization in their inquiry into nature.

Yet this closed system was not sufficient unto itself: we have here what we might call the second adaptation to Parmenides' criticism. Everything that is moved is set in motion by a mover, which was set in motion, in turn, by another mover. The ultimate of these movers to be set in motion, the one on whose motion all other motions depend, directly or through mediation, is the "first sky," the set of fixed stars that Aristotle thought were affixed to a sphere, the last one in his geocentric and finite Universe. But the first sky itself received its motion from an unmoved mover, which, for Aristotle, was divinity. This paradoxical concept of the unmoved mover shows clearly the status Aristotle accorded physics. Being immaterial and having no other possible activity—that is, no activity compatible with its preeminent dignity as pure act, except for the activity of thinking about itself—the Prime Mover cannot move in a physical sense. The first sky is thus moved by *desire*, because the perfection of the Prime Mover makes it also supremely desirable. The physical world therefore draws its motion, and even its possibility of a beyond-itself, from a reality that is "metaphysical" in the etymological sense of the term. The higher domain of being lies outside the domain of physics.

Thus the unity of the ancient *physis* was not restored. Moreover, in the cosmos itself certain domains of being are inaccessible to physics. This is true for everything connected with human technologies, and perhaps for certain animal behaviors as well. It is also true in the domain of what Aristotle was the first to call the "practical sciences," i.e., those that take actions resulting from human free will as the objects of ethics and politics. It is perhaps justifiable to speak of nostalgia here as well; in opposition to some Sophists, Aristotle upheld the natural basis of politics and certain social ties. Humans assemble naturally in societies that come to form city-states (poleis); family ties and slavery are also natural, for some people are naturally destined to serve. But this naturalness is not enough to make social and political ties the objects of physics; as those ties are based on human free will, they are subject to a different type of scientific discourse. Finally, phenomena that come about fortuitously, and not always or most of the time, remain outside the science of physics, although they cannot be declared unnatural in every case.

It is at the price of such drastic limitations that Aristotle preserves the status of scientific discourse for physics. The regularities on which this discourse depends are certainly not perfect, whence the reservation noted above: the phenomena studied by physics occur "always or most of the time." But the physicist must uncover the *causes* of these phenomena, and display these properties through demonstrative discourse.

The teleological character that Aristotle attributes to natural phenomena—"nature does nothing in vain," "it always produces the best," he repeats incessantly in his treatises on natural philosophy—is the aspect of his physics that has earned him the most criticism, and interpretation of this teleology remains the object of lively argument among scholars to this day. To understand this Aristotelian position, we should perhaps relate it to what was said above concerning Aristotle's cosmos. If the cosmos is eternal and unchangeable overall, it lacks the possibility of *constructing*, in the past, the perfection—all-encompassing but not total—that we see in it. Moreover, being uncreated, the cosmos cannot derive this perfection from the intelligent intention of a demiurge. It must then be good in and of itself, this goodness being the imperfect imitation of the absolute excellence of the Prime Mover.

The fate of Aristotle's physics, and notably his cosmology and its dynamics, is a paradoxical one. At odds with the past and adopted by none of his successors (even the loyal Theophrastus, who succeeded Aristotle at the head of the Lyceum, criticized his master's teleology), this system is undoubtedly the approach to physics that had the most enduring posterity. Its longevity is largely due to the "Christianization" of Aristotle by certain medieval writers.

Later physicists abandoned Aristotle's eternal and immutable cosmos to return to a more cosmogonic conception of the science of nature. Even if their visions of the universe were radically opposed on several important points, Stoics and Epicureans had in common the conception that worlds form, develop, and finally disappear. Stoic teleology took the providentialist form, which was not part of the Aristotelian cosmos, despite some recent assertions to the contrary, while Epicureanism adopted a modified form of Democritean atomism based on chance. But Aristotelianism obviously left traces. On the fundamental point of the structure of physical discourse, for example, we note that Lucretius, following perhaps the order of exposition of Epicurus's treatise *On Nature,* rather than beginning his poem with the creation of the universe and going on to deal with the genesis of the various entities that compose and inhabit it, first outlines the pertinence of atomic theory, deduces from it the various properties of entities, and then moves on to an "application" of the results of this procedure by examining each category of entities.

Physics from then on was a *part* of philosophy. The first Stoics maintained, emphatically enough to make clear that it was no longer accepted by everyone, the idea that the study of physics was necessary for any would-be philosopher. But from the end of the Hellenistic era on, philosophy began to privilege its ethical side. In his *Naturales quaestiones,* a long treatise on natural science exploring subjects that would have come under the heading of inquiries into nature a few centuries earlier, Seneca justifies his enterprise to Lucilius (to whom the work is dedicated) in terms of an apologetic aim: "You say: 'What good will these things do you?' If nothing else, certainly this: having measured god I will know that all else is petty" (I, Preface, 17). In the context of a polemic with the Epicureans for whom the ultimate object clearly relates to the "art of living," the goal is to have Stoic providentialism triumph over Epicurean atomism, which is based on chance.

THE GREAT DEBATES OF ANCIENT PHYSICS

Such, then, are the principal episodes in the development of ancient speculation concerning *physis.* Let us now look briefly at what we might term the great divisions within ancient physics. At the end of antiquity, the drama whose important events we have just described was played out again more or less synchronically: the theories that had grown out of the difficulties of earlier doctrines coexisted alongside the latter, which took on entirely new forms, as we shall see with the Neoplatonist commentators on Aristotelian physics. In this way, too, ancient physicists bequeathed to the Middle Ages and modern times a set of opposing points of view. Even though these oppositions were of course always outside of physics in the modern sense, the "conflicting matrices" still have plenty of meaning for the Postgalileans that we are. Let us look at two of them.

It is a commonplace to say that, unlike the physics of Galileo's day, the ancient physics was not a physics of engineers. Certainly the Greeks, and through them the Romans, possessed a body of technical thought. The authors of technological treatises made reference to physical science, principally Aristotelian, but knowledge of the available physical theories could not have helped them in the least. No doubt the point was to provide inventions arising from skill and determination with an a posteriori theoretical foundation. The machines described in these treatises were related to physics only by virtue of being *material:* they were presented as a direct application of mathematics. The same held true for optics and acoustics, aptly described by Aristotle along with mechanics as "the most physical fields of mathematics" (*Physics* II.2.94a7). It is in the margins of physics, then, and one might say in the shadow of mathematics, that the speculations that are the most interesting from the point of view of physics in the modern sense arose. As for Archimedes' treatises, which unquestionably constitute for us the most remarkable and fertile production of physics in antiquity, the ancients unanimously located this work in the realm of mathematical speculation.

These remarks bring us to the first significant opposition, which has to do with the role of mathematics in physics. This question must be handled with the greatest caution, because here we run the greatest risk of being misled by statements by ancient philosophers that have a modern ring. We may recall once again to what extent the aims of mathematical physics were alien to the spirit of the ancient physicists; nevertheless, there is a tradition of mathematical analysis of nature that goes back, if not to Pythagoras himself, at least to the first Pythagoreans. It is difficult to pin down the exact nature of the affinity they posited between things and numbers. But what interests us here is that a Pythagorean-Platonist tradition developed a mathematical approach to natural phenomena from which Renaissance and modern scientists explicitly drew their inspiration. Certain Neopythagorean and particularly Neoplatonic texts, notably those of Iamblichus (ca. 245–ca. 325 C.E.) and Proclus (412–485), appear to outline a veritable program for the mathematicization of nature. These texts remained purely programmatic, although it would take too long to show why this is so. They are all based, in the final analysis, on Plato's *Timaeus,* where geometric figures (triangles and squares) are the ultimate components of all corporeal entities. Running counter to this tradition is Aristotle's qualitative approach, adopted by, among others, the Stoics, who felt, on the one hand, that mathematics concerned objects less ontologically rich than those of physics, from which they were derived via abstraction of their sensible qualities, and, on the other hand, that mathematical explanation of the qualities of bodies—as according to the properties of atoms in Democritus or to those of elementary triangles in Plato—derived color, for example, from entities that had no connection to it. For Democritus, it was in fact the form and structural arrangement of atoms that produced color, atoms themselves being colorless. Aristotle did not reject the use of mathematics and measurement in physics, since bodies are mixtures of elements in certain proportions. He even states explicitly in *Physics* (III.iv.202b30) that physical science is concerned with magnitudes, which are by definition measurable. But this avenue of research was of no interest to the Aristotelians for various reasons, chief among them being perhaps that in their view the qualities of bodies—colors, odors, and so on—are among their objective properties.

The second great opposition in the history of ancient physics also divided physicists into two camps, albeit with certain exceptions. On one side were the partisans of a finite world, who adopted a continuous conception of matter and space. This world is, in the majority of accounts, full, or if it does contain some emptiness, it does so in small quantity. On the other side were the partisans of an infinite universe, inhabited by innumerable worlds wandering in the intercosmic void; these thinkers professed an atomist theory of matter and posited the chance encounter of atoms as the basis of all reality. Those who belonged to the first camp, of whom Aristotle was the "purest" representative, had a tendency, entirely consistent with their cosmological presuppositions, to view the universe as the product of an intention or, at the least, of final causes, while the atomists criticized this physical recourse to teleology. The study of "mixed" forms is particularly interesting. The Stoics, for example, as partisans of an absolute providentialism and a determinism so strict that they thought that after its destruction the same world was identically reborn, and that the same Socrates would walk on the same day in the same agora an infinite number of times, shared with Aristotle the idea of a spherical and geocentric world. But not only is this world not eternal, although eternally re-created, nor invariant, since it is susceptible of expansion and retraction, it is also immersed in an infinite void.

This second opposition is of much greater historic importance than the first. At the end of antiquity it formed a background to all physical investigation, pitting Aristotelians and Democriteans against one another. Christians would bring crucial reinforcements to the first camp, but not without undermining the actual organization of Aristotelian physics, which required that the world be eternal. And up to the end of antiquity concepts arising from these physical traditions were studied; a remarkable example is furnished by Aristotle's Neoplatonist commentators, whose richness and intellectual audacity we are only now rediscovering. Primacy of place belongs to the two great 6th-century commentators Philoponus and Simplicius. Let us look at the former. The fact that Philoponus was a Christian led him to criticize the overall conception of Aristotle's eternal universe, but he undertook to rectify or replace certain concepts of Aristotelian physics. Thus he developed the notion of internal momentum that is transmitted from the outside, and that would later be termed *impetus,* to explain the persistence of motion in something mobile that is no longer in contact with its mover. This notion allowed Philoponus to posit a unity of the laws of dynamics: although he preserves the Aristotelian distinction between natural and forced motion, the same kind of impetus explains the motion of heavenly bodies, heavy bodies, and animals. In the same vein, Philoponus abolished the difference in nature between the superlunary and sublunary worlds, maintaining that they are made up of the same matter. In both cases, religious considerations led him to these views: impetus derives ultimately from God, and the fact that the stars were no longer divine but created and destined for destruction removed all their divine character. Philoponus pushed the unification of the universe even further by proposing a definition of matter as extension, which has Cartesian overtones. Through polemics of remarkable theoretical force and subtlety, the notions of space and time were very carefully worked out. All later philosophical and scientific tradition could only return to the same oppositions between absolute or relative space and time.

It seems, then, as if this body of research, based on ancient—and particularly on Aristotelian—notions, which commentators at the end of antiquity handed on to the Middle Ages, constituted a reserve of the principal ideas on which modern physics would draw for its own development. Not that there was theoretical continuity between Philoponus and Galileo, but Galileo could have done nothing without the reelaboration by Philoponus, and his friends and adversaries, of the concepts of Aristotelian physics.

PIERRE PELLEGRIN
Translated by Selina Stewart and Jeannine Pucci

Bibliography

Texts and Translations

Anaxagoras. In *The Presocratic Philosophers*, 2nd ed. Ed. G. S. Kirk, J. E. Raven, and M. Schofield. Cambridge and New York: Cambridge University Press, 1983.

Anaximander. *Fragments et témoignages*. Ed. M. Coche. Paris: Presses Universitaires de France, 1991.

Aristotle. *Meteorologica*. Trans. H. D. P. Lee. Loeb Classical Library.

———. *On Coming-To-Be and Passing-Away*. Trans. E. S. Forster. Loeb Classical Library.

———. *Parts of Animals*. Trans. A. L. Peck. Loeb Classical Library.

Empedocles. In *The Presocratic Philosophers*, 2nd ed. Ed. Kirk, Raven, and Schofield.

Parmenides. Ibid.

Plato. *Timaeus*. In *Timaeus; Critias; Cleitophon; Menexenus; Epistles*. Trans. R. G. Bury. Loeb Classical Library.

Seneca. *Naturales quaestiones*. Trans. Thomas H. Corcoran. Loeb Classical Library.

Studies

Brisson, Luc, trans. Introduction and notes to French ed. of Plato, *Timaeus and Critias*. Paris: Flammarion, 1992.

Burnet, John. *Early Greek Philosophy*. London: A. and C. Black, 1930.

Kahn, Charles. *Anaximander and the Origins of Greek Cosmology*. New York: Columbia University Press, 1960; Philadelphia: Centrum Philadelphia, 1985.

Naddaf, Gérard. *L'origine et l'évolution du concept grec de phusis*. Lewiston, N.Y.: E. Mellen Press, 1992.

Sambursky, Samuel. *The Physical World of the Greeks*. Princeton: Princeton University Press, 1956.

Solmsen, Friedrich. *Aristotle's System of the Physical World*. Ithaca, N.Y.: Cornell University Press, 1960.

Sorabji, Richard, ed. *Philoponus and the Rejection of Aristotelian Science*. Ithaca, N.Y.: Cornell University Press, 1987.

Vernant, Jean-Pierre. *Myth and Thought among the Greeks*. London and Boston: Routledge and Kegan Paul, 1983.

Related Articles

The Question of Being; Cosmology; Aristotle; Epicurus; Milesians; Observation and Research; Anaxagoras; Democritus; Aristotelianism; Stoicism

POETICS

From the beginning, poetry has been recognized for its power and strength, owing to its capacity to evoke and communicate certain emotions. We can recall in Book 1 of the *Odyssey*, at the start of the suitors' banquet, how unbearable Penelope finds the evocation, by the minstrel Phemius, of the return of the Achaeans from Troy: "Phemius, many other things you know to charm mortals, deeds of men and gods which minstrels make famous. Sing them one of these, . . . and let them drink their wine in silence. But cease from this woeful song which always harrows the heart in my breast, for upon me above all women has come a sorrow not to be forgotten" (337–342).

Similarly in Book 8, during Alcinous's feast, when the Phaeacian minstrel sings a prelude and, at Odysseus's request, begins to recount the city's capture and fall, Odysseus, hearing about his companions and their exploits, cannot hold back his tears. This leads him to betray himself and to reveal his true identity to his hosts. Thus anamnesis or anticipation can lead to tears, and can likewise awaken a truth.

What better homage can we imagine than this double testimony to the affective power woven into the very fabric of the story being told? What is more modern, too, than this reflection in a mirror in which the narrative work naturally comments on itself and justifies itself, even as it gives impetus to the story in progress? Moreover, it is not insignificant that specific testimony to the irrefutable emotional and affective power of poetic diction is brought us by Odysseus and Penelope, the two protagonists of the *Odyssey*.

A second element to which the poets themselves bear witness is the will to style, *Kunstwollen*, conceived as an inseparable component of their expressive undertaking. Theognis of Megara is perhaps the first to speak of it, when he refers to the inimitable "stamp" he has imposed on each of his works: "For the sake of my art, let a seal be placed on these verses, Cyrnus, so no one can steal them or replace the noble original with inferior copy. All will say, 'These are the words of Theognis of Megara, famous everywhere'" (I.19–23). Phocylides, for his part, uses an authentic signature in many of his compositions, in a familiar formulaic hemistich: "Here is this work, another by Phocylides."

Finally, in a different realm, the art of pastiche as Plato practiced it in *Menexenus, Phaedrus,* and the *Symposium,* for example, is like a repeated mirroring of the effect of style, since it constantly refers to another textual image emerging from the text's fabric or framework. Of course we are dealing here with prose and oratory, but, as we shall see, the factors involved in artful prose, like those involved in the psychagogic—and not merely the argumentative—effect of oratory, belong to poetry.

The theories of the Sophist Gorgias of Leontion evoke the same two aspects of poetry when he formulates the rules for speech making. The argumentation, always brilliant and relative, not to say relativistic, must be accompanied, as in Gorgias's *Encomium of Helen,* by more concerted stylistic effects: the quantitative balance among the parts of a sentence *(kola),* the use in proximity of words with the same root *(paronomasia),* rhymes or assonances at the end of the phrase *(homoeoteleuta),* and so on.

As for Plato himself, playwright and stage manager of his own dialogues, how can we take him seriously when he has Socrates say, in Book X of *The Republic,* that Homer must be banished and the poets, guilty of fictions, are to be thrashed? We may be inclined to read this as a muted echo of the philosophical rigorism that, since Xenophanes' day, had stigmatized the "immorality" of the Homeric gods, rather than as a serious and definitive condemnation, though it is often presented as such. Otherwise, how could we account for the subtle, self-directed irony with which its author says, on several occasions, that the ideal model of a just state, as it is sketched out in the ten books we have just read, constitutes nothing less than the exercise of a verbal fantasy, analogous therefore to poetic and literary fictions? Moreover, is there any better apology for poetry and for the poet than *Ion,* confronting the rhapsodist with his inspiration?

In this dialogue, Plato presents the case of a bard reciting Homeric works. Accompanying himself on the *kithara,* he travels from city to city to give public recitals of parts of the *Iliad* and *Odyssey.* The problem raised is the entirely sophistic one of his competence and technical prowess. Must he be a warrior, a hunter, a fisherman, a strategist, or an artisan if he wants to evoke those diverse activities convincingly for us? Or is it enough for him to be a good interpreter of Homer, persuasive by virtue of his enthusiastic verve alone? The second option is obviously the one retained, accompanied and enriched by the clause that has him share in the power of the gods. The Muses, indeed, are the first to express this; they breathe their grace into the poet, while the interpreter, in this case the rhapsodist Ion, and all those who see and hear him, are participants in the strong sense of the term. This is how the rings attracted by Heracleus's stone are linked, Plato comments, resorting to the rightly celebrated metaphor that represents the poetic attraction exercised by the artist over his public as a force analogous to that of magnetism. The problem of competence, necessarily Protean, was thus a false problem, since the only real role for Homer's interpreter is to be available to transmit the poet's message well, a message that comes from the Muses and thus from the gods. As Socrates says to the rhapsodist: "And when you ask me the reason why you can speak at large on Homer but not on the rest, I tell you it is because your skill in praising Homer comes not by art, but by divine dispensation" (*Ion* 536d). When Hesiod invoked the Boeotian Muses of Mount Helicon on the threshold of his work, his request for protection had the same meaning.

Democritus, in his day, had affirmed that poetic form of enthusiasm. To be *entheos*, "full of the god," is a characteristic that the poet shares with other inspired individuals: prophets, bacchantes, pythonesses. As he puts it, "Everything a poet writes inspired by enthusiasm and a sacred spirit becomes a masterpiece" (frg. 18).

This sort of sacred delirium is not without a relationship to poetry, as Plato's *Ion, Symposium,* and *Phaedrus* attest; we may think in particular of the prayer addressed to Pan and the Nymphs that opens and closes this last text, one of Plato's most inspired dialogues, one that also speaks to us of love and true eloquence. Thus poetic "madness" figures, alongside the madness of Eros or of sacred inspiration, as a high ontological value, proceeding both from myth itself and from the underlying truth expressed in myth. Euripides' *Bacchae* offers an exemplary embodiment of this irrational and inspired aspect of the Greek soul. Let us not forget that Dionysus, god of ecstasy, is the source of the dithyramb and of tragedy. As for Orpheus, whose myth is so frequently invoked, he is the very incarnation of lyricism, which complements the orgiastic music proper to the Dionysian cult. The Thracian bard stands out as an initiate as early as the archaic period, since the purity of his song enables him to cross the portals of death. Thus he is the avatar of the Apollonian theme of continuous creation, for his song, capable of charming all the realms of the living, from craggy rocks to the wildest beast, suffices to ensure the cohesiveness of the cosmos and universal harmony.

Pythagoras belongs in the same company; another Apollonian, he measures and calculates the musical gaps between the various tones in the scale and uses them to measure, in equally harmonic terms, the distance that separates and makes proportionate the orbits of the planets that give the world its rhythm as they gravitate around us. The mathematical model thus guarantees the music of the spheres, establishing and justifying every other form of melody, through the adjustment of gaps in sound, and every other form of rhythm, by recurrences, periods, or returns. In every era, poetry and music are hard to dissociate. They both take their authority from the Muses; they are similarly psychagogic and measurable in their prosodic or harmonic manifestations. The separation of the media comes about only with the first prose writers, with Hecataeus or Herodotus, in other words relatively late, at the beginning of the 5th century. Other genres, however, remained faithful to the ancient alliance.

With Aristotle, reflection on poetry ceases to be circumstantial. In more than one youthful hypothetical treatise devoted "to the poets," of which we have a few fragments, the Stagirite is the author of a *Poetics* that we can rightly call the first handbook of literary theory in the history of Western literature. Without naming it, Aristotle even manages to designate the literary reality that is still seeking a name: "the art which uses either plain language or metrical forms (whether combinations of these, or some one class of metres) remains so far unnamed" (*Poetics* I.7–8).

Thus in his characteristic concern with making distinctions he separates the plastic, musical, and "literary" arts according to the means they use to bring about what he calls imitation. The key term *mimesis* in fact characterizes any artistic production, any figurative representation, whatever the genre. Thus what is at stake is not simply imitation understood as a copy of an external and anterior reality; rather, what is at stake is the very essence of artistic activity. Moreover, when Aristotle tells us that "art imitates nature," he implies that the process of art *(techne)* is analogous to that of nature *(phusis)*. Just as the ancient natural entity of *phusis* ceaselessly produces beings of all sorts and brings them to life, in the same way art produces and creates, bringing into existence a quantity of artifacts that are no less imbued with ontological density than the things that exist "by nature." They may even be considered preferential, owing to their "fabrication" *(poēisis)*, which weighs them down with intellectuality and sometimes saturates them with emotional content. This is how the previously defined literary products appear, for example, and they are clearly distinguished from others. The epic and tragic genres count among these literary products, and the Stagirite speaks of these first of all, at least in the part of his *"ars poetica" (techne poietike)* that has come down to us.

With the initial definitions established relative to the means, objects, and manner of imitation *(mimesis)* or, more precisely, the representation through which literary fiction is exercised, Aristotle is ready to give us his definition of tragedy in chapter VI. Along with *mimesis* we find *katharsis*, the other key term of his aesthetics: the emotional liberation of affects provoked by the dramaturgical act. Here is the rightly celebrated text: "Tragedy, then, is mimesis of an action which is elevated, complete, and of magnitude; in language embellished by distinct forms in its sections; employing the mode of enactment, not narrative; and through pity and fear accomplishing the catharsis of such emotions" (*Poetics* VI.2–3).

This affirmation of the literary fiction that constitutes the tragic genre, allied to that of the liberating—and properly psychagogic—effect that emanates from it, allows us to rediscover our two elements: style, achieved through appropriate shaping of the text, and emotional impact, here placed under the seemingly ambiguous sign of purification. The term used *(katharsis)* indeed evokes the religious or philosophical lexicon in the sense of lustration and prelude to a ritual or moral purity, and at the same time it refers to the Hippocratic (and more generally medical) vocabulary, in the sense of purge or purgation. In fact, without denying the possibility of multiple meanings, it seems that the term must be endowed here with a meaning sui generis, related to the aesthetic definition of tragedy, the literary genre whose essential and foundational efficacy it represents.

If we return briefly now to the content and outline of *Poetics*, we shall recall that while the treatise posits imitation or representative fiction *(mimesis)* from the outset as the common denominator for all the arts, Aristotle quickly makes his statement more specific, inflecting it in the direction of the arts of speech (I). He spells out the noble subjects that are required by the epic and tragic genres (II) before contrasting narrative and direct action as differential modes of imitative suggestion (III). To complete this fine exordium, he returns to *mimesis,* emphasizing its epistemological role, its hedonic source, and its paradoxical status, which enables us to like even images of corpses (IV).

Next, he evokes comedy and its origins, promising to return to the topic later on. He adds, as if in passing, the theatrical requirement of a fictional action that would take place in the time of one revolution of the sun. He does not return to this point, but his remark leads to the well-known principle of the unity of time (V).

Plunging into the heart of a first argument here, Aristotle seeks to encompass the essence *(ousia)* of tragedy in the definition we have seen, before he goes on to enumerate its component parts: plot, characters, diction, argument, music, staging. From here on, our teacher confines himself to the plan he has outlined, and speaks to us in an orderly fashion of the arrangement of facts *(sustasis tōn pragmatōn)* that will be necessarily unified around a single master action and a single main character (as in the *Iliad,* the *Odyssey,* or *Oedipus the King*). These considerations, which are dealt with in chapters VII through XIV, include important notations such as the indispensable marriage of verisimilitude with internal necessity in plot development (IX), and the differentiation between simple and complex schemas accompanied by vicissitudes and instances of recognition (X–XI). Such dramatic turns of events, arising from the very way the facts are arranged, are designed to produce reactions of pity and fear; as we have seen, these are the hallmarks of the tragic genre (XIII–XIV), whose formal elements (prologue, *parados, stasima,* and so on) have just been reviewed (XII).

We then come to an examination of characters. We are reminded that they are required to be elevated and noble, just as the source is necessarily mythical and aristocratic (XV). Our instructor now goes back to clarify some earlier points. Returning to the subject of recognition (XVI), he distinguishes among its various possibilities, preferring those that arise directly out of the arrangement of the facts. He reaffirms the preeminence of unity of action, the condition for successful staging (XVII), before applying this principle once again to the denouement (XVIII). A proper outcome, as we recall (XIII–XIV), will bring an average—though noble—individual who had once been guilty of a notorious and forgotten crime *(hamartia)* from happiness to unhappiness, as if through an internal necessity of which he alone is unaware. We recognize the shadow of the redoubtable and pitiable Oedipus.

Once the staging has been reduced to its dependence on the play's unitary composition as well as to the result of a good overall visualization (XVII), along with music, which has been sufficiently evoked in the earlier chapters (and it will come up again in the eighth book of *Politics*), all that remains to be considered is argument. Argumentative discourse must be given a logical form according to the places from which the actors are speaking and according to the actors' conditions. Aristotle refers us here to *Rhetoric*.

As for the play's diction, concerning the writing per se and its stylistic effects, the author allows himself an ample digression (XX–XXII) in which he deals in turn with phonetics, linguistics, grammar, and prosody. He then examines effects as such: rare words, ornaments, metaphor. Metaphor is admirably defined (XXI) as a mixture attributable to the passage of a single term into the categories of genre and species, or even to an analogy grouping disparate terms in pairs: thus with reference to Ares, it will be said that the cup is Dionysius's shield, or with reference to the revolution of the sun, that evening is the old age of day, just as old age is the sunset of life. Chapter XXII presents the outline of a series of "problems" in which examples of barbarisms and solecisms are juxtaposed with ingredients of the elevated style, such as extensions, inversions, and insertions of dialectal expressions.

After those three rich and difficult chapters (which cannot be separated from a perfectly explicit development), the author moves on to examine the epic genre. The rhythm of the exposition is amplified even as it is accelerated, from the criteria defining the genre to unity of action (XXIII–XXIV), again passing through the sketch of a series of historical and technical "problems" (XXV) up to the lovely aesthetic comparison of the respective merits of the two genres at issue (XXVI). What results is the preeminence of tragedy, owing to its greater liveliness of presentation and the fact that unity of action is more natural in tragedy: "tragedy possesses all epic's resources (it can even use its metre), as well as having a substantial role for music and spectacle, which engender the most vivid pleasures. Again, tragedy has vividness in both reading and performance. Also, tragedy excels by achieving the goal of its mimesis in a shorter scope; greater concentration is more pleasurable than dilution over a long period: suppose someone were to arrange Sophocles' *Oedipus* in as many hexameters as the *Iliad*" (*Poetics* XXVI.9–13). And the text concludes, a few lines further, with a familiar refrain: "As regards tragedy and epic, . . . let this count as sufficient discussion" (XXVI.16). The developments that were to follow, concerning comedy, dithyrambic verse, and—perhaps—poetic and musical lyricism, seem to be irremediably lost.

Through certain of its technical aspects, especially the examination of specific problems raised by various passages in the *Iliad* and *Odyssey*, Aristotle's

Poetics announced and in part inspired the works of Homeric philology to which we must now turn. As early as the 3rd century B.C.E., in Alexandria, in the context of the Museum and its sumptuous Library, a whole literary school flourished; its principal representatives, following Zenodotes and Callimachus, became specialists in the works of Homer. They produced editions and commentaries of which we have only indirect traces, but these are nonetheless revealing.

The principal scholar of the group was Aristophanes of Byzantium, the author of a critical edition of the two epics; he corrected the texts, which were apparently riddled with errors. In the following century his illustrious successor, Aristarchus of Samothrace, produced the first vulgate of the Homeric text, with its division into books and into the number of verses that would thenceforth be traditional. There is general agreement that traces of this work are present in the principal medieval manuscripts, especially the 10th-century *Venetus* A, and the 11th-century *Venetus* B. The abundant scholia that accompany the text of these manuscripts represent the state of Aristarchus's Alexandrine commentary, especially in the case of *Venetus* A. *Venetus* B is thought to have retained traces of more symbolic commentaries that came from the Pergamene school, a rival of the Alexandrian school. The author is thought to have been one Crates of Mallus, Aristarchus's contemporary and Pergamum's rival.

Thus an entire philological and historical corpus of knowledge developed around Homer, not without some connections to the logical and linguistic preoccupations of early Stoicism. There is evidence of the same preoccupations, moreover, during the imperial period (from Augustus to Hadrian), in authors such as Didymus, Aristonicus, Herodian, and Nicanor. In any event an anonymous text, known as the "Résumé of the Four," was circulated under those four names; this text too found its way in part into the famous scholia of *Venetus* A. Along the same lines, I should also mention the *Homeric Questions* of Porphyrus of Tyr, in the 3rd century C.E.

Let us turn now to two important treatises on literary aesthetics in which we shall once again encounter the two major ideas of style and inspiration. These are Demetrius's *Peri hermeneias (On Style),* from the end of the 2nd century B.C.E., and an anonymous text entitled *Peri hupsous* (On the Sublime), very probably dating from the 1st century C.E.

The first of these should not be attributed to Demetrius of Phalerum, one of the founders of the Alexandrian Library, but to a less well-known grammarian from Syria who was active in both Alexandria and Athens, where the young Cicero, the future defender of the poet Archias, may have heard him as a very old man. Despite the title, which might be understood as announcing a theory of interpretation, the treatise deals directly with what we term "style." The author offers us four approaches to the topic. He sorts out the various stylistic possibilities and characterizes them briefly, examining typical examples of each and identifying the forms of excess to avoid. He always uses the same schema and the same order of presentation. The examples are distributed evenly among the great classical authors, from Homer to Thucydides and Demosthenes; they include, as Aristotle had proposed, "plain language" and "metrical forms." We can see that the effect of art in literature decidedly exceeds the bounds of mere versification or "poetic art" in the restricted sense of the term.

Thus Demetrius reviews in turn "grand style," warning us against the coldness it may entail; "elegant style," which charms but must avoid falling into affectation; "plain style," a sort of "zero degree of writing," occasionally risking dryness; and, finally, "forceful style," or, more explicitly, "vehement [deinos] style," which seems to be given preferential treatment by the author. Of course, the interest of the undertaking lies more in the distribution of styles than in the examples, which are circumstantial and sometimes repetitive. Thus the work of Sappho, mentioned several times, is celebrated repeatedly under various headings: its hyperbole ("more golden than gold") keeps it from being cold (127), and its use of anaphor or repetition leads to effects always touched with grace and elegance, whether the poet is speaking to us of nuptial bonds or addressing the Evening Star (141):

> Evening Star, you bring everything home,
> You bring the sheep, you bring the goat, you bring the child to its
>   mother.

The last characteristic, "vehemence," may be the most difficult of all; it needs to be defined briefly here, or, rather, its mechanisms need to be spelled out. The first of these, brachylogy, is entirely Spartan; it must never lapse into enigma. The best example would be the laconic declaration, "Dionysius, at Corinth," the goal of which is to recall that the tyrant of Syracuse, defeated and overthrown, had been reduced to earning his living as a schoolmaster in Corinth (V.241). Then there are figures such as antithesis, imitative harmony, anaphora, extreme gradation (klimax), certain compound words, true (non-"rhetorical") questions, emphasis, and, finally, certain euphemisms or figurative allusions: these are all devices, ways of taking recourse to figures of speech, that make it possible to approach or achieve a form of the "sublime" that has not yet been articulated, which the author classifies under the heading of vehemence, or deinotes (251–300). It is clear that the art of Demosthenes is often invoked as an example or as a representative sampling of this maniera. The "repulsive style," which would be its negative excess, is hastily evoked at the end of the treatise, as if in remorse or through anticipation.

As for the sublime, properly speaking, it appears as early as the title of the anonymous text mentioned earlier. That text was for a long time attrib-

uted to Cassius Longinus, a rhetor from the 3rd century C.E., or, more prudently, to a pseudo-Longinus whom we would do better to put back on the
shelf of historical errors or cultural approximations. Boileau may well have
believed in him; the occasional imprudent contemporary commentator (certainly not a well-trained Hellenist) may resort to that opinion; still, we shall
do better to yield to the arguments of internal criticism as well as to those of
cultural coherence. In the authoritative opinion of Henri Lebègue, those arguments indicate that the author of the treatise on the sublime wrote early in
Tiberius's reign.

However this may be, and without neglecting the influence of middle Stoicism in the writings of two scholars from Rhodes, Panaetius and Posidonius,
we must now turn to the well-documented establishment of this new aesthetic category, the sublime (*to hupsos*, "the highest"). The author of the text
begins by defining his object as a devastating force equally present among poets, prose writers, and orators. This force aims more at creating overwhelming
delight or ecstasy than at deploying any power of reason or persuasion. It is
like a bolt of lightning, he says, which shatters everything (I.4). Its means and
its forms then remain to be defined. Loftiness of thought is the first criterion
proposed, but to this must be added pathetic effects and expressions of enthusiasm. The vividness of the text's imagery and its power of suggestion guarantee its authenticity. Certain tropes and figures are privileged for creating
the effect of surprise: the absence of liaisons (asyndeton), breaks in construction (anacoluthon), the disruption of logical order in phrasing (hyperbaton),
augmentative repetition and the effect of accumulation (epanaphoron and
amplification), and, finally, hyperbole and apostrophe, which are to be discreet
and must hide their effects as much as possible. All this is to be counterbal-
anced by a major concern with construction, with the unity of the whole, and
with the successive order of presentation of terms.

Such textual construction is the principal quality recognized by the author
in the beautiful poem by Sappho evoking the torments and physical pains of
love, a poem that has been preserved thanks to him. If only on this account,
the treatise would deserve to be called "the little golden book," as the humanist Casaubon dubbed it. Here is the excerpt and the accompanying commentary:

> I think him God's peer that sits near you face to face, and listens to
> your sweet speech and lovely laughter.
> It's this that makes my heart flutter in my breast. If I see you but
> for a little, my voice comes no more and my tongue is broken.
> At once a delicate flame runs through my limbs; I see nothing with
> my eyes, and my ears thunder.
> The sweat pours down: shivers grip me all over. I am grown paler
> than grass, and seem to myself to be very near to death.

Here the commentator interrupts: "Is it not wonderful how she summons at the same time, soul, body, hearing, tongue, sight, skin, all as though they had wandered off apart from herself? She feels contradictory sensations, freezes, burns, raves, reasons, so that she displays not a single emotion but a whole congeries of emotions. Lovers show all such symptoms, but what gives supreme merit to her art is, as I said, the skill with which she takes up the most striking and combines them into a single whole" (*On the Sublime* X.2–3).

Moreover, the models the author proposes remain Homer, Thucydides, Plato, Euripides, and Demosthenes, in preference to the orators Lysias, Isocrates, or Hyperides. The latter may be the principal champions of Atticism, but their only merits are their correctness (deemed mediocre) and their seemingly smooth, well-disciplined style, in which all the effects are diluted under the emollient action of overly obvious syntactic links. Even Cicero's ample cadences are only a vast wildfire compared to Demosthenes' phrasing, which strikes like lightning (XXXIV.4).

It is clear that one of the aims of this short treatise was polemic in nature. It was first directed against a certain Cecilius who had, shortly before, spoken ploddingly on the subject, but it also targeted an Atticist tendency, anticipating Dionysius of Halicarnassus, who preferred to the brilliant imperfections of the advocates of the sublime in literature the monotony and impeccable demeanor of works with more modest—not to say more mediocre—ambitions and intonations.

Finally, I shall mention the *Chrestomathy* of Proclus, a writer of the 2nd century C.E. who owes a good part of his celebrity to someone who remains, after the patriarch Photios, his best critic and biographer: Albert Severyns, the learned editor, translator, and commentator of the precious relics of Proclus's work of literary theory. The work is actually a "short course" or "literary handbook" in which the author declares at once that prose and poetry have similar qualities, particularly where style is concerned. Style is of three orders, with no other specification: abundant style, pared-down style, and middle style. However, the surviving summary of the first two books of the treatise deals essentially with poetry. Chronology thus requires that one begin with the epic, in which what is at issue is mainly the content of the various works in the Trojan cycle, from the "Cyprian songs" to the Telegony. Then come definitions and historical evocations of the various poetic genres: elegy, iamb, and lyric.

The latter is subdivided into sacred lyric, including hymns, paeans, dithyrambs, and nome, and secular lyric, covering elogy, epinicia or homage to the conquerors, scholia or alternating songs used in banquets *(symposia)*, and assorted variants of love songs: epithalamia, wedding songs, and other drinking songs. Various choral genres, such as partheneia or daphnephoria, are evoked at the end, before the conclusion of this summary of the first two books of Proclus's "literary handbook"; it leaves us wishing for more.

462 ❖ THE PURSUIT OF KNOWLEDGE

The summary itself, the work of Photius, contained in codex 239 of his "Library," is an entirely fortuitous windfall. Let us recall that the patriarch, accompanying a Byzantine embassy to the Middle East in the 9th century, had with him a shipment of books; he seems to have spent most of his time drafting summaries of these works for the benefit of his brother, who had remained in the capital, unless he did the work after his return to Constantinople. Although he does not mention any poet by name, the place he reserved for Proclus's handbook has allowed me to discuss it here, with all the respect it is due. This "Library," dating from the first renaissance, was indeed a remarkable and irreplaceable conservatory of Greek and Byzantine letters.

To return to Proclus, another part of his work, which is actually a "life of Homer," has been transmitted to us by the scholia of the medieval manuscripts mentioned above. As anecdotal as one could wish, and highly colorful, this brief *Vita Homeri* gets lost in calculations concerning the place of origin as well as the cause and modalities of the poet's death, before offering, in a few brief pages, the best summaries we have of the now-lost epics of the Trojan cycle: the "Cyprian songs" concerning the most remote prodromes of the Trojan war, going back to the wedding of Peleus and Thetis and to the apparition of Eris that led to the quarrel over the golden apple and the three goddesses. We recall Aphrodite's poisoned gift to Paris: he was to marry the beautiful Helen and incite war. The episode of the pseudo-sacrifice of Iphigenia and her rescue among the Taurians, owing to Artemis's intervention, is very clearly presented, along with Odysseus's feigned madness and the role of Telephus, who guides the fleet to Troy. The other lost epics—which were to give Virgil the inspiration for his *Aeneiad*—are also summarized clearly, the "little Iliad" and the "capture of Troy" in particular, where the "traitor" Sinon appears, along with the wooden horse and a certain priest called Laocoon.

Finally, to return to our starting point—namely, to Homer—let me evoke Eusthathius's Byzantine commentary on the two epics, in a text dating from the late 11th or early 12th century, i.e., from the beginning of the second Byzantine renaissance, as well as the statements of his contemporary Tzetzès, whose praise to the poet begins with a good summing up of the great Homeric devotion of his time, echoing our own, at least in its best moments:

> Homer,
> Learned in all things
> Ocean of words replete with nectar
> Entirely free of salt.

PIERRE SOMVILLE
Translated by Catherine Porter and Dominique Jouhaud

Bibliography

Texts and Translations

Aristotle. *Poetics*. Trans. Stephen Halliwell. Loeb Classical Library.

Chiron, Pierre. *Introduction, édition et traduction de "Demetrios, Du style."* Paris: Les Belles Lettres, 1993.

Demetrius. *On Style.* Trans. Doreen C. Innes, based on trans. of W. Rhys Roberts. Loeb Classical Library.

Homer. *Odyssey.* Trans. A. T. Murray, rev. George E. Dimock. 2 vols. Loeb Classical Library.

Lebègue, Henri. *Introduction, édition et traduction de "Du sublime."* Paris: Les Belles Lettres, 1939.

"Longinus" (Dionysius or Longinus). *On the Sublime.* Trans. W. Hamilton Fyfe, rev. Donald A. Russell. Loeb Classical Library.

Somville, Pierre. *Platon: Ion, texte et bref commentaire,* 5th ed. Liège: Dessain, 1974.

Plato. *Ion.* Trans. W. R. M. Lamb. In *The Statesman; Philebus; Ion.* Loeb Classical Library.

Proclus Diadochus. *In Platonis Cratylum commentaria.* Ed. Georgius Pasquali. Leipzig: B. Teubner, 1908.

Theognis. In Mulroy, David. *Early Greek Lyric Poetry.* Ann Arbor: University of Michigan Press, 1995.

Studies

Boyancé, Pierre. *Le culte des Muses chez les philosophes grecs.* Paris: De Boccard, 1937.

Delatte, Armand. *Les conceptions de l'enthousiasme chez les philosophes présocratiques.* Paris: Les Belles Lettres, 1934.

Dodds, Eric Robertson. *The Greeks and the Irrational.* Berkeley: University of California Press, 1968.

Labarbe, Jules. *L'Homère de Platon.* Liège and Paris: Les Belles Lettres, 1949.

Lanata, Giuliana. *Poetica pre-platonica (testimonianze e frammenti).* Florence: "La Nuova Italia," 1963.

Motte, André. *Prairies et jardins dans la Grèce antique.* Brussels: Palais des Académies, 1973.

Norden, Eduard. *Die antike Kunstprosa.* Leipzig and Berlin: Teubner, 1909.

Schamp, Jacques. *Photios, historien des lettres.* Liège and Paris: Les Belles Lettres, 1987.

Segal, Charles. *Singers, Heroes and Gods in the Odyssey.* Ithaca, N.Y.: Cornell University Press, 1994.

Severyns, Alvert. *Le cycle épique dans l'école d'Aristarque.* Liège: H. Vaillant-Carmanne, and Paris: E. Champion, 1928.

———. *Recherches sur la Chrestomathie de Proclos.* Vols. 1 and 2, Liège: Faculté de philosophie et lettres, and Paris: E. Droz, 1938; vol. 3, 1953: vol. 4, 1963. Repr. Paris: Les Belles Lettres, 1977.

Somville, Pierre. *Essai sur la Poétique d'Aristote.* Paris: Vrin, 1975.

———. "Ironie platonicienne à la fin de la *République.*" In *Serta Leodiensia secunda:*

Mélanges publiés par les Classiques de Liège à l'occasion du 175e anniversaire de l'Université. Liège: Ulg, 1992. Pp. 445–450.

Vernant, Jean-Pierre, and Pierre Vidal-Naquet. *Mythe et tragédie en Grèce ancienne.* Paris: Maspero, 1972.

Related Articles

Myth and Knowledge; Aristotle; Language

RHETORIC

In the contemporary usage of all modern European languages, outside the specialized vocabulary of certain antiquarian and literary critical coteries, the word *rhetorical* is unfailingly pejorative. Rhetoric now roughly connotes the dissembling, manipulative abuse of linguistic resources for self-serving ends, usually in a political context: witness the routine coupling of "rhetoric" with "propaganda" in the dismissal of an opponent's speech. Yet from the time of the Roman republic down to at least the beginning of the 19th century, rhetoric so dominated both general and political culture (albeit with certain periodic eclipses), that a person without rhetorical training could hardly pretend to education at all. What is rhetoric, that it could suffer so curious a fate? During its ascendancy the answer, enshrined in a multitude of handbooks that first appeared in the ancient world and were propagated tirelessly down the centuries, is obvious and uncontentious: rhetoric is "the tool of persuasion," and an education in rhetoric is an education in the elaborate technical expertise needed to produce and appreciate persuasive discourse, oral and written, sometimes stretched to include the visual arts, architecture, and music.

But the great Latin exemplars of the rhetorical tradition, primarily Cicero and Quintilian, did not live and work in a vacuum. As in so much else, the Romans inherited the very idea of rhetoric, at least as a self-reflective concept, from the Greeks. In the classical Greek world there was no consensus on either the nature or the value of rhetoric: instead there was a fierce and profound debate, ignited by the late 5th-century figure Gorgias of Leontini and cast in its enduring form by Plato, whose polemic insists that rhetoric be defined in contrast to philosophy, and seeks to persuade us that the comparison is all to the disadvantage of rhetoric. Since his formulation of the issue so dominates the earliest Greek phase of the history of rhetoric, only an examination first of Gorgias himself, and then of Plato's dialogue named after him, can help us understand what Cicero and ultimately we ourselves inherited, and what was done with it.

Who was Gorgias? Philostratus, a hack writer of the Second Sophistic, reports that Gorgias is the man "to whom we believe the craft of the sophists is to be traced back as it were to his father" (Buchheim, test. 1). Philostratus's mediocrity is precisely what renders his opinion valuable: it reveals how Gorgias typically appeared to later antiquity. But why did he appear as the father of sophistry? First, because of rhetorical innovations at a basic technical level that Gorgias is supposed to have made, involving both structure and ornamentation. Second, and of considerably more interest, because he introduced *paradoxologia*, which embraces both paradoxical thought and paradoxical expression. On the occasion of his famous embassy to Athens seeking military aid for his home city, Leontini, in Sicily, his skill in speaking *extempore* reputedly brought nearly all the leading politicians and intellectuals under his influence. Of the three most striking claims preserved in the largely anecdotal biographical reports, one is that he pioneered improvisation, so that "on entering the Athenian theater, he cried out 'Give me a theme!' . . . in order to demonstrate that he knew everything" (test. 1a); a second, that his pupil Isocrates claims in an apparently neutral tone that Gorgias accumulated relatively great wealth by traveling about unwed and childless, thus avoiding the civic and educational expenses of the paternal citizen (ibid. 18); and the third, that "among the Thessalians 'to orate' acquired the name 'to gorgiasie'" (test. 35).

Clichéd as they are, these fragmentary portraits raise all the important questions about Gorgias. Why is Gorgias a "sophist"? Whatever sophistry might be, is it necessarily connected with rhetoric? Need a sophist/rhetor really claim omniscience? What does the performative aspect of rhetoric (Gorgias impressing his public in the theater) reveal about its nature? Isocrates' denial of familial and civic identity to Gorgias does not sit easily with Gorgias's role in obtaining Athenian aid for his fellow citizens: how, then, does rhetoric connect with political activity? Finally, to compound the confusion, many scholars lengthen the list of characterizations of Gorgias by adding the title philosopher, albeit usually only for the early stages of his career. A reading of Gorgias's immensely provocative texts, *On What Is Not* and *The Encomium of Helen*, will show that this difficulty in classifying him, so far from being a mere pedant's problem, goes to the heart of his unparalleled contribution to the history of rhetoric. But, since Gorgias unmistakably challenges us to react to both works against one specific philosophical background, that of Parmenides' great argument, we must first extract some vital information from the figure dubbed by Plato the father of philosophy, to match Gorgias, the father of sophistical rhetoric.

Parmenides' goddess (the figure of authority in his poem) announces: "You must hear everything, both the unmoved heart of persuasive *alētheiē* and the opinions of mortals, wherein there is no *alēthēs* conviction" (Coxon, frg. 1). *Alētheiē* is conventionally rendered either "truth" or "reality," and often context clearly favors one over the other: the problem here is that Parmenides seems not only to fuse the real with the true but also to suggest that truth/reality is *objectively* persuasive.

"Never will the strength of conviction permit something extra to come to be from what is not; that is why justice has released neither generation nor destruction by loosening their bonds, but holds them fast" (frg. 8). This later declaration adds the paradoxical dimension that persuasion, standardly opposed to compulsion, actually shares in constraining necessity: thus judicial imagery recurs in the famous claim that "powerful necessity holds what is in the bonds of a limit." Not only that, but rational conviction also seems to act on or at least with what is, as the goddess associates reality with reason ever more intimately.

Yet when she passes from truth to human delusion, the goddess implicitly acknowledges that reality is unfortunately not alone in swaying minds, although she emphatically divorces falsity from conviction: "Now I put an end to persuasive *logos* and thought about reality/truth, and from this point do you learn mortal opinions by listening to the deceptive *kosmos* of my words" (frg. 8). *Logos* here resists translation even more than *alētheiē*. First, although it often means "verbal account," it stands here in polar opposition to the "words," thus highlighting the logical, rational character of truth. Second, and crucially, the debate between philosophy and rhetoric can be formulated as a conflict over the very meaning of *logos*. What is *"kosmos?"* Anything ordered or harmonious, but also, by an obvious extension, anything adorned by virtue of arrangement—hence *cosmetics*. Just as a painted face deceives the onlooker, so the goddess's phrase suggests the disturbing possibility that a *kosmos* of words—a *logos*, perhaps—might mislead precisely in that it wears an attractive appearance of order.

These features of Parmenides' discourse make an essential context for the appraisal of Gorgias, since together they formulate questionable conditions on argument that he deftly exploits. In the first place, even if the goddess insists that it is the force of her *logos* to which the auditor must yield, the fact remains that Parmenides puts his argument into the mouth of an authoritative divine figure. Is this not a rhetorical rather than a strictly philosophical device? Again, Parmenides fuses reality with persuasive truth by way of rational compulsion, but Greek culture traditionally opposes force and persuasion; thus the difficulty in aligning conviction with necessity, as Parmenides does so forcefully. Perhaps no one can simply will to believe (rationally): one must be *made* to believe, ideally by valid argument (cf. Descartes: "I move the more freely toward an object in proportion to the number of reasons that compel me," letter to Mersenne of February 9, 1645). Of course, rational constraint does not necessarily equal compulsion; both Gorgias and Plato will, however, return to the problematic relation between them. Next, when Parmenides contrasts *logos* with (mere) words, he must intend us to understand that the only vehicle of authentic conviction is rational argument, whereas Gorgias will systematically subvert the claims of philosophical *logos* to this monopoly. Finally, the goddess's exhortation to "decide by *logos* the controversial test enjoined by me" (frg. 7) encapsulates in philosophical form the salient competitiveness of Greek culture. Controversy normally entails a victor and a vanquished: does a successful persuader then inevitably victimize his audience?

Gorgias's *On What Is Not* has come down to us in two versions, one preserved by the skeptical philosopher Sextus Empiricus, the other in the Peripatetic mélange *About Melissus, Xenophanes, and Gorgias*. Although we should not believe we have access to the Gorgianic original, we can nevertheless maintain with due caution that what we read is a reasonable extrapolation from *On What Is Not* itself. Our purpose is not to investigate *On What Is Not* in its entirety, but rather to focus on its exemplification of *paradoxologia*, its discussion of communication, and its problematic relation to philosophical thought.

In the very title we confront our first paradox: it actually bears a disjunctive name, *On What Is Not, or About Nature* (Sextus, *Against the Professors* 7.65). Unfortunately the alternatives might both be later impositions, but they could preserve a significant Gorgianic joke. For an ancient philosopher or scientist, "nature" is what really is, so that *On Nature* became the standard designation awarded to Presocratic writings by Hellenistic librarians. If the alternative titles are original with Gorgias, then he is blithely equating what really is with nothing; taken together, the titles constitute a self-negating claim, a saying that unsays itself. This phenomenon of arrested or self-destructive communication, introducing semantic convention only to flout it, will emerge as the hallmark of the entire work. All the same, even if the doubled label is not original it remains of interest, since it then so clearly betrays the difficulty later readers experienced in attempting to pigeonhole Gorgias's text alongside less arresting Presocratic works.

The text begins disconcertingly: "He says there is nothing; even if there is something, it is unknowable; even if it both is and is knowable, nevertheless it is not showable to others" (979a12–13). We shall not pause over the details of Gorgias's "proof" of nihilism and unknowability beyond remarking that it deliberately overturns Parmenides' denial that "is not" is either sayable or thinkable, and that at this early date Parmenides' deduction was the paradigmatic, almost unique, example of logical progression, as manifested in Gorgias's conditional sentence. Parmenides had argued that reality is single and changeless; when Gorgias maintains that reality is not, is he any less credible? If both thinkers marshal deductions to reach contradictory but equally incredible conclusions, what becomes of Parmenides' theme that conviction unfailingly accompanies truth?

"Even if things are knowable," the text continues, "how could someone, Gorgias says, reveal them to another? For how could he say in *logos* what he has seen? Or how could a thing the listener does not see become clear to him? For just as vision does not recognise speech, so neither does hearing hear colours, but rather speech; and the speaker produces a *logos*, not colour or the thing" (980a2–b3). Gorgias is assuming that the sense modalities exclusively apprehend their own objects: a heard *logos* cannot convey anything not aural. The argument is puzzling, because the special object of hearing is surely sound in general, not speech. In fact the word translated as *speech* can, albeit rarely, mean just sound, but this gives rise to a dilemma: if *speech* is widened to *sound*, then the passage presumes that one simply hears *logoi* as one hears any noise, and the essentially meaningful character of *logos* is repressed; if, however, speech *is* what is meant, then Gorgias may well not be repressing the fact that *logoi* have semantic content—but then our simply hearing *logoi* as we see colors loses all plausibility.

"When a person does not have something in his thought, how will he acquire it from another through *logos* or some sign different from the thing . . .? For to begin with, the speaker produces neither noise nor colour, but *logos*; so it is possible to have neither colour nor noise in thought, only to see or hear them" (980b3–8). Gorgias now identifies *logos* as the tool with which we fruitlessly attempt to convey our thoughts to one another (notice that the mere act of hearing or reading and understanding *what Gorgias says* is enough to show that this cannot be true). Two considerations against successful communication are adduced. First, a sign is necessarily different from its object. As experience must (it is assumed) be direct, all symbols, by definition different from what they represent, inevitably fail. As for the (admittedly noncommunicable) *logoi* in our thoughts, these will also presumably be non-representational, for they cannot be signs *of* anything from which they differ. Second, "noise" rather than "sound/speech" is now the proper object of hearing, so that no means remain whereby we might perceive *logoi*. Gorgias caps his case against *logos* as a medium of communication by making it a condition for conveying information that one and the same *logos* be present in both speaker and auditor, which is impossible (980b9–11); thus he assimilates *logos* to a unique physical object that cannot be reproduced.

What are we to make of these amazing propositions? Parmenides' philosophy issues in the "rational" conclusion that all that is, is a unique, homogeneous, timeless entity, but it does not explain how, then, he can engage us in dialogue. In parallel, Gorgias's exercise in argumentation, a reaction to Parmenides, suggests that successfully *saying* that communication cannot occur must lead to self-contradiction and paradox. If *On What Is Not* is a perfectly acceptable piece of philosophy and this is its message, then philosophical *logos* will by itself carry precious little conviction, despite Parmenides' attempt to monopolize persuasion.

But *is* it philosophy? Or is it merely a cerebral joke? (We cannot dismiss it as a game on the evidence of the argumentative flaws I have only partially catalogued, since by that criterion a large proportion of early Greek philosophy would disappear from the canon.) To decide if it really is philosophical requires analysis of its arguments (or pseudo-arguments). But perhaps this analytical response presupposes just what we want to find out. Scholars have claimed too that *On What Is Not* formulates a *theory* of *logos* that liberates both rhetoric and literature from the supposed constraints of representational discourse: if language is not *about* the world, then poets and orators are free to influence us in disregard of the inaccessible facts. This sadly mistaken reading overlooks the most obvious consequence of Gorgias's *paradoxologia:* his message refutes itself, and in consequence, so far from constituting a theory of *logos,* it confronts us with a picture of what language cannot be, with what we must not assume it should aspire to be. I propose instead that the significance of *On What Is Not* resides in our very uncertainty over whether Gorgias is in earnest. As indicated in our reading of Parmenides, philosophy pretends to an impersonal authority deriving from *logos.* But the fact that any honest attempt to determine whether Gorgias's text has the status of "authentic" philosophy seemingly presupposes an affirmative answer to that question suggests that its actual genre is to be discovered only in the obscure intentions and pretensions of its author and not in or from the *logos* itself. That is to make the decision a very personal, contingent matter indeed, and thus to undermine the philosophical drive beyond personal authority. *On What Is Not* seriously threatens philosophy because philosophy cannot tell whether to take it seriously without dangerously compromising its fundamental commitment to a reason that is no respecter of persons. We shall see that Gorgias redeploys the weapon of the joke in *Encomium of Helen,* and that Plato's *Gorgias* hammers away inexorably at the problem of the (im)personal generated by Gorgias's challenge to Parmenides.

In the technical handbooks, rhetoric came to be divided into three main genres, forensic (speeches of defense or accusation before a law court), deliberative (political advice to a legislative and executive body), and epideictic (speeches in praise or blame of some individual or institution). *Encomium of Helen* ostensibly falls in the last category. Although scholars now appreciate that epideictic oratory in the civic context played a prominent role in the construction and maintenance of civic identity in the Greek city-state, a casual attitude toward *Helen* still prevails; since Helen herself is no more than a figure from mythology, it is typically felt that a composition about her could only have been a display piece intended to advertise Gorgias's craft and perhaps to serve as a model for students. In fact *Helen* masterfully complements Gorgias's maneuver to wrest the *logos* out of philosophical control in *On What Is Not,* and it further develops his challenge by uncompromisingly opening up the political dimensions of rhetoric.

Who is Helen? Wife of Menelaus, lover of Paris, she is an adulterous and infinitely desirable anti-Penelope. Even in her first, Homeric incarnation, she arouses profoundly ambiguous feelings. Although in the fourth book of the *Odyssey* she initially appears as a reinstated spouse entertaining Telemachus with stories, Menelaus recounts an unsettling anecdote that casts a shadow on her verbal skill: at the moment of maximum danger, when the Achaean warriors were concealed within the wooden horse, she mischievously imitated the voices of their wives to lure them out. Her association with *logos* is implicit from the beginning: she yielded to the verbal importunity of Paris, and she herself possesses a bewitching, deceptive tongue. So what would it mean to speak in *praise* of Helen? In fact Isocrates in his own *Helen* upbraids Gorgias on this very score, asserting that despite his express intention, Gorgias actually wrote not an encomium, but rather a defense of her (*Helen* 14–15). I shall argue that as concerns Helen, Gorgias's text is indeed forensic, but that it crosses genres by mounting this defense within the scope of its true epideictic purpose, the glorification of *logos*.

At the outset Gorgias announces: "The *kosmos* . . . of *logos* is *alētheia*" (*Helen* 1). All these key words are featured in Parmenides, where, however, deceptive *kosmos* was opposed to *logos* as argument. Will Gorgias, too, seek to persuade us by means of logical reasoning? And does *alētheia* here signify truth, with the implication that Gorgias's *Helen* in particular can achieve the excellence of *logos* only if it tells us a *true* story? If *kosmos* regularly connotes ornamentation and artifice, is there not the danger that a cosmetic *logos* may disguise rather than represent reality?

Gorgias excuses his passing over the events leading up to Helen's departure for Troy by saying that "to tell those who know what they know carries conviction, but conveys no pleasure" (5). Plato's Gorgias will concede that the orator *cannot* communicate knowledge, and that his utterances carry no conviction for knowers. Here, in contrast, the real Gorgias declines to retail common knowledge on the grounds that it brings no pleasure: if his *logos* is to be pleasing, then at the very least it must be novel. Granted, novelty is not incompatible with truth, but commitment to the principle that the criterion of pleasure (at least partially) governs what will be said surely renders problematic Gorgias's other commitment, that to *alētheia* (only a philosopher would even pretend to take pleasure in the truth alone). What we will get are causes making Helen's behavior *eikos*. Perhaps the most important word in Greek rhetoric, *eikos* can be rendered as likely, plausible, probable—often, as here, with the positive normative connotation of reasonable. It is a commonplace of subsequent rhetorical theory that the orator's task of instilling confidence in the likelihood of his case depends on achieving verisimilitude that might, but need not, coincide with the facts. It is because the orator occupies the ineliminable gap between the likely and the true that he can serve flexibly pro or contra. Thus Gorgias's intention to deliver a "likely" *logos* in conjunction with his promise to please distances him yet further from *alētheia* in Parmenides' sense of truth/reality.

Gorgias will exculpate Helen by running through each of the possible causes for her elopement with Paris and suggesting in each case that she cannot be held accountable; thus, if the catalogue is exhaustive, her defense will be successful (it is perhaps to this methodical procedure that he refers when he speaks of the *logismos* in his *logos*). "Helen did what she did through either the wishes of chance and the intentions of the gods and the decrees of necessity, or because she was seized by force, or persuaded by *logoi*, or captured by love" (6). At this stage Gorgias presents force and persuasion as categorically distinct, but his rhetoric will operate to erode this hallowed distinction. "How would it not be *eikos* for a woman forced, deprived of her country, and bereaved of her family to be pitied rather than reviled in *logos*? He acted terribly, but she suffered; thus it is just to feel sorry for her, but to hate him" (7). Here *eikos* must have normative force, as a plea for a *reasonable and just* reaction to the victim's plight from the listener or reader—but the reasonable response is *emotional:* does this mixture of compassion and indignation also afford us the promised pleasure? The opposition of "he acted . . . she suffered" invokes a second fundamental polarity, that between action and passion; when the first opposition between force and persuasion comes under pressure, the scope of the role of sufferer will enlarge to threaten us as well.

The heart of Gorgias's text comes in section 8: "But if *logos* persuaded and deceived her soul, it is also not difficult to construct a defense." Helen went to Troy: if this action was not inherently bad, its consequences indubitably were. A conventional piece of forensic rhetoric would be to plead compulsion on Helen's behalf; if she was forced to go with Paris, she deserves to be exonerated, maybe even pitied. What one therefore anticipates is an argument that she did *not* yield to persuasion. The standard polar opposition of force and persuasion entails that succumbing to a merely verbal seduction is altogether blameworthy. Instead—and here, surely, we find the most illuminating example of the *paradoxologia* to which Philostratus attributed Gorgias's fame—he unnervingly collapses the polarity. The process is begun by simply juxtaposing "persuasion" and "deception," as if persuasion too, by its very nature, victimizes, and by introducing the concept of the soul into the argument, a tactic with the most far-reaching consequences.

"*Logos* is a great *dynastēs*, which accomplishes divine deeds with the smallest and least apparent of bodies; for it is able to stop fear, remove pain, implant joy, and augment pity" (8). With this ringing affirmation the political implications of Gorgias's rhetoric break cover. *Dynastēs*, like *tyrannos* (applied in section 3 to Zeus), need not carry sinister, "tyrannical" overtones, but it certainly can. The rallying cry of Athenian democratic ideology is "free speech": a citizen is supposedly free in that his access to political power is limited only by his ability to persuade his fellows in the Assembly; it is not limited by brute force or by the handicaps of low birth or poverty. But if *logos* confers such power, the chief mechanism for the maintenance of a democratic polity may actually subvert it. Anxiety at this point is deepened in the original by the fact that the verb "is able" in Greek is etymologically related to *dynastēs*, permitting Gorgias a clever word play: verbal ability in and of itself creates political dominance. And the ramifications of this elaborate sentence spread wider still. Another traditional Greek polarity is that between word and deed: Gorgias's claim that *logos* performs superhuman deeds erases it. The illustrations of divine accomplishments, which presumably exemplify persuasion/deceit, are all of emotional rather than intellectual change, and the ability to instill rational conviction is not even mentioned. An almost universal inclination in Greek thought conceives of the emotions as *pathē*, states that happen to us, before which we are passive. In retrospect we realize that Gorgias's own *logos* (which enjoined us to "pity" Helen) may already have exerted an impact on our souls, in which *logos* can "augment pity." If Paris seduced the hapless Helen, by the same token we, in responding emotionally to Gorgias's rhetorical seduction, are equally passive, equally impotent before his active and divine power.

Gorgias's first species of omnipotent *logos* is poetry, which he famously defines as "*logos* with meter" (9): its auditors literally experience "sympathy" with depicted characters when poetic *logoi* cause their souls to "suffer." Later traditions in literary criticism will tend to discriminate among various poetical (especially theatrical) devices, and *not* to attribute to *logos* as such the predominant, let alone exclusive, responsibility for moving the emotions. Gorgias's monistic conception of *logos*, in contrast, should warn us that his definition is not intended to suggest that the emotional power of poetry resides extrinsically in the meter; while Parmenides was at pains to separate superior *logos* from deceptive "words," Gorgias strives to fuse all aspects of *logos*, irrational as well as logical, into a single overwhelming force.

The second species of logos is magic, which also has the ability to change feelings: "Inspired spells working through *logoi* effect the attraction of pleasure and the repulsion of pain; for by coming together with the opinion of the soul, the power of the spell enchants and persuades and moves it by wizardry" (10). The words "coming together" and "moves" strengthen the impression—not to be exaggerated into a theory—of the soul as a quasi-concrete object open to manipulation. That idea that spells work "through *logoi*" makes them into uniquely effective tools, but any choice between *logoi* as meaningful, persuading by their meaningful content, and *logoi* as instruments, shaping by their quasi impact, is rejected by the collocation "enchants and persuades and moves." The reason for this is clear: if a spell contains a linguistic message, it is one addressed to the god or daemon whose aid is being sought, not to the intended beneficiary or victim on whom the spell works. By so artfully intertwining brutely physical and semantic features, Gorgias refuses to admit categorical differences between species of *logos*. He is at work systematically obliterating distinctions between *logoi*, which are all alike in being emotionally manipulative, and different only in mode of operation and, presumably, effectiveness.

In section 12 comes the turning point of the text, where Gorgias explicitly denies the difference between force and persuasion—indeed actually identifies them—so as to complete his defense of Helen: "*Logos* in persuading the soul it persuaded forced it to obey what was said and approve what was done. Therefore in persuading, that is forcing, he commits injustice, but in being persuaded, that is being forced by the *logos,* she wrongly has a bad reputation." In the original Greek, because "*logos*" is grammatically masculine and "soul" *(psyche)* grammatically feminine, an immediate transition can be made from the asymmetric relation between *logos* and soul to that between Paris and Helen: the "he" and "she" in the last sentence refer indifferently to *logos*/Paris and soul/Helen. Grammar is being used not only to persuade us to apply the model to this particular compulsion but also to associate characteristics of one mythological case with the persuasive/compulsive situation in general. All the verbal forms of *logos*/Paris are active, while all the forms of soul/Helen are passive, as we have come to expect. But further, the deliberate feminization of the soul plays on Greek culture's assumption that the female is a passive object shaped at will by a dominating, masculine force. Thus, perhaps, every male citizen who yields to rhetorical *logos* is comparable to a man who suffers the physical violence of another, and whose masculinity is thereby humiliated: the successful orator performs psychic rape.

Gorgias adduces further examples of *logos* "molding" the soul as it wishes: "One should notice . . . necessary contests through *logoi,* in which a single *logos* written with skill, not uttered in truth, pleases and persuades a great crowd; and the conflicts of philosophical *logoi,* in which swiftness of judgment is also shown to make the conviction of opinion readily changeable" (13). These "necessary" conflicts are legal battles, and "necessary" in both a passive and an active sense: such speeches are delivered under compulsion by defendants, but they compel the jury to yield. The opposition of a single *logos* to a great crowd will be turned against rhetoric in Plato's *Gorgias;* and now Gorgias's promise to retail pleasure rather than (known) truth is fulfilled when persuasion results from a misleading pleasure induced by rhetorical skill inimical to truth. In making philosophical argument just another species of *logos,* Gorgias is deliberately ignoring Parmenides' epoch-making insistence that deductive *logos* is sui generis: *all* varieties of *logos* are displays of persuasive contention; despite its pretensions, philosophy does not establish stable, well-founded judgment but only demonstrates the mutability of passive belief as now one, now another participant in philosophical contests gains the upper hand.

"The power of *logos* has the same ratio *(logos)* to the order of the soul as the order of drugs has to the nature of bodies. For just as different drugs expel different humours from the body, and some put a stop to illness, others, to life, so too some *logoi* cause pain, some pleasure, some fear, some induce confidence in the auditors, some drug and bewitch the soul with a certain bad persuasion" (14). This passage assimilates *logos* to an irresistible drug administered either to heal or harm at the whim of the practitioner, and the drug itself to an occult agent. The same *logos* that, as white magic, gives pleasure, creates pain in the guise of "bad" persuasion/compulsion, but in either case the defenseless soul is drugged, not offered a rational invitation to react. Gorgias elicits an analogy between rhetorician and doctor, *logos* and chemicomagical agent; Plato will both insist on a sharp distinction between healing doctor and amoral wizard, and deny that the rhetorician deserves comparison with the doctor properly understood.

We have hardly plumbed the riches of *Helen*, passing over without comment its fascinating account of erotic and visual attraction, but enough has now been assembled to permit meaningful comparison with Plato's *Gorgias* so as to reconstruct the challenges that rhetoric and philosophy presented to each other in ancient Greece. The text ends: "I wished to write the *logos*, an encomium of Helen, but an amusement for myself" (21). Of course what we have is a text in praise of *logos* itself. Too many pedestrian critics take refuge from Gorgias by understanding this sting in the tail as a simple disclaimer: *Helen* is just a harmless joke. But when we recall how *On What Is Not* dislocated philosophy by obstinately hovering between "serious" and "playful" intentions, we can recognize that *Helen*'s joke is on us. When we ourselves are made to pity Helen and execrate Paris, are persuaded (perhaps) that persuasion is manipulation, and enjoy the deception with which Gorgias amuses us even as we discern it, we feel in our own souls the seduction of rhetoric.

Plato's response to Gorgias in his dialogue *Gorgias* is to present us with the most emphatic reaffirmation of the Parmenidean ideal, a scheme of philosophical dialectic utterly distinct from and immeasurably superior to rhetoric, which is fiercely castigated as nakedly exploitative emotional manipulation. The terms of the contrast are of course by now thoroughly familiar; what Plato does is to reinstate systematically all the great polarities that Gorgias just as studiously, if with profound ambiguity, chose to occlude. The running theme of our investigation has been the paradoxical skill with which Gorgias encourages us to place his very own words within the scope of his rhetoric about rhetoric. In consistency we must ask how *Gorgias* itself fares according to its author's strictures on the use and abuse of language. Gorgias insists that his *logos* constitutes no exception to the way words work, because they all work to the same purpose, but Plato's writing is informed by an incomparably higher degree of tension, because his Socrates pretends that there is all the difference in the world between a philosopher and a rhetorician. To avoid damning inconsistency, this had better not be just another rhetorical claim.

Gorgias falls little short of *The Republic* in the continuous influence it has exerted on Western intellectual and political history, and it has stimulated voluminous scholarship. Largely because in it Socrates propounds his celebrated paradox that no one does wrong willingly, and embarks on the psychological theorizing that attains full expression in *Phaedo*, the majority of its students concentrate on the second two-thirds of the dialogue, in which Gorgias himself does not feature as the chief interlocutor. We shall instead limit our attention to the first portion, where Plato most obviously addresses rhetoric in rhetoric's own terms; even so, our analysis will be highly selective, omitting everything not directly germane to an appreciation of why Gorgias matters so much to the history of persuasion.

In the very first lines of the dialogue Socrates prepares his attack. Depicted as arriving shortly after Gorgias's performance, he asks if he is too late for the "feast," introducing a metaphor that will not lie dormant for long (447a). When he is assured that Gorgias will gladly "display" for him again (the word is cognate with the label "epideictic" for the rhetorical genre exemplified by *Helen*), Socrates requests something else: will Gorgias instead engage in "dialectic," explaining what the "power" of his skill might be (447b–c)? Gorgias readily agrees, confidently making the boast recorded in Philostratus, that no question whatsoever exceeds his ability to answer. After Socrates again discriminates between dialectic and "so-called rhetoric" (448d), Gorgias affirms that rhetoric is to be defined as "knowledge of *logoi*" (449e). But Socrates immediately demands clarification, and elicits the admission that *logoi* concerning matters of health are the exclusive preserve of the doctor, the physician *rather than* the rhetorician. His point hangs on a conception of expertise shared by the Platonic Gorgias that *knowledge* alone confers mastery of a given domain; Gorgias's specialism has already been distinguished from that of his medical brother, Herodicus (448b), disposing of *Helen*'s likening of global *logos* to a physician's enchanting drug.

Under increasing pressure to explain what rhetoric is about *in particular*, Gorgias finally makes the grandiloquent pronouncement that its *logoi* concern "the greatest and best of human affairs" (451d). Socrates objects that this claim is doubly contentious: there is disagreement over what is greatest and best, and there are rival claimants for the role of purveying it, specifically the traditional contenders for the supreme good, health, beauty, and wealth, and their matching specialists, the doctor, the trainer, and the moneymaker. Gorgias's reply is a subtle reworking of the real Gorgias's *logos*, but one endowed by Plato with a newly explicit political emphasis, for rhetoric now imparts freedom to the man who can wield it, together with control over everyone else in his city (452d). (Cf. "A Athènes, tout dépendait du peuple, et le peuple dépendait des orateurs," Fénelon.) Gorgias thus aggressively enunciates the antidemocratic possibilities incipient in "*logos* the great ruler." Rhetoric is the power to persuade with *logoi* people assembled in any *political* gathering whatsoever; it makes "slaves" of all the other experts to the expert empowered to persuade "the masses," who appropriates their products and profits (452e).

Socrates expresses satisfaction with the completeness of Gorgias's disclosure, and quietly encapsulates it in the definition that has echoed down the centuries: rhetoric is "the craftsman of persuasion"; the power of rhetoric is "to produce persuasion in the soul" (453a). Socrates will demolish Gorgias by taking issue with the Gorgianic conceptions of both persuasion and psychology.

Before pushing the argument a stage further, Socrates interjects a methodological aside bearing directly on his attempt to prise apart philosophical dialectic and rhetorical display. He insists that more clarification come from Gorgias, rather than himself, "not for your sake, but for the *logos*, so that it will advance in the fashion best able to render what is under discussion clear to us" (453c). Gorgias had represented rhetoric as an asymmetric, exploitative relation: the active individual uses his *logos* to enslave the passive multitude. Now, while Socrates does not substitute individual concern for his interlocutor—his procedure is not for Gorgias's sake (alone)—the dialectical *logos* does not fall within the scope of a personal pronoun; it progresses through the phases of argumentative development to the intellectual benefit of questioner and answerer together. Dialectic is ultimately for the sake of knowledge. If it appears either to attack or to spare the interlocutor, that is a mere appearance. The *logos* itself is not just our chief but our sole concern: we interact with our partner in the investigation only because and insofar as he contributes to it. By the same token, we do not care about our own dialectical fate as such, that is, whether whatever fragment or figment of truth emerging from the discussion is "ours." Truth on this Socratic conception is not a commodity accessible at some points within a hierarchy at the expense of the occupants of other positions; all participants in the discussion share the truth communally. It hardly needs pointing out that in this remark Plato provides the starkest possible contrast to Gorgias's definition of rhetoric as ideological manipulation for the sake of personal political power.

Socrates suggests that the definition "craftsman of persuasion" is successful only if rhetoric is unique in producing conviction, but as a matter of fact all experts by teaching persuade us of matters falling within their specialty, so that the variety of persuasion to which rhetoric lays claim remains obscure. Gorgias repeats that specifically rhetorical persuasion is aimed at "crowds," and adds that it concerns justice and injustice, a topic embracing deliberative politics as well as legal conflict (454b). His earlier reference to "the masses" could but need not carry pejorative implications, but "crowds" most definitely does. Plato puts in Gorgias's mouth a word unmistakably intended to exacerbate any democrat's suspicions of his indispensable but dubious ally, the orator. "Democracy" means "rule of the *dēmos*," and *dēmos* neutrally means "the common people," as opposed to the affluent and aristocratic few. Only an enemy of the people would designate them "the crowd," a term of opprobrium at home in oligarchic polemics. This is not to pretend that the Platonic Socrates is by any means a democratic champion; in the last portion of the dialogue, he will contentiously disparage the achievements of the greatest Athenian heroes and astonishingly reserve for himself the title of the city's only authentic politician, albeit in his own special sense. Socrates is not at all concerned to deny that the Athenian civic body is a "crowd"; his aim is to demonstrate that Gorgias's advertisement for the omnipotence of rhetoric is indeed justified within a democratic political structure, and thus to damn rhetoric rather than defend democracy. But to jump to the conclusion that he therefore stands revealed as the enemy of freedom would be highly premature. If—a very large "if"—his vision of dialectic as enquiry aimed at shared truth can be sustained, then liberty, if not unqualified equality, is to be found within the limits of philosophical *logos,* and there alone.

Socrates now exploits, lethally, Gorgias's earlier admission that teaching issues in persuasion. He extracts the agreement that learning and conviction are distinct; there is false conviction as well as true, but knowledge is always true. Therefore there are two species of the genus persuasion, one convincing with knowledge, the other without it, and Gorgias volunteers that rhetorical persuasion falls within the latter (454d–e). "Then neither does the rhetor teach juries and other crowds about justice and injustice, but only persuades them; for certainly he could not teach such great matters to so many people in a short time" (455a). Philosophical insistence on knowledge as opposed to mere fallible belief shows that the Gorgianic identification of *logos* with power is falsified by the rhetorician's incapacity to convey knowledge within his special context of adversative debate on political and legal matters before the masses. In *Helen* Gorgias had not ignored philosophers, but there they were yet another type of fighter contending in the battle of *logos,* compelling rather than instructing their passive auditors' souls.

The question of abiding interest to us is not whether the most scathing critique of Athenian participatory political and judicial practice is warranted, but rather whether the category "persuasion without knowledge" has contemporary, worrying, validity. (In passing I note that in Athens a tragedian was conceived of as "teaching" the entire assembled city, and that his production was evaluated by a jury selected on egalitarian principles; Plato's denial in *Gorgias* that instructing a multitude is possible thus effectively robs of all legitimacy an Athenian institution we regard as one of radical democracy's signal triumphs.) Socrates' denigration of democratic decision-making relies on two presuppositions about which we moderns might feel rather differently. The first is the supposed impossibility of "true" education on a mass scale. If anything, subsequent history has given us far greater reason for profound pessimism on this score (and about there being one "true" education for all). But the second is the proposition that there is or could be "instructive persuasion" in politics. Anyone who claims to possess political "expertise" (unless he means Gorgias's antidemocratic power politics) must believe that there is. Thinking democrats, however, should insist that although there is a recognizable sphere of public interest, it does not define a corresponding specialist; no one is *authoritative* about justice. Plato has Protagoras expound how this could possibly be so in his eponymous dialogue. If we wish to resist the second assumption in *Gorgias,* we must be prepared to explain how modern democratic ideology is compatible with the political "expertise" its inaccessible institutions encourage and the propagandistic manipulation they invite.

Socrates goads Gorgias into delivering an extended defense of and panegyric on omnipotent rhetoric by making a deliberately naive claim about the Athenian manner of implementing public programs—surely the advice of the relevant expert, the architect, will prove persuasive, rather than that of the rhetorician? Gorgias retorts that as a matter of verifiable historical fact, it was Themistocles and Pericles who, through rhetoric, were responsible for Athens's imperial projects. He insists that if a competent orator such as himself were to compete against a doctor or other knowledgeable specialist in convincing a recalcitrant individual to submit to painful treatment, or for a civic medical position, the orator would invariably win—"for there is nothing concerning which the rhetor could not speak more persuasively than any other craftsman among the masses" (456c6; the damning "crowds" has now discreetly disappeared). So much for panegyric. His apology on behalf of rhetorical experts, only dubiously consistent with the implications of his former characterization of rhetoric as the means for tapping ultimate political power, rests on the plea that in itself it is a neutral capacity. It can be exploited to good or ill effect, but that is a decision for the individual skilled speaker, not his rhetorical teacher. Rhetoric is intrinsically an amoral weapon. This position is inherently unstable, since Gorgias classes rhetoric together with the maritial arts as a combative skill; surely this entails that it is intrinsically aggressive. The defense is culturally specific and wholesomely conventional. Greek society enthusiastically cultivated expertise in all sorts of competitive physical combat. It is of course no part of the job of the physical trainer to encourage his student to unleash that deadly expertise against friends and family. Gorgias piously assures us that rhetoric analogously is to be used justly, that is, only defensively against enemies and wrongdoers (456e); the worthy rhetorician could but would not rob the physician of his reputation.

Gorgias now pretends that the proper exploitation of rhetorical power is invariably morally correct—the word *just* and its cognates run right through his speech. He nowhere specifies what this actually means, but given his repeated appeal to conventional mores, he must intend to rely on the popular Greek conception of right and wrong, familiar from *The Republic,* that right action benefits or protects members of one's "own" group, not outsiders; harm to enemies is positively encouraged. However, a Greek's sense of his affiliations, the ground for even minimal moral consideration, was notoriously fluid and easily capable of generating unresolvable contradictions; most Athenian political dissension was the direct upshot of individuals' pursuing the ambitions of their "own" clan or class against those of the large body politic.

Thus Gorgias's proviso guarantees very little. It leaves the potentially lethal orator free to speak against the interests of anyone beyond what might prove a desperately narrow social limit. Furthermore, Gorgias's reference to disciples who pervert rhetoric of course concedes that the uninhibited, selfish exertion of rhetorical power is a fact of realpolitik.

Before returning to the attack, Socrates interjects a further declaration of the essential distinction between philosophical and rhetorical conflict: "I am afraid to push through my examination of you, lest you imagine that my purpose in competing is not clarification of the issue, but your defeat . . . I am one of those who would gladly be refuted on saying something not true, gladly refute someone else uttering falsehood, but bearing refutation no less gladly than administering it" (458a). In *Helen* Gorgias had undertaken to refute her slanderers, but his exaltation of a *logos* that pleases and deceives left no room for construing refutation as anything other than personal defeat. Socrates' reaffirmation of truth as the supreme good, falsehood as the ultimate evil, opens a space for unselfish "competition," where dialectical "victor" and "victim" alike share the spoils of discovery.

Socrates' renewed onslaught addresses the implications of the idea that the audience (once again a pejorative "crowd") in the rhetorician's sway is ignorant; if a speaker is more persuasive in this context, this is only because a man who does not know has the advantage over one who does among people as ignorant as he. As the real Gorgias had proclaimed, rhetorical power consists in deception, since it has its effect on the foolish by *appearing* more knowledgeable than expertise (459c). Plato's Gorgias is made to concede the point and with embarrassing fatuity extol the convenience of besting legitimate experts without the inconvenience of learning anything but meretricious rhetoric.

This is the philosopher's damning representation of Gorgias's boast that he can extemporize with equal facility on any topic whatsoever thrown at him in public display. It is mere display, because only the readiness of the ignorant "crowd" to be amused by the equally ignorant blandishments of rhetorical *logos* assures his success. Now, a basic strategy of the real Gorgias in both *On What Is Not* and *Helen* had been playfulness: are these texts *jeux d'esprit*, and any the less effective for it? High Platonic seriousness will brook none of that. But notice how Socrates' indictment turns on a rationalist presumption that comes all too easily to thinkers, such as Parmenides and perhaps Socrates himself, for whom the supposed fact that *"logos* is a great ruler" entails that logic must be omnipresent in discourse and in reality. Of course a *manifest* fool would be unpersuasive in political debate, but that is no reason to conclude that rhetorical authority uniquely appeals, or even pretends to appeal, to the intellect. Political discourse need not mimic ratiocination, as the authentic Gorgias indicated in his global catalogue of *logos;* only in Socrates' wholly rational world would even fools require specious *knowledge* to be impressed.

We shall not pursue Gorgias's discomfiture any further, as Socrates argues that this moralized rhetoric is inconsistent with Gorgias's previous admissions (457e) and constructs a definitive refutation from the impossibility of simultaneously maintaining both that a teacher is not at fault if his students turn morally neutral rhetorical power to evil ends, and that a teacher, such as Gorgias, is capable of imparting ethical and political expertise to his students. Does Socrates win? Most of the premises Plato feeds into the argument would strike most of us as, at best, intensely problematic, since the dialectic depends on an extreme form of Socratic rationalism. It is not just that both Socrates and Gorgias are committed to an intellectualist conception of expertise extending throughout the area of politics. The development of the theme that the rhetorician will "teach" ethics, which is crucial for the refutation, cannot be sustained without the Socratic thesis that true knowledge suffices for virtue. That is a paradox that Plato himself will come to reject as his psychology develops, and accordingly he will modify his vehement rejection of rhetoric as the indefensible manipulation of ignorant emotion.

But the point is not simply the tenability, or otherwise, of the substantive theses of the argument in *Gorgias;* rather, the confrontation with Gorgias takes shape in the very opposition of methods, "display" versus "dialectic," regardless of whether the philosophical method in this particular instance succeeds in divulging truth. Does Socrates "bewitch" Gorgias, does Plato seduce us, into haplessly conceding that the *logos* that is proper argument logically compels a conviction distinct from the psychic impress of a brute force? Later in the dialogue Plato will reanimate the Parmenidean imagery of logical necessity, the necessity that Gorgias in turn had conflated with a uniform persuasion before which our passive souls must yield. If Descartes was right to assert, paradoxically, that the compulsion of reason enhances rather than inhibits freedom, then we should take a stand against both Gorgias and his modern ideological heirs, such as Foucault. Gorgianic psychology is bleakly reductive; Socratic psychology is overweeningly rationalistic. Yet if we are to resist a portrait of ourselves as passive Helens, we cannot allow that species of power reflect mere superficial variations in mode and effectiveness, rather than essential differences in nature.

This introduction to Greek rhetoric works within the narrowest constraints: using the paradigm of Gorgias, it seeks to involve the reader in the *problematic* of the rhetorical tradition rather than to supply a substantive exposition. Nevertheless, a complete omission of Aristotle would be unacceptable, on two grounds: first, and simply, his enormous historical import; second, his intimate connection with the seminal conflict I have sketched between philosophy and rhetoric. One might contend that it is precisely by virtue of that connection that Aristotle occupies his prominent position in the development of rhetoric.

The Socrates of *Gorgias* rejects rhetoric so resolutely and in its entirety be-

cause he conceives of it as at once pandering to and exploiting vulgar ignorance; thus his reaction flows immediately from a provocative philosophical
psychology of extreme rationalism. This attitude undergoes drastic revision
in *Phaedrus,* which, importantly, presupposes and elaborates on the famous
division of the soul into three components introduced in *The Republic.* This
pluralization of the psyche is, in part, specifically designed to accommodate
the genuine occurrence of conflict between reason and passion that Socrates
had previously refused to recognize, but, more positively, it also clears a theoretical space for a conception of the passions that need not automatically condemn them, on condition that they obey the dictates of independent reason.
Most pertinently, the way is now open for the vindication of at least a properly regimented rhetoric, since the irrational components of the soul are susceptible to distinctive, irrational modes of persuasion. If there is more to a
human being than more or less defective rationality, then rhetoric has found
its proper voice: it speaks to the emotions in the only accents they can hear.

Thus the evolution of Plato's philosophy of mind exonerates the rhetorical
project, if only as an "ideal" and "scientific" rhetoric. But the rehabilitation is
hardly unqualified. Even an "ideal" rhetoric, deployed skillfully and with the
best intentions, would remain firmly subordinated to philosophy. This follows inevitably from the very condition permitting the partial rehabilitation
of rhetoric, the pluralistic model of the soul. If the irrational psychic components are legitimately susceptible to distinctively rhetorical persuasion, by
the same token they are deaf to the purely rational, philosophical persuasion
that the highest, rational part of the soul heeds. Emotion has independent reality but remains markedly inferior to reason; analogously, rhetoric is authentic but is ranged well below philosophy.

This is the juncture at which Aristotle makes his decisive contribution to
the debate. Aristotelian philosophy of mind flatly rejects any Platonic scheme
of psychic pluralization. For Aristotle, thought and desire combine in the act
of deliberation to constitute the choices that are the precondition for fully rational human behavior. Philosophical analysis detects intellectual and affective aspects in deliberation, but this analytical distinction is just that—it does
not reflect a categorical division between reason and passion in the soul.

The consequences for rhetorical theory could not be more radical. Platonic
emotions are irrational, not in the sense that they are reducible to, e.g., simple
tastes or tactile feelings, but rather because they are, by definition, unmoti-
vated and unmodified by the full-blown, active rationality most evident in
philosophical *logos.* In complete contrast, Aristotelian emotions are permeated by reason. When I, for instance, unhappily perceive a state of affairs as
unfortunate and react accordingly, I do indeed perceive it *as* unfortunate: cognitive, evaluative, and affective responses are, apart from pathological cases,
typically indissoluble. This is not, of course, to pretend that misperception
(along any of these dimensions—cognitive, evaluative, affective) does not oc-

cur, but it is to insist that emotion as such must not be prised apart from *logos* and then, inevitably, disparaged.

"The *pathē* are those things because of which people change their judgements, and are accompanied by pain and pleasure" (*Rhetoric* II.1)—so Aristotle defines emotion before issuing subtly detailed analyses of the passions, together with prescriptions for arousing and stilling them. Gorgias had refused to discriminate between modes of persuasion; Plato's reaction was to make distinctions with a vengeance, all to the discredit of rhetoric. With characteristic dialectical agility, Aristotle deliberately revives and revitalizes the terms of our primary encounter: "Rhetoric is the power of discovering potential persuasion about everything. This is the function of no other skill; for each of them can instruct and persuade about its own subject, e.g., medicine about health and sickness . . . But rhetoric seems to be able to discover persuasion about any given subject. That is why we say that its expertise does not concern some specific, separate class" (*Rhetoric* I.2). Aristotle here draws from Gorgias not only the conception of rhetoric as power but also the explosive claim of universality. Evidently the assumption that a skill provides persuasive instruction within the field of its proprietary expertise comes straight from *Gorgias,* as witnessed by the perennial example of medicine. Yet, unlike the Platonic Socrates, Aristotle does not infer that such particular expertise precludes the existence of a quite general rhetorical faculty founded on legitimate technique, not ignorance. It is not that Aristotle simply returns to Gorgias: his dialectic achieves a truly novel synthesis. *Rhetoric* hardly suggests that there is nothing to choose between a philosophical argument and a rhetorical plea. But Aristotle does not merely maintain, as does the Plato of *Phaedrus,* that rhetoric is, after all, acceptable in its (unavoidable) place. He further insists that, when in the rhetorical forum we induce emotions in others and, in turn, are emotionally swayed, this is not an unfortunate *pis aller* we follow only under the compulsion of political exigency.

"There are three kinds of persuasive means furnished by the *logos:* those in the character of the speaker, those in how the hearer is disposed, and those in the *logos* itself, through its demonstrating or seeming to demonstrate" (*Rhetoric* I.2). This critical tripartition will play a major architectonic role in *Rhetoric:* Aristotle not only acknowledges that rhetoric includes aspects irreducible to argument (that is, *ostensible* argument) but also recognizes that these divisions enjoy a certain independence. Explicating the second, emotive means of persuasion, he says that "the orator persuades through his hearers, when they are led into emotions by his *logos*" (ibid.), while his metaphorical description of rhetoric as an "offshoot" of dialectic and politics indicates a refusal either to assimilate or to rip asunder reasoning and affective motivation: this intricate scheme is intended at once to divide and to unify. Although rhetoric is a "part and likeness" of dialectic, in general its arguments, even when valid, do not meet the high (and inappropriate) standards of theoretical investigation, but they are *real* arguments for all that. There are also, of course, rhetorical appeals to the emotions, but the orator in arguing and in influencing our feelings is not precariously engaged in disparate activities. Just as the perception of something *as* unfortunate is a unitary state, so my persuading you to see it as so is a single, if highly complex, act of rhetoric.

At the outset I remarked on the curious fate of the word *rhetoric,* suggesting that our negative conception of it displays closer affinities to the original Greek contention in which the very idea of rhetoric was born than to the vast stretch of history in which it came close to epitomizing culture itself. What happened in between? Anything less than a grotesquely oversimplified response would have to mention almost all aspects of Western intellectual and political evolution, but our reflection on the formative battle between rhetoric and philosophy can at least provide a useful hint. Isocrates, that genius of mediocre compromise, synthesized Protagoras's paean to human progress with the Gorgianic conception of *logos:* it is responsible for all civilization, with the telling detail that political concord is maintained by those "we call capable of speaking to the masses" (*Antidosis* 256). Isocrates quite deliberately equates *logos* in the sense of "right reason" with *logos* in the sense of rhetoric, and he is surely challenging Plato when he insists that one and the same man persuades others and judges right for himself, by engaging in an internal discourse (he artfully employs the very word *dialectic,* which the philosopher reserved for his special, rational discourse). Isocrates makes the next move in the game by returning to Gorgias's position that *logos* is unitary, but with the blandly moralistic conception of rhetoric offered by the chastened Platonic Gorgias, rather than with the infinitely more arresting idea of the real Gorgias's *Helen.*

Through the conduit of Cicero this anodyne conciliation of the quarrel achieved an authority that set the seal on rhetoric's official status as universal culture. The Gorgianic boast of universal fluency is a salient topic in the first book of *De oratore.* Cicero prevaricates. He does not affirm that the profession of rhetorical skill promises ability to orate *knowledgeably* on any subject but rather, "elaborately and abundantly." Yet by tempering the Platonic rejection of a rhetorical *scientia universalis* to a commonplace admission of its extreme rarity, he in fact keeps alive the middlebrow Isocratean vision of the political orator who indeed "knows," but only because this knowledge is polymathic competence, rather than the all-demanding, all-conquering *logos* to which Gorgias and Plato alike responded with pure extremism.

The complementary extremism of our century has revitalized the original terms of the quarrel. For us, no issue burns more fiercely than the attempt to impose a civilizing distinction between force and persuasion. If we no longer formulate it precisely as the difference, if any, between rhetoric and philosophy, the fact remains that the primal scene between Gorgias and Plato provides our intellectual and political debates with their fundamental structure, and that meditation on it continues to offer one of our best hopes of understanding, if not resolution. If we can ultimately accept even a heavily modified version of Aristotelian psychology, we might aspire with him to transcend the conflict opposing Gorgias to Plato. For many centuries the verdict went in Aristotle's favor; our age is characterized by its indecision over this issue of the gravest political moment.

ROBERT WARDY

Bibliography

Brunschwig, Jacques. "Gorgias et l'incommunicabilité," in *La communication: Actes du XVe congrès des Sociétés de philosophie de langue française*. Montreal, 1971. Pp. 79–84.

Buchheim, Thomas. *Gorgias von Leontini: Reden, Fragmente und Testimonien, Herausgegeben mit Übersetzung und Kommentar*. Hamburg, 1989.

Cassin, Barbara. *L'effet sophistique*. Paris, 1995.

Coxon, A. H. *The Fragments of Parmenides: A Critical Text with Introduction, the Ancient Testimonia and a Commentary*. Assen/Maastricht, 1986.

Desbordes, Françoise. *La rhétorique antique*. Paris, 1996.

Loraux, Nicole. *The Invention of Athens: The Funeral Oration in the Classical City*. Trans. Alan Sheridan. Cambridge, Mass., 1986

Newiger, H.-J. *Untersuchungen zu Gorgias' Schrift über das Nichtseiende*. Berlin, 1973.

Plato. *Gorgias: A Revised Text with Introduction and Commentary*. Ed. E. R. Dodds. Oxford, 1959.

Romilly, Jacqueline de. "Gorgias et le pouvoir de la poésie." *Journal of Hellenic Studies* (1973): 155–162.

Segal, Charles. "Gorgias and the Psychology of the Logos." *Harvard Studies in Classical Philology* (1962): 99–155.

Vickers, Brian. *In Defence of Rhetoric*. Oxford, 1989.

Vlastos, Gregory. "The Socratic Elenchus." *Oxford Studies in Ancient Philosophy* (1983): 27–58.

Wardy, Robert. *The Birth of Rhetoric*. London, 1996.

Related Articles

Schools and Sites of Learning; Demonstration and the Idea of Science; Language; Sophists; Inventing Politics; Poetics; Aristotle

TECHNOLOGY

A REMARKABLE PASSAGE in Sophocles illustrates the respect that the Greeks reserved for *tekhne*. It is an encomium on skillfulness, an exaltation of the powers of human beings, of the tricks and tools by which these singular animals are able to alter their condition and escape, for better or for worse, the laws common to all species:

> Many things are formidable, and none more formidable than man! He crosses the gray sea beneath the winter wind, passing beneath the surges that surround him; and he wears away the highest of the gods, Earth, immortal and unwearying, as his ploughs go back and forth from year to year, turning the soil with the aid of the breed of horses.
>
> And he captures the tribe of thoughtless birds and the races of wild beasts and the watery brood of the sea, catching them in the woven coils of nets, man the skilful. And he contrives to overcome *[kratei mechanais]* the beast that roams the mountain, and tames the shaggy-maned horse and the untiring mountain bull, putting a yoke about their necks.
>
> And he has learned speech and wind-swift thought and the temper that rules cities, and how to escape the exposure of the inhospitable hills and the sharp arrows of the rain, all-resourceful; he meets nothing in the future without resource; only from Hades shall he apply no means of flight; and he has contrived escape from desperate *[amechanon]* maladies.
>
> Skilful beyond hope is the contrivance of his art *[to mechanoen technas]*, and he advances sometimes to evil, at other times to good. When he applies the laws of the earth and the justice the gods have sworn to uphold he is high in the city; outcast from the city is he with whom the ignoble consorts for the sake of gain. (Sophocles, *Antigone* 332–371)

The underlying theme of this hymn, interrupting the initial plot development of *Antigone,* is the ambivalence of human invention: humans are so cunning that their audacity affords them the capacity for good and evil. Once free of nature's constraints, man is at maximum risk, and the laws of the polis may conflict with the unbreakable edicts of the gods. Despite the grave possible consequences of such action, the step is taken and man emancipated. Sophocles gives a comprehensive list of the skills in which material tools coexist alongside the intellectual faculties of speech and law: navigation, agriculture, hunting, domestication, language, social life, and construction.

PRACTICAL INNOVATIONS AND
WRITTEN TRADITIONS

The originality of the Greek contribution probably lies beyond particular inventions or techniques. What is most noteworthy about Greek technology, rather, is a conceptualization of *tekhne,* and the rational principles underlying machines and technical procedures.

Every civilization cultivates its own forms of technical skill, and the principal inventions of which the Middle Ages took increasing advantage derive from many sources. Crucial innovations can very probably be credited to the Greek world, although it is often impossible to disentangle fact from legend. Traditions that are extremely difficult to verify generously attribute notable inventions to the legendary heroes of ancient times. Plato, for example, lists Thales among the *eumekhanoi,* men skillful in invention *(The Republic),* and the anchor and potter's wheel are attributed to Anacharsis, the screw and the pulley to Archytas, and the arch to Democritus. The figure of Archytas symbolizes the very ideal of the philosopher capable of technological invention.

At a later period various inventions are associated with the name of Archimedes, without definite historical proof, and it is still a matter of dispute whether Archimedes was as great a technician as he was a mathematician. The two principal incidents that illustrate his technical genius, the revelation of the fraud perpetrated by the royal goldsmith and the defense of Syracuse against the Romans, are attested only in much later writings, and we have no precise and reliable text concerning his actual procedures—if they existed.

More precisely and more credibly, the catapult may have been invented around 400 B.C.E. by engineers in the service of Dionysius of Syracuse (Diodorus of Sicily).

Such inventions, often difficult to date or to attribute to a particular inventor with any certainty, are unlikely to represent the principal, original contribution of Greek culture in technical matters. In the field of technology, as in many others, the remarkable fecundity of Greek culture consists largely in the organization of knowledge, and in the sustained and stubborn effort to discover logical principles and present them through written exposition. The Greek world has left behind a rich heritage of theoretical outlines and treatises, transmitted to the West under the names of Aristotle, Philon of Byzantium, Archimedes, and Hero, to name only the most important.

A broad selection of literary works, including the *Iliad* and *Odyssey,* offers all kinds of precious information concerning weaponry, agriculture, metallurgy, the transportation of water, navigation, and so forth. In *Works and Days,* Hesiod mentions in passing the type of wood to be used in plow making, and in *Oeconomika* Xenophon discusses the most appropriate methods of seeding, planting, and harvesting wheat, and compares the characteristics of different soils. Thucydides describes a few war machines, for instance the hol-

low engine used by the Boeotians for setting fire to the ramparts of Delion during their conflict with the Athenians.

But these isolated instances, while indications of a technical culture, do not constitute a technology per se, that is, an organized discourse on tools and methods. We do, however, find accounts in Greek texts that, linked together, form series of writings that transmit and refine the description of certain instruments or methods. It is these series or written traditions that we shall focus on here: mechanics, optics, and alchemy.

These technical treatises exhibit one remarkable characteristic: they include little or nothing concerning the most vital or basic techniques—nothing about roofing, pottery, textiles, or agricultural work. The texts frequently describe apparatuses without any practical or everyday use: automata for the theater, complex toys, gear systems that are probably unworkable and entirely theoretical, distorting mirrors for the amusement of princesses, stills for a chimerical transmutation of metals. The only apparatuses of any real importance in these texts are the war machines: assault engines, tortoise-shell shields, watchtowers, mines, and catapults.

It is extremely difficult for us, surrounded as we are by technological artifacts, not to project our own habitual categories and classifications onto ancient Greek culture. The Greek categorization of knowledge is different: its tenets are hidden from us. For whom were these treatises on technology (if that is the right word) written? What did the Greeks mean, in different periods, by the term *mechanics?*

Although the texts in question may have had little to do with everyday life and with practical human needs at the time, this is not to say that their impact has been negligible. Historians of technology hypothesize that the Romans put into practice certain Greek innovations (an apparatus consisting of multiple pulleys for use on construction sites, siphon pipes for aqueducts, arch construction); it is possible that certain Greek "machines" that had retained the status of prototypes or fictions were actually constructed within the larger framework of the Roman empire.

But the texts also achieved an even more brilliant and fertile destiny later on. Cardan, Tartaglia, Galileo, and Newton were inspired by the *Problemata mecanicae* of (Pseudo-)Aristotle and by the books of Hero, Pappus, and Vitruvius. Greek mechanics contributed fundamentally to the renewal of the theoretical science of forces in Europe in the 16th and 17th centuries.

THE ARTS OF WAR

One skill not included in Sophocles' list of technological accomplishments is of all the arts perhaps the most favored by those in power and the most productive of innovations: war. The realm of the art of warfare is also one of the best represented in our surviving texts.

The invention of the catapult is an element in the transformation of the martial arts that appears to have taken place about 400 B.C.E., in particular during the campaigns of Dionysius of Syracuse, Philip of Macedon, and Alexander and his immediate successors. The catapult is a kind of enlarged crossbow attached to a pedestal (stationary or mobile); the bow is replaced by two arms that pass through a bundle of twisted fibers, and when the apparatus is stretched, the fibers twist and recoil. Naturally, care must be taken to ensure that the force of the recoil is the same on each side; otherwise, the arrow or stone will fire at an angle.

The use of this new weapon spread widely between 400 and 350; highly effective, the catapult made a strong impression at the time and brought about new methods of attack. At about the same time, we find other indications of a profound alteration in the techniques of warfare (attack, siege, entrenchment), as Herodotus attests somewhat earlier in regard to the Phoenicians' skill in digging a canal for Xerxes' troops. It is hard to say which of these inventions actually did originate with Greek-speaking inventors. The perfecting of military techniques in this period, especially projectile armaments, is echoed in a series of descriptive, more or less theoretical texts by Aeneas Tacticus, Philon of Byzantium, and other authors whose writings are lost (Ctesibius, for one).

At the same time, a class of men who can be termed military engineers began to emerge, especially in the entourages of Philip and Alexander. A passage in Vitruvius (10.16) sets forth the characteristics of this class of military experts and attests to their new importance: the Rhodians dismiss Diognetes, their military architect, who is a native of the island, and allow themselves to be seduced by a newcomer, Callias, who presents them with a superb description *(akroasis)* of his new machines; Callias claims to be able to withstand the assault towers of Demetrius Poliorcetes, or rather of Epimachus, the military architect in Demetrius's service. But it turns out that Callias's machines do not work, and the previous architect, Diognetes, is recalled and entreated to save his country. Finally Diognetes uses the old hydraulic methods, rerouting water channels so that Demetrius's assault towers become unusable. This example is a clear indication of the new requirements of the city-states and the emergence of the figure of the architect or mechanic, who combines the old architectural capability with more recent know-how involving various machines. Such a man can sell himself to the highest bidder and must be able to convince princes and statesmen of his own expertise and the originality of his techniques: he gives a lecture, provides models, promises a technology superior to that of the enemy (one may wonder whether the arms trade has changed significantly).

In this context, a literature of military technology begins to flourish. The first author whose book has survived is Aeneas Tacticus (about whom we know very little). He left a treatise called *Poliorcetica* (The Art of Siege War-

fare), illustrated with allusions to events that took place between 400 and 360 B.C.E. He also mentions other works he had written on the arts of war: a book on supply *(poristika)* and on fortifications or preparations for war *(paraskeuastika)*. The book that has survived describes various aspects of siege tactics: the choice of sites and hours when watches should be set, means of reconnaissance, passwords and secret messages, and precautions to be taken against plots and mutinies. It also describes some technical procedures: the use of mines and countermines, incendiary devices, and so forth. Machines per se occupy little space. There is an apparatus for toppling assault ladders whose description and usage are somewhat unclear.

Shortly after Aeneas, other authors (a certain Diades, for example) wrote works on war machines that have not survived, though some elements appear to have been used by Philon of Athens around 300 in his own (lost) treatise *Poliorcetica*, which Philon of Byzantium used in turn around 225 for a new treatise on the same subject. It was at this point that the field of military technology was expanded and reorganized: Philon also wrote a book on projectile armaments in which he proposed several improvements for catapults (replacing the twisted fibers with metal springs, or even a system of compressed air, inspired by Ctesibius). Thus a corpus of technical texts on the art of war and projectile and siege machines was developed.

FROM MILITARY ARTS TO MECHANICS

With Philon of Byzantium, however, the theory of war machines became part of a larger technical corpus, within what Philon termed a *syntaxis mechanike*—in other words, a treatise based on mechanical procedures. On the basis of the order of Philon's surviving works, A. G. Drachmann has been able to reconstitute the general organization of this "mechanical syntax":

1. preamble
2. levers
3. the construction of ports
4. catapults
5. pneumatics
6. automat theaters
7. the construction of fortresses
8. the siege and defense of cities *(poliorcetica)*
9. stratagems

The book on catapults (4) has been preserved in Greek, as well as portions of those on fortresses (7) and sieges (8); pneumatics (5) exists only in Arabic. Except for a few fragments cited by other authors, the rest has been lost.

The arts of war thus became part of a larger discipline called mechanics,

with a more systematic form of presentation. Connections appeared among several branches: new catapults presupposed levers and even pneumatics. Mathematics acquired a privileged position. The element of theory in Philon had rational foundations at least up to a certain point, if what is indirectly attested in the preamble can be believed (Book 1). To calculate the dimensions of a catapult with twice the capacity of a given model, Philon has to solve the problem of the duplication of the cube (Catapults, Book 4); he discusses the conditions for making a tool starting from a different-size model, and proposes using a graduated ruler to effect the change of scale. On both occasions, Philon mentions that he has treated these questions in his preamble. His treatise on mechanics thus opens with the rudiments of applied mathematics. Likewise when he reports on his predecessors and their efforts to construct projectile armaments, Philon reproaches them for being ignorant of the whys and wherefores, and of having proceeded by trial and error without an overall perspective. Aristotle's influence can be felt in Philon's theoretical requirements and even in his vocabulary.

IN SEARCH OF MECHANICS

Thus the arts of war are integrated into mechanics. But what is mechanics? In Europe, from the 18th century on, mechanics meant the science of movements and forces. Previously, between the end of antiquity and roughly the 1700s, mechanics was the theory of machines (sometimes "simple machines"; the same theory is sometimes improperly called "statics"). These simple machines, or "mechanical powers," were listed by Hero of Alexandria: the wheel, the lever, the multiple pulley, the wedge, the screw (Pappus, VIII). This is a quite restrictive interpretation of mechanics, much narrower than that of Philon of Byzantium.

To understand the subject matter of mechanics in the 3rd century B.C.E. we must turn to etymology. We have already encountered the term *mekhane* in Sophocles; if man rules over other living species, if he delves unremittingly and without respect into the venerable earth, if he has created shelters for himself, and cities with their own laws, it is thanks to all kinds of *mekhane*. Here the word is used in a very broad sense, similar to its use in the *Odyssey*, where Odysseus is termed a master of tricks *(polymekhanos)*.

Before it was used to designate a specific body of doctrine (whose outline, moreover, is difficult to trace), *mekhane* referred in general terms to expedients, remedies, artifices, tricks, machinations, and skilled resources—processes or even modes of behavior rather than things. The word has undergone an evolution comparable to that of Old French *engin:* the Latin term *ingenium* became the medieval "engine," trick or machination, and finally came to designate the technological object itself, independent of the mind that "manufactured" or "machined" it.

Mechanics was established as a distinct science before Philon's time; a specific science designated "mechanics" is found in the Aristotelian corpus, for example. It is listed among the "physical components of the mathematical sciences," along with optics, harmonics, and astronomy (Aristotle's two lists in *Physics* III and *Metaphysics* M can be combined). These four disciplines study objects or concrete phenomena, considering them, according to Aristotle, as mathematical objects: the light or visual ray as a geometric line, sound vibration as a relationship between numbers, the movement of stars as a circular orbit. The status of the object of mechanics is more difficult to pin down. What, according to this perspective, is the proper object of mechanics, and in what respect is that object mathematical?

The answer probably lies in a text that belongs, marginally, to the Aristotelian corpus: the *Problemata mecanicae* (*Mechanical Problems*, or simply *Mechanics*), attributed to Aristotle, which was rediscovered in the Renaissance and which stimulated discussions among scientists on the most important questions of physics. Galileo, for example, held the *Problemata mecanicae* in high esteem and drew from it on several important points.

The *Problemata mecanicae* begins with a definition of *mekhane:*

Remarkable things occur in accordance with nature, the cause of which is unknown, and others occur contrary to nature, which are produced by skill *[techne]* for the benefit of mankind. For in many cases nature produces effects against our advantage; for nature always acts consistently and simply, but our advantage changes in many ways.

When, then, we have to produce an effect contrary to nature, we are at a loss, because of the difficulty, and require skill. Therefore we call that part of skill which assists such difficulties, a device *[mechane]*. For as the poet Antiphon wrote, this is true: "We by skill gain mastery over things in which we are conquered by nature."

Of this kind are those in which the less master the greater, and things possessing little weight move heavy weights, and all similar devices which we term mechanical problems. These are not altogether identical with physical problems, nor are they entirely separate from them, but they have a share in both mathematical and physical speculations, for the method is demonstrated by mathematics, but the practical application belongs to physics.

Among the problems included in this class are those concerned with the lever. For it is strange that a great weight can be moved by a small force, and that, too, when a greater weight is involved. For the very same weight, which a man cannot move without a lever, he quickly moves by applying the weight of the lever.

Now the original cause of all such phenomena is the circle. (Aristotle, *Mechanical Problems* 847a10–b16)

Mechanics is similar to the other sciences that are "common" to physics and mathematics (astronomy, optics, and harmonics): its object is material and physical, yet it is considered mathematically. At the same time there is a difference: the movements of stars, light rays, and sound vibrations are considered as simplified mathematical objects—curves, lines, numerical relationships—while in the case of mechanics the object itself remains indefinite, and it is the mode of explanation that is mathematical (mathematics provides the reason).

We learn more about the variety of objects of mechanics by pursuing the thirty-five questions of the collection. First: why are larger scales more accurate? The questions that follow—in an order that is difficult to justify—have to do with standard instruments (the sling, the pulley, the steelyard, forceps), with common technical devices (rowboats or sailboats, bedsprings), with reflections on everyday situations that involve the distribution of force (carrying by several persons, the posture of a person rising), or with natural phenomena (why are pebbles by the seashore round? the study of projectiles and the continuation of movement, whirlpools). There are even questions that might be considered as stemming from pure theory: the study of the composition of movements according to the parallelogram, and the paradox known as Aristotle's wheel. The mixture of everyday, practical situations and speculations in the realm of mathematics or dynamics is striking, and appears to be new in the history of technological literature as we know it.

The unknown author puts forward answers to these questions, often in interrogative form ("Is it because . . . ?"); sometimes he even suggests several responses. The theory of mechanics thus appears relatively "open" and unsystematic. But the majority of machines derive from the lever, which derives in turn from the circle. The initial principle is the following: a larger circle is more powerful than a smaller one because an identical force produces a larger effect if it is less distorted or disturbed, and because the force is distorted to a greater extent if it is exercised on a trajectory that is more sharply curved (see François De Gandt, 1982).

This general foundation of mechanical theory is probably connected to Aristotle's arguments on forces in *Physics* (VII.v). However, it seems exaggerated to deduce from this, as Pierre Duhem did, that Aristotle is the father of rational mechanics.

DEVELOPMENTS IN MECHANICS

As the generations passed, mechanics was enriched, further developed, and refined. In particular, we have an Arabic translation of a book by Hero of Alexandria, who probably lived about 60 C.E.: *Mechanics, or Elevator*. Otherwise the *Mathematical Collection* of Pappus (ca. 300 C.E.) is a precious compilation, containing in its eighth book a collection of propositions on mechanics,

drawn from Hero among others. Finally one must mention Vitruvius's treatise *On Architecture*, which despite being composed in Latin (ca. 30 B.C.E. in all probability), passes on elements of mechanics and architecture taken from Greek authors and practitioners, particularly in Book X, which is devoted exclusively to mechanics.

In Hero and Pappus, mechanics is occasionally extremely theoretical (for example, in the calculation of the gearing necessary to raise a given weight with a given force; Hero calls this a *baroulkos*, which would allow—theoretically—a weight of 1,000 talents to be balanced by another of 5 talents). But one also finds remarks dealing with quarries or construction sites, and Hero gives detailed instructions about transportation by wheel bearings, different types of cranes, and even wine and oil presses (Book III).

The sources of the theory are multiple. The authors seem to have hesitated to follow the dynamic reasoning of *Problemata mecanicae*, and here and there they presuppose a different kind of foundation: Archimedes' geometrical theory of levers and centers of gravity, which has nothing to do with the consideration of forces (see, for example, Hero's *Mechanics* I.24 and II.7).

The beginning of Hero's *Pneumatika*, where the author discusses the composition of air and possible explanations for the elasticity of gases, was also influential. Hero envisaged a multitude of tiny voids disseminated throughout matter (this text inspired authors of the Renaissance, particularly Galileo). On the other hand, *Pneumatika* is particularly poorly organized and difficult to read, and one is apt to remember only a few toys or amusing devices, some magic tricks, and an astonishing water organ. Hero's work was held in high regard during the Middle Ages.

OPTICS AND ALCHEMY

The two remaining corpuses of the technological tradition are not very closely related to mechanics or to machines of war or construction; they warrant an overview here.

Greek optics is principally represented by Euclid's *Optica* and his *Catoptrica* (preserved in Greek, edited by Heiberg in 1895 with a Latin translation) and Ptolemy's *Optica* (by indirect transmission, preserved in a Latin translation issuing from a lost Arabic version). In Ptolemy's case, it is difficult to uncover the original argumentation behind the successive versions of the text.

Euclid's *Optica* is a strictly geometrical theory of light rays, presented in axiomatic form and proceeding from definitions. The light ray is thought to originate in the eye, and the object of study is the cone whose summit is in the eye and whose base rests on the contours of the object seen. Euclid discusses and justifies effects of perspective and the illusions created by distort-

ing mirrors, but makes no physical study of either light or color. (On the status and limitations of this view of optics, Gérard Simon demonstrates that it would be wrong to confuse the geometrical study of visual rays undertaken by Euclid with a theory of the propagation of light; it is only with Al-Hazen in the 11th century that the physiological study of the eye as an optical apparatus begins, opening up new paths for instrumental optics.)

Ptolemy, so far as one can judge from the highly unsatisfactory text that has come down to us, enters more into physical and psychological considerations, discussing cases of altered vision (myopia, presbyopia) and the role of the mind in visual illusions. He is interested in reflection and refraction, and he even presents numerical tables for calculating the angle of refraction starting from the angle of incidence.

The alchemical corpus is completely separate: it consists of later texts written in a far less rational mode than the mechanical ones. A *Collection des anciens alchimistes grecs* was published by Marcellin Berthelot in the 19th century, but the choice of manuscripts is somewhat idiosyncratic, and the absence of a commentary makes this edition difficult to use. A more systematic publication has begun at the Editions des Belles Lettres (*Les alchimistes grecs*, volume 1, covers the Leiden Papyrus, Stockholm Papyrus, fragments of formulas; edited by R. Halleux). The texts are heterogeneous and fairly obscure, mixing the theory of matter with blueprints for dyeing, metallurgy, and magic charms. Subsequent volumes will include the writings of Pseudo-Democritus *(Physica* and *Mystica)*, the *Opusculae* of Zosimus (thirteen texts, edited by M. Mertens), and finally the writings of the commentators Synesius, Olympiodorus, and Stephen of Alexandria.

Alchemists often quote the Presocratics and other philosophers in the Greek tradition, imbuing them with mystical signification, and it is difficult to tell which conception of matter is the underlying one. Certain texts are veiled in figurative language. The intellectual ambiance is that of the magical and occultist religiosity that is linked to Neoplatonism and Hermeticism (Zosimus cites Hermes and Zoroaster).

Zosimus, originally from Pannopolis in Egypt (ca. 300 C.E.), is the first in this chain of authors to be historically identifiable. He is cited as an authority by his successors, and even as an inspired soothsayer. His writings put forward a symbolics of the liberation of the soul, while describing in enigmatic form certain operational procedures and apparatuses difficult to reconstruct exactly (stills, and so on). Metals are made of spirit and body, and matter dies in order to be reborn. Jung and historians of religion are particularly interested in the "vision of Zosimus" (*Opusculae* X): "I fell asleep, I saw a sacrificer standing before me above an altar"; "the said altar had fifteen steps up to it" (X.2); "he whom you saw as a man of copper and who vomited his own flesh, this one is both he who sacrifices and he who is sacrificed" (X.3). These

accounts have the strange beauty of dreams or surrealist poems, but interpretation is indispensable for determining what is meant by each symbol (are the fifteen steps the fifteen days of the rising of the moon, the heavenly body that rules over waxings and wanings?). It is too early to form an accurate idea of the content of these texts and to evaluate their subsequent influence.

FRANÇOIS DE GANDT
Translated by Selina Stewart and Jeannine Pucci

Bibliography

Texts and Translations

Aeneas Tacticus. *Poliorcetica.* In *Aeneas Tacticus, Asclepiodotus and Onasander.* Trans. members of Illinois Greek Club. Loeb Classical Library.

Aristotle. *Mechanical Problems.* In *Minor Works.* Trans. W. S. Hett. Loeb Classical Library.

Hero of Alexandria. *Les mécaniques, ou l'élévateur des corps lourds.* Trans. Carra de Vaux. Paris: Les Belles Lettres, 1988.

Pappus of Alexandria. *La collection mathématique.* 2 vols. Trans. Paul Ver Eecke. Paris: Librairie scientifique et technique A. Blanchard, 1982.

Philon of Byzantium. *Traité de fortification, d'attaque et de défense des places.* Trans. Rochas d'Aiglun. Paris: Ch. Tanera, 1872.

Sophocles. *Antigone.* Trans. Hugh Lloyd-Jones. Loeb Classical Library.

Zosimus. *Historia nova.* Trans. Ronald T. Ridley. Canberra: Australian Association for Byzantine Studies, 1982.

Studies

Daumas, Maurice, ed. *Histoire générale des techniques,* vol. 1. Paris: Presses Universitaires de France, 1962.

De Gandt, François. "Force et science des machines." In *Science and Speculation: Studies in Hellenistic Theory and Practice.* Ed. Jonathan Barnes et al. Cambridge and New York: Cambridge University Press, 1982. Pp. 96–127.

Drachmann, A. G. *The Mechanical Technology of Greek and Roman Antiquity: A Study of the Literary Sources.* Copenhagen: Munksgaard; Madison: University of Wisconsin Press, 1963.

Duhem, Pierre. *Les origines de la statique.* 2 vols. Paris: A. Hermann, 1905–1906.

Ferrari, G. A. "Meccanica allargate." In *La scienza ellenistica.* Ed. Gabriele Giannantoni and Mario Vegetti. Naples: Bibliopolis, 1985. Pp. 225–297.

Frontisi-Ducroux, Françoise. *Dédale: mythologie de l'artisan en Grèce ancienne.* Paris: F. Maspero, 1975.

Gille, Bertrand. *Les mécaniciens grecs: La naissance de la technologie.* Paris: Seuil, 1980.

Jacomy, Bruno. *Une histoire des techniques.* Paris: Seuil, 1990.

Rose, P. L., and S. Drake. "The Pseudo-Aristotelian Questions of Mechanics." *Renaissance Culture: Studies in the Renaissance* (1971): 65–104.

Simon, Gérard. *Le regard, l'être et l'apparence dans l'optique de l'antiquité.* Paris: Seuil, 1988.

Related Articles

Images of the World; Observation and Research; Hellenism and Judaism; Myth and Knowledge; Archimedes

THEOLOGY AND
DIVINATION

HECTOR IN THE *Iliad* has an alter ego, his prudent adviser Polydamas, "who alone saw before and after." Polydamas's counsel is ordinarily full of carefully articulated calculation. But on one occasion he grounds his advice in augury: the portent of an eagle carrying a snake that bites its captor and thus effects its escape. Hector's response is to reject reliance on "long-winged birds." He does not care whether they fly to the right or to the left. His trust is in the plan of mighty Zeus, lord of all mortals and immortals. He sums the matter up in the most famously skeptical remark about divination in all Greek literature: "One omen is best—to fight for one's country" (*Iliad* 12.243).

Augury, oracles, and prophetic dreams are dominant features of the literature of the classical period, and nowhere more so than in the plots of Greek tragedy and the narratives of Herodotus's history. They are usually portrayed as true but ambiguous or unbelievable divine communications, although Herodotus is clear that the Delphic oracle was sometimes subject to political manipulation. When properly explained, they can normally be seen to have encapsulated authoritative advice and correct predictions, but often so obscurely or counterintuitively that those who can interpret them—the wild visionary Cassandra, the blind seer Tiresias—are distrusted and abused.

Despite its troubled prominence in literature, divination probably played a more restricted role in the key decision-making processes of the Greek city-state than it did either in Rome or, for example, among Africa's Azande in Evans-Pritchard's account. Argument in a council or assembly could settle most political issues. But there remained certain momentous choices fraught with uncertainty that required guidance that merely human resources could not supply. Thus the need for favorable auguries in deciding when to join battle was universally accepted. And while the international status of the Delphic oracle placed it outside the institutional framework that defined the civic community, it was nonetheless consulted on matters of state, albeit mostly for specifically cultic questions: e.g., the foundation of colonies, regulations for sacrifices, purificatory procedures for sacrilege or epidemics.

If reason in these various ways limited the scope or questioned the power of divination, there is no evidence of general doubt about *whether* the gods would indicate to humans what they should or should not do, still less about

the existence of a divine order itself. The worry was whether humans in general or "experts" in particular really had the ability to decipher what were alleged to be signs of divine intention or approval. This apprehension actually presupposes a belief in divine beings, and that belief was expressed in the complex and disparate religious structures that governed the rhythms of the public calendar of the city-state. The greatest authority on the nature of the many divinities who presided over different aspects of the life of the polis, or the greatest "theologian," as Aristotle calls him, was Homer. For later generations, the *Iliad* (ca. 725 B.C.E.) and *Odyssey* (ca. 700) came to constitute a cultural encyclopedia that, amid other information, told of the names, natures, responsibilities, and interrelations of the gods. Homer is often linked with Hesiod, the contemporary author of a poem entitled *Theogony,* which attempts, in a sequence of creation and succession myths, genealogies, and tales of war in heaven, to bring some order to the bewildering variety of deities and divine forces attested in stories—many newly imported from the Near East—about the gods.

Our first evidence of philosophical speculation dates to the following century: Thales, regarded by the Greeks as its originator, was active in Miletus in the first half of the 6th century. When philosophers started to engage explicitly with the beliefs and practices of traditional religion, what they confronted was the whole structure of polytheism and its claims to make sense of the natural world. And dealing with Homer and Hesiod was a central part of that enterprise.

XENOPHANES

Indeed, Greek philosophical theology begins with a celebrated lampoon: "Homer and Hesiod have attributed to the gods everything that is a reproach among men, stealing and committing adultery and deceiving one another." Like mortals in general, they cast divinities in their own image. The Ethiopians make them black and snub-nosed; the Thracians give them blue eyes and red hair. No doubt lions or horses would represent them as lions or horses if they were capable of art.

This brilliant critique was the work of the traveling philosopher-poet Xenophanes (ca. 570–470 B.C.E.), born in Asia Minor but mostly active in the Greek colonies of southern Italy. It made a deep impact on Plato, who develops its attack on Homeric theology (partially preserved in Xenophanes, frgs. 11, 14–16) in Books 2 and 3 of *The Republic,* and subsequent Greek philosophers were agreed—with the notable exception of Epicurus—that the gods were not to be conceived as anthropomorphic. In place of these traditional conceptions Xenophanes proposed monotheism: "one god . . . in no way similar to men either in body or in thought" (frg. 23). We must rid ourselves of

the notion that divinity needs limbs and sense organs. This god causes things to happen by thought alone, without moving a muscle; all of him sees, hears, thinks (frgs. 24–26).

Xenophanes insisted that he did not claim the status of knowledge for his proposal: "No man knows, or ever will know, the clear truth about the gods and about all the things I speak of" (frg. 34). Yet he was doubtless confident that it was eminently more rational than the ideas he was attempting to displace. The same goes for his naturalistic demythologizing explanations of phenomena traditionally associated with divine intervention in the world. Iris, the rainbow, for example, who features as a goddess in Homer, is construed by Xenophanes like other meteorological and celestial phenomena as a particular variety of cloud. It comes as no surprise to find him reported as rejecting the validity of divination.

In other parts of Xenophanes' fragmentary oeuvre evidence survives of prescriptions for moral and religious reform complementing his onslaught on traditional belief. In particular, frg. 1, on the proper conduct of a symposium, focuses on the nature of true piety. After advising cleanliness, purity, and simplicity in all the material aspects of the occasion, the poem turns to what is to be said. "Reverent words and pure speech" hymning the god are to precede talk of virtue, of right and noble deeds—not tales of giants, Titans, and centaurs, nor of conflicts between men in which there is no profit: nothing, presumably, at all like *Theogony* or *Iliad*.

The main elements in Xenophanes' thinking about the nature of divinity and proper religious practice were what remained the dominant ingredients of most later philosophical treatments of these subjects: namely, a radical conception of god or gods; rationalizing explanations of phenomena traditionally explained in religious terms; and new notions of piety.

LATER PRESOCRATICS

So far as we can tell from their surviving fragments, few of the later Presocratic philosophers made theology the explicit focus of their writing and thinking. If we may use modern categories to describe their preoccupations, what primarily concerned them was metaphysics, theory of knowledge, and cosmology and natural philosophy. Their theories might or might not recognize a function for some particular conception of the divine, but understanding the nature of god or gods was not their main purpose.

Anaxagoras (ca. 500–428 B.C.E.) and Diogenes of Apollonia (late 5th century) illustrate the point. With them physics, not metaphysics or epistemology, takes center stage. In their systems god is introduced as first cause: transcendent in Anaxagoras, immanent in Diogenes. Anaxagoras never actually names his first cause "god." He identifies it as mind, unlimited, self-governed, and free from mixture with any other substance (frg. 12). In virtue of these

attributes it has the ability to control everything else, and to order nature as it decides. But the language in which Anaxagoras speaks of mind is hymnic, and when Diogenes repeats the same phraseology with reference to his very similar immanent principle (intelligent air) he has no qualms about explicitly identifying it with god (frg. 5), conceived as author of cosmic order, as evidenced, e.g., in the disposition of the seasons of the year (frg. 3). This identification supplied Aristophanes—on the premise that all intellectuals have more or less the same ideas—with ammunition for caricaturing Socratic philosophy as a form of atheistic materialism in his comedy *Clouds* (423 B.C.E.). Even if theological concerns were not uppermost in Diogenes' mind, the radically antitraditional theological consequences of his theory were not lost on his readers. The same goes for Anaxagoras's claim that the heavenly bodies were nothing but incandescent rocks, which prompted his prosecution by the Athenians for impiety around 433. The antireligious reputation he retained throughout antiquity is typified by the anecdote that has him giving an entirely naturalistic explanation of the portent—produced for divinatory diagnosis—of a ram with a single horn in the middle of its forehead.

Heraclitus (probably active around 500 B.C.E.) is closer in time and spirit to Xenophanes. He too lambastes Homer and Hesiod: Homer as a fool, despite his reputation (frgs. 42, 56), Hesiod as one of a number of practitioners of intellectual inquiry who are dismissed as charlatans (frgs. 40, 57). Humans in general are consistently presented as benighted and confused, in their religious practices as elsewhere (e.g., frg. 15). Many of Heraclitus's sayings talk about god or divine understanding or "the one wise willing and unwilling to be called by the name of Zeus" (frg. 32). As this interest in understanding and wisdom indicates, Heraclitus's notion of the divine is geared to the epistemological preoccupations that pervade his fragments. God is for him the complete vantage point, from which every opposition is comprehended as a unity—even if that generally eludes the grasp of human understanding—and indeed the locus of a perspective in which *all* oppositions are simultaneously apprehended in a single vision (frg. 63). Heraclitus has no *theory* about this transcendent perspective: its very transcendence ensures that it cannot be adequately captured or explained in human language. But the *logos* or structure of the universe and of everything in it expresses the unity and identity of opposites, and as such is conceived as conforming to divine law (frg. 114). So the divine perspective apparently exercises a prescriptive function both in cosmic organization and in the human ethical and religious spheres. But those of Heraclitus's remarks on these themes that mention divinities or the divine continue to be informed primarily by epistemological concerns.

The Presocratic who most resembles Xenophanes in the theological and religious orientation of his philosophy, and in his concern with practice as well as theory, is someone who writes with a passionate commitment as far re-

moved as could be imagined from Xenophanes' coolly critical tone. This is the extraordinary Sicilian thinker Empedocles (ca. 495–435): philosopher-poet, political leader, medical man, and magician. In Empedocles, physical and cosmological concerns are fused with intense moral and religious preoccupations. The life cycles of the biological realm are for him echoed both in an overarching pattern of disintegration and reconstitution predicated on the universe itself, and in the fall of the soul, its incarnation and successive reincarnations as an exile from god, and its eventual restoration to peace and harmony. There can be little doubt that his whole complex system is elaborated ultimately in an attempt to make sense of the human condition.

Empedocles seems to have introduced talk about some of the principal deities of traditional Greek religion at a fairly early stage in his major poem, later known as *On Nature*. He offers radical reinterpretations (frg. 6): Zeus is really one of the four natural elements (probably air), and Hera likewise (probably earth). Similarly Aphrodite, or Love, is the motive force of harmony at work in the natural world, causing combinations of elements that then constitute the huge variety of living forms (frg. 17). For his conception of *true* divinity Empedocles borrows heavily from Xenophanes. He speaks of a holy mind, "darting through the whole universe with swift thoughts," and attacks the idea that it might possess limbs, genitals, and the like (frg. 134). Indeed at the time of most complete cosmic harmony it makes up a perfect sphere, subsuming into one unit all the diversity of the world with which we are familiar (frgs. 27, 31). Is Empedocles' god a first cause? Love and the opposing principle of strife play that role in his system. Perhaps, like Heraclitus's god, it is rather the locus of perfect understanding.

In a powerful sequence that inspired later writers, such as the Neoplatonist Porphyry (3rd century C.E.), in their arguments against animal sacrifice and meat eating, Empedocles imagines a mythical time when Aphrodite ruled over nature as undisputed queen. Then man and beast lived as friends (frg. 130), and sacrifice involved no bloodshed: Aphrodite was worshipped with images and incense and gifts of honey, and "the altar was not drenched with the unspeakable slaughter of bulls" (frg. 128). Implicit in this vision is a deep-seated belief in the Pythagorean doctrine that all life is akin, which is taken to dictate a law of nature against bloodshed (frg. 135). Empedocles diagnoses man's primal sin as the infraction of this law, brought about by "trust in raving strife" and punished by a sequence of incarnations (frg. 115).

In his later poem *Purifications* he seems to announce his recall from spiritual exile and his transcendence of that gulf between god and man that had been a powerful theme in Homeric theology: "An immortal god, mortal no more, I go about honored by all" (frg. 112). This claim echoes the words of self-disclosure employed by Hermes in the *Iliad* (24.460) and by Demeter in the Homeric *Hymn to Demeter* (120). But they are deployed in service of a

new form of religion preoccupied with the fate of the individual soul, as in the greeting with which the deceased initiate of the mystery cults is received (apparently by Persephone) in the formula recorded in the "golden plates" recovered at the southern Italian site of classical Thurii: "Happy and blessed one, you shall be a god instead of a mortal."

ETIOLOGY AND ALLEGORY IN
THE AGE OF THE SOPHISTS

The Sophists of the mid- to late 5th century B.C.E. are generally associated in our sources with various forms of theological skepticism. Thus, on record is a famous remark by Protagoras, portrayed by Plato as the leading Sophist of the period (frg. 4): "About gods I cannot know either that they are or that they are not. For many things prevent one from knowing—the obscurity of the question, and the life of man, which is short." This has a Xenophanean ring to it, and indeed the limitations of human understanding are a constant theme of the Presocratics and other early Greek writers. Protagoras's notoriety came from his boldness in focusing agnosticism explicitly on the existence and nature of the gods. A more obscurely celebrated figure, apparently active in Athens at the same time as Protagoras, was Diagoras of Melos, frequently designated "the atheist." Most of the evidence about him is anecdotal. It suggests that he earned his reputation by his expressions of contempt for religious practices, and by his cynicism about the idea that the gods have any concern for human affairs in general and for justice in particular.

Other Sophists were more confident than Protagoras of what to say about religion. Prodicus offered an anthropological account of the origins of belief in gods, as did the atomist philosopher Democritus (born ca. 460 B.C.E.). A sophisticated political explanation—put in the mouth of a character in a fragmentary drama called *Sisyphus*—of how religion was invented as a tool of law enforcement also originated in this milieu. But these theories are antitheological, not exercises in theology, although the line between the two genres became increasingly hard to draw. From around 500 B.C.E. onward, allegorical interpretations of Homer were proposed that represented his understanding of the Olympian deities as much more like that of Prodicus or Democritus than might superficially appear. It was suggested that a distinction should be drawn between what Homer said and the meaning he was conveying by what he said. Thus, for example, when the *Iliad* portrays the gods at war with each other, this is Homer's way of indicating the opposition of fire (Apollo and Hephaestus) and water (Poseidon and Scamander), or again between wisdom (Athena) and folly and desire (Ares and Aphrodite, respectively).

To Plato's disgust, the allegorization of Homer was particularly popular in

his time. Its most systematic philosophical exponents in antiquity were the Stoics. The fullest early specimen of the method, belonging probably to the early 4th century B.C.E., is in the Derveni papyrus, which contains extensive fragments of a commentary in this style, although not on Homer but on an Orphic hymn. The poem itself evidently presented a variant of a Hesiodic succession myth, and told of Zeus swallowing an earlier generation of deities. According to the commentator it is not really about creation at all. He explains it as a statement of the philosophy of Anaxagoras (in Diogenes' version): the poem is taken to be expounding how air or mind governs all the things by reason. The author's technique is essentially arbitrary, but interestingly includes appeals to etymology, grammar, common usage, and the principle that one thing can have several different names.

SOCRATES, PLATO, ARISTOTLE

Did Socrates have a theology? According to Xenophon, yes; readers of Plato would infer no. In *Memorabilia* (1.4 and 4.3) Xenophon ascribes to Socrates a set of proofs for the existence of god, including an argument from design, that were later appropriated by the Stoics. But their Socratic credentials are generally disbelieved, as incompatible with his determination to have nothing to do with natural philosophy. What Socrates did introduce—if we are prepared to trust Plato's *Apology*—was a novel and highly individual religious position.

He was charged at his trial with disbelieving in the city's gods and introducing new divinities. The charge was probably correct. At any rate, in *Apology* Socrates represents himself as living his life like a soldier under orders imposed on him by an authority higher than the state. Practicing philosophy and what it entails—submission by himself and others to moral and intellectual examination—"has been commanded me, as I maintain, by the god through oracles and dreams and every other means through which divine apportionment has ever commanded anyone to do anything" (33c). And Plato often has Socrates appealing to the "divine sign" that would restrain him from action. How this conviction of a divine mission so described relates to the austere critical rationality of his ethical method is a matter for debate. It is perhaps significant that the one dialogue of Plato's wholly devoted to a theological question—the early *Euthyphro*, on piety—explores a problem of just this sort: is piety loved by the gods because it has some moral characteristic independent of their loving it, or does it count as piety precisely because it is behavior loved by the gods?

Plato's dialogues are designed to conceal as much as to disclose their author's mind. Nonetheless he evidently writes from a deep sympathy for a religious outlook on life and, particularly in his later works, enunciates a number of strong theological positions, crucial for the moral or theoretical projects

being undertaken in the contexts in which they appear, and in the case of *Timaeus* greatly influential in later antiquity and the Middle Ages. Part of the difficulty of evaluating his contribution to theology comes from not knowing whether some uses of the notion of divinity are revolutionary or merely figurative. The Forms in their otherworldly eternity and perfection are often characterized as "divine," and the language of mystic initiation is used to describe the soul's approach to them—*Theaetetus* speaks of "assimilation to god" (176b). The Form of Good, ultimate cause of all there is, has often been thought to function as Plato's supreme deity, notably by the Neoplatonists (3rd to 6th centuries C.E.) in their grand synthesis of Platonic and Aristotelian theology. Another problem is that most of Plato's uncontroversially theistic propositions leave the identity and attributes of the god or gods he speaks of un- (or at any rate under-) determined. At one point he goes so far as to make Socrates insist that we know nothing about the gods (*Cratylus* 400d).

For evidence of Plato as theologian, four dialogues are particularly important. The first chronologically is *Phaedo*, which sees humans as subjects or possessions of the gods, benefiting from their providential care and destined to fall under divine judgment after death. *Phaedo* expresses the wish for a convincing teleological explanation of all things in terms of the dispositions of mind, and this is supplied in *Timaeus*, where Plato argues, first, that as something perceptible the world must have been created, and, second, that its order and beauty are such that its creator must be a "good craftsman," "the best of causes." He is subsequently called "the god" in Plato's comprehensive teleological account of the way the universe is constructed—using relatively sophisticated mathematics—as a living being. Plato stresses the god's goodness and generosity; and goodness and incapacity of deceit are the main attributes of god insisted on in the attack on Homeric theology in *The Republic*.

Book 10 of Plato's last work, *Laws*, deals with the place of religion in the ideal state. Its theological interest consists in the proofs of the existence and providence of gods that Plato presents as weapons to be used against atheist materialists not persuaded of the need for piety. He argues that soul is causally and ontologically prior to body, because only soul is capable of the fundamental form of movement, namely self-motion. The heavenly bodies, as perfect paradigms of self-motion, must therefore be governed by perfect souls. Such causal powers can in fact be exercised only by gods, so the argument effectively demonstrates the existence of gods. But it is important to appreciate that this equation of "souls" with "gods" is for popular consumption. It suffices to refute atheism, not to unlock a true philosophical understanding of the supreme form or forms of deity.

In theology, as in other areas of thought, Aristotle is both at odds with Plato and very close to him. The opposition in their modes of thought comes

out very sharply in their approach to divination. While despising the arts of augury and their claims to knowledge, Plato treats as a gift of god those forms of divination that were regarded as divine possession or madness. He construes dreams in particular as giving the irrational part of the soul access to truths, which can only be interpreted, however, when reason returns. Aristotle, by contrast, like Democritus and the Hippocratic treatise *On Regimen*, argues for a completely naturalistic account of dreams. If they came from god, they would be experienced during the day and by the wise. As it is, they resemble the hallucinations of the sick in telling us much more about the physiological or psychological condition of the dreamer than about the future. Sometimes they *are* precognitive: e.g., someone preoccupied with some present or future project may find his waking thoughts causing him dreams on the same subject, and these may in turn become starting points for actions to be performed on rewaking. In this sense some dreams may be "signs and causes." But for the most part any correspondence between a dream and its apparent fulfillment is pure coincidence.

All the same, Aristotle's principal theological arguments have much in common with the ideas of *Laws* 10, although since in his physical system the universe has no beginning, he has no interest in *Timaeus*'s conception of a creator god. The nature and causes of the perfect movements of the heavenly bodies were topics to which he returned again and again, usually with a view to drawing theological conclusions. His final position on these issues is given in Book 12 of *Metaphysics,* where he argues that since everything in the sublunary world sooner or later perishes, that world would eventually collapse if it were not sustained by an eternal motion, namely that of the heavenly bodies, or rather the fixed stars. These he construes in Platonic fashion as self-movers. At this point he diverges from Plato, for he has argued exhaustively in Book 8 of *Physics* that ultimately no self-motion is self-explanatory, but can be caused only by a mover that is not itself moved: by a pure actuality not subject to change of any kind. This is Aristotle's god. He explains that it moves the stars because its mode of being is the object of their desire, and he identifies its activity or life as the self-reflexive exercise of thinking. As Aristotle himself insists, this means that if physics is the study of the changeable, theology—now for the first time formally located on a comprehensive map of the sciences—has to be a quite different discipline, devoted to understanding unqualified being.

EPICUREANS, STOICS, AND SKEPTICS

In the dominant philosophical systems of the Hellenistic age, questions about the existence and nature of gods acquired an established place among the fundamental topics of philosophy. Epicurus believed that without a proper under-

standing of what the gods were like there was no prospect of attaining the *ataraxia*, freedom from anxiety, to which his whole philosophical teaching was directed. For the Stoics, theology, conceived as cosmology (and so as part of physics), constituted the final and, from some points of view, most important chapter in their favored sequence of philosophical topics.

Both schools summarized the key elements of their teaching on the subject in pithy syllogisms easy to memorize. The first two prescriptions of Epicurus's "fourfold remedy" *(tetrapharmakos)* against anxiety are directed toward allaying fears of divine punishment before or after death. The argument relating specifically to the gods runs as follows (in the version of *Key Doctrines* 1): "That which is blessed and imperishable neither suffers nor inflicts trouble, and therefore is affected neither by anger nor by favor. For all such things are marks of weakness." The Stoics, for their part, produced whole batteries of arguments in this style. Most of those attributed to Zeno of Citium (334–262), founder of the school, aimed to establish pantheism: e.g., "If something generates from itself life and rationality, it is itself alive and rational. But the world generates living rational creatures. Therefore the world is alive and rational." The cosmic *logos* or reason on which the rationality of the world is properly predicated is also conceived as its creator, regularly reconstituting it after periodic destructions, and Chrysippus (ca. 280–206), third head of the school, propounded a cosmological argument for such a divine creator: "If there is something in nature which human mind, reason, strength and power cannot make, what *does* make it must be superior to man. But the things in the heavens and all those whose regularity is everlasting cannot be created by man. Therefore what creates them is superior to man. But what more appropriate name is there for this than 'god'?" Zeno even propounded what has sometimes been construed as the first ontological argument for the existence of god or gods: "It would be reasonable to honor the gods. It would not be reasonable to honor what does not exist. Therefore gods exist."

Epicurean cosmology is constructed on mechanistic principles that leave no room for divine agency in the world. The conclusions reached by physical inquiry therefore turn out to be consistent with the general preconception of the blessedness and invulnerability of the gods on which Epicurus relies in *Key Doctrines* 1. Whether he actually believed in their *existence* was controversial in antiquity and remains so today. Some texts support the idea that Epicurean gods were envisaged as inhabiting interstices between universes, where they would be relatively protected against atomic collisions. Others suggest that they are nothing more than our own instinctive, self-projecting thought constructs. Stoic theology is a more ambitious theoretical undertaking. It too draws on what are claimed to be common notions about the gods, but it builds these into a systematic construction incorporating much earlier

philosophical thought. Indeed Stoic theological cosmology can be viewed as a rewriting of *Timaeus*, but with the divine craftsman converted into an immanent principle of creative reason embodied in Heraclitean fire, and with periodic cosmic bonfires replacing the imperishability of the Platonic cosmos. Divine reason "encompasses all the seminal principles whereby everything comes about in accordance with fate": "god, intelligence, fate and Zeus are one."

More original is the Stoics' explication of the concept of providence, to which their commitment was no less fierce than the Epicureans' hostility. Here, three ideas in particular are worth mentioning. First is the Stoic doctrine of the cosmic city. Because, according to the Stoics, humans and gods are unique in *sharing* the capacity to love according to reason, so constituting a community under the same moral law, it must be supposed that the universe and its contents were designed for the sake of men as well as gods—just as cities are designed for their inhabitants. Here the Homeric gulf between god and man has yielded to an outlook that manages to be simultaneously theocentric and anthropocentric. Second, because the gods care for men, we must expect them not only to give us signs serving as premonitions of the future, where this is to our advantage, but also to put in our hands the means of understanding such signs. In other words, disbelief in divination is incompatible with belief in providence, and natural theology itself indicates the necessity of revelation. Third, the Stoics recognized that their belief in providence obliged them to attempt a theodicy, i.e., an explanation of why a deity who cares for humans should allow evil in the world. They seem to have canvassed a number of possible answers, but their favored argument was the contention that there cannot be good without evil. In his *Hymn to Zeus* Zeno's successor Cleanthes (331–232) says: "No deed is done apart from you except what bad men do in their folly. But you know how to make things crooked straight and to order things disorderly. You love things unloved. For you have so welded into one all things good and bad that they all share in a single everlasting reason."

Not surprisingly this and every other doctrine of Stoic theology provoked counterargument and often mockery and parody by opponents, notably from the Skeptic Carneades, head of the Academy in the mid-2nd century B.C.E. Each of the three syllogisms quoted above was attacked. Using arguments parallel with Zeno's, one could prove that the world is not only alive and rational but also a harpist and a flute player; or, again, that since it would be reasonable to honor the wise, wise persons exist—which the Stoics denied. As for Chrysippus, the Academics complained that he relied heavily on notions like "superior," which are hopelessly vague. In making their criticisms they disclaimed atheistic intentions. Custom and tradition were, they said, a sufficient basis for accepting the existence of gods. Reason—especially in its guise as Stoic demonstration—was neither necessary nor sufficient.

Are natural theology and the study of religion the proper province of metaphysics, cosmology, anthropology, or physiology and psychology? The question is still disputed, and the cacophony of answers given by ancient Greek thinkers has not been improved on. Can we know anything about the gods? And if so, by what means? Here, too, it is the variety of incompatible answers proposed by Greek philosophy that constitute one of its most impressive and characteristic legacies to theology.

Agnosticism took different forms: we simply have no means of knowing (Protagoras); reason cannot establish theological truths, but that should not threaten customary belief (Skeptics); we don't know, but we can make reasonable conjectures (Xenophanes). It was no doubt the very existence of articulate agnosticism, and indeed atheism, that prompted the general philosophical project of offering *proofs*—elaborate or otherwise—of the existence of gods: this is explicitly acknowledged by Plato in *Laws* 10. To put the point another way, theology as a specialized philosophical discipline was born from philosophical doubt about the gods. At the same time theistic philosophers, notably Aristotle and the Stoics, were anxious to insist that the common belief in gods, universal among humankind, was already a testimony to their existence. The Stoics seem to have gone so far as to claim that the existence of gods is obvious, as indicated, for example, by the order of the universe in general and the heavenly bodies in particular. We should accordingly interpret philosophical demonstrations of their existence or nature in line with Aristotelian and Stoic theories of science: as attempts to advance us from the bland certainties of belief to true understanding or, more specifically, to articulate common notions in ways that exhibit and analyze the deep truths about the universe that they encapsulate.

Philosophy therefore came to claim for theology and (in the Stoic case) divination a more secure epistemic status than either traditional belief or rational reflection had earlier thought possible. If this historical outcome of the ancient debate about the gods is a dubious achievement, we can at least grant that Greek thinkers identified many of the perennial problems of theology, and pioneered many strategies for handling them that have proved attractive in the long history of inquiry in this field.

MALCOLM SCHOFIELD

Bibliography

Bouché-Leclercq, Auguste. *L'astrologie grècque.* Paris, 1899.
———. *Histoire de la divination dans l'antiquité.* 4 vols. Paris, 1879–1892.
Dodds, E. R. *The Greeks and the Irrational.* Berkeley, 1951.
Dragona-Monachou, Myrto. *The Stoic Arguments for the Existence and Providence of the Gods.* Athens, 1976.
Festugière, A. J. *Epicure et ses dieux,* 2nd ed. Paris, 1968.

————. *La révélation d'Hermès Trismégiste.* 4 vols. Paris, 1944–1954.

Gerson, L. P. *God and Greek Philosophy.* London, 1990.

Kenney, J. P. *Mystical Monotheism: A Study in Platonic Theology.* Hanover, N.H., 1991.

Kirk, G. S., J. E. Raven, and M. Schofield. *The Presocratic Philosophers,* 2nd ed. Cambridge, 1983.

Lloyd, G. E. R. *Magic, Reason and Experience.* Cambridge, 1979.

Long, A. A., and D. N. Sedley. *The Hellenistic Philosophers.* 2 vols. Cambridge, 1987.

Solmsen, Friedrich. *Plato's Theology.* Ithaca, N.Y., 1942.

Vernant, J. P., ed. *Divination et rationalité.* Paris, 1974.

Related Articles

Myth and Knowledge; Ptolemy; Platonism; Stoicism; Theories of Religion; Milesians; Pythagoreanism

View of the Agora.

Athens: View of the Acropolis,
the Odeon, and the Theater of
Dionysus.

The Pnyx. An open space where
all citizens could gather to make
laws, the Pnyx was a key site for
Athenian democracy.

Theater of Dionysus, Athens. This theater was as political a space as the Agora or the Pnyx. Aristophanes had his comedies performed there; in these plays, the ideology and practice of Athenian democracy were openly criticized. The statuary is a much later addition, dating from the time of Nero.

Construction of the wall of the Acropolis. Skyphos attributed to the "Penelope painter," ca. 440 B.C.E. (Paris, Louvre.)

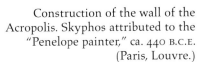

Bust of Solon (640–560 B.C.E.). Marble, after a Greek original from the 4th century B.C.E. (Naples, Museo Archeologico, Farnese Collection.) The reforms Solon carried out in Athens in 594–593 extended the right to vote to the poorest citizens and reinforced democracy.

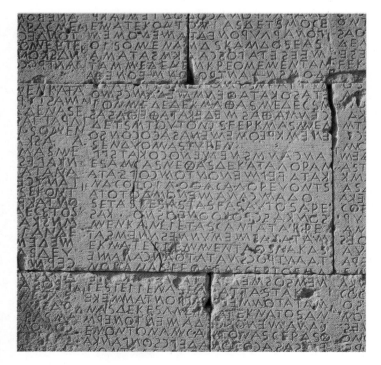

Law code of the city of Gortyn, on Crete. First half of the 5th century B.C.E. One of the oldest and most important legal texts of Greek antiquity.

Decree of Callias. Marble, 418 B.C.E. (Paris, Louvre.) The many decrees engraved in stone bear witness to the effective workings of democracy.

Democracy crowning Demos (the people). Bas-relief decorating the stele of the law on tyranny, 337–335 B.C.E. (Athens, Agora Museum.) This law was promulgated to protect democracy against the machinations of the oligarchs.

Klerōterion, or machine for drawing lots. 3rd century B.C.E. (Athens, Agora Museum.) Tokens and white and black balls allowed voters to choose, by *deme*, the citizens who would be members of the *boule*.

Ostrakon (ostraka). 5th century B.C.E. (Athens, Agora Museum.) These ceramic shards were used for ostracism by members of the assembly, indicating the name of the individual who was to be banished.

Tokens for drawing lots. (Athens, Agora Museum.) Used to designate the holders of public positions.

Ballots for voting by judges. (Athens, Agora Museum.) With crosspiece: not guilty; without: guilty.

Bust of Pericles (495–429 B.C.E.). Marble, copy of a Greek original from 430 B.C.E. (Berlin, Pergamum Museum.) The leader *(strategos)* of Athens for fifteen consecutive years, his reforms contributed to the democratization of the regime.

Bust of Herodotus (484–424 B.C.E.). Marble, copy of a Greek original from the 4th century B.C.E. His *Histories* tell the story of the Persian Wars.

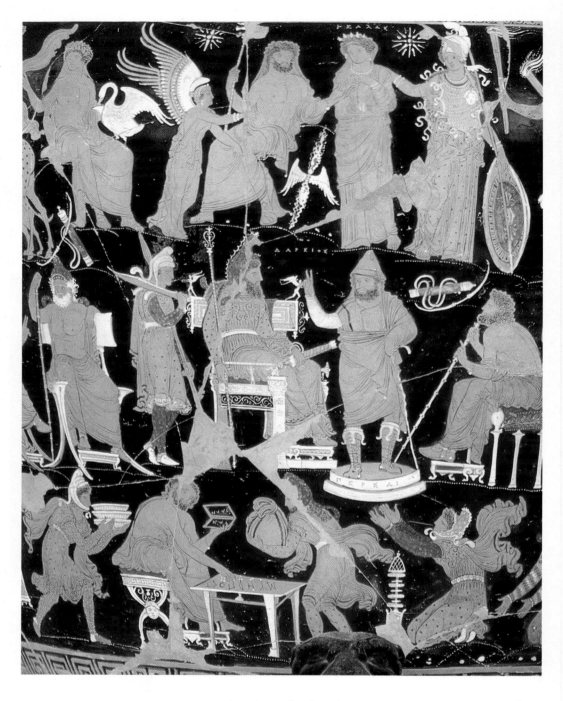

Volute-krater by the "Darius painter," 340–320 B.C.E. In the
center, Darius and his councilors; on the lower level,
one of the king's councilors receiving tribute.

Gravestone of two young hoplites, Chairedemos and Lykeas, who died during the Peloponnesian War. Ca. 400 B.C.E. (Athens, Museum of Piraeus.)

Bust of Thucydides (460–406 B.C.E.). Marble. (Paris, Louvre.) The principal witness to the Peloponnesian War, he was also a theoretician of democracy.

Head of Alexander (356–323 B.C.E.). Gilded bronze, 2nd century B.C.E. (Rome, Museo Nazionale Romano.) A pupil of Aristotle, he founded Alexandria and extended his empire into the Far East.

THEORIES OF RELIGION

From its very inception, philosophy thrived by breaking with tradition and—although total respect was the rule in such matters—evaluating cults and beliefs on the basis of innovative criteria that later became entrenched. A reader of the early thinkers discovers a jubilant and stimulating energy that is apparent even in a domain as ordinarily austere as religion. This initial spark gave rise to all subsequent thinking on the subject.

Aside from the usual problems (gaps in sources, length of the period studied, and so on), one difficulty in particular is of concern in the present study: practices and beliefs may have varied from city to city and from epoch to epoch, in ways about which we have no information; thus there is a considerable risk of oversimplification. The main hurdle, however, is methodological. Often, philosophers did not begin by interpreting factual data but took the opposite course: they analyzed or evaluated religion on the basis of their own concept of divinity. As a result, it can be difficult for us to define the role of their own theology with respect to both their analysis of religion and their understanding of it.

Although Homer, Hesiod, and Pindar developed some themes in what amounted to early reflections on religion, it seems preferable here to present only judgments formulated by philosophers; these provide a critical perspective in the very broadest sense of the term. Moreover, the opinions of Greek philosophers, while they do not actually constitute a system, do allow for a methodical approach to religion. After Anaximander, who regarded the gods as natural beings, the Presocratics included them in their investigations, and some examined the validity of beliefs and cults surrounding the gods. This was the beginning of the history of the relationship—often a discordant one—between religion and philosophy. The principal questions, from the outset, concerned the conception of the gods, ritual practices, mythology, and divination.

Xenophanes was the first to articulate a line of thinking that looked at religion objectively. His thinking was based on a particular hypothesis that later became widespread: the impossibility of knowing the divine with certainty. In a famous passage, Xenophanes criticized the anthropomorphism that was the basis of Greek religion: "But if cattle and horses or lions had hands, or were able to draw with their hands and do the works that men can do, horses would draw the forms of the gods like horses, and cattle like cattle, and they would make their bodies such as they each had themselves" (frg. 169). Along

the same lines, he also attacked the belief that gods were born and died, and moved around like people; he denounced the myths of Giants and Titans, linked to certain cults, as "pure fiction created in remote times." More broadly, he condemned immoral myths. Finally, he rejected divination entirely. Despite his critique of beliefs, he advocated respect for traditional forms of piety: he recommended prayers and hymns, "holy respect for the gods." Here, too, in his conciliatory language, he was a pioneer. But it would be a mistake to limit Xenophanes' contribution to these few fragments. His scientific interpretation of celestial phenomena took them out of the realm of superstition: for example, he explained rainbows, usually viewed as apparitions of the goddess Iris, as multicolored clouds. In this he was following a path opened up by Anaximander, and he had illustrious successors in Anaxagoras and Democritus. Some forty years after his death, a decree promulgated by Diopeithes in Athens around 433 B.C.E. prohibited "speaking of celestial things," at the risk of being tried for impiety.

Heraclitus's even more radical critique concerned cult itself: "The secret rites practised among men are celebrated in an unholy manner" (frg. 242, p. 209). His well-known statement that cadavers are no more than manure reflects his complete indifference toward funeral rites, which were regarded as most sacred of all. Heraclitus ridiculed official purification rites, the cult of statues, and prayers: "They vainly purify themselves of blood-guilt by defiling themselves with blood, as though one who had stepped into mud were to wash with mud; he would seem to be mad, if any of men noticed him doing this. Further, they pray to these statues, as if one were to carry on a conversation with houses, not recognizing the true nature of gods or demi-gods" (frg. 241, p. 209). In ancient Greece, questioning such official practices was more revolutionary than challenging the beliefs behind them: not only were there no theological dogmas, but the only expression in classical times for belief in gods, *theos nomizein*, originally meant simply to honor the gods as custom *(nomos)* ordained.

By attacking religious customs, Heraclitus demonstrated an audacity paralleled only by that of the Cynics. However, the essential feature of his contribution to the field of religion does not lie in his criticisms, which, considered in isolation from the rest of his theory, might take on a positivist aspect running counter to the spirit in which they were formulated. By striving to adapt religious representations borrowed from traditional beliefs to his own conception of the divine, Heraclitus shed light on those representations. His puzzling statement, "One thing, the only truly wise, does not and does consent to be called by the name of Zeus" (frg. 228, p. 202), goes to the very heart of religious thought. The Greeks in effect measured the distance between the divine and its human representation (or name): they emphasized the ambiguous relationship between gods and men, a relationship symbolized in par-

ticular by Apollo Loxias (the Oblique), so called because the meaning of his prophecies was never obvious. For Heraclitus, the "Logos" is "common"; it can be clearly heard. Thus "men should try to comprehend the underlying coherence of things" (frg. 193, p. 186), that which links men objectively to one another, but the very meaning of Logos remains unheard, because "men always prove to be uncomprehending" (frg. 194, p. 187). Clarity and obscurity are thus components of human experience and discourse. This duality applies in particular to religion. An anecdote reported by Aristotle is revealing. A group of foreigners who had come to visit the sage in Ephesus did not dare to approach because they saw that he was "warming himself by the fire" (a euphemism designating a more trivial occupation). Heraclitus encouraged them to come in, saying: "The gods are found here as well." Thus a mysterious aspect of the sacred, echoes of which are found in Greek ritual, is expressed with the greatest clarity by one of the harshest critics of tradition. Heraclitus was also the first to reveal the role of the sign in divination: "The Lord whose oracle is in Delphi neither speaks out nor conceals, but gives a sign" (frg. 244, p. 209). Last, and most important, Heraclitus influenced the understanding of the religious phenomenon itself by showing that what is self-evident, even when it is derived from cult practice, is merely the visible pole of a symbolic system whose meaning the mind cannot encompass as a whole.

Democritus proposed an approach to religion that might be called, anachronistically, anthropological. He tried to account for the origin of the common belief in the gods by adopting an approach that was new in philosophy but pursued also by contemporary Sophists: Democritus did not refer to theology but relied solely on phenomena, although without attributing any truth-value to them. According to a later account, he believed that the experience of celestial phenomena, such as thunder, lightning, and eclipses, so terrified the ancients that they were convinced that only the gods could have caused them. Stobaeus tells us that Democritus imagined hell as a fable inspired by the fear of punishment after death. On the scientific origin of the concept of God, Sextus Empiricus has recorded this explanation: "Democritus says that certain images impinge on men, and of these some are beneficent, others maleficent—whence also he prayed that he might have 'propitious images'—, and these images . . . signify the future to men beforehand, as they are visible and utter sounds. Hence the ancients, on receiving a presentation of these images, supposed that God exists, God being none other than these images, and possessed of an indestructible nature" (*Against the Physicists* I.19). So we have the remarkable conception of a divinity whose only reality consists in images. According to Cicero, Democritus would have approved of the examination of the entrails of animals offered as sacrifices: their shape and color provided "signs" predicting good health or epidemics, or the fertility or steril-

ity of the land (Cicero, *On Divination* I.131). In other words, for Democritus divination rested on the purely natural correspondence between the state of the entrails and that of the place where the animal had lived and grazed.

Rapid though the present survey is, it may seem surprising that the names of several great Presocratics, such as Pythagoras, Parmenides, and Empedocles, are absent from it. However, there are very few fragments on the subject of civic religion that can be attributed to them, no doubt because their conception of the divine was too far removed from popular belief. Their philosophy, on the other hand, had considerable influence in the religious sphere. The Pythagoreans, through many ritual observances, undermined religion. Empedocles took up their condemnation of animal sacrifices on the basis of the following argument, according to Aristotle: "In fact, there is a general idea of just and unjust in accordance with nature, as all men in a manner divine, even if there is neither communication nor agreement between them . . . And as Empedocles says in regard to not killing that which has life, for this is not right for some and wrong for others 'But a universal precept, which extends without a break throughout the wide-ruling sky and the boundless earth'" (*Rhetoric* I.xiii.2.1373b). Here the contract between men and gods — the basis for Greek sacrifice — is called into question.

Ancient tradition often regarded the Sophists as atheists. Only the first sentence of Protagoras's treatise *On the Gods* has survived, and it testifies to his agnosticism. However, he did not reject all forms of popular religion: in a passage from Plato's *Protagoras,* apparently reflecting the thinking of the great Sophist (325a, d), religion is taken as an element of "human virtue," indispensable to civic life. Skepticism and the cultural enhancement of religion have generally gone hand in hand in the Greek tradition. Another Sophist, Prodicus, stated that people regard as divine, and worthy of honor, whatever ensures their livelihood: the sun, the moon, rivers, springs, the fruits of the earth. Among other examples, he cited wine, which takes its name from Dionysus, and water, named after Poseidon, to show that these divinities always correspond to elements of nature. This allegorical method, developed further by Metrodorus of Lampsacus, was to enjoy lasting popularity. In addition, according to Daniel Babut, Prodicus anticipated modern theory concerning the origin of religion by claiming that all religious practices were derived from agriculture and were expressions of man's gratitude for the blessings he received from the earth.

Critias took a decisive step forward in the debate on the origin of the gods when he declared that "a wise and clever man invented fear [of the gods] for mortals, that there might be some means of frightening the wicked, even if they do anything or say or think it in secret. Hence he introduced the Divine saying that there is a God flourishing with immortal life, hearing and seeing with his mind . . . who will be able to see all that is done" (frg. 25, in Freeman, *Ancilla,* p. 158). This view of religion as a factor in political stability

was shared and advanced by many others, particularly by historians such as Polybius. According to ancient sources, Critias wrote a satirical play, *Sisyphus* (now sometimes attributed to Euripides); Sextus Empiricus quotes some forty lines of it in which the writer makes fun of theologians and popular beliefs alike. Critias's reputation as an atheist appears to be fully justified.

Thus, at the end of the 5th century B.C.E., the principal lines of thought about religion were established: an anthropomorphic conception of the gods, polytheism, the value of rituals and cults, and their historical origins, along with the historical origins of belief in gods. These themes were addressed by Xenophanes, Heraclitus, Democritus, and the Sophists in particular, but we should also keep in mind the works of the tragic poets in these areas. Their analyses are essential to our understanding of certain key concepts that are derived from ritual, such as notions of purity and impurity. In *Philosophy of Religion,* Hegel grants preeminence to Sophocles for the depth of his reflection on religion, and in particular for his demonstration of the close connection between freedom and necessity. As for Euripides, whose views were close to those of the Sophists, the critique he formulated took into account the diversity of cults and beliefs and thus contributed to a better understanding of them.

The remarkable legacy of Presocratic thought provided the foundation for the subsequent attitudes of philosophers toward religion. These later attitudes favored, in a more systematic fashion, three principal options: first, the coexistence of philosophy and religion, either as two separate fields or with certain traditional elements integrated into philosophy; second, the annexation of religion by philosophy; and third, the total rejection of religion. Socrates may be said to be the pivotal figure in this evolution. Xenophon portrays him as the systematic defender of religious tradition. Socrates himself appears not to have foreseen the conflict between his rationalist approach in philosophy and a scrupulous respect for tradition. However, it was the rationalist approach that led him to criticize the conception of piety that was generally accepted in Athens at the time, what he called a "commercial technique, governing exchanges between gods and men." In Plato's *Euthyphro* Socrates, on the way to his trial on charges of impiety, shows that the pious gesture is not pious because it is pleasing to the gods, as his interlocutor the priest Euthyphro believes; on the contrary, it is pleasing to the gods because it is pious. This is a crucial distinction, because it affirms the intrinsic value of piety. When, at the end, Socrates declares to his judges: "I will obey the gods rather than you," he breaks the fundamental connection between the gods and the state. Daniel Babut stresses this "striking paradox," pointing out that "Socrates, the unconditional defender of traditional state religion, is also the one who first calls into question its fundamental principle." Socrates thus inaugurated two major trends: on the one hand, respect for religion, notwithstanding the triumphs of theoretical knowledge, and on the other hand, the control, in-

deed the domination, exercised by philosophy over religious thought. Plato was to develop in depth this second trend more than any other.

In his very first dialogues, Plato reveals that the Greek religion of his time suffered from a lack of spirituality, a spirituality that he tries to instill in the ideal religion described in his last work, *Laws*. However, in earlier works he examines various aspects of the state religion. Thus, in *Cratylus*, he considers "what kind of correctness" the names of the gods have. He first remarks that "we, if we are sensible, must recognize that there is one most excellent kind [of correctness], since of the gods we know nothing, neither of them, nor of their names, whatever they may be, by which they call themselves, for it is clear that they use the true names. But there is a second kind of correctness, that we call them, as is customary in prayers, by whatever names and patronymics are pleasing to them, since we know no other" (*Cratylus* 400d–e). Then he goes on to explain at length the etymologies of the names of various gods; these appear to be based on views formed by men in accordance with tradition. But this play on the gods' names that Plato somewhat ironically attributes to Socrates conceals a critique of etymological interpretation. This practice, widespread in ancient Greece, was brought back into fashion by Max Müller with his famous maxim: "Mythology is a disease of language." According to *Critias*, recourse to myths and the search for aspects of the past appeared quite late, at about the same time as leisure, when some people were able to free themselves from the harsh necessities of daily life. The representation of the gods also conformed to social status. The armed figure of Athena appeared at a time when "the activities of warriors were shared by men and women alike": "The people of that time, in accordance with custom, depicted the goddess armed as a dedicatory offering." This attempt at historical explanation can be seen as the counterpart to a rejection of traditional myths, expressed most notably in the second book of *The Republic*, as well as a rejection of the rationalization of myths through allegorical method. There is no hidden meaning to be found in mythology that might lead to some Idea of the divine. However, in *Phaedrus* the value of inspired divination is affirmed: "The greatest of blessings come to us through madness, when it is sent as a gift of the gods" (244b). For Greece, prophecy of this kind "has conferred many splendid benefits" (ibid.). In contrast, Plato sees the art of augury (prophecy based on the flight of birds), which he considers somewhat inferior, as arising out of a purely human rationality. Finally, *The Republic* and *Laws* specifically advise consultation of the oracle of Delphi about the cult of the gods and about funeral customs.

Laws accords religion a central position. As Olivier Reverdin points out, religion in Delphi and in the city-states seemed to Plato to be a valuable inheritance that, in the absence of dogma, was at risk of succumbing to the attacks of skepticism, atheism, and foreign superstitions. Plato tried to provide what

was lacking and to make religion the basis for moral and civic life in the best of all city-states. But the status of belief, as Plato conceived of it, called into question the role of theology: "For we needs must be vexed and indignant with the men who have been, and now are, responsible for laying on us this burden of argument, through their disbelief in those stories which they used to hear, while infants and sucklings, from the lips of their nurses and mothers—stories chanted to them, as it were, in lullabies, whether in jest or in earnest; and the same stories they heard repeated also in prayers at sacrifices, and they saw spectacles which illustrated them, of the kind which the young delight to see and hear when performed at sacrifices; and their own parents they saw showing the utmost zeal on behalf of themselves and their children in addressing the gods in prayers and supplications, as though they most certainly existed" (Plato, *Laws* 887c–d).

Here Plato affirms that belief in the divine is inherent in cult practice and is transmitted through tales, not unlike fables for children, which constitute a more solid ground for religion than any rational discourse. Denied this naive faith, citizens must be induced to obey religious laws and be threatened with punishment if they disobey.

Cronos, the divine legislator, justified recourse to such measures: he is said to have originally imposed exemplary laws of piety. However, as Plato stresses, the story of Cronos is a myth, whereas the Athenian in *Laws* goes so far as to state that, if there were an individual of pure intellect, it would be a *sacrilege* for him to obey any law, since the intellect is "master of all." How better to suggest that religious obligations and prohibitions serve, above all, to maintain the stability of the city-state? From this political perspective, Plato allows no private cults, thereby denying the fundamental link between public cults and family cults that was essential to Greek religion. Last, in the ideal city-state the legislator prohibited the mystery cults that Isocrates celebrated for offering "the sweetest hopes for the end of life and eternity." Plato, in contrast, feared their excesses, their shadowy, magical character. Thus, following in the footsteps of his master, Socrates, the disciple Plato believed that piety consisted first and foremost of a moral and intellectual attitude. But by giving preeminence to religion in the ideal city-state, he also showed that it provided the best paradigm of Law, and that it offered, through the Olympians, a credible conception of the divine, in a realm where the truth cannot be known. Plato's work therefore marks a decisive turning point in the history of the relationship between philosophy and state religion: it defined for the first time the terms and the stakes in each field, what they had in common, and where they diverged.

Aristotle's approach, in the treatises that have come down to us, is characteristic of the tendency to present religion and philosophy as coexisting independently. The question of the divine is approached through metaphysics

with the concept of the "Prime Mover." In *Nicomachean Ethics*, Aristotle states that it would be ridiculous to reproach God for not returning love, since love and friendship exist only among beings of the same species. Nevertheless, Aristotle does not object to the beliefs and institutions of popular religion; on the contrary, he recognizes their necessity. In *Politics*, in his list of the functions that are essential to the life of a state, he includes "a primary need, the service of religion, termed a priesthood" (VII.vii.4.1328b). In *Topica* he asserts that "those who feel doubt about whether or not the gods ought to be honoured and parents loved, need castigation" (I.xi). Following Plato's example, Aristotle too believes that religious festivals are moments of relaxation for the citizens.

This conservatism in religious matters seems to be based primarily on the principle, already recognized by Plato, according to which "what is most ancient is most revered" (*Metaphysics* I.iii.6). Aristotle formulates a new argument favoring belief in the gods, that of universal consensus: "All men have a conception of gods, and all assign the highest place to the divine, barbarians and Hellenes" (*On the Heavens* I.iii.270b). This argument will be heard over and over again. On other subjects, mythology and the anthropomorphism of the gods, Aristotle adopts Xenophanes' position. Finally, he takes up divination in a manner that reflects his own thinking more deeply. In *Parva naturalia*, he challenges the supernatural origin of dreams *(On Prophecy in Dreams)*, but, in accordance with tradition, which is "based on experience" (462b), he accepts the truly prophetic nature of some of them. "For quite common men have prescience and vivid dreams which shows that these are not sent by God; but that men whose nature is as it were garrulous or melancholic see all kinds of sights" (468b). Prophecy is therefore natural. If Freud makes room for Aristotle in *The Interpretation of Dreams*, it is because the latter explains religious belief without reference to theology.

The absolute rejection of religion, a view first formulated by Critias, is illustrated by the Cynics. They spared no quarter, neither the conception of the divine, nor mythology, nor the cults (least of all the mystery-cults that provoked Antisthenes' mockery), nor divination. This rejection of popular religion rested on the principle that whatever conforms to custom *(nomos)* is worthless compared to what is natural *(phusis)*; hence the Cynics, and especially Diogenes, modified and intensified an opposition that had been preeminent in the thought of the Sophists.

Then there is Euhemerus (ca. 340–260 B.C.E.), a strange author who defies categorization and whose conception of religion is better known than any other. He held that the gods were divine men. If one judges by the long extract that is preserved in the work of Diodorus of Sicily, his *Sacred History* is a strange tale about a marvelous imaginary island, Panchaea. Various mythical sites appear in this text along with the ancient descendants of deified men. "There is also on the island [of Panchaea], situated upon an exceedingly high

hill, a sanctuary of Zeus Tripylius, which was established by him during the time when he was king of all the inhabited world and was still in the company of men" (Diodorus, VI.I.6). "Around the world, Jupiter spread the sympathy for his cult and provided an example for men to imitate" (Lactantius, *Divine Institutions* I). "Venus established the art of the courtesan" (Quintus Ennius, "Euhemerus," 134–135). In short, all the quotations from *Sacred History* are in the same vein. Perhaps owing to its apparent ingenuousness, Euhemerus's story enjoyed great success not only in Greece but also in Rome, where it was revived and circulated by Ennius.

The Hellenistic period was characterized by profound changes: the accelerated decline of traditional religion, the growth of individualism, and, last, the increasing importance of practical concerns, particularly those relating to the cults. More than ever before, philosophy sought to include religion in its purview. The major systems, such as those of Epicurus and the Stoics, attest to this radicalization. In the Epicurean doctrine, paradoxically, the popular representation of the gods was included and granted some legitimacy. People have a true "preconception" of the gods derived from images, some perceived in dreams (which are the source of belief, according to many philosophers), others appearing by day. These images take the traditional form, and Lucretius's picture of the gods in their "calm abodes" is the same as the picture presented in Homer's *Odyssey*. However, for most people this conception is distorted because of their ignorance of the causes of natural (in particular, heavenly) phenomena. They thus think, mistakenly, that the gods govern the world, and in this way do themselves the greatest harm.

Epicurean doctrine held that, on the contrary, the gods embody the ideal of happiness and the absence of troubles. They can be perceived only through images that strike the mind directly. According to Epicurus, it is the "mind directed toward these images, and concentrated on them" that obtains knowledge of the "blissful and eternal nature" of the divine (Cicero, *On the Nature of the Gods* I.49). Thus, while most philosophical schools tended toward a monotheistic view, the philosophy thought to be most hostile to religion was in fact the only one both to accept Greek polytheism and to supply concrete arguments for the traditional view of the gods. However, Epicureanism repudiates divination and deprives worship of its traditional purpose. Myths, particularly those of the underworld, are rejected: since death means annihilation, myths of the underworld are merely projections of the fears felt by the living. According to Lucretius, the primary function of Epicureanism is to dispel "this terror of mind . . . and this gloom" (*On the Nature of Things* I.146–148). He concludes his description of Iphigenia's sacrifice with a well-known statement about the miseries produced in the name of religion ("often . . . superstition has brought forth criminal and impious deeds," *On the Nature of Things* I.82–83). No ancient author offers a better denunciation than Lucretius of the violence embedded not only in blood sacrifice but also in

other rituals. Lucretius exposes the sexual aspect of this violence by revealing the orgiastic displays of the cult of Cybele. In Rome, the connection established between *religio* and *religare* (to tie), according to a commonly accepted "etymology," helped to denounce the alienating character of religion. Neither Epicurus's *Letters* nor the fragments of his other writings reveal the same virulence; he encouraged participation in traditional cults and participated in them himself.

In contrast to Epicureanism stands Stoicism. According to Plutarch, in all their written works the Stoics "railed" against Epicurus, whom they accused of overturning the common view of the gods by eliminating the role of Providence. However, Stoicism, so closely linked to religion, had constructed its own system in this domain as well, which explains the harshness of Stoic criticism of cults and popular beliefs. The Stoics rejected myths, calling them "futile and inconsistent"; they denounced the irrational character of anthropomorphism and the triviality of some of the gods venerated in cult practices. All of these criticisms stem from the Stoics' belief in a single god, the Reason *(Logos)* inherent in the universe. However, by means of etymological explanation, the Stoics tried to identify popular religion with their doctrine. Thus, through a process that was the opposite of Prodicus's approach, the Stoics saw the various divinities as metonyms for a universal god: Demeter is the earth mother *(Ge meter)*, Hera is air *(aer)*, and so on. Most Stoics even defended divination, which became a science based on the Stoic theory of signs. Cicero, in his *On the Nature of the Gods*, not only presented these various aspects of Stoicism but also showed that they were hotly contested, especially by the philosophers of the New Academy. Their spokesman in Cicero's dialogue, taking up Carneades' arguments, accused the Stoics of misinterpreting and perverting religion. As a follower of the Skeptic academy, Cicero accepted tradition without committing himself and recognized some intrinsic value in the cults of different societies. In his view, writers who study myths provide important evidence of the various representations of divinity. A method was thus established for analyzing religious practices and beliefs as sociocultural data. This method was further developed by Plutarch, although in a very different spirit, for he attempted, through allegorical exegesis, to find in religion a nucleus of transcendent truth.

The "challenge" that philosophy posed from its very beginning is particularly applicable to the area of religion. The validity of philosophers' opinions consists in the depth and variety of the points of view presented as much as in the accuracy and coherence—at least within each system—of the methods used to pin down the nature of religion. But cults were rarely analyzed in their own right and on the basis of the details that enable modern scholars to pursue a phenomenological approach to the sacred. Owing in particular to the critical distance required by theology, most Greek philosophers aspired to a

general understanding of practices and beliefs. While this was one source of their greatness, it was also a limitation.

José Kany-Turpin
Translated by Elizabeth Rawlings and Jeannine Pucci

Bibliography

Texts and Translations

Aristotle. *Art of Rhetoric.* Trans. J. H. Freese. Loeb Classical Library.
——. *Metaphysics.* Books I–IX. Trans. Hugh Tredennick. Loeb Classical Library.
——. *On the Heavens.* Trans. W. K. C. Guthrie. Loeb Classical Library.
——. *Parva naturalia.* Trans. W. S. Hett. Loeb Classical Library.
——. *Politics.* Trans. H. Rackham. Loeb Classical Library.
——. *Topica.* Trans. E. S. Forster. Loeb Classical Library.
Freeman, Kathleen. *Ancilla to the Pre-Socratic Philosophers: A Complete Translation of the Fragments in Diels.* Oxford: Basil Blackwell, 1948.
Kirk, G. S., J. E. Raven, and Malcolm Schofield. *The Presocratic Philosophers,* 2nd ed. Cambridge: Cambridge University Press, 1983.
Lactantius. *The Divine Institutions.* Trans. Sister Mary Francis McDonald. Washington, D.C.: The Catholic University of America Press, 1964.
Plato. *Cratylus.* Trans. H. N. Fowler. Loeb Classical Library.
——. *Euthyphro.* Trans. H. N. Fowler. Loeb Classical Library.
——. *Laws,* vol. 2. Trans. R. G. Bury. Loeb Classical Library.
——. *Phaedrus.* Trans. H. N. Fowler. Loeb Classical Library.
——. *Protagoras.* Trans. W. R. M. Lamb. Loeb Classical Library.
Sextus Empiricus. *Against the Professors.* Trans. R. G. Bury. Loeb Classical Library.

Studies

Babut, Daniel. *La religion des philosophes grecs.* Paris: Presses Universitaires de France, 1974.
Burkert, Walter. *Greek Religion.* Cambridge, Mass.: Harvard University Press, 1985.
Decharme, Paul. *La critique des traditions religieuses chez les Grecs.* Paris: Picard, 1904.
Détienne, Marcel. *Les jardins d'Adonis: La mythologie des aromates en Grèce.* Paris: Gallimard, 1972.
Morel, Pierre-Marie. "Le regard étranger sur la cité des Lois." In *D'une cité possible: Sur les Lois de Platon.* Ed. J. F. Balaudé. 1. Nanterre: Université Paris X–Nanterre, 1995. Pp. 95–113.
Obbink, Dirk. "Epicurus 11(?): Sulla religiosità e il culto popolare." In *Corpus dei papiri filosofici greci e latini,* vol. 1. Florence: Olschki, 1992. Pp. 167–191.
Pépin, Jean. *Mythe et allégorie: Les origines grecques et les contestations judéo-chrétiennes.* Paris: Montaigne, 1958.
Reverdin, Olivier. *La religion de la cité platonicienne.* Paris: De Boccard, 1945.

Vernant, Jean-Pierre. *Mythe et pensée chez les Grecs.* Paris: Maspéro, 1965; La Découverte, 1985.

————. *Mythe et religion en Grèce ancienne.* Paris: Le Seuil, 1990.

Related Entries

Images of the World; Plutarch; Socrates; Heraclitus; Hellenism and Judaism; Theology and Divination; Epicurus; Protagoras; Cynicism; Hellenism and Christianity

MAJOR FIGURES

ANAXAGORAS

Anaxagoras was born around 500 b.c.e. in Clazomenae in Asia Minor. But he spent a great part of his life in Athens, and in a sense it is thanks to him that philosophy became the Athenian specialty it would thereafter remain. A friend of Pericles, who had gathered around him a prestigious group of artists and intellectuals, Anaxagoras was the target of political attacks. The adoption in 438/437 of a decree proposed by the soothsayer Diopeithes allowing charges to be brought against "those who deny divine things or who in their teaching spread theories about celestial phenomena" (Diels-Kranz, A16) was directly aimed at Anaxagoras, and led to his prosecution in 437/436. Condemned, he was forced to leave Athens, and he passed the last year of his life in Lampsacus, on the Hellespont, where he died in 437/436.

Since antiquity, Anaxagoras has represented the enlightened rationalist struggling against superstition (Plutarch, *The Parallel Lives* 3.IV.4), and he is remembered for predicting the fall of a meteorite at Aigospotami in 467/466. But because he took Mind (Nous, a term that was also used as his nickname, according to Diogenes Laertius) as the basis for his philosophy, he also embodied better than anyone the type of the contemplative philosopher. The same Anaxagoras whom Aristotle criticized for holding that it is owing to his hands that man is the most intelligent of animals was also said to have declared that man was born to contemplate the heavens (Diogenes Laertius, II.10; cf. Plato, *Phaedrus* 269e).

Anaxagoras is the author of a single treatise which, according to a well-known episode in Plato's *Phaedo* (97b), was the object of a public reading in Athens, in the presence of Socrates (we can date the event to around 450). Like numerous other Presocratic writings, the work is known only from fragments (a little more than twenty), almost all preserved by Simplicius in his commentary on the first book of Aristotle's *Physics*, and by an important series of testimonies (117 entries in the Diels-Kranz collection). Since the treatise was probably a short one, our information is less incomplete than it might seem. In any event, it is not at all certain that, had we more texts at our disposal, we would be in a better position to resolve the formidable problems of interpretation posed by a complex system of thought—the first to have exploited, if not explored, the paradoxes of infinity.

Anaxagoras's philosophy, in accordance with its geographically mediating position, has sometimes been presented as an attempt at synthesis between a physics of the Milesian type and Parmenides' (Western) ontology. It would

probably be more accurate to see it as an attempt, prompted by Parmenides' poem itself, to overcome the scandal represented, in the latter, by the leap from the sphere of being and truth (in the first part of the poem) to that of becoming and opinion (in the second part). Still, such a story hardly accounts for the central role played by the Mind in Anaxagoras's system. Heraclitus's universal reason is sometimes cited in this regard, or Xenophanes' god. But these links are too loose to be really enlightening, even if we were to acknowledge their pertinence. To understand the function of Mind in the harmonious arrangement of the treatise, we must start with what is known, following Aristotelian terminology, as the Anaxagorean doctrine of "matter."

In this domain, the Eleatic heritage seems self-evident. Like Parmenides, Anaxagoras dismisses the use that men—or, as he writes, "the Greeks"—make of the terms *birth* and *destruction*. To come into being is just as impossible as to be annihilated, for nothing arises from nonbeing, nor does being return to nonbeing. This first principle nevertheless does not exclude local change, as it does for Parmenides. The "things that are" are not born, nor do they die, but they reunite *(sunkrisis)* and dissociate *(diakrisis)* themselves. Anaxagoras can thus conceive of the history of the world not as the faded reflection of ontological discourse but as the very site of its deployment. His treatise, of which the beginning has been preserved, starts right out describing the original state, characterized by indistinction: "All things were together, infinite in regard both to number and to smallness; for the small too was infinite. Since all things were together, nothing within was clear because of smallness" (Diels-Kranz, 1). From this primordial mix, which seems to be not a state of fusion but of juxtaposition (whence the infinity of "smallness"), visible things emerge by a process of "separating off," which, from another point of view, is also a process of "mixing"—for the "decomposition" of the primitive mass coincides with the "formation" of composite entities.

From the point of view of a strict Eleatism, such a redistribution represents a major concession to the world of the senses. But being, in Anaxagoras, gains in extension what it loses in intension. In Parmenides, *nothing* of what constitutes the world of opinion *is* in the strict meaning of the term (not even the two fundamental components, fire and night); for Anaxagoras, on the other hand, *everything* that constitutes the world, by the same token, *is*. It follows that every existing thing preexists and survives itself. If we do not see this and fall under the illusion of births and destructions, it is only because, disseminated, things remain indistinct, as they were in the primordial mix.

The problem, then, is to enumerate and define the members of the primitive ontological population. Nothing in principle precludes reducing fundamental entities to a small number of elements. In Empedocles, for example, whose argument coincides up to this point with that of Anaxagoras, only four elements, called "roots," are necessary to account for the totality of things

that have come into being (subject, of course, to a definite "organization," whose role is more important to the extent that the elements by themselves are more amorphous). In Anaxagoras, the "things that are" are numerous and disparate, already much closer to the world that will eventually result from them; bones and blood, for example, two typical creations of Empedocles' artisan Aphrodite, are already present in the primordial mix. Even if it seems difficult to maintain that Anaxagoras, anxious to leave the least possible space for nonbeing in a world that already presupposes local change, abolished every distinction between "ingredients" and "composites," the fact remains that his position combines a stricter interpretation of Parmenides' interdict than that of Empedocles; hence his incomparably more generous ontology.

It is very difficult to set up an exhaustive list of the "things that are." In the succession of fragments, we find first air and aether (these are more abundant than the other ingredients in the primordial mix), then the moist and the dry, the hot and the cold, the bright and the dark (the "opposites" of Aristotle's doxography, *Physics* 187a); then the earth, isolated; and finally a mysterious category of seeds *(spermata)*, which are said to be infinite in number. This list is manifestly open-ended: one should probably add to it, on the basis of other fragments or accounts, the "dense" and the "rare," the sweet and the salty, as well as organic composites such as hair or flesh. (According to one possible reading of some very controversial passages, it is this last group of substances that Aristotle calls by the technical name *homoiomeres*; however, this term, which certainly does not go back to Anaxagoras, ended up referring in post-Aristotelian doxography to Anaxagoras's principles in general.) Finally, Mind should certainly be counted among the things that are, since it is, in Anaxagoras's terms, "the finest" and "the purest" among them (Diels-Kranz, 12).

The profile of the series depends in great part on the extension one gives the term *seeds*. If we take the term literally as referring to seeds of organisms, we must acknowledge that animals and plants are already included in the primordial mix. Such a view fits an interpretation that seeks to minimize the difference between ingredients and composites (an extreme version would even include in the primordial mix all the individuals that would ever come into existence). As its defenders realize, this concept is not unproblematic: organisms, in fact, do not develop through the addition of substantially identical parts. Two options seem to arise at this juncture. We may suppose that organic development is subject to more complex mechanisms than the terms of association and dissociation suggest. This approach would highlight the fact that, in addition to the vocabulary of association and dissociation, Anaxagoras uses a terminology of organic differentiation *(apokrisis)*. Alternatively, we may suppose that the term *seeds* is used here metaphorically to refer to nonorganized entities, whether we take it as a general term or, more nar-

rowly, as corresponding to the Aristotelian *homoiomeres*. In support of the latter hypothesis (and likewise of the second option), one can emphasize that natural substances are unquestionably part of the primordial mix.

Moreover, only a limitation of the primitive population to nonorganized substances allows us to give an acceptable meaning to the formula—fraught with difficulties in any event—of universal inherence ("in everything there is a portion of everything"), which appears in several fragments. It is generally thought that this second principle, from which Mind alone is excluded, as is revealed in the course of the treatise, derives from the application of the initial principle of conservation of being to biological phenomena, and in particular to nutrition, which unquestionably interested Anaxagoras. Observing that blood, hair, bones, and so forth come from the food we eat, Anaxagoras would have concluded that "in everything there is a portion of everything." The conclusion, however, does not follow. What the phenomenon of nutrition allows us at most to claim is that *certain* things are contained in others. To be able to affirm on the basis of an empirical observation that "everything" is in "everything," it would be necessary for everything to come from everything. Such is in fact the argument that Aristotle lends to Anaxagoras in *Physics* (187b). But this is so manifestly contrary to observation that we may wonder whether it is not a rather desperate reconstruction on Aristotle's part.

Two paths open up here once again. We can try to weaken the scope of the formula "everything comes from everything," by supposing it to be true only under certain circumstances that we can try to specify; or we can admit that the principle "everything is in everything" is not based on a simple empirical observation. The first solution was adopted by Simplicius; trying to justify Aristotle even more than Anaxagoras, he suggests that everything comes from everything not in the sense that everything could at any moment come from anything whatsoever, but in the sense that, granted a certain number of steps, one could start from any entity whatsoever and arrive at any other (according to Anaxagoras [Diels-Kranz, 16], stones derive from clouds through the intermediary of water and earth, at the end of a process of progressive solidification).

However, in worrying about realism we run the risk of considerably reducing the range of a thesis that really seems to be above all "metaphysical." Taken literally, the second principle reverses the meaning of the very thesis from which it derives. While for Parmenides the predicates of being are so many aspects of self-identity, forms that his poem progressively unfolds up to the point where the homogeneous "sphere" of being is constituted, Anaxagoras's beings are characterized by their radical heterogeneity. Universal inherence in fact implies an infinite regression in the search for an ultimate identity: the earth contains gold, which in turn contains earth, which contains gold, and so on. This self-embedding structure, which defies all representation, becomes even less comprehensible as the size of the initial popu-

lation increases. We can see why his interpreters devoted considerable energies to "saving" Anaxagoras from his own doctrine, whose consequences appeared logically unacceptable.

Thus some have tried to show, on the one hand, that Anaxagoras's "things" must have been pure after all (which is true in a certain sense, as we shall see) and, on the other hand, that their fundamental ingredients included only opposites. As a general rule, the basis for these solutions, which are often technically complicated, goes back to antiquity. Simplicius draws a distinction between quantitative divisibility, which alone could be pursued to infinity, and qualitative indivisibility, which permits the isolation of an ultimate element; he also remarks that Anaxagoras's fragments mention only the separation of opposites.

However, the principle of universal inherence (in other words, the thesis according to which there is no such thing as an element, properly speaking), repeated in the fragments in different ways, seems to be a fundamental tenet of the system. Even if its only value is indicative, the comparison with Leibniz (*Monadology* 67s) can help us overcome the uneasiness aroused by its paradoxical consequences. Anaxagoras was perfectly capable of measuring the resources inherent in the notion of the infinite, even though he obviously lacked the conceptual apparatus needed to resolve the logical difficulties the system produces (it requires, for example, that certain infinites be larger than others). It is important to stress, in this context, that Anaxagoras's qualitative infinite is not on the same footing as Zeno's quantitative infinite. One essential consequence of the principle of universal inherence is that, in some sense, the world in its present state does not differ from the initial mix: "Just as in the beginning now too are all things together" (Diels-Kranz, 6). It is in this sense that one might argue that there really exists in Anaxagoras a general principle of "homoiomery," each part of the primitive constituents, as Aristotle puts it, being a mix similar to the whole (*Physics* I.iv.187a). What differentiates the actual state from the initial state is not the existence of the mix but rather the internal equilibrium of its distribution, governed by the principle of domination.

By virtue of the first principle, "separation" from within the mix produces not things themselves, but their visibility. Still, this visibility is deceptive, for the thing separated off is no less mixed, or "impure," than the mixture from which it is detached. Instead of all things being invisible, it is now the mixture that has become so, as it were. The illusion of identity comes from the fact that in every detached thing, one thing, or rather a series of things, "predominates" over the other ("of things of which there is the greatest quantity, every one of these things is most manifestly these things, and was so," says Anaxagoras; Diels-Kranz, 12, end of frg.). Thus one can say of an entity that it is hot, heavy, or white because it contains a greater quantity of the hot, the heavy, or the white.

It follows from the principle of domination that the characteristics we predicate of things, useful as they may be pragmatically, are the source of a categorical illusion: in fact, they turn simple quantitative superiority into a criterion of ontological identity. A number of specific explanations in Anaxagoras's treatise can be interpreted as attempts to restore to the mix, and especially to their contrary, all those constitutive entities of our world that seem to have escaped it and to which we give a definite name: thus Anaxagoras maintains that snow is no less black than white, and that every sensation is painful, tracking down in every phenomenon what it is not *manifestly*; or else, in Anaxagoras's paradoxical language, one can say that "the visible existence is a sight of the unseen" (Diels-Kranz, 21a)—a formula Democritus praised, although he understood it differently. As for the senses, of which linguistic predication is an accomplice, they are limited, on their own, to establishing surface identities. Thus it is not surprising that Anaxagoras criticized our sensory faculties, incapable as they are of *distinguishing* between two closely related phenomena (like two shades in a gradation of colors).

The principle of domination exacerbates the logical difficulties already raised with regard to universal inherence, so much so that it has given partisans of the elementary character of ingredients one of their best arguments. The problem clearly arises from the example by which Simplicius illustrates the principle: "What has much gold in it appears to be gold, though there are numerous things in it." If it is really impossible to isolate a pure state of gold, one in which gold would be nothing but gold, the description of a piece of gold as "that which contains the most gold" seems to be circular: by virtue of the principle of the mixture, the *definiens* is neither more nor less gold than the *definiendum*. The difficulty is real. There is no solution for it compatible with the principle of universal inherence unless we are willing to distinguish between inherence in fact and independence in principle, where the status of the latter can be explained only in relation to the role of Mind in the dissociation of the original mixture.

We learn about the cosmogonic process through a long fragment of about thirty lines (Diels-Kranz, 12), the oldest example of continuous philosophical prose that has come down to us. We may be struck by a certain hieratic quality in the expression, owing to the abundance of paratactic relations, the repetition of the same terms, and, in the first lines, a "hymnic" character (as Deichgräber calls it) in the enumeration of the attributes of Mind (which Anaxagoras, however, does not appear to have called a god). We can see why the ancients must have been sensitive to the beauty and grandeur of this style. While the writer's effort to produce a syntax of justification is unmistakable, interpreters have insisted on the obscurities of the text's form, which is better suited to the expression of a dogmatic "archaic wisdom" than to the

needs of argumentation. However, the fact remains that Anaxagoras's argument, taken in conjunction with the principle of universal inherence to which he explicitly refers, contains all the elements necessary for an adequate understanding of the function of Mind.

The primordial mix seems to have been held in place at first by the domination of air and aether (which suggests perhaps a natural but thwarted tendency on the part of matter toward movement). Mind gave it the initial thrust, imparting to it a rotary motion that was at first restricted in amplitude, then gradually expanded, and it will continue to expand—perhaps until the world in which we live is destroyed. Although the term signifying rotation *(perichōresis)* means nothing more than circular movement (it applies to the course of the stars today as well as to the initial disturbance), it is likely that the crucial stages of the formation of the world were explained by a physics of whirling movement. The first separation out of the primitive mix was that of air and aether, which are opposed, as cold and wet are to hot and dry; this separation must have been accompanied by the concentration, at the center, of the heavy mass of the earth, which as a result of rotation itself would presumably have taken the form of a flat disc. The action implies a force capable of liberating the enormous mass of opposing "elements" from their own "weight." The existence of incandescent stars, carried along by the celestial rotation, also proves the violence of a process that, in a second phase, tore enormous masses from the earth and projected them into the aether, where they burst into flame (thus the stars are stones, not gods). Anaxagoras derived this force (explicitly called violence, *bia*) from the extreme rapidity of the circular motion. Thus we see here how, through the intermediary of rotation, Mind made of its own constitutive weakness (it is the "finest" of all things in this sense too) the very instrument of its domination *(kratos).* Other aspects of the cosmogonic process are more difficult to grasp. We know that the universe tilted, probably owing to the effect of an imbalance created by the play of concentrations once living beings emerged from the earth, surely because of the effect of heat acting on a mass still damp in the center.

Like the other Presocratics, Anaxagoras went into the details of cosmology and zoology. His explanation of eclipses and meteors, in relation to the thesis of the stony nature of the stars, must have been striking to his readers' minds. We are thus informed about rainbows, the flooding of the Nile, and the sensory mechanisms of living beings. In all these cases, it would be interesting to speculate about the extent to which the particular explanations illustrate the great systematic principles of universal inherence or the phenomenal visibility of hidden things. This task, which remains to be carried out, would develop, with very different presuppositions, an approach of which the doxography has left us a few traces, when it inquires, for example, whether the tilting of the universe might not be attributable to providence *(pronoia)*

rather than to mechanical factors, "so that certain parts of the universe are uninhabitable and others habitable" (Diels-Kranz, A67).

This last, typically Stoic interpretation of a cosmogonical episode raises the central question of the status of Mind within the system. We are indebted to Plato, in *Phaedo,* for providing a strong formulation of the problem in the famous intellectual autobiography of Socrates (96a6–100a7). On hearing one passage of the treatise (which we can identify with confidence as the beginning of frg. 12), Socrates is said to have conceived the "hope" of having discovered in Anaxagoras a philosopher of the final cause; breaking radically with the characteristic mechanism of traditional cosmogonies, Anaxagoras would explain everything through the principle of the best. Is Mind not in fact determined, from a Platonic point of view, by an end that can only be the good? It was all the more disappointing to find, in reading the rest of the treatise, that Anaxagoras was in fact appealing only to material pseudocauses, the very ones that the elevation of Mind to the level of "cause of everything" ought to have at least subordinated to the action of the final cause—a program that *Timaeus,* which is outlined in this passage of *Phaedo,* will undertake to realize.

This schema determines the whole history of the interpretation of Anaxagoras. Depending on which aspect of the Platonic reading we stress, Anaxagoras will be thought either to have provoked a decisive break in the history of philosophy or else to remain within the frame of a traditional physics—however original in other respects his views may be. While the first position is dominant in antiquity (see Aristotle, *Metaphysics* 984b11–21), modern interpreters tend rather to adopt the second (which Aristotle also mentions, in *Metaphysics* 985a18–21). Still, the opposition is henceforth situated less between Mind and the mechanism of elementary masses, following the presentation in *Phaedo,* than at the core of Mind itself, between a cognitive-intentional function, on the one hand, and a kinetic function, on the other. This duality, which Aristotle addresses again in the doxographic section of the treatise *On the Soul* (405a17), does create a tension within fragment 12 itself. While possessing understanding and will (two aspects intimately blended in the archaic usage of the word Nous), Mind is not conceived in Anaxagoras in an anthropomorphic manner, on the model of the artisan, but as a simple principle of movement. Kurt von Fritz has sought to provide a historical explanation of this strange conflation of two antithetical perspectives, seeing in it an ultimate and, so to speak, uncompromising compromise between two major evolutions of Presocratic philosophy: one tends to make Mind the supreme organ of knowledge and deliberate organization, while the other tends to explain the cosmogonic and cosmological processes in terms that leave very little room indeed for teleology.

Nevertheless, it seems that the very structure of Anaxagoras's treatise, entirely determined by the theme of mixture and separation, justifies a different

approach. The first step is to recognize that the cosmogonic process is not only one of mixture and separation but also, and perhaps above all, the material projection of what is the activity of a mind, an intelligence—essentially a "critical" activity, like the process of dissociation that it initiates.

It is indispensable, in this regard, to understand the privileged bond that unites (according to a schema that was to prove enormously successful) Mind with circular movement. The relation can be analyzed on two levels. First, the setting into rotation of a point in the primordial mix can be seen as resulting from a vast hypothetical syllogism: *if* a vortex is created in the mass of mixed things, *then* the things will dissociate in such a way as to reproduce the world we know. Between conception and realization, there is room for something that we may call a scientific law, by virtue of which a foreseeable set of effects (including our world) will follow by a process enmeshed in defined conditions (those of the primordial mix). From this point of view, Anaxagoras's Mind is indeed a teleological power, not in the sense that it organizes the world and its parts in view of the Good (according to the Platonic expectation), but in the sense that it is capable of drawing the maximum effect from a minimum of means (rotation). We have already seen how the intelligence of Mind consisted in giving itself all the strength it needed.

Then—and this is the most important feature—the cosmic rotation tends, by dissociation from the primordial mix, to form identical entities. Of course Mind creates nothing (except the "composed things," if we acknowledge that they have to be excluded from the initial ontological population), since everything exists prior to Mind. And the identities that it "assembles" are never complete, precisely by virtue of the principle according to which "in everything there is a portion of everything." (If the end of our universe were the same thing as the wholesale dissociation of primitive identities, henceforth identified in their purity, our sources would probably have mentioned it.) One of the fascinating aspects of Anaxagoras's system consists precisely in the fact that, contrary to what Plato's criticism in *Phaedo* might lead us to expect, this double limitation finally brings Anaxagoras's system fairly close to the Platonic cosmogony of *Timaeus*.

The existence of affinities between the systems of Anaxagoras and Plato, beyond the pretense of teleology, has occasionally been noted. One can stress, for example, in an epistemological perspective, that the notion of the integral "inherence" of everything in everything was a first expression of the problem of predication (this reading probably goes back to the Platonic Academy: see Aristotle, *Metaphysics* 991a6ff). But still more striking is the fact that the Anaxagorean entities, which exist before Mind's intervention, combine the functions that, in *Timaeus*, are those of the paradigmatic Forms and of the principle of disorder (the *chora*). The Anaxagorean ingredients, which have been there forever, are in principle identifiable by Mind, which "knows" them. By this token (insofar as they are intelligible, one might say), they

should be able to be conceived in their "purity." In this noetic sense, they are then indeed separable. But the fact remains that, unlike the Platonic Forms, they always exist in a mixture, as if a force of resistance analogous to the one the *chora* opposes to the demiurgic ordering of the universe prevented the "critical" work of Mind not only from ever reaching completion but even from making real progress. It is worth noting that, while allowing us to see the results of separation in the realized cosmos, Anaxagoras's treatise emphasizes this incapacity. Even the keenest knowledge, that of the cosmic Mind, is unable to inscribe into the world the ideal identity of things.

ANDRÉ LAKS
Translated by Rita Guerlac and Anne Slack

Bibliography

Texts and Translations

Anaxagoras. *Anassagora: Testimonianze e frammenti.* Ed. Diego Lanza. Florence: La Nuova Italia, 1966.

———. In *Die Fragmente der Vorsokratiker,* 6th ed., vol. 2. Ed. Hermann Diels and Walther Kranz. Berlin: Weidmann, 1952. Pp. 5–44.

———. *The Fragments of Anaxagoras.* Ed. David Sider. Meisenheim am Glan: Anton Hain, 1981.

———. In *Die Vorsokratiker.* Ed. Jaap Mansfeld. Stuttgart: Reclam, 1987. Pp. 482–555.

Aristotle. *Physics.* Trans. Philip H. Wicksteed and Francis M. Cornford. Loeb Classical Library.

Plutarch. *The Parallel Lives.* Trans. B. Perrin. Loeb Classical Library.

Studies

Babut, Daniel. "Anaxagore jugé par Socrate et Platon." *Revue des études grecques* 91 (1978): 44–76.

Deichgräber, Karl. "Hymnische Element in der philosophischen Prosa der Vorsokratiker." *Philologus* 42 (1933): 347–361.

Fritz, Kurt von. "Der Nous des Anaxagoras" (1964). In *Grundprobleme der Geschichte der antiken Wissenschaft.* Berlin and New York: W. de Gruyter, 1971. Pp. 576–596.

Furley, David. "Anaxagoras in Response to Parmenides" (1976). In *Cosmic Problems.* Cambridge: Cambridge University Press, 1989. Pp. 47–65.

Laks, André. "Mind's Crisis: On Anaxagoras' Nous." *The Southern Journal of Philosophy* 31 (supplement, 1993): 19–37.

Lanza, Diego. "Il pensiero di Anaxagora," *Memorie dell'Instituto Lombardo* 29 (1965): 223–288.

Mansfeld, Jaap. "The Chronology of Anaxagoras' Athenian Period and the Date of His Trial." *Mnemosyne* 32 (1979): 39–69.

Schofield, Malcolm. *An Essay on Anaxagoras.* Cambridge: Cambridge University Press, 1980.

Strang, Colin. "The Physical Theory of Anaxagoras" (1963). In *Studies in Presocratic Philosophy,* vol. 2. Ed. R. E. Allen and David J. Furley. London: Routledge and Kegan Paul, 1975. Pp. 361–380.

Related Articles

The Question of Being; Theology and Divination; Cosmology; Democritus

ANTISTHENES

ANTISTHENES, SON OF AN ATHENIAN and a Thracian slave, is said to have used his own social status as the impetus for critiquing the ideology of the "well-born" (eugeneia). (His polemics were probably directed against the Athenian democracy: under laws established by Pericles in 451–450 and reestablished in 403, Athens granted citizenship only to children of two Athenian parents.) Antisthenes' status as illegitimate may account for the place he chose to do his teaching, the Cynosarges gymnasium: according to one of the many a posteriori explanations provided by the ancients, the gymnasium, which was reserved for illegitimate children and dedicated to Heracles, gave its name to Cynicism. This piece of information, like the other biographical elements that have been handed down largely in anecdotal form, is not easy to assess. In particular, the reports that establish a master-pupil succession from Antisthenes to Zeno the Stoic by way of Diogenes of Sinope and Crates have been called into question many times, for good reason. But whatever their historical accuracy may be, these reports show that the ancients—who, unlike ourselves, read Antisthenes' works—found in them significant features indicative of affinity with the Cynico-Stoic tradition. Socrates' reported praise of Antisthenes' actions in the battle of Tanagra (426), a witty remark about the battle of Leuctra (371), and the fact that Diodorus of Sicily thought that Antisthenes was still alive in 366/365 lead us to place his life span roughly between 445 and 365 B.C.E. Moreover, he is described as one of Socrates' faithful followers in Xenophon's *Symposium*, set in 422. Thus we cannot accept the idea that his life was divided into two phases, in the first of which he practiced rhetoric under the influence of Gorgias, while in the second he became one of Socrates' disciples. The "Gorgian phase" is a construct of the Hellenistic period, apparently based on little more than the "rhetorical character" of some of Antisthenes' works. However, we can credit Diogenes Laertius's report that Antisthenes "heard" Gorgias (who came to Athens as an ambassador in 427): the few remaining examples of his style (in particular the fictional discourses *Ajax* and *Odysseus*, the only texts by Antisthenes that have survived intact) are full of stylistic figures such as antitheses, parisoses (parallelisms among parts of sentences), and homeoteleutes (similarities in grammatical endings), and they do in fact betray the influence of the artistic prose associated with Gorgias.

Diogenes' catalogue of Antisthenes' works (*Lives of Eminent Philosophers* VI.15–18) seems to point to an authentic critical edition paralleling editions

of Democritus's and Plato's works. It confirms what other accounts also suggest: among the Socratics, Antisthenes' importance in ancient culture was second only to Plato's. The list of the titles of his works, grouped in ten thematically unified volumes (with some exceptions possibly attributable to distortions introduced in the transmission process), constitutes the most important trace we have of his activity and interests, given the almost complete disappearance of his writings and the small number of surviving fragments. In the 3rd century, Timon of Phlius defined him as a "chatterbox who produced everything," alluding to the "countless books" St. Jerome would mention later, and also to the variety of topics addressed. Alone among all the Socratics, Antisthenes earned the praises of the anti-Platonician Theopompus, in the 4th century. Cicero admired him, and his works continued to be read into late antiquity. From the philosophical point of view, he is much more present in the writings of Dion of Prusa or of Epictetus than the infrequent mentions of his name might suggest; these writings bear witness to Antisthenes' impact on the Cynico-Stoic tradition. In the 4th century c.e., Julian and Themistius knew and cited his writings; in the imperial era, grammarians (Demetrius, Fronton, Phrynichus, Longinus) compared him to Xenophon and Plato as a model of stylistic purity.

Antisthenes' highly regarded writing style may account for the fact that, of all his immense production, the two texts that remain are fictional orations: they have been preserved in a manuscript that also includes orations by Lysias, Alcidamas, and the pseudo-Demades, along with Gorgias's *Encomium of Helen*, confirming that Antisthenes figured among the authors read in schools. He cultivated literary genres other than dialogue, but his best-known works (*Truth, Protreptics, Heracles*, among others) were written in that form. Socrates must have played an important role in them, since Panaetius unhesitatingly included Antisthenes among the authors of authentic *logoi sōkratikoi*. Unfortunately, the traces of Antisthenes' Socrates are extremely sparse, and one must be very cautious in attempting to reconstruct what has been lost on the basis of Xenophon's *Memorabilia*, or later works whose authors might have had access to Antisthenes' writings. Antisthenes takes on sharply contrasting contours in modern reconstructions: he is sometimes extravagantly praised, as a result of an extensive and often overly casual use of the sources, and he is sometimes harshly disparaged, as if the obliteration of his works over time sufficed to prove his philosophic insignificance. The vicissitudes he has undergone in these reconstructions are presented clearly and evaluated judiciously in the notes Gabriele Giannantoni prepared to accompany the most recent collection of fragments, and they warrant careful attention by future scholars in the field.

The titles of his works, to which we can link only a few fragments with certainty, point, significantly, to a number of themes frequently encountered in the culture of the second half of the 5th century. In addition to Homeric

exegesis, to which Antisthenes applied himself in a systematic way, writing commentaries on numerous episodes in the *Iliad* and *Odyssey*, he also took up themes from the mythological and historico-biographical traditions (Heracles, Cyrus the Great). From a social background quite unlike that of Plato or Socrates' other followers, Antisthenes had to win prestige and fame through a socially recognized and remunerated pedagogical enterprise, although his self-portrait (Xenophon, *Symposium* IV.34ff; see also Isocrates, *Against the Sophists* 3) indicates that he did not use his teaching to build wealth. He may have earned his reputation by offering a philosophical reinterpretation of the familiar figures of the Greek *paideia*, such as Heracles and Odysseus, rereading the Homeric poems in the light of Socratic teaching and thus entering into competition with a diffuse but well-established tradition.

Antisthenes seems to have possessed the art of "knowing how to deal with men" to the fullest; he undertook to teach through dialogue and example, drawing on dialectical gifts reinforced by a refined rhetorical technique and great moral rigor. His polemics against Lysias and Isocrates, on the one hand, and against Plato, on the other, which are explicitly attested by other titles, outline the cultural space he sought to occupy. Typically Socratic themes appear in the titles of works devoted to virtues (courage, justice), goodness, law, liberty, and slavery; other works, such as *Aspasia, Alcibiades,* and *Archelaos,* also refer to ongoing discussions in the Socratic circle. An important group of writings was centered on logico-linguistic and gnoseological themes: *Truth* (a title that, after Parmenides, had been adopted by Protagoras and Antiphon); a text on dialectical argument; a work whose title, *Sathon,* involved a play on Plato's name; five volumes called *On Education, or On Names;* and still other works on the use of names, on the art of questioning and responding, on opinion *(doxa)* and science *(episteme),* to mention just a few of the subjects addressed.

Diogenes Laertius's life of Antisthenes (*Lives* VI.1–19.103–105), to which we owe the preservation of the catalogue, is constructed and oriented in such a way as to highlight the elements of continuity between Antisthenes, Cynicism, and Stoicism. Diogenes refers primarily to *Heracles,* from which he excerpts statements in a form that quite manifestly reveals the influence of Hellenistic terminology. Even though in most cases we have no justification for rejecting them, the choice of these particular excerpts and the way they are formulated clearly tend to project Antisthenes into a period that is not his own; the way he may have responded to the questions and problems of his own day remains obscure. We are told—to cite only the most important themes—that for Antisthenes, the sovereign good is life lived according to virtue; virtue can be taught; once achieved, it cannot be lost; virtue suffices for happiness and requires only the Socratic "force"; it is manifested in actions and can dispense with speeches and theories. Heracles' saga and Cyrus's vicis-

situdes illustrate the idea that "effort" *(ponos)* is a good thing and leads to virtue; at the same time, pleasure is to be avoided (but perhaps less drastically than we are led to believe by the celebrated dictum, "I would rather go mad than experience pleasure"). Antisthenes the sage has many features in common—perhaps too many—with the Stoic sages. Antisthenes is also said to have been the first to define *logos* as "that which shows what things were or are" (Diogenes Laertius, *Lives* VI.3), but even that isolated assertion may reflect the Stoics' desire to establish a link with Socrates via his intermediary, since Alexander of Aphrodisias considers Antisthenes' use of the imperfect as a precedent with respect to the Stoics (*Stoicorum veterum fragmenta* II.228).

In any event, the Antisthenian doxography seems to indicate that Antisthenes had taken the Socratic message in a direction of his own, propounding an ethics based on exemplary action, relegating dialectics to marginal status, and rejecting the study of the sciences. However, in addition to the anecdotes that show the importance he attached to reasoning, the intellect, and *phronesis* (which is not practical wisdom but the instrument that makes it possible to construct a rampart of unassailable arguments), the very titles of Antisthenes' works preclude accepting this image: we must be careful not to confuse the models of virtue he proposed with the arguments intended to justify the choice of those models or with the method he used in his teaching.

Comparing him to Socrates, Epictetus (*Discourses* I.17.10) tells us that Antisthenes thought the basis of education was the study of names; we may assume that this expression designates, in the first place, the study of the meaning of terms pertaining to moral life. However, there are few surviving accounts of this aspect of Antisthenes' thinking, which must have resulted from his personal interpretation of Socratic methodology and philosophy, and these accounts are so difficult to interpret that the conclusions drawn from them have been quite divergent and often unfounded. The adequately documented facts are the following: Antisthenes was engaged in a polemic against Plato's Forms, declaring that he could perfectly well perceive a horse, but not "horse-ness," or, more abstractly, he could perceive what was "qualified" *(poion)* but not the "quality" *(poiotes)*. This amounted to rejecting Plato's ontology; Antisthenes (or perhaps his disciples: Aristotle refers to the "followers of Antisthenes"; *Metaphysics* VIII.iii.1043b) rejected the possibility of defining essence *(to ti estin)*, because the definition is nothing other than an extended *logos*; however, he acknowledged the possibility of teaching "how a thing is" *(poion ti estin):* from the context, it is clear that this aporia concerned only simple substances, and, indirectly, that the predicates constituting the definition were understood as part of the *definiendum*, namely, as that *of which* a thing is constituted. Aristotle uses the example—on the whole a rather unclear one—of silver: one cannot say what it is, but only that it is

similar to tin. Antisthenes also denied the possibility of contradicting *(ouk estin antilegein)*, with the argument (strongly criticized by Aristotle, *Metaphysics* V.xxix.1024b26) that nothing can be said except with the proper *logos*, and that there is only one *logos* for each thing *(tōi oikeiōi logōi, hen ephhenos)*; consequently, it is impossible to contradict, and it is virtually impossible even to say untruths. Proclus justifies this view, perhaps wrongly, as follows: "Every *logos* says the truth; for whoever speaks says something; whoever says something says what is; whoever says what is says the truth" *(In Platonis Cratylum commentaria* 37). To this we must add the previously mentioned definition of *logos* (Diogenes Laertius, *Lives* VI.3), a term that, given the way it is presented, must have had a technical value—if not the Aristotelian sense of "definition," which seems presupposed by Alexander Aphrodisias *(Stoicorum veterum fragmenta)*, then surely at least the restrictive sense of the "proper" *logos*, the only one that expresses the object in accordance with its own intrinsic nature, and that is therefore not open to contradiction.

Whatever meaning one may attribute to these scattered fragments (which appear, for the most part, in highly polemical contexts), a few facts seem reasonably certain. A fundamental theme of Antisthenes' investigations was reflection on being, truth, and language; his primary reference was to Parmenides. Yet the centrality of the ethical theme and the methodology that the fragments allow us to glimpse lead us back to Socrates as well; the latter thus remains the chief reference point for any reconstruction. Furthermore, it is illegitimate to interpret the term *logos*, which recurs repeatedly in the fragments, as an equivalent of "name," on the basis of the obscure passage in *Metaphysics* (VIII), and thus to identify Antisthenes with the thinkers who recognized only judgments of identity; in reality, Antisthenes' name never comes up in conjunction with them. This is a crucial point, because this presupposition, an overconfident use of Diogenes Laertius's doxography, and the underestimation of the attention Antisthenes paid to problems of language, dialectical argument, and rhetoric, have led to a widely accepted historiographical schema (one only recently subjected to revision, on the basis of rigorous analysis of the sources). According to this schema, Antisthenes, who was confined within the bounds of a tautological logic that was deprived of the Platonic metaphysical referent and unable to ground itself in any other way, had to fall back on an ethics based on action, setting aside all "logico-scientific" problematics (even in the sense these expressions may have had before Aristotle).

This position reintroduces, in terms that are more veiled in form but analogous in substance, the old idea according to which the figure of Antisthenes can be understood only if it is split into two phases or aspects. The first phase is oriented toward the past, dominated by rhetorical interests and by attempts

at logico-dialectical analyses confined within bounds that were archaic, potentially self-destructive, and at all events incapable of responding to the great Socratic problem of the scientific foundation of ethics. In the second phase, Antisthenes is represented as committed to "living" according to virtue, seeking to outline the model of a "path toward virtue" that, inspired more than embodied by Socrates and by Antisthenes himself, took as its reference—not coincidentally—Heracles, a hero admitted among the gods after he had conquered the "tasks" (ponoi) that had tested, and proved, his virtue, and Cyrus, who rose from obscure origins to supreme royal power.

However, while these figures were indeed the protagonists of some of the works that contributed most prominently to Antisthenes' fame, we must not forget his other works if we are to avoid a distorted perspective; even in the few fragments that remain to us, we find traces that complicate the foregoing picture and make it relatively unconvincing. In particular, there is the Odysseus figure, about which, fortunately, we have information from sources independent of the biographical and philosophical tradition: the discourse attributed to Odysseus in his conflict with Ajax over Achilles' weapons, and a scholium in the first line of the *Odyssey*, preserved by Porphyrius, constitute invaluable testimony. Here Antisthenes defends the thesis according to which the adjective Homer used to characterize Odysseus, *polytropos*, "the man of a thousand tricks," has a positive meaning. He supports his argument with a complex analysis that starts with the double meaning of *tropos*, an attitude of character and a form of discourse. These two meanings are analyzed separately to begin with; later, their combination gives rise to the idea that the distinctive feature of wise men who are skilled at speaking and conversing (*dialegesthai*) is that they know how to express the same concept in many different ways, and that this ability is necessary if they are to act effectively on their diverse listeners. Only such differentiated use of *logoi* can lead the multiplicity of the listeners' *tropoi* back to unity, because "only one thing is proper to each" (*hen gar hekastōi oikeion*). This theory presupposes a subtle reflection, applied here to a specific case, on the relations between the one and the many and on the art of *dialegesthai*; it also refers to the art of "dealing with men," in which Antisthenes excelled. It lets us glimpse the complexity of the path leading to the discovery of the "proper *logos*" belonging to each thing, which transforms multiple truths into a single truth; by means of a well-conducted dialogue, this *logos* will tell us the nature of the object (which, in a Socratic inquiry, manifests its nature as good or evil).

By becoming the common patrimony of master and disciple, *logos* is in a position to transform our lives, as an effective medicinal drug might do; it allows us to distinguish between what belongs to us and what does not (rejecting anything evil as "foreign"), and thus to attain true freedom. This inner freedom supports the praise Antisthenes offers of his own wealth in Xeno-

phon's *Symposium;* it is based, on the one hand, on tireless inquiry into the nature of things, thanks to an adequate use of the instrument of language governed by reason, and, on the other hand, on the Socratic force that prevents the body from asserting its hegemony over the rational soul and over truth.

FERNANDA DECLEVA CAIZZI
Translated by Catherine Porter and Jeannine Pucci

Bibliography

Texts and Translations

Antisthenes. *Antisthenis fragmenta.* Ed. Fernanda Decleva Caizzi. Milan: Cisalpino, 1966.

Aristotle. *Metaphysics.* Trans. Hugh Tredennick. 2 vols. Loeb Classical Library.

Epictetus. *Discourses.* Book I. Trans. Robert F. Dobbin. Oxford: Clarendon Press, 1998.

Giannantoni, Gabriele, ed. *Socratis et socraticorum reliquiae.* 4 vols. Naples: Bibliopolis, 1990.

Paquet, Léonce, ed. *Les Cyniques grecs: Fragments et témoignages.* Ottawa: Editions de l'Université d'Ottawa, 1975, 1988; Paris: Le Livre de Poche, 1992.

Stoicorum veterum fragmenta. Ed. Hans Friedrich August von Arnim. 4 vols. Leipzig: B. G. Teubner, 1903, 1924.

Xenophon. *Symposium.* In *Anabasis, Books IV–VII, and Symposium and Apology.* Trans. D. J. Todd. Loeb Classical Library.

Studies

Brancacci, Aldo. "Dialettica e retorica in Antistene." *Elenchos* 17 (1996): 359–406.

———. *Oikeios logos: La filosofia del linguággio di Antistene.* Naples: Bibliopolis, 1990.

Decleva Caizzi, Fernanda. "Antistene." *Studi urbinati,* n.s. 1–2 (1964): 48–99.

Diogenes Laertius. "Antisthenes." In *Lives of Eminent Philosophers,* vol. 2, book 4. Trans. R. D. Hicks. Loeb Classical Library. Pp. 2–23.

Eucken, Christopher. "Der schwache und der starke Logos des Antisthenes," *Hyperboreus* 3 (1997): 251–272.

Gillespie, G. M. *The Logic of Antisthenes: Archiv für Geschichte der Philosophie* 19 and 20 (1913 and 1914): 479–500 and 17–38.

Goulet-Cazé, Marie-Odile. "L'*Ajax* et l'*Ulysse* d'Antisthène." In *Chercheurs de sagesse: Hommage à Jean Pépin.* Paris: Institut d'études augustiniennes, 1992. Pp. 5–36.

Höistad, Ragnar. "Cynic Hero and Cynic King: Studies in the Cynic Conception of Man." Thesis, University of Uppsala, 1948.

Luzzatto, Maria Tanja. "Dialettica o retorica? La *polytropia* di Odisseo da Antistene a Porfirio." *Elenchos* 17 (1996): 275–357.

Natorp, Paul. "Antisthenes." *Realencyclopädie* 1 (1894): 2538–2545.

Patzer, Andreas. *"Antisthenes der Sokratiker: Das literarische Werk und die Philosophie, dargestellt am Katalog der Schriften."* Dissertation, Marburg, 1970.

Rankin, H. D. *Antisthenes Sokratikos.* Amsterdam: Hakkert, 1986.

Romeyer Dherbey, Gilbert. "Tra Aiace e Ulisse: Antistene." *Elenchos* 17 (1996): 251–274.

Related Articles

Socrates; Stoicism; Cynicism

ARCHIMEDES

GEOMETERS IN THE 16TH AND 17TH CENTURIES, in aspiring to the title of the "new Archimedes," revealed a major source of their technical endeavor. It was hardly different in antiquity, when geometers in the generation immediately following Archimedes engaged in research directly modeled on his, while the impact of his achievement remained evident even centuries later, in works of Hero, Pappus, Eutocius, and Anthemius.

At the same time, Archimedes emerged as a figure larger than life in the popular imagination, legendary for the seeming miracles he performed through his mechanical inventions. Referring to the (apocryphal) tradition of Archimedes' use of gigantic burning mirrors for destroying the Roman fleet, the Byzantine mechanician Anthemius of Tralles (early 6th century), while voicing his skepticism about its possibility, nevertheless is compelled to admit that "one cannot gainsay the reputation of Archimedes," and so contrives some way by which "the most divine [theiotatos] Archimedes" could have done it.

On the life of Archimedes we are better informed than about any other figure of the ancient exact sciences, for it happens that military devices of his invention, including catapults and ship haulers, as well as fortification designs, proved significant in the defense of his native city, Syracuse, when it was besieged by the Romans during the Second Punic War (215–212 B.C.E.). Accordingly, from the historians Polybius, Livy, and Plutarch we learn of Archimedes' dealings with his patron, King Hieron of Syracuse, of the fearsome impression his siege engines made on the Roman attackers, and of the honor in which he was held by the Roman general Marcellus, against whose orders Archimedes was slain by a Roman soldier during the final sack of the city.

A substantial body of Archimedes' writing is extant through collections assembled in the 9th and 10th centuries during the Byzantine revival. The principal codex (lost in the 16th century but represented by a half dozen copies derived from it) includes the five treatises addressed to Dositheus at Alexandria (*Quadrature of the Parabola*; the two books of *On the Sphere and Cylinder*; *On Spiral Lines*; and *On Conoids and Spheroids*), plus *Dimension of the Circle, Sand Reckoner,* and the two books of *On Plane Equilibria*. In the 13th century Willem of Moerbeke prepared a literal Latin translation from this codex, collated with a second one that also included a text of the two books *On Floating Bodies*. Heiberg exploited this in his second critical edition (1910–1915), in which he also made valuable use of the evidence from yet a third co-

dex (then at Constantinople), a palimpsest whose Archimedean underwriting was first identified by Heiberg at the beginning of the 20th century. In addition to most of the works already known in Greek, the newly identified codex provided most of the Greek text of *On Floating Bodies*, as well as texts of *Method* and *Stomachion*. This codex passed surreptitiously into private hands during the 1920s and has been inaccessible for scholarly examination ever since. A few minor works, held in other codices or in medieval versions, or attested in fragments, are included in Heiberg's second edition. Since then, studies of the Arabic tradition of the corpus have revealed an additional work, *Construction of the Regular Heptagon*, and alternative versions of works extant in Greek (*Dimension of the Circle, Sphere and Cylinder*, and fragments of *Floating Bodies*).

From Archimedes' writings we learn a few additional personal details. In *Sand Reckoner* he cites his father, Pheidias, as an astronomer. This same tract, addressed to "King Gelon" (apparently then coregent with his father, Hieron, at Syracuse), seems to be a popular lecture for the court. Archimedes takes as his theme a certain misconception about the infinite—that, for instance, the number of grains of sand is infinite—and proceeds to show how one can express a number that greatly exceeds the grains of sand, that would even fill the entire cosmos. Along the way, Archimedes alludes to his own system of nomenclature for large numbers (expounded in a tract now lost), and to his invention and use of a special sighting instrument for measuring the angular width of the sun. Archimedes here also provides our sole substantial testimony of the heliocentric cosmos of Aristarchus (cited for its being vastly larger than the conventional geocentric systems).

From the prefaces to his works, we learn that Archimedes maintained collegial contact with several scholars in Alexandria, notably Conon of Samos, an eminent astronomer in the court of Ptolemy III Euergetes; the geometer Dositheus; and Eratosthenes of Cyrene, noted for his contributions to geometry and other sciences, for literary scholarship, and for his directorship of the Alexandrian Library. "Publication" in the case of most of Archimedes' writings consisted of their being forwarded to Alexandria, with an explanatory preface addressed to one or another of these men. Hints of their personal relations emerge: that Archimedes held Conon in high esteem for his mathematical acumen, that he was impatient over Dositheus's insistence on fully elaborated proofs, and that with Eratosthenes he perceived (rightly or wrongly, we do not know) a potential for making his own geometric discoveries. It becomes clear that for Archimedes himself the *heuristic* effort to expand the domain of known results in geometry takes precedence over the criticism of proofs, but in this respect he seems already to be confronting a certain scholastic temperament among his Alexandrian colleagues.

At a few places Archimedes provides hints of his views on the nature of mathematics. In the preface to *Sphere and Cylinder*, for instance, he distin-

guishes between the properties of figures per se and our knowledge of them: remarkable results, like Eudoxus's theorems on the pyramid and cone or his own on the sphere, however simple in form, might long evade recognition even by most acute intellects. In *Method* he separates heuristic strategies, like his own "mechanical method," from rigorous demonstrations. The latter are obligatory if one is to claim the right actually to know or to have established a result. Nevertheless, informal methods have an indispensable role to play, for they bring to light results that might not otherwise be evident and offer guidance in the working out of proofs. To the extent that such statements may seem obvious to us, they define how deeply the Archimedean conception of research is engrained in the Western tradition of mathematical science.

The core of Archimedes' work builds directly on the "exhaustion" technique first developed by Eudoxus. Indeed, Archimedes' citations provide valuable testimony to Eudoxus's work. They suggest that Archimedes could refer firsthand to Eudoxus's writing, rather than through an intermediary version, but that Eudoxus's methods are generally well represented by the formulations in Euclid's *Elements,* Book XII.

Archimedes' most elementary geometric effort is his study of the circle, as presented in the short tract *Dimension of the Circle.* The version of this tract that survives in Greek cannot represent the original version, for commentators—among them Hero, Pappus, and Theon—cite the work according to a significantly different text form. In fact, it appears that the medieval Arabic translation (made in the 9th century) is founded on a Greek prototype superior to the extant Greek version, although even that text is at best an adaptation. Nevertheless, collating the extant versions with citations in earlier commentaries, we can piece together with reasonable confidence the content and technique of Archimedes' treatment.

Its two essential results exploit the Eudoxean method of polygonal approximation to establish measures for the area and circumference of the circle. By the first, in proposition 1 (as stated in the Greek and medieval versions) Archimedes demonstrates that any circle equals a right triangle whose two legs equal, respectively, the radius and the circumference of the circle. As cited by Hero and Pappus, however, an alternative phrasing is used: that the area of the circle equals half the product of its radius and circumference. The technique of proof follows the model of Eudoxus's theorem on the circle, as given in *Elements* XII.2, that circles are as the squares on their diameters.

Archimedes' proof falls into two cases, in accordance with an indirect mode of reasoning: if this product *(Z)* does not equal the circle *(C)*, then it is either less than it or greater. If less, we can construct, via continued bisection of arcs, beginning from the square inscribed in the circle, an inscribed regular polygon P such that the difference $C - P$ is less than the difference $E = C - Z$. That this is possible is known from the Eudoxean bisection principle: since the procedure of forming the octagon from the square, for instance, dimin-

ishes the remainder from the circle by more than half, and this applies in each subsequent stage of the construction, the remainder can be made arbitrarily small (cf. *Elements* X.1, as invoked in XII.2), and thus, in particular, less than the hypothesized difference E. Thus, *P* must be greater than *Z*. But the perimeter of the polygon is less than the circumference of the circle, while its apothem (the line drawn from the center perpendicular to any side) is less than the radius. Thus, the area of the polygon, equaling half the product of its perimeter and apothem, must be less than *Z*. This contradiction thus excludes that *Z* can be less than *C*. Similarly, if *Z* is supposed greater than *C*, a contradiction is inferred by considering a sequence of regular polygons circumscribed about the circle. Thus, since *Z* can be neither greater nor less than *C*, it must equal *C*.

By the same process of polygonal approximation, in proposition 3 Archimedes calculates that the ratio of the circumference to the diameter of the circle (namely, the constant we represent by π) is less than $3\frac{1}{7}$ but greater than $3\frac{10}{71}$. The computation is among the finest specimens of arithmetic procedure from ancient mathematics outside the astronomical literature. To derive the upper bound, Archimedes works out the sequence of circumscribed polygons, from the hexagon to the dodecagon and so on, ending with the 96-gon; for the lower bound, he takes the corresponding inscribed figures. The values for the initial hexagons require estimates of $\sqrt{3}$, for which Archimedes cites, without explanation, $\frac{1351}{780}$ as upper bound and $\frac{265}{153}$ as lower bound. An extensive literature supplying possible reconstructions has arisen among modern commentators, tantalized by these odd-looking but extraordinarily good approximations (for instance, they are optimal values within the sequence of continued fraction approximations to the root). Each subsequent polygon requires application of the equivalent of a trigonometrical rule for half-angles, namely, $\tan(\varnothing/2) = \tan\varnothing/(1 + \sec\varnothing)$, which is here proved in a geometric form. Applying the rule requires the taking of irrational square roots; although the text does not explain how its cited values are derived, they appear to depend on applications of the so-called Heronian rule: $\sqrt{A} < (a + A/a)/2$, for any convenient initial estimate *a*. Thus, Archimedes' computation displays not only geometric ingenuity in its basic organization but also considerable arithmetic ingenuity in its execution.

With this effort, the estimate $3\frac{1}{7}$, which Archimedes here derives as an upper bound, enters the history of mathematics for the first time. Through the geometric manual by Hero of Alexandria (1st century C.E.), if not earlier, it becomes a fixture in practical geometry. But Archimedes is reported to have improved these estimates in another writing, now lost, which is also mentioned by Hero. One possible reconstruction of his result (for the stated figures are corrupt) leads to a lower bound of $3\frac{15}{106}$ and an upper bound of $3\frac{17}{120}$, which could be obtained via inscribed and circumscribed 640-gons. By a simple averaging technique, these bounds suggest an intermediate estimate of

$3\frac{16}{113}$. This value, which was derived independently by the Chinese geometer Tsu Ch'ung-chih in the 5th century and in the Renaissance by the Flemish computist Adriaen Anthoniszoon, as cited by his son Adrian Metius (1625), exceeds the true value of π by less than $\frac{3.7}{10}$, and would require polygons of no fewer than 10,000 sides to be established rigorously.

The Eudoxean procedure also underlies Archimedes' measurement of the parabolic segment, as being equal to $\frac{4}{3}$ the triangle having the same altitude and base as the segment (*Quadrature of the Parabola*, prop. 24). Archimedes forms a sequence of polygons inscribed in the segment *(S)* via successive bisection of the base and shows that these tend arbitrarily close to the segment. Since, further, the inscribed triangles, constituting the successive increments from each polygon to the next, decrease in the ratio 1 to $\frac{1}{4}$, each inscribed polygon is the sum of the initial triangle *(T)* plus its 4th, 16th, 64th, and so on. Archimedes shows that the sum of finitely many parts in this ratio is always less than four-thirds of *T* by an area equal to one-third the last term in the series. Since that term can be taken as small as desired, the polygonal sequence (which converges to the segment) must also converge to $\frac{4T}{3}$. By a standard two-part indirect proof, Archimedes then shows that either hypothesis—that *S* is greater than $\frac{4T}{3}$ or less than $\frac{4T}{3}$—leads to contradiction. One observes that the basic plan of this argument lies completely within the Eudoxean manner, employing only inscribed polygonal figures converging to the limit from below.

As Archimedes himself observes, his measurement of the parabolic segment marks the first case where a curved figure in the class of the circle or the conics has been found equal to a rectilinear figure. The problem of circle quadrature, whose history among the Greeks extends back at least to Hippocrates of Chios, some two centuries before Archimedes, seems to have attracted Archimedes' attention. While, as we now know through researches by Lindemann in the 19th century, no quadrature by means of algebraic functions (hence, by constructions via circle and straightedge) is possible, nevertheless a quadrature is possible by means of transcendental curves. One such is the Archimedean spiral, whose first definition appears to be due to Archimedes' mentor Conon. In the treatise *On Spiral Lines,* Archimedes establishes the condition for drawing the tangent to a spiral, which, conversely, provides a solution for the circle quadrature: the intercept of the tangent with the line drawn at right angles to the radius vector through the point of tangency equals the arc of the circle subtended by the angle lying between the initial position and the radius vector and having as its radius that same radius vector.

A natural extension of these measurements of plane figures is the consideration of curvilinear solids. One result is so remarkable in this context that Archimedes is said to have commanded its diagram to be engraved on his tombstone: a sphere inscribed in a cylinder, representing his discovery that

the two solids, both in volume and in surface area, have to each other the ratio of 2 to 3.

In his *Sphere and Cylinder* Archimedes sets out the formal demonstrations of the corresponding theorems: that the surface of the sphere equals four times the area of any great circle (prop. 33); that its volume equals that of a cone whose altitude equals the radius of the sphere and whose base equals its surface area (prop. 34). Analogous results are given for the surface of spherical segments and the volume of spherical sectors and segments. Characteristic of the demonstrations of these results is the use of a variant form of convergence method, where the one-sided Eudoxean approximation is replaced by a two-sided manner. For an example one can consider the treatment of the circle in *Sphere and Cylinder* (props. 1–6), which provides an alternative to the Eudoxean manner of *Dimension of the Circle*. Archimedes shows that it is possible to construct two regular polygons, one circumscribed about the given circle, the other inscribed in it, such that their ratio is less than any preassigned ratio greater than 1 : 1. For using two lines in the given ratio as hypotenuse and leg of a right triangle, one takes the angle contained by them and constructs by successive bisection of a right angle an angle less than it; taking this as the central angle of a circumscribed and an inscribed regular polygon drawn in the same circle, one shows that the ratio of their perimeters is less than the given ratio. Similarly, one can construct two such polygons whose areas have a ratio less than any preassigned ratio greater than 1 : 1. From this it becomes possible to construct inscribed polygons exceeding any area that is less than the circle, and circumscribed polygons less than any area that exceeds the circle. Such polygons are required as auxiliaries in the indirect proofs of the measurement theorems.

This two-sided convergence typifies all the Archimedean measurements, save for the circle measurement of *Dimension of the Circle* (prop. 1) and the second of the two parabola measurements given in *Quadrature of the Parabola* (prop. 24). For these proofs Archimedes states a special principle of continuity (now sometimes called the Archimedean axiom), which, he says, fills a gap in the Eudoxean proofs, namely their assumption of a "lemma" (that any finite magnitude, on successive bisection, can be reduced to less than any preassigned finite magnitude of the same kind). This Archimedes reformulates in a manner more flexible for application in proofs, as in *Quadrature of the Parabola*, prop. 16: that of two finite homogeneous magnitudes, the lesser, by being added to itself a suitable, finite number of times, can be made to exceed the greater. This is often noted as the appropriate condition for excluding infinitesimal magnitudes, since no zero magnitude, however many times multiplied, can ever exceed any finite magnitude of its kind. But the bisection lemma provides an adequate condition for the same end. In context one sees that Archimedes' intent is to replace the bisection lemma with a more evident condition. One infers that he does not have before him the Euclidean treat-

ment of this material, since Euclid's definition of "having the same ratio" (*Elements* V, def. 4), his proposition on the bisection (X, prop. 1), and their applications in the "Eudoxean" propositions of Book XII, would have rendered Archimedes' lemma superfluous.

Biographical anecdotes celebrate Archimedes' exploits in the practical fields of mechanics. Recognizing the principle of leverage, for instance, and deploying it in the form of compound pulleys for the hauling of ships, Archimedes is said to have extrapolated his feat, boasting "Give me a place to stand and I will move the earth." In some reports, the device associated with this earth-moving ambition is called the *charistiōn*. This heightens the audacity of the boast, as Archimedes' theory-inspired imagination outruns the physical evidence at hand, since the device is nothing other than the humble steelyard (often known as the Roman balance) used by merchants for weighing goods.

Pappus mentions an Archimedean tract *On Balances (Peri zygōn)* for a dynamic conception of the principle of leverage: that the greater circle overpowers the smaller circle when the turning is about the same center. This latter conception underlies the proof of the balance principle (that weights balance each other when they are inversely proportional to their respective distances from the fulcrum) that in certain medieval tracts forms the basis for a geometric account of the action of the unequal-armed balance (the steelyard). Although in the Arabic and Latin versions of the tract the author is named as Thabit ibn Qurra, the names employed for the balance (*garastūn* and *karaston*, respectively) and nuances in the technique of proof indicate their ultimate dependence on a Greek treatment of the *charistiōn* based on an Archimedean tradition. The key result is to show, via an indirect proof much like that used for the quadrature of the parabola, that if a section of a uniformly weighted beam in equilibrium is replaced by an equal weight suspended at its midpoint, there is no change to the equilibrium. From this one can work out the weight needed to bring into equilibrium a beam suspended off center, the theoretical correlate of the steelyard.

The medieval texts thus furnish insight into a lost portion of Archimedes' mechanical work—indeed what appears to be an early stage of his efforts in mechanics—for absent from them is the principle fundamental for Archimedes in all his extant mechanical writings, the concept of "center of gravity." No explicit definition of the barycenter is given in these works, but the commentators Hero and Eutocius, relying on other lost works, provide two formulations. In the topological sense, the barycenter is taken as that point at which a given figure or body, if supported there, will maintain its disposition relative to the horizon. Alternatively, in the quantitative sense, the barycenter of two figures is that point that divides the line joining their respective barycenters such that the weights will be inversely proportional to their distances from it. A geometric proof of the latter is given in *Plane Equilibria* I, props. 6–7. From this Archimedes determines that the barycenter of any par-

allelogram lies on the line bisecting its parallel sides (props. 9–10), that the barycenter of any triangle lies on the intersection of its medians (props. 13–14), and that the barycenter of the trapezium divides the line bisecting its parallel sides in a given ratio (prop. 15). In *Plane Equilibria* II, Archimedes determines the barycenter of the parabolic segment as being the point dividing its axis into segments in the ratio 2 : 3 (prop. 8).

Archimedes extends these results to the determination of barycenters of solids: e.g., that the barycenter of the cone divides its axis in the ratio 1 : 3; that the barycenter of the paraboloid divides its axis in the ratio 1 : 2; and similarly for segments of the sphere, ellipsoid, and hyperboloid. The formal demonstrations are now lost, but some of them are presented in a heuristic manner in the extant *Method*. This writing is devoted to examples of what Archimedes calls his mechanical method, a procedure for the determination of the content and center of gravity of figures by means of a conceptual weighing.

For the parabola, for instance, Archimedes considers an arbitrary section of the segment, taken parallel to the axis, and shows that since its length is to that of the section of the containing triangle as the abscissa to the base of the segment, if the base of the segment is extended and conceived as an equal-armed balance with the segment suspended along one arm, then the line in the segment, upon being transposed to the opposite end, will exactly balance the line in the triangle in its given position. Then, if all the lines in the segment are so transposed, the entire segment, now set at the opposite end of the balance, will balance the entire triangle in its position. Since, further, the barycenter of the triangle lies one-third the distance of its arm from the fulcrum, and the areas of the segment and the triangle are inversely proportional to the distances of their barycenters from the fulcrum, the segment is thus found to be one-third the triangle.

Employing the same procedure of sectioning and weighing, Archimedes shows how to find the volumes and barycenters of spherical and conoidal segments. At the end he employs it toward the measurement of two types of solid formed by sections of the cylinder. In all these cases, Archimedes insists that the method has only heuristic value, the theorem requiring its formal geometric demonstration to be considered rigorously established. In *Method* he includes such proofs for the cylindrical solids, but for the others defers to prior demonstrations. Modern critics have been especially impressed by Archimedes' application of indivisible sections, a method richly exploited by Cavalieri, Kepler, and their followers in the 17th century, and so have focused on this feature as what must disqualify it, in Archimedes' mind, from being a valid demonstration. But in the first account of the parabola in *Quadrature of the Parabola*, Archimedes replaces the indivisible sections with narrow trapezia in an indirect proof that still requires the mechanical assumptions, and he follows this with the alternative, strictly geometric treatment, involv-

ing only summations (as sketched above). This duplication of proof would hardly be called for if the first quadrature were considered adequate. Further, by naming his procedure the *mechanical* method Archimedes emphasizes that the barycentric elements are its essence, the indivisibles being merely an auxiliary feature to facilitate its execution.

Resonating far beyond the narrow domain of mathematical history is the story of Archimedes' discovery of the basic principle of hydrostatics. According to the account in Vitruvius, Archimedes was asked by King Hieron to determine whether a certain dedicatory wreath was worked of pure gold, rather than of gold alloyed with silver. Pondering over the problem, Archimedes happened to notice, as he entered the bath, how the level of the water rose higher the more deeply he immersed himself in it, and then suddenly realized the general principle involved. Elated by the discovery, he rushed out, naked, crying, *"Heurēka!"* ("I have found it!").

The more sober exposition of these principles is given in the writing *On Floating Bodies.* Postulating an incompressible fluid medium, Archimedes proves two basic properties of immersed bodies: if a solid is lighter than the fluid (that is, of a lesser specific gravity), then it will float, and the floating body will displace a volume of the fluid equal to its own weight (props. 4–6); if the body is heavier than the fluid, it will sink, such that its weight in the fluid is diminished by that of an equal volume of the fluid (prop. 7). From the latter principle one can reconstruct a method for solving the "wreath" problem. The design of an actual device, a hydrostatic balance for determining the specific gravity of bodies, is transmitted and attributed to Archimedes by Arabic writers following the authority of Menelaus (2nd century).

A miscellany of Archimedean results are attested outside the corpus. His construction of the regular heptagon by means of a sophisticated variant of *neusis* is extant in an Arabic version. A solution of the angle trisection, also by *neusis,* is reported in Arabic sources, and appears to have inspired the method via conchoid devised by Nicomedes. A method of cube duplication, this too via *neusis,* presented by Hero and related to a Nicomedean construction via conchoid, may be related to an Archimedean precedent. The rule for finding the area of a triangle from its three sides, presented by Hero, is referred to Archimedes by Arabic commentators. Pappus summarizes Archimedes' description of the thirteen semiregular solids. In a remarkable document, the epigram on the "cattle number," addressed to Eratosthenes, Archimedes sets out a deceptively simple arithmetic problem whose solutions require solving a quadratic form of the "Pellian" type and would be numbers running into hundreds of thousands of digits. It is doubtful, however, that Archimedes himself possessed the means to complete that solution.

In one account of Archimedes' death reported by Plutarch, as the Roman invaders finally breached the defenses of Syracuse, Archimedes, alone, "having given both mind and gaze" to the investigation of a certain geometric

construction, failed to notice the coming of the Romans and was killed by a soldier for refusing to follow him before completing the problem and its proof. The stereotype favored by the intellectual Plutarch portrays Archimedes as possessed of "such mind and depth of spirit and richness of theorems" that despite a reputation for superhuman ingenuity, through his mechanical inventions, he saw the latter pursuits as contemptuous and base and instead devoted himself only to the beauty and precision of pure inquiry. In modern judgments, by contrast, not only Archimedes' practical inventions but also his masterful insights into the applications of geometry in mechanics and hydrostatics are esteemed as paradigms of the fruitful liaison of theory and practice that underlies great achievement in the physical sciences.

WILBUR KNORR

Bibliography

Heiberg, J. L. *Archimedis opera omnia,* 2nd ed. 3 vols. Leipzig, 1910–1915; repr. Stuttgart, 1972. The English version by T. L. Heath (Cambridge, 1897; suppl. 1912) is based on Heiberg's first edition.

Dijksterhuis, E. J. *Archimedes.* Copenhagen, 1956; repr. (with corrections and a bibliographical supplement by W. R. Knorr) Princeton, 1987.

Knorr, Wilbur. *Ancient Sources of the Medieval Tradition of Mechanics.* Florence, 1982 (supplement of the Annali dell'Istituto e Museo di Storia della Scienza).

———. *The Ancient Tradition of Geometric Problems.* Boston, Basel, and Stuttgart, 1986; repr. New York, 1993.

———. "Archimedes and the Elements: Proposal for a Revised Chronological Ordering of the Archimedean Corpus." *Archive for the History of Exact Sciences* 19 (1978): 211–290.

Schneider, Ivo. *Archimedes: Ingenieur, Naturwissenschaftler und Mathematiker.* Darmstadt, 1979.

Related Articles

Demonstration and the Idea of Science; Technology; Mathematics; Euclid

ARISTOTLE

MANY SOURCES OFFER US INFORMATION about Aristotle's life. Certain accounts, owing to their temporal proximity, seem to carry more weight than others. Hermippus of Smyrna, for example, an Alexandrian who lived during the 3rd and 2nd centuries B.C.E., wrote *Lives* and a work on Aristotle; he seems to be one of the chief sources for Diogenes Laertius's collected *Lives of Eminent Philosophers* (2nd or 3rd century C.E.). At the same time, like the biographies of all great men, Aristotle's is accompanied by a string of anecdotes, often unfounded and sometimes malevolent. What philosophical meaning can we grant to certain aspects of Aristotle's biography that we may reasonably consider well documented? Three of these aspects will be considered here, though not in chronological order: the influence on Aristotle of his father's profession, Aristotle's role as tutor of Alexander the Great, and his relations with Plato within the Academy.

Aristotle was born in 384 B.C.E. in Stagira, a Greek colony situated in Thracian Chalcidice. His father, Nicomachus, was physician to Amyntas III, king of Macedonia, whose grandson Amyntas IV, too young to reign, was to be supplanted by his uncle Philip II, father of Alexander the Great. Why was Aristotle born in Stagira and not in Pella, residence of the Macedonian court? Was it because Stagira was a colony of Chalcis, his mother's native town? We do not know for sure. Polybius says Stagira was a colony of Andros. Was Aristotle's father, as some suggest, on a spying mission in Chalcidice, a region coveted by Macedonia, which wanted access to the sea? His parents were both Asclepiads, members of one of the lineages that claimed descent from Asclepius, god of medicine, and that passed down a medical tradition.

Aristotle's partiality for the natural sciences is generally attributed to this family origin. Although in the 4th century B.C.E. it was possible to acquire a medical education by paying for it, medical knowledge was transmitted principally within families. Thus Hippocrates, who was born three-quarters of a century before Aristotle, was the son and grandson of physicians: he had two sons who were also physicians and who taught medicine to their own sons; they all claimed to be descendants of Asclepius through his son Podalirus. A well-established tradition discloses privileged ties between the family of Hippocrates and the court of Macedonia, since Hippocrates had attended King Perdiccas II. These ties lasted until 310, the year in which a grandson of Hippocrates was assassinated by a son of Antipater, twelve years after Aristotle's death. The historian Dionysius of Halicarnassus (1st century B.C.E.) and sev-

eral other biographers maintain that Aristotle's father was a descendant of Machaon, the other son of Asclepius. But this raises two questions. Why was a Machaonite present in the king's court, when the dynasty's doctors ordinarily came from Cos and were descendants of Podalirus? And why did Aristotle not become a physician? The usual response to the second question is that he was orphaned too early to have been influenced by his father. However, such a response fails to take into account the importance of lineage, of the extended family—which, in Aristotle's case, passed along the medical tradition. As for the first question, perhaps we should minimize the medical importance of Nicomachus, and when Diogenes Laertius writes that Nicomachus "resided with Amyntas, the king of Macedon, in the capacity of physician and friend" (*Lives* V.1), we should probably stress the latter term. Moreover, if we give some credence to the testimony of the *Suda*, a 10th-century Byzantine encyclopedia that assigns two articles to Nicomachus, one on medicine, the other on physics, the image that emerges shows Nicomachus as more of a theoretician than a practitioner of the art of medicine. In other words, from this viewpoint, the intellectual breach between Aristotle and his father was considerably less profound than it is ordinarily thought to have been: Aristotle explicitly makes the healing art depend on knowledge of causes, the best physicians being also "physical philosophers" (*Of Sense and Sensible Objects* I.436a19; *On Respiration* 21.480b24).

Around 343 Aristotle was called to Mieza by Philip II of Macedonia to undertake the education of Philip's son Alexander. If this pedagogical connection between "the greatest of philosophers" and the "greatest of conquerors" has struck many as peculiar, the explanation lies chiefly in a retrospective illusion: Aristotle, then in his forties, had doubtless not yet founded his own school, and contrary to what Plutarch says in his *Alexander*, he was certainly not "the most famous and learned of philosophers" in his day (*Lives* VII.2). Alexander at the time was thirteen years old. Aristotle's tutorship seems to have lasted seven years, until Philip's death and Alexander's rise to power. Although Philip wished to give the young prince a Greek education, it is likely that for numerous reasons, mostly political, he had no desire to send the boy to Athens; we may also suppose that teachers as important as Plato or Isocrates would not have come to Macedonia to spend several years. The friendly relationship between Nicomachus and the Macedonian dynasty must have had a decisive effect on the king's choice. As to the later tradition, which shows Alexander reproaching Aristotle for having made his *Metaphysics* available to the public, asking his teacher's advice before undertaking his expeditions, and sending him specimens of exotic animals, they are all entirely without historical foundation.

All of these details finally put into even more striking relief one essential fact: of the association between Aristotle and Alexander, of the life they shared for several years, we know almost nothing. Aristotle mentions Mace-

donia in *Politics* only in connection with other barbarian warlike peoples, pointing out one of their strange customs: a man who had killed no enemy would wear a harness as a belt. What seems certain, however, is that relations between master and pupil deteriorated. In 327 Alexander put to death Callisthenes, a relative of Aristotle who was the historian of his expeditions. Callisthenes had ridiculed the king's pretentiousness in obliging his subjects, and also his Greco-Macedonian companions-at-arms, to prostrate themselves before him in the Oriental manner. The anecdote reveals an essential point: Aristotle shows himself reserved, to say the least, toward Alexander's grand project of merging Greek and Persian customs and characteristics under a single political system. For Aristotle, a natural difference forever separates the Greeks, who are destined to live free under *political* institutions, from the barbarians, who are fated to live in servitude under despotism and slavery. This is what Aristotle allegedly explained in a work now lost, *Alexander, or the Colonies*. The complete disruption that separates the Hellenic from the Hellenistic period, in our way of scanning history, was produced, in contradiction with Aristotle's firm convictions, by the one whom he had probably taught that the city was the natural framework for perfect political life.

When he arrived in Athens at the age of seventeen, Aristotle attended classes at Plato's Academy. It is not certain that Plato was present at that time, but later encounters must have been frequent, since Aristotle remained at the Academy for twenty years, and the Platonic school was a veritable society of philosophers and scholars leading in large part a common life. Echoing a more ancient tradition, Theodoret, a 5th-century bishop of Cyrrhus, wrote that "even during Plato's lifetime, Aristotle openly opposed him and made war on the Academy, without respect for the school of which he had been a fervent disciple." But testimony that is probably more reliable gives us an almost diametrically opposed image of the relations between Plato and Aristotle. The incontestable differences between master and disciple seem not to have spoiled Aristotle's attachment to Plato, and it appears that he did not found his own school, the Lyceum, until after the death of Speusippus, nephew and successor to Plato as head of the Academy. Perhaps he finally decided to make this institutional break when the members of the Academy chose Xenocrates as head over Aristotle himself. Aristotle seems to have remained, if not a Platonist, at least a member of the Platonist "sect" as long as he could. But his fidelity to the school proves nothing about the relationship between Plato's doctrines and his own, for within the Academy, at least in Plato's time, there was no orthodoxy to which its members were obliged to submit.

The doctrinal relations between Plato and Aristotle have also been the subject of opposing opinions. Thus the great Neoplatonist commentators on Aristotle see more continuity than rupture between the two philosophers; among the Neoplatonists of the 5th and 6th centuries C.E., Aristotelian doctrines are taught as a sort of introduction to Platonism. The fact remains,

nonetheless, that tradition has had an undeniable tendency to deepen the differences between Plato and Aristotle. In Raphael's *School of Athens,* the idealist fascinated by mathematics and the realist student of biology gesture in opposite directions. The same opposition appears in every realm. In politics, for example, it was common until recently to contrast a visionary totalitarian with a pragmatic centrist endowed with good sense. Thus the problem of "Aristotle's Platonism" is generally approached by interpreters in narrow terms: on what points and to what degree has Aristotle accepted a certain Platonist doctrine? The question is a fruitful one, and it led to a recent turnabout in Aristotelian studies. But in any account of Aristotelian philosophy a larger question must be faced at the outset, and implicitly asked again at every turn. In continuing a fundamentally Platonist enterprise by other means, was Aristotle not the best possible spiritual son Plato could have had?

This turnabout was the work of Werner Jaeger and his book *Aristoteles: Grundlegung einer Geschichte seiner Entwicklung,* published in 1923. Challenging the usual presentation of Aristotelianism as a system, Jaeger offered a genetic vision of the Stagirite's thought. Although he was not the first to suggest that the contradictions in the Aristotelian corpus could be explained by further rearrangements of texts from different epochs, Jaeger pursued this research much more thoroughly than any of his predecessors, and he based it, above all, on the hypothesis that Aristotle, who had once strongly adhered to Platonism, had gradually moved away from it. Thus the Aristotelian texts could be arranged over time in terms of a decreasing "coefficient of Platonicity." Used in specific instances, this method can be productive: it is clearly significant, for example, that in *Topica* Aristotle takes the Platonic tripartite division of the soul for granted, though he disavows this doctrine in other works. But in using the method systematically as he does, Jaeger actually relies on an implicit psychological hypothesis. It seems self-evident to him that Aristotle would inevitably embrace the teaching of someone as charismatic as Plato *before* breaking free of it. However, the contrary, more Oedipean assumption—held, for example, by Ingemar During—is no less plausible: overwhelmed by a Plato at the height of his powers, the young Aristotle might well have done all he could to distance himself from his master's teaching before returning, after the master's death, to more Platonic positions on certain issues.

The very status of the Aristotelian corpus that we have at hand precludes us, doubtless forever, from choosing among hypotheses of this kind. It is often said that Plato and Aristotle, along with Plotinus, Epictetus, and Sextus Empiricus, differ from the other ancient philosophers in that they left us entire texts, whereas the Presocratics, the Stoics, and the Epicureans left little but fragments and evidence cited by later writers. In fact, the texts of Aristotle that have come down to us belong to neither category. According to a story reported by Strabo, the library of Theophrastus, which contained works

by Aristotle, among others, was placed by ignorant heirs in a cave for safe-keeping. It was only at the beginning of the 1st century B.C.E. that Aristotle's texts were published by the peripatetic philosopher Apellicon of Teos, who repaired the damage done by time as best he could. Sulla had Apellicon's library moved to Rome, where it ended up in the hands of a grammarian, Tyrannion, who published Aristotle's work at least in part. Plutarch tells the same story, adding that Andronicus of Rhodes, head of the Lyceum, acquired Aristotle's works and published them, after reorganizing them in a "corpus" accompanied by "tables." This is still the form, more or less, in which we read Aristotle today.

This story is probably not without some romantic accretions. Andronicus has even been suspected of having originated it, to convince his contemporaries that the texts he published had not been published previously. Nevertheless he reports a troubling but undeniable fact: after Theophrastus, who succeeded Aristotle as head of the Lyceum, the texts of "our" Aristotelian corpus seem to have been unknown. What is more, in Cicero's day—and Cicero was a contemporary of Andronicus—a whole set of works by a *different Aristotle* was in circulation among cultivated groups: these were often dialogues in the Platonic style, and their readers gave them high marks for their literary qualities. They were intended for publication, but they have survived only in the form of citations or allusions in the works of later writers—sometimes ample enough to allow us to reconstruct their structure and content. These works may be what numerous ancient authors, and Aristotle himself, called the exoteric writings, as opposed to the treatises reserved for members of the Lyceum.

The texts that have come down to us under Aristotle's name have thus undergone a double series of interventions. In the first place, Andronicus (who may simply be the spokesman for a group) corrected, rearranged, and occasionally rewrote the texts, suppressing some passages and adding explanatory glosses to others. Such practices, which offend our sense of textual authenticity today, were in widespread use until the modern period. The "written" writings, such as poetry, or the texts that Plato or Aristotle produced for publication, may well have escaped such editorial violence, generally speaking. But what was the initial state of Aristotle's scholarly treatises as edited by Andronicus? A second intervention comes into play here. The texts of the corpus are very probably not course notes jotted down by students or handed out by Aristotle, as some have claimed. But we may have to see them as the result of a collective endeavor in which the master incorporated certain critiques and remarks offered by his assistants—who were actually colleagues rather than students. The collective character of the development of these texts must have removed the last scruples (assuming there were any) on the part of later editors when they took over the corpus that had been transmitted to them.

These basic assumptions about the texts put the chronological hypotheses of today's commentators in an inescapable vicious circle. Since the texts of our Aristotelian corpus are not, properly speaking, *from Aristotle's own hand*, they cannot be studied objectively, that is to say, according to stylistic criteria like those that have allowed interpreters to be in general agreement about the chronology of Plato's dialogues, or at least groups of dialogues. Even the rare historical allusions, as well as the internal references contained in texts that may have been revised over and over, can be used only for very imprecise dating. Chronological hypotheses must therefore depend on *doctrinal* criteria. If we judge that texts in which we think we find some Platonic resonances were written before other passages in which such are missing, it is because we are convinced that Aristotle, at first a faithful Platonist, later distanced himself from Platonism. At the same time, interpreters who think that Aristotle distanced himself from Platonism claim to rely on textual divergences attributable to the different dates of composition. The most exasperating factor in the whole affair is perhaps that it is difficult to deny that Aristotle's positions evolved over time.

The Aristotelian corpus now in our libraries thus offers a deceptively systematic form, which does not mean that Aristotle did not intend to construct such a system. The systematic order imposed from the outside on Aristotle's texts is partly canceled out by one of the fundamental characteristics of Aristotelian learning: the relative autonomy, theoretical and methodical, of the various "branches" of Aristotelian speculation. But when this autonomy is recognized for what it is, it gives us a remarkable freedom—that of beginning the exposition of Aristotelianism *at any point at all.*

Post-Andronican editors adopted the custom of putting a collection of logical and epistemological treatises, written at different times, at the head of their editions; they group these under the title *Organon.* This title bears the trace of a polemic in which Aristotle himself could have taken no part: contrary to the Stoic thesis that logic, or dialectic, was a science, and more precisely one of the three parts of philosophy along with physics and ethics, the Peripatetics—partisans of Aristotle who earned that label owing to their master's habit of philosophizing while strolling about *(peripatein)*—maintained that it was an *instrument* (the meaning of the Greek word *organon*) for the sciences and philosophy. This instrumental quality is not the only factor to justify grouping together the various treatises that constitute *Organon.* Although it is a grouping that cannot be attributed to Aristotle himself, it is nevertheless compatible with an Aristotelian perspective. Two philosophic movements, Sophistics and the Eleatic movement followed by Plato, stand out against the background of the Stagirite's epistemological enterprise.

Sophists knew how to make the weakest discourse stronger, and thus to make it prevail. *Topica,* which is probably one of Aristotle's earliest works, codifies the dialectical discussion (its last book is traditionally published sepa-

rately under the title *On Sophistical Refutations*). When a topic is proposed for discussion, one of the interlocutors declares that he wishes to defend a position that the other will undertake to demolish by his questions. This confrontation takes place before one or several arbiters, whose role is to declare the winner. An examination of the different situations that each of the protagonists in the dialectical confrontation can encounter leads Aristotle to distinguish the different forms of argumentation and, more precisely, of reasoning. The most effective form of reasoning, and for the ancients the most compelling, is the scientific syllogism, which deduces from true premises a necessary conclusion that inherits the truth of the premises. But it would be mistaken to think that Aristotle has only the theory of scientific discourse in view. He means to work out the rules of argumentative discourse in general. The dialectical syllogism, for example, would not have the same "force" as the scientific syllogism, because it rests on what Aristotle calls "valid opinions" *(endoxa)*. By the term *endoxos*, which comes from *doxa* (meaning both opinion and good reputation) and means of good reputation, illustrious, Aristotle indicates opinions that have a certain weight, a certain force, because they are shared by everyone or by eminent persons—"by all, or the majority, or the most distinguished among them." Finally, deductive reasoning is not the only method through which Aristotle seeks to form a theory. What he calls *epagōge*, a term translated only approximately as induction—because it is a question of passing from particular cases to general definitions—also has its place in the Aristotelian overview of forms of reasoning.

The aim of argumentation is to persuade. Aristotle sought to codify the rules of persuasion, that is, to make them rules of an art *(techne):* the art of rhetoric, the subject of the treatise by the same name. For Aristotle, rhetoric is not so much the art of convincing as the art of "considering in each situation what is calculated to convince." It is not a science with a definite object but an art that can be applied to all domains. Even science does not always find a way to be convincing, Aristotle tells us, and the scholar should not disdain rhetoric. Several ancient witnesses tell us that *Rhetoric,* and also *Poetics,* which presented the theory of literary "genres" and of which only one book remains, have sometimes been included in *Organon;* at all events, the problem of their inclusion in *Organon* has arisen. Ammonius, for example, a Neoplatonist commentator at the end of the 5th century C.E., thinks we should distinguish between a syllogistic component and a nonsyllogistic component in Aristotle's logic; *Rhetoric* and *Poetics* should be included in the latter.

The fact remains that, in the eyes of posterity, Aristotelian logic has been almost exclusively reduced to the theory of scientific discourse. Scientific discourse is a true discourse that bears on necessary, therefore eternal and unalterable, objects. Through Plato and his distinction between science and opinion, Aristotle is a direct heir of Parmenides on this fundamental point. Two criteria allow us to say that we have knowledge *(episteme):* when we know

the cause of the thing of which we claim to have knowledge, and when we know the thing by means of demonstration *(apodeixis)* or "scientific syllogism." The articulation between these two criteria is one of the most delicate problems in the interpretation of the Aristotelian theory of cognition. We will come back to the issue of causality in discussing Aristotelian physics; for the moment, let us look at demonstration. Aristotle saw the syllogism, a form of deductive reasoning in which, once certain things are posited, others necessarily follow from the data, as the form adequate to all demonstration in the theoretical sciences, including mathematics. A syllogism is a set of propositions in which the conclusion (Greeks are mortal) is deduced from two others, called premises (all human beings are mortal, all Greeks are human beings), that have a common element (human beings), called the middle term. This definition presupposes a preliminary reduction. For Aristotle, a proposition, a statement that must be either true or false, can always be reduced to the *attribution* of a predicate to a subject by the intermediary of the copula *is:* "Socrates walks" can be reformulated as "Socrates is walking." We shall not study here the different kinds of propositions distinguished by Aristotle.

This theory of proposition presupposes an inventory and a study of simple terms. This is why, in the traditional, systematic, and nonchronological order that comes from Andronicus of Rhodes, the first treatise in *Organon* is the one we call *Categories*. Here we find what may be one of the fundamental presuppositions, and, in any case, one of the principal enigmas, of Aristotelian thought. The term *category*—from the verb *katagorein*, which means to speak against someone, to accuse, impute to, hence to attribute, predicate—is used to label what Aristotle describes as "the things that are *meant*, when we . . . speak of uncombined words" (*Categories* II); he gives the following list: substance (man), quantity (two cubits long), quality (white), relation (double), where (in the Lyceum), when (yesterday), posture or position (seated), state or condition (has shoes), action (cut), affection (be cut). But with Aristotle, categories are not only irreducible semantic units. They also express the different meanings of "being," all of which relate to the fundamental meaning of the term, which is substance *(ousia)* in the ontological sense. For Aristotle this correspondence between logic and ontology is unproblematic; the difficulties are left to his interpreters.

Thus a special way to articulate the attributive propositions among themselves is what constitutes the language of science. To be scientific, a syllogism must first be formally valid. Accordingly, in a treatise later known as *Prior Analytics,* Aristotle studied the various ways to combine different types of propositions. Thus to say, "If A is affirmed of all B and B of all C, then A is affirmed of all C" is valid, while the syllogism "A is affirmed of all B; A is affirmed of all C; therefore B is affirmed of all C" is not valid. There are 256 possible forms of the syllogism, of which only 24 are valid.

But a valid syllogism, to be scientific, must also be true, that is to say, as we

have seen, it must rely on true premises that are causes of the conclusion. At the core of every science there are premises that are absolutely primary, not deduced from any anterior premise: these are the principles (*archai,* plural of *arche*). The way Aristotle intends to establish these principles is, for his interpreters, a long-standing subject of controversy. Among the different sorts of principles, Aristotle is interested above all in definitions. He devotes lengthy developments to them in his epistemological treatise known as *Posterior Analytics.* Aristotle discards two solutions: the argument according to which everything is demonstrable, including the principles, an argument that leads to an infinite regression; and the argument in *Meno* on recollection of knowledge acquired by the soul before its incarnation. The modalities of the construction of definitions in Aristotle are very complex, if only because there are several types of definitions, one of which has particular scientific importance for him, the one that posits a definition as language that "exhibits the essence" of a thing at the same time that it reveals the cause of the thing. Thus to define thunder as a noise in the clouds is to give a merely descriptive and ultimately verbal description; to define it, instead, as the noise caused by "an extinction of fire in a cloud" is to reveal its cause and its essence, at least according to Aristotle's meteorology. However rigorous and elegant the syllogism may be, one must acknowledge its sterility: the syllogism, a deductive procedure, is not an instrument of discovery or creation of information. What seems to us the main point of the scientific work accomplished in the Aristotelian framework will thus be the construction of definitions. This epistemological practice is perfectly in accord with the ontological nature of Aristotle's world; we shall see that that world is composed of autonomous entities, the substances *(ousiai).*

Of the difficult doctrine concerning the establishment of the principles of each science, there is one thing we can remember. It is through a process of reascending from particular cases to general notions and propositions, a process called inductive (though improperly, for Aristotle does not think that a general notion necessarily emerges from the consideration of all particular cases, or even from many of them), that the spirit moves from immediate experience to abstract thought. The basic condition of our ability to constitute the general principles of the sciences is thus fundamentally rooted in a "power" that we share with the other animals, sense perception, which Aristotle then describes as "an innate faculty to discriminate." Only a difference of degree between human beings and the other animals allows the former, notably because they are endowed with superior memory permitting them to agglomerate many sense impressions from different periods into one unique idea, to undertake this kind of theoretical elaboration. Thus Aristotelian science depends on a biological reality, arranged by a beneficent Nature. Man's biological (and especially sensory) perfection is the basis for his destiny as a theoretical animal.

This bond between science and human nature leads us to consider what we might call the other face of Aristotelian science, one that has been neglected by modern interpreters. Science is both a body of doctrine (thus we speak of "physical science") and a systematic construction of which we have just given the broad outlines. But science is also a state *of the subject who knows:* Aristotle defines it in this sense as a disposition that makes one qualified to demonstrate. At the end of one of the most famous passages devoted to the definition of science (*Posterior Analytics* I.ii.71b27–35) Aristotle repeatedly associates knowledge *(eidenai)* with conviction *(pisteuein),* coordinating them by a strong tie *(te kai),* the use of which serves, in Greek, to mark the bond between two realities of the same nature. While for Plato conviction *(pistis)* is an inferior form of knowledge, when Aristotle writes that "the required condition of our knowledge or conviction of a fact consists in grasping a syllogism of the kind which we call demonstration" (ibid. I.ii.71b26–28), he is representing the two faces of knowledge as complementary and equally worthy. The learned man is one who has succeeded in giving a necessary, hence unshakable, form to what he knows. This is the aspect stressed by the Stoics: they go so far as to say that knowledge is the soul of the wise man—this soul being a body—organized in a particular way. One who knows causally or demonstratively, or both, may very well not know more things than one who knows empirically and accidentally, but he knows them in a different way. If, for example, what he knows are natural phenomena, the syllogistic formulation of his knowledge reveals nothing new to him, but it allows him to form propositions that reflect necessary connections existing in nature. Thus, speaking of the following syllogism: "all broad-leafed plants are deciduous"; "all vines are broad-leafed"; therefore "vines are deciduous" (ibid. II.xvi.98b4–11), Aristotle remarks that this syllogism should be preferred to an equally valid one that would demonstrate that vines are broad-leafed plants because vines are deciduous ("every deciduous plant is broad-leafed"; "all vines are deciduous"; "therefore all vines are broad-leafed"; I.xvi.98b11–16). In fact, the first gives the causes of the conclusion, not the second. A passage in *Generation of Animals* and some post-Aristotelian texts reveal that Aristotle thought the lack of warm humidity was what caused leaves to fall (as well as hair, and so on); one can assume that, for him, winter cold congealed warm sap. Now, a broad-leafed plant has a greater circulation of sap. The syllogism thus has no part in the *discovery* of the cause of a phenomenon: these are probably observations, as well as lines of reasoning of the at once hypothetical and generalizing sort that allowed Aristotle to arrive at his theory about why leaves fall.

In "Aristotle's Theory of Demonstration," a well-known article published in 1969, Jonathan Barnes concluded that if all Aristotle's writings on syllogisms had been lost, our idea of Aristotelian science would not have been affected; thus syllogistics had a pedagogical and not a heuristic objective. While

this is true, we must be more specific: the objective was pedagogical not in the sense that syllogisms would serve to help a student acquire more knowledge, but in the sense that to relate the different objects of knowledge syllogistically with one another allows the student to re-form his knowledge (in the etymological sense of the word *reform*), that is, it gives him the form of the immutable necessity that gives knowledge some resemblance to the divine.

Aristotle occupies a primary place in the history of natural science. Taking up the torch of speculation on *physis,* which Aristotle says the Socratics had tried to extinguish, he claims to have brought the line of "natural scientists" to a close, notably through his "discovery" of the theory of the four causes. In another respect, he puts an end to research on nature *(historia peri physeos)* as an all-embracing enterprise.

The Aristotelian doctrine is a sort of recollection of earlier speculations; this is very apparent in the article entitled "Nature" published in Book V of *Metaphysics,* which is a sort of dictionary of philosophical notions. In this book Aristotle distinguishes, as he did with other ideas, several valid meanings of the word *nature.* The term *physis* describes first the growth of things that are capable of growth: the same term is used to designate the growth process itself, that from which a thing grows (the seed, for example), or that which provokes the growth process (the stock of the vine is, in this sense, the nature of the bunch of grapes). In other respects, the nature of a statue is also the bronze on which the sculptor practices his art; but the nature of a thing, as Empedocles was well aware, is also the manner, proper to that thing, in which its constituents are mixed and arranged among themselves. More precisely, the nature of a being is its *ousia,* its essence or substance, which Aristotle calls its form *(eidos).* For Aristotle, the primary and fundamental meaning of "nature" will then be "the essence of those things which contain in themselves a source of motion" (*Metaphysics* V.iv.1015a12–14). This passage calls for several observations.

First of all, the integrative capacities of Aristotelian philosophy are manifest here in the highest degree. The old Presocratic *physis,* a bottomless reservoir from which everything comes and to which everything returns, as well as Nature itself as the set of manifold combinations of elements, is not relegated to the shadows of myth. On two conditions the ancient physics continues to tell its share of the truth. First, in Aristotle's closed, finite, and eternal world the very idea of the emergence of the total being of things from nonbeing, or of cosmic order from chaos—which Parmenides had shown we could not even envisage—disappears. Second, nature is no longer either all of being or even the most important part of being. The whole of nature, a closed system of self-propelling realities, draws its movement from outside itself. The immovable prime mover moves the "high heavens" but is itself neither moved nor material. It is *pure actuality*—that is, it contains no potentiality, nothing it has to bring about. The eternal heavenly bodies themselves are

marred by a certain potentiality, which betrays itself by change, if only movement in space. According to this difficult doctrine, an incorporeal mover moves a corporeal sphere that it has not created, and in which, owing to the fact of its own completeness, it can have no interest. Aristotle's solution raises as many difficulties as it resolves: the heavens move because they are animated by a movement of desire toward the prime mover. The supernatural is thus necessary for the existence and the coherence of nature.

The heavenly bodies are composed of a special element (which was later called quintessence, because it is different from the four elements present in our region of the universe; according to later accounts, Aristotle called it "aether") that is affected by an *eternal* movement of circular translation. In contrast, in the "sublunar" region—that is, the one under the orbit of the moon, which is the nearest to us of the heavenly bodies—change is eternal, but at the same time it is more complex and less regular. By the word *change (metabole)*, Aristotle means change in terms of substance (coming to be, or generation, and disappearance), quantity (increase and decrease), quality (alteration), or place (movement in space). All natural bodies in the sublunar region are composed of four elements—Earth, Water, Fire, and Air—which eternally transform themselves into one another, each body having a *natural* movement owing to its elementary composition: heavy ones move downward (hence, if nothing prevents them, toward the center of the earth), while light bodies move upward. These movements are less regular than the movements of the heavenly bodies; in addition, the beings involved in such movements are not eternal. Accordingly, beings that have in themselves the principle of their movements are natural. A dog is a natural being; a bed is not, at least judging by its form, which is given it by the cabinetmaker—for by its matter, wood, a bed is also in a certain respect a natural reality.

Natural science, then, will be knowledge of self-propelling beings. Aristotle delimits his territory in a programmatic passage at the beginning of his *Meteorologica:* "We have already dealt with the first causes of nature and with all natural motion; we have dealt also with the ordered movements of the stars in the heavens, and with the number, kinds and mutual transformations of the four elements, and growth and decay in general. It remains to consider a subdivision of the present inquiry which all our predecessors have called Meteorology. . . . After we have dealt with all these subjects let us then see if we can give some account, on the lines we have laid down, of animals and plants, both in general and particular" (I.1.338a20–339a8).

Every attentive reader of the Aristotelian corpus will easily recognize the treatises to which the author is alluding here: *Physics, On the Heavens,* and *On Coming-to-Be and Passing-Away,* as well as *Meteorologica,* the zoological works, and the treatise on plants that is lost (or that may never have been written). In these scientific works we find no trace of the syllogistic form, one of the criteria that defined science for Aristotle. This omission confirms our

idea that syllogistics had no heuristic function for Aristotle. At the same time, causality is omnipresent, in the form of a systematic account of causes in *Physics,* and actively in the other treatises that seek the causes of the phenomena they are studying.

It was certainly not Aristotle who introduced the word *cause* into philosophy (a word that translates the feminine noun *aitia,* or the neuter adjectival noun *aition*). But he gave the search for causes an unprecedented development by a triple move. First, he identified a sure understanding of science with knowledge of the cause; next, he limited interrogation about the cause to a finite number of four questions; finally, he made the theory of the four causes the secret mover of all human thought, since these are the causes that, consciously or not, his predecessors, philosophers and also "mythologists," were seeking. If we read carefully the celebrated third chapter of Book II of *Physics,* in which Aristotle examines the notion of cause in itself, we see that he turns to "manners of speaking" for the various ways to say that something is an *aition.* In Greek the adjective *aitios* means responsible, often in the sense of guilty, and *aitia* means both the responsibility accruing to a thing, and especially to a person, in a result or an action, and the accusation, the cause for complaint.

According to Aristotle, there are four ways in which something "is said to be" responsible for something else. In one sense, the responsible element in the statue is the bronze from which it is made; in another sense, a certain numerical relation is responsible for the octave; in still another sense, the one who has promulgated a decree is responsible for it; finally, the health I would like to recover is responsible for the fact that I waste my time at sports. Thus it turns out that a complete analysis of our ways of speaking furnishes us with the four causes that are actually at work in nature: taken in the order of the above examples, these are the material, the formal, the efficient, and the final.

We must say "in nature," because it is to certain physical beings that Aristotelian causality applies *completely.* God, in fact, is not really answerable to causality: without matter, nothing affects him or sets him in motion, and he has no end but himself. Perhaps a formal cause might be found for him that would be nothing other than himself. Certain natural beings are only partly dependent on causality. The heavenly bodies have as causes only the desire that connects them to the prime mover and their own nature. We must presumably resist an excessively teleological explanation of nature in Aristotle: to be sure, the meteorological phenomena obey the necessary "laws," but they exist to no purpose. As for fabricated things, one can apply causal analysis to them only indirectly: it is because there is a nature that the bed has a material cause in the natural beings that are trees, and formal and efficient causes in the mind and muscles of cabinetmakers, who are natural beings. Causality is thus the trace both of nature's grandeur and its misery. Causes

are fully causes only in the case of natural beings. Paradoxically, this claim appears in Aristotle's remarks about the coalescence of the different causes. In a frequently cited passage from *Physics,* he writes: "Clearly, then, the 'becauses' being such and so classified, it behoves [*sic*] the natural philosopher to understand all four, and to be able to indicate, in answer to the question 'how and why,' the material, the form, the moving force, and the goal or purpose . . . But in many cases three of these 'becauses' coincide; for the essential nature of a thing and the purpose for which it is produced are often identical . . . and moreover the efficient cause must bear some resemblance in 'form' to the effect . . . for instance, man is begotten by man" (II.vii.198a22−29).

Reading such a passage shows us what Aristotle has immediately in mind when he speaks of natural beings: they are living beings, and in particular, animals. Aristotle's "biology," the supreme achievement of his natural history, constitutes such an imposing enterprise that it is hard to find anything comparable in the history of science. When he indicates that the essential nature of a thing and the purpose for which it is produced are identical—his examples could include statements such as the following: "the definition [the essence] of the lung is to be an organ intended to cool the organism" (*Parts of Animals* III.vi; cf. *On Respiration* 475b, 476a, b)—Aristotle in fact provides several of the principal keys to his biology. Far from being descriptive, his biology is explanatory. This is one of the reasons his principal object is not whole animals but their "parts"; his project is to define the functions common to all animals—respiration, for instance—and to study the variations in organs intended for these functions. Aristotle's zoology is fundamentally *teleological.*

Aristotelian teleology has often been caricatured by those who have not made the effort to appreciate its subtlety. It rests on a radical tension. Aristotle's finite and eternal world is perfect, and perfection and eternity are in a sense interchangeable, since only that which cannot improve or degrade itself can continue to be what it is for eternity. This perfection can be seen also in "our" world where, as Aristotle often reiterates, "Nature always produces the best." But we must remember that the sublunar world is a tissue of regularities that imitate the eternal and perfect round of the stars; therefore this world cannot claim absolute perfection. The presence of matter, which is indeterminate in that it is potentially the various beings, brings an irreducible element of irregularity into the sublunar world.

Thus Aristotle is the first philosopher from whom we have retained a theoretical analysis of chance—which is in itself a sort of cause. In Aristotle's phallocentric view of animal reproduction, for example, the male provides the form and the female the matter. The "resistance" of matter to being given form is the origin of "deviations," that is, of monsters, as Aristotle remarks in *Generation of Animals,* the first of these deviations being the birth of a female. Here, eternity plays the regulating role: because the reproduction of

species is eternal, genetic monstrosities are drowned in a flood of "normality." In this manner, deviations cancel one another out. The image that makes Aristotelian finalism most comprehensible may be the one proposed in *Generation of Animals:* Nature is like a good head of household who arranges things for the best—one is tempted to call it a tinkerer. To take a well-known example, *it so happens* that animals of great size have a superabundance of earthy matter; thus Nature profits by it to make horns that will serve as weapons for self-defense. But since this quantity of earthy matter is not unlimited, it is impossible to provide these animals both with horns and with many teeth. That is not a problem: Nature alleviates this inconvenience by providing several stomachs—Aristotle meticulously describes the digestive system of ruminants—to convert nourishment that would otherwise be insufficiently masticated into useful food.

Nature's tendency toward perfection must also "play tricks" with the teeming abundance in the living world. Although the *History of Animals* counts more than five hundred species, Aristotle never intended to enumerate all the animals, nor to classify them as the 17th- and 18th-century taxonomists undertook to do. While he sketched out a sort of scale of living creatures, nowhere does he claim that this diversity is in itself a debased image of divine unity. For Aristotle, to be sure, man is the most perfect animal—in a remarkable formula, he refers to him as "the animal the most in accordance with nature" (*Progression of Animals* IV.706a18)—and according to him, with respect to man the other animals are "like dwarves," that is, they are ill-proportioned copies. But it is important to note that no teleological principle can account for the diversity of living things. There must, of course, be prey for predators, but that is not enough to explain this diversity. Everything happens, then, as if nature were trying out all possible organic combinations without a fixed objective. Aristotelian biology is thus far from being entirely teleological. Not only is it impossible to explain all the characteristics of living things through final causes, but Aristotle never misses an occasion to remind us that the biologist must also study the vital *mechanisms,* owing to the necessary interaction of the properties of matter.

It is then well within this domain of nature, and first in the domain of living nature, that causality functions completely. Cause, which is a cause of something, is the trace of a splitting that is itself a sign of imperfection, but it takes on its full meaning only in the domain of natural regularities. This is the image that posterity has retained of Aristotelian natural history: Diogenes Laertius, in his cursory and disappointing résumé of Aristotle's philosophy, does not fail to note that "in the sphere of natural science he surpassed all other philosophers in the investigation of causes" (*Lives of Eminent Philosophers* V.32). Aristotle's "scientific" treatises reveal an astounding desire for knowledge. Our perception of this largely neglected part of his work has been distorted for too long by a naive continuist prejudice: certain of Aris-

totle's "exact" observations aroused enthusiasm, but they clearly did not weigh heavily in the balance against the "errors" of a biology that is not comparable to ours in its objectives, its methods, or its theoretical or material resources.

In Aristotle, the domain of physics is thus *defined* by metaphysics, though this term was not introduced until the 1st century C.E., when Aristotle's editors used it to designate what ought to be studied "after physics," whether this "after" indicates a difference in the dignity of the objects or simply a pedagogical order of exposition. To define means both to limit and to explain. Yet Aristotle's metaphysics gestures in two directions: toward theology and toward ontology.

Aristotle speaks of God, the immovable prime mover, in quasi-mystical terms. God is pure actuality and, as such, perfect; he is alive, but he is impassible, since it is the desire that the highest heaven feels for him that makes heaven move, while God himself loves nothing and no one; it would be detrimental to his perfection to act on something other than himself, or to think of something other than himself: God is "thought thinking itself." Theology is in contact with natural science, as we have seen, through the intermediary of the celestial bodies. These share with God individual eternity, of which all the cyclical or recurrent phenomena of the sublunary world are imitations; this is the case, for example, with the specific—not the individual—eternity of animals and plants. The concept of *imitation* allows Aristotle to account for the behavior and the coherence of the sublunary world. The distance is no less great between the Aristotelian divine and sublunary, on one hand, and the Platonic intelligible and sensible, on the other. But there is, as it were, a world between the Aristotelian imitation of superior realities by sublunary beings and the Platonic participation of realities inferior to eminent realities. Weak as they are, the terrestrial substances do not have a delegated reality; they are not simply shadows cast by the ideal world, and thus they deserve to be considered in themselves. All the more so in that whatever imitates teaches us about what it imitates.

It is precisely because the universe, and especially our sublunary region, is neither an emanation nor a copy of God that metaphysics is not reduced to theology, and that we need a discourse about being *(ontology)*. The absolute simplicity of God means that he is not subject to such a discourse. But nondivine beings are characterized by division and dispersal, as the very way we talk about these things reveals. In fact, our discourse combines elements of varying status. This is something the Sophists did not realize when they affirmed that, as Plato's *Euthydemus* had already claimed, to teach Clinias was to make the ignorant Clinias disappear, thus to kill Clinias. Others were similarly unaware of this feature of discourse: this was the case with Antisthenes, and with the Eleatics, for whom every predication is necessarily tautological, and for whom to say about something anything other than "it is" amounts to

saying that being is not. These difficulties, which had fascinated—that is to say, partially paralyzed—Greek thinkers prior to Plato, were resolved by Aristotle thanks to his distinction between essence and accident. In the sentence "Clinias is learned," "Clinias" signifies the essence *(ousia)*, which can be affected by different accidents, like "learned," "white," "here." Thus we rediscover the ontological side of the doctrine of categories. As for the impossibility of movement, which, according to the Eleatics, amounted to having being proceed from nonbeing, Aristotle reduced that by his distinction between act and power: the ignorant Clinias is potentially a learned man. But this distinction is accompanied by a condition, which is why Aristotle took the Eleatic objection fully into account: fundamentally, actuality is anterior to potentiality. An embryo, for instance, becomes an infant and an infant becomes an adult because the embryo has the potential to develop the characteristics that an adult has transmitted to it. "Man begets man" because there have always been men; Aristotle sometimes explains this assertion by saying that man is *by nature* anterior to the infant, even if infants are chronologically anterior to the adults they will become.

Thus, "there is a science which studies Being *qua* Being, and the properties inherent in it in virtue of its own nature" *(Metaphysics* IV.i.1003a21–22). For us, this claim presents many difficulties; let us consider just one of them. According to Aristotle, being is not a genus that can be divided into species, as, for example, the genus "figure" can be divided into rectilinear figures and curvilinear figures. In *Sophist*, Plato had already felt compelled to acknowledge this, in part by making being a sort of "transversal" genus. Now, one of the underlying features of Aristotelian epistemology is that there is one science corresponding to one genus. This means, in particular, that if form and sound are two different species, propositions concerning knowledge of forms (geometry) are not transferable to sounds (acoustics), except by analogy, as when one says that a certain sound is "sharp." Any attempt to describe the science of being in strictly "scientific" terms, then, cannot help but be inadequate. Are we encountering, here, the specter of the universal science that had up to that point claimed to be philosophy, and of which Aristotle was the first to reject the possibility?

Aristotle gave this science of being as being two different but complementary contents. In Book IV of *Metaphysics,* where he assumes its existence, he declares its object to be the great principles common to all the sciences, such as the principle of noncontradiction, which is established in the "dialectic" manner, that is to say, by remarking that even the discourse of anyone who would oppose this principle is impossible. But elsewhere in the same book and especially in the books considered to be central to *Metaphysics* (Books VII, VIII, IX), Aristotle reduces the study of being to that of the first of its categories, substance or essence *(ousia)*. This "ousiology" is the very heart of Aris-

totelian metaphysics. The *ousia* is characterized by three essential properties: it exists by itself; it is separate; it is "cause and principle." Several realities can, in differing degrees, claim the title of *ousia*. The universal and the species can be considered *ousiai*, but in a secondary sense, because the universal exists as a logical (intellectual) entity.

On this point, the break with Plato is very clear. In one sense, matter is *ousia*, but matter does not exist by itself, and the *ousiai* that we perceive most immediately in our concrete experience—sensible substances—are what they are more by virtue of their form than by virtue of their matter. Form alone is nevertheless not fully *ousia*, because to describe the ontological units that are natural substances only by their form is to give a schematic knowledge of them. To indicate their form, Aristotle uses the terms *eidos* (which indicates the visibility of a thing) and *schema* (which refers to its contour), for there is a complex and nonarbitrary relation between form and matter. Not just anything can be made of anything. The term *ousia* applies most properly, in the end, to what Aristotle designated in a formula that has retained a great part of its mystery: the *ti en einai*. This expression, which the medievals translated as *quiddity*, seems to be a question turned, as it were, into a substantive, as is also the case with the expression *to ti estin* (the what-it-is), used to designate the essence of a thing. But in relation to the *ti estin*, the *ti en einai* indicates a superior degree of properness. Aristotle suggests in *Posterior Analytics* that the *ti en einai*, the "essential definition of a subject," is constituted by the elements that are proper to the essence *(ti estin)*, or, following a correction proposed by a modern editor, by what is proper among the things that are in the essence (II.vi.92a7).

Nevertheless, Aristotle claims that the *ti en einai* of natural substances does not contain their matter, because matter is to a certain extent accidental. Thus the quiddity of a (sensible) natural being, while not a part of that being, is something other than the being. Let us pursue the paradox, at least that of the expression, right to the end: the *ti en einai* of a thing is, in a way, more truly that thing than the thing itself is. Thus it is with the soul, which is the vital active force of the animate body: it is more truly the living thing than the living body itself. Platonism is thus actually reversed: there is indeed something else more really "this" than "this" thing I see and touch: but the former reality is not outside or "above" the latter.

The case of the soul is an interesting one. In his treatise *De anima*, Aristotle carefully skirts the problems that the whole philosophic tradition presumably expected to see him address, particularly the problem of the immortality of the soul. The soul consists of embedded "faculties": for example, an animal that has a body adequately constituted for this purpose is able to grow and reproduce itself, to discriminate among the types of information provided by its environment, and to act in that environment. Thus the soul plays a

greater role in defining the living body than does the living body itself, because the soul gives the *causes* of vital manifestations, which anatomical and physicochemical knowledge of organs, tissues, and so on, does not do.

But the sublunary world is not simply the domain of living beings. It is also the domain of those animals capable of deliberation and rational choice that we call humans. The opening of Aristotle's *Politics* has a tone we would identify as sociobiological: the human tendency to associate in cities is given as the result of the other natural tendencies that lead to sexual union for reproduction, and to the association between inferior and superior beings. However, the "realm of human affairs" is controlled by its own rules, and "practical philosophy" does not propose to transpose laws developed in the field of theoretical knowledge into its own realm. Here, too, we are far from Plato. To grasp the peculiar characteristics of Aristotelian practical philosophy, let us confine ourselves to examining two of its key ideas, that of virtue and that of excellent constitution.

The translation of *arete* by virtue, while it has a long tradition of its own, still remains dangerous because of the connotations of the word. For Aristotle, *arete* is the excellence of some thing. He remarks that we can speak of the *arete* of a tool or a horse. Nevertheless, he uses the term most particularly in the ethical realm. Now "ethical" comes from *ethos*—character—which, Aristotle tells us, "comes from a slight modification of *ethos*," a word that means the habitual way to be, the one that results from experience and education. If someone has acquired the habit, from childhood, of being intemperate, intemperance will become for him a habitual, almost natural, way to be. Ethical virtue then will be a state of being virtuous, rooted in the human subject by long experience. But while Aristotle acknowledges that immorality and vice can procure satisfactions, he posits as the basis for his ethics the principle that virtue, which implies moderation of tendencies and self-mastery, is the principal—though not the only—element in happiness *(eudaimonia):* no one can be happy in suffering or misery. Now happiness is every human being's *natural end.* To be virtuous, then, for human beings, is to give themselves the best opportunity to realize their human nature fully. Still, in most cases people do not spontaneously choose virtuous conduct, and the best way to lead them to conform to what is basically their nature is to constrain them to virtue by imposing "good habits" on them from childhood. But, in contrast to the Christian sinner for whom the practice of virtue does not suppress temptation, and who is, therefore, yoked to an indefinite task of self-mastery, the virtuous Aristotelian, once established in virtue, is no longer tempted by vice, since virtue gives him the happiness that is his natural end. Consequently, as Pierre Aubenque showed very well in *La prudence chez Aristote,* although Aristotle denies ethical relativism—good and evil really do exist— he also refuses to set absolute objective moral standards. The virtuous man,

master of himself, who allows the capacities of his human nature full scope to flourish, does not conform to standards but is himself the standard. The Stoic wise man, who is always upright because there is a wise way of doing everything, including lying or killing, is not far removed; the wise man is the standard of virtuous action because he alone can determine what he should do, to whom, at what moment, and by what means.

This brief account shows the importance of education in the acquisition of virtue. For Aristotle, as for Plato, education is essentially a *political* matter. Life under good laws is what serves to anchor the good habits that lead to virtue in the minds of citizens, and especially in their children. Finally, then, public virtue, and consequently the public well-being, lie in the hands of legislators. But the practice of virtue itself, and not its mere acquisition, is political: against conventionalist theories of the social bond, Aristotle maintains that man's character is naturally political. This means that the city, in the Greek meaning of the term, is, for the individual, the place of his perfection. Hence all peoples and all individuals who cannot live in cities are excluded from this perfection.

Aristotle's political philosophy has long been distorted by interpreters. In fact, one cannot use the pretext that Aristotle separates himself from the Platonic project of the "ideal city" to conclude that he renounces political excellence. Every city, to make its citizens virtuous and therefore happy, must endow itself with an excellent constitution. For Aristotle, however, excellence is multiple. The type of constitution that can lead a city to virtue depends on the characteristics of the people involved, both psychological (these stem from a number of factors, including the climate) and historical. To a people barely emerged from a patriarchal society, royalty is acceptable, so long as it consecrates the preeminence of a man who prevails over the rest in virtue. But a good king is a king who spreads virtue and happiness throughout the social body. Consequently he digs the grave of royalty, for when virtuous people manage to form a group (a minority, to be sure, but a rather important one), it would be *unjust* for them to continue to obey a king whom they equal in virtue. It is just, however, for them to take in hand the affairs of the city and establish an aristocracy. When the majority of the citizens, owing to their virtue, deserve to exercise power, it will be necessary to establish a politeia, a word that designates in turn, in Aristotle, the constitution, whatever it is; the mere fact of living in a city; and a particular form of constitution in which a significant body of virtuous citizens holds power. This form of government could be called constitutional. It is clear, therefore, that laws correspond to constitutions and not the reverse: a given law requiring the sharing of wealth, for example, which would be just in a constitutional government, would be completely unacceptable under a monarchy. To each of these excellent constitutions there corresponds a deviant form: tyranny, oligarchy, and democracy

(which we would call demagogy). Under these regimes, the man or the group in power governs to his own advantage and not "with the common advantage in view": the very purpose of politics, which is the development of virtue in the bosom of a group of free and equal citizens, is then called into question.

For Aristotle, the philosopher should no longer govern. He should not even make laws. However, he can help train legislators, who will have to establish an excellent constitution or rectify a bad one and make it excellent. It is principally to this end that Aristotle wrote his ethical and political treatises. The Platonic Academy was intended to produce kings. Aristotle's Lyceum is content to turn out professors of political virtue.

Aristotle's posterity and influence have been immense. Despite the brief eclipse that his work suffered, antiquity did not cease to consider him one of the "divine geniuses" of philosophy (Cicero). The reorganization of learning and scientific research that was accomplished in Alexandria in the 3rd century B.C.E. incontestably bears an Aristotelian stamp. While Aristotle's work was almost entirely unknown to thinkers of the Latin West from the 7th century on, it was the principal force behind the development of Arab philosophy and science, through Arabic and Syriac translations, which were translated, in turn, into Latin starting in the 12th century. The rediscovery of Greek texts by Aristotle in the 13th century, which gave birth to the Scholasticism of Albertus Magnus and Thomas Aquinas, was a revolution whose scope we have difficulty measuring even today. Modern philosophy and science have been constructed in harmony with Aristotle or in opposition to him, but never without him. But more than the survival, recognized or unacknowledged, of a given Aristotelian doctrine, what Aristotle bequeathed to following generations is a way of thinking. If it is true, as the poet Coleridge claimed, that humanity is divided between Platonists and Aristotelians, the whole history of thought might be understood as a sometimes mute, sometimes violent confrontation between Platonic thought and Aristotelian thought. The latter might be defined by several invariables: respect for concrete reality, the understanding of which is the basis of all later theoretical elaborations; the autonomy of that reality, which bears in itself the rules of its own intelligibility; a systematic articulation among different domains that retain their own rationality. The theoretical frenzy provoked by the birth of physics in the 17th century did, to be sure, impose on Aristotelianism a theoretic purgatory of three centuries. The present era, on the contrary, is auspicious for Aristotle's thought: many of today's scholars are rediscovering an Aristotelian inspiration at the foundation of their own theoretical enterprises.

PIERRE PELLEGRIN
Translated by Rita Guerlac and Anne Slack

Bibliography

Texts and Translations

Aristotle: Opera. Ed. Immanuel Becker. 5 vols. Berlin: Academia Regia Borussica, G. Reimer, 1831–1870.

Aristotle. *Works.* 23 vols. Loeb Classical Library.

Studies

Aubenque, Pierre. *Le problème de l'être chez Aristote.* Paris: Presses Universitaires de France, 1962.

———. *La prudence chez Aristote.* Paris: Presses Universitaires de France, 1963.

Goldschmidt, Victor. *Temps physique et temps tragique chez Aristote.* Paris: Vrin, 1982.

Gotthelf, Allan, and James A. Lennox, eds. *Philosophical Issues in Aristotle's Biology.* Cambridge: Cambridge University Press, 1987.

Granger, Gilles Gaston. *La théorie aristotélicienne de la science.* Paris: Aubier, 1976.

Hamelin, Octave. *Le système d'Aristote.* Paris: Alcan, 1920.

Irwin, Terence. *Aristotle's First Principles.* Oxford: Clarendon Press, 1988.

Jaeger, Werner. *Aristotle: Fundamentals of the History of His Development* (1932). Trans. Richard Robinson. Oxford: Clarendon Press, 1948.

Lear, Jonathan. *Aristotle: The Desire to Understand.* Cambridge: Cambridge University Press, 1988.

Le Blond, Jean-Marie. *Logique et méthode chez Aristote.* Paris: Vrin, 1939.

Patzig, Günther. *Aristotle's Theory of the Syllogism.* Trans. Jonathan Barnes. Dordrecht: Reidel, 1968.

Pellegrin, Pierre. *La classification des animaux chez Aristote.* Paris: Les Belles Lettres, 1982.

Robin, Léon. *La théorie platonicienne des Idées et des Nombres d'après Aristote.* Paris: Alcan, 1908.

Related Articles

The Philosopher; Epistemology; The Statesman As Political Actor; Demonstration and the Idea of Science; Logic; Poetics; Theology and Divination; Language; The Question of Being; Ethics; Observation and Research; Cosmology; Physics; Rhetoric; Theories of Religion; Aristotelianism

DEMOCRITUS

THE ATOMIC THEORY OF MATTER was invented in the late 5th century B.C.E., during the lifetime of Socrates and about the time of the birth of Plato. Ancient writers attributed its invention to two men: Leucippus and Democritus. Leucippus is a mysterious figure of uncertain date and provenance. It is impossible from the surviving evidence to detach the contributions of Leucippus from those of Democritus; Democritus was better known and much more often quoted, and this article will make no attempt to distinguish the contributions of the two men.

Plato never mentions Democritus—a remarkable omission, since there is evidence in *Timaeus* that he was acquainted with Democritean atomism. Aristotle, on the other hand, frequently discusses his theories, occasionally associating him with Leucippus but usually mentioning only Democritus's name. Simplicius refers to a monograph by Aristotle entitled *On Democritus,* and books with this title are also attributed to Theophrastus, Heraclides Ponticus, Epicurus and his disciple Metrodorus, and the Stoic Cleanthes. According to the biographer Diogenes Laertius, fifty-two books by Democritus were arranged by Thrasyllus (who gave the same treatment to Plato's books) into tetralogies grouped by subject: ethics (two), physics (four), mathematics (three), music (two), and technical (two). There was also a miscellany of unclassified writings.

Not one of these books survives. The atomist tradition of Democritus and Epicurus proved to be notably antithetical to the interests of those who ensured the preservation of chosen portions of the classical heritage, especially in the period when education was in the hands of learned Christians. We are dependent for our knowledge of Democritus on quotations and summaries in other classical writers, many of them "hostile witnesses"—though it is worth noting that Aristotle himself, and Theophrastus, both treated his work with great respect, however much they disagreed with it.

Democritus was born around 460 B.C.E. and lived to an advanced old age. Several sources mention extensive travels in the course of his life—to Egypt, Persia, Babylon, "the Chaldaeans," even Ethiopia and India. He is said to have visited Athens and commented, "But no one knew me." Later sources began to give more and more stress to his cheerfulness of character, until he eventually became known and pictured as the Laughing Philosopher.

The achievement with which he will forever be associated is the theory that the universe is made of atoms and void. The arguments with which he

supported the theory were metaphysical, and drew virtually nothing from sense perception, nor (of course) experiment. An *"a-tom"* is something that cannot be cut. The earliest use of the word in surviving Greek literature is as an adjective applied to the grass in a sacred meadow. If Aristotle's testimony is right, Democritus's proof of the need for atoms in physics went like this. The contradictory of the proposition "There are atoms" is "All bodies are cuttable into smaller pieces ad infinitum." Suppose, then, that a finite body is actually cut up ad infinitum. What will be left? It cannot be small bodies of finite size, since the hypothesis was that the cutting is completed ad infinitum. It cannot be points with no size, since the original body could not be composed out of points. And it cannot be cut up in such a way as to be nothing at all. The contradictory thus being proved false, it remains that there are atomic bodies—bodies of finite size that in principle cannot be cut up. (The argument, paraphrased, is attributed to Democritus by name in Aristotle's *De generatione et corruptione* 1.2.316a11ff).

There is much modern controversy about the nature of Democritus's atomism. Basically there are two irreconcilable positions. One is that the argument outlined above was intended to apply only to "body," and the kind of division in question was simply the cutting up of bodies into smaller pieces. Nothing, then, was implied about theoretical or mathematical division: one might speak about half an atom or a quarter of an atom without talking nonsense. The second interpretation takes the atom to be a theoretically minimum quantity: a point with size.

There are advantages and difficulties in both interpretations. The first has the advantage that it is easy to understand how atoms may differ in shape, as they are required to do by the theory: parts of the atom may be distinguished in thought, so that one may be shaped like an H and another like an A. What is in favor of the second is that it appears to answer the Eleatic argument from which it plainly derives, whereas the other does not; and that the argument as given by Aristotle would apply just as well to a mathematical quantity as to a physical atom. Indeed, Aristotle says in another place (*De caelo* 3.4.303a20–24) that those who talk of atomic bodies (meaning Democritus and his school) clash with the mathematical sciences. This might perhaps be regarded as conclusive, since an atom that is only physically unsplittable does not clash with mathematics; but Aristotle is in a peculiar position on this subject, since he himself held that there is no "magnitude" except corporeal magnitude.

There are some slight but ambiguous indications that Democritus may have worked out a geometry that was not based on infinite divisibility. Plutarch (*De communibus notitiis adversus Stoicos* 1079.Eff) discusses at length a problem raised by Democritus: if a cone is sliced along a plane parallel to its base, what are we to say about the surfaces of the two resultant segments? If they are equal, and this applies to every such cut, then the cone has the properties of a cylinder. If they are unequal, then the sides of the cone are not

smooth but stepped, each step being one atom in thickness. Since all atoms are below the level of sense perception, the sides of the cone would appear smooth. It may be that Democritus proposed the stepped version as correct, and suggested that below the level of perception geometrical magnitudes are composed of indivisibles. There is no agreement among scholars, but the majority view now appears to be that Democritean atoms are physical bodies, and that mathematical extension was allowed by him to be infinitely divisible.

The atoms of Democritus have a strictly limited set of properties: they have shape, size, and (probably) weight, but no qualities such as color, heat, taste, and so on. There is no such thing as an atom of iron, as distinct from an atom of water. As to size, there are some texts that say that atoms may be of enormous size ("as big as the cosmos," Aëtius, in DK 68.A.47), although it is evident that all the atoms in our cosmos are below the level of perception. It is clear that they vary in shape, since the compound bodies that they form take on perceptible qualities according to the varieties of the component atoms. Indeed, we are told (Aristotle, *De generatione et corruptione* 315b8) that the perceptible varieties of compounds are infinite, and therefore the number of different atomic shapes is infinite.

Weight is a more problematic property. Aristotle and Theophrastus both report that the weight of atoms varies with their size; the doxographer Aëtius denies that Democritus's atoms have any weight, but although some interpreters accept this, and claim that weight is a property that emerges only when atoms are in some kinds of motion, Aëtius is heavily outnumbered. But it is still not an easy matter to decide what Democritus meant by weight. Aristotle defined it as a tendency to move toward the center of the universe. But Democritus's universe, being infinite, had no center. Democritus's follower Epicurus, a century later, took weight to be a tendency of all atoms to move parallel to each other in a particular direction through the infinite void. That is a theory that depends on a belief that our earth is more or less flat: the "downward" direction is simply the direction of free fall of a heavy body perpendicular to the earth's surface. Democritus too believed the earth to be flat, and it can be argued that his view of weight was the same as Epicurus's. (What other explanation did he give for the fall of heavy bodies in our cosmos?) Some scholars take the weight of Democritean atoms to be equivalent to their resistance to blows from collisions with other atoms. There is still no certainty about this.

What is certain is that Democritus described the atoms as moving in all directions, colliding and rebounding, and forming compounds whenever atoms of suitable shape and size happened to meet and join together. This is the way that worlds are formed. In the infinite void, infinitely numerous atoms are moving in all directions. Sometimes, a collection of atoms moves into "a great void," where they are caught up together in a vortex. The vortex acquires a

kind of skin or membrane around its outer surface (like the embryo of an animal?), thus confining a quantity of atoms within a finite perimeter. The vortex motion brings about a sorting of atoms by size and shape (as we can observe that the churning motion of breakers on the seashore sorts pebbles into groups by size and shape), and thus the heavier atoms congregate together in the middle to form an earth, in the shape of a flat disk (though some texts report that it was not round but elongated), and the lighter and more mobile atoms are extruded so as to form the air and the heavens. This idea gives rise to a problem that troubled many of the early philosophers, and survived to Epicurus's day: if earth is heavy, and if a piece of earth when detached from the parent body and dropped from a height falls until it hits the ground, what prevents the whole earth from falling through the air beneath it? The answer given by Democritus, and most of the others, was that its breadth prevents it from falling: it floats on the air underneath it, rather as a flat plate will float on water, although it will sink if tipped up sideways.

The details of the cosmogonic process are not clearly described in the surviving literature, but there are several important features that can be regarded as being beyond doubt. Since the universe is infinite, there is no limit on the number of worlds that can be formed by this process: we must take it that there are infinite worlds. (It is probable that Leucippus and Democritus were the first to hold this view, although some attribute it to Anaximander and others of the Presocractics.) All atomic compounds, including the worlds, come into being as a result of random collisions, and perish in the course of time by the dispersion of their component atoms. The cause of creation and destruction is "necessity"—that is to say, it has to happen as it does whenever the atoms fall into the appropriate patterns. There is (and this is crucial) no plan or design.

It is particularly disappointing that none of the texts about the formation of the cosmos has survived. The pressing need for a good description of Democritus's theories in this area has led scholars to attribute a great variety of texts to him—parts of book 3 of Plato's Laws, the early chapters of Diodorus, book 5 of Lucretius, and so on. But convincing arguments are lacking.

Democritus proposed a system in which none of the fundamental components of the world is perceptible: we are asked to believe that all the rich variety of impressions taken in by our senses in our dealings with the physical world is missing from the "real" world, which consists only of atoms and void. The paradox is made sharper by Democritus's vocabulary: he refers to the basic components of the universe as "the full" and "the empty," or as "beings" and "not-being." This is to go back to the language of the Eleatics, Parmenides and Melissus—but with a remarkable difference. The Eleatics insisted on a strict interpretation of "what is not." It is equivalent to nothing, and to talk about it is to say nothing rational. Leucippus and Democritus, on

the other hand, claim a kind of being for "what *is not*." It has no properties of its own except extension, it is just what separates one piece of being from another, it is contrasted with the "beings" that are atomic bodies, but nonetheless it is said to have a kind of being.

This dualism marks a retreat from the richer ontology of Democritus's predecessors. Anaxagoras classified a huge range of physical entities among the basic ingredients of the universe, and added a separate moving agent, which he called Mind; Empedocles reduced the physical substances to the four that came to be regarded by subsequent natural philosophers as the elements of all things: earth, water, air, and fire, together with the agents of change postulated in his own system, Love and Strife. Democritus banished the moving agents altogether and reduced the basic ingredients to the imperceptible pair, Being and Not-Being. The paradox that Not-Being itself has a kind of being is not explained.

There is some question about whether it is right to identify Democritus's "void" or Not-Being with space. The suggested alternative (Sedley 1982) is that it is not space itself but an occupant of space: thus there is space (for which we have no name in Democritus's terminology) that may be occupied by either "the full" or "the empty," both of which may move around and change places with each other. But Aristotle, at least (*De generatione et corruptione* 1.8.325a30), interpreted the void as the locus of the movement of "beings" (i.e., atoms) — that is, as being identified with space rather than as an occupant of space. That is certainly what the void meant to Epicurean atomists in the following century, and it is likely that Democritus had the same view of it.

The attention of philosophers has in recent years been directed at Democritus's epistemology. It is obvious that a philosopher who claims that the basic constituents of the universe are imperceptible must provide a link between human experience and his proposed ontology. There are in fact many remarks in the ancient literature about Democritus on this subject, and quotations of his own words, but they are by no means clear or unambiguous. We may begin with the most famous quotation, given in somewhat different forms by Galen and Sextus: "By convention [*nomōi*], sweet; by convention, bitter; by convention, hot; by convention, cold; by convention, color; but in truth, atoms and void" (frg. 9, cf. frg. 125). The problem is to interpret the meaning of Democritus's "by convention." The contrast between *nomos* and *physis* (convention and nature) was familiar from the teaching of the Sophists: it is a contrast between rules of behavior that have been decided on by the agreement of human beings, and those that are inevitably imposed by natural conditions such as the limits of human strength and endurance. But that contrast hardly seems applicable in this case. People do not decide by agreement whether they are experiencing heat or cold, or red or green; what

they may decide is whether the object itself has these qualities. The question, in other words, is one of ontology.

Sextus—a Skeptic himself—was able to find several other remarks by Democritus to reinforce his own position. Man is "separated from reality" (frg. 6); "in reality we know nothing about anything: belief is, for each of us, a reshaping" (frg. 7). "Of knowledge there are two forms, one legitimate, the other bastard; of the bastard breed are all these—sight, hearing, smell, taste, touch; the other is legitimate, but separate from these" (frg. 11).

But there are ample indications to show that Democritus was not in any strict sense a Skeptic; he was far from advocating the "suspension of belief" characteristic of later Skeptics. The text of Theophrastus's *De sensibus*—of which we fortunately have a long consecutive portion—shows that Democritus worked out a careful causal account of sense perception. The text gives details of the sizes and shapes of atoms that according to Democritus regularly produce this or that effect *(pathos)* in the perceiver. It is true that according to his theory we cannot directly perceive the elements of reality. But we can, he thought, work out the causal relations between the shapes and behavior of atoms of different shapes and sizes, and the sense impressions caused by their impact on the sense organs.

This is a simple-minded story, based on our large-scale sense experience. Democritus works with generalizations, such as that rough surfaces are unpleasant, smooth surfaces soothing. But it is notorious that people differ in their sense impressions of the same objects; according to Theophrastus, Democritus explains this by assuming that the objects themselves are made up of atoms differing widely in shape and size, and different observers are receptive of and respond to different shapes among the collection. He avoids saying that the same atomic shapes produce different results in different people: the causal link between atomic shape and the perceiver's *pathos* seems to be preserved intact.

But how did Democritus offer a causal account of our perception of objects at a distance? He constructed a theory of "images" *(eidōla* or *deikela)*, made of atoms, that flow from the surfaces of all compound objects. They produce their effect on the perceiver by direct contact with the sense organs—hence, sight and hearing are in fact a kind of touching. Democritus is quoted by Aristotle *(De anima* 419a12) as saying that if the intervening space were empty, one might have an accurate view of an ant in the heavens. There are traces in the sources of a more complicated theory of sight, too, according to which a stream passes from the eye of the beholder, meets and interacts with the stream of images from the object to produce a revised image, which is then received by the eye. The former theory is worked out and recorded in much greater detail in the Epicurean texts, especially Lucretius, *De rerum natura* 4.

To sum up, Democritus was clear that only the properties of shape, size,

and weight (and we should add motion) are properties that exist at the basic level of reality; we have no direct acquaintance, by sense perception or by any other means, with the atoms and void that are alone "real." But by making analogies between our experience of the properties of large-scale objects and our perception of them, we can infer what kinds of atoms are the causes of particular sensations in us. Our inferences about the nature and behavior of atoms are not fanciful and arbitrary.

It is striking that Aristotle often quotes Democritus for his observations in the field of biology, especially in embryology. True, he has no time for Democritus's notion that the soul, the essential feature of life, is made of spherical atoms, as fire is. The reason for Democritus's choice is that spherical atoms may be thought of as especially mobile, and thus able to transmit motion to the parts of the body almost instantaneously. Aristotle objects that this is much too simple: how could spherical soul-atoms also be responsible for the body's being at rest? A completely different set of concepts is needed, such as desire and intention. But he enters into debate on terms of equality with Democritus on many embryological problems, such as the contributions of the male and female parent to the embryo, the cause of monstrous births, the infertility of mules, and so on. There are also fairly extensive references to Democritus in Aelian's *Natural History*. The random citations do not enable us to put together any body of theory.

What is most paradoxical is that Aristotle never once mentions Democritus in any of his ethical writings, and yet the vast majority of the surviving quotations of Democritus's words are on subjects that might loosely be called moral. In the anthology of Stobaeus there are 130 maxims or sayings attributed to Democritus. A work called *The Golden Sayings of Democrates* turned up in a 17th-century manuscript, and since some of them overlap with the collection in Stobaeus, they have all from time to time been attributed to Democritus, with little authority.

Most of the fragments are of the character of *gnōmai*—that is to say, short, memorable, self-contained sayings, often phrased in the form of a balanced antithesis or a telling simile, presenting a bit of moral advice. A few examples will be enough to illustrate the genre: "Fine speech does not hide a bad act, a good act is not damaged by defaming speech" (frg. 177). "There is good sense in the young and nonsense in the old; for it's not time that teaches wisdom, but seasonable education and nature" (frg. 183). "Health is the object of men's prayers to the gods, but they don't realize they have power over it in themselves. They attack it with intemperance, and become traitors to their own health through lust" (frg. 236).

The gods play no very serious part in Democritus's philosophy, either in the field of cosmology or in morality. It is no part of his intention to dismiss altogether the popular idea of the gods. Our fullest source is Sextus (*Math.*

9.19), who tells us that Democritus spoke of great "images" *(eidōla)*, some well intentioned, some not, durable but not indestructible, which come to men and foretell the future. But the absence of textual evidence makes it impossible to attribute a worked-out theory to Democritus. Shortly after the passage just referred to, Sextus quotes Democritus as deriding the men of old who attributed thunder and lightning and eclipses to the gods. At least the negative side of his theology is clear: the gods are not the makers or manipulators of the physical world.

Much of the content of the moral fragments of Democritus is strongly reminiscent of Epicurus (and to some extent suspect for that reason). The goal is "good spirits" *(euthymiē)*. It comes to men, Stobaeus reports, "through temperate enjoyment and balance in life; deficiencies and excesses tend to change around and to bring about great commotions in the soul. And souls that are extensively moved are neither in good balance nor in good spirits" (frg. 191). There are other witnesses to the demand for moderation "both in private and in public" (frg. 3). Perhaps there is a hint here of an Epicurean reluctance to engage in public life. But unlike Epicurus, Democritus was ready to offer a spirited defense of democratic institutions: "Poverty in a democracy is as much to be preferred above what the powerful call 'happiness' as liberty is above slavery" (frg. 251). "It is from consensus *(homonoiē)* that great deeds, and wars, become possible for cities to undertake; without it, not" (frg. 250). The following has been called by Eric Havelock "the most remarkable single utterance of a political theorist of Hellas": "When those in power take it on themselves to be generous to the have-nots and to help them and to please them, then there is compassion and the end of isolation and the growth of comradeship and mutual defense, and agreement among the citizens, and other good things beyond anyone's capacity to count" (frg. 255).

Is there any connection between Democritus's morality and his physics? It is certain that his theory of the soul is in harmony with his moral views. We have no detailed account of the working of the Democritean soul, such as Lucretius (books 3 and 4) gives us in the case of Epicurus. But there are fragments that indicate the power of the soul over the body (it is to have such power that the soul is made of mobile, spherical atoms), and hence the priority of thought and intention over physical needs and longings. The goal of life is sometimes expressed in almost physical terms, as "balance" and the absence of violent motion. Moral education is described in remarkable words: "Nature and teaching are akin. For teaching re-forms a person, and by reforming, creates his nature" (frg. 33). It can hardly be doubted that *some* materialist theory of moral psychology lies behind such sayings, but it is hard to be more specific than that.

No one in the history of classical philosophy has been so badly treated by tradition than Democritus (unless indeed it is Leucippus). He covered many

subjects, from embryology to music to mathematics, and we know hardly anything about what he wrote. He was ignored by one of the two greatest philosophers in the next generation and opposed by the other. His great physical theory was transmitted through the medium of Epicureanism, which was received with prejudice because its morality was conceived (wrongly, but in part excusably) to be nothing more than selfish hedonism. In the Roman period, Democritus offended the Stoics; in postclassical times, his ideas were anathema to the Christians.

Yet the atomic theory is a mighty achievement, and Democritus's name has deservedly remained famous. He constructed a system that was to become the greatest challenge to Aristotelianism. He showed how worlds might occur by accident in the infinite void, how matter might be corpuscular instead of continuous, how qualities might be derived from atoms that lacked all qualities but shape, size, and weight. In vain he struggled to defend the flat earth, but in the process he demonstrated the possibility of a unified theory of motion.

DAVID FURLEY

Bibliography

Texts and Translations

Diels, Hermann, and Walther Kranz. *Fragmente der Vorsokratiker,* vol. 2, 6th edition. Berlin, 1952. (Cited as DK.)
Luria, S. *Demokrit.* Leningrad, 1970.

Studies

Alfieri, V. E. *Atomos Idea.* Florence, 1953.
Bailey, Cyril. *The Greek Atomists and Epicurus.* Oxford, 1928; repr. New York, 1964.
Barnes, Jonathan. *The Presocratic Philosophers,* vol. 2. London, 1979.
Benakis, L. G., ed. *Proceedings of the First International Congress on Democritus.* Xanthe, Greece, 1984.
Cherniss, Harold F. *Aristotle's Criticism of Presocratic Philosophy.* Baltimore, 1935; repr. New York, 1964.
Cole, T. *Democritus and the Sources of Greek Anthropology.* Cleveland, 1967; repr. Atlanta, 1990.
Furley, David J. *Two Studies in the Greek Atomists.* Princeton, 1967.
Guthrie, W. K. C. *History of Greek Philosophy,* vol. 2. Cambridge, 1965.
Havelock, Eric A. *The Liberal Temper in Greek Politics.* London, 1957.
Langerbeck, Hermann. *Doxis Epirysmiē: Studien zu Demokrit's Ethik und Erkenntnislehre.* Berlin, 1935; repr. Zurich, 1967.
Lasswitz, Kurd. *Geschichte der Atomistik* (1890). Hildesheim, 1963.
Mau, J. *Zum Problem des Infinitesimalen bei den antiken Atomisten.* Berlin, 1954.
O'Brien, D. *Theories of Weight in the Ancient World,* vol. 1: *Democritus: Weight and Size.* Paris, 1968.
Sedley, David. "Two Conceptions of Vacuum." *Phronesis* 27 (1982): 175–193.

Vlastos, Gregory. "Ethics and Physics in Democritus." In *Studies in Presocratic Philosophy*, vol. 2. Ed. R. E. Allen and D. J. Furley. London, 1975.

Related Articles

The Question of Being; Schools and Sites of Learning; Physics; Epicurus; Ethics; Cosmology; Theories of Religion

EPICURUS

EPICURUS WAS BORN in 342/341 B.C.E. on the island of Samos, where his father, an Athenian colonist, had settled in 352. According to Diogenes Laertius in his *Life of Epicurus,* he asserted that he had been introduced to philosophy at the (not unusual) age of fourteen, apparently by a local Platonist called Pamphilus. If we are to believe Cicero, Epicurus, whose followers were afraid of nothing so much as that they should appear to have learned anything from somebody else (*De natura deorum* I.viii.18), later referred to Pamphilus in scornful terms. The claim to autonomy, confirmed by other accounts, probably targets not only those who taught Epicurus directly but also and especially Democritus, who was incontestably his principal source of philosophical inspiration. Rather than revealing a pathological trait, the self-portrait of Epicurus as self-taught shows an original—and perhaps healthy—awareness of the difficulty raised by attempts to trace a philosophical lineage: how can borrowing be measured, when the borrower completely changes the meaning of the material used?

The fact that Epicurus weighed the question of philosophical debt does not make it any easier to interpret certain details of his intellectual biography. Thus the question of whether or not he followed the teaching of Xenocrates (who had succeeded Speusippus as head of the Academy in 338), as he would surely have had the opportunity to do during the two years he spent in Athens on his military duty (323–321), depends on how one reads the denial reported by Cicero: had Epicurus spent time with Xenocrates without learning anything from him, or did he simply ignore him?

Forced by the outcome of the Lamian War to leave Samos when he returned from Athens, he settled with his father at Colophon, on the coast of Asia Minor, a little north of Samos. It is presumably at this time (rather than before his Athenian sojourn) that he studied at Teos (north of Colophon), with an unquestionably able philosopher, the Democritean Nausiphanes. We know almost nothing of the period that preceded the foundation of an independent school in 311/310, first at Mytilene (on the island of Lesbos) then at Lampsacus on the Hellespont. We may suppose that Epicurus devoted his time primarily to reading and to the enrichment of a philosophical culture that there are good internal and external reasons to think was extensive: among all the Presocratics, Anaxagoras and Archelaus (but not Democritus) seem to have been Epicurus's favorite authors; several aspects of his physics and ethics are much clearer if we grant that he knew not only Aristotle's exo-

teric works but also his technical works, particularly *Physics.* This last text is mentioned, along with *Analytics,* in a fragment of a letter preserved by Philodemus (*To [the friends of the school],* frg. 111 [Angeli]).

During Epicurus's first years of teaching, the philosophical friendships were formed that would be associated with the later development of the school. Hermarchus, first successor to Epicurus as head of the Garden, was a native of Mytilene; Colotes, Idomeneus, Leonteus and his wife, Themista, Metrodorus and his renegade brother, Timocrates, Polyaenus, and Pythocles, all well known figures in the Epicurean circle, were from Lampsacus.

Sometime around 306 Epicurus decided to settle in Athens, where, with the restoration of democracy, the law of Sophocles of Sunium controlling the opening of philosophical schools had just been abolished. Alexandria notwithstanding, Athens remained the center of philosophical activity (Zeno arrived in Athens in 312/311, and he founded the Stoa there a few years later). For twenty-four minas Epicurus acquired a small property, probably in the northwest section of Athens, which quickly became well known as the Garden. The school was not simply an institution for study and teaching, or even for "symphilosophy" (the members of the school were fond of saying they "philosophized together"). It harbored a genuine living community, based on economic solidarity, intellectual exchange, and an ideal of friendship that the doctrine exalts—a community probably unequalled in the history of ancient philosophy (as a comparison with the Pythagorean school and Plotinus's circle would show). As has often been noted, the organization of the Garden resembles in more than one respect that of a religious sect: significant in this regard are the existence of neophytes and more advanced students (the hierarchy is reflected at the beginning of *Letter to Herodotus,* which is addressed to several types of recipients), the presence of "guides," the recourse to pedagogical and psychagogical techniques based on the repetition and memorization of texts, and above all the cult of Epicurus, celebrated at a fixed date according to the traditional forms of the rite, as was done for a divinity or a hero (a surprising but essential aspect of Epicureanism). If we add that the bonds with disciples and friends in Asia Minor were systematically maintained by correspondence (Epicurus also traveled back and forth on several occasions), we can understand how it has been possible—though not without forcing the comparison—to evoke the life and missionary proselytism of the first Christian communities in connection with the Garden. One can only be struck, in any case, by the role played in the Epicurean corpus by personal address, exhortation, and more generally the defense and illustration of the behavior of the school's members. The fact is that Epicurus's teaching, emphasizing the therapeutic ambitions that animate most ancient philosophies, unquestionably sought to be the bearer of salvation.

Epicurus managed to make an emblem of his death, in 271/270, as he had of his life. The famous *Letter to Idomeneus,* which seems to have been writ-

ten in agony, tells us that Epicurus's end, marked by terrible suffering, was a happy one according to the criteria of hedonism properly understood, which he had made the foundation of his teaching.

Through an exceptional set of circumstances, we are better informed about the Epicurean philosophy than about any other Hellenistic school. Several original texts by Epicurus and by certain of his disciples have in fact survived, along with the usual doxographical résumés or polemical summaries, and other citations from lost works. To begin with, Diogenes Laertius, in the tenth book of his *Lives of Eminent Philosophers*, which is devoted entirely to Epicurus, quotes in full three letters of Epicurus (to Herodotus, Pythocles, and Menoeceus), each of which represents a major aspect of his philosophy (respectively, physics, the theory of atmospheric and celestial phenomena, and ethics), as well as a collection of forty fundamental propositions or "Principal Doctrines," which complement the *Letter to Menoeceus* on the subject of moral and social theory. Finally, the eruption of Vesuvius in 79 c.e. partly charred—but by the same token partly preserved—numerous papyri belonging to the library of the Epicurean Philodemus (from about 100 to sometime after 40 B.C.E.). Badly damaged and often difficult to read, they still give us access to a number of otherwise unknown treatises that are quite varied in nature (not only philosophical but also biographical and apologetic works). Thus we possess some fairly substantial fragments of Epicurus's major work, *On Nature*, in thirty-seven books, along with important works of the second generation of disciples, like the treatise *Against Those Who Irrationally Despise Popular Beliefs* by Polystratus (Hermarchus's successor as head of the Garden, ca. 250), as well as numerous writings by Philodemus himself, writings that doubtless reflect in large part the teaching of Zeno of Sidon, a leading scholar of the preceding generation (ca. 100). Finally, *De rerum natura*, or *On the Nature of Things*, a didactic epic in six books that Lucretius, a contemporary of Philodemus and Cicero, composed to glorify Epicurus for a Latin public, constitutes a precious and sometimes irreplaceable source of information (it presents, for example, the case for the famous doctrine of atomic "declination"). Still, the properly literary ambition that animates it sometimes makes its use for the purpose of systematic reconstruction rather tricky. To this list of direct sources we could add, for the record, a collection of maxims and excerpts found in 1888 (the *Vatican Collection*) and, more surprisingly, the portico that a certain Diogenes, in the 2nd century c.e. (ca. 125 according to Smith's dating), erected at Oenoanda in northern Lycia (in what is now Turkey), and on which he had engraved the aids to salvation, for the sake of passersby—that is, for humanity in general. This public monument is probably the best symbol of the persistent vitality of Epicureanism and the extraordinary strength of its influence when the school had long before disappeared (the last great scholar we know of is Patron, at the end of the 1st century B.C.E.).

Contrary to Platonic-Aristotelian contemplation, which is an end in itself, philosophical thought in Epicurus bears the stamp of instrumentality. The individual, immersed in bodily suffering and mental fears, finds in Epicurean thought the means to attain, once and for all, a security that members of the species have been seeking from the start—for a sense of danger, which is natural at first, is nurtured above all by the exercise of spontaneous, and erroneous, speculation as to the nature of the world and our own needs. Whence the well-known maxim, whose counterfactual formulation entails a certain degree of provocation (a characteristic feature of Epicurus's philosophical style): "If we were not troubled by our suspicions of the phenomena of the sky and about death, fearing that it concerns us, and also by our failure to grasp the limits of pains and desires, we should have no need of natural science" ("Principal Doctrines" XI [Oates, p. 37]). Philosophy is like one excrescence designed to eliminate another, to reestablish the only "limits" within which a happy life can be lived.

It has often been stressed that the subordination of knowledge to the search for security did little to foster the development of theoretical sciences, mathematics for example. But, paradoxically, it also led Epicurus to examine for itself, and more systematically than any philosophy had previously done, the question of the validity of our knowledge. *Canon* (a word that denotes, in Greek, the straightedge that enables us to ascertain the verticality of a wall) may not be the first full-fledged epistemological treatise in the history of philosophy (Nausiphanes, using a different metaphor, had written *Tripod*), but it seems to have contributed in a decisive manner to the formation of a technical vocabulary on the subject. Thus the term *criterion*, which was to become so important, is a key concept of Epicurean philosophy. Faced with the infinite number of false judgments and unfounded opinions that feed our fears, criteria are the only bases that allow us to orient ourselves securely.

The doxography distinguishes two criteria of knowledge: sensations and prolepses ("affections," the third term on the list, does not have any independent value; in this epistemological usage, it refers to the internal aspect of our perceptions). Both terms, and the pair they constitute, are difficult to interpret, though for different reasons. Concerning sensation, the problem stems from the very restrictive use Epicurus makes of the word. To be able to serve as criteria, sensations must *all* be "true." This affirmation, well attested in our sources, is at first surprising. Do not the senses in fact often deceive us? However, the formula "all sensations are true" does not mean that the things of this world are, in themselves, such as one perceives them. To quote the two best-known examples, the Erinyes Orestes sees (in Euripides' tragedy, for example) are not present in person, and the fact that a tower appears short and round to me does not mean that it is not actually tall and square (Lucretius, *De rerum natura* IV.353–363; Sextus Empiricus, *Against the Mathematicians* VII.203–210 and VII.63f; frgs. 247 and 253 [Usener]). Neither the presence of

the Erinyes nor the circularity of the tower forms the content of the sensation, according to Epicurus. There are, rather, inferences, in this case illegitimate, on the basis of a piece of information that is in itself incontestable. Something has gotten through to Orestes from the external world, something that has the form of the Erinyes, or is rounded. But the Erinyes themselves may be far away, and the round form may not be that of the tower. For between the experience I undergo and the world of solid objects, there is an imperceptible process by which these objects affect me. The mysterious "conjoined movement" that, paralleling the movement of the sensation, is at the source of the error, according to the *Letter to Herodotus*, now comes into play: it reflects what might be called a presumption of immediacy. This presumption is responsible not only for the error of our first-order judgments, for example about the existence of the Erinyes or the shape of the tower, but also, on the level of theory, for the destructive opinion according to which certain sensations can be erroneous.

These two illusions can be corrected only by an appropriate analysis of the sensorial process. In other words, natural science enters very early into the canonic—so early, indeed, that we can understand why the Epicureans did not generally consider it an independent discipline. Every object in the world is an aggregate of atoms from which a dense and continual flow of pellicles emanates, extremely tenuous particles that Epicurus calls images (we can call them doubles or idols, if we want to preserve the technical character of the term), and that come to strike the organs of the senses. Now these images live a life of their own, and a sometimes risky one. Exposed to injury, they can cease to correspond to the properties of the object of which they are an emanation (this is the case of the square tower that appears round); having become autonomous, they continue to act independently of the emanating source (this is the case in Orestes' vision and, more generally, of our dreams and fantasies). This in no way detracts from the truth of the feeling they provoke, but it implies that we cannot incautiously draw conclusions about the world from our sensations, if by world we mean exclusively the set of "solid" aggregates, as opposed to the (fluid) images that also fill it, and that are no less objective (nor any less numerous) than those aggregates. The truth of sensations may well be infrangible, but it probably leads us less far than we might be tempted to suppose at first glance, and in any case it leads elsewhere.

The difficulties connected with the doctrine of prolepsis are of a different sort. Here, our understanding of the term, which cannot be guided by any familiar representation (this is one of Epicurus's numerous neologisms, suggesting the idea of a "preliminary grasp"), depends on heterogeneous sources, characterized by extreme concision. The problem arises from the fact that prolepsis seems to play two completely distinct roles. On the one hand, it gives access to types of objects, or types of concepts, that do not spring from sensation. Thus it is thanks to a prolepsis that we know the divinity to be an

immortal and blessed being, and that justice stipulates what is useful in the area of community relations. Given the propositional form of these contents, and their abstract character, it is tempting to see prolepsis as knowledge of an analytical and conceptual type. Yet, beyond the fact that such an interpretation does not fit well with what we otherwise know of Epicurean empiricism, it does not explain why there are also prolepses of sensible objects, whether it is a question of their form (seeing a man, we recognize him as a man on the basis of the prolepsis we have of him) or of propositional predicates (we know proleptically that the body as body is endowed with mass and the property of "resistance," or again that man is a rational animal—cf. Philodemus, *On Signs* 34.7–11). Neither does it account for the fact that Epicurus rejects the idea of a prolepsis of time while he accepts a prolepsis of cause (*On Nature* 35.26 [Sedley 1938, p. 19]).

The solution must be linked to the fact that between sensations and prolepses there is a certain dissymmetry. Although proleptic knowledge covers a realm of objects that lies outside sensorial knowledge, it is in no way defined by it. What distinguishes it, rather, is the nature of the relation it maintains with objects whose provenance can be mental as well as perceptual. For in Epicurus, along with sense perception there is a "mental perception" (the images that penetrate the mind are simply more tenuous than those that make up the sensible flow). Only its absence from the initial list of criteria— an absence that certain disciples wanted to remedy by adding to the list "the imaginative projection of thought"—accounts for the fact that some have been tempted by an intellectualist interpretation of prolepsis. If, on the other hand, we make mental perceptions an independent category, the specificity of the proleptic function stands out more clearly. Unlike perceptions, the two forms of which—sense perceptions and mental perceptions—are after all confined to the present (even if, in the texts we are considering, only sensation is viewed as "without memory"), prolepses are empirical concepts, traces that accumulated experience has deposited in us, and that guide us, as well, in the recognition of perceptible objects (the senses for men, the mind for the gods) and in understanding, at a higher level of generality, of concepts of experience such as justice or cause. We consequently understand that prolepsis possesses a linguistic function (we speak most often of things we do not have before our eyes). Interpreters have rightly recognized a reference to the criterion of prolepsis, even though the term is not used, in the first rule set forth in *Letter to Herodotus*, "grasp the ideas attached to words" (Oates, p. 3). (It is significant, moreover, that prolepsis occurs even before sensations in the order of the argument: in a certain sense, the use of words constitutes an absolute precondition for inquiry into the nature of things.)

Beyond the kernels of certitude that the criteria define, there is the whole world of "obscure" things, a world that cannot be grasped except indirectly, and through reference to what possesses immediate clarity (*enargeia*). It is no

accident that the operation of referring the invisible to the visible, the unknown to the known, plays a central role in Epicurean philosophy: philosophical activity consists essentially in "relating" what we say and think, as well as what others say or may have said, and which forms the cultural horizon of our convictions, to these pockets of ultimate certainty, to see whether, or to what extent, the prevailing assumptions can be upheld, or whether they are "empty" instead. This movement of perpetual confrontation, characteristic of Epicurus's writings and often even of his sentence structure (a "form of thought" might be identified here) explains how some interpreters have been able to see Epicurean philosophy as an essentially "critical" enterprise. The critique in question can take an aggressive turn, in the face of the scandal constituted—given what is at stake—by the distance between the positions we take and what would justify our taking them.

The realm of obscure things, including everything that falls neither under sense perception nor under intellectual perception and thus is not the correlative of a prolepsis, comprises two vast domains: the set of everything that is too far distant in space for us to apprehend it directly (atmospheric and celestial phenomena) and the set of everything that is too minute to be grasped by the senses and thus is not the object of a mental perception either (only aggregates give forth images, not atoms nor, of course, the void). These are the subjects covered, broadly speaking, in *Letter to Herodotus,* devoted to basic physics, and *Letter to Pythocles,* devoted to "meteorology" (in the sense of Aristotle's *Meteorologica*) and celestial physics. But there are few subjects that are not at first "obscure," and fewer still that are not made so by the very process of clarification, with the subsidiary questions the process necessarily raises. What falls outside the temporal limits of our life, for example (past history and what will come after our death), must be just as much the object of analogical reconstruction as what is remote and what is infinitesimal. The function of the psychic faculties, and even more the exercise of our freedom, must consequently be explainable on the basis of atomic physics. *Letter to Herodotus* briefly addresses certain of these themes (along with the propositions of a basic physics, it includes the outlines of a psychology and a section devoted to the theory of civilization). Detailed analysis and the treatment of more complex questions (such as that of free choice) also appear in the treatise *On the Nature of Things* (of which *Letter to Herodotus* and *Letter to Pythocles* are partial "summaries") or are developed in other specialized treatises.

Philodemus's treatise *On Signs* sheds light on the mechanism and stakes of Epicurean inference, even if the terminology and the problematics are influenced by the debates of the 3rd and 2nd centuries. Arguing against the Stoic critics, Philodemus aims essentially to establish that the method called "by suppression" *(anaskeue),* by virtue of which we prove the existence of an invisible entity (the void, for example) by showing that its suppression would

entail a visible phenomenon (movement, in this case), is not a process independent of an "inference through likeness," to which it can always be reduced. The most interesting case of inference through likeness is plainly that which applies only mutatis mutandis—that is, analogy. For example, it is not because—by analogy with the sensible body, where the eye distinguishes a perceptual minimum—one posits the existence of parts on the body of the atom (the so-called *minima*) that the atomic body thereby becomes divisible, as is the perceptual body. Analogy thus often leads to paradoxical results: the world of atoms and the void obeys laws foreign to the world of composite forms, laws in which the eye and the mind cannot immediately find their bearings. Atoms, whose progress nothing can impede, move at a speed that defies the imagination; in infinite space, there is neither up nor down; and so on. Epicurean physics, the physics of likeness, is based first of all on the rejection of false likenesses.

This does not mean, of course, that the propositions it establishes can ever be incompatible with the criteria, and in particular with the data of the senses. In every case, and notably in the most paradoxical among them, assertions about the invisible, which by definition cannot be the object of any direct "confirmation" *(epimarturesis)*, must be able to pass the test of "noninvalidation," or *ouk antimarturesis*. Despite what certain formulas may suggest, noninvalidation seems to have been not a method of discovery but a simple means of control, guaranteeing that a proposition established on the basis of independent considerations is actually possible.

It is therefore essential to understand the nature of the procedure that guarantees the correct use of the analogical method by imposing necessary restrictions on our spontaneous manipulation of likenesses. In this regard, David Furley is right to cast aside the idea that the ultimate propositions of Epicurean physics rely on a purely conceptual type of analysis (that is how Bailey understood the "imaginative projection of thought"). The impossibility of conceiving of a given affirmation, which Epicurus often uses as an argument, is always ultimately based on a fundamental datum provided by experience. Still, the fact remains that, once established, one proposition can lead to the rejection of other ones that likeness would nevertheless seem to suggest. If the fact that atoms include parts does not make them composites, it is because the ultimate indivisible elements, in order to account for the visible world, must contain a series of properties that can be attributed only to a resistant mass, of which a "minimum" is deprived. At the same time, the indivisibility of the atom will be explained by a new property, "impassibility," which Democritus, who saw no difference between the atom and the minimum, could dispense with. Here it is very clear how a fundamental principle has precedence over a possible and, under the circumstances, erroneous application of the principle of likeness.

Thus the order in which the propositions of physics are established is im-

portant. This is why the "pedagogical" presentation of fundamental physics under the form of a whole made up of propositional "elements," or *stoicheia* (Diogenes Laertius, X.30), also corresponds to an internal necessity. It is remarkable, in any case, that the term *stoicheiōsis* (rudimentary introduction), destined to play an important role in the mathematical sciences as well as in philosophy, is attested for the first time in Epicurus.

Physical *stoicheiōsis* consists of ten propositions (nine, according to a different breakdown) that make up the infrangible framework of the discipline, and the frame of reference which, once established, can serve as a second-degree criterion. (1) Nothing is born out of what does not exist. (2) Nothing dissolves into what does not exist. (3) The universe has always been such as it now is and will always remain the same. (4) The universe is composed of bodies and space. (5) Bodies are of two sorts, atoms and composites of atoms (the aggregates). (6) The universe is infinite. (7) The atoms are infinite in number and space boundless in extension. (8) Atoms of identical form are infinite in number, but their differences in form are indefinite in number, and not infinite. (9) The atoms are in constant motion. (10) Atoms have but three properties in common with perceptible bodies: form, volume, and weight.

These statements deviate in several respects from the ancient atomism of Democritus: for example, Epicurus acknowledges that atoms are endowed not only with form and size but also with weight. Atomic forms cannot be infinite in number, or else they would need, in order to have infinite variety, to cross the threshold of the perceptible (according to testimony as famous as it is difficult to fathom, a Democritean atom can be the size of a world). Several of these modifications can be attributed to the intention to defend the atomic doctrine against the objections that Aristotle raised, specifically in Books IV and VI of *Physics*. But they must all be understood as an effect induced by the application of the canonic rules to a theory with regard to which Epicurus turns out to be the more critical the closer he stays to it. This is particularly the case for the atom's property of deviating minimally from its trajectory. Although neither *Letter to Herodotus* nor any other work that has been preserved makes any mention of this "declination," which is mentioned for the first time in Lucretius, it is very likely that the doctrine goes back to Epicurus himself *(clinamen)*. In its cosmogonic function, it explains the fact that a world can come into being in the infinite void: atoms, which can be represented by analogy with bodies falling in parallel through space, would never meet, since they move at equal speed, if at least one did not depart from its course (Lucretius, *De rerum natura* II.216–250). But the principal object of the doctrine must have been to account for voluntary movements and human freedom, although the way it fulfills this function remains open to discussion: the unforeseeable and arbitrary deviation of an atom on the microscopic level seems ill-suited to "explain" the phenomenon of the will, which is by definition governed by an end. The idea that Epicurus could have imagined a model

of "emergent properties" (David Sedley) is not borne out by the text of Book XXXV of his *On Nature* (our principal source of information on the subject, along with Lucretius). Finally, the purely analogical interpretation, which sees in the atom's "freedom" with regard to mechanical determinations the equivalent of a voluntary movement of which it would certify only the possibility or the nonimpossibility, does not entirely do justice to the explanatory dimension of the theory, which is strongly emphasized by Lucretius (II.286).

Elsewhere we can see more clearly how the Epicurean universe is entirely reducible to the fundamental properties of atoms and the void. In infinite space the relatively concentrated pockets of matter are released, protected by an envelope beyond which we find the "interworlds," where the gods live in tranquility (at least according to accounts subsequent to Epicurus's). Inside the perishable worlds, aggregates are formed that are no less perishable. The cohesion that makes them "solids" at the macroscopic level results from the constant vibration of elements that, at the microscopic level, impede each other inside a more or less dense network; their manifest velocity is likewise only an effect, since in the interior of the aggregate, the atoms continue to pass through the void "at the speed of thought." A violent pulsation, which conceals the relative stability of bodies, is responsible for the emission of the flow of "images." Finally, the three primary properties, which are for all bodies (elementary or composite) form, size, and weight (designated by the term Aristotle uses for accident, *sumbebekota;* in Latin, *conjuncta*), account for the infinite variety of properties and secondary "occurrences" (*sumptōmata;* Latin *eventa*): colors and flavors, but also war and peace, which result from their interaction and make up the world in which we live.

The status of the gods in this physics of composition and dissolution naturally constitutes a challenge. Their existence and their indestructibility, known proleptically, would require a special explanation that must have been developed, but about which we have very little information beyond a few columns in Philodemus's treatise *On the Gods:* we can just begin to glimpse how the interworld space might guarantee, beyond the absence of perturbations, the inextinguishable renewal of the divine body. Whether and how the images emitted by the body of the gods reach us is a thornier question. The answer depends on the interpretation of a particularly difficult account by Cicero, who suggests, at least in the reading of the manuscripts *(ad deos),* that the gods could, in a certain way, be nothing but the product of an abundant flow of images projected by man's thought (Long and Sedley). If such a conception seems at first glance compatible with the presuppositions of a resolutely realist doctrine, we must emphasize that for Epicurus, the mind, at first receptive, finally succeeds in exercising all but complete control over its own productions. The idea that the god is our own product, in a sense that would need to be specified, should therefore not be ruled out too quickly. It is significant in any case that Epicurus's gods are anthropomorphic, and that

Epicurus could proclaim his own divinity and have it revered. The strangeness of the doctrine converges with the strangeness of the cultic practice.

Letter to Pythocles, like the letter addressed to Herodotus, shows how the canonic allows us to filter and remodel an earlier philosophical tradition. But the data here are different. Meteorological and celestial phenomena are in effect "hidden," though not in the same sense that the ultimate constituents of the world are hidden. First, we perceive these phenomena with our senses, although at a distance. Then, the "nearby" phenomena of which we have direct experience suggest a plurality of explanatory models for the distant ones. Now the canonic, according to Epicurus, makes it impossible to choose among the various explanations, for that would amount to rejecting, in a necessarily arbitrary manner, some of the information we get from the senses, information that by definition is also all true. The seriousness of such a transgression is shown by the fact that Epicurus does not hesitate to equate the adoption of one single explanation, while sensory data suggest a plurality of explanations, with the form of "myth," itself conceived as a source of terror. Whence the formulaic constructions that punctuate the letter: "It is possible that such a phenomenon occurs for *these reasons;* it is also possible that it happens for *these other reasons.*" Thunder, for example, will result either "from the [compression] of wind in the hollows of the clouds, as happens in vessels [of our bodies], or by the [rumblings] of fire [stirred up by the] wind, or by the rending and tearing of clouds, or by the friction and bursting of clouds when they have been congealed into a form like ice" (Oates, p. 23). The vocabulary of "possibility" notwithstanding, Epicurus is not suggesting that we should welcome all possible hypotheses without distinction or preference. The thesis is a stronger one—namely, that all the possible explanations are actually true (even if not simultaneously). We more easily grasp the significance and also the philosophical foundation of such an affirmation if we acknowledge that the infiniteness of matter and of time guarantees the realization of all possibilities (Lucretius, V.526–533).

Theories about meteorological and celestial phenomena thus present a striking contrast with the propositions of elementary physics, which have an absolute value, whether they belong to the initial *stoicheiōsis* or derive from it. We may wonder whether Epicurus is justified in exempting explanations governing the realm of distant phenomena from the principles of limitation and organization at work in the field of fundamental physics: why would certain hypotheses not exclude others here too, and why would certain apparent similarities not be discarded as erroneous opinions? After all, Epicurus thought he had enough information at his disposal to affirm that the real size of the sun and stars was, if not what it appears to us to be, at least not a great deal larger or smaller. Be that as it may, the picture of the world Epicurus presents to us is not one of a unified cosmic mechanism (the equivalent

of physical *stoicheiōsis*) but of a dispersed multiplicity of independent phenomena.

Such epistemological naïveté, which claims to be in the service of an ethic of tranquillity, may sound the more embarrassing at a time when contemporary astronomy was making spectacular progress, thanks to the astronomic "investigation" that Epicurus dismissed so scornfully. One fascinating aspect of the doctrine of multiple causes must be emphasized, however. Readers have long been struck by the fact that the explanations offered in *Letter to Pythocles* for each of the phenomena studied often converge with the views of the Presocratic physicists. This is understandable, since those earlier views most often rely on analogy. We must add that Epicurus could find in his contemporary Theophrastus a fully developed theory of multiple causes in the field of meteorology. The relation between the two strains of thought remains to be studied, but it is clear that the relation of Epicurean meteorology to the philosophical tradition is no different from the relation that characterizes the field of elementary physics. Here and there, the doctrine looks like a reworking of opinions already advanced by others but renewed in their content or meaning by the requirements of a canonic that is Epicurus's alone.

Despite what *Letter to Pythocles* may suggest, and despite the attitude of Epicureans toward the sciences more generally, the subordination of physics to the practical side of philosophy is not the mark of any "lack of interest" in physics. On the contrary, it situates the nature of this interest, which is deep and necessary, in refusing to see in it anything but the expression of a fundamental need. This is why the part of the doctrine that defines the nature of this need in a reflective way is not less primary than the canonic. Commonly called ethics, it bears, in fact, though in another sense, on the "choices" and "refusals" that determine the course of our life. We thus understand why *Letter to Menoeceus*, setting forth the outlines of a doctrine of human action, takes the form of an invitation to philosophize, and why, in contrast to the two other letters, its treatment is deliberately exoteric. The opening of *Letter to Menoeceus*, even though it belongs to the tradition of Aristotle's *Protrepticus*, thus perfectly expresses the universal and, so to speak, catholic aspect of Epicurus's philosophy. "Let no one when young delay to study philosophy, nor when he is old grow weary of his study. For no one can come too early or too late to secure the health of his soul" (*Letter to Menoeceus* [Oates, p. 30]).

The content of the good life is circumscribed by four fundamental propositions (again called elements), famous from antiquity on as the "quadruple remedy" *(tetrapharmakon)*. They open both the collection of *Principal Doctrines* and the *Vatican Collection*. In a modified form, so far as the last two are concerned, they also provide the structure of *Letter to Menoeceus*. A full conception of (1) the nature of the gods, (2) death, (3) pleasure, and (4) suffering

are the base for a "strong" life, sheltered from harm. The fact is that the three domains of theology, eschatology, and the affections encompass the sources of all our fears, and consequently define the space wherein a serene life can be attained. The certitude that the god, minimally defined as "the blessed and immortal nature," is "never constrained by anger or favour" (*Principal Doctrines* I [Oates, p. 35]) is the first condition of human felicity, for it suppresses the fears, as well as the vain hopes, that belief in their intervention would inspire. At the same time, the life of the anthropomorphic god supplies man with his paradigm, since it is only tranquillity carried to its highest point of perfection (thus the letter promises man that he can live "like a god among men"). The terror aroused by the thought of the beyond, which feeds the fables of mythology, vanishes if death, the simple dissolution of the perceptive aggregate, "is nothing to us" (*Principal Doctrines* II [Oates, p. 35]). But the suppression of terror is also the condition for a concentration on life itself (according to a fine oxymoron in *Letter to Menoeceus*, it "makes the mortality of life enjoyable" [p. 30]). Finally, without a clear awareness of the nature of pleasure and suffering—that is, of their "limits"—we would be incapable of leading our lives as they ought to be lived. The "affections" *(pathe)* in fact guide our choices and our refusals, and serve as ultimate criteria for action.

The Epicurean theory of action is based on the Aristotelian model, common to all the Hellenistic schools (with the notable exception of the Cyrenaics), according to which all our actions tend toward an ultimate end *(telos)* called happiness. The specificity of the theory, which is also the source of its difficulty, stems from the manner in which it determines the content of happiness. On the one hand, the end, which concerns both body and soul, depends on a complex relation in which each of the two terms can claim a certain priority. On the other hand, and more important, this end is defined in negative terms: when the body is not suffering and when the soul is not tormented, "all the tempest of the soul is dispersed, since the living creature has not to wander as though in search of something that is missing, and to look for some other thing by which he can fulfil the good of the soul and the good of the body" (*Letter to Menoeceus* [Oates, p. 31]). Because pleasure, corporal and psychical, is itself defined negatively as the absence of pain (in the body) or affliction (in the soul), Epicurus can maintain that "pleasure is the beginning and end of the blessed life" (ibid.) The beginning, because even before becoming the ultimate criterion for our choices and rejections it is what the living being seeks from its birth onward. The end, because the serenity that ataraxy procures (*ataraxy* is Epicurus's term for the absence of all psychical disturbance) is a particular form of pleasure—the greatest form conceivable.

While, on the one hand, this negative conception of pleasure shields the doctrine from the accusations of vulgar hedonism that it encountered from the outset (Epicurus was already answering such charges in *Letter to Menoeceus*), on the other hand it poses the problem—which is articulated

perfectly in Cicero's critique in *De finibus*—of the relation between the ordinary sense of the term *pleasure* and its Epicurean redefinition. It is not certain that the gap between them can be entirely filled in, nor even that it should be: why would Epicurus not maintain that the common concepts of the nature of pleasure are erroneous, as in the case of the gods? Still, there is every reason to think that Epicurean pleasure is not a negative state. It is not enough to recall—even though this is an important element in our understanding—that the Epicurean doctrine stands out among classic conceptions of pleasure (Platonic or Cyrenaic) in that it does not admit a median state between pleasure and suffering. Although this model implies that the absence of suffering must, ipso facto, be identical with pleasure, it does not rule out the possibility that Epicurus may have simply rebaptized as "pleasure" what others had called the "median state." Now, the disappearance of suffering certainly leaves room for a state of positive contentment or satisfaction that Epicurus occasionally describes in terms of "health," or "well-being," or even "serenity." Whether or not the comparison goes back to Epicurus, Seneca succeeds in conveying what the dissipation of the tempest implies: not the dead calm that the Cyrenaics blamed Epicurus for setting up as an end, likening it to the state of a corpse, but the pure brilliancy of a sky cleared by the disappearance of all that darkened it (Seneca, Epistle 66.45).

Underlying the "negative" definition of pleasure is the distinction between pleasure "in movement" (or kinetic pleasure) and pleasure at rest (or catastematic pleasure). While the opposition may well owe something to the Aristotelian analysis of the nature of pleasure in Book X of *Nicomachean Ethics,* it is difficult, given the nature of our information, to arrive at a firm picture of the systematic relation between the two terms. Epicurus distinguishes between two phases of pleasure that correspond to two aspects that are connected in reality but distinct in theory; more technically, they are related to an important categorial difference. Pleasure is in fact measured quantitatively by the process leading to the suppression of lack, or catastematic pleasure. Beyond this it "varies" only qualitatively, without increasing. It seems clear that the existence of an ongoing qualitative variation, once catastematic pleasure has been secured, serves to show the duality inherent in the earlier phase of repletion, when the (quantitative) pleasure of the suppression of need is inextricably entangled with "kinetic," qualitative pleasure. We may admit that this lack of distinction is responsible for an illusion equivalent to the one that taints our sensory judgments, when we think that a delicate dish brings more pleasure than bread does: the error is categorial, inasmuch as the true measure of pleasure is the satisfaction of an "objective need." The methodical concentration on the quantity and state of pleasure, to the detriment of its "variety" and movement, explains the ascetic aspects of the Epicurean doctrine, which are well attested, and which had seduced the Stoic in Seneca.

Epicurus's hedonism, however, does not in principle exclude variation. In fact it does not operate in a binary system where the necessary, with which one ought to be satisfied, would simply be opposed to the nonnecessary, which one ought to reject. The model is tripartite, as we can see from the classification of desires: these are either "natural and necessary" or "natural and nonnecessary" or "not natural and not necessary" (this is "empty"). Only the third category, that of artificial desires deriving from opinion, should be rooted out. The status of the second category, on the other hand, is more complex. Since they are natural, desires cannot be blameworthy in themselves: delicate dishes do taste good, and sex is a source of pleasure. However, the consequences stemming from the abandonment of the sphere of necessity can turn out to be alienating and even destructive, in that they give rise to false needs, which will have less chance of always being able to be satisfied, or even of remaining "within our power," in that they will be more diversified and demanding (cf. *Vatican Collection* 51). "Variation" thus falls within the province of prudence *(phronesis)*, which *Letter to Menoeceus*, if we do not amend the text, identifies with philosophy itself. The fact remains that delicate Epicureanism, which Horace's carpe diem emblematically represents, is a possibility structurally inscribed in the doctrine. Contrary to what Epicurus himself suggests, it is not on the basis of a simple misunderstanding that the enemies of pleasure condemn its philosophy.

In Epicurus himself, warning nevertheless takes precedence over authorization, and abstinence unquestionably tends to be endowed with intrinsic value. The deliberate confinement to the sphere of necessity, which could be explained by the harshness of the times (the siege of Athens by Demetrius Poliorcetes in 294), is also the result of an intellectualism profoundly anchored in the ancient philosophical tradition going back to Socrates, a tradition to which Epicurus was heir no less than the Stoics.

Here we must explore the complex relationship that, beyond the parallelism marked by their common "negativity," links pleasures of the body with pleasures of the soul. On the one hand, Epicurus admits the "superiority" of the latter over the former. This superiority, which is of a quantitative nature, is due to the exclusive connection the soul maintains with time: while the body's affections are limited to the present, the soul, which embraces the past and the future, multiplies their intensity (the Cyrenaics, on the contrary, in insisting on the qualitative difference between actual affection and affection anticipated or remembered, maintained the superiority of corporal affections over psychical ones). Consequently we find a first shift from body to soul: false opinions on death and, within the limits of life, uncertainty about the future are infinitely harder to bear than any corporal pain. Conversely, the power of serenity is in proportion to anguish, more than to pain. But at the same time, the satisfaction of psychical pleasures always depends, in the last analysis, on the satisfaction of bodily pleasures. For the psychical pleasures al-

ways refer to the bodily pleasures as their final object: certainty about the future is first of all certainty about the possibility of always satisfying one's elementary needs. It is in this sense that not being hungry, thirsty, and cold, and expecting that this will remain the case in the future, allows one to "rival even Zeus in happiness" (*Vatican Collection* 33 [Oates, p. 41]).

Thus there is no question that psychical pleasures will ever substitute for corporal pleasures. Still, some of Epicurus's assertions unquestionably point in that direction, for example when he maintains that the wise man will be happy under torture. The last of the four remedies accounts for this paradox: "Pain does not last continuously in the flesh, but the acutest pain is there for a very short time, and even that which just exceeds the pleasure in the flesh does not continue for many days at once. But chronic illnesses permit a predominance of pleasure over pain in the flesh" (*Principal Doctrines* 4 [Oates, p. 35]). The idea is that, so long as life continues, the quantity of corporal pleasure, understood here as a factor of organic cohesion, prevails de facto over the destructive force of suffering, which gets the upper hand only at the very moment when it vanishes with the dissolution of the aggregate in death (whence the opening of *Letter to Idomeneus* mentioned above). This analysis of the quantitative relation between suffering and pleasure also accounts for the central role played by reflection in the Epicurean doctrine of pleasure: only the thought of the "limits" of pleasure and suffering is capable of transforming survival in the most miserable conditions into the equivalent of life, and even a happy life, to the point of abolishing the distinction, which remains true in principle, between the desires "necessary for happiness," those necessary "for the repose of the body," and those necessary "for very life" (*Letter to Menoeceus* [Oates, p. 31]). It is just as though, now, the ultimate source of pleasure were less the satisfaction of the body than reflection on the minimal conditions for such satisfaction. Put back in this perspective, the idea that it is "easy" to satisfy the needs of the body takes on a second sense, since the absence of bread can always be compensated by the certainty that pleasure still prevails over the suffering of the stomach. Thanks to the concept of limits, everything can always virtually step down a rung on the ladder of needs, and the modest pot of cheese can become the equivalent of the greatest luxuries. A number of Epicurean paradoxes that have been found shocking, like the idea that a premature death does not diminish the quantity of lived pleasure, are also explained by this: the soul is the organ of time, but it is also, by the force of the thought that it shelters, the instrument of time's abolition.

Given these conditions, we shall be less surprised that the idea of a "natural variation" plays an even more discreet role in the case of the pleasures of the soul than in that of the pleasures of the body. It is as if the psychical energy concentrated in thinking about limits had eliminated even the pleasure linked with other intellectual enjoyments. Still, one can understand that later Epicureans (such as Philodemus) could feel entitled by the logic of the system to

rehabilitate music. Besides, Epicurus himself seems to have recognized the legitimacy of certain aesthetic pleasures: the wise man takes pleasure in spectacles, and even "more than the others."

The fact remains that the life outlined by Epicurus is dominated by an idea of autonomy that is capable of confining gratifications to their proper place. The essential point—and on this, too, Epicurus is close to the Stoics—is that we must be masters of our own lives and responsible for our actions. The most serious reproach Epicurus addresses to "the destiny of the physicists," by which he means chiefly, if not exclusively, the ancient atomism of Democritus, is that, in demolishing human freedom, it was unable to give meaning either to the practice of blame and praise—two fundamental aspects of social life too obvious to question—or to the use of argumentation, which presupposes that the opponent can change his mind. Whatever the challenge to atomism raised by the obligation to account for human liberty, it is clear that Epicurus had to take it on. Epicurean man is only very provisionally a receptive being subject to the flood of images. Through the exercise of thought, the memorization of principles, and work on his own character, he is capable of developing a capacity for selection, so that he can become master of what he sees as well as of what he decides.

It is not surprising, given the role it plays in physics and ethics, that the idea of security also dominates the final aspect of Epicurean doctrine, which is devoted to the theory of society and the relation of friendship. It has long been the standard view, undoubtedly sustained by the famous injunction to "live unknown" (to which Plutarch consecrated one of his three anti-Epicurean treatises) that Epicurus was not interested in problems of social organization. Still, the rejection of political ambition as well as renown—quintessential examples of "empty," destructive desires—is perfectly compatible with an analysis of the basis of human society and particularly of justice, which is well represented in the last ten *Principal Doctrines* as well as in a long fragment of Hermarchus (cited in Porphyry's treatise *On Abstinence* 1.7–12).

Although justice is defined as a "contract," Epicurus is not a conventionalist, because the content of such a contract, according to the prolepsis of justice, is objectively defined by "utility." This utility touches essentially on the preservation of life, at the expense of animals and other men, and it does not seem that Epicurus or his disciples sought to analyze the way it was translated into the multitude of arrangements that form the specific infrastructure of societies and political systems. The central aim of the theory seems to have been to show—once again, in opposition to a precipitous conclusion—that the variability of norms of justice does not constitute an argument against the objectivity of justice. On the contrary, it is because utility is always identical to itself "from a general point of view" that institutions resulting from

the accord can vary in the function of circumstances and remain open to revision. The resultant distinction between justice and laws is not without originality in the context of Greek thought, strongly marked as that thought is by conventionalism: laws are just only to the extent that they are useful. From Hermarchus's fragment we can draw a second distinction that is not attested for Epicurus himself but that allows us to cast light on an important aspect of his social theory. Laws are formulated, in a perspective that is partly pedagogic and partly prophylactic, for the sake of those incapable of understanding the usefulness of their provisions on their own. A society of wise men would thus have no need for laws. We can understand better now how Epicurus could declare that "the laws exist for the sake of the wise, not that they may not do wrong, but that they may not suffer it" ("Fragments from Uncertain Sources" 81 [Oates, p. 51]), and that he recognized the existence of an organic bond between virtues and pleasure. In particular, contrary to what Cicero suggests in *De finibus* (II.51–59), the wise man has every reason, at least under normal circumstances, not to commit injustice, independently of threats that the laws bring to bear on him. Thus we see taking shape, within the very limits of society, the program for a community ruled by the imperatives of wisdom alone. Thanks to the inscription at Oenoanda, we know that later Epicureanism developed a genuine social utopia on this basis. In Epicurus himself, the idea takes the more limited form of a community of friends who represent, at the heart of an imperfect society ruled by the constraint of law, what would be the ideal for that society.

Given the importance attached to the practice of friendship in Epicurus's philosophy, it is paradoxical that the doctrine of friendship is also the doctrine (if we except declination) whose philosophical justification raises the most difficulties: how do I move from a utilitarian concept locating the end of my actions in the acquisition of pleasure that can only be my own to an "altruistic" perspective that accords as much value to my friend's pleasure as to mine (Cicero, *De finibus* I.68)? The problem, apparently, had already preoccupied certain disciples. Cicero mentions two solutions supported within the school: either that friendship properly so called develops progressively on the basis of an original interest that it surmounts at a certain point in its evolution, or that it is based on a form of contract. Without minimizing the philosophical difficulty of the position, we can acknowledge that if Epicurus's philosophy culminates, in a way, in a paradoxical doctrine of friendship, this is because the relation of friendship combines the fundamental features of Epicurean man and brings them to their point of greatest intensity: friendship is at once the site of the greatest dependency and that of the greatest certainty.

ANDRÉ LAKS
Translated by Rita Guerlac and Anne Slack

Bibliography

Texts and Translations

Arrighetti, Graziano, ed. *Epicuro: Opere,* 2nd ed. Turin: G. Einaudi, 1973. Includes papyrological fragments.

Bailey, Cyril, ed. *Epicurus: The Extant Remains.* Oxford: Clarendon Press, 1926; repr. New York: Hildesheim, 1975.

Gigante, Marcello, ed. *La scuola de Epicuro.* Naples: Istituto italiano per gli studi filosofici, 1982.

Long, Anthony A., and David N. Sedley. *The Hellenistic Philosophers.* Cambridge: Cambridge University Press, 1987.

Oates, Whitney J., ed. "The Complete Extant Writings of Epicurus." Trans. Cyril Bailey. In *The Stoic and Epicurean Philosophers.* New York: Random House, 1940. Pp. 3–66.

Seneca. *Epistles.* Trans. Richard M. Gummere. Loeb Classical Library.

Smith, Martin F., ed. *Diogenes of Oenoanda: The Epicurean Inscription.* Naples: Bibliopolis, 1993. *La Scuola di Epicuro,* suppl. 1.

Usener, Hermann, ed. *Epicurea.* Leipzig: Teubner, 1887. Repr. 1966.

Studies

Alberti, Antonina. "The Epicurean Theory of Law and Justice." In *Justice and Generosity,* ed. André Laks and Malcolm Schofield. Cambridge: Cambridge University Press, 1995. Pp. 161–190.

Asmis, Elisabeth. *Epicurus' Scientific Method.* Ithaca, N.Y.: Cornell University Press, 1984.

Brunschwig, Jacques. "The Cradle Argument in Epicureanism and Stoicism." In *The Norms of Nature,* ed. Malcolm Schofield and Gisela Striker. Cambridge: Cambridge University Press, 1986.

Clay, Diskin. "The Cults of Epicurus." *Cronache Ercolanesi* 16 (1986): 11–28.

———. *Lucretius and Epicurus.* Ithaca, N.Y.: Cornell University Press, 1983.

Furley, David J. "Knowledge of Atoms and Void in Epicureanism." In *Cosmic Problems.* Cambridge: Cambridge University Press, 1989. Pp. 161–171.

———. *Two Studies in the Greek Atomists.* Princeton: Princeton University Press, 1967.

Glidden, David K. "Epicurean Prolepsis." *Oxford Studies in Ancient Philosophy* 3 (1985): 175–217.

Goldschmitt, Victor. *La doctrine d'Epicure et le droit.* Paris: Vrin, 1977.

Mitsis, Philip. *Epicurus' Ethical Theory: The Pleasures of Invulnerability.* Ithaca, N.Y.: Cornell University Press, 1988.

Schmid, Wolfgang. "Epikur." In *Reallexikon fur Antike und Christentum* 5 (1961): 681–819.

Sedley, David. "Epicurean Anti-Reductionism." In *Matter and Metaphysics,* ed. Jonathan Barnes and Mario Mignucci. Naples: Bibliopolis, 1988. Pp. 297–327.

———. "Epicurus' Refutation of Determinism." In *Suzetesis: Studi sull' epicurismo greco e romano offerti a Marcello Gigante.* 2 vols. Naples: G. Macchiaroli, 1983. Pp. 11–51.

————. *Lucretius and the Transformation of Greek Wisdom*. Cambridge: Cambridge University Press, 1998.

Striker, Gisela. "Kriterion tes aletheias." *Nachrichten der Akademie der Wissenschaften in Göttingen*, Philologische-historische Klasse (1974: 2): 47–120.

Van der Waerdt, Paul A. "The Justice of the Epicurean Wise Man." *Classical Quarterly* 37 (1987): 402–422.

Related Articles

The Philosopher; The Sage and Politics; Cosmology; Language; Ethics; Observation and Research; Theories of Religion; Democritus

EUCLID

Across the centuries and up to our own day, Euclid's name has endured in the minds of thinkers and scholars as synonymous with mathematics. What exactly was his work? What has been its place in the history of science for more than twenty centuries? What problems does it raise for scholars today, and what new research has sprung from it?

EUCLID AND HIS WORK

We know very little of the life of Euclid the mathematician—who must not be confused with his homonym, the philosopher of Megara. Only by crosschecking sources can we surmise his birth and death dates. It is fairly certain that these dates place him between the mathematicians who worked at the Academy after Plato's death and Archimedes' early scientific work. His institutional position provides us with more specific information. Euclid taught mathematics at Alexandria; he was probably drawn there, along with other scientists, by Ptolemy I Soter when the Museum was founded. It is safe to say that Euclid's scientific work was carried out during the first decades of the 3rd century B.C.E.

According to ancient sources, the Euclidean corpus comprised about ten titles relating to the "mathematical sciences" as that term was used by the Greeks (including, for example, astronomy and optics). Six of these works have come down to us; however, some important texts have been lost.

Pappus of Alexandria, for example, cites Euclid's four books on *Conics*, apparently an ordered presentation of everything that had been learned about the question since the discovery of these curves (parabolas, ellipses, hyperbolas) by Menaechmus and, later, the treatment of curves as conic sections by Aristaeus (*Pappi Alexandrini*, II.672.18–678.24). This is probably the work to which Archimedes refers on several occasions. Pappus provides the most likely explanation for the disappearance of this work when he states that Apollonius of Perge (latter half of the 3rd century) completed the four books of Euclid's *Conics* and added four others, to form his own famous eight-volume treatise of the same name.

The second important work that has been lost is *Porisms*, in three volumes, mentioned by Pappus and Proclus. Its subject matter is disputed. It appears to have been a work preparatory to a theory of geometric loci. Since this theory

was developed for the most part during the Hellenistic period, we may infer that its very successes led to a loss of interest in Euclid's initial work. In 1860, Michel Chasles published an attempt to reconstruct the work, based on fragments found in Pappus.

A third treatise, *Surface Loci* in two books, is also cited by Pappus as being part of a *Treasury of Analysis*, but its purpose is also a matter of conjecture. Did it deal with surfaces treated as loci of certain characteristic lines, for example surfaces in rotation limiting certain solids? Archimedes did brilliant work on these bodies, which may explain why, once again, Euclid's work itself has not survived.

According to Proclus, the corpus also included a didactic treatise intended to teach students to avoid paralogisms, entitled *Pseudaria* (Fallacies).

Of the works that have survived, the most important, and the source of its author's age-old fame, are the thirteen books of *Elements*. However, in the field of plane geometry we should not overlook the extant collection of *Data*, which provides the elementary foundation for all analytical reasoning; this text shows what can be determined about a figure when certain information is given. We must also note the treatise *On Divisions (of Figures):* the Greek text is lost, but fragments have reached us via the Arab-Latin tradition; here figures are divided proportionately by lines subject to certain restrictions.

To this collection we must add three other texts that stand apart from geometry, strictly speaking. *Phaenomena* provides a description of what is visible in the celestial sphere in motion, in other words the rising and setting of the stars, not including planetary movements. Starting from the hypothesis of visual, rectilinear rays, *Optics* determines what is actually seen of a distant object, and its argument depends in reality on perspective. The *Sectio canonis* contains the arithmetic theory of musical intervals, in the spirit of Pythagorean tradition, and is perhaps only a fragment of the more complete *Elements of Music*. These three treatises are presented in the Euclidean form that governs *Elements*.

Besides these ten titles, others attributed to Euclid include several fragments of *Mechanics* (of dubious authenticity), a *Catoptrica* that is not genuine, and an *Introduction to Harmony* that is by Cleonides, a disciple of Aristoxenes.

ELEMENTS

The tradition of composing *Elements* extends back to Hippocrates of Chio (ca. 435); the texts were revised on several occasions by geometricians who were probably from the Academy. Euclid's edition seems to be the fifth, and while the four preceding versions have been forgotten, his had no successor—a clear indication of its success.

The *Elements* were not "elementary" works, not in the sense that their mathematical content had been simplified for beginners. According to Proclus's analysis, they contained necessary and sufficient propositions for the advancement of science beyond the results obtained, and they permitted further exploration of unsolved problems. They constituted the body of the central doctrine of mathematical sciences from which all the rest could be derived. Though they gave an accounting of acquired knowledge, they adhered to essentials and were not a demonstration of all extant mathematical knowledge to date. As theoretical works, they did not introduce the art of calculation, called "logistics"; they bore instead on the two fundamental mathematical sciences, arithmetic and geometry. The composition of *Elements* was thus a matter of complex choices: specialized questions were eliminated; both prolixity and excessive brevity were avoided; a general guideline for the deductive process was provided.

Elements developed during a period of major advances in Greek mathematics, between the time of Hippocrates of Chio and Euclid, and one might expect to find traces of that period in Euclid's text. The chronological order in which knowledge was acquired was not necessarily the order adopted by the treatise in its exposition. Thus there is a large historical question about the genesis of *Elements*.

Euclid's exposition is divided into propositions, each one demonstrated by means of the preceding one, and each being either a theorem or a problem, all of which are connected according to the order of a deductive synthesis. This approach presupposes certain initial statements serving as starting points, or principles. These form three groups. First, definitions of terms appear each time new objects are introduced. Second, certain statements that are true for all mathematical sciences, called common notions, deal with the properties of equality and inequality, and correspond to what Aristotle considered "judgments of reason" (axioms), indubitable by their very nature. Finally, for geometry alone, there are hypotheses formulated as "claims" (or postulates), especially concerning the possibility of using an "ideal" ruler or compass, and—most famous of all—the meeting of straight lines the sum of whose angles with a common secant is inferior to two right angles (the Fifth Postulate).

Several theories or subtheories are distributed, in a somewhat complicated order, among the thirteen books. Book I opens with the theory of plane figures, but beginning with proposition 35 and throughout Book II, the subject is a theory of equivalence in measurements for rectilinear areas, a theory of great importance because it allows for transformation of a given figure into a different, equivalent one. This leads most notably to the so-called Pythagorean theorem on right triangles, and the solution of the problem of the squaring of a rectangular figure. Then, in Book III, the theory of plane figures re-

sumes with the study of the circle; in Book IV the subtheory of regular polygons results in the application of the knowledge acquired in Book II to that of Book III. This collection of results is applied to the case of solids in Book XI.

Up to this point, the author of *Elements* does not allow himself recourse to the idea of proportion among geometric magnitudes. This idea is a very general one, since it applies to any ratio between magnitudes, even if it cannot be expressed numerically. The theory is developed in Book V, a pivotal book in the organization of *Elements,* for it takes the reader to a further level of abstraction. Its first application to plane figures leads, in Book VI, to the subtheory of similar figures that allows one to find, in a generalized form, the results obtained in Books I and II by means of the equivalence of areas. One should note that, in this generalized form, the arguments involving ratios between the areas of polygons lead beyond *Elements* to the theory of conics. In addition, the theory of proportions opens the way to a sophisticated method for measuring areas and volumes that prefigures infinitesimal calculus by using progressive approximations of the magnitude to be estimated; known ever since the 17th century as the exhaustion method, it does not appear, in essence, until the beginning of Book X, and it comes into its own in Book XII. Archimedes made important advances in this area and provided brilliant applications.

Books VII, VIII, and IX contain Euclidean arithmetic, the theory of whole numbers and their ratios; proportions here constitute in effect a special case, and the notion of "continuous proportion" leads to the development of a subtheory of the powers of whole numbers.

When two magnitudes of the same type have a number-to-number ratio between them, they are mutually commensurable. The case of incommensurables thus remains to be examined in Book X, where incommensurable straight lines and the rectangles that they can form are classified.

The last three books are devoted to stereology, or solid geometry. Book XI lays the foundation by generalizing plane geometry for the third dimension. Book XII treats the measurement of circles, pyramids, cones, and spheres by applying the exhaustion method. Book XIII describes the construction of the five regular convex polyhedra in a given sphere; this argument presupposes in particular some results from Book X.

The text of *Elements* is remarkable in its form. Basically, each proposition is developed according to a precise and unchanging formal process consisting of six steps, the most important being the statement, the construction, the demonstration, and the conclusion; each step has a set function, either heuristic or logical.

Elements can be seen as a treatise on the measurement of geometric objects, using only straight lines and circumferences. This metric geometry is

created without recourse to the notion of rational numbers, nor real numbers; without a clearly defined notion of "operation" (despite its use) and without recourse to an algebraic form of literal and operative symbolism. Finally, we should note that in no case did Euclid employ any processes that might suggest actual infinity.

THE HISTORY OF THE WORK

Since ancient times, as we can see from any number of the great works, Euclid's *Elements* has been the object of many commentaries. The work of Heron of Alexandria has been partially preserved in Arabic; it is shaped by Heron's desire to complete and perfect Euclid's treatise. The Neoplatonist logician Porphyry of Tyre seems to have been interested in the forms of Euclid's argumentation, the precision of his propositions, and the rigor of his proofs. The mathematician Pappus of Alexandria left an important contribution to the discussion that is known through an Arabic version as his *Commentary on Book X*. The Aristotelian Simplicius examined the principles, in particular—that is, the initial propositions—and his commentary became an introduction to geometry; excerpts have been preserved in Arabic. Finally, there remains in Greek, from the 5th century C.E., the very important *Commentary on Book I* by Proclus of Lycia, the diadochus (head of the Academy); treating all aspects of the text and its historical, logical, epistemological, and philosophical context, *Commentary* remains an irreplaceable document on the position of *Elements* in Greek science, the intentions of its author, the progress that culminated in *Elements*, the criticism it encountered, and the difficulties it contained.

Elements was the chief means of transmission of basic mathematical knowledge in Hellenic and Roman times. In the 4th century C.E., the mathematician Theon of Alexandria put out a new edition, somewhat enlarged for didactic purposes, from which all the known Greek manuscripts before the 19th century were derived. The tradition continued in the Byzantine empire. For example, in the year 888 Arethas, the archbishop of Caesarea, had *Elements* copied and annotated the text in his own hand: today this codex is in the Bodleian Library at Oxford. The Greek manuscripts, actually still quite numerous in Europe, contain a total of 1,440 scholia from various periods.

Before it was resurrected during the Renaissance, Euclid's work followed a different course in the countries that had been converted to Islam. From the very beginning of the 9th century, educated people in Baghdad knew the Greek text, and the caliphs encouraged its translation into Arabic. Two traditions appeared, one from the two successive editions of the first translation by Al-Haggag, the other stemming from a work of the second half of the 9th century by Ishaq ibn Hunayn and revised by Tabit ibn Qurra. Although these translations indicate an interest in the sources and in comparing manuscripts,

they made no secret of their aim to improve on the text, either for didactic purposes or for logical and mathematical ones. Starting with these versions, an entire "Euclidean" literature developed, consisting of critical analyses, summaries, précis, emendations, and, finally, commentaries on *Elements*, as a whole or in part. From the 9th century to the 13th, the greatest mathematicians and philosophers of the Arab world studied Euclid, and principally concerned themselves with the question of parallels and the Fifth Postulate, with the theory of proportions in Book V, and with the theory of incommensurable lines in Book X. These debates were important for the development of mathematical thought in the Arab world, while the translations figured in the transmission of *Elements* to medieval Latinists in the West.

The early Middle Ages knew *Elements* only through collections containing altered fragments of a Latin translation probably done by Boethius. In the 12th century a Latin translation of a Greek text appeared in Sicily but apparently had little influence. However, a translation of a manuscript from the Ishaq-Tabit school is attributed to Gerard of Cremona, who was famous in Toledo in the 12th century; in the same period, Adelard of Bath is credited with three successive versions of *Elements*: a translation, a condensed commentary, and a complete collection in the tradition of Al-Haggag, of which some fifty manuscripts survive. This was the beginning of a tradition that lasted up to the 15th century with some fifteen revisions, including the translation by Campanus of Novare, appearing in 1259, the best Latin version of the Arabic from a mathematical point of view. So it is not true that people of the Middle Ages were ignorant of Greek mathematics; in the later centuries several versions of *Elements* were available. These presented some notable differences from the Greek, since they came through the Arabic tradition, but they nevertheless allowed for comparison and discussion. Medieval scholars were interested in logic and principles, in the problems of infinity, real or potential; and thus in the question of the divisibility of magnitudes and of geometric continuity. Philosophical preoccupations outweighed mathematical inventiveness. Afterward, as Latin continued for a long time to be the language of scholars, the practice of accompanying the Greek text with a Latin version continued until the beginning of the 20th century.

Since the invention of the printing press, there have been more editions and translations of Euclid's *Elements* than of any work except the Bible. The first printed edition of Euclid appeared in Venice in 1482: this was Campanus's Latin text, which brought the work into the modern age. It was soon followed in 1505, again in Venice, by the complete Euclid of Zamberti, this time a Latin version of the Greek text. Editors and scholars were divided about the merit of these two editions throughout the 16th century, even though the first printed edition of the Greek appeared in Basel in 1530; unfortunately, this edition was based on two of the poorest manuscripts. The quarrel continued until the appearance of Commandino's Latin version in 1572 in

Pesaro. This was the first one based on an acceptable Greek original, and it served as the basis for many later works.

Besides these key facts, the 16th century stands out for the great number of publications throughout Europe; these reflected various choices, but their common goal was to provide a working instrument adapted for students. The first vernacular translations also appeared at this time: for example, the one by Pierre Forcadel in French (1564–1566). Finally, in the 16th century a whole genre of commentaries emerged that often dealt with the logical structure of *Elements,* and also with the mathematical implications of the theory of proportions in Book V. The masterful work of Christopher Clavius fell within this genre; an extremely detailed Latin review that appeared in 1574, it was frequently reissued: rewriting, notes, additions, critiques, and explanations all combined to provide an instructive and stimulating mathematical approach to the Hellenistic legacy. There is every reason to believe that it was from Clavius's Euclid that Descartes first taught himself mathematics at the college of La Flèche.

The history of the Greek text was next punctuated by Gregory's edition at Oxford in 1703; by Peyrard's discovery of the Vatican manuscript, indicating a tradition that antedates the edition of Theon, and which allowed him to publish a trilingual edition (Greek, Latin, French) in 1814–1818; and, finally, by Heiberg's critical edition, which became the authoritative modern version (1883–1916). In addition, the tradition of publishing texts for teaching purposes—the commentaries and handbooks used in schools—persisted throughout the 17th and 18th centuries, and even into the 19th in some countries, for example in England. This is the source of the view of *Elements* as an elementary pedagogical text, even though the mathematical discussions it introduces are of the first rank. At the same time, Euclid was translated into every language of Europe, and the influence of his work extended to China and India.

ELEMENTS AND MODERN MATHEMATICAL THOUGHT

The development of modern mathematics has occurred not via a rejection of *Elements* but in a dialogue permitting a better elaboration of new concepts by integrating ancient knowledge destined to be surpassed. For example, in the 17th century mathematicians drew on every possible aspect of the theory of proportions and its key ideas, including infinitesimal geometrical analyses, before the discovery of the differential calculus algorithms; one could say the same of the exhaustion method, which works in conjunction with proportion before the introduction of integral calculus.

Between the time of Henry Savile, who studied implicit postulates in 1621, and the time of Girolamo Saccheri, who tried to prove the Fifth Postulate in

1733, the work of the best commentators, such as Isaac Barrow (1655), Robert Simson (1756), or John Playfair (1795), offered a host of indicators on the means of perfecting proofs. In England in particular, until the 19th century, *Elements* remained the basis for teaching and continued to spark productive critical work. Logicians such as Augustus De Morgan studied the text closely. That England should be the home of so many innovators in modern mathematical logic is perhaps owing to research into the laws of logic in standardized discourse in search of proof, the discourse of mathematics, of which *Elements* was still the classic example.

This work, moreover, was to have an impact on mathematics itself. In effect, the logical analysis of arguments progresses naturally to axioms. Since Descartes, the epistemological status that Aristotle had given axioms developed amid differences between philosophical doctrines. Instead of relying on self-evidence, Leibniz sought to derive axioms from the principle of noncontradiction. Moreover, since Pascal's day, the discussion of definitions of primary terms that Aristotle had initiated took a different course. The 19th century was characterized by more technical reflections, in which more adequate reformulations were sought. Correlatively, the distinctions between axiom and postulate, indeed between definition and postulate, began to be questioned. The discussions of the Fifth Postulate contributed substantially to this reconsideration. Launched anew by Saccheri, the attempts to prove the famous proposition ended with the appearance of some ten equivalent propositions, assumptions implied in the so-called new demonstrations. The result is well known: the failure of the attempts to prove via the absurd led to the appearance of diverse non-Euclidean geometries. The notion of mathematical theory and that of mathematical truth changed; the status of preliminary principles changed as well. Increasingly, the logical properties were brought out that should belong to any collection of propositions that could be called axiomatic.

At the very end of the 19th century, in 1899, David Hilbert brought modern axiomatics to Euclidean geometry, completing the developments begun a century earlier. Since the presentation of the mathematical content of the other theories figuring in *Elements* had been profoundly transformed by the generalization of the idea of "number" and the growth of analysis, it is clear that, by the end of the 19th century, the debate about Euclid's work and its fecundity for the development of science was over, and its place in history was definitively established.

What this work has contributed to the history of human thought is nothing less than one form of scientific rationalism. This is characterized by applying universally recognized rules in furnishing proof. The proof of the falsity of a proposition can be obtained in two ways, either because the facts refute it, or because it can be found to be in contradiction with propositions

taken as true. In the first case, the furnishing of the proof is experimental, while in the second it is entirely logical—in other words, it is linked to the structure of the standardized discourse written in technical language that the Greeks called *logos*. *Elements* furnished the signal example of this second type, one adopted by all great mathematicians since antiquity. Such a mode of rationalism corresponding to what Aristotle described as "demonstrative science" demands not only that one define the objects on which knowledge rests, but also that one specify a small number of propositions initially taken as true in reference to the universe containing these objects and that one allow oneself certain manipulations of these objects (in geometry, "constructions") compatible with the structure of that universe. It is the function of the postulates to be hypotheses assuring the applicability of Euclidean mathematics in a world where physical bodies are invariable for the group of displacements (translations, rotations, or both). This choice assured it the privilege of appearing to be "natural" for hundreds of years, well into the 19th century. Moreover, concerning what measure of "truth" came from intuition of first principles, it was permissible for mathematicians to continue to reduce the role of intuition more and more, and this tendency toward ever-increasing abstraction was the main line of historical development in mathematics. This was perfectly compatible with the type of rationalism that *Elements* offered; thus *Elements* continued to be the ideal pursued even in periods when new methods focused attention on the proliferation of results obtained by the strength of calculus more than by the rigor of the demonstration. When, under the influence of non-Euclidean geometries, reference to "the natural world" ceased to be exclusive, we saw a change in the meaning of the initial hypotheses. Mathematical theories appeared as paradigms of possible worlds, divided between the demand of noncontradiction and the demand of constructibility. Although singularly refined, *Elements'* model of rationalism endured. In the 17th century, Giles de Roberval wrote a new *Elements of Geometry*; in the 20th, the Bourbaki group entitled its great work *Elements of Mathematics.*

ELEMENTS AND CONTEMPORARY RESEARCH IN THE HISTORY OF SCIENCE

Just when *Elements* had lost its power to inspire mathematicians, a new area of interest in it began to appear. Under the influence of philological scholarship and studies in the history of universal thought after the manner of Hegel and Renan, the ancient Greek world, its culture, and its thought were the focus of attention for all those who were searching for the roots of Western civilization. Greek reason engaged the mind. The history of science began to replace philosophy in the search for the birth process of these canons of ra-

tionality in Greek mathematics that people in every century had admired. The 20th century has been punctuated by works by the historians of Greek mathematics: Zeuthen, Tannery, Heath, Becker, Loria, Mugler, Abel Rey, Van der Waerden, to name only the principal authors in the first half of the century. Thanks to their works, a more accurate vision, a deeper comprehension, of the history of Greek science has been achieved. This historical enlightenment has modified the understanding of the text itself, some of whose details can be explained only by the intellectual and linguistic practices, modes of thought, and cultural features of the period. This historical interest was entirely lacking in the classical approach to *Elements*.

Contemporary research centers on a few principal themes, which can be only briefly stated. First of all, it involves reconstituting, so far as possible, the origin of *Elements*, the mathematical advances that preceded Euclid. This project raises the extremely complex problem of determining the role of the Pythagoreans, cited by Aristotle but burdened with the weight of later legends that call for intense scrutiny. In particular, one aspect of the reconstruction is the question of the antecedents of the theory of ratios: was this theory based in ancient times on the sophisticated definition that Euclid gave it, or on a calculation procedure known as Euclid's algorithm? Linked to this question of origins is the important problem of the influence that doctrines advanced by Plato or Aristotle to define "science," which at the time constituted what we would call the epistemology of mathematics, might have had on Euclid. Bearing on this problem is also the question of the deductive structure of the collection of *Elements:* to what extent was Euclid able to complete effectively and accurately the logical outline of a perfect deductive theory and an entirely coherent technical language?

If we turn to the history of the civilizations that preceded or followed that of the Greeks, we must take into account the recent challenge to a "classical" interpretation built up by early 20th-century historians, who saw a "geometric algebra" in certain Euclidean methods for transforming areas; this question also bears on the interpretation of the codes for calculation revealed by the cuneiform tablets of Mesopotamia, as well as on the history of mathematics in the Islamic countries. Another historical question, which has been studied surprisingly little, involves the way geometricians of the Hellenistic period used Euclidean techniques and methods. Finally, owing to the recent discovery of manuscripts, a new interest in medieval Latin versions of Euclid is emerging; this returns to the forefront the need for critical editions of the Arabic translations, which are still lacking. Euclid's *Elements* remain a locus for dynamic research; in this respect, the work's career is far from over.

MAURICE CAVEING
Translated by Elizabeth Rawlings and Jeannine Pucci

Bibliography

Texts and Translations

Busard, H. L. L. *The First Latin Translation of Euclid's Elements Commonly Ascribed to Adelard of Bath.* Toronto: Pontifical Institute of Medieval Studies, 1983.

———. *The Latin Translation of the Arabic Version of Euclid's Elements Commonly Ascribed to Gerard of Cremona.* Leyden: Brill, 1984.

Chasles, Michel. *Les trois livres de porismes d'Euclide rétablis.* Paris: Mallet-Bachelier, 1860.

Euclid. *Les eléments.* Ed. and trans. Bernard Vitrac. 3 vols. Paris: Presses Universitaires de France. Vol. 1: *Introduction générale,* by Maurice Caveing, and *Géométrie plane* (Books I–IV), 1990. Vol. 2: *Proportions, Similitude: Arithmétique* (Books V–IX), 1994. Vol. 3: *Grandeurs et Incommensurables* (Book X), 1998.

———. *The Thirteen Books of Euclid's Elements.* Ed. and trans. Thomas Little Heath. 3 vols. Cambridge: Cambridge University Press, 1908; 2nd ed. revised and supplemented, 1926; repr. New York: Dover, 1956.

Euclidis Elementa, post Heiberg ed. Evangelos Stamatis. 5 vols. Teubner: Leipzig, 1969–1977.

Euclidis Opera omnia, ed. Iohannes Ludovicus Heiberg and Henricus Menge. 8 vols. Teubner: Leipzig, 1883–1916.

Heron of Alexandria. *Anaritii in decem libros priores Elementorum Educlidis Commentarii.* Ed. M. Curtze (an. Nayrizi). Leipzig: Teubner, 1899.

Pappus of Alexandria. *Pappi Alexandrini collectionis quae supersunt.* Ed. Friedrich Hultsch. Berlin: Weidmann, 1876–1878; repr. Amsterdam: Hakkert, 1965.

———. *The Commentary of Pappus on Book X of Euclid's Elements.* Ed. G. Junge and W. Thomson. Cambridge, Mass.: Harvard University Press, 1930; repr. New York and London: Johnson Reprint Company, 1968.

Proclus: A Commentary on the First Book of Euclid's Elements. Trans. Glenn R. Morrow. Princeton: Princeton University Press, 1970.

Thomas, Ivor. *Selections Illustrating the History of Greek Mathematics.* Vol. 1: *From Thales to Euclid;* vol. 2: *From Aristarchus to Pappus of Alexandria.* Loeb Classical Library.

Studies

Caveing, Maurice. *La figure et le nombre: Recherches sur les premières mathématiques des Grecs.* Lille: Presses Universitaires du Septentrion, 1997.

———. *L'irrationalité dans les mathématiques grecques jusqu'à Euclide.* Lille: Presses Universitaires du Septentrion, 1998.

Hilbert, David. *The Foundations of Geometry* (1899). Trans. E. J. Townsend. 2nd ed. La Salle, Ill.: Open Court, 1971.

Knorr, Wilbur Richard. *The Evolution of the Euclidean Elements.* Dordrecht and Boston: Reidel, 1975.

Michel, Paul-Henri. *De Pythagore à Euclide: Contribution à l'histoire des mathématiques préeuclidiennes.* Paris: Les Belles Lettres, 1950.

Mueller, Ian. *Philosophy of Mathematics and Deductive Structure in Euclid's Elements.* Cambridge, Mass.: MIT Press, 1981.

Mugler, Charles. *Dictionnaire historique de la terminologie géometrique des Grecs.* 2 vols. Paris: Klincksieck, 1958–1959.

Taisbak, Christian Marinus. *Division and "Logos," A Theory of Equivalent Couples and Sets of Integers Propounded by Euclid in the Arithmetical Books of the Elements.* Odense: Odense Universitetsforlag, 1971.

Related Articles

Demonstration and the Idea of Science; Geometry; Mathematics; Archimedes

GALEN

As much a philosopher as a physician, Galen was viewed by his contemporaries as garrulous, brilliant, and intolerable. For us, the image of the physician has won out over that of the philosopher. Galen lives in history as an exceptional figure distinguished by a combination of great speculative power and passionate investigation of medical phenomena. His prolixity as a writer, too, explains the influence he has exerted throughout the centuries. Handed down through the Oriental world and later in the West, his vast work—of which the twenty volumes of the Kühn edition offer only a part—remained the basis of medical teaching until the beginning of the 18th century. This success was also the reason for the decline of Galen's influence. Because his work was tied to a science, it gradually fell out of fashion, and Galenism became synonymous with a way of thinking judged both dogmatic and sterile. It was only when it could be completely detached from science and restored to history that the Galenic corpus could finally be studied in its own right. From the hands of physicians it passed to those of historians and philologists at the beginning of the 19th century. Despite their efforts, however, Galen's thought is still not fully known. The reasons for this are the very large size of the corpus, the fact that access to it is still difficult, and the problem of mastering its complexity and scope. Moreover, a good number of his writings have disappeared, as have many of the works to which Galen refers. Others survive only in Arabic or in bad Latin, and in translations of translations. In the last analysis, we know the man better than his work.

As part of Galen's work is autobiographical, we have a good deal of information about his life and career. Born in 129 C.E. in the wealthy town of Pergamum, the gifted young man was educated under the attentive care of his father, Nicon, a learned architect. A taste for mathematics and rigorous demonstration, a thorough grounding in philosophy acquired without loss of intellectual freedom, and rigorous standards on the intellectual and moral planes remained associated, for Galen, with this revered and noble paternal figure. About his mother, however, Galen says only a few harsh words. When a dream suggested to Nicon that he should let his son pursue the path of medicine, he offered the young Galen a medical education at the hands of the best masters. After his initial training in Pergamum, Galen went to Smyrna, where he could hear Pelops and also the Platonist philosopher Albinos, then to Corinth, where he arrived too late to encounter the great anatomist Numisianus, and finally to Alexandria, a major center for the study of anat-

omy in particular; this was the only place one could study human skeletons. His study tour completed, he returned to Pergamum, where he became a physician to gladiators, a prestigious job for a young practitioner. He saved many, by his own account. But political troubles in 166 led him to leave his native city for Rome, the imperial capital, where he stayed initially for four years (162–166). This was an exciting period. Galen built up a high-level practice and devoted himself to intense anatomical research. Nevertheless, for a number of reasons, among which he mentions the fierce jealousy of his colleagues, he left the city for his homeland, stopping along the way at various places to gather medicinal material. Pharmacology remained one of his chief interests.

He had scarcely arrived home when he had to leave again, called back by the emperors Marcus Aurelius and Lucius Verus to join them at their winter camp in Aquileia, the base for their expeditions against the Marcomans. Nevertheless Galen, who had nothing to gain from cold military stations, obtained permission to remain at Rome with Commodus, the son of Marcus Aurelius. He spent eight years there, devoting his time to intense study and writing, before Emperor Marcus Aurelius returned. Galen remained in favor at court from then on. This period was clouded, though, by a huge fire in Rome in 191; it destroyed the house in which he had stored numerous unpublished manuscripts. Despite this blow Galen, already advanced in years, had the courage to begin several of his projects all over again. He went on to write important treatises, and seems to have lived and continued writing to an advanced age.

Galen's work undeniably represents a major achievement, owing to its encyclopedic nature. It is encyclopedic in the fields it covers—medicine, of which he had explored almost all the branches—as well as logic, philosophy, philology, and so on. It is comprehensive, too, in its pedagogical interest, pointing out in what order subjects should be taken up, from the beginning to the highest level. But it is a masterwork also because Galen saw himself as continuing the entire Hippocratic and Hellenistic medical tradition; he did not view himself as an innovator, a claim he detested. Such an attitude on his part implied that he took the history of doctrines into account. In this respect, Galen was often a historian or doxographer. Even when he truncates or distorts his adversaries' thought, or interprets them in a tendentious manner, we are indebted to him for transmitting crucial accounts of medical and philosophical history, Stoic in particular—accounts that, without him, would have disappeared.

A MEDICAL PHYSICS

To analyze the essence of Galen's doctrine, we may begin with what forms the basis of his "physics," the substance of which living creatures are made, according to him, and with what animates them. Galen's thought depends, to

begin with, on a theory of the constitution of matter that is presented as a holdover from the ancients. It is on them, in particular on Hippocrates, that he bases his thesis of a continuous and noncorpuscular matter, made up of four fundamental elements *(stoicheia)*. By the term *element*, he explains, he does not mean an element in itself in an absolute form (fire), or a pure quality (warmth); he is referring to what is dominant in a particular body. It is this last form that interests medicine, which is concerned with living bodies. In these bodies, the elements, or qualities, always appear mixed *(krase)*, and in proportions that make up the uniqueness of individuals. Similarly, and in conformity with the Hippocratic tradition, Galen's humoral theory is based on four humors: yellow bile, black bile, phlegm, and water, each formed of a mixture of qualities. Although it will play no role except in pathology, this humoral theory will become one of the key elements in late Galenism.

Galen's theory of the constitution of matter allows him to explain phenomena relating to health and illness. It is in fact the nature of the mixture (or temperament) that determines the performance of bodily functions and their disorders. In a general way, the state of health, or the unimpeded performance of the functions of the body, depends on a good mixture *(eukrasia)* and the good proportion of qualities. Illness, on the contrary, is principally attributable to a bad mixture, a *dyskrasia*. Galen develops these notions, which he sees as essential for the vital processes and their disorders, in the two treatises that set forth the bases of this medicophilosophical physics, *On the Elements according to Hippocrates* and *On Temperaments*. He adds the Aristotelian notion of quality, active (warm) or passive (cold), in the tradition of physicians who attribute an important role to innate heat and to "breath" or *pneuma*, especially in the process of generation. Moreover, at the end of his long career, Galen continued to posit these notions as the foundation of a knowledge of nature that he considered absolutely necessary for any good doctor.

The second theoretical stage, in which medicine and philosophy are still allied, is that of the dynamic properties issuing from the mixtures of elements or humors. The notion of faculty *(dynamis)* is complemented by that of activity *(energeia)*, or function. Physiology as a whole depends on two types of faculties: those that preside over involuntary or "natural" functions, and those that rule over voluntary or "psychic" movements. The issue of the natural faculties raises the essential problem of finalism in nature. For Galen, the natural functions—which can ultimately be summed up under four headings: attraction, assimilation, retention, expulsion—are each attributed to an innate faculty required by nature and inscribed in bodies. For example, the attraction that allows the body to draw nourishment essential for its growth is an innate faculty. Here, Galen opposes any corpuscular or mechanistic vision, or any vision that is simply less goal-oriented than his own, one that would depict digestion, for example, as the result of a pulverizing of the ele-

ments, and filtering and urinary excretion as a purely mechanical process. On this point, he never stops taunting his favorite adversaries, the Alexandrian Erasistratus and especially Asclepiades (1st century B.C.E.).

The other faculties, the so-called psychic ones, also bring Galen into some of the basic arguments of his day: debates over the place of sensations and the role of the heart and brain. The problem touches on the question of the soul in its nature, its parts and their localizations. Galen adopts an unwavering position: he chooses not to take a stand on questions he deems unanswerable through physiological investigation and useless to medicine. Conversely, the concrete question of the hegemonic seat of the soul, responsible for sensation and movement, remains a fundamental issue for him. In this realm Galen, like Plato, locates the hegemonic soul and its activities in the brain, or rather in the psychic *pneuma*, which allows for their realization and which fills its ventricles (let us recall that the cavities of the brain are thought more important than its substance, during this period). The heart plays a secondary role: through the carotid arteries, it supplies the brain with the aeriferous blood that contributes to the formation of the psychic *pneuma*, the one that belongs to the higher functions. Whence the idea of ligating the arteries to see what damage is done.

Just how, then, are sensation and movement produced? The example of the electric ray, which transmits a shock to the fisherman through an iron-tipped harpoon, is an example of a "qualitative transmission" from the brain to the muscles via the nerves. The hypothesis of the transmission of *pneuma* through the nerve canal, adopted by other physicians, applies for Galen only to the optic nerve, the only one that appears to be hollow. In his treatise *On the Doctrines of Hippocrates and Plato,* in which he does his best to show that Plato and Hippocrates are in agreement on the soul, he sharply attacks the belief of Chrysippus the Stoic, who saw the heart as the seat of the *hegemonikon,* especially in its function as producer of the voice and of discourse. Galen shows that, on the contrary, the voice is tightly linked to respiration and that respiration is achieved by muscles moved by the nerves themselves, under the direction of the brain. In the course of his ongoing arguments with his adversaries, Galen used his favorite tactics: he liked to point out the way an author contradicted himself (Chrysippus on the soul) or the way he habitually "denied the evidence." For Galen, failing to acknowledge what is self-evident means falling into error or skepticism.

ANATOMY AND PHENOMENA

The importance attributed to visible facts, or "phenomena," explains the preeminent role of anatomical knowledge for Galen. Here again he sees himself as his masters' heir, continuing the work of Hippocrates. Against all reason, he even goes so far as to consider Hippocratic anatomy an infallible source of

truth—all the while claiming credit for himself, to be sure, for some important discoveries, such as his famous recurrent laryngeal nerve.

Anatomical knowledge overall has, for Galen, several goals. It is indispensable for practice, whether that involves surgery or a simple bleeding; it is necessary for physiological knowledge; and finally, it offers access to the understanding of nature in general, and to natural philosophy. These various levels of interest are reflected in specific works. At the beginning of his career Galen wrote short works for strictly pragmatic purposes, such as a treatise for midwives on the anatomy of the uterus and several treatises intended for beginners. These useful studies of anatomy are designed to prevent physicians from making serious mistakes not only in their actions but also in their diagnoses. In this regard, Galen defends the theory of "affected spots" in pathology, a theory that attributes local causes to many ailments, and that therefore requires sound anatomical knowledge. Whether it remains situated in a precise spot or affects other structures through "sympathy," the ailment will be the more curable if its place of origin is treated. This brought Galen many therapeutic successes: for example, he cured a man with paralyzed fingers by working on the spinal column and not—as did his more ignorant colleagues—on the fingers themselves.

Aside from its practical value, Galen saw anatomy as the chief means of access to an understanding of physiological processes. Nevertheless, the step from structures to functions remains tricky. Not everything is as simple as demonstrating that the hand is perfectly adapted for grasping. In any case, Galen discarded the oversimplistic principle of "anatomical deduction," that is, the direct deduction of function from form, and he also rejected the topological argument that draws on the organ's position in the body. Moreover, he took advantage of the opportunity to attack the "anatomical indolence" of the Stoics once again. Nevertheless, in his writings the form and the other characteristics of organs (texture, density, composition, relations, and so on) are inseparable from their functions, because they have been perfectly adapted to them by a provident Nature. And an understanding of functions, even the most complex, such as respiration or digestion, will in turn permit an advance in the understanding of particular structures. Thus it is clear that Galen refers to anatomy at every turn. We find in anatomy the most visible sign of Nature's providence, Nature having chosen the best possible forms and dispositions for the accomplishment of the functions in question. The great treatise in fourteen books *On the Use of Parts* spells out this functional and providential anatomy for each part of the body.

The principal means of acquiring anatomical knowledge is dissection. Galen devoted a magisterial work, *Anatomical Procedures,* to animal dissection—the only kind he envisaged and practiced. This treatise also contains an account of practical experiments on animals or, better, "still living" animals—swine, monkeys, and other animals whose suffering did not trouble him inor-

dinately. Galen's most famous experiments, which go back to much of his teachers' repertory, concern the neurological and vascular system: compressions of the cerebral ventricles, serial section of the spinal nerves, experiments on thoracic nerves and muscles responsible for respiration and the voice, ligatures or sections of vessels such as the carotid artery and an experiment with a tube in the femoral artery, and many experiments performed in embryology. These are all aimed at proving the existence of phenomena that are not directly accessible to the senses: the responsibility of the brain and not the heart for movement and sensation, the production and function of the pulse, and so forth. The strength of his experiments, for Galen, lies precisely in their demonstrative power. As a matter of fact, he performed many of these experiments in public sessions during his first stay in Rome, playing on the curiosity and surprise of the spectators.

The understanding of complex phenomena, such as those having to do with major bodily functions, implies not only observation but also other means that are theoretical in nature. Galen refers to a variety of concepts, and especially to the Aristotelian type of causality (the Stoic causal system turns out to be useful to him in pathology). He also resorts to many other notions, such as balance, proportion, and exchange, or "sympathy." The more difficult the function is to understand—for example, the exchange between blood and *pneuma* through the pulmonary vessels—the stronger the presence of these models becomes. They sometimes lead Galen to go beyond observation, as when, from the pores visible on the lining separating the two cardiac ventricles (interventricular septum), he infers the existence of passages allowing the blood to pass directly from the right ventricle to the left. Later acknowledged as an intangible truth, this "error" was hard to refute because it was linked to a coherent explanatory system and to the implacable principle that Nature does nothing in vain. This explains the minimal importance Galen gave to quantitative measures. In this regard, scholars have long been intrigued that Galen "missed" the circulation of the blood when he had all the elements necessary to understand it. The only real example of quantitative measurement was the production of urine, which was measured and compared to the quantity of liquid ingested, a model in which Owsei Temkin saw a possible source of inspiration for Harvey. Actually, Galen had no need to know objective quantities, since his system was based on a balance of exchanges that he judged satisfactory. And he attached much more importance to the demonstrative method.

THE THEORY OF DEMONSTRATION

Even if Galen uses many ad hoc arguments whenever the need arises, he gives his developments a character that is at least formally rigorous, so persuaded is he that the discovery of truth comes through sound methodical rea-

soning. A major treatise entitled *On Demonstration*, which has disappeared, attested to the importance Galen attributed to the art of logical demonstration. He sought to provide an accesssible explanation of it for specialists as well as a broader public, including the medical profession in particular. For Galen, as for Aristotle, the basis of knowledge rests on principles *(archai)* that are facts or axioms recognized by everyone and accessible through evidence. From that starting point, truth lies in deducing, from general but more specific statements, "theorems," which can comprise empirical or practical elements. Logical operations also call for definitions and divisions. The question of definition and nomination holds little interest for Galen. He says he cares nothing for designations, so long as they are clear and understood by everyone, and that what is interesting is the esssence of the "thing." And nothing irritates him more than sterile discussions with the "sophists" or "logickers" he often meets on his way. Of his abundant logical work, nothing remains but *Logical Education*, a manual of elementary teaching. In this field Galen is particularly exacting in the choice of propositions. Among the classes of premises discussed in his treatise *On the Doctrines of Hippocrates and Plato*, he follows Aristotle in considering scientific premises the only acceptable ones. And on that point he once again vents his dislike of the Stoics, who use the most common phenomena, gestures, and ordinary expressions in their deductions. Galen's competence extends to other areas such as language and the various forms of error in expression: he devotes an entire work to linguistic ambiguity. A preoccupation with logic, in the larger sense, pervades all of Galenic medicine. And he uses this competence as a criterion of excellence and a "war horse" against his adversaries, whether they are ignorant, like the Stoics, or negligent, like the Empiricists.

THE THERAPEUTIC AND PHARMACOLOGICAL METHOD

Pathology and therapeutics offer more propitious terrain than physiological knowledge for observing Galen's stance between speculation and empiricism. He makes an initial choice, which is not to follow the Empiricists, who refuse to know or even to name maladies, on the pretext that to do so is of no use. Second, he rejects any theoretical element that might have an explanatory function, and he even renounces any inductive or deductive procedure linked to theoretical notions. A first sign of this attitude is that Galen sees pathology as the opposite of physiology and considers it necessary to know the latter to understand any pathological issue. Next, he applies logical procedures to pathology as he has done for physiology: definitions and divisions like those of genus and species and the proper use of differences are indispensable instruments for the physician in this area as well. Thus pathology is anchored in theory, as the method of healing will be.

Speculation alone can grasp causes. As a matter of fact, for Galen, all pathology comes down to two generic causes, breaks in continuity and *dyskrasiai*. Ruptures are wounds or ailments, such as ulcers that destroy the skin. *Dyskrasiai* are an excessive predominance of one of the four qualities in the tissues or homoiomerous bodies, or in the *pneuma* or innate heat. The result is damage to the functions, which only work thanks to a good *eukrasia* of the body and its parts. This is why Galen defines pathology in general as damage occurring to a specific function (vision, stride, digestion) or to the whole body. The same explanation holds good for the soul and certain of its ailments. In his treatise *That the Habits of the Mind Follow the Temperaments of the Body*, certain psychological disorders, like delirium and melancholy, are attributed to a poor bodily temperament.

Therapeutics, for Galen, is directly derived from this principle: an illness gives the "instructions" for its own treatment. In its generality, these instructions are of a logical nature, like the reasoning one follows to establish that a person who suffers from a rupture will be cured by the renewal of continuity. Nevertheless this "theorem" must be completed by others to lead to particular therapeutic acts. For example, to treat an open wound, rules must be considered for the replacement of flesh, that is, the mechanism of its formation, its duration, the supplementary effects (formation of residues that make the wound damp and unclean), the age and constitution of the patient, and so on. The same approach is to be followed in the case of defective "diathesis." The choice of treatment, its strength and duration, is then a function of many specific considerations drawn from the general principle. This constitutes the "therapeutic method," a logical approach radically distinct from that of the medical empiricists. But it is clear that, in actual practice, experience is of prime importance for Galen.

This is particularly the case in pharmacology. Knowledge of the actual effects of a medicine on the patient seems to Galen still more important than knowledge of the nature of the medicine itself. In extreme cases, pharmacology can dispense with theory, especially when compound medicines are involved. All the same, the pharmacologist should not ignore the test results, whether he does the testing himself or profits by others' experience. Galen did a number of experiments on himself, such as burning his skin in several places to find the best remedy for burns. As for experiments with dangerous products, it was safer for him, he admits, to have them tried by some country doctor, on sturdy peasants. A respected doctor should take certain precautions. Whenever he could, Galen went off to gather vegetal, mineral, or organic substances with local uses or those handed down by the pharmacological tradition. Thus he built up huge reserves of substances of superior quality, in which he took pride. His pharmacological works are full of picturesque accounts: how he found a given medication by chance or used certain others,

such as animal or human excrements he recognized as having remarkable efficacy. But he expresses with horror his revulsion for the use of "vile and shameful" substances, especially if they are dangerous, of which he found many examples in the pharmacological tradition. In this field we inevitably touch on the outer frontiers of science. Local beliefs, true or mythic accounts, symbolic materials, social distinctions are all part of this body of knowledge. And the dividing line between what is rational and what is irrational, despite all Galen's efforts, is not always easy to perceive. Nevertheless, pharmacology was the principal route by which the name of Galen spread throughout the Occident.

ETHICS AND RELIGION

Being a good doctor depends on paying close attention to things and ideas. But for Galen, the ideal also explicitly entails a moral dimension. When he states that *A Good Doctor Must Also Be a Philosopher* (the title of one of his treatises), he is indeed using the term in the moral sense. In the first place, rigorous training of thought and work give the practitioner a general aptitude to distinguish what is true from what is false. The excesses and lies of the "sophists" are detected by authentic learning. The trained physician thus avoids wasting his time, avoids talking nonsense, and can concentrate on his art. Better still, study itself strengthens him against corruption. The asceticism it imposes is incompatible, for Galen, with the striving for wealth and patronage that characterize his contemporaries. Conventional as this type of social diatribe against the luxurious life in Rome may be, we cannot discount the strong connections that Galen established between education, practice, and virtue. Constant practice is the surest guarantee of an upright life devoted to learning and virtue.

Nor is Galen's medicine detached from all religiosity. For him, as for the Hippocratic doctors, science goes hand in hand with piety. It does not exclude the intervention of the gods in cases where, for example, the doctor is helpless before the severity of the disease. Among the gods, Galen feels a particular devotion to Asclepius. He believes in his revelations during dreams, even when they conflict with his scientific activity. Thus Galen accepts certain medical prescriptions that come to him through dreams, such as performing a bloodletting through an artery in the hand. In his experience, the god generally approves or confirms rational medicine, or informs it, conferring on it a supplementary supernatural element. Moreover Galen acknowledges that temple medicine constitutes a specific form of medicine. He expresses neither skepticism nor irony with regard to it, as certain doctors of his time seem to have done, such as his contemporary Aelius Aristides. He remains halfway between the skeptics and the devout.

Galen manifests a more intellectual veneration for the divine power that sometimes he calls the Demiurge, sometimes Nature, the source of a very strongly teleological representation of nature. Galen's Demiurge, who in certain ways very much resembles Plato's in *Timaeus*, willed that the entire body, like its parts, should have the best possible predisposition. But this teleology is not without restrictions or hierarchy, and Galen explicitly opposes the conception, which he attributes to Jews and Christians, of an all-powerful divinity capable of extracting anything from nothing, while his god takes into account natural constraints such as the separation of species or the existence of organic materials. Nevertheless, the action of Nature retains a certain mystery for him, as he acknowledges in particular, concerning the process of generation, in his treatise *On the Formation of Fetuses;* in his intellectual testament *On My Own Opinions*, Galen himself acknowledges that in this field he sometimes has no answers.

GALEN THEN AND NOW

Galen was much concerned with the transmission of medical knowledge. He annotated Hippocrates copiously, and worked to ensure the future of his own work. In this transmission, the role of the second school of Alexandria (4th to 6th century C.E.) was of prime importance; it made possible the diffusion of this work among scholars who came to study in Alexandria from all parts of the empire. Translated into Syriac, then into Arabic, Galen's work never ceased to be taught and studied in the course of the brilliant centuries of Arab domination in Baghdad and Ispahan, by scholars such as Rhazes, Haly Abbas (al-Magusi), or Avicenna, and in Muslim Spain. In Córdoba, Averroës played a critical role in the transmission of Galen's work; his own work, translated into Latin, was to exercise a lasting influence. Even after the Christian reconquest, the city of Toledo continued to be a great center of teaching, manuscript copying, and translation. In the Latin Occident the tradition had been weak in antiquity and had been passed on through bad translations. But Galen resurfaced in the Middle Ages, owing to new translations made from the Arabic by such scholars as Constantine the African at Monte Cassino in the 11th century, or Gerard of Cremona at Toledo in the following century. Along with the works of Arab doctors, Galen's works made a definitive entrance into the curriculum of medieval universities. In the Renaissance, the rise of Hellenism meant a new departure for the history of the Galenic corpus, marked by the *princeps* edition of the Greek text of his complete works. The Aldine edition of 1525, the result of considerable work by humanists, was greeted by contemporaries with indescribable enthusiasm as a return to the pure sources of antique knowledge, and as a means of liberation from a barbarous period for thought. New Latin translations, made directly from the

Greek, were to result in a diffusion of Galen's work in various European countries. Thus his work became known by great scholars such as Vesalius and Harvey, who were nourished by this rediscovery before they brought their own decisive renewal to medicine.

Modern interest in Galen is marked, on the contrary, by the retreat of the medical perspective, if not its disappearance. Even if medical doctors like Charles Daremberg, in the 19th century, were interested in Galen for apparently practical purposes, as Littré was in Hippocrates, the enterprise ceased to have the slightest practical value. Approaches to Galen were nevertheless not uniform; they varied according to national traditions in the history of medicine, philology, and science. Until the middle of the 20th century, the principal studies of Galen's work were undertaken in the fields of anatomy and physiology (notably on the question of pulmonary circulation). But within the past twenty years, a renewal of Galenic studies has led to a rediscovery of this great figure. Preoccupied at first with shedding light on the least known aspects of Galen's work, such as its clinical, epistemological, and religious aspects, recent research has concentrated on two principal fields: Galen's historical environment and his philosophy. Placing Galen back in his own time, the better to know his life, his contemporaries, the position of medicine, and the medical customs of the period, among other things, helps draw him out of his splendid isolation and helps integrate him better into the society and the cultural milieu of the Second Sophistics, and the very diverse practices of his era. Studies on Galen's epistemology and various other aspects of his philosophy not only help reveal in a precise manner the importance of this aspect of his work, but also help counter the image of his eclecticism or, worse, of his philosophical syncretism, that had prevailed earlier. Whether causality, logic, empiricism, or doxography is at issue, we discover what Galen, and thereby also medicine, contributed to ancient thought. This revised view has the additional effect of giving new meaning to certain notions, including eclecticism; it invites speculation about the transmission of Plato or Aristotle; it helps clarify Galen's importance in the formation of commentary as a genre, and it allows us to look at empiricism in a new way. In fields other than philosophy, too, the revised approach to Galen opens up unexpected paths. For historians of science, medicine, and philosophy, as for historians in general and philologists, the Galenic lode is still full of treasure.

Armelle Debru
Translated by Rita Guerlac and Anne Slack

Bibliography

Texts and Translations

Galen. *Opera omnia*. Ed. and Latin trans. C. G. Kühn. 20 vols. Leipzig: 1821–1833; repr. Hildesheim: Olms, 1964–1965.

————. *Oeuvres anatomiques, physiologiques et médicales de Galien*. Trans. Charles Daremberg. 2 vols. Paris: Baillière, 1854–1856; partial repr. A. Pichot, Paris: Gallimard, 1994. 2 vols.

————. *Scripta minora*. Ed. Johann Maquardt, Ivan Müller, and Georg Helmreich. 3 vols. Leipzig: B. G. Teubner, 1884; repr. Amsterdam: Harrert, 1967.

————. *On Anatomical Procedures*. Trans. Charles Singer. London and New York: Oxford University Press, 1956.

————. *Galen on Anatomical Procedures: The Later Books*. Trans. W. L. Duckworth. Cambridge: Cambridge University Press, 1962.

————. *On the Doctrines of Hippocrates and Plato*. Ed. and trans. Phillip De Lacy. Berlin: Akademie Verlag, 1978–1984. *Corpus medicorum graecorum* 5, 4, 1–2.

————. *Three Treatises on the Nature of Science. On the Sect to Beginners. An Outline of Empiricism. On Medical Experience*. Trans. Richard Walzer and Michael Frede. Indianapolis: Hackett Publishing Co., 1985.

————. *On Semen*. Ed. and trans. Phillip de Lacy. Berlin: Akademie Verlag, 1992. *Corpus medicorum graecorum* 5, 3, 1.

————. *On the Therapeutic Method*, Books I and II. Trans R. J. Hankinson. Oxford: Clarendon Press, 1994.

Galen. *Selected Works*. Trans. and annotated P. N. Singer. Oxford: Oxford University Press, 1997.

Moraux, Paul. *Galien de Pergame: Souvenirs d'un médecin*. Paris: Les Belles Lettres, 1985.

Studies

Debru, Armelle. *Le corps respirant: La pensée de la physiologie chez Galien*. Leiden: Brill, 1996.

Haase, Wolfgang, ed. *Aufstieg und Niedergang der Römischen Welt*, Series 2, vol. 37, books 1–2. Berlin: W. de Gruyter, 1993, 1994 (numerous articles on Galen).

Harris, Charles Reginald Schiller. *The Heart and the Vascular System in Ancient Greek Medicine from Alcmaeon to Galen*. Oxford: Clarendon Press, 1973.

Kollesch, Jutta, and Diethard Nickel, eds. *Galen und das hellenistische Erbe*. Proceedings of the 4th International Galen Symposium at Humboldt University in Berlin, September 1989. Stuttgart: F. Steiner, 1993.

Kudlien, Fridolf, and Richard Durling, eds. *Galen's Method of Healing: Proceedings of the 1982 Galen Symposium*. Leiden: Brill, 1991.

Lloyd, Geoffrey E. R. *Greek Science after Aristotle*. London: Chatto and Windus; New York: Norton, 1973.

López-Férez, Juan Antonio, ed. *Galeno: Obra, pensamiento e influencia*. Colloquio internacional celebrado en Madrid, March 22–25, 1988. Madrid: Universidad Nacional de Educación a Distancia, 1991.

Manuli, Paula, and Mario Vegetti. *Cuore, sangue e cervello: Biologia e antropologia nel pensiero antico*. Milan: Episteme Editrice, 1977.

————. *Le opere psicologiche de Galeno: Atti del terzo Colloquio galenico internazionale.* Pavia, September 10–12, 1986. Naples: Bibliopolis, 1988.

Nutton, Vivian, ed. *Galen, Problems and Prospects: A Collection of Papers Submitted at the 1979 Cambridge Conference.* London: The Wellcome Institute, 1981.

Temkin, Owsei. *Galenism: Rise and Decline of a Medical Philosophy.* Ithaca, N.Y.: Cornell University Press, 1973.

Related Articles

Observation and Research; Medicine; Demonstration and the Idea of Science; Hippocrates

HERACLITUS

HERACLITUS OF EPHESUS lived at the end of the 6th century B.C.E. Nothing is known of his life (the ancient "biographies" are fiction). There is no sign that he ever left his native city, which at that time was part of the empire of the Achaemenid dynasty of Persia. (Iranian influences on his thinking have sometimes been suggested.)

The book written by Heraclitus was famous in antiquity for its aphoristic obscurity. About a hundred sentences survive. The obscurity is a calculated consequence of Heraclitus's style, which is usually compact and often deliberately cryptic. He believed that what he had to say went beyond the limits of ordinary language. Combined with the meagerness of other testimony, this obscurity is a formidable obstacle to understanding.

Interpretation of Heraclitus has been a controversial matter since at least the late 5th century B.C.E. Both Plato and Aristotle attempted to fit Heraclitus into the mold of Ionian "natural philosophy" and accepted the view of Cratylus, who attributed to Heraclitus his own doctrine of "universal flux." Later ancient interpreters, notably Theophrastus and the Stoic Cleanthes, influenced (and clouded) the later testimony; but Cleanthes at least took a broader and more sympathetic view of Heraclitus than Aristotle had done. It is probable that Heraclitus intended and anticipated some of the difficulties of his interpreters, since the understanding of language, cryptic or otherwise, is itself a guiding theme in his thinking.

Since he was "rediscovered" at the end of the 18th century, and rescued from crude misunderstandings, Heraclitus's appeal has grown, in spite of his obscurity. Hegel explicitly acknowledged his indebtedness; Heidegger gave a lengthy exegesis. Wittgenstein's *Tractatus* is rather similar to Heraclitus in style and perhaps partly in method.

There are certain requirements that necessarily constrain and guide any serious attempt to interpret Heraclitus. First, one must keep in mind the intellectual context within which Heraclitus found himself. The new so-called natural philosophy of the Milesians, with its abstract approach, claimed to make the universe intelligible as a whole. It had already given rise to problems both epistemological (how could anything be known or plausibly conjectured about matters far beyond human experience?) and systemic (how was it possible convincingly to account for the variety of the experienced world in terms of only one or two fundamental components?). Xenophanes of Colophon, earlier in the 6th century, can be seen already grappling with these

problems, and though Heraclitus speaks slightingly of Xenophanes, he may have learned from him.

Second, one must respect the systematic unity of thinking that lies behind the aphoristic form and is implicit in the correspondences of language and meaning by which the individual remarks are tied together. It is clear that Heraclitus's book was meant to form a comprehensive and systematic whole, covering every aspect of human experience, of which each part was connected with every other. Hence, as in a jigsaw puzzle, each statement of Heraclitus must be compared and contrasted with many others, in order that something like a map of his thinking can be constructed, within which each remark can then be located. One must also take note here of the difference between the examples drawn from everyday experience and the generalizations expressed in more abstract terms.

Third, one must be sensitive to the linguistic clues given by the fragments. These are of many different kinds. There is ambiguity of meaning in single words and phrases, and ambiguity of construction in sentences. Words, by their form or associations, carry deliberate allusions to other senses. Passages of Homer and Hesiod are implicitly referred to. In some cases it seems that Heraclitus's statements are intended to be self-applicable: their linguistic form exemplifies the very structure of which they speak.

Fourth, one must be guided by what Heraclitus himself says and implies about the business of interpreting difficult statements, and about all understanding as consisting of interpretation. "The prince to whom the oracle at Delphi belongs neither speaks nor conceals: he gives a sign" (frg. 93, Diels-Kranz). Another remark (frg. 56) tells how Homer was "deceived" by the terms of a riddle that he could not solve; just so are human beings generally "deceived" in their attempts to understand what is given in their own experience. For "bad witnesses to men are eyes and ears, if they have souls that do not understand the language" (frg. 107); they will not even be given what they need, for their very eyes and ears will distort their testimony to accord with their mistaken presuppositions, just as we misread and mishear the words of a foreign language to accord with our mistaken expectations. Therefore, "If one does not expect it, one will not discover it, undiscoverable as it is and unreachable" (frg. 18). Deciphering the "account" *(logos)* of Heraclitus himself is, for Heraclitus, the same operation as deciphering the meaning of experience, for both consist of the very same statements. One must listen to the *logos*, but it is equally "not understood" by most hearers.

A GENERAL HYPOTHESIS: THE INWARD TURN

The hypothesis on which the present account is founded is as follows. Heraclitus's thinking resulted from the turning-in on itself, the self-application, of the abstract theorizing invented by the Milesians. This introjection of the

theoretical enterprise was a response to the problems encountered in trying to discover the nature of the universe as a whole. By this "turn" Heraclitus hoped to transform and to solve the original problems.

The inward turn was not in any way intended as a retreat from the immediate realities of ordinary experience. On the contrary, Heraclitus insists on the primacy of these realities: "All of which there is seeing, hearing, learning: those things I rank highest" (frg. 55). This programmatic statement is supported, most obviously, by his repeated appeals to familiar situations of ordinary experience, and by the direct and vivid language in which they are described. Ordinary experience includes, also, what is experienced by the mind when it inspects reflexively its own contents and operations. This, for Heraclitus, is not a separate realm of experience but an area continuous with the rest.

Immediate experience has an inherent structure and meaning, which it is Heraclitus's concern to explore, and which is identical to the structure and meaning of the universe. Language has a special place as the vehicle of both.

STRUCTURE: THE UNITY IN OPPOSITES

The abstract notion of structure is omnipresent, sometimes explicitly (in the word *harmoniē*), more often implicitly. In general, the structure that is indicated is one that may conveniently be described as "unity in opposites." This appears in the surviving fragments in many shapes.

In the first place, there are many examples drawn from everyday life, with no comment or elaboration. "People step into the same rivers, and different waters flow onto them" (frg. 12). "A road, uphill and downhill, one and the same" (frg. 60). "Sea is water most pure and most polluted: for fish drinkable and life-giving, for human beings undrinkable and deadly" (frg. 61). These, and the other such remarks, are not meant to infringe the law of noncontradiction. They rely for their first impact on the appearance of a contradiction, which is removed when we have recourse to our own experience to add the necessary qualifying phrases. But the paradox remains: how is it that these oppositions cohere so closely that they are mutually inseparable in thought or in experience, that they need one another? The traditional approach to representing opposites (e.g., Day and Night) in Homer and Hesiod was to make them separate persons in a state of mutual enmity or avoidance. Heraclitus explicitly rejects such a representation: Hesiod "did not know Day and Night: they are one thing" (frg. 57).

But at the same time, Heraclitus does not, as it might at first seem from these words, proclaim the identity of opposites. It turns out that Day and Night "are one thing" only in the sense that they are different temporary states of one and the same thing. To each pair of opposites, Heraclitus supplies an "underlying unity" in which the opposites are present.

In the case of Day and Night, the opposites are successively but not simultaneously present in the unity. In many other cases the opposites are simultaneously present. It is therefore clear that the unity in opposites does not depend on time and change: rather, the temporal aspect of things is for Heraclitus only one among many aspects that allow the manifestation of the fundamental structure. This is the first indication that (as will be seen later) the temporal dimension, though not denied by Heraclitus, becomes in effect of limited interest, because the cosmos and the soul pass through repeated cycles of change. "Beginning and end are together on the circle" (frg. 103). Each unity, then, exhibits in these examples a systematic ambivalence, as between the two opposites; it is an ambivalence that belongs to its essential nature. And in each pair of opposites there is typically one "positive" and one "negative" term.

Besides the examples drawn from everyday life, explicit generalizations, containing more abstract statements of the same structure, also appear. "People do not understand how what disagrees comes to agree: back-turning structure like that of the bow and the lyre" (frg. 51). "Comprehensions: wholes and not wholes, agreeing disagreeing, consonant dissonant; and from all things one and from one thing all things" (frg. 10).

These generalizing statements apply to all examples and therefore also to themselves, if we may regard sentences, and particularly statements containing opposed predications of the same thing, as examples of unity in opposites. This is an example of the self-reference in some of Heraclitus's remarks, and it is a particularly interesting one, because it suggests the infinite regress generated by generalizations that try to encompass everything, or by theories that try to explain everything, including themselves. Another remark says that "the soul has a *logos* which increases itself" (frg. 115), which again suggests awareness of the infinite regresses engendered by self-reference.

The notion of unity in opposites appears also to be used by Heraclitus as a theory-guiding idea, for yet another class of remarks contains examples of unity in opposites that are manifestly not derived directly from ordinary experience. They are rather to be understood as parts of a theory: of the physical transformations of the cosmos, or of the parallel transformations of the soul.

REASON, KNOWLEDGE, UNDERSTANDING

It has often been recognized that for Heraclitus there is a parallelism or structural identity between the operations of the mind, as expressed in thought and language, and those of the reality that it grasps. This parallelism implies that understanding any part of reality is like grasping the meaning of a statement. The "meaning," in this case, like that of a cryptic statement in words, is not obvious but yet is present in the statement, and can be worked out provided one "knows the language." Human reason has the power to know the

"language of reality," precisely because its own operations are conducted in the very same way.

A prominent place is given by Heraclitus to what he calls "this *logos*" or "the *logos*." It is evident that he is here starting from the most basic and familiar sense of the word: "this *logos*" is his own account, what he has to say. It is what is given by his own words. Yet it is also evident that, characteristically, Heraclitus packs much more meaning into the word *logos*. "Of this *logos* which is always people prove to have no understanding" (frg. 1). "When one listens not to me but to the *logos*, it is wise to agree *[homologein]* that all is one" (frg. 50). "While the *logos* is public *[xunou]*, the many live as though they had a private source of understanding" (frg. 2). "Those who speak with sense *[xun nōi]* must affirm with what is public *[xunōi]* for all, as a city does with law, and much more firmly" (frg. 114).

These remarks, and the extension of sense of the word *logos,* fall into place if we note that here it is the *logos* that supplies the independent authority to which Heraclitus appeals. In attacking traditional beliefs and the authority of sages, Heraclitus, like the other 6th-century thinkers, was implicitly setting up and appealing to a standard independent of tradition and personal authority. What could this be? It could not be the empirical standard of immediate experience, as suggested by Xenophanes. Heraclitus prized experience, but (as we have seen) he knew that it needed interpretation. For this, "insight" *(noos)* was needed. The *logos* provides a *public* test of insight: it can only, therefore, be something like reason. And in fact the sense "reason" is well attested for the word *logos* in the next hundred years.

Having appealed to reason as something to which all have access, Heraclitus has to explain why it is that the fruits of reason are (in his opinion) gathered by so few: why, in fact, his teaching has so far not been accepted by others, let alone independently discovered.

It is first of all clear that the acceptance of the *logos* as such is not something automatic. On the contrary, "of this logos which is always people prove to have no understanding, both before they have heard it [they do not discover it independently] and when once they have heard it [they do not accept it from Heraclitus]. For though all things come to be according to this *logos*, they are like inexperienced people though they experience the words [Heraclitus's sayings] and the deeds [the facts of experience] such as I set forth, as I take apart each thing according to nature *[kata phusin]* and show how it is. But other people do not notice what they do when awake, in the same way as they do not notice all the things that they forget about when asleep" (frg. 1).

The image of sleepers, who "forget about" the public world of shared experience, shows that the mistake of most people consists in "living as though they had a private source of understanding." They do in some sense experience things, but they force on their experience some private interpretation,

just as a dreamer distorts in his dream the external stimuli that impinge on him. Several other images suggest the same conclusion. Most people are like children (frgs. 70, 74, 79); like dogs (frg. 97), and perhaps other animals; like fools (frg. 87); like deaf people (frgs. 19, 34).

The process of "waking up," of becoming conscious of one's reason and deliberately exercising it, is also far from automatic. It requires strenuous self-exertion to get any distance. Besides, "the nature of things likes to lie hidden" (frg. 123). To free oneself of error is presumably just a matter of self-discipline, though hard and painful for those who are not used to it. But to attain positive understanding is a matter of solving enigmas, for which a guide or an unforeseeable insight is needed.

"Human character does not have knowledge, but divine character does" (frg. 78). This remark may seem to put an unbridgeable gulf between human beings and any worthwhile insight. But at a closer view it can be read encouragingly. "Character" *(ēthos)* is not what is essential but what is determined by habit. To shake off all-too-human habits is to move halfway toward acquiring "divine character." What exactly may be implied by that must be left at present in suspense, but at least it is clear that the divine intelligence in the cosmos is named by Heraclitus "the wise" or "the only wise."

THE INTERPRETATION OF EXPERIENCE: THEORIES OF COSMOS AND SOUL

Reason has to be applied to immediate experience. This implies the existence of general principles of interpretation. What these may be, Heraclitus does not tell us explicitly. But a reconstruction of them can, with due caution, be attempted. We have to be guided by (1) the general analogy of understanding with interpretation of language; (2) the results of the interpretation as evidenced by what we know of Heraclitus's cosmology and his theory of the soul.

These guides lead us to suppose that Heraclitus followed two principles: "No Cancellation" and "No New Sensibles." These may already have figured in the epistemology of Xenophanes. The principle of No Cancellation requires that no part of immediate experience may be discarded; everything that is experienced must be accounted for in theory, and must appear in the theoretical account exactly as experienced. This is analogous to the demand that every part of a sentence must be interpreted, and the interpretation must account for it as it functions in the sentence and not otherwise. The principle of No New Sensibles sets limits to what may be added to experience by the interpretation. It requires that nothing extra may be postulated as existing but not experienced unless it is not the sort of thing to be an object of experience at all. This corresponds to the requirement of interpretation of language, that

we must not postulate unspoken or unwritten words in addition to the ones that are expressed.

The result of applying these two principles to sensory experience of the world is a characteristically parsimonious empiricism, like that of Xenophanes. The observed cosmos is all there is. The physical constituents are the obvious ones: earth, sea, atmospheric vapor, fire. Their transformations are governed by the characteristic physical opposites: hot-cold, wet-dry. The sun is not even a persisting object but a regularly repeated process, in which a container of modest size is carried up into the heavens by the power of fire after its contents have ignited.

There are indications that for the individual soul there was a parallel theory. In the physical theory, two pairs of opposites (hot-cold, wet-dry) give a system of transformations between four states or stages of the underlying fire, which must be thought of as a process rather than as a "material." In the more cryptically expressed theory of the soul the pair wet-dry reappears, but there are also the oppositions alive-dead and awake-asleep.

The reconstruction is in both cases controversial, and the nature of the analogy between the two systems still more so. One fundamental question concerns the nature of the "measures" or "proportions" that are said to be preserved throughout the transformations of fire. Do these represent an equilibrium between actual amounts of physical opposites in the cosmos? Or do they indicate the conservation of some quantity less closely tied to observation? In the latter case, it is possible that the cosmos goes through long-term cyclical oscillations of state, as the Stoic interpretation asserted.

In any case, though, the interest, for Heraclitus, lies not so much in the theory itself as in subsumption of these aspects of experience under the general structure of unity in opposites. Unlike Xenophanes, Heraclitus insists that the cosmos (and analogously the individual soul) is something that makes sense as a whole. (Understanding is literally "putting together," *xunienai*, the creating of a unified whole.) It remains, therefore, to see how cosmology and psychology were intended to be subordinated to Heraclitus's general metaphysical concerns. This depends on the identification of the underlying unity in both cases with "fire" in the sense of an intelligent process: the divine intelligence.

MEANING, STRUGGLE, AND THE DIVINE IN COSMOS AND SOUL

It follows from the principles already explained that the key to understanding the nature of the world is *introspection:* "I went looking for myself" (frg. 101). The human self ("soul," *psukhē*) is variously occupied: it is combatively active, physically, emotionally, and intellectually; it is reflectively self-discov-

ering and self-extending; and it is constantly self-reversing in the swings of circumstances or passion or thought. Yet it needs firm frameworks (objective truths, fixed rules of conduct) to be at all, or to make sense of its own existence. For Heraclitus, all this is true of the world too. Here also there is no sharp line between what it is and what it means. As already mentioned, the behavior and structure of the world and of the soul are seen as closely analogous, if not the same.

In fact there is good reason to suspect an underlying identity. In the series of physical changes between opposites, fire (in the sense of a cosmic process that is also a self-transforming force) is given as the underlying unity. "All things are got in exchange for fire, and fire for all things; just as all goods are got in exchange for gold, and gold for goods" (frg. 90). "This cosmos . . . an everliving fire which is kindled in measures and is quenched in measures" (frg. 30).

In the soul, too, wet and dry appear as the important opposites, with negative and positive values: "Dry beam of light is soul at its wisest and best" (frg. 118), while the stumbling drunkard "has his soul wet" (frg. 117). The underlying unity is not named, but the association with light, and some other slight indications, might suggest that here, too, it is seen as fire. What adds force to this suggestion, and completes the chain of links, is that the divine intelligence controlling the cosmos is certainly identified as a kind of fire. "Thunderbolt steers all things" (frg. 64); the traditional attribute of Zeus is given as a name for the divine intelligence, elsewhere "the wise." "For one is the wise to be versed in the knowledge of how all things are steered through all" (frg. 41). "The one only wise is unwilling and willing to be called by the name of Zeus" (frg. 32). The traditional role of Zeus—to be the cunning supreme governor of the cosmos—is taken over by "the wise."

If these identifications are right, it follows that the divine intelligence is not something remote from human understanding; on the contrary, it is, at least qualitatively, the same as human intelligence itself. True, Heraclitus emphasizes that it is different in nature from anything else: "Of all those whose words I have heard, none has got so far as to recognise that the wise is separated from all things" (frg. 108). It is in fact the underlying unity of "all things" that are given in experience, and therefore necessarily different in nature from them. But "the wise" is a term that can be applied to both human and divine intelligence, and there are indications that Heraclitus saw no essential difference between them. This is intelligible if they are both, in the best state, fire.

But human intelligence is often unable to function at its best, as it is impeded by "wetness." It is possible for human beings to take possession of their inheritance of intelligence; otherwise Heraclitus's preaching would be pointless. It needs, however, a choice, and a struggle, for a human being to become

truly wise, as Heraclitus claimed to be. The same should therefore be true of the divine intelligence; that, too, must have its moral struggles, and its periods of "death" and "sleep" produced by the excess of moisture, followed by re-newed vigor. We can understand of both soul and cosmos the cyclic process implied in this remark: "The same thing is present inside as living and dead, as sleeping and awake, as young and old; for these change to become those and those change to become these" (frg. 88).

This hypothesis, that the cosmos, too, goes cyclically through processes of decay and renewal, and that these are accompanied by struggles, is confirmed by various evidence. The Stoic reconstruction of Heraclitus contained long-term oscillations between the extremes of cosmic conflagration and cosmic deluge. Even if this cosmic cycle is doubted, the oscillations of day and night, winter and summer play the same role. That the cosmos is the arena of "war" or "strife" is stated explicitly. "War is the father of all things and the king of all things" (frg. 53). "One must know that war is shared in by all, and that strife is justice, and that everything comes to be according to strife and neces-sity" (frg. 80).

It seems to be this struggle, in the individual soul and in the cosmos, that for Heraclitus gives meaning to both. Certainly there are some remarks remi-niscent of the heroic ideal of Homer. "The best choose one thing in place of all: glory ever-flowing of mortals; but the many are glutted like cattle" (frg. 29). "Those slain in war are honoured of gods and men" (frg. 24). It seems even possible that for Heraclitus the individual struggle to achieve (and to spread?) the use of intelligence may be a contribution to the cosmic struggle on the side of the hot and the dry. Certainly war and peace are mentioned as cosmic as well as merely human opposites. And the actors on the human stage are, though mortal (because subject to periods of being dead), just as mortal and just as immortal, too, as the actor or actors on the cosmic stage. "Immortals mortals, mortals immortals: alive in the others' dying, dead in the others' living" (frg. 62).

IMAGES AND GENERALIZATIONS

Heraclitus, in spite of his deliberate obscurity, was a lucid and ambitious thinker. We may expect that he would have been aware that a system of thought, such as has been outlined, raises certain crucial questions. How, above all, are we to understand the equation of strife or war, on the one hand, with justice (and perhaps necessity) on the other hand? It is reasonable to suppose that this is one more example of the structure of unity in opposites, but saying that is not enough for understanding. We need also some sort of explanation—*how* such opposites are capable of forming a genuine unity. (The difficulty is deepened if we accept as genuine the remark: "For the god,

all things are fine and good and just; but men suppose some things to be just and others unjust" [frg. 102]. In fact, there are independent reasons for doubting the authenticity of this fragment.)

In the same way, we wish to have better insight into how it is possible for the underlying unity, the cosmic intelligence, to conduct strife against itself. It may be that Heraclitus took the fact of such internal strife to be immediately acceptable as a possibility, on the model of "the mind divided against itself." Yet that does not make it any more intelligible.

As indications for dealing with such crucial questions, Heraclitus provided not explicit statements but images. Some of the remarks drawn from everyday life may have been intended also to serve as thought-guiding images of a general kind. The remark about rivers (the river persists though the waters change) is capable of being taken, and has often been taken, as an image of the permanence through change of the cosmos or the individual soul.

As the supreme image of the coexistence of justice and strife, Heraclitus describes a child playing both sides of a board game. "*Aiōn* ["Lifetime" or "Time everlasting"] is a child playing, playing at tric-trac; a child's is the kingdom" (frg. 52). The child pits his wits against themselves, by alternately playing both sides in the game. The game is thus a genuine struggle, though conducted by only one person. And it is conducted according to rules; the lawlike moves are the conflict. The outcome is determined perhaps by the chances of war in any one case, but in the long run, if the child plays equally well on both sides, the honors will be even. The image captures the opposites that stand at the highest level in Heraclitus's thinking and helps us to understand their fundamental coexistences: those of conflict and law, of freedom and regularity, of intelligence and its lapses, of opposition and unity.

EDWARD HUSSEY

Bibliography

Diels, Hermann, and Walther Kranz. *Die Fragmente der Vorsokratiker.* Berlin: Weidmannsche Verlagsbuchhandlung, 1956.

Dilcher, Roman. *Studies in Heraclitus.* Hildesheim and New York: Olms, 1995.

Heidegger, Martin. "Logos (Heraclitus Fragment B 50)." In *Early Greek Thinking.* Trans. D. F. Krell and F. A. Capuzzi. San Francisco: Harper and Row, 1984. Pp. 59–78.

Hölscher, Uvo. "Heraklit." In *Anfängliches Fragen.* Göttingen: Vandenhoeck and Ruprecht, 1960. Pp. 130–172.

Hussey, Edward. "Epistemology and Meaning in Heraclitus." In *Language and Logos: Studies in Ancient Greek Philosophy Presented to G. E. L. Owen.* Ed. Malcolm Schofield and Martha Nussbaum. Cambridge: Cambridge University Press, 1982. Pp. 33–59.

Kahn, C. H. *The Art and Thought of Heraclitus: An Edition of the Fragments with Translation and Commentary.* Cambridge: Cambridge University Press, 1979.

Kirk, G. S. *Heraclitus: The Cosmic Fragments.* Cambridge: Cambridge University Press, 1962.

Vlastos, Gregory. "On Heraclitus." In *Studies in Presocratic Philosophy,* vol. 1: *The Beginnings of Philosophy.* Ed. D. J. Furley and R. E. Allen. London: Routledge and Kegan Paul, 1970. Pp. 413–429.

Related Articles

The Question of Being; Theology and Divination; Cosmology; Theories of Religion

HERODOTUS

HERODOTUS WISHED to rival Homer; what he became, ultimately, was Herodotus. In other words, he drew from the epic the courage, or the temerity, to begin. Like the epic, the recording of history always starts with conflict, with war. Herodotus set out to do for the Persian Wars what Homer had done for the Trojan War. As the famous opening sentence of *Histories* begins, "What Herodotus the Halicarnassian has learnt by inquiry is here set forth: in order that the memory of the past may not be blotted out from among men by time, and that great and marvellous deeds done by Greeks and foreigners and especially the reason why they warred against each other may not lack renown" (Herodotus, *Histories* I.1).

Of Herodotus the man (roughly 480–420 B.C.E.) we know very little. He came originally from Ionia, the birthplace of the earliest Greek thinkers (such as Anaximander, the creator of the first map of the world, and Hecataeus of Miletus, sometimes considered the first historian). Herodotus traveled throughout the Mediterranean, experienced exile, learned what it meant to be an outsider (at least until he arrived at Thurii, the new colony that Pericles wished to make Panhellenic), and spent time in Athens. Some traditional sources present him as a lecturer, visiting the great centers of Greece and collecting speaker's fees. Thus he appeared as an itinerant historian, a peddler of stories, not unlike the rhapsodes who traveled from contest to contest, or those other, better-known travelers, the Sophists. However, at that time "history" did not refer to a sphere of knowledge, nor was it regarded as a profession.

The life of Herodotus unfolded between two major conflicts. The Persian Wars (which he had not known firsthand but which he chose to relate) were a period of threats to, and consolidation of, the polis, and the Peloponnesian War, inextricably linked to Thucydides' account, was also a perilous time of profound questioning. The period Herodotus describes in his work (550–480, with several additional flashbacks) saw important changes. To the east, the Persian empire arose and prospered; in Greece, first Sparta and then Athens came to prominence. Politically, the ancient ideal of "eunomy" was replaced by that of "isonomy" (equality of political rights for all citizens), and finally by an entirely new notion, that of democracy.

Histories is divided into nine books, but these divisions were introduced much later. Herodotus himself spoke only of his "account" or "accounts." The last five books are largely devoted to the history of the Persian Wars proper,

starting with the revolt of Ionia against the Persians (500 B.C.E.) up to the capture of Sestos in Chersonese. The Persians were defeated, the Ionians liberated, and the bridges that the overambitious Xerxes built across the Hellespont were destroyed. The first four books, in contrast, deal with the barbarians: Lydians, Persians, Babylonians, Massagetes, Egyptians, Ethiopians, Arabs, Indians, Scythians, Libyans. However, these books are not so much ethnographic or geographic notes as they are an account of the emergence of these various peoples as they were confronted by the advancing power of the Persians (or of the still earlier Medes), for the Persians, as Herodotus describes them, were incapable of staying put. Thus *Histories* is also a meditation on the drive for conquest and the destiny of the conquerors.

THE INVENTION OF THE BARBARIAN AND THE INVENTORY OF THE WORLD

When *Histories* opens, the barbarians were already situated geographically, forming, with the Greeks, a pair of opposites. To Herodotus, the division between them is obvious: there was no need to explain or justify it, although it was absent from Homer's poems. The distinction had appeared between the 6th and 5th centuries, starting with the Persian Wars, which territorialized the barbarians geographically (opposite Europe, in Asia) and gave them a face: first of all, that of the Persian. In *Histories* Herodotus bore witness to this phenomenon and actively contributed to it. He went even further, however, in constructing a political rationale for distinguishing between Greeks and barbarians, which also offered a political perspective on the Greek past. As a result, the word *barbarian* came to signify not primarily, or necessarily, barbarism (cruelty, excess, laxity) but political difference; it separated those who chose to live in city-states from those who never managed to get along without kings. The Greek is "political"—in other words, free—while the barbarian is "royal," meaning submissive to a master *(despotēs).*

Between the world of the barbarian and the city-state stands the tyrant. It was in opposition to this Greek figure of power, typical of the end of the archaic period, that the "isonomic" city-states were developed. Herodotus's account establishes the ties that link king and tyrant: by highlighting the overlap of the two images (each borrowing from the other), the representation of despotic power appears barbarian. The king is a barbarian and the tyrant is a king; thus, the tyrant is a barbarian, or barbaric.

The despot (king or tyrant) exercises excessive power. Prey to hubris, which Herodotus borrows from the lexicon of tragedy, he is incapable of moderation and is guilty of every transgression: spatial transgression, in that a king always overreaches his space, and transgression against the gods (who, according to Themistocles, "deemed Asia and Europe too great a realm for one man to rule" [*Histories* VIII.109]). He violates the *nomoi* (laws and cus-

toms) not only of other cultures but of his own as well. In *Histories,* three despots vie for first place: Cambyses, the mad king; Periander, the tyrant of Corinth; and Cleomenes, the king of Sparta, who was also mad. One Persian and two Greeks: are we to conclude, then, that the distinction between Greek and barbarian is no longer pertinent? No, on the contrary, for the great kings, tyrants, and ordinary kings spring from a common ground (that of despotic power) or lean toward barbarism. In contrast to this world of the outsider, and also, from this point on, to the past, stands the city-state. Between the Greeks and the "other," *Histories* tells us, the new frontier is above all political. This frontier separates Asia and Europe, but it also cuts across Greece itself, shaping and explaining the brief period when tyranny flourished and the isonomic city-state was established (it perhaps even stigmatizes the city-state that later became democratic and that, in the years around 430, was accused of behaving in a "tyrannical" fashion: Athens?).

The "political" division proposed by Herodotus is consistent with a worldview in which the fundamental categories of Greek anthropology are still at work (divisions between animals, men, and gods, as they were set down in the stories of Homer and Hesiod). Herodotus, the curious traveler, like a Lévi-Strauss of his time, presents a broad canvas on which all the different cultures are arranged systematically. The concept that best expresses this attitude of openness toward the world is *theōria,* traveling in order to see. The Athenian legislator Solon appears in *Histories* as a thinker and a traveler, for whom the project of "seeing" the world and the effort to "philosophize" (the first use of that word) are linked. King Croesus greets him with those words and questions him in the name of that knowledge. In a larger sense, wise men (of whom the best known are the Seven Sages) undertake travel as a way of life, even if they generally do so more to teach than to learn. In fact, *Histories* represents a time in Greek culture that is both confident and curious: Herodotus travels less to construct his representation of the world than to confirm it.

Once he has established the Otherness of people and places, he uses a variety of narrative strategies to reveal his grasp and mastery of the subject. He exploits a whole series of expressions and figures of speech that I have referred to elsewhere as "the rhetoric of Otherness": the category of the *thōma,* or marvelous; play on symmetry, oppositions (hot/cold, courage/cowardice, and so on), and inversions (a useful form that transforms the difference of the other into the inverse of the self); the omnipresent concern for counting and measuring; the use of analogy; validation of the notions of "blending" and "center." This rhetoric allows him to speak the Other, or rather to write it, and to encompass it as he depicts the cultures and draws a map of the known world. Mindful of his limits, the investigator intends to expand his story as far as possible, up to the point where extreme heat or cold prohibits his going any farther and learning more. But up to that point he makes it his task to investigate, to enumerate customs, to name peoples, to define space, construct-

ing in the process, *more geometrico,* so to speak, a representation of the world.

If Herodotus, quoting Pindar, declares that custom is the queen of the world, his ethnology shows just as clearly that all customs are not equal (and that in all cases, absence of laws or of rules is a sure criterion of inhumanity). Above all, *Histories* reminds us constantly that around the notion of *nomos* there is always something essentially and inherently Greek. The famous dialogue between Xerxes, the barbarian king, and Demaratus, the exiled Spartan king, is a perfect demonstration: Spartans, Demaratus says, are at once free and submissive to a "master," the law. The laughter with which Xerxes greets this declaration indicates his total lack of understanding. Whereas this Spartan "contract" clearly shows that, while non-Greeks may have their *nomoi* (sometimes very fine ones), the Greeks alone have "politicized" their *nomos.*

THE BEGINNINGS OF HISTORY

Did the writing of history begin in Greece? For many years the answer from scholars of the ancient civilizations of the East has been an emphatic no, expressed with the impatience of those who have had difficulty making themselves heard, so strong was the habit of regarding Greece as the place of all beginnings. To take just one important example: Mesopotamian historiography, linked directly to royal authority, is as ancient as it is rich. The Greeks did not invent history; in fact, they rediscovered writing rather late, borrowing the Phoenician alphabet. However, it was with the Greeks, beginning with Herodotus, that the historian as a subjective figure first appeared. In the service of no particular power, with his very first words he begins to define and claim the narrative form that begins with the use of his own name: "Herodotus the Halicarnassian . . ." He is the author of his "account," and it is this account *(logos)* that establishes his authority. The paradox lies in the fact that, at the same time, this newly claimed authority has yet to be fully constructed. Such a narrative strategy, characteristic of this moment in Greek intellectual history, marks a break with the Eastern historiographers. If the Greeks were inventors of anything, it was less of history than of the historian.

This new form of discourse and this singular figure did not emerge from a vacuum. Both the epic and the bard were still present, close at hand and yet very old, in the prologue to *Histories,* which answered, for the most part, the question: How can one be a bard in a world that is no longer epic? The answer: by becoming a historian. Like the bard, the historian deals with memory, oblivion, and death. The bard of old was a master of glory *(kleos),* a dispenser of immortal encomia to the heroes who died gloriously in war, and the organizer of the collective memory. Herodotus sought only to ensure that the traces and the markings of men, the monuments that they produced, would

not disappear (like the colors of a painting that fade with time), would not cease to be recounted and celebrated (he used the term *aklea*, stripped of glory). The shift from *kleos* to *aklea* indicates that the historian refers continually to the epic, but also that he makes more modest claims than the bard. It is as if he knew that the ancient promise of immortality could never again be uttered except as a negative: as the promise to delay oblivion.

Similarly, where the bard's area of expertise covered "the deeds of heroes and of gods," the historian limits himself to the "deeds of man," in a time that is itself defined as "the time of man." He adds one principle of selection: to choose what is great and elicits astonishment *(thōma)*. Thus he gives himself a means of measuring difference in events and of ordering multiplicity in the world.

"Tell me, O muse, of the man of many devices" (*Odyssey* I.1) was the inaugural pact of the epic. The Muse, daughter of memory and source of inspiration, was the guarantor of the poet's song. With the first history, the realm of the spoken word is over. Prose has replaced verse, writing dominates; the Muse has disappeared. In its place we find a new word and a new narrative economy: "What Herodotus the Halicarnassian has learned by inquiry *(historiē)* is set forth." This emblematic term took hold, little by little (although Thucydides, for his part, took pains never to use it). It was Cicero who gave Herodotus the lasting title "father of history." *History* is an abstract word, formed from the verb *historein*, to inquire, originally in the sense of judicial inquiry; *historia* is derived from *histōr* (which itself is related to *idein*, to see, and *oida*, I know). The *histōr* is the I, the "one who knows by having seen or learned." Thus the *histōr* is present in the epic, where he appears, always in a context of dispute, as arbiter (never as an eyewitness): he has not seen with his own eyes, but, in terms of the process, it is he who will reveal what has happened, or, still more probably, who will be the guarantor of the decision made.

Herodotus is neither bard nor arbiter. He lacks the natural authority of the latter (he is not, like Agamemnon, a "master of truth"), and he does not benefit from the divine vision of the former (the bard is an inspired seer); he inquires. He has only *historiē*, a certain method of inquiry, which I offer as the starting point of his practice of historiography. Produced as a substitute, this inquiry operates in a way analogous to the omniscient vision of the Muse, who was able to know because her divine nature allowed her to be present everywhere and to see everything. The historian, acting on no authority but his own, intends from this point to "go forward with my history, and speak of small and great cities alike [we remember what was said about Odysseus in the *Odyssey*: "Many were the men whose cities he saw"], for many states that were once great have now become small" (*Histories* I.5).

If the historian's inquiry (thus defined) both evokes the wisdom of the bard and breaks with it, Herodotus also appeals to a second register of knowledge:

that of prophecy. He investigates, but he also "signifies," *sēmainei:* he "designates," "reveals." The term *sēmainein,* for example, is used for someone who sees what others do not, or could not, see and makes his report. The verb specifically designates oracular knowledge. In the epic, the seer, who knows present, future, and past, is already portrayed as a man of knowledge. Epimenides of Crete, a famous seer, was reputed to apply his gift of prophecy not to what ought to be but to what, having happened, still remained obscure. We are also reminded of Heraclitus's formula, according to which the oracle neither says nor hides, but "means" *(sēmainei).*

Thus, beginning with the prologue, at the very moment when Herodotus speaks for the first time, saying "I," he signifies *(sēmainei):* drawing on personal knowledge, he reveals who first took offensive action against the Greeks: Croesus, the king of Lydia. The first to subjugate the Greeks, Croesus is "designated" as "responsible," or "guilty" *(aitios).* By assigning responsibility in this way, Herodotus appeals to a level of knowledge that is inherently oracular.

The verbs *historein* and *sēmainein* form the junction where ancient and contemporary knowledge come together and intertwine, as attested by the work of Herodotus himself. These verbs—both functions of "seeing clearly," of seeing further, beyond the visible, into space and time—characterize the style of the first historian. He is neither bard, nor prophet; he is between bard and prophet: he is Herodotus.

FRANÇOIS HARTOG
Translated by Elizabeth Rawlings and Jeannine Pucci

Bibliography

Texts and Translations

Herodotus. *Histoires.* Ed. and trans. Philippe-Ernest Legrand. Paris: Les Belles Lettres, 1932–1954.

———. *Histories.* Ed. and trans. T. E. Page. Loeb Classical Library.

———. *L'enquête.* Ed. and trans. Andrée Barguet. 2 vols. Paris: Gallimard, 1985.

———. *Libro I: La Lidia e la Persia.* Ed. David Asheri. Trans. Virginia Antelami. Milan: Mondadori, 1988.

Studies

Burkert, Walter. "Hérodote et les peuples non grecs." In *Entretiens sur l'antiquité classique,* vol. 35. Geneva: Vandoeuvres, 1990.

Corcella, Aldo. *Erodoto e l'analogia.* Palermo: Sellerio Editore, 1984.

Darbo-Peschanski, Catherine. *Le discours du particulier: Essai sur l'enquête hérodotéenne.* Paris: Editions du Seuil, 1987.

Hartog, François. *The Mirror of Herodotus: The Representation of the Other in the*

Writing of History. Trans. Janet Lloyd. Berkeley: University of California Press, 1988.

————. "Myth into Logos: The Case of Croesus, or The Historian at Work." In *From Myth to Reason: Studies in the Development of Greek Thought.* Ed. R. Buxton. Oxford and New York: Clarendon Press, 1999. Pp. 183–195.

"Herodotus and the Invention of History." *Arethusa* 20 (1987):1–2.

Hunter, Virginia. *Past and Present in Herodotus and Thucydides.* Princeton: Princeton University Press, 1982.

Marincola, John. *Authority and Tradition in Ancient Historiography.* Cambridge and New York: Cambridge University Press, 1997.

Meier, Christian. "An Ancient Equivalent of the Concept of Progress: The Fifth-Century Consciousness of Ability." In *The Greek Discovery of Politics.* Trans. David McLintock. Cambridge, Mass.: Harvard University Press, 1990. Pp. 186–221.

Momigliano, Arnaldo. "The Herodotean and the Thucydidean Tradition." In *The Classical Foundations of Modern Historiography.* Berkeley: University of California Press, 1990. Pp. 29–53.

Nagy, Gregory. *Pindar's Homer: The Lyric Possession of an Epic Past.* Baltimore: Johns Hopkins University Press, 1990.

Payen, Pascal. *Les iles nomades: Conquérir et résister dans l'Enquête d'Hérodote.* Paris: Editions de l'Ecole des Hautes Etudes en Sciences Sociales, 1997.

Sauge, André. *De l'épopée à l'histoire: Fondements de la notion d'historié.* Frankfurt: Peter Lang, 1992.

Thompson, Norma. *Herodotus and the Origins of the Political Community.* New Haven: Yale University Press, 1996.

Related Articles

Inventing Politics; Language; History; Utopia and the Critique of Politics; Geography

HIPPOCRATES

Hᴵᴘᴘᴏᴄʀᴀᴛᴇs, often called the father of medicine, represents a semilegendary figure for many people, just as Homer does. In fact, he was a real historical figure who lived in Pericles' time; he was famous even in his own day, as his contemporaries attest. If he was not the founder of Greek medicine, strictly speaking, he gave it an influence it had never had before, probably owing to his personality and to his teaching. What helped in particular to assure his lasting fame, from antiquity to the present, was the existence of an important collection of medical texts attributed to him and designated today by the title *Hippocratic Collection* or *Hippocratic Corpus*. Although they could not all have been written by Hippocrates himself, these texts nevertheless allow us to discover Hippocratic thought in the broadest sense and to measure the decisive influence of his legacy on the history of Western medicine and, more generally, on how we think about science and about human beings.

What we know about Hippocrates' life we owe to a variety of sources of unequal reliability. The oldest account (and the most interesting) is that of his young contemporary Plato, who refers to Hippocrates on two occasions: first, in *Protagoras,* as the exemplar of a great physician whom Socrates' interlocutor should approach if he wishes to learn the art of medicine, just as he might go to Polyclitus of Argos or Phidias of Athens to learn the art of sculpture. The second reference is in *Phaedrus,* where Socrates (ambiguously) praises Hippocrates' thought. Some forty years later, Aristotle, himself the son of a doctor, refers to Hippocrates in his *Politics*—somewhat incidentally, to be sure—as an example of a man who is great because of his medical science and not because of his size.

Besides these important, although allusive, references, we find more detailed biographical data in a variety of texts. The *Letters* purported to be by Hippocrates (or to him) in the *Collection* are certainly apocryphal, if not fictional; still, they may contain a certain amount of authentic information. Similarly, the *Ambassadorial Speech,* or *Presbeutikos,* which also appears in the *Collection* (a speech that Thessalos, the son of Hippocrates, is believed to have given before the Athenian Assembly toward the end of the 5th century) contains some information on Hippocrates' family—information confirmed, in part, by recent epigraphic discoveries. Besides the *Collection,* there are two *Lives* of Hippocrates, one by Soranus of Ephesus (a physician of the 1st and 2nd centuries ᴄ.ᴇ.), the other by the so-called Pseudo-Soranus (this

Vita Hippocrati is in fact anonymous and incomplete); both draw on earlier sources. Finally, the immense work of Galen of Pergamum (2nd century C.E.), a great admirer of Hippocrates and an authority on his work, contains numerous allusions to the physician from Cos, who was a role model for the physician in Pergamum. All these sources enable us, after a critical examination, to extract a few proved or probable facts about Hippocrates' life. This information is divided fairly distinctly into two periods, before and after his departure from Cos.

In ancient cities there was no organized, public instruction such as we have today, nor were there titles authorizing the practice of medicine; thus the teaching that took place in the city-states was still clearly organized along familial and aristocratic lines. Hippocrates is a perfect case in point. Born around 460 B.C.E. on the Dorian island of Cos, close to the coast of modern Turkey, he descended on his father's side from the Cos branch of the Asclepiades family; another branch had settled just opposite Cos, at Cnidus, on a promontory of Asia Minor. Doctors in general were sometimes called "Asclepiades," and Hippocrates actually was born into a great aristocratic family that claimed direct descent from Asclepius and, more significantly, from the latter's son Podalirius, who is mentioned in Homer along with his brother, Machaon. This family played an important role on the island of Cos in both politics and medicine. Hippocrates, far from being the "inventor" of medicine, actually belonged to a long line of physicians who passed down their medical knowledge from father to son. One of Hippocrates' ancestors, Nebros, became famous as a doctor at the time of the first holy war (600–590 B.C.E.). Hippocrates' grandfather and his father, Heraclides, were also doctors, and in his turn, Hippocrates passed down to his sons, Thessalus and Draco, the knowledge that he had acquired within his family. Hippocrates was actually a link in a long family tradition, rather than the founder of the "school of Cos."

We know that he remained in Cos during the early years of his career, married there, and had three children (two sons, Thessalos and Draco, and a daughter who married one of his students, Polybius). The *Letters* link two anecdotes to this period, anecdotes that bear witness to Hippocrates' renown in both Greek and barbarian lands. He is supposed to have been summoned by the inhabitants of Abdera to tend to the mad philosopher Democritus, who laughed at everything for no apparent reason, and Hippocrates found that, far from being a sign of madness, Democritus's laughter showed the philosopher's wisdom. True or false, the anecdote enjoyed great popularity even beyond antiquity, as attested by one of La Fontaine's fables *(Democritus and the Abderians)* and by an allusion Stendhal makes in his *Life of Henry Brulard*. In another, the king of Persia, Artaxerxes I, is said to have made Hippocrates a magnificent offer to employ him at a time when a plague was devastating his country; however, Hippocrates spurned the king's offer, for he was unwilling

to aid the enemies of Greece. This second story, already well known to Plutarch in the 2nd century C.E., survived for centuries, as we know from a painting by Girodet housed in the Ecole de Médecine in Paris.

But Hippocrates' fame would not have been what it was had he not left his native island for continental Greece. The career of a physician in antiquity was different from that of his modern counterpart who, once established in an office, rarely leaves it. A Greek doctor could, by contrast, practice in different city-states throughout his career, either as a public doctor or in private practice. Like the great Sophists, important doctors traveled to perfect their medical training, and also to profit financially from their reputation abroad. The most famous example before Hippocrates is that of Democedes of Croton, whose brilliant and eventful career is reported by Herodotus. It is in the context of this type of medical career that we can understand Hippocrates' departure from Cos for Thessaly, where he spent the second part of his life surrounded by his sons and his disciples (his practice probably extended throughout the north of Greece). Certain geographic indications preserved in a few of the Hippocratic treatises identify areas of activity of the Hippocratic school after Hippocrates' departure for Thessaly.

In the treatises entitled *Epidemiology*, for the first time in the history of medicine we find individual case studies that track the course of a disease day by day. The geographic origin of the patients is sometimes mentioned, which allows us to trace on a map the places where Hippocrates himself, or a doctor associated with his school, must have practiced. In a few of these cases, the patients lived in the cities of Thessaly (Larissa, Melibeus, Crannon, Pharsale, Pheres), but they are also found in cities of the Propontis (for example, Cyzicus and Perinthus), Thrace (Abdera and Thasos), and Macedonia (Pella).

Hippocrates' biographers link two events to his Thessalian period. The first relates to Macedonia: called to the bedside of Prince Perdiccas II of Macedonia, who was thought to have consumption after the death of his father, Alexander I, Hippocrates is said to have diagnosed him as lovesick for one of his father's courtesans. While the story may not be entirely believable, one can see in it some traces of the bonds of hospitality between the Asclepiades family and the kings of Macedonia that are found in the *Ambassadorial Speech.*

The second event is mentioned only in the *Ambassadorial Speech:* at some time during the years 419–416, Hippocrates apparently refused (again) to help the barbarian princes in the north of Greece (Illyris and Paeonia) combat the plague; however, thanks to the information he had gained from them on the nature and course of the disease, he was able to alert the Greek regions threatened, and to treat those already afflicted. This attitude won him compensation from various city-states, including Delphi; inscriptions found at Delphi indicate that Hippocrates paid a visit there, and that special privileges were extended to the Asclepiades of Cos and of Cnidus.

Hippocrates died at an advanced age in Larissa, perhaps around 377 B.C.E.

His biographers disagree as to his age at the time of death: he may have been 85 years old, or perhaps 109. Buried near Larissa, he became a legendary healer after his death, and at Cos he became the object of a public hero cult. He is figured on coins from Cos as a bald and bearded old man, sometimes in association with Heracles.

If Hippocrates' name became so famous that he was called the father of the art of medicine, it is chiefly because he made the school of which he was a product known far and wide. The school's influence was undoubtedly due in part to its expansion during Hippocrates' lifetime. A true revolution in medical training occurred at a moment that is difficult to date: the family training program in Cos was opened to students from outside the island, for a fee. It was at that point, according to Galen, that the art of medicine spread beyond the Asclepiades' line. Did this revolution occur before Hippocrates' arrival, or was he in fact responsible for it? We do not know, but it is certain that the change took place during his lifetime, since Plato, in *Protagoras*, suggests to a young Athenian that he pay Hippocrates to teach him medicine; and we know that Hippocrates had such students, since his son-in-law, Polybius, although not a direct male descendant of the Asclepiades, was nevertheless a student in Cos. The *Oath* itself confirms this dramatic change: while the second part contains the well-known code of medical ethics, the entire first part reveals that there was in fact a partnership agreement to which only the new students outside the Asclepiades family had to subscribe. The disciple agreed, under oath, to accept his teacher as a father, and eventually to offer free medical training to his teacher's sons. The biographies then name a dozen or so students, some of whom ensured the school's reputation over that of Cnidus, its neighbor and rival, even after Hippocrates' departure.

What contributed more than anything else to the fame of the Cos school and of Hippocrates are the written medical treatises in which the medical teaching was recorded. Here, however, we have to proceed with caution: although tradition has handed down to us some sixty treatises under Hippocrates' name, they are not the work of a single man, nor of a single school, nor even of a single epoch. We cannot go into the "Hippocratic question" in detail here; it is just as thorny and debatable as the Homeric question. We must refrain from unequivocally attributing any particular treatise to Hippocrates himself; but, by the same token, we must not be unduly skeptical. An important core subset of these treatises is undoubtedly the product of Hippocrates himself or his immediate followers; to this original core other treatises were added from outside Cos, often from a later period.

The central core traditionally linked to the school of Cos includes a number of well-defined groups. One group, the "surgical treatises," offers carefully edited texts describing with precision either various head injuries and their treatment—there is an especially detailed description of trepanation *(Head Wounds)*—or different methods for reducing dislocations and fractures; the

search for effective treatment is based on respect for the natural conformation of the limb rather than on sensational effects *(Fractures and Articulations)*. These treatises, while technical, are the work of a strong personality, remarkable for both his human and his scientific qualities, and it is perfectly possible that this figure was Hippocrates himself. These works, apparently intended for publication, are associated with others, edited in a rather terse style, that may simply be notes: for example, *Mochlicon* (the title comes from the Greek word for the "lever" used in surgery), which is a reworked summary of *Fractures and Articulations*, and *Doctor's Dispensary*, which spells out the rules for dressings and operations in the doctor's office.

Another important group consists of *Epidemics*, texts linked, as we have seen, to Hippocrates' and his disciples' Thessalian period of activity. Actually, this collection of seven treatises brings together texts written at different times, and it also artificially breaks up some obvious groupings. Three groups can be reassembled (*Epidemiology* I and III, *Epidemiology* IV and VI, and *Epidemiology* V and VII), extending from the last decade of the 5th century to the middle of the 4th; of these, only the first group can credibly be attributed to Hippocrates himself. Another well-known treatise, *On Airs, Waters, and Places*, also focuses on the activity of the itinerant doctor. Its first, scientific section explains the various external factors the physician must observe when he moves into an unfamiliar city, in order to anticipate the local diseases and treat them successfully (wind direction, water quality, climate). A second, wholly original section shifts from medicine to ethnography and explains the differences between Asians and Europeans through differences in climate and soil, and secondarily in political organization (Montesquieu will echo this argument in *Spirit of the Laws*). The importance attributed to climate reappears in a brief but remarkable treatise, *Sacred Disease*, probably by the same author, which strongly suggests that the disease in question (epilepsy) is no more sacred than others and can be explained, like any other disease, by natural causes. This treatise offers a vigorous polemic against doctors who attribute a divine origin to epilepsy and claim to treat it with magic.

Whether the physician was itinerant or stationary, to provide the best treatment he had to know how to interpret symptoms and predict the course of a disease: this is the object of the famous *Prognostic*, some of whose descriptions are canonical, for example that of a face transformed by illness and announcing imminent death (the "Hippocratic facies"). The therapeutics of acute diseases is treated in *Regimen in Acute Diseases*, a large part of which is devoted to the use of a barley brew, but it also contains prescriptions concerning the use of drinks and baths, and warnings against abrupt changes in diet. In addition, the treatises whose aphoristic style ensured that Hippocratic learning would circulate very widely are also linked to the Cos school. The collection called *Aphorisms* is the most widely read, cited, published, and discussed of all the Hippocratic treatises (the best-known being the first, "Life is

brief, art is long," echoed in a verse by Baudelaire, "Art is long and time is short"). *Coan Prenotions* also received wide circulation. It constitutes a sort of critical encyclopedia of Hippocratic diagnosis. To this by no means complete list must be added, lastly, the famous *Oath,* attesting to the time when the Cos school was opened to include students from the outside, and a treatise—which Aristotle tells us is the work of Polybius, Hippocrates' son-in-law—called *The Nature of Man,* which contains the famous theory of the four humors that was subsequently attributed to Hippocrates himself.

The school of Cnidus, Cos's rival, also left some writings that have come to be included in the *Hippocratic Corpus.* They are referred to in the polemic that the author of *Diet in Acute Diseases* develops against a now lost Cnidian work entitled *Cnidian Lines;* in it he addresses some specific criticisms to the authors (he viewed it as a collective work): their list of diseases was too specific and too limited; their cursory treatments placed too much emphasis on purges like milk and whey, and they neglected the issue of diet. These charges allow us to identify, within the *Corpus,* the texts that meet these criteria. They include the nosological treatises such as *Diseases* II, *Diseases* III, and *Internal Conditions,* to which we may also add the treatises on gynecology, *Nature of Woman* and a complex group on *Female Diseases* (I, II, and III). These treatises can be identified not only by their content but also by their consistent expository style. They generally consist of a sequence of notes about different diseases or types of disease considered according to an ordering principle called *ad capite ad calcem,* from head to toe. Each note contains three main parts: symptoms, diagnosis, and treatment; the very sentence structure in the notes appears to follow an established pattern. These treatises preserve a medical tradition that seems not to have been shaped by the experience of an itinerant doctor nor to have been enlivened by any general reflection on the art of medicine, as was the case at Cos. This is not to say that the Cnidian tradition is without merit: its description of symptoms is very detailed, and in it we find for the first time in the history of medicine a description of the procedure for direct auscultation.

Over time, other treatises independent of Cos and Cnidus came to enlarge the *Corpus.* The most important are the medical treatises with a philosophical bent, like *Winds, Weeks, Flesh,* and *Diet.* In these works man appears as a microcosm reflecting the universe and composed of one or more fundamental elements: air in the case of *Winds,* fire and water in the case of *Diet,* ether, air, and earth in the case of *Flesh,* and up to seven elements in the case of *Weeks.* Two doctors in the *Corpus* argue vigorously against this sort of cosmological medicine. One is Hippocrates' disciple and son-in-law, Polybius, who, in a famous preamble, takes on the philosophers who believe that human nature is made up of a single primordial element. The other is the author of *Ancient Medicine,* who denounces the "modern doctors" who oversimplify notions

Statue of Chrysippus (281–205 B.C.E.), 3rd century B.C.E. (Paris, Louvre.) A great logician and a great dialectician, Chrysippus is shown here in mid-debate; he appears to be gesturing with his hand to enumerate the points in his argument.

Mosaic of a group of philosophers. Pompeii, Villa of Siminius Stephanus, 1st century B.C.E. (Naples, Museo Archeologico.) The figures are identified sometimes as the Seven Sages, sometimes as the members of Plato's Academy.

Bust of Socrates (469–399 B.C.E.) with a passage from Plato's *Crito*. Marble, after a Greek original from the second half of the 4th century B.C.E. (Naples, Museo Archeologico, Farnese Collection.)

Bust, thought to be of Plato (487–347 B.C.E.). (Naples, Villa dei Papiri.)

Plato and Aristotle. Detail from the center of *The School of Athens,* fresco by Raphael (1483–1520). (Vatican, Stanza della Segnatura.) Here Plato is pointing to the heaven of Ideas; tradition often opposes his idealism to Aristotle's realism and to the latter's interest in understanding the order of the world as it is.

Bust of Aristotle (384–322 B.C.E.). Marble attributed to Lysippus. (Vienna, Kunsthistorisches Museum.)

Relief of Diogenes (404–323 B.C.E.) and Alexander the Great. (Rome, Villa Albani.) The insolent Cynic is asking the master of the world not to stand in his light.

Crates and his wife Hipparchia. Fresco in the Villa Farnesina, 4th century B.C.E. (Rome, Museo delle Terme.) The Cynics, along with the Epicureans, were among the few groups of philosophers to admit women.

Diogenes. Engraving after F. Mazzola, 1540. (Paris, Bibliothèque Nationale.) Known for using a lantern in broad daylight to look for a "man" in the streets of Athens, Diogenes is also known for having mocked Plato's characterization of man as a "featherless biped."

Antisthenes (444–365 B.C.E.).
Terra cotta statuette, Pompeii.
(Naples, Museo Archeologico.)

Bust of Epicurus (341–270 B.C.E.).
(Naples, Museo Archeologico.)

Cup from the Boscoreale hoard.
Silver, late 1st century B.C.E. to early
1st century C.E. (Paris, Louvre.)
Depicted are Zeno (325–264 B.C.E.)
and Epicurus, the latter accompanied by his "swine."

Helios. Mosaic from the Synagogue
of Hammath near Tiberias,
4th century C.E.

Christ represented as Sun
God. Mosaic from the
necropolis located under the
Basilica of St. Peter in Rome,
3rd century C.E.

David playing the *lyra*, portrayed as Orpheus. Synagogue of Gaza, 6th century C.E. (Jerusalem, Museum of Israel.) The association of the biblical king with the Thracian bard appears to date from the 1st century B.C.E.

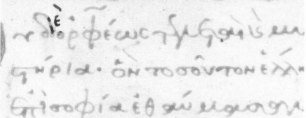

Orpheus represented with a halo and playing the *lyra*. Illustration from Gregory of Nazianzen, *Orations*. Constantinople, 12th century. (Paris, Bibliothèque Nationale.) The Christian Orpheus presented here is a transposition of the David-Orpheus of the Jewish tradition.

Sarcophagus of Prometheus, 3rd century C.E. (Rome, Museo Capitolino.) In this Neoplatonic depiction, Prometheus shapes the body of man while Minerva breathes into him his soul, divine in origin, in the form of a butterfly chrysalis.

Biagio d'Antonio, *Allegory of the Liberal Arts,* 15th century. (Chantilly, Musée Condé.) Below, the arts of the Trivium (Grammar teaching children before the door to Wisdom, then Rhetoric and Dialectic), followed upward by the arts of the Quadrivium (Music, Astronomy, Geometry, and Arithmetic); at the very top, Theology. The figures are accompanied by corresponding symbols; before each one, the author who best represented the art is depicted. Thanks to parallel examples in which these authors are explicitly identified, it is possible to identify here, from bottom to top, Priscian, Cicero, and Aristotle; then Pythagoras, Ptolemy, Euclid, and Boethius; finally, Bishop Pierre Lombard.

6th century with the thinkers of Miletus (Thales, and Anaximander and his disciple Anaximenes) and Samos (Pythagoras, who later emigrated to Croton in southern Italy) and continued in Athens with the brilliant "age of Pericles," which saw the birth of rationalism, humanism, and arts and science *(technai)*. Like other thinkers of their time, physicians reflected on their art and about science in general.

Hippocratic medicine is characterized above all by its rational approach to illness. Even if we can detect here and there the legacy of the archaic mentality that held disease to be an external demonic force, Hippocratic thought vigorously denied any divine intervention in the progress of illness, and rejected magical treatment by prayer, incantations, or purification. Many doctors reacted forcefully against seers and charlatans who attempted to act as healers. This fact is all the more remarkable because popular belief in Hippocrates' day held that disease was caused by the gods, and because religious medicine as practiced in the temples of Asclepius—and in particular in Cos—had experienced unprecedented growth. However, the rationalism of the Hippocratic doctors was not a form of atheism. The *Oath* and other pointed remarks in several treatises all acknowledge a notion of the "divine," but with a new definition: all the essential elements of the universe were considered divine, independent of man and capable of influencing both health and illness. The divine is thus called on to explain a pathological phenomenon, but it lacks any anthropomorphic content. It is a sort of rational divinity that looks very much like nature.

In this respect, Hippocratic rationalism approaches that of Thucydides: the concept of nature *(phusis)* is a central one for Hippocrates, as it is for the historian. The art of medicine, like the understanding of historical facts, is based on knowledge of the laws of human nature. But for the doctor there is the added notion that "human nature" varies according to the external environment. For example, according to the author of *The Nature of Man*, every humor in the body increases or decreases as a function of the season. For the author of *Airs, Waters, and Places*, the physical characteristics and intelligence of human beings vary as a function of the climate and the winds to which they are exposed. The doctor even becomes an ethnographer, comparing the characteristics of Europeans and Asians; he offers in passing an original depiction of the lacustrian villages of Phase (today's Rioni) and describes their inhabitants as indolent, soft, and thick, like their environment, which is swampy, hot, humid, and foggy. In this treatise we also find for the first time the opposition between *phusis* (nature) and *nomos* (custom, law): it is offered not to support the subversive theories that Callicles would develop later in order to undermine the law, but to explain how something acquired by usage—for example, the elongated head of a macrocephalic, an artifact of birth—can come to modify nature.

Greek doctors did not stop at defining the place of human beings in their

environment when they reflected on the causes of disease. They also reflected on the art of medicine and on the place it occupied in human history. The author of *Ancient Medicine*, for example, regarded the doctor's art as a civilizing force thanks to the discovery of dietary principles, following on the introduction of cooking. Cooking was a process of adapting raw food to human nature by a sequence of operations, primarily heating and mixing; it was medicine that showed how cooked food could be adapted to the diets of both healthy and sick people. Thus cooked food was the mark of a superior humanism, and one that was not shared by everyone, since certain barbarians continued to feed themselves after the fashion of savages. But medicine was also seen as an art that could be called the model for all other arts. For the author of *The Art*, medicine is an elevated art, a fact only professional skeptics would dispute. In defending his argument, he launches into a reflection that might qualify as the earliest general epistemological essay left to us by antiquity. Not only does the author affirm, in the style of Parmenides, that it is impossible for science not to be, and for nonscience to be, but he also bases his arguments on both a philosophy of language and a theory of knowledge (opposing science and randomness, chance and necessity) that bring to mind the well-known Sophists and Plato. Other treatises, however, are vehemently opposed to this confusion of medicine with philosophy, and the *Hippocratic Corpus* offers valuable testimony to the identity crisis that medicine experienced at the end of the 5th century, at the moment when the art of medicine began to affirm its independence from philosophy. This independence was so fully achieved in medicine that it served in turn as the model Plato would use to define authentic history or authentic politics. And Galen later associated Hippocrates' reflection with Plato's to describe the ideal physician.

Hippocrates has shaped medical thinking for more than twenty centuries; his influence can be compared to that of Aristotle on philosophical thought. Sometimes disputed, often admired, and very often twisted to suit individual purposes, the work of the Hippocratics remained a constant reference in Western medicine from antiquity to the 19th century.

JACQUES JOUANNA
Translated by Elizabeth Rawlings and Jeannine Pucci

Bibliography

Texts and Translations

Hippocrates. *Oeuvres complètes d'Hippocrate.* Ed. Emile Littré (Greek text with French translation). 10 vols. Paris: J. B. Baillière, 1839–1861.

———. *Works.* 8 vols. Ed. and trans. W. H. S. Jones, E. T. Withington, Paul Potter, Wesley D. Smith. Loeb Classical Library.

Studies

Ayache, Laurent. *Hippocrate.* Paris: Presses Universitaires de France, 1992.

Bourgey, Louis. *Observation et expérience chez les médecins de la Collection hippocratique.* Paris: Vrin, 1953.

Di Benedetto, Vicenzo. *Il medico e la malattia: La scienza di Ippocrate.* Turin: G. Einaudi, 1986.

Duminil, Marie-Paule. *Le sang, les vaisseaux, le coeur dans la Collection hippocratique: Anatomie et physiologie.* Paris: Les Belles Lettres, 1983.

Grensemann, Hermann. *Knidische Medizin.* Vol. 1, Berlin and New York: Walter de Gruyter, 1975. Vol. 2, Stuttgart: F. Steiner Verlag, 1987.

Grmek, Mirko. *Diseases in the Ancient Greek World.* Trans. Mireille Muellner and Leonard Muellner. Baltimore: Johns Hopkins University Press, 1989.

———. *Les maladies à l'aube de la civilisation occidentale.* Paris: Payot, 1983.

Grmek, Mirko, ed. *Western Medical Thought from Antiquity to the Middle Ages.* Trans. Antony Shugaar. Cambridge, Mass.: Harvard University Press, 1998.

Joly, Robert. *Le niveau de la science hippocratique.* Paris: Les Belles Lettres, 1966.

Jouanna, Jacques. *Hippocrate.* Paris: Fayard, 1992; 2nd ed., 1995.

———. *Hippocrate: Pour une archéologie de l'école de Cnide.* Paris: Les Belles Lettres, 1974.

Lloyd, Geoffrey E. R. *Magic, Reason and Experience: Studies in the Origin and Development of Greek Science.* Cambridge: Cambridge University Press, 1979.

———. *Science, Folklore and Ideology: Studies in the Life Sciences in Ancient Greece.* Cambridge: Cambridge University Press, 1983.

Pigeaud, Jackie. *Folie et cures de la folie chez les médecins de l'antiquité gréco-romaine: La manie.* Paris: Les Belles Lettres, 1987.

Smith, Wesley D. *The Hippocratic Tradition.* Ithaca, N.Y.: Cornell University Press, 1979.

Thivel, Antoine. *Cnide et Cos: Essai sur les doctrines médicales dans la Collection hippocratique.* Publications de la Faculté des lettres et des sciences humaines de Nice 21. Paris: Les Belles Lettres, 1981.

Related Articles

Observation and Research; Medicine; Galen

PARMENIDES

Among the earliest Greek thinkers, it was Parmenides who gave philosophy the object that has remained central to it ever since, namely, being. He thus inaugurated the history of what is called ontology, or the science of being.

According to Diogenes Laertius, biographer of the ancient philosophers, Parmenides reached his "acme" (one's culminating point, traditionally located around the age of forty) in the sixty-ninth Olympiad (504–501 B.C.E.). This observation, based on the *Chronicles* of the chronologist Apollodorus (a text generally considered reliable), thus indicates that he was born between 544 and 541. However, that chronology appears incompatible with the account Plato gives in the *Parmenides* dialogue (127a). According to Plato, Parmenides, accompanied by his disciple Zeno, came to Athens when he was sixty-five years old, and met Socrates when the latter was still quite young. Socrates was born in 469, so the meeting Plato imagined could have taken place around 450; in that case, Parmenides would have been born about 515. But most specialists tend not to take Plato's account literally; they are inclined to credit Apollodorus's chronology instead.

Also according to Diogenes Laertius, Parmenides, son of a certain Pyres, was born in Elea, a Greek colony founded by the Phocaeans in southern Italy about 540. He is said to have given his fatherland excellent laws (this information comes from Speusippus, and it is confirmed by Strabo and Plutarch). These details have come into sharper focus since the finding in 1962, in Elea (Velia in Latin), of a headless herm dating from the first half of the 1st century C.E. and bearing the following inscription: "Parmenides, son of Pyres, Ouliades, physician." Scholars hold that "physician" means doctor here, and "Ouliades" means a descendant of Apollo Oulios, that is, Apollo the Healer, viewed as the father of Asclepius, the mythical inventor of medicine.

According to Aristotle, Parmenides was a student of Xenophanes of Colophon (*Metaphysics* I.5.986b22), while Diogenes Laertius borrows another detail from Sotion: Parmenides was a student of Ameinias, the Pythagorean. The two assertions are not incompatible: Parmenides probably had contacts with Xenophanes, who is said to have participated in the foundation of Elea, as well as with the Pythagoreans, whose school was flourishing in southern Italy at the time. At all events, Parmenides' philosophy is wholly original with respect to the teachings of his supposed masters. According to Plato, as

we have seen, Zeno was one of his disciples; others claim that Empedocles of Acragas was also among his pupils.

All the ancient doxographers agree that Parmenides wrote a single work, a poem in hexametric verse entitled *On Nature*. Owing above all to citations by Sextus Empiricus and Simplicius (the latter relying on Theophrastus), about one hundred sixty verses from this poem, spread over some twenty fragments, have survived, and we have good reason to consider them authentic, since, beyond the guarantee conferred by metric analysis, they are often confirmed by citations in Plato and Aristotle. In addition, we also have some fifty statements by ancient authors attesting to Parmenides' life and his doctrine.

THE PROEM

Parmenides' poem begins with a proem of thirty-two verses (frg. I), in which the author, speaking in his own name, tells how he has been transported on a chariot drawn by docile mares and driven by young girls, identified as the daughters of the Sun, on a "many-voiced way" *(hodos poluphemos)*. This road, characterized also as "the resounding road of the goddess" and as able to lead "the man who knows" everywhere, is said to proceed from "the realm of the night" to the light, that is, to "day," while the author claims to have encountered along the way "the gate [separating] the ways of day and night." The keys to this door are said to be held by a goddess called Justice. Persuaded by the words of the daughters of the Sun, the goddess is said to have unlocked the door, thus allowing the traveler, his chariot, and his horses to enter the "high road"—the path of day.

The proem goes on to say that the goddess, presumably the same Justice, then greeted the traveler cordially, rejoicing with him that he had arrived on a road so little traveled by men but one in conformity with divine law and justice; and she described in advance the path followed by that road: "You must hear about all things, both the still heart of persuasive truth and the opinions of mortals, in which there is no true conviction. But even so, these things too you shall learn: how the things that appear would have to have real existence" (frg. I.28–32).

This narrative is manifestly inspired by the mythical tradition, in particular by travel myths, which are common in ancient epics. But there is no opposition here between myth and *logos,* or reason; Parmenides presents the myth as a true discourse, as the divine revelation of a truth. At the center of the myth is the image of the path, a trajectory leading from darkness to light, and this is presumably the symbol of the trajectory of human knowledge moving toward truth. This image subsists in later Greek philosophy: the "way" *(hodos)* becomes the "method" *(met-hodos),* the trajectory of knowledge. The content of the revelation, which is prefigured in the proem and will constitute

the body of the poem as a whole, entails first a presentation of the "truth," through the description of the way things really are, then a presentation of the "opinions of mortals," that is, of what men believe (but which is false), and also an explanation of the way "the things that appear would have to have real existence."

The meaning of these last words, which clearly allude to the final section of the poem, is controversial; some recent studies (Couloubaritsis; Reale and Ruggiu) suggest that the phrase presents the final section not as an uncovering of what is false but as a valid explanation of appearances—that is, the reconnecting of physical phenomena, beyond all the erroneous opinions of mortals, with their true origin, which is a blend of two opposing principles, light and darkness. This interpretation appears to be supported by the fact that Aristotle views the last part of Parmenides' poem as an authentic expression of his thought; he even seems to appreciate it, since he discovers in it on two occasions an allusion to the discovery of the source of motion (*Metaphysics* I.3.984b2; 4.984b25).

THE REVELATION OF TRUTH

According to the unanimous interpretation of the scholars, fragments II–VIII (1–49) of Parmenides' poem contain a revelation of truth, and these fragments include more than half of the lines that have been preserved, doubtless because the ancient doxographers thought it was less important to cite the poem's last part. In the opening lines, which seem to come directly after the proem, the goddess formulates the following revelation: "I shall tell . . . just what ways of enquiry there are, the only ones that can be thought of. The one <way, which tells us> that 'is' [*hopōs estin*], and that it is not possible not to be, is a path of persuasion, for <persuasion> accompanies truth. The other <way, which tells us> that 'is not' [*hōs ouk estin*], and that it is necessary not to be; this I tell you is a road of which we can learn nothing. For you could hardly come to know what is not—for <what is not> is not accessible—nor could you tell <it to others>" (frg. II.1–8).

Here, the paths designated earlier as "the way of day" and "the way of night" seem to reappear in the form of an alternative, the one that separates the thought "is" from the thought "is not." Of the two alternatives, however, only the first, namely, the thought "is," is in conformity with truth. The second, the thought "is not," does not make it possible to learn anything; on the contrary, it even amounts to thinking nothingness, that is, to not thinking. This does not mean that the second path is absolutely impossible to follow: it is devoid of truth, and that is why all those who find themselves on it—as was doubtless the case for Parmenides himself before he was brought into the presence of the goddess—are in a state of ignorance or in error.

The fragment that comes immediately afterward seems to express the same doctrine as well: "For there is the same thing for being thought and for being" (frg. III). This does not mean that being is reduced to thought, after the manner of idealism, which is a concept foreign to the most ancient Greek philosophy and whose application would thus be totally anachronistic; it means that to think is the same thing as to think being, or else that to be is the same thing as to be thought. Indeed, the fragment is sometimes translated as follows: "To think and to be are in fact the same thing," or even: "The possibility of thinking and the possibility of existing are in fact the same thing." In any case, however the fragment is translated, the meaning indicated above is accepted more or less unanimously.

By identifying the first way, that is, the way of truth, with the thought "is," Parmenides was probably referring to all the thoughts expressed by true affirmations and containing the verb "to be," whether that verb is in the position of copula or predicate. It would be anachronistic indeed to suppose that he clearly conceptualized the distinction between a copula and a predicate, or the distinction between a predicate of the simply attributive type, a predicate of the existential type, and a predicate of the so-called veritative type (x is = x is true). Furthermore, if we may judge by the reason he gave for declaring the second path impossible to follow, Parmenides considered that such thoughts or statements were equivalent, respectively, to thinking and to expressing "being" *(to eon)*. In this way, the copula or the predicate *is* turned out to be transformed, so to speak, into indications of an object existing in itself, or of an objective reality—that is, precisely, being, which became in turn the subject of the verb *to be*.

We can see this clearly in a later fragment, in which Parmenides declares: "See <them>, though they are absent, as firmly present to the mind *[nooi]*. For <the mind> will not cut off what is from holding onto what is: <what is will not cease to hold onto what is> either by <its> scattering in all directions everywhere across the world, or by <its> coming together" (frg. IV.1–4). In short, even what is not present to the senses is thought of as being, inasmuch as it is an object of thought, and thought can think only that it is; in other words, it cannot separate being from its own being, it cannot say that being is not. Here thought, or mind *(noos)*, is viewed as true thought, capable of guaranteeing the existence of its object, even in the absence of other attestations stemming, presumably, from the senses.

The same doctrine is affirmed once again further on, when the goddess declares: "It is necessary to say this, and to think this, <namely> that there is being *[eon emmenai]*; for it is possible to be, while it is not possible for <what is> nothing <to be>" (frg. VI.1–2). Here, thinking and saying "is" become thinking and saying that "there is being," where "being" or "existent" is that which is, i.e., it is the subject about which being, as predicate, un-

derstood as a verb, is affirmed. If one must think and say that being is, the reason for this is the impossibility of thinking and saying nothingness—i.e, nonexistent, nonbeing—or better, the impossibility of thinking and saying that nothingness is. The idea is repeated in yet another fragment, one that is famous because both Plato and Aristotle cite it verbatim: "For never shall this <wild saying> be tamed, <namely> that things that are not, are" (frg. VII.1). It is not clear what "tamed" may mean here: we may understand it as "imposed by force," or else "made acceptable." In any case, the overall meaning of the sentence is that it is impossible for nonexistents to be.

Why did Parmenides consider the verb *to be* the only one capable of expressing the truth, and thus as being the sole possible object of thought? Probably because this verb is the only one that makes it possible to express, in Greek, all truths as predicate or copula. Indeed, Aristotle indicates later on that expressions such as "the man walks" or "the man cuts" are perfectly equivalent, respectively, to expressions such as "the man is walking" or "the man is cutting" (*Metaphysics* V.7). This function of universal vicariousness, so to speak, with respect to all verbs, a function belonging to the verb *to be*, must have been a phenomenon already known to Parmenides.

What is striking, nevertheless, in Parmenides' doctrine is not only that discovery—the discovery that to think and speak truly always means to think and express being—but also the affirmation, immediately linked to the preceding one, that the truth of thinking and speaking is always and only a necessary truth; in other words, thinking and expressing being not only to affirm how things are but also affirm that they are that way necessarily, that they cannot be otherwise. In fact, for the philosopher of Elea the first path, the only way endowed with truth, consists in thinking "is" and also in thinking "it is not possible not to be." If such a thought is expressed in the formula "it is possible to be" (frg. VI), by virtue of the preceding declaration this formula also signifies that "it is not possible for <what is> nothing to be," i.e., that there is necessarily being. In short, at the very moment when he is discovering being, Parmenides conceives of it as necessary, whether what is in question is copulative being, existential being, or veritative being. For Parmenides, all true knowledge is what Plato and Aristotle will later call science (*episteme*), that is, knowledge endowed with necessity.

What is the reason for this conception? What led Parmenides to think that being—everything that is, or everything that is something—is necessary, cannot not be, or cannot not be what it is? The answer is not clear. Some have found an explanation in the fact that the verb *to be* in Greek, like the equivalent verbs in the Indo-European languages, possesses a meaning—perhaps arising from a contamination of its various roots—that could be synthesized around the idea of enduring presence, permanence, which would contrast it with becoming (Aubenque). Perhaps the very opposition that Parmenides es-

tablished between being and nonbeing led him to believe that being cannot in any way not be, that is, to use post-Parmenidean terms, that a being is a being by essence, which has as its unique essence being itself.

Immediately after affirming the necessity of saying that being is, the goddess adds: "For this is the first way of enquiry which *I hold* you *back* from [eirgō], and then next from the <way> which mortals fabricate, knowing nothing, double-headed" (frg. VI.3–5). And right afterward, she characterizes the position of these latter as consisting in admitting that being and nonbeing are identical and nonidentical, and that for all things (or for them all), the way is "one that turns back upon itself" *(palintropos)*. In fact, the expression "hold back" is not found in any surviving manuscript; it was inserted by Diels on the basis of the so-called Aldine edition, which probably drew on manuscripts that are no longer available. The expression presupposes that that "first way" is not the one that has just barely been mentioned, the one that says "is," but the one that has remained implicit in the fragment, the one that says "is not." Furthermore, it implies that the goddess holds the traveler back from not just one but two paths, and thus that she is speaking of three paths, whereas earlier she mentioned only two paths between which the traveler had to choose.

That is why some interpreters (Cordero, for example) have preferred to introduce another expression, "you will begin" *(arxei)*, meaning that the traveler has to begin by learning the way of truth, and then must learn the way of error as well. In this view, the ways of which the poem speaks would remain two in number. However the text might best be completed (and there is unquestionably a gap here, as the metric structure proves), the consensus among contemporary scholars is that the ways mentioned by the goddess are only two in number, that of being and that of nonbeing; a possible third path, which affirms at the same time being and nonbeing, can be reduced to the second, inasmuch as the second affirms that being is not, and thus is condemned by the goddess as devoid of truth.

The same fragment raises another difficulty: who are the "double-headed" men? Some scholars have identified them with Heraclitus, a contemporary of Parmenides, by virtue of the fact that the Ephesian speaks of a harmony "that turns back upon itself" *(palintropos, frg. VIII)*; others associate them with the earlier philosophers (Ionians, Pythagoreans, and so on); still others equate them with the common man, influenced by sensations. Whoever the "double-headed" men may be, however, it seems clear that Parmenides condemns their way as an erroneous interpretation of perceptible appearances; in the second section of the poem, he presumably reserves for himself the right to supply what he deems to be the best explanation of these appearances.

The condemnation recurs in the subsequent fragment, in which the goddess declares, referring precisely to the affirmation that "things that are not,

are": "But do you turn away your thought from this way of enquiry. Let not habit <too> full of experiences, drag you along this way <and force you> to exercise an aimless eye, an echoing ear and tongue; but judge by reason *[logōi]* the refutation that has been uttered by me, <a refutation> arousing much controversy *[poluderin elenchon]*" (frg. VII.2–3, frg. VIII.1). Here the senses, the eyes and ears, the source of error, and reason *(logos)*, the source of truth, are clearly contrasted; the exposition of reason is presented as a refutation *(elenchos)* of the opposing way, even if the refutation in question seems to have to be repeated several times.

After ruling out the way of error, the goddess moves on to present the path of truth, the one that says "is": on this path, she declares, are found numerous "signs" *(semata)*, that is, signals indicating direction, expressing an equivalent number of characteristics of being. These are listed in advance: unborn *(ageneton)*, imperishable *(anolethron)*, whole of limb *(oulomeles)*, unshaking *(atremes)*, unendable *(ateleston)*, one *(hen)*, continuous *(suneches)* (frg. VIII.1–6). The reason for being to be unborn and imperishable is that it cannot have an origin: if it had one, it would have to have gotten it either from nonbeing or from being; but nonbeing is not, it is neither thinkable nor expressible; and being is already, thus it cannot be that from which being takes its origin. This is why, according to the goddess, being is firmly bound up, as it were, in the chains of Justice (frg. VIII.6–15).

Of being, then, one can say neither that it was nor that it will be, but only that it "is now, all <of it> together." If in fact one were to say that it was, one could no longer say that it is, and also if one were to say that it will be, one could no longer say that it is. In short, being is eternal; it subsists in a sort of timeless present. Furthermore, it is one and continuous in the sense that it is not divisible, because it is not more in one place and less in another: it is the same everywhere, and there is nothing that can prevent it from being unified, because it is entirely full. In short, "Since staying both the same and in the same <place>, it lies by itself and stays thus fixedly on the same spot" (frg. VIII.29–30).

Finally, the goddess continues, being is limited: "for <a> powerful Necessity holds <it> in the chains of a limit *[peiratos]* which shuts it in all around," because it lacks nothing; it is complete, perfect. By virtue of the limit that encloses it, it is complete in all respects: thus it is like the mass of a well-rounded sphere, equal in all its parts, starting from the center throughout its limits (frg. VIII.30–49). Here we can clearly see the emergence of the typically Greek concept according to which limitation is not a flaw but a form of perfection, because it is synonymous with completeness. The limited nature of a sphere is only an image, which makes it possible to emphasize the perfection and the homogeneity of being without any connotation of materiality. It is probably because of this doctrine that Aristotle, though he is one of

Parmenides' harshest critics, nevertheless credits him with having conceived of being as one "in concept" *(kata ton logon)*, not "according to matter" *(kata ten hulen)*, as did Melissus *(Metaphysics* I.5.986b18−21); Aristotle approves of Parmenides for conceiving of being as limited, and he will reproach Melissus for having conceived of it as unlimited *(Physics* III.6.207a15−17).

If being is eternal, immobile, one, undifferentiated, then any expression such as "coming into being and passing away," "being and not <being>," "changing place and altering <their> bright color"—in other words, any expression indicating change, alteration, difference in place and quality, any expression created by a "mortal" in the belief that it was true—is merely a "name" *(onoma)* devoid of truth (frg. VIII.38−41). Thus Parmenides denies the reality of change and of difference, or else he relegates change and difference to the level of simple appearances, which "mortals," that is, all those who follow the path of error, are incapable of explaining in a satisfactory way.

Given these characteristics, we can understand how Parmenides' being was viewed—by his disciples Zeno and Melissus as well as by his critics Plato and Aristotle—fundamentally as "one," even if Parmenides does not place particular emphasis on this feature and stresses instead the eternal and homogeneous nature of being. Some interpreters have even explicitly denied that Parmenides' text contains the term *one (hen),* so far as the "signs" of being are concerned; they lean toward a manuscript variant that speaks only of its homogeneity (Untersteiner). Still, it is undeniable that this homogeneity rules out the existence of true differences at the heart of being: such differences would imply differing degrees or modes of being, and that is something Parmenides quite clearly disallows.

THE EXPLANATION OF APPEARANCES

The second part of Parmenides' poem is presented by the goddess herself as the account of the "opinions of mortals"; nevertheless, these latter must be learned in the proper order. According to the goddess, mortals "have set their minds on naming two forms, one of which is not right <to name>; <that is> where they have strayed <from the truth>. They separated <the two forms, so as for them to be> oppositely <characterized> in body, and they set up signs independently one from the other" (frg. VIII.50−56). Whatever the precise translation of line 54 may be, it is clear that for Parmenides it is a mistake to posit two opposing realities, and that, on the contrary, it is necessary to posit only one.

The two forms posited by mortals are fire (designated later also as light), which is tenuous and light in weight, identical to itself and opposed to the other, and night, which is dense and heavy, it, too, identical to itself and opposed to the other. "This division and ordering <of the cosmos> I tell you

looks good enough, in every way *[eoikota panta]*, for no mortal ever to be able to overtake you in the conclusion he has come to" (frg. VIII.60–61). This phrasing seems to entail an affirmation that the opinion presented by the goddess, although false (because of the opposition it establishes between two realities), remains the best of all explanations that mortals can offer for perceptible appearances.

The central thesis of the second part is then stated by the goddess in the following terms: "All is full alike of light and of night invisible, both of them equal, since <there is> nothing <that> falls to the lot of neither" (frg. IX.3–4). Here it appears clearly that the true explanation for perceptible things, that is, for appearances, is that they are all the result of a mixture between two opposing principles, one positive and the other negative, and that neither one can do without the other.

The goddess then announces an explanation of the origin, and thus of the nature *(phusis)*, of the aether, which seems to be the element that constitutes "the sky which embraces all," the stars, the sun, the moon, and all the other heavenly bodies (frgs. X–XI). But this explanation has been preserved only in a very fragmentary fashion: the text speaks in fact of certain things that the doxographers designate as rings or "coronas," that is, circles or spheres; some are narrower, full of pure fire; these are followed by others, full of night mingled with fire; amid these spheres there is a divinity who governs all things and who presides over all unions, such as that of the male and the female toward the end of reproduction (frg. XII). This divinity would have conceived, as the firstborn of all the gods, the god of love and of generation, Eros (frg. XIII).

According to the doxographers, these entities are precisely concentric coronas, formed alternatively of light (that is, of fire) and night (earth), between which are interposed coronas made up of a mixture of both elements; on the outside there is a solid corona, and in the center there is a solid body surrounded by fire. Among the mixed coronas, the central one is the cause of movement and generation; it is a divinity known as Justice and Necessity. At all events, we encounter a grandiose cosmology that conceives of the universe as a system of concentric spheres formed by two opposite realities, a system governed by a divinity that presides over all generation by uniting and blending opposites.

Parmenides must have dwelt at length on the idea of mixture as exemplified by sexual union, for other fragments describe in detail the mixture of male and female seed, specifying that if this mixture produces a true union, well-constituted bodies result, while if the mixture gives rise to conflict, the bodies that result are tormented (frg. XVIII). Some doxographers report as one of Parmenides' doctrines the idea that if the female seed comes from the right side of the uterus, the offspring will resemble its father, whereas if it comes from the left side, it will resemble its mother; according to others, the two

seeds, male and female, will struggle against each other, and the offspring will resemble the parent who produced the victorious seed.

In this context, the soul and its faculties, thought and sensation, also had to be mentioned. One fragment asserts, in fact, that thought (*noos*) is arranged in men in the same way the mixture of members takes place, "for what there is more of is thought" (frg. XVI.4). The doxographers, for their part, report that for Parmenides the soul, too, consists of a mixture of fire and earth; the soul coincides with intelligence; sensation and thought are the same thing; and knowledge is achieved through resemblance. We may conclude from this, apparently, that the soul, or thought, is constituted by a mixture of the two opposing principles, and that this is why it is capable of knowing the various realities, which are constituted by the same mixture.

Finally, in what must have been the last fragment of the poem, we read: "That then, I tell you, is how these things were born to be and now are and shall from this <time> onward grow and die, in the way that <people think of them and that> they appear <to them to be>. To them men have assigned a name, peculiar to <and distinctive of> each <and every> one" (frg. XIX). This seems to confirm that the account just produced has to do with opinions held by men: what is at issue, in other words, is not real truth but the world of perceptible appearances. At the same time, the goddess repeats that what is in question is the most plausible explanation of the origin and the nature of these appearances, and thus also of the names that men have given them. In short, it seems that, in the second part of his poem, Parmenides intended to offer us what would later be called a physics, the best physics possible, even while he remained convinced of the purely illusory character of perceptible appearances.

PARMENIDES' LEGACY

Parmenides' doctrine had an enormous influence over all of ancient philosophy. His disciples, Zeno of Elea and Melissus of Samos, left the second part of the poem completely aside; they abandoned the effort to produce a theory of nature, and they interpreted the first part of the poem as the assertion of a being that is essentially one and immutable. Zeno set out to refute multiplicity and becoming, with his celebrated arguments by way of the absurd; that is why Plato and Aristotle view him as the founder of dialectics. Melissus, in contrast, interpreted being as a unique mass of matter, and consequently conceived of it as infinite in space as well. That is why Aristotle saw Melissus as a crude thinker.

The other philosophers of nature, Empedocles, Anaxagoras, and the Atomists Leucippus and Democritus, fell under Parmenides' influence to a similar extent. At the base of all things, they posited realities (respectively, the four elements, the "seeds" of all things, the atoms) that were permanent, although

multiple. Moreover, in their opposition between plenitude and multitude, the Atomists reproduced the Parmenidean opposition between being and nonbeing. Parmenides' doctrine was contested later in a thoroughgoing way by the Sophist Gorgias, who affirmed what being is not, that it is not thinkable and not communicable. Among his various arguments, one in particular stands out: being, since it is uniquely identical to itself, has nothing more than nonbeing, which is also identical to itself; for this reason, one cannot say that it is, that it is thinkable, and that it is communicable, any more than nonbeing is.

Reference to Parmenides is a central feature in Plato's writings. Plato describes Parmenides as "one to be venerated" and also "awful" (*Theaetetus* 183e); he gives his name to one of the dialogues, presenting Parmenides above all as a proponent of oneness; and he refutes him in *Sophist*, where he presents his critique of Parmenides as a form of parricide. This critique consists in positing nonbeing alongside being, but nonbeing understood not as absolute nonbeing (after the fashion of the void introduced by the Atomists), but as an "otherness" that belongs to every being, together with "sameness." In this way Plato paves the way for Aristotle's critique, which accuses Parmenides of having conceived of being in only one sense, namely as univocal, and Aristotle opposes his own conception of being as plurivocal, as something that has several meanings (*Physics* I.2–3).

In modern and contemporary philosophy, because Parmenides said that being is identical to itself, he has been viewed as having discovered what is called the principle of identity, according to which every existent is identical to itself; and because he said that being cannot not be, he has been viewed as having discovered the principle of noncontradiction. In reality, the latter principle, formulated by Plato and Aristotle, simply says that each existent cannot have opposite characteristics at the same time and under the same aspect. The most appropriate modern interpretation may remain Hegel's: because Parmenides took as his object the philosophy of being, which is the first of all concepts, he is, for Hegel, the true initiator of all Western philosophy. Hegel nevertheless also took up Gorgias's critique, by observing that being, by being simply identical to itself, that is, devoid of all determination, has nothing more than nonbeing and is thus reduced to the latter, thereby giving rise to becoming. More recently Parmenides was exalted by Heidegger, who interpreted the identity of being and thought, affirmed by the philosopher from Elea, as an opening of being to thought, and thus as truth *(aletheia)* in the original sense of nonconcealment, a truth that precedes the logical form of the proposition and all the representative thought based on that form (*Introduction to Metaphysics*, 1953).

ENRICO BERTI
Translated by Catherine Porter and Jeannine Pucci

Bibliography

Texts and Translations

Parmenides. *Fragments: A Text and Translation*. Intro. David Gallop. Toronto: University of Toronto Press, 1984.

———. *The Fragments of Parmenides: A Critical Text*. Trans. and ed. A. H. Coxon. Assen: Van Gorcum, 1986

———. *Le poème de Parménide: Texte, traduction, essai critique*. Trans. and ed. Denis O'Brien. Vol. 1 of *Etudes sur Parménide*. Ed. Pierre Aubenque. 2 vols. Paris: Vrin, 1987.

———. "The Proem." In G. S. Kirk, J. E. Raven, and M. Schofield, *The Presocratic Philosophers: A Critical History with a Selection of Texts*. 2nd ed. Cambridge: Cambridge University Press, 1983.

Studies

Allen, R. E., and David J. Furley. *Studies in Presocratic Philosophy*, vol. 2. London: Routledge, 1975.

Aubenque, Pierre, ed. *Etudes sur Parménide*. 2 vols. Paris: Vrin, 1987.

Barnes, Jonathan. *The Presocratic Philosophers*, 2nd ed. London: Routledge, 1982.

Beaufret, Jean. *Le poème de Parménide*. Paris: Presses Universitaires de France, 1955.

Conche, Marcel. *Parménide: Le Poème: Fragments*. Paris: Vrin; Brussels: Ousia, 1996.

Cordero, Nestor-Luis. *Les deux chemins de Parménide*. Brussels: Ousia, 1984.

Couloubaritsis, Lambros. *Mythe et philosophie chez Parménide*. Brussels: Ousia, 1986.

Dumont, Jean-Paul. *Les présocratiques*. Paris: Gallimard, 1988.

Guthrie, W. K. C. *A History of Greek Philosophy*, vol. 2: *The Presocratic Tradition from Parmenides to Democritus*. Cambridge: Cambridge University Press, 1965.

Heidegger, Martin. *An Introduction to Metaphysics*. Trans. Ralph Manheim. New York: Doubleday, 1961.

Kirk, J. S., J. E. Raven, and M. Schofield. *The Presocratic Philosophers*, 2nd ed. Cambridge: Cambridge University Press, 1983.

Mourelatos, Alexander. *The Pre-Socratics: A Collection of Critical Essays*. Garden City, N.Y.: Anchor Press, 1974.

Reale, Giovanni, and Luigi Ruggiu. *Parmenides: Poema sulla Natura: I frammenti e le testimonianze indirette*. Milan: Rusconi, 1991.

Reinhardt, Karl. *Parmenides und die Geschichte der griechischen Philosophie*. Bonn: Cohen, 1916.

Tarán, Leonardo. *Parmenides: A Text with Translations, Commentary and Critical Essays*. Princeton: Princeton University Press, 1965.

Untersteiner, Mario. *Parmenide: Testimonianze e frammenti*. Florence: Nuova Italia, 1958.

Related Articles

The Question of Being; Cosmology; Anaxagoras; Sophists; Demonstration and the Idea of Science; Rhetoric; Zeno of Elea

PLATO

Plato of Athens (429–347 B.C.E.) descended from a wealthy and distinguished Athenian family; on his mother's side he had Solon, the great lawgiver, as an ancestor. His family, like many, was divided by the disastrous political consequences of the Peloponnesian War. Plato's stepfather, Pyrilampes, was a friend of Pericles and a democrat who even called his own son Demos; but two of Plato's uncles, Critias and Charmides, became members of the Thirty Tyrants, infamous for their reactionary, antidemocratic, and lawless rule. Plato probably grew up expecting to play a prominent role in public life, but so far as we know he did not do so either under the Thirty or under the restored democracy.

At some point in his life Plato decided to devote his life to philosophy, and he took two steps that decisively detached him from his family and political context. He rejected marriage and the normal duty to family and clan of producing citizen sons. (To the performance of this duty one's personal sexual preferences were irrelevant, so we cannot ascribe this rejection to Plato's being homosexual in temperament, something that seems evident from much of his writing.) He also founded a philosophical school, called the Academy after the public gymnasium where it held its discussions and instruction. The Academy, something new in the Greek world, soon became famous and attracted many students, the most noteworthy being Aristotle. We have almost no evidence as to its organizational structure, but the founding of this new institution, inward-looking and "academic" by comparison with the public activities of the Sophists, marks an important point in the history of philosophy. Thenceforward, philosophical schools would be distinguished by different doctrines, approaches, and arguments.

Ironically, the motivation for this momentous step came in large part from the influence on Plato of Socrates of Athens, someone who himself wrote nothing and founded no organized school. Socrates was a charismatic figure of undistinguished background, and by the end of his life he was poor because of his devotion to philosophical activity; earlier he had served as a heavily armed soldier, or hoplite, a duty requiring substantial financial means. Socrates attracted a great variety of pupils and became the ideal figure of the philosopher. Many of his followers wrote dialogues including him; the later dominance of Plato's dialogues should not make us lose sight of the fact that many different writers and philosophers claimed Socrates as the inspiration and symbol of their ideas. He was regarded as the "patron saint" of ascetic

Cynics, hedonistic Cyrenaics, Stoics, and Skeptics, as well as of the ideas that Plato presents in his works. Socrates' deep influence on Plato is clear from the fact that most of Plato's works take the form of dialogues between Socrates and other people, even where, as in some later dialogues, this is plainly unsuitable and the actual role of Socrates shrinks. Also influential, of course, was the fact of Socrates' execution by the restored democracy, on the vague and inflammatory charge of introducing new divinities and corrupting the young men. It has always been suspected that the charge was politically motivated and stemmed from Socrates' association with some of the political leaders who had destroyed the democracy during the closing years of the Peloponnesian War. But whatever the truth of this, Plato was certainly moved to spend much of his own philosophical activity defending the memory of Socrates.

The ancient biographical tradition about Plato offers much romantic detail to fill in the sparse outline I have given of a life lived teaching philosophy, mainly in Athens. The ancient accounts of Plato's life ascribe to him, for example, extensive travels. Scholarly study of the accounts' sources, however, should incline us to suspend judgment about most of what they contain, for much of the detail is tailor-made to fit with aspects of the dialogues. In *Laws*, for example, Plato discusses Egyptian art and its high degree of stylization (656–657), and the ancient biographies tell us of a trip to Egypt. We may suppose that the latter is historical fact that explains the former. But we may equally well suppose that it is an example of a common tendency to explain something in Plato's writing by giving it a personal reason or association.

Part of this reconstructed biography, of uncertain date, took the form of alleged "letters," a recognized literary genre that probably did not originally intend to deceive. One of them, the seventh, which gives an account of Plato's relationships with Dionysius II of Syracuse and his relative Dion, has been accepted by many scholars and even turned into an account of historical fact explaining Plato's political writings, particularly *The Republic*. This is surely unsafe; the authenticity of the "Seventh Letter" remains controversial, and it is regarded by many as created later to illuminate *The Republic*.

The tendency to accept "biographical" background about Plato has been particularly strong in the 20th century. However, it has also been influenced by a constant desire to find *something* that straightforwardly expresses, or explains, Plato's views on a topic. For Plato differs strikingly from most philosophers: deliberately spurning the standard format of the prose philosophical treatise, he chose to use the form of dialogues, in none of which he appears as an interlocutor, thereby formally distancing himself from what is expressed in any of his works. The desire for a "Life and Letters of Plato" undoubtedly springs in part from the frustration that many readers feel at this detachment.

In the Academy Plato probably did some oral teaching, and he gave one

unsuccessful lecture, "On the Good," but his only preserved works were a number of dialogues. Since the 19th century, great effort has been expended on establishing the chronology of their composition, but in spite of much computer-based analysis, no stylistic test serves to establish any precise order. However, there is a general consensus on three roughly marked groups: (1) the short "Socratic" dialogues, in which Socrates is the main figure, questioning others but putting forward no philosophical theses himself; (2) the "middle" dialogues, notably *Phaedo, The Republic*, and *Symposium*, marked by large, confident metaphysical schemes; (3) the later dialogues, in which the dialogue form is used merely for exposition, Socrates retires as the chief figure, and Plato deals with philosophical issues in a way that is more piecemeal and more "professional," paying serious attention to other philosophers' views. Some dialogues are difficult to place; *Theaetetus* and *Euthydemus* seem, in different ways, to postdate *The Republic,* but both return to the Socratic format and examine Socratic method. *Timaeus* and its unfinished companion, *Critias*, belong thematically with *The Republic* but fit stylistically with later dialogues, such as *Laws*. Plato is a skilled and versatile writer whose works cannot be listed chronologically by any simple stylistic criteria.

The dialogues are not only bewilderingly varied but are also more interpretatively open than other ancient philosophical works. From antiquity onward there has been an unceasing debate as to whether Plato put forward any systematic positive ideas. Arcesilaus (315–240 B.C.E.), who became the head of the Academy, initiated a period during which Plato's philosophical legacy was taken to be one of debate and argument, not doctrines. This "skeptical" or investigative way of reading Plato gave great emphasis to *Theaetetus*, the dialogue in which Socrates compares himself to a barren midwife who draws philosophical ideas out of others and criticizes them, but puts forward none himself. On this conception, it is all right for the philosopher to hold positions, as Socrates emphatically does, but these are not advanced to be argued for, nor as the basis for further argument. The philosophical impulse is to "follow the argument where it leads," to destroy the ill-conceived views of others, as Socrates does, not to put forward a system of one's own.

However, while the skeptical reading of Plato can account excellently for the Socratic dialogues and *Theaetetus,* it does not seem to do as well with the confident positive pronouncements of dialogues like *The Republic* and *Laws*. It can, of course, regard these as mere presentations of positions for argument, but from antiquity onward this reading has had to compete with the "dogmatic" reading, according to which the dialogues should be read as presenting pieces of doctrine that the reader is encouraged to put together in systematic ways. The dogmatic reading has, historically, been by far the more popular one, and most of the discussion of Plato's thought has taken the form of arguing about how, not whether, it should be systematized. In the 1st

century B.C.E. we find the writer Arius Didymus insisting that "Plato has many voices, not, as some think, many doctrines" (*ap.* Stobaeus, *Eclogae* II.55.5–6). The dogmatic reading has to cope with the diverse and unsystematic nature of the dialogues, with some conflicts between passages in different dialogues, and with the changing role of Socrates. In the 20th century, few interpreters have doubted that Plato's thought undergoes development, but for the most part this has been traced as a development of doctrine. Often it is assumed that in the early dialogues Plato is reproducing the thought of the actual Socrates, while in the middle and later dialogues he goes on to develop his own ideas.

As is clear by now, there is no uncontroversial way of presenting Plato's thought. Some aspects of his thought invite the reader to open-ended investigation of the philosophical issues. Others present the reader with worked-out positions. These can always, of course, be regarded as *merely* presentations of positions for argument, but still they are substantial enough to characterize a number of views as distinctively "Platonic." Any brief introduction to Plato risks losing either the emphasis on continuing investigation and argument or the importance of adopting certain positions and rejecting others. In what follows I shall focus on certain prominent themes and their development in Plato's writings, rather than either presenting Plato's ideas as finished doctrines or merely listing the arguments without systematizing their conclusions.

Much of Plato's discussion clusters around two recurring themes: knowledge and the conditions for it (and, concurrently, claims about the metaphysical nature of what is known) and the importance of morality in the best human life (and the proper conditions for society to produce the best life). I shall follow through these themes in turn, seeking to bring together, in mutually illuminating ways, a number of Plato's most central arguments. Inevitably this approach is selective and omits much of independent interest—for example, Plato's view of *eros,* his differing positions on art, and his views on the soul and its afterlife. But with Plato, even more than other philosophers, a listing of his concerns misses the point of his activity as a philosopher, something that a selective discussion can bring into sharper focus.

In the early dialogues, Socrates is constantly in search of knowledge. He supposes that his interlocutors have it but discovers by questioning that they do not. Sometimes the supposition is patently insincere, and provides comedy (often rather cruel) at the interlocutor's expense. What is immediately striking is that Socrates is not afflicted with modern epistemological doubt about ordinary knowledge claims; he shows no hesitation in claiming to have knowledge about a variety of ordinary matters, but this is seen as irrelevant to his need for a kind of knowledge that he frequently calls wisdom *(sophia).* When he disclaims knowledge, it is this kind that he disclaims, so that there is no inconsistency with his retaining ordinary knowledge claims. (Nonetheless, this

sets up a somewhat awkward situation in which there are two standards for knowledge, the ordinary and the higher.)

Wisdom is not a lofty or meditative state; the people who have it, Socrates agrees, are simple craftspeople. They are cobblers, weavers, ordinary working people whom Socrates is scornfully accused of constantly dragging into the discussion. What Socrates admires as a paradigm of knowledge is *expert* knowledge, *techne* or expertise. Right from the start, therefore, Socrates assumes that knowledge of the kind he seeks can be found, for everyday examples of it exist. There is no attempt to meet the skeptic who denies that there is knowledge. Socrates' complaint is rather that actual experts are insufficiently aware of the limits of their expertise; his own goal is a global expertise over one's life as a whole, a knowledge of how best to live. Such knowledge has ethical implications and, as we shall see, is taken to be the essential aspect of virtue.

An expertise extends over its field as a whole; it is not an aggregative knowledge of matters of fact. When Ion says that he has expert knowledge of poetry, but only of Homer, Socrates takes it as obvious that if he lacks knowledge of other poets, he also lacks (expert) knowledge of Homer. This point, untrue of our familiar notion of knowledge, shows that expert knowledge is a unified understanding. It also involves a grasp of principles rather than just memory of facts. A plausible comparison might be understanding a language; if one knows the indicative but not the subjunctive, then one just does not know Latin. Also of great importance is the characterization of expertise offered in *Gorgias*. Socrates sharply distinguishes "experience," our ordinary way of getting by unsystematically on the basis of memory and observation, from expertise, a unified intellectual grasp based on *logos*, reasoning, enabling the expert to say what it is that he knows, and to justify his judgments in particular cases. The expert, unlike the person who proceeds unsystematically on the basis of experience, has something that he understands, and can explain and justify what he understands.

This is an attractive model of knowledge. The basic demand is for the explanation and justification that only the person with understanding can provide; a different model from the post-Cartesian demand for certainty and absence of doubt that has dominated modern discussions of knowledge. A problem arises, however, in that Socrates' method for achieving his goal, the famed Socratic "testing," or elenchus, does not seem a promising way to achieve it. In dialogues like *Laches*, Socrates declares that what is being sought is expertise, but what he then proceeds to do is to argue negatively against his interlocutors' suggestions. When Laches and Nicias offer answers to the question, What is bravery? Socrates draws them into committing themselves to other theses, and then points out that these conflict with the original suggestion. All that has been shown, of course, is that the interlocutor is committed to inconsistent premises; he could reject any of the theses

that lead to the problem. In fact, however, the discussion is always focused on the original suggestion, and the result of the elenchus is that the interlocutor, and Socrates, end up knowing more about what bravery or friendship or piety is not, but no nearer to knowing what it is.

Not only is the elenchus an irritating procedure that makes several interlocutors lose their temper, but also it is hard to see how it could get Socrates any nearer the goal of expert knowledge. As a technique, it is appropriate to the investigative, "skeptical" Socrates, concerned to destroy ignorant pretension. But it does not have the potential to produce expert knowledge of the required kind. There is a systematic mismatch between Socrates' goal and his method of achieving it. In one dialogue, *Gorgias,* the elenchus appears in a somewhat different light, and Socrates makes rather different claims about it. It is characterized as a way of uncovering a person's real beliefs: argument forces you to admit what you really believed all along, although before the argument with Socrates you rejected it—usually because the thesis in question is counterintuitive, even absurd to most people. This much stronger conception of the role of argument goes along with increased claims by Socrates that the argument has *forced* the interlocutor to a conclusion, and that the arguments are as unbreakable "as iron and adamant" (508e–509d). But no grounds are given for these increased claims about the elenchus, and they are most implausible, and not repeated in other dialogues.

The mismatch between goal and method is at its most striking in the dialogues of "Socratic definition," where the goal is to answer the question, What is *X* (bravery, etc.)? Socrates is not concerned with definitional questions as such, and it is misleading to think of these dialogues as concerned with meaning; the question What is *X*? applies where there is, in Socrates' view, expert knowledge to be had. From *Laches,* where the preferred answers turn out to be either too broad or too narrow, we find increasingly more stringent initial conditions on an acceptable answer. In *Euthyphro* and *Hippias Major* we find that the answer to the question, What is piety (etc.)? has to be in some way explanatory of our claims that certain kinds of things or actions are pious. Further, we find that grasping such an answer is described metaphorically as "looking toward the form" of the notion in question, "form" (*eidos,* idea) being the ordinary Greek for the appearance of a thing. And an acceptable answer to the question What is *F*?, we find in *Hippias Major,* has to meet two more conditions: it must be itself *F,* and it must be in no way the opposite of *F.* The demand that what explains particular cases of being *F* must be itself *F* comes from a generally accepted conception of explanation: only something that is itself *F* could do this job. The demand that it be in no way the opposite of *F* comes from a desire to evade counterexamples. Plato is concerned that things that are *F* by some standard turn out to be the opposite of *F* by some other standard; faced by even a well-established example of justice, or piety, an opponent can show it to be unjust or impious by clever counter-

examples appealing to some other standard. We do not have to look far for the source of this worry; it is the sophistic practice of producing arguments on both sides of an issue, illustrated dramatically for us in *Double Arguments (Dissoi logoi)*. Plato is convinced that where expert knowledge is possible, its object cannot be the object of this kind of counterclaim. Taken together, these conditions push Plato away from accepting empirically based claims as knowledge, since such claims are always open to counterexamples of the kind he produces. But this point is not made explicitly.

In *Meno*, elenchus is dramatically replaced by a new idea—knowledge is really "recollection." For the person to acquire knowledge is for his soul to recollect what it already knew before incarnation. This new account of knowledge is tailored for the acquisition of a priori knowledge, and is introduced by an example in which Socrates gets an uneducated slave boy to understand a mathematical proof. Since the proof requires the introduction of a counterintuitive idea, Plato is also introducing a basis for his demand that knowledge of some topics requires revision or discarding of everyday empirical beliefs. Plato's demands on knowledge have got him to raise the standards so that now only intellectually graspable objects, like mathematical proofs, meet them. However, he develops one feature of the *techne* conception of knowledge: knowledge, characterized as understanding, is something that each knower has to achieve for him- or herself: it is only when the boy can do the proof for himself that he will know it.

Further, it is in *Meno* that Plato, having raised the standards for knowledge, clearly distinguishes it from true belief, a status to which he now relegates what were previously taken as everyday-level knowledge claims. Later in the dialogue he distinguishes knowledge from true belief with the condition that the knower can "tie down" the true belief by "reasoning out the cause," a plausible development of the explanatory side of the expertise model. However, although this process is said to be recollection, Plato unambiguously produces an example of empirical knowledge—knowledge of the road to Larisa. Scholars have been much exercised by this seeming slip—for what can my soul be recollecting when I come to know the road to Larisa? It seems that Plato is working with a broad conception of knowledge, for which the conditions are that the knower come to understand what is known *for himself*, and be able to justify and explain his knowledge claims; but at the same time he is drawn (doubtless under the influence of mathematics as an example of an undisputed body of knowledge) to the thought that knowledge proper is to be found only in fields where this kind of justification can be found entirely from within the knower himself—that is, entirely a priori.

In the well-known "middle" dialogues *Phaedo* and *The Republic*, we see the convergence of Plato's different lines of thought about knowledge and its objects, and the formation of a grand, ambitious conception of both, one that has dominated interpretation of Plato, perhaps excessively. Two lines of

thought hitherto developed separately are brought together. On the one hand, *Meno* argues that some knowledge, at least, must be a priori, obtained "from within" the person by use of his or her mind, without reliance on the empirical world; but the only examples of this knowledge are mathematical proofs. On the other hand, Socratic dialogues such as *Euthyphro* and *Hippias Major*, which call the desired objects of expert knowledge "forms," set up conditions for their achievement that seem to rule out ordinary empirical access (since any empirical account we can give of justice, piety, and so on, seems vulnerable to empirical counterexample) but leave the reader in the dark as to how actually to get knowledge of such forms, especially since the only available instrument, the elenchus, seems to be inadequate in principle. In the middle dialogues we find that the objects of knowledge are forms, and that they are taken to be nonempirical.

At the end of the fifth book of *The Republic* Plato gives us an argument to show that knowledge has forms as objects. He claims that, since the person with knowledge cannot be wrong, the objects of knowledge must be "fully" or "purely" what they are; otherwise knowledge would not be "of what is, to know it as it is." This idea is clarified by means of the same kind of example as in *Hippias Major*: everyday instantiations or characterizations of what is just, pious, good, and so on, all have the defect that they also turn out to be unjust, impious, bad, and so on. The examples of forms are familiar from early dialogues in their search for accounts of moral terms; here, and in the analogous passage of *Phaedo,* they are joined by mathematical and quantitative examples (half, double, straight, equal) reflecting the new confidence in mathematics as a field of knowledge.

Plato's argument falls far short of showing that *only* forms can be objects of knowledge, for the condition is that what is known be "fully" what it is, in a way that precludes error and precludes its being called the opposite of whatever it happens to be. The cases Plato has in mind are clearly disputable ethical terms, and mathematical terms like *equal.* Plato does not acknowledge the point that the problems arise when there is an opposite to the term in question and do not apply to terms with no opposites. Since, as Aristotle was later to observe, substance has no opposite, substances such as people, horses, and the like would seem to be possible objects of knowledge. And they could be, so far as Plato's actual arguments go, although he undoubtedly writes, in the middle dialogues, as though he had consigned the entire world as we perceive it to the realm of belief rather than knowledge.

It remains a large problem for Plato's position on forms that the only argument for forms in the middle dialogues is the "argument from opposites," which cannot be extended to other terms. In the tenth book of *The Republic* Plato talks of a form of bed, but this is generated by the framework of the argument, which represents artworks, artifacts, and forms as all being examples of things made (either by skill or by copying). It is unclear how serious

this argument is, and likewise unclear how Plato believes himself entitled to think, as he sometimes does, as though forms corresponded to all the terms we use, not just terms with opposites. Nor is it easy to see how he could do this without trivializing the grounds for introducing forms. (A passage in *The Republic*, 596a, sometimes thought to introduce a form for every general term, is in fact quite controversial, and the Greek has been construed in very different ways.) It is not surprising that in a presumably later dialogue, *Parmenides*, Plato has Socrates express doubt as to whether there are forms for substance terms and shrink from commitment to forms of hair and mud, while having no doubt as to forms for the kinds of terms to which the argument from opposites is applied in the middle dialogues.

The knowledge that Plato envisions in *The Republic* is, as we shall see, practical. However, it is also theoretical, bringing to a culmination Plato's increasing interest in mathematics from *Meno* through *Phaedo*. The two strands are not brought together very convincingly. Plato insists that his ideal rulers will direct practical matters in a way that is based on unified insight into principles, as the doctor and the navigator do. Yet he insists that this insight must be based on lengthy abstract intellectual training, founded on mathematical reasoning, which decreases dependence on the senses and encourages the person to rely on abstract thinking.

Mathematics gives us confidence that there is knowledge that is not dependent on sense experience. However, it also serves as a model in its methods and structure. Plato takes from mathematics the notion of hypothesis, a protean idea that figures rather differently in *Meno, Phaedo,* and *The Republic* and, more important, develops the idea that the understanding that knowledge involves has the structure of the understanding that someone would have who had mastery of the relations holding in a field where results are obtained deductively using a set of primary principles. Given the evidence for interest in mathematics in Plato's Academy, it is likely that he would have in mind an embryonic form of what was to become Euclidean geometry. Knowledge, in *The Republic*, has the form of mathematics (geometry, that is) writ large; to have knowledge is to have the understanding that someone has of an abstract field and the relations of derivation and dependence holding within it. Nothing less counts as knowledge; anything short of this is mere true belief. Few accounts of knowledge have been as ambitious.

But we have more surprises yet. Because Plato is insistent that the knowledge that concerns him, however abstract, must issue in practical directions, he holds that the ultimate ground of the whole system, the basis for all the abstract derivation, is the form of the Good, which is the source of everything, not merely intelligibility but the very being of things (509a–b). Plato leaves this suggestive thought, deliberately, at the metaphorical level. It does not seem to solve the potential tensions between the theoretical and practical aspects of this grand conception of knowledge.

Finally, there remains a constant element at the heart of Plato's grand synthesis. The philosophers in his ideal state will do mathematics as a preparation for philosophy proper, the intellectual discipline that comes to understand everything in the light of the form of the Good. Although Plato's account is sketchy, we get some idea of the method to be employed at this crucial point. And it is the same as the philosophical method visible since the early dialogues—argument.

In dialogues that are traditionally regarded as later than *The Republic*, we find that its grand metaphysical and epistemological synthesis has fallen apart. We do not find trenchant criticisms of it, but we do not find it recurring either. Plato no longer has one concern with knowledge and its objects, but several. One striking development is that the practical and theoretical strands in Plato's account of knowledge become separated. In *Statesman* we find, unchanged, the view that directive practical knowledge has the structure of a *techne*, but its abstract and mathematical underpinnings have disappeared. Plato has not lost interest in the distinctive nature of mathematical thinking. In *Laws* the capacity for mathematical thinking is what distinguishes those who have a serious claim to intellectual activity from those who do not, and in *Philebus* the mathematical method is contrasted sharply with the empirical. Mathematics continues to be important to Plato for its potential for improved effectiveness in skills and techniques, and because it represents for him a way of thinking intrinsically superior to any that relies on the empirical world. But, deprived of its place in the grand synthesis, mathematical thinking shrinks in significance; in *Laws*, for example, there is a tension between the continued praise of mathematical thinking and a new, more Aristotelian stress on the importance of learning from experience.

The nature of Plato's continued interest in forms is more elusive. Partly because of the dominance of *The Republic* in Plato studies, forms have been far more prominent in Plato interpretation than they are in Plato, who says strikingly little about them and presents a few arguments without ever trying to bring them together in a connected theory. The one passage of Plato devoted to sustained discussion of forms is wholly negative: the first part of *Parmenides,* where various powerful arguments are brought against forms, and no answers are supplied. Whatever Plato's opinion of these arguments (some bear a strong resemblance to arguments in early Aristotle), forms in the later dialogues revert to a role more like their earlier one. Plato takes it that some kinds of things have an objective nature, and that the way to discover it is to bring the mind actively to bear on the data of experience. His attention has shifted, however, from the problematic moral and mathematical concepts of the early dialogues to a more general concern with the definition of natural-kind terms. Large parts of the later dialogues *Sophist* and *Statesman* are devoted to the search for definitions that will mark out the objective divisions of reality. Plato calls this process "collection and division"; his char-

acterizations of it are difficult and contentious, as is the question of its relation to basic philosophical discussion and argument.

Further, Plato is now inclined, sometimes in a rather professorial way, to stress the need for pedagogical practice before embarking on important topics, and so spends large amounts of time on illustrative definitions of subjects like weaving. However, one central point remains the same: Plato still holds that there are, in the world, objective natures and real divisions between kinds, and that to grasp these requires active thought and inquiry, not just passive reliance on phenomena. Any idea that forms might correspond to general terms is exploded by a passage that declares that language can be misleading; Greeks like to divide the world up into Greeks and barbarians, but this is merely the projection of Greek prejudice: there is no form of barbarian, since the word simply means "not Greek," and this is not a unifying characteristic. Which of our words do, then, pick out real kinds? We cannot say in general; there is no single method, only the use of inquiry in each case *(Statesman)*.

Plato's concern with knowledge continues, and is shown in one of his finest dialogues, *Theaetetus*, but in a way that bypasses rather than explores the conceptions of knowledge brought together in *The Republic*. *Theaetetus*, by raising the question, What is knowledge? brings into question the assumptions of the early dialogues, and pursues difficulties in the everyday notion of knowledge, leaving mathematics and higher philosophical flights aside. One aspect of this pursuit is that Plato's concern, in much of the dialogue, is to argue for the existence of objective knowledge, against various forms of relativism and subjectivism represented by Protagoras. The other is that he has expanded his view of knowledge to include types that have hitherto interested him not at all. Right at the end of the dialogue we find some examination of the idea that knowledge might be true belief *plus* some extra factor, which he calls "an account." He explores different construals of this, without success. This notion of knowledge, that it is some kind of improved true belief, is otherwise glimpsed only at the end of *Meno*, and is in general upstaged in Plato's thought by the idea of knowledge as some kind of expertise. It is an indication of the continued fertility of Plato's thought that he should at this point raise an essentially fresh view of knowledge—one that lays more weight on the justification for particular knowledge claims. We find this further developed in the Hellenistic period, as well as in much of modern epistemology.

Plato's concerns with knowledge and its objects thus display a pattern: in the Socratic dialogues a number of lines of thought are developed separately, brought together in the grand synthesis of *The Republic*, and later developed separately once more. In this, as in other areas, the dominance of *The Republic* can distract attention from the interest and subtlety of Plato's treatment of the distinct strands.

Plato's concern with morality and the good life likewise shows continuity of concern coupled with dramatic shifts of interest from the early to the mid-

dle and from the middle to the late dialogues. Plato shifts on the relation of individual and social morality, and on issues like the relation of happiness to pleasure, but on the importance of morality in the individual's life, and insistence on the objectivity of values, he is consistent from beginning to end.

In a passage in *Euthydemus* Socrates undertakes to show to a young boy why wisdom is worth pursuing; he recommends a serious commitment to learning, and to argument as an intellectual tool, as opposed to the shallow, and ultimately naive and clownish, arguments of the Sophists with whom he is confronted. It is not merely a matter of intellectual fashion whether one follows Socrates or the Sophists. The choice between them is presented as a choice between ways of life: on the one hand there is trivial competitiveness; on the other, Socrates' wisdom, a wisdom that in recognized worldly terms constitutes pathetic failure—failure to achieve wealth, success, even to save his own life—but that the thoughtful can recognize as true virtue. Socrates' search for knowledge is also a search for virtue; knowledge is not taken to be a purely cognitive state isolated from the rest of one's life.

Socrates begins from the assumption that everyone seeks happiness. Given the ancient notion of happiness, a vague and capacious one, this is taken to be trivially true. It is not itself a Socratic thesis but a commonplace that Plato relies on as late as *Laws*. Plato never spells out for us, as Aristotle would do later, the structure of this initial thought: we all seek an overarching final end in all we do, and we agree that this is happiness (since happiness is the only end that, intuitively, we seek for its own sake and not for the sake of any further end) though we disagree as to what happiness is. Nonetheless, it is reasonable to see Plato as working intuitively with the basic structure of eudaemonistic ethics, which Aristotle was the first to articulate. But since Plato does not articulate it, and he tries out several variations within the basic structure, it is difficult and hazardous to extract a "Platonic" or even a "Socratic" ethics understood as a fixed system of doctrines.

Socrates does not rest content with an ethical commonplace but shows that, rightly understood, the idea that we all seek happiness has important implications. For happiness comes from good things, but a little thought shows us that the things themselves, just sitting there, do nothing for us; it is from using them that we benefit. Thus we find that the only thing that is really good, and that really benefits us, is the knowledge that ensures right use of the other conventionally respected goods. It is not health or wealth that we should be seriously aiming to get, but the wisdom that enables us to make a right use of health and wealth. This wisdom, moreover, is virtue—for it is essential to virtue, the other, emotional or dispositional aspects of virtue being likewise regarded as so much raw material that can be put to good or bad employment (*Meno* 87d–89a).

This argument prefigures rather strikingly a central thesis in Stoic ethics, but whereas the Stoics develop the theory fully, Plato leaves it at a suggestive

stage. Nothing is said, for example, to meet several points that arise at once if virtue and other things have different kinds of value: why should we, for example, value other things except insofar as they contribute to our virtuous activity? Plato does not face this problem, but he makes Socrates reiterate the point in *Apology*, his speech defending his life: ordinary people's values are completely wrong, since they most value things like money, and value virtue and knowledge only insofar as they produce things like money. This is to get it the wrong way round, he says: "Virtue does not come from possessions; it is from virtue that possessions and all the rest become good for people, both in private and in public."

In the Socratic dialogues Socrates is constantly trying to get people to rethink their priorities. He does this in a variety of ways, something that may reflect the protean quality of the historical Socrates' own ideas (they inspired both hedonism and asceticism) as well as Plato's own dissatisfaction with the various ethical ideas he works out. In *Apology* Socrates urges the jury to consider him not a subversive wrecker of established values but the gods' gift to Athens, someone whose actions deserve public support. In *Gorgias* he stresses that he has no idea how to perform the simplest administrative task, but that he is nonetheless the only person in Athens who has knowledge of how politics should be carried out. In *First Alcibiades* he urges the young politician to forget about making his way in public life until he first comes to understand himself. The two *Hippias* dialogues are scathing in their portrayal of a person who is the epitome of fashionable success as being really a pompous and empty fool, someone whose ideas are contemptible beside those of Socrates, who is, in worldly terms, unattractive and a failure.

We should rethink our values and priorities, then, and the message of the early dialogues is that we shall do so only if we achieve the wisdom that can give us a correct assessment and use of everything else. As we have already seen, there is a built-in problem with Socrates' pursuit of this wisdom. What he has, to achieve it, seems to be merely the elenchus, which does not seem capable of achieving the desired positive goal. The wisdom he seeks has the structure of a skill—a unified grasp based on the principles defining the field, enabling the person to explain and justify her particular decisions and actions. We do not see Socrates claiming that he does in fact have this skill; nor could he, given the repeated failure of his attempts to achieve answers to questions about the nature of bravery, piety, and other controverted moral notions. However, we do find Plato developing some aspects of the idea of moral knowledge, considered as a skill.

In one very striking dialogue, *Protagoras*, we find Socrates claiming that the skill that will preserve and improve our lives is a skill of a calculating kind—and we find that it is purely instrumental to achieving pleasure. Moreover, in a somewhat Benthamite fashion, pleasure is construed as something that can be measured in an entirely quantitative way. We always aim at get-

ting the most pleasure, it is assumed, and the major problem in our lives comes from faulty perspective: we imagine future pains, because they are future, to be less than they in fact are, and so on (354e–357a). It is, to say the least, surprising to find such a mechanical and crude conception of the role of moral reasoning in Plato, and those who dislike it are fortified by the fact that we find, in *Phaedo,* strong rejections of the idea that our final aim could be pleasure, or that moral reasoning could be limited to calculating amounts of it.

The solution to this apparent contradiction seems to be more complicated than Plato's simply changing his mind, being a hedonist in *Protagoras* and an antihedonist in the other two dialogues. The theory in *Protagoras* is not put forward as Socrates' own; it is a theory that Socrates examines in an inquiring spirit. But it is not ascribed to Protagoras either, and it is not definitively rejected. And in Plato's last dialogue, *Laws,* we find strikingly hedonistic passages, enough to make a 1st-century B.C.E. author compare Plato with Democritus as a kind of hedonist. It seems, then, that Plato is tempted toward a form of hedonism at times, perhaps for the reason that is aired in *Laws:* it is trivially true that we all seek happiness, and surely this must involve a search for pleasure in some form. Plato gives several accounts of pleasure in different dialogues (*The Republic,* most of *Philebus*) and seems to have been exercised throughout his life by the question of its role in the good life. Whatever the reasons for his trying out the hedonist theory in *Protagoras,* he shows himself willing, on that occasion, to cast wisdom in the role of minister to pleasure. But it is possible that the reason that this form of hedonism is not more widespread in Plato's work is precisely that it forced on him an unacceptable role for moral reasoning.

There is some wavering, then, as to the instrumental and noninstrumental roles for moral reasoning. There is also a tendency for Plato to expand the scope of moral reasoning from the agent's own life to the lives of others. The eudaemonist appeal is to the structure of the agent's own life. However, we find that the skill of dealing well with one's own life will also be the skill of excellently managing the lives of others *(Lysis).* The skill of living well thus comes sometimes to be characterized as *politikē technē,* the "political skill" or skill exercised in political activity. We find this in *Euthydemus:* later in the dialogue we return to the theme of the protreptic passage, and a problem is found in it, but in the process this skill is casually identified as the "kingly" skill and the skill of directing and ruling. The same wholly casual identification of personal virtue with justice, understood as the virtue of ruling over others, characterizes *Alcibiades* and *Lovers.* In *Gorgias,* Socrates treats the question of individual virtue as being essentially the same as the question of what is the best state for someone to be in who is to exercise political power. Plato seems to feel no need for argument to make this identification; this is part of a general cluster of attitudes that we shall turn to, about the organiza-

tion of society and the relationships of people within it. By the time of the later *Philebus* and *Laws* he has shown that he can separate the questions of how best an individual should live and how best political power should be exercised, but earlier he shows no concern to separate them, and indeed in *The Republic* he provides one of the most famous of the theories that take the two issues to be necessarily interconnnected.

Plato's treatment of what we would call social or political matters is always marked by a tension between two strands in his thought. One is his conviction that what most matters is the exercise of expert judgment: just as in an individual life it is an overall grasp based on understanding that is crucial, so in a community what is required is an overall direction based on an understanding of what is in the common good. Plato also, however, is alive to the dangers of relying on expert insight in running society and thereby undermining the rule of law. There are disadvantages, but also advantages, in being able to rely on the stability provided by obedience to law. Plato's position changes dramatically in several respects, but we can trace a continuing engagement with the problem of obedience to law.

In *Crito* the laws of Athens are introduced, telling Socrates why he should not, as his conventionally minded friend Crito suggests, evade his unjust condemnation to death. The laws stress two grounds for this, grounds that, on their face, have very different implications. One is that a citizen's obligation to his laws and government is like his obligation to his parents; he is bound by a relationship that he has not chosen but may not reject. Further, it is a notably asymmetrical relationship: the laws may inflict punishment on you, or make demands, while you are not entitled to respond in kind; in this context the relationship is even likened to that of master and slave. (Like any Greek, Plato is ready to see a relationship where one side exercises power and the other has no control over it as one of master and slave.) The laws, however, also stress that Socrates will be breaking his "agreements" with them. They regard him as having made an implicit agreement to obey the laws by his having undergone the *dokimasia,* or vetting, when admitted to the citizen body, and by having stayed in Athens when it was open to him to go elsewhere. Having shown his satisfaction with Athens, they claim, by staying and raising a family, he has shown himself satisfied with its laws. The conflict between these two grounds for compliance is patent: one set appeals to obligations that one has not chosen to have, the other appeals to obligations that one has chosen to have. Socrates' obligation to obey the laws of Athens can hardly be both of these things at the same time—not, at least, without further argument, which is lacking here.

Crito also creates a well-known problem when taken together with the passage in *Apology* where Socrates says that if the court releases him on the condition that he stop practicing philosophy, "I will obey the god rather than you." The laws in *Crito,* however, demand obedience; Socrates must "per-

suade them or obey." This has been taken to mean that one must obey the law unless one succeeds in changing it; more realistically, it could mean that one must obey unless one persuades the jury. Either way, Socrates has clearly failed to persuade; how can his resolve in *Apology* not conflict with the demands of the laws in *Crito?* If the laws were *ideal* laws, there would be no problem; Socrates could not then be in the right in defying them. But how the unideal laws of Athens can make the claims that the laws do, remains obscure. In *The Republic* Plato moves on to considering an ideal state in which the rule of law is considerably reduced. He does not return to the *Crito* situation until *Laws,* when he finally gives the laws a better answer to Socrates.

The Republic begins with the question, starkly posed, of why I, the individual agent, should be just, but here Plato sees an adequate answer as requiring an entire sketch of a just society. *The Republic*'s double focus, which has led to widely different types of interpretation, is the culmination of Plato's previous tendency to conflate individual moral reasoning with the skill of ruling over others. But at the end of Book 9 he suggests firmly that it is the individual that is his primary concern: the just state, Socrates says, may well be merely a pattern laid up in heaven, but it is still possible for the person who is determined to become just to think about it, and develop his character accordingly. (As against this, the suggestion that one could start off an ideal state with people under the age of ten may be merely a vivid way of saying that it is not a practical possibility.) Still, to know what it is to be just, we need to know what it would be for a state to be just.

Plato's state, it is important to stress, is not a utopia; it is an ordinary Greek city, transformed so as to become just but otherwise subject to normal Greek conditions such as the assumption of warfare with other states, dependence on slavery, and normal economic processes. It is within this context that Plato develops his idea that a just city is one in which our inevitable interdependence is organized in a rational way, so that conflicts are eliminated.

Conflict is to be eliminated by ensuring that people are educated, and function, only in ways appropriate to their nature. This will come about, it is claimed, if there are three classes in the state: the Guardians, who rule in the general interest; the Auxiliaries, who help to put that rule into practice; and the Producing Class, who have no unifying characteristics but are just normal citizens of a Greek state, pursuing their private business, but with no political power. These three classes must function together in such a way that the Producing Class obey the political directives of the Guardians, whose exercise of power in the common interest is institutionally unconstrained. Plato is somewhat ambivalent about the attitude of the Producing Class. At times he is confident that they have enough sense of the general good to appreciate that it is best for them to go along with what the Guardians think, and they are presented as deferential. At other times, however, Plato seems to think that resentment and lack of cooperation on the part of the Producing Class are in-

evitable, given their inability to understand what is in the general good, and will have to be repressed by the Guardians.

The Republic is based on the idea that the individual soul will exhibit the same sort of three-part relationship as the state: reason, which seeks the truth and realizes overall good; spirit, which provides the energy for rational considerations to be acted on; and the desiring part of the soul, marked by no unifying factor other than the fact that all desires aim merely at their own satisfaction, without regard for overall good. People will fit into one of the three political classes according as reason, spirit, or desire dominates in their souls. But all are alike in having all three parts of the soul, and the unified and harmonious state that results from all three parts' "doing their own," as Plato puts it, will differ in members of the three different classes. In the Guardians reason dominates, and so those people will have love of truth and devotion to the common good as their major aims; their spirit and desires have been reformed and restructured by these priorities. Similarly with the Auxiliaries. The members of the Producing Class are dominated by their desires, and so reason and spirit function in them mostly as instrumental to the achievement of their desires, though (in a way parallel to the political problem with the Producing Class) their reason is sometimes taken to have enough implicit grasp of the general good to approve of what the Guardians do.

Plato, against all Greek intuitions, identifies this state of harmony of soul with the virtue of justice. It is a radical redefinition, and his solution as to how to produce justice is a radical departure from any strategy hitherto envisaged. It can be understood only in terms of his desire to make reason paramount in political organization. Just government is to be brought about by putting people in charge whose souls are ruled by reason. Plato sneers at the idea of improving states by modifying laws or institutions; this is, he thinks, a useless waste of energy. True improvement can come only by trying to conform ourselves to the rational pattern "laid up in heaven" and accessible only to those who use their reason. Hence Plato relies entirely on the Guardians' education (first of character, then of intellect) to ensure the correctness of their reasoning. Laws serve a limited and pragmatic function and do not constrain the results of the Guardians' reasoning.

Reason in its capacity as what discerns the general good demands much that is outrageous by both Greek standards and our own. The Guardians will have no property, no private life, no lasting personal relationships. Women as well as men will be Guardians, since the demands of reason overrule convention. Reason in its capacity as what aims at the truth turns out to require similarly radically revised standards. For the Guardians to be entitled to rule, they must *know* what is right, and Plato now conceives of knowledge, as we have seen, in a way depending on mathematical method. To rule, the Guardians must spend several years perfecting their techniques of philosophical thinking. And Plato faces the paradox that results: by the time they are fit to

rule, the Guardians are unwilling to rule, because they alone appreciate the overwhelming value of philosophical study for its own sake. The only truly just people, then, will not want to rule the just state and will have to be in some way "compelled" to do so.

The Republic represents the most thorough working-out ever attempted of the principle that knowledge is what entitles rulers to rule. Plato accepts the extreme consequences both for the rulers and for the ruled, although later he comes to have doubts about both aspects. In *The Republic* Plato is alive to the corrupting power of money and ambition but ignores the corrupting force of power itself. Later he allows that it is not a possibility for human nature to have absolute power and remain selfless *(Laws)*. And he comes to rethink the role that absolute, knowledge-based rule assigns to its subject. Rulers are constantly compared to experts, such as doctors and pilots. But people are not like a craftsman's material; in a political community, each citizen is a distinct person with needs and desires that should be given a hearing, if they are to consider themselves members of a genuine community rather than slavelike subjects whose labor is exploited. In *Laws* Plato comes to hold that "masters and slaves can never be friends" and so cannot, as he thought in *The Republic*, form a community together. In *Laws* the doctor who treats free people, as opposed to the doctor who treats slaves, has to convince his patient to undergo the treatment and argue with him by rational means, persuading him and not merely threatening him (*Laws* 719e–720d, 857c–e).

Laws thus presents a considerably changed ideal state from that of *The Republic*. But it would be a mistake to ascribe this simply to the increased pessimism of old age (despite the many rather tedious references in *Laws* to the wisdom of the old). Rather, Plato's final thoughts about politics are marked by a more profound treatment of themes that were previously treated in too simple a way. Over a number of areas he shows himself ready to recognize the necessity of compromise and complexity.

The most immediately striking is the question of the status of law. While earlier Plato had given expertise total priority over law, he comes to appreciate the advantages of the sovereignty of law. A long passage in *Statesman* develops this. Law is a blunt instrument, falling far short of the precision of expertise, but if the expert is not available, his prescription is a lot better than nothing, or guesswork. In the world as it is, in which an ideal statesman is not a realistic prospect, we should make use of the stability and rationality that laws offer. Hence, in *Laws*, we find Plato producing an ideal state by drawing up a legal code.

Plato is in fact surprisingly empirical in his second great political work. Rather than sketch a fundamentally new form of life, he takes an existing institution and modifies it in the light of a new, moral aim he takes to be achievable by it. (Unafraid of ridicule, he claims that drinking parties can be transformed to achieve an educational, moral goal, and tries to transfer the public

honors and glamour of military heroes to aged public officials who have served the state in undramatic ways.) In particular, he takes over many existing Athenian laws, aiming to make them coherent and rationally acceptable to the citizens by prefacing them with philosophical preambles giving their rationale. Many of these laws frame democratic institutions, and the ideal city of *Laws*, Magnesia, is in many ways, and quite deliberately, like Athens. However, it also retains the feature insisted on earlier, that all citizens be educated in a way appropriate to their capacity. Now this has a far more egalitarian result than previously, but there is still a heavy emphasis on the common good and shared community goals. Indeed, in some respects Plato goes further than ever: pregnant women have to do daily exercises; everyone must be trained to be ambidextrous; and, most alarmingly, all citizens must get up early and get used to as little sleep as possible.

Laws stresses both the communal education that instills in the citizens a strong consciousness of the common good and the democratic institutions that give them a space for individual political activity. *Laws* can be read as authoritarian, but it can also be read as developing a far more individualistic and egalitarian strand than hitherto seen. The virtue characteristic of the citizen is "self-control" *(sophrosune)*, the virtue of recognizing the dominance of the common good over one's own good. But Plato proposes here a "mixed" constitution: the principle of "monarchy," or obedience to authority, must now be constrained by the principle of "democracy," each citizen living according to his own plan of life. Democratic institutions are taken over, but they are modified in ways that in ancient terms bring them closer to oligarchy— though we should note that the result is often much closer to democracy in the modern sense of the term than is ancient democracy. Plato, for example, removes most direct political decision making from the assembly, which functions instead more like a modern electorate, electing officials and ensuring that they are responsible to it for their actions.

The increase in Plato's willingness to use empirical method in ethics and politics is remarkable; it comes out most strikingly in his attitude to history. While *The Republic* is totally ahistorical, *Statesman* makes use of collective memory to develop the truths in folktales and myths about the past. *Critias*, an extension of the frame-dialogue of *Timaeus*, contains an extraordinary kind of unfinished historical fiction about the cities of ancient Athens and Atlantis, designed to teach political morals about the superiority of land-based cities over sea-based ones, and the importance of abiding by the law. And the third book of *Laws* is an extended exercise in drawing political lessons from history. Although Plato's actual history is selective and biased, it is recognizably a first step toward the study of political history that we find in Aristotle's *Politics* and the studies of constitutions that lie behind it.

The increased empiricism of *Laws* is reflected in different ways in the other late dialogues. In *Timaeus*, Plato constructs a strange and elaborate cosmol-

ogy, showing a remarkable degree of interest in issues that had previously been dismissed as trivial. In *Statesman* he is on the way to a pragmatic interest in political institutions, although he retains an interest in the idea of the ruler with knowledge. Whereas earlier Plato had used the dialogue form to begin discussion of philosophical issues from a fresh point of view, one owing little or nothing to the state of the contemporary debate, *Sophist, Philebus,* and *Theaetetus* are occupied in answering problems, or furthering debates, initiated by other philosophers, while *Parmenides* is partly occupied with problems that Plato himself has produced. Again Plato is moving in a direction that will be followed further by Aristotle, who begins from problems that are already philosophical and positions himself in a debate that has already begun.

In these later dialogues Plato makes less use of the figure of Socrates, as though recognizing that the anachronism is too striking. He also seems to realize the distance that he has come from the new beginnings that Socrates makes in the early dialogues to the far more developed and academic discussions of the late ones. Plato never abandons the dialogue form; to the last he retains the position of the person who puts forward the arguments without committing himself to them or their premises. But in the later dialogues this position makes less and less sense; we do not really feel a distance between the author and the arguments of *Sophist* or *Timaeus*. These dialogues are, however, strikingly difficult to fit into any overall account of "Plato's thought." This is because in them we find Plato going down avenues opened up by the work of others—cosmology, Parmenides' problem of being and not-being, Protagoras's account of truth and knowledge. In recent years much energy has been spent in trying to determine whether and how Plato is being self-critical in the late works. A more fruitful approach, however, is probably one in which we see Plato as moving, in the late works, toward a different way of doing philosophy, one to which the dialogue form is increasingly irrelevant, a problem-based approach to philosophy that takes account of the work of others—a way of doing philosophy recognizably like Aristotle's.

Owing to these features of the later dialogues, their appeal has been primarily to philosophers. Some of the middle dialogues, like *Phaedo* and *The Republic,* have had a literary life of their own, and the Socratic dialogues have always been an attractive introduction to philosophy; few but philosophers will get through *Sophist* or *Parmenides.* Because of this, they resist brief summary or evaluation; each deals with a difficult philosophical issue in a complex but focused and complete way. Also, because they are relatively independent from the set of concerns that dominate the early and middle dialogues, they have fitted less well into overall accounts of Plato's thought; from antiquity to the 20th century, an account of "Plato's ideas" is bound to feature *The Republic* more than *Critias* or *Philebus.* It would, however, be wrong to think that a fine system of ideas peters out into academic detail in

the late dialogues; to think that is to undervalue the practice of philosophical investigation and argument that we see in these works. They will always be less attractive to nonphilosophers, and more compelling to philosophers, than works like *Phaedo* and *The Republic*.

Plato is possibly the most original philosopher who ever lived. He begins by adopting a radically new way of doing philosophy, one which consciously makes a break with previous approaches to the subject. We also find him, over the course of a long lifetime, gradually traveling a long road back to more conventional ways of doing philosophy. Throughout, however, he never wavers in certain respects, such as in formally distancing himself from the argument by the dialogue form. Even the last works maintain an elusive quality that distinguishes Plato from other great philosophers. It is this combination of daring ideas presented in elusive form—locally clear but globally fragmented and disjointed—that makes Plato perennially frustrating, challenging, and fascinating.

JULIA ANNAS

Bibliography

Annas, Julia. *An Introduction to Plato's Republic.* Oxford: Oxford University Press, 1981.

————. *Platonic Ethics Old and New.* Ithaca: Cornell University Press, 1999.

Canto-Sperber, Monique. *Les paradoxes de la connaissance: Essais sur le Ménon de Platon.* Paris: Editions Odile Jacob, 1991.

Chatelet, François. *Platon.* Paris: Gallimard, 1965.

Goldschmidt, Victor. *Platonisme et pensée contemporaine.* Paris: Aubier-Montaigne, 1970.

————. *Questions platoniciennes.* Paris: Vrin, 1970.

Irwin, T., ed. *Classical Philosophy: Collected Papers,* vol. 2: *Socrates and His Contemporaries;* vol. 3: *Plato's Ethics;* vol. 4: *Plato's Metaphysics and Epistemology.* New York and London: Garland Publishing, 1995.

Kahn, Charles. *Plato and the Socratic Dialogue.* Cambridge: Cambridge University Press, 1996.

Kraut, R., ed. *The Cambridge Companion to Plato.* Cambridge: Cambridge University Press, 1992.

Schuhl, Pierre-Maxime. *L'oeuvre de Platon.* Paris: Vrin, 1954.

Vlastos, Gregory. *Platonic Studies,* 2nd ed. Princeton: Princeton University Press, 1981.

Vlastos, Gregory, ed. *Plato: A Collection of Critical Essays.* 2 vols. Garden City, N.Y.: Doubleday, 1971.

Related Articles

The Philosopher; Ethics; Cosmology; Theology and Divination; Language; Plutarch; The Academy; The Question of Being; The Statesman As Political Actor; Physics; Theories of Religion; Anaxagoras; Plotinus; Platonism

PLOTINUS

PLOTINUS WAS BORN IN EGYPT about 205 C.E. and is rightly regarded as the founder of Neoplatonism. The first of these statements he would have found trivial, the second puzzling. His biographer Porphyry, whose *Life of Plotinus* supplies almost all our information about his career, begins by telling us that "Plotinus was ashamed to be in the body." That attitude may have led to some reticence about his life, even if it is to be understood as a manifestation of the philosopher's concern to avoid more than the necessary involvement with either his own body or the sensible world of which it is a part; it is in any case not unparalleled at this period. Nevertheless, Porphyry gives us a series of invaluable stories about the philosopher's life and teaching—and even about his illnesses.

As for Neoplatonism, it is important to realize that the word does not exist in ancient Greek; it was invented by English and French writers in the fourth decade of the 19th century. It is important because Plotinus, like all the Neoplatonists who came after him, regarded himself simply as a Platonist. From Plotinus in the first treatise of the fifth *Ennead* through to Proclus in his massive *Platonic Theology*, the Neoplatonists claimed that everything they said was already there, even if not explicitly, in the text of Plato. Here it should be said that it was the text of Plato as it is accessible to us, and not some alleged esoteric Platonic doctrine, that they took as the basis of their philosophy. It was not, of course, a reading of his texts that Plato would have understood. Plotinus may have learned at least some of his approach to Plato from the mysterious figure of Ammonius Saccas, who Porphyry tells us was the first teacher of philosophy whom Plotinus found satisfactory after much searching in Alexandria, and with whom he stayed for some eleven years. Porphyry reports that Plotinus brought the mind, or the thinking, of Ammonius into his own philosophy. Unfortunately we can only speculate about what that thinking was, and in spite of many attempts to discover facts about Ammonius or reconstruct his ideas, we know nothing further about him.

Apart from his standpoint as a Platonist, two other points about Plotinus's philosophy should be borne in mind. The first is that he was a metaphysician rather than a mystic. Though he has for long and often been thought of as a mystic, and had certainly had mystic experiences, these appear only rarely in his writings and do not control his philosophy. Indeed one of the few texts in which he has been thought to refer to them, the beginning of *Enneads* IV.8, has recently been recognized as having to do with Intellect rather than with

the One. The other point is that, like all Greek philosophers, his philosophy was not disinterested enquiry but a search for the way to achieve the best life for the individual. A consequence of this was that it could be seen as a kind of religious practice, though it would be misleading to think of it as a "religious philosophy," an expression that embodies a distinction that neither he, nor Plato or Aristotle before him, would have been able to appreciate. This remains true even if strictly ethical discussion occupies a relatively small proportion of Plotinus's output that survives in its entirety. His philosophy is represented by the *Enneads,* so called because they consist of six groups of nine treatises, arranged by his pupil, colleague, biographer, and editor, Porphyry. These fifty-four treatises are not, however, fifty-four separate works by Plotinus: they have been forced into this numerologically significant framework by the dismemberment of some of the longer treatises, such as that on the soul, which appears as IV.3, 4, and 5, or the one on issues raised by Plotinus's conflict with the Gnostics, which has been distributed over three *Enneads* as III.8, V.8, and V.5 and II.9, and occasionally the amalgamation of short pieces to form others such as III.9. The six *Enneads* group treatises mainly concerned with ethics, physics, the physical world and our life within it, Soul, Intellect, and the One, but this is only roughly true, since many works do not fit well into these categories, and in any case Plotinus is notorious for tending to introduce large parts, or even all, of his philosophy into many of his works that are ostensibly directed to a single topic, a direction that is only rarely followed. This is probably a result of his method of practicing philosophy by discussion, against a background of philosophical reading, a method described for us in the *Life,* rather than a conscious attempt to follow this tendency as it is already manifest in the writings of Plato.

Being a Platonist, Plotinus did, however, follow Plato in dividing his world into sensible and intelligible, or material and immaterial, forms of existence. He differed from Plato in having a more complicated structure for his intelligible world and a different status for his material one. The structure and operation of both, moreover, were heavily dependent on ideas that Plotinus, following the tradition of one tendency in Hellenistic and later Platonism, had adopted, and often adapted, from Aristotle. These were particularly important in the construction of the second hypostasis, Intellect, and also in his exposition of the functioning of the human soul.

Apart from the mysticism, what most people who know anything about Plotinus are aware of is his division of the intelligible world into three hypostases, namely One, Intellect, and Soul. Though the boundary between the latter two was sometimes blurred and transgressed, and though some have found a fourth, in which nature *(phusis)*, as a lower form of soul corresponds to the higher form *(psukhe)*, which is the third, Plotinus is firm about there being no more than three and, equally important, no fewer. In this he may be contrasted with his Platonist predecessors who, with the possible exception of

Numenius, had no One above their Intellect. Plotinus's One is the basis and origin of the whole system. Both these terms must be understood in an unusual sense, because the One is "above" rather than underlying, and it is the origin only in the sense that all else depends on it, for in Plotinus's philosophy there can be no question of any beginning in time. Thus any expressions suggesting temporal succession must be understood as referring only to causal sequence or stages of exposition. Though some Platonists did—as do an increasing number of modern scholars—understand Plato's account of the genesis of the world in *Timaeus* in a chronological sense, Plotinus followed what was always the majority view, that the succession of events in it was merely an expository device.

With these cautions we may consider the status and characteristics of the One, always bearing in mind that, strictly speaking, there is nothing that can be said about it: it is, as most translators have it, ineffable *(arrhēton)*. That is because it transcends Being and can be defined only by the negation of all the characteristics of Being that, however, derive from it, or by the use of words applicable to Intellect prefixed with "super-" *(huper-)*, for example superintellection *(hupernoēsis)* or "superexistently" *(hyperontōs)*. The common description of it as "beyond Being" goes back to Plato's description in *The Republic* of the Form of the Good as being on the far side of the things that exist *(epekeina tēs ousias)*, but while Plato used this as an indication of the position of the Good at the head of the hierarchy of the Forms, which were for him what truly has being, for Plotinus and all Neoplatonists it meant that it was something transcending, and other than, the Forms. Nevertheless Plotinus's One, which he also calls the Good, has this in common with the Platonic Form, that it is responsible for the being and, though Plotinus has less to say about this, the intelligibility of everything in the intelligible realm. One of the most difficult problems about Plotinus's philosophy is how the One relates to everything else and, in particular, whether or not it can be said to take any interest in its products. The view that it can has been advocated mainly by Christian interpreters who have perhaps wished to assimilate Plotinus's thought to their own, but the more austere interpretation, according to which the One is responsible for the existence of the others and their various levels of unity but has no other relation to them except insofar as it is an object of aspiration, is probably correct. This problem is connected with others about the nature of the One and its role as the source of all else. The most important is why there should be anything else at all, and it can be argued that this is a fundamental defect in Plotinus' philosophy, notwithstanding the fact that the philosophical reason for positing a One will have been the wish to have a completely simple unitary first principle for the soul and intellect, which were part of the now Aristotelianized Platonic heritage. The next problem is whether the One can be said to have will, a question to which Plotinus devotes the long and difficult treatise VI.8, and whether, if it does,

that will is involved in its causation of the others. This question tends to be answered positively by those who think that the One is somehow personal, like a Judeo-Christian God, and negatively by those who deny this, inter alia, on the grounds that to equip the One with will, or self-knowledge, would infringe its unity. For them what is "below" the One emerges automatically as a consequence of its supreme power and intrinsic infinity. A further problem, which relates to the others rather than to the One, is how the atemporal process by which they arise is to be described. The word *emanation* has often been used for this purpose, indicating that the others flow from the One as from an inexhaustible spring, but though commonly used by writers on Plotinus, the relevant words are far less common in the text of Plotinus himself.

The first product of this coming into being of other things is the second hypostasis, Intellect. Though it is essentially Form and Being, at its first appearance it is unformed and indeterminate, and so preexistent. It acquires its characteristics by turning back to the One and contemplating it. Thereby it acquires the Form and Being that the One bestows without itself having them. This acquisition of characteristics from the One by means of contemplation is based on a piece of Aristotelian rather than Platonic thought, namely the notion that in thinking, the intellect, be it human or divine, is assimilated to its objects, a notion that is a crucial element in the structure of Intellect itself and of the relationship, on more than one level, of what is below with what is above. It might be as well to state that above and below are merely metaphorical, if frequently utilized, ways of talking about the hierarchical or causal relationship of things that are conceived, qua immaterial, as not being in place at all. Another way of describing the relationship is to talk about lower entities being in higher ones: here Plotinus follows a suggestion in Plato's *Timaeus*. Intellect falls short of the unity of the One by virtue of the duality that Plotinus insists exists between what knows and what is known. With that qualification the Intellect is a unity insofar as its contents are not only Forms with the enhanced characteristics of Form as described in a famous passage of Plato's *Sophist* (248–249), but also intellects that have each other as objects and, by virtue of the Aristotelian theory of intellectual cognition, are thereby identified, and identical, with each other. A problem about the genesis and structure of the hypostasis Intellect lies in whether its Being, or its being Forms, is in any way prior to its being Intellect or intellects. It can be argued with adequate support from the texts that Being must come first for there to be an object of the intellects, but an equally good case can be made for its intellectual aspect's being prior, insofar as it is necessary for the as yet unformed Intellect to receive its being by contemplation of the One. The best solution is that neither is prior since both are eternal.

As Intellect corresponds to the model used by the Demiurge, or divine maker, in *Timaeus*, it should contain Forms of everything that exists in the

sensible world: "Everything that is here comes from there, and exists there in a better way." In fact Plotinus was not entirely sure about the universality of this principle, which receives lengthy discussion in a late and rightly admired treatise titled, "How the Multiplicity of Forms Came into Being, and the One" (VI.7). Though he argues, for example, that even though there is no conflict in the intelligible world, the Forms of animals require the parts necessary for conflict, since they will be part of the world that these Forms produce, he does not introduce forms of undesirable things nor, a fortiori, of evil though, strictly speaking, Intellect should include them in some appropriate form. This is only one of the problems and inconsistencies relating to evil that will be discussed below. These difficulties, just like the principle that Intellect should contain everything that appears in the physical world, are a result of Plotinus's strict monism, which allows no room for matter as an independent principle such as most would find in Plato. The amalgamation of Platonic Forms and Aristotelian Intellect to produce a new kind of Platonic intellect had been made by certain so-called Middle Platonists of the preceding period, who saw this as a solution to the notorious problem about what would be the object(s) of the eternal intellection of the self-thinking Intellect that is Aristotle's supreme principle. They thus added to the Aristotelian description of its activity that it thinks itself "and its own thoughts," which are the Forms. For Plotinus this solution required special care to avoid importing duality into the unity of Intellect, and we learn from Porphyry that much time was spent in his circle on showing that the intelligibles, namely the Forms, are inside the Intellect, a matter that is the subject of treatise V.5. This was one of a number of questions on which Plotinus's Aristotelian solution was prepared by the precisions brought to Peripatetic thinking by the commentator Alexander of Aphrodisias, the best known of those whose work was studied in Plotinus's philosophical group. The unity of the Intellect was encapsulated in a description drawn from Plato's *Parmenides*, namely that it was a one-many or one and many, to be distinguished from the third hypostasis, which was many and one. In most, though perhaps not all, of Plotinus's work, where the question arises, the human individual may be part of this unity by having the highest part of his soul permanently at this level. This was one of the points on which most later Neoplatonists were not prepared to follow Plotinus, who by his own admission in IV.8 was taking a line that was unorthodox. A problem that is connected with our presence in Intellect, and that has received much discussion recently, is whether or not there must therefore be a Form of each individual. In general those who favor a personalizing interpretation of the nature of the One tend to accept the existence of Forms of individuals on the grounds that they are a reflection of the high value Plotinus placed on the individual. Those who do not, and who find that Plotinus's writings appear to be inconsistent on this point, would say that this was a matter on which he did not come to a final decision. Certainly some of

the later treatises suggest, even if they do not prove, that Plotinus then thought that the highest part of the individual existed at the level of Soul rather than Intellect. This interpretation has the further advantage that it fits with a new way of looking at Plotinus—not so much, as has been the custom, as a systematic philosopher, but as one who was prepared, in the manner of Aristotle, if to a lesser degree, to put forward ideas tentatively and then reconsider them later if and when a better solution came to mind.

The hypostasis Soul is the link between the intelligible and sensible worlds. Soul, as Plotinus puts it, stands on the boundary. It is in the middle, having the intelligible in the fullest sense on one side, the sensible on the other. As with the generation of Intellect, so with the generation of Soul it is difficult to explain why it should happen at all. Again one must resort to the explanation that the infinite power of the One requires the existence of everything else. If, moreover, the world is to exist, then there has to be some part of the intelligible that both proximately gives it form and controls it. The difficulty of the controlling function increases as one descends from what all Platonists and Aristotelians regarded as the higher kind of physical existence to be found in the heavens to the lower kind that exists on earth. Thus Soul's function of governance is exercised effortlessly in respect of the heavens but not in respect of what is on earth, where it risks being affected, in some sense, by the unsatisfactory nature or behavior of what it controls.

Soul "comes into existence" by a process similar to that which lies at the origin of Intellect—though occasionally Plotinus will attribute a personal motive in the form of boldness or daring *(tolma),* a concept possibly acquired from Gnostic opponents that recurs in other contexts, such as the descent of the human soul, but that he does not seem to have taken very seriously. But just as Intellect falls short of the unity of the One, which it contemplates to finalize its own existence, so Soul falls short both of the unity and the level of being to be found in Intellect. Thus all its formal elements exist at a greater level of diffusion than they do in Intellect. Another way of expressing this disunity is to say that the contents of Soul are not all simultaneously present in and to each other, as are those of Intellect by virtue of the reciprocal identity of intellects and intelligibles.

Related to the difficulty of justifying the coming into being of Soul is another, well known to students of Plotinus and also his pupil Porphyry: the problem of keeping the two hypostases separate and distinct. At times when Plotinus is concerned to stress the tripartite nature of the intelligible world and the existence of neither more nor fewer than three hypostases, he distinguishes Intellect from Soul in some or all of the following ways: Intellect is a one-many, while Soul is a many and one. In Intellect all cognition is simultaneous and immediate, whereas in Soul there is transition *(metabasis)* from one component to the next, as in reasoning from premise to conclusion. Intellect is characterized by eternity, whereas in Soul there is time, which is gener-

ated along with Soul itself—an anomalous position insofar as Soul qua hypostasis is no less eternal than Intellect itself. Soul stands to Intellect as an unfolding or unraveling of what exists in a more compact form there, a relationship that Plotinus, at this and other levels, describes by calling the lower form of being the *logos* of the higher, meaning it is a representation of it in a lower mode—an unusual use of *logos*, but one frequently found in Plotinus. Soul is also causally dependent on Intellect, which in itself makes it different by virtue of a Plotinian principle, stated in the early treatise VI.9, that the cause is other than the effect. In addition Soul has the responsibility of being involved with, and in charge of, what is below, a responsibility that Intellect does not share because, when it is considered as being responsible for the existence of the world, it has assigned to Soul the duty of maintaining it. These distinctions include some in which Soul is defined by not being Intellect, and when Plotinus on one occasion says that the two differ by otherness alone, without defining what this otherness might be, we must assume that he himself saw the philosophical difficulty of having two entities that are immaterial but required to differ from each other. At times this difficulty is too much for him, and we find that he has removed the distinction between the two, tending to import characteristics of Soul into Intellect when he wishes to emphasize its dynamic and even creative nature, and conversely attributing characteristics of Intellect to Soul when he is concerned to stress its transcendence above the material world, or the contrast between immaterial and material existence—as, for example, in his treatise "The Simultaneous and Identical Omnipresence of What Is" (VI.4–5)—or even the untroubled nature of Soul's control of the world. At such times he also denies to Soul the discursive and progressive nature of thought by which he normally distinguishes it from Intellect; when he makes this distinction he will say that when we have finished with discursive thinking and arrive at immediate intuition of its results, we have passed from Soul to Intellect.

Another context in which similar language to that used of Intellect is applied to Soul is when Plotinus is trying to show that Soul remains unaffected by its involvement with body. Here we have reached the level of existence at which we are talking not about the intelligible hypostases on their own, but about Soul's function of organizing and controlling the body, be it the superior body to be found in the heavens or the ordinary kind found below. Before we look at how Soul functions in this capacity, we must look at the distinctions Plotinus makes between different kinds of soul. While he asserts that all souls are one, the subject of one of his earlier treatises, IV.9, this assertion applies only to two of the three kinds of soul he distinguishes: Soul as a hypostasis, the World-soul, and the souls of individuals. Though it sometimes appears that all these are coextensive "parts" of one single Soul, closer inspection reveals that the hypostasis is not a part of this unity but stands above it, differing precisely by its having no direct involvement with matter or body.

Those souls that do, and that may be seen as a reflection or image of Soul itself, just as Soul is sometimes seen as a reflection or image of Intellect, are to be seen as one. World-soul differs from the individual souls only by having a better body to govern and so being exempt from the problems that may trouble any one of the souls of individuals—that is, human individuals, since Plotinus takes no great interest in the souls of other kinds of living beings. Inevitably he will have problems in explaining how the theoretically identical souls of different individuals are not the same.

With this problem we move into the area where Plotinus's monism causes difficulties. Since everything has its being from above, with what is above causing what is below to be such as it is, different individuals should be identical, insofar as they are caused by souls. And yet Plotinus explains their differences as being due to body rather than matter, which has no characteristics until it is informed by a soul and thereby becomes a body. Though he sometimes speaks in terms of a soul's being short of informative and controlling power by virtue of its distance from its origins, and so unable fully to control a body, or even matter, which can influence a soul as it descends to them, a basic inconsistency remains. Plotinus on occasion tries to alleviate this inconsistency by treating bodies as if they were part of a whole preformed by Soul so that individual parts of Soul can become embodied in parts of that whole.

Plotinus's account of the human soul is another area where Platonic and Aristotelian ideas are fruitfully combined. As a Platonist, Plotinus believed that the soul was separate from and superior to the body, which it used as an instrument. How it did so, or, from another point of view, how the individual functioned, was explained on lines that generally follow Aristotle's account of the soul in *De anima*, omitting only the crucial concept of the soul as the formal element in a single substance for which body provides the matter. Only at the level of the intellect, to which Aristotle was at least prepared to give a separate existence, did the two philosophers' views virtually coincide. Given his Platonist and dualist approach to psychology, Plotinus naturally found it difficult to explain how the soul related to the body at all. After examining various possibilities in his long treatise *On the Soul* (IV.3–5), once again in the light of Alexander's treatment of Aristotelian ideas, Plotinus concludes that the soul is present to the body, rather than in it, after the manner of heat in air: heat may affect the air, by warming it, without itself being affected. Though he envisaged the nerves as somehow transmitting instructions from the soul and sensations to it, Plotinus never gave a clear account of how soul and body act on each other. That he did allow body to act on soul, in spite of his principle that it was inferior to and controlled by it, is clear on more than one occasion, for he was sufficiently realistic to see that some explanation of other than ideal behavior needed to be given. In holding that the unsatisfactory condition of the body, or excessive attention to it, could drag down at least the lower "part" of the soul, Plotinus again allowed matter and body a

degree of autonomy that realism requires but strict adherence to his own principles would forbid. It was partly to avoid these difficulties that Plotinus, like all the later Platonists, divided the soul into a lower and a higher part, which they generally but he less often referred to as irrational and rational. The higher was generally immune to affections from the body, and the individual who succeeded in not concentrating on the body and its demands lived at the level of the higher soul; whether that level was the discursive reason, or the intellect, which transcended the individual and had a permanent place in the intelligible, is not always clear. To preserve this immunity from corporeal interference, and also to make it possible to have reincarnation for the "respectable" part of the soul only, Plotinus doubled the imaginative (or representative: *phantastikon*) faculty that lay on the border between the two, thus allowing to each part of the soul the appropriate kind of memory, since memory was a function of the imagination. An important addition to traditional Greek views about perception and memory was the idea that unconscious memories could be stronger and longer-lasting than conscious ones. This, combined with the notion that our personality is formed by what we have seen and remembered, is one of the clearest anticipations of modern thought in ancient psychology.

We have already seen that it is desirable for the human to turn his attention away from the body. The immediate result of this is that he may live at the level of higher rather than lower soul, thus embarking on that process of aspiration to higher reality that is shared by everything in Plotinus's hierarchy. In this way, contemplation, which focuses on what is above and results in assimilation to it, is the most important activity for a philosopher: the Greek word for contemplation was the same as one of the terms for philosophical enquiry. The term of this process is normally the Intellect, but on rare occasions the One itself, which can be known only by means of a sort of touching.

From all this, matter stands apart, since the creative processes that have produced it are by then so weak that matter is devoid of all the formal and other characteristics that might have caused it to join in the upward aspiration of everything else. It is described as sheer negativity, being as devoid of features as the One itself. Somehow this negativity is the cause of evil, thus making evil a metaphysical rather than a moral problem; in a few texts, however, it is explained in moral terms as due to weakness in the soul.

Though later Platonists differed from Plotinus in numerous ways, their systems were a development of his, so that all Neoplatonism to a greater or lesser extent absorbs his influence. In the West, Plotinus, or his pupil Porphyry, provides the Platonic elements in the Latin philosophical tradition of late antiquity, both pagan and Christian. In the East it was generally mediated by later Platonists like Proclus and the Aristotelian commentators. More directly influential was the work known as the *Theology of Aristotle*, which appeared to provide the missing theology for Aristotle's metaphysic but ac-

tually consisted of selections from Plotinus, possibly first organized by Porphyry, but in any case known only in Arabic. Through Syriac and, later, Arabic translations of Neoplatonic works, Plotinus's thought became a crucial part of the Islamic, and the Jewish, philosophy that was written in Arabic and through Latin translations found its way back into the Western tradition in the Middle Ages. It is now generally recognized that much of the so-called Aristotelianism of the later Middle Ages was strongly influenced by Neoplatonism, and in particular the Platonizing interpretations of the Greek commentators of late antiquity mediated by Averroës and other commentators of the Arabic tradition. Similarly the Platonism of the Augustinian tradition owed much to Plotinus, either directly or through Porphyry. Thereafter Plotinus was more influential in art and literature than in philosophy, this influence receiving its greatest impetus from the 1492 Latin translation by the Florentine Marsilio Ficino. The Greek text of Plotinus remained unpublished for nearly another century, and it was not till 1973 that the first edition on modern principles was completed.

HENRY BLUMENTHAL

Bibliography

Texts and Translations

Plotinus. Ed. A. Hilary Armstrong. 7 vols. Loeb Classical Library.
———. *Enneads.* Ed. Paul Henry and Hans-Rudolf Schwyzer. 3 vols. Oxford: Clarendon Press, 1964–1982.

Studies

Armstrong, A. Hilary. "Plotinus." In *The Cambridge History of Later Greek and Early Medieval Philosophy.* Ed. A. H. Armstrong. Cambridge: Cambridge University Press, 1967. Pp. 195–268.
Blumenthal, Henry J. *Plotinus' Psychology: His Doctrines of the Embodied Soul.* Amsterdam: Nijhoff, 1971.
Bréhier, Emile. *The Philosophy of Plotinus.* Trans. Joseph Thomas. Chicago: University of Chicago Press, 1958.
Emilsson, Eyjólfur K. *Plotinus on Sense-Perception: A Philosophical Study.* Cambridge: Cambridge University Press, 1988.
Gerson, Lloyd P., ed. *The Cambridge Companion to Plotinus.* Cambridge: Cambridge University Press, 1996.
Hadot, Pierre. *Plotinus, or, The Simplicity of Vision.* Trans. Michael Chase. Chicago: University of Chicago Press, 1993.
Himmerich, Wilhelm. *Eudaimonia: Die Lehre des Plotin von der Selbstverwirklichung des Menschen.* Forschungen zur Neueren Philosophie und ihrer Geschichte n. F. 13. Würzburg: Konrad Triltsch Verlag, 1959.
Igal, Jesús. *Porfirio, Vida de Plotino; Plotino, Enéadas I–II.* Madrid: Editorial Gredos, 1982. Pp. 7–114.

O'Meara, Dominic J. *Plotinus: An Introduction to the Enneads.* Oxford: Clarendon Press, 1993.

Rist, John M. *Plotinus: The Road to Reality.* Cambridge: Cambridge University Press, 1967.

Schroeder, Frederic M. *Form and Transformation: A Study in the Philosophy of Plotinus.* Montreal and Kingston: McGill–Queen's University Press, 1992.

Trouillard, Jean. *La procession plotinienne.* Paris: Presses Universitaires de France, 1955.

———. *La purification plotinienne.* Paris: Presses Universitaires de France, 1955.

Wallis, Richard T. *Neoplatonism.* London: Duckworth, 1972. Pp. 37–93.

Related Articles

The Question of Being; Hellenism and Christianity; Plato; Platonism

PLUTARCH

For anyone interested in Greek learning, Plutarch is an obvious reference, so rich and varied is the prolific work left us by this Pico della Mirandola of antiquity. Modern scholars rely heavily on him for information about lost authors or obscure periods of the Hellenistic and Roman epochs. Still, to portray him as a "guardian of the temple," or even to limit his Hellenism to mere learning, would give too reductive an impression of a man who explored tradition for an answer to the questions of his time, drew vital strength from that tradition, and sought to revive it. In this sense, Plutarch is an exemplary representative of the period in which Trajan tried to revitalize the former city-states and Hadrian worked to restore the Temple of Delphi.

A DOUBLE ANCESTRY: CHAERONEA AND PAIDEIA

Plutarch was born around 45 C.E. in Chaeronea, in the region of Boeotia, near the two great historic poles of Hellenism, Athens and Delphi. In his youth, he went to Athens, storehouse of the classical intellectual heritage, to study philosophy with the Platonist Ammonios; later, he returned frequently to see his friends and to take advantage of the "many books and all manner of discussions" (*Moralia, The Epsilon at Delphi* 384e). He was even made an honorary citizen of the Leontian tribe. Toward the end of the 90s he became a priest at Delphi, which had remained the major center of the religious tradition, despite the decline of its oracle. In this favorable geographical setting, Plutarch's moorings in the tradition were reinforced by his immense learning. In addition to the knowledge of rhetoric and literature a classical education implies, and in addition to philosophy, he himself tells us of his youthful passion for mathematics. He displays his knowledge in a variety of other fields as well: in music (even though the treatise *On Music* preserved under his name is spurious), in the physical and biological sciences (largely drawn from the Aristotelian school), and in medicine, which he may have studied during his stay in Alexandria. Following the custom of the time, he effectively completed his education while traveling throughout the Roman empire before giving the successful lectures that brought him to Rome toward the end of Vespasian's reign (69–79) and probably again when Domitian was in power (81–96). Nevertheless, around the year 90, before the expulsion of the philosophers in 93–94, he chose to return to Chaeronea, where he served as magistrate and where he taught philosophy. The major portion of his work dates from this

second part of his life, during which he continued to travel to see his friends. The very form of his work gives us some idea of the way he and his circle must have lived.

The prefaces to Plutarch's treatises not only introduce us to members of that circle, distinguished Romans and eminent Greeks to whom the works are dedicated, but they also echo these men's concerns and the debates that informed Plutarch's writing. Once allowances are made for the literary shaping that minimizes controversy and suppresses anything that is not of intellectual interest, the learned banquets of *Table-Talk* show us, more than anything else, the ideal of urbane sociability that prevailed in Plutarch's cultivated milieu, the varieties of fields of knowledge in which he and his interlocutors were interested, and the spirit in which they approached those fields. So when each guest in turn is prevailed upon to develop a personal theory, he makes a point of respecting the categories of the probable *(eikos)* and the credible *(pithanon)*, in the spirit of the line by Xenocrates with which Ammonius liked to punctuate his accounts: "Let this be our opinion, with the look of truth" *(Moralia, Table-Talk* IX.14.746b). Here, as in so many passages in Plutarch's work, we find the spirit of the New Academy, anxious to refrain from manifesting "excessive confidence" *(to agan tes pisteōs)*, and this encouragement of probabilism—but not of skepticism—partly accounts for the polyphonic form of philosophic dialogues like *The Oracle at Delphi No Longer Given in Verse* and *On the Sign of Socrates* (which are quite different in this respect from Plato's dialogues), as well as the difficulty commentators sometimes have in appreciating the interest of every contribution.

One other feature is evident in *Table-Talk* and characteristic of imperial paideia: a taste for learning and commentary. This feature underlies works like *The Roman Questions* and *The Greek Questions,* which deal with the customs of various peoples, and, in the realm of philosophy, it inspires *Platonic Questions;* more curiously, it also turns up in *Parallel Lives.* The biographer does not hesitate to interrupt his account to detail his sources, retrace a history of mechanics, or comment on the attitude of his heroes. While this procedure appears quite natural, it is also very revealing of the way Plutarch looks at the past and at history.

THE LESSONS OF HISTORY: POLITICS ACCORDING TO PLUTARCH

It is remarkable that Plutarch should have composed *Parallel Lives,* about a Greek and a Roman; it is a sign that, for him, Greeks and Romans shared a common moral universe in the framework of a single civilization. This is clear in the priority he gives to moral values, and in his manifest desire to discern the nuances of virtue or to look in the mirror of the history of great men "to

try to rule his [own] life and make it conform to the image of their virtues" ("Aemilius Paulus," *Parallel Lives* VI.1.2). This effort brings to mind the passage in the treatise *How a Man May Become Aware of His Making Progress in Virtue* where we are invited to wonder: "What would Plato have done in this case? What would Epameinondas have said? How would Lycurgus have conducted himself, or Agesilaus?" (*Moralia* I.85.15b). Plutarch's emphasis on morality and virtue reveals the profound unity that links the moral treatises and the *Lives;* the works are distinguished from one another only for the convenience of classification. Moreover, the word *Bios* (life) may apply, as it does in *Gorgias* and the Myth of Er, to the "way of life" that everyone must choose, or it may designate the literary genre of Peripatetic origin that is used to describe the "way of life" chosen; but in both cases, the idea belongs to the philosopher's domain, not the historian's.

Writing as a moralist, in numerous prefaces Plutarch affirms the exemplary quality of great men, but he does not deceive himself about the imperfection of man in general and of his heroes in particular. While he claims not to dwell on the latters' defects, his *Lives* do not become hagiography any more than they become indictments when he chooses such antimodels as Demetrius and Anthony, stressing that there is no moral conduct without knowledge of good *and* evil. Instead, Plutarch sets out to enumerate the myriad "struggles of virtue *[arete]* pitted against fortune *[ta syntynchanonta]*" (*On the Sign of Socrates* VII.575c), and in the guise of a chronological account, he develops a fragmented narrative in which a historical fact is stripped of its properly historical substance and treated the way orators treat literary quotations taken out of context, using them in support of a particular feature or idea. Thus historical facts tend to turn into exempla: using a mimetic style, Plutarch allows them to speak for themselves, or else he comments on them the way he comments on literary texts in the treatise *How the Young Man Should Study Poetry.*

He claims to arrive in this way at an instructive portrayal of the character of a statesman, since, in keeping with his own choice of lifestyle, he considers only "practical" and not "theoretical" lives, even if he never fails to emphasize his heroes' philosophical training and affinities. He does not conceal his partiality to his compatriot Epaminondas, who knew how to combine politics and philosophy. In Plutarch's portrayal of a statesman, the first characteristic called for is absolute devotion to the city-state, and we have to understand the amount of space Plutarch gives to wartime exploits in this context. At first glance, this emphasis seems out of keeping with the reality of the imperial city, and it contradicts even the *Precepts of Statecraft*, where Plutarch advises speech makers to avoid recalling past victories and encourages them rather to extol the virtues of peace. However, his stress on valor in war allows him to give contemporary leaders examples of men who were ready to serve the city

everywhere and under all circumstances, ready to sacrifice their lives, their interests, and their personal attachments, even their honor and their principles, to their community.

But many dangers lurk in the struggle *(agōn)* we know as political life, and in all epochs (which he often neglects to differentiate), Plutarch finds the passions that he denounces in the *Precepts of Statecraft:* ambition *(philotimia)*, a necessary spur to action but which can degenerate into party strife *(philoneikia)* and thirst for power *(philarchia)*, and jealousy *(phthonos)*, a sword of Damocles suspended over the head of the powerful, who need prestige and popularity in order to act.

This is why the politician must follow Pericles' example and combine the teacherly qualities of firmness and persuasiveness. He must be able to resist the attractions of the crowd, and he must be aware of his responsibility as a leader whose duty it is to ensure the safety of those he governs. If he wishes to have followers, he must also persuade people to like him, and Plutarch attaches the greatest importance to the contacts the hero establishes with his fellow citizens or subjects. Smiling and affable, shunning the ostentation of a luxurious style of living that would alienate others, accommodating and accessible to all, he remains very much a man of the city, even if Plutarch's text occasionally resonates with Plato's theory of the philosopher-king, or with Pythagorean reflections. We see evidence of Plutarch's ideals in his discomfort with the Hellenistic kings, whose arrogance, greed, and perfidy he stigmatizes. His heroes fully deserve to be called *politikoi*, that is, both "belonging to" and "befitting" the city-state, because in fact they both serve the city-state and respect its values of humanity and tolerance.

THE LESSONS OF PLATONISM: REASON AND ANCESTRAL FIDELITY

Devoted to Chaeronea, Plutarch is also the servant of philosophy and of the god of Delphi. These two elements are indispensable for understanding a body of thought that is often difficult to grasp. In the first place, Plutarch's thought is never presented systematically; the variations inherent in the needs of the subject under consideration lay it open, accordingly, to accusations of incoherence. In the second place, while Plutarch repeatedly proclaimed his attachment to Platonism and assailed Stoics and Epicureans in his polemical works, and while his disciple and friend Favorinus chose to give his name to a defense of the New Academy's method, against Stoic assaults, we do not know for sure whether there was still a New Academy school in Plutarch's day, nor do we know what is implied by the fuzzy term "Middle Platonism." Some scholars even deny Plutarch the label Platonist, charging him with an eclecticism for which he is sometimes blamed and sometimes praised,

but it is difficult to determine how much he himself contributed and how much he received from a philosophic tradition that had been nourished on five centuries of reflection since Plato and Aristotle.

Some critics, too, are willing to see Plutarch only as a moralist, a sort of Greek Seneca who, like the Roman writer, drafted advice on how to control anger or attain spiritual tranquillity. And the *Lives,* which, like Plutarch's pedagogical and moral treatises, manifest great psychological refinement, undoubtedly offer strong evidence of his qualities as a moralist. Still, in his eyes, if philosophy is to be truly the "mistress of life," it cannot neglect the beginning and the end of life. Thus the thought of God is at the heart of his reflection, and it underlies his differences with the other schools of thought. He is no more willing to accept the immanence of the Stoic *logos* than he is to accept Epicurean "atheism": the transcendence of the divine being is an essential truth that he has his teacher Ammonius proclaim in the discussion on the Epsilon at Delphi. The letter *epsilon* is pronounced *"ei"* (thou art); this votive offering to God should remind us that He alone possesses the plenitude of being, since He escapes the vicissitudes of time (*The Epsilon at Delphi* 392e). On the contrary, the precept "Know thyself," which the god confers on us, reminds us of the fragility of our nature and our inability to comprehend God in a consistent way (cf. *The Oracle at Delphi No Longer Given in Verse, Moralia* V.409d, or *On the Delays of the Divine Vengeance, Moralia* VII.549e). This transcendence precludes our bringing the divine being at random into our human world, and reason, like respect for divinity, condemns the excesses of superstition. But the limits of our knowledge in turn mean that we must not reject traditional faith in heavenly signs for the sake of a narrow rationalism, or scoff at the prerogatives of Providence. Providence can inspire us to action, but only by way of representations that stimulate the active and volitional part of our soul; it does not make our arms and legs move. To see Providence at work, a crucial distinction is required, one that Plutarch attributes to Plato: the distinction between the final or higher cause and the material or natural cause (*The Obsolescence of Oracles, Moralia* V.435e–436e). Pericles' unicorn ram offers a striking illustration of this: the anomaly had physical causes that Anaxagoras brought to light, but it also revealed that its owner would become the sole master of Athens, as the soothsayer Lampon saw.

This general framework helps us situate two highly debated points, Plutarch's dualism and his demonology. Inspired by *Timaeus,* Plutarch's cosmology deviates from Plato's precisely through the role attributed to the divine being. Instead of conceiving a demiurge intermediary between form and matter, Plutarch identifies God with the paradigm and develops the idea that "universal nature, disordered before, became a 'cosmos'; it came to resemble after a fashion and participate in the form and excellence of God" (*On the Delays of the Divine Vengeance,* 550d). But once Ideas are left aside and the

world has become a reflection of the *Nous* (eternal mind), what about evil? Must one make God its cause—an intolerable blasphemy—or deny its existence against all evidence?

The preexistence of anarchic matter—which a temporal interpretation of *Timaeus* implies—lets us escape from this dilemma and suppose the existence of a precosmic and disordered evil soul (*On the Generation of the Soul in the Timaeus, Moralia* XIII.1.1014f–1015f) whose strength could not compare with divine power (*Isis and Osiris, Moralia* V.371a); this evil soul is more like a resistance to order and intelligence than a maleficent will. Apart from this theologico-physical analysis, there still remains the question of evil spirits, which is the focus of some recent studies on Plutarch's religion. But any consideration of evil spirits in isolation is unfaithful to a much broader demonology, which has to be put back within the framework of the destiny of the soul as it is treated in three great myths *(Concerning the Face Which Appears in the Orb of the Moon; On the Delays of Divine Vengeance; On the Sign of Socrates).* In his commentaries on *Timaeus*, Plutarch distinguishes between the irrational principle in the soul, a remnant of primordial disorder, and the divine *nous*. In *On the Sign of Socrates,* he reserves the term *soul* for the part immersed in the body and makes *nous* the term inappropriately applied to the part inaccessible to corruption, which is the *daimōn* (VII.591e). Once liberated by death, depending on whether vice has weighed it down or virtue lightened it, the *daimōn* can rise to unite itself with pure Intelligence, according to *Concerning the Face Which Appears in the Orb of the Moon.* It is no longer a matter, as in Plato, of contemplating Ideas, which have already been separated from cosmological speculations, and so demonology brings an answer to eschatological questions and the anguish of salvation. In certain cases, demonology also allows us to preserve the transcendence of the divine being in a plausible manner: thus, by assuming the intervention of demons in the operation of oracles, one can avoid the dilemma of "[making] the god responsible for nothing at all" (*On the Obsolescence of Oracles* V.414f), or seeing divine intervention in everything, and one can exonerate divine goodness from responsibility for human sacrifices by considering that sacrifices are demanded by demons that have not yet been purified of their evil worldly sentiments.

Owing in part, but only in part, to his monumental learning, Plutarch embodies the essential features of the Hellenic tradition: service to the city-state, the virtues of civilization, the requirements of reason introduced by Socrates, ancestral faith, and respect for divine grandeur. The man Montaigne celebrated for holding opinions that were "Platonic, mild, and accommodated to civil society" reminds us that the classical ideal put no distance between learning and life.

FRANÇOISE FRAZIER
Translated by Rita Guerlac and Anne Slack

Bibliography

Texts and Translations

Plutarch. *Moralia.* 15 vols. Loeb Classical Library.

————. *Parallel Lives.* Greek-Italian ed. Mondadori, in progress.

————. *Plutarch's Lives.* Trans. Bernadotte Perrin. 11 vols. Loeb Classical Library.

Studies

Aalders, Gerhard J. D. *Plutarch's Political Thought.* Amsterdam and New York: North-Holland Publishing Co., 1982.

Aalders, Gerhard J. D., and Lukas de Blois. "Plutarch und die politische Philosophie der Griechen." *Aufsteig und Niedergang der Römischen Welt (ANRW)* II, 36, no. 5 (1992): 3384–3404.

Babut, Daniel. *Parerga: Choix d'articles 1975–1993.* Lyon: Collection de la Maison de l'Orient Méditerranéen, 1994.

————. "Plutarque et le Stoïcisme." Dissertation, Paris, 1969.

Boulogne, Jacques. *Plutarque: Un aristocrate grec sous l'occupation romaine.* Lille: Presses Universitaires de Lille, 1994.

Brenk, Frederick E. "An Imperial Heritage: The Religious Spirit of Plutarch of Chaironeia." *ANRW* II, 36, no. 1 (1987): 248–349.

————. *In Mist Apparelled: Religious Themes in Plutarch's Moralia and Lives.* Leyden: E. J. Brill, 1977.

Dörrie, Heinrich. "Le platonisme de Plutarque." *Actes du VIIIème Congrès de l'Association Guillaume Budé.* Paris: Belles Lettres, 1969. Pp. 519–530.

————. "Die Stellung Plutarchs im Platonismus seiner Zeit." In *Philomathes: Studies and Essays in the Humanities in Memory of Philippe Merlan.* Ed. Robert B. Palmer and Robert Hamerton-Kelly. The Hague: Nijhoff, 1971. Pp. 35–36.

Frazier, Françoise. *Histoire et morale dans les Vies Parallèles de Plutarque.* Paris: Belles Lettres, 1996.

Hershbell, Jackson P. "Plutarch and Epicureanism." *ANRW* II, 36, no. 5 (1992): 3353–3383.

————. "Plutarch and Stoicism." *ANRW* II, 36, no. 5 (1992): 3336–3352.

Jones, Christopher P. *Plutarch and Rome.* Oxford: Clarendon Press, 1971.

Montaigne, Michel de. *The Complete Essays of Montaigne.* Trans. Donald M. Frame. Stanford, Calif.: Stanford University Press, 1958.

Mossman, Judith, ed. *Plutarch and His Intellectual World.* Oxford: Clarendon Press, 1997.

Panagopoulos, Cécile. "Vocabulaire et mentalité dans les Moralia de Plutarque." *Dialogues d'histoire ancienne* 3 (1977): 197–235.

Pavis d'Escurac, Hélène. "Périls et chances du régime civique selon Plutarque." *Ktèma* 6 (1981): 287–300.

Pelling, Christopher. "Aspects of Plutarch's Characterization." *Illinois Classical Studies* 13:2 (1988): 257–274.

————. "Plutarch's Adaptation of His Source Material." *Journal of Hellenic Studies* 100 (1980): 127–140.

————. "Plutarch's Method of Work in the Roman *Lives*." *Journal of Hellenic Studies* 99 (1979): 74–96.

Puech, Bernadette. "Prosopographie des amis de Plutarque." *ANRW* II, 33, no. 6 (1992): 4831–4893.

Stadter, Philip A. "Life of Pericles." *Ancient Society* 18 (1987): 251–269.

———. "The Proems of Plutarch's *Lives*." *Illinois Classical Studies* 13, no. 2 (1988): 275–295.

Van der Stockt, Luc. *Twinkling and Twilight: Plutarch's Reflections on Literature.* Brussels: Paleis der Academien, 1992.

Vernière, Yvonne. *Symboles et mythes dans la pensée de Plutarque.* Paris: Les Belles Lettres, 1977.

Ziegler, Konrat. *Paulys Realencyclopädie der classischen Altertumswissenschaft.* Stuttgart: J. B. Metzler, 1894–1972. XXI.1, col. 639–961.

Related Articles

The Statesman As Political Actor; Xenophon; The Academy

POLYBIUS

POLYBIUS EXEMPLIFIES one of the crowning achievements of classical historiography. His importance is the product of several factors: Polybius's moment in history, during which the end of the autonomy of Greek city-states coincided with the onset of the *pax romana;* his exceptional role as witness to the events he recounted; the object of his work—to explain Roman expansion and Rome's domination of the Mediterranean world; his experience as someone destined to exist between two worlds, Greek and Roman, which enabled him to adopt a clear and somewhat detached point of view of both. Moreover, he had a distinctive approach to the writing of history, and he maintained throughout a reflective and critical view of the meaning of his work.

Polybius was born around 208 B.C.E. at Megalopolis in Arcadia, and spent his youth in the Achaean Confederacy. The son of a high-ranking politician, he served as Hipparch of the Achaean Confederacy in 170. The Greek world was torn by factions at the time, and the confederacy did not align itself decisively enough with the Roman side in the struggle against Perseus of Macedonia. After the victory of Pydna (168 B.C.E.), between 167 and 150, the Romans deported to Italy some one thousand Achaean hostages suspected of treachery; Polybius was among them. While living in Rome, he became a friend of the young Scipio Aemilianus. His circumstances there were ambiguous: he was both a hostage and a member of an important philhellenic society (the "Scipionic circle"), and he enjoyed a privileged position from which to observe Roman civilization, its institutions, the role of religion in maintaining cohesion within the state, and the organization of the army. Having become a trusted ally of the Romans, Polybius accompanied Scipio in 147–146 B.C.E. during the siege of Carthage. He continued to play an active role in the political life of the Greek world, especially in the context of the administrative reorganization that followed the sack of Corinth. It seems likely that the major part of his *Histories* was written during the last twenty years of his life. Polybius is also the author of a *Life of Philopoemen,* a treatise on tactics, and a work on the Numantine War.

Polybius's intention was to answer the question, "Who is so worthless or indolent as not to wish to know by what means and under what system of polity the Romans in less than fifty-three years have succeeded in subjecting nearly the whole inhabited world to their sole government—a thing unique in history?" (*Histories* I.1.5) A dual objective is thus set forth: he sought to

understand the unfolding of events that led first to the pursuit of world supremacy and then to its realization (from 223 to 168 B.C.E.); basing his research on a comparison between Greece and Rome, he also looked at their political systems and institutions, in search of a key to understanding this great historical process and the military success of the Romans. Starting with Book III of *Histories*, Polybius broadened his chronological scope to include the period immediately following the sack of Corinth and the destruction of Carthage (146 B.C.E.).

It is a dizzying panorama: in Greece, there were chronic conflicts among Achaeans, Aetolians, and Spartans, and the city-states were powerless to form a coherent policy in the face of the rising power of Rome and the Macedonians, whose Panhellenic ambitions led first Philip V and then Perseus to confront the Romans (in the three Macedonian wars that ended in the defeat of Persia at Pydna in 168 B.C.E.). There was also the conflict with Carthage, which took place in the western Mediterranean (Sicily, Spain, and Italy) before concluding in Africa. Last, there were conflicts with the eastern kingdoms, including Pergamum, Seleuceia, and Ptolemaic Egypt, and the Roman war against Antiochus III.

Polybius's work was written with the advantage of hindsight and was constantly revised, even during the final phases of editing, when the author further modified the early books. Polybius had by then returned to Greece, where, according to legend, he died after 118 B.C.E. following a serious riding accident. By that time, his very readable history had already been completed.

A project such as his demanded a particular form of historiography. Clearly, in choosing to limit himself to the events of the recent past, and in emphasizing politics, Polybius adhered to the tradition of Thucydides, Xenophon, and Theopompus. His history is an exercise in memory, made up of his interpretation of events experienced firsthand, testimony taken from participants (from the preceding generation as well as his own), archival research, and critical readings of earlier historians.

In contrast with his predecessors, however, Polybius sought to write a universal history; his project went beyond the formal framework of a historiography centered on the Greek world and Greek history. As a result, he could not conform to Thucydides' strict chronological principles. He had to find a connecting thread that would allow him to organize the whole and that was consistent with his ambitions, stated in the opening lines of the work: to reconstruct the course of historical process in a condensed time frame, but encompassing the entire Mediterranean world. It was less a matter of retracing a chain of events than of providing the reader with an overview of the whole that would include those events and reveal their underlying relationships. To do that, Polybius had to reconcile the chronology of events—from one Olympiad to the next—with the broad geographic framework: in other

words, he had to relate the continuity of a particular event, its causes, and its consequences, to the simultaneous outbreak of events, the playing out of the same action in different parts of the world. Such a writing of history aims at total isomorphism with the dynamics of the events that it recounts.

This spatial dimension is evident not only in the purpose of *Histories* but also in the form and organization of the text. Rome was undertaking to unify the world under its authority. To do so, it had to operate on several fronts and to impose its law on distant regions over a period of time. Polybius sought to retrace the process by which history is fulfilled through an organic unification of space (I.1.3). In choosing the 140th Olympiad (220–216 B.C.E.) as his starting point, he points to the dawn of a period when "the affairs of Italy and Africa have been interlinked with those of Greece and Asia, all leading up to one end" (I.1.3). The history repeatedly attempts to show how the sequence of local events contributes to this final end; in other words, it tries to reveal the connections between what appear to be separate events and the consequences of those linkages. Polybius chose to write a universal history, rejecting a method that juxtaposes regional monographs in favor of one that aims at grasping the interconnectedness of events. The universality of the work derives not from a history that reaches into the distant past and continues up to the present time (like those of Ephorus or Diodorus Siculus) but from an ecumenical dimension, and, embedded in this, from the exposure of links between events that had previously appeared unconnected.

Keeping in mind this goal, which is restated at several key points in *Histories*, and also Polybius's unflagging interest in geography (to the point that he dedicated Book XXXIV to "continental topography"), we may reflect on the almost cartographic organization of a work that articulates many disjointed parts within an organic whole, and constantly refers regional information to the overall structure. Starting with the 140th Olympiad, Polybius covers the inhabited earth according to a determined order: Italy, Sicily, Spain, Africa, Greece, Macedonia, and Egypt. As the organizing principle of his narration, he adopts the form of a journey around the Mediterranean. Like a cartographer, Polybius seeks to construct a synoptic point of view, from which it would be easy to see the coherence and profound unity of an action "with a recognized beginning, a fixed duration, and an end which is not a matter of dispute" (III.1.5). Also like a cartographer, he has to draw out the correlation among distant places or phenomena. Here, synchronicity is the equivalent of the relations of commensurability established by means of the Euclidean grid of parallel and perpendicular lines that organized Eratosthanes' Alexandrian map. Polybius's conception of historical action ultimately converges with the theory of tragic action outlined in Aristotle's *Poetics:* unity and coherence as criteria, the body as metaphor.

The narrative challenge before Polybius is to reconcile chronology and to-

pology: in other words, to situate each event in its proper place, and yet to respect the antithetical demands of describing the connectedness and continuity of events. The divisions by Olympiad and the method of describing events year by year (XIV.3.12) have to be adapted to a narrative that covers events occurring in different theaters of action—Greece, Asia, Africa, Spain, and Italy. This necessity sometimes leads Polybius, depending on the geographical progression, to relate the outcome of an event before describing its beginning (XV.3.24). The general rule lends itself to a variety of adjustments, made to avoid breaking the flow of events by fragmenting the account (for example, XXXII.C.2.ll). Such a principle of composition assigns an active role to the reader, who has the task of tying up the threads of this rhapsodic tale and restoring continuity: "But I myself, keeping distinct all the most important parts of the world and the events that took place in each, and adhering always to a uniform conception of how each matter should be treated, and again definitely relating under each year the contemporary events that then took place, leave obviously full liberty to students to carry back their minds to the continuous narrative and the several points at which I interrupted it" (XXXVIII.1.6). The form of the work and the evolution of a principle of composition thus had to reflect the very dynamics of history, in which theaters of action that seem independent at first become progressively interrelated within a universal configuration (IV.1.28). The discontinuity of the narrative, a consequence of the universal dimension of the particular historical process being investigated, while posing a difficulty for the reader against which Polybius defends himself in advance, also establishes an aesthetic of diversity (XXXVIII.1.5–6).

Another aspect of Polybius's work is the combination of historical narrative with continuous reflection on the task of the historian. The writing of history itself is accompanied by epistemological and ethical reflections on the issues at stake in this practice, the principles to be respected, and the pitfalls to be avoided.

Histories highlights Polybius himself, as both actor and author. He speaks of himself sometimes in the third person, sometimes in the first, to introduce some variety and to keep the reader interested; he even refers to himself by name, since "no one as far as I know, up to the time in which I live at least, has received from his parents the same proper name as my own" (XXXVI.12.5). He does not fail to recall his own political activity and the carefully argued support that he gave the Roman policy in Greece. More broadly speaking, his military and political experience give Polybius an essential advantage as a historian. As he notes (XII.13.25g and h), it is quite impossible to retrace these kinds of incidents if one has not been personally involved in the events themselves. History is done well, he adds, only when politicians themselves undertake to write it (XII.14.28).

Instructed by his fieldwork, Polybius takes every opportunity to reinforce his account by recalling the circumstances of his investigation and his sources of information. Very often these involved site visits (in Italy, Gaul, Spain, and Africa: most notably, following Hannibal's itinerary across the Alps) and personal encounters with people who had made history. Polybius's travels, which recall those of the polymath Ulysses, come across as the way he substitutes truth for the approximations and errors of armchair historians (III.2.48 and III.2.59, for instance). Examples include his interviews with Massinissa about Hannibal and with Laelius about Cornelius Scipio. However, it was his friendship with Scipio Aemilianus in particular that placed him at the center of events.

Polybius also inserts himself into the picture as the author of *Histories*, commenting frequently on the progression of his narrative, underlining the connections between cause and effect and crucial moments, and justifying his choices. Throughout the account he defines the objective of history, what it is that he must construct in his narrative: not the tedious detail of the actions, but their general features and the effects they produced (I.1.57, II.1.l). He does not hesitate to rank events or to restore chronological continuity when it has been interrupted by the shift from one theater of action to another.

One of the means Polybius adopts to affirm his conception of history is critical reading; at times he even corrects his predecessors. Underlying these controversies we see Polybius engaged in drawing a negative portrait of the ideal historian, that is, of Polybius himself. The reader is the final judge: often directly challenged, he is ultimately the only one in a position to determine the reputation and the future success or failure of the work.

Polybius's critiques of earlier historians define, in contrast, his own conception of history. On several occasions Polybius distances himself from the tradition of historical pathos that seeks to excite emotion in the reader by fueling the imagination with spectacular images (II.3.56) or even supernatural events. He aims his criticism at a form of history influenced by the rhetorical effects of tragedy, even though he himself resorts at times to the same stylistic expedients. Book XII devotes a lengthy argument to a critique of Timaeus of Tauromenium in which Polybius is attempting as much to reestablish the facts as to undermine the reputation of an author who might be called, with some justification, the first great Greek historian of the West and of Rome. Polybius severely criticizes Timaeus's factual errors, and also his systematic lies, his lack of historical ethics, the uncritical acceptance of witnesses that leads him to introduce unbelievable elements, and his propensity for polemic. Polybius also denounces the emotion that led Timaeus to present a partisan portrait of certain individuals, without a balanced dose of praise and blame. But the opposition is most clearly stated where it contains the two authors' conception of history. Polybius reproaches Timaeus for basing his research

entirely on books, for visiting libraries instead of sites (XII.14.27): "But to believe, as Timaeus did, that relying upon the mastery of material alone one can write well the history of subsequent events is absolutely foolish, and is much as if a man who had seen the works of ancient painters fancied himself to be a capable painter and a master of that art" (XII.12.25e). It is impossible, Polybius believes, to describe a battle without ever having experienced warfare. By the same token, without having personally been there it is impossible to describe a scene of action or the configuration of a city. Truth and the ability to bring words to life are beyond the reach of the armchair historian, and it is impossible to spark the interest of readers when one has not been personally involved in the events.

Polybius's emphasis on the reader is striking. His entire work reflects his preoccupation with a public whose interest must be captured, readers who must be motivated to pursue a work forty volumes long (forty papyrus scrolls) and who must be aided by frequent summaries, by the addition of a preface for each Olympiad, and by the inclusion of a chronological table in the final volume (which has been lost). Polybius belonged to a world in which books were beginning to circulate, in which the historian had to "publish" his work by having the manuscript copied and put in circulation through libraries (see, for example, XVI.3.20).

The presence of the reader also shaped Polybius's philosophy of history. Unlike those authors who spared no effort to seduce their readers by resorting to anecdotes of the supernatural and appealing to a sense of pathos, Polybius's aim was primarily practical: he wanted to inform. But he was not pursuing knowledge for its own sake. He saw history as a storehouse of experiences, examples, and lessons that could help a reader avoid the mistakes of the past. The lessons of history can be applied to the present (XII.2.25b), provided that one pays attention to the similarities between different situations. Thus, he presents reading history as a means of acquiring political, military, and ethical experience by proxy: one can draw the lessons of history without running the attendant risks (I.1.35). In consequence, there is a gap between Polybius's narrative itself and his ethical and political discourse, which systematically recalls the overall stakes involved in a given situation, the strategic principles behind a military maneuver, and the vigilance required in interpreting human behavior. *Histories* constitutes a dissertation on the art of war and a treatise on political science that fills in a portrait of the ideal statesman with repeated brush strokes. However, it also explores a vast range of situations—battles, sieges, ambushes, betrayals, reversals of fortune, and so forth—all of which, if they are thoroughly learned by heart, will provide the reader with a kind of wisdom and experience. Particularly striking are Polybius's emphasis on commanders' mistakes, which often precipitate the catastrophic outcome of a battle (X.5.32), and his analysis of the reasons for

success as well as failure, an analysis that transcends the pleasure of the text to extract useful lessons (XI.4.19a). In the same way, the actions of statesmen are painstakingly scrutinized: "It will be, I think, of some service to examine into the principles of the leading politicians in each place and decide which of them prove to have acted in a rational manner and which to have failed in their duty" (XXX.2.6).

At times these lessons take the form of structured developments that Polybius analyzes according to categories of Greek political philosophy (Peripatetics, Stoics), as in Book VI, for example, which is devoted to the army and to Roman institutions. The political life of a state is subject to a quasi-biological cycle of growth and decline, in which royalty, aristocracy, and democracy follow one after the other, as do their corrupted forms, tyranny, oligarchy, and mob rule. To escape this cycle, which sees a return of monarchy after a period of decadence, in the course of its political development Rome adopted a form of "mixed constitution," a synthesis of the three constitutions of the cycle, in which power is shared among the consuls, the Senate, and the people. But while Carthage, another example of a mixed constitution, left the greatest power to the people, in Rome the Senate dominated the other two components. Certain Greek states, such as Achaea, Sparta, and Crete, which possessed similar political organizations, failed to derive the same historical benefit from this break in the cycle. Polybius's account of the Roman constitution and its military organization attempted to explain the singularity of Rome to the Greeks in the framework of their own political thought, and also sought to present the Romans with a global interpretation of their institutions.

This insistence on the useful lessons of history suggests that Polybius's historical project is indeed twofold: to reconstruct the mechanism of the rise of Rome, and also to understand the reasons for the decline of Greece, a disaster parallel to that of Carthage—worse, even, since the Greeks had no extenuating circumstances to excuse their errors (XXXVIII.1). Moreover, his political and pragmatic approach to history suggests a dual readership: on the one hand, statesmen, or those who aspire to be statesmen, and on the other hand, Greeks of the city-states, to whom he offers an explanation of the principle mechanisms that brought about the final result. The unfolding of recent history is intended to enlighten his contemporaries: is life under Roman rule acceptable or intolerable? As for praise, credit, and blame, it will be for future generations to evaluate the Romans, by studying Polybius's account as well as by observing how they managed their victory (III.1.4).

Histories paints the portrait of a good leader. Such a leader adapts his decisions to an accurate evaluation of the circumstances, he shows moderation in victory, and he is honest. Among the more remarkable examples, Polybius offers Philopoemen, Scipio, Hadrusbal, and Hannibal. But one of the primary

qualities of a leader is his awareness that fortune brings about unforeseeable changes, and for that reason Polybius has all the more admiration for Scipio who, at the moment of victory over Carthage, felt a certain anxiety for his own fatherland (XXXVIII.4.21).

A meditation on the responsibility of men and the role of Fortune in the unfolding of history runs throughout Polybius's work. History appears as a field where Fortune—the power that brings all events together toward a unique end (I.1.4)—can act, or even experiment; Fortune would thus be the principle of underlying order behind events. She embodies the instability of things, and can even overturn a seemingly certain outcome at the last moment, thus creating unexpected opportunities. Fortune is the only enemy that even the best generals cannot vanquish. She is also the least dependable ally, and a cautious general deserves greater credit than a lucky one who gambles. Fortune is generous in her warnings, and it is wise not to provoke her capricious moods. According to Hannibal, speaking to Scipio before the battle of Zama, Fortune "behaves as if she were sporting with little children" (XV.6.8). Nevertheless, she appears as a form of justice, punishing excess and the worst crimes—it was Fortune that brought on all the ills resulting in the defeat of Philip and the Macedonians (XXII.2.10). Fortune also urges those she favors to moderation, for fear of unpredictable outcomes. Thus she might be compared to the historian, who reads about events long after they transpired and knows how they came out. She can almost personify the unlimited inventiveness of the play of circumstances that always introduces the unpredictable into human actions.

Enlivened by the author's exceptional ability as a storyteller (his descriptions of Hannibal crossing the Alps, the battle of Cannes and the meeting between Hadrusbal and Scipio before the last battle at the gates of Carthage have become set pieces in anthologies) and by a surprising sense of portraiture, Polybius's work is a major source for historians today who seek to understand this crucial period. It has been required reading in the modern epoch, both for its instruction in the art of governing and for the political theory that emerges from its analysis of the Roman constitution—as attested, for example, by Machiavelli.

CHRISTIAN JACOB
Translated by Elizabeth Rawlings and Jeannine Pucci

Bibliography

Texts and Translations

Polybius. *Histories.* Trans. Walter Paton. Loeb Classical Library.

Studies

Ferrary, J.-L. *Philhellénisme et impérialisme: Aspects idéologiques de la conquête romaine du monde hellénistique.* Rome: Ecole française de Rome, 1988.
Pédech, Paul. *La méthode historique de Polybe.* Paris: Les Belles Lettres, 1964.
Wallbank, F. W. *Polybius.* Berkeley: University of California Press, 1972.

Related Articles

Geography; History

PROTAGORAS

PROTAGORAS WAS BORN around 492 B.C.E. in Abdera, a Greek colony in Thrace, and died at the age of about seventy. He seems to have begun his working life by practicing a manual trade and then had the idea of teaching for fees *(misthos)*. He thus established the social status of the Sophist, someone who lived by transmitting his learning and who traveled from town to town doing so.

The Sophists' earnings seem to have depended on the results they obtained, as we can see from the suit that Protagoras brought against his disciple Euathlos, an advocate. It had been agreed that Euathlos would pay fees to his master only when he had won his first case. However, Euathlos was in no hurry to plead and hence paid nothing, and Protagoras eventually felt obliged to sue him. Euathlos then explained to the judges two possible outcomes of the suit: either he would win the trial, and that would mean that Protagoras would not be justified in demanding payment from him; or he would lose, and then Protagoras, by the very terms of their agreement, would have no grounds for claiming fees from him. If this story is true, we see that it is not quite right to call the Sophists the first teachers, since they were formally obliged to achieve results! Moreover, this explains the great difficulty the Socratics had in exonerating their master for having had as disciples two men of such questionable behavior as Alcibiades and Critias.

Protagoras came to teach in Athens, where he was a friend of Pericles, but his treatise *On the Gods* created a scandal there (rightly or wrongly; we shall try to decide), and Pythodoras brought a suit against him for impiety. Protagoras was condemned to leave Athens, and his works were burned on the Agora. This key event in his life prompts us to begin with a study of the scandalous treatise, or at least what remains of it, fragment B4.

From the famous affirmation according to which "of all things the measure is Man" (frg. B1; *Ancilla,* p. 125) the question of the existence of the gods seems to follow quite naturally, and Protagoras's agnosticism would thus follow from his relativism. In turn, the interpretation of the famous fragment B1 on man the measure *(anthropos metron)* would depend on the interpretation of the equally famous fragment B4, which deals with the impossibility of knowing the gods: "About the gods, I am not able to know whether they exist or do not exist, nor what they are like in form; for the factors preventing knowledge are many": their invisibility "and the shortness of human life" *(Ancilla,* p. 126).

This fragment was nothing other than the exordium of a book, *On the Gods,* which probably constituted the first part of Protagoras's great treatise on *Antilogies.* The general plan of this book seems to be indicated by a passage in Plato's *Sophist,* where the Sophist is defined as being essentially an *antilogikos,* a manipulator of contradictions. The Stranger invites Theaetetus to investigate the fields in which the Sophist reveals antilogies, that is to say the fields in which one finds "two contradictory discourses," as Protagoras would put it. At the end of the account, Theaetetus recognizes the allusion to Protagoras's writings.

The first of these fields was that of the invisible: the problem of the gods. Protagoras also studied the fate of the soul after death; we know he had written an essay titled *On the Underworld.*

The second field concerned the visible. Here, Protagoras explored the following. (1) Cosmology, "what the sophists call the cosmos" (Xenophon, *Memorabilia* I.1 [11]). No fragment of this text has survived. (2) Ontology (being and becoming): Protagoras opposed Parmenides and the argument for the unity of being. (3) Politics, that is to say, the study of various bodies of law. This section probably included the discussion on the death of Epitimus, who was accidentally killed by a javelin. The discussion presumably determined the responsibility for the death: was it the javelin, the thrower of the javelin, or the organizer of the games? (4) Art *(techne):* included in this part were reflections on mathematics, which for Protagoras was an art form (frg. B7 on tangents).

To understand fragment B4, it is essential to *situate* it within the totality of Protagoras's thought and not take it as an absolute. It is a fragment, and it is but one phase—the first—of Protagorean analysis. Indeed, Diogenes Laertius is careful to remind us of this: "For this *introduction* to his book, the Athenians expelled him; and they burnt his works" (*Lives of Eminent Philosophers* IX.52; emphasis added). Moreover, if we extend the context still further, we perceive that the treatise on the gods was the subject of a certain publicity: "The first of his books he read in public was that *On the Gods* . . . ; he read it at Athens in Euripides' house" (ibid. IX.54).

This last circumstance is important because fragment B25 DK, attributed to Critias by some scholars and to Euripides by others, is likely to have been written by Euripides. This fragment declares that the existence of the gods is a fable invented by a "far-seeing man" so that fear would prompt every man to respect the law of his own accord. But it is probable in other respects that a discourse that entirely rejected traditional piety could not have been the subject of a reading attended by such publicity.

We should in any case be well aware of one fact: if we had only a single passage of Descartes's *First Meditation,* we might thereby conclude that the author in question was casting doubt on the existence of the external world,

whereas Descartes sought on the contrary to establish it, albeit in his own way. Similarly, in the rest of the work Protagoras too may have been establishing, in his own way, the existence of the gods. The finest fragment in the world can offer only what it contains, and fragment B4 is simply the first step in Protagoras's undertaking. Now by good fortune we also have an account of the *outcome* of Protagoras's reflection on the gods: the myth of Epimetheus and Prometheus in Plato's *Protagoras.* The fact that we are dealing with myth should not cast suspicion on its content; Protagoras in fact gives his listeners a choice as to the form of the account, scientific argument or myth, and he implies that the underlying content will be the same in either case.

Thus, having started from a position of doubt, Protagoras seems to have ended with belief in the gods. Can we trace the outline of the path the Sophist followed in his thinking? To do so we would use the general outline of Protagoras's approach, which would have allowed him, starting from the establishment of "double discourses," to end by affirming the statement of a "Truth." This outline would have three stages: the antilogies; man the measure; strong discourse.

THE ANTILOGIES

We cannot say, with respect to the gods, that "either they exist, or they do not exist." I prefer to translate the passage as "neither that they are, nor that they are not," instead of "neither how they are nor how they are not," for it is hard to find meaning in the expression "how they are not." It has been pointed out, moreover, that we should not give *eisin* (they are) an existential meaning; it would in fact be absurd, we are told, to wonder about the "appearance" of the gods while their existence remains uncertain. It is easy to answer this last remark, and Protagoras's thinking seems to be the following: even if we could prove that the gods exist, we could not know how they look (Gorgias will use a similar argument in his *Treatise on Nonbeing:* being does not exist, and even if it does, it is unrecognizable).

The expression "either they exist, or they do not exist" unquestionably puts before us an antilogical formulation. This theme of the double nature of reality and of hesitation before two divergent paths is not peculiar to Protagoras. It is first of all a tragic theme (we may think here of Aeschylus's Orestes in the *Choephorae*), and it is also a moral theme (here the example is the famous choice made in Prodicos's *Herakles,* when the hero is invited to choose between a life of pleasure and life ruled by excellence). It is an aesthetic theme as well: we may refer to an account by Pliny the Elder *(Natural History)* of a picture by the painter Parrhasios: "His picture of the People of Athens also shows ingenuity in treating the subject, since he displayed them as fickle, choleric, unjust and variable, but also placable and merciful and com-

passionate, boastful . . . , lofty and humble, fierce and timid—and all these at the same time" (IX.xxxv.69). This last account shows us that we are also dealing with a political theme.

But this theme of the fundamental ambiguity of reality turns out to be partially reabsorbed, in the tradition, by the reference to the gods. Here the very existence of the gods comes within the provisions of antilogy instead of making us depart from it. What is the source of this crisis in the belief in the traditional gods? It appears that we cannot attribute it to the loss of confidence in civic gods, since this crisis was brought about by the defeat of 404 (on this point, see Edmond Lévy's *La défaite de 404*), and Protagoras in fact died around 422. There is one other possible cause: at about this time people began to look closely at the texts of the poets, especially Homer, discovering contradictions and improprieties. We can see the critical spirit developing; for example, Protagoras reproaches Homer, chiding him on his language and for giving orders to the goddess in the guise of a prayer, when he began the *Iliad* with "Sing, goddess, the wrath."

The formula "nor how they look" clearly sets the stage for the gods' *invisibility*, to which it is related. The problem of the gods' visible form surprises the modern reader, who conceives of the deity rather as the Christian hidden God: the church is highly skeptical about "apparitions," while the Greek gods are manifest gods. Doubt about the existence of gods thus means, first of all, for a Greek, doubt about their perceptible manifestation. Herodotus tells us that Homer and Hesiod, who were the founders of polytheism, were concerned not only with naming the gods but also with determining their forms: "These they are who taught the Greeks of the descent of the gods, and gave to all their several names, and honours, and arts, and declared their outward forms" (*Histories* II.53). And while Plato would later protest against the liberties the poets took in their presentation of the gods, he rejected the idea that the gods were in the habit of changing their form. "A god," Plato wrote, "abides for ever simply in his own form" (*Republic* II.381c). Thus the god has a form, and that form is changeless.

In fact, as Jean-Pierre Vernant recalls in *L'individu, la mort, l'amour* ("Le corps divin"), the gods have bodies. Of course a god's body is "glorious," if I may use Christian terminology here. In comparison with the human body, the gods have a "superbody," an eternal body, according to Vernant. A god's body has blood, but a wound does not cause him to die; a special diet of nectar and ambrosia provides him with the elixirs of immortality. Gods also feed on the fumes of sacrifices; this is why the Pythagoreans will say that one can feed on odors. The body of a god is resplendent and radiant, with a strength far superior to that of a mortal. A god can intervene without becoming visible, concealing her body in a cloud (as Aphrodite did when she spirited Paris away from combat in the *Iliad*), or he can reveal himself in majesty—although an excess of light can be as obscuring as darkness.

From Vernant's analysis, then, we shall retain the notion that the gods have bodies that can be totally invisible without ceasing to be bodies. This ambiguity of the divine superbody, one of whose powers is to make itself invisible at will, is not unproblematic. Problems arise with regard to statues, for example, when it is a question of representing a god: let us recall, for instance, Phidias's statue of Zeus, a chryselephantine statue at Olympia; fifteen meters tall, it was unanimously admired for its truly divine bearing (Phidias, like Protagoras, was a contemporary of Pericles). This statue, like that of Athena, has a human aspect. Similarly, we may recall Polygnotus's paintings, with their mythological subjects. These representations perhaps contributed to reviving the criticisms of Xenophanes, who challenged their anthropomorphism as early as the 6th century: "But mortals suppose that gods are born, wear their own clothes and have a voice and body" (frg. 14). "Ethiopians say that their gods are snub-nosed and black; Thracians that theirs are blue-eyed and red-haired" (frg. 16). "But if horses or oxen or lions had hands or could draw with their hands and accomplish such works as men, horses would draw the figures of the gods as similar to horses, and the oxen as similar to oxen, and they would make the bodies of the sort which each of them had" (frg. 15). This text is a good example of a Protagorean antilogy, a century in advance, and it shows the impossibility of having *knowledge* based on the presentation of a form, so far as the nature of the gods is concerned.

The series of problems about existence and form was to take up again a question already posed, one that would be canonical in Stoicism, for example. In Cicero's *De natura deorum*, Cotta the Academician says to Balbus the Stoic, "First you designed to prove the existence of the gods; secondly, to describe their nature" (III.iii.6).

The justification for the difficulty of knowing the gods, namely that human life is short, has troubled commentators with its facile air. And yet it does not seem to harbor irony. One might explain it this way. The gods are the "immortals"; really to know the gods, to understand their nature, would require verifying this immortality. Now our life—that is, the life of a mortal—is always too short for that; we cannot measure our lifespan against that of the gods, who thus remain outside our comprehension in time as they remain in space.

But there is another possible, and perhaps more plausible, explanation of the formula about the brevity of human life. Here we are presumably dealing with a literary reminiscence in Protagoras, an allusion to a "saying" of the poet Simonides, who was in many respects Protagoras's favorite author. Indeed, if we turn to Cicero's *De natura deorum*, we will be able to understand Protagoras's allusion: "Inquire of me as to the being and nature of god, and I shall follow the example of Simonides, who having the same question put to him by the great Hiero, requested a day's grace for consideration; next day, when Hiero repeated the question, he asked for two days, and so went on sev-

eral times multiplying the number of days by two; and when Hiero in surprise asked why he did so, he replied: 'Because the longer I deliberate the more obscure the matter seems to me'" (I.xxii.60).

Thus man's life is too short with respect to the extraordinary difficulty of knowing whether the gods exist and, if they exist, what they look like. With Simonides, as with Protagoras, the obscurity of the question of the visualization of the gods takes a very long time to dissipate.

MAN THE MEASURE

We must read the famous fragment B1 all the way through: "Of all things the measure is Man, of the things that are, that they are, and of the things that are not, that they are not" (*Ancilla*, p. 125).

We find once again the terms used in the fragment on the gods, on their being and their nonbeing, but we go a step further with regard to the balanced hesitation of fragment B4, "whether they exist or do not exist," since with regard to this being or nonbeing, it is man who will decide. The being or nonbeing of the gods will have man as its measure; that is without doubt the real blasphemy of Protagoras, who makes the gods depend on man, and not the reverse. That is why Plato will oppose him in *Laws*, where he writes: "The measure of all things" is God (IV.716c).

That man is the measure of the being or nonbeing of a god means that man may be either a believer or an atheist (like Diogoras or Theodorus of Cyrene), and if he is a believer, that he may have a quite different "idea" about *what* this god is. (We may recall that in his youth Protagoras had spent time with the magi of Persia, for whom the gods are personifications of natural phenomena; that is a different conception of traditional polytheism.) However, we are still left with a division of opinions, since "man" in Protagoras's formula has both an individual and a generic meaning. In the debates that this division produces over time, the adherents to one set of opinions come to outnumber the others. Thenceforth, one of the two discursive strategies used to express these divergent viewpoints (the discourses of existence and nonexistence, the discourses of "like this" and "like that") will be weak and marginal, the other powerful and majoritarian.

Now the strong discourse, that is to say the most widely accepted one, expresses a reality: it affirms the existence of the gods and sees them as the tradition of the city-state dictates.

STRONG DISCOURSE

The theory put forward by the strong discourse, though it was used, after Protagoras, for eristic ends, and though it uses rhetoric to persuade, is not the manipulation of opinion to which it will later be reduced. Instead it expresses

a large *consensus*. It has been wrongly believed that Protagoras contested the tradition, while in fact he was its most ardent supporter: the existence of the gods rests entirely on tradition, which has the stability of our renewed adherence.

To this some may object that Protagoras accepts and exploits the *belief* in the existence of the gods more than the existence of the gods itself. But in fact, in his philosophy, these amount to the same thing, since Protagoras suppresses the distinction between knowledge and opinion. What is true is collective adherence, which constitutes strong discourse. Such is truth, according to Protagoras.

Of course against this Protagorean conception it will be argued that this truth is not truth at all, that it is completely relative, that it is changing and far from universal. To be sure, Protagorean truth is not justified by its absoluteness (the Absolute and, a fortiori, a transcendent absolute do not exist for Protagoras), but it justifies itself by its quality of *usefulness*. It is a useful truth, to borrow an idea applied to Nietzsche by Jean Granier. The explanation of Protagoras's thought in Plato's *Theaetetus* is clear on this point: all appearances are not of equal value; appearance has a greater or lesser value according to its degree of usefulness (167a). The symptoms of health and those of illness are both real and true, but those of health are more useful than those of sickness, which are harmful. In the same way, all opinions are not to be considered on the same level: the Sophist, that is to say, the man who knows, is more clever than other men to the degree that he is able to replace a harmful appearance by a useful one: men of the skilled professions also do this, artists, doctors, and farmers. A doctor, with his remedies, replaces the symptoms of sickness with those of health; the farmer, with his fertilizers, allows plants to thrive instead of remaining sickly. In the same way, those who have mastery of the great art of rhetoric—the Sophists—properly speaking, by their lucidity and oratorical talent, will carry a better measure *(beltion)*, that is, a more useful one *(chrestos)*, and thus triumph in the eyes of the city-state by making their discourse into a strong, unanimous one, thereby giving it the appearance of truth.

Now the discourse that affirms the existence of the gods is more useful than the discourse that denies it, especially in the field of politics, as is shown by the myth of Epimetheus and Prometheus in Plato's *Protagoras*, the myth that was part of Protagoras's text called *Truth*. This famous myth shows that while Prometheus may be able to steal fire (that is to say, *techne*) and give it to men, he nevertheless cannot steal civic wisdom *(sophian politiken)*: "This was in the possession of Zeus" (321d). And the intervention of Zeus is necessary to give men, through Hermes, the art of politics, without which men either remain dispersed and are destroyed by other animals, who are better equipped than they with natural defenses, or they gather together and destroy each other, because they are unjust, and so they still perish. The politi-

cal art cannot be developed until men receive "shame and justice" from Zeus. These alone make the city-state possible, because they bring about order and the bonds of friendship. We must conclude, then, that for Protagoras not only is the existence of the gods posited but even divine Providence is restored. Belief in the gods is the necessary condition for solving the political problem, human survival. Thus, for Protagoras, a society cannot exist in which the majority of the people are atheists. The religion in question, then, is pragmatic and not mystical: it is a religion necessary for humanity if humanity is to survive.

If the existence of the gods is an appearance created by the persuasive art of the Sophist (as in the famous fragment attributed to Critias, but which is probably by Euripides, as we have seen, an echo of Protagoras's teaching in the tragic poet's work), through an immediate reaction, the organization of men in city-states—that is, political and social life—is achieved, and humanity is saved. It is only when man has created the gods that the gods can create man. That, perhaps, is what the succession of two moments suggests in the myth. After the invention of technology and before any attempts to found city-states, "man was the only creature that worshipped gods, and set himself to establish altars and holy images" (*Protagoras* 322a). Then, in a second phase, Zeus granted man the political virtues and thereby saved humanity. Belief in the simple *existence* of the gods has as a consequence the appearance of *providential* gods: thus the two degrees of Greek theology are established.

Here is a grandiose theory, a remarkable union of transcendence and immanence. Without this foundation of the divine, man cannot be man; this is why, in the myth of Epimetheus and Prometheus related by Plato, man is presented as being the work of the gods, which means that when he becomes aware that he is the work of the gods, man, by strong discourse, begins to create gods.

By quite different paths, Protagoras arrives at the same conclusion as Socrates, who says to a disciple: "And that I am speaking the truth, you, too, will know, if you do not wait until you see the shapes of the gods, but if it is enough for you when you see their works, to revere and honor the gods" (Xenophon, *Memorabilia* IV.3[13]). It is in this sense that, in Plato's *Protagoras*, impiety, with the injustice it entails, is the opposite of political virtue.

Plato, in a passage of *Laws* where the Sophists are under attack, seems to allude to the theology of Protagoras and Euripides when he writes: "The first statement, my dear sir, which these people make about the gods is that they exist by art and not by nature—by certain legal conventions" (889e). All in all, for Protagoras, the gods are the creatures of man, and if by mischance the gods do not exist, we must hasten to invent them.

GILBERT ROMEYER DHERBEY
Translated by Rita Guerlac and Anne Slack

Bibliography

Texts and Translations

Cicero. *De natura deorum.* Trans. H. Rackham. Loeb Classical Library.

Diels, Hermann, and Walther Kranz. *Ancilla to the Pre-Socratic Philosophers; A Complete Translation of the Fragments in Diels Fragmente der Vorsokratiker.* Trans. Mary Fitt. Oxford: Basil Blackwell, 1948. Cited in text as DK.

Diogenes Laertius. "Protagoras." In *Lives of Eminent Philosophers.* vol. 2. Trans. R. D. Hicks. Loeb Classical Library.

Herodotus. *Histories.* Trans. A. D. Godley. 4 vols. Loeb Classical Library.

Plato. *Laws.* Trans. R. G. Bury. 2 vols. Loeb Classical Library.

————. *Protagoras.* Trans. W. R. M. Lamb. Loeb Classical Library.

Pliny. *Natural History.* Trans. H. Rackham. 10 vols. Loeb Classical Library.

Poirier, Jean-Louis. "Les Sophistes." In *Les Présocratiques.* Coll. La Pléiade. Paris: Gallimard, 1988.

Untersteiner, Mario. *Sofisti: Testimonianze e frammenti,* fasc. 1. Florence: La Nuova Italia, 1949.

Xenophanes of Colophon. *Fragments.* Trans. and commentary by J. H. Lesher. Toronto: University of Toronto Press, 1992.

Xenophon. *Memorabilia.* Trans. Amy L. Bonnette. Ithaca, N.Y.: Cornell University Press, 1994.

Studies

Adorno, Francesco. *La filosofia antica,* vol. 1. Milan: Feltrinelli, 1991.

Bayonas, Auguste. "L'art politique d'après Protagoras." *Revue philosophique* 157 (1967): 43–58.

Bodéus, Richard. "Réflexions sur un court propos de Protagoras." *Les études classiques* 55 (1987): 241–257.

Dupréel, Eugène. *Les Sophistes: Protagoras, Gorgias, Prodicus, Hippias.* Neuchâtel: Editions du Griffon, 1948.

Granier, Jean. *Nietzsche.* Paris: Presses Universitaires de France, 1982.

Guthrie, William Keith Chambers. *The Sophists.* London: Cambridge University Press, 1971.

Isnardi-Parente, Margherita. *Sofistica e democrazia antica.* Florence: Sansoni, 1977.

Jaeger, Werner. *Paideia: The Ideals of Greek Culture.* Trans. Gilbert Highet. New York: Oxford University Press, 1939.

Kerferd, George Briscoe. *The Sophistic Movement.* Cambridge: Cambridge University Press, 1981.

Lana, Italo. *Protagoras.* Publicazioni della Facoltà di Lettere e Filosofia. Vol. 2, fasc. 4. Turin: Universita di Torino, 1950.

Levi, Adolfo. *Storia della sofistica.* Naples: Morano, 1966.

Lévy, Edmond. *La défaite de 404: Histoire d'une crise idéologique.* Paris: De Boccard, 1976.

Romeyer Dherbey, Gilbert. *La parole archaïque.* Paris: Presses Universitaires de France, 1999.

————. *Les Sophistes,* 4th ed. Paris: Presses Universitaires de France, 1995.

Romilly, Jacqueline de. *The Great Sophists in Periclean Athens*. Trans. Janet Lloyd. Oxford: Clarendon Press; New York: Oxford University Press, 1992.

Untersteiner, Mario. *Les Sophistes*, vol. 1. Trans. A. Tordesillas, preface G. Romeyer Dherby. Paris: Vrin, 1993.

Vernant, Jean-Pierre. *L'individu, la mort, l'amour: Soi-même et l'autre en Grèce ancienne*. Paris: Gallimard, 1989.

Zeppi, Stelio. *Protagora e la filosofia del suo tempo*. Florence: La Nuova Italia, 1961.

Related Articles

Ethics; Theology and Divination; Language; Utopia and the Critique of Politics; Theories of Religion; Sophists

PTOLEMY

ALTHOUGH THE ACHIEVEMENTS of Claudius Ptolemaeus represent the very peak of Hellenistic astronomy, remarkably little is known of the precise way in which the subject developed during the three centuries between him and the astronomer to whom he owed most, namely Hipparchus, who died sometime after 126 B.C.E. Ptolemy himself remains a shadowy figure. His synthesis of the work of his predecessors, together with his own considerable additions, continued to influence Greek, Islamic, and Western civilizations for more than fourteen centuries after his death, and yet our knowledge of his life is slight and uncertain. We know from his principal astronomical work, *Almagest*, that he made series of observations between 127 and 141 C.E., during the reigns of the emperors Hadrian and Antoninus, and the existence of subsequent writings from his pen is compatible with the statement of a later writer that he died during the reign of Marcus Aurelius (161–180).

Ptolemy's name tells us a little about his forebears. "Claudius" indicates Roman citizenship, possibly granted to his family by the emperor of that name, or by Nero. "Ptolemaeus" shows that he was an inhabitant of Egypt, descended from Greek—or at least Hellenized—stock. His writings give many indications that he worked in Alexandria, and none suggests any connection with any other place. He promised in *Almagest* that he would list the geographical positions of towns with reference to Alexandria's meridian, but when he came to write *Geography*, he took the meridian through the "Isles of the Blest" (the Canaries), since they had the advantage of being at the western extreme of the known world.

Beyond these trifles gleaned from his name and his works, we know almost nothing about him of a personal nature. The scholarly advantages of life in Alexandria, and in particular of access to its Museum, do not need to be repeated here. The Museum had entered a period of renewed prosperity under the Pax Augusta, had been well patronized by Hadrian, and would survive two generations after Ptolemy's death before suffering under the depredations of Caracalla. Although Ptolemy must have been indebted to this institution, we know nothing of his associates there. From *Almagest* we know that he was provided with observations by a certain Theon, and several of his works are presented to a certain Syrus. These persons are no more than names to us. In the last analysis, it is through Ptolemy's works that we must know him. Numerous legends that cluster round his name in Arab and later Western sources are without value. One theme is particularly common,

namely his royal ancestry. The idea stems, of course, from the fact that Ptolemy was the name of all the Macedonian kings of Egypt. By the 2nd century it had become an extremely common boy's name—just as Cleopatra was common for girls.

GREEK ASTRONOMY BEFORE PTOLEMY

Especially since the time of J.-B. Delambre (1817) it has been customary to disparage Ptolemy's contribution to astronomy and to suggest that he did no more than report on the achievements of his predecessors, in particular Hipparchus. This is unjust and is ironic to the extent that it is almost entirely through Ptolemy's personal testimony in *Almagest* that we know the foundations on which he built, and that he is supposed to have purloined. *Almagest* is the work on which his reputation chiefly rests. His writings on geometrical projection, on geography, and on optics would undoubtedly have given him an important place in history on their own account. His *Almagest* is his great synthesis, however. Its very name is from the Greek for "the greatest compilation" *(he magiste)*. The Arabs turned this phrase into *al-majisti*, which became *almagesti* or *almagestum* in medieval Latin. This summary of the whole of mathematical astronomy is presented from a very Greek standpoint, with its characteristically geometrical form, although it is now known to contain a strong Babylonian component of astronomical data—and the Babylonians had built their astronomy on what were primarily arithmetical foundations.

The first Greek attempts to represent the movement of the Sun, Moon, and planets by mathematical models used simple rotational movements that failed to account for the variations in the velocities of the bodies concerned as they move against the background of fixed stars. The planetary motion that gave the most trouble was retrograde motion, to which all planets then known (Mercury, Venus, Mars, Jupiter, Saturn) are subject. Their general drift round the sky is in a direction opposite to that of the daily rotation. However, as a consequence of the fact that we view the planets from Earth, which is revolving round the Sun just as they are, each planet appears from time to time to reverse the direction of its long-term motion. In other words, although each planet moves (with direct motion) in the general direction of the Sun, from time to time it slows down to a stationary position (with respect to the fixed stars), reverses its path for a relatively short period (retrograde motion), and then again returns to direct motion.

To explain this retrogradation, the geometer Eudoxus of Cnidos, early in the 4th century B.C.E., devised a system of spheres concentric with Earth ("homocentric spheres"). He found that he could produce a figure-of-eight motion by pivoting one sphere inside another, both of them rotating, so long as the axes were inclined to each other. To get a retrograde motion, it was

necessary only to carry this figure-of-eight around the sky on yet another concentric sphere. The details of this brilliant geometrical device are less important than the fact that, as a model to predict precisely the observed motions of the planets, it can have achieved very little. It was adopted by Aristotle, who was attracted to it by the thought that it mirrored the physical workings of the universe. In the form of the Aristotelian spheres, Eudoxus's model remained in intellectual currency until the 17th century and even later—almost two millennia after it was superseded astronomically. Even Ptolemy found it physically appealing.

The great change in geometrical approach to the problem of retrogradation came with the twin concepts of the eccentric and the epicycle. The idea of the eccentric is essentially simple: if a body—and the Sun was the body for which the scheme was devised—is moving at constant speed round a circle, then its speed as seen from a point at some distance from the center of the circle will be variable over the cycle. The Sun's annual motion is known to be nonconstant—in other words, the seasons were known to be of different lengths. It was found that a simple eccentric model can give a very reasonable approximation to the Sun's annual motion, if the scale of the model is carefully chosen.

The eccentric alone will not explain the retrogradation of the planets, but there is a very simple model that may be used to do so: the epicycle. If a planet moves around a small circle, and the center of that circle moves around Earth, then the resulting apparent motion will represent appearances in a qualitatively acceptable fashion. By choosing the values of the two speeds, the starting points of the motions, and the relative scale of the two circles, it is possible to get quite respectable empirical results for the movements of any particular planet. The same model may be used to explain to some extent the notorious irregularities in the Moon's motion. (This is so even though the Moon never enters a retrograde phase. In this case the sense of rotation of the Moon on the epicycle is the reverse of that of the planets.)

With Hipparchus (2nd century B.C.E.) Greek astronomy became a more rigorously quantitative science. Hipparchus was in possession of Babylonian materials—for example, Babylonian eclipse records and lunar and planetary theories—and through Hipparchus's writings Ptolemy obtained the same invaluable material. The Babylonian theories, arithmetically based, were of a level of sophistication unparalleled in any other civilization. Hipparchus's achievement was to combine the merits of the two different mathematical outlooks, for instance in his epicyclic theories of the Sun and Moon, using Babylonian parameters. He measured the parallax of the Moon (its apparent shift in place due to the fact that we observe this relatively nearby object from places at a distance from Earth's century) and found ways of measuring the distance of the Sun and Moon. His most important discovery, however, was that the so-called fixed stars do not hold their position but seem to drift

around the sky along courses parallel to the zodiac. This they do at a very slow rate: by comparing his own observations of the star Spica with those of Timocharis 160 years earlier, he found that the rate was greater than a degree per century. (It is roughly half as much again as this.)

By Ptolemy's time, the mathematical tools of the astronomer were highly developed. Although we think of trigonometry as a self-sufficient subject, at an elementary level having to do with figures in two dimensions, this is to overlook its origins. It grew out of the geometry of three dimensions, as that part of geometry that was needed for solving astronomical problems. As such, although Hipparchus had advanced it considerably, some of its most important results were made available only a generation or so before Ptolemy, by Menelaus. Ptolemy codified all this brilliantly, added a number of results of his own, and so put astronomy in his debt for more than a millennium.

ALMAGEST

Ptolemy's *Almagest* is in thirteen books, the first of which gives the necessary mathematics, including the theorems of Menelaus for solving triangles on the surface of a sphere. He uses the chord function where we would use sines, but this first book translates very easily into modern terms, and it set the pattern for future works on "spherical astronomy." He made full use of the sexagesimal notation of the Babylonians, dividing the degree into 60 minutes, each minute into 60 seconds, and so forth.

From the extremes of the Sun's declination he found a figure for one of the fundamental parameters of astronomy, the inclination of the ecliptic (the Sun's path) to the equator. His instruments were imperfect, and his figure was indifferent—in fact he probably allowed his admiration for Hipparchus to influence his judgment. In Book III of *Almagest* Ptolemy accepts Hipparchus's solar theory, and again there was little incentive to change what was a relatively successful theory. When he came to the theory of the Moon, however, in Book IV of *Almagest*, he showed his mastery of planetary theory. Starting from a careful discussion of the lunar theory of Hipparchus, he compared it with his own observations and found that it fitted well only when the Sun, Earth, and Moon were in line (at conjunctions and oppositions). He added extra elements to earlier explanations and produced a geometrical model that produced far better results for the Moon's celestial longitude than any before it. *Almagest* Book V ends with a discussion of the distances of the Sun and Moon, and includes the first known theoretical discussion of parallax, that is, of the correction it is necessary to apply to the Moon's apparent position to obtain its position relative to Earth's center. In Book VI, Ptolemy uses the solar, lunar, and parallax theories of the preceding books to construct tables for solar and lunar eclipses.

Before dealing with the planets, Ptolemy turned to the longitudes, lati-

tudes, and magnitudes (in six classes of brightness) of the fixed stars. His catalogue of 1,022 stars in 48 constellations, and a handful of nebulae, provided the framework for almost all others of importance in the Islamic and Western worlds until the 17th century. It was based on materials by Hipparchus that are no longer extant and took into account his theory of precession, but it was more extensive than anything before it.

Books IX, X, and XI of *Almagest* account for the longitudes of the inferior planets (Mercury and Venus) and the superior (Mars, Jupiter, and Saturn). Two different arrangements of the epicycle in relation to the deferents are needed, and since Mercury gives rise to difficulties of its own, further refinements were needed in that case. He extended in important ways the epicycle principle developed by Apollonius of Perge and others. One new technique was especially important to him, and yet it gave rise to much controversy in later periods. The epicycle had always been thought to move around the deferent circle at a constant rate along the circumference. Ptolemy introduced the idea of a motion that was constant as seen from a point that was neither the center of the universe (Earth) nor the center of the deferent circle. This, his "equant" principle, was all the more commendable because it meant breaking with the traditional dogma that all must be explained in terms of uniform circular motions. The power of his method did not save him from criticism, and fourteen centuries later we find that even Copernicus found the equant distasteful. Ptolemy's final two books deal with predicting planetary phenomena, such as first and last appearances, and latitudes.

Ptolemy was concerned not only to explain observed planetary motions but also to make it easy to calculate them. His *Almagest* includes tables to this end, and other tables he issued separately *(Tables manuelles)* had enormous influence on the later progress of astronomy, for they set the style for astronomical technique, first in the Islamic world and later in Europe. Ptolemy taught posterity the art of selecting and analyzing astronomical observations for theoretical purposes, although it has to be said that in this supremely important aspect of astronomy he had no real equal until Johannes Kepler came to analyze the observations of Tycho Brahe.

TETRABIBLOS

For astrology Ptolemy wrote what also became a standard text, *Tetrabiblos*. Babylonian astrological schemes were known in Roman Egypt. Hellenistic astrology was flourishing, and astronomical methods that were easier to apply than Ptolemy's, however inaccurate, were called for. *Tetrabiblos* is a masterly book, and in many respects a scientific one. Where Babylonian and Assyrian divination had mostly concerned public welfare and the life of the ruler, the Greeks applied the art in large measure to the life of the individual. The activ-

ity had been unintentionally encouraged by the teachings of Plato and Aristotle on the divinity of the stars, and in late antiquity many astrologers regarded themselves as interpreting the movements of the gods. With the rise of Christianity this attitude was of course repressed, although it flourished as a literary device throughout Roman antiquity and has been a characteristic of Christian Europe almost until the present day. Ptolemy's *Tetrabiblos* was thus a handbook for people of many different persuasions.

It opens with a defense of astrology and is ostensibly written around the idea that the influences of the heavenly bodies are entirely physical. In the end, however, it amounts to a codification of unjustified superstition, largely inherited from Ptolemy's predecessors. Book II deals with cosmic influences on geography and the weather, the latter a popular and spiritually safe subject in later centuries. Books III and IV deal with influences on human life as deduced from the state of the heavens, but they are oddly lacking in any of the mathematics of casting the houses that so obsessed astrologers in later centuries.

OTHER WRITINGS

Ptolemy's extensive writings suggest that he was engaged in assembling an encyclopedia of applied mathematics. One work of considerable interest is his *Planetary Hypotheses*, which went a long way toward providing a more sophisticated version of Aristotelian cosmology than the original. It made use of the paraphernalia of circles—eccentrics, epicycles, and so forth—but added the requirement that there should be no empty spaces in the universe. This led to a curious model in which the planetary distances were automatically deducible. They were of course wrong, but to our eyes they were impressively large (on the order of millions of miles). Of Ptolemy's books on mechanics, only the titles are known.

Much of his *Optics* and *Planetary Hypotheses* can be pieced together from Greek or Arabic versions. *Optics* includes some important semiempirical work on refraction, and it inspired the monumental study by Ibn al-Haytham (d. 1039). Some minor works on projection (his *Analemma* and *Planisphere*), as well as the monumental *Geography*, survive in Greek, as does his great treatise on astonomy, *Almagest*. A treatise on musical theory by Ptolemy was never directly influential, but Boethius placed much reliance on it, and so at secondhand it entered the European tradition.

Geography was essentially an outgrowth of astronomy, and apart from its comprehensive lists of places and their latitudes and longitudes, covering the known world, it is noteworthy for the ingenious map projections it introduces. For his data, Ptolemy acknowledges the work of Marinus of Tyre. Ptolemy corrects many of Marinus's errors but of course leaves many uncorrected, especially in regard to India and Africa. The influence of *Geography*

was considerable in the Islamic world (where it was translated into Arabaic ca. 800), but in Europe it was surprisingly slight until the 15th century. It was translated from the Greek ca. 1406, and thereafter a Renaissance interest in Greek literary works gave it a certain cachet. New exploration soon rendered it obsolete, but through the work of Mercator (1554) and others, Ptolemy's map projections greatly affected later practice.

A purely philosophical work that has survived under Ptolemy's name has the title *On the Kriterion and Hegemonikon*. By *kriterion* the author means not only judging but also analyzing the process of judging, while *hegemonikon* denotes a principle of acting, or exerting power. The aim of the work is to investigate the *kriterion* of reality, and the procedure followed makes use of an analogy with legal procedures and institutions, so that the human desire for truth, for example, is made analogous to the human desire for social harmony.

The epistemology is in no respect strikingly new. The act of judging is analyzed into sense perception, the impression and transmission to the intellect *(phantasia)*, thought (internal *logos*), and speech (uttered *logos*). Internal *logos* may in turn be mere supposition, or it may be firmly grounded knowledge and understanding. Like Plato—who is briefly mentioned—and Aristotle, the writer holds that knowledge, when clear scientific distinctions are made, is always of the universal. The work has a strong admixture of physiology and psychology, and betrays a concern to come to grips with the mind-body problem. Thus a distinction is drawn between the *hegemonikon* of the body and that of the soul, between the cause of mere life (especially the lung-heart system) and "the chief cause of living well" (the brain, "through which we direct our impulses towards what is best"). In regard to the second cause, the heart is said to be not even next in importance. The writer believes rather that the senses, in particular, sight and hearing, contribute more to "living well" than does the heart.

The brief text of this philosophical work has clarity and succinctness rather than philosophical depth. In subject matter it has scarcely any point of contact with Ptolemy's generally accepted writings, but in its didactic qualities— for instance its businesslike brevity—it does have a slight resemblance to *Tetrabiblos*, and no completely convincing grounds for rejecting it have yet been given.

All told, there are very few scientific writers, whether from antiquity or any other historical period, whose work so strongly influenced posterity as did Ptolemy's. Through him the mathematical methods of the astronomical sciences passed into the domain of the natural sciences generally, and this must be counted as one of the most significant of all events in the entire history of Western science, even outweighing in importance the technical brilliance of Ptolemy's individual results.

JOHN DAVID NORTH

Bibliography

Barker, Andrew. *Greek Musical Writings,* vol. 2: *Harmonic and Acoustic Theory, Ptolemy.* Cambridge, 1989.

Bouche-Leclercq, Auguste. *L'astrologie grecque.* Paris, 1899; repr. Brussels, 1963.

Goldstein, Bernard R., ed. *The Arabic Version of Ptolemy's Planetary Hypotheses.* Philadelphia, 1967.

Heiberg, Johan Ludwig. *Claudii Ptolemaei Opera quae existant omnia: Syntaxis mathematica.* 2 vols. Leipzig, 1898–1903.

Huby, Pamela, and Gordon Neal, eds. *The Criterion of Truth: Essays Written in Honour of George Kerferd Together with a Text and Translation . . . of Ptolemy's On the Kriterion and Hegemonikon.* Liverpool, 1989.

Lejeune, Albert. *L'Optique de Claude Ptolémée,* 2nd ed. Leiden, 1990.

Neugebauer, Otto. *A History of Ancient Mathematical Astronomy.* 3 vols. Berlin, 1975.

North, J. D. *The Fontana History of Astronomy.* London, 1994.

Pedersen, Olaf. *A Survey of the Almagest.* Odense, 1974.

Ptolemy. *Tetrabiblios.* Ed. and trans. F. E. Robbins. Loeb Classical Library.

Toomer, Gerald James. *Ptolemy's Almagest.* London, 1984.

Related Articles

Observation and Research; Astronomy; Harmonics; Demonstration and the Idea of Science; Geography

PYRRHON

LIKE SOCRATES, Pyrrhon (ca. 365–275 B.C.E.) wrote nothing. However, he played a major role in the history of philosophy, owing to his singular personality, his eccentric way of life, and his electrifying presence as a speaker; for those close to him he held a fascination that has been transmitted to later generations through the relatively stylized accounts of his followers. He gave his name to Pyrrhonism, a term that is broadly applied to the various strains of Skepticism, even today. He owes his renown no doubt in large part to the fact that the principal formulation in which the arguments of the Skeptical school are preserved—that is, in the writings of Sextus Empiricus (2nd century C.E.), one of whose works is entitled *Outlines of Pyrrhonism*—takes him as its patron. Sextus, moreover, was writing in an older tradition, that of Aenesidemus (1st century C.E.), himself the author of *Pyrrhonian Arguments*.

Pyrrhon's historical position has encouraged this equation between "Pyrrhonism" and Skepticism. The period he lived in was a turning point both in philosophical history and in history as such. With his teacher and friend Anaxarchus, he joined the eastern expedition of Alexander the Great, whose tutor had been Aristotle. Some twenty years younger than Aristotle, Pyrrhon belonged to the generation preceding Epicurus and Zeno of Citium, founders of the new philosophical schools of the Hellenistic period, generally said to have begun with the deaths of Aristotle and Alexander, which occurred a few months apart (about 323–322 B.C.E.). Before that period, there had certainly been no absence of critics to point out the shortcomings of human knowledge, but it is safe to say that various triumphs in the sciences, particularly in mathematics, had enabled philosophers, when they focused their inquiry on knowledge as such, to concentrate on questions about its nature, its origin, its instruments, and its structures of research and exposition, rather than on the question of its existence or possibility. The Hellenistic period, by contrast, was a period in which philosophers, particularly the Epicureans and the Stoics, became suddenly and vitally preoccupied with establishing that knowledge is possible, that our cognitive access to the world rests on an infallible base, which they called the "criterion of truth." They attempted to identify and describe that criterion in such a way as to demonstrate the accessibility of knowledge. This preoccupation, apparently a new one, leads us to suppose that in the intervening period an unheard-of and radical challenge had been issued, aiming to deny or question the very possibility of knowledge. And if

one were to ask who could have initiated this challenge, Pyrrhon, living when he did and with the reputation attributed to him, would seem to be the ideal candidate.

The scenario is perhaps too good to be true. We do not need to take the logic of Skepticism to the extremes of Theodosius, a 2nd-century physician, who reasoned that "if the movement of the mind [in someone else] is unattainable by us, we shall never know for certain what Pyrrhon really intended, and without knowing that, we cannot be called Pyrrhoneans" (Diogenes Laertius, IX.70), but we have to admit that the figure of Pyrrhon is shrouded in obscurity. His thought has been the object of many fairly divergent attempts at reconstitution. All the testimonies about his life and thought that do exist (and until 1981 these had not been collected) come principally from Book IX of *The Lives of Eminent Philosophers* by Diogenes Laertius (3rd century C.E.). This material contains biographical information about Pyrrhon and his disciples (the best known, Timon, is a satirical poet-philosopher of whose work a fair number of fragments have been preserved), about Pyrrhon's way of life and the impression he made on those who knew him. Many anecdotes—perhaps too many—about Pyrrhon are to be found there; these are often piquant, at times astonishing, always meaningful, but their historical value is clearly subject to reservation.

In these accounts we discern the beginning of a split between two images of Pyrrhon—corresponding to two versions of Skepticism—which will continue to vie with each other for a long time. According to the first, Pyrrhon is equally indifferent toward others and toward himself; he takes no care to stay out of harm's way; he finds no value in the sensory information and daily assumptions that ordinarily guide human conduct; thus he behaves as a bizarre eccentric. This image may have given credence to the idea that he had been influenced by the gymnosophists (the so-called naked sages) of India, fakirs whose exploits he had perhaps witnessed admiringly in his travels; this is also the image by which he prefigures what has been called "rustic Skepticism," the refusal to accept any belief or assumption, even of the most ordinary sort. According to the second image, which remains just as alive in the tradition, Pyrrhon is on the contrary a quiet and unassuming country man, rather conventional, living with his sister and his chickens, going about his chores, respected by his fellow citizens; this second image presages the "urbane" variant of Skepticism, which rules out any belief that could be characterized as dogmatic: the dogmata of philosophers and scholars who claim to know the true nature of things, the hidden aspect of phenomena. These two images may well come from a common root in Pyrrhon himself, and they may express a conflict between his deep desires and his awareness of the limited prospects for realizing them. According to one particularly good story, he had once fled from an attacking dog, and when he was reproached for having violated his principles of indifference, he replied that it "was not easy entirely to

strip oneself of human weakness" (IX.66)—which is another way of saying both that he was striving to adhere to his principles and that he should be forgiven if he did not always succeed in his efforts.

What seems certain is that Pyrrhon aimed to find, for himself as well as for others, an infallible recipe for happiness by adopting an attitude of *adiaphoria,* or indifference, with respect to conventional values. Though it may be true that, since antiquity, some people have seen this indifference as verging on *apatheia,* a complete absence of feeling (this is the rustic slant of the Pyrrhonian ethic), and others have seen it as verging on *praotēs,* or mildness (this is its urbane slant), the end to be achieved by these various means remains the same and is of an ethical order. Timon sees his master as a guide on the path of life and exalts him, asking him for the secret of his superhuman serenity. And Cicero, finally, depicts Pyrrhon uniquely as a moralist—one of the most imperturbable ever, with respect to what men consider good or evil.

The problem posed by the necessarily conjectural reconstitution of Pyrrhon's thought lies in knowing whether to include, among the means that Pyrrhon musters toward this ethical end, a line of argument that could be considered genuinely Skeptical, in the traditional sense of the term—that is, a critique of the possibility of knowledge and a systematic development of the arguments and experience that can produce and endorse what later Skeptics will call the *epochē,* or the suspension of judgment (the impossibility or refusal to choose between yes and no) with respect to all possible assertions.

The tight interweaving of the project of happiness and the critique of our ways of knowing seems to be solidly attested by a text that all historians of Pyrrhon consider fundamental because of its synthetic character, its philosophical content, and the fact that it comes, via two intermediaries, from Timon. The text is too long to be cited in its entirety here, but it is articulated clearly enough so that a summary, accompanied by a few comments, should not greatly misrepresent it.

To be happy, says Timon, three points, or questions, must be considered. "First, what are things like by nature? Second, in what way ought we to be disposed toward them? And third, what will be the result for those who are so disposed?" (Eusebius, *De evangelica praeparatione,* XIV.16.3). The order in which these three points are enumerated is already surprising: a Skeptic of the type that would become traditional would not inquire into the nature of things before having asked whether we have the means to know that nature. If he is true to the principle of the *epochē,* he will carefully abstain from any opinion about that nature, even if only to say that it is unknowable. (According to Sextus, such a "metadogmatic" statement is foreign to genuine Skepticism.)

To the first question, however, Pyrrhon has an original answer, which occurs in the only sentence in the text that Timon expressly attributes to him. His reply is that "things" are indifferent, indeterminate, and undecided, a

statement that seems to imply that it is we who introduce between and among things the distinctions that apparently differentiate them for us (for example, good things from bad ones—perhaps also white things from black ones, and anything that we may in general describe as being "thus, rather than otherwise"). The text goes on to say, strangely, that "for this reason, neither our sensations nor our opinions tell the truth or lie." Unless we change the text to reverse the logical connection between the two propositions—that is, to make the fallibility of our cognitive means the cause and not the consequence of the indeterminacy of things (a correction suggested by some of the most knowledgeable commentators)—it seems to mean that our sensations and our opinions, being in some respects "things" themselves, suffer from the same indeterminacy as things in general, and such a condition means, in the case of sensations and opinions, that what they tell us is neither always true nor always false. The grammar of the text suggests that this line of thinking is spelled out not by Pyrrhon but by Timon. One could conclude that Pyrrhon's thought has been inflected in the direction of a critique of knowledge as a result of an intervention by Timon, a disciple who was undoubtedly less devoid of philosophical personality than has sometimes been believed, and whose interest in these questions, hotly debated in his own generation, is amply attested elsewhere.

The second question in Pyrrhon's program, according to Timon, bears on the appropriate attitude to adopt with respect to those things that are not differentiated by their own nature. The "indifference" of the sage is a consequence that must be inferred from the "indifferentiation" of things: the correct response is to treat things as they are, and thus to be "without opinions and without inclinations and without wavering" in one direction more than another. The verbal translation of this attitude is to say of each single thing that "it no more is than is not" or else (if one must say something at all costs), to recant immediately by saying that it "both is and is not" or that it "neither is nor is not."

According to the third point of Pyrrhon's program, man will find the reward for his training in the leveling of his practical attitude toward things (he neither chooses nor rejects them) and in the balancing of his discourse about things (he neither affirms nor denies them). Timon uses two terms to describe this reward: the first condition attained by the Pyrrhonian adept will be *aphasia*, speechlessness, or at least an abstention from any assertory use of language; the next will be *ataraxia*, a complete absence of the trouble and anxiety that constitute human unhappiness. The order in which these two terms are presented suggests that the Pyrrhonian manner of speaking is only a stage on the way to a Pyrrhonian manner of living.

This analysis of a crucially significant account, which obviously leaves the door open to discussion, widens the distance that modern historians have often sought to establish between Pyrrhon and the Pyrrhonians who have

claimed him as their model. The quiet reserve of Alexander's wise, taciturn companion, this enigmatic observer of the legendary Alexandrian enterprise, isolated from other philosophers by his refusal to write, by his indifference to the tumultuous relations among the various Athenian schools, and by his scorn for the rules of the dialectical game, contrasts with the festering animosity of Sextus, who packs into his voluminous writings the entire argumentative arsenal, accumulated over centuries, against "professors," scholars, and "dogmatic" philosophers of every ilk. Moreover, is it not striking to note that the main target of Sextus's attacks, the Stoics, are philosophers clearly younger than Pyrrhon?

Perhaps Pyrrhon was not the first of the Pyrrhonians; perhaps his name has only been conferred on Pyrrhonism on the basis of a more or less contrived legend. But there must have been in him, as in Socrates, the matter and the occasion for such a legend. If the only surviving accounts were those by the sarcastic and biting Timon, from whose criticism Pyrrhon alone was spared, we might already credit him with exceptional charisma, but Diogenes Laertius tells us that he had many "disciples" (if we may apply this word to followers of a master who taught nothing) who tried to rival him in their scorn for humankind's futile agitations, and who passed on to their own pupils—who were intrigued by Pyrrhon's reputation—what they themselves had been able to grasp of the man. No doubt this was how the myth of Pyrrhon was forged, from one person to the next, initially by word of mouth: a myth that finally made him, through the centuries and right up to our own day, the silent Greek hero of nonknowledge.

JACQUES BRUNSCHWIG
Translated by Emoretta Yang and Anne Slack

Bibliography

Texts and Translations

Decleva Caizzi, Fernanda. *Pirrone: Testimonianze.* Naples: Bibliopolis, 1981.
Di Marco, Massimo. *Timone di Fliunte: Silli.* Rome: Edizioni dell'Ateneo, 1989.
Diogenes Laertius. *Lives of Eminent Philosophers,* vol. 2. Trans. R. D. Hicks. Loeb Classical Library.
Sextus Empiricus. Vol. 1: *Outlines of Pyrrhonism.* 2: *Against the Logicians.* 3: *Against the Physicists; Against the Ethicists.* 4: *Against the Professors.* Trans. R. G. Bury. Loeb Classical Library.

Studies

Ausland, Hayden Weir. "On the Moral Origin of the Pyrrhonian Philosophy." *Elenchos* 10 (1989): 359–434.

Bett, Richard. "Aristocles on Timon on Pyrrho: The Text, Its Logic, and Its Credibility." *Oxford Studies in Ancient Philosophy* 12 (1994): 137–181.

Brochard, Victor. *Les Sceptiques grecs.* Paris, 1887; repr. Paris: Vrin, 1923, 1981.

Brunschwig, Jacques. "Once Again on Eusebius on Aristocles on Timon on Pyrrho." In *Papers in Hellenistic Philosophy.* Trans. Janet Lloyd. Cambridge: Cambridge University Press, 1994. Pp. 190–211.

Conche, Marcel. *Pyrrhon ou l'apparence.* Paris: Presses Universitaires de France, 1994.

Dal Pra, Mario. *Lo scetticismo greco.* Milan, 1950; repr. Rome and Bari: Laterza, 1975.

Giannantoni, Gabriele, ed. *Lo scetticismo antico.* 2 vols. Naples: Bibliopolis, 1981.

Hankinson, R. J. *The Sceptics.* London: Routledge, 1995.

Long, Anthony A. "Timon of Phlius: Pyrrhonist and Satirist." *Proceedings of the Cambridge Philological Society* 204, n.s. 24 (1978): 68–91.

Robin, Léon. *Pyrrhon et le scepticisme grec.* Paris: Presses Universitaires de France, 1944.

Stopper, M. R. "Schizzi pirroniani." *Phronesis* 28 (1983): 265–297.

Related Articles

Ethics; Skepticism; The Academy

SOCRATES

SOCRATES' NAME ALONE suggests an image of the philosopher. Yet nothing that contributes to his reputation today applies to philosophic activity. Socrates wrote nothing, nor did he teach. He spent most of his time on the Agora, endlessly questioning his fellow citizens. The philosophers who came after him did write or teach, for the most part; they appear to owe him nothing. Plato was the author of the first philosophical opus ever written, the founder of the first school of philosophy; thus in his life and his philosophic activity he had little in common with Socrates. Yet Plato promoted Socrates as the embodiment of the philosopher.

This paradox reveals Socrates as the model—however inimitable—for philosophic life and thought, and it shows how hard it is to isolate the historical figure of Socrates, an Athenian citizen of the 5th century B.C.E. about whom we have a limited amount of relatively solid information, from Socrates the first philosopher, acknowledged by Plato and by the Cynics, the Skeptics, and the Stoics as their philosophic hero. Determining who Socrates really was is not just a modern concern: the question was being asked as early as the 4th century B.C.E. Addressing it twenty-four centuries later, we are not unduly handicapped, since we can benefit from the rigorous critique to which the various source materials offering testimony about Socrates have been subjected. A presentation of "the problem of Socrates" presupposes a preliminary portrait of the individual as he emerges from the points of agreement among the four major sources available to us, each more or less contemporaneous with Socrates' life.

The oldest—and also the most hostile—source, which gives us the only portrait of Socrates known to have been written during his lifetime (at least twenty-seven years before his death) is Aristophanes' *Clouds*. Two other major contributions, from Plato and Xenophon, came later; their accounts are more detailed, and vastly more favorable to Socrates. Plato knew Socrates during the final years of the philosopher's life, while he himself was in his early twenties. His earliest dialogues, doubtless written after Socrates' death, are called the "Socratic" dialogues; they include *Apology, Crito, Lysis, Laches,* and *Gorgias*. In these texts, Plato seems bent on reproducing his master's philosophical approach and ideas. Xenophon's testimony is quite different: in *Memorabilia, Economics, Apology* ("Socrates' Defense to the Jury"), and *Symposium*, Xenophon shows us Socrates arguing about concrete ques-

tions with a common sense that is often quite conventional. For a long time, moreover, the very ordinariness of the character Xenophon presents was taken to confirm the authenticity of his portrait. Last, in *Metaphysics* and *Eudemian Ethics* Aristotle provides information that is not derived from direct knowledge of Socrates; its value is based on Aristotle's close dealings with the Academy in his youth. While these four sources are sometimes difficult to reconcile, and do not allow us to draw an entirely coherent picture of Socrates the philosopher, we still need to acknowledge the many areas of agreement, especially regarding Socrates' intellectual biography.

SOCRATES, CITIZEN OF ATHENS

Socrates was born in Athens around 469 B.C.E. His father, Sophroniscus, was a sculptor, born in the deme of Alopece. His mother, Phaenarete, is said to have been a midwife. Although Socrates may have been trained as a sculptor in his youth, no evidence indicates that he practiced any craft at all. This does not mean he was idle: on the contrary, he spent his days carrying out the task a god had prescribed for him "through oracles and dreams and in every way in which any man was ever commanded by divine power to do anything whatsoever" (Plato, *Apology* 33c). His responsibility was to examine every human being he encountered, "young and old, foreigner and citizen," to incite them "not to care for [their] persons or [their] property more than for the perfection of [their] souls, or even so much" (ibid. 30a). As Socrates makes clear in addressing his fellow citizens, such an examination bears first on "the manner in which [they] now spend [their] days, and . . . the kind of life [they have] lived hitherto" (*Laches* 187e–188a), but it also allows him to test the reality of some knowledge that his interlocutor claims to possess, some quality with which he credits himself or some behavior of which he boasts. As he reminds his fellow citizens, he is "a gadfly . . . I go about arousing, and urging and reproaching each one of you, constantly alighting upon you everywhere the whole day long" (*Apology* 30e–31a). Xenophon's testimony is even more explicit: Socrates "was always visible . . . he used to go on walks and to the gymnasia"; he was prepared to spend the day "where he might be with the most people" and where all those who wanted to hear him could do so (*Memorabilia* I.i.10). Socrates' philosophic activity thus was a form of systematic interrogation applied to whoever agreed to submit to it, whether out of bravado, conviction, or a desire to save face. Plato's first dialogues capture the public essence of these conversations perfectly: we see Socrates confronting an interlocutor, but the two are surrounded by attentive listeners. Even if the exchange is protreptic—that is, even if it is intended to transform the respondent's soul—its goal is not so much to teach as to supply a model for any listener capable of profiting from

it. This condition justifies Socrates' claim that he was never anyone's master, for, he says, "if any man says that he ever learned or heard anything privately from me, which all the others did not, be assured that he is lying" (*Apology* 33b). Such a passion for the improvement or elevation of souls is no doubt the principal form of the love that Socrates said he felt toward young people (*Memorabilia* IV.i.2).

The divine injunction that assigned Socrates the task of constant examination is frequently confused with the inner signal that Socrates often called his *daimonian,* or demon: "It is a sort of voice that comes to me, and when it comes it always holds me back from what I am thinking of doing, but never urges me forward" (*Apology* 31d). This form of divine inspiration (which can incite as well as dissuade, according to Xenophon's texts) has remained one of the most popular features of the Socratic persona; it has also helped shape the image of a Socrates inspired by the god. But it may be advisable to think of the "demon" as a form of moral awareness that came to be attached, especially in Plato's account, to the divine forms of delirium and inspiration.

Apart from this philosophic occupation, we know very little about Socrates' life. At the time of his death, he was married to Xanthippe, with whom he had at least two sons. He may have been married earlier to the daughter or granddaughter of Aristides. He fought courageously during the Peloponnesian War, at Potidaea, at Amphipolis, and at Delium, where he served as a hoplite. This detail is important, for the citizen hoplites, who had to pay for their own arms, belonged to the first three classes of the census. The poverty to which Socrates so often referred was thus relative to the wealth of others of his class and to that of the Athenians who kept him company; it must by no means be mistaken for the destitution of a cynical sage. Socrates' frugal and modest way of life, his legendary ability to withstand cold and hunger, his temperance, his indifference to physical discomfort, and his deliberate asceticism (Diogenes Laertius tells us that "he used to say . . . that he was nearest to the gods in that he had the fewest wants," "Socrates" 27) must have been thought more plausible when credited to extreme poverty. It may be, too, that the modest antecedents traditionally attributed to Socrates (at first glance hardly compatible with the fact that he served as a hoplite) were depicted as humbler than they really were for the same reason.

Socrates boasted, it seems, that he had never left Athens, except when he was participating in a military campaign and when he attended the Isthmic Games (just once). He accepted the political assignments that fell to him as a citizen, although he did not have much taste for them (as he recalls in *Gorgias:* "When I was elected a member of the Council and, as my tribe held the Presidency, I had to put a question to vote, I got laughed at for not understanding the procedure," 474a), nor did he have any ambition to hold power. But when Socrates disapproved of the Assembly's decisions, he seems to have

opposed them without hesitation. Two incidents bear witness to this. In 407, as a member of the Council and while his tribe held the presidency, he objected to the Assembly's illegal move to pass collective judgment on six generals who had succeeded with great difficulty in disengaging the Athenian fleet from Sparta's blockade in the battle of Arginusae, but who had failed, after the battle, to retrieve the corpses and shipwrecked sailors from the sunken boats, as religious law required (*Apology* 32b; Xenophon, *Hellenica*). And a few years later, summoned with four other citizens by the Thirty Tyrants and ordered to bring Leon back from Salamis so he could be put to death, Socrates refused to obey and returned home, leaving his companions to carry out their grim task. These acts demonstrate his resolution "not to do anything unjust or unholy" (*Apology* 32d). During his trial, Socrates in fact recalled that he had preferred to take the side of "law and justice" (ibid. 32c) rather than support the Athenians and their unjust designs "through fear of imprisonment or death" (ibid. 29a). It is easy to understand how he could have credited the repeated interventions of his "demon," aimed at deterring him from political action, for the fact that he could live in Athens until the age of seventy without ever betraying his resolution to act justly.

Socrates' personality cannot be evoked without mention of the friends that surrounded him, friends whose fidelity was especially apparent during the events leading up to his death. Socrates referred to the value of friendship in many contexts, and he described the model of excellence that two friends eager to improve their souls can represent for each other. Socrates doubtless never had such a perfect friend, but the devotion and admiration of Crito, a rich landowner, and of his son Critobulus, the loyalty of Chaerephon, exiled among the Thirty as a "friend of the people," the fidelity of Hermogenes, Callias's brother, and of Aeschines, called the Socratic, all attest to the outstanding character of Socrates' personality. These men admired Socrates without reservation and imitated his behavior, to the point that Aeschines of Spettos, who later became a philosopher, was accused of stealing texts supposedly written by Socrates. Several foreigners were also devoted to Socrates (Simmias and Cebes of Thebes, Euclid and Terpsion of Megara, Aristippus of Cyrene); some of these men later founded schools (the Megaric school, the Cyrenic school) in which the Socratic influence was pronounced. Finally, another, less stable element of the "Socratic circle" consisted of a group of well-to-do young men closely associated with the most dramatic events in Athenian politics at the time. They must have felt a similar fascination with Socrates, and they sought his company over a period of several years. Among their ranks were the immensely wealthy Callias, Agathon, Critias, and Charmides, who later figured among the Thirty Tyrants, and most notably Alcibiades, who may have sought to seduce Socrates through his beauty, his noble birth, his powerful intelligence, and the force of his personality. The praise he offers at the end of Plato's *Symposium* attests to Socrates' clearly exceptional influ-

ence: Alcibiades says that when he is in Socrates' company he cannot keep from being ashamed of himself.

The major event in Socrates' life was the trial of which he was the victim in 399, at the age of seventy. An accusation of impiety was lodged with the archon-basileus by three Athenian citizens: Meletus, a mediocre poet; Anytus, a politician; and Lycon, an otherwise unknown orator. Anytus was the real instigator of the trial. A moderate democrat from Theramene's entourage, he had been forced into exile under the Thirty before rejoining Thrasybulus. He then became one of the most powerful men in Athens in the period following the restoration of democracy. The hatred he felt for Socrates was probably fanned by personal motives (rivalry for Alcibiades' love, rancor owing to the influence Socrates had had for a time over his own son) as well as political ones. The principal accusation against Socrates, as reported by Diogenes Laertius (who in turn is citing Favorinus of Arles, a historiographer from Hadrian's time), was worded as follows: "Socrates is guilty of refusing to recognize the gods recognized by the state, and of introducing other divinities. He is also guilty of corrupting the youth" ("Socrates" 40; we find a different formulation in Xenophon, "Defense" 10). The trial was conducted by the Heliaea, a popular tribunal made up of 501 judges. Plato seems to have been present, as well as all of Socrates' friends, among them Hermogenes—who may have been Xenophon's informant, for the latter was absent from Athens at the time.

After Meletus had developed the main points of the accusation, Socrates probably spoke out in his own defense. Considering that he had no proof of his innocence to supply, beyond a life totally devoted to justice, Socrates rejected the services of the orator Lysias, according to Diogenes Laertius. It is highly unlikely that the dialogue Plato reports in *Apology* between Socrates and his official accuser, Meletus, actually took place, but it is certain that Socrates sought neither to win the judges' pity nor to justify himself. After he made his plea, Meletus and Anytus, fearing that the judges might have been persuaded, apparently intervened to reiterate their accusations. On the first ballot Socrates was condemned by a vote of 281 to 221. Given the unusual nature of the complaint, the accused and the accuser were urged to propose the penalty themselves. Meletus asked for death, but Socrates, considering the services he had rendered the city-state, asked that he be given his meals in the prytaneum or, short of that, that he pay a small fine. The judges decided in favor of death. Before the sentence was carried out, Socrates was detained for about a month in the prison of the Eleven. He could easily have escaped, but he apparently refused to do so. His friends came to visit daily (*Phaedo* 59d); they were with him when he drank the hemlock. As the poison was beginning to take effect, Socrates raised the veil that covered him and spoke what, according to Plato, were his last words: "Crito, we owe a cock to Aesculapius. Pay it and do not neglect it" (118a).

THE PROBLEM OF SOCRATES

A critical examination of the accusations brought against Socrates brings us to what is conventionally called "the problem of Socrates." This term actually covers several problems having to do with Socrates' role in Athens, the specificity of his philosophic thought and practice, and the question of whether there exists an authentic Socratic philosophy. As it happens, the solution to this problem is closely tied to the critique of the sources of the information we have about the Socratic persona.

The charge that Socrates corrupted youth was in part inspired by the portrait Aristophanes drew of him in *Clouds*. In the play Socrates is perched in a gondola suspended in the air, his head in the clouds; arguing like a Sophist, he persuades the young Phidippides that it is legitimate to beat one's father. But the accusation can also be explained by the fact that the young people who sought Socrates' company, most of them idle and wealthy, found it entertaining to hear him examine the Athenians, and they tried to imitate him by subjecting their relatives and friends to the same sort of examination. As Socrates recalls in *Apology*, it is understandable that "those who are examined by [the young people] are angry with me, instead of being angry with themselves" (23c). The hostility toward Socrates that such exchanges reveal also betrays the uneasiness felt by the upper reaches of Athenian society at the idea that the city's traditional values were being subjected to rational examination, criticism, and evaluation. Moreover, in this regard Socrates was often confused with the Sophists, who had also carried out a form of critical reflection while professing to teach virtue.

However, another, more aggressive reproach accuses Socrates of leading a life unworthy of a citizen of Athens. Here is Callicles accusing Socrates in *Gorgias:* "This person . . . is bound to become unmanly through shunning the centres and marts of the city . . . he must cower down and spend the rest of his days in a corner whispering with three or four lads" (485d). The examples Socrates uses (he speaks of "pack animals, blacksmiths, shoemakers, and tanners" [*Symposium* 221e], since they always seem to be saying "the same things with the same means") also appear contemptible; Hippias remarks that they are "mere scrapings and shavings of discourse" (*Greater Hippias* 304a). Ridicule and scorn of this sort helped transform Socrates into a comic character.

Finally, a third complaint, more difficult to appreciate today, tended to depict Socrates as a sorcerer who, by asking questions that were at once simple and unexpected, left his interlocutors paralyzed, reduced to confusion or silence; in short, he bewitched them *(Meno)*. This charge may account in part for the accusation of impiety, which is otherwise hard to explain, given what is known of Socrates' conformity in religious and ritual matters. Rather than reproaching him for introducing new divinities (toward whom the city of

Athens was actually fairly tolerant) or for believing in his demon as if it were a new god, the accusation of impiety expresses disapproval of Socrates' critical attitude toward the values of the city. Even if it was not aimed at religion, Socrates' critique was probably perceived as antireligious. The same accusation of impiety was regularly brought against philosophers: Anaxagoras was subject to it, and perhaps also Protagoras and Euripides.

While each of these accusations at least confirms that in the eyes of the Athenians, Socrates "was doing something other than most people" (*Apology* 20c), another motive for hostility, not mentioned in the official charges, has been offered in several recent critical works as the real reason for his death: out of hatred for democracy, Socrates is alleged to have favored tyrants and tyranny. Socrates was unquestionably opposed to several of the principles and aspects of Athenian democracy as it was actually practiced (for example, the drawing of lots, or majority rule). The power acquired by rhetoric in the place of knowledge, the contempt in which real competence was held, the ignorance of those in power, the practice of pandering to the demos are indeed characteristic of all those who "manage the city's affairs" (Plato, *Alcibiades* 119b). But Socrates' criticisms are aimed more at the new men of democracy (rhetoricians and socially ascendant artisans) than at the regime itself. Probably exaggerated in the accounts of Plato and Xenophon, who were both rather hostile to democracy, Socrates' criticisms did not express a condemnation of the democratic regime as such, still less a declaration of faith in the oligarchy. His praise of the Spartan regime in *Memorabilia* and *Crito* bears only on minor questions and hardly allows us to deduce that he really admired the way Sparta was governed.

The proponents of the thesis that accuses Socrates of being a friend of tyrants are thus reduced to a single argument, based on Socrates' friendship with Critias and Alcibiades and the influence his teaching had on them. Xenophon himself explains that the Athenian democrats condemned Socrates because of his friendship with tyrants, an accusation that could not be included explicitly among the official charges because of the amnesty of 403. But such friendship, even though it may explain the circumstances of Socrates' trial, could in no way prove that he was sympathetic to the oligarchy; one could counter with the long friendship between Socrates and the democrat Chaerephon, and, even more tellingly, with the fact that Socrates did not turn away any listeners and that he taught no one anything that he did not teach everyone. If the lives of Critias and Alcibiades cannot be used as an argument in favor of the master who trained them, Socrates, who refused to be anyone's master, cannot be held responsible.

As for the other pieces of evidence presumed to prove Socrates' antidemocratic leanings (Polycrates' pamphlet against Socrates, published several years after his death, and the end of *Gorgias,* where Plato seems to be justifying Socrates against Polycrates' attacks), they emerged for the most part from

the enterprise of justifying and critiquing the Socratic persona that helped form the legend of Socrates; it would be imprudent at the very least to use such indications to assess the reality that those same pieces of evidence seek to inflect in one direction or another. To be sure, Socrates was condemned to death by a democracy, but that does not suffice to establish that he was condemned as an enemy of democracy. Nor does the hatred that a good number of democrats felt toward him prove anything. That hatred was doubtless directed at all intellectuals, and it attests most of all to the conformity that reigned in the years following the Athenian defeat. Since Socrates himself recognized that he would not have been able to live as long under any regime other than democracy (and since he himself was not the philosophical reformer in political matters that Plato was to become), he must have thought that, despite its failings in practice, it was no doubt the least undesirable of regimes.

Thus we have moved gradually toward an examination of Socrates' thought. This aspect, too, of the problem of Socrates is tied to the critique of sources, for our four major sources differ widely as to the definition of the objects or theses of Socratic thought. Aristophanes speaks of a Socrates who speculates about "the things in the air and the things beneath the earth" (*Apology* 23d), but such a characterization has a somewhat predictable cast, and, since other accounts contradict it, we can readily abandon the image of a chiefly "meteorological" Socrates. Aristotle's indications, on the other hand, have given credence to the thesis according to which Socrates was concerned only with "human things," morality and politics; they confirm the portrait that emerges from the earliest Socratic dialogues. As for Plato's and Xenophon's accounts, they disagree both on the conceptions found in Socrates' philosophy and on its style.

If the Socrates we see in Plato's first dialogues deals only with moral notions (justice, piety, the beauty of men and actions) and human affairs, Xenophon's Socrates, on the contrary, speaks of theology or theodicy and seeks to prove the existence of a divine spirit. In other respects, if Plato's Socrates opposes the ordinary morality of the era (in which virtue is conceived as the capacity to fulfill one's role as man and citizen and in which justice consists in part in returning evil for evil and good for good), Xenophon's Socrates basically expresses the moral values of his day. Furthermore, this Socrates implacably wins over his adversaries and always seems to accomplish the protreptic function that Socrates advocated for philosophy. In contrast, however conclusive the arguments of Plato's Socrates may be, they rarely persuade: Polos, Callicles, Thrasymachus, and Meno seem briefly troubled but do not abandon their own convictions. Finally, Plato's Socrates wields irony and double meaning; for example, after a long and wholly vacuous presentation by Hippias, he exclaims: "Bravo, bravo, Hippias!" (*Greater Hippias* 291e). This Socrates, who constantly plays on a two-pronged way of understanding

utterances (in their everyday sense and in philosophical terms), is absent from Xenophon's account. Xenophon defends a Socrates who is so conventional and whose responses are so predictable that one wonders how such a character could ever have troubled the Athenians.

Where, then, is Socrates the philosopher to be found? Hegel was one of the first to attempt to show that the real Socrates could not be the one Plato used as the main character in most of his dialogues. However, he did not succeed in establishing that the real Socrates is Xenophon's, for the Socrates of *Memorabilia* in no way resembles the philosopher we have legitimate reasons to seek. Still, it is not very plausible that in his dialogues Plato would have created a Socrates very different from the one all his contemporaries still remembered vividly. In addition, starting with *Meno, Phaedo,* and *The Republic* a new thematic cluster appears (the interest in mathematics, the conception of Forms) that seems to belong to Plato himself (and that cannot be attributed to Socrates, contrary to the views of Burnet and Taylor). The presence of these new themes and the implementation of new methods give us, within Plato's thought itself, a way of differentiating between Socratism and Platonism. Thus we shall end up with a solution that closely resembles the conventional definition.

It is perfectly plausible that the critique of the Sophists or the rhetoricians should belong to the historical Socrates. We can readily grant that the irony of the Socratic persona bears Plato's mark. But there is a body of Socratic thought that includes a set of theses in moral and political philosophy, that carries out the search for meaning and truth according to a certain protocol (which Aristotle's account describes reasonably well, as does Xenophon's, on occasion), and that can be fairly clearly differentiated from the set of "Platonic" theses. Whether this set of theses belongs to the historical Socrates (as is probable) or whether it expresses the first state of Plato's thought, influenced in varying degrees by that of Socrates (a hypothesis that cannot be ruled out), is a dilemma that, in the current state of affairs, remains intact. What I shall proceed to present is the core of this thought, conventionally called Socratic, whose primary methods are dialectics and maieutics.

SOCRATIC DIALECTICS: *ELENCHOS* AND MAIEUTICS

His refusal to allow himself to be credited with any knowledge is one of the most striking features of the Socrates who appears in Plato's early dialogues. Socrates reports in *Apology* how astonished he was to learn that the oracle of Delphi had designated him the most learned of men. It was out of a desire to understand the oracle, he says, if not to put it to the test, that he undertook to interrogate learned fellow citizens: politicians, poets, authors of tragedies, and artisans. At the conclusion of these conversations, which he himself calls "Herculean labours" (*Apology* 21a), he had to admit that what these men

know masks an ignorance that is unaware of itself; he also had to recognize, as he put it in *Apology*, that "what I do not know I do not think I know either" (21d). The connection between his systematic examination of others and the task assigned by the god is self-evident. But the fact remains that examining the lives and beliefs of one's fellow citizens and showing the vanity of the political or "technical" knowledge they claim to possess are two different enterprises. In the one case, it is a matter of refuting ill-founded or unfounded moral beliefs and of showing the connection between moral knowledge and moral behavior. In the other, it is a matter of critiquing the major forms of knowledge to show that they do not represent, or do not adequately represent, true knowledge.

This last Socratic critique is all the more astonishing in that it seems to be conditioned on setting aside several areas of knowledge (such as mathematics and astronomy) that Socrates, like Plato after him, might have recognized as models. Yet it seems that Socrates took no interest in that sort of knowledge. As Xenophon notes: "He did not converse about the nature of all things in the way most of the others did—examining what the sophists call the cosmos: how it is, and which necessities are responsible for the coming to be of each of the heavenly things" (*Memorabilia* I.i.11). No doubt he had good reasons to dismiss studies leading in that direction as vain occupations, even though he himself had undertaken such studies in considerable depth. ("He said that one should learn geometry up to the point of being competent" in measuring, but "he disapproved of geometry as far as the diagrams that are hard to comprehend. For what benefit these might have, he said he did not see," *Memorabilia* IV.vii.2–3.) But it is regrettable that the critique to which Socrates chose to subject politicians, poets, and artisans does not really tell us what reservations he had regarding mathematical or astronomical knowledge. Socrates indicates that the forms of knowledge he is criticizing do not satisfy the *kata ton theon* examination, an examination that is conducted in conformity with the order of the god and that undoubtedly aims to identify the conditions that make a body of knowledge authentic. These conditions seem to select for the only form of knowledge that Socrates does not deny possessing, a form of *anthropine sophia*, a human science or a science having to do with humankind. That such a science does not bear on any specific content, however, could explain why Socrates sometimes calls it nonknowledge.

It is important to stress that Socrates' interlocutors never interpret his profession of nonknowledge as indicating real ignorance; on the contrary, they continually solicit his advice *(Laches).* It is true that in a famous passage of *Memorabilia* Xenophon attributes specific objects of investigation to Socrates: "He himself was always conversing about human things—examining what is pious, what is impious, what is noble, what is shameful, what is just, what is unjust" (I.ii.16), but the essential element in this account is still the idea of examination. The fact that "human things" are the proper object of

Socratic study must not be interpreted, then, in the strictly anthropological sense of "human affairs."

The autobiography Socrates gives us in *Phaedo*, when he recalls his own interest in the "investigation of nature" (96a), and his disappointment with explanations using matter as a cause, seems to suggest that he could have conceived a theory of the soul in connection with a cosmological representation (to which the last myth in the same dialogue may also refer). There remains essentially no trace of such a conception, the expression of which is influenced in *Phaedo* by Platonic philosophy, but one may suppose that it shored up the Socratic conception of the immortality of the soul, of retribution after death, and of the possibility of knowing. If Socrates' philosophical contribution remains particularly closely tied to morality and politics, the hypothesis that he sketched out a theory of the soul makes it possible to explain how "human knowledge" in the sense in which Socrates understood it relates to criticism and the establishment of certainties, which is the proper object of dialectics.

In Plato's early dialogues, dialectics is defined as the art of questioning and answering. But this definition is accompanied by a well-defined procedure for questioning, *elenchos,* or Socratic refutation, which helps to make dialectics an art and to determine its capacity for truth. *Elenchos* starts from a thesis affirmed by an interlocutor who believes it to be true; the technique consists in showing that the thesis is in contradiction with a set of beliefs held by the same interlocutor. *Elenchos* thus proves to be particularly well suited to assessing the coherence of individuals' moral beliefs, and it helps bring to light the links between the various moral qualities that stem from virtue. But this form of refutation cannot really contribute to the conceptual definition of the notion being studied, nor can it help define the characteristic differences between the various virtues. Furthermore, the truth of the conclusion of an *elenchos* has no guarantee except the validity of a generally accepted formula (for example, all men desire happiness) that represents the starting point for the procedure. *Elenchos* thus can reach only moral certainty; it does not manage to achieve the foundation in truth that Plato's later philosophy will find in the intellectual apprehension of Forms.

The same requirement of consistency among the beliefs of a given individual allows maieutics, or the art of giving birth to minds—in *Theaetetus* Socrates says he learned the art from his mother, a midwife—to distinguish true conceptions from those that are merely illusory. The beliefs brought to light form a true conception when they are linked together in a coherent whole, one that can confront established certainties or moral "axioms" without contradiction and that entails no contradictory consequences. However, maieutics, which is a discovery procedure, cannot suffice to establish the truth of the set of beliefs thus disclosed.

Socrates usually begins his questioning, which shapes the material of his

refutations, by requesting a definition. "What is courage?" in *Laches*. "What is beauty?" in *Greater Hippias*. "What is virtue?" in *Meno*. But however celebrated the request for a definition may be—to the extent that it is referred to as the question "What is X?"—it still remains somewhat obscure. The definition Socrates asks for is not a lexical definition (which would give equivalents for the term and conditions for its correct use). It is not a causal definition either, but rather an essential definition aiming to exhibit a real essence endowed with the same sort of being as the particular phenomena to which it belongs and which are known by its name. This property, called *eidos* or idea, is probably the object of the "universal" definition, which, as Aristotle reminds us, Socrates was believed to have sought *(Metaphysics)*.

In another account, Aristotle assures us that these real properties, which belong to a collection of individuals, have no independent existence. This is an additional reason not to attribute to Socrates a theory of Forms similar to the one Plato will propose (Forms as permanent, independent, nonperceptible realities, the only ones available to knowledge); Aristotle, removing Socrates from the picture, will attribute the origin of the theory to a systematization of Heraclitus's legacy. But from another standpoint, the Socratic definition is not universal in the sense that it would proceed from a conceptual inquiry (Socrates is often content with a characteristic mark), or in the sense that it would provide a procedure allowing the justification of beliefs and the establishment of bodies of knowledge. In fact, the definition of a thing cannot be constructed from knowledge of its properties; on the contrary, as *Meno* teaches, one must first know the essence of virtue before determining whether it possesses the property of being teachable. This is the main reason one would hesitate to acknowledge a Socratic epistemology. A related reason is that, as a procedure for seeking certainty, *elenchos* seems limited to the specific domain of moral objects.

MORALITY

The Socratic conception of morality has remained famous because of the radical form of intellectualism it defends. Indeed, not only does it reserve to reason (rather than to conventions or desires) the task of defining the goals of human action, but it also defines the goals themselves as forms of knowledge. Aristotle, whose opposition to this Socratic thesis is well known, formulates one of its consequences clearly: "Socrates . . . thought that the End is to get to know virtue . . . he thought that all the virtues are forms of knowledge, so that justice and being just must go together" (*Eudemian Ethics* I.15).

Socrates' conception takes its validity from the paradigm of technical activity. Happiness, to which all human beings aspire, is generically defined as the goal of human action. But such a certainty, which figures in the Socratic conversations as a practical axiom, applies not to happiness conceived as internal

satisfaction or beatitude, but rather to happiness conceived as a form of accomplished action *(eupragia)* or success *(eutykhia)*. The import of one of the
best-known "Socratic paradoxes" (it suffices to know the good in order to do
good, and no one does evil knowingly) is easier to understand if one compares
moral action to technical action. Like the artisan who is concerned with carrying out his task to the best of his ability and who commands the means for
doing so, the moral agent, whose desire for happiness is also a desire for
eupragia, for straightforward successful action, and who knows that knowledge, intrinsically defined as virtue, is the only means for achieving his goal,
cannot deliberately choose to act badly.

Socrates repeatedly stresses the sovereignty of virtue and the fact that it is
a component of happiness. Virtue is knowledge, for the good of the soul that
it represents can only be knowledge; it is at once the principle of internal order and the means for correct usage, success, and accomplishment. Socrates
does not spell out the aspects or the objects of such knowledge, but one may
suppose that virtue represents, first of all, the exercise of a certain cognitive
activity whose effect is to maintain within the soul the optimal state that corresponds to its good and inspires actions destined to consolidate that good.
Such an identification of virtue with knowledge frees the latter from goods
that depend on the body and also from external goods (such as wealth, honor,
or power, which are essential to the practice of political virtue). Socrates
sometimes seems to want to assign an object to this knowledge, one that
would represent the content common to all the moral qualities, but it is hard
to see what kind of common knowledge would make true virtues of the various virtues—piety, justice, courage—that designate optimal forms of action
under specific circumstances. Socrates seems to indicate that such knowledge
has to do with good and evil *(Charmides)*, but he does not specify in what
way it allows each of the virtues to be characterized. It is true that Socrates
helped introduce a certain requirement of universality in virtuous behavior
by detaching it from the circumstances or from consideration of its beneficiaries, but that requirement results more from the conception of virtue as
"successful action" than from an ethical demand. In addition, detachment
from conventional morality is also the consequence of an increased requirement of reflexivity. Above all, Socrates does not depart at all from Greek morality conceived as exclusively centered on the agent.

The Socrates of Plato's early dialogues defends a fairly explicit conception
of human motivation. On the basis of the thesis that reason defines goals and
motivates agents, Socrates is commonly credited with a bipartite conception of the soul in which a rational component and an irrational component
(which incorporates desires of all sorts) are in opposition, along with a mechanistic moral psychology in which motivation results from a power relation
between reason nourished by knowledge and by desire. But this conception
does not correspond very well with what is implied by the Socratic thesis of

virtue as knowledge. For while Plato's moral psychology seems to recognize an irreducible set of desires, Socratic psychology tends instead to depict the rational soul as the true nature of the human soul. Ignorance of the passions and of the importance of moral character justifies the Socratic certainty that the improvement of moral knowledge would lead to the improvement of moral character.

The impossibility of acting against one's better judgment stems from the commensurability postulated among all the elements of the soul that contribute to human motivation. Socrates shows that *akrasia* (weakness of the will) does not exist, because one cannot be "overcome by pleasure" *(Protagoras)*. While pleasures may promise satisfactions, they yield, if need be, to considerations that demonstrate their uncertain or ephemeral character and weigh them against other more stable satisfactions. Virtue is then identified with an activity of assessment that compares the claims of the various pleasures without actually distinguishing them according to their origin. More than the reality of a Socratic hedonism, as it is presented in *Protagoras* in particular, this conception attests to the sovereignty of reason and to the specifically moral value of rational deliberation. A similar tendency to define moral behavior through rational deliberation—as Socrates said of himself, "I am not only now but always a man who follows nothing but the reasoning *[logos]* which on consideration seems to me the best" *(Crito,* 46b)—is precisely the object of Aristotle's criticism in *Nicomachean Ethics.* The same use of rational argument also justifies the belief in a future life and the immortality of the soul, even though Socrates acknowledges that he has no arguments to prove it. Still, even if the soul is not immortal, Socrates insists on the necessity of improving it, for the improved soul allows one to live with a better self, and the prospect of future pleasure is a good reason to prefer virtue.

SOCRATIC POLITICS

The foregoing conceptions lie behind Socratic politics. Socrates repeatedly emphasizes that he has not participated a great deal in the political life of the city, and he evokes the dangers he would have incurred had he been more active. But he also reminds us that, despite his remoteness from the political scene, he is the only man in Athens who is truly devoted to politics and concerned with the affairs of the city. How are we to understand the fact that Socrates saw his mission—that of questioning his fellow citizens and exposing their ignorance—as a plausible reason for declaring that he was "the most political" man in Athens? A study of *Crito* and *Apology,* along with part of *Gorgias,* allows us to suggest an answer.

The improvement of the soul, which is the goal of Socratic conversation, has political implications. Its result, a better state of the soul as a form of order or harmony, is in the first place the product of rational deliberation and

choice. It is also the true work of the art of politics, or the art "that has to do with the soul" (*Gorgias* 464b), since rational persuasion, intended to convince citizens to take care of their soul and to be just, can exist on a broad scale and in an effective way only in the framework of a city-state. Thus the moral quality of individuals is the very object of politics. When a just government, concerned not with enriching the city but with improving it, uses such persuasion as the foundation for political consensus, it "accomplishes" justice in a way that no one could with private exhortation alone. Socrates' moral intellectualism, or the conviction that if citizens have access to knowledge of the justice that the government is meting out, they will act justly, supports this hope.

Since political competence is comparable to any other technical competence, those who possess it should be entrusted with the governance of human affairs. Xenophon's Socrates defends the same idea, although the knowledge he speaks of consists largely in knowledge of the city's income and expenses, the military forces at its disposal, or its problems of provisioning and resources. Such a "scientific" conception of politics must have been surprising in an Athens in which people justified democracy by stressing that the essence of political community lay in the institutionalization of public discussion. But in Socrates' eyes, such discussion, unless it is illuminated by knowledge of the public good, consists merely in pandering to citizens' desires by means of political rhetoric.

Socratic "politics" can also be credited with proposing one of the first formulations of political obligation. In *Crito,* when one of his friends suggests to Socrates that he should avoid death by escaping from prison, Socrates insists on submitting the proposition to rational examination. If flight is just, he will flee; if it is not, he will stay in prison and accept his punishment. The Laws of Athens then come on stage to remind Socrates of his civic responsibilities. The duties of citizens toward the state are similar to those of children toward their parents; there exists no "right" to dissent or to disobey; Socrates' flight would thus be an injustice. Sufficiently convinced, Socrates then gives up the idea of escape. This decision seems hard to reconcile with the passage in *Apology* where Socrates informs his judges that if they want to let him live on condition that he will no longer practice criticism, he will be compelled to disobey. But this latter case in fact makes the limits of the duty of civic obedience quite clear; its benefit will be devoted in this instance to convincing the state of its injustice and its error. The duty of the individual toward the state stops at the point where the accomplishment of that duty threatens to alter the quality of his soul. In all other cases, the individual is obliged to submit to the punishment prescribed by the state, even if that punishment is unjust, for in fact it is never just to mistreat those under whose protection we have agreed to live. Political obligation results from a form of "tacit consent" that is freely given and confirmed by the mere fact of living in the city. On this point,

nothing is more contrary to Socratic politics than the theses presented in *The Republic* and *Laws*. There, improvement of citizens remains the ultimate political goal, but Plato no longer sees moral autonomy, to which each individual could accede through rational persuasion, as the way to reach that goal. For him, specifically political resources (the definition of a constitution, the organization of society, coercion), of which Socratic politics makes no mention, are what will make it possible to achieve justice in the city-state.

SOCRATES IN HISTORY

This brief evocation of Socrates' political thought will perhaps help nuance the conventional image of untrammeled confrontation between the philosopher and his city, an image that is still attached to the Socratic legend. For even though it is commonly believed that Socrates' trial and death at the hands of the Athenians account by and large for his fame, we must recall that virtually no mention of the event can be found either in the works of contemporary dramatic authors or in those of the orators Lysias, Andocides, or Isocrates, even though the latter were intimately involved in the political events of the early 4th century. Diogenes Laertius's remark ("Not long [after Socrates' death], the Athenians felt such remorse that . . . they banished the other accusers but put Meletos to death," *Lives of Eminent Philosophers* II.43) is of dubious accuracy, and it already belongs to the constitution of the Socratic legend.

Xenophon and Plato were the first to give Socrates' death the exemplary sense of the execution of a courageous man, a victim of his city's injustice. After them, Cicero calls the Athenian judges "scoundrels," and Marcus Aurelius labels them "vermin." In the Renaissance, the image of Socrates as a free spirit and a victim of intolerance is definitively forged. Rabelais, Montaigne, and Erasmus see in him a "perfect soul," a "great light of philosophy" whose attachment to truth and independence of spirit led to his death. But the myth of Socrates' martyrdom is constituted during the Enlightenment: "The death of Socrates," Condorcet says, "is an important event in human history. It was the first crime that marked the beginning of the war between philosophy and superstition, a war which is still being waged amongst us between this same philosophy and the oppressors of humanity" (*Sketch*, p. 45). Likewise Rousseau and Diderot (who, when he is locked up in Vincennes, calls himself a prisoner of the Eleven) see Socrates as a victim of intolerance and fanaticism. Moses Mendelssohn makes him the figurehead of the Enlightenment. The history of philosophic interpretations of Socrates culminates with Hegel (who stresses the "tragic" character of Socrates' death, the unfortunate outcome of the conflict between the legitimacy of the state and that of philosophy) and Kierkegaard. At the end of the 19th century—indeed, with the development of Greek history as a discipline and the more general understanding of the in-

tellectual world of democratic Athens—interpretations of the Socratic persona change in nature, becoming less "philosophic," and relying more closely on the critique of sources.

Socrates' philosophic posterity is found first of all in the groups known as "the Socratics" (Megarics, Cynics, Cyrenaics). Our knowledge of their thought is fragmentary, owing to the disappearance of many of the writings of those who were influenced by Socrates (Aeschines, Phaedo, Antisthenes), authors of "Socratic speeches" *(logoi sokratikoi)* or erudite dialogues that have come to constitute an authentic literary genre.

There remains Plato, whose thought developed in close contact with that of Socrates. Far from being a Socratic author himself, he is perhaps the one whose creative power did the most, involuntarily, to conceal Socrates' own thought, or to make it hard to disentangle. The effort to pinpoint the theses that constitute Socratic thought is an enterprise of modern criticism, begun in the 19th century; it is still basically a question of looking for Socrates behind Plato. The enterprise is nevertheless undoubtedly less hopeless than it would be in the case of the Sophists or Antisthenes, for Plato's philosophy and Socrates' are similar, in a way: they have in common the freedom and the isolation that Plato described as philosophy's share in unforgettable pages of *Theaetetus.*

MONIQUE CANTO-SPERBER
Translated by Catherine Porter and Dominique Jouhaud

Bibliography

Texts and Translations

Aristophanes. *Clouds.* In *Clouds; Wasps; Peace.* Trans. Jeffrey Henderson. Loeb Classical Library.

Aristotle. *Eudemian Ethics.* In *Aristotle,* vol. 20: *Athenian Constitution; Eudemian Ethics; On Virtues and Vices.* Trans. H. Rackham. Loeb Classical Library.

———. *Metaphysics.* Trans. Hugh Tredennick. 2 vols. Loeb Classical Library.

———. *Métaphysique.* Trans. J. Tricot. Paris: Vrin, 1953, 1970.

Condorcet, Antoine Nicolas de. *Sketch for a Historical Picture of the Progress of the Human Mind.* Trans. June Barraclough. London: Weidenfeld and Nicolson, 1955.

Diogenes Laertius. "Socrates." In *Lives of Eminent Philosophers,* vol. 1. Trans. R. D. Hicks. Loeb Classical Library. Pp. 148–177.

Plato. 12 vols. Loeb Classical Library.

———. *Lettre VII.* Trans. Luc Brisson. Paris: Flammarion GF, 1987.

Socrates: A Source Book. Compiled by John Ferguson. Open University Set Book. London: Macmillan, 1970.

Socratis et Socraticorum Reliquiae. Ed. Gabriele Giannantoni. 4 vols. Naples: Bibliopolis, 1990.

Xenophon. *A History of My Times (Hellenica)*. Trans. Rex Warner. London: Penguin Books, 1979.

———. *Memorabilia*. Trans. Amy L. Bonnette. Ithaca, N.Y.: Cornell University Press, 1994.

Studies

Benson, Hugh H., ed. *Essays on the Philosophy of Socrates*. Oxford: Oxford University Press, 1992.

Canto-Sperber, Monique, ed. *Les paradoxes de la connaissance: Essais sur le Ménon de Platon*. Paris: Odile Jacob, 1991.

Finley, Moses I. "Socrates and Athens." In *Aspects of Antiquity*. London: Chatto and Windus, 1968. Pp. 58–72.

Grote, George. *Plato and the Other Companions of Socrates*. London: J. Murray, 1865.

Guthrie, W. K. C. *Socrates*. Cambridge: Cambridge University Press, 1971.

Humbert, Jean. *Socrates et les petits socratiques*. Paris: Presses Universitaires de France, 1967.

Magalhaes Vilhena, V. de. *Le problème de Socrate: Le Socrate historique et le Socrate de Platon*. Paris: Presses Universitaires de France, 1952.

Mossé, Claude. *Le procès de Socrate: A Collection of Critical Essays*. Notre Dame: University of Notre Dame Press, 1971.

Vlastos, Gregory. *Socrates: Ironist and Moral Philosopher*. Cambridge: Cambridge University Press, 1991.

Wolff, Francis. *Socrate*. Paris: Presses Universitaires de France, 1985.

Related Articles

The Statesman As Political Actor; Utopia and the Critique of Politics; Rhetoric; Theories of Religion; Plato; Ethics; Physics; Theology and Divination; Anaxagoras; Xenophon

THUCYDIDES

THUCYDIDES OBLIGES READERS by supplying all the information on his own life that he considers relevant for this purpose. What he volunteers is, from our point of view, sparse. It is confined to his opening statement, that he was an Athenian and began writing on the Peloponnesian War as soon as it broke out in 431 B.C.E.; that he lived to see its end, and that he was mature enough at the time to understand what was going on; that he was in Athens and afflicted by the plague in 429 B.C.E. (*History of the Peloponnesian War* II.48.3); that he was a general in 424/423 B.C.E., serving in the vicinity of Thasos and Amphipolis, where he had some interest in gold mines and thus considerable influence among the local upper classes; and that he spent twenty years in exile after his service at Amphipolis. We learn his father's name, Olorus, only incidentally, when he identifies himself by his full name in connection with his generalship. In short, Thucydides tells us just enough to establish his credentials as a historian—or more precisely, as an accurate reporter of the events of his own time—specifically because he personally experienced the Peloponnesian War in its entirety. We know the date of his birth only by inference from the date of his generalship: since it is likely that a general had to be at least thirty years of age at the time of his election, Thucydides cannot have been born later than 454 B.C.E. Similarly, he will have died after the end of the Peloponnesian War (404/403 B.C.E.), since he tells us that he lived through the whole of it. For other data about his life—that he came from an aristocratic family related to that of Miltiades and Cimon, which had Thracian connections, and that he belonged to the deme Halimous (not far from the modern airport of Athens)—we depend on what later biographers, especially Marcellinus (4th to 5th century of our era), have preserved for us. Thucydides himself apparently did not consider these details relevant to his enterprise.

Although Thucydides is more forthcoming with biographical data than is Herodotus, many aspects we should have liked to hear about remain unaddressed in any credible fashion even by later authors. What kind of education did he have? Who were his friends? Was he married, and if so, to whom? Did he have children? What did he do before the Peloponnesian War broke out? What did he do between his recovery from the plague and his generalship? What mechanism sent him into exile? What were his movements during his twenty years of exile? Who were his major informants?

A question that has occupied modern scholars for a long time is the chro-

nology of the composition of his work. Even a superficial reader will notice that Thucydides' opening statement, namely that he began his work as soon as the war broke out, cannot mean that he wrote what he did at the time that each event happened and in the sequence in which it has come down to us: statements such as those about the Sicilian Expedition and the end of the war, which are appended to his estimate of Pericles (II.65.11–12) or appear at the opening of the so-called second preface at V.26, presuppose that he outlived some of the events he described. At what time did he write these sections? When did he compose the introductory section on past events, the *archaiologia*, through which he wishes to prove the greatness of the Peloponnesian War? When was the so-called *pentekontaēteia* written, which describes the growth of Athenian power? All we can know is that he must have revised at least part of his work before he reached the end point he had envisioned for it but never attained: his account breaks off abruptly in the middle of a sentence in his narrative of events of 411 B.C.E. and is taken up precisely at that point by Xenophon's *Hellenica*. Intensive research has shown us what passages must have been inserted at certain points, but it has not been and cannot be definitively established at what period larger sections were composed. Moreover, attempts at detecting changing historical perspectives, which might help differentiate earlier strata from later, have not been successful, since it is difficult to demonstrate that Thucydides ever changed his mind on fundamental historical principles.

Unlike his only major predecessor, Herodotus, Thucydides selects as a theme not the recent past but the history of his own time, as he and his contemporaries experienced it. What prompted him to do this can be reliably inferred from his insistence on accuracy and precision in his own account of the Peloponnesian War and his protestations that these criteria cannot be expected of a study of the past. This suggests that the present was the only period on which it was possible to get precise and controllable information. That he was an Athenian is as important as the fact that the Athenians exiled him: it explains any bias—for Athens as well as against it—that a reader might detect in his writing. Moreover, he treats his exile not as the hardship it undoubtedly was, as it would have been for anyone in antiquity, but as an opportunity, in his quest for accuracy, to gain access to both sides in the Peloponnesian War. For apparently no other reason than to establish his credibility, he emphasizes his intellectual maturity at the outbreak of the war and the fact that he lived to see its end twenty-seven years later. He offers no apology for his failure at Amphipolis despite his military experience and his standing among Thracian tribes, even at the risk of giving his political or personal enemies ammunition for censure. There is no complaint and no self-pity; the information is given to supply his reader with a clue to his competence. Similarly, his statement that he succumbed to the plague bolsters his authority to speak about that. In short, Thucydides refers to only those of his

vital statistics that establish his credentials as an accurate reporter; the data he regards as important are given without concern for their consequences on the reader's estimate of Thucydides' personal culpability.

Consistent with this penchant for dry objectivity is Thucydides' statement of his aim and methods. He discusses his method under two headings, speeches and narrative. What he has to say about his narrative is more easily understood than his statement about speeches: "As for the factual side of what happened in the war, the right thing to do seemed to me to base my report not on information gathered from just any witness, nor on my own impressions; but to follow up with all possible accuracy in every detail both what I myself witnessed and what I learned from others. This procedure was laborious, because those present at any given event did not say the same thing about the same points, but their statements were colored by sympathy or memory favoring one side or the other" (I.22.2−3).

The speeches are more problematic because the modern reader is unaccustomed to having so much importance attached to a direct report of public utterances. Moreover, accuracy in reporting speeches was infinitely harder to attain in an age without radio, television, and tape recorders. Thucydides was aware of this problem: "It was as difficult for me to remember accurately the language used in the speeches I myself heard delivered as it was for those who reported to me from elsewhere" (I.22.1). Why, then, did he find it important to include speeches in his work at all? There is no explicit answer to this question anywhere in his eight books, suggesting that he took the importance of including them for granted. Accordingly, we must try to find our own answer by combining his methodological statement on speeches with his practice in the body of his work.

"I have included in my work how each speaker seemed to me to come to grips with the issues that faced him, keeping as closely as possible to the general thrust of what he actually said." This constitutes a disavowal of verbatim accuracy and claims merely (a) that a given speech in the written text accurately reflects the attitude of a speaker toward the course of action he advocated; (b) that it was addressed to the situation that is its context in Thucydides; and (c) that it adheres as literally as possible to the spoken text of the speaker. But what are we to make of the phrase "seemed to me to come to grips"? Is this not an admission on the part of Thucydides that it was ultimately he who composed the speeches he put into the mouth of others? And if so, what objective historical value can we attach to them?

The response to these fundamental questions is decisive for our estimate of Thucydides as a historian. A partial answer emerges from his usual (but not universal) practice of presenting speeches in antithetical pairs: when the point has been reached at which a major decision needs to be taken, he frequently has a representative of one of the interested parties look at the situation from his vantage point, to be followed at once by a speech presenting the counter-

arguments raised by the opposing interested party. A few examples will help to illustrate the point.

The first pair of speeches in his work (I.31–44) sheds light on the problems facing the Athenians as a result of Corcyra's request for an alliance against Corinth in 433 B.C.E. Interestingly enough, no Athenian speech is reported. The first speech (I.32–36) is attributed to unnamed Corcyreans, who not only air their grievances against Corinth and argue that by complying Athens would help an injured party, but also hold out as a lure the advantages that an alliance with the second most powerful navy in the Greek world would bring to Athens, without violating the terms of the Thirty-Years' Peace. The complementary speech (I.37–43) is given by unnamed Corinthians. After refuting the Corcyreans' charges against them, they point to the dire consequences an Athenian alliance with Corcyra would have on Athens's relations with Corinth. They impress the Athenians sufficiently that they accommodate the Corcyreans by agreeing to only a defensive alliance with them, which, in the immediate sequel, leads to a naval encounter between Athenians and Corinthians at the Sybota Islands (I.54), but ultimately leads to the outbreak of the Peloponnesian War.

Are these two speeches historical? Although there is no external evidence to confirm or refute Thucydides, there is no reason to reject their historicity. Similarly, we have no way of checking whether the arguments Thucydides attributes to the speakers here were actually made by them. But it is clear that the Corcyreans make out the best possible case to tempt the Athenians with their offer, and that the equally cogent counterarguments of the Corinthians are borne out by the events that followed. Furthermore, no narrative could have depicted the Athenian dilemma as graphically as these two speeches.

There are two further points. First, the decision on what speeches to insert into his narrative from among the many that were given can only have been Thucydides' alone, and his choices must have been motivated by considerations other than the desire to be complete as well as accurate in his account. Evidently his view of "accuracy" included making as precise a presentation as possible of a situation whose full significance could be communicated only by having the living arguments of both sides involved supplement his own narrative. By proceeding in this way he also isolates the issues in each situation, but—and this is important—it is the situation as seen through the historian's eyes.

The second point is: why did Thucydides choose the speeches of the Corinthians to oppose the Corcyreans when he could equally well have chosen, for example, the speech of an Athenian opposed to foreign entanglements on the ground that they would ultimately lead to war with Sparta? Thucydides may have chosen the Corinthians not only to remain faithful to historical reality but also to demonstrate how a local quarrel between two states on the periphery of Spartan-Athenian relations could lead to the general conflagration that

it did. The fact that he motivates the presence in Athens of the Corinthians merely by their awareness of the possible consequences of an Athenian-Corcyrean alliance stresses the urgency of an issue that the Athenians themselves did not fully recognize. In addition, the two speeches enable Thucydides to make an indirect "philosophical" statement on the general historical truths he sees embedded in the concrete situation: momentous results may come from small local beginnings.

All paired speeches in Thucydides serve similar purposes. The proper treatment of allies, for example, presents a fundamental problem of imperial policy to the Athenians after the suppression of the revolt at Mytilene: would a harsh treatment of subdued rebels or a more compassionate one be more conducive to deterring recurrence? The former course of action had already been voted by the Assembly when it was decided to reconsider the issue. Thucydides reports none of the speeches that must have been delivered at the first debate; although he tells us that "different views were expressed by different speakers" at the second debate (III.36.6), he reports only those of the influential demagogue Cleon and of Diodotus (otherwise unknown) at the second Assembly meeting, even though both had already presented their opposing views in the earlier debate. Why he did this can only be guessed; presumably the second debate established a sharper contrast between their opposing views than the first had done. Cleon, maligned by Thucydides as "the most violent citizen," attacks excessive discussion and argues that only the fear of harsh treatment can teach the allies to accept Athenian rule. Diodotus welcomes deliberation and discussion as a prelude to intelligent action; no law, he argues, and not even the death penalty, has ever inhibited human nature from pursuing its impulses. A peaceful solution, he suggests, will not deprive Athens of its future revenue from Mytilene, and a policy of generosity toward the lower classes, the demos, who, he claims, are sympathetic toward the Athenian democracy in all the states of the empire, will prevent the upper class from any future attempts at rebellion.

By choosing these two speakers, Thucydides achieves a multiple effect. In the first place, he pinpoints the issue as centered on the question of the politically most effective way of handling rebels. Second, by excluding other speeches made on this occasion, some of which will doubtless have pleaded for a gentler treatment of the captured Mytileneans on humanitarian grounds, he shows that Cleon's motion could be refuted and defeated only by another tough argument based on the rebels' usefulness to the state. Third, by branding Cleon as "violent" before reporting his speech and by presenting him as opposed to discussion, he reveals his own sympathy for the rational argument of Diodotus against the blind emotionalism of Cleon. Fourth, at the same time he also wistfully notes the tragic aspect of the human condition, which has to hide its nobler moral impulses behind a curtain of political usefulness in order to prevail. In other words, a debate on a practical political problem is

manipulated in a way also to yield a "philosophical" statement on human nature, which remains impervious to conventional laws or penalties, and on the human condition, which permits moral action only when it is also politically advantageous.

Issues have no objective existence. They have reality only once they are recognized as issues by an intelligent observer. The observer in this case is, of course, Thucydides, who has his identification of an issue confirmed by two of the agents involved in it. Since it would have been impossible as well as undesirable for Thucydides to report any and every speech delivered during the Peloponnesian War, his activity compelled him to select the events that he regarded as crucial enough to be presented as issues. To the extent that he has to work under this constraint, an element of subjectivity is bound to appear in his report.

Moreover, what applies to speeches also applies (in a way not explained by Thucydides) to the narrative. However good Thucydides' own memory may have been, and however accurately he may have checked it as well as the information he received from others, the decision on which facts to include as relevant to the whole can only have been his. This means that, as modern readers, we depend for our knowledge of the past on the judgments of a historian who experienced it, and the relevance of what is to be included is subject to his choice; only rarely can we check his judgment against external sources. The great merit of Thucydides lies in his serious effort to stay within the limits of objective historiography and his recognition of the subjective element necessarily inherent in his enterprise. The sum total of issues identified and the observations made on them in speeches enables us to isolate the view of history taken by the historian. His selection of facts, the way he relates them to one another, the occasions he selects for the insertion of speeches, and the persons he selects for delivering arguments, which, though partly their own, nevertheless bear the historian's stamp—all these factors enable Thucydides to convey to the reader what significance he sees in the historical process.

This leads us to the question of what significance Thucydides saw in his history. While he is explicit in his estimates of such men as Pericles, Cleon, Brasidas, Hermocrates, Nicias, Antiphon, and some others, most of his views are so firmly embedded in his narrative of events or in the words he attributes to the speakers that the facts themselves speak more powerfully than the interpretation an outsider living centuries later can give to them. What can interpretation say about the significance of the plague, described at II.47.3–53? How can we express the meaning of civil discord *(stasis)* beyond what we read about it in Corcyra, at III.82–83? The meaning is unequivocal, even though it is communicated only through a statement of the unadorned facts. It is different with other questions he seems to address, and to which only close interpretation or juxtaposition of different passages and contexts can give an uncertain answer. To what factors does Thucydides attribute the out-

break of the Peloponnesian War? Could it have been avoided? Could it have ended differently than it did? To what extent is man master of his fortune? Does Thucydides believe that human morality declined as the war went on? What role does reason play, and what role do emotion and passion play, in human affairs? Is democracy reconcilable with empire?

We know from Thucydides' own opening statements that he sensed from the beginning that the Peloponnesian War would be the most momentous disturbance the Greek world had ever seen, and he spends the first nineteen chapters of his work proving the point. Moreover, he censures past historians for having been too cavalier in not ferreting out facts from reliable evidence, and for having shown more concern to make their tales arresting and entertaining (I.20). Against them he maintains that he has meticulously sifted what evidence he found, to present an account that may indeed be less enjoyable but nevertheless useful to those "who will wish to gain a clear view of the events of the past and, in future, of the events which, human affairs being what they are, will again be like or very similar to them" (I.22.4).

He does not imply that history has a circular movement but merely suggests that the immutability of the very humanity of man will guarantee that future generations can learn from the experiences of his own. Some of Thucydides' general observations are unremarkable, e.g., that man is fallible, that life takes many unexpected turns, that hardships will always beset men in times of civil strife, that men have the tendency to exaggerate their assets. But there are some interesting views on the parameters that limit human existence. No human inventiveness, he tells us, could cope with the plague; the fall of Torone could not be explained in human terms; and he has Hermocrates brand as "beyond human power" the realization of the desire of some Sicilians to see Syracuse both humbled and preserved. It is in these passages, if in any, especially in his description of the fall of Torone, that Thucydides comes close to recognizing the existence of a transcendent power against which human efforts are of no avail. Other human limitations are inherent in the biological nature of man: the plague is said to have been too severe for "human nature" to endure, and Nicias's troops, "having achieved what humans can, have suffered what they cannot endure."

By far the most momentous use of the "human" element in history, however, is in the explanation of the development of empire. The locus classicus is the Athenians' defense of their empire in their address to the First Lacedaemonian Congress: "We have done nothing extraordinary or different from the way men act, if we have accepted an empire that was given to us, and if we did not give it up under the pressure of the [three] most potent motives: prestige, fear, and self-interest. We were not the first to display this attitude, but it has always been a rule that the weaker must be kept down by the greater power. At the same time, we regarded ourselves as worthy and were so regarded by you, until in calculating your interests you are now using the

argument from justice, which no one has ever advanced to inhibit his lust for more when he had the chance of gaining his ends by force. Those men deserve praise, who once they have made use of human nature to establish control over others, follow justice more than the power at their disposal requires" (I.76.2–3).

The Athenians thus ground imperialism in a force that is ineradicably given as a constant element in the human animal. Since prestige, fear, and self-interest are ingrained in human nature, we expect them to explain not only Athenian imperialism or even imperialism as such, but also all personal and social human conduct. This raises the question of whether Thucydides means his readers to take the convictions articulated to be only those of leading Athenians as filtered through his mind, or as convictions of his own that he regarded as objectively true, and that he used the Athenians to express. Obviously Thucydides gives no explicit answer to this question. But the frequent reappearance of prestige, fear, and self-interest, and related expressions, as mainsprings of personal and political action and reaction in the bulk of his work leaves little doubt that he has the Athenians at the First Lacedaemonian Congress expressing something of the truth of which he was himself convinced.

To prove this point philologically is made difficult not only by Thucydides' indifference to a strict technical vocabulary but also by the consideration that he is not and does not pretend to be a philosopher whose aim is to offer to his readers a coherent and consistent theory of historical development. If he has such a theory, we find it embedded in the details of his narrative and in the arguments he attributes to his speakers; and we do find it embedded so deeply that it is fair to say that these motives formed a pattern in Thucydides' thinking. Appeals to all three motives, jointly or separately, pervade the entire work, from its opening account of early history *(archaiologia)* to the aftermath of the oligarchical revolution of 411 B.C.E. at its end, in speeches as well as in the narrative. Fear *(deos, phobos)* is the most common, and references to it range from the emotion felt on the field of battle to Thucydides' own statement of his own deepest conviction about the cause of the Peloponnesian War: Athenian expansion and the fear it engendered in the Lacedaemonians made its outbreak inevitable, but the Athenians also fear the Spartans (I.91.3). Mutual fear of the use the other side might make of the captured island of Sphacteria determines the policies of both Athens and Sparta. The actions of the Plataeans against the Thebans are prompted by fear (II.3.1,4), and fear makes the Sicilian cities resist Athenian expansion and prompts the Syracusan attack on Messana. But fear also prevents Nicias from attacking Syracuse immediately after landing in Sicily.

Self-interest enters Thucydides' argument as *ōphelia* (benefit), *kerdos* (gain), *pleonexia* (greed), *to xymphoron, to chrēsimon, to lysiteloun* (advantage), and similar expressions. Together with fear, self-interest appears as

a motive in the attempt by the Corcyreans to persuade the Athenians to become their allies, and in the Corinthian argument at the Second Lacedaemonian Congress, that the Greek cities will rally to the Peloponnesian cause; Hermocrates looks on Sicilian fear of Athenian aggression as "useful" *(chrēsimon)* to effect a united Sicily, and a similar argument is used by Gylippus when he warns his men that the Athenians will not reap any advantage *(ōphelia)* from the size of their navy if the Sicilians do not fear them.

Prestige *(timē)* is somewhat harder for us to understand. It includes a sense of personal or national "dignity," the esteem or honor in which a person or state is held by another person or state *(doxa, axiōsis, axiōma)*. As a motive in interstate affairs, it is the sense in which a more powerful state feels that it cannot afford to yield to the claims, demands, or interests of a weaker state in matters where it believes its own vital interests affected. Together with fear *(phobos)*, it enters the Melian Dialogue at several places in the Athenians' argument that they have to assert themselves among their allies, and that they cannot project an image of weakness or fearfulness in dealing with them.

Of special relevance are four passages in which fear, self-interest, and prestige combine to explain the complex dynamism of a given situation. The first of these is the revolt of Mytilene. What the Athenians most resent about it is that the Mytileneans had occupied a privileged position among Athens's allies and that Mytilene had respected Athens. But at the same time, the Athenians feared the strength of Mytilene's fleet, just as Mytilene feared the Athenian navy. The combination of these two motives goes some way toward explaining the narrow vindictiveness with which Cleon proposes to handle the situation. Against him, Diodotus argues that discussion is beneficial *(ōpheleitai)* and fear *(phobos)* detrimental to the city, and that a good citizen ought not to be dishonored *(atimazein)* for giving the city the benefit of his advice.

A second passage has Hermocrates argue for Sicilian unity at the Congress at Gela on the grounds that "no one is compelled to go to war by ignorance, or prevented by fear from going into it, if he thinks he will gain anything by it; in some cases, the gain appears greater than the danger; in other cases, people are willing to undertake risks rather than face an immediate humiliation. But if both sides miss the right moment for acting, the advice to come to terms is profitable" (IV.59.2–3, cf. 61.6, 62.2). A similar confluence of the three motives is found in the third passage, Euphemus's defense of Athenian policy at Camarina. He begins by reminding his audience of Athenian prestige *(axioi ontes)* won by her past leadership of the Greeks; he affirms that the presence of the Athenians will be advantageous *(xympheronta)* for Sicily; and he asserts that they have nothing to fear *(phoberōteron, perideōs, deos)*.

The fourth passage shows that Thucydides believes (as, indeed, he has Diodotus suggest at III.45.3) that this triple motivation applies to individuals as well as to states. All three motives enter his description of Alcibiades' character: "Desirous to be general and hoping to be instrumental in capturing Sic-

ily and Carthage, and, if successful, to profit personally in wealth and reputation *[chrēmasi te kai doxēi ōphelēsein]*. For the prestige *[axiōma]* he enjoyed among the citizens made him gratify desires greater than the means he had allowed, both in keeping horses and in his other expenditures. This became later a considerable factor in bringing Athens down: fearing *[phobēthentes]* the extent of his lawlessness in his personal lifestyle and in the design pervading every single action of his, most people became his enemies, convinced that he wanted to be tyrant" (VI.15.2–4, cf. 17.1). As a contrast, Pericles' power is earlier attributed to his prestige *(axiōma, axiōsis)*, through which he could bring an overconfident populace back to reality by instilling fear in it *(kateplēssen epi to phobeisthai)* (II.65.8–9).

The preceding is only a very small part of the evidence that shows how the three factors adduced by the Athenians to explain their empire pervade the whole of Thucydides' *History*. To interpret this evidence, as is still fashionable, as explaining Thucydides' fascination with imperialism is only partly true. He leaves no doubt that he sees fear, prestige, and self-interest as the mainsprings of all human action, anchored by an inescapable necessity *(anankē)* in human nature.

Thucydides defines his fascination with the unprecedented dimensions of the Peloponnesian War as his motive for writing its history, and he spends the first nineteen chapters of Book I demonstrating that it was indeed the "greatest movement that ever shook the Greek and part of the non-Greek world" (I.1.2). It is tempting to see this greatness less merely in terms of imperialism than as affording Thucydides a large canvas to explore the actions and reactions of the human animal in extreme situations. As to what benefit future generations will be able to derive from his accurate account, the only possible answer is knowledge. But not the kind of knowledge that will enable a person to prevent the mistakes of the past: if Thucydides is convinced that fear, prestige, and self-interest are ingrained in the nature of man, nothing will ever free human beings from the necessity that this unholy trinity lays down for them. What knowledge can do is alert future generations to the workings of fear, prestige, and self-interest, so that when they observe these or similar symptoms in the future, they can recognize what is in store for them and, if possible, initiate measures to soften the blow that is sure to come.

One example of this is Thucydides' description of the plague. He introduces his painstakingly detailed and precise account by saying: "All speculation as to its origin and its causes, if causes can be found adequate to produce so great a disturbance, I leave to other writers, whether lay or professional; for myself, I shall simply set down its nature, and explain the symptoms, which will enable an observant student, if it should ever break out again, to know what is coming and not be ignorant. This I can the better do, as I had the disease myself, and watched its operation in the case of others" (II.48.3, trans. adapted). Thucydides makes clear his doubts that future generations

will be any more successful than his own at discovering the cause of the disease (and, perhaps, in that way finding a cure). He is content if he can describe the symptoms—and not merely those that he experienced himself—accurately enough to enable members of future generations "to know what is coming and not be ignorant."

Thucydides' celebrated comments on the civil upheaval in Corcyra corroborate that this is his purpose: "Many hardships befell the cities in the course of civil war, things which have been happening and will always be as long as the nature of man remains the same; but changing in form from severe to mild, depending on the changes of fortune that determine them. In peace and prosperity states as well as individuals have better judgement, because they are not faced with conditions they cannot control and that are not of their own making. But war, in removing easy provision of daily needs, is a violent schoolmaster and brings most people's tempers to the level of their situation" (III.82.2). Again the purpose of a detailed and gruesome description, here of the events in Corcyra, is not to prevent a recurrence (which is impossible inasmuch as it is determined by human nature) but "to know what is coming and not be ignorant." It is no accident that this same insight characterizes such great statesmen in Thucydides' account as Themistocles and Pericles (I.138.3; II.65.5–6, 13).

The conviction that human actions are primarily motivated by fear, prestige, and self-interest gives Thucydides a hard-nosed, "realistic" attitude toward the events he so graphically describes. Nothing relieves his stark description of the plague; nothing embellishes the partisan attitudes and actions rampant during the Corcyrean revolt. No considerations of humanity or compassion enter into the debate about the prisoners from Mytilene, either on Cleon's side or on the part of Diodotus. The *raison d'état* alone governs all interstate relations.

This comes out most unequivocally in the Melian Dialogue (V.85–114). According to Thucydides, the Melians, though ethnically related to the Lacedaemonians, had remained neutral in the war until the Athenians decided to incorporate them into their empire as the only islanders who were not yet part of it. In other words, the Athenians felt that their own prestige as a superpower demanded their incorporation of a small island that might possibly be used as a base against them and that refused to surrender voluntarily. In the debate that follows, the Athenians rule questions of right and wrong out of order and deprecate appeals to past achievements or to Spartan kinship for help; they invite the Melians to consider nothing but the hard fact that their survival depends on surrendering without bloodshed to the more powerful enemy: "You know as well as we do that what is right is a criterion in human calculation only when both sides are equally powerful to enforce compliance; but a preponderant power exacts what it can and the weak have to concede" (89); "In the case of the divine it is our opinion and in the case of humans our

clear conviction that by a constraint inherent in nature they rule wheresoever they have the power" (105.2). This seems to be the underlying principle in the historical process that Thucydides sees at work not only in the passages just discussed but throughout his *History*. That its recognition constitutes a landmark in cultural history is beyond question, and is the basis on which some modern scholars have called him a "scientific" historian who, like Machiavelli or Marx, has contributed to discovering the dynamics of human history.

But this is not the whole story: Thucydides did not see himself in this light alone. What we regard as his principles are for him mainsprings of particular actions embedded so deeply in the nature of man that they will of necessity shape whatever man does. But the effect they have on the human condition is nothing short of tragic. Since, in facing them, man is subject to a necessity inherent in his own nature, they inhibit the exercise of free choice: where self-interest *(to xympheron)* asserts itself, the voice of morality *(to dikaion)* is stilled. Again and again Thucydides makes a point of showing that moral stirrings, which also animate human thought and aspiration, are suppressed by the overriding demands of fear, prestige, and self-interest. From the arguments of the Corcyreans at Corinth we may glean that arbitration of disputes rather than resorting to war constitutes one set of moral desiderata, and the Corinthian speech at Athens suggests that adhering to the terms of a treaty is another. We learn from the Melians and from the list of Athenian allies who joined the Sicilian expedition that kinship ought to be a motive for states to help each other in an emergency, and that the decision to go to war should be taken by autonomous states on the basis that it is morally right to do so. Statements by the Athenians at Sparta as well as at Melos, that arguments from justice are eclipsed when one side is stronger than the other, suggest that moral considerations ought to carry more weight than considerations of relative strength and weakness. That judicial proceedings, even if they result in injustice, are preferable to violent treatment and that gentle treatment of allies is preferable to harshness are implied by the Athenian speech at Sparta and by Alcibiades' justification of the Sicilian campaign.

Moral considerations dominate especially what is normal in personal (as opposed to collective) behavior. This is shown most vividly in Thucydides' account of civil discord in Corcyra: morality is suppressed as soon as fear, prestige, and self-interest appear on the scene. Thucydides regrets that partisanship imported foreigners to interfere in internal matters, and that vindictiveness, atrocity, greed, and personal ambition prevailed. What emerges as desirable is a situation in which daily needs are satisfied, in which words retain their normal meaning and are not perverted into slogans, and in which kinship counts for more than partisan loyalty. He values obedience to laws and respect for the sanctity of oaths; public interests should have a higher priority than private; verdicts must be just; violence must be shunned; gods and

parents must be respected; and unsophisticated openness must not be ridiculed.

The impression that this list does not significantly differentiate Thucydides' values from those of a conventional Greek is confirmed by an inquiry into his views on religion. In his account of the settlement of the Pelargikon with evacuees from the Attic countryside he mentions an oracular injunction that prohibited its settlement. Thucydides attacks the interpretation of the oracle current at the time, which attributed the disasters befalling Athens to the unlawful occupation of the place, by asserting that "the war constituted the necessity of settling it; though the oracle did not name the war, it knew in advance that its habitation would never bode any good" (II.17.1–2). This shows that he regarded the inviolability of religious injunctions as desirable; while he questions the interpretation of an oracle, he does not reject its basic veracity. Similarly, in the dispute between Athenians and Boeotians about the sacred water that the Athenians had used for mundane purposes during their occupation of the Temple of Apollo at Delium, the fact that the Athenians defend themselves by saying that they had disturbed the water not in wanton disregard of its sanctity but prompted by necessity, and that, accordingly, their act does not constitute a transgression (IV.98.5), shows that religious sanctions ought normally to be respected, regardless of one's own opinions about them.

There has been a tendency in recent scholarship to emphasize Thucydides' more humane side and to see in him a moralist who views with regret how the pursuit of self-interest leads to the eclipse of human values. This interpretation seems to be as one-sided as its opposite, the view that he was first and foremost an exponent of hard-nosed realpolitik. To regard both views as aspects of the same person seems to me closer to the truth. Their combination gives us a Thucydides who knew and felt the tragic side of the human condition: man has the power to recognize the forces that shape human behavior, but his knowledge does not enable him to change their course; he has to ride roughshod over the more conventional social values that make life civilized.

If we were to interpret Thucydides only on the basis of what we learn from him about the moral social values of his time, he would at best be a polemicist who put his great artistic gifts into the service of preaching how the horrors of war barbarize the human animal, and whose own values differ little from those of his fellow citizens. But this would ignore the much greater and more profound dimension of Thucydides the intellectual. His respect for conventional values does not conceal the fact that intellectually Thucydides accepts the antithetical principles of realpolitik, which he sees as pervading the entire Peloponnesian War, from the Athenians' defense of their empire in Book I to the Melian Dialogue in Book V, the speeches of Hermocrates and of Euphemus in Books IV and VI, and the oligarchical maneuverings in Book VIII. It informs his method, his passion for accuracy and precision, his chronological

division of the year into summers and winters, his use of (usually antithetical) speeches, and his constant search for deeper realities behind the events. These preoccupations, in addition to his disinclination to accept the transcendent explanations of human events found in Herodotus, suggests that he had been exposed to the sophistic teaching that had captured the minds of young Athenians in the second half of the 5th century, and which favored an enlightened, rational view of the world over an older more religiously informed attitude.

This assumption also explains certain Thucydidean attitudes and apparent contradictions that have baffled modern scholars. How can an author whose avowed aim is accuracy and precision in reporting so consistently denigrate Cleon? He describes him at his first appearance as "the most violent citizen and far more trusted by the people at this time than anyone else" (III.36.6; IV.21.3). Cleon's spectacular success at Sphacteria is presented as the result of intrigue and prevarication because his own motives for opposing peace were under suspicion, and even his death in battle in Thrace is attributed to cowardice and lack of judgment. But how popular can Cleon have been, if, as Thucydides tells us, his offer to resolve the Pylos affair within twenty days was met "with laughter at his irresponsible talk, while serious persons greeted it with delight, reckoning that they would gain either way, either in getting rid of Cleon (which was their greater hope), or in unexpectedly reducing the Lacedaemonians" (IV.28.5)? Is popularity a bad thing in a democracy? Or is democracy itself a bad thing in the eyes of Thucydides? A number of narrative passages—that is, passages in which Thucydides speaks in his own name—might suggest as much: the fickle "crowd" reelects Pericles as general after just having fined him; the "mob" eggs on Nicias to surrender his generalship to Cleon while Cleon prevaricates; the people are crazy with emotion as the ill-fated campaign against Sicily is launched; panic-stricken, they hear of the desecration of the Herms (VI.60); the "mob" at Syracuse gets overconfident when an expected Athenian attack does not materialize. At the same time, democracy is extolled in Pericles' great Funeral Oration (II.36–46, esp. 37), and Diodotus praises, as Pericles had done, "democratic" discussion as a prelude to action.

The assumption that Thucydides was influenced by sophistic teaching implies what is also implied by his service as general. He must have been a member of the upper class; as a beneficiary from gold-mine concessions, he could well have afforded the fees charged by the sophists for their instruction. His training and his social class, together with his personal temperament, would have made him sympathetic to rational political discourse, freed from emotionalism as far as possible, regardless of the political orientation of those who used it. Therefore, he would have favored the intellectual attitude of a Pericles, a Diodotus, or a Hermocrates to the rabble-rousing of a Cleon and the unreasoning sentiments with which the common people reacted to events.

This stance does not characterize Thucydides' attitude to democracy alone: he is equally averse to the machinations and strong-arm methods with which the oligarchs established their regime in 411 B.C.E. But there, too, Antiphon, "the person who had organized the method by which the whole affair should come to this issue," is praised as "second to none of the Athenians of his time in excellence and most forceful in conceiving ideas and in communicating his conclusions"; this despite (or because of?) the fact that "his formidable talent rendered him suspect in the eyes of the masses" (VIII.68.1).

This would suggest that Thucydides was indifferent to what kind of regime prevailed in a given state, so long as it gave the state intelligent leadership that governed in the interest of all. This is perhaps also the reason why the only regime that elicits his unqualified praise is the short-lived government that briefly ruled Athens after the overthrow of the oligarchy of the Four Hundred: "It was a judicious blend geared to the interest of the few and the many, and this fact first buoyed up the city after the wretched condition into which it had fallen" (VIII.97.2).

Thucydides' view, embodied in his account of the Peloponnesian War, cannot be translated into partisan politics. What he favors is a politics of human intelligence, a product of human rationality, operating without appeal to transcendent powers but open to an understanding of what the limits of rationality are, and also aware of the obstacles that stand in the way of attaining it.

MARTIN OSTWALD

Bibliography

Texts and Translations

Thucydides. *History of the Peloponnesian War*. Trans. Richard Crawford. Everyman Library. Citations in the text are to this edition.

———. *History of the Peloponnesian War*. Trans. C. F. Smith. 4 vols. Loeb Classical Library.

Studies

Adcock, F. E. *Thucydides and His History*. Cambridge, 1963.

Cochrane, C. N. *Thucydides and the Science of History*. Oxford, 1929.

Cogan, M. *The Human Thing: The Speeches and Principles of Thucydides' History*. Chicago, 1981.

Connor, W. R. *Thucydides*. Princeton, 1984.

Cornford, F. M. *Thucydides Mythistorichus*. London, 1907.

De Romilly, Jacqueline. *Histoire et raison chez Thucydide*. Paris, 1956.

———. *Thucydides and Athenian Imperialism*. Trans. Philip Thody. Oxford, 1963.

Finley, J. H. *Thucydides*. Cambridge, Mass., 1946.

Gomme, A. W., A. Andrewes, and K. J. Dover. *A Historical Commentary on Thucydides*. 5 vols. Oxford, 1945–1981.

Hornblower, Simon. *Thucydides*. London, 1987.

Ostwald, Martin. *Anankē in Thucydides*. Atlanta, Ga., 1988.

Parry, Adam. Logos *and* Ergon *in Thucydides*. Salem, N.H., 1981.

Rood, Tim. *Thucydides: Narrative and Explanation*. Oxford and New York, 1998.

Schwartz, Eduard. *Das Geschichtswerk des Thukydides*. Bonn, 1919.

Stadter, P. A., ed. *The Speeches in Thucydides*. Chapel Hill, N.C., 1973.

Stahl, H.-P. *Thukydides: Die Stellung des Menschen im geschichtlichen Prozess* (= *Zetemata* 40). Munich, 1966.

Strasburger, H. "Die Entdeckung der politischen Geschichte durch Thukydides." *Saeculum* 4 (1954): 395–428.

Related Articles

Observation and Research; Utopia and the Critique of Politics; Polybius; Inventing Politics; History; Xenophon

XENOPHON

XENOPHON THE ATHENIAN (ca. 430–after 355 B.C.E.) was a brilliant military strategist, an accomplished man of letters, and a devoted follower of Socrates. Xenophon could be called the first journalist: he recorded his personal adventures in wartime, and expressed himself on the leading moral, social, and political issues of his day.

Xenophon's intelligence was more practical than theoretical. He was not interested in abstract philosophical argument for its own sake, but he had a keen practical interest in many of the questions raised by Socrates, such as what is justice, and how might the good life be reliably secured, not only for an individual but also for a household, a city-state, or an empire. On these topics Xenophon has much to say that is interesting and even wise. Thus, although Xenophon is not a major figure in the history of philosophy, if philosophy is viewed (as Plato viewed it) as a comprehensive and professionalized theoretical discipline, he is nonetheless a major figure in the history of social thought. To use a modern parallel, Xenophon is more a Camus than a Sartre.

Opinions of Xenophon have varied greatly through the ages. To some, Xenophon has seemed like a dull and boring pious old uncle, a man far too unphilosophical to have understood Socrates. To others, Xenophon's rival Plato appears to be a dangerously alienated intellectual, a man who is a genius at abstract philosophy but who has very little concrete understanding of ordinary human life. Xenophon, by contrast, is sensible and insightful and wise.

Although Xenophon was not a professional philosopher, his works are permeated with philosophy. Here is one example. Xenophon repeats many times the traditional Greek view that one should help one's friends and harm one's enemies. By contrast, Plato's Socrates insists that it is never right to harm anyone. Here it may seem that Xenophon is resting content with prephilosophical common sense, but this is not truly the case. Xenophon's Socrates also holds the philosophically grounded views that good people should be friends to good people and enemies to bad, and that it is in everyone's interest to become good. When combined with those views, the traditional maxim, Help your friends and harm your enemies, is transformed into a thoroughly moral principle. It now signifies roughly the same as Promote the good and oppose evil.

Over the centuries, Xenophon's works have served as models of the "simple" style of Attic prose. From ancient times down to 20th-century Europe, generations of schoolchildren have been taught to imitate him. Fluent, lucid,

779

and unpretentious, Xenophon's style of writing can seem easier and less carefully crafted than it is. Underneath the apparent casualness of Xenophon's prose there lies a skilled and intelligent author who chooses words with great care and organizes each work with a deliberate, though subtle, plan.

The most controversial aspect of Xenophon's significance is the value of his testimony concerning Socrates. In antiquity his portrait of Socrates was quite influential, for example on the Stoics. Leading scholars, especially in the last century, have argued that Xenophon is our most reliable source for the historical Socrates, since Plato was too creative to be a good historian. Other equally prominent scholars have argued that Xenophon was too dull or unphilosophical to understand the real Socrates. No scholarly consensus concerning "the problem of the the historical Socrates" exists today.

Plato and Xenophon were not the only authors of Socratic dialogues. Many of Socrates' followers contributed to this genre. The conventions of the genre seem to have allowed authors considerable freedom to reshape Socrates, idealize him, and put their own views in Socrates' mouth. Therefore the cautious and reasonable view is that certainty about the historical Socrates is lost to us—and, in a way, not very important. The most important fact about Socrates was his influence: the extraordinary fertility of his ideas and the moral example he set for his followers. The richness of the Socratic movement is a fascinating subject for which we do have good evidence, and Xenophon's Socratic writings are a precious resource.

The variety and literary originality of Xenophon's works are remarkable. He wrote, among other things, a history, a military memoir, Socratic dialogues, a biographical novel, and technical treatises on horsemanship and hunting. In fact Xenophon's main contribution to Greek thought is not any set of doctrines but rather the many literary genres that he either created or to which he gave a new impulse.

The *Cyropaedia,* or *Education of Cyrus,* is a biographical novel or historical romance about the life and character of Cyrus the Great, founder of the Persian empire. Xenophon's chief aim is to use Cyrus as a vehicle for portraying the ideal ruler. Thus the work does not aim at historical accuracy but is a kind of utopia—Xenophon's counterpart to Plato's *Republic. Cyropaedia* is Xenophon's longest and most comprehensive work, incorporating ideas from all his other writings. It covers not just Cyrus's boyhood but his entire career, thus implying that education is a lifelong process. *Cyropaedia* is perhaps the most influential of all mirrors of princes. It had great influence in Roman times, and again in the Renaissance, for example on Machiavelli. As the first historical romance, it has affected the history of Western imaginative literature, particularly influencing the ancient Greek novel and literature in the 16th and 17th centuries.

Whereas in *Memorabilia* Xenophon portrays Socrates as the ideal example of one who does not seek to rule others, in *Cyropaedia* he portrays Cyrus as

the ideal example of one who has a large or unlimited desire to rule others. (In between these complementary opposites lie Ischomachus of *Oeconomicus*, the ideal ruler of a household, and the fictionalized Agesilaus of *Agesilaus*, who is the ideal ruler of a kingdom.) The problem Cyrus faces is that human beings, unlike sheep or cattle, by nature resist those who try to rule them. Cyrus's solution is to rule justly, i.e., to rule over willing subjects in accord with law. He persuades people to follow him through two main methods: the display of his own virtue, and benefaction—treating his subjects well and making them better off. Thus Cyrus is merciful and kind to those he conquers, to convert them into loyal subjects. Part of Cyrus's virtue as a leader is his great skill at manipulating other people for his own ends.

Xenophon opens *Cyropaedia* by declaring that a central problem of politics is instability, the tendency of people to overthrow their government. Xenophon was no democrat: the solution he offers to this problem is monarchy by a brilliant and virtuous leader like Cyrus. But the limits of this solution are revealed when, after Cyrus's death, the empire breaks up due to his sons' inadequacies. Just as the famous question Is virtue teachable? inspires the beginning chapters of *Cyropaedia*, so its corollary, Why do virtuous fathers so often fail to pass on their virtue to their sons? haunts the end.

Memorabilia, or *Recollections of Socrates,* is Xenophon's major Socratic work. *Memorabilia* 1.1–2 presents a formal defense of Socrates, who was condemned to death by Athens, against the charges lodged against him at his trial. These chapters present a revised and expanded version of Xenophon's independent work, *The Apology of Socrates.* The rest of the *Memorabilia* continues this defense by showing that Socrates' words and deeds were beneficial to his companions and to Athens. Plato's Socrates claims to know nothing. If that were true, then Socrates would be acting immorally in spending so much time with young people, as he would not know whether his influence on them was bad or good. Xenophon's Socrates has a great deal of moral wisdom, which he generously shares with his young associates, thereby improving their lives. *Memorabilia* is a rich and episodic work, portraying Socrates in conversation with a great variety of people on a great variety of subjects.

For the historian of philosophy *Memorabilia* can be frustrating, since Xenophon has Socrates discuss or assert many interesting philosophical theses, but—in contrast to Plato's dialogues—the arguments for these theses are often entirely missing or else condensed or weak. The interpreter's difficult but rewarding task is to reconstruct the philosophical arguments and outlook that underlie the claims.

According to Xenophon, Socrates benefited his companions in large part by his outstanding moral example. But in addition, by means of argument and advice, Socrates made his young associates more pious and just, and he discouraged overambitious and ignorant young men from seeking power. Xenophon stresses more than Plato does Socrates' concrete practical wisdom

and his intense interest not only in abstract definitions of moral concepts but also in helping the people around him live better lives.

Symposium, or *Dinner Party,* is Xenophon's most polished and enjoyable Socratic work. Whereas the *Symposium* that Plato wrote is magnificent and profound, Xenophon's *Symposium* is light and charming, but with the serious purpose of presenting philosophical views on love, virtue, and education. Of those present at the dinner gathering, Socrates has the most *kalokagahia*—an untranslatable Greek term meaning something close to virtue or nobility of character. Nobility of character is a central concern in all of Xenophon's Socratic and political writings, but *Symposium* highlights an underappreciated feature of Socrates' noble character: his urbanity. Socrates displays the exact mixture of humor and seriousness, irony and tact, and frivolity without a hint of coarseness that make for an ideal dinner companion. Other more familiar Socratic themes are also stressed. What one should love in another person is not money or power or physical beauty but rather virtue and nobility of character. In the case of the young, one should love their *potential* for nobility of character. The sexual urge behind ordinary Greek homosexual attraction is spiritualized by Socrates into a force for moral education.

Although overshadowed by Plato's, Xenophon's *Symposium* was greatly admired in antiquity, as it has been admired by others since. A work of philosophy, it also has historical value in giving us a more realistic picture than Plato's does of what an actual Athenian dinner party might have been like.

Oeconomicus, or *Estate Manager,* is not about economics in the modern sense but rather household or estate management. Its moral and political importance is obvious: relations between husband and wife, parents and children, and (in ancient Greece) master and slave all fall within its scope. *Oeconomicus* was thus pathbreaking as the earliest work devoted to this vitally important branch of practical philosophy. The dialogue shows Socrates in the unusual role of student: Ischomachus, a perfect country gentleman, teaches Socrates the basic principles of managing or ruling a country estate. While the historical Socrates spent all of his life in the city of Athens, Xenophon had considerable experience as an estate manager. Toward the end of the 390s, perhaps because of his pro-Sparta activities, Xenophon was banished from Athens. He then settled down at an estate near Olympia, where he led the life of a country gentleman, farming, hunting, and also writing. Just as Plato put his own ideas into Socrates' mouth in *The Republic,* so in *Oeconomicus* Xenophon puts his ideas into the mouth of Ischomachus.

A basic theme of the work is that the art of ruling others begins with the art of ruling oneself. Xenophon and Plato agree on this thesis. They also agree, against Aristotle, that the art of ruling oneself, the art of ruling a household, and the art of ruling a city are fundamentally the same.

The section of the work in which Ischomachus describes how he taught his

young wife her domestic duties is the longest and most detailed classical Greek portrayal of the role of women in the household. Although written from the point of view of a man, it is an important source for women's history.

From a literary point of view, Xenophon's *Anabasis*, or *March Up Country*, is his most successful work. *Anabasis* is a "good read," combining entertaining narrative with vivid and colorful details. In 401 Xenophon decided (ignoring advice from Socrates) to join a Greek militia accompanying Cyrus the Younger on an expedition to overthrow Cyrus's brother Artaxerxes, ruler of Persia. *Anabasis* recounts these experiences. At Cunaxa near Babylon, Cyrus was killed and his army collapsed. The Greek mercenaries (the Ten Thousand) found themselves far from Greece and surrounded by powerful enemies. Xenophon played a chief role in rallying the dispirited troops, eventually leading them on their march through 1,500 kilometers of unknown and hostile territory until they reached the Black Sea. The chant of the troops as they sighted shore has become famous: *"Thalatta! Thalatta!"* ("The sea! The sea!")

This successful retreat was a brilliant military exploit. It was also a significant turning point in world history, since it demonstrated the weakness of Persian military power in the face of superior Greek tactics and discipline. The success of Xenophon and his band of mercenaries gave grounds for hope that the Greeks might conquer Persia—a dream realized three-quarters of a century later by Alexander the Great.

Generations and generations of schoolmasters assigned *Anabasis* to generations and generations of schoolboys, partly to teach them Greek, but also to teach them virtue. As Xenophon recounts the military adventures of the Ten Thousand, the virtues of the ordinary Greek soldier shine through: courage, determination, piety, independence of spirit combined with a capacity for teamwork. These are just the virtues that schoolmasters aimed to teach their charges. Historians of military strategy have also always valued *Anabasis* highly. The tactics of retreat fighting and techniques for commanding a rear guard that Xenophon described (and presumably helped to invent) were major and enduring contributions to military science.

Xenophon's *Hellenica* is a history of Greek affairs from 411 to 362 B.C.E., although the chronological limits are accidental to the narrative. Thucydides died before completing his great history of the Peloponnesian War, so Xenophon began his history where Thucydides' history ends. In *Hellenica* Xenophon writes the political and military history of his times. It is valuable as the only surviving complete, contemporary account of the period. Xenophon's narrative is highly selective, however, and shows marked pro-Sparta and anti-Thebes bias. It is therefore important to supplement and correct Xenophon's history with such other sources as *Hellenica oxyrhynchia* and the works of the later authors Diodorus Siculus and Plutarch. Overall, *Hellenica* is one

of Xenophon's least successful works. As a product of the historian's craft, *Hellenica* is dramatically inferior to the works of his predecessors Herodotus and Thucydides, and also to his own *Anabasis*.

DONALD MORRISON

Bibliography

Texts and Translations

Bowen. A. J., ed. and trans. *Symposium*. Warminster: Aris and Phillips, 1998.

Marchant, E. C. *Xenophontis opera omnia*. Oxford: Oxford University Press, 1900–1920 (in Greek).

Xenophon. 7 vols. Loeb Classical Library.

Studies

Anderson, John K. *Xenophon*. New York: Scribner, 1974.

Breitenbach, Hans R. *Xenophon von Athen*. Stuttgart: Druckenmuller, 1966. (Published separately and as vol. 9, A2 of *Pauly's Realencyclopädie der classischen Altertumswissenschaft*.)

Gera, Deborah. *Xenophon's Cyropaedia: Style, Genre, and Literary Technique*. Oxford: Clarendon Press, 1993.

Gil, Juan, ed. and trans. *Economico*. Madrid: Sociedad de Estudios y Publicaciones, 1966.

Gray, Vivienne. *The Framing of Socrates: The Literary Interpretation of Xenophon's Memorabilia*. Stuttgart: Steiner, 1998.

Guthrie, W. K. C. *A History of Greek Philosophy*, vol. 3: *The Fifth-Century Enlightenment*. Cambridge: Cambridge University Press, 1969.

Morrison, Donald R. *Bibliography of Editions, Translations, and Commentary on Xenophon's Socratic Writings, 1600–Present*. Pittsburgh, Pa.: Mathesis Press, 1988.

Patzer, A. *Der historische Socrates*. Darmstadt: Wissenschaftliche Buchgesellschaft, 1987.

Pomeroy, Sarah, ed. and trans. *Oeconomicus: A Social and Historical Commentary, with a New English Translation*. Oxford: Oxford University Press, 1994.

Strauss, Leo. *On Tyranny*, rev. and expanded ed. New York: Free Press, 1991.

———. *Xenophon's Socrates*. Ithaca, N.Y.: Cornell University Press, 1972.

Tatum, James. *Xenophon's Imperial Fiction*. Princeton: Princeton University Press, 1989.

Vander Waerdt, Paul, ed. *The Socratic Movement*. Ithaca, N.Y.: Cornell University Press, 1994.

Related Articles

Inventing Politics; Socrates; Utopia and the Critique of Politics; Thucydides

ZENO

Zᴇɴᴏ ᴏғ Eʟᴇᴀ ɪs ʀᴇᴍᴇᴍʙᴇʀᴇᴅ ᴛᴏᴅᴀʏ thanks to a fairly large number of accounts. Those of Diogenes Laertius, Diodorus Siculus, Plutarch, Clement of Alexandria, and Philostratus are limited to unverifiable biographical events. In addition to these, there are a few maxims attributed to Zeno. The sources for his contributions to philosophy are Plato, Aristotle, and Simplicius, who in turn cites Alexander of Aphrodisias, Eudemus of Rhodes, and Porphyry of Tyre, as well as Themistius and Philoponus, who simply reiterate Simplicius. Clearly, on this front, the Aristotelian tradition prevails.

According to the doxographers, whose accounts differ slightly, we can estimate that Zeno reached maturity around 460 B.C.E. and surmise that he rarely left his native Elea in southern Italy. Although the *Suda* credits him with four works, only one was known in antiquity, between Plato's time and Simplicius's. Proclus describes this text as a dry collection of forty "arguments." Of these, Aristotle discusses six, at times only through allusion and without citing the texts; Plato may refer to one. Simplicius, however, quotes passages of Zeno's book treating two additional arguments, and Diogenes Laertius adds another. We can therefore recreate, with more or less precision depending on the case, roughly ten of Zeno's arguments.

Plato's account is found in *Parmenides* (127e6–128d6, 135d8–136b), where he confirms that Zeno, as a supporter of the philosophy of Parmenides of Elea, conceived all of his arguments for the purpose of refuting the existence of "plurality," and claimed success. Although their works were not organized according to the same principle (Parmenides argued for monism and Zeno against pluralism), they were both defending the same thesis, and Zeno sought to demonstrate the absurdity in the position of those who found Parmenides' monism absurd. Skeptical though we may be about the scenario described in Plato's dialogue, where Parmenides, Zeno, and Socrates all meet in Athens, we may nevertheless accept Plato's interpretation of the doctrine in the light of the very learned discussion that has taken place among specialists on this point. It is plausible that a passage from a different dialogue (*Phaedrus* 261d6–8) gives a very brief summary of the aporias (paradoxes) that Zeno derived from the hypothesis of plurality: if one wants to refute a thesis by reducing it to an absurdity, one must show that, taken as a hypothesis, it leads to contradiction. Popular tradition has held, for example, that Zeno denied the existence of motion. This is an oversimplification that ignores the meaning that this negation had in the context of his work in its entirety. I

propose to examine those of Zeno's arguments that have come down to us, grouping them thematically.

THE ARGUMENTS AGAINST THE PLURALITY OF BEINGS, ACCORDING TO SIMPLICIUS

If, like the Greeks, we agree to make a substantive of the present participle of the verb *to be*, to designate that which is permanent by itself and identical to itself, as opposed to changeable and unreliable appearance, then we can say that "being" is properly what Parmenides wanted to characterize in his doctrine. He did this in the negative, by excluding "what is not": in other words, becoming (for how can something become without ceasing to be, or without not yet being?), difference (for how can something be other without yet ceasing to be the same?), and division (for how can something be divided if nothingness and emptiness do not exist?). Thus being, or what exists absolutely, is immutable and permanent, one and identical to itself, indivisible, all of a piece, a fullness of being that is motionless and unique.

If the adversaries of the doctrine reject as absurd the affirmation of a unique being beyond appearances, they also have to deny that it is all of a piece and indivisible; and if it is divisible, then it is in fact divided, since any gap between the possible and the actual would imply a "becoming" that is excluded from being. Thus, in this hypothesis, there is a plurality of beings, each one existing absolutely, each one immutable and permanent, each one all of a piece and identical to itself, each one indivisible, for if it were divisible, then it would in turn be divided, and so on. Zeno set out to test the consistency of this thesis of a plurality of indivisible beings.

Zeno and his contemporaries doubtless knew that every segment of a straight line is divisible into two at its midpoint (which they probably knew how to determine with a ruler and compass): each half can also be divided in half, and so on, indefinitely; in addition, while a geometric magnitude is divisible in this way, the same word, *magnitude*, is applied in Greek to a physical body as well, to designate not only its size but also the body itself.

Once this had been posited, according to texts quoted by Simplicius, Zeno then raised two questions about the plurality of beings, the first concerning their number and the second their size, leading us to suppose that the adversaries he was addressing took pride in mathematics. With regard to number, if the existent is reduced to a multitude of indivisible beings, how many will there be, for example, in a given length? It is logical, on the one hand, that there should be twice as many in its entire length as there are in half of its length: thus there will be just as many beings as there must be, in each part of the length, and therefore the total number of beings will be finite. But, on the other hand, since what exists is not indivisible, it is therefore divisible everywhere. Thus the dichotomy of the length at its midpoint can be repeated on

each half, and so on to infinity, so that between two beings there will always be others, and consequently beings will be infinite in number. Thus, if beings are a plurality, they will be, at the same time and in the same object, both finite and infinite in number, which is a contradiction.

Next, from the standpoint of size, nothing indivisible can have any parts, for if it did, it would be divisible; thus indivisibles can have no size, for everything that has size has parts. But even an infinite number of indivisible entities without magnitude, which are therefore nothing, could never constitute something of finite magnitude. Thus it is necessary for each of the ultimate products of infinite division to have magnitude; that means that each one contains at least two parts exterior to one another, contiguous, and with no point in common; hence these parts are in contact at at least two points, and these points are not without magnitude, since otherwise they would be nothing. Now, what we have said about an indivisible entity having magnitude will also be true about each of the parts mentioned above, and so on to infinity. To put it in more modern terms, each being contains at least a double infinity of points of contact that are not without some measure and is therefore infinite in magnitude. All finite magnitude, being made up of an infinity of such "indivisibles," is formed of an infinite number of infinite magnitudes, which is absurd. If this were the case, then the same things could be at the same time without magnitude and of infinite magnitude, which is a contradiction.

What Zeno shows is that the thesis of the plurality of beings contains an intrinsic incompatibility. It implies both the actual infiniteness of the division of a fixed magnitude (for once the indivisibility of the whole is rejected, division cannot be stopped) and the additive composition of this magnitude by means of the ultimate indivisible parts (for the physical composition of existing things is conceived by means of the mathematical additivity of magnitudes).

Another of Zeno's arguments seems to deal with the question of plurality as well (Aristotle, *Physics* VII.5.250a19–25; Simplicius, 1108.18): if a bushel of millet spilling creates noise, then a single grain or a tiny fraction of a grain must also make a noise, if it is true that the ratio of noises to one another is the same as the ratio that exists between the objects. Such an argument is directed against an adversary who maintains that facts that are sense-data are in themselves mathematical facts, arithmetical in this case, and that things form a divisible, physical reality, so that the elements that make up this real plurality are always additive and constitute, by their addition, physical magnitudes. This supposed adversary thus rejects the Eleatic distinction between being and appearance and grants an ontological meaning to arithmetic by allowing a plurality of beings whose magnitude or physical effect must add up in every case.

Finally, Plato's argument, succinctly reported in *Parmenides* (127d6–127e4), also concerns plurality: if beings are a plurality, they cannot fail to be

both alike and unlike at the same time, which is impossible and contradictory. In fact, if beings are the ultimate and shared constitutive elements of tangible things, they must all be the same, identical, for otherwise they would not be ultimate but could be broken down into more fundamental elements. But if tangible things are varied—and if there is no distinction between appearance and being—then beings are necessarily dissimilar, for otherwise they could not account for this diversity. Those who seek to relate the diversity of appearances to an ontological plurality transform into a rigid, absolute, and irreparable contradiction an opposition that, in the world of appearance, differing from being, fades into the relativity of different points of view.

"KINEMATIC" ARGUMENTS ACCORDING TO ARISTOTLE

In *Physics,* Aristotle echoes four of Zeno's aporias concerning movement, aiming to prove that despite what the senses tell us, movement is impossible.

The first of these asserts the impossibility of movement, on the ground that the moving object must arrive first at its halfway point before reaching its final goal (Aristotle, *Physics* VI.9.239b9–14; cf. VI.2.233a21–32; VIII.8.263a4–11 and 263a23–263b6). We are back to the midpoint that divides a distance to be covered into two equal parts; this argument is known in English as the "Racecourse" or the "Dichotomy." Obviously, in the elliptical form the argument is given by Aristotle, it is important to understand that the same reasoning process is applied to the first half of the course, and so on. Thus the argument embraces infinity. It goes as follows: if you actually divide a continuous line in half, the point of division is used twice, once as the end point of the first half, and again as the starting point of the second; thus the moving object must both reach this point and depart from it. Since the dichotomy repeats itself ad infinitum, the moving object has to cross an infinite number of actual points, achieve an infinite number of contacts, or, rather, accomplish an infinite number of tasks of the arriving/departing type. Now, this is impossible in a finite amount of time, since each task, when it is actually carried out, requires a constant amount of time, however short, and an infinite number of tasks requires an infinite amount of time.

Hence we can see that if motion is impossible, it is so under particular hypothetical conditions similar to those of the preceding arguments. The distance to cover (as a physical object) is viewed as made up of indivisible beings all actually given, separate and therefore contiguous. The length of the trajectory results from an additive process of composition, starting with real, indivisible "elements," and at the same time the infinite divisibility of a finite magnitude is recognized. Hence the contradiction: a finite distance demands an infinite amount of time to be covered.

The second kinematic argument reported in Aristotle is well known as the "Achilles" (Aristotle, *Physics* VI.9.239b14–29): the faster of two runners

(Achilles) can never overtake the slower (the tortoise) for the faster must first reach the point from which the slower left, and so on, in such a way that the latter will always have a head start. We must keep in mind that the aporia does not concern the lengths of the intervals, the infinite number of which introduces a limit that ancient Greeks could calculate very easily once Achilles' handicap and the ratio n of the distances covered in the same time were known: the ratio of Achilles' total distance to the handicap, is $n/(n-1)$, the well-known *epimorphios* ratio. Commentators who assert that Zeno did not know how to compute geometric progression are missing the point. The question once again concerns the points Achilles must cross, and it is quite true that the point at which the faster moving object actually catches up with the slower is none of those belonging to the infinite sequence of points defined by the argument, points that the faster object must cross one after another: if the points are actual physical entities, Achilles must indeed complete an infinite task before even reaching the point that "closes" the line, where he would overtake the tortoise. In substance, therefore, the argument is identical to the Racecourse paradox and it obeys the same implicit hypothesis: it would take Achilles an infinite amount of time to complete all the steps that make up this infinite sequence.

Besides the fact that, to divide the course, the Racecourse argument employs the ratio 1/2, and the Achilles the ratio of $1/n$, where n can be any whole number, we can imagine that the Achilles answers the following objection to the Racecourse dichotomy: if one repeats the division as often as necessary, one must be able to reach a segment of the distance so small that to cover it a moving object—even a very slow one—would take only an instant, and therefore the entire distance would be covered in a finite number of instants. This objection misses the point of the argument; it is possible only because the intervals considered successively in producing the dichotomy, if taken in the direction of the moving body's motion, are *overlapping* intervals: if the moving object manages to cover an interval of a given length "in an instant," however small that length may be, it will have succeeded in beginning its race, and it will have before it only a finite number of tasks to accomplish, whatever they may be. Thus, if only for didactic reasons, Zeno had to show successive intervals that did not overlap but that were juxtaposed in succession, and that is what the Achilles manages to do. Moreover, the Achilles argument divides time as it does space, and rejects the "instant" at the end of the indefinitely repeated division. The structure of the argument does not allow for the problem to be resolved by "forcing" the matter, a "final" interval crossed "in an instant." The presumed adversary is compelled to agree that one and only one "point" on the trajectory must correspond to one and only one "moment," and to recognize that in a single moment one can cross only a single point.

Zeno then counters with his third argument: the "Arrow." Aristotle sum-

marizes it by saying that the arrow in its flight—a moving object, we notice, even faster than Achilles—is stationary (*Physics* VI.9.239b29–33; cf. 239b5–9). This conclusion is reached by considering time as made up of instants, that is, by extending to time one of the implicit hypotheses that we have identified with respect to space. This argument can be compared to a proposition that several accounts attribute to Zeno: "A moving body moves neither [in a place] where it is nor [in a place] where it is not" (Diogenes Laertius, *Lives of Eminent Philosophers* IX.72). As a whole, the argument most probably took the following shape: everything is at rest whenever it is in a space equal to itself, and everything is, for a given instant in time, in such a space; now, at any instant, a moving body is in the moment and consequently the arrow—in mid-air, flying—is immobile.

Attaching a single instant of time to every point in the trajectory, and vice versa, is pointless if time is "composed" of instants—in other words, if these instants are consecutive, and if the points are contiguous. At every instant, the "moving object" can be located in one point of its trajectory, where it is at rest, and no real movement is produced by juxtaposing immobilities. The argument applies whether the indivisibles of time and space are finite or infinite in number.

There is only one recourse left to the adversary attempting to defend the idea of movement: to argue that, in a moment in time, a moving object passes from one point to another one immediately next to it. Called the "Moving Blocks," or the "Stadium," Zeno's last argument is his response: the term *stadium* proves useful for talking about rectilinear and parallel trajectories (Aristotle, *Physics* VI.9.239b33–240a18). Let us imagine three such trajectories, A, B, C, and on each of them are "blocks" arranged in rows. Each block is treated as though undivided; each is equal to every other; all are identical in shape; and each row has an equal number (an even number), which we shall call $2n$. Row A remains immobile in the middle of the stadium; B and C move in opposite directions passing A; the first block of each row, at the start, is lined up with the middle of row A. Then let us suppose that at the end of the movement, the first B has reached one end of row A while the first C has simultaneously reached the other end, and the first B has thus passed before n A, the first C before $2n$ B, so that the time of one is half the time of the other, but, at the same time, the first B has passed before $2n$ C, so that the time of the first B is equal to that of the first C, even though it is only half of it. Consequently, a given time is the same as its double, which is absurd.

It has been said that Zeno had no concept of relative speed; the question is, rather, the following: what structure of space and time is necessary to make the notion of relative speed intelligible? As Aristotle emphasized, the validity of the argument rests entirely on the following axiom: the time it takes for a B to pass every A and for a C to pass every B is the same. But this axiom itself presupposes that the blocks are treated as indivisible—in other words, that

space is made up additively of contiguous points and time of successive instants. The Stadium argument "stages" the cost of imagining for every point another point that is immediately contiguous in space, and for every instant another instant that follows it immediately in time, and motion as the passage from one element to the next: the instant of a B passing an A splits into two "instants," in which the B passes 2 C's (as well as from one C to another). Now, contiguity and the additivity of constitutive elements are what we get if we presuppose magnitudes and physical bodies that can be reduced to indivisible entities that really exist: the beings in the arguments summarized by Simplicius.

Another of Zeno's arguments, mentioned by Aristotle, illustrates this point well (*Physics* IV.1.209a23–26 and IV.3.210b23–37; cf. Simplicius, 562.3–6 and 563.17–19). It involves "place," and it can be understood as follows: if a "place," for example the trajectory of the moving body, is made up of "points" existing in reality, in short, of beings, and since every being is in a place, there must be a place of the place, and so on indefinitely, which is absurd; consequently, "space" constituted in this way does not exist.

All of this corroborates Plato's claim that all of Zeno's arguments were directed against the plurality of beings. In his "kinematic arguments" Zeno shows that if those who argued for the existence of motion (as anything other than mere appearance) thought they could base the argument on the thesis of plurality as opposed to Parmenidean immobility, they failed, and that ontologically, in any case, motion, change, and becoming are impossible.

RESOLUTIONS OF THE APORIAS

Zeno reasons within the framework of a physical world where there exists in actuality an infinite number of real and distinct "points," in pairs, a world that is actually ontologically plural. This framework is characteristic of the thesis that he means to refute as absurd, it being, a contrario, out of the question that the Parmenidean being should contain in actuality an infinity of distinct elements, since it is not divisible.

From a modern point of view, the aporias are resolved in the following way. We can consider the (ideal) points that divide a continuous line, such as a straight segment, according to a given iterative law; hence, they are separate from one another and form an infinite, enumerable sequence that we can number. The set of these points can be ordered as the set of whole numbers can, but it is not measurable; all we have left to do is to add up the series of lengths of intervals, producing a sum limited to the length of the segment. Alternatively, we can consider the totality of points of the segment that form an infinite and nonenumerable set, but then the set is not ordered like a set of whole numbers: there are no two contiguous points (the points cannot be numbered, or no point has an immediate successor), and there is no question

of considering the length of the line as resulting from some sort of addition of all the points-elements. What is true of points in a line is also true of instants in time. The paradoxes developed by Zeno result from the assumption of the double hypothesis: there is an infinite set of elements, the end result of repeated division, and there is a possibility of adding the magnitudes of the indivisible entities together to obtain the magnitude of the segment of the continuum under consideration.

Aristotle saw very clearly that he had to accept the infinite divisibility of a continuum, even a physical one, of time on the same pattern as space, as the "Achilles" argument had shown. But he rejected the second premise of the aporias, repeating that a line is not "composed" of points, nor time of moments. What, then, would prevent one from "composing" a finite line by adding an infinite number of points? Aristotle's reply consists of eliminating actual infinity. Never is the totality of points of one section of a continuous line given in actuality and simultaneously. Only certain specific points, the ends, the middle, and so on, are given in actuality. The others exist only potentially, for division is never achieved and will never reach the ultimate element; it is infinite to be sure, but only potentially infinite. It suffices for a continuum to be indefinitely divisible, in other words, for division always to be capable of being taken beyond the point it has reached. Continuity does not boil down to contiguity of elements: in a continuum, these exist only potentially, blended together in some way. The doctrine of potential infinity has in fact been found by mathematicians to be sufficient. It was not until the end of the 19th century that infinity became conceivable as actual infinity through concepts developed by modern mathematics.

However, the Aristotelian distinction between the actual and the potential, beginning with actual infinity and potential infinity, came after Zeno's time. Starting from premises that his contemporaries took for granted in an attempt to understand the measurement of distance and time in motion, and more generally the texture of a physical continuum, Zeno, as a faithful Eleatic, could show only their intrinsic contradictions.

ZENO AND THE HISTORY OF PHILOSOPHY

Diogenes Laertius reports, and Sextus Empiricus confirms, that Aristotle viewed Zeno as the inventor of dialectics (Diogenes Laertius, *Lives* IX.25, VIII.57; Sextus Empiricus, *Adv. Math.* VII.6). Dialectics, he explained, takes accepted beliefs as premises to deduce consequences and to submit the beliefs to debate by examining whether or not the consequences were coherent. Already in Plato's work, the testing of a hypothesis by examining the non-contradiction of its consequences was part of dialectical training, as seen in *Parmenides* in the example of Zeno himself. This process of refutation by

showing the absurdity of the opposite thesis would be rightly a technique of logic whose invention we owe to Zeno.

What, then, were the "accepted ideas" that Zeno took as targets in defending the Eleatic doctrine against its detractors? Many answers have been proposed, some maintaining that these targets concerned merely "common sense," which grants the plurality of things and the existence of movement as an immediate given, based on the senses, while others maintain that the targets were one or another of the various "pluralist" theories that predated the Eleatics or were contemporary with them. But an analysis of the set of arguments themselves suggests that Zeno sought to refute an idea that was still quite foreign to the distinctions between the perceptible and the intelligible, between the physical and the mathematical, between the physical and the ontological, between the potential and the actual, between arithmetic unity and the ultimate element of the division of magnitudes. This idea grew out of syncretic, archaic thought. Now, the confusion among ontology, physics, geometry, and arithmetic is quite obvious in Aristotle's summary—which shows signs of perplexity, moreover—of the old Pythagorean doctrine prevailing in southern Italy during the period when Zeno was defending Parmenides. Moreover, it is most likely that the Pythagoreans were critical of Parmenidean monism. However, this historical interpretation has largely lost the credit it had gained from the work of Paul Tannery. While it is not possible to go into the details here, the debate is worth recalling.

After Zeno, it was hard not to take into account the aporias to which he had drawn attention. Some aspects of doctrines from later times seem designed to avoid those questions. For example, Democritean atomism rejects the infinite divisibility of physical magnitudes: it posits atoms as unbreakable and varying in shape and size, and it conceives of the continuum as a vacuum in which the movement of atoms nevertheless exists. Platonism, for its part, makes a radical distinction between mathematical entities and the things of the perceptible world, by positing the former as ideals; this may be no more than a partial response, but it is nevertheless a decisive first step. Aristotle maintains this distinction by presenting mathematical entities as abstractions of the physical world, and his doctrine of potential infinity, valid for both the geometrical continuum and the physical continuum (Aristotle is no atomist), resolves for good—as we have seen—Zeno's aporias. The Aristotelian and even the Scholastic traditions were content to adopt this position; however, it entails a distinction between the actual and the potential that has been challenged in modern times.

If we set aside the misunderstandings that we can attribute to lack of knowledge of the historical doctrinal context, all the greatest thinkers have kept Zeno's arguments in mind. We see this, for example, in Spinoza, in the "Letter to Louis Meyer" (April 20, 1663), in which he explains that time,

measure, and number exist only in the mind, as modes of thought; we see it in *The Principles of Descartes's Philosophy* (II, VI, scholia) in which Spinoza contests the existence of a minimum of time. There is also Pascal, who criticizes the indivisibles in depth at the end of the first section of the treatise *On the Geometrical Mind;* and there is Kant, who evokes Zeno with regard to the "cosmological conflict of reason with itself," a conflict linked to the assumption that the world is an entity in itself (*Critique of Pure Reason* I, II, 2.2.7). At the end of the 19th century and in the 20th, discussion of Zeno of Elea regained its vigor, owing to the influence of neo-Kantianism, to mathematical theorizing on the actual infinite, and to the development of the history of Greek science. Those debates have not always shed any new or relevant light on the topic, and they have led some to conclude that the famous aporias constitute an eternal defiance of human reason. I hope to have shown that that is not at all the case.

Maurice Caveing
Translated by Elizabeth Rawlings and Jeannine Pucci

Bibliography

Texts and Translations

Diels, Hermann. *Die Fragmente der Vorsokratiker.* Ed. Walther Kranz. Berlin: Weidmann, 1968.

Lee, H. D. P. *Zeno of Elea: A Text, with Translation and Notes.* Cambridge: Luzac, 1936.

Simplicius. *In Physica.* Ed. Hermann Diels. 2 vols. Berlin, 1882–1895.

Untersteiner, Mario. *Zenone: Testimonianze e Frammenti.* Amsterdam: Hakkert, 1967.

Studies

Brochard, Victor. "Les arguments de Zénon d'Elée contre le mouvement." *Comptes-rendus de l'Académie des sciences morales* 29 (1888): 555–568. Repr. in *Etudes de philosophie ancienne et de philosophie moderne.* Paris: Alcan, 1912; Vrin, 1974.

———. "Les prétendus sophismes de Zénon d'Elée." *Revue de métaphysique et de morale* (1893): 209–215. Repr. in *Etudes de philosophie ancienne et de philosophie moderne.*

Caveing, Maurice. *Zénon d'Elée: Prolégomènes aux doctrines du continu.* Paris: Vrin, 1982.

Fraenkel, Hermann. "Zeno of Elea's Attacks on Plurality." *American Journal of Philology* 63 (1942): 1–25, 193–206.

Fritz, Kurt von. "Zenon von Elea." In *Paulys Realencyclopädie der classischen Altertumswissenschaft.* 2nd ser., 19.2. Stuttgart: Metzler, 1972. Pp. 53–83.

Grunbaum, A. *Modern Science and Zeno's Paradoxes.* London: George Allen & Unwin, 1967.

Koyre, Alexandre. "Remarques sur les paradoxes de Zénon." Trans. from *Jahrbuch für Philosophie und Phänomenologische Forschung* 5. Halle, 1922. Repr. in *Etudes d'histoire de la pensée philosophique.* Paris: Gallimard, 1971. Pp. 9–35.

Lachelier, Jules. "Note sur les deux derniers arguments de Zénon d'Elée contre l'existence du mouvement." *Revue de métaphysique et de morale* 18 (1910): 345–355.

Raven, J. E. *Pythagoreans and Eleatics.* Chicago: Argonaut, 1967.

Solmsen, Friedrich. "The Tradition about Zeno of Elea Reexamined." *Phronesis* 16, no. 2 (1971): 116–141.

Tannery, Paul. "Le concept scientifique du continu: Zénon d'Elée et Georg Cantor." *Revue philosophique de la France et de l'étranger* 20, no. 2 (1885): 385ff.

Vlastos, Gregory. "Plato's Testimony concerning Zeno of Elea." *Journal of Hellenic Studies* 95 (1975): 136–162.

———. "Zeno of Elea." In *The Encyclopedia of Philosophy.* Ed. P. Edwards. New York and London: Macmillan, 1967. Vol. 8, pp. 369–379.

Related Articles

Demonstration and the Idea of Science; Mathematics; Parmenides

CURRENTS OF THOUGHT

THE ACADEMY

THE HISTORY OF THE ACADEMY seems better suited than that of any other school to illustrate the creative freedom that is a hallmark of Greek thought. For this reason, the bond of tradition is particularly difficult to discern when one seeks to define an Academic. From an institutional point of view, the matter is a simple one: an Academic philosopher is someone who belonged to the school founded by Plato, a school that functioned without significant difficulties under a series of scholarchs, or heads, up to the 1st century C.E. But if we want to bring even a modicum of philosophical coherence into correspondence with this historical unity, we find ourselves with a real problem. What type of continuity could there have been, for example, between Plato, the inventor of the theory of Forms, and Speusippus, who denied their existence? How can we include in the same lineage the dogmatic philosopher Xenocrates, whom the ancients credited with inventing the tripartite division of philosophy (physics, ethics, logic), and Arcesilaus, who preached suspension of judgment in all circumstances?

INSTITUTIONAL HISTORY

Even in antiquity, some writers attempted to solve the problem just raised: preferring to emphasize differences rather than commonalities, they distinguished among several Academies. The most complete classification is that of Sextus Empiricus. Referring to sources he does not cite, Sextus identifies three distinct Academies: the Early, that is, Plato's; the Middle, that of Arcesilaus; and the New, that of Carneades and Clitomachus. He even points out that others added a fourth, that of Philon, and a fifth, that of Antiochus of Ascalon. Despite its apparent rigor, this classification has no absolute value: it is confirmed neither by Cicero, who knew the Academy from the inside, as a pupil of Philon of Larissa, nor by Plutarch, who identified with the Academy and knew it well. Sextus's account proves only that the ancient historians of philosophy had dwelt on genuine differences to justify the discontinuity in their presentation of the Academy. But what Sextus does not make clear is that these philosophical changes never disturbed the institutional unity of the school.

We know that at the age of twenty-eight, after Socrates' death, Plato traveled through various regions in the Mediterranean Basin; when he returned to Athens he began to teach in a gymnasium located in a zone outside the

walls. This site was named after the hero Hecademus, whose legend, passed down in various versions, is connected with the account of the arrival of the Dioscurides in Greece. Some time later Plato set up his school in a small garden near the gymnasium. The Academy was founded in 387, and it was long believed that this institution had the status of an association. However, such a status did not exist under Athenian law, nor was the school defined by Plato's ownership of the property. Institutionally, then, the Academy existed only through the selection of a scholarch; by this means, an Academic chosen by his peers was designated a successor to Plato. The first succession seems to have been arranged by Plato himself, who chose his nephew Speusippus as scholarch. The election, if there was one, was merely a ratification of the master's choice. After Speusippus's death, however, a real electoral process was adopted. One might have expected that the choice would be Plato's most brilliant student, Aristotle, but whether by chance or as the result of some maneuvering, Aristotle was traveling in Macedonia at the time. Xenocrates just barely won the election over two other candidates who, after their defeat, chose to found other schools rather than remain in the Academy. Xenocrates was not the most brilliant philosopher: Plato himself had said that Aristotle needed a rein and Xenocrates a goad. The election seems to have been based on a moral criterion, Xenocrates having qualities in this realm that Speusippus was said to have lacked. Was the selection of other scholarchs the object of such close competition? The sources are silent on this point. We may suppose, in any case, that no scholarch tried to impose his own successor himself, even though some let their personal preference be known: according to Diogenes Laertius—but how credible is he?—Crates and Arcesilaus were made scholarchs because they were special favorites of Polemon and Crantor.

According to the most rigorous chronology, the dates of election of the principal scholarchs of the Academy were as follows: 348/7, Speusippus; 339/8, Xenocrates; 314/3, Polemon; 270/69, Crates; 268/264?; Arcesilaus; 244/3, Lacydus; 167/6, Carneades; 127/6, Clitomachus; 110/9, Philon of Larissa.

Until fairly recently, it was generally thought that the Academy had functioned without interruption from Plato's day until the Athenian schools were closed by Justinian. In fact the history of the school founded by Plato ends in 88 B.C.E., the year in which the last scholarch, Philon of Larissa, sought refuge in Rome, fleeing an Athens besieged by Mithridates. This date marks a break in the institutional line, and the efforts of Philon's dissident disciple, Antiochus of Ascalon, to substitute what he believed to be philosophical legitimacy for institutional legitimacy proved vain. At various times, philosophers claimed to be representing the Academy—Plutarch, for example—or founded Platonic schools. However, these thinkers were never Academics in the historical sense of the term.

THE EARLY ACADEMY

The designation Early Academy was of course given a posteriori to the scholarchs in the line from Speusippus to Crates, to emphasize the importance of modifications introduced after their time by Arcesilaus. It is only recently that the Early Academy has been studied in depth, and these efforts have run into considerable difficulty. No works by the scholarchs of the Early Academy have survived, and Aristotle, our most complete source for an understanding of their thought, is by no means an objective historian. Committed to refuting Plato and the Academics, he proceeded with his demonstration without troubling to give precise references. Speusippus, for example, while very important in *Metaphysics,* is cited only twice. It is thus difficult to know what can be attributed to each of the philosophers of the Early Academy. An additional difficulty arises in connection with learned controversies over Plato's "oral teaching." The group of exegetes known as the Tübingen school (Konrad Gaiser, Hans Joachim Kramer) used some passages from Aristotle to construct the theory according to which Plato's oral teaching was more important than his writings; an understanding of that teaching was indispensable, according to the theory, for an analysis of the philosophy of Speusippus and Xenocrates.

Speusippus

The Early Academy was characterized from the outset by one fundamental feature: the abandonment of the theory of Forms as Plato had conceived it, and the search for what we may call a "substitute transcendence." Indeed, although Speusippus remained faithful to the Platonic dogmas, according to Diogenes Laertius, a reading of Aristotle's *Metaphysics* suggests that Plato's first successor did not maintain the doctrine of Forms, which had evolved over time in its conception but which the master had never completely renounced.

Why did Speusippus dissociate himself from Plato on such an essential point? We have no information about his motivations, but we may suppose that this decision did not merely express a desire to affirm his philosophical originality after the disappearance of Plato's overpowering personality. It probably resulted above all from a reckoning with all the objections to the Platonic Forms raised within the Academy. Does Aristotle not say that the school of Speusippus "abandoned Ideal number and posited mathematical number because they perceived the difficulty and artificiality of the Ideal Theory"? (*Metaphysics* XIII.9.1086a.3–6). These objections are analyzed by Plato himself in *Parmenides;* they are presented differently in the critiques formulated by Aristotle in *Metaphysics,* which takes up the themes already expressed in his book on ideas, prior to the founding of the Lyceum. In the

Platonic dialogue that bears his name, old Parmenides shows Socrates what difficulties await him when he considers the multiple world of the sensible as the copy of these Forms, which are absolute realities situated apart from the things that belong to them. Without going into the details of a very complex demonstration, we can recall some of the arguments here. If sensible things belong to separate Forms, do they belong to form as a whole? This would assume that each Form, present in each of its representations, is separate from itself. But if we abandon this hypothesis and assert that a sensible thing participates in only one aspect of Form, Form loses the essential unity that was presented as one of its characteristics.

Just as serious a difficulty arises with the argument that Aristotle calls the "third man." As expressed by Parmenides, the objection goes as follows: when we look at a collection of objects that appear great, there is in them a common characteristic by which we infer that greatness is one thing. But when we include in our thought at the same time greatness and things that appear great, there will also appear a greatness in relation to which all these appear great. Accordingly, as Parmenides tells Socrates, "each of your ideas will no longer be one, but their number will be infinite" (*Parmenides* 132b). It is quite likely that, in Aristotle's day, the objections expressed in *Metaphysics* were also debated in the Academy. In that text, the Stagirite condemns what he calls *ekthesis,* the Platonic separation between the world of Forms and the world of sensible realities, in which he sees the source of insuperable contradictions. For example, if each Idea constitutes a separate reality, this reality is impossible to define, for the definition will be made up of common nouns, and this implies that the definition will apply equally to other things. Moreover, how could Forms be, as Plato would have it, the cause of movement and change? By virtue of their immutable nature, they must rather be causes of repose. And if we seek to define the relation between a sensible object and the equivalent Form, we still find ourselves in a quandary: if a Form is identical to a thing both by nature and by name, it constitutes a useless doubling of the thing; and if a Form has nothing in common with a thing but a relation of homonomy, in what sense can the two belong together, given that there is an essential difference between the two realities? It is also possible that for Speusippus the theory of Forms was incompatible with the method of division *(diairesis)* by which Plato had believed he could surmount the objections put before him.

Speusippus thought he was escaping these difficulties by equating the absolute that Plato had found in the Forms with mathematics. His recourse to mathematics was not made ex nihilo, for mathematics already had an important place in Platonic philosophy. But whereas Plato viewed mathematical objects as intermediary beings between Forms and sensible things, Speusippus saw in numbers the characteristics that Plato attributed to Ideas.

According to Aristotle, Plato recognized three substances: Ideas, mathemat-

ical objects, and sensible things. For him, then, mathematical objects were intermediary between Numbers and ideal Figures, which did not differ essentially from any other Form, on the one hand, and the numbers and figures of the sensible, on the other. For example, between the necessarily imperfect circles of the sensible and the Idea of a circle, there exists the circle insofar as it is a mathematical object, defined by its perfect roundness. This intermediary status of mathematical objects explains the difference that Plato establishes in *The Republic* between mathematicians and dialecticians: the former reason from hypotheses, for which they seek verification, while the latter seek to attain an unconditional *(anhypotheton)* that will guarantee them absolute knowledge.

We know for certain from Aristotle that Speusippus rejected the theory of Forms: he believed neither in absolute numbers nor in absolute figures. If numbers and figures constituted for him the only absolute realities, this was not insofar as they were Forms but insofar as they were mathematical entities. It would be too simple to suppose that Speusippus reserved for numbers and figures the status that Plato assigned to all Forms. The matter is much more complex, for it is in the very conception of number that he expressed his difference in relation to his predecessor. For Plato, each ideal number, by virtue not of its nature as number but of its status as Form, constitutes a unity that is separate both from the numbers of the sensible world and from the other ideal numbers. Speusippus, on the contrary, defines each number not as a unique entity but as a set of units, since he derives them from two principles: One and multiplicity. The Speusippean number is, like the Platonic Ideas, an eternal reality, separate from the sensible world, and the figures are derived from it by analogy, the analogy of the point being number one, the line number two, and the plane number three. One of the principal problems that arise here is the status of the One: has it a substance different from that of the other numbers, or is it only the first of numbers? Aristotle writes: "Speusippus assumed still more kinds of substances starting with 'the One,' and positing principles for each kind: one for numbers, another for magnitudes, and then another for the soul" (*Metaphysics* VII.ii.1028b). Taken literally, the text implies that One is of a different nature from the other numbers, but in another context the same Aristotle says that, for Speusippus, mathematical numbers are the first entities. The explanation of this problem may lie in the ingenious solution proposed by Leonardo Tarán, who stressed the difference between Aristotle and Speusippus with regard to One. For Aristotle who, like Plato, begins the series of numbers with two, One is not a number but the principle of numbers. For Speusippus, on the contrary, One is identical with the number one, and it is for this reason that it is the principle of numbers. The contradiction that can be discerned in Aristotle concerning the Speusippean One can thus be explained by interference on this point between his own thought and that of the Academic.

As far as the second principle of number, multiplicity, is concerned, there is a paucity of evidence, and it is quite possible that Speusippus himself was not very explicit on this point, since Aristotle reproaches him for not having stated precisely how number can be composed of One and of Multiplicity. In any event, it is especially important to know how Speusippus moved from numbers, which he saw as the primary entities, to sensible objects. As we have already seen, he established a relation of likeness between figures and mathematical numbers. But according to Aristotle's account, Speusippus identified several substances: in addition to numbers and figures, the soul—which he claimed to be immortal—and others he did not specify, until he came to sensible objects, which he also apparently construed as a substance. Thus Aristotle criticizes him for representing the universe as a series of episodes lacking any relation one to another. This charge has to be assessed in relation to the fact that Speusippus did not equate the One with the Good; he asserted that for plants and animals the beautiful and the perfect did not meet in the seed but in the products derived from it. In thus refusing to give an essential status to the Good, he diverged from Platonism on a fundamental point of doctrine. According to Aristotle, in so doing he sought to avoid the difficulties involved in identifying the One and the Good—for example, the resultant need to equate Evil with Multiplicity. But how is one to conceive of this universe, which is made up of different substances and which reveals its perfection only at the end of its course?

For Aristotle, numbers cannot be the cause of anything, and that is one reason he viewed the Speusippean universe as a discontinuous series of "episodes." But we know that Speusippus himself established a relation of similarity, or *homoiotes*, between the different levels of reality. This concept is unquestionably inherited from Plato, for whom a thing is defined by a relation of similarity to the corresponding Form. But its use by Speusippus poses at least two problems. On the one hand, what can this similarity be when the first entities are no longer Forms, but numbers? On the other hand, if we recall that similarity goes hand in hand in Plato with causality, since *Phaedo* indicates that Ideas are at once models and causes of being and becoming, what does this really mean for Speusippus?

On the first point, Tarán emphasizes that each individual object turns out to be, for Speusippus, the center of a network of relations, the set of which constitutes its essence. If knowledge of numbers, which are the only eternal and immutable entities, is direct, knowledge of sensible realities requires that we allow concepts of similarity and difference to come into play, for these concepts are derived from this direct knowledge of number, and they allow us to determine the relation of the object in question to other objects. The classification of sensible objects thus presupposes a dichotomy, which arises when we establish whether two things are alike or unlike, and Speusippus applied this method to the classification of words, plants, and animals.

As for the second problem, that of the unity of the Speusippean universe, the volume of criticisms formulated by Aristotle show that this was the locus of a cluster of quite significant difficulties. As Léon Robin justly writes: "Speusippus, preserving the One as principle, considered it not as something real and actually in existence, but as an imperfect and indeterminate principle that is itself gradually determined and enriched" (p. 510). In considering that One is all in potentiality and nothing in actuality, the Academic left himself open to the objection formulated in *Metaphysics:* if One is not a substance, how could number exist as an independent reality? Aristotle also reproached the Platonists in general and Speusippus in particular for failing to define with adequate precision how numbers derive from principles. Finally, he rejected the Speusippean theory of similarity, which he criticized for confusing genus and species. As even the exegetes most favorable to Speusippus emphasize, it is hard to see how his system can end up with concepts such as "man" or "plant."

Another aspect of Speusippus's philosophy warrants mentioning precisely because it is responsible for a great deal of confusion, and that is its relation to Pythagoreanism. Speusippus was unquestionably interested in this philosophical doctrine, since according to Iamblichus he had written a "nice little book" on numbers, inspired by Philolaus's writings, a good half of which was consecrated to the decade. The question of just what in Iamblichus's account really comes from Speusippus is controversial. However much influence Pythagoreanism may have had on Speusippus, an essential divergence between these two philosophical beliefs persists: for the Pythagoreans, numbers were inherent in matter, while for Speusippus, they had a transcendent status.

The philosophy of Speusippus, who claimed to have gotten around the difficulties of Platonic idealism, itself drew numerous objections. Thus it is not surprising that Xenocrates did not maintain the same positions, and that he developed a system that he undoubtedly thought allowed him to avoid the contradictions with which his two predecessors were charged.

Xenocrates

Xenocrates' attempt at renewal found no favor in Aristotle's eyes. In fact the Stagirite seems to have thought that Xenocrates, instead of producing a satisfactory solution, had developed the most erroneous doctrine of all, since he combined the incoherent aspects of both Plato and Speusippus. Speusippus had been charged by Aristotle with "episodism." Xenocrates, for his part, placed special emphasis on the articulations of philosophic thought and on the definition of the nature of relations between the different levels of reality.

According to Sextus Empiricus, Xenocrates was the first to divide philosophy into three parts: physics, ethics, and logic. To be sure, Sextus, reclaiming a tradition that was to be echoed again in a passage of Cicero's *Academica,* says

that this tripartite division was already implicitly present in Plato. The fact remains that Xenocrates was the one who provided a clear definition of this method, which played an important role in the constitution of the great Hellenistic documents, notably those of Stoicism.

Concerning the way reality is organized, several sources show us with what care Xenocrates sought to eradicate the Speusippean doctrine of a world made of mutually independent substances. Sextus Empiricus—whose testimony does seem to be contradicted by a much more allusive text by Theophrastus—tells us that Xenocrates identified three substances, the sensible, the intelligible, and the mixed, and that he situated the first inside heaven, the second outside, and the third in heaven itself. According to Sextus, Xenocrates had at least one thing in common with Speusippus: he affirmed the existence of intelligible realities external to the world. But while Speusippus identified these intelligible realities with numbers, Xenocrates went back to the theory of Ideas, which must have struck him, all things considered, as less subject to difficulties than the doctrine of his immediate predecessor. As further evidence of a tendency toward systematic simplification, one can point to the fact that Xenocrates criticized the multiplicity of Aristotelian categories and affirmed that all realities could be encompassed within the categories of the in-itself and the relative.

Relying on the testimony of Theophrastus, Léon Robin points out that Xenocrates was the first of the Platonists to pursue deduction from principles to its logical end, "and to determine, by their means, everything in the Universe" (p. 297, n. 272). This systematic use of deduction explains why Xenocrates has been viewed as the one of the Academics who most clearly foreshadowed Neoplatonism.

We actually know very little about the way Xenocrates conceived of principles. Aristostle refers at some length in *Metaphysics* to the various ways the Academics named the principle opposed to the One, but he does so without identifying the philosophers by name, and this allows for divergent interpretation on points of detail. We know from other sources that he opposed the *aenaon* to the One *(en)*; ancient Pythagoreanism, for which the *aenaon* was an important concept, interpreted it as "not-one," whereas the meaning was probably "always fluid." Did Xenocrates define this principle of multiplicity in terms of the Platonic dyad of the Large and the Small? This is entirely possible, but the anonymous character of Aristotle's discussion rules out any certainty on this point.

Nor do we know how Xenocrates explained the derivation of Ideas, which Plato said escape becoming, on the basis of the principles of the One and the Multiple. In contrast, we are better informed about the way he conceived of these Ideas, which were restored under his scholarchate after Speusippus's mathematical approach. Xenocrates defined the Idea as being "the exemplary cause of all the things that always subsist in the order of nature" (Proclus, *In*

Plat. Parm. IV.888). This definition, considered suspect by certain commentators owing to the fact of its inclusion in one of Proclus's texts (several passages of which are indeed foreign to the Early Academy), seems, on the contrary, characteristic of the Xenocratean effort to avoid the objections that had been raised to Speusippus. Indeed, the definition of the Idea as being inextricably model and cause constituted a display against the Aristotelian reproach of episodism. The reference to "things that always subsist in the order of nature" can be understood in opposition to the products of technology, which for their part are not included in this narrow relation to ideas and, beyond these, to principles. But Xenocrates' return to idealism does not mean that he is confined to an attitude of Platonic orthodoxy. His mature innovation in the domain of Ideas was in fact to develop more fully an alternative that Aristotle called "the worst" (*Metaphysics* XIII.viii.1083b), namely, the equation of ideal Number with mathematical number. For Aristotle, this way of thinking involves arbitrarily attributing to mathematical number properties that do not belong to it, and encountering anew all the difficulties of the ideal Platonic Number. Aristotle also reproaches Xenocrates for constructing magnitudes on the basis of matter and ideal Number, each geometric figure deriving from a Number-Idea. What is the status of these magnitudes? he inquires. Are they Ideas, and in what way will they contribute to establishing the existence of sensible things? As Margherita Isnardi Parente has rightly remarked, Aristotle criticizes Xenocrates both for his mathematical concept of Ideas and for endowing these with a kind of "intrinsic capacity for dynamic deployment in the spatial dimension" (*Senocrate,* p. 346). This was the point of view from which Aristotle and the Peripatetics vigorously criticized the Xenocratean theory—already present in Plato, according to certain scholars—of the indivisible line. Xenocrates, who, contrary to Speusippus, did not conceive of every number as deriving from the One (at once principle and first number), defended the thesis of indivisibility of all the magnitudes, each of them referring to a Number-Idea.

So far as cosmology is concerned, Xenocrates affirmed that in *Timaeus* Plato had evoked a creation of the world to clarify his thought, and he compared this method to the construction of a geometrical figure designed to make clear what the essence of a triangle is, for example, even if the triangle itself does not correspond perfectly to this transcendent reality. With regard to this interpretation, Aristotle critizes Xenocrates for seeking to "come to Plato's aid," and this concept of "aid" *(boetheia)* does not necessarily have a polemical origin; it can be interpreted as demonstrating genuine historical solidarity between the Early Academy and Plato. This solidarity left a great deal of room for interpretation (the little we know of Xenocrates' cosmology reveals significant differences from that of *Timaeus*), but it can be defined as the determination not to leave the last word to Aristotelian criticism on fundamental points. This dual aspect, original creation against a background of

faith in the Platonic inspiration, appears with particular clarity in Xenocrates' definition of the soul as being a "number moving by itself" (*On the Soul* I.ii.404b27–28). In this definition we find both a Platonic element—the soul is defined in *Phaedrus* as self-moving—and the mathematical idealism characteristic of Xenocrates. Following the lead of Aristotle, who had criticized this definition, Simplicius claimed to demonstrate that the soul, for Xenocrates, was an intermediary between the Idea and the sensible, but there is every reason to believe that Xenocrates, who like Plato proclaimed the immortality of the soul, did not establish any difference between the soul and the ideal Number. Moreover, the fact that an entire doxographic tradition, perhaps inaugurated by Xenocrates himself, attributes this definition of the soul to Pythagoras changes nothing so far as the equivalency of this definition with the general orientation of the Xenocratean philosophy is concerned. After all, a text by Plutarch shows how the Academic—who had abandoned the tripartite division of the soul described in *The Republic* for the bipartite division of Pythagorean origin (reason, passion)—could invoke *Timaeus* in support of this definition, by interpreting in a very personal manner the passage in which Plato explains how souls are constructed.

But Xenocrates was also particularly careful to explore all the possible articulations between philosophy and theology, and this aspect of his thought had a lasting influence; Varro (116–27 B.C.E.) drew on it when he sought to give the Roman religion a philosophical foundation. We know that Xenocrates, who attributed a certain notion of the divine even to irrational animals, had explained that the One and the Dyad are gods, the first corresponding to Zeus, king of heaven, the second to Hera, mother of the gods, sovereign of all things under heaven and soul of the universe. In the same way he identified heaven and the stars with the fire of the gods of Olympus, and he declared that the sublunary world is peopled with invisible demons, intermediaries between gods and men. Using a mathematical metaphor, he compared the gods with an equilateral triangle (a symbol of the invariable), man with a scalene triangle, and demons with isosceles triangles. Through his reflection on religion, Xenocrates seems thus to have preceded the Stoics in their identification of the mythological gods with philosophical concepts. Still, no source attributes explicitly to him, as do certain exegetes, the invention of the theme—so present in Middle Platonism—of ideas as thoughts of God.

The Ethics of the Early Academy

In the realm of ethics, too, Xenocrates asserted his own strong philosophical personality, opening the way for Stoicism with his reflection on happiness. A number of accounts of his moral thought bear the mark of the rereading of his work by Antiochus of Ascalon and should thus be interpreted with great prudence, but the presence in Xenocrates of pre-Hellenistic themes, and most

particularly pre-Stoic ones, is difficult to contest: the search for inner serenity as the ultimate end of ethics, the importance of voluntary submission to the law, the invention of the category of indifferents, a reflection on virtue in its relation to nature and happiness. Now the little we know about Polemon, his successor as head of the Academy, has to do almost exclusively with the field of ethics. Polemon stressed moral action and criticized those who devoted themselves to logical speculation, comparing them to people who might have learned a manual of harmony by heart but would be incapable of putting it into practice. Polemon defined the sovereign good as a life in conformity with nature, and he seems to have strongly influenced his student Zeno, who was to be the founder of Stoicism. We find this same priority granted to ethics in Crantor, another Academic who was the author of a commentary on *Timaeus* (of which only a few fragments have survived), but who was especially well known in antiquity for his *Consolation*, addressed to a friend after the death of his child, in which he urged the distraught father not to fight suffering in a radical way—as the Stoics would do later on—but rather to moderate it. In this work, Crantor developed the theme of the survival of the soul after death, proof that the Early Academy's stress on the natural foundations of ethics had not cut it off from Platonic transcendence.

THE SKEPTICAL ACADEMY

It has long been a commonplace of the history of ancient philosophy to affirm that, with Arcesilaus, the Academy passed from dogmatism to Skepticism. This dualist vision of the history of the Platonic school is justified: Arcesilaus claimed to be unable to know anything, and he made the universal suspension of judgment *(epoche peri pantōn)* the key to his philosophy. Moreover, unlike the scholarchs of the Early Academy, who had written a great deal, those of the Middle and New Academies most often restricted themselves to the oral practice of philosophy, which had its origin at least partly in the Socratic model. Nevertheless, to characterize this period of the Academy as Skeptical is problematic, inasmuch as this does not correspond to the genealogy of the concept of Skepticism. Indeed Skepticism, in the sense in which we understand it today, does not appear as an autonomous philosophy until the 1st century B.C.E., when Aenesidemus criticized the New Academy, too dogmatic in his eyes, for quoting Pyrrhon—and recent research has shown that Pyrrhon did not correspond very well to the common image of a Skeptic.

The Neopyrrhonism of Aenesidemus is the philosophy that, by way of Sextus Empiricus, is at the origin of the skeptical ideas that have proliferated from antiquity to our day. However, it would never have occurred to Arcesilaus to use the term *skepticism* in connection with himself; the word was not applied to him until much later, and there is every reason to believe that he described himself first and foremost as an Academic. Here much

more than a label is at stake. Indeed, even though Arcesilaus preceded the Neopyhrronians in the universal suspension of judgment, this suspension occurred in his case against the background of his Platonic philosophical identity; this is the principal difficulty for those who study his thought. We may even wonder whether Aenesidemus's decision to take Pyrrhon as an emblematic figure of Skepticism—a Pyrrhon of whom the only traces were the memory of a moralist indifferent to everything that was not the moral good—was not the result of the difficulty inherent in professing a philosophy of universal doubt while attempting to integrate oneself, if only by institutional tradition, with the posterity of Plato.

This problem of the coexistence in the same line of thought of the suspension of assent and the reference to Plato was already intriguing to the ancients. Some, evidently not very happy with the course the Academy had taken under Arcesilaus's direction, explained the mutation by proclaiming the existence of an esoteric teaching: according to them, the Academics concealed the positive side of Plato's philosophy, revealing it only to a small number of students. Thus their skepticism was only a tactical maneuver, intended to counter the development of the dogmatism proper to Hellenistic schools and notably to the Stoics. St. Augustine himself, in *Contra Academicos*, comes to the defense of this thesis, but it appears chiefly as the caricature of an unquestionable reality: in the Academy of Arcesilaus and Carneades, Plato continued to be studied, and even to serve as a source for universal doubt. But precisely what of Plato's was being read? Although the thesis of a selective reading, retaining only the dialogues in which Plato claims he himself had arrived at no result, may be immediately attractive, it is not confirmed by any source, and several indications allow us to suppose, on the contrary, that the New Academics had taken over the entire Platonic corpus. While they clearly could not claim that Plato had come up with the theory of the suspension of judgment himself, they announced that they had found in him a refusal of certainties, a universal questioning in which they saw the anticipation of their own intellectual undertaking.

Arcesilaus

Arcesilaus's complex personality is too often muddled by the fact that we refer almost exclusively to the account of Sextus Empiricus, who, while not recognizing Arcesilaus as a genuine Skeptic, still speaks of him in the framework of Neopyrrhonism. Now, in seeing Arcesilaus only as the philosopher of the *epoche,* we neglect important aspects of his thought. Thus we are too often unaware that this philosopher, to whom we generally attribute the responsibility of a real break in the history of the Academy, was seduced in his youth by a very dogmatic Platonism, since he compared the school of his master, Polemon, to a place that would have provided refuge for survivors of the

Golden Age. A few traces remain of his attachment to this teaching: we know from Tertullian that he worked out—it would be nice to know at what period in his life—a theology in which three types of divinities derived from heaven and earth. In any case, the importance that this "Skeptic" saw in the articulation between philosophy and religion, in the tradition of the Early Academy, is confirmed for us by the fact that, in interpreting a verse from Hesiod in a very personal way, replacing the word *bion* (life) with the word *noon* (mind), he liked to repeat that the gods concealed intelligence from man. All this shows that Arcesilaus's aporetic philosophy still retained something of the transcendental orientation of Platonism. There is even a late but on the whole well-informed text, *Prolegomena in Platonis philosophia,* in which we are told that among the arguments raised by the New Academy to justify its philosophy of doubt there was a reference to *Phaedo,* a dialogue in which it is said that the soul can never reach truth so long as it is intertwined with the body. But whereas Plato, in the most famous of his myths, compared the life of men with that of prisoners who perceive only shadows on the walls of the cave, Arcesilaus declared that the world was entirely covered with darkness, and he claimed to go further than Socrates, who had at least the certainty that he knew nothing.

Arcesilaus's aporeticism, which led him to claim that the senses, and also reason, are incapable of reaching any certain knowledge, and that the wise man should suspend his judgment under all circumstances, gave rise to very different interpretations. Some have found Pyrrhonian or Peripatetic influences, though these are not very likely. Much more interesting is the thesis advanced by Pierre Couissin in 1929, for whom the fundamental concepts of Arcesilaus's thought resulted from the dialectical subversion of Stoic concepts. The Stoics maintained that most representations are "cataleptic," that is, that they correspond to at least part of reality and produce assent almost automatically. In proclaiming that man lives in a world of darkness, Arcesilaus thus transformed into a rule what was the exception for his dogmatic adversaries; in this way he made *epoche* the very essence of wisdom. Similarly, the concept of the probable *(eulogon),* which he advocated as a guide for the wise man's action, resulted from the ironical generalization of a concept that, for the Stoics, characterized "middle" morality, precisely that of the man who has not attained wisdom. Couissin's thesis accounts for many aspects of Arcesilaus's philosophy, but it does not reckon with all the sources, especially those that tell us that he based suspension of assent on the principle of isosthenia, that is, the equal force of opposed discourses.

Thus there really was in Arcesilaus a personal philosophy of the impossibility of knowing that could not be reduced to his anti-Stoic dialectics, even if the struggle against Stoicism was his major cause, as it was of the scholarchs who followed him. Yet Arcesilaus did not claim originality: we know from Cicero and Plutarch that he had built up a genealogy of the philosophy of

doubt that included not only Socrates and Plato but also such Presocratics as Parmenides, Heraclitus, Democritus, Anaxagoras, and Empedocles. It would be a mistake to see in this enumeration nothing but a confused amalgamation. In bringing together in a single tradition thinkers whose profound divergences he could not have failed to recognize, Arcesilaus was trying above all to emphasize an old way of philosophizing that was exempt—whatever dogmatic aspects were manifested by one philosopher or another—from the criticisms he directed at the Hellenistic, and especially the Stoic, philosophies, namely, the claim to absolute certainty, the obsession with a perfect system, the exaltation of the sage, who was equated with a god. This is especially clear in the way in which he elaborated the criticism of "cataleptic" representation. In the Stoic system, this has three characteristics: it is actual—that is, it derives from a real object; it is in conformity with that object; and it is such that it could not be the same if it came from anything other than that object. In concentrating his whole dialectic on this last provision, which he himself—if we can believe Cicero—obliged the Stoic Zeno to formulate, Arcesilaus was not merely attacking the sensualism of the Stoics. Indeed, when he strove to demonstrate that to every representation there may be a corresponding one that is in every respect identical to the first and that derives from a different object (this is what happens when twins are confused with one another) or from a nonbeing (dreams, hallucinations), he called into question a whole system that was based on the instinctive trust in fundamental ideas about nature and that established a continuity of certainty, from initial confidence in the senses to the perfect and unshakeable reason known as wisdom.

Carneades

Arcesilaus's inspiration was perpetuated, and in certain respects modified, by Carneades. One of the few things we know about Carneades is that he took part in an embassy sent by Athens to Rome in 155 in an attempt to lower a fine that had been imposed as a result of the sack of the village of Oropos. This embassy was unusual in that it consisted of three philosophers: in addition to Carneades, scholarch of the Academy, it included Critolaus and Diogenes of Babylon, scholarchs of the Lyceum and the Stoa, respectively. Carneades fascinated the Roman public with his oratorical virtuosity in defending, then in criticizing, the virtue of justice, or rather its diverse philosophical definitions. The Roman episode was a diplomatic success: Cato the Censor, fearing that the philosophers would turn Roman youth away from their ancestral virtues, asked the Senate to settle the affair as quickly as possible, and this was done to the benefit of Athens. Yet for a long time the embassy of 155 gave credence to the idea that Carneades was close to the Sophists, since he shared with them the quite undiplomatic practice of antilogy.

Considerable recent research has established that, despite some superficial re-semblances, Carneades had nothing in common with the Sophist Gorgias.

From the standpoint of epistemology, Carneades is presented as the founder of probabilism, a system of hierarchization of representations in terms of their degree of resemblance, since he judged that one cannot state with certainty about any representation that it is true. However, the term *probabilism* should be used with caution, for it possesses all the modern con-notations, mathematical connotations of probability in particular, whereas Carneades reasoned solely on the basis of the feeling of truth that representa-tions produce in us. The term *probable* comes to us from Cicero, who created the philosophical language used in Latin, and who chose a term he had al-ready used a good deal in his reflections on rhetoric. But with *probable*, Cicero was translating both *eulogon* and *pithanon*, and these terms corre-sponded to different phases in the philosophy of the New Academy. It has long been remarked that in sources dealing with Carneades, in place of the concept of *eulogon*, which Arcesilaus used, we find *pithanon* (literally, per-suasive), a term that referred directly not to the activity of reason but to the feeling of truth that one experiences in the face of most representations. Carneades returned to Arcesilaus's critique of "comprehensive" representa-tion and developed it further, pointing out in particular that no criterion for the truth of representations exists, since representation, which should simul-taneously reveal the condition of the subject and the reality of the external object, is often a source of error. But he also called into question the capacity of reason to arrive at truth and claimed to doubt the very principles of mathe-matics. His dialectics used *sorites* as its privileged instrument, that is, the sophism making it possible to pass imperceptibly from a thing to its contrary. However, this radical refusal to recognize the existence of a criterion for knowledge elicited from the Academy's adversaries the accusation that all life was being made impossible. Thus Carneades defined a practical criterion based on the feeling of truth that representations produce, and also on the ca-pacity of reason to carry out the task of verification. He thereby established a hierarchy, placing at the top the representation that gives a feeling of truth, that is not contradicted by any other, and that has been subject to verification.

Did Carneades himself espouse probabilism, or should his probabilism be interpreted only in terms of anti-Stoic dialectics, since the concept of *pithanon* also belonged to the gnoseology of that school? To tell the truth, the two aspects of Carneades' thought are inseparable. Dialectically, he certainly wanted to prove to the Stoics that at the very heart of their system they possessed elements that allowed them to do without a dogmatism that was impossible to espouse, since it was regularly contradicted by experience. But beyond this anti-Stoic dialectics, the Academic probably also wished to reha-bilitate, at a point when philosophy was heavily dogmatic, a concept of the act

of thinking in which uncertainty no longer appeared as a defect, but on the contrary as the sign of a requirement and as the condition of progress.

Carneades was not only a philosopher of knowledge. His reflection also bore on the other two parts of philosophy, ethics and physics. In the first of these fields, he struggled unceasingly to show the contradictory consequences that resulted from the Stoic claim to base morality on the natural impulse that makes every living thing seek from birth to persevere in being. For the Stoics, ethics was nothing but the passage from an instinctive harmony with nature to a harmony grounded in reason. Carneades responded, from within a certain Platonic tradition, that this natural tendency is not the source of wisdom but of self-centeredness and violence. Similarly, where physics was concerned, he demonstrated that if the Stoics were as rigorous as they claimed to be, they would start from their own premises—the observation of nature, a reckoning with beliefs about nature and the gods—and would cease to believe in the existence of a universal reason governing the world for man's benefit, reaching the conclusion that God does not exist and that everything is made and unmade through a straightforward dynamics of forces. For Carneades, the Stoic rooting of reason in feeling and instinct led to the negation of any really rational order. Though no source notes any dogmatic reference to Plato on the part of the Academic, it is certain that the systematic questioning of the Stoics' immanent rationalism left as a possible way out the recourse to a philosophy of transcendence. In this sense, one might say that Middle Platonism, which began to develop in the 1st century C.E., situates itself within a certain continuity in relation to the New Academy.

Carneades' Successors

The very long duration of Carneades' scholarchate and the philosopher's exceptional dialectical power were bound to lead to divergences as to the interpretation of a teaching which, like that of Arcesilaus, was exclusively oral. Clitomachus, Carneades' third successor as head of the Academy (we know nothing about the first two, and their scholarchates were very brief), abandoned this tradition of orality and indeed proved to be quite a prolific writer: he is credited with more than four hundred works. Comparing Carneades to Hercules, Clitomachus expressed his gratitude to his predecessor for liberating the human soul from what he considered a monstrosity, namely, assent, a source of opinions and lack of reflection. He gave a highly detailed presentation of his master's thought, insisting particularly on the absolute character of the suspension of judgment and on the viability of *pithanon* as a practical criterion. Clitomachus, some of whose writings have been passed along by Cicero, declared that, contrary to his adversaries' claims, the Academy in no way suppressed sensations. "The Academic school holds that there are dissimilarities between things of such a nature that some of them seem probable

and others the contrary; but this is not an adequate ground for saying that some things can be perceived and others cannot, because many false objects are probable but nothing false can be perceived and known" (Cicero, *Academica* II [*Lucullus*], xxxii.103).

Clitomachus has been described as standing in the same relation to Carneades as Xenophon did to Socrates: as an attentive disciple, but lacking significant originality or depth. The fact is, despite the importance of his written work, he did not succeed in convincing the majority of other Academics that he had given an irrefutable representation of his master's thought. In particular, Metrodorus of Stratonicea, who had gone from the Epicurean school to the Academy, claimed that he had been the only one who understood Carneades' teaching, and he expressed his differences with Clitomachus on two essential points. While Clitomachus placed absolute value on suspension of judgment, Metrodorus claimed that it had been only a weapon against Stoicism. Moreover he maintained that, contrary to Clitomachus's assertions, Carneades had acknowledged that in certain cases the sage himself gives his assent to an opinion. How can we assess these Metrodorean interpretations? The relativization of the suspension of judgment contained at least a partial truth, in that the Skepticism of the New Academy was principally a form of anti-Stoicism. As a matter of fact, Metrodorus posed a problem that has been given new currency by Pierre Couissin's research, and which contemporary specialists of this period of the Platonic school continue to debate: how is the game of dialectics, in which one only pretends to accept the adversaries' positions in order to draw contradictory or absurd consequences from them, articulated with personal beliefs in the thinking of the New Academics? So far as the problem of the sage's assent is concerned, Metrodorus's exegetical position expresses the same wish to define a New Academic thought independent of the fascinating Stoic model. Indeed, in the "orthodox" interpretation of Clitomachus, the New Academic sage is the mirror image of the Stoic sage: in admitting that the wise man sometimes does gives his assent by mistake, the scholarch departed from the Hellenistic conception of the *sophos* to return implicitly to the figure of the philosopher, a seeker of wisdom who thus accepts his own fallibility.

Metrodorus was never a scholarch, so his original position, which he pronounced with a certain arrogance, could be considered that of one of the dissidents who were regularly churned up by the system of philosophical schools. The conflict of interpretation between Clitomachus and Metrodorus would thus have assumed much less importance if Philon of Larissa, who was the last institutional scholarch of the Academy, had not adopted a position close to Metrodorus's. Despite the affirmations of some, no source authorizes us to suppose that it was in Athens itself that Philon, who had at first been in Clitomachus's camp, changed his opinion. He was already acquainted with Metrodorus's theses, but if he had accepted them while he was still scholarch

at Athens, the books he wrote after his arrival in Rome, where he went into exile after the siege of Athens by Mithridates, would not have astonished his friends as well as his adversaries. On this point, Cicero's account in *Academica* is devoid of ambiguity: the Roman books of Philon scandalized his old pupil Antiochus of Ascalon, who had seceded from the New Academy to recover what he insisted was the authentic inspiration of the Early Academy, as well as Heraclitus of Tyr, who had remained faithful to Carneades' philosophy insofar as Clitomachus had understood it. Unfortunately Cicero's *Academica* has come down to us in mutilated form, and the exact content of the Philonian innovations are the subject of debate among specialists. These innovations were of such importance that, in antiquity itself, some scholars saw Philon as the founder of a fourth Academy. More recently, Harold Tarrant has sought to give this philosopher an importance that he had never before had in philosophical research, by presenting him as the real promoter of the passage from Academic Skepticism to Middle Platonism. This is probably an excessive magnification of the role of someone who did no more than give official sanction to an evolution that would have taken place without him. What points did he develop in his Roman books? Certainly he insisted much more than his predecessors had on the unity of the Academy, from Plato to himself. This stress on the theme of unity does not mean that Arcesilaus and Carneades considered themselves foreign to the Platonic tradition, and we have seen that the former, in any case, had included Plato and Socrates among the inspirations of his philosophy. But in their day it was simply not as crucial to affirm the historic unity of the Academy as it was at a time when the philosophical and institutional continuity of the Academy might appear to have been shaken by the break with Antiochus of Ascalon and by the fact that, for the first time, a scholarch of the Platonic school found himself in exile, far from Athens.

It is in the field of epistemology that it is hardest to pinpoint the Philonian innovations. One thing at least is certain: he continued to fight the Stoic doctrine in this field, using the dialectical tools forged by his predecessors. There is no doubt that, even in his Roman books, there were sections in which he went back to the Academy's arguments against the Stoic criterion of knowledge, the "cataleptic" representation. But this criticism, traditional in its form, was no longer integrated into a vision of the world in which all certainty was considered impossible. Philon declared, in effect, that if the Stoic criterion does not allow knowledge of reality, the latter is none the less knowable by nature. Thus with Philon the skeptical arguments of the New Academy took on new meaning. They no longer expressed aporia, but instead reflected prudence and the need for truth in a cognitive process presented as conforming to the very nature of things. The problem that confronts the historian of the Academy is that the accounts that have Philon as their source do not tell us how he conceived of this knowledge, whose possibility he clearly affirmed.

Reading Cicero, in particular, leaves the impression that Philon, after giving the Academy this new orientation, had chiefly devoted himself to perpetuating the anti-Stoic dialectics that had prevailed since Arcesilaus. Certain recent research has nevertheless emphasized the concept of evidence *(enargeia)*, which would constitute Philon's personal contribution to Academic epistemology. Yet if we take into account the fact that he pugnaciously pursued his criticism of the criterion of self-evidence, and if we also recall that Carneades had already constructed his hierarchy of probability on the basis of the feeling of self-evidence, we must conclude that Philon was not being truly innovative in the appreciation of sensorial knowledge. In reality, he seems not to have been capable of giving a concrete content to the theoretical revolution that his Roman books expressed. Although no account credits him explicitly with a return to Platonic idealism, it is likely that he gave a more positive interpretation of Plato than Carneades had done. Having limited Academic Skepticism to a form of anti-Stoicism, he could demonstrate without contradicting himself that the Platonic corpus had contained something other than aporias concerning knowledge. Perhaps it was he who began to emphasize a theme that was starting to arise in Cicero and that flourished notably in Middle Platonism: "to become like God, so far as this is possible," which Plato develops in the digression in *Theaetetus* (176b). I would add that, in the area of relations between rhetoric and philosophy, Philon also showed his capacity to establish a new spirit. While Clitomachus had perpetuated only the Platonic tradition of hostility to rhetors, Philon introduced a radical innovation by offering his own courses in rhetoric alongside his teaching of philosophy; we may suppose that in this enterprise he drew on a personal interpretation of *Phaedrus.*

Antiochus of Ascalon

Even before Philon's exile in Rome, the Platonic school had undergone a significant schism with the departure of Antiochus of Ascalon. Antiochus claimed to have recaptured the inspiration of the Early Academy, over and beyond that of the New Academy, which he ended up considering an aberrant parenthesis in the history of Platonism. Things would have been relatively simple for the Academics if Antiochus had been content to comment on the works of Speusippus or Xenocrates. But his aim was not simply to reestablish a dogmatic interpretation of Platonism. His ambition was actually to restore the Academy's preeminence over the Hellenistic schools, primarily the Lyceum and the Stoa, by demonstrating that they had by and large contributed nothing but terminological innovations. The consensus on these schools, which Antiochus had made a key point of his philosophy, corresponded to goals that were hardly innocent: it meant reducing Aristotle and Zeno to talented and rather unruly successors of the unsurpassable Plato. This strategy

was not foolproof: Antiochus himself risked being viewed as more of a Peripatetic or a crypto-Stoic than a real Academic. In fact, Cicero, who held him in high regard, but who in *Academica* revives the arguments of the New Academy against him, did Antiochus no favor in characterizing him as an "authentic Stoic"; the theme has been repeated by many scholars interested in him. Now the least one can say is that such a formula does not account for Antiochus's philosophical personality.

In the field of ethics and physics, his method consisted in demonstrating that the Peripatetics and the Stoics had been satisfied to offer a new presentation of what already existed in Plato and in his successors in the Early Academy. Antiochus did not hesitate to claim as discoveries of the Academy concepts that were foreign to the Platonic school, such as *oikeiosis,* the immediate adaptation of the living being to its own nature. In the same way, his presentation of the physics of the Early Academy contains a good number of propositions derived much more from Zeno than from Speusippus or Xenocrates. But Antiochus, allegedly close to Stoicism, carried on an implacable polemic against the Stoics on all the points of doctrine that he could not really attribute to the Academy. For example, Book IV of Cicero's *De finibus* shows how relentlessly he attacked the specifically Stoic idea that the happiness of the wise man is totally independent of his external environment.

In the field of knowledge, our perception of Antiochus's philosophy is somewhat blurred by the fact that, to combat the Skepticism of the New Academy, he used the arguments of the Stoics themselves. This has led certain historians of philosophy to think that, on this point, Antiochus had completely gone over to the Stoic doctrine, judging that this doctrine really represented progress with respect to the Early Academy. Taken all together, our sources inspire more caution. Antiochus gave a sympathetic account of Platonic idealism, and he attributed to the Early Academy the idea that certainty should not be sought in the senses independently of reason, an implicit condemnation of the Stoic theory of "comprehensive representation." There is thus reason to believe that, in this field too, Stoicism was for him only an instrument in an overall strategy that he thought would incontrovertibly demonstrate the superiority of Platonism.

Antiochus, who purported to have recovered the true doctrine of the Academy, was never recognized as head of the Platonic school, because the institutional bond that, above and beyond any doctrinal changes, had connected the scholarchs from Plato to Philon of Larissa, was broken with Philon's departure for Rome. The school founded by Antiochus in Athens survived for a time after his death; then, for more than a century, no source mentions any Academic philosophers in Athens. During this whole period Middle Platonism was spreading in various parts of the Roman world; one of its features was that it functioned without the central core constituted by the Hellenistic

schools. Was the Academy restored in the 2nd century C.E. thanks to Ammonius, Plutarch's master? The question is controversial, and the fact remains that with the departure of Philon of Larissa, a certain mode of organization of philosophical reflection disappeared once and for all.

We can now try to respond to the initial question: what, notwithstanding the changes that occurred in the Academy, distinguishes an Academic from any other Greek philosopher? Part of the answer lies, first of all, in the reference to Plato. This is apparent in the Early Academy. It is a little more problematic in the New Academy, insofar as there is still a scholarch—and not least since the scholarch in question is Carneades—for whom no source indicates any loyalty to the figure of the founder. There is even a passage (whose source is open to question) in Cicero's *De republica* in which we are told that Carneades criticized the Platonic conception of justice. These difficulties must not be underestimated. Still, the fact that Arcesilaus and Philon of Larissa explicitly claimed a relationship to Plato, and the reference in *De oratore* to the study of *Gorgias* under the direction of Charmadas, one of Carneades' disciples, allow us to suppose that the Platonic corpus remained, from the beginning of the Academy's history to the end, a living source of inspiration.

If admiration for Plato and the sense of being the legitimate repository of his work constituted the basic elements of the Academy's identity, these factors were never understood as implying a duty of adherence to any point of doctrine whatsoever. All the same, Platonic thought—so diverse, so difficult to establish—preserved from the beginning for the Academics the almost religious respect for a body of doctrine that was commonly found in the Hellenistic schools. That this freedom of inquiry has been perceived as essential to the tradition of the Academy was never in doubt. But in the Early Academy this inquiry seems often to have been oriented by the desire to "come to Plato's aid"—reserving the right to contradict him—on questionable points of his thought. It is also important to stress that the Academy's thinking was always dialectic, in the sense that it always developed in confrontation with a privileged adversary: Aristotle for the Early Academy, Stoicism for the New. Yet in each case, the interlocutor is a philosopher not radically foreign to the Platonic tradition but a product of that tradition, someone who won his own autonomy by using criticism of Plato to define himself.

Is it possible to find in the history of the Academy not a dogma but a philosophical orientation common to all the scholarchs? The reference to transcendence is very clear in the Early Academy—if we except Polemon (about whom we know very little), who was concerned with expressing the extrauniversal character of essential realities. In contrast, there is only marginal reference to transcendence in accounts of the New Academy. Still, we may imagine that transcendence made itself felt through its absence, for if on the one hand the New Academy carried on an unremitting battle against Stoic

immanentism, on the other hand it never criticized the Plato of the Forms. For this reason, idealism remained an outlet for the aporias that the Academics denounced in the Stoic confusion over the nature of reason.

The extreme complexity of the evolution of philosophical systems makes it difficult to draw up a "balance sheet" for the Academy. Let us simply recall that the Early Academy, which we might think had been forgotten after Arcesilaus and Carneades, was one of the sources of inspiration for Neoplatonism, which itself strongly influenced Christian thought. And the concepts developed by the New Academy were useful to Neopyrrhonism, whose role was so important in the history of Western thought—especially in the Renaissance—and also, to a lesser degree, in Middle Platonism, that is, among authors as diverse as Philon of Alexandria, Apuleius, and Plutarch. The inability of the Platonic school to settle on a body of doctrine could seem a disadvantage in the era of the great Hellenistic dogmatisms. Over time, this drawback has turned out to be a source of richness and variety.

CARLOS LÉVY
Translated by Rita Guerlac and Anne Slack

Bibliography

Texts and Translations

Aristotle. *Metaphysics.* Trans. Hugh Tredennick. 2 vols. Loeb Classical Library.
———. *On the Soul.* In *On the Soul; Parva naturalia; On Breath.* Trans. W. S. Hett. Loeb Classical Library.
Cicero. *Academica.* In *De natura deorum; Academica.* Trans. H. Rackham. Loeb Classical Library.

Studies

Barnes, Jonathan. "Antiochus of Ascalon." In *Philosophia togata.* Ed. Miriam Griffin and Jonathan Barnes. Oxford: Clarendon Press; New York: Oxford University Press, 1989. Pp. 51–96.
Burnyeat, Malcolm, ed. *The Skeptical Tradition.* Berkeley: University of California Press, 1983.
Cherniss, Harold. *The Riddle of the Ancient Academy.* New York: Russell and Russell, 1962.
Couissin, Pierre. "L'origine et l'évolution de l'*épochè.*" *Revue d'études grecques* 42 (1929): 373–397.
———. "Le Stoïcisme de la Nouvelle Académie." *Revue d'histoire de la philosophie* 3 (1929): 241–276.
Dorandi, Tiziano. *Filodemo: Storia dei filosofi Platone e l'Academia.* Naples: Bibliopolis, 1991.
Gaiser, Konrad. *Platons ungeschreibene Lehre.* Stuttgart: E. Klett, 1968.

Glucker, John. *Antiochus and the Late Academy.* Göttingen: Vandenhoeck and Ruprecht, 1978.

Inwood, Brad, and Jaap Mansfeld, eds. *Assent and Argument: Studies in Cicero's Academic Books.* Leiden: E. J. Brill, 1997.

Ioppolo, Anna Maria. *Opinione e scienza.* Naples: Bibliopolis, 1986.

Isnardi Parente, Margherita, ed. and trans. *Senocrate-Ermodoro, Frammenti.* Naples: Bibliopolis, 1982.

———. *Speusippo-Ermodoro: Frammenti.* Naples: Bibliopolis, 1981.

———. *Speusippo: Frammenti.* Naples: Bibliopolis, 1980.

Kramer, Hans Joachim. *Platonismus und hellenistische Philosophie.* Berlin: De Gruyter, 1971.

Lévy, Carlos. *Cicero Academicus: Recherches sur les "Académiques" et sur la philosophie cicéronienne.* Rome: Ecole française de Rome, 1992.

Mette, Hans Joachim. "Philo von Larissa und Antiochus von Askalon." *Lustrum* 28–29 (1986–1987): 963.

———. "Weite Akademiker heute . . . von Lakydos bis zu Kleitomachos." *Lustrum* 27 (1985): 39–148.

———. "Zwei Akademiker Heute: Krantor von Soloi und Arkesilaos von Pitane." *Lustrum* 26 (1984): 7–104.

Robin, Léon. *La théorie platonicienne des Idées et des Nombres d'après Aristote.* Paris: Félix Alcan, 1908.

Tarán, Leonardo. *Speusippus of Athens: A Critical Study with a Collection of the Related Texts and Commentary.* Leiden: E. J. Brill, 1981.

Tarrant, Harold. *Scepticism or Platonism?* Cambridge: Cambridge University Press, 1985.

Related Articles

The Question of Being; Logic; Plato; Platonism; Schools and Sites of Learning; Mathematics; Plutarch; Skepticism

ARISTOTELIANISM

THE HISTORY OF PERIPATETIC PHILOSOPHY after Aristotle falls into two phases, divided by the renewal of interest in the works we now possess after their publication by Andronicus in the 1st century B.C.E.

Initially, Aristotle's own associates in the Lyceum and their successors carried on the work of the school. When Aristotle left Athens for Euboea at the news of the death of Alexander the Great in 323 B.C.E., the scholarchate passed to Theophrastus of Eresus, who had collaborated with Aristotle at least since the latter's stay in Assos in Asia Minor in 347–345 B.C.E. When Theophrastus died in 288/7 or 287/6 B.C.E., he was succeeded by Strato of Lampsacus, who remained head of the school until his own death eighteen years later.

The early activity of the school was characterized, as it had been in Aristotle's lifetime, by the collection and interpretation of information in every field, and by the raising and attempted resolution of theoretical difficulties. Two very different examples of the collection of information are provided by the best-known of the surviving works of Theophrastus. The first example, *Characters,* is a series of sketches of more or less imperfect personality types; it has been variously interpreted as material for a study of comedy, for the presentation of character in rhetoric, or for that study of character that the ancients called "ethics," but that we might rather classify as psychology; these purposes are not mutually exclusive. The second example is found in Theophrastus's botanical writings, which are the earliest systematic botanical texts to survive. The botanical subject matter calls some aspects of the Aristotelian theoretical framework into question; what is unnatural, Theophrastus says, may become natural with time, and the way in which art helps nature in the cultivation of plants prompts consideration of whether the true end of a tree's growth is to produce fertile seed or edible fruit (edible by humans, that is, and Theophrastus is prepared, in discussing wild and cultivated species, to speak about natural kinds in a flexible way, describing reversion from cultivated to wild varieties as changes of kind *[genos]).* But Theophrastus does not—in the extant texts anyway—explicitly present his approach to natural history as different from that of Aristotle.

The Lyceum was also active in collecting the views of earlier scholars: Eudemus compiled a history of mathematics, Menon of medicine, and Theophrastus the opinions of earlier philosophers about the natural world and about sense perception. Theophrastus's concern with earlier writers was not,

however, purely historical; like Aristotle himself, he discussed their views as a basis for establishing his own, though he does seem to have gone into more detail than Aristotle, and some interest in historical detail for its own sake cannot be excluded.

It has often been held that Theophrastus, and to an even greater extent Strato, changed the emphasis of Peripatetic philosophy, placing a progressively greater emphasis on empiricism and materialism. There is some truth in this view, but it has been overstated. For our knowledge of much of Theophrastus's activity and all of Strato's, we are dependent on fragmentary reports by later writers. Writers like Plutarch, a Platonist, and Cicero, emphasizing the differences between philosophers of the same school in the interests of neo-Academic skeptical debate, may not be the best guides to whether or not Strato is a good Aristotelian. Plutarch presents Strato as denying any purpose in nature, but the sense in which Aristotle himself admits it has not been uncontroversial either.

To show that there is a basis in *some* passages of Aristotle for a position adopted by Theophrastus or Strato does not establish that it is not in some sense un-Aristotelian; divergence can take the form of selective emphasis and omission as well as of straight contradiction. But such divergence may be unconscious and unintentional, and since selective emphasis of particular aspects of Aristotle's thought is not confined to Theophrastus and Strato, or even to Plutarch and Cicero, but is found among modern interpreters as well, we need to be aware of the standpoint from which a modern judgment of what is or is not Aristotelian is being made. Those who regard metaphysics as the central philosophical issue, and theology—in the sense of the study of incorporeal principles—as central to metaphysics, may well regard not only Theophrastus and Strato but later ancient Peripatetics too as neglecting what *they* regard as Aristotle's chief contributions. In a recent masterly short account of Aristotle, Jonathan Barnes devoted just two pages out of eighty-eight to Aristotle's theology and the theory of the Unmoved Mover. This might have surprised Thomas Aquinas; Theophrastus and Strato might have found Barnes's Aristotle more familiar than Aquinas's.

One of the Theophrastean works to survive is his so-called *Metaphysics*. This has often been described as a "fragment"; it seems in fact to be complete, but it comes to no conclusions and raises questions rather than answering them. In questioning the explanation of natural phenomena in terms of purpose and the theory of the Unmoved Mover, it can easily be seen as indicating Theophrastus's rejection of central Aristotelian doctrines—especially when Theophrastus can be seen as paving the way for Strato. However, Glenn Most has shown that some (but only some) of the examples of purpose in nature apparently rejected by Theophrastus are ones equally rejected by Aristotle himself, and he has suggested that Theophrastus's discussion is aimed not against Aristotelian teleology but against a more thoroughgoing Platonist

version. And though Theophrastus's treatise has no definite conclusions, it does have a positive message, which is that the universe is an organized system in which the same degree of purposefulness and goodness should not be expected at every level—a theme we shall find recurring in later Peripatetics too.

That Theophrastus did reject Aristotle's Unmoved Mover seems probable enough; but Aristotle did not accept the theory of the Unmoved Mover throughout his career, and in any case, raising objections is a thoroughly Aristotelian way of proceeding. Critics have been too ready to forget the problematic and exploratory nature of much of Aristotle's own surviving works, and too ready to interpret his successors as abandoning supposedly crucial features of Aristotelianism rather than as continuing Aristotle's enquiries (or sharing in them, for there is no reason to suppose that Theophrastus's *Metaphysics* was not written in Aristotle's lifetime). Even where Aristotle's own position can be easily stated, it is not always clear how we should interpret his successors' relation to him. Theophrastus certainly begins his surviving treatise *On Fire* by raising general questions about the Aristotelian theory of the elements, but, characteristically, he then turns aside from the general questions to investigate particular phenomena. Some of his remarks about these do seem to reveal un-Aristotelian assumptions. At this point we may suppose that Theophrastus did indeed develop a distinctive theory of his own, and look for other reports of Theophrastus's views that seem to confirm this; or we may suppose that Theophrastus couples a general adherence to an Aristotelian framework with a flexibility and readiness to speculate on particular details.

One reason why the question of Theophrastus's and Strato's loyalty to Aristotelianism has received attention has yet to be mentioned. After Strato, the Lyceum, and with it Peripatetic philosophy, rapidly fell into decline. Strato's successor Lyco (head of the school for forty-four years, from 270/69 or 269/8 B.C.E.) was notable for his oratory, social standing, and love of luxury rather than for science or philosophy; his successor Ariston of Ceos was noted chiefly for his biographical studies. (It is probably to Ariston that we owe the preservation of the wills of Aristotle and Theophrastus, and perhaps the list of Aristotelian titles in Diogenes Laertius.) In the 2nd century Critolaus, who accompanied the Academic Carneades and the Stoic Diogenes of Babylon on their visit to Rome in 156/5 B.C.E., was philosophically active, chiefly in defending Aristotelian positions (the eternity of the world, the fifth heavenly element, and the inclusion of external goods as a constituent of happiness) against the Stoics. Those for whom the most important aspects of Aristotelianism are those that they see Aristotle's immediate successors as questioning, rejecting, or neglecting have tended to see the decline of the Peripatetic school as a natural consequence of the change of emphasis. Others, themselves favoring an empiricist approach to the natural world, have seen

Theophrastus and Strato as advancing scientific inquiry where Aristotle's attitudes hindered it; this equally seems to overstate the contrast between Aristotle and his successors.

The real reasons for the decline of the Lyceum may be harder to recapture. Certainly the special sciences in the Hellenistic period developed an impetus of their own in institutions other than the Lyceum—notably medicine in Ptolemaic Alexandria—but this does not explain why zoology and botany, the sciences Aristotle and Theophrastus had made their own, declined in the Lyceum without developing elsewhere. Where philosophy in a narrower sense is concerned, the answer may be easier. Aristotle's own thought is guided indeed by clear structures and assumptions, but within that framework it is characteristically questioning, open-ended, and provisional. Moreover Aristotle explicitly stressed, against Plato, the relative independence of the different branches of philosophical enquiry. For those who were attracted by comprehensive and dogmatic philosophical systems, the Lyceum had nothing new to offer that could compare with Epicureanism or the Stoa, while for those who rejected dogmatism, the tentative and questioning approach of Aristotle's "unpublished" writings, such as *Metaphysics,* proceeding within the context of an assumed general framework and clearly supposing that there were answers to be reached, must have seemed a poor second best to the aggressive skepticism introduced to the Academy by Arcesilaus in the middle of the 3rd century B.C.E. Strato's successors emphasized those aspects of the school's activity—present indeed from the outset—that related to the general literary and rhetorical culture of the period, and this too may have lessened the distinctive appeal of the school. There is nothing un-Aristotelian in paying attention to the views and concerns of people in general, as a glance at the *Nicomachean Ethics* will show, but for Aristotle himself it was only the foundation on which he built.

To speak of how Aristotle's "unpublished" writings might have seemed to Hellenistic readers assumes, indeed, that those who might have wanted to read them could have done so. (I use "published" and "unpublished" as equivalents for the traditional "exoteric" and "esoteric," respectively; the latter, in particular, could have misleading connotations.) The decline of the Lyceum is linked by Strabo and Plutarch with the story that Aristotle's and Theophrastus's writings, left by Theophrastus not to Strato but to Neleus of Scepsis in the Troad, passed from Neleus to his descendants. They, having no interest in philosophy, hid the works in a cellar to preserve them from the kings of Pergamum, who wanted to create a library to rival the one in Alexandria and were not too scrupulous about their methods of acquiring materials. Thus, according to the story, the unpublished works of Aristotle—those which we now have, the published works having been lost later in antiquity—were inaccessible until rediscovered in the 1st century B.C.E., and the Peripatetics were unable to "do philosophy in a systematic way" without

them. The manuscripts were eventually recovered by the bibliophile Apellicon, who took them to Athens and published them, but inaccurately; they were then seized by the Roman general Sulla when he sacked the city in 86 B.C.E., and taken to Rome, where they were copied by the grammarian Tyrannio. From his copies a new edition, which established the arrangement of Aristotle's writings that still exists today, was produced by Andronicus of Rhodes; this also included some works of Theophrastus.

It is true that the revival of Aristotelianism dates from Andronicus, and that it is different in character from what had preceded; where the earlier Peripatetics had sought to continue Aristotle's work, later writers essentially look back to it and comment on it. It is significant that Strabo supposes that one *could not be* a Peripatetic philosopher without access to the texts of Aristotle himself. Concentration on the study of canonical texts was not a development confined to Aristotelianism; it was characteristic of the imperial period. What is much less certain is that Aristotle's works were ever as inaccessible as the story suggests. It is unlikely that even the unpublished works existed in only one copy; we know that different, and differing, copies of Aristotle's *Physics* existed in the lifetime of Theophrastus, and Strato left to Lyco "all the books, apart from those I have written myself" (Diogenes Laertius, 5.62). H. B. Gottschalk suggests that the books inherited by Neleus may never have left Athens and speculates that Apellicon may have stolen the books and made up the whole story to conceal the fact. If Aristotle's works were little read in the Hellenistic period, this may be not because they were unavailable but because—however strange this may seem to modern interpreters, for whom Aristotle is a central figure in the whole history of philosophy—they were not considered of great interest. Aristotelian doctrines were still discussed and referred to, but characteristic of the Hellenistic period is not the study of Aristotle's own works but the compilation and use of summaries of the sort that underlie Cicero's knowledge of Aristotle and the accounts of Areius Didymus and Diogenes Laertius.

The writing of such summaries of Aristotelian doctrines did not cease after Andronicus's edition. Nicolaus of Damascus, a courtier of Herod the Great, compiled, in addition to historical and ethnographical writings, a summary of Aristotle's philosophy, including the biological works, which survives in a Syriac summary and in other fragments. This brought together material on similar topics from different Aristotelian texts edited by Andronicus. Nicolaus also made use of Theophrastus's *Metaphysics,* unknown to Andronicus, and other material from Theophrastus and later Peripatetics. A treatise by Nicolaus on plants, possibly part of the compendium, was translated from Syriac into Arabic in the 9th century C.E., thence into Latin in the second half of the 12th century, and thence back into Greek. In the process it became misattributed to Aristotle himself, and it is this retranslation that ap-

pears as *On Plants* in modern editions of Aristotle, though the falsity of the attribution was already realized in the Renaissance.

Areius Didymus, a Stoic and "court philosopher" to the emperor Augustus, wrote summaries of the teachings of the various schools. Of his treatment of the Peripatetics we possess the section on ethics, quoted at length by Stobaeus, and fragments of the section on physics. Areius sometimes used the Aristotelian texts, but the terminology and emphases reflect Hellenistic preoccupations; with regard to the section on ethics in particular, while the doctrine is basically Aristotelian, it appears in a guise and with emphases that owe more to Hellenistic preoccupations and to Areius's own concern to stress the similarities between Peripatetic and Stoic ethics.

Other scholars, however, directed their activities toward the writing of commentaries on the newly popular Aristotelian texts. The earlier commentaries are now lost except for scattered quotations, having been replaced by later, often Neoplatonic commentaries. Andronicus and his pupil Boethus commented on *Categories* and other works; so too did Alexander of Aegae, teacher of the emperor Nero. The earliest surviving complete commentary is that of Aspasius (first half of the 2nd century C.E.) on *Nicomachean Ethics*. But the earliest author from whom a considerable number of commentaries survives is Alexander of Aphrodisias, described as *"the* commentator" by his successors, though even of his works only a part survives, much having been superseded by later commentaries. Interest in Aristotle's published works declined as that in the unpublished works in Andronicus's edition developed; for Cicero, who either did not know of or was not interested in the texts published by Andronicus, Aristotle still meant the Aristotle of the published works, but he is perhaps the last major writer for whom this is true.

It is possible that the Lyceum ceased to exist as an institution at the time of Sulla's sack of Athens. But Athens continued to be a center for philosophers of all schools. In 176 C.E. Marcus Aurelius established posts there for teachers of the four principal philosophies (Platonic, Aristotelian, Stoic, and Epicurean), and it may be to an appointment in Athens that Alexander refers in the dedication of his treatise *On Fate*, written between 198 and 209. The institution of the imperial appointments only confirmed a situation that already existed; philosophers of the different schools were teaching in Athens—and engaging in lively polemic against each other's schools—throughout the 2nd century.

Alexander's commentaries do not yet show the adaptation to a context of formal teaching apparent in the later, Neoplatonic commentaries. They are discursive and open-ended, presenting alternative interpretations without always indicating a preference between them. We also possess some collections of short discussions attributed to Alexander; once there were more, but they are now lost. Some of these take the form of problems in Aristotelian doc-

trine, or in the interpretation of particular texts, followed by solutions; others are expositions of particular passages, or summaries of texts or doctrines, which seem to derive from a teaching context. Whether they were written by Alexander himself has to be considered text by text; it is unlikely that they all were. Since many of these texts are connected with themes dealt with in Alexander's commentaries or in monographs by him, it is natural to assume that they at least originate from his school. But it has recently been suggested that some of them may be considerably later in date, though still concerned essentially with Aristotelian issues. This highlights a problem: that of the *second* disappearance of Aristotelianism in antiquity, or rather its absorption into Neoplatonism.

We know the names of Alexander's teachers and can identify some of their doctrines and his reaction against them. But we do not know the names of any of his pupils; with one exception, all ancient commentators on Aristotle after Alexander whose writings are known to us are Neoplatonists. There had long been a tendency on the part of Platonists to incorporate Aristotelian ideas into their expositions of Plato; some, notably the 2nd-century Platonist Atticus, rebelled against this, but they were in the minority. Plotinus himself had the works of Aristotle and the commentaries of Alexander, among others, read in his school. Subsequently, with the formalization of the Neoplatonic philosophical curriculum, selected works of Aristotle were studied as a preliminary to the reading of Plato. The emphasis was on the logical and physical treatises and the work *On the Soul;* this explains why Aspasius's commentary on *Ethics* survived and why we have to wait until the 12th century for commentaries on *Parva naturalia* or any of the zoological works, and on *Rhetoric.*

The exception to the general dominance of Platonists after Alexander is Themistius, who in the 4th century combined epideictic rhetoric with the production of explanatory paraphrases of Aristotle's works. But Themistius's Aristotelianism has no clear heritage; we cannot trace either its immediate antecedents or his successors. There are occasional references to other individuals as Peripatetics, but none of this amounts to the continued existence of a distinctive Aristotelian tradition.

Before considering the reasons for this second decline of Aristotelianism, it will be convenient to consider developments throughout the period of five centuries separating Aristotle from Alexander in each branch of Aristotelian philosophy in turn, following the order of topics in the standard arrangement of Aristotle's writings that goes back to Andronicus.

LOGIC

Theophrastus and Eudemus continued and developed the study of formal logic that Aristotle had instituted in *Prior Analytics*. There are two areas in which they made a particular contribution. The first is modal logic, the logic

of necessity and possibility. Aristotle had utilized a notion of possibility according to which "possible" excludes not only what is impossible but also what is necessary; while this is intuitive (it is not natural to say, "It is *possible* that 2 + 2 = 4," for example), it removes the expected parallelism between statements of possibility and statements of fact. For with this type of possibility, "It is possible that all B are A" implies "It is possible that no B are A," and "It is possible that no B are A" does not imply "It is possible that no A are B" (for it may be that all B have the possibility of being A or not being A, but that there are some other A that cannot be B at all). Moreover, while it may seem natural to suppose that a conclusion cannot be stronger than the weakest of the premises from which it follows—the "weakest link in the chain" principle, or, as medieval logicians put it, *sequitur conclusio partem deteriorem*—for Aristotle it made a difference which premise was concerned; he regards as valid that "Necessarily all B are A" and "All C are B" yield "Necessarily all C are A," while "All B are A" and "Necessarily all C are B" yield only "All C are A" and not "Necessarily all C are A."

On both these issues Theophrastus and Eudemus, who are regularly cited together, adopted the opposite view; and in both cases the effect is to make modal logic simpler and tidier. Statements of possibility now behave like statements of fact, and the modality of the conclusion in all syllogisms is determined by a simple rule. If Aristotle was influenced in taking the view he did by extralogical considerations (for example, that being as a matter of fact a member of a group implies possessing necessarily the properties that all members of the group possess necessarily), the changes made by Theophrastus and Eudemus may indicate a move from logic conceived in terms of its applications in the real world to logic as a purely formal system. It is, however, one thing to assert this with hindsight and quite another to claim that Theophrastus and Eudemus would have seen the change in these terms.

Theophrastus also developed the study of argument forms mentioned by Aristotle but not fully discussed by him. It seems highly probable that these included the forms of argument with conditional, conjunctive, and disjunctive premises that were to form the basis of both Stoic logic and modern propositional logic. But it also seems likely that Theophrastus did not realize the significance of what he had discovered, and did not see that propositional logic was actually more fundamental than the Aristotelian logic of terms.

The contribution of Aristotelian writers after Theophrastus and Eudemus to the development of logic was not great. The innovations came from writers outside the school, such as Galen (even though it is not true, as once thought, that Galen discovered the fourth figure of the "Aristotelian" syllogism). Alexander of Aphrodisias wrote an extensive commentary on *Prior Analytics* and a separate monograph, now lost, on *Syllogisms with Mixed Premises* (that is, premises of differing modalities); characteristically, he endorsed Aristotle's view on the latter topic against that of Theophrastus and Eudemus.

PHYSICS AND METAPHYSICS: FATE AND PROVIDENCE

Aristotle defined time as the numbered aspect of motion (*Physics* 4.11.219b5) indicated most clearly by the movement of the heavenly sphere, though not to be identified with it (*Physics* 4.14.223b23). Theophrastus and Eudemus followed Aristotle's view, but Strato rejected it on the grounds that motion and time are continuous whereas number is discrete, and defined time as quantity or measure both in motion and in rest, thus giving it an existence independent of motion. He was followed on the latter point by Boethus (Simplicius, *In Cat.* 434.2ff). Alexander explicitly rejected such a theory, attributed to Galen; indeed, Alexander identifies time as the number of the motion of the outermost heavenly sphere more definitely than Aristotle himself had done. Aristotle had suggested that there could be no time without soul, as without soul there could be no numbering (*Physics* 4.14.223a21ff); Alexander argues that time is in its own nature a unity and is divided by the present moment only in our thought. This suggests that time itself can exist without any actual *numbering*; and Alexander appears to identify time in this sense with the continuous *numerable* movement of the outermost heavenly sphere. Characteristically, Alexander's approach combines a claim to be simply setting out the Aristotelian position, and an attempt to defend it, with a new development and emphasis of his own.

Though Theophrastus did not challenge Aristotle's view of time, he assembled a whole series of difficulties for Aristotle's definition of place as the innermost unmoved limit of what surrounds a thing. We do not, however, know whether these difficulties led Theophrastus to reject the Aristotelian conception of place altogether. The Neoplatonist commentator Simplicius, after outlining the view of place held by his predecessor Damascius, mentions in passing that Theophrastus seems to have anticipated this, interpreting place as the proper position of a part in a complex whole. What is not clear is whether Theophrastus, like Damascius, already extended this concept to the place of things in the universe as a whole. Strato certainly rejected Aristotle's view of place and defined it as the interval or extension delimited by the outermost surface of what is contained or the innermost surface of what contains it— which amounts to saying that the place of a thing is not, as for Aristotle, what contains it, but the space that it occupies.

For Aristotle, sublunary things are composed of the four elements, earth, air, fire, and water (which can be and are transmuted into each other), while the heavenly spheres are composed of ether, the fifth element, which has the capacity for movement but for no other kind of change. It has been argued that Theophrastus both rejected the fifth element and maintained that fire requires a substrate in a way that the other elements do not. It is true that in the opening section of *On Fire* Theophrastus draws attention to the fact that

terrestrial fire needs a constant supply of fuel, which might be thought to conflict with its status as a primary element; and he also speculates over whether the sun, if not fire, may not be at least hot. Such thoughts might indeed lead to a world picture radically different from Aristotle's; but it is not clear that they did so for Theophrastus. The introductory discussion in *On Fire* ends inconclusively and, as already mentioned, Theophrastus turns to more specific questions, but not before pointing out that the need for replenishment applies not just to fire but to all the sublunary elements. As for the fifth element, Philoponus suggests that Theophrastus retained it. Strato certainly rejected the fifth element and held that the heavens are composed of fire, and the Stoics rejected the fifth element and gave a major role to fire and—later, with Chrysippus—*pneuma* as embodiments of the active principle in the universe.

It has also been suggested that Theophrastus emphasized the role of heat, especially that of the sun, in causing physical change, and that he modified the Aristotelian theory of the dry and moist exhalations, reducing the dry one to mere reflection of the heat of the sun. But both Theophrastus's *Meteorology* and his *De igne* suggest less divergence from Aristotle's views than this interpretation supposes. And, once again, there is the question of Aristotle's own consistency. Theophrastus treated fire as active and the other three elements as passive, and both this and his distinction between the generative heat of the sun and terrestrial fire develop themes that are already present in Aristotle's physiological and biological writings, as opposed to his general physical theory.

Although Theophrastus denied the existence of the Unmoved Mover, he continued to hold, like Aristotle, that the heavens are ensouled. (That the heavens are ensouled was later the belief of Alexander of Aphrodisias, and of his teacher Herminus.) Theophrastus, like Aristotle, upheld the doctrine of the eternity of the world, and engaged in polemic against the Stoic Zeno on this issue—if we can trust an early work of Philo Judaeus.

Aristotle maintained the infinite divisibility of matter and the absence of any void. Scholars have drawn particular attention to contexts where Theophrastus, in the explanation of physical processes, makes use of the notion of passages or pores. There is, however, no inconsistency between this and Aristotelian physical theory, unless we are to suppose that the pores contain a vacuum; they may well be thought of rather as containing more tenuous matter than what surrounds them. Strato, but not, it seems, Theophrastus, was prepared to allow the temporary existence of completely empty voids within material bodies. Theophrastus *did* apparently employ the principle of "nature abhorring a vacuum" in the explanation of winds. But all this is still far removed from the Atomist conception of discrete particles of matter moving within an otherwise empty space. A tendency toward materialistic expla-

nations can be seen in Theophrastus's introduction of material effluences into the explanation of odor, which Aristotle had interpreted as the propagation of a change in the intervening medium.

On issues of physical theory such as these, the Peripatetics of the Roman empire, concerned as they were to explain the Aristotelian texts, returned to orthodox Aristotelian positions. But on other aspects of the organization of the natural world, later Peripatetics found themselves constrained to develop "Aristotelian" positions on issues to which Aristotle himself had devoted little or no direct attention. The Stoics, in particular, had made fate and divine providence central topics of philosophical debate. Aristotle himself had little to say about the former, and his account in *Metaphysics* XII of the Unmoved Mover as engaged in self-contemplation, causing movement as an object of desire without itself being affected, seems like a complete denial of divine providence, though there is evidence to suggest that in his published works he may have taken a less uncompromising view.

The nature of divine involvement with the universe forms the climax of the treatise *On the World (De mundo)*, attributed to Aristotle (and contained in our standard editions) but probably in fact a composition of the Roman period. In it God is likened to the Persian king, ruling by delegated authority; divine influence is present in the world, but God himself is remote in a way that is appropriate to his dignity. Other interpreters, however, took a harsher line, and the standard view attributed to Aristotle in both pagan and Christian sources—among them, Areius Didymus and Diogenes Laertius—is that the heavens are the objects of divine providence while the sublunary region is not. The Platonist Atticus attacked Aristotle vehemently for holding such a view (and also for denying the immortality of the soul); Aristotle's views, he argued, are really no different from those of Epicurus, but at least Epicurus had the courage of his convictions and denied providence altogether, whereas Aristotle allows its existence, but only in a context where it cannot directly benefit us.

It was apparently in reply to Atticus that Alexander of Aphrodisias developed an alternative "Aristotelian" theory of providence, preserved in part in his treatise *On Providence*, which survives in two Arabic versions, and partly in various of the short texts attributed to him. Providence is located in the heavens, he argues, in the sense that it is exercised from the heavens over the sublunary region, which is subject to coming-to-be and passing-away, and so is the only part of the universe that actually needs providential care. However, providence extends to the sublunary only in preserving the eternity of natural kinds; there is no involvement of providence in the lives of individuals (as contemporary Platonists, for example, were arguing). By adopting this position Alexander can account for the occurrence of misfortunes in the lives of individuals, and also avoid an involvement of the divine in things that

would be beneath its dignity—something for which he repeatedly criticizes the Stoics.

Alexander's theory of providence is a reworking of authentically Aristotelian materials in a new guise. That the movements of the heavens, and especially the seasonal movements of the sun, preserve the continuity of sublunary coming-to-be, and hence of natural kinds, is argued by Aristotle himself in the penultimate chapter of his *De generatione et corruptione,* and the eternity of natural kinds had been used as an argument for that of the world by Critolaus (frg. 13, Wehrli). Moraux, before the Arabic text of *On Providence* was known, criticized Alexander's theory of providence for being "mechanistic." In fact the Arabic text makes it clear that Alexander does want to assert that the divine is aware of its beneficial effects on the sublunary, though how he reconciled this with *Metaphysics* XII we do not know.

Similarly, where fate is concerned, Alexander's position is an adaptation of Aristotelian themes. For Aristotle, what is natural applies for the most part but not always; and Alexander, in his treatise *On Fate,* argues that individuals' fate is their nature or, quoting Heraclitus, their character, which for the most part determines what happens to them, but not always. Alexander may not have been the first to put forward this view; certainly one of the texts attributed to him endeavors to read such a notion of fate back into Aristotle's own two uses of the adjective *fated,* into Theophrastus, and into an otherwise unknown Polyzelus.

What Alexander's view of fate emphatically rules out is the Stoic concept of fate as inexorably determining everything. The unity of the universe, he argues, is preserved not by the chain of causes and effects, but by the regular movement of the heavens; as in a household, so in the universe, minor variations in matters of detail do not affect the orderliness of the whole (Alexander, *On Fate,* chap. 25). The similarity to Alexander's theory of providence is apparent; so too is the recurrence of the idea, already encountered both in Theophrastus's *Metaphysics* and in *De mundo,* of the Peripatetic universe conceived as a hierarchy in which the same degree of order, goodness, and perfection is not to be expected at every level. It is tempting to see the remoteness of God in *De mundo,* and Alexander's attacks on the Stoics for involving God in every detail of the management of the world, as reflecting the increased remoteness of earthly rulers when the Greek city-state was replaced, first by the Hellenistic monarchies and then by the Roman empire, but the fact that the hierarchical picture is already implicit in Aristotle (*Metaphysics* XII.10) may argue for caution here.

Theophrastus and Strato devoted little attention to such problems of general metaphysics as the status of universals. With the revival of Aristotelianism and the placing of *Categories* at the beginning of the whole sequence

of Aristotle's works, the status of universals became a central issue. Once again the thinker on whose views we are most fully informed is Alexander, though his views were anticipated by Boethus, and some of the evidence comes from short texts that may not all be by Alexander himself. Definitions, it is argued, are of specific or generic forms, which do not include any of the pecularities of individuals, such as Socrates' snub nose—these being due to matter—and yet they are not universal in themselves; the nature of human being would be the same even if only one human being existed. Socrates exists because "human being" exists, and not the other way round; yet "human being" would not exist if no individual human being at all existed. It seems reasonable to suppose that each human being has the same nature or form, the form of the species human being, but that my form and yours are the same only in kind (or "form"; the Greek is the same), not numerically; or, putting it another way, to speak of "the same form" does not mean that there is a single numerically individual form that you and I share. The first way of putting it suggests a doctrine of individual forms (not, of course, in the sense that each person's form will include individual *peculiarities,* just that my form and yours are two tokens of the type "form of human being"); the second, that a form is the sort of thing to which questions of numerical identity or difference do not apply. The question of whether *Aristotle* believed in "individual forms," and if so in what sense, has been a major topic of contemporary debate.

Alexander's position has been criticized both in ancient and in modern times for being nominalist and hence un-Aristotelian. Some of those criticisms come, however, from a Platonist standpoint, and thus are suspect so far as the assessment of what is and is not Aristotelian is concerned. For Aristotle as well as for Alexander, universals have their existence as *post rem* mental constructs; but it is important that those mental constructs are not arbitrary but reflect the fundamental reality of the specific forms. The latter are indeed the product of the abstracting power of intellect, but that does not mean that it is up to us which features we abstract. On the contrary, the important thing about every human being, as it were, is that he or she is a *human being,* the various accidents due to matter being secondary to this. This explains why texts attributed to Alexander can say that the universal is prior to any *particular* individual; and while it may be questionable whether we should use ideas from one area of Alexander's philosophizing to settle an issue in another, the emphasis in his theory of providence on the preservation of the species agrees with an emphasis on the reality of specific form.

Alexander has also been regarded as un-Aristotelian in diminishing the role of form in comparison with that of matter. But this is chiefly in the context of his doctrine of soul, to which we shall now turn.

SOUL

Aristotle defined the soul as the form of the living creature. It is thus neither a separable immaterial entity (as Plato had supposed) nor a distinct material ingredient in the whole creature (as Epicurus, for example, was to argue). But neither is it, for Aristotle, simply a product of the arrangement of the bodily parts and thus reducible to the latter; body is to be explained in terms of soul, and in general, compounds of matter and form are to be explained in terms of form. A human body has a certain structure to enable the human being to function in the way that human beings do.

However, that body is to be explained in terms of soul and not vice versa need not mean that a certain arrangement of bodily parts is not a necessary condition for the existence of a certain type of soul. In the case of perceptive soul, indeed, the bodily organ that relates to a particular soul-faculty is evident: the eye in the case of sight, the ear in that of hearing. It is less obvious how we are to relate the soul to the body in general—both in terms of how soul and body interact, and in terms of whether some part of the body plays a particularly vital role. Aristotle had seen "connate spirit" (pneuma) as the physical means by which soul operated, and the heart as the particularly vital organ, the first to develop in the embryo. He had also asserted that intellect, alone of the soul-faculties, was not correlated with any particular organ, and had spoken, in the notorious chapter 3.5 of De anima, of a distinction in intellect between "that which makes everything" and "that which becomes everything," apparently presenting the former as imperishable in a way in which the latter was not. The history of subsequent Peripatetic discussion of the soul is largely that of attempts to clarify these issues, attempts that were affected to varying extents by contemporary attitudes and the positions of other philosophical schools. It will be convenient first to discuss the nature of the soul as a whole and its relation to the body, and then to consider the question of intellect separately.

Among Aristotle's immediate pupils, Dicaearchus is said to have regarded the soul as a "harmony," or mixture of the four elements in the body, a view that some reports present as equivalent to denying the existence of the soul at all. Aristoxenus, too, is said to have regarded the soul as simply a harmony or attunement of the body.

Strato emphasized the role of pneuma, breath or spirit, in the functioning of the soul. Aristotle and Theophrastus had used pneuma to explain bodily processes, and for Strato soul-faculties were explained by pneuma's extending throughout the body from the "ruling part," which he located not in the chest (as both Epicurus and the Stoics did) but in the head, or more precisely in the space between the eyebrows. Tertullian illustrates Strato's theory with the analogy of air in the pipes of an organ (the Stoics were to use that of the tentacles of an octopus). Strato was influenced here by developments in

contemporary medicine and anatomy. All sensation, he held, was felt in the ruling part of the soul, rather than in the bodily extremities, and all sensation involved thought. Some have drawn a contrast between Strato's views on thought itself and those of Aristotle, emphasizing Strato's view that all thought is ultimately derived from sensation; but the contrast sometimes depends on attributing to Aristotle himself a belief in intuition as a mode of cognition distinct from the senses, and this is at best questionable.

Lyco's successor Ariston of Ceos may have stressed the distinction between rational and nonrational soul, against the Stoics, but perhaps in an ethical rather than a psychological context. Critolaus described the soul as made of ether, the fifth element. Cicero says that Aristotle himself identified the soul with ether, but this may reflect a misunderstanding, aided by the familiarity of materialistic theories of soul in other schools.

Andronicus defined the soul as the power arising from the mixture of the bodily elements, and he was followed in this both by Alexander's teacher Aristoteles of Mytilene and by Alexander himself. Alexander has been criticized for interpreting Aristotle in a materialist way, treating soul as form, indeed, but making form secondary to matter. His treatment of soul as the culmination of an analysis that starts from the simple physical elements and builds up through successively more complex structures does suggest that he sees form in general, and soul in particular, as the product of material arrangement. However, it is not un-Aristotelian to say that a certain bodily arrangement is a *necessary condition* for the existence of soul. Indeed, Alexander may have intended to defend an authentically Aristotelian position against more materialist interpretations. Alexander's view does indeed exclude any personal immortality, but so does Aristotle's own, with the possible exception of his cryptic remarks in *De anima* 3.5 about the Active Intellect. Alexander compared soul as a principle of movement with the nature of the simple bodies, for example the weight of earth. It was by appeal to this conception of nature (itself Aristotelian enough; Aristotle, *Physics* 2.1.192b21) that Alexander explained the application to the simple bodies of Aristotle's claim that everything that moves is moved by something (Aristotle, *Physics* 8.4.254b24), defending it against Galen's attack in a treatise surviving only in Arabic. Alexander's view can be seen as an ancestor of the impetus theory used by Philoponus to explain the forced motion of projectiles (on which Alexander holds the orthodox Aristotelian view that it is caused by the transmission of movement through the air behind the projectile) and passed on by him to medieval science.

INTELLECT

Discussion of Aristotle's theory of intellect begins with Theophrastus. A major difficulty was how intellect—which can have no nature of its own if it is

to be able to receive all intelligible forms—can ever begin to perform the task of abstraction by which it separates forms from their matter (cf. Theophrastus, frgs. 307, 309, 316–317; Fortenbaugh et al.). Alexander (*De anima* 84.24–27) later expresses the point by saying that our intellect, at birth, is not so much like a blank wax tablet as like the blankness of the wax tablet, and Xenarchus, an Aristotelian in the Augustan period, suggested, whether seriously or as a reductio ad absurdum, that potential intellect was to be identified with prime matter. It was natural to see Aristotle's remarks in *De anima* 3.5 about an Active Intellect that "makes all things," contrasted with the passive intellect that "becomes all things," as indicating some solution to this problem.

In the treatise *De generatione animalium*, moreover, Aristotle refers, in passing and with no very clear explanation, to intellect, alone of our soul-faculties, as entering into the father's seed "from outside" (2.3.736b27). At some point this was linked with the Active Intellect of *De anima*. One of Alexander's predecessors, possibly his teacher Aristoteles of Mytilene, is recorded in one of the minor works attributed to Alexander, *De intellectu (On Intellect)*, as answering the objection that such an intellect could not "come from outside" since, being immaterial, it could not change place at all.

Before answering the objection, the author of *On Intellect* first explains the role of the Active Intellect. For him, it is not an element in the soul of each individual separately; rather, it is identified with the supreme intelligible, the Unmoved Mover, and acts on our intellect to develop its potential through our thinking of it. The objection concerning movement is answered by the argument that the Active Intellect is present everywhere throughout the world, but can produce intelligence only in those parts of matter that are suitable— i.e., human beings (and any superior intelligences there may be). To this the author of *On Intellect* himself replies with objections similar to those that Alexander elsewhere brings against Stoic pantheism, complaining that involvement of the divine in the sublunary world is inconsistent with the divine dignity.

The author of *On Intellect* does, however, retain the basic explanation of the way in which the Active Intellect acts on our intellect: it is by our becoming aware of it so that it becomes, as it were, a paradigm of the intelligible for us. The difficulty with this is that it suggests that God is the first thing we actually think of, whereas it would be more plausible for awareness of him to be the culmination of our understanding. And in Alexander's own certainly authentic *De anima* we find two other explanations of the role of the Active Intellect; being the supreme intelligible itself, it must be the cause of other things' being intelligible, and it is also the cause of things' being intelligible because, as Unmoved Mover, it is the cause of their having being in the first place. Neither argument, however, indicates *how* the Active Intellect causes us to have intelligence; they simply provide ingenious grounds for asserting

that it does so. Such concentration on solving the immediate problem is typical of Alexander, naturally enough for a commentator. An explanation would indeed be available if we were to suppose that the divine intellect already contained within itself the thoughts that we can come to apprehend, but that is essentially the position of Plotinus, and while he may be indebted to Alexander's account of intellect, there is no indication that Alexander himself took this step.

It has been debated whether Alexander's *De anima* is an attempt to improve on *On Intellect*, or the reverse. Both accounts, by identifying the Active Intellect with God rather than with a part of the individual's soul, deny personal immortality. Since thought, for Alexander as for Aristotle, is identical in form with its objects, and the Unmoved Mover is pure form without matter, our mind in a sense becomes the Unmoved Mover while it thinks of it, and can thus achieve a sort of temporary immortality; but that is all. Whether such a claim is to be seen in mystical terms, or whether it is simply the by-product of Alexander's undoubted ingenuity in attempting to clarify Aristotelian doctrine, is debatable. It is also questionable as exegesis of Aristotle; Aquinas was later to argue, against Alexander and against Averroës (who adopted Alexander's interpretation of the Active Intellect but differed from him in holding that the passive or potential intellect, too, was one and the same for all individuals), that Aristotle *had* intended the Active Intellect to be a personal element in each individual's soul and had thus intended a personal immortality. Alexander's interpretation became a focus of discussion of the question of immortality in Renaissance Italy.

ETHICS, POLITICS, RHETORIC

Throughout the period under discussion, Peripatetic ethics are characterized by a contrast with the paradoxical extremes of Stoicism. Rhetorical contrast may play a part; Cicero repeatedly portrays Theophrastus as weakening virtue by recognizing external goods, subject to fortune, as necessary for happiness. Theophrastus's position is not that far removed from some aspects of Aristotle's; after all, Aristotle had said that to call someone being tortured happy is absurd (*Nicomachean Ethics* 7.13.1153b19).

The claim that happiness is "completed" by the three classes of goods—of the soul, of the body, and external—is attributed also to Critolaus, though he argued that if virtue were placed on one side of a balance and bodily and external goods on the other, the former would far outweigh the latter. The account of Aristotle's views in Diogenes Laertius agrees with Critolaus in regarding bodily and external goods as *parts* of virtue (Diogenes Laertius, 5.30). Areius Didymus, however, seeking to reconcile Peripatetic and Stoic ethics, explicitly rejects Critolaus's view and regards bodily and external goods as *used by* virtuous activity.

Opposition to extremist Stoic ethical views played a part in the renewed interest in Aristotelianism on a popular level in the imperial period. It is particularly notable in the treatment of *pathos*, or "emotion," which Aristotle had regarded as fundamental to ethics. The Stoics confined the term to emotional reactions that went beyond right reason, and therefore regarded *pathé* as such as uniformly bad (though also recognizing a class of good feelings, *eupatheiai*, such as watchfulness by contrast with fear). The Peripatetics characteristically recommended not the absence of passions, *apatheia*, but *metriopatheia*, moderation in the passions. As Aristotle himself had taught, failure to show anger when anger is due is a shortcoming.

According to Areius Didymus, Aristotle regarded *pathos* not as an excessive movement of the soul but as an irrational movement *liable* to excess. Andronicus shared with the Stoics the view that all *pathos* involves a supposition that something is good or bad, and Boethus held that it was a movement possessing a certain magnitude. Aspasius rejected both these points, distancing the Peripatetic position further from the Stoic one. Aspasius's role in the development of Aristotelian ethics as a subject of study has been a topic of recent debate. His commentary on *Nicomachean Ethics* includes the "common books" that are transmitted both as part of *Nicomachean Ethics* and part of *Eudemian*. It has been shown that it is from the time of Aspasius that *Nicomachean Ethics*, rather than *Eudemian*, has been the work regularly studied and cited (as in the *Ethical Problems* attributed to Alexander, for example). Given the immense influence of the study of *Nicomachean Ethics* on ethical discussion up to and including the present century (it and Plato's *Republic* were the two works of ancient philosophy that were for a long time central to the Oxford philosophy curriculum, for example), the significance of this change can hardly be overstated.

The Stoics based their ethics on the appropriation *(oikeiōsis)*, or recognition, by living creatures of their own selves. The most fundamental impulse was that to self-preservation, which developed in two ways in human beings as they grew older, first by the person's coming to recognize virtue and reason as true self-interest, and second by the recognition of other people as akin to oneself. Attempts have been made to trace the origin of this Stoic doctrine to the post-Aristotelian Peripatos. It was indeed attributed to Aristotle by Areius Didymus, Boethus, and Xenarchus, but this may simply reflect Stoic influence and, in the case of Areius at least, a desire to assimilate Stoic and Aristotelian thought to each other. Theophrastus spoke of affinity *(oikeiotēs)* between all human beings and animals, but this is not really the same as the process of appropriation described by the Stoics. Some, however, have argued that a major part of Cicero's *On Ends*, including the account of moral development in terms of appropriation at 5.24–70, derives from Theophrastus, though book 5 as a whole represents the views of Antiochus of Ascalon.

Dicaearchus in his *Tripoliticus* set out the doctrine of the mixed constitu-

tion, a combination of monarchy, aristocracy, and democracy superior to each of these. The concept was already present, applied to Sparta, in Plato (*Laws* 4.712d) and Aristotle (*Politics* 2.6.1265b33); it was later to be applied to Rome by Polybius (6.11.11) and Cicero (*Republic* 1.69–70, 2.65), and it appears in Areius Didymus. Theophrastus developed Aristotle's study of rhetoric, elaborating from Aristotelian materials a doctrine of the four virtues of style (correctness, clarity, appropriateness, and ornament) that became standard for later writers, and dealing with rhetorical delivery, a subject Aristotle had neglected. Subsequently, however, the study of rhetoric became a subject in its own right and grew apart from Peripatetic philosophy.

The history of Aristotelianism as a separate tradition in the ancient world comes to an end with Alexander and Themistius. It has already been suggested that one reason for the first decline of Aristotelianism, in the Hellenistic period, was that it lacked a clear program to rival the attractions of Stoic or Epicurean dogmatism, on the one hand, and Pyrrhonian or Academic skepticism on the other. It is tempting to suppose that the reason for the second decline of Aristotelianism was the reverse of the first; the revived Aristotelianism of the empire was too closely tied to the exposition of texts, and lacked the scope and appeal of revived dogmatic Platonism. More might indeed have been made of the Aristotelian texts: Alexander's discussion of intellect might have shown the way here, whether he realized it or not. But further development of his ideas would have led to a position not unlike that of the Neoplatonists themselves. And this may indicate a further reason for the decline of the Peripatetic tradition.

Some scholars assess Alexander in terms of a tension between naturalism and mysticism. Indeed it has been suggested that the whole history of the Peripatetic tradition in antiquity can be seen in terms of an uneasy oscillation between a materialism insufficiently distinct from Stoicism and a belief in immaterial principles insufficiently distinct from Platonism. The school declined because it lacked a distinctive enough position of its own.

The end of a purely Peripatetic tradition was not, however, the end of Aristotelianism, in two ways. Aristotle's works continued to be studied by the Neoplatonists, although they were interpreted as applying to the sensible world as opposed to the higher, intelligible realm, and where that higher realm was concerned, the influence of Aristotelian doctrines and concerns, transmitted through the Peripatetic school, was felt. The placing of the Platonic Forms within the Divine Intellect may well go back to Xenocrates, the third head of Plato's Academy; but the way in which the theory of intellect was developed by Middle Platonists and Plotinus owes not a little to the Aristotelian doctrine of the Active Intellect and the interpretation of God as self-thinking immaterial thought. The Neoplatonic commentators did not all adopt the same approach to Aristotle's works—Philoponus, in particular, was

ready to reject Aristotelian positions—but even a critical reaction reflects a type of influence.

It may also have been the type of reaction Aristotle would himself have welcomed. For the second legacy of ancient Aristotelianism to subsequent thought is a problem-solving approach to philosophy, structurally in texts like the *quaestiones* attributed to Alexander and the medieval format of responses to objections, and more generally in a certain cast of mind and way of proceeding. It is a thoroughly Aristotelian approach, for it is Aristotle himself who says that it is an advantage in any inquiry to "state all the difficulties well" (*Metaphysics* III.1.995a28). What we will never know is how definitive he regarded his own achievement as being, and how he would himself have regarded the ways in which his successors continued the process he had begun.

R. W. Sharples

Bibliography

I would like to acknowledge my considerable debt to the writings of Paul Moraux and Hans Gottschalk. A longer version of this article appeared in the *Routledge History of Philosophy*, vol. 2 (1999).

Texts and Translations

Aspasius, Alexander of Aphrodisias, and the Neoplatonic commentators on Aristotle: *Commentaria in Aristotelem Graeca (CAG)*. Berlin: Reimer, 1883–1909. Alexander's minor works in *Supplementum Aristotelicum* 2.1–2 (ibid., 1887–1892); annotated English translations in the *Aristotelian Commentators* series edited by R. Sorabii (London: Duckworth, 1987–).

Theophrastus. *De causis plantarum*. Ed. B. Einarson and G. K. K. Link. Loeb Classical Library.

———. *Historia plantarum*. Ed. S. Amigues. 4 vols. Paris: Budé, 1988–.

———. *Metaphysics*. Ed. W. D. Ross and F. H. Fobes. Oxford: Oxford University Press, 1929.

———. *Theophrastus of Eresus*. Ed. W. W. Fortenbaugh, P. M. Huby, R. W. Sharples (Greek and Latin) and D. Gutas (Arabic). 2 vols. Leiden: Brill, 1992; commentaries, 1995–.

Wehrli, F. *Die Schule des Aristoteles*, 2nd ed. Basel: Schwabe, 1967–1978.

Studies

Barnes, Jonathan. *Aristotle*. Oxford: Oxford University Press, 1982.

Fortenbaugh, W. W., et al., eds. *Rutgers University Studies in Classical Humanities*. New Brunswick, N.J.: Transaction, 1983–.

Gottschalk, H. B. "Aristotelian Philosophy in the Roman World." In *Aufstieg und Niedergang der römischen Welt (ANRW)*, II, 36, no. 2. Berlin: De Gruyter, 1987.

Hahm, D. E. "The Ethical Doxography of Arius Didymus." In *ANRW*, II, 36, no. 4.

Lynch, J. P. *Aristotle's School.* Berkeley: University of California Press, 1972.

Moraux, Paul. *Der Aristotelismus bei den Griechen.* Berlin: De Gruyter. Vol. 1, 1973; vol. 2, 1984; vol. 3, forthcoming.

Regenbogen, Otto. "Theophrastos." In *Paulys Realencyclopädie der Classischen Altertumswissenchaft,* suppl. 7. Stuttgart: Metzler, 1940. Pp. 1354–1562.

Repici, Luciana. *La natura e l'anima: Saggi su Stratone di Lampsaco.* Turin: Tirrenia, 1988.

Wehrli, Fritz. "Der Peripatos bis zum Beginn der römischen Kaiserzeit." In Friedrich Ueberweg, ed. Hellmut Flashar, *Grundriss der Geschichte der Philosophie: Die Philosophie der Antike,* vol. 3. Basel: Schwabe, 1983. Pp. 459–599.

Related Articles

Schools and Sites of Learning; Aristotle; Cosmology; Plotinus

CYNICISM

Cynicism was an antiestablishment philosophical movement that arose in Greece in the 4th century B.C.E. around Diogenes of Sinope, called the Dog, and his disciples. It lasted until at least the 5th century C.E.; the last known Cynic philosopher, Sallustius, was connected with the circle of the Neoplatonist Proclus. Acting in all realms—political, moral, religious, literary, and philosophical—to contest traditional values in a radical way, Cynicism offered a "shortcut" to happiness: physical asceticism in pursuit of a moral end. In a period when speech was an instrument of power, Cynicism preferred the power of acts and testimony to the subtleties of discourse and, in this respect following the path opened up by Socrates, it gave priority to the existential experience of the wise man.

Study of this movement is hampered by a lack of documentation. Virtually nothing remains of ancient Cynic literature. We know these philosophers principally through anecdotes and sayings (passed down by Greek tradition but also by Arab gnomologies) whose historical value is impossible to verify. Some Cynic *Letters* have been preserved; unfortunately, they are pseudepigraphical. Moreover, the sources on which we depend are not unbiased: these include not only opponents of Cynicism, such as the Epicureans or certain Church Fathers, but also figures such as Epictetus and Julian, whose idealized views of Cynicism were shaped by their own personal convictions. Moreover, even when we have no reason to suspect bias, it is difficult to determine to what degree we can depend, for an understanding of Diogenes, on late sources like the five very substantial discourses (IV, VI, VIII, IX, and X) in which Dio Chrysostom presents the philosopher. Finally, because of the very nature of this movement, texts with doctrinal content are quite rare, and this is aggravated by the fact that our principal source, Book VI of Diogenes Laertius's *Lives of Eminent Philosophers* (in particular the doxographic sections 70–73 and 103–105), has been influenced by a Stoic outlook that has unquestionably distorted some of the theoretical aspects of Cynicism.

We must nevertheless try to discover behind the anecdotes, apothegms, and slogans not a system—for nothing is more contrary to the spirit of Cynicism—but at least a guiding thread, a homogeneous philosophical inspiration expressed in a coherent manner.

HISTORICAL SURVEY

We cannot speak of Cynicism without first exploring the meaning of this label. Two explanations were already available in antiquity, based on two different etymologies. The first, which certainly derives from a need for similarity with the Academy, the Stoa, or the Lyceum, links the movement to a place well known to Athenians of the period, the Cynosarges gymnasium, which housed a temple dedicated to Hercules and was where Antisthenes, one of Socrates' disciples, taught. This gymnasium was reserved for *nothoi*, that is, sons of an Athenian father and foreign mother, as well as for illegitimate children and freedmen. The etymology of the word *cynosarges* is itself uncertain: it may mean dog food, white dog, or fast dog. Partisans of this explanation of the word *cynicism* maintain that Antisthenes was the founder of the movement. The second explanation comes from a jest that compared the cynics to dogs *(kunes)* owing to the freedom and simplicity of their behavior and the shamelessness and impudence of their lifestyle, which led them to declare that acts ordinarily judged morally shameful were "unimportant": masturbation or copulating in public, eating in the public square, sleeping in empty earthenware jars or on street corners. The name "Dog" perfectly suits our philosophers, who took pains to "bark" loud and long; they would not only have accepted it, they would have adopted it proudly.

Cynicism was never a school. Is it even reasonable to speak of Cynicism or Cynics? This philosophical movement indeed readily located itself outside the traditional framework of school life: it had no fixed place of teaching, no succession of famous scholars, no courses or lectures; instead, it hurled disruptive "barkings" into the street, in squares, at temple doors, at the entrance to the stadium while the games were on, voiced by strong personalities who knew how to give weight to their message by flaunting their actions and their way of living.

Who was the founder of the movement? Was it Antisthenes, who, after studying with the orator Gorgias, became one of Socrates' well-known disciples, and was nicknamed *haplokuōn* (perhaps "plain dog," in an allusion to cynical frankness, or "dog with a plain coat," because of his *tribōn* [worn cloak], or else "natural dog," that is, one whose behavior was based on natural requirements and not on social conventions)? Or was it perhaps Diogenes of Sinope (412/403–324/321), the man in the tub who, while sunning himself in the Craneum gymnasium in Corinth, calmly asked an astounded Alexander to "stand out of [his] light" (Diogenes Laertius, *Lives* VI.38), and who used a lantern to look for men in broad daylight? The ancient tradition leans toward Antisthenes, but the sources on which it is founded are late (Epictetus, Dio Chrysostom, Aelian, Diogenes Laertius, Stobaeus, and the *Suda*), and the moderns suspect, perhaps rightly, that some Stoics in search of a Socratic lineage forged a pedigree extending through Socrates to Antisthenes, Diogenes,

and Crates to Zeno, one that the authors of *Successions* would hasten to adopt, since it made their task so much easier. In fact the chronological and numismatic data are not unanimous, and we still do not know for sure whether Diogenes, exiled from Sinope, spent time with Antisthenes in Athens. Whatever role Antisthenes may have played (and he did play one, if only through the decisive influence his writings were to have on the earliest "Dogs"), there is no doubt that it was Diogenes who launched Cynicism as a movement and who determined its principal directions.

How could such a philosophy arise in 4th-century Athens and develop in the Hellenistic period? The society in which Diogenes lived was acquainted with all the refinements of luxury, as attested by the numerous anecdotes that show the philosopher castigating the behavior and gluttony of his contemporaries; we may conclude that Athenian society was in need of harsh censors. But we should not see Diogenes as an ignorant and unpolished man, inclined by his social origins to scorn the effects of civilization. He was the son of a banker, born in Sinope, a Greek city-state on the Euxine Sea in the Pontus region. Sinope was very active in the commercial realm and very advanced, owing to the numerous contacts it maintained with other centers. Diogenes apparently received a solid education there, to judge by the works he produced, whose titles Diogenes Laertius has preserved.

But 4th-century society was also one of contrasts. Around the edges of a brilliant civilization that was responsive to luxury, a world of the disadvantaged was growing: impoverished citizens, slaves, exiles, the victims of pirates, and so on. In such a context, an individual really was prey to terror; compelled to face Tuche, or Fortune, the only active divinity in this troubled world, with only his own resources, he felt helpless, condemned to individualism and a personal search for happiness. Thus we can imagine the effects of the vociferous Dog, exempt from complacency but extremely bracing, on individuals whose everyday existence was precarious. Like the other Hellenistic philosophies, but with extraordinary vigor, Cynicism thus set itself the goal of securing individual happiness.

Two major periods in the history of the movement have to be distinguished: the ancient Cynicism of the 4th and 3rd centuries B.C.E. and the imperial Cynicism of the 1st to 5th centuries C.E. The first period is dominated by the exceptional figures of Diogenes and his disciple Crates. The former was intransigent and in many respects heroic; he had chosen to shock, both by his way of life and by his caustic language. The latter was just as committed but perhaps more humane and more approachable in his manner. People admired Diogenes, the "heavenly dog," but they also feared him; they admired Crates, the "dear hunchback," and they liked him, too. We know that Diogenes left Sinope and took the path of exile after a murky adventure involving counterfeit money about which we shall never know the true story, or even whether it really happened. He went to Athens, where he may have fre-

quented Antisthenes; captured by pirates on a sea voyage, he was sold as a slave to one Xeniades of Corinth, who made him his children's teacher. Diogenes had the chance to prove his never-failing frankness when he met Philip of Macedon, and later Philip's son Alexander. The numerous stories that circulated about his death attest to his wish to conform as much as possible to rules dictated by nature. Among his disciples, Crates of Thebes, born to a rich family, deliberately gave away all his resources to dedicate himself to Cynicism and live a real dog's life with his wife, Hipparchia of Maronea, even going so far as to make love in public. Crates, too, had his disciples, notably Metrocles of Maronea (Hipparchia's brother), Monimus of Syracuse, who began as the slave of a banker, and the famous Menippus of Gadara, also a slave, whose literary influence on writers such as Varro, Seneca, Petronius, Apuleius, and of course Lucian was very important.

In the following century, two people who were atypical, but who were unquestionable strong personalities, turned to the Cynic movement: Bion of Borysthenes (ca. 335–245 B.C.E.), son of a freed merchant of salting equipment and a courtesan, whose completely eclectic philosophical education led him in turn to the Academy, the Cynics, the Cyrenaics, and finally the Peripatetics; and Cercidas of Megalopolis (ca. 290–217 B.C.E.), a friend of Aratus of Sicyon, who was at once a statesman, a general, a legislator, and a poet. In addition to these colorful figures, thanks to Stobaeus we can mention Teles, a modest professor of philosophy who lived in Athens and Megara and who appealed to a circle of young people. We are indebted to Teles for passing on to us, in his *Diatribes* (the oldest testimony we have on the Cynico-Stoic diatribes), some sayings by several Cynic philosophers, including Crates, Metrocles, and especially Bion, the model Teles preferred.

During the next two centuries, Cynicism seems to have undergone a certain eclipse. In Greece, one can cite only the poet Meleager of Gadara (ca. 135–50 B.C.E.) and the *Pseudepigraphical Letters* of the Cynics, some of which date from this period; among the Romans, we see almost no one but the senator Marcus Favonius, an intimate of Cato of Utica, whose bearing and speech conformed to the Cynic style. However, beginning with the 1st century of the Christian era, that is, during a period when Rome was experiencing an economic prosperity that fostered the development of wealth and luxury, we see such an extraordinary revival of Cynicism that Diogenes' philosophy became the popular philosophy par excellence in Rome, Alexandria, Constantinople, and Athens. To be sure, exceptional personalities emerged: Demetrius of Corinth, a friend of Seneca and of Thrasea Paetus, was banished from Rome by Nero, then by Vespasian, and remained faithful to the short path of asceticism; Demonax of Cyprus professed a milder Cynicism that appealed to his laudatory biographer, Lucian. The latter adopted a very different tone, in contrast, with regard to Peregrinus Proteus, who professed both Cyn-

icism and Christianity; with crudely slanderous insinuations, Lucian relates many piquant but unedifying anecdotes about Peregrinus that can be held quite suspect, thanks to the very different and even contradictory testimony left by Aulus Gellius. In the 2nd century we encounter Oenomaus of Gadara, whose highly audacious opinions would be criticized harshly later on by the Emperor Julian. Among other works, Oenomaus wrote one that we know under two titles: *Against the Oracles* and *Charlatans Unmasked,* in which he launches attacks of a rare violence against gods whom he pronounces unjust, against soothsayers whom he treats as ignorant charlatans, and above all against oracles whose fraudulent character he delights in stressing.

Peregrinus was not the only example of a Christian Cynic. In the 4th century we also know Maximus Hero of Alexandria, a friend of Gregory Nazianzus who became the latter's worst enemy when he surreptiously got himself named bishop of Constantinople one night (Gregory had hoped to assume that office himself). Maximus Hero practiced frugality, made use of Cynic frankness, wore the *tribōn,* the rough little cloak characteristic of Cynic dress, and claimed to be a citizen of the entire universe. Finally, in the following century, the figure of Sallustius stands out. Damascius tells us that after studying law, Sallustius attended the rhetorical schools of Alexandria and devoted himself to Cynicism, practicing a rigorous and austere asceticism. He succeeded in diverting one member of Proclus's circle, Athenodorus, from philosophy; later, Sallustius quarreled with Proclus himself.

But the Cynicism of the imperial period was not confined to these prominent figures. It was above all a popular philosophy that attracted its adepts from the most disadvantaged regions of the large cities, from among poor citizens and slaves. It was also a philosophy practiced collectively, yet outside of any school framework; in fact, along with those who, like Oenomaus, produced literary texts, groups of Cynics roamed the streets of Rome and Alexandria, begging on street corners and taking up stations where the crowds were thickest: on squares swarming with people, in ports, or outside the stadiums. These beggars harangued an undefined public that changed from day to day. We can imagine that charlatans, relying on the principle that clothes make the philosopher, were not in short supply; they were the targets of the criticisms leveled by Epictetus, Lucian, and Julian. All the same, imperial Cynicism on the whole remained faithful to the tradition of the Dogs, to the extent that it remained faithful to the practice of asceticism.

The Cynics have often been compared to members of the most rigorous Christian sects, such as the Encratites and the Apotactites. It is certainly easy to see the resemblances between these two movements: they both defended poverty, criticized false values, vaunted the universality of their message, and, although their ultimate goals were different, they shared the same aspiration to self-abnegation. Nevertheless, while Peregrinus and Maximus Hero were

Christians, it was Crescens, a Cynic, who was responsible for the martyrdom of Justin in 165, and Church Fathers such as St. Augustine and Sidonius Apollinaris did not hide the fact that they were shocked by the Cynics' impudence and their rejection of the most widely shared moral values.

Cynicism did not disappear with the Roman empire. It aroused great interest, and it has even undergone an occasional resurgence in the modern period and in our own era. Thus the reader of Montaigne's *Essais* often comes across a reference to Diogenes, a Diogenes whom Montaigne came to know through Diogenes Laertius. But it was in the 18th century, in the atmosphere of the Enlightenment, that Cynicism came back into prominence most compellingly. In 1770, in Germany, Christoph Martin Wieland, an Enlightenment philosopher, published a work titled *Sokrates mainomenos oder die Dialogen des Diogenes von Sinope (Socrates out of His Senses, or Dialogues of Diogenes of Sinope)*; it was a great success. In France, Rousseau was nicknamed "Diogenes," quite to his own disliking, by a number of his contemporaries—with respect by Kant and Wieland, with sarcasm and spite by Voltaire. The latter used this appellation to make fun of him yet again: under his pen, Rousseau became "Diogenes' monkey," a "little would-be Diogenes who hides the soul of a scoundrel under the cloak of Diogenes," and even a "Diogenes without a lantern," which was the ultimate insult in a period when everyone aspired to Enlightenment. D'Alembert, for his part, thought that every age, and especially his own, had need of a Diogenes. However, it is unquestionably with the Diderot of *Le neveu de Rameau* that we can best measure the attraction exerted by the spirit of Cynicism. Both of the satire's protagonists, Moi and Lui, quote Diogenes as their authority. Moi, the narrator, represents a Cynicism faithful to the ancient tradition, while Lui, the Nephew, the incarnation of a parasite who despises society and voluntarily chooses a kind of ethic of abjection, already heralds cynicism in the modern sense of the term.

The 19th century had its own version; it witnessed the flowering of what Ludwig Stein called Nietzsche's "Neocynicism." In fact, the *Umwertung der Werte*, the inversion of values extolled by Nietzsche, was deliberately rooted in "the Diogenean counterfeiting of money." Today the word *cynicism* conveys a rather different reality from the ancient *kunismos*. We use the term *cynics* for those who deliberately flaunt an attitude of impudence, of bold contempt for propriety and systematic immorality. Today cynics care nothing about helping their contemporaries on the way to happiness; their provocation is purely negative, and the mere idea of asceticism has no part in their way of life. If there is any link connecting the philosophy of Diogenes to the present cynicism, it seems to be only superficial, external. Even when the attitude is identical, the underlying motives and aim are not at all the same. It is worth noting that the German language, in an attempt to avoid confusion—at least since the 19th century—has used two distinct terms: *Kynismus*, des-

ignating the ancient Cynic philosophy, and *Zynismus,* specifying the modern attitude. German philosophers have focused recently on resemblances and differences between the two notions; pertinent here are Heinrich Niehues-Pröbsting's *Der Kynismus des Diogenes und der Begriff des Zynismus* and Peter Sloterdijk's *Kritik der zynischen Vernunft.* The latter text, which has been extraordinarily successful in Germany, explains why *Kynismus* liberates while *Zynismus* oppresses, why the one warrants respect while the other should be condemned, and it proposes *Kynismus* as the only alternative to the generalized *Zynismus* of the present day.

THE PRINCIPLES OF THE CHALLENGE

Diogenes makes a point of asserting difference. "He was going into a theatre, meeting face to face those who were coming out, and, being asked why: 'This,' he said, 'is what I practise doing all my life'" (*Lives* VI.64). "When people laughed at him because he walked backward beneath the Portico, he said to them: 'Aren't you ashamed, you who walk backward along the whole path of existence, and blame me for walking backward along the path of the promenade?'" (Stobaeus, III.iv.83).

Diogenes had taken up "counterfeiting money" as a slogan, perhaps as the result of a personal experience of counterfeiting for which he (or his father) may have been responsible. The phrase referred to the idea of reversing the currently respected values in all realms of human activity, individual and collective, and replacing these false values with new ones based on the Cynics' view of humankind and of life—an undertaking of systematic subversion.

For the Cynic, only the individual matters, with all his singularity: to ensure his happiness, he must be shown the way to individual revolution. From this perspective, the Cynic rejects all the prohibitions that ordinary social life requires and urges a radical return to nature. Emboldened by a heightened lucidity, he understands that man's unhappiness derives from his intrinsic weakness, which is attributable to his passions, to pride, fear, and the attraction to pleasure, and also to the aggressions of the world around him that lead him to sacrifice to illusory values. A slave to fame, to social obligations, and to wealth, which leaves him insatiable, man spends his life engaged in feverish activity directed toward the emptiest of goals. Thus Diogenes points out an athlete who trains like a madman in the stadium in order to triumph in the Olympic games, or a politician prepared to make any sacrifice to win power, not to mention rich men, or committed gourmets who expend great energy so that their table can provide countless pleasures for the most delicate palate. For such men, prey to all sorts of desires and anguish, Diogenes, like a doctor with his patient, wants to make him understand that the real struggle does not lie where he thinks it does, and that a conversion is in order. Given that

the ultimate goal is happiness, man must create three indispensable conditions in himself to achieve it: autarchy, that is, the ability to be self-sufficient and completely independent; apathy, which allows him to be impassible under all circumstances; and, finally, freedom. Whereas people traditionally deem a man happy when he is provided with abundant material goods, Diogenes shows on the contrary that happiness is achieved when one manages to limit one's needs to the maximum degree and to reach a total serenity that makes it possible to face the whims of fortune without any difficulty. From this perspective, the Cynic proposes animals as concrete models of autarchy, for animals are able to support themselves with what nature offers, and God as a theoretical model, according to the principle that "it was the privilege of the gods to need nothing and of god-like men to want but little" (*Lives* VI, 105). In one of his poems, Crates proclaimed: "Far be it from me to pile up fabulous treasures! I scheme only to achieve the happiness of the beetle, and the ease of the ant" (Julian, *Discourse* VII.9.213c).

THE SOCIAL CHALLENGE

The most obvious form is the social challenge Diogenes posed in his everyday lifestyle. Its symbol was his dress: the cloak *(tribōn)*, folded in two, generally filthy, which served as a wrap in all seasons and also as a blanket at night; the staff, at once a voyager's staff, beggar's rod, and royal scepter; the double sack into which the cynic put everything he needed for daily life. To complete the picture, the philosopher had a long beard, his hair was long and dirty, and he went barefoot. This negligent appearance was one of the components of the practice of asceticism: it showed a deliberate intent to practice social nonconformity and also an ardent desire to return to nature. Perhaps it was derived from tragedy, since the Cynics had taken as models not only Heracles, but also Telephus, his son, whom Euripides put on stage in the tragedy that bears his name, and who arrived at Aulis dressed in rags, carrying a little basket.

The Cynic opposed the society of his own time by hurling invectives and using frankness to the point of insult. He took to task those around him who tried to avoid him at all cost for fear of his sarcasm. Everything in which his contemporaries took pride was systematically belittled: Olympic victories, the exercise of power, intellectual success. Moreover, Diogenes did not hesitate to play the parasite and beg for alms, thinking he was reclaiming in this way only what was his due. But what most shocked the people who encountered him was his shamelessness. It was more than distasteful to see Diogenes in the public square, unembarrassed, doing anything he wanted to do: eating, urinating, masturbating. For their part, Crates and Hipparchia created a scandal by consummating their union in the sight of all, to the great embarrassment of poor Zeno, the Stoic philosopher, who tried as best he could to hide them from prying eyes with an old cloak (Apuleius, *Florides* 14).

THE POLITICAL CHALLENGE

Diogenes, who lived at the time Alexander went off to conquer the world, declared himself *a-polis* (without a city), *a-oikos* (homeless), and *kosmopolites* (a citizen of the universe), and Crates declared: "Not one tower has my country nor one roof / But wide as the whole earth its citadel / And home prepared for us to dwell therein" (Diogenes Laertius, *Lives* VI.9). Yet their contemporaries were not yet ready to give up the traditional markers of civic and political life, especially as cynical cosmopolitanism appeared rather negative: in being a citizen of the world, the philosopher is a citizen nowhere, and Diogenes advocated abstention with regard to all political commitment; the very notion constituted an impediment to individual liberty, in his eyes. In keeping with this stance, as he explained in his *Republic,* he rejected the law that was the cornerstone of the city-state, and he opposed to it the law that rules the universe, otherwise called natural law. His work, as one might well imagine, created a scandal, for he encouraged people to drop all taboos, to reject every impediment to individual freedom, and thus potentially to practice anthropophagy and incest, to hold women and children in common, and finally to practice complete sexual liberty. In the Cynic republic, there would no longer be room for weapons, and knucklebones would take the place of money. Diogenes' text produced such a scandal that some Stoics, contemporaries of Philodemus, an Epicurean philosopher of the 1st century B.C.E., judged it too brash and declared, to avoid being tainted by such theories, that it was not by Diogenes.

THE RELIGIOUS CHALLENGE

It should come as no surprise that Diogenes challenged the religious practices of his time in just as radical a manner. He relentlessly called attention to the lack of morality his contemporaries displayed in their way of honoring the gods and in the demands they made on them; he showed that popular religion came from custom and convention, not from nature, and that it was in fact an obstacle to the apathy he sought, because of the fears it inspired in people, particularly the fear of death and infernal punishment. Diogenes rejected all anthropomorphism and criticized religious institutions and traditional forms of the cult, notably the mysteries, prayer, interpretation of dreams, and ritual purifications. It was unacceptable to him that human happiness should depend on practices that have nothing to do with man's moral disposition. But his challenge went even further. He had no rational image of the world, no providential concept of nature. He did not think that the universe was made for man or that there was a mystery of the world to penetrate. His vision of things showed the gods to be, in a sense, insignificant. By imitating animals, man would come to know only animal happiness and would be able to accept

the inevitable. Thus the Cynic drew his strength from his impassibility in the face of destiny, not because he accepted its superior or mysterious rationality, but simply because he himself asserted his will to be impassible. Noting the artificiality of the world in which we live, he resigned himself to it. His realism and his desire to refuse all illusions required him to submit to the laws of nature and to refrain from making pronouncements on questions that were beyond him. Thus one could define the Cynic's overall position as an agnosticism that allowed him to preserve his apathy and to achieve his own happiness, day after day, by willpower alone.

THE PHILOSOPHICAL CHALLENGE
AND ITS CONSEQUENCES

Perhaps it was with regard to the traditional notion of philosophy that Cynicism offered its most radical challenge. When a new philosophy offered solutions, these were generally formulated in opposition to the ones offered by existing schools. Cynicism was no exception. It was not an improvised reaction; it proceeded to evaluate the choices offered by contemporary philosophies, all of which it grouped together into an overall stance whose inefficacy and intellectualism it denounced. But at the same time, Cynicism was not purely and simply a denunciation of philosophy, since it proposed a new kind of philosophy, one deemed more authentic and more effective at ensuring human happiness. Cynicism represented itself, indeed, as a "short-cut" (Diogenes Laertius, *Lives* VII.121), accessible even to those who lacked education, those who had not had the means to frequent the renowned schools of philosophy. It did away with the notion of an intellectual elite that took itself too seriously. Diogenes was aware of the pretension it takes to proclaim oneself a philosopher, and "to one who says to him, 'You know nothing and yet you philosophize,' he replies: 'Even if I am but a pretender to wisdom, that in itself is philosophy'" (*Lives* VI.64). To counterfeit traditional philosophy, that is, to philosophize without claiming to know anything, was, from the Cynic's standpoint, the only legitimate practice.

In a period when speculative philosophy was in the process of acquiring its elitist credentials, Cynicism played the spoilsport with its distrust of study, reason, and debate. While the Platonic dialogues were offering a dazzling demonstration of superior intelligence, while Aristotle was broadening his research into all fields of learning and the Stoics were about to work out a vast systematic construction, the Cynics threw themselves into provocation, deliberately breaking with the intellectual component of philosophy and insisting on existential experience. Why this rejection of paideia? First because, in their eyes, virtue depended on actions, and then because the disciplines traditionally taught—music, geometry, astronomy, and so on—were not useful for the acquisition of virtue. What is the use of tuning the strings of one's lyre if

one leaves untuned the temper of one's soul? As a general rule, the Cynics did not value book learning; they far preferred practice to study. One day when Hegesias begged him to lend him one of his works, Diogenes replied: "You are a simpleton, Hegesias; you do not choose painted figs but real ones; and yet you pass over the true training and would apply yourself to written rules" (*Lives* VI.48).

The path to virtue recommended by Diogenes was thus that of a purely corporeal asceticism, based on daily training, and its aim was the health of the soul. This asceticism was conceived as a preventive method: anyone who practices *ponoi* (suffering) daily, by drinking only water, eating very frugally, sleeping on the bare ground, and enduring the cold and heat of the seasons, feels no fear, because he knows that one day when suffering is imposed on him by *Tuche* (Fortune) in the form of exile, poverty, or dishonor, he will be trained to bear it and will be able to meet it with serenity. Thus poverty appears to be "an instinctive support for philosophy." If one submits to the law of Cynic asceticism, that is, to a lifestyle based on frugality and to satisfying only life's bare necessities, one becomes autarchic, apathetic, free, and therefore happy, like Diogenes, "a homeless exile, to his country dead, / A wanderer who begs his daily bread" (*Lives* VI.38). "Nothing in life, . . . he maintained, has any chance of succeeding without strenuous practice; and this is capable of overcoming anything. Accordingly, instead of useless toils men should choose such as nature recommends, whereby they might have lived happily. Yet such is their madness that they choose to be miserable" (VI.71). If happiness is the result of such strenuous asceticism, we may suspect that Diogenes also falsified the idea of pleasure. For him, true pleasure came from contempt for pleasure and had nothing to do with the way civilized life commonly defines it. This is why, even as a prisoner of pirates, Diogenes continued to be happy, for owing to his asceticism he was able to preserve a sphere within himself that no external aggression could disturb. Whereas philosophers such as Aristotle sought truth through the intermediary of learning, the Cynic philosopher sought internal peace and serenity by training his will and submitting his body to the harsh law of asceticism.

Such a conception of philosophy could not help but seem provocative and give rise to criticism. In fact, Cynic philosophy seems to have been challenged fairly early, perhaps as early as the period of classical Cynicism. In any event, it was challenged in the 2nd century by one Hippobotus, the author of *On the Sects*, who explicitly excluded the Cynic sect from his list. Among the complaints leveled against Cynicism, the absence of coherent dogmas and of a specific end, of a clearly defined *telos*, seem particularly noteworthy. Certain critics, as Diogenes Laertius recalls (*Lives* VI.103), thus thought they could reduce the Cynic movement to a simple way of life, and they refused to grant it the status of a *hairesis* (school).

The antiestablishment positions of the Cynics aroused discomfort among

the Stoics, though not among those of the earliest generations. For Zeno of Citium, a disciple of Crates of Thebes, and probably also for Chrysippus, Stoicism seemed in fact to be Cynicism's heir. One can nevertheless perceive a considerable divergence, for as some of the Cynic attitudes were reinterpreted within Stoicism, they took on quite different meanings from the initial inspiration. For Zeno and Chrysippus, the overturning of customs and taboos, scandalous as it was, would serve to affirm a natural law valorized in itself insofar as it expressed the rationality of the universe. For the Cynic, however, these attitudes marked a break with society and its laws, without going beyond this critique to manifest an idealization of the order of nature.

Later on, certain Stoics influenced by Panetius, hoping to avoid being linked to the scandalous positions of the Dogs, declared that Diogenes did not write the *Republic* attributed to him; others also saw Zeno's *Republic* as an inauthentic work (Diogenes Laertius, *Lives* VII.33–34), or else as an error of his youth (Philodemus, *De Stoicis* col. IX). One approach was as good as another to wipe out the scandal. The procedure could be less flagrant, more subtle. Epictetus, for example, rejected the Cynicism of his contemporaries and admired that of the past. It was certainly easier to refer to a Diogenes remote in time, by then a quasi-legendary figure, than to address the Dogs who were very much alive, dirty, biting, "barking," and begging.

THE LITERARY CHALLENGE

It may well seem surprising that the Cynics produced an abundant body of literary work (which has unfortunately been lost), given that they rejected every form of learning. But here again, in order to understand their position, we must fall back on the notion of "falsification." Diogenes and his followers succeeded in practicing subversion at the very heart of writing itself. While they borrowed the framework of traditional genres, they marked these with their own imprint. We attribute dialogues, letters, and tragedies to Diogenes, and to Crates letters and tragedies as well; however, the latter won fame especially in the poetic genre, with elegies such as his *Hymn to the Pierian Muses*, in which he parodied Solon, and poems such as *Pera (The Beggar's Sack)*, in which he imitated Homer. Crates' poetry, especially his Homeric parodies, seems to have had a decisive influence on Timon of Phlius, author of *Silloi*. Moreover, the Cynics invented new literary genres that achieved great success later on: these included diatribe (Bion of Borysthene), satire (Menippus of Gadara), and the *chreia* (Metrocles, and perhaps before him Diogenes), generally rather short philosophical remarks often accompanied by a flash of wit. Above all, the Cynics practiced a new style, so characteristic of their writing that it was called the *kunikos tropos* (Demetrius, *De elocutione* 259); one of its compositional principles is the *spoudaiogeloion*, a mixture of humor

and seriousness honored in the light verse of Monimus of Syracuse and Crates of Thebes. Despite their preference for acts, these philosophers knew how to use words in new ways, practicing humor and making skilled use of piercing sallies or multilayered wordplay. Their writing had playful elements, even as it remained, paradoxically, powerfully serious.

THE PEDAGOGICAL CHALLENGE

A doctor of souls, like every philosopher of the Hellenistic period, the Cynic, though in many respects a misanthrope, was a man of crowds and assemblies; he needed a public receptive to his "barkings." A missionary in his own way, he sought to convince, to get his message across. To this end, he used three weapons: frankness, which led him to scold and use biting words; humor, or, rather, sarcastic sallies that could take the form of derision, light joking, or buffoonery, and that were designed to force the interlocutor to react; and, finally, provocation, gratuitous only in appearance, which allowed the Cynic to bring his interlocutor to ask himself questions directly, to emerge from his lethargy. Diogenes was at once the guilty conscience of his time and the midwife of scandal.

Not only have Cynics not disappeared from view, as we can tell from the numerous publications devoted to them in recent years, but they seem be undergoing a revival. Why? Cynicism can be reproached for proposing a reductive morality that offers a totally negative happiness consisting in experiencing no sorrow and acknowledging no difficulties. One can also stress that this happiness is offered to truncated human beings, mutilated in their aspirations, who practice an attitude of retreat with regard to engagements of all kinds and who renounce every project of an intellectual nature. One can finally judge that the morality in question is too narrow, too centered on the individual, and that the tribute paid to independence and to happiness is too great. Still, the Cynics continue to exert their fascination. Among these philosophers, lived experience entails such dynamism, such passion for life and happiness, that one remains captivated even if one does not share their manner of "making life wild."

Cynicism challenges the historian of philosophy in particular, for it reveals that philosophy, contrary to all expectations, is not just an exercise of reason. Diogenes was said to be "a Socrates gone mad." With the Cynics, one is always at the limit of madness, on the line between laughter and sobriety, between comedy and tragedy: in other words, in an uncomfortable, ambivalent position. Thus it was more convenient to ridicule them or to forget them. But for all that, Diogenes has not put down his stick or put out his lantern. He continues, and will continue, to stroll backward through porticoes.

MARIE-ODILE GOULET-CAZÉ
Translated by Rita Guerlac and Anne Slack

Bibliography

Texts and Translations

Billerbeck, Margarethe, ed. *Epiktet: Vom Kynismus.* Philosophia Antiqua 34. Leiden: E. J. Brill, 1978.

————. *Der Kyniker Demetrius: Ein Beitrag zur Geschichte der frühkaiserzeitlichen Popularphilosophie.* Philosophia Antiqua 36. Leiden: E. J. Brill, 1979.

Diogenes Laertius. *Lives of Eminent Philosophers.* Trans. R. D. Hicks. Loeb Classical Library.

————. *Vies et doctrines des philosophes illustres.* Ed. Marie-Odile Goulet-Cazé. Paris: Librairie Générale Française, 1999.

Dorandi, Tiziano. "Filodemo: Gli stoici (PHerc 155 e 339)." *Cronache Ercolanesi* 12 (1982): 91–133. (In particular, Dorandi edits, translates, and comments on the accounts of Diogenes' *Politeia* preserved in Philodemus's *De Stoicis.*)

Giannantoni, Gabriele. *Socratis et Socraticorum Reliquis,* 2nd ed., expanded. 4 vols. Naples: Bibliopolis, 1990. Vol. 2, pp. 135–589; commentary in vol. 4, nn. 21–55, pp. 195–583.

Kindstrand, Jan Fredrik. *Bion of Borysthenes: A Collection of the Fragments with Introduction and Commentary.* Acta Universitatis Upsaliensis—Studia Graeca Upsaliensia 11. Uppsala: University of Uppsala, 1976 (distributed by Almquist and Wiksell International, Stockholm).

Malherbe, Abraham J., ed. *The Cynic Epistles: A Study Edition.* Society of Biblical Literature, Sources for Biblical Study, no. 12. Missoula, Mont.: Scholars Press, 1977.

Paquet, Léonce. *Les Cyniques grecs: Fragments et témoignages.* Philosophica 4. Ottawa: Editions de l'Université d'Ottawa, 1975; Philosophica 35, new ed., rev. and expanded, Ottawa: Les Presses de l'Université d'Ottawa, 1988; shortened version with foreword by Marie-Odile Goulet-Cazé, Paris: Librairie Générale Française, 1992.

Studies

Billerbeck, Margarethe, ed. *Die Kyniker in der modernen Forschung: Aufsätze mit Einführung und Bibliographie.* Bochumer Studien zur Philosophie 15. Amsterdam: B. R. Grüner, 1991.

Brancacci, Aldo. "I *koine areskonta* dei Cinici e la *koinōnia* tra cinismo e stoicismo nel libro VI (103–105) delle *Vite* di Diogene Laerzio." *Aufstieg und Niedergang der Römischen Welt (ANRW)* II, 36, no. 6 (1992): 4049–4075.

————. *Oikeios logos: La filosofia del linguaggio di Antistene.* Elenchos 20. Naples: Bibliopolis, 1990.

Branham, R. Bracht, and Marie-Odile Goulet-Cazé, eds. *The Cynics: The Cynic Movement in Antiquity and Its Legacy.* Berkeley: University of California Press, 1997.

Döring, Klaus. "Sokrates, die Sokratiker und die von ihnen begründeten Traditionen." In *Grundriss der Geschichte der Philosophie: Die Philosophie der Antike,* vol II. 1. Ed. Helmut Flashar. Basel: Schwabe, 1998.

Dudley, Donald R. *A History of Cynicism: From Diogenes to the 6th Century A.D.* London: Methuen, 1937; repr. New York: Gordon Press, 1974.

Goulet-Cazé, Marie-Odile. *L'ascèse cynique: Un commentaire de Diogène Laërce VI*

70–71. Histoire des doctrines de l'Antiquité classique 10. Paris: Librairie Philosophique J. Vrin, 1986.

———. "Le Cynisme à l'époque impériale." *ANRW* II, 36, no. 4 (1990): 2720–2833.

———. "Le Livre VI de Diogène Laërce: Analyse de sa structure et réflexions méthodologiques." *ANRW* II, 36, no. 6 (1992): 3880–4048.

Goulet-Cazé, Marie-Odile, and Richard Goulet, eds. *Le Cynisme ancien et ses prolongements.* Actes du colloque international du CNRS (Paris, 22–25 July 1991). Paris: Presses Universitaires de France, 1993.

Niehues-Pröbsting, Heinrich. *Der Kynismus des Diogenes und der Begriff des Zynismus.* Humanistische Bibliothek I, 40. Munich: Wilhelm Fink Verlag, 1979.

Onfray, Michel. *Cynismes: Portrait du philosophe en chien.* Paris: Grasset, 1990.

Sloterdijk, Peter. *Critique of Cynical Reason.* Trans. Michael Eldred. Minneapolis: University of Minnesota Press, 1987.

Related Articles

Ethics; Schools and Sites of Learning; Antisthenes; The Sage and Politics; Theories of Religion; Stoicism

HELLENISM AND CHRISTIANITY

To STUDY THE RELATION between Christianity and Hellenism is to think simultaneously of harmony and contrast. This ambivalence is perfectly illustrated by Paul's sermon to the Areopagus: a missionary sermon addressed to the Athenians and a reflection of the Hellenistic approach to true knowledge of God, it combines a Stoic conception of the relation of man to God with the doctrine of salvation by the resurrected Christ. The scene also sets in place the roles of partners and antagonists: in their approach to a new form of doctrine, the Greeks are torn between mocking rejection and curiosity; the disciple of Christ contrives to pour his preaching into the mold of their culture, to minimize the differences while at the same time contriving to draw his audience into a movement of radical conversion. On the Christian side, there will be no end, in the following centuries, to the alternation of conciliation and rupture. Paul himself will not persevere in his pacifism. He knows how to proclaim brutally the incompatibility between the wisdom of the Greeks and his message, "A crucified Christ: to the Jews an obstacle that they cannot get over, to the pagans madness" (1 Corinthians 1:23).

Still, one fact must be stressed. Christianity has had a strong tie with Hellenism from the beginning, in that it was spread by means of Greek. The oldest Christian writings, the authentic letters of Paul, were written in Greek. Whatever may have been the linguistic form of the oral traditions and underlying sources of the canonical Gospels, these, too, were composed in Greek. The choice of this language is not limited to the mission of the "Apostle to the Gentiles." It is inherent in the usage of the communities that produced the texts that were later canonized as a coherent set, the New Testament. The Jews of the Diaspora were speakers of Greek. They adopted the *koine*, the language of communication throughout the Orient from the time of Alexander's conquests. Galilee was strongly marked by Hellenistic civilization, and even in Judaea, Greek was widespread.

Koine left its imprint on the religious expression of the authors of the New Testament, who used as their Bible the Septuagint, that is, the Greek translation of the Bible begun in Alexandria in the 3rd century B.C.E. and followed up largely in Palestine. It is also the language in which revisions were made, and in which various writings called "intertestamentary" were produced, forming the multiple Jewish traditions well known to the first Christian authors.

858

It is precisely these Jewish origins of Christianity that draw our attention toward Hellenism in the larger sense, in its cultural and intellectual dimensions. The mindsets, the ways of thinking, the literary products of the first Christian centuries bear witness to the meeting that had already taken place between Hellenism and Judaism. A process of Hellenization began with the Greek translation of the Torah, the Pentateuch, and continued with the works written directly in Greek, like the Book of Wisdom. It grew more vigorous in Alexandrian Judaism, owing to contributions by authors such as Aristobulus and especially Philon; the latter consciously adapted Greek philosophical concepts to his understanding of the Bible by means of allegory, producing a theology, a cosmology, and an anthropology that profoundly influenced the first church fathers.

This Hellenized Judaism plays an important role starting with the earliest Christian missions, as attested by the figure of Apollos, born in Alexandria, who definitively joined the new faith at Ephesus, before preaching the "Way of the Lord" to the Jews of Corinth (Acts 18). The exegesis of the Letter to the Hebrews shows some resemblance to Philon's style. The horizon of thinking found in John's Gospel is clearly apparent in the religious and philosophical writings of the same Philon. It also has some affinity with the intellectual universe of the properly Hellenistic current that produced the hermetic writings. This literature dates from the 2nd and 3rd centuries, but it reveals a more ancient religious trend and, in its way, the reciprocal fruitfulness of Greek and oriental thought.

Among the so-called apostolic works of the Fathers, the *Letters* of Ignatius of Antioch take their place in the tradition of Johannine theology. Barnabus's *Epistle* makes use, in his exegesis of Moses' dietary prescriptions, of the moral allegories already suggested by Hellenized Judaism. The *Epistle to the Corinthians* of Clement of Rome, who witnessed the variety of intermingling currents in the Christian community of Rome at the end of the 1st century, abounds in traces of Hellenistic culture. Clement was well versed in the methods of contemporary rhetoric. At the same time, he had access to the images and themes of what has come to be called the Cynico-Stoic argument; he drew on these to invoke the combat of virtue, to recommend voluntary exile out of devotion to the group, and to give examples of self-sacrifice among the Gentiles. Some of his ideas recall Stoic notions about divinity, as being exempt from anger, or the harmony of the world, a model for human concord. In his writings, one can find echoes of the Pythagorean theme of friendship and communion among men and between humankind and the divine. Still, all these turns and motifs derive only indirectly from Hellenism. They are rooted first of all in Jewish homiletic, which had already absorbed them, and they were modified by specifically biblical concepts.

Starting in the middle of the 2nd century, the confrontation between Christianity and Hellenism, provoked by the expansion of the new religion

into a pagan milieu and by the resistance of Greco-Roman philosophers and governors concerned with political control, led, among Christian apologists, to explicitly formulated problematical questions that are related to Paul's sermon to the Areopagus. The first to confront the difficulty with the requirement of thinking as a philosopher and as a Christian was Justin Martyr. In his *Apologia*, written around 153 to 155 C.E. on the pretext of defending his religion against slander, he sought to transform the Greco-Roman world following the model of his own intellectual and spiritual itinerary, which had led him from philosophy to Christianity, according to the narrative he offered at the beginning of another work, *Dialogue with Tryphon*. In reference to Plato, the Stoics, the poets, and prose writers, he dared to proclaim: "Whatever good they taught belongs to us Christians" (*II Apologia* 13.4). This triumphal gesture implies a favorable judgment on Greek thought. Justin saw Greek thought as capable of presenting real entities, at least confusedly. According to him, there is a kinship between the partial generation of the Logos in the intelligence of the philosophers and the Logos born of the unbegotten and ineffable God. A Platonist by training, Justin remained one, appearances notwithstanding, after his conversion. His knowledge of Plato did not depend simply on doxographic collections or anthologies. He makes precise references in his work to the texts of Plato himself. In his exchanges with the Christian master who is thought to have led him to the faith, he carries over the critical method set forth by Plato in his dialogues. And having become a Christian, he refuses to grant any propositions except those that could be deduced rationally. His system even seems very close to that of the most original Platonist of his time, Numenius.

This did not prevent Justin from borrowing from the Jewish apologetics of the Alexandrian tradition the theory that the teachings of philosophy proceed from the prophets of the Bible, or from affirming, in particular, that Plato found his material in Moses. This theory was not without parallel on the Greek side in this period of infatuation with "barbaric wisdom," as we learn from Numenius's famous remark: "Who is Plato, if not Moses speaking Greek?" The coexistence of a rational explanation and a myth of plagiarism affirming that Christian revelation fulfills Greek philosophy is found again at the end of the 2nd century in the writings of Clement of Alexandria, who praises the progress achieved by the Greeks in learning, all the while excoriating their "larceny."

Clement is certainly the most "Greek" of the church fathers. In his *Hortatory Address*, exhorting Greeks to conversion, he transforms the language of Homer, Pindar, and the Euripides of *Bacchantes*. In *Pedagogue*, he presents Christian virtue as the perfection of the successful man, as modeled by the rules for good living in a well-regulated society and the ethical ideal of the philosophers. *Miscellanies* leads toward the "aphorism," which brings Platonic contemplation to its culmination in the illumination dispensed by the

divine Logos, the Son, mediator between a transcendent God the Father and man. In the first stage of this progression, Clement puts into play an idea of the unity of learning, subordinated to real philosophy, that is typically Platonic, and that has already been adopted by Philon. An "encyclical education" thus consists in four mathematical sciences and dialectic. These are auxiliaries that contribute to awakening the soul and exercising it in view of grasping intelligible matters. As for the alteration that must transform Hellenism into Christianity, it begins with philosophical eclecticism. No more than "Middle Platonism," a vigorous movement of which Clement is a good representative, is the "eclecticism" of the author of *Miscellanies* to be taken in a pejorative sense. It is not a question of combining heterogeneous elements in the confusion of flabby thinking. Clement took unequivocal responsibility for the eclectic course of his method: "When I speak of philosophy, I do not mean Stoic philosophy, or Platonic philosophy, or Epicurean or Aristotelian, but all that has been well said in each of these schools, through the teaching of justice accompanied by pious knowledge: it is this whole ensemble resulting from pious choice that I call philosophy" (*Miscellanies* I).

To be sure, Greek philosophy is conceived as propaedeutic. Still, if it appears inferior to "real philosophy," Christian wisdom, it is what determines Clement's doctrinal program (dominated by the tripartite division of philosophy), which provides a large part of the instruments of his research (for example, the rules of argument, the theory of causes, the path of abstraction leading to the incorporeal principle) and which characterizes even the content of his Christian gnosis. In fact he discovers in the Bible the message of the "best of the Greeks" in his eyes, Pythagoras and Plato.

Even when he claims to contrast the virtues of the "barbarian" wisdom of the prophets and the Apostles with the defects of Hellenism, Hellenism preserves a preponderant importance. Clement wants to reduce "Greek speech" to the style of artifice, which distracts, by way of "tropes," from the propriety of sense. The "dialect of the Hebrews," on the contrary, whose emblematic form is the "parable," is set forth as a model of truthful expression because it is first of all obscure: setting out to identify, through resemblance, it leads to the thing itself. Now this dialect of the Hebrews was in fact "prophecy in Greek," the Septuagint. The displacement brought about thus has the effect of justifying a double movement of translation, which has allegory as its driving force: the cryptic language of the Bible contains statements that can be expressed in philosophical terms, and the "best of the Greeks" use the same veiled diction as "prophecy."

This attempt at assimilation does not go as far in the writings of other apologists. For Athenagoras, who addresses his *Petition* to Marcus Aurelius and Commodus in 177, the recourse to Greek accounts and the philosophical formulation of Christian dogma has as its chief aim the defense of the rationality of Christianity against attacks from the outside, without minimizing

the differences between Christianity and Hellenism. This moderate attitude is found again in the *Contra Celsum* of Origen, whose ample and powerfully erudite response to the pagan pamphleteer Celsus attests to an acute sense of the singularities of civilization and systems of thought.

Not all Christians, not even all educated Christians, were sympathetic to Hellenism. Clement had to fight against those who represented philosophy as an invention of the devil. If he often takes up the myth, grafted onto the interpretation of Genesis 6 in the Book of Enoch, that associates philosophy with the union of angels and the daughters of men, he is more prone to speak about reflection and imitation. Tatian, on the contrary, indulges in a violent polemic against Hellenism in his *Oration to the Greeks,* produced around 165. Not content with condemning—along with other apologists—the pagan religion as idolatrous, or with denouncing the immorality of Greek myths and affirming the anteriority and superiority of Moses, he accuses the Greek philosophical systems of inanity; he deems them absurd, owing to their internal contradictions.

The variety of opinions held by the Fathers on the subject of Hellenism, and also the ambiguity of the relations between Christian thought and Greek tradition, surface again in the internal controversies of Christianity. Justin invented the idea of heresy, to combat tendencies considered deviant. It was a major part of the procedure devised to control dissension, and was borrowed from the heresiography of the time, which defined a school in terms of allegiance to doctrines ascribed to the patronage of a great thinker of the past, and not as an organized institution endowed with rules of succession. The malleability of the concept makes it easy to define a sect, and to trace a doctrinal filiation from tenuous indications. The effectiveness of the system is strengthened by another factor, the Christian tradition of the demonic origin of quarrels, built around the figure of the false prophet. Still, in Justin, the comparison with trends in Greek thought does not go beyond analogy. His entire offensive strategy lies in his ability to hold in check the tactic ascribed to his adversary, in denying him the attribution of "Christian." Other heresiologists handle Justin's weapon quite differently: Greek philosophy becomes the source of heresies. This is already the case with Irenaeus of Lyon, and the polemic reaches its height and approaches absurdity in the *Refutation of All Heresies,* attributed to Hippolytus of Rome, who likens the doctrine of such and such a heresiarch to the system of a Greek philosopher. Thus Marcion is viewed as depending on Empedocles, Basilides on Aristotle, and Noetus on Heraclitus. Still, for the historian of Hellenism, the author deserves credit: not only does he preserve fragments of the Presocratics, but also his knowledge allows him to bear witness to ancient Greek doxography, which he exploits with great skill.

Christians borrowed the instruments of allegory from the Greeks and put them to use in their understanding of Moses and the Bible as a whole. Here

again, they had been preceded by Alexandrian Judaism. Still, the New Testament writings also provided decisive rules and models. The church fathers exploited to the maximum the exegetic devices that were at work in these texts: the story of Jesus and his followers brings to fruition the figures sketched by the institutions, events, and individuals referred to by the law and the prophets; Paul gives examples of the method and specifies its purpose; the veil that hid Moses' face was removed through conversion to Christ (2 Corinthians 3:12–16). The Christians appropriated the Bible, which became an immense allegory whose meaning was reserved for them. The two wives of Abraham, Hagar and Sara, represent two covenants and are thus thought to stand on the side of slavery and freedom, respectively. "This can be regarded as an allegory," writes Paul (Galatians 4:24). The parables of the synoptic Gospels, beyond their narrative content, have a symbolic meaning to unveil. In the Gospel according to John, too, Jesus's language is presented as enigmatic. Moreover, Paul uses the term *type;* this term will be the focus of lengthy developments in the "typology" of the church fathers, who stripped it of its literal meaning and discovered in every element of the Old Testament the "figure" of an element of the New and, by extension, of the church. The question of the Greek legacy comes up again here, but it bears more directly on the Jewish hermeneutic that dominates the writings of the New Testament and that continues, despite the break, to nourish the interpretation of the Fathers. However, the role of Hellenism is hard to appreciate in the rabbinical traditions and in the conventional methods of the adepts of Qumran, whose similarities with Christian "typology" and "allegory" are striking.

Moreover, a major difference separates Greek allegory from that of the Christians. As found in Homer and other poets, Greek allegory is devoid of the historical aim that characterizes Christian allegory, which sees prophetic signs realized in the recent past or in the present time. This sense of progress, related to a divine plan, is often reinforced by the eschatological perspective, which gives hope for the perfect fulfillment of promises at the end of time.

The fact remains that certain features of Christian allegory depend directly on Hellenism. Recourse to etymological meaning, in the style of Plato's inventions in *Cratylus,* the taste for Neopythagorean numerology, the quest for the moral meaning and for the cosmological and theological significance of the stories all go back to the Greek allegorism of the period. For Clement of Alexandria, the symbolic exegesis of the Greeks was the way to uncover the secret meaning of the messages handed down by the great civilizations. He consciously transposed these procedures to the study of the Bible, a divine perquisite of the most noble of the "barbarian" cultures.

A number of apologists, on the contrary, considered Greek allegory a ruse to mask the noxiousness of pagan fables. As for the writings of the Pseudo-Clement, which retain, well into the 4th century, the expression of a Christianity close to Judaism, they go so far as to reject the "typology" of the Pau-

line tradition, because in wishing to prove the divinity of Jesus, that typology compromises monotheism and multiplies rival interpretations. For other reasons, from the 4th century on, the Fathers of the Antiochian tradition differentiate typology from allegory: they disapprove of the latter but recognize the validity of the former. The separation is thus expressed in their vocabulary, which had been rather vague before: the terms *image, type, symbol,* and *enigma* were used indiscriminately, and the technique of allegory had a very wide range.

One other attitude appears that seems contradictory. Origen used the procedures of Greek allegory abundantly in his biblical exegesis, but rejected it when it applied to his own subject, the texts and myths of Hellenism. We can find a similar approach among adversaries of Christianity, such as Celsus, Porphyry, and the emperor Julian. It must be said that Origen's scorn for the allegory practiced by the Greeks stems from his condemnation of the pagan myths, taken literally, while he always finds the literal meaning of the Bible useful. As for his personal hermeneutic, it brought together the traditions stemming from Judaism, Hellenism, and the earlier church fathers so forcefully that it mapped out the paths Christian interpretation would follow for centuries to come. The Greek part of his theory and practice is important, even if it does not play the preponderant role with which it has too often been credited. The reasons Origen gives for the obscurity of the Scriptures (to stimulate research, to protect the unprepared from dangerous illusions) have their equivalents in the Greek pedagogical practice of reading the great texts. The images he uses to describe the articulations among the historical, "psychic," and "spiritual" meanings do not refer to Scripture alone. They also refer explicitly to the tripartite division of philosophy and the composite structure of human beings. The comparison between the harmony of the Scriptures, which is hard to perceive at first glance, and the coherence of the world, which is often invisible, is grafted onto Greek representations of the cosmos. The fundamental principle according to which the Bible is to be explained by way of the Bible corresponds to the "golden rule," formulated quite late by Porphyry but followed by the first masters of Alexandrian philology, decreeing that "Homer is to be explained by way of Homer." When Origen finds gaps in the historico-legislative record inviting a search for spiritual meaning, he falls back on a precept illustrated by Greek exegesis of poets, oracles, and myths: absurdities and contradictions are signs calling for allegorization. The fact that Origen refers to these breaks in continuity as "impossibilities" may even be evidence that the encounter must have taken place, in the Greek tradition, between the allegorical justifications of Homeric passages that had been judged unbecoming and an examination of "impossibilities" in poetic texts—an operation like the one Aristotle carried out for a different purpose in *Poetics* and in his *Homeric Problems.*

Origen also adapts to his commentaries the rules used in the schools to ex-

plicate Aristotle and Plato. The prologue to his treatise on the Song of Songs contains certain elements of schemas that would become known in a later period as introductions to the works of the two philosophers. This evidence shows that the establishment of such schemas began in the 3rd century in the Platonic commentaries. Furthermore, this ingenious allegorist is a proven "grammarian." Origen is one of the best representatives of his time of the discipline of textual explication. This discipline is divided into four parts: lexical and syntactic decoding of the text, explanation of its contents (history, topography, physical data, and so on), textual criticism, and examination of the text's aesthetic and moral value. He demonstrates complete mastery of the rules and concepts relevant to these fields. The same knowledge is put to work, in the 4th century, by the Christian interpreters of the Antiochian movement, who are for their part hostile to allegorization. The Cappadocian Fathers—Basil of Caesaraea, Gregory of Nazianzus, and especially Gregory of Nyssa—reflect, on the contrary, all the dimensions of the Origenian hermeneutic.

For Origen the strenuous work of hermeneutics ultimately conflates his understanding with the very inspiration of the Scriptures; this is for him the highest, and probably the only, mystical experience. A similar alliance of rational urgency and affective tension appears in Christianity through another form of spiritual exercise, which also bears the mark of Hellenism, the way of thinking that defines Christianity as a philosophy. It is a question of the way the church fathers understood "ascesis" in the philosophic sense: as an internal activity of thought and will that leads to a life conducted according to reason. From Justin to John Chrysostomos, by way of Clement, Origen, and the Cappadocians, we see Christianity conceived as "true philosophy" and as lived wisdom. It appropriates the spiritual practices of ancient philosophy, substituting the divine Word for universal Reason. The techniques of introspection, attention to the self, concentration on the present moment, and examination of one's conscience, along with continual practice of the presence of God and constant recourse to the principles of life (which are always available), are aimed at attaining tranquillity of soul and self-mastery. The Greek heritage is thus imprinted on Christian behavior and goes as far as monachism, where reference to the fundamental "dogmas" of the philosophic schools is replaced by constant reference to the ancients' words and "commandments," which were preserved in the *Apophthegmata* and *Kephalaia*. These exercises undoubtedly included properly Christian features: they always presuppose the help of God's grace, and humility, penitence, and obedience on the part of the sinner; renunciation is experienced as a way of participating in Christ's suffering and divine love. But they also contribute to the partial Hellenization of Christianity, especially when Christian "philosophy" becomes a rehearsal for death, in view of separating the soul from the body and liberating it from the "passions," in the Platonic manner.

If we limit our inquiry to the role of Hellenism in the development of Christian doctrines, two fields in particular stand out, anthropology and theology. Meditating on human nature and destiny, the church fathers spun out endless versions of the analogy between the biblical motif of creation "in the image and likeness" of God and the Platonic theme of identification with God (*Theaetetus* 176b). They also rediscovered in Genesis 2:7 Greek theories on the quickening of the embryo and various classical descriptions of the way human beings are constituted. However, the passage from Genesis 2, associated with other scriptural formulas (Wisdom 15:11, Joel 3:1, John 20:22), is related by some exegetes to the gift of the Spirit and to baptism as a second creation. Similarly, the focus on redemption transforms the Greek representations when it brings the Adam-Christ typology into play. Faith in the resurrection of the body, furthermore, never ceases to assert its singularity. Its apologists strive, at best, to prove that it is not unreasonable. But Origen's attempt, employing Greek concepts to imagine the permanence of corporeal "form," was not well received by the church, because it was suspected of diminishing the reality of the resurrected body. It was quite probably the reflection on free will and human responsibility that most advanced the influence of Hellenism. To refute the determinism attributed to the gnostics, first of all, and, more generally, astral fatalism, the church fathers borrowed Aristotle's analysis of free will, or the Stoics' doctrine of "assent." A leitmotiv of this reflection is also found in the famous line from Plato's myth of Er (*Republic* X): "Virtue is free . . . the responsibility lies with the one who chooses—God is justified." It is a principal reference for Gregory of Nyssa, later on. To be sure, the church fathers took on the task of harmonizing the importance of human choice with divine omniscience and foreknowledge, but their insistence on the capacity of reason distances them from Paul's teaching and gives their doctrine of salvation an entirely different cast from the doctrine of occidental Augustinianism.

In theology, the question of the relations between Christianity and Hellenism is particularly controversial. At least since the Reformation, the debate has centered on the "Platonism of the Fathers," which has been viewed as the pinnacle of Christian "Hellenism." Ecclesiastical positions and differing ideas on the essence of Christianity have interfered with scientific examination of the facts. Historians of dogmas have oscillated between partial inquiries, which set forth the use the early church fathers made of the concepts of Greek philosophy, and interpretations that reopen the controversy over the compatibility of the two systems. Heinrich Dörrie has sought to reduce "Christian Platonism" to a means of propaganda for the apologists: at worst metaphorical, at best a correction that renewed the model in question from top to bottom. Even as he has helped identify borrowings, Dörrie has deemed the Christian doctrine of grace and revelation contrary to the Platonic hierarchy of being. Endre von Ivánka, more sensitive to the complicities between

Platonic and Christian theology, ends up reaching similar conclusions, stressing the unassimilable singularity of the concepts of creation and grace. He has even given new life, paradoxically, to the old slogan "Plato purveyor of heresies," by purporting to indicate just how far the theologian can follow Platonism without falling into error. On the opposing side, the learned research of John Whittaker and others tends to blend the ancient Christian doctrines with the moral and intellectual ambiance of the Hellenistic culture of the time.

It is undeniable that the Fathers, to think through their faith and construct their doctrine conceptually, turned toward Platonic "theology," the most prestigious of their era. In so doing, they did not cease to confront a crucial difficulty: how to reconcile the biblical notion of a God endowed with will and acting in a contingent fashion, going so far as to incarnate himself, with an ontology that assumes God's immutability? One of the historian's tasks is to study the successive solutions found by the ancient scholars, or to note the aporias in their work. Contemporary studies, based on a critical knowledge of the sources used by the church fathers, have brought to light the kinship between the latters' hypotheses about the relations between Father and Son, up to the beginning of the 5th century, with Platonic propositions concerning the relations between the demiurgic intellect, the intelligible world, and the transcendent One. The Christian theologians who went farthest along the path to Platonism, far enough to sketch, as Origen did, the disjunction between the supreme principle and the Intellect that was imposed by Plotinus, continue to attribute intellective and voluntary activity to the Father. And, according to Rowan Williams, if Arius radicalizes the difference between the Father and the Son, in terms that the Plotinian decision best illuminates, it is to affirm the perfect independence of God's will. The Arian crisis marks the culmination of the theology of the Logos, which implicated the Son in the cosmic process while subordinating him to the Father. But the new problematic, based on the consubstantiality of the Father and the Son, raises the question of the divine will once again. If the Father is the cause of the Son, and if his will intervenes in the eternal generation of the Son, how can this causality include equality between Son and Father? Such is the difficulty envisaged by Gregory of Nazianzus.

The development of trinitarian theology led the Fathers, from Eusebius of Caesaraea to Cyril of Alexandria, to seek in the Platonists the equivalent of the doctrine of the "three hypostases." Their efforts succeeded so well that a number of commentators on Plotinus, even among the moderns, carried over into philosophical works the Christian sense of "hypotheses" (existing persons, and not "substantial products" of a transcendental reality), and wrongly applied these terms to the Good, the Intellect, and the Soul, terms that have been misused in their turn by the title given to treatise V.1.10: "On the Three Hypostases That Have the Rank of Principles."

We obviously cannot reduce the encounters between Christian and Hellenistic theology to misunderstandings, nor can we conclude, as Adolf Harnack did, that the springtime of the alliance between orthodoxy and philosophy was followed not by a summer but by devastating storms. Far from making any value judgment, we would do well to recognize that the development of Christian dogma took place in a Hellenistic context, and that the questions raised by philosophy and by Greek ideas about God, man, and the world have influenced the system of Christian thought in a decisive manner.

ALAIN LE BOULLUEC
Translated by Rita Guerlac and Anne Slack

Bibliography

Texts and Translations

Justin Martyr. *An Early Christian Philosopher: Justin Martyr's Dialogue with Trypho, Chapters 1 to 9.* Ed. J. L. M. Van Winden. Leiden: Brill, 1971.

———. *The First and Second Apologies.* Trans. and ed. Leslie William Barnard. New York: Paulist Press, 1997.

———. *The Works Now Extant of S. Justin the Martyr.* Oxford and London, 1861.

Sources chrétiennes. Paris: Editions du Cerf, 1940–. Numerous works by the church fathers translated into French, with the Greek or Latin texts, introductions, and notes.

Wiles, Maurice, and Mark Santer, eds. *Documents in Early Christian Thought.* Cambridge: Cambridge University Press, 1975.

Studies

Armstrong, Arthur Hilary. *Hellenic and Christian Studies.* London: Variorum, 1990.

Aubin, Paul. *Plotin et le christianisme: Triade plotinienne et Trinité chrétienne.* Paris: Beauchesne, 1992.

Brown, Peter. *The Making of Late Antiquity.* Cambridge, Mass.: Harvard University Press, 1978.

Chadwick, Henry. *Early Christian Thought and the Classical Tradition: Studies in Justin, Clement, and Origen.* Oxford, 1966, 1984.

Dodd, Charles Harold. *The Interpretation of the Fourth Gospel.* Cambridge: Cambridge University Press, 1953, 1970.

Dorival, Gilles. "L'originalité de la patristique grecque." In *Las humanidas grecolatinas e a civilicao do universal,* Congresso internacional, Coimbra, 1988. Pp. 383–420.

Dörrie, Heinrich. *Platonica minora.* Munich: W. Fink, 1976.

Festugière, André-Jean. *L'idéal religieux des Grecs et l'Evangile.* Paris: Gabalda, 1932.

Gnilka, Christian. *Chresis: Die Methode der Kirchenvater im Umgang mit der antiken Kultur.* Vol. 2, *Kultur und Conversion.* Basel: Schwabe, 1984–.

Hadot, Pierre. *Philosophy As a Way of Life: Spiritual Exercises from Socrates to Foucault.* Trans. Michael Chase. Oxford: Blackwell, 1995.

————. *Porphpyre et Victorinus.* Paris: Etudes augustiniennes, 1968.

Ivánka, Endre von. *Plato Christianus.* Einsiedeln: Johannes Verlag, 1964.

Mansfield, Jaap. *Heresiography in Context: Hippolytus' Elenchos as a Source for Greek Philosophy.* Leiden: E. J. Brill, 1992.

Meijering, E. Peter. *God Being History.* Amsterdam: North-Holland Publishing Company, 1975.

Pépin, Jean. *Mythe et allégorie: Les origines grecques et les contestations judéo-chrétiennes.* 2nd ed. Paris: Etudes augustiniennes, 1981.

————. *De la philosophie ancienne à la théologie patristique.* London: Variorum, 1986.

————. *La tradition de l'allégorie: De Philon à Dante.* 2nd ed. Paris: Etudes augustiniennes, 1987.

Rist, John M. *Platonism and Its Christian Heritage.* London: Variorum, 1985.

Whittaker, John. *Studies in Platonism and Patristic Thought.* London: Variorum, 1984.

Williams, Rowan. *Arius: Heresy and Tradition.* London: Darton, Longman and Todd, 1987.

Related Articles

The Philosopher; Physics; Platonism; Cosmology; Hellenism and Judaism

HELLENISM AND JUDAISM

THE ENCOUNTER BETWEEN Hellenism and Judaism, a complex phenomenon that is sometimes difficult to pin down, will be discussed here from two different perspectives. The Greeks—or *some* Greeks—were able to discover a people, a culture; we may wonder what they really knew and thought about it. But these Greeks were also bearers of a body of learning, which spread (without the Jewish world being necessarily eager to receive it). We shall try to gauge the effects of this process.

It is in the Hellenistic period that contacts between Greeks and Jews are most significant, in Judaea and Egypt; thus our search will take us to Paul of Tarsus, to Philon of Alexandria, and later to Flavius Josephus. It was Christianity that recovered the work and intellectual heritage of these three Jews.

Did the Greeks know anything about the Jewish people? Were the Jews worthy of attention and interest in their eyes? We would search in vain for an unambiguous mention of any exchange with Jews in a Greek text from the archaic period. The poet Alcaeus cites the exploits of his brother Antimenidas of Lesbos, who went off to offer his services to the Chaldaean armies. Antimenidas may have been a mercenary under Nebuchadnezzar: he may have besieged Ashquelon (604 B.C.E.) and even Jerusalem (598–597). But we are already in the realm of historical fiction: Alcaeus does not mention the Jews, nor do his contemporaries. What meaning could there be for them in a small, crushed, vassal kingdom lacking even access to the sea during this period? The picturesque voyage was as yet an unknown genre.

Still, in the early 1960s, archaeologists in the neighborhood of Yavne (between Jaffa and Ashdod) uncovered the remains of a military fortress. The garrison that lived there used a great quantity of Greek pottery, exclusively from the Orient, all of it dating from the last third of the 7th century. This is enough to allow us to infer the direct presence of Asian Greeks. The architecture and masonry of the place offer no evidence of restoration; it seems logical to suppose that the pottery is contemporary with the walls. One hesitates to identify these Greeks as mercenaries in the service of the pharaoh, since no trace of Egyptian equipment has been found. Were they not rather in the service of Josiah (king of Judah from 640 to 609)? One shard found on the site apparently bore a Hebraic character. If this was the case, the Greek garrison was probably powerless to prevent the raid by the pharaoh Nekaon in 609. If the first hypothesis is correct, the garrison was swept away in 605 or 604 by Nebuchadnezzar's army. These Greeks, whichever their faction, unquestion-

ably knew of the Jews' existence (and may have been acquainted with their culture). But of the Greeks who survived, it is likely that a certain number settled in Egypt or Phoenicia and that very few returned home; they were not numerous enough to spread knowledge of the Jewish people and their culture in Greece.

Writing in the second third of the 5th century B.C.E., Herodotus discusses the dissemination of the Egyptian people and their customs in the Orient. Speaking of circumcision, he asserts in particular that "the Colchians and Egyptians and Ethiopians are the only nations that have practised circumcision from the first" (II.104). Thus the Phoenicians and the Syrians of Palestine allegedly owe this practice to these three groups, through imitation. The historical validity of such reasoning is not important here; still, we can ask what the term "Syrians of Palestine" may have meant to a Greek traveler. Circumcision is known to be a Jewish practice, but it is not limited to Jews. The Greek term for Palestinians corresponds to the term *Philistines* in the Bible, though the Bible calls them uncircumcised, like the Phoenicians. Did Herodotus confuse Jews and Philistines? Possibly, but according to our sources, the term *Philistines* was politically outdated in the 5th century. Is it a reference to circumcised Nabataean immigrants? The term *Palestine,* which is ordinarily used for the Syrian coast, comes up again in Herodotus (VII.89), when the historian indicates that "the Syrians of Palestine" (the same ones?), together with the Phoenicians, supplied ships for the Persian army. It is hard to imagine the Judaeans furnishing a battle fleet, even as a tributary obligation. Here, the term can only mean the cities of the coast, once known as Philistia. None of this is very clear. But we can hardly expect Herodotus, who had apparently never gone into Syria, to think in terms of a cultural mosaic in describing a region and peoples that he had been led—by the Persian administration, as well as by the atavistic contempt of the Egyptians (his informants) for Asiatics—to call Syria. It is highly probable that Herodotus knew nothing at all of the existence of a Jewish people.

Moreover, in the Bible Isaiah seems to indicate that this general lack of knowledge was reciprocal (66:19). There are numerous traces of active commerce—direct or indirect—between Greeks and Jews, starting in the 7th century B.C.E. and continuing more or less indefinitely thereafter; but this by no means signifies that Jews and Greeks were acquainted except in the vaguest way.

Writing in the second half of the 4th century, Aristotle refers in his *Meteorologica* to the properties that the Dead Sea owes to its high salinity. But he warns his reader that the anecdotal account is to be taken, as it were, *cum grano salis:* "If there were any truth in the stories they tell about the lake in Palestine . . ." (II.iii.359a18–19). Such a reservation tells us not only that Aristotle is not personally acquainted with the region and does not know the term *Judaea,* but also that no really reliable source has gone to see it. In

the framework of Greek ideas, this means that the author has collected (directly or indirectly) the tales of some merchant, one of a breed notoriously given to exaggeration and falsehood in the eyes of the ancient geographers and scholars. Furthermore, this informant, if he himself has seen the Dead Sea, may well have seen it from the east bank, following the route of Nabataean commerce, rather than from the Jewish oases. A Greek of that period would have no reason to associate the Dead Sea with Jews rather than with Nabataeans (this is the connection the historian Jerome of Cardia makes at the end of the 4th century). However that may be, we still have no trace of Jews in Greek literature.

It is thus surprising and interesting to come across the following anecdote. Clearchus of Solis reports that his master Aristotle told him one day of his encounter in Asia Minor with a Jew from Coelo-Syria. His exceptional people, whose capital city bore the "tortuous" (sic) name of Jerusalem, is somewhat comparable to Brahman sages from India (!). This man, in any case, "was Greek, not only in language but also in soul." It must be said unequivocally that this testimony, which dates from the beginning of the 3rd century, is inadmissible for historical reasons: according to what is known about his life, Aristotle lived at Atarneus, in Asia, between 347 and 342. Now it is very unlikely that there was a Jewish community settled in Asia Minor, in Pergamum (neighboring city of Atarneus) or elsewhere, at this time. The first Jews of the Diaspora did not appear much before the beginning of the 3rd century, and they lived more to the south, toward Sardis and Ephesus. The first attested communities in Asia Minor go back to Antiochus II (261–247), who ensured a collective migration of his Jewish subjects, since he granted them citizenship in the cities of Ionia, where they settled. Furthermore (for one might object that a given Jew could have traveled independently, coming from Judaea), the notion of a perfectly Hellenized Jew is completely anachronistic with regard to the period to which the anecdote is thought to refer. Clearchus's account is equally unacceptable on literary grounds: the passage includes numerous devices meant to alert readers to the dreamlike and prodigious nature of such an encounter (reported in a treatise on sleep), or to make them laugh at this awkward people with philosophical pretensions. It shows only that Clearchus was aware that Jews existed as a separate people, and that he had enough (or little enough) understanding of their customs to see them as a people as exotic as the Indians.

Until the end of the 4th century, then, the Jews were neither within the scope of the Greeks' acquaintance nor of concern to them. In Arnaldo Momigliano's formula, "The Greeks lived happily in their classical age without recognizing the existence of the Jews" (p. 78). The converse is also true, and even more so: Jewish isolationism must be taken into account. Unquestionably, individual adventurers must have encountered Jews at least as early as the 7th century, and Clearchus himself, who may well have been a great

traveler, could have known some in the Orient, in Ionia, or in his native Cyprus. But up to that point, such an encounter had never produced any hint of a collective preoccupation, not even an interest limited to a circle of educated men. In this respect, Clearchus marks a turning point.

Indeed, not long before, in 332, an event occurred that was fundamental in many respects, and certainly for the question at hand: the conquest of the Orient by Alexander the Great. The Greeks and Jews really discovered each other at this point. If Alexander's voyage to Jerusalem stems from legend, it is nonetheless true that Judaea came to be administered by Macedonia and that its inhabitants had to learn, if not to speak Greek, at least to recognize the existence of the language and to acknowledge a new institutional reality. The Greeks, for their part, were to discover this small vassal nation (among many others), and they were to learn of the Jews' unshakable attachment to strange customs. But they also encountered a prodigiously rich culture and an unexpected field of knowledge that was to spread throughout the Orient.

At this point in our study, it is time to pause. For as the contacts between Hellenism and Judaism developed under quite particular geographical conditions (in Palestine and Egypt principally; probably in Mesopotamia as well, but these contacts are more difficult to estimate) and in specific chronological circumstances (after the Macedonian victory over the whole of Greece), Hellenism now looked quite different from the way it had appeared half a century earlier. Hellenism as a vital force was no longer a phenomenon bound up with Greece itself. The conquerors did not come from all of Greece: they were for the most part Macedonians. The men who had won control of the known world were the grandsons of those whom the rest of the Greeks regarded as semibarbarians. Now, in the course of a few short years, they burst open the geographical and mental confines of Hellenism to an extraordinary extent. They displaced the core of its activity, principally toward Lagid Egypt and its new city-state, Alexandria (the great intellectual center of the epoch), and toward the Seleucid Orient to a lesser degree. Palestine was at the heart of this "new world." But they did not bring Hellenism to the Orient as a museum piece, unalterable and frozen in its classical grandeur. The Hellenism they offered had been renewed, profoundly modified, often by the conscious and voluntary action of the king. The model of the city-state, which was never the only viable political form in Greece but which constituted the norm for most Greeks, with its system of assemblies in which the government—whether democratic or oligarchic—took shape through the ongoing practice of verbal exchanges, was replaced by the hegemonic model of monarchy, incontestable but familiar in the Orient. Absolute, the embodiment of power, monarchy soon extended its reach over vast territories, blending countless peoples in a common subjection. United in a shared dependence on the same sovereign, these peoples and lands came to be ruled by written laws, in a process that fostered the juridical unity of the great kingdoms that emerged as Alexan-

der's successors divided up the realm. Administration and war (which had remained essentially the duty of citizens, thus of amateurs) were already becoming professionalized. Cults and supplicants' pleas came to be addressed to the person of a monarch, who looked more and more like a god, greatly scandalizing most Jews, whose intransigent monotheism was viewed as an oddity, and gaining ground on the old civic or regional cults.

In the intellectual domain, too, things changed: intensifying a development initiated by the Sophists, the educated man, the scholar, also became a professional and at the same time a specialist. Science, pure or applied, was most often dissociated from philosophy. Unlike Plato, Euclid and Archimedes did not mix philosophy, and still less political philosophy, with their work as mathematicians. Astronomy, geography, and agronomy, as well as philology, gave rise to technical treatises written by specialists. To grasp the originality of the (often conflicted) relations between Hellenism and Judaism, it is important to understand that this new culture, which we call Hellenism, is not "a Greek surface plastered onto a non-Greek base" (even though, elsewhere, mechanisms for segregating Greeks from indigenous peoples were also present). This new culture was the original fruit of an epoch, of circumstances, of the actions of some great men, but especially of the encounter—not uniformly successful or far-reaching, but always complex—between a Greek model in full mutation and oriental milieus capable of changing in the same direction: in Jerusalem itself, in the 2nd century B.C.E., an aristocratic minority (?), although it originated in the priesthood, sought to transform the traditional theocratic Jewish state into a Greek city-state (a polis).

The primordial vehicle for learning is language, and it was the local populations who had to learn Greek, not the other way around. This relation was to determine the direction of cultural transmission. Until the Christian mission got under way in the course of the 1st century C.E., it was essentially Greek culture that spread throughout the Oriental world—which happened to be Jewish. There was very little movement in the opposite direction; what there was corresponded to an infatuation with the exotic. The Greeks were not interested in the Jews until fairly late, and even then their audience was Roman (Posidonius and Strabo, for example).

No more than it had in Egypt did Greek ever become the language of exchange common to all levels of the Jewish population. In any case, the Greeks had no tradition of "cultural missionaries." Ordinary people used Aramaic. But the religious milieus, though often hostile to the culture of the new masters, did not necessarily remain apart from the Greeks. The new language spread, by and large, through aristocratic urban environments: yesterday's masters, if they wanted to conserve any part of their privileged status, had to be in a position to approach the masters of the day and earn at least some respect. Little by little, a whole class of administrators and educated men, including the priestly circles, absorbed the Greek language; they became fully

bilingual, even trilingual, starting in the 2nd century B.C.E. at least, and in some cases as early as the end of the 3rd century.

In fact, while the author of Ecclesiastes (or Quoheleth) still wrote in Hebrew during the 3rd century, he was nourished on Greek culture. Jesus ben Sirach, the cultivated scribe of Jerusalem, wrote—also in Hebrew—at the beginning of the 2nd century; but (if we are to believe the preface attached to his work) his grandson translated him into Greek at the end of the 130s. Shortly afterward (around 124), an abridger rewrote the second book of Maccabees, by Jason of Cyrene (a Jew with a Hellenized name), directly in Greek. This flowering implies that at least a core of educated men had given their children a Greek education of high quality, sometimes motivated by the stamp of nobility and purity conferred by its Atticizing tint. "Supplementary education" at first, it often became the only education, to the point that Philon of Alexandria, on the threshold of the Christian era, is thought not to have known Hebrew. Without the existence of such a Hellenized class, we could not understand an enterprise like the Septuagint Bible, the translation into Greek of the Hebrew text of the Pentateuch, perhaps starting in the second quarter of the 3rd century, then later the other books, by scholars working in Egypt and more precisely in Alexandria. If the sacred text was translated, counter to the entire Near Eastern tradition, it was surely because a not inconsiderable segment of Jewish society, principally in the Diaspora, felt the need for a Greek text, for want of being able to read the Hebrew one (the curiosity of learned Greeks and the mistrust of the Lagid power with regard to a text capable of governing a community may have played a supporting role). Now translation itself, by obliging its authors to approach it from philological and religious standpoints simultaneously, fixed the text, increased its importance at the expense of the living practice, and made it known in this new form; hence Elias Bickermann's remark that Judaism became the religion of the Book when the Bible was translated into Greek.

The existence of a strong Jewish Diaspora, especially in Alexandria, a city-state created by the Greeks, is a primordial factor in the diffusion of Greek thought and knowledge in a Jewish milieu and in Judaea. We know that in the Hellenistic period Alexandria became the principal center from which Hellenism radiated, and we know of its famed Library, which was thought to have brought together all literature written in Greek or translated into Greek. The Hellenistic epoch represents the high point of the empirical and technical sciences: it is scarcely possible to imagine that this library and the centers of intellectual activity that comprised the glory of the Egyptian city-state failed to have repercussions, in Judaea and elsewhere. Moreover, Judaea does not seem to have been exempt from the economic expansion that stemmed from the logical and technical enrichment characterizing this period. The problem lies in the difficulty of measuring these repercussions. Varro lists some fifty authors of technical treatises, a specifically Greek genre; a treatise on agronomy

by a certain Bolos of Mendes, for example, enjoyed great renown throughout antiquity and even later; there were also treatises on gardening, farming, and so on. Yet it seems quite impossible to find a trace of any of these where Judaea is concerned. We can only note that Apollonius, minister of finances under Ptolemy II, who was passionately interested in agricultural and arborial experimentation, owned a vineyard in Galilee. It would be indeed astonishing if this had not had some impact on the growing techniques of the local peasantry, especially in this region scorned by pious Judaeans for its lack of attachment to Jewish formalism and traditions. But we know virtually nothing about this. The same could be said about botanical treatises, those dealing with zoology, medicine, architecture, and especially treatises on manufacturing techniques. At most, we could mention the probable introduction by the Greeks of artificial irrigation in the 3rd or 2nd century B.C.E., attested in Ecclesiastes (2:6), in Ecclesiasticus (24.30–32), and in the use in the Talmudic language of the word *ntly*, Greek *antlia* (irrigation wheel); or, in the text of the Greek Bible of the Septuagint, the distinctions made among the various stages of fetal development, unknown in the Hebraic lexicon.

In contrast, it is easier to follow the introduction by the Greeks of technologies related to the exercise of power: in particular to warfare, administration, and tax collection. The overwhelming, crushing, universal victory of the Greek armies offers the best proof of the excellence of their technologies. The Hellenized aristocracy of Jerusalem not only had a gymnasium built in order to conform to a cultural model, it also recognized the superiority conferred by the premilitary or paramilitary training acquired there. Syria bristled with fortresses constructed in conformity with Hellenistic techniques, built through the good offices or on the order of the Hellenistic powers, first Lagid, then Seleucid. But although neither Polybius nor the Books of the Maccabees describe for us the tactics used by the Jewish armies in the Hellenistic period, most of the Jewish mercenaries who enlisted in the Hellenistic armies, and who came to constitute a not inconsiderable vehicle for Greek values and knowledge, also offered the Maccabees, when the time came, an abundance of skills that were decisive for the Maccabees' ability to hold the Greek armies in check (even if their revolt also allowed them to develop guerrilla techniques specifically adapted to the Jewish situation).

In the interim before these periods of crisis, thanks to tax farming (a typically Greek system), the rise of the Tobiades family proves that from the Lagid period (the 3rd century) on the Jewish aristocracy had integrated Hellenistic techniques into its tax collecting and administrative practices. In the absence of a manual of ancient fiscal practices, it is difficult to evaluate the innovations with any precision. But it is certain that the Hellenistic monarchies were responsible for constructing a bureaucratic system—a ponderous one, certainly, but also, as it developed through elaboration, one capable of real efficiency. We can judge the value of these innovations by observing the pro-

gressive replacement of tribute in natural goods by tax revenue in cash, and also, probably, by the relative satisfaction of the Jews—at least the urban Jews—with a system that was sufficiently rational to function without major difficulty until the Romans arrived. Thus, according to Artapanos, a 2nd-century Judaeo-Egyptian author, the biblical Joseph and Moses are known as the "first financial ministers" of Judaea: this is a way of legitimizing the new fiscal techniques both by biblical precedent and by the antiquity that such a precedent confers on them.

The discretion of our sources about the contributions of Greek technical knowledge may, at least for the Jewish sources, have to do with an intellectual tradition. For we clearly cannot refer to the encounter between Hellenism and Judaism without mentioning the source par excellence of their collective survival: their historical, moral, and religious productions.

The problem posed by the conjunction of these two cultures is first of all epistemological. Greek knowledge is divided into several domains that, in the period that concerns us, are quite distinct. Traditional myths provide the key to certain fundamental revealed bodies of knowledge, for example, agricultural myths such as that of Eleusis, or the myth of Prometheus; other areas of knowledge and skill have an intermediary status that one might call "patronage": the Muses inspire the poet—without them, there would be no poetry—but they do not reveal or "inspirit" texts as the Holy Spirit does for Pope Gregory; finally, even if they are theoretically under the patronage of the Muses, history, geography, astronomy, politics, the various intellectual *technai*, and even philosophical speculation are bodies of knowledge produced or acquired by the human spirit: they lend themselves more and more to a dual movement of theorization and empirical verification (thus Hipparchus will do his best to measure the dimensions and the distances of the Moon and Sun to verify the heliocentric system posited theoretically by Aristarchus of Samos). Eratosthenes is the teacher of a pharaoh who subsidized the scholarly and literary life; Archimedes frequented the palace of the king of Syracuse; Hellenistic scholars have much more to do with the circle of temporal power than with the realm of the sacred. In contrast, "Jewish knowledge" stems from God and from revelation—all the more so because the scribes and the priestly hierarchy are historically its only vehicles in Judaea, and we do not see in the Diaspora any writer who could be called secular (not even—especially not—Flavius Josephus).

If these two cultures had anything in common intellectually, it is that they each constructed a long historiographical tradition, one that was particularly lively among the Greeks of the Hellenistic period (even though in this matter Alexandria probably did not play a major role) and very ancient among the Jews, since its first elements may go back to the 11th century B.C.E. However limited literary diffusion in antiquity may have been, both cultures also distinguished themselves from the annalistic Egyptian and Mesopotamian tradi-

tions, in that they did not limit the use of texts to the powerful monarchies and their clergy.

Between the two, not much had to change for the Books of the Maccabees and then, at the end of the 1st century C.E., Flavius Josephus to appear as examples of a historiography that could be called Judaeo-Hellenistic. Even though it retained phraseology of a prophetic type (the epiphany of a god is not foreign to Greek historical literature), from that point on the Jewish chronicle, like that of the Greek historian, produced justificative texts, diplomatic in particular (1 Maccabees 10:25ff). The traditional practice of dialogue or discourse (often brief, except for Isaiah 36:4–10) leads quite naturally to its rewriting according to the canons of Greek rhetoric.

Willingly or not, Jewish authors had to come to terms with the idea that even the divine manifests itself in history, through institutions that had developed more or less gradually and that were to take on a given secular form at a given time; thus the law of Moses was a codification of principles, an ancient one to be sure, and yet Abraham and the generations that followed him before Moses had had to act without the support of such a code. This question of historical evolution is an "import." The Talmudic treatise *Pirke Abot* is meant to show the triumph of rejection, of rigidity: "Moses received the Torah from Sinai and handed it on to Joshua . . . and Hillel and Shammai took over from them" (in Bickermann, p. 299). But such a citation also shows, on the contrary, the religious and epistemological malaise that arose in the Hellenistic period from contact with Greek historical thought.

This led, then, to the integration of the Bible with the renewed historical genre; the process was completed by the end of the 3rd century by a certain Demetrius (a Samaritan?), then by Flavius Josephus. Paradoxically, this literary convergence adapted itself to a fundamental divergence in the philosophy of history that each of the two cultures professed. To differing degrees, depending on the authors, the Greeks attributed to history a double driving force: human action on the one hand, either destiny or fortune *(tyche)* on the other (this distinction is particularly characteristic of Polybius, but it is a banality in Greek thought). If such a conception is discernible in the high Hellenized sacerdotal aristocracy (which wagered on a solely political and later military but purely *human* dimension when, in the 2nd century, it attempted to integrate the Jewish world with the Greek), the Jewish tradition as a whole recognized as the driving force of history nothing but God and the piety of the human actor. Jesus ben Sirach, in the 2nd century, is no exception. Whereas in Hellenistic historiography the divine sign, consulted by soothsayers, is merely indicative, and moreover scantily reported by the authors, in the Jewish world history is driven by the conformity of human action to the teaching of the prophets and the covenant concluded by God with man; in his preamble to *Jewish Antiquities*, Josephus still holds this view. We can speak, then, of a consciously accepted competition between two visions of the world.

Itinerant "sages" in the Greek mode began to appear, devoting themselves to spreading their moral and religious views (on this point, Jesus is their heir). Perhaps this is the way the mysterious title Quoheleth, the Hebrew title of Ecclesiastes, should be translated: he who stirs up a crowd (of listeners). Like their Greek counterparts, such sages dispensed their wisdom in public, in a highly logical discourse that did not share in what was characterized as biblical discourse up to that point. Whether their moral philosophy was marked by Greek influences or nourished by more or less universal principles remains a controversial question. Nevertheless, the celebrated "All is vanity" has been compared with an identical apothegm of Minumus of Syracuse (4th century); his morality of "Carpe diem" and his skepticism about the morality of retribution have brought to mind Euripides, Archilochus, and Theognis. Even his major opponent, Jesus ben Sirach, professed a morality in conformity with Aristotle's ethics and cited the fable of the two routes that, through Prodicos of Ceos and Xenophon, supposedly came from Pythagorean circles. The historical analysis of this evolution is complicated. On the one hand, the tradition of Jewish exclusivity probably slowed it down; on the other, it was considerably facilitated, first, by the almost monotheist option of Platonic philosophy (which in *Timaeus,* for example, calls to mind the creation of the cosmos by a single, demiurgic god), then by the convergent evolution of oriental thinking and Greek philosophies. These latter could be compared in some respects with the "sects" (the different currents of Judaism); Stoicism was the most influential, if only through the idea of a cosmos organized by a rational power that merges with divinity. The idea of a hidden, incomprehensible God, closely related to an impersonal force like Destiny, could then circulate at the same time as dualist notions, such as the allegories of time and fortune used by Quoheleth, or divine personifications of Wisdom and Science, auxiliary hypostases of God. The convergence of the reflections was given vigorous expression by a gnostic of the 2nd century C.E., Numenius of Apamaea: "Who is Plato, if not Moses speaking Greek?" The god of the Greek philosopher blended, for some, with the God of the Jews.

And in fact Philon was very familiar with Plato's work (*Timaeus,* in particular) and with the Presocratics (Heraclitus, for example); his Moses was every bit a match for the Greek physicists, those scholars who studied nature and its laws. Others openly professed a philosophical ecclecticism in which the Stoa often remained the dominant component: thus Aristobulus defined wisdom as "the knowledge of things human and divine" (ca. 160 B.C.E.). It is Aristobolus who inaugurated the reading of the biblical text according to the allegorical method (taken up again by Philon). They practiced *interpretatio Graeca:* Yahweh was a local form of a great universal divinity worshipped elsewhere under the names of Pan (the All) or Dionysus. Enoch was nothing but an avatar of Atlas, also the inventor of astrology; Kronos crystalized the figures of Noah and Nimrod, the founder of Babylon and the builder of its

tower. These associations may conceivably point to the influence of Euhemerism, for which the figure of the gods perpetuates the transfigured memory of particularly eminent and beneficent men. Presenting the patriarchs as teachers of humanity, as Triptolemus did, is a clear sign of Hellenization.

But we must not be misled: this intellectual attitude, mostly limited to certain intellectual circles, carried with it new ways of thinking, but they always served to glorify Judaism as the true philosophy. Greek philosophy was only a way of rereading the testamentary revelation: the Jews remained the only ones who truly "know God." Pythagoras, Socrates, and Plato were sometimes portrayed as Moses' disciples in monotheism; the Jewish religion had to retain its primacy.

The Greek influence was nevertheless sufficiently powerful that, from this period on, the figure of the Hellenistic king strongly influenced that of the Messiah to come. The Greeks, for their part, remained full of disdain for what they saw as one more oriental superstition, about which they knew essentially nothing (only the Romans would violate the *soreg,* the sacred enclosure that marked off the Square of the Gentiles at the entrance to the Temple).

In every realm, it is clear that evaluating the Greeks' knowledge of Judaism, like assessing the diffusion and reception of the branches of learning the Greeks conveyed, remains a delicate task. As a model, Hellenism was ignored by the great majority and adopted by a numerically weak but socially powerful minority, and even among those who approached it, a certain number did so to infiltrate the enemy. The practical disciplines presumably spread more readily. Be that as it may, after the destruction of the Temple in 70 C.E., the principal authorities of the pharaonic faction rebuilt a crushed Judaism while abandoning the Neoplatonist heritage, and on the basis of an ahistorical line of thinking. The divorce was to be more or less gradual, and it allowed etymologically Greek terms to become established in the Talmudic language. But it was not through Judaism that Greek culture would live outside of Greece: it was through Christianity, by way of Rome and the labyrinth of gnostic sects, until the Arabs took it to Spain, where Jewish intermediaries translated it in turn for Roman Europe.

SERGE BARDET
Translated by Rita Guerlac and Anne Slack

Bibliography

Texts and Translations

Aristotle. *Meteorologica.* Trans. H. D. P. Lee. Loeb Classical Library.
Herodotus. *Histories.* Trans. A. D. Godfrey. Loeb Classical Library.

Studies

Bickermann, Elias Joseph. *The Jews in the Greek Age*. Cambridge, Mass.: Harvard University Press, 1988.

Genot-Bismuth, Jacqueline. *Le Scénario de Damas: Jérusalem hellénisée et les origines de l'essénisme*. Paris: F. X. de Guibert, 1992.

Hengel, Martin. *Judaism and Hellenism: Studies in Their Encounter in Palestine during the Early Hellenistic Period*. Trans. John Bowden. 2 vols. Philadelphia: Fortress Press, 1974.

Isaac, Jules. *Genese de l'antisémitisme*. Paris: Calmann-Lévy, 1956.

Michaud, Robert. *Qohélet et l'hellénisme*. Paris: Le Cerf, 1987.

Momigliano, Arnaldo. *Alien Wisdom: The Limits of Hellenization*. Cambridge: Cambridge University Press, 1976.

Rostovtzeff, Michel. *The Social and Economic History of the Hellenistic World*. 3 vols. Oxford: Clarendon Press, 1953.

Will, Edouard, and Claude Orrieux. *Ioudaismos-Hellenismos: Essai sur le Judaïsme judéen à l'époque hellénistique*. Nancy: Presses Universitaires de Nancy, 1986.

Related Articles

History; Hellenism and Christianity; Technology

THE MILESIANS

THREE CITIZENS OF MILETUS in the 6th century B.C.E.—Thales, Anaximander, and Anaximenes—are conveniently grouped together under the term *Milesians*. They were apparently approximate contemporaries, as well as sharers (and rivals) in a new intellectual enterprise: the science of nature.

This brief description rests principally on the interpretation due to Aristotle. The writings of the Milesians themselves have not survived (apart from one or two possibly authentic quotations). The scanty reports by later ancient authors derive almost entirely from Aristotle or from the tradition of doxography (writing about philosophers' doctrines) established by Aristotle's pupil Theophrastus. The first step toward understanding the Milesians therefore consists in understanding Aristotle's own conception of physical science, within which his interpretation of the Milesians is framed. The next is understanding the method of dialectical examination of previous opinions that Aristotle applied to help establish and clarify the principles of his own physics.

Once Aristotle's interpretation of the Milesians is understood, it must next be subjected to critical examination. Here there is other evidence to be taken into account—indirect evidence, it is true, but not negligible. The Milesians were at the fountainhead of the study of "natural science," which was continued into the 5th and 4th centuries by others (both cosmologists and medical theorists), and which was criticized by philosophers (notably Heraclitus, Parmenides, Plato, and Aristotle) who reflected on its underlying assumptions. The historians Herodotus and Thucydides show traces of its influence. Even in the tragedies of Euripides and the comedies of Aristophanes, some echoes of the scientific enterprise can be heard. Enough is known to allow us to grasp, at least in outline, the aims and methods of natural science, as it was understood and practiced in the 200 years *after* the Milesians. With due caution, it is legitimate to argue backward from this later evidence to the Milesians themselves.

The path toward an understanding of the Milesians is therefore, unavoidably, a tortuous one. It is also beset by the danger of unconscious anachronism. Here as elsewhere, it is only too easy to import into the study of ancient Greece mistaken assumptions derived from our own era. In particular, it is necessary to examine with caution both the similarities and the dissimilarities between Milesian science and modern science. By calling the enterprise of the Milesians physical science, we do not imply that they shared all the aims, methods, and programmatic assumptions of modern physics. Rather, it is

meant that their activities are best understood, when allowances are made for differences in knowledge and conceptual tradition, as something closely akin in some essential respects to the modern natural sciences.

Aristotle recognized the Milesians as his first true predecessors in natural science. For him, Thales, the pioneer of this kind of investigation, marks the boundary before which there were only theologians and writers of stories. He recognizes in the Milesians a new respect for *system*. Aristotle was well aware that Hesiod, and other earlier cosmogonical authors, had general ideas governing their constructions. But they used them "in a storylike way" *(muthikōs)*: that is, their aims, guiding concepts, and substantive theses were not stated clearly and explicitly, and were not used systematically. By contrast, Aristotle implies, the Milesians professedly inquired into *phusis*, the nature of individual things and of things collectively. They aimed at a system of knowledge that would cover that realm completely and systematically.

There is no reason to doubt the correctness of Aristotle's account thus far; no evidence exists that would support an attempt to undermine it, and there is a good deal to confirm it. Much more difficult to evaluate is Aristotle's report on the substance of the Milesian theories. This hinges on the Aristotelian concept of "cause" *(aition* or *aitia)*, of which the interpretation is perennially controversial. It is at least clear that the four types of cause serve to identify the types of relationship within the structure of physical processes and the types of understanding of such processes by the human intellect. The close tie between structure and understanding is, as will be suggested later, already implicit in the Milesian concept of *phusis*.

In *Metaphysics* I Aristotle seeks to show historically that physics has always consisted in the search for these causes. But he himself is forced to admit that the evidence is not straightforwardly in favor of his reading. He therefore sees the Milesians and their successors as beginners; they were like children who cannot pronounce their words distinctly, or amateur boxers who sometimes land good punches by chance. They do not make clear and conscious use of any of the four causes, but they do in a way use all four.

With these qualifications, Aristotle identifies the Milesians as using the "material cause," and that type of cause alone. He gives examples: Thales said that everything was made of water; Anaximenes, of air. Some skepticism is required here. Like all philosophers, Aristotle is constantly pressed in the direction of anachronism when he interprets earlier thinking. Only a full examination of all the other evidence for Presocratic science can, in the end, tell us how far Aristotle is correct. But it is very important to note that even if Aristotle's testimony is accepted in full, it does not have the implications that have often been supposed. In particular, it does not imply that the Milesians were materialists, or that they employed anything like any modern concept of *matter*. It does not imply that they excluded from consideration other kinds of explanation that correspond to Aristotle's other causes. It implies

only, in that respect, that Aristotle could not find in their writings an *explicit* recognition of such "causes." In *Metaphysics* I, Aristotle is in fact judging his predecessors, not like a physicist judging earlier physicists but like a philosophy professor judging his own students. For the purposes of the Aristotelian dialectic, all interlocutors are considered to be contemporary, and what is not said clearly and explicitly does not count as having been said at all.

Aristotle's testimony in *Metaphysics* I turns out, therefore, to be much less certain and positive than it may appear. Fortunately, Aristotle's own evidence in other places may be combined with the indirect evidence already mentioned to produce a reasonably consistent picture of Presocratic science in general and (if some backward inferences are permitted) of the Milesians in particular.

The Milesians took, as the object of their thinking, "all things" *(ta panta)* or "the universe" *(to pan, to holon)*. This in itself was, it seems, a novelty. Earlier cosmologies (those of the ancient Near East and Hesiod's *Theogony*) do aim at some kind of completeness in their coverage; they give accounts of the origins and functioning of the whole of the presently observable world order. But they do not seem to raise explicitly the question of whether that order is "everything there is"; correspondingly, the spatial and temporal boundaries of the world order, and whatever may lie beyond, are left ill-defined or wholly unspecified.

The Milesians' search for an account of "everything"—that is, of whatever there may be—led them to push back the boundaries of thought. The conscious intent to consider everything leads immediately to the question of whether the limits, in space and in time, of human observation, are also the limits of the universe. One of the most significant facts about the Milesians (attested by Aristotle) is that they asked this question, and answered it by postulating the spatial and temporal infinity of the universe. For, as Aristotle observes, given any limited space or stretch of time, one can always conceive of a space or a time stretch outside of it and containing it; and why should one stop anywhere in particular?

It might seem hopeless, though, to aspire to knowledge of anything about the universe generally, particularly if it is infinite in space and time. What guarantee could there be that this vast totality is knowable or intelligible as a whole to human minds? Such epistemological doubts were expressed explicitly as early as Xenophanes, in the late 6th century B.C.E. It is not certain how the Milesians met them, but what must be true is that they held their theorizing to be probable and in some sense an advance toward the truth: it was not meant as an idle game.

Necessarily, then, they assumed not only that the universe was a possible object of study but also that it was, at least in principle and in outline, knowable and intelligible *as a whole*. This assumption is implicit in the concept of

natural science that Aristotle attributes to them. It is another powerful assumption, and a revolutionary step in contrast to what had preceded. Earlier cosmologists, like Hesiod, normally specified a unified *origin* for the observable world order, but no kind of unity beyond that.

The Milesian enterprise was constituted by "the rules of the game." By this is meant both the rules governing the construction of theories and the corresponding rules of argument by which those theories were criticized and justified. Once again, the scanty earlier evidence has to be supplemented from the practice of the late 5th and the 4th century, so that there is always the danger of reading too much back into the Milesians.

The foundation of each Milesian theory was the single "fundamental entity" (what Aristotle wished to see as the "material cause"), the entity of which, ultimately, the universe consisted, and in terms of which it was to be understood. It was also implicit that this fundamental entity was of necessity essentially *uniform*, in the large scale and the long term.

Closely linked to this functional unity of the theory was its explanatory economy and power. Everything had to be explained, and explained easily, in terms of the fundamental entity and its essential properties.

But how was such explanatory power to be achieved? The aim was to represent many diverse phenomena as variations on one underlying theme, and many complex entities as the result of intelligible complications of a single one. The theory's merit was to be judged by how well it functioned explanatorily as a whole. The systematic effort to achieve explanatory economy and power by these means is evident in the Milesians, as in their successors.

The demand contained in the "principle of sufficient reason"—namely, that there should be no unexplained asymmetries or ad hoc features—was just one particular facet of the demand for explanatory efficiency. It finds extensive application in a maximally uniform universe, and it was connected to the demand for "equality" and "justice" in nature. These may have been partly intended as analogies with human political systems. They can also be understood as recognitions of the importance of symmetry and efficiency of explanation. Here symmetry is meant in its widest mathematical sense (including not only reflection symmetry but also radial symmetry and uniformity in space and time generally).

The argumentative form of the principle of sufficient reason is the question, Why this particular thing/time/place rather than any other? The most striking early application is Anaximander's explanation of why the Earth rests in the middle of the cosmos: it stays at rest because the symmetry of its position within the cosmos gives it no reason to move one way rather than another (Aristotle, *Cael.* 2.13.295b11–16). But the essential overall uniformity of the Milesians' whole universe, in both its spatial and its temporal extensions, is even more important structurally.

According to the interpretation followed here, the Milesians postulated a universe not only infinite (as already mentioned) but also filled at any time with an infinite number of "worlds" *(kosmoi)*. The word *kosmos* here (although the usage is not directly attested for the Milesians) signifies an ordering of the world (of Earth, atmosphere, celestial bodies and outer heavens) like that which is observable by humans on Earth. If the universe is infinite, it is obviously contrary to the principle of sufficient reason to assume that the particular *kosmos* that happens to contain us is in a privileged position. Therefore there must be infinitely many *kosmoi,* scattered approximately uniformly throughout the infinite extent.

These formal requirements are only one aspect of the constraints on Milesian theorizing. The other aspect, the appeal to experience, is represented by the use of analogies and by the concept of nature *(phusis)*. For in the end it was "ordinary experience" that the theories (however abstract and intellectually elegant their construction) had to look to, to command understanding and assent.

Here, one must always recognize the inherent indeterminacy of the notion of ordinary experience. It is doubtful whether "our" notion of ordinary experience corresponds at all closely or unambiguously to that of Ionians in the 6th century B.C.E. A naive appeal to common sense as a source or touchstone of Milesian theories is unilluminating. It must be true, of course, that Milesian theorists felt themselves constrained by what they took to be "the facts." But they will have found, as scientists always do, that what the facts are, and how they should be appealed to, is already an ambiguous and contestable matter. Even the most basic aspects of everyday life, and the results of the most careful experiments, are always open to reinterpretation.

The Milesians used analogies from ordinary experience. But their intentions are not self-explanatory, and are not reliably reported. We can imagine that analogies might be used in justifying and expounding the theoretical setup and the account of the total system, or in giving accounts of particular phenomena. In either case, the analogy might be a substantive part of the *justification* for the theory, or it might be a *heuristic,* theory-building, explanation-suggesting device; or it might be no more than an *expository* device, a way of supplementing the lack of technical terminology. Mixed and intermediate cases are also, obviously, possible.

It is reasonable to assume that, in theorizing about the universe as a whole, overall analogies were used heuristically, and as argumentative supports. In any case, what the Milesians aimed at was certainly not an *explanation* meeting modern scientific (or even Aristotelian) standards of explanation, but an intelligible and plausible outline that fitted into the chosen overall framework. The three types of Greek cosmic "model" apparently used by the Milesians—the living organism, the artifact, the political entity—all have obvious appeal to a cosmologist. Living organisms, artifacts, and political

structures are complex things but as a rule fairly predictable, and with a distinct overall individuality and unity.

To complete the understanding of Milesian theorizing, what is needed is the concept of nature *(phusis)*. The Ionian enterprise was, in the 5th and 4th centuries, often referred to as speaking (or writing or inquiring) about the *phusis* of everything, of the universe. So it is no far-fetched hypothesis that the concept of *phusis* was central.

The nontechnical early usage of the word *phusis* makes it correspond systematically to the uses of the verb *be (einai)*. The *phusis* of anything is what supplies the answer to the question "What is it?"—in any sense of "is." The concept of *phusis*, for the Milesians, involved a compound of empirical content and theoretical interpretation. The *phusis* of any (type of) thing comprised all those properties that were observed in nature to be its invariable properties. These were then theoretically "baptized," i.e., they were specified, within the theory, as being (all of) its essential properties.

This notion of *phusis*, though it was a constraint, did not determine by itself the specific form that the theories took. It did not determine the number and the identity of the fundamental entities, nor the general nature of their interaction within the (usually infinite) universe. Yet if explanations were required to be given in terms of *phusis*, that demand already severely limited the possibilities for ultimate entities. They had to be either (1) directly observable things, (2) "enriched" entities combined out of observables, or (3) entities formed by "impoverishment" of observables. The Milesians' ultimate entities, water, the infinite, and air, are examples of case 2: combinations from observables. Thus, Thales' water and Anaximander's air were not just ordinary water and air, but water and air enriched by the properties of life and intelligence. Anaximander's infinite was not just "something infinite" but something infinite that was also living and intelligent.

In this way the notion of *phusis* gives Milesian theorizing its empirical anchorage. The essential properties of the fundamental entities were understood to be those that are known to belong to the *phusis* of the entity in question. At the same time, the concept of *phusis* grounded a notion of natural *necessity*, for the "nature" of a thing was always understood as a constraint upon it.

Naturally, this notion of *phusis* was never unproblematic. It remained, of necessity, a concept of debatable application. It was originally intended to indicate the aspects of the external world that we seem to be able to grasp immediately as objectively regular in their behavior. But it is always debatable what should count as "external" or as "regular." Are colors, for example, or rainbows, part of the external world? Is the stability of the earth something "regular"? The notion of *phusis* was bound to focus debate on the questions (scientific and philosophical) of the nature and reliability of sense perception. These questions become, in fact, steadily more prominent after the Milesians.

Like modern science, the Presocratic enterprise tended to transform the understanding and delimitation of its own empirical basis, and to generate philosophical questions in the process.

The concept of *phusis* was also the structural tie that held together and balanced the demands of formal theorizing and those of empiricism. There was, as there always is, a natural *internal* tension between the "top-down" and the "bottom-up" approaches, between the exhilarating generalities and the awkward particular facts. It is possible, for example, even with the wretchedly incomplete evidence we have, to trace the Milesians' efforts to reconcile their grand theoretical vision of the unity of the universe with the apparently irreducible multiplicity of everyday experience. In so doing, they invoked the *phusis* of everyday things—water and air, animals, human societies—and made it carry a heavy theoretical load.

There is no reason in principle why Milesian cosmology should not have operated with a notion of god or the divine, provided of course that that notion satisfied the rules of the game set out above. In particular, if the divine was to be fundamental in the explanatory setup, it had to be both genuinely unified and well defined, and its *phusis* had to contain essential properties having a clear connection with ordinary experience. Also, to be functionally efficient, it would have to be in principle wholly intelligible to human minds. Therefore it had to be rather unlike any traditional Greek conception of a god or of the gods collectively.

In fact, a "scientific theology," in which the divine formed part of the natural world, was seen, at least from the late 5th century on, as characteristic of the Milesians and their successors in natural philosophy. Later commentators, from Plato and Aristotle onward, found the scientific theology of the Milesians difficult to understand. In modern times it has often been treated with skepticism or discussed in anachronistic terms.

The concept of nature *(phusis)* and the rules of the game, as explained above, can provide insight into this theology without the danger of anachronism. Yet it must be admitted that the evidential basis for this reconstruction consists almost entirely of the reports of Aristotle, with some help from Plato and other incidental indications. (The post-Aristotelian doxographic reports about the Milesians' theology are probably worthless.)

The essence of Milesian "natural theology" is that the basic item (or one of the basic items) in the explanatory setup is taken to have, among its basic properties, those of being alive, intelligent, purposeful, and able to act with infinite power on the contents of the universe, including itself. It seems further to have been taken to be omniscient and (within the limits imposed by the theory itself) omnipotent. Hence this, the divine and its purposes, is the ultimate explanation of the large-scale spatial and temporal structure of the universe, insofar as that, too, is not dictated by the explanatory setup itself. There is therefore a form of teleology inherent in this kind of theory.

The explanatory economy of this type of theory is fairly obvious. It enabled the Milesians to give a kind of explanation for certain centrally important phenomena:

1. The existence in our cosmos of living, intelligent, and purposive beings. To explain this, it is easier to begin with something living and intelligent, from which the other beings are derived.
2. The existence of change and movement generally. The divine was, as a living thing, naturally a source of movement.
3. The existence of order and apparent purposefulness in the cosmos. This was derived from the purposeful planning of the divine.

(The assertion of an *overall* teleology of this kind must be sharply distinguished from the assertion of a divine providence directly involved in the planning of *particular* features of the world.)

Hence this concept of the divine unites everything that is needed to complete the explanatory task. It may have seemed to the Milesians that it promised the only kind of unity reasonably to be hoped for in the universe. The unity of living beings, and the unity of minds, are impressive kinds of unity. Animals unite dissimilar components, and involve change and yet stability through change. So too with the conscious mind, which also unites dissimilars and involves change and stability, and therefore may seem more promising as a model to explain the universe than mere material unity. This is particularly so if the lawlike behavior of the contents of the universe is taken not only as part of the explanation but also as one of the things to be explained. Thus the divine, with its intelligence and justice, is meant as a substantive and functional part of the whole theoretical construction. (This does not imply that Milesian theorizing was substantially continuous with any earlier theology. Nor does it imply that Milesian theorizing was a priori, or *dictated* by theological or teleological considerations.)

Such a theology obviously has its difficulties. It may be asked, in particular, how one is supposed to understand the idea of, say, "intelligent water" or "purposive air." But to put the question thus is to look at matters the wrong way round, from the point of view of a theory based on *phusis*. The claim is that the *phusis* of (e.g.) water includes life and intelligence, a claim that in itself is no more and no less difficult to understand than the observed fact of life and intelligence inhabiting animal bodies. The difficult question that the theorist faces is, rather, the following one: Why then are there no signs of life and intelligence in ordinary everyday water or air? And on this question there is room for argument; perhaps in fact there are such signs, but they are overlooked or misinterpreted.

Milesian theorizing turns out to have been like modern science in important respects, and unlike it in other important respects. There is no simplistic,

one-dimensional story to be told. It is often claimed that rationality (as opposed to the alleged irrationality of myth or of "mythical thinking") is the principal characteristic of the Milesians as against their predecessors. Yet the concept of rationality is elusive and contested, and it is not clear that prescientific thinking is in any sense irrational. It is clear that 6th-century Miletus produced something that was genuinely and strikingly new. Whatever influences there may have been from the ancient Near East (and none have been firmly proved), it is not possible to claim that the Ionians were merely continuing ancient Near Eastern or other cosmologies by other means.

It has been suggested that the Milesians had: (1) a notion of "objective reality," (2) a programmatic demand that it should be intelligible as a whole, and (3) the outlines of a method for finding and representing it as intelligible. It cannot be stated dogmatically that no one before them had had this combination of aims and methods. Apart from the obvious point that our evidence for earlier thinking is excessively scanty, it might plausibly be argued that some of the speculative cosmogonies and theologies of the ancient Near East are products of a similar program. Yet the fact remains that the ancient Near East saw no explosive outburst of theorizing like the one seen in 6th-to-4th-century Greece, nor did it produce philosophy or anything like science, apart from specialized accumulations of knowledge in restricted areas.

What seems different in 6th-century Miletus is not the activity of the theoretical intellect as such, but its adoption of a naturally "self-developing" program of investigation. Can we identify the decisive ingredient of such a program? The freedom enjoyed by the Greeks in the face of traditional and generally accepted ideas must be relevant. The Presocratics are clearly associated with frank and radical criticisms of the most revered authorities known to the Greeks on religious matters: Homer and Hesiod. Such freedom, however, is only a negative matter, and in any case there cannot be forthright criticism of tradition unless one is already sure enough of an alternative "Archimedean point" from which to criticize. We may see the achievement of freedom in the face of tradition, as well as the advent of literacy, as the removal of external obstacles.

The positive new ingredient was presumably closely connected with (and almost defined by) the adoption of the *formal* demands on theories, as listed above. To give a central place to completely formal, abstract, logically absolute properties of theories and theoretical entities (for example, essential unity or universal uniformity of behavior) creates a new kind of freedom from the phenomenal world. This is not, of course, inconsistent with *respect* for the phenomena as such.

The formal demands are the product of an *abstract* manner of conceiving of reality as a whole. This is not the same as conceiving of reality as itself entirely abstract (which the "natural philosophers" obviously did not). It means

going behind the phenomena to a "hidden structure" that is postulated as something abstract, such as, for example, the structure shown by a geometrical diagram. It is no accident that this period also sees the beginnings of mathematics as a systematic and abstract study.

We do not, then, need to assume any polarity between myth or mythical thinking, on one side, and rationality or rational/logical thinking, on the other. The transition was rather between less and more abstract styles of theorizing. It was a reform of thinking, a freeing of the mind from traditional habits. It also implied a new self-awareness of the abstracting theoretical mind as something autonomous, recognizing no court of appeal higher than itself, and as something universal, capable in principle of investigating anything whatever.

The application of the rules of the game led to abstract accounts of the concrete realities of nature. The underlying abstract structure was, perhaps, guessed rather than fully grasped. It was modeled by the behavior of a mind or a city, or by that of a pebble or a wheel. Such teleology as was involved did not exclude "mechanical" explanations, which did most of the detailed work. Though there was little or no systematic experiment, a corpus of ideas about the mechanical workings of the material world began to be accumulated.

The rules of the game also necessarily led to critical debate of the most fundamental kind. As noted above, they already contained, like every scientific and philosophical enterprise, tensions, circularities, and ambiguities that led to conflict and dissension: about methods and aims, about the appeal to "reasonableness" and to "experience," about the dual commitment to both overall simplicity and respect for the detail of the phenomena. By the very nature of their enterprise, the Presocratic natural philosophers were led, from the Milesians onward, further and further into debates about first principles with their colleagues. Their bare, abstract style of theorizing made the existence and the nature of disagreements more obvious than before, while at the same time the shared appeal to intrinsic reasonableness or explanatory efficiency (rather than authority or tradition) made disagreements less theoretically tolerable. It is in these self-developing theoretical tensions that we can recognize the forerunner of modern science and philosophy.

EDWARD HUSSEY

Bibliography

Barnes, Jonathan. *The Presocratic Philosophers*. London: Routledge, 1982.

Fränkel, Hermann. *Dichtung und Philosophie des frühen Griechentums*. Munich: Beck, 1962.

Furley, David, and R. E. Allen, eds. *Studies in Presocratic Philosophy,* vol. 1. London: Routledge, 1970.

Gadamer, Hans-Georg, ed. *Um die Begriffswelt der Vorsokratiker*. Darmstadt: Wissenschaftliche Buchgesellschaft, 1968.

Guthrie, W. K. C. *A History of Greek Philosophy*, vol. 1: *The Earlier Presocratics and the Pythagoreans*. Cambridge: Cambridge University Press, 1962.

Heidegger, Martin. "Der Spruch des Anaximander." In *Holzwege*. Frankfurt: Klostermann, 1950.

Hölscher, Uvo. "Anaximander und der Anfang der Philosophie." In *Anfängliches Fragen*. Göttingen: Vandenhoeck and Ruprecht, 1968. Pp. 9–89.

Jaeger, Werner. *The Theology of the Early Greek Philosophers*. Oxford: Clarendon Press, 1947.

Kahn, Charles. *Anaximander and the Origins of Greek Cosmology*. New York: Columbia University Press, 1960.

Kirk, G. S., J. E. Raven, and M. Schofield. *The Presocratic Philosophers: A Critical History with a Selection of Texts*, 2nd ed. Cambridge: Cambridge University Press, 1983.

Lloyd, G. E. R. *Magic, Reason, and Experience: Studies in the Origin and Development of Greek Science*. Cambridge: Cambridge University Press, 1979.

———. *Polarity and Analogy: Two Types of Argumentation in Early Greek Thought*. Cambridge: Cambridge University Press, 1966.

Maddalena, Antonio. *Ionici: Testimonianze e Frammenti*. Florence: Nuova Italia, 1963.

Snell, Bruno. *Die Entdeckung des Geistes*. 3rd ed. Hamburg: Claasen Verlag, 1955.

Stokes, Michael C. *One and Many in Presocratic Philosophy*, Cambridge, Mass.: Harvard University Press, 1971.

Vernant, Jean-Pierre. *Mythe et pensée chez les Grecs*. Paris: La Découverte, 1985.

———. *Les origines de la pensée grecque*. Paris: Presses Universitaires de France, 1962.

Vlastos, Gregory. "Equality and Justice in Early Greek Cosmologies." In *Studies in Presocratic Philosophy*, vol. 1: *The Beginnings of Philosophy*. Ed. D. J. Furley and R. E. Allen. London: Routledge and Kegan Paul, 1970. Pp. 56–91.

Related Articles

The Question of Being; Cosmology; Anaxagoras; Schools and Sites of Learning; Physics; Heraclitus

PLATONISM

In ANTIQUITY, and especially in the Hellenistic period, a Platonist *(Plato-nikos)* was either a commentator on Plato or one of his disciples. Members of the first group, such as Panaetius of Rhodes, a Stoic commentator on *Timaeus,* may well not have shared the Platonic positions. Whether they claimed the critical heritage of the early dialogues or presented what they viewed as the doctrines developed in the other dialogues, Plato's followers pursued their activity primarily within the framework of schools, where reading and explanation of the master's works, along with commentary on them, were based on an exceptionally strong manuscript tradition and were closely linked with the practice of virtue. As a school-based phenomenon that took its inspiration very early from the Pythagorean tradition, Platonism showed an astonishing diversity through the ages; innovation did not appear to be irreconcilable with true fidelity.

This diversity originated in the Platonic corpus itself. After an initial critical period during which, with Socrates as spokesperson, Plato called into question his contemporaries' opinions and values, he adopted a more dogmatic approach, staking out a certain number of positions in the fields of ethics, epistemology, and ontology. In all these domains, one idea was stressed above all others: that of transcendence, implying on the one hand the division of reality into two realms—the sensible, the realm of individuals that is continually changing, and the intelligible, the realm of the absolutely immutable—and on the other hand the distinction, within each human being, between a mortal body endowed with five senses and an immortal soul that can grasp the intelligible.

PLATO

In the early dialogues, up to *Meno,* Socrates makes use of the method called *elenchos:* a thesis is refuted if, and only if, its negation is deduced from the interlocutor's opinions. In fact, the *elenchos* presents four essential features: (1) from a formal point of view, this method is negative: Socrates does not defend a thesis of his own but limits himself to examining a thesis advanced by his interlocutor; (2) since Socrates seeks to discover the truth while realizing he knows nothing, he must derive this truth from premises his interlocutors hold to be true; (3) he must accept as provisionally established that truths are

involved; and (4) it follows that the *elenchos,* as a tool for seeking out the truth, cannot guarantee certainty.

To arrive at certainty, that is, at the confidence that results from possessing truth, Plato will, in view of the overwhelming success of the geometrical method, use mathematics, considered as a paradigm of all methods. A truly demonstrative method should present the following logical structure: to link the truth of a proposition to the truth of a hypothesis, one must try to prove the proposition true (or false) because it is a necessary consequence of the hypothesis in question, which is considered true (or false) in the final analysis, for the latter (or its contrary) is the necessary consequence of the axioms of the system—that is, of the propositions whose truth is immediately and incontrovertibly self-evident within the framework of the system.

Plato's use of this method suggests that the philosopher had a "doctrine," even though it was subject to a continuous and significant process of elaboration. Now the doctrine in question is paradoxical, characterized as it is by a double reversal. First, for Plato, things perceived through the senses are only images of intelligible Forms, which themselves conceal the principle of their existence and constitute true reality. Second, man is not reduced to his body; his true identity coincides with the soul, an incorporeal entity that explains every movement, whether material (growth, locomotion, and so on) or spiritual (emotions, sense perceptions, intellectual knowledge, and the like).

The hypothesis of the existence of intelligible Forms, which Plato never defines and which he evokes only in terms of their negative features, allows him to lay the foundations for an ethics, a theory of knowledge, and an ontology.

Given the confusion that reigned in Athens, where the classical city-state was crumbling under the assaults of its adversaries and where citizens spoke in diametrically opposed terms about common values, Plato, in an effort to prolong Socrates' activity, sought to establish a different political order based on absolutely sound moral principles; this explains why the early dialogues deal with ethical questions. It was a matter of defining the essential virtues of the perfect citizen, a requirement that implies the existence of absolute norms depending neither on the tradition transmitted by the poets nor—as the Sophists claimed—on arbitrary conventions, norms that could serve as reference points for evaluating the human condition.

But this hypothesis, which makes an ethical system possible, refers back to the epistemological sphere, as *Meno* in particular makes clear. To grasp the absolute norms that ethics requires, we must hypothesize the existence of a faculty distinct from opinion: the intellect. Now a distinction between intellect and opinion implies a distinction between their respective objects; whereas opinion has as its domain sensible entities immersed in becoming, the intellect can grasp immutable and absolute realities. In short, to provide a foundation for the epistemology required by his moral system, Plato is led to hypothesize the existence of realities that he calls intelligible Forms.

Intelligible Forms account for the processes of intellectual knowing; still, perceptible reality does not depend on these processes. If, in the sensible world, objects and their features are reduced to transitory results of compound movements, no ethics or epistemology can be developed, and from this standpoint the hypothesis of the existence of a world of intelligible Forms presents itself as empty and gratuitous. Accordingly, independently of the needs that ethics and epistemology impose, an ontological foundation must be found that will allow us to take into account sensible phenomena, which, left to themselves, would dissolve in an incessant becoming. We can only know these sensible phenomena, we can only speak of them, if they present a certain stability, which derives from their participation in the intelligible. In short, in creating the universe while keeping his eyes fixed on intelligible Forms, the artificer or demiurge guarantees the existence, in the sensible world, of a certain stability that allows us to know the world and to talk about it, and in the city-state, the existence of norms serving to orient both individual and collective human conduct. This indeed must have been Plato's intention in writing *Timaeus* in particular.

THE OLD ACADEMY

This doctrine, which is formulated more or less explicitly in the dialogues from *Meno* on, must have been the object of intense discussion in the context of the Academy that Plato is believed to have founded in 387 B.C.E. He had just returned from his first tour of Magna Graecia (southern Italy), where he had met some Pythagoreans, among them Archytas, and Sicily, where he had been received at the court of Dionysius the Elder, tyrant of Syracuse, and had made the acquaintance of Dion. Plato established his school in Athens, at his own expense, in a tree-shaded setting freshened with springs, a park devoted to the hero Academos. The park was on the road to Eleusis, near the Cephissus River and not far from Colonos; a gymnasium stood at its center. The school was intended above all to prepare young people to play an active role in politics by giving them a philosophical education according to the program set forth in Books VI and VII of *The Republic*. The Academy rapidly achieved great success; it soon became the principal rival of Isocrates' school, which focused on teaching rhetoric.

Plato seems to have been surrounded by friends and associates, each responsible for a particular discipline. The best known are Aristotle of Stagira, Speusippus of Athens, Xenocrates of Chalcedon, Philippus of Opus, Hermodorus of Syracuse, Heraclides of Pontus, Eudoxus, Hestiaeus of Perinthus, and Theaetetus. We should also include in this group a certain number of other mathematicians and astronomers, such as Menaechmus, his brother Deinostratus, Amphinomus, Amyntas, Athenaeus, Hermotimus, Callipus (who is thought to have refined the system of the spheres), and Theodius of Magne-

sia, to whom *Elements* in the style of Euclid are generally attributed. Other persons mentioned in the *Letters* include Euphraius *(Letter V)*, Erastus, and Coriscus of Scepsis *(Letter VI)*.

From the outset, the Academy seems to have been a place of intense discussion rather than an instrument for the dogmatic transmission of a body of privileged doctrines. It is important to keep this in mind: neither Aristotle nor any of Plato's successors as head of the Academy maintained the core of the founder's thought in its orthodoxy, that is, the doctrine of intelligible Forms. If we consider the relations Plato and Speusippus maintained with Dion, who, after listening to Plato's talks and even frequenting the Academy, returned to Sicily to try to seize power, political action must have occupied an important place, along with the development of astronomical theories and geometry.

Moreover, we have every reason to believe that, as the geometric method prescribed, a search for the highest principles was undertaken within the framework of the Academy. This quest, of which *Philebus* may have supplied an early sketch, could well have given rise to the system of principles that, according to some modern authors and some contemporaries, constitutes the heart of the "esoteric doctrines." In this esoteric context, the true Plato is the one Aristotle criticized, a Plato whom only his closest disciples knew. The figure of Plato conveyed by the Platonic tradition was thus from the beginning an "Aristotelized" Plato, a Plato whose doctrine had already been discussed within the framework of the Academy and in terms that in many instances were fixed once and for all by Aristotle.

This school, which defined itself neither by the possession of the property bought by Plato nor by a particular status as an association, existed institutionally only through the election of a scholarch, or head, an Academic named by his peers who thus became a successor to Plato. The Academy remained faithful to the directions set by its founder; however, the heart of the Academy's activity seems to have been the systematization and diffusion of the master's thought, as opposed to the competing views professed by other schools. Aristotle's philosophy was taught in the gymnasium of the Lyceum; that of Antisthenes, who was viewed as the founder of Cynicism, was expounded in the Cynosarges gymnasium. Later, two new schools were established, also in Athens: Zeno's Stoic school, and the Epicurean school.

If, for the Sophists and for Plato, philosophical training was intended to prepare young men for life as citizens, by teaching them to master their external discourse and their internal dialogue by dialectic or rhetorical methods and to understand all the rational principles that these could involve, later philosophical instruction was designed instead to prepare for life in general, either public or private; still, in one way or another, mastery of discourse was always involved.

This means that the method of teaching consisted, above all, at least among the Platonists, Aristotelians, and Stoics, in dialectical exercises by means of

which the interlocutors learned to carry on a dialogue with others and also with themselves. Although master classes did exist in these schools, probably resembling the classes that resulted in Aristotle's *Physics* and *Metaphysics*, the philosopher's monologue was not the presentation of an entire system, for the speaker was always responding, if not to a listener's question, at least to a specific problem. The teaching generally included three distinct areas, thought to have been introduced by Xenocrates, the Academy's second *diadoch* (successor to Plato). The first area might be said to correspond both to logic and epistemology, in the sense in which these terms are used today; it was called logic by the Stoics, canonics by the Epicureans, dialectics by the Platonists and by the Aristotelians, though these two schools had given a very different content to dialectics; all the schools called the second area physics and the third ethics.

THE NEW ACADEMY

With Arcesilaus of Pitane, who succeeded Crates as diadoch in 268/264, the Academy transformed itself into the "New" Academy, in that all effort at systematization was abandoned. Suspension of judgment became the cardinal principle of philosophy; the refusal of certainty led to universal questioning. Arcesilaus symbolizes this crucial shift in his own person. He began by studying mathematics with Autolycus, and spent some time at the school of Theophrastus before becoming acquainted, at least through their writings, with some of the dialecticians of Megara and Eretria. Turning away from Xenocrates' grandiose system, which was largely inspired by the dialogues of Plato's maturity, Arcesilaus went back to the practice of Socrates, which the earlier dialogues illustrate. This is why he gave primacy to critical dialogue and to the affirmation of ignorance; this is the sense in which he understood Plato's dubitative formulas and mythical narratives. His principal target was quite naturally Stoicism, the most widespread dogmatism of the period; starting from overall conceptions based on certainty and extending to the universe, Stoicism presented itself as the necessary precondition of wisdom.

Like Socrates, Arcesilaus wrote nothing and never dogmatized; he engaged his interlocutors in lively conversation and asked them for advice. His students were to be guided not by the master's authority but by their own reason; Arcesilaus's replies were in turn new questions. The spirit of Arcesilaus's teaching was perpetuated by Carneades, who sought to establish a hierarchy of representations according to their degree of verisimilitude, since he maintained that one cannot assert with certainty of any given representation that it is true.

At all events, the history of the Academy seems to have ended in 88 B.C.E., when Philo of Larissa fled Athens, under siege by Mithridates, to seek refuge in Rome. But even before Philo's exile, the Platonic school had undergone a

major schism with the departure of Antiochus of Ascalon, who claimed to find the inspiration of the Old Academy outside of this New Academy, which he himself finally wrote off as an aberrant parenthesis in the history of Platonism. He had a dual purpose: to reestablish a dogmatic interpretation of Platonism, and to demonstrate the preeminence of the Academy over the Lyceum and the Stoa, making Aristotle and Zeno epigones of Plato. Thus his Platonism was strongly influenced by Aristotelianism and especially by Stoicism. Antiochus was never recognized as head of the Academy, whose institutional lineage had been disrupted. The school taken over by Antiochus outlived its founder by nearly a century.

MIDDLE PLATONISM

The period just described, which lasted from the 4th to the 1st century B.C.E., is characterized by two features: the presence of philosophical institutions in Athens and teaching intended as training in the arts of speaking and living. The major schools—Platonic, Aristotelian, Epicurean, and Stoic—had been set up in different parts of the city of Athens. Instruction consisted in dialectical exercises and discussions designed to train students for political action enlightened by knowledge (Platonism), for a life devoted to science (Aristotelianism), or for moral life (Epicureanism and Stoicism).

On their last legs during the final years of the Roman republic, these philosophical institutions were virtually defunct in the early years of the principate. The disappearance of the philosophical schools of Athens and the formation of numerous philosophical institutions throughout the Mediterranean basin inaugurated a new phase in the history of philosophy.

To affirm their loyalty to the tradition from which each took its inspiration, the four philosophical schools—which by that time were spread among various oriental and occidental cities—could no longer turn for support to the Athenian institutions created by their founders; thus they carried on an oral tradition. Platonic philosophy, in particular, became essentially textual commentary, focusing on *Phaedo, Alcibiades* I, *Gorgias, Phaedrus, Symposium, Theaetetus, The Republic, Laws, Statesman,* and, especially, *Timaeus.*

The existence of philosophical commentaries had its origins in the remote past; indeed, Crantor very probably commented on Plato's *Timaeus* around 300 B.C.E. But at the beginning of the Roman empire, this practice took on a newly systematic character. In the past, students had learned to speak, and in learning how to speak they had learned how to live. Now, they learned not so much to speak as to read, even if, in learning how to read, they were still learning how to live. The philosophic enterprise thus became exegetic. If one were to inquire, for example, what relations pertain among "the Living Thing," the intelligible Forms, and the intellect, one would be seeking to grasp the meaning of the following phrase from *Timaeus:* "Reason perceives

Forms existing in the Living Thing" (39e). Reflection bears directly not on a given problem, but on the problem as it is addressed by Aristotle and Plato.

From the end of the 1st century B.C.E. and during the early stages of the Roman empire, the dominant philosophy continued to be Stoicism, which permeated even a cultivated, eclectic, relatively undogmatic Platonism that was strongly influenced by Aristotle. But gradually the need for a more religious philosophy made itself felt. Platonism then appeared as a means to accede to another order of reality, that of the divine, which only the soul could grasp. This is the context that produced, among the Platonists, a renaissance later known as Middle Platonism.

In the middle of the 1st century C.E., Potamon is considered to have been the father of eclectic Platonism, following the model of Philo Judaeus (first half of the 1st century C.E.), the most prolific and most intelligent representative of a syncretism in which Platonism played a decisive role. Plutarch of Chaeronaea (ca. 50–125) has his place within this new stream of thought; after him, in the second half of the 2nd century, came the Sophists Maximus of Tyre and Apuleius of Madaurus, and a little later Galen the physician, who may have studied with Albinus (the latter, in turn, may have been a disciple of Gaius in Smyrna), Celsus (the virulent refutation of whom by the Christian Origen allows us to reconstruct in part his *Real Discourse*), Numenius of Apamea (who rediscovered Moses behind Plato), and also Alcinous in his *Didaskalikos* (The Handbook of Platonism). All these Platonists either interpreted Plato in a theosophic spirit, using the allegorical method without hesitating to invoke astrology, demonology, and even magic, or else, at the very least, they compared Platonism with Aristotelianism, with Stoicism, or—as did the first apologists—with Christianity.

One institutional sign of this renaissance, which also touched the other schools, is Emperor Marcus Aurelius's establishment in Athens in 176 of four chairs of philosophy: Platonic, Aristotelian, Stoic, and Epicurean. Atticus, who may have belonged to the family of Herod Atticus, may have been the first chair of the Platonic school; this would explain his openly anti-Aristotelian attitude.

The Pythagorean influence, which had already been exerted over Platonism in the Old Academy by Speusippus and Xenocrates, became decisive at this point, although the details of its historical transmission remain obscure. This tendency is clearly discernible in Eudorus, who is thought to have lived in Alexandria during the 1st century B.C.E., and who may have commented on *Timaeus,* and in his compatriot Philon. Pythagorean thought, significant in the work of Thrasyllus (an astrologer under Tiberius and a philosopher at the court of Nero), is transformed in Plutarch's writings into a philosophical presupposition.

The Pythagorean influence made itself felt not only on the level of doctrine but even on the material level. The order in which Plato's writings were pre-

sented reflects the order adopted by Thrasyllus, who may himself have written about the principles of Plato and Pythagoras. In fact, this rearrangement of Plato's works into nine groups of four (tetralogies), which can perhaps be attributed to Dercyllides, may go back to the annotated edition that Cicero's friend T. Pomponius Atticus arranged to have produced in Rome. This edition may already have had the benefit of the work of revision carried out in Alexandria by Aristophanes of Byzantium (271–180 B.C.E.). And the Alexandrian edition, in which Plato's works were organized in groups of three (trilogies) is thought to have been based on the Academic edition published while Xenocrates was scholarch, some thirty years after Plato's death.

The Pythagorean influence on Platonism had many facets, but one of them, secrecy, took on crucial importance. Secrecy applied to two elements that came into play in the communication of Platonism: the means of transmission, and coding. The privileged means of transmission of fundamental truths was supposed to be the spoken word, for writing put information within everyone's reach, at least in theory. Whence the use of the term *akousmata* to designate the Pythagorean doctrines; writing was used only to produce memoranda *(hupomnēmata)*, or memory aids. As the relation to writing never ceased to be problematic in the Platonic tradition, the ties between Platonism and Pythagoreanism were strengthened. And this first restriction bearing on the means of transmission was accompanied by another, one that concerned the symbolic and enigmatic fashion in which these doctrines were formulated; indeed this is why they were described as *sumbola* and *ainigmata*.

Timaeus and *The Republic* were the key dialogues used initially to construct this new dogmatism. In the early stages at least, they were not the object of extensive commentary, but their interpreters looked to them for viewpoints on divinity, the world, man, and society, in the context of a system articulated around three principles: God, the Model, and Matter.

For Atticus as for Plutarch and Alcinous, the God in question has to be identified with the Good of *The Republic* and with the demiurge, the Constructor of the Cosmos, of *Timaeus*. Since this God is first among all gods, and the supreme principle, nothing can be superior to him. Such supremacy determines the type of relation that this God maintains with the second principle: the paradigm, or Model.

The Middle Platonists were accustomed to envisaging the problem by recalling the passage in *Timaeus* where "the artificer of any object . . . keeps his gaze fixed on that which is uniform" (28a.6–7). This led them to the conviction that, in a way, the intelligible Forms were God's "thoughts," which did not prevent them from having existence in themselves, apart from the Intellect. Consequently, the Model, which corresponded to the Intelligible, was, as the object of God's thought, at once external and internal to the Intellect, that is, to the first God.

Atticus declares that Plato was merely perpetuating the opinions of his pre-

decessors and that, like them, he recognized only four elements, from which all the other bodies were formed as a consequence of transformations and combinations according to clearly defined proportions. These elements are earth, water, air, and fire, and the positions they occupy in space are determined by the very constitution of the universe. They emerged from a single, homogeneous, and undifferentiated matter—probably what Plato, in *Timaeus*, called the third principle, an extended, wandering cause, a receptacle. He was probably referring here to that in which or upon which figures and bodies are outlined, but he never views this reality as corporeal matter. Atticus had been to a school other than Plato's. He must have studied with Plutarch, from whom he took this very idea (unless it was from Alcinous). Atticus in fact understood the third principle in the sense of a corporeal and sensible reality, a sort of undifferentiated chaos, in which all the elements of the universe are merged: like Plato, he still called it "a receptacle, nurse, mother, substratum, elusive to the senses, having as a property only the power to receive forms, all the while being itself without quality, without form; matter, which is neither corporeal nor incorporeal, which is only potentially a body"; but he definitely regarded it as "matter," a notion that Plato never adopted. Atticus could have been influenced on this point by Posidonius or Galen the Aristotelian, who, like Posidonius, also recognized a universal matter in which all the elements are resolved, a "primal substance that provides the basis of all bodies born and perishable." The fact remains that in making a material reality of the third principle, Atticus seems to have gone far beyond his master Plato.

Beyond this doctrine of the three principles, the representatives of Middle Platonism interpreted the soul of the world in *Timaeus* in a quite original manner. Probably in reaction against the Stoics' material monism, they hypothesized that the world has an irrational soul. Having made the distinction between a transcendent divinity and a totally indeterminate primary matter, these interpreters of *Timaeus*, who were seeking in this way to account for the chaos and the irregularity of the movement that permeates corporeal nature, considered that the soul of the world, irrational at first, would later be ordered, insofar as possible, by the demiurgic intelligence. In Middle Platonism, the constitution of the universe thus took on the aspect of a drama, while in Neoplatonism it would be considered within the framework of a system in which the Intellect deployed, without intentionality, all the possibilities inherent within it.

The best way to get a sense of this interpretative strategy is to read Alcinous's *Didaskalikos* (ca. 150 C.E.). The author was closely linked with the branch of Middle Platonism that interpreted Plato in the light of Aristotle; it has recently been established that he must be distinguished from Albinus, another Middle Platonic philosopher and the author of *Introduction to the Dialogues of Plato*, with whom Galen the physician may have studied. The title *Didaskalikos* designates a more or less well defined principle of philosophical

Introduction

Definition of philosophy
Qualities of an aspirant to philosophic study
The two ways: contemplative and active
Division of philosophy into its parts: dialectical, theoretical, and practical, with
    their subdivisions

Development

I   Dialectical philosophy
    Epistemology
    The aim of dialectics and its parts
    Division
    Definition
    Analysis
    Induction
    Propositions
    Syllogisms
    Categories
    Knowledge required of an accomplished orator
    Sophisms
    Etymology and the accuracy of names
II Theoretical philosophy
    a The mathematical sciences
    b Theology: first principles
       Matter
       Forms
       God
       The incorporeality of qualities
    c Physics
       A The universe
          The generation of the world
          The geometric structure of the elements and the world
          The structure of the soul of the world
          The stars and the planets
          The created gods
          The earth

discourse consisting in the account of a philosophy that had previously been
reduced to a body of doctrine.

The accompanying outline of Alcinous's work in *Didaskalikos* highlights
the principal vectors that allow us to define Middle Platonism. Grounded in
the opposition between the Philosopher and the Sophist thematized in *Sophist*, which extends into an opposition between being and nonbeing, truth and
error, this account of the Platonic doctrine is developed in terms of the three
major components of philosophy in the Hellenistic period: dialectical, physi-

cal integrated with theoretical, and practical. Theoretical philosophy actually includes three areas: mathematics, as a method; theology, which concerns first causes; and physics, which deals with the universe and its contents. Theology is in fact concerned with the three principles that structure the Middle Platonic interpretation: God, the Model, and Matter; these account for the macrocosm and the microcosm alike.

The passage from Middle Platonism to Neoplatonism, illustrated by the polemic launched by Porphyry at Plotinus's school in Rome, is played out in the relation between God and the Model, that is, more precisely, in the question of knowing whether the Model, the Intelligible, is at the same level as the Demiurge, at the same level as the Intellect, before it or after it. In his *Commentary on the Timaeus of Plato,* Proclus recapitulates the positions of Plotinus, Porphyry, and Longinus on this: "For among the Ancients, some, like Plotinus, have represented the Demiurge as containing the Forms of all things, while others, rejecting that view, have situated the Forms either before the Demiurge, as Porphyry did, or after him, as Longinus did" (II.1.322c). Longinus thus defended a position in conformity with the Middle Platonists' doctrine on God and the Model; since the Demiurge was the supreme principle, the Model could only be inferior to him.

At the same time, positions like that of Plotinus and Porphyry result from an approach to interpreting Platonic doctrine that apparently goes back to Numenius. In identifying the Good with the first Intellect, Numenius construed it as a principle superior to the Demiurge, which he identified with a second Intellect. From that point on, as the Demiurge was no longer the ultimate principle, the Model could be situated either prior to it, as Porphyry maintained, or in it, as Plotinus affirmed. Porphyry, who had just arrived from Athens, went on to defend Longinus's doctrine in Rome in Plotinus's school. In the ensuing polemic, Amelius, Plotinus, and of course Longinus all had their say. Longinus reaffirmed his positions, but in vain, for Porphyry joined forces with Plotinus. The story of Neoplatonism was beginning.

But this story was paradoxical from the very outset, for in separating the ultimate source of being from being itself, the Neoplatonists raised a redoubtable problem. If the Absolute is determined by nothing but itself, if it transcends being and reason, it can intervene at any level it chooses, independently of any preexisting rational order. Moreover, the Absolute is free to reveal itself to human beings, independently of their behavior and their efforts in the field of reason. That was the problem Plotinus raised in his fascinating treatise *On the Freedom and Will of the One* (*Enneads* VI.vi.39). Hermeticism, Gnosticism, and the Chaldaeans would offer a soteriological answer to this problem that the Neoplatonists would try, for better or worse, to solve by appealing to reason.

NEOPLATONISM

The story thus begins with Plotinus, who was inspired by Ammonius, his teacher in Alexandria (about whom we know very little). Plotinus undertook to explain Plato's principles, which had previously been identified with those of Pythagoras; he took his inspiration from what we now call the later dialogues, and primarily from *Parmenides,* a difficult text that had either been

neglected until then or interpreted superficially. This vast enterprise led to a renaissance that would leave a decisive stamp on Platonism.

Plotinus founded a true school of philosophy in Rome that functioned on a strictly private basis for twenty-five years, from 244 until 269. Porphyry, who attended this school for less than five years (from 263 to 268), describes its operations succinctly in his *Life of Plotinus*, which he wrote as a preamble to his edition of the master's treatises collected in six *Enneads*, or groups of nine. (The number six was obtained by multiplying the first uneven number by the first even one, and the number nine, by multiplying the first uneven number by itself; all these numbers and operations presented a profound metaphysical meaning in the framework of Neopythagoreanism.)

Probably born to a family of high Roman officials in Egypt, Plotinus settled in Rome, after a misadventure at the court of the emperor Gordian (to which he belonged during an unfortunate campaign against the Persians), to take advantage of the opportunities his family ties afforded him. The school, which he founded shortly after his arrival in Rome, met in the home of a noblewoman who may have been the widow of the emperor Trebonianus Gallus. Senators sat in on the courses, during which Plotinus discussed problems raised by Plato and Aristotle in a polemical anti-Stoic context; he eschewed rhetorical staging and paid close attention to the major commentators. Two of the master's pupils soon became his favorite disciples and collaborators: Amelius, who functioned as his assistant before leaving to take over Numenius's school in Apamaea, and Porphyry, who later prepared a systematic edition of Plotinus's writings.

In metaphysics, Plotinus brought the break with Middle Platonism to its culmination on the level of principles, by extracting all the consequences of the position held by Numenius. As we have seen, Numenius identified the Good with the first Intellect and made it a principle superior to the Demiurge, which he considered a second intellect. Since Aristotle's divine intellect did not suffice to explain the world of beings, Plotinus maintained that there must be a principle beyond being, which is the One, and which must be identified with the Good. In Plato's *Parmenides*, which for this reason supplants *Timaeus* as Platonism's key dialogue, Plotinus found not only the theory of the One but also theories of the Intellect and of the Soul. This led him to oppose the Gnostics as well, by elaborating an entire architecture of the intelligible world that accounts, in a different way, for the presence of the intelligible in the sensible world. But in the case of Plotinus, as well as all the other philosophers who followed, the effort to maintain a rationalistic attitude within the framework of a system whose principle is located beyond reason constituted a source of inexhaustible difficulty.

So far as the soul is concerned, Plotinus held a view that he himself described as paradoxical. One part of the soul—and even a part of the human soul—remains on the divine level of intelligible realities. It is thus through

only a part of itself that the human soul is united with the body. A thesis of this sort leads, moreover, to the view that there is also an intermediate part of the soul between the two extreme parts; its task is not only to resolve conflicts between soul and body but also to allow knowledge of Forms, for it is an intermediate part of the soul that becomes conscious of what the superior part contemplates eternally. This intermediate part is in fact self-awareness. This thesis is also related to problems concerning the movement of the soul, its immortality, its purification through virtues, and its mystical life, which consists in making our empirical "I" coincide with the transcendent "I," without falling back on grace or ritual. Supreme wisdom can thus operate on a purely philosophical level.

In Rome itself, Plotinus's teaching remained without influence. Even before the end of his life, his two best disciples had already abandoned their master: Porphyry had gone to Lilybaeum in Sicily, and Amelius to Apamaea in Syria. Nevertheless, Plotinus had established the foundation for all of Neoplatonism and had initiated its evolution: the preference for *Parmenides* over *Timaeus* as the key Platonic dialogue; the Platonic One taken as the very first principle beyond the Aristotelian Intellect; all the degrees of being set forth in a hierarchy starting from the One. What is more, Plotinus had inquired into the nature and the structure of the soul. And above all, as we know from Porphyry, it was Plotinus who reread the principal texts of the great philosophers, giving them new currency and commenting on them in relation to his own fundamental project: to achieve an original synthesis between the Platonic and the Pythagorean principles.

Porphyry was the agent of transmission of Plotinus's philosophy. His work, which must have been immense, is largely lost. Born in Tyre, he studied at first in Athens with Longinus, a Middle Platonist who made no distinction between philosophy and literature. Then he went to Rome to study at Plotinus's school. From the start he had to repudiate Longinus's typically Middle Platonic doctrines concerning the relations between the Intellect and the Intelligible in favor of Plotinus's views. Plotinus used his polemical skills against the Gnostics and, according to Porphyry—who was thereby justifying his own work as editor of the *Enneads*—entrusted Porphyry with the revision of his work. But five years after his arrival in Rome, Porphyry suddenly broke with Plotinus, perhaps because of the latter's anti-Aristotelian outlook.

This is the hypothesis that comes readily to mind if we assume that it is in Sicily that Porphyry plunged into the production of commentaries on Aristotle. He wrote on *Categories, Peri hermeneias, Physics,* and *Metaphysics* (XII); he also wrote *Isagoge* and, in particular, *That the Schools of Plato and Aristotle Are Only One,* a treatise that proclaims Aristotle's agreement with Plato. He also drafted an enormous treatise called *Against the Christians,* which earned him the wrath of the Christian emperors. Of course, he dedi-

cated himself to the study of Platonic philosophy by composing commentaries on *Timaeus* and *Parmenides*. He even commented on Plotinus and based the manual called *Sentences* on his work. He was also a historian of philosophy *(Life of Pythagoras, On the Soul)*, and he took part in controversies on several subjects *(On Abstinence, Letter to Anebo)*.

Porphyry seems not to have had a school. Visitors spent limited periods of time with him. The most famous of these is Iamblichus, the originator of Syrian Neoplatonism. But Porphyry also influenced the rhetor Marius Victorinus in Rome, and Chalcidius, whose translation and Latin commentary on part of *Timaeus* had a critical impact throughout the Middle Ages. Having become a Christian, Marius Victorinus was to be the intermediary between Plotinus and the Christian Neoplatonism illustrated by St. Ambrose and St. Augustine.

Porphyry's essential contribution to the history of Neoplatonism is a double one. He reintroduced the literary genre of commentary—on Aristotle first of all, then on Plato—into Neoplatonism. He also spread Plotinus's doctrine through his own works, in particular in 301, when he produced a standard edition of Plotinus's treatises in the form of the *Enneads*, which have survived. Porphyry commented on the *Enneads* in *Sententiae*, a work of which only fragments remain, but in which Porphyry develops for the first time the doctrine of levels of virtue (civic, purificatory, contemplative, and paradigmatic), a doctrine that played an essential role in later Neoplatonism. In fact, the way the *Enneads* were organized in three volumes ensured a progressive order of reading designed within a pedagogic perspective to elevate the soul to knowledge of the highest realities.

Volume One
Ennead I: treatises with a moral focus
Ennead II: treatises on physical reality
Ennead III: treatises relating to the world

Volume Two
Ennead IV: treatises on the soul
Ennead V: treatises on the intellect

Volume Three
Ennead VI: treatises on the One

Also, Porphyry went on to defend what he took to be his master's doctrine against what he viewed as Iamblichus's deviations.

We know practically nothing about Iamblichus's family (the name comes from a transcription from the Syriac or Aramaic *ya-mliku*, "he is king" or "let him be king"). Iamblichus was born in Chalcis in Syria-Coele, probably Chalcis ad Belum, the present Quinnesrin, around 240. He studied first with

Anatolius, then with Porphyry. He probably founded a school in Syria at Apamaea. His best-known pupil is Sopater. After Sopater was executed by order of Constantine, Iamblichus was succeeded by Aidesius, who is thought to have settled in Pergamum, then by Eustathius. Theodorus of Asine and Dexippus were also among his disciples.

No clear-cut criterion allows us to propose a chronology of Iamblichus's works. His most significant production seems to have been a collection of ten books on Pythagoreanism, only four of which have survived. The first, intended to serve as an introduction, is *Life of Pythagoras*. This book is followed by three others: *Exhortation to Philosophy*, *On Common Mathematical Science*, and *On the Introduction to Nichomachean Arithmetic*. The missing books dealt with physics, ethics, theology, geometry, music, and astronomy. Psellus preserved excerpts from Books V through VII, of which two fragments survive: "On Physical Number" (Book V), and "On Ethical and Theological Arithmetic" (Books VI–VII). In the same vein there is a curious book called *The Theology of Arithmetic*, which turns out to be a compilation of passages from a work with the same title by Nicomachus of Gerasa and from a work by Anatolius (probably Iamblichus's teacher), *On the Decade and the Numbers Contained in It*. After such a massive effort, Platonism could no longer be dissociated from Pythagoreanism.

Iamblichus's most original work nevertheless remains his response to Porphyry's *Letter to Anebo*, which, in the manuscripts, bears the title *Abammo's Reply to Porphyry's Letter to Anebo and Solution of the Difficulties Inherent in It*. This work comprises two volumes that appeal to Chaldaean and Egyptian wisdom to promote the "true" theurgy.

Stobaeus preserved lengthy fragments of *On the Soul*, a treatise that deals with the nature of the soul, its powers, and its peregrinations, whether it is in a body or separated from it; in this text, Iamblichus evokes the positions of several other contemporary and more ancient philosophers. He comments on the *Chaldaean Oracles* in a work comprising twenty-eight books, of which only fragments remain; we also have fragments from *On the Gods*, a treatise that became the basis for two discourses (IV and V) by the emperor Julian and for *On the Gods and on the Universe*, a book by Synesius.

In the area of commentary, Iamblichus seems to have developed the doctrine according to which each dialogue has a single theme, which is its end, its design *(skopos)*, and to which everything else must be related (Anon., *Prolegomena* 26; Westerink, pp. 13–44). On the strength of this conviction, he proposed an order for reading the Platonic dialogues that takes the student through the three traditional divisions of philosophy, ethics *(Alcibiades* I, *Gorgias, Phaedo)*, logic *(Cratylus, Theaetetus)*, and physics *(Sophist, Statesman)*, to lead him to the height of these studies, theology *(Phaedrus, Symposium)* and even to bring him to the summit of theology, the Good *(Philebus)*. *Timaeus* and *Parmenides* come last, recapitulating all of Plato's teaching in

the fields of physics and theology. This approach to reading Plato, which Iamblichus must have followed in his teaching, remained the rule for all later Neoplatonists.

A fairly large number of fragments of a *Commentary on Timaeus* survive, along with several fragments of a *Commentary on Parmenides* and a *Commentary on Phaedo*. We find exegetic remarks on specific points in passages from *Alcibiades* I, *Phaedo*, and *Philebus*. And, in a scholium on *Sophist*, we find an allusion to the *skopos* that Iamblichus attributed to this dialogue. Iamblichus occupied a unique position in the interpretation he proposed of the hypotheses of *Parmenides*, into which the Neoplatonists read the organization of the first principles. To ensure a position—very high up in the hierarchy of the gods—for the actors in the theurgy whom Iamblichus called "superior beings" (archangels, angels, demons, and heroes), he shifted the entire hierarchy of the gods up a notch and even went beyond *Parmenides*, since he was obliged to posit an ineffable god not included among the hypotheses found in that dialogue; Damascius later adopted this crucial interpretive detail.

At bottom, Iamblichus's philosophical system resulted from an elaboration of Plotinus's, carried out within the framework of an original interpretation powerfully influenced by Neopythagoreanism and the *Chaldaean Oracles*. Iamblichus postulated a totally ineffable principle prior to the One. In addition, between the One and the Intelligible he imagined a pair of principles, the limited and the unlimited. Thus the One-Being, which is at the summit of the intelligible triad, is a mixture resulting from these two principles. In this manner Iamblichus may have opened the way to the doctrine of units *(henads)*, which played an important role in later Neoplatonism.

After the domain of the One, we find the domain of Being, that is, that of the Intelligible and the Intellect. At this level, according to Proclus (*On Timaeus* I.308.17ff), Iamblichus hypothesized seven triads: three triads of intelligible gods, the first being that of the One-Being (*hen on*), three triads of the intelligible and intellective gods, and one triad, the seventh, of intellective gods. This last triad may have included Kronos, Rhea, and Zeus, who was the Demiurge for the Neoplatonists. There is reason to doubt that this was the case, however, because Proclus introduces this development to show that Iamblichus expressed himself too summarily when he gave the entire intelligible world the name of Demiurge in his controversy against Porphyry (*On Timaeus* I.307.14–308.17ff).

Then comes the domain of the Soul, the hypostasis of the Soul as well as all other sorts of souls. Concerning particular souls, Iamblichus distanced himself from Plotinus and Porphyry on one essential point. He refuted the thesis according to which a higher part of the soul dwells at the level of the Intelligibles. For him, the soul was completely one with the body. This was the Aristotelian position, and it implies that salvation of the soul must necessarily

come from elsewhere. The gap between Porphyry's position and Iamblichus's on this specific point widened: while Porphyry remained faithful to Plotinian rationalism, Iamblichus gave priority over philosophy to theurgy, understood as a spiritual movement through which one appeals directly to the gods according to well-established rites in order to obtain the union of the soul with the gods. Hence the importance of the *Chaldaean Oracles* in Iamblichus's works.

As far as nature is concerned, Iamblichus, who was less optimistic than Plotinus on the capacities of the Intellect, nevertheless maintained that destiny exercises its power only over the inferior (nonrational) soul, and that the superior soul can liberate itself through the practice of theurgy.

Finally, matter, which can perhaps be traced back to the dyad in the realm of the One, should be viewed as that which introduces otherness into the *logoi,* which are the manifestations of Forms in the soul and in the sensible.

Iamblichus taught in Apamaea during the first quarter of the 4th century, and his school flourished. One of his disciples, the highly talented Theodorus of Asinaea, set himself up as a rival of his master. Iamblichus remained under the influence of Numenius and Porphyry, and continued to maintain the Plotinian thesis according to which one part of the soul is not transmitted through generation. After his death (around 326), Sopater succeeded him in Apamaea, and Aedesius founded a new school in Pergamum that was to have special historical importance, since the future emperor Julian had his first contact with Neoplatonism there in 351.

Aedesius's disciples went in three different directions: Maximus left to teach in Ephesus, Chrysanthius went to Sardis, and Priscus to Athens. The emperor Julian turned to these philosophers to ensure his restoration of the pagan cult: he brought Maximus to his court and he named Chrysanthius high priest of Lydia, while Priscus, who had refused to come with Maximus to join the emperor, preserved the Iamblichean tradition of Neoplatonism in Athens. It was to Priscus that Julian wrote: "I entreat you not to let Theodorus and his followers deafen you too by their assertions that Iamblichus, that truly godlike man, who ranks next to Pythagoras and Plato, was worldly and self-seeking" (letter to Priscus, 358–359, from Gaul). Thus the respective merits of Iamblichus and Theodorus were debated in Athens in the 350s. Priscus's presence in Athens ensured a victory for Iamblichus in the second half of the century.

Neoplatonism was given a powerful impetus in Athens, where a Platonic school could quite naturally claim the legacy of the Academy. Iamblichus's successors ensured the establishment of a new dynasty of philosophers who, more than any other group, could view themselves as Plato's successors: Plutarch, Syrianus, Proclus, and Damascius. We know that, every year, Proclus took it upon himself to go to the Academy to celebrate the memory of his philosophical ancestors, Plato and all his successors.

Under the reigns of the emperors Theodosius (379–395) and Justinian (527–565), two waves of antipagan legislation gradually put in place increasingly repressive measures directed against non-Christians. Centers of cult practices had to be destroyed or transformed into Christian churches, and their rites were banned. Philosophers felt that they were the last custodians of a religious tradition that had been practiced in the Greek Orient for nearly a thousand years.

Athenian Platonists reacted by initiating a return to the sources of their religious spirituality, the *Orphic Rhapsodies* and the *Chaldaean Oracles* (which were viewed at the time as testimony to a fabled antiquity), and also by undertaking a theological rereading not only of the ancient poets Homer and Hesiod but also of Plato, construing the second half of *Parmenides* as a systematic theological treatise that described the hierarchy of classes of gods by means of "hypotheses." For these philosophers, *epopteia* was no longer the result of the Eleusinian initiation, but rather of the reading of Plato's *Parmenides*. From this point on, the entire Neoplatonic school in Athens took up the task of reconciling these theological traditions with one another. To this end, the Athenian masters wrote a work, unfortunately lost, called *The Harmony of Orpheus, Pythagoras and Plato with the Chaldaean Oracles*, which was based on the following "myth": "All Greek theology is the progeny of the mystic tradition of Orpheus; Pythagoras first of all learned from Aglaophamus the initiatory rites providing access to the gods; then Plato received the all-perfect science of the gods from the Pythagorean and Orphic writings" (Proclus, *On the Theology of Plato* I.5.25–26). The Platonic school in Athens went as far as it was possible to go in associating Platonism with Pythagoreanism, a Pythagoreanism that claimed to be the repository of the Orphic mysteries.

We do not know very much about the Athenian philosopher Plutarch, who is viewed as the founder of the Neoplatonic school in Athens. None of his writings has been preserved, and we are aware of his importance only through the respect in which he was held by his successors. He set up his school in a large house, discovered by archaeologists south of the Acropolis, which remained its site to the end. He deserves particular credit for training Syrianus—probably the most prolific mind in the school—as a teacher.

Syrianus offered his students the following program of study. During the first two years, they would read all of Aristotle. They would then study Plato's dialogues in turn, in the order established by Iamblichus; finally, they would be shown the harmony between the Orphic and Chaldaean theologies. This was achieved through detailed commentary on *Timaeus*, for the philosophy of nature, and on *Parmenides*, for the theology.

Traces of this teaching have been preserved in Syrianus's commentary on four books of Aristotle's *Metaphysics* (III, IV, XIII, and XIV), and in his commentary on *Phaedrus*, which is known only via notes made by Hermias, one

of his pupils. Syrianus had time to carry out only part of his program, for he limited himself almost entirely to establishing harmony between Plato, Pythagoras, and the Orphic texts. He did not take the *Chaldaean Oracles* into account to the same degree, and he died before he could undertake a scholarly presentation of the Oracles.

But Syrianus is famous above all for his exegesis of the hypotheses of *Parmenides*. In studying the structure of the hypotheses, he had noticed a perfect correspondence between the negations of the first hypothesis and the affirmations of the second. He concluded that the first hypothesis contained the negative theology of the first god, the One, while the second enumerated, in order, the characteristic properties of each degree in the hierarchy of the gods. He reached fourteen conclusions that matched the fourteen classes of the transcendent and cosmic gods. Proclus, who adopted this remarkable result, always attributed it to Syrianus. Proclus presented his master as the one "who, as our guide in all that is beautiful and good, had received in its purest state the most genuine and pure light of truth in the bosom of his soul. He made us partaker in Plato's philosophy as a whole, he made us his companions in the traditions he had received in secrecy from his predecessors, and he brought us into the group of those who sing the mystic truth of divine realities" (*On the Theology of Plato* I.1.7).

Of all the Neoplatonists, Proclus is certainly the best known, because a large part of his work has been preserved. Syrianus had foreseen this and named him as his successor; Proclus led the school in Athens for more than fifty years. As Marinus relates: "without stint did he give himself up to his love for work, daily teaching five periods, and sometimes more, and writing much, about 700 lines. Nor did this labor hinder him from visiting other philosophers, from giving purely oral evening lectures, from practicing his devotions during the night, for which he denied himself sleep; and further, from worshipping the sun at dawn, noon, and dusk" (*The Life of Proclus* 22). Under Proclus's leadership, the school experienced a period of intense activity.

Considerable portions of Proclus's commentaries on *Alcibiades*, *Timaeus*, *The Republic*, *Cratylus*, and *Parmenides* have been preserved. These texts show with what rigor Proclus practiced scientific commentary. He divided each text into pericopes (excerpts), subjected it to a general explanation by discussing the opinions of his predecessors, and produced a word-for-word exegesis. This procedure had two phases, *theoria* and *lexis*. The school produced commentaries composed in this way on all the canonical Platonic dialogues, and the same method was applied to the end. In fact, the method outlived the Athenian school, as it is found in Simplicius's commentaries on Aristotle, and in medieval Arabic and Latin commentaries.

But Proclus's importance lies essentially in the fact that he achieved the most important synthesis of late Neoplatonism, in a vast work titled *On the Theology of Plato*. This text contains, first of all, the formula for what we

must call "theology as science," a Neoplatonic creation. Indeed, Proclus wrote: "Plato alone, as it appears to me, of all those who are known to us, has attempted to make correct distinctions in the regular progression of all the divine classes, and to describe their mutual differences and the properties common to all these classes and those which are peculiar to each one" (*On the Theology of Plato*, I.4.20). And it is in *Parmenides* that he finds this result. Proclus also wrote: "If it is necessary to have an overview, in a single Platonic dialogue, of the entire series of the gods from first to last, my formulation will perhaps appear paradoxical; it will be self-evident only to those of our own persuasion. We ought to dare, however, since we have begun to use such arguments, to affirm against our opponents: the *Parmenides* is what you need, and you have in your mind the mystic revelation contained in this dialogue" (*On the Theology of Plato* I.7.31). Here is a very schematic representation of this divine hierarchy:

The One, first god
The monads
The intelligible gods
The intelligible-intellective gods
The intellective gods
The hypercosmic gods
The hypercosmic-encosmic gods
The encosmic gods
The universal souls
The intelligible souls: demons, angels, heroes
The partial souls: those of men and beasts
Bodies
Matter

This gigantic construction thus sums up the tripartite scheme inaugurated by Plotinus: the One, Intellect-Intelligible, Soul. But it multiplies the intermediaries while introducing, on the one hand, the monads between the One and the simultaneous multiplicity of the Intellect-Intelligible, and on the other, the reign of the hypercosmic divinities, hypercosmic-encosmics, and encosmics between the Intellect-Intelligible and the Soul. Moreover, it makes very clear how even matter emanates from the One; this produces an optimistic vision of the sensible world and all it contains. Indeed, all reality is thus integrated into this metaphysical continuum that proceeds from the One to matter, and that for this reason construes even the sensible world and matter as participating to some degree in the Good.

Starting with the conclusions of *Parmenides*, then, Proclus confirmed them by turning to parallel texts drawn from the other Platonic dialogues or from other traditions: those of the Theologians, the Orphics, and the *Chaldaean*

Oracles: in six books he offered a reasoned explanation of the whole of Platonic theology. At the same time, he designed, in the geometrical manner, the architecture of the first principles in the short work titled *The Elements of Theology;* in *The Harmony of Orpheus, Pythagoras and Plato with the Chaldaean Oracles,* a treatise whose paternity he attributed in part to Syrianus, he argues that these theologies are in concord. Indeed, the final impetus that Proclus gave Syrianus's theology consisted in confronting it systematically with the *Chaldaean Oracles,* of which he also offered a complete interpretation in an extensive commentary (more than a thousand pages) that has unfortunately been lost.

The work of Proclus can be characterized as the culminating point of Neoplatonism. Damascius, who succeeded him, was the last head of the Athenian school. Damascius came from Alexandria, where another Platonic school defended virtually the same doctrine as that of the Athens school, but in a different style. Hermias, who had studied in Athens with Syrianus, and who included notes on the latter's course on *Phaedrus* in his own *Commentary on the Phaedrus,* had introduced the doctrines of the Athens school to Alexandria several decades earlier.

Ammonius, one of the sons of Hermias and his wife, Aidesia (who was also related to Syrianus), wrote a commentary on Aristotle's *De interpretatione.* His successor as head of the school was a certain Eutocius, none of whose writings has survived. But it was Philoponus, who seems not to have had any official function in the school, who published notes on Ammonius's course, and all the evidence suggests that there was a connection between the publication of his most important work, *Against Proclus on the Eternity of the World,* and the closing of the Athenian school in 529. The last pagan *diadoch* of the Alexandria school was Olympiodorus, three of whose commentaries on Plato—on *Alcibiades, Gorgias,* and *Phaedo*—and two on Aristotle—on *Categories* and *Meteorologica*—have survived. His Christian successors were Elias, David, and Stephen, all of whom commented on Aristotle.

As head of the Athenian school, Damascius preserved the essential elements of the Platonic doctrines as represented by Proclus, although Damascius's works are filled with endless discussions of Proclus's teaching, in most cases marking a return to Iamblichan theses. Taking his cue from Iamblichus, in his own key work, which is a commentary on Plato's *Parmenides,* Damascius demonstrates his originality, especially by establishing a principle prior to the One, the Ineffable, which is totally buried in an abyss of silence. Although derived from the Ineffable, the One remains extremely close to it. But in removing itself from all distinctions, the One projects itself on the near side of the Ineffable in three monadic principles: the One-All, the All-One, and the Unified. In addition, Damascius is the only Neoplatonist to prolong the procession across the negative hypotheses of the *Parmenides;* they consti-

tute for him the structure of the sensible. In all other respects, Damascius remains faithful to the system set forth by Proclus.

The closing of the school in Athens by Justinian in 529 brought to a definitive end this specifically Greek attempt to assert and maintain authentic transcendence both in reality and in human beings. In all antiquity, Platonism alone proved to offer an escape outside the universe, thus offering one of the rare glimmers of hope traversing philosophy.

The idea of transcendence was of course maintained by Christianity, which had institutionally eliminated Neoplatonism, even while appropriating the principal elements of its doctrine. But this transcendence was put within the reach of all and no longer reserved for a small group of thinkers leading a specific way of life in the context of a school. Moreover, transcendence was now no longer based on the use of reason in search of certainty in the application of a method inspired by the one used in mathematics; instead, it was based on recourse to such emotions as love. And above all, it no longer had as its "end" *(telos)* the dissolution of the individual within an absolutely universal Unity; its end lay in individual immortality.

Luc Brisson
Translated by Rita Guerlac and Anne Slack

Bibliography

Texts and Translations

Alcinous. *The Handbook of Platonism.* Trans., introduction, and commentary John Dillon. Oxford: Clarendon Press, 1993.

Atticus. *Fragments.* Ed. and trans. Edouard Des Places. Paris: Les Belles Lettres, 1977.

Damascius. *Traités des premiers principes.* 3 vols. Ed. L. G. Westerink. Trans. Joseph Combès. Paris: Les Belles Lettres, 1986–1991.

Iamblichus. *Iamblichi Chalcidensis in Platonis dialogos commentariorum fragmenta.* Ed. and trans. John Dillon. Leiden: E. J. Brill, 1973.

———. *On the Pythagorean Way of Life.* Ed., trans., and notes John Dillon and Jackson Hershbell. Atlanta, Ga.: Scholars Press, 1991.

———. *Vie de Pythagore.* Ed. and trans. Luc Brisson and A. Ph. Segonds. Paris: Les Belles Lettres, 1996.

Julian. *Letters; Epigrams; Against the Galileans; Fragments.* Trans. Wilmer C. Wright. Loeb Classical Library.

De Laodamos de Thasos à Philippe d'Oponte. Ed. and trans. François Lasserre. La Scuola di Platone 2. Naples: Bibliopolis, 1987.

Marinos of Neapolis. *The Life of Proclus.* In *The Extant Works.* Ed. A. N. Oikonomides. Chicago: Ares, 1977.

Plato. *Complete Works.* Ed. John M. Cooper. Indianapolis: Hackett, 1997.

Der Platonismus in der Antike: Grundlage, System, Entwicklung. Vol. 1: *Die Ge-*

schichtlichen Wurzeln des Platonismus. Ed., trans., and commentary Heinrich Dörrie (posthumous work published under the direction of Annemarie Dörrie). Vol. 2: *Der hellenistische Rahmen des kaiserzeitlischen Platonismus*. Ed., trans., and commentary Heinrich Dörrie (posthumous work published under the direction of Matthias Baltes and Annemarie Dörrie). Vol. 3: *Der Platonismus im 2. und 3. Jahrhundert nach Christus*. Ed., trans., and commentary Matthias Baltes. Vols. 4 and 5: *Die philosophische Lehre des Platonismus*. 2 vols. Ed., trans., and commentary Matthias Baltes. Stuttgart and Bad Cannstatt: Frommann-Holzboog, 1987–1998.

Plotinus. Trans. A. H. Armstrong. 7 vols. Loeb Classical Library.

Porphyry. *Life of Plotinus*. In *Plotinus*, vol. 1. Trans. A. H. Armstrong. Loeb Classical Library.

————. *La vie de Plotin*. Vol. 1: *Travaux préliminaires et index complet*. Luc Brisson, Marie-Odile Goulet-Cazé, and Denis O'Brien et al. Vol. 2: *Etudes d'introduction, texte grec et traduction française, commentaire, notes complémentaires, bibliographie*. Luc Brisson et al. Paris: Vrin, 1982, 1992.

Proclus. *Commentaire sur le Timée*. Trans. and notes A. J. Festugière. 5 vols. Paris: Vrin/CNRS, 1966–1968.

————. *Commentary on Plato's Parmenides*. Trans. G. R. Morrow and J. Dillon; introduction and notes J. Dillon. Princeton: Princeton University Press, 1987.

————. *Elements of Theology*. Rev. text, trans., introduction, and commentary E. R. Dodds. Oxford: Clarendon Press, 1933; 2nd ed., 1963.

————. *In Timaeum*. Ed. E. Diehl. Leipzig: Teubner, 1903–1906; repr. Amsterdam: Hakkert, 1965.

————. *Proclus's Commentary on the Timaeus of Plato*. Trans. Thomas Taylor. London, 1820; repr. Frome, Somerset: Prometheus Trust, 1998.

————. *The Six Books of Proclus . . . on the Theology of Plato*. Trans. Thomas Taylor. London, 1816.

————. *Théologie platonicienne*. 6 vols. Ed. and trans. H. D. Saffrey and L. G. Westerink. Paris: Les Belles Lettres, 1968–1997.

Prolégomènes à la philosophie de Platon. Ed. L. D. Westerink. Trans. J. Trouillard with A. Ph. Segonds. Paris: Les Belles Lettres, 1990.

Speusippus. *Frammenti*. Ed. and trans. Margherita Isnardi Parente. La Scuola di Platone 1. Naples: Bibliopolis, 1980.

Speusippus of Athens: A Critical Study with a Collection of the Related Texts and Commentaries. Ed. Leonardo Tarán. Leiden: E. J. Brill, 1981.

Xenocrates and Hermodoros. *Frammenti*. Ed. and trans. Margherita Isnardi Parente. La Scuola di Platone 3. Naples: Bibliopolis, 1982.

Studies

Dillon, John. *The Middle Platonists*. Ithaca, N.Y.: Cornell University Press, 1977; rev. ed., 1996.

Görler, Waldemar. "Älterer Pyrrhonismus, Jungere Akademie, Antiochus aus Askalon." In *Die Philosophie der Antike*, vol. 4: *Die hellenistische Philosophie*. Basel: Schwabe, 1994. Pp. 717–1168.

Krämer, Hans-Joachim. "Altere Akademie." In *Die Philosophie der Antike*, vol. 3: *Die hellenistische Philosophie*. Basel: Schwabe, 1983. Pp. 1–174.

Lévy, Carlos. *Cicero Academicus: Recherches sur les Académiques et sur la philosophie cicéronienne*. Rome: Collection de l'Ecole française de Rome, no. 162. 1992.

O'Meara, Dominic. *Plotinus: An Introduction to the Enneads*. Oxford: Clarendon Press, 1993.

Rosán, L. J. *The Philosophy of Proclus: The Final Phase of Ancient Thought*. New York: Cosmos, 1949.

Saffrey, Henri Dominic. *Recherches sur le Néoplatonisme après Plotin*. Paris: Vrin, 1990.

Siorvanes, Lucas. *Proclus: Neo-Platonic Philosophy and Science*. New Haven: Yale University Press, 1996.

Smith, Andrew. *Porphyry's Place in the Neoplatonic Tradition: A Study in Post-Plotinian Neoplatonism*. The Hague: Nijhoff, 1974.

Related Articles

The Philosopher; Mathematics; Plotinus; Hellenism and Judaism; The Question of Being; Plutarch; Hellenism and Christianity

PYTHAGOREANISM

PYTHAGORAS IS THE MOST WIDELY KNOWN of the Presocratic philosophers, yet modern scholars often view Pythagoras and Pythagoreanism with considerable suspicion. Instead, the history of Presocratic philosophy is told in terms of the great figure of Parmenides, his rejection of earlier accounts of reality, and the response to his challenge by figures such as Anaxagoras and Democritus. This ambivalent attitude toward Pythagoras is mirrored in the ancient evidence as well. Plato and Aristotle, writing one hundred to one hundred fifty years after his death, hardly mention Pythagoras himself. Aristotle is famous for reviewing the work of his predecessors in each field of philosophy before presenting his own views. Yet, although he discusses at some length the Pythagoreans of the 5th century, who were active fifty years after Pythagoras's death, he never in his extant works mentions Pythagoras himself as an important figure in any branch of philosophy. Aristotle did write a treatise on the Pythagoreans, surviving only in fragmentary form, in which he deals directly with Pythagoras himself, but only as a wonder-working religious teacher. Plato likewise shows influence from 5th- and 4th-century Pythagoreanism but mentions Pythagoras himself only once, as a famous teacher who left a way of life for his followers. However, if we jump six hundred years to the Neoplatonist Iamblichus writing in the 2nd century C.E., we find Pythagoras presented as a semidivine figure who brought all true philosophy from the gods to men and from whom Plato and Aristotle stole all their best ideas. So by 300 C.E. Pythagoras is viewed in some circles as the philosopher par excellence, while in the 4th century B.C.E. Plato and Aristotle could discuss the important philosophical issues of the day with no reference to Pythagoras.

Recent scholarship (most notably the work of Walter Burkert) has made enormous progress in unraveling the complex tradition about Pythagoras and Pythagoreanism, but inevitably much remains uncertain and controversial. Before giving a detailed assessment of Pythagoras and specific Pythagoreans, it is necessary to give a brief overview of the whole Pythagorean tradition, to identify the unique problems in arriving at an accurate portrayal of Pythagoras and his philosophy. Pythagoras spent his early years on the island of Samos off the coast of Asia Minor; probably around the age of forty (ca. 530 B.C.E.), he emigrated to Croton in southern Italy, and he spent the rest of his life there, dying around 490 in the town of Metapontum. One of the crucial things to remember about him is that he wrote nothing. It is true that by the

2nd and 3rd centuries c.e. books were attributed to him, and the seventy-one lines of the *Golden Verses* were confidently accepted as his on into the Renaissance, but these forgeries were part of the phenomenal growth of the Pythagoras legend. The first book written in the Pythagorean tradition was by Philolaus of Croton (ca. 470–390 B.C.E.). Fragments of this book survive, and it seems to have been the primary basis for Aristotle's reports on the Pythagoreans. The other important name in early Pythagoreanism was Archytas (fl. 400–350 B.C.E.), who was a contemporary of Plato and who is connected to serious mathematical work, particularly in relation to music theory.

Aristotle is careful to distinguish the Pythagoreans from Pythagoras himself and refers to them as the "so-called Pythagoreans," probably to show that this is the name commonly given them but to express doubts about the exact connection between their thought and Pythagoras himself. However, among the immediate successors of Plato in his school the Academy, Speusippus and Xenocrates, an important new attitude toward Pythagoras arises. Many of Plato's most mature ideas, and particularly his positing of the One and the indefinite dyad as the basic principles of reality, come to be regarded as simply developments of ideas that Pythagoras had originated. It is not completely clear why Plato's followers should want to see his philosophy as simply a development of Pythagoras's thought, but it seems to be part of a mind set that sees philosophy as a divine revelation given to a chosen man (Pythagoras). Such a view, of course, gives the authority of divine revelation to the philosophy of Plato insofar as it unfolds ideas of Pythagoras.

This attitude toward Pythagoras comes to dominate the entire later tradition, and Aristotle's distinctions both between Pythagoras and later Pythagoreans and between the Pythagoreans and Plato are ignored. One important result of this dominant attitude toward Pythagoras is that by the 2nd century c.e. a very large collection of writings had been forged in the name of Pythagoras and early Pythagoreans. These pseudepigrapha are full of Platonic and Aristotelian ideas and terms and are clearly meant to provide the "early" texts from which Aristotle and Plato supposedly derived their whole philosophy. A few short treatises survive intact; the most famous is the purported original of Plato's dialogue *Timaeus,* supposedly written by Timaeus of Locrus. It is largely a précis of Plato's *Timaeus,* and like most of the pseudepigrapha it adheres very closely to the doctrine of its model while possessing little of its literary merits. Plato's own dialogue *Timaeus,* with its powerful description of the structuring of the cosmos by a divine craftsman, was more frequently quoted but regarded as simply a report of Pythagorean doctrine. Many more fragments from spurious Pythagorean works survive than fragments that are likely to be from genuine works by early Pythagoreans.

It is not until the 3rd century c.e. that we have the appearance of the first detailed accounts of the life of Pythagoras and the Pythagorean way of life that have survived intact. These lives by Diogenes Laertius (fl. 200–250), Por-

phyry (232–ca. 305), and Iamblichus (ca. 250–325) are the sources that were used in the Renaissance and by many later scholars to provide a picture of Pythagoras and his accomplishments. They drew heavily on sources from the 4th century B.C.E. that have not survived. In particular they drew on Aristotle's two-volume work on Pythagoreanism and on works on Pythagoras by Aristotle's pupils Aristoxenus and Dicaearchus, as well as works by the Platonist Heraclides and the historian of southern Italy, Timaeus. Since these lives are rather uncritical compilations of earlier sources, they must be used with utmost caution. However, it is their portrait of Pythagoras as a philosopher of almost divine status that dominates the late antique world and carries over even into many modern interpretations.

The present overview of the Pythagorean tradition is necessarily drastically simplified and selective. However, the crucial lesson to be learned is that from the time of Plato's successors in the Academy onward (ca. 350 B.C.E.), the Pythagorean tradition is dominated by a school of thought that assigns back to the divine Pythagoras all that is true in later philosophy. If we want to get behind that view to gain an appreciation of the actual significance of Pythagoras's thought in the late 6th century B.C.E., we must begin by looking only at the early evidence for Pythagoras. Initially, then, we must look only at the evidence of authors up to and including Plato and Aristotle, but not their pupils.

By modern standards there is not much evidence from this early period, a collection of twenty or so brief references in works of early philosophers, poets, and historians, apart from the fragments of Aristotle's book on the Pythagoreans, but this is in fact much more evidence than we have for many other early thinkers, and to some extent it is a reflection of Pythagoras's fame. What emerges most clearly from this evidence is that Pythagoras was famous for his knowledge of the soul and its fate after death, and more specifically for his belief in metempsychosis, the doctrine that our soul is reborn in another human or animal form after our death. Even these early reports about Pythagoras often have a polemical tone, either attacking some aspect of his doctrine or portraying him as possessing superhuman wisdom. Thus his contemporary Xenophanes (ca. 570–480) is clearly having fun at Pythagoras's expense when he reports the story that Pythagoras pitied a puppy that was being beaten by a man and said to the man, "Stop, don't keep beating it, for it is the soul of a friend of mine, I recognize his voice" (frg. 7). On the other hand, Ion of Chios (b. ca. 490 B.C.E.) is clearly serious in his praise of Pythagoras for his knowledge of the fate of the soul after death (frg. 4).

Heraclitus attacks Pythagoras, among others, for being a polymath without having attained any real understanding (frg. 40), calls him "the chief of swindlers" (frg. 81), and says that he practiced inquiry beyond all other men, making a wisdom of his own by picking things out of the writings of others, a wisdom that was in fact "a polymathy and evil trickery" (frg. 129). Some

scholars have thought that since Heraclitus links Pythagoras with Xenophanes and Hecataeus as polymaths (frg. 40), Heraclitus must have regarded Pythagoras as being engaged in the same sort of rational inquiry about the world that they pursued and that had arisen around the city of Miletus in Asia Minor, close to Pythagoras's home of Samos, in the 6th century. However, the fragment of Heraclitus in fact joins him more closely to Hesiod the poet, who was famous for his mythical account of the origin of the gods in *Theogony*. Nevertheless, the overall tone of Heraclitus's reports is clear. He regards Pythagoras as a charlatan of some sort. Empedocles (ca. 493–433), in a fragment that most agree refers to Pythagoras (frg. 129), adopts the exact opposite tone toward Pythagoras and begins by praising him in general terms as a man who knew "extraordinary things" and possessed "the greatest wealth of wisdom." He then goes on to praise him specifically for "wise deeds" and says that "whenever he reached out with all his intellect he easily beheld all the things that are in ten and even twenty generations of men." It is not necessary, but it is tempting, to see this last phrase as a reference to the idea of rebirth, and the mention of "wise deeds" calls to mind the image of a wonder-worker of some sort who here is venerated but who might well also elicit Heraclitus's description of him as a charlatan.

Other early evidence about Pythagoras shows a close connection to religious ritual. His connection with Orphism in Ion of Chios and Herodotus underlines his close connection to ritual (initiations) and his expertise on the soul and the afterlife. Plato's contemporary Isocrates says (*Busiris* 28) that Pythagoras journeyed to Egypt and makes the vague point that "he first brought other philosophy to the Greeks" before going on to say that he was particularly zealous about the matters of sacrifice and rites of the temple.

Other early evidence suggests that in connection with his interest in the soul and its afterlife and religious ritual Pythagoras showed a broader interest in how we should live our lives. Thus the atomist Democritus (b. 460) is reported as having been very influenced by Pythagorean ideas and as perhaps having studied with Philolaus. However, it seems clear that this influence was on his ethical views, since we are told that he wrote a book on Pythagoras and that this book was classified with Democritus's ethical works. Isocrates in the passage mentioned above said that Pythagoras's reputation was so great that young men wanted to be his pupils and that their parents were happier to have them associate with him than to attend to family affairs. Isocrates comments that even in his day, Pythagoreans were more marveled at for their silence than great orators for their speech. This statement suggests that the later tradition of a rule of silence among Pythagoras's pupils has some foundation. The 4th-century rhetorician Alcidimas gives what is probably an apocryphal report, but which nonetheless represents early 4th-century attitudes, that Empedocles studied with both Pythagoras and Anaxagoras, and that while he got knowledge of nature from Anaxagoras, he got the dignity of

his bearing from Pythagoras. Once again it is striking how consistently Pythagoras is associated with the manner in which we live our lives rather than with theoretical knowledge.

The most famous evidence for Pythagoras as an influential teacher and founder of a way of life is Plato's only reference to him, which is found in *The Republic.* Pythagoras is not included in the list of those who have contributed to the good government of a city, as the lawgivers Lycurgus and Solon did, nor among the good generals, nor among the men wise in practical affairs and the producers of ingenious inventions, such as Thales. Instead Plato places Pythagoras's activity in the private sphere and presents him as the model of the sort of figure who was particularly loved as a teacher and whose followers even now are famous for their Pythagorean way of life (600a9–b5). Thus, the early evidence consistently portrays Pythagoras as a figure with an extremely loyal following who can tell you how to live your present life to best satisfy the gods and to ensure the best fate for your soul in the next life. At the same time, outsiders such as Heraclitus and Xenophanes could well view his pretensions to knowledge about ritual and the fate of the soul, as well as the glorification of him by his followers, as foolishness or even quackery.

Particularly problematic for nonbelievers would have been the "wise deeds" to which Empedocles refers and which may well be the miraculous actions that Aristotle assigns to Pythagoras. Aristotle reports that Pythagoras was supposed to have appeared in both Croton and Metapontum at the same hour on the same day; that when he crossed a river it gave him the greeting, "Hail, Pythagoras"; that he bit and killed a poisonous snake; and that he had a golden thigh. This last report probably picks him out as the favorite of the god and is tied to initiation rites in which a part of the body is dedicated to the divinity. Indeed, Aristotle reports that the people of Croton called him the Hyperborean Apollo. The other reports stress his special control over the animal and natural world. Often these miraculous stories are rejected as useless in understanding the historical figure of Pythagoras, but this attitude is mistaken because the stories show how he was conceived by his early followers and are thus crucial in understanding the type of figure he was.

The biggest lacuna in the picture of Pythagoras presented in the early evidence is the precise nature of the way of life he handed on to his followers. Once again some details can be filled in from Aristotle and other later 4th-century witnesses, but these sources contradict each other in important ways; accordingly, the following description of the Pythagorean life is very problematic. Particularly important are the many Pythagorean maxims preserved by Aristotle. Some of these are likely to go back to Pythagoras himself because they fit well with the picture of Pythagoras derived from the earliest evidence. These maxims are called *acusmata* (things heard) or *symbola* (passwords, or things to be interpreted) in the later tradition. Iamblicus gives a

very large collection of them in his work *On the Pythagorean Life* (82–86), which is surely based primarily on Aristotle.

In Iamblichus's collection the maxims are broken up into three classes, corresponding to the three questions: (1) What is it? (2) What is best? (3) What must be done? Of the first sort are the maxims reported by Aristotle: "The ring of bronze when it is struck is the voice of a daimon trapped in it" or "The planets are the hounds of Persephone." Of the second sort Iamblichus lists, "What is wisest? Number"; "What is the most just? To sacrifice"; "What is the loveliest? Harmony." But the biggest number of maxims are of the third sort, which often have clear ties to rules of religious ritual. Aristotle is given as the authority for maxims against eating certain fish (red mullet and black tail) and certain parts of animals (heart and womb). Iamblichus gives a long list, including the injunctions that one must beget children, one must put the right shoe on first, one must not sacrifice a white cock, one must not use public baths. As early as 400 B.C.E. a tradition sprung up according to which these maxims were not to be taken literally but interpreted to find a deeper meaning. Thus the prohibition not to eat the heart is interpreted as meaning that one should not grieve. However, this is likely to be the attempt of later generations to explain away seemingly bizarre rituals rather than the original import of the maxims. Their connection with ritual and magical practices elsewhere in Greece shows that they were probably meant to be taken quite literally and also that many of them were hardly original to Pythagoras but were adopted by him.

One of the most famous of the maxims is the one that prohibits the eating of beans. All the early evidence supports the authenticity of this maxim except Aristotle's student Aristoxenus, who reports in his book on Pythagoras that "Pythagoras especially valued the bean among vegetables saying that it was laxative and softening. Wherefore he especially made use of it." This is probably an attempt on Aristoxenus's part to eliminate the stranger aspects from early Pythagorean doctrine, and it is likely that we should follow Aristotle's report that the eating of beans was prohibited. Aristotle gives several obscure explanations for the prohibition: that beans were like the genitals, or the gates of Hades, or the universe, or connected to oligarchy. It is also plausible that the problems beans cause for digestion, or indeed the fact that many people are allergic to a certain amino acid that is in this type of bean, was behind the prohibition.

Slightly more complicated is the issue of vegetarianism. There would seem to be a natural connection between the belief in metempsychosis and vegetarianism; the philosopher Empedocles writing in the generation after Pythagoras made the connection clear in graphically condemning the eating of all animal flesh as cannibalism. Moreover, Eudoxus of Cnidus, a famous mathematician and member of the Academy in Plato's day, reports that Py-

thagoras not only did not eat any meat but also even avoided the company of butchers and hunters. Aristoxenus, however, takes the iconoclastic view again and asserts that although Pythagoras avoided plow oxen and rams, he was particularly fond of young kids, suckling pigs, and cockerels. Moreover, in this case there is considerable support for Aristoxenus's view that Pythagoras was not a strict vegetarian. Some *acusmata* reported by Aristotle only ban eating specific parts of animals. Moreover, there is the maxim mentioned above that says that the most just thing is to sacrifice, and Iamblichus reports among the *acusmata* one to the effect that souls do not enter into sacrificial animals. Some scholars have argued that to reject animal sacrifice totally would be such a complete overturning of traditional ways as to be unthinkable, while others have tried to argue that sacrifice was acceptable but that the Pythagoreans limited themselves to a simple sacramental tasting of the victim. The fact that Pythagoreans were recognized as so distinctive in their way of life suggests that a prohibition on animal sacrifice is not so unthinkable and that, with Empedocles as the model, we should believe that Pythagoras was a strict vegetarian. This issue is an excellent example of the complexity of determining the actual nature of the Pythagorean way of life and shows the already contradictory nature of the evidence even in the 4th century B.C.E.

One way of trying to reconcile the contradictions in the testimony about vegetarianism both in the ancient world and among modern scholars has been to suppose that there were different grades among the followers of Pythagoras, as the later tradition suggests, and to argue that vegetarianism was practiced to different degrees by members of different grades. This explanation raises directly the broader question of whether Pythagorean societies in a strict sense ever existed at all. Some have suggested that the notion of a community separated from regular society and governed by a strict rule along the lines of a monastery would be an anachronism in the 6th century B.C.E., and that such an idea was introduced into the tradition at a later point and perhaps even by Iamblichus. However, some of our early evidence, the reports of Plato and Isocrates, make it very clear that Pythagoras attracted a loyal following and showed them a way of life that made them easily distinguishable from ordinary citizens even as late as the 4th century. How strict the way of life was and how the community was related to the rest of society may remain open questions, but this evidence surely justifies our talking about Pythagorean communities as groups of people who lived a way of life that clearly set them apart from other people.

A number of reports from the 4th century B.C.E. indicate that Pythagoras and his followers had significant impact on the politics of the Greek city-states in southern Italy. It is difficult to derive any coherent Pythagorean political views out of these reports, which contradict one another on a number of points. Since Plato seems to clearly distinguish Pythagoras from lawgivers and other public figures, it seems most likely that there were not many spe-

cific Pythagorean political policies. Rather it was probably the case that many of the talented and prominent members of the communities became followers of the Pythagorean way of life while at the same time participating in the government of the city-state. Of course the Pythagorean societies may have looked like political organs to their opponents, and we know that there were two major attacks on them. One seems to have occurred in the lifetime of Pythagoras himself and to have led to the deaths of many of his followers in a fire set in the house where they were meeting in Croton, and to the flight of Pythagoras himself to Metapontum. Another attack on the societies seems to have occurred in the mid-5th century and to have led once again to many deaths and to the apparent dispersal of many of the communities.

A common feature of an exclusive society is some sort of secrecy associated with initiation and grades of membership. Isocrates' report lets us know that the Pythagoreans were famous for their silence, but it is unclear whether this refers simply to their self-restraint in not speaking too much, or to a sort of novitiate in which new members were not allowed to speak for the first five years, as mentioned already by the historian Timaeus in the 4th century. It is also possible that it refers to some sort of specifically secret doctrine. Both Aristotle and Aristoxenus give evidence that at least some doctrines were not for all ears. Aristotle reports that among their very secret doctrines was the division of rational animals into three groups, men, gods, and beings like Pythagoras. Aristoxenus says that the Pythagoreans used to say that not all of Pythagoras's doctrines were for all men to hear, which suggests both secret doctrine and perhaps grades of initiates. All the same, neither Aristotle nor Plato hints that the Pythagorean philosophy of the 5th and 4th centuries was in any way secret. The most likely scenario is that the Pythagoreans, like most exclusive societies, did have secrets such as Aristotle and Aristoxenus suggest. However, these were limited to a certain group of maxims, without putting any restriction on the publication of philosophical ideas such as we find in the book of Philolaus, or on mathematical proofs such as those that appear in Archytas. It is true that Hippasus, a Pythagorean active in the generation after Pythagoras, is supposed to have been killed for the impious act of publishing a construction of a dodecahedron. However, in terms of the history of mathematics it is unlikely that Hippasus gave a strict construction of the dodecahedron at this date; the story may instead relate to the dodecahedron as a cult object.

Hippasus is also connected to the problem of the existence of different sects of Pythagoreans. A report in Iamblichus that seems to go back to Aristotle suggests that in the 5th century there were two groups referred to as the *acusmatici* and the *mathematici*. The *acusmatici* were clearly connected with the *acusmata* and were said to be recognized as genuine Pythagoreans by the *mathematici*. However, the *acusmatici* argued that the *mathematici* were not true Pythagoreans but in fact stemmed from Hippasus rather than Pythago-

ras. The *mathematici* in turn argued that Pythagoras himself had presented his views to some people in simple commandments, while to others who had time for more study (young men), he had given the explanations. Hippasus, as they presented him, was publishing views that were originally Pythagoras's own, only for his own aggrandizement. Thus it is clear that by Aristotle's time, and probably earlier, there was already debate about what ideas in fact went back to Pythagoras himself, with the *mathematici* seeming to adopt the view found among the successors of Plato, that all ideas really go back to the master.

At this point we must confront the most controversial of all issues regarding Pythagoras: Was he a natural philosopher and mathematician as well as the founder of a way of life and expert on the gods, ritual, and the afterlife? After all, he is most famous among the educated public for his connection to the so-called Pythagorean theorem (see below). However, it should be clear from the evidence given above that, up to and including Plato and Aristotle, there is no direct evidence that shows him to be either a mathematician or a natural philosopher. The example of Empedocles shows that the roles of religious wonder-worker and natural philosopher can well be combined in 5th-century Greece, but were they so combined in the figure of Pythagoras? Pythagoras grew up on Samos, which was the site of great technological achievements involving the application of mathematics (most notably the tunnel of Eupalinus, which went under a mountain and was dug from both sides, missing only slightly in the middle). Samos was an easy journey from the city of Miletus, on the coast of Asia Minor, which was home to a series of early natural philosophers, such as Anaximander and Anaximenes. Accordingly some scholars argue that it is impossible to imagine that Pythagoras was not aware of such work or that he could have become famous in such a milieu if he were simply a wonder-worker. However, this argument fails spectacularly since, however probable it may be that Pythagoras knew of the natural philosophy that grew up at Miletus, this argument says nothing about whether or not he was interested in that sort of inquiry himself. Surely an expert on the fate of the soul after death might achieve as much or more fame as someone who speculates about whether water or air is the original state of the cosmos.

The strongest reason for believing that Pythagoras had special interest in mathematics and the structure of the natural world is that Aristotle's evidence and Philolaus's book make clear that in the 5th century people called Pythagoreans gave an account of the natural world that showed it to be structured according to pleasing mathematical relationships. Furthermore, Archtyas, the contemporary of Plato, who is also identified as a Pythagorean, was a distinguished mathematician. We must remember that Philolaus and Archytas may have been Pythagoreans only insofar as they followed a Pythagorean way of life, and that their views on the natural world and mathe-

matics may have been primarily influenced by non-Pythagorean writers such as Anaxagoras, or Hippocrates of Chios. However, it is legitimate to ask if the seeds of this interest in mathematics and the mathematical structure of the world were planted by Pythagoras himself.

The connection between Pythagoras and proposition 1.47 of Euclid's *Elements* (ca. 300 B.C.E.), popularly known as the Pythagorean theorem, is based on the commentary on Euclid written by Proclus in the 5th century C.E. It is reported that Pythagoras, on making a geometric discovery of some sort, sacrificed an ox. This tradition seems to rest on an epigram by an obscure Apollodorus: "When Pythagoras found the famous figure, for which he carried out the noble ox-sacrifice." This Apollodorus might date back to the 4th century, which would give the story considerably more authority, but this dating is far from certain. The story was actually as famous in the ancient tradition for the apparent contradiction with vegetarianism represented by the ox sacrifice as it was for its connection to a geometrical theorem. However, even if we accept the story as genuine 4th-century tradition, there are serious problems. First, it is clear from the history of Greek mathematics that it is unlikely that Pythagoras could have proven the theorem. A strict proof would have required some sort of structure of theorems and definitions, and the first hint of such a structure that we have is connected to Hippocrates of Chios in the later 5th century. However, it is known that the Pythagorean theorem had been part of Babylonian arithmetical technique for centuries, although the Babylonians had given no general proof of it. One might say that Pythagoras was the first Greek to discover the truth of the theorem or the first Greek to bring the knowledge from Babylon to the Greeks, but the truth of the theorem is likely to have come to Greece through several sources. Indeed the reports about Pythagoras do not stress that he was the one who discovered the theorem, and it is tempting to take the reports to emphasize the value he put on knowledge of the theorem. He was so impressed when he found out that the sides of the right triangle were related according to this precise mathematical rule that he sacrificed an ox, something that an ordinary Greek might do to celebrate a more material success, such as a safe voyage home.

Another set of late stories associated Pythagoras with the discovery that the basic musical concords of the octave, fourth, and fifth could all be expressed in terms of whole-number ratios of string lengths ($1 : 2$, $3 : 4$, and $2 : 3$, respectively). Supposedly he heard the musical concords in the sounds made by a blacksmith's hammers and discovered that hammers whose weights were in the ratios given above produced the musical concords when struck one after the other. He is also said to have hung weights equal to the hammers by strings so that the strings also produced the concords. However, none of these observations or experiments correspond to physical reality. The earliest full versions of the stories come from Nicomachus in the 2nd century C.E., but in the 4th century B.C.E. Xenocrates had already reported that "Py-

thagoras discovered that the musical intervals did not arise without number"
(frg. 9). At the same time, there is a report that ascribes an experiment to
Hippasus that does in fact work and thus may well be true. It is important to
note that another report associates Lasus of Hermione with such an experiment. Lasus is in fact a contemporary of Pythagoras, although he is not a Pythagorean. In conclusion, it seems best to say that Pythagoras himself did not
discover the whole-number ratios that underlie the musical concords, but that
the knowledge may well have been available in his day and that Hippasus
may have demonstrated it with a valid experiment in the next generation. As
in the case of the Pythagorean theorem, it may well be that what was important was the value Pythagoras attached to this information when he learned
of it from others.

What then can we conclude about Pythagoras's connection to mathematics? The key may be found in the maxims attested for the early Pythagoreans.
One says that the wisest thing is number, and yet another reports that the oracle of Delphi is "the tetractys which is the harmony in which the Sirens
sing." In the later tradition the "tetractys," the tetrad consisting of the numbers one through four whose sum equals the "perfect" number ten, was central to Pythagoreanism but clearly had become contaminated with ideas derived from Platonism. The Pythagoreans were supposed to have sworn oaths
by Pythagoras as "the one who handed on to our generation the tetractys,
which has the source and root of everflowing nature." It is doubtful that the
oath in this form can go back to the time of Pythagoras, but the tetractys itself as mentioned in the *acusmata* might. The connection of the tetractys to
the Sirens, who were famed for their singing, suggests a connection to music,
and it becomes just possible that the tetractys was in part venerated because
its four numbers were all involved in the whole-number ratios that govern
the musical concords. If we connect the Sirens in turn with the famous doctrine of the harmony of the spheres, which says that the heavenly bodies produce musical concords as they move (as Plato does in *The Republic*), then Pythagoras starts to emerge as someone impressed with the power of number—
particularly as embodied in the first four numbers, which seem to be the basis
of the musical concords, which in turn seem to structure the cosmos. The doctrine of the harmony of the spheres is discussed by Aristotle in *De caelo* but
once again is ascribed only to Pythagoreans and not to Pythagoras himself; it
remains quite possible that it too belongs to 5th-century Pythagoreanism and
not to Pythagoras. It was never worked out in any mathematical detail by the
early Pythagoreans but was, rather, a very general conception.

It should be clear that the evidence does not support the conclusion that
Pythagoras was any sort of serious mathematician or that he was a natural
philosopher or scientist. Instead he is to be seen as a charismatic teacher who
attracted a large group of followers for whom he prescribed a way of life that
included instruction about the future life of the soul, the gods, ritual, and a

bewildering variety of rules that applied to many aspects of daily life, including what foods to eat and how to dress. Some of this instruction encouraged certain moral virtues (such as silence) and probably included the memory training and emphasis on friendship attested in the later tradition. It may be that it also instilled a certain attitude toward the cosmos and promoted reverence for the concept of number and particularly for certain significant numbers. The followers of Pythagoras stood out in the communities of which they were a part, attracting both praise and ridicule as well as having some influence on the politics of southern Italy.

The real significance of Pythagoras, as Walter Burkert points out, is that he was the first person to establish a set of rules that apply not just to the special moments of life that are marked by religious ritual but that give direction as to how each day of our life ought to be lived, as well as how our life in this world relates to the life in the next. It is in this sense that he is a great moral teacher and a true precursor of Socrates and Christ, however bizarre to modern sensibility some of the teachings of the *acusmata* may seem to be. It is with the so-called Pythagoreans of the 5th century B.C.E., and in particular with Philolaus of Croton, that we see the important contributions of Pythagoreanism to natural philosophy.

We know virtually nothing about Philolaus's life (ca. 470–390) except that he came from Croton (or perhaps Tarentum) in southern Italy and visited Thebes in mainland Greece sometime before 399. Nonetheless he is the central figure in early Pythagoreanism, since his book was the first to be written by a Pythagorean. The book was still available in the late 4th century B.C.E. to Aristotle's pupil Meno, who reports Philolaus's medical views in his history of medicine. The whole book has not been handed down to us, although more than twenty fragments and a number of secondhand reports (testimonia) have survived. A consensus has emerged that, although more than half of the fragments that survive in his name are from spurious works, a central core of fragments from his genuine book survive (1–7, 13, 17). These fragments show that, although Philolaus's book was the primary source for Aristotle's account of Pythagoreanism, Aristotle recast Pythagoreanism in important ways to fit his own purposes, and that Aristotle's evidence thus must be used with caution. In addition it becomes clear that Philolaus's book was a significant influence on Plato's *Philebus*.

The book appears to have followed a typical Presocratic pattern in that it presents an account of the natural world, beginning with a cosmogony, and goes on to present astronomical, psychological, and medical theories. It is striking that in the fragments there is no discussion of morality or how to live one's life, although Philolaus is mentioned in Plato's *Phaedo* as arguing that suicide is not permissible. Philolaus explains the cosmos in terms of two basic types of things, limiters and unlimiteds. Unlimiteds include the elements, such as water and air, that had been used by earlier Presocratics to ex-

plain the natural world, but Philolaus does not focus on any one specific element or group of elements of this sort. Instead he argues simply that a supply of such unlimiteds (continua that are in themselves without any limit, including water, air, earth, and also things like void and time) must be presupposed in order to explain the world that we see. But Philolaus's most noteworthy innovation is his claim that earlier thinkers had been mistaken to think that the world could be adequately explained in terms of such unlimiteds alone. He argues that limiters, things that set limits in a continuum—e.g., shapes and other structural principles—must also be regarded as basic principles. Objects that we observe in the world, such as a tree, are manifestly combinations of continua that are unlimited in their own nature (the wood) and structural principles (the shape and structure of the tree). Thus individual objects in the world and the cosmos as a whole are combinations of limiters and unlimiteds.

However, limiters and unlimiteds alone are still not sufficient to explain the world. Limiters and unlimiteds are not combined in a chance fashion but are instead held together by a *harmonia,* a fitting together in accordance with pleasing mathematical relationships. The first sentence of Philolaus's book sets out his basic view of the world: "Nature in the cosmos was fitted together both out of limiters and unlimiteds, both the cosmos as a whole and everything in it" (frg. 1). Philolaus gives as the model of this fitting together a musical scale. The unlimited continuum of sound is limited by certain notes picked out in that continuum. However, these notes are placed not at random intervals but in accord with the whole-number mathematical ratios that govern the basic intervals of the diatonic scale. Thus, to really understand the world or anything in it, we must not only observe the limiters and unlimiteds that make it up but also the number in accordance with which those limiters are fitted together. Writes Philolaus, "And indeed all things that are known have number. For it is not possible that anything whatsoever be understood or known without this" (frg. 4). Of course he is putting forward a grand scheme here and was unable to specify many of the numbers that governed the structure of individual things. It is to his credit that there is little evidence that he tried to postulate an arbitrary set of numbers that governed all things.

Aristotle recasts this emphasis on number as giving us knowledge of things into the claim that the Pythagoreans thought that things were made up of numbers in some way, but Philolaus says nothing of the sort. In trying to distinguish the Pythagoreans from Plato, who thought that numbers had existence separate from things, Aristotle supposed that the Pythagoreans must have identified numbers with things. However, this anachronistically supposes that the Pythagoreans had asked the questions, what sort of existence do numbers have, and how are they related to things? These questions probably first directly arose in the 4th century in Plato's Academy. Philolaus was content to argue that numbers give us knowledge of things in the world,

without focusing on the ontological status of numbers. What is crucial is the insight that, in principle, both the cosmos as a whole and also everything in it are knowable with the determinacy of perspicuous numerical relationships.

The cosmos began with a fire (an unlimited) in the center of a sphere (a limiter). This central fire then breathed in another group of unlimiteds (time, void, breath), which were fitted together with limiters to produce Philolaus's famous astronomical system. With this theory, for the first time the Earth is made a planet, and Copernicus refers to Philolaus as one of his precursors. However, rather than orbiting around the Sun, the Earth orbits around the central fire along with the Sun, the Moon, the five planets, the fixed stars, and a counter-Earth that was evidently introduced to bring the number of orbiting bodies up to the perfect number ten. The system thus combines a reverence for principles of order that fly in the face of observation with a desire to accommodate the basic observable facts. Night and day are explained by the Earth's moving around the central fire in one twenty-four-hour period, while the Sun takes a year, thus turning our side of the Earth away from the Sun for a portion of the twenty-four-hour period. The Earth rotates so that our side of the Earth is always turned away from the central fire and counter-Earth, explaining the fact that we never see them. This is also the first astronomical system that identifies a set of five planets and arranges them in proper order according to observations of their periods.

After presenting his view of the generation of the cosmos as a whole, Philolaus turned to a discussion of life. Just as he was interested particularly in the structure of the cosmos, so he emphasizes the structure of the animate world, in ways that prepared for the later Platonic and Aristotelian systems. He regarded all life as ordered in the hierarchy of plant, animal, and human beings, where each higher level shares the abilities of the lower but has a unique ability of its own. All life shares the ability to reproduce itself; plants have the ability to send out roots (which is paralleled by the human umbilical cord), animals can move and have sensation, but humans alone have reason. Philolaus saw a clear analogy between the birth of the cosmos and the birth of individual human beings. Humans were seen as initially consisting of just the hot, which then at birth naturally breathes in the cold, just as the central fire breathed in to generate the cosmos. The health of the human body seems to have depended on the proper limitation of the hot by cooling breath. Philolaus is said to have explained disease in terms of the three humors, bile, blood, and phlegm, which are also prominent in the contemporary theories of medicine found in the Hippocratic writings.

Philolaus's view of the cosmos is recognizably Presocratic, just as his medical views employ the same concepts as the early Hippocratic writings. However, the thematic emphasis on the structural features of the cosmos (limiters) and on the role of number in making the cosmos intelligible are important original steps that had influence on both the great philosophers of the next

century, Plato and Aristotle. Indeed, Philolaus is the first philosopher to present a coherent view of the natural world that calls for its explanation in
terms of mathematical relationships. However, the growth of the Pythagoras
legend that began in Plato's Academy made it imperative that the Pythagorean cosmos appear to be not merely an important precursor of Plato and Aristotle but the true revelation of reality. Hence, Philolaus's system, after being
relatively faithfully represented by Aristotle, was pushed aside and neglected,
and Plato's mature presentation of the cosmos in *Timaeus* came to be regarded as in reality the work of Pythagoras; accordingly, the term *Pythagorean* in the Renaissance usually in fact refers to the Platonism of *Timaeus*.

Archytas (fl. 400–350), who belonged to the generation after Philolaus and
who was a contemporary of Plato, is the Pythagorean who comes closest to
matching the modern stereotype of a Pythagorean as the master mathematician. Whereas there is no evidence that Philolaus made any contribution to
the advancement of Greek mathematics, Archytas is primarily known for important mathematical proofs and as the founder of the discipline of mechanics. There are in fact only three fragments (1–3) that can with some confidence be regarded as coming from genuine works, amid a much larger group
of fragments that derive from spurious works. We know of his mathematical
achievements through secondhand reports.

Archytas came from Tarentum in southern Italy, and the details of his life
are largely unknown to us. He has tended to be better known than Philolaus
because he is closely associated with Plato in several Platonic letters, whose
authenticity, however, is controversial. He sent a ship to rescue Plato from the
clutches of the tyrant Dionysius II of Syracuse in 361. However, even if we
accept the Platonic letters as providing accurate information, the exact relationship between Plato and Archytas and the nature of their influence on one
another is unclear. He is never mentioned in the Platonic dialogues.

As in the case of Philolaus, and in contrast to the tradition about Pythagoras himself, we have little information about Archytas's views on moral issues or the proper way to live one's life. Two anecdotes suggest that he emphasized the importance of acting solely on rational judgments and never in
anger or under the influence of the enticements of pleasure. When Archytas
came back from war to find his lands neglected, he reportedly told his slaves
that they were lucky that he was angry, because otherwise they would have
been punished. In another case, when someone had argued that pleasure was
the ultimate good, Archytas responded that reason was the greatest gift of the
gods to human beings, but that in the throes of pleasure we are unable to use
it. In fragment 3 he praises "correct calculation" as the source of political harmony.

It is not unlikely that Archytas did have something to say about the basic
principles of the cosmos, but we have very little evidence about his views on

this topic. There is nothing in the tradition about Archytas that mentions limiters and unlimiteds. However, Aristotle does say that Archytas gave definitions that appealed to both form and matter. Thus, calm weather is defined as "lack of movement in a mass of air," where the air is the matter and the lack of movement is the form. Such a definition could well have arisen out of the Philolaic distinction between unlimiteds and limiters. Again it is unclear whether Archytas accepted Philolaus's view of the structure of the cosmos or not. He is reported as arguing that what is outside the cosmos is unlimited in extent, by asking, "If I were at the extremity, for example at the heaven of the fixed stars, could I stretch out my hand or my staff into what is outside or not?" The study of such sciences as astronomy, geometry, arithmetic, and music is for him crucial to the understanding of reality. His reference to these sciences as "sisters" may have influenced Plato (*Republic* 530d). But the fragment goes on to present a theory of acoustics rather than discussing the cosmos as a whole.

It is for his work in the specific sciences that Archytas is particularly famous. Ptolemy (2nd century C.E.) in his *Harmonics* reports that Archytas was the most dedicated of all the Pythagoreans to the study of music and then presents Archytas's mathematical accounts of the diatonic, enharmonic, and chromatic scales. Archytas's proof that numbers in a superparticular ratio ($n + 1/1$) have no mean proportional is important for ancient musical theory in that it shows that neither the whole tone ($9 : 8$) nor the central musical intervals of the octave ($2 : 1$), fifth ($3 : 2$), and fourth ($4 : 3$) can be divided in half. Fragment 2 shows Archytas working with the arithmetic, geometric, and harmonic means that are also important in music theory.

He was regarded as the founder of mechanics and was said to have given method to the discipline by applying mathematical principles to it. This interest is manifested in the charming reports of his making toys for children, including a flying wooden dove. It is also reported that he was the first to use mechanical motion in geometrical constructions. Thus, in his proposed solution to the famous problem of doubling the cube, which was supposedly first posed by inhabitants of the island of Delos, who were commanded by the god to double the size of an altar, he used a striking construction in three dimensions that determined a point as the intersection of three surfaces of revolution.

After Archytas there are no prominent Pythagoreans. Aristotle's pupil Aristoxenus says that the Pythagoreans of the first half of the 4th century were the last Pythagoreans. However, this is not in fact the end of Pythagoreanism in the ancient world, although it is probably the end of the Pythagorean societies. As has been mentioned above, there was a strong revival of what were regarded as Pythagorean ideas in the 2nd and 3rd centuries C.E., although there were some important figures even earlier. The revival was

connected with Neoplatonism to such an extent that it is sometimes hard to know whether to call an individual thinker a Neopythagorean or a Neoplatonist.

Some Neopythagoreans focused primarily on Pythagoras's special connection to the gods, his wonder-working, and his way of life. Most prominent is Apollonius of Tyana (1st century C.E.), whose writings are largely lost but whose way of life is described in Philostratus's *Life of Apollonius*. Apollonius was a wandering ascetic wonder-worker who claimed a divine wisdom derived from Pythagoras. Some of his miraculous achievements were clearly modeled on stories about Pythagoras, such as his ability to be in two places at one time and the ability to speak the language of animals. Most Neopythagoreanism, however, focused on Pythagoras as the archetypal philosopher to whom the divine revelation of the true philosophical doctrine had been given. Two figures will serve as central examples of this tradition, Nicomachus and Iamblichus.

Nicomachus (ca. 50–150 C.E.), who wrote a very influential *Introduction to Arithmetic*, is a good example of the tendency to treat Platonism as if it were in fact Pythagoreanism. Nicomachus begins his book with Pythagoras and presents him as the first person to correctly define philosophy as knowledge of the immaterial and unchangeable reality that lies behind the flux of bodily existence. He is thus ascribing to Pythagoras Plato's central distinction between the world of unchanging forms and the constantly changing phenomena. Nicomachus then illustrates Pythagoras's supposed philosophy by quoting from Plato's *Timaeus*, thus exemplifying a pattern that will be repeated many times in the later tradition. While some authors do quote the Pythagorean pseudepigrapha to illustrate Pythagorean doctrine, it is more common to treat Plato's *Timaeus* as the central text for Pythagorean doctrine. Nicomachus also portrays Pythagoras as the master mathematician and scientist who instituted the quadrivium of mathematical studies that must be mastered to understand reality. These are the studies of arithmetic, music, geometry, and astronomy. Nicomachus himself wrote works on at least three of the sciences in the quadrivium.

The Neoplatonist Iamblichus (ca. 250–325 C.E.) wrote a ten-volume work entitled *On Pythagorean Doctrine*. The first volume, *On the Pythagorean Life*, was, as its title suggests, more than a biography of Pythagoras. Iamblichus's goal was to show Pythagoras as the archetype of the sage who had close contacts with divinity, and to present the way of life that he handed on to his followers. Many scholars have suggested that it would not be inappropriate to call Iamblichus's work a gospel, and it may be that Pythagoras was consciously set forth as a competitor to Christ. Iamblichus went on to write a volume on each of the four sciences in the quadrivium and then a volume each on the role of mathematics in physics, in ethics, and in theology. These last three works are lost and known only secondhand. But a later treatise of

uncertain authorship entitled the *Theologumena arithmeticae* seems to have drawn extensively on Iamblichus's and Nicomachus's work on the theology of number and comprises a discussion of the properties of each of the first ten numbers, including their connection with various divinities. Iamblichus had a number of important predecessors in his work on Pythagoreanism, including Nicomachus and a 2nd-century Neopythagorean named Numenius. Iamblichus's teachers Porphyry, who was the pupil of the great Neoplatonist Plotinus, and Anatolius, who wrote a work titled *On the Decad,* also fostered his Pythagoreanism. But Iamblichus himself is a crucial figure insofar as he appears to be responsible for the Pythagoreanizing and mathematizing of Neoplatonism that is still prominent in the important Neoplatonists Proclus and Syrianus in the 5th century C.E.

Neopythagoreanism has some connections to early Pythagoreanism: the inspiring figure of the semidivine sage is based to some extent on the historical Pythagoras; the picture of the cosmos ordered according to number does go back, in spirit at least, to Philolaus; and the notion of a set of sciences necessary to understand reality is found in Archytas. However, it was only in Platonism that these general ideas were given a sophisticated metaphysical foundation and a compelling literary embodiment. Neopythagoreanism is not so much a revival as a transformation of Pythagoreanism.

CARL HUFFMAN

Bibliography

Barker, A. D., ed. *Greek Musical Writings,* vol. 2. Cambridge: Cambridge University Press, 1984.

Barnes, Jonathan. *The Presocratic Philosophers,* rev. ed. London: Routledge & Kegan Paul, 1982.

Burkert, Walter. *Lore and Science in Ancient Pythagoreanism.* Trans. E. L. Minar, Jr. Cambridge, Mass.: Harvard University Press, 1972.

Guthrie, W. K. C. *A History of Greek Philosophy.* 6 vols. Cambridge: Cambridge University Press, 1962–1981.

Huffman, Carl. "The Authenticity of Archytas Fr. 1." *Classical Quarterly* 35, no. 2 (1985): 344–348.

———. *Philolaus of Croton.* Cambridge: Cambridge University Press, 1993.

Iamblichus. *On the Pythagorean Way of Life.* Ed. and trans. John Dillon and Jackson Hershbell. Atlanta, Ga.: Scholars Press, 1991.

Kahn, Charles. "Pythagorean Philosophy before Plato." In *The Pre-Socratics: A Collection of Critical Essays,* rev. ed. Ed. A. P. D. Mourelatos. Princeton: Princeton University Press, 1993.

Kirk, G. S., J. E. Raven, and M. Schofield, eds. *The Presocratic Philosophers: A Critical History with a Selection of Texts.* 2nd ed. Cambridge: Cambridge University Press, 1983.

Lloyd, Geoffrey E. R. "Plato and Archytas in the Seventh Letter." *Phronesis* 35, no. 2 (1990): 159–174.

O'Meara, Dominic J. *Pythagoras Revived: Mathematics and Philosophy in Late Antiquity.* Oxford: Oxford University Press, 1989.

Thesleff, Holger. *An Introduction to the Pythagorean Writings of the Hellenistic Period.* Åbo: Åbo Akademi, 1961.

————, ed. *The Pythagorean Texts of the Hellenistic Period.* Åbo: Åbo Akademi, 1965.

Zhmud, Leonid. *Wissenschaft, Philosophie und Religion im frühen Pythagoreismus.* Berlin: Akademie Verlag, 1997.

Related Articles

Schools and Sites of Learning; Harmonics; The Academy; Zeno; Cosmology; Mathematics; Platonism

SKEPTICISM

LIKE MANY PHILOSOPHICAL TERMS that end in "-ism," the word *skepticism* does not exist as a word in ancient Greek, even though it combines a Greek root and a Greek suffix. There was indeed a group of thinkers who called themselves *skeptikoi*, among other things; however, when they wanted to designate their "school" (in which nothing was taught), they used the word *skepsis*, with a suffix evoking an activity and not a doctrine. "Skeptics" did not profess a system that we might call Skepticism; they practiced an activity known as *skepsis*.

The philosophical positions of the *skeptikoi* were not unrelated to what we call Skepticism, but they were not identical to the modern version, either. Many philosophers whom we would describe as skeptics were not viewed in the same light by the *skeptikoi*; indeed, it was enough to adopt certain positions, which for us are characteristic of Skepticism (for example, to say that one cannot know anything), to distinguish oneself from the *skeptikoi*. Any introduction to classical Skepticism consistent with the ancient criteria would be incomplete from today's standpoint; if it were consistent with modern criteria, it would be historically unfaithful. The most delicate issue, in this regard, would be how to situate the New Academy, that phase of the school Plato founded during which, under the leadership of teachers such as Arcesilaus and Carneades, it adopted positions that we would classify as skeptical: the *skeptikoi*, for reasons whose validity has been controversial since ancient times, did not view them in the same way. Still, it is generally acknowledged today that the two tendencies were mutually influential; most modern historians argue at the very least that the "external analogies" between them "suffices to make it impossible to write a history of Skepticism without speaking of the New Academy" (Victor Brochard).

If we restrict ourselves to the vocabulary of the ancients, however, we may be tempted to concentrate here on so-called Pyrrhonist Skepticism—which means not so much on Pyrrhon himself as on later thinkers who claimed to be his heirs and who should rather be called Neopyrrhonists. This means dealing essentially, on the one hand, with two great philosophers whose texts have been lost and whose lives and personalities are obscure, but whose work is relatively well known: Aenesidemus (active toward the middle of the 1st century B.C.E.) and Agrippa (probably active at the end of the 1st century C.E. and at the beginning of the 2nd), and, on the other hand, with Sextus Empiricus (probably active at the end of the 2nd century and at the very begin-

ning of the 3rd), a prolific writer whose works, largely intact, constitute the richest and most influential source of information about ancient Skepticism.

But adopting this approach would still not solve all the problems. Nothing in the activity of *skepsis* itself necessarily associates it with what we mean by Skepticism. First of all, *skepsis* designates the activity of looking attentively at something, of observing, examining with the eyes: the verb *skeptesthai*, the frequentative form of the verb *skopein*, refers to the idea of seeing and looking (as in the words *microscope* and *telescope*); then, through a metaphor that is a familiar one in the vocabulary of epistemology, it designates the activity of examining with the mind, reflecting, studying. The terms in question are thus not the exclusive property of Skeptics; they characterize all philosophers as such. Who could in fact claim to be a philosopher in ancient Greece and say that he did not reflect, that he did not examine things, that he accepted a system of belief without testing its claims? In one sense, all Greek philosophy is skeptical, and words from the *skepsis* family regularly appear in the work of philosophers whom the Skeptics do not count among their own, such as Plato and Aristotle. The philosophers of the New Academy represented themselves as faithful to Plato, and their arguments in favor of Plato as a Skeptic could not be discounted out of hand; the *skeptikoi* themselves, although they did not agree that the New Academy was skeptical, were willing to consider the possibility that Plato may have practiced skepticism. As for Aristotle, his theory and his practice of dialectical discussion "for" and "against" provided the Academics with a model that they appropriated as their own.

SKEPTIC NOMENCLATURE

What, then, constitutes the specifically skeptical method of practicing *skepsis*? To answer this question, let us examine the other names the Skeptics gave themselves. One in particular warrants attention: *zetetikoi* (zetetics, or seekers: *zetesis* designates the activity of seeking). Sextus Empiricus does not hesitate to acknowledge that all philosophers are seekers. But at the very beginning of his *Outlines of Pyrrhonism,* he specifies the properly skeptical manner of seeking as follows: "The natural result of any investigation is that the investigators either discover the object of search or deny that it is discoverable and confess it to be inapprehensible or persist in their search. So, too, with regard to the objects investigated by philosophy, this is probably why some have claimed to have discovered the truth, others have asserted that it cannot be apprehended, while others again go on inquiring" (I.i.1–2).

The first group is that of the Dogmatics (not the authoritarian teachers who propound their doctrines dogmatically, in the contemporary sense of the term, without providing any supporting arguments, but philosophers who hold doctrines that they deem perfectly reasoned and rationally teachable);

this group is represented, in Sextus, by Aristotle, Epicurus, the Stoics, "and certain others."

The second group is that of the philosophers who despair of searching and declare truth to be inherently ungraspable. This "negative metadogmatism" (Jonathan Barnes) consists in proffering dogmatic assertions in the second degree (having to do not with the real itself, but with the possibility of knowing the real), and assertions that are negative (the real is not knowable). Logically, there is nothing unacceptable in negative metadogmatism: if one specifies the degree of what is unknowable, or the type of statements that one rules out presenting as true or false, nothing precludes one from saying that one knows that something is unknowable, unverifiable, or unfalsifiable. However, a good part of the history of classical Skepticism stems from the fact that it was considered self-contradictory to say, "I know that nothing is knowable"; philosophers thus always tried to attribute this contradiction to their adversaries, and to demonstrate that they themselves made no such claim. Sextus (after Aenesidemus) thus associates philosophers who renounced all inquiry with the New Academy, the better to differentiate himself from them.

As for true Skeptics, they do not say that truth is ungraspable, and they do not give up its pursuit; they profess "to pursue the quest." Those whom we would probably call Skeptics, because they do not believe in the possibility of reaching truth, are thus the ones whom Sextus, for this very reason, refuses to call by that name. As for those who, like Sextus, say neither that truth is unattainable nor that it is not, we would be more likely to call them open-minded agnostics. The zetetic is therefore not simply someone who seeks or who has sought: he is someone who up to this point has done nothing but seek without finding, and who has the intention of continuing to seek, without giving up hope of finding. The label Skeptic can be explained in the same way: all philosophers devote themselves to inquiry, or have done so; only Skeptics "go on inquiring" because they have so far found no good reason to adopt any one position rather than another, and thus no good reason to break off their inquiry to settle on some particular position.

The Skeptics gave themselves two other labels as well: "aporetic" and "ephectic." An aporia, literally, is an impasse, a dead end, an "embarrassing" situation that one can experience oneself in the face of an obstacle that one has taken into account, or that one can produce in others by raising obstacles that one brings to their attention. An aporetic philosopher is thus, one might say, both embarrassed and embarrassing. The term is not the exclusive property of the Skeptics. With his questions, Socrates led his interlocutors into aporias; when they complained, he said that he reduced them to this situation only insofar as he himself was reduced to it; most of Plato's early dialogues, traditionally called aporetic, end with the acknowledgment of failure, at least on the surface. But aporia can be fertile, whether because it provokes reflection, because it eliminates ignorance unconscious of its own existence and

reinvigorates the investigation, or even because it makes possible its own surpassing. All of Plato's philosophy is, in one sense, the result of Socratic aporias. And Aristotle was careful, before resolving a given problem, to review all the difficulties that earlier considerations of the problem, and his own reflections, brought to the fore: he trusted that "diaporia," the systematic examination of all relevant aporias, would finally lead to "euporia," a way out of the impasse.

What is unique to the skeptical aporia is that it is unacquainted with this outcome, or even with the hope of finding in itself the possibility of such an outcome. The Skeptic is aporetic, it seems, in a double sense: he experiences passive aporia in a lasting way (he presents himself as more sensitive than anyone else to conflicts of appearances, to the contradictions and anomalies of all kinds that the world offers us), and he simultaneously cultivates active aporia (he identifies *skepsis* with the power of making these contradictions appear, by developing arguments capable of counterbalancing, "with equal force," arguments that support any given position). Is it inconsistent on his part to claim that he "goes on inquiring" while he is doing everything in his power to perpetuate the aporia in which he encloses himself and in which he wants to enclose others? Probably not: he freely admits that nothing keeps him from possibly stumbling onto the truth one day; but in the meantime, whenever a candidate for "truth" comes along, he examines it carefully to see if he can shoot it down, and experience shows him that, in any event up to the present moment, none has stood up to the shock. If ever some truth were to end up imposing itself on his mind, it would not be because the maieutic practice of aporia had "given birth" to it, but because it had been unexpectedly spared by the infanticidal practice of aporia.

The label "ephectic," for its part, is related to the only outcome that the Skeptic expects from his aporetic attitude, and the only one that he does hope for it: not an advance in his knowledge, not a positive step forward in the search for the truth, but rather the state of suspension of judgment (*epochē*) from which the word *ephectic* comes. *Epochē* is not to be confused with doubt (despite the association usually made today between doubt and skepticism), if one views doubt as a state to which, according to the current expression, one "is prey"—which means that one is its passive victim, in a state of indecision or even anguish, wavering endlessly between a belief and its opposite. If *epochē* resembles doubt, it would be the deliberate and methodical doubt through which Descartes, taking up on his own account and carrying to the extreme "all of the Skeptics' most extravagant suppositions," tried to see if there were anything undoubtable that could hold up against it. Historically, in fact, it is probable that the word *epochē* and the corresponding attitude originated, independently of the Pyrrhonist tradition, in the course of a fundamental debate between the Stoics and the Academics. The former maintained that the sage must abstain from giving his assent to any representation

that is not absolutely self-evident, but the latter retorted that no representation possesses such self-evidence, and that thus the sage must always, and in all matters, abstain from giving his assent. On this point, the *skeptikoi* seem to be indebted to the Academics, even if they disguise this by accusing them of a metadogmatism that is incompatible with the generalized *epochē*. This latter is, in sum, a state of immobile equilibrium: there is no topic at all on which the Skeptic is inclined toward affirmation or denial, and he finds in this equilibrium not only intellectual tranquillity but also the peace and happiness of his soul.

This ethical stake in the skeptical approach leads us to examine one last name that the *skeptikoi* gave themselves (the only one, along with the label Skeptics, that has withstood the test of time): the label Pyrrhonists. Unlike the others, this designation is not drawn from the Skeptics' manner of philosophizing, or from the methods they used, or from the results they claimed they had achieved, but from history, and from a precise and crucial moment of history, since Pyrrhon lived at the turning point between two historical eras, the classical and the Hellenistic, periods separated by the expedition of Alexander the Great and all the accompanying upheavals. Even if the coincidence is accidental, it is symbolic that Aristotle, the last of the great classical Dogmatics, and Pyrrhon, officially the first of the Skeptics, had each had a personal relationship with Alexander: the former was the prince's preceptor before Alexander's accession to the throne, while the latter was an obscure member of the conqueror's intellectual entourage. Since Pyrrhon wrote nothing, as it happens, and since he was manifestly an extraordinary individual, all the conditions were at hand to enhance his place in history—or in legend.

PYRRHON AND NEOPYRRHONIST SKEPTICISM

Does Greek Skepticism really begin with Pyrrhon? This question, which seems simple enough, nevertheless raises several others. The first is whether we can consider Pyrrhon as the first of the Pyrrhonists; the next questions are whether, when, and why he was considered a Pyrrhonist by the ancient Skeptics themselves.

As to the first question, one can say briefly that the accounts of those closest to him (in particular, that of his disciple Timon, a brilliant poet-philosopher who spent some twenty years in Pyrrhon's circle of intimates, and that of Cicero) present Pyrrhon first and foremost as a master of happiness, as a moralist for whom the surest ways to achieve happiness are through insensitivity *(apatheia)* and imperturbability *(ataraxia)*. Plausibly enough, Pyrrhon did not view the problem of knowledge as fundamental, and he was not primarily concerned with refuting the claims of scientists and philosophers; "human instability, vain concerns, and puerility," which he denounced with the help of citations from Homer, were his chief targets. There are reasons to

believe that Timon was the first person responsible for the shift in his master's thought toward a questioning of cognitive powers. The alliance between the search for happiness and the critique of knowledge, which is found in Pyrrhon in a preparatory stage at most (and which seems to be absent, on the contrary, from the preoccupations of the Neoacademics), is in any case clearly confirmed in Timon.

This alliance will subsist among the later Skeptics, including those indefatigable collectors of antidogmatic arguments, Aenesidemus and Sextus; in this sense, Pyrrhon's ethical message survives in the Neopyrrhonists. But we can identify several shifts of emphasis showing that determining the exact nature of the link between cognitive Skepticism and the conquest of happiness remains problematic. According to Timon (as reported by Aristocles), the attitude Pyrrhon recommended—that is, "life without beliefs," the absence of any inclination toward a given opinion rather than its opposite—has as its effects, first, abstention with respect to any assertion *(aphasia)* and, second, imperturbability, or *ataraxia.* As these effects are expected and desired, *ataraxia* seems to coincide with the ethical goal pursued by Skeptics, and with respect to which Skeptics knowingly make use of the means recognized as most appropriate.

In other texts, where Timon is associated with Aenesidemus, *epochē* is designated as being itself the end *(telos)* sought by Skeptics; *ataraxia* is said to follow "like its shadow." This image seems intended to disconnect cognitive Skepticism from ataraxic happiness: by setting himself a goal of an intellectual nature, *epochē,* the only goal in view of which the deployment of appropriate means depends on the Skeptic himself, the latter achieves a different goal of an ethical nature, *ataraxia;* but he achieves it as a supplement, as it were, and by a stroke of good luck. (In this connection, Sextus tells the story of the painter Apelles: one day, furious that he was not managing to portray a horse's foam, he threw his sponge at the canvas and in so doing produced the very result that he had given up hope of achieving.) This development is completed by Sextus himself, who differentiates clearly between two separate goals, one having to do with matters of judgment, *ataraxia* (taken here in a strictly intellectual sense), and the other concerning affectivity: the latter goal no longer entails complete insensitivity *(apatheia)* but rather moderation of affect(s) *(metriopatheia). Ataraxia* is what makes moderation possible: in fact, if the Skeptic cannot escape the inevitable perturbations to which external needs give rise, at least, thanks to his intellectual *ataraxia,* he can avoid making them worse by ill-considered judgments. One suffers more from pain when, not content with experiencing it, one deems it an evil in itself; Sextus notes astutely that observers have more difficulty tolerating a surgical operation than the patient does.

As for the Skeptics' own opinion of Pyrrhon's thought and its originality, there are distinctions to be made. Timon, Pyrrhon's direct disciple, uses his

full poetic powers to present his master as a unique and peerless man whose example is comparable to that of the sun-god, man's eternal guide. To enhance his teacher's prestige even further, in a kind of jovial parody of Homer, in a poem titled *Silloi,* Timon indulges in lively attacks on virtually all philosophers past and present, although he makes a few exceptions or near exceptions (Xenophanes in particular). Let us also note that a figure about whom we know nothing, Ascanius of Abdera, attributed Pyrrhon's radical originality in the context of the Greek tradition to his experiences in the East: in Ascanius's view, Skepticism is an import, brought back by Pyrrhon from India and Persia. Not all modern scholars dismiss this hypothesis; but the fact that Timon says nothing about it, whereas his testimony on this point would presumably have been preserved if it had existed, is an invitation to try to do without it.

The fragments of *Silloi* that have survived allow us to suppose that the poem's message was not completely destructive. In the scenario Timon offers, Xenophanes may have played the role of an intercessor of sorts, soliciting indulgence for some of his colleagues; this would explain why some philosophers who are treated very badly in one fragment receive better treatment in another. Thus Timon's partial amnesties may have paved the way for the construction of a portrait gallery of the ancestors of Skepticism.

SKEPTICISM BEFORE PYRRHON

The ancients' effort to insert Pyrrhon into a plausible genealogy took several forms. The most serious consisted in introducing him into one of the "successions" *(diadochai)* of masters and disciples that scholars at the end of antiquity constructed, more or less artificially, to create some order in the burgeoning field of Greek philosophy. Timon's suggestions may have been used, among other materials, to construct the succession given in the structure of Book IX of Diogenes Laertius's *Lives of Eminent Philosophers.* The book's headings appear in the following order: Xenophanes, Parmenides, the Eleatics, the atomists Leucippus and Democritus, then, after several more obscure intermediaries, Anaxarchus, Pyrrhon's teacher and Alexander's friend, Pyrrhon himself, and, finally, Timon. This succession established a filiation between Pyrrhon and Democritus, whose complex and still-controversial theory of knowledge presented some skeptical aspects; the relationship was probably both an effect and a cause of the interpretation of Pyrrhon's thought in gnoseological terms.

Another trend, probably less "scientific" in its claims, sought to show that Skepticism was less the distinctive feature of a specific philosophical line of thinking than a diffuse and very old tradition characteristic of virtually all Greek thought. This approach thus challenged Pyrrhon's right to be viewed as the "founder" of Skepticism; however, it did not necessarily stem from an in-

tent to denigrate him (novelty was rarely taken as a positive value in antiquity, and it was thought to be more useful to a philosophy to endow it with prestigious ancestors than to underscore its revolutionary character). Once again it is Diogenes Laertius who provides us with a list of "honorary Skeptics" (*Lives* IX.71–73) along with one or two citations apiece by way of justifying their inclusion: Homer, the Seven Wise Men, Archilochus, Euripides, Xenophanes, Zeno of Elea, Democritus, Plato, Euripides again, Empedocles, Heraclitus, Hippocrates, and Homer once more (the repetitions may indicate that the list results from an amalgam of several sources).

If we think solely about the desire for and the intoxication with knowledge that are so manifest in the Greeks, the attempt to portray Greek thought as a generalized Skepticism, through several of its seminal figures, may seem absurd. And yet it is not completely so, for we also have to take into account the sort of gnoseological pessimism that in some ways constituted the terrain out of which Greek dynamism (or, more precisely, the dynamism of certain Greek thinkers) was extracted, and onto which that dynamism collapsed on more than one occasion.

Thus, for some of the ancients, Skepticism began with Homer. This affirmation seems eccentric to us, and the arguments that have been offered in its defense are unquestionably weak. However, in the Homeric poems we can readily find a strong sense of the limitations of human knowledge as contrasted with the extent and quality of divine knowledge, and this sense is unquestionably characteristic of the most ancient Greek wisdom (the dogmatic thinkers understood that that sentiment had to be reckoned with, and that they had to overcome it). In a celebrated invocation, the poet beseeches the Muses to inform him about the distant past that he is preparing to describe: "For you are goddesses and are present and know all things, but we hear only a rumor and know nothing" (*Iliad* II.484–486). The human mode of knowledge is made fragile by our enclosure within a narrow space and an ephemeral time: considered individually or even collectively, human beings have a field of vision that is necessarily linked to, and therefore limited by, a particular point of view.

Countless echoes of this call to order run through Greek thought: man is not God, and to seek to ignore the fact is a culpable and dangerous excess (the celebrated hubris). There is probably not yet any skepticism here, even in the broadest sense of the word. If it is imprudent to want to gain access to the knowledge the gods keep for themselves (for example, what goes on in heaven and in the underworld), this does not rule out the possibility that such knowledge is in principle attainable: quite to the contrary, indeed, since we must be warned of its dangers. A seed of practical skepticism, as it were, appears when transgression of the forbidden is presented as useless: the famous anecdote about Thales falling in a well while looking at the stars is only one illustration of a widespread antitheoretical theme according to which scien-

tific knowledge of nature adds nothing—indeed, quite the opposite—to the modest knowledge needed for daily life. A metadogmatic form of skepticism is finally attained when the desire for knowledge appears not only dangerous or useless but impossible to satisfy, and above all when arguments in support of this thesis are provided, instead of mere assertions that man is not God.

This path was quickly followed to its end. The proliferation of theoretical research in the pre-Socratic era had given rise almost as rapidly to skeptical reactions. Several limited experiments and some bold arguments had led thinkers of that era to construct ambitious doctrines on the broadest and most difficult subjects: "nature"; the origin and foundation of reality; the principles of being and becoming; the genesis and structure of the world; the origin of the elements, stars, and living beings—for them nothing seemed inaccessible to the enterprises of knowledge, and they did not hesitate to present their results in solidly self-assured tones. The trouble was that these doctrines were numerous, and mutually incompatible; in a very short time and with staggering theoretical imagination, the principal options had been tested and confronted with their competitors (the one and the multiple, the finite and the infinite, the continuous and the discontinuous, movement and rest, mechanism and finality). Aristotle sought to discern signs of progress in this proliferation, but more superficial ears heard in it only discordance and cacophony *(diaphonia)*, which were well suited to give rise to Skepticism.

However, it is one thing to take note of cacophony, quite another to prove that it is inevitable. On this point, we need to reckon with a famous fragment by Xenophanes of Colophon, a poet-philosopher and a powerful personality whose long life spanned the late 6th and early 5th centuries. We need to do so for several reasons. Remarkably precocious in terms of its date, the fragment may prefigure a famous argument against the very possibility of the search for truth; this argument was presented as "eristic" by Plato in *Meno,* and it played an essential role in the later history of theories of knowledge. In addition, Xenophanes' fragment unquestionably explains the particular position that Timon had attributed to the Colophonian in his *Silloi;* finally, the question of whether it contains a skeptical argument, and if so, just which one, gave rise to many debates in late antiquity and continues to do so in our own day. Here is an approximate translation: "No man has seen the exact truth, and no man ever will, about the gods and everything else I am discussing. For even if, in the best case, someone should by chance stumble across what is actually happening, he would still not know it himself: it is an opinion that is elaborated for everyone" (Xenophanes, in Diels-Kranz, frg. 21.B.34). In the absence of context, it is difficult to know what scope Xenophanes assigned to the domain in which he claims, for his discourse, only the status of true belief and not that of exact knowledge, but he seems to endow it with this status thanks to an argument according to which, in the domain under consideration, no verification criterion is available. One might happen on a truth by

chance, but one would have no way to know whether it was a truth or not. One would then be in possession of a belief that could be true, but what would be missing, not by chance but of necessity, is the justification that alone would transform it from belief to knowledge.

Xenophanes thus brought himself to the attention of the future Skeptics. For those who were less demanding about the criteria for filiation, the search for the ancestors of Skepticism became even easier. The most extreme dogmatic thinkers could figure in the genealogical tree. Not only were their violently counterintuitive theses about "the nature of things" contradictory among themselves, but in addition, taken in isolation, their theses exploited the conflicts between perceptible appearances (this was the case for Heraclitus, the Eleatics, and Democritus); thus they made it possible to nourish the aspect of skeptical thought that also made use of these conflicts. For their part, the Sophists—Protagoras and Gorgias, for example—each in his own manner and with arguments that the Skeptics could also put to good use, had undermined the notions of objective truth and absolute knowledge. The candidates for the status of precursors to Skepticism were rapidly presenting themselves in serried ranks. Sextus Empiricus himself, who was not overly interested in Pyrrhon and who obviously knew little about him, grants him only relative and comparative originality: others, Sextus admits, had devoted themselves to *skepsis* before Pyrrhon's time, but "Pyrrhon appears to us to have applied himself to Scepticism more thoroughly and more conspicuously than his predecessors" (*Outlines* I.iii.7). Once Neopyrrhonist Skepticism had succeeded in defining itself clearly, well after Pyrrhon's day, it was no longer urgent for it to find guarantees of historical authenticity; on the contrary, it was necessary to keep authentic Skepticism from being confused with the "neighboring philosophies" that resembled it.

NEOPYRRHONISM AND THE "NEIGHBORING PHILOSOPHIES"

Sextus Empiricus undertakes the confrontation between Skepticism and other philosophies in a long and important section of *Outlines of Pyrrhonism* (I.xxix), where he studies in turn Heraclitus, Democritus, the Cyrenaics, Protagoras, the Middle Academy (Arcesilaus) and the New Academy (Carneades), and the empiricist physicians. In each case, he attempts to determine, along with the reasons that might have led to the idea that these philosophers were Skeptics, the differences that proved to him that they were not. His criterion for differentiation is quite strict: "The man that dogmatizes about a single thing, or ever prefers one impression to another in point of credibility or incredibility, or makes any assertion about any non-evident object [that dogmatic philosophers claim to know] assumes the dogmatic character" (*Outline* I.xxxiii.223).

The Skeptic thus appears to present himself as more "radical" than those from whom he wishes to be distinguished. This description is not completely accurate, however. Without examining each of the "neighboring philosophies" that Sextus summarizes, we shall choose one of them, the philosophy of the Cyrenaic school (developed by one of Socrates' direct disciples, Aristippus), because its theory of knowledge, less well-known than its moral hedonism, is of great philosophical interest.

If, among the ancient theories of knowledge, it were necessary to choose one that was "radically skeptical" in the sense in which we are using the term, Cyrenaic theory would probably be an even better candidate than Neo-pyrrhonist Skepticism. Its sole text is contained in a single formula: "Our affects *(pathe)* alone are graspable." These "affects" are the impressions of all sorts—tinged with pleasure or pain, according to circumstances—that we experience in an entirely passive manner. As we do not produce them ourselves, agents outside of ourselves that produce them in us must exist. But we can know nothing about the identity or nature of these agents; nothing guarantees that they actually and intrinsically have the properties that correspond to the feelings that they make us experience, or that the affects they produce on people other than ourselves are identical to ours. I am "affected whitely," says the Cyrenaic; but is what affects me this way something white or not? I cannot know, since I would have to go look, and this is by definition impossible: I have no relation with the things that affect me except by way of the affects that they produce in me. To seek to grasp them independently would be to seek to leap over my own shadow; as Plutarch says about this theory, we are in a city under siege, cut off from the rest of the world.

The Cyrenaics do not seem to have identified the positive side of their thesis, namely, the infallible, incorrigible, and indubitable character with which we "grasp" our own affects (in antiquity, it seems, only St. Augustine had the already Cartesian idea that this thesis can lead to an argument against Skepticism rather than for it); this is probably because the idea of knowledge, for the ancients, implies grasping an object that (at least before its cognitive appropriation) is other than the knowing subject. By stressing the fact that the causes of affects are ungraspable, rather than the fact that affects themselves are graspable, Cyrenaic theory thus developed a remarkably powerful argument. Though many philosophers up to our own day have sought to refute it in various ways, it readily springs back to life from its own ashes, drawing as needed on resources appropriate to each era (including those of science fiction: how can I be sure, for example, that I am not a brain in a jar, covered with electrodes, through which an army of scientists supplies me with precisely the impressions that I have?). This argument tends to establish that, as a matter of principle, anything other than my own modifications is radically inaccessible to me.

To distinguish them from the Skeptics, Sextus criticizes the Cyrenaics, first,

for their dogmatism in ethics. For the Skeptic, nothing is good by nature; pleasure is no more so than anything else. On the gnoseological level, the same argument holds up against most of the "neighboring philosophies": Cyrenaic theory asserts, and even claims to demonstrate, that external things are unknowable; the Skeptic says only that he knows nothing about that, and he denounces the manifestation of negative metadogmatism in the Cyrenaics' assertion. There may appear to be very little difference between the Cyrenaic who takes note of his own modifications and declares their causes unknowable and the Skeptic who denies suppressing appearances *(phainomena)* by saying that he does no more than ask whether things are as they appear to be. However—and in this sense, Skepticism is less "radical" than Cyrenism—it would be hard to say about the Skeptic, even with ill will, that he is locked up in a fortress under siege. The *phainomenon,* the subject of the verb *appear,* is still a sort of object for the consciousness to which it appears, and this distinguishes it subtly but clearly from feeling *(pathos),* which is only a modification of the subject itself. There is an eloquent difference between typically Cyrenaic statements, such as "I am affected whitely," and typically Skeptical statements, such as "a certain thing appears white to me." This difference allows us to understand another, crucial difference: while it would appear absurd to speak of assent given by a subject to his own modifications, it is not absurd (at least not for a Skeptic) to speak of a weak form of assent that the subject can give to what appears in front of him: assent without deep-seated commitment, a kind of instinctive adherence that Sextus compares to a pupil's distracted acceptance of his master's discourse. According to the Skeptics, *epochē* is not at all incompatible with this weak form of assent.

NEOPYRRHONISM AND STOICISM

To determine how and why the specifically skeptical position was able to define and maintain itself, it is at least as necessary to give an account of the opposing philosophies as of the neighboring ones. Negative metadogmatism is one reaction, comprehensible enough, to positive dogmatism: whether one takes a position on the level of the certainties of naive consciousness or on the level of the arrogance of scientific theories, the fact that appearances conflict and that doctrines contradict one another readily gives rise to the idea that the reality of the world is, in its very nature, inaccessible to human knowledge. For something like a Skepticism that is itself exempt from negative metadogmatism to appear, a little higher up on the scale of reflection what could be called a positive metadogmatism had to appear in the meantime, that is, a doctrine tending to justify, on a theoretical level and in a closely argued fashion, the possibility of knowing the external world. In other words, just as, in the first degree, the opposition of positive and negative dogmatisms (for example, "Everything is in movement," "Not everything is in movement")

favors the appearance, in the second degree, of negative metadogmatism ("It is impossible to know whether everything is in movement or not"), so the opposition to this negative metadogmatism by a positive metadogmatism ("It is possible to know whether everything is in movement or not") favors the appearance, in the third degree, of a Skepticism that is careful to stay out of the traps of each of the two opposing metadogmatisms. This Skepticism has to take pains not to assert, for its part, either that it is possible or that it is impossible to know whether everything is in movement or not and, more generally, whether the real is knowable or not.

From this point on, it is not Pyrrhon's existence that ought to be seen as the crucial event in the history of Neopyrrhonist Skepticism; it is the appearance of a dogmatism that was refined and reflective enough to have created a metadogmatic theory from the foundations of its own certainties. This dogmatism that deemed itself capable of establishing itself on its own has a name: Stoicism. In fact there is no better candidate to be found. Plato could not play this role: the Academies of Arcesilaus and of Carneades, both of which were inclined toward Skepticism, claimed Plato, no less than Socrates—not without cause—as their founding father. Aristotle may well be placed, by Sextus Empiricus, in the first rank of dogmatic philosophers, but he is not one of Sextus's habitual interlocutors, and in any case, his most important works were not well known during the period in which Neopyrrhonism emerged. Epicureanism had long been marginalized by its hedonist ethic, by its requirement of political abstention, by its affectation of lack of culture, and by several doctrines viewed as logically scandalous (the theory of the *clinamen*); it does not have the appearance of a respectable partner, and Sextus is careful to stress his distance from it when he touches on points against which Epicureanism and Skepticism are waging war in common (for example, against the traditional mode of education).

Stoicism, on the other hand, inaugurates a new type of thought in which dogmatism no longer seeks to be excused but declares itself and shores itself up with arguments. For what is probably the first time in so decisive a manner, the Stoics free themselves from the ancient fear of arousing the jealousy of the gods; in this view, human reason is homogeneous with the divine reason that governs the world, and the sage is Zeus's equal. The only vestige the Stoics retain of the ancient divisions is the distance they put between the sage, a phoenix nowhere to be found, and the rest of us, ignorant fools all. However, philosophically speaking, this factual difference does not count: however rare he may be, the Stoic sage is a man; to draw his portrait, as the Stoics never tired of doing, is to describe what man can be when he is fully human.

Now, the base on which this unprecedented dogmatism stands is the famous "cognitive impression" *(phantasia kataleptike)*, the essential characteristic of which, from the standpoint that interests us, is that it contains its own

self-certification. According to the Stoics, among the "impressions" that affect us, some have the privilege both of being causally produced by the states of external things and at the same time of representing these states of things, in their content, with absolute precision and exactitude, to the point that these impressions cannot arise from any state of things other than the one from which they have arisen. In other words, a cognitive impression caused by a given state of things is inherently distinguishable from any impression caused by a different state of things; it cannot be false. As Cicero says when he is describing Stoic theory, cognitive impressions possess "a sort of inherent power to bring to full light the things that are manifested in them"; they include an intrinsic "note" that guarantees their truth. Such is, indeed, the most heroic element in the Stoic solution: some of our impressions certify by themselves that they are not merely our impressions, but that they also allow us to know what is.

Over several generations, the early Stoics argued against contemporary adversaries on the subject of cognitive impressions; the early Pyrrhonists were not involved. In these disputes, the Stoics made out fairly well, since the successive Academics had an increasing tendency to moderate their Skepticism; they even ended up thinking, as did Antiochus of Ascalon (1st century B.C.E.), that the two schools differed in form alone. The disputes had several consequences that concern Neopyrrhonist Skepticism.

On the historical level, we know very little about what went on between Timon and Aenesidemus. Ancient scholars evoked either an uninterrupted succession of masters and disciples, whose names mean nothing to us, or else an eclipse brought to an end by a predecessor of Aenesidemus. We have very little information about Aenesidemus himself. It was thought for a long time (though some scholars question this today) that he had started out as a member of the Academy, and that owing to his disagreement with the school's dogmatic drift, he had sought to resuscitate a pure, hardline Skepticism with Pyrrhon as his patron, Pyrrhon being a shadowy, legendary figure at the time. In any event, Photius, patriarch of Constantinople in the 9th century C.E., who was a reader of Aenesidemus's *Pyrrhonian Arguments,* attests that, according to Aenesidemus, it was necessary to renew the struggle against Stoic dogmatism: the Academics had watered down the doctrine to such an extent that in the final analysis it was a matter of "Stoics fighting against Stoics." The formula eloquently reveals to what extent, for Aenesidemus, the philosophic landscape had been literally invaded by Stoicism.

The whole effort of Aenesidemus's Neopyrrhonism was thus aimed at forging an apparatus capable of destroying the Stoics' self-certifying mechanism. It was not enough to deny the existence or the possibility of cognitive impressions, as the Academics had done with tireless ingeniousness: to do that was once again to pit one metadogmatism against another. To refute a dogmatism that claimed to justify itself by including itself in its own field of

application, Aenesidemus presented Pyrrhonist thought, with a symmetry that was perhaps deliberate, as a Skepticism that succeeded in eliminating itself by including itself in its own domain. Although Aenesidemus was probably not the originator of this approach, Photius's testimony shows rather touchingly that he was still aware of submitting language and thought to an acrobatic test: "For the Pyrrhonist determines absolutely nothing, not even this very claim that nothing is determined. (We put it this way, he says, for lack of a way to express the thought)" (Long and Sedley, *The Hellenistic Philosophers*, p. 469). When he says: "I determine nothing" (that is, I answer no question in the affirmative or in the negative), the Skeptic professes not to "determine" further the question of whether he determines anything or not.

This way of turning the typical formulas of Skepticism ("in no way more," "all things are indeterminate," "for every argument there is an opposing argument of equal weight") back on themselves becomes systematic with Sextus Empiricus; to the extent that Sextus expresses less circumspection than Aenesidemus toward his own language, the difficulties of the skeptical position are manifested more clearly in his case. The Skeptic, we are told, for example, gives his assent "in no way more" *(ouden mallon)* to *p* rather than to non-*p*; but if this formula is applied to itself, it is also necessary to understand that the Skeptic privileges the attitude expressed by "in no way more" over the attitude expressed by the opposite formula, "in some way more," which is the very negation of the Skeptic *epochē*. Would Skepticism be condemned by its very logic to refuse to choose between itself and dogmatism? Some of Sextus's well-known images attempt to make arguments out of comparisons: Skepticism is like a fire that consumes itself as it consumes its fuel; it is like a ladder that one tosses aside after climbing a wall (this image will be passed along all the way to Wittgenstein); finally (less poetically, but very much in the spirit of a late Skepticism that had forged an alliance with medical empiricism), it is like a purgative that evacuates itself along with the matter that it is intended to evacuate. Whatever logical and psychological difficulties these images may dissimulate (and what if a purgative eliminated itself *before* eliminating what it was supposed to eliminate?), Neopyrrhonism considered that it was freed, through this device that was a mirror image of the Stoic mechanism, from the risks of contradiction that negative metadogmatism entails.

THE STATUS OF SKEPTICAL DISCOURSE

This freedom implies several other benefits, first of all in the theoretical realm. By protecting himself from dogmatism at all levels, the Skeptic believes he has found a way of speaking without asserting anything, a way of being "aphasic" without remaining silent. He thus expresses weak assent, which allows him to avoid extravagance. He gives this sort of assent to his

bodily sensations: it is not a problem for him to say that he is hot. He also gives weak assent to his inferences, through an association of ideas: if he sees smoke without seeing fire, he concludes that there is fire, because he has already seen the two things associated; he has no objection to the use of such "commemorative" signs, whereas he does object to the use of "indicative" signs, by means of which dogmatics believe they can infer, on the basis of observable phenomena, the existence of realities that are in principle unobservable. The same type of assent is valid for his own philosophic utterances: at the beginning of his *Outlines,* Sextus Empiricus takes pains to warn his readers that nothing in what he is about to say is to be taken as "affirmed," nothing is presented decisively as expressing exactly the way things are; the Skeptic only "records" facts as they have appeared to him *(phainetai)* up to the present moment. As he does not record just anything at all, however, one may argue that he has "beliefs," in an appropriate sense of the term. The beliefs he avoids are not those that our nature leads us to maintain but the artificial and hasty beliefs that dogmatics think they can profess on their own behalf and instill in others, and that claim to reach beyond appearances to the hidden nature of things themselves.

Several recent publications have distinguished between two varieties of Skepticism: a "rustic" Skepticism, which submits all beliefs to *epochē,* including those that govern ordinary people's daily lives, and an "urbane" Skepticism, which condemns only the dogmatic beliefs of scientists and philosophers. In this respect, and even if some more or less legendary aspects of Pyrrhon's personality (which Aenesidemus contests, moreover) have placed him at the origin of a tradition of rustic Skepticism, we may say that Neopyrrhonism is on the whole an urbane Skepticism.

There is not enough room here to examine all the means the Skeptics used to arouse and justify *epochē:* Aenesidemus's ten "tropes" or devices; his eight specific tropes against the possibility of knowing the causes of phenomena; and finally Agrippa's five tropes, which form an admirable network in the form of a spider's web in which dogmatics can be caught. We shall look briefly to see whether any belief incompatible with urbane Skepticism is presupposed by one of these devices and arguments or another.

Aenesidemus's tropes do not pose too many problems in this regard, because they lead precisely to not taking what appears as the criterion for what is. They draw attention to the diversity presented by phenomena, chiefly perceptible ones, according to a whole series of dimensions that involve either the subject or the object or the relation between the two. The diversity of phenomena is itself, in some cases, a phenomenon that can be observed directly; in other cases, it can be inferred on the basis of commemorative signs, that is, signs of the type that Skeptics allow themselves to use. To take just one example (this is Aenesidemus's first trope), the sensory organs of many

animals are not the same as ours; now, we observe that when our own organs are modified in one way or another, our perceptions are likewise modified; we may thus infer, without claiming to know what animals different from ourselves perceive, that they do not perceive in the same way we do. And there is no reason to think that our perceptions discover the nature of things "in any way more" than theirs do.

Agrippa's tropes raise other, quite fundamental questions. They presuppose that a certain number of intellectual situations are intolerable: first, contradiction (Pyrrhon is sometimes thought to have rejected the principle of noncontradiction, but it is clear that the Neopyrrhonists do not do this); next, all formal defects (infinite regression, circular reasoning, arbitrary hypotheses) to which the demonstration procedures that attempt to escape from contradiction are condemned, according to Agrippa. What is the epistemological status of these logical interdictions? Let us take the example of infinite regression: we may suppose that the Skeptics would justify its interdiction by invoking either the empirical impossibility, for the human mind, of going back indefinitely from each statement to the one that proves it, or else the logical impossibility, for every possible mind, of considering as proved a statement whose proof would require an infinite series of prior statements.

THE PRACTICAL QUESTION

It is necessary to go back to the empirical component of Skepticism to describe the crux of its response to an objection that is constantly raised, among the ancients as well as the moderns, against all forms of Skepticism: the charge of "making life impossible." According to this view, Skeptics are condemned, unless they are inconsistent, to inaction *(apraxia)*, but is it not impossible to live "without beliefs" *(adoxastos)*, as Skeptics claim they can live? To live in the world of things and of people, can one do without a certain number of beliefs having to do either with the state of things here and now or with the values that make it possible to choose between various possible courses of action? Neopyrrhonism does not consider itself to be affected at all by these criticisms; quite the contrary. The phenomenon, to which it gives the weak assent it permits itself, appears to Neopyrrhonists to be a sufficient criterion for action, and an effective guide for "nonphilosophic" life. Must we say that Skeptics, like Sartre's *salauds*, act like everyone else and think like no one else? But do ordinary people themselves adhere dogmatically to the beliefs that govern their behavior? The Skeptic does not think so, and he would prefer to say that he acts and thinks like everyone else, except for the small, stubborn core of dogmatists. By giving in to his natural reflexes, he meets his own needs and keeps himself out of danger; giving up the illusory quest for universal and objective values, he obeys the laws and follows the customs of

his country. He is capable of abandoning his professional inactivity, so long as we do not imagine that technical action requires objective knowledge of the area in which he operates.

The Skeptic's conception of technical action owes a great deal to the model of so-called empirical medicine. As early as the 3rd century B.C.E., a school of empirical physicians appeared; in opposition to rationalist physicians, the empiricists thought they could base effective practice on experience alone, without any recourse to a supposedly scientific knowledge of the human body, its hidden mechanisms, the objective causes of illness and health, or the intrinsic reasons why remedies and treatments are effective for one illness and not for another. The medical field is probably the one in which a balanced rivalry between empirical and rational practices was established in the most clear-cut and well thought out way (in other areas, the struggle was more uneven: the successes of reason were manifest in mathematics, and the experience of a sailor or a farmer was hard to challenge when it came to predicting the weather). The debate between the schools of medicine thus took on an epistemological and philosophical significance whose importance the philosophers were quick to measure: the Skeptics could see in medical empiricism a model for renouncing dogmatism that did not imply renouncing action, and that could even justify the idea of a nondogmatic form of practical knowledge.

Between Skepticism and the assorted variants of medical empiricism, not only did there exist a sort of preestablished harmony, but also, starting from a date that is difficult to pin down, both philosophies ended up being embodied in the same individuals, such as Menodotus (probably active in the 2nd century C.E.) and several of his successors. Sextus Empiricus himself, as his nickname indicates, was a physician as well as a philosopher; he presented himself as a therapist dealing with illnesses of both mind and soul; he wrote works on medicine that have been lost. Other texts, those of Galen in particular, allow us to clarify the interferences and the debates over epistemological problems that took place between physicians and philosophers of the various schools.

Should we be disappointed that the waters of Skepticism ended up mingling with those of medical empiricism? All this, for such an outcome? A centuries-long effort aimed at critical reflection, at vigilance against illusions, at mastery of the mind over itself, only to end up advocating renunciation of all intellectual ambition, acceptance of a life of dull conformity and the weary exercise of a routine trade? Before giving in to disappointment, we should perhaps ask ourselves whether medical empiricism was as woefully sterile as one might think. The method of empirical physicians, according to Galen, does not rely on direct personal observation alone ("autopsy," in the strict sense of the term); it also calls on the testimony of predecessors (history), a source of enrichment of experience and also an instrument of critical reflection, and on an operation of "passage from like to like," which probably does not purport to explain the similarity of particular cases through a com-

mon cause, but which, motivated and governed by experience, can succeed in establishing laws of regular association between the two. If it is difficult to expect therapeutic progress from a purely empirical medicine, in our sense of the term, we may readily expect progress from experimental medicine; and the empirical medicine of the ancients came to resemble experimental medicine more and more closely.

What is certain is that Skepticism itself, at least as a thought experiment, has not been sterile in the history of Western philosophy. Rarely taken up again as such (it would hardly be very skeptical to adopt Skepticism as a received doctrine) but frequently revisited and rethought, sometimes attenuated, sometimes radicalized, sometimes taken up as a challenge, it has proved capable, by way of Montaigne, Descartes, Pascal, Bayle, Hume, Kant, Nietzsche, and many others, of arousing thought from its "dogmatic slumber." Perhaps it would succeed, if needed, in arousing it from its antidogmatic slumber as well. Let us say that it can lead to anything, on the condition that, if one leaves it behind, one does not do so too quickly.

JACQUES BRUNSCHWIG
Translated by Emoretta Yang and Catherine Porter

Bibliography

Texts and Translations

Diogenes Laertius. *Lives of Eminent Philosophers*, book 9, vol. 2. Trans. R. D. Hicks. Loeb Classical Library.

The Hellenistic Philosophers. Ed. Anthony A. Long and David N. Sedley. Cambridge: Cambridge University Press, 1987.

Sextus Empiricus. *Works*. Trans. R. G. Bury. Loeb Classical Library.

Studies

Annas, Julia, and Jonathan Barnes. *The Modes of Skepticism: Ancient Texts and Modern Interpretations*. Cambridge: Cambridge University Press, 1985.

Barnes, Jonathan. "The Beliefs of a Pyrrhonist." *Proceedings of the Cambridge Philological Society* 28 (1982): 1–28; *Elenchos* 4 (198): 5–43.

———. "Diogenes Laertius IX 61–116: The Philosophy of Pyrrhonism." In W. Haase, ed. *Aufsteig und Niedergang der römischen Welt* II, 36, no. 6 (1992): 4241–4301.

———. *The Toils of Scepticism*. Cambridge: Cambridge University Press, 1990.

Bett, Richard. *Pyrrho: His Antecedents and His Legacy*. Oxford: Oxford University Press, 2000.

Brochard, Victor. *Les sceptiques grecs*. 1887; repr. Paris: Vrin, 1981.

Burnyeat, Myles. "Conflicting Appearances." *Proceedings of the British Academy* 665 (1979): 69–111.

———. "The Sceptic in His Place and Time." In *Philosophy in History: Essays on the*

Historiography of Philosophy. Ed. Richard Rorty, J. B. Schneewind, and Quentin Skinner. Cambridge: Cambridge University Press, 1984.

Burnyeat, Myles, ed. *The Skeptical Tradition.* Berkeley: University of California Press, 1983.

Dal Pra, Mario. *Lo scetticismo greco.* Repr. Rome-Bari: Laterza, 1975.

Frede, Michael. *Essays in Ancient Philosophy.* Minneapolis: University of Minnesota Press, 1987.

Giannantoni, Gabriele, ed. *Lo scetticismo antico.* 2 vols. Naples: Bibliopolis, 1981.

———. "Sesto Empirico e il pensiero antico." *Elenchos* 13 (1992): 1–366.

Hankinson, R. J. *The Sceptics.* London: Routledge, 1995.

Robin, Léon. *Pyrrhon et le scepticisme grec.* Paris: Presses Universitaires de France, 1944.

Schofield, Malcolm, Myles Burnyeat, and Jonathan Barnes, eds. *Doubt and Dogmatism.* Oxford: Clarendon Press, 1980.

Stopper, M. R. "Schizzi Pirroniani." *Phronesis* 28 (1983): 265–297.

Related Articles

The Philosopher; Ethics; Language; Pyrrhon; Epistemology; Medicine; Plato; The Academy

SOPHISTS

In the Presocratic dawn of philosophy, the intellectual movement known as sophistic seduced and scandalized all Greece. Indeed, the sophists were the "masters of Greece," according to Hegel's apt expression. Instead of reflecting on being, like the Eleatics, or on nature, like the Ionian physicists, they elected to be professional educators, through whom "culture itself came into being." They were itinerant foreigners who traded on their wisdom and skills like courtesans trading on their charms. However, they were also men of power who knew how to convince judges, sway an assembly, lead a successful embassy, give a new city its laws, build democracy—in short, they were engaged in politics. This dual mastery was rooted entirely in their command of language, from linguistics (the morphology, grammar, and synonymy that made Prodicus famous) to rhetoric (the study of tropes, sonorities, and opportuneness, at which Gorgias excelled); above all, according to Hegel's diagnosis, the sophists were "masters of eloquence."

This type of connection to language constituted, for better or for worse, the line separating the "sophist," *sophistēs,* an expert in wisdom, from the "philo-sophe," who loves his subject but dares not claim to possess it completely. Consider the following example that shows, in symptomatic fashion, the double meaning of the word *sophistic* as found in one of the most current dictionaries of philosophy (translated from André Lalande, *Vocabulaire technique et critique de la philosophie*): "Sophistic: A. Collection of doctrines, or, rather, the intellectual attitude shared by the principal Greek sophists (Protagoras, Gorgias, Prodicus, Hippias, etc.). B. Said of a philosophy of verbal reasoning that is neither sound nor serious." The first meaning situates the Greek sophists of the 5th century B.C.E. within the framework of intellectual history: powerful personalities who constituted something like a movement. In this sense, sophistic is a way of thinking that, with increasing appreciation, we define today as relativist, progressivist, concerned with phenomena and the human world, even humanistic. By contrast, in the second definition, in a way that is timeless and somewhat mysterious, the name serves to designate one of the nonphilosophical modes within the field of philosophy, that of "verbal reasoning." And so we are obliged to conclude that sophistic came into being, and has been constituted, as philosophy's alter ego: it is not only a historical fact but also a structural effect.

The evidence for this duality is found first of all in the texts. Owing to the vagaries of transmission, only a few original fragments have survived. Al-

most all of these are contained in statements or interpretations that sought to discredit them.

Hermann Diels and Walther Kranz, and later Mario Untersteiner, assembled the fragmentary writings of the sophists. By looking at this collection, we can measure the sparseness of the authentic works, those that can be attributed *expressis verbis* to the sophists. There are two clear tendencies: on the one hand, the work of Gorgias, with the ontology, or "meontology," of his *Treatise of Non-Being* and the rhetoric of his *Encomium of Helen* and *Defense of Palamedes;* on the other hand, the work of Antiphon, new fragments of which have recently been discovered, with its focus on ethics and politics in the papyrus *On Truth* and with the model speeches presented in the *Tetralogies.* The surviving fragments are insignificant, however, compared with the number of accounts and dramatizations that they generated. Reconstructing these theses and doctrines resembles a kind of paleontology of perversion, since the same texts supply both reliable knowledge and distorted representations of sophistic.

The starting point, and Plato's point of fusion of history and structure, is as follows: sophistic is a historical reality and at the same time an artifact, a by-product of philosophy, which always represents it as the worst of the alternatives. Let us take the example of Protagoras, who is said to have been the first sophist. We possess only two statements made by him. One refers to the gods: "I can neither know that they are, nor that they are not" (Diogenes Laertius, IX.51); the other, the more famous, deals with the *khrēmata*, normally translated as "things": "Man is the measure of all things: of those that are, that they are, of those that are not, that they are not" (Plato, *Theaetetus,* 151e–152e). It is significant that the context for the transmission or interpretation of this phrase is none other than Plato's *Theaetetus* and Book IV of Aristotle's *Metaphysics,* as well as Book VII of Sextus Empiricus's *Adversus Mathematicos.* The dialogue between Socrates and Theaetetus alone doubtless suffices to give credence once and for all to the relativist and subjectivist meaning of "Protagoras's proposition," and to strip it of all pretension: if truth is reduced to what each person feels it to be, Protagoras might just as well have said that "a pig or a baboon is the measure of all things."

The now traditional image of sophistic first appears in Plato's dialogues. It is discredited on all grounds: ontological, because the sophist is not concerned with being but takes refuge in nonbeing and the accidental *(Sophist);* logical, since he does not seek truth or dialectical rigor but only opinion, superficial coherence, persuasion, and victory in oratorical jousting *(Euthydemus);* and on ethical, pedagogical, and political grounds, since he does not strive for wisdom and virtue, either for the individual or for the city, but aims at personal power and money *(Gorgias).* Sophistic is discredited even on literary grounds, since its stylistic devices are nothing more than the swelling of an encyclopedic emptiness (as illustrated throughout *Protagoras,* for example). If mea-

sured by the yardstick of being and truth, sophistic must be condemned as pseudophilosophy: a philosophy of appearances and the appearance of philosophy. Plato invents the sophist as the alter ego of the philosopher, continually imitating and pretending to be a philosopher. They resemble one another, according to the remark of the Stranger in *Sophist*, "as the wolf resembles the dog, the fiercest resembles the tamest." Yet from the use of grammatical cases alone we understand that resemblance is "the slipperiest of genres," for (although this normally goes unnoticed) in the exchange between Theaetetus and Socrates, the dative case clearly puts the sophist in the position of the dog, thus putting the philosopher in the position of the wolf. They resemble one another so closely that, even when you grasp them with both hands, whenever you think you have caught one, you find yourself holding the other: Socrates' cathartic maieutics, his method of refutation, thus constitutes the *genei gennaia sophistikē* ("the authentic and truly noble sophistics"), and generates the possibility of Socrates as a sophist or quasi sophist. Conversely, when all the dichotomies that have served to trap the sophist and construct a definition of him are recapitulated at the end of the dialogue, the final branch leaves us on the same side, opposite the demagogue, with the alternative "sage or sophist?" (268b10), and the answer is determined by just one thesis: "But we have posited"—says Theaetetus—"that he knows nothing." The sophist is not only an imitator but also a paronym of the "sage," designated by a word of the same family, neither more nor less than the philosopher himself. Consequently—and this is of course what surfaces in *Sophist* and completely disrupts its tight organization—the artifact is, conversely, a producer of philosophy; it leads inevitably to parricide and prompts a reflection on being and nonbeing, the major genres, and syntax.

Aristotle, in turn, refutes those who use Protagoras's "man is the measure" to claim that "all phenomena are true," and who believe that they can thus escape the principle of noncontradiction: like Heraclitus and in fact like all the Presocratics, they simply confuse thought with feeling, and feeling with alteration (*Metaphysics* IV). To trust exclusively in the perceptible and in feelings, and to seek to translate faithfully this perpetual becoming in words, is like trying to catch a bird in midflight, and it means condemning oneself to silence, like Cratylus who, simply by moving his finger, designates the river that is never the same and that no one can ever enter (Aristotle, *Metaphysics* IV.5.1010a10–15). If the sophist perseveres with consistency in his so-called phenomenology of all that is fleeting and relative, he condemns himself to silence and disqualifies himself single-handedly. But what if he prefers to continue speaking, and knowingly contradicts himself? Unlike Plato, Aristotle cannot be content to reduce sophistic to a shadow cast by philosophy—a harmful one, since it is both misled and misleading: he has to elaborate a veritable strategy of exclusion. This time, the impossibility of subverting the principle of noncontradiction lies in the proper demonstration of the principle

itself, since this demonstration is a refutation. Starting with what the adversary of the principle maintains, if only to deny it, the demonstration reveals the surprising consequence that the adversary is obeying the principle at the very moment he is contesting it. Sophistic taken at its word is Aristotelian, and if Protagoras speaks (which sophists ordinarily do), he can speak only as Aristotle does. The core of the refutation depends on a series of equivalencies that, once articulated, are as obvious as ontology itself: to speak is to say something, something that has a single meaning, the same for everyone, speaker and listener alike. Therefore, all I have to do is speak; the principle of noncontradiction is thereby proven and established. The same word cannot simultaneously have and not have the same meaning. All I have to do is speak, or, to quote Aristotle, have "the adversary say something." Aristotle seals the argument by incorporating that necessary and sufficient condition in the very definition of man as an animal endowed with *logos*: this excludes a priori from humanity all those who choose not to participate in the demonstration, since then "such a man, inasmuch as he is [such], is from the outset equal to a plant" (*Metaphysics* IV.4). Those who refuse to accept this condition are thus reduced to a prelinguistic stage: silence or noise. They are free to take an interest in "what is in the sounds of the voice and in words," such as the barbarian's bla-bla-bla; they are left to focus on the signifier, inasmuch as it does not signify. The need for meaning, thus confused with the goal of univocity, can then become, throughout Aristotle's *Sophistical Refutations*, a formidable weapon against homonymy (a single word with several meanings) and amphiboly (homonymy in syntax, when a single phrase may be construed in several ways). But, more radically, by making the necessity of noncontradiction, the necessity of meaning, and the goal of univocity equivalent, Aristotle marginalized the resisters, equating them with "talking plants," and relegated them to the fringes not only of philosophy but also of humanity.

If the sophist is the philosopher's other, and if philosophy systematically excludes sophists from its own field, the philosopher can only define himself as the sophist's other, an other that sophistic never stops pushing further into a corner. Philosophy is the daughter of wonder, and, according to the first sentence of *Metaphysics*, "all men by nature desire understanding" (Aristotle, *Metaphysics* I.980a). However, "those who feel doubt about whether or not the gods ought to be honoured and parents loved, need castigation, while those who doubt whether snow is white or not, [just need to have a look]" (Aristotle, *Topica* I.xi). The sophist (Protagoras on the gods, Antiphon on the family, Gorgias on what is) exaggerates: he always asks one question too many, draws one conclusion too many. This insolence (*hybris*, shameless excess, and *apaideusia*, the ignorance of the ill-bred, are the two Greek terms that characterize the sophist's philosophical perception) succeeds in putting philosophy literally outside itself; it forces the love of wisdom to transgress

the limits that it assigns itself and to perform a certain number of gestures—to come to blows—that are definitely not of the same order as the rest of its approach. Sophistic marks the boundaries of philosophy.

In this light, we can understand the value of studying the repeated resurfacing of sophistic, the way in which it constantly outwits philosophical censure, particularly with the movement that called itself, at the height of the imperial period five centuries after Protagoras and Gorgias, the second sophistic. It is something other than philosophy, different from the metaphysics extending from Plato and Aristotle to Hegel and Heidegger, and yet there is nothing purely and simply irrational in it. This is why sophistic remains very much an issue today.

SOPHISTIC AND THE CRITIQUE OF ONTOLOGY: THE PRIMAL SCENE, OR GORGIAS VERSUS PARMENIDES

If philosophy seeks to silence sophistic, it is probably because, conversely, sophistic produces philosophy as an artifact of language. Witness, first and foremost, a remarkable little treatise by Gorgias, a Sicilian born at Leontium around 485 B.C.E. (We have two versions of this text, one transmitted by Sextus Empiricus, *Adversus mathematicos* VII.65–87, the other constituting the third part of an anonymous doxographic text, *On Melissus, Xenophon and Gorgias [M.X.G.]*, traditionally published within the Aristotelian corpus.)

On Nonbeing, or On Nature: the title of Gorgias's treatise, passed on by Sextus, is provocative. It is precisely the title given to the works of almost all Presocratic philosophers who wrote treatises on nature. But it is also the exact opposite, since what these physicists, or physiologues, especially Parmenides, call *phusis,* or "nature," as Heidegger will insist, designates whatever grows and hence comes into presence: being. Gorgias's treatise, emblematic of sophistic in this respect, must be understood as a secondary discourse, as the critique of a previous text—in this case, Parmenides' poem, which potentially contains the ontology.

"Nothing is." "If it is, it is unknowable" (or, as Sextus puts it, "it cannot be grasped by man"). "If it is and if it is knowable, it cannot be communicated to others" (or "formulated and explained to one's fellow man"). In addition to the title, Gorgias's discursive gesture, in its very form, runs counter to the poem's development. Instead of the self-unfurling of the "is" in the circular fullness of its very present and represented identity, instead of "nature" as progress, as a self-revelatory accretion, the treatise offers a structure of retreat, setting forth the main thesis at the outset, then dwindling according to the characteristics of antilogy, of defense, of discourse that remains forever secondary. This structure is illustrated quite masterfully by Freud, who refers to the sophists in *Jokes and Their Relation to the Unconscious* and is often invoked by their interpreters: A has borrowed a copper pot from B; when A re-

turns it, B complains that the pot has a large hole that makes it useless. A's defense: (1) I never borrowed the pot from B; (2) it had a hole when I borrowed it; (3) I returned the pot intact.

Each of Gorgias's three theses appears to be an ironic or crude overturning of the conventional reading of Parmenides that everybody since Plato must have learned by heart: first, that there is being because being is and nonbeing is not; next, that being is by nature knowable, since being and thinking are the same. This means that philosophy, and more precisely the primary philosophy we call metaphysics, has been able quite naturally to follow its own course: to know being as such, and to trade in doctrines, disciples, and schools. To be, to know, to transmit: not to be, to be unknowable, to be untransmissible.

With his first thesis, Gorgias's whole strategy is to make us understand that Being, Parmenides' hero just as Ulysses is Homer's hero, is never anything but the effect of the poem. By following the way the key word *Is* at the beginning of the poem suffices through a series of infinitives and participles to conceal the entire subject, *being* (in Greek *to on*, "the being," fully identified by means of the definite article), the sophist dissects the way syntax creates semantics. Such a reading is sufficient to overturn the evidence of the poem, for nonbeing can be expressed in a sentence just as well as being. Plato's Stranger will return to this Wittgensteinian argument: Parmenides should not have spoken of nonbeing, should not have pronounced the word or even thought it, for unless it accomplishes the inhuman feat of making sounds like a chiming bell, language propels us, and whoever says *ouk esti* ("is not") will, before he knows it, borne by the very syntactic force of the language he is speaking, reach the point of saying *ta me eonta* (literally, "the nonbeings"; *Sophist* 237a–239b). Gorgias explains it perfectly: "If Not-being is Not-Being, Not-Being IS no less than being. For Not-Being IS Not-being, and Being IS also Being, so that things exist no more than not exist" (*M.X.G.* 979a). Hegel suggests, in *The Science of Logic,* that "those who insist on the difference between being and nothingness ought to *tell* us what the difference is." But Gorgias reveals something else again, in a way that leads this time rather more from Aristotle to Kant and Benveniste: not only can nonbeing be expressed in a sentence just as being can, it can be expressed better than being: better in the sense of being less "sophistic," because it allows less room for ambiguity between the copula and existence. In fact, when someone says "the being is being," the two meanings of the verb *to be* are confirmed in one another and risk becoming indistinguishable; conversely, the proposition of identity applied to nonbeing ("the non-being is non-being") does not lead one to conclude, in the absence of error or bad faith, that nonbeing exists; it simply leads to a distinction between the two meanings of "is": the ontologist is, as it were, more sophist than the sophist.

The catastrophe is complete with the second premise of the poem — "being,

thinking: the same," to borrow the paratactic translation that Heidegger occasionally proposes for the controversial Fragment 3—where truth as unveiling, and then as adequacy, finds its moorings. It suffices in fact to think something, and, a fortiori, to say it, for that thing to be; if I say, "Chariots are fighting in the middle of the sea," then chariots are fighting in the middle of the sea. This series of reversals does not belong to rhetorical—hence external—virtuosity, but to catastrophe, in the etymological sense of the word: it is a radical internal criticism of ontology. If it is impossible to say what is not, then anything one says is true. There is no room for nonbeing, nor any room for error or lies; it is Parmenides' ontology alone, taken at its word and pushed to its limits, that guarantees the infallibility and the efficacy of speech, which is thereby sophistic. Gorgias's procedure, his treatise against Parmenides' poem, thus simply consists in drawing attention, somewhat insolently, to all the maneuvers (even those of language and discursive strategies themselves) that allow the relationship of unveiling between being and saying to occur. The effect of limit or catastrophe thus produced consists in showing that, if the ontological text is rigorous, in other words if it does not constitute an exception with regard to the rules it lays down, then it is a sophistic masterpiece.

In place of ontology, which is now only one discursive possibility among others, quite patently self-legitimated, the sophist proposes something like a "logology" by his "performances" (as early as in Plato's dialogues, *epideixeis* designates the lectures and presentations characteristic of the sophistic style). The term *logology* is borrowed from Novalis, to indicate that being, inasmuch as it is, is first produced, performed, by speech. This is readily verified in *Encomium of Helen*, which is the model for epideictic oratory, the rhetorical genre par excellence: *epideixis* again, but this time in the rhetorical terminology adopted by Isocrates and especially by Aristotle, in the narrower sense of "eulogy." Far from giving us an adequate picture of Helen of Troy, the "dog face," a traitress twice over—to her first and second homelands—who left Greece scorched and bloodied, both in actual wars and in Homer's poems, Gorgias fabricates for future generations (from Euripides, Isocrates, and Dio Chrysostom to Offenbach, Claudel, and Giraudoux) an innocent Helen who will make him famous. He imagines four scenarios: Helen is innocent, obviously, if "she did what she did" owing to the will of fortune, the whim of the gods, and the decrees of necessity—"fatality," as Offenbach will have her say; she is innocent again if, as a weak woman confronted by male strength, "she was taken violently" (*Encomium of Helen* 6–7). But Gorgias adds that she is also innocent if—his third hypothesis—she was persuaded by words, or if—in the fourth case—she was simply in love. How can her crime itself—letting herself be seduced—make her blameless? Very simply because it is not Helen's fault if she has eyes and ears. Just as her eyes beheld Paris's beautiful body, her ears heard his speech. Now "speech is a great master [lo-

gos dunastēs megas estin] which, [by the means of] the smallest and most imperceptible bod[ies] achieves the most divine acts, for it has the power to end fear and banish pain, to produce joy and increase pity" (ibid. 8). Gorgias goes on to analyze the results of discursive tyranny in different areas of speech and its deep causes, anchored in human temporality. In the end, Helen's innocence depends on just that power of the *logos:* seduced by Paris's words, Helen is not guilty because words are, in the strictest sense, irresistible, and the encomium becomes both a hymn to the *logos,* and an encomium of the encomium itself. Gorgias deploys the eulogy like a toy (*emon de paignion,* "my game" or "my toy," as the final words of the *Encomium* crudely state): it is a matter finally of a performance, both codified and creative, that enables the orator not only to strengthen the consensus but also to create it. Appealing to opinion, starting with banalities, those things everyone agrees on (everyone says "with a single voice and a single heart" that Helen is the guiltiest of women [ibid.]), he plays with the *logos* to make these objects exist differently, to produce them as different, to produce different ones ("in every case she escapes accusation": Helen is worthy of praise). Or again, there is a moment in every encomium when language overtakes the object, when language becomes the maker of objects, when description, commonplace statements, open up. This is the moment of creation, including the creation of values: the moment of rhetorical convergence between critique of ontology and institution of politics.

If being is an effect of speaking, then the immediacy of nature and the evidence of words that have the duty of expressing it adequately disappear together: *phusis*—nature—revealed by words, gives way to politics created by speech. Here, thanks to the sophists, we reach the political dimension: the city appears as the continual creation of language. If it is a game, sophistic is a game that produces the world just as the game of the Heraclitean child does.

ETHICS AND POLITICS: PROTAGORAS, ANTIPHON

Once confidence in Plato's artifact is lost, it is difficult to speak of sophistic, especially with regard to politics: taken individually, according to all accounts, the sophists held very contradictory views. The first generation, that of Protagoras of Abdera (ca. 490–421 B.C.E.), a friend of Pericles and legislator of Thourioi who was finally exiled for impiety, is sometimes thought to have consisted of democrats and freethinkers. The second generation, that of Critias, who was allied with the Thirty and conspired with Sparta to turn Attica into "a desert left to the sheep" (Philostrates, *Lives of the Sophists* I.16), is thought to have turned away from this sort of equality. Sophistic seems to value contradiction, not just in logic or ontology, but throughout the political and social domain. The sophists somehow managed to appear both as the "new wise men" who sought to do away with prevailing ideas and traditional

values, and as promoters of orthodoxy in the city-state, champions of the most conventional and stereotypical behavior.

The difficulty is most pronounced in the case of Antiphon. Projecting contemporary contradictions, some scholars have believed, based on their reading of the doxographers and biographers, that there must have been several Antiphons, and in fact, for many years a distinction was made between two Antiphons in particular (and some still make the distinction today). Antiphon of Rhamnus, born around 470 B.C.E. and known as an oligarchic aristocrat, was condemned to death in 411 for high treason following his involvement in the affair of the Four Hundred; he was a logographer and mainstream orator of whom Thucydides gives a highly favorable portrait. The second Antiphon, whom Hermogenes, relying on Didymus of Alexandria, introduces for stylistic reasons as "the other Antiphon" (*De ideis* II), was the author of *Peri aletheias* and *Peri homonoias*. A later tradition identified him as Antiphon the Sophist, who, as an anarcho-democrat, was able to maintain that Greeks and barbarians were of the very same nature.

The paradox is partially explained if we agree to return to a position that antedates our own antitheses (democracy/conservatism, revolution/reaction): to the very constitution of the polis that signals the "Greek miracle" of the 5th century. Polis, *logos*, sophistic: the eminently political character of sophistic is first of all a matter of *logos*, a term that in Greek ties together thinking and speaking. The sophists would certainly not have existed without the city-state par excellence, Pericles' Athens, where they could establish their reputation, and where they could recruit their wealthy students from the assembled crowds. But, for better or worse, the Greek city-state itself could not have existed without these troublesome strangers—the city-state that Aristotle defines as composed of animals who are simply more political than the others because they can speak.

We can verify the strength of the bond between *logos* and politics through Protagoras's statement, the one that forced Socrates, as if he were ashamed of his relativistic interpretation, to make an "apology" for its author. Protagoras does not simply mean that a phenomenon is only what it appears to be to those to whom it appears, man or pig, but also that from that point on there can be no distinction between being and appearance, opinion and truth. Hence, the wise man will not be in the right, nor will he ever persuade anyone to give up a false opinion in favor of a true one, but he will, like a physician with his medications or a sophist with his speech, produce "inversions" or "reversals" and bring his interlocutor from an inferior state to a better one. Thus "the wise and good orators make the good [things that are useful to their states], instead of the evil [harmful ones], seem to be right" [Plato, *Theaetetus* 167c]. In perfect agreement with *Encomium of Helen*, the *logos* of the sophists is not an *organon*, a tool needed to show or demonstrate what is, but a *pharmakon*, a remedy for improving souls and cities—even if, follow-

ing Plato, no one can forget that *pharmakon* means, indissolubly, poison. Like Gorgias's so-called nihilism, what is called Protagoras's relativism takes its meaning only if interpreted in light of political life when related to eloquence as its very foundation.

Thus, instead of an opposition between true and false, there emerges a question of value; and not in the form of a new alternative between good and evil, but, according to the plurality inherent to the comparative, as a quantification of "the best," understood as useful and, more exactly, useful for. It is on this basis that we must understand, in the phrase about man the measure, the meaning of *khremata*, which Protagoras uses to designate exactly that of which man is the measure. *Khrema*, from the same family as *khrē* (it is necessary, it must) and *khraomai* (to desire, to lack, to use), is understood as linked to *kheir*, the hand. In contrast to *pragmata* (things as resulting from action, the state of things) and *onta* (things inasmuch as they are there, present, as beings), it designates what one needs and uses—a "deal," an event, and, in the plural, wealth and money. This key word of sophistic launches, in the face of an accumulation of being as presence, the temporalized spread of usage, of usury, of expenditure. "Whatever someone has not used, nor will not use, whether or not it belongs to him, will have neither more nor less effect," says Antiphon (frg. 87B.54, *Die Fragmente des Vorsokratiker* 2, p. 362), for example, to console the miser in the fable who, instead of "pouring as much as possible," like Callicles, into his punctured vessels, had buried his treasure (thus *khremata*) in the garden and was robbed. Some interpreters, like Aristotle, will link this notion to the infinite evil of the chrematistic, where money, just by circulating, produces money independently from any need; they may even read into it a model for a general economy in which accumulation and exchange yield to flux and to what Georges Bataille calls "consumation." Whether it is a matter of *logos* or of *khremata*, we understand in any case that sophistic chooses time and flux over space and presence.

While calculating what is best, "the line between good and evil disappears: there is where the sophist is found" (Nietzsche, *Posthumous Fragments* 87–88). Yet Protagoras claims that he teaches "virtue" (at least that is how *arete* is normally translated), despite Socrates' protestations in *Protagoras* and in *Gorgias*. Socrates never stops fighting that claim, using examples drawn from fathers and statesmen celebrated for their virtue but unfortunately surrounded by unworthy sons and compatriots. The famous myth of Protagoras would seem to give credence to this goodwill on the part of the sophist, and to make it plain that a politics worthy of the name, in the stable form of a city-state, depends on ethics, for politics is inconceivable without the participation of all in *aidōs* and *dikē*, two fundamental virtues usually translated as respect and justice. This interpretation of a major text of political philosophy, which offers the conventionally minded a good Protagoras to redeem the insufferable Callicles or Thrasymachus, warrants a more serious reexamination,

starting with the literal text of the myth and of the sustained speech that explicates it (Plato, *Protagoras* 320c–328d).

We know that Prometheus, to compensate for Epimetheus's carelessness, steals "knowledge of art along with fire" from Hephaestus and Athena, and that these gifts are enough to procure for men "all the abilities they need to live": not only can they build houses, clothe themselves, and cultivate the land, but they can also honor the gods and speak words; faced with aggressive beasts, they even try to "gather together" and "build cities." Yet they need the art of politics for two reasons: to triumph over animals, and to stay together without letting the injustices they commit against one another divide them from the start. Hence the intervention of Zeus, worried about our species' survival, who sends Hermes bearing *aidōs* and *dikē*, "so that the cities might have the structures and bonds of friendship necessary for [gathering people together]" (Plato, *Protagoras* 322c3), with instructions to divide them up among all men, and to destroy all those incapable of sharing in *aidōs* and *dikē* as constituting a "disease of the city" (ibid., 322d5).

If we take the terms more literally, *aidōs*, respect, represents the feeling produced by others' scrutiny and expectations, a respect for public opinion and, as a result, self-respect; similarly, *dikē*, before it meant justice, hence trial and punishment, signified rule, custom, everything that one might "display" *(deiknumi):* a standard of public behavior. *Aidōs* is thus simply the reason to respect *dikē*, and *dikē* is strong insofar as human beings feel *aidōs:* in this combination of respect and custom there is nothing suggesting an ethical intention, and even less the autonomy of a moral subject; the terms refer only to the rules of public action, always mediated by the gaze of the other. What is more, this kind of behavior necessarily demands hypocrisy: when Protagoras comments on his myth, he reinterprets the "disease" condemned by Zeus, and stresses that "all men must call themselves just, whether they are or not, and anyone who doesn't feign justice is a fool" (*Protagoras* 323b). Such a myth cannot be purely and simply the ethical basis for politics.

If we read closely, it becomes apparent that the model for political "excellence" (the most literal translation of *arete*) is once again nothing other than *logos* itself. The two teachings converge when the child begins to practice the convention represented by words, later when he learns to read, write, and make music, and finally through the written texts of the laws (indeed, a magistrate, on finishing his term, has to submit a report to show that he has copied the laws well). To seek a teacher of virtue is the same as to seek someone who teaches one to *hellenizein:* "Why, you might as well ask who is a teacher of Greek," concludes Protagoras (327e–328a): politics and language, or more exactly teaching the Greek language, thus make common cause. This is just what Aelius Aristides, a sophist of the second sophistic, will demonstrate forcefully, rewriting the myth seven centuries later and substituting for *aidōs* and *dikē* the single term *rhetorical virtue* (*Orations* II.394–399). While hu-

man beings in the Prometheus myth had the means "to articulate sound and words" (*Protagoras* 322a), according to Aristides, they obviously did not know either Greek or the art of speaking well: the myth of Protagoras, reread in light of Protagoras's explication in Plato's *Protagoras,* makes the institution of politics an *analogon* of discursive excellence.

The paradox inherent in Protagoras's teaching as well as in his myth thus appears very clearly. Everyone in the city teaches virtue, just as everyone teaches Greek, and everyone is an expert; however, some students are more gifted than others, and some teachers, like Protagoras, ask to be paid. Without exception, they all participate in politics, just as they all speak: Protagoras's myth is clearly the founding myth of democracy. But certain people are differentially "better," are recognized as such, and therefore must be listened to, so the same myth is after all a founding myth of aristocracy—which means that democracy and aristocracy are linked by pedagogy, by paideia. To prefer to be a teacher who is paid rather than a philosopher-king who subjugates is perhaps the truly sophistic—and surprisingly modern—way to separate ethics from politics while reinforcing democracy.

Logos produces the continuous creation of the city-state, because it is the crafter of the *homonoia* (literally, identity of spirit, of feeling) to which both Gorgias and Antiphon, among others, devote a treatise. In Plato's *Republic,* where politics and ethics are one and the same, subjected to the same idea of the Good, *homonoia* determines one of the four virtues that characterize the individual's soul as well as the expanded soul that constitutes the city-state: it is defined as a sense of hierarchy, and, along with justice, is a virtue of structure, determining the proper function of each class within an organic whole. In contrast, a consensus of the sophistic type is always the precarious result of a rhetorical exercise of persuasion, which produces, time after time, an instantaneous unity made entirely of dissension, of differences (this opportunity, *kairos,* is represented in the guise of a young man who is balding in back and who must be seized by the front hairs). The model of the city-state, unified only as a plurality in progress (*homonoia:* consensus), extends to the way in which each individual, in order not to be "at war against himself," relates to himself (*homonoia:* "accord of the self with the self" [Stobaeus, II.33.15; 87B.44a Diels-Kranz]). The unity implied by "with" becomes the matrix of singularity.

The scraps of *Peri homonoias, On Consensus* (on concord, on agreement, as we might say) that have been attributed to Antiphon are too fragmentary to allow us to make much progress: often in the form of a proverb or a fable (that of the miser, discussed earlier, for example), they lead us to take time and usage into account when actual behavior is at stake, but in the surviving fragments the term *homonoia* appears only in the title.

In contrast, Antiphon's *On Truth,* which has to be reevaluated in light of some recently discovered fragments, constitutes the longest authentic text we

have on the political thought of a Sophist. The object of a multitude of interpretations (it has been associated with the names of Hobbes, Rousseau, Kant,
Sade), it establishes the opposition between nature and law, probably for the
first time—an opposition taken up again later, with contradictory evalua-
tions, by Plato's Socrates and Callicles in *Gorgias* and by Thrasymachus in
The Republic. In Antiphon's text, nature and law are differentiated not by the
ideas on which they are based but by the way they are used, their utilization
and their usefulness, and in particular by the consequences their transgression entails. The transgression of natural necessity does harm "according to
truth" (*di alētheian,* frg. B, col. II and III; 87B.44, Diels-Kranz frg. A): as the
etymology suggests, one cannot "escape" (*lāthei,* from *lanthanō,* to be hidden) nature, and punishment always follows. By contrast, the transgression of
a conventional rule produces only an effect "according to opinion"; thus the
effect is radically different depending on whether one is acting under public
scrutiny or in the secrecy of the private realm. With secrecy, clearly, we come
back to the natural, but nature is then no longer primary: it is a simple
break—which Antiphon describes in a tone sometimes evocative of Sade—
with the imperialism of the legality that claims to limit even our senses and
to prescribe, for example, "what the eyes may and may not see." But the laws
that define the city-state in which one lives are themselves "the result of an
agreement" or "consensus" (*homologethenta):* such is the role of *homonoia,*
in all the force of its novelty and its separation from the natural order.
Antiphon even invents a neologism to say that man, from the beginning, is
no longer a creature of nature but of culture: "one is citizenized" (*politeuetai
tis,* behaves like a citizen), in other words, one is immersed in a "there is" of
politics. Hence man-as-citizen is confronted with laws from the outset, although it might be in his interest, yet again, to have as little to do with them
as possible, especially if the laws are powerless to defend him against ensuing
violence. Thus, in a manner that allows criticism of the law once its effectiveness has been overwhelmingly established, politics again substitutes for
physics as it typically does in sophistic, and the definition of political legality
is simply sharing, agreement, and even—in the true meaning of *homologia*—linguistic agreement.

Antiphon, in the very controversial and conjectural fragment A (44, Diels-
Kranz frg. B, col. II) is quite probably the inventor of another neologism: to
barbarize. "The laws of those who live far away are unknown to us and we do
not respect them. In this behaviour we have become like barbarians [*bebar-
barometha*] to one another, whereas, by nature, we all find ourselves in all respects naturally made to be both Barbarian and Greek." This simple sentence
has contributed to the view of Antiphon as a subversive and modern partisan
of absolute equality among all men. It is a matter of replacing the natural basis for the difference between Greek and barbarian—a difference invalidated
by the universality of the characteristics of the species ("we all breathe air

through the mouth and nostrils" (44, Diels-Kranz frg. B, col. II)—with a cultural basis, even a political one: Greeks and barbarians have a different way of relating to laws. We know that the term *to barbarize* will later come to mean (and it is the irrefutable sign of ethnocentrism) to speak in an unintelligible manner, to commit barbarisms. We should understand that, for Antiphon, we "barbarize" and lose our identity as "Greeks" whenever we relate to the law in a manner that is purely idiosyncratic and thus renounce the intelligibility and universality of both the *logos* and the *homologia*. This view is confirmed by, among other things, the relationship between Antiphon and certain texts of sophistic learning, including Euripides' *Orestes* (to barbarize is to reject, like Orestes, the "common law"—which happens to be precisely that of the Greeks, who are thus champions of the universal—and to fall back into bestiality as a result) and the dialogue between Socrates and Hippias as reported by Xenophon (*Memorabilia* IV), in which Socrates distinguishes Greece from the rest of the world because one law, valid for all, demands that the citizens "take an oath of *homonoia*." If we sought to find something of Kant in Antiphon, as all the major interpreters have attempted to do, it would have to be not the Kant of the autonomy of moral conscience but rather the Kant of the typic of pure practical reason, who recommends acting as if the law were universal, that is to say, as universal as a natural law.

But we must always keep in mind this "as if," which has to do with the fabrication of the universal and the legal. Apart from the historical and philological reasons, this is no doubt the best argument for believing that the two Antiphons are in fact only one. Indeed, *Tetralogies* provides textbook cases for the fabrication of law. For example, in the second *Tetralogy* a young man has killed his friend while practicing with the javelin. A specialist in Athenian law such as Glotz cannot comprehend why Antiphon fails to invoke that law, which provides for acquittal in precisely such a case of involuntary murder. Instead, in what happens it is as if the law, and not just jurisprudence, had to be invented, along with both the meaning and the understanding of the concepts that define and delimit causation *(un état de cause)*. Thus the father of the javelin thrower stipulates that his son acted voluntarily, in throwing, but suffered involuntarily, by being prevented from reaching his target; the agent responsible for the involuntary murder turns out to be the victim himself, whose fault *(hamartia)*, with respect to himself, has already been punished by death (*Tetralogies* III.B.7–8). *Nomimon* and *dikaion,* that which conforms to the law and to justice, are nothing more than the effect of a convention whose judgment will provide the ultimate content until the next trial. To the surprise of jurists, but not of readers of Aristotle's *Rhetoric*, the orator only shows the elaboration that suits the *kairos*: he can call on the *jus sacrum* (religious law), miasma and revenge, to reestablish purity, or upon *jus civile* (civil law), which he can apply in one direction or another ("the law that serves to pursue me absolves me," *Tetralogies* IV). Aristotle will elaborate

without scruples on this practice, under the name of "nontechnical proof" (atekhnos pistis), in chapter 15 of the first book of his *Rhetoric*. Laws, like witnesses' accounts, conventions, confessions under torture, and oaths, must be used with skill. One must be able to determine their "spirit"; one can and must play written law against common law, the legal against the equitable, one text against another, one interpretation against another. In short, it is all a matter of discourse.

Thus we measure the sophistic power that *Tetralogies*, a series of four speeches, possesses as a model of judicial rhetoric: an accusation, a defense, a new accusation that takes into account the first defense, then a final defense, each offering its own narrative and its own version of the same event, according to the immediate tactical demands. The identity of the individuals and of the behaviors in question is diffracted in a perfect illustration of the fact that "truth" always comes second. Just as, in the papyrus *On Truth*, the immediate is nothing other than the legal, in view of which the primacy of nature is only secondary, in the same way the *Tetralogies* immerse us in the *eikos*, the probable, the plausible, so that the true becomes a simple trope of the *eikos*. On the one hand, both *eikos* and *nomos* are first and foremost the product of a discourse that succeeds in obtaining agreement about what it presents, thus constructing the public sphere. On the other hand, truth (*alētheia*) does not exist any more than nature (*phusis*) does: whether logical or physical, *alētheia* and *phusis* can only appear as hollow, as a break or a way out, as a secret for which, by definition, no public proof can ever be definitively given.

So it is for solid theoretical reasons, linked to sophistic as a starting point for politics and to a definition of the conventional and the legal as logic or language, that a single Antiphon is at least capable of having been both orator and sophist, without our having to search history for a pretext to split him in two.

The thematic order of sophistic offers the best means of understanding the rift—a rift that sheds light on a number of contemporary antagonisms—between the two major political philosophies of classical antiquity, those of Plato and Aristotle. Hannah Arendt is especially sensitive to this rift when, bent on distinguishing herself from the tragic Platonism of Heidegger and his political philosophy, she attempts to characterize in her own way the *bios politikos* (the political "type of life") and the "Greek solution" to the fragility of human affairs. It is easy to see that the Platonic *theōria*, along with the total submission of politics to philosophy that it implies, is wholly developed against a politics of the sophistic type and its Athenian practice; on the contrary, several fundamental principles of Aristotle's *Politics* constitute, de facto, an anti-Platonic rehabilitation of traditional sophistic themes. We can readily recapitulate the features by which Aristotle, in one of his guises, in order not to be a Platonist, makes himself a sophist: the city-state, which implies a distinction between economics and politics, private and public, defines itself as a

"plurality of citizens" whose diversity or "symphonic" quality must be maintained—it is far from being a "homophonic" unity of an organic or hierarchic type that does away with the specifically political dimension. This is why the flaws or anomalies of individuals become—as in the case of a contest judged by the public, or a potluck supper—more qualities to go into the mix; and democracy is the only system finally to be awarded the unqualified name of "Constitution" (cf. *Politics* II.5; III.1; III.4; III.11; IV.2). Armed with the critical and doxastic virtue known as prudence, citizens are thus trained in the Agora, with Euripides, Isocrates, or Thucydides, in the school of the sophists (among whom one could legitimately include one version of Socrates), where they learn the place of appearances, the combative plurality of speech, the exchange and criticism of different points of view—what Arendt calls judgment.

One's assessment of the sophists' politics obviously depends on the position one occupies. And if today we all call ourselves democrats, the sophists can still be called—by writers ranging from Grotius to Finley—precursors of the Enlightenment; or, on the contrary, by such writers as Croiset in his *Démocraties antiques,* and by more than one connoisseur of Plato, they can be called demagogues who need to be eliminated to preserve a healthy democracy, that is, a nonrhetorical one. But the process of conceptualizing politics and democracy has always involved the sophists.

FIRST AND SECOND SOPHISTICS

The first sophistic lost the philosophical war: Plato and Aristotle reduced it to *pseudos* (nonbeing, fake, falsification) and relegated it to the status of bad rhetoric, whether it usurps the status of true rhetoric, which is philosophy (this was Plato's thesis in *Phaedrus*) or is a combination of recipes incapable of amounting to theory (this was Aristotle's opinion at the end of *Sophistical Refutations*). It was a successful expulsion: the second sophistic, so called by Philostrates in the 3rd century C.E., belongs not to the field of philosophy but to that of oratory. If no one quibbles today about whether or not the second sophistic has a real, separate existence, we must nevertheless acknowledge that the importance attributed to it, particularly among Anglo-Saxons, has never been anything but literary, or even merely historical.

However, the second sophistic demands, like the first, to be evaluated, or reevaluated, by the yardstick of philosophy. Its first gesture, with Philostrates, who signals its birth, is to turn the accusation of *pseudos* against philosophy itself. For Philostrates, answering Plato's *Phaedrus,* the old sophistic is a "philosophizing rhetoric" (*Lives of the Sophists* I.480) and only the best philosophers can attain the name and status of sophists: while sophistic defined itself in *Metaphysics* as "[looking] like philosophy, without being so"

(III.2.1004b.26), it is now the philosophers "who are not sophists, but just [look like them]" (*Lives of the Sophists* I.484). Thus, in the palimpsestic replies of the second sophistic to Plato and Aristotle, sophistic becomes both a model for and an eponymous genre of philosophy. The first sophistic, as Philostrates presents it with Gorgias as its founder, covers the gamut of themes that philosophy only attempts to broach, whether with cunning or caution. But the second sophistic—which is as old as the first, for traces of it go back as far as Aeschines—produces "hypotyposes" instead; that is, it describes types (the poor, the noble, the tyrant) and composes case studies. It has more to do with *historia,* as inquiry and narrative, than with philosophy.

Under the Roman empire, sophistic triumphed: if in the early pages of the *Protagoras* Hippocrates blushed with shame at the very idea of being called a sophist, the emperor Trajan in his victory chariot leaned over to Dio Chrysostom and whispered: "I don't understand what you are saying, but I love you as myself," while in the chapel of Alexander Severus there were four portraits, representing Christ, Orpheus, Abraham, and Apollonius of Tyana, the hero of Philostrates' "biography." The triumph of sophistic is rooted in the hegemony of paideia, i.e. of sophistic education, and the development of a literary culture: in schools where the director was a sophist, "rhetorical imitation" encouraged appropriation of all the works of classical antiquity throughout the curriculum. This generalized rhetoric is above all creative: the palimpsest displaces, diverts, changes the meaning and even the literary genre of the texts it appropriates. Alongside a multitude of ancient genres, new genres were gradually identified, in particular one that was to become for us literature par excellence: the novel.

In fact, we can argue that the novel constitutes a completely original response to the philosophical prohibition against fiction. For the novel is a *pseudos* that acknowledges and claims its status as *pseudos,* speech that renounces any ontological equivalency to follow its own "demiurgy": it speaks not to mean something but for the pleasure of producing a "world-effect," a novelistic fiction. The popularity of novels, restoring a link with the founding tradition of Homeric poems, ends up constituting the cultural avatar of a political consensus that has spread, by virtue of the Pax Romana, throughout the inhabited world. As Dio said, not everyone sees the same sky, but even the Indians know Homer.

The paradigm of truth has thus been transformed. Sophistic is no longer judged by the yardstick of philosophical authenticity, but rather by that of the accuracy of the historical facts. Now the historians, in their turn, are the ones accusing sophistic, and its philosophical and literary kin, of being *pseudos.* Evidence of this new conflict is seen in Lucian's text, *How to Write History:* the historian, whose judgment must be a "clear mirror, unblemished and well-centered" (50.1), is the complete opposite of the poet, who, unlike Thucydides,

has the right to "overturn the fortress of Epipolae with a stroke of the pen" (38.27). In other words, the historian defines himself as having nothing to do with fiction. However, Lucian is being sophistic about sophistic itself: his irony, in *The True History*, ultimately calls his own practice into question: "I decided to lie, but with greater honesty than others, for there is a point on which I will tell the truth, and [it is] that I am lying" (1.4.8). "True" history thus returns to the paradox of the liar, and it counters the history of the chroniclers and the faithful account of events with the incomparable power of fiction *(plasma)* and invention. The first sophistic, when confronted with philosophy, preferred consensus-building speech to speech in conformity with reality, or with the substance of reality. This very shift, from conformity to political and cultural consensus, parallels a shift in the relevant opposition: the second sophistic can be understood through its difference from history and not, like the first, through its difference from philosophy. We have moved from ontology to the human sciences, and from sophistic to literature.

We can understand—as Gorgias asserts in connection with tragedy—why "he who seduces [i.e., he who deceives, *ho apatāsas*] is more just than someone who does not seduce," and why "he who is seduced [i.e., he who agrees to be deluded, *ho apatētheis*] is wiser than someone who is not seduced." *Apatē* is, in short, the sense of the power of speech, in all its forms: ontological, political, and cultural. What sophistic may, in its own way, help to bring to light in philosophy, politics, and literature is the loss and gain constituting such a discursive autonomy, in other words, constituting a *logos* that is an alternative to the Platonist-Aristotelian logic that has always been ours.

BARBARA CASSIN

Translated by Elizabeth Rawlings and Jeannine Pucci

Bibliography

Texts and Translations: First Sophistic

Antiphon. *Corpus dei papiri Filosofici Greci e Latini.* Ed. and trans. G. Bastianini and Fernanda Decleva-Caizzi. Florence: Olschki, 1989. Vol. 1, 1, pp. 176–236.

———. *Tetralogies.* In *Discours.* Trans. Louis Gernet. Paris: Les Belles Lettres, 1923.

Aristotle. *Metaphysics.* Trans. H. Tredennick. Loeb Classical Library.

———. *On Sophistical Refutations.* In *On Sophistical Refutations; On Coming-to-be and Passing Away.* Trans. E. S. Forster. Loeb Classical Library.

———. *Topica.* Trans. E. S. Forster. Loeb Classical Library.

Cassin, Barbara. *Si Parménide: Le traité anonyme De Melisso Xenophane Gorgia.* Lille: Presses Universitaires de Lille, Maison des Sciences de l'Homme, 1980.

Diels, Hermann. *Die Fragmente des Vorsokratiker,* vol. 2. Berlin: Weidmann, 1903; 6th ed. rev. Walther Kranz, 1952. Pp. 252–416, 425–428.

———. *The Older Sophists.* Columbia: University of South Carolina Press, 1972.

Plato. *Euthydemus* and *Protagoras*. In *Laches; Protagoras; Meno; Euthydemus*. Trans. W. R. M. Lamb. Loeb Classical Library.

———. *Gorgias*. In *Lysis; Symposium; Gorgias*. Trans. W. R. M. Lamb. Loeb Classical Library.

———. *Greater Hippias* and *Lesser Hippias*. In *Cratylus; Parmenides; Greater Hippias; Lesser Hippias*. Trans. H. N. Fowler. Loeb Classical Library.

———. *Theaetetus; Sophist*. Trans. H. N. Fowler. Loeb Classical Library.

Untersteiner, Mario. *Sofisti: Testimonianze e frammenti*. 4 vols. Florence: Nuova Italia, 1949–1962.

Texts and Translations: Second Sophistic

Aelius Aristide. *Orations I, Orations I–II*. Ed. and trans. C. A. Behr. Loeb Classical Library.

Dio Chrysostom. Ed. and trans. J. W. Cohoon and H. Lamar Crosby. Loeb Classical Library.

Lucian. Ed. and trans. A. H. Harmon, K. Kilburn, and M. D. Macleod. Loeb Classical Library.

Philostratus. *Lives of the Sophists*. Ed. and trans. W. C. Wright. Loeb Classical Library.

Romans grecs et latins. Ed. and trans. Pierre Grimal. Paris: Gallimard, 1958.

Studies

Anderson, Graham. *The Second Sophistic: A Cultural Phenomenon in the Roman Empire*. London: Routledge, 1993.

Bowersock, G. W. *Greek Sophists in the Roman Empire*. Oxford: Clarendon Press, 1969.

Cassin, Barbara. *L'effet sophistique*. Paris: Gallimard, 1995.

Cassin, Barbara, ed. *Le plaisir de parler*. Paris: Minuit, 1986.

———. *Positions de la sophistique*. Paris: Vrin, 1986.

Classen, C. J. "Bibliographie zur Sophistik." *Elenchos* 6, no. 1 (1985): 75–140.

Classen, C. J., ed. *Sophistik*. Darmstadt: Wissenschaftliche Buchgesellschafts, 1976.

Détienne, Marcel. *The Masters of Truth in Archaic Greece*. Trans. Janet Lloyd. Cambridge, Mass.: Zone Books, 1996.

Dupréel, Eugène. *Les Sophistes*. Neuchâtel: Ed. du Griffon, 1948.

Gomperz, Heinrich. *Sophistik und Rhetorik: Das Bildungsideal des eu legein in seinem Verhältnis zur Philosophie des V. Jahrhunderts*. Leipzig and Berlin: Teubner, 1912; repr. Darmstadt: Wissenschaftliche Buchgesellschaft, 1965, and Aalen: Scientia, 1985.

Grote, George. *History of Greece*, vol. 8. New York: Harper, 1850. Pp. 151–204.

Hegel, G. W. F. *Lectures on the History of Philosophy*, vol. 2. Trans. E. S. Haldane and Frances H. Simson. London: Routledge and Kegan Paul; New York: Humanities Press, 1974.

Kerferd, George B. *The Sophistic Movement*. Cambridge: Cambridge University Press, 1981.

Perry, B. E. *The Ancient Romances: A Literary-Historical Account of Their Origins*. Berkeley: University of California Press, 1967.

Reardon, B. P. *Courants littéraires grecs des IIème et IIIème siècles après J.-C.* Paris: Les Belles Lettres, 1969.
Rocca-Serra, G. "Bibliographie de la seconde sophistique." In *Positions de la sophistique.* Ed. Barbara Cassin. Paris: Vrin, 1986. Pp. 301–314.
Untersteiner, Mario. *The Sophists.* Trans. Kathleen Freeman. Oxford: Blackwell, 1954.

Related Articles

Aristotle; Ethics; The Statesman As Political Actor; Protagoras; Rhetoric; Schools and Sites of Learning; Theology and Divination; Language

STOICISM

If Zeno of Citium (ca. 334–262 B.C.E.), Cleanthes of Assos (ca. 331–230), and Chrysippus of Soli (ca. 280–208) were to return among us today, they would probably have mixed feelings on seeing what has become of their thought and their work. They would not be displeased to see that the name of the *Stoa poikile* (Porch of Paintings), the Athenian portico where they taught and that gave its name to their school, has gloriously survived, not only in academic terminology, where it designates Stoic philosophy, but also in the vernacular, where it refers to the "stoic" attitude, which for many is identical with philosophy itself. They would rejoice to see that study of their thought is not strictly limited to specialists, and that their philosophy has formed a sort of ideal type in the Western tradition; it has continued to play a powerful role in the self-definition of doctrines, particularly in ethical philosophy. They would be flattered and intrigued by the title of Michel Spanneut's book, *Permanence du Stoïcisme* (1973).

But aside from these reasons to be pleased, the first Stoics would also find some cause for melancholy. They wrote a great deal, Cleanthes more than Zeno, and Chrysippus even more than Cleanthes; they would find to their dismay that almost all of their works have disappeared in the turbulence of the centuries. Apart from Cleanthes' famous *Hymn to Zeus* (whose survival could provide an argument for those among the early Stoics who actively valued the educational role of poetry), we have access today only to lists of titles and some short textual citations, accompanied or not by a more or less precise reference. They would realize that to inform ourselves about them, we have to resort to the texts of much later writers who may well be their adversaries (such as Cicero and Plutarch), and we must often turn as well to the texts of more or less intelligent and well-informed compilers, authors of manuals, résumés, or collections of opinions (called doxographies, of which the best-known surviving example is the work of Diogenes Laertius).

Adversaries and doxographers alike tend to speak of Stoics in general, without going into detail concerning the thought of individuals. The risk in this approach is that it may give an exaggerated idea of the homogeneity of the Stoic school. The extended and lasting success of that school in antiquity surely rests in part on the fact that it was governed by a spirit of liberty along with fidelity (in the eyes of its partisans), of dissension and of competition (in those of its adversaries). Those who are often described as dissident Stoics were not shunted aside because of their lack of orthodoxy; they were consid-

ered unorthodox because their competitors within the school had prevailed. Besides, the doxographic literature tends to hold on to theses without reproducing the arguments that uphold them. Stoic philosophy, undeniably dogmatic in the antique sense of the term (in the sense that it had "dogmas," positive doctrines that it thought itself in a position to prove and to teach), thus runs the risk of appearing, despite its passionate rationalism, just as dogmatic in the modern sense of the word, that is to say, authoritarian, rigid, little concerned with arguing.

Another surprise would await our long-lost friends. They would learn that the works of their successors have known quite contrasting destinies. Those of the 2nd- and 1st-century Stoics, like Panaetius of Rhodes (born around 185) and Posidonius of Apamea (born around 135), have been swallowed up in the same shipwreck as theirs (which is particularly unfortunate in the case of Posidonius: if his numerous scientific works had been preserved, we would have a different image of the Stoic contribution to Greek learning). But even today we find few famous Stoics in bookshops; they differ considerably from philosophy's founding fathers, and also from one another. No longer intellectual heads of schools, teaching in Athens, passing along the official direction of the Stoa, they include a member of the imperial Roman court, Seneca (ca. 8 B.C.E.–65 C.E.), Nero's teacher and minister; a freed slave, Epictetus (ca. 50–130), exiled in Epirus, where he taught before an audience that fortunately included a competent stenographer; and, for a beautiful finish, the master of the world in person, Emperor Marcus Aurelius (121–180). In contemplating these very dissimilar descendants, the first Stoics might well feel a certain pride: their diversity bore witness to the universality of Stoicism, its capacity to give an intellectual and moral frame to a wide range of vocations. But if they were to read their successors' works, in the form in which we have received them, the earliest Stoics might also be rather astonished, if not scandalized.

Why so? Because if there is anything in their philosophy of which Stoics have been proud, it is surely its systematic unity, which reflects in the register of discourse the very unity of the great system we know as the world. Of course everything cannot be explained all at once; thus it is inevitable that the explanation of Stoic philosophy is spread among several chapters or "places," the most extended of which are logic, physics, and ethics. Plato's successors had probably already used the same classification to put their master's teaching in order; indeed, it dominates all Hellenistic philosophy. But this categorization does not affect the philosophy itself, the organic unity of which is such that nothing in it could be changed or withdrawn, the Stoics claim, without overthrowing the whole system.

Now imperial Stoicism, at least at first glance, puts its entire emphasis on ethics—its theoretical principles and its practical applications. The earliest Stoics could thus complain that their descendants, more favored than they by

the accidents of history, have transmitted to posterity only a deformed or truncated image of Stoicism. They themselves certainly did not fail to teach a moral code, to which they attributed great importance, nor did they fail to practice it to the best of their ability. Nevertheless, they wanted to make that code inseparable from the rest of their doctrines: they thought they had anchored it solidly to a dogmatic system with a high level of coherence and technical adequacy. And now these distant successors, however respectable they may have been personally, were turning Stoic morality into spiritual counseling, popular philosophy, or solitary meditation.

Zeno and Chrysippus might have remembered, in this context, that they had already encountered philosophers who, believing they held fast to the lesson of Socrates, had scorned theoretical research, and who had adopted "ethics only" as their motto. The Cynics were the radical representatives of this tendency; Zeno had had among his masters the Cynic Crates, and the influence of the *Republic* of the Cynic Diogenes had been sufficiently strong on his own *Republic* to have embarrassed certain of his successors, so much so that they sometimes suppressed it, declared it inauthentic, or represented it as a youthful error. The slogan "ethics only" was taken up by one of Zeno's disciples, Ariston; a 2nd-century Stoic, Apollodorus of Seleucia, described Cynicism as "a shortcut to virtue." But if Zeno and Chrysippus were the founders of Stoicism and not simply Cynics succeeding other Cynics, it was to the extent that they refused this shortcut and adopted a "long path" toward virtue, implying not only physical and moral asceticism but also intellectual effort, the critical acceptance of the legacy of earlier philosophies, the development of techniques of language and reason, knowledge of the physical world, and the elaboration of a theology. Was this immense work, recorded in the veritable library that issued from the fertile pen of Chrysippus, forgotten in the imperial era? We might well think so, seeing that a small, practical, portable selection of Epictetus's maxims was in circulation under the title *Manual*—a title that Simplicius justified, when he annotated the work, by saying "that it should be always at hand for those who want to live well, as we call the short swords of soldiers 'daggers' or 'manuals,' because they must always be at hand for those who want to fight."

But given a closer look, the founders of Stoicism might well perceive that they had not been betrayed by their successors. Even if the latter admired Diogenes the Cynic, they did not imagine the primacy of ethics according to the model he established. Despite the disdain he showed for the subtleties of the school, Seneca put together an austere collection of physical and meteorological studies, the *Quaestiones naturales*. Epictetus's *Conversations*, transcribed by Arrian and handed down to posterity in this form, reproduce only the part of his teachings in which, after a course of a more scholarly nature (Chrysippus would have been happy to learn that the students did exercises in logic and explicated his own texts), the master exhorted his followers in a

familiar manner to put their philosophy into practice; even these "diatribes," with their supple and often digressive air, are based on a more rigid doctrinal framework than it would appear. As for Marcus Aurelius, who wrote down his famous *Meditations* for his own use, he had internalized the fundamental spirit of Stoic physics and theology, even though he made no display of it, and even though he dared consider the possibility that the Stoic principles might be incorrect. Were they to read his sublime reaction to this hypothesis ("If there is a Providence, all is well; and if the world operates by chance, do not you, yourself, behave by chance") would not Zeno and Chrysippus, harsh schoolmasters though they were, be won over?

Moreover, if the Stoic ethic had evolved into a relative autonomy, they would not have anyone but themselves to blame. In the person of Zeno, despite his exotic demeanor and his flirtation with Cynicism, the Athenians, good judges in the matter since Socrates' trial, recognized a perfectly respectable master of morals: they awarded him official honors because he had "for many years been devoted to philosophy in the city and ha[d] continued to be a man of worth in all other respects, exhorting to virtue and temperance those of the youth who come to him to be taught, directing them to what is best, affording to all in his own conduct a pattern for imitation in perfect consistency with his teaching" (Diogenes Laertius, *Lives* VII.10–11). The Stoics used many different images to symbolize the various aspects of their doctrine and their intimate unity (the white, yolk, and shell of an egg; the fences, trees, and fruits of an orchard); in most of these images, if not all, ethics held the place of honor. Chrysippus himself, undoubtedly the most theoretical head of the whole school, certainly brought his teaching to its climax with the most speculative parts of the doctrine, physics and its theological culmination; he professed nonetheless, in terms Epicurus would not have rejected, that "physical speculation is to be undertaken for no other purpose than for the discrimination of good and evil" ("On Stoic Self-Contradictions," *Plutarch's Moralia* 1035d). This instrumental relation between physics and ethics contained the seeds of a potential split, for if some other instrument should appear as a basis for Stoic ethics—one more economical than the vast detour by way of knowledge of the world, one less tightly bound, at least for the centuries to come, to a specific state of science—it could enter into competition, or at least into coexistence, with the instrument of physics.

This rapid sketch of the history of ancient Stoicism, from its founders to its last representatives, is intended to shed light on a structural characteristic of Stoic philosophy: the factors of systematic unification of the doctrine and the factors of relative autonomization of its elements coexist in a relatively unstable equilibrium. This tension among centripetal and centrifugal forces (similar to the type of unity that the Stoics discovered in living organisms; in the world, which is itself a living organism; and in their accounts of the

world) is not necessarily a weakness: on the level of historical longevity and philosophical seductiveness, it has allowed Stoicism to offer "a big tent," as we say today of ideologies flexible enough or comprehensive enough to adapt themselves to the needs of quite varied clienteles. It is this tension that will serve here as our guideline.

Having decided, as they left their Cynic inheritance behind, that they would have something to teach, and not just rely on provocative examples or edifying exhortations, the Stoics needed an infallibly solid pedestal on which to base their dogmatism. According to an authorized and justly famous account, "'The Stoics agree to put in the forefront the doctrine of presentation [*phantasia*] and sensation, inasmuch as the standard by which the truth of things is tested is generically a presentation, and again the theory of assent and that of apprehension and thought, which precedes all the rest, cannot be stated apart from presentation. For presentation comes first; then thought, which is capable of expressing itself, puts into the form of a proposition that which the subject receives from a presentation'" (Diogenes Laertius, *Lives* VII.49). On a first reading, this text argues in favor of the primacy of the theory of knowledge over all knowledge of any domain of objects whatsoever: before offering any dogma at all as true, we must know whether we possess a "criterion," a means of access to "the truth of things." By giving priority to their strongly affirmative reply to this crucial question, the Stoics exposed their response to vigorous polemical attacks, but they defended their position with all their might.

The Stoics' principal criterion is not named in the text just cited; we are told only that it belongs to the genus *phantasia*. This first specification leads us to identify the criterion with a psychophysical event, described in material terms as the action of external bodies on the soul, itself a body, with the soul playing a purely passive role. The order of the account thus reproduces the very genesis of the human mind, which is a tabula rasa at birth and is bombarded thereafter with sense impressions whose sedimentation eventually produces speech and reason, both of which are expressed by the key word *logos*. When we analyze the mechanism of perception, however, we find that the passivity of the initial moment leaves room for an active moment, that of the acceptance or "assent" through which the perceiving subject adheres to the content of the impression. Subjects can do this more or less decisively, some to a lesser extent than they might, others to a greater extent than they should. From Zeno on, assent is held to "reside within us and be a voluntary act" (Cicero, *Academica* I.xi.40): this means not that it results from a deliberate and conscious choice (certain impressions are "so obvious and striking they almost grab us by the hair and impel us to assent"), but that it is attributable to us, and that if, owing to haste or bias, we give or refuse our assent unwisely, the responsibility is ours, as well as the responsibility for the conse-

quences of our mistake. We are responsible for organizing our entire set of beliefs in a more or less coherent way; we are responsible for making "use of our impressions" as best we can, to use one of Epictetus's favorite expressions; and we are morally accountable for them.

Moreover, this is not the only moral dimension of the theory of knowledge. Indeed, the very notion of impression is not limited to the reception of perceptible qualities: things give us the impression not only of being white, or sweet tasting, but also of being worthy of choice or not. Our assent to such impressions results in a belief, and also in an action, in which we express both the kind of person we are and the responsibility that is ours for having consented to the impression.

Since on the dual levels of knowledge and action we can thus see that assent can be given or refused, and since we can also judge whether it has been given or refused wisely or unwisely, it should respond, well or ill, to the intrinsic characteristics of the impression. In this connection, the type of impression that stands out among all others is the one the Stoics call cognitive or comprehensive *(phantasia kataleptike)*. This kind of impression has three distinctive features: it comes (causally) from a real object; it reproduces the relevant particular characteristics of the object adequately; it is such, finally, that it could not come from any object that is not exactly the one from which it comes. This last provision, added by Zeno to stave off an objection (drawn from the alleged indiscernibility of impressions provoked, for example, by a pair of twins), is crucial: if no impression fulfilling this condition existed, there would be no possibility, either theoretical or practical, of an infallible knowledge of reality. Hence the Stoics' determined efforts to defend this point against all objections. With the theory of cognitive impressions, they had found a philosophical goose laying golden eggs: something self-evident that carries in itself the unfalsifiable certificate of its own truth. On this theory the very foundation of their dogmatic system was to stand or fall.

Once assent is given, as it should be and normally is, to a cognitive impression, the result is cognition, a grasping or comprehension *(katalepsis)*. Although such a grasping cannot be erroneous, what is important is that at this stage Stoicism refuses to speak of knowledge or of science *(episteme)*: if we are to situate the grasping "between science and ignorance," and consequently are not to count it "among either goods or evils," it is because the cognitive impression is a grasping of only an isolated state of affairs; hence it runs the risk of being "shaken" by some seductive argument or some unexpected occurrence, while science can be only unshakable. There is no knowledge until the precarious morsels of what is "true," picked up here and there, are integrated into a "truth," into a coherent system of rational convictions where they support one another like the stones of an arch.

To say and think the "true" is thus accessible to every human being, but the "truth," for which the standards of satisfaction are much higher, is found

only in an ideal human being, which no Stoic claimed to incarnate: the *sophos* (at once learned and wise), a perfect figure of human beings such as they can be. In contrast, people as they really are, are all equally "worthless" (*phauloi*, of no use, both ignorant and mad). The whole analysis of the cognitive process and its stages—impression, assent, comprehension, science—as Zeno represented it, accompanied by a famous series of gestures in which a hand closes little by little, had the explicit function of showing that no one "except the wise man *knows* anything" (Cicero, *Academica* II.xlviii.145).

This is a decisive strategy, it seems, that allows Stoicism to remain flexible: instead of setting the bar of human knowledge at a single height, the Stoics set up a range of levels, while ensuring the possibility of passing from one to another. This is probably why their philosophy has sometimes seemed contradictory. Thanks to its idea of *katalepsis,* a cognitive moment accessible to the mad as well as to the wise, it claims that our perceptual and rational equipment gives us direct access to knowledge of reality. We are not fallen souls, exiled in a world that is not our true homeland; we are the inhabitants of a world made for us, parts of a world that is a living being, sensitive and rational as we are, made of the same substances as we are. Thus Stoicism can be a popular philosophy, universal by right, intent on presenting itself as the simple "articulation" of the "common notions" that nature implants in everyone. Rejecting the symmetrical paradoxes of Epicureanism and Skepticism, the Stoics believe that there are hosts of things that are clear as day, and on which we can lean as we attempt to shed light on the realm of those that are not clear. It is no accident that "There is daylight" (literally, there is light, *phōs esti*) is their favorite example of an elementary statement, for through an etymological figure they find this light *(phōs)* again in the very name *phantasia,* which "shows itself at the same time as the object that produces it," exactly as light "shows itself simultaneously with the objects on which it shines" (Aetius IV.12.2).

What benefit, then, does the doctrine derive from having reserved for the wise man, a bird "rarer than the phoenix," the privilege of knowledge? More generally speaking, in a philosophy that is opposed by its materialism and its nominalism to all aspects of Platonic "idealism," what is the use of invoking the chimerical figure of the wise man at every turn, and accumulating with respect to him the famous "Stoic paradoxes"? Not only does the wise man "know everything," but he also has all virtues, all skills, and he enjoys perfect happiness under all circumstances; he is "the equal of Zeus." But the important point is that he is never presented as the favorite of Zeus, as a man permitted by a special gift to transcend the limits of the human condition. He remains a man, the only man, indeed, who is wholly human, the only one in whom man's rational nature is fully developed. On these grounds, we other *phauloi* can benefit from the lesson he teaches, even if we do not run into him on the street: through the intermediary of teachers who are no less *phauloi*

than we are, even though they may be less remote from wisdom than we are, the wise man teaches us that it is not owing to some inherent defect that we are not what we should be, nor what we could be if we had not let our natural development be impeded or perverted. Plato and Aristotle invited us to imitate God "insofar as possible": they implied that no one is expected to do the impossible. In showing us what a perfect man would be like, if such a man existed, the Stoics implied that no one is authorized to renounce the possible. From his own viewpoint, then, Pascal is right to find in Epictetus not only the marks of man's greatness but also, for want of a counterpart on the side of man's misery, the marks of a "diabolical pride." This is perhaps why Stoic philosophy was able to exalt the most exacting consciences of antiquity, yet without discouraging in the process men of goodwill.

Let us look, now, in the field of logic to begin with, at how the articulation between factors of unification and factors of autonomization is worked out. The Stoics identified two disciplines in this field: dialectic, the art of argumentation through questions and answers, and rhetoric, the art of continuous discourse. They devoted by far the most energy to dialectic. In the time of the earliest Stoics, dialectic had already undergone remarkable developments at the hands of subtle and willfully paradoxical "dialecticians." Far from thinking, like the Cynics (whose work on this point will be developed by Ariston), that logic is "nothing that concerns us," Zeno joined the dialectic school. But he did not cultivate it for its own sake. Ever faithful to his gestural approach to teaching, he summed up his own conception of dialectic by comparing it to a closed fist (as opposed to rhetoric, symbolized by an open palm): in other words, dialectic was to serve to protect his mind, and his disciples', against the risk of being shaken in their theoretical or practical convictions by some fallacious argument. This defensive function of logic, like a remedy one would not have to use if the malady for which it is the antidote did not exist, turns up in several of the images that symbolized the unity of Stoic thought: logic is like an eggshell, like a fence around an orchard, like a rampart protecting a town.

Once the Stoics were launched on this path, however, there was no turning back. Zeno, enamored of "laconic" formulas, left the core of the school's characteristic doctrines to his successors; however, many of these doctrines remained indefinite in their meaning and uncertain in their argumentative foundations. Zeno's principal adversaries, the skeptical Academics of the period, set out to exploit all the school's weaknesses. Thus Zeno's successors had to make the meaning of their master's formulas explicit (without always agreeing among themselves on their proper interpretation), and they had to strengthen their rational foundations. Cleanthes, a faithful disciple but a mediocre debater, put the legacy at risk. Chrysippus took it upon himself to restore the school's foundations, to be a second founder, as it were ("But for Chrysippus, there had been no Porch"; Diogenes Laertius, *Lives of Eminent*

Philosophers VII.183—or so the saying went). He is said to have told his master Cleanthes, with some condescension, "that all he wanted was to be told what the doctrines were; he would find out the proofs for himself" (*Lives* VII.179). This is a fine example of *ben trovato*: the saying makes clear that the dogmas, specific truths that, in the aggregate, sum up the doctrine, can doubtless be transmitted without proof (they have a meaning that everyone can grasp), but that it is possible and useful to demonstrate them (they have a content of objective rationality that permits them to be logically linked with a network of other statements).

Chrysippus put all his talent into strengthening the logical framework of the doctrine, so much so that he is like an architect who is as absorbed by the construction of the scaffolding as by the straightening up of the building. Through the scarce remnants of his work, we can still see him as one of the three or four great names in the entire history of logic, and we can understand why it was said that "if the gods took to dialectic, they would adopt no other system than that of Chrysippus" (*Lives* VII.180). It is a matter not simply of a logic, in the narrow sense of a theory of formally valid reasoning, but of a grand theory of the *logos*. In brief, it consists of an effective and subtle theory of signification, a stratified analysis of the signifiers of language (whose development exercised a considerable influence on the theories of the ancient grammarians); a theory of signifieds, incomplete or complete (the most fundamental of these last being the proposition, the bearer of truth or falsity); a theory of propositions, simple or composite (here we find in particular a remarkable analysis of interpropositional connectors *and, or, if . . . then,* an analysis that is essential for the construction of a propositional logic, which is itself logically anterior to the Aristotelian logic of terms), assertoric or modalized according to possibility or necessity (notions whose manipulations entail profound consequences with respect to the contingency of the future and the moral responsibility of the agent); an analysis of lines of reasoning and the different properties they can or cannot have (validity, truth, demonstrativity); a thorough reflection on sophisms and paradoxes, which are powerful motors of logical and philosophical creativity. In the hands of the Stoics, logic becomes a full-fledged discipline. It is no longer, as it was in the Aristotelian tradition, an *organon*, an instrument for science, something such that one knows nothing so long as one knows nothing else; it is an integral part of science, and when one knows it, one knows something.

The rigor and the "formalism" with which this grand theory is constructed have long been considered defects, justifying the scorn in which Stoic logic was held. However, these defects turned into assets for those who succeeded in rehabilitating it in the light of modern logic—to the point that many have felt the need to react, more recently, against a too anachronistically assimilative enthusiasm. In these debates we find again the effect of our axial prob-

lematic. Might Chrysippus (who led the studious life of an "academic," even if he felt a little guilty about it) have been caught in his own game? In constructing a timelessly true logic, might he not have forgotten that he was a philosopher, and a Stoic philosopher? The definition of dialectic as the "science of statements true, false, and neither true nor false" (Diogenes Laertius, *Lives* VII.42), which was probably his, is curiously ambiguous: at first sight, it seems to identify the dialectician with the wise man who "knows all things, divine and human," but it should most probably be read in a different sense, that is to say, as the science of what is capable of being true or false (propositions) and what is not (nonpropositional and incomplete signifieds). In this second sense, dialectic corresponds well with the logical enterprise as it was in fact undertaken by Chrysippus.

Yet we must not overestimate the independence of Stoic logic, even for Chrysippus, with regard to the doctrine as a whole. It is worth pointing out, in any case, that after a brief series of dialecticians succeeded Chrysippus, Posidonius, a Stoic inclined to empirical research rather than pure logic, criticized ideas that attributed to logic a role of external protection with regard to the doctrine as a whole: he preferred to compare philosophy to an animal, in which logic was symbolized by the bones and tendons, the internal mechanisms responsible for the body's solidity and movement. The fact is that dialectic, whatever the scope and rigor of its formal architecture, does not constitute a closed system. In exploring the structures of language and reason, dialectic explores not only the structures of the thinking and acting human mind but also, and quite legitimately, those of the divine mind, and those of the world, which is not really distinct from God. Nor are the ties between dialectic and ethics lost from sight. The virtues required by the dialectical exercise of reason—the absence of haste, the rigorous control of terms and connections, the mastery of internal order—are the same as those presupposed by moral virtue ("Let us strive to think well: that is the principle of morality"; this saying of Pascal is very Stoic), and Diogenes Laertius concludes his account of Stoic logic by saying that the fundamental objective of the school, in this sphere, was to show that "the wise man is the true dialectician," including when he applies himself to physics or ethics, because he considers all things "by means of logical study" (Diogenes Laertius, *Lives* VII.83).

Epictetus, too, warned his students against the dangers of an insularization of logic, of which the beginner can be a victim in two opposite ways: either he prides himself on "knowing how to analyze syllogisms like Chrysippus" (Epictetus, *Discourses* II.xxiii.44), or else he minimizes the importance of his mistakes in logic, suggesting that they are not tantamount to parricide (I.vii.31). Questioning a student of the first sort, who is led by the delights of logical virtuosity to forget the primacy of ethics, Epictetus asks: "What prevents you from being wretched, mournful, envious—in a word, bewildered

and miserable?" As for the second, who forgets the ethical signification of the practice of reason itself, Epictetus teaches him a concise lesson with the famous paradox of the "equality of errors": "You have committed the one error which was possible in this field" (I.vii.32). Thus, far from being abandoned (and even if it does not benefit from any more technical improvements), logic remains firmly anchored in the ethical totality of Stoicism.

Stoic physics also reveals a paradoxical alliance between the accessibility of *katalepsis,* which is a matter of fact, and that of *episteme,* which is a matter of right. What the Stoics meant by physics has little relation with modern physics. What would come closest is what they called etiology, the search for and knowledge of the causes that account for natural phenomena. The Stoics did not hesitate to engage in this, but it was not their most characteristic activity: Posidonius, the most expert among them in this type of study, was labeled an "Aristotelizer" for this reason. In their era, one could not escape from the "philosophical" agenda as it had been drawn up long before by the Presocratics: a self-respecting school had to have not only a theory of the principles and elements of nature and a theory of the structure of matter, but also a cosmology, an astronomy, a meteorology, a zoology, an anthropology, a psychology, and even a theology, since the gods were not "supernatural." Still, one of the striking features of Hellenistic culture is that many branches began to detach themselves from the philosophic tree. More and more specialized scholars, mathematicians, astronomers, physicists, medical doctors, scholars, and philologists began to appear—learned men who were not philosophers and did not wish to be considered as such.

The Stoics took note of this tendency even while trying to control it. In the realm of explanations of specific phenomena, a field that requires observation and experience, the collection of facts, and the recognition of signs, they were willing to leave the detailed work to "experts"; but as they saw it, philosophers could qualify as experts, and had to keep themselves abreast of the others' work. Above all, it is the philosopher's task to determine the principles that establish the framework in which the expert's work is to be developed, and to reflect on the methodological conditions of this work. The Stoics made important contributions (in collaboration or in polemic with Epicureanism, empirical medicine, and Skepticism) to debates over the acceptability of intellectual acts that, starting from observable effects, trace back to the causes that these effects may signify—debates that in the last analysis raise the problem of the degree to which knowledge of nature can be scientific. To avoid modernizing these reflections too much, we must nevertheless keep in mind that one of the disciplines to which the Stoics most readily turned to illustrate their thinking was divination, the prediction of the future through the interpretation of signs supplied by the gods—a subject on which we are likely to share the skepticism of their adversaries.

This division of roles between philosophers and experts makes it possible to say that there is, all things considered, a kind of immanent justice in the classification made over the centuries among the works of authors of the Stoa. We can regret having lost Chrysippus's *Logical Inquiries,* while the elementary dialectic doxography of Diogenes Laertius survives; in the same way, we can regret having lost Posidonius's treatises on winds, tides, and the flooding of the Nile, while Cicero's *De natura deorum* lives on, which makes clear the theological resonances of his conception of a universe tied together by cosmic "sympathy." But what survives is, in one sense, what was destined to survive: the fundamental, elementary core.

The heart of Stoic physics, then, consists of principles whose determination depends on conceptual decisions rather than empirical considerations. At the center of their ontology the Stoics, taking Plato's analyses in *Sophist* literally and turning them inside out like a glove, equate with being, body, the ability to act and the ability to suffer. Only what is capable of acting and suffering exists, properly speaking; only what is tangible and corporeal has these capabilities. The principles that are necessary and sufficient to account for the totality of being are thus, once isolated in their pure polarity, a wholly active principle, identifiable with God, and a wholly passive principle, identifiable with matter stripped of all qualities. The object of the science of being is therefore the object of physics, that is, the entire set of bodies, for which forming a totality and acting and reacting one on another amount to one and the same thing. Nevertheless, pairing once again the sturdy assumption of common notions and the paradoxical subtleties of the technical apparatus, the Stoics carve out a special ontological niche for a collection of "incorporeals" (the void, time, place, and also, for reasons that are not at all foreign to physics, the *lekta,* immaterial significations of the vocal signs of language), which do not fulfill the necessary conditions for being actual beings, although they cannot be said to be nothing, either; they are "something." This two-level ontology finds a cosmological translation in the representation of a world that fully exists, a finished and unified totality of bodies, and that is surrounded to infinity by a "something" that does not exist, the void. This void is not philosophically superfluous: too perfectly empty to make room for the innumerable worlds of the atomists, or to harbor the extraworldly residence of the Epicurean gods, it metaphorizes the exclusion of any "intelligible place" of the Platonic type, as it does that of any transcendent God. In Stoicism, no object offers itself to a "first philosophy" in relation to which physics would be, as it is for Aristotle, a "second philosophy."

The Stoic image of the world, even in its details, derives from this strong intuition of the *kosmos,* which precedes all proofs and finds as many as it needs in the moral and religious impetus that never ceases to support it. The litanies of the world, in the rhetoric of the Stoa, are like the litanies of the wise man: in effect, they are the same, for there are not two different ways to

be perfect, one for man and one for the universe. From the starting point of this intuition, Stoicism takes to the logically coherent extreme one of the two great worldviews that characterized ancient thought, the other being perfectly represented by atomistic and mechanistic Epicureanism. The skein of attributes of the Stoic world is so closely woven that it comes all together no matter on which strand one tugs: this world is a totality, not a simple sum; it is one, finite, spherical, geocentric, full, continuous, ordered, organized. The events that take place in this world are not mutually independent; this world's temporal and causal unity is summed up in the notion of fate, an orderly and inviolable arrangement of causes, a notion to which the Stoics held no less than to that of moral responsibility, which the notion of fate seemed to put at risk. To articulate their physics and their ethics, they elaborated a complex and differentiated theory of causes that made Chrysippus "sweat," according to Cicero, who relates this discussion in his treatise *De fato*.

The parts of the world are not more foreign to one another than are the events that take place in it; quite to the contrary, the Stoics recognize the possibility of a "total mixture" among bodies, a notion that explicitly transgresses the principle according to which two bodies cannot occupy the same space. The Stoics can consequently conceive of the parts of the world as connected by a vertical and horizontal network of complicities and "conspiracy" (from corespiration, *sumpnoia*), the agent of which is seen as a sort of energetic substance, or substantial energy, penetrating bodies and passing through the whole universe, for which various physical models have been tried, including fire, principally represented by vital heat, and the breath of life *(pneuma)*, a mixture of fire and air. The composition of the *pneuma*, in particular, makes it possible to attribute to it a control of the forces of expansion and contraction, whose result, called *tonos* (tension), accounts in varying degrees for the qualities that differentiate natural beings (inanimate, vegetable, and animal substances). From this standpoint, the cosmic picture is clothed in biological and vitalist colors: the differences between natural beings are of degree rather than of nature, and the world itself is imagined, according to the ancient analogy of the microcosm and the macrocosm, as possessing the properties that its most perfected parts possess: life, to begin with, but also the sensitivity characteristic of an animal and the rationality characteristic of man. It would not be contrary to the spirit of the Stoa to say that man is "at home" in this great warm cocoon that resembles him, where everything that is not man is made for him, where evil is but an illusion, a detail, or an inevitable ransom for the good. Still, we must add that man himself, a rational but mortal animal, does not achieve fulfillment except by acknowledging the whole of which he is a part, a great, perfect, rational being—that is, God. Fate is a form of providence, and at the last stage of initiation to the mysteries (the image is from Chrysippus), physics turns out to be a theology.

The Stoic ethic, a total part of the doctrine, shows in an exemplary manner

the dual structure that serves us here as guiding thread, to such an extent that this ethic has often been accused of incoherence or contradiction. In identifying not only human nature but also universal nature with reason, the Stoics still gave themselves the means to give ethics both a natural and a rational foundation. Cicero, in his account of Stoic ethics (*De finibus* III), provides an admirably telling image: nature gives us a letter of recommendation addressed to wisdom and, as often happens, we become more closely attached to the letter's addressee than to its sender.

To pull the rabbit of a singularly powerful moral rigor out of the hat of nature, the Stoics found, both in experience and in theory, a remarkably ingenious instrument. Contrary to what a superficial observation would suggest to their Epicurean adversaries, natural instinct does not lead the small living being, either animal or human, toward the search for pleasure or the avoidance of pain: it leads it to self-preservation and the development of inborn possibilities, even at the cost of effort and pain. This process makes manifest the somewhat maternal providence (foresight or preintelligence, *pronoia*) of a nature that would not put a being in the world without endowing it with this "adaptation" to itself, this "familiarity" with itself, this "attachment" to itself, which is called *oikeiōsis* in Greek, and which makes all the values distributed among external objects, among other individuals, among specific acts of choice or rejection, depend on the contribution they make to the agent's own maintenance and fulfillment. This reading of natural behavior makes it possible to see in it something like the primitive model of a unified organization of the active life.

One must add, nevertheless—and here we see how the paradoxical alliance occurs, in Stoicism, between the legacy of Cynicism and conformity—that the notion of *oikeiōsis* is not, appearances to the contrary, strictly egocentric. The living being, originally "appropriate" to itself, is also appropriate to the parts of which it consists; it has the "feeling" of its own constitution. When it reproduces, its own parts take on autonomous life, but it remains attached to them, as the parental behavior of animals shows. By this expedient the Stoics thought they could lay the foundation in nature, by a progressive movement of expansion whose outline outlasted many objections and many refutations, of a familial and civic altruism and, to top it off, a cosmopolitan philanthropy supported by the idea of a natural human justice. In this respect, I must at least mention in passing the way Stoicism was grafted onto Roman law, particularly with regard to the idea of an international "people's law"; it was a Roman jurist, Marcian, who transmitted the Chrysippian definition of the law, "queen of all things divine and human," "rule of the just and unjust, which lays down for naturally political animals what they must do, and forbids what they must not do" (*Stoicorum veterum fragmenta* III.314).

But let us return to the primitive model of unified organization of practical life that *oikeiōsis* provides. This model is accessible to the observer, not to the

agent itself; the agent is aware only that he is seeking his own preservation and his own maintenance in his natural state, as well as the things and actions that promote those ends. Still, as man develops and as his activity of choosing and refusing progresses in assurance and systematicity, he comes to see (and here I am paraphrasing Cicero, who makes the image of the letter of recommendation quite explicit) that the order and harmony of actions have more value than the actions themselves, that they are the end to which the actions are only the means. To act in accordance with nature, but *in a certain manner* (finalized, selective, regular), *is* to act in accordance with reason, the specific nature of man. *Homologia*, the unification of practical life under the rule of a unique and dominating *logos*, the formal consistency and rational coherence of activity, is thereby qualified as the sovereign good or ultimate end *(telos)*, as that in view of which is sought everything that is sought. The rationalist rabbit was not hidden in the naturalist hat; the rabbit is the hat itself, turned neatly inside out, seen from an entirely new and different perspective; there is a reversal of relations between the matter and form of behavior, between what one does and the manner in which one does it, between the verb and the adverb, just as, in certain optical games, there is a reversal of relations between figure and background.

The historical and theoretical gains of this well-conducted operation turned out to be considerable. First of all it made it possible to conceive of the notion of the good in strictly moral terms: if Stoicism preserves the idea, common in Greek morality, that what is good is what is good for the agent (what is "beneficial" or useful to him), it also defends the idea, a much more paradoxical one (when it is compared, for example, to the Aristotelian ethic, which deliberately focuses on making ordinary common moral intuitions explicit), that the only thing that is good for the agent himself is what is morally good (the beautiful, the honorable, *to kalon* in Greek, *honestum* in Cicero's Latin), that is, the perfection (or virtue, *arete*) of his practical reason, unchangeable and unshakable through all the choices it brings about and all the acts it controls, its absolute nonconflictuality, its infallible constancy. Virtue thus understood suffices for happiness, because being happy is less a subjective state of satisfaction than an objective state of "success," of full efflorescence of the nature of the agent in what is specific to that nature. This is a paradox that nourishes many others, and the Stoics never tired of developing it. The thesis rests not only on the model of the god, in whom is displayed, for anyone who has followed the Stoic teaching of physics and theology through to the end, a complete coincidence between reason, beneficence, and happiness, but it also claims to be in accord with the innate intuitions of good and evil such as they would develop naturally in common humanity, if they were not perverted or obscured by society and its false values. In spite of everything, these intuitions retain enough strength to subsist in the form of moral concepts, which we all have even if we do not apply them; the philosopher has only to gather

them up in our common sense and "disarticulate" them to find his theory again. In characteristic fashion, the Stoics justify a very paradoxical thesis (virtue is enough for happiness) paradoxically, by saying that that is really what everyone has thought all along.

Thus defined by its formal characteristics of rational coherence, moral perfection nevertheless does not leave in its wake the matter it needs to be practiced and made manifest. Strictly speaking, everything that is neither virtue—which is the only good—nor vice—which is the only evil—is precisely "indifferent"; this is the case for everything that valorizes and everything that normally governs ordinary behavior: life and death, health and illness, pleasure and sorrow, wealth and poverty, liberty and slavery, power and submission. Nothing in all this, however intensified, contributes to or alters moral perfection. However—and here is where Stoicism parts company with Cynicism, relayed in vain by Ariston—these "indifferent" elements are such only from the point of view of morality, which is not the only view from which they can and should be considered; from the point of view of natural tendencies, which morality transcends without abolishing them, they maintain a value of selection, that is to say, a relative value: other things being equal, it is reasonable to prefer the ones that are "in conformity with nature," like life or health, to their opposites; as for those—for example, death or illness—it is preferable to avoid them, because they are "contrary to nature." Only a small category of things that are neither in conformity with nor contrary to nature, such as having an odd or even number of hairs, are indifferent from the double viewpoint of virtue and nature. Epictetus quotes a statement by Chrysippus that sums up very well the Stoic attitude toward the things "in conformity with nature," which are pursued "with the reservation" (hupexairesis) that they not show themselves contrary to the providential plan of Zeus: "Inasmuch as the future is unknown to me, I always cling to what is most naturally apt to help me obtain what is in conformity with nature: it is God himself who has made me capable of making these choices. But if I knew that my fate was now to be ill, my inclination would be to give way to illness; in the same way my foot, if it were intelligent [if it could understand that it is, for the man of whom it is a part, the means of arriving at his end] would have a tendency that would lead it to get dirty." The Stoic notion of fate leaves no room for the "lazy argument" (it is useless to see the doctor or take medicine if in any case it is written that I shall die from this illness or that I shall be cured): in the book of fate are written not only isolated sentences, but also connected sentences (I shall be cured *if* I see the doctor), conjugations of events that are conjointly subject to fate *(confatalia)*, in which my own initiatives are implicated.

In the capacity of raw material for moral behavior, "things in conformity with nature" are thus explicitly introduced into Stoic formulations of the *telos,* starting with Chrysippus and continuing with his successors Diogenes

of Babylon and Antipater. These formulations are continually reworked to ward off the ceaseless criticism, and they always strive to preserve the essential: what counts is not to obtain these things but to choose those that it is reasonable to choose, and to do everything in one's power to obtain those. Without going into the detail of the complex polemics these formulations elicited, I shall simply recall the famous image by which the spokesman of Stoicism in Cicero's *De finibus* sums up the connection between the absolute value of the good and the relative value of "things in conformity with nature": the image of the archer whose *aim* is doubtless to hit the target, but whose *end* is to do all in his power (more precisely, in his power as an expert in archery) to hit it. Let us develop the image somewhat freely: it is preferable to hit the target rather than to miss it, but as this result does not depend entirely on the archer, expert though he is, we may say quite precisely that the only end that unquestionably lies within his power is to do everything he can to hit the target that it does not unquestionably lie within his power to hit. The archer who thinks only of being successful risks being unhappy; the one who thinks only of trying his best and aiming with the greatest precision holds his happiness in his own hands.

Our archer is a hypocrite: he seems to want something other than what he really wants. The Stoic is also a hypocrite, at least in the sense of the Greek word *hypokrites*, which means "theatrical actor." Stoics could not reject this image, which they themselves often use. Ariston (in no way heterodox in this respect) compares the wise man to a good actor who plays his role to perfection, whether he is playing Thersites or Agamemnon. The theoretical translation of this alliance between the actor's professional conscience and his refusal to identify completely with his character can be found in the interplay between two crucial and difficult notions of the Stoic ethic, *katorthōma*, a proper, rigorously correct action, and *kathekon*, an action that it is appropriate (to the nature of the agent) to accomplish, and that can therefore be reasonably justified if this nature is that of a rational being—the word has been translated fairly well in Latin by *officium*, less well in French and English, often, by *devoir*, duty. It is not a question of two materially different classes of action. The relation between the two notions is more like the one just noted between the "grasping" of the true, which belongs to the wise and the non-wise man alike, and its integration into a "knowledge" of the truth, which belongs only to the wise man. An action of a given type, such as honoring one's parents, is in itself neither good nor bad. In conformity with the animal and social nature of man, as it is, such an action is a *kathekon*, and only a *kathekon*, when it is the nonwise man who carries it out. But an action of the same type becomes a *katorthōma* when it is the wise man who carries it out, because he does it in a different way, purely owing to his virtuous disposition, solely on the basis of his own wisdom. The wise man is like a moral genius in whom reason, fully in charge, finds at its own level the infallibility of animal

instinct. If this moral genius can be put to work in the "perfect" accomplishment of the ordinary functions of natural and social man, it is still not bound by a conventional list of these functions: for certain men and under certain circumstances, it is reasonable to act otherwise than is reasonable for other men, under ordinary circumstances, to act. This distinction creates a new bridge between the seductions of nonconformism and concessions to conformism. The extreme example is that of suicide, which the theory justifies in terms of expediency, and which was practiced in a spectacular way by several masters or disciples of the school.

With its supple force, and owing to its very ambiguities, the contours of Stoicism allowed it not only to spread throughout broad layers of the Hellenistic and Roman world but also to survive over the centuries. It has been reproached for painting resignation in the colors of fervor, for sublimating human powerlessness by transforming it magically into a purely inner liberty. An image attributed to Zeno and Chrysippus seems to justify this interpretation: the figure of a dog attached to a cart, the animal's only choice being to trot along behind the cart willingly or to be dragged along by force. As Seneca puts it more nobly, "the willing soul Fate leads, but the unwilling drags along" (Seneca, *Ad Lucilium Epistulae Morales* CVII.11). Stoicism thus gained its reputation as a philosophy for hard times: in private distress and public calamities, it offers the impregnable help of the "interior citadel" of which Marcus Aurelius spoke. The description of the dog and cart is not quite right: the dog follows the cart of his fate, but it can also be his fate to have his own little cart to draw. Stoicism is not a school of inaction; rather, it teaches man to live and to act with adverbs, so to speak: in a certain manner, serious and detached at the same time, with the conviction that his intentions are pure, and with a relative indifference to results that may eventually belie his intentions. We have the right to dream of a humanity that would no longer have any need of the smallest scrap of Stoicism. But we are not likely to see our dream come true tomorrow.

JACQUES BRUNSCHWIG
Translated by Rita Guerlac and Anne Slack

Bibliography

Texts and Translations

Arnim, Hans von, ed. *Stoicorum veterum fragmenta*. 4 vols. Stuttgart: Teubner, 1903–1924.

Bréhier, Emile, and Pierre-Maxime Schuhl, eds. *Les Stoïciens*. Paris: Gallimard (Pléiade), 1962.

Cicero, Marcus Tullius. *De finibus.* Trans. H. Rackham. Loeb Classical Library.

———. *De natura deorum; Academica.* Trans. H. Rackham. Loeb Classical Library.

———. *De officiis.* Trans. Walter Miller. Loeb Classical Library.

———. *Tusculan Disputations.* Trans. J. E. King. Loeb Classical Library.

Diogenes Laertius. *Lives of Eminent Philosophers.* Trans. R. D. Hicks. 2 vols. Loeb Classical Library.

Epictetus. *The Discourses and Manual, Together with Fragments of His Writings.* Ed. and trans. P. E. Matheson. 2 vols. Oxford: Clarendon Press, 1916.

———. *The Discourses As Reported by Arrian; The Manual, and Fragments.* Trans. W. A. Oldfather. Loeb Classical Library.

Inwood, Brad, and L. P. Gerson, eds. *Hellenistic Philosophy: Introductory Readings,* 2nd ed. Indianapolis: Hackett Publishing Company, 1957.

Long, Anthony A., and David N. Sedley, eds. *The Hellenistic Philosophers.* 2 vols. Cambridge: Cambridge University Press, 1987.

Marcus Aurelius. *The Communings with Himself of Marcus Aurelius Antoninus, Emperor of Rome.* Trans. C. R. Haines. Loeb Classical Library.

Seneca. *Epistulae morales.* Trans. R. M. Gummere. Loeb Classical Library.

———. *Moral Essays.* Trans. J. W. Basore. Loeb Classical Library.

Sextus Empiricus. Trans. R. B. Bury. Loeb Classical Library.

Studies

Annas, Julia. "Stoic Epistemology." In *Epistemology.* Ed. Stephen Everson. Companions to Ancient Thought, 1. Cambridge: Cambridge University Press, 1990. Pp. 184–203.

Barnes, Jonathan, et al., eds. *Science and Speculation.* Cambridge: Cambridge University Press, 1982.

Bréhier, Emile. *Chrysippe et l'ancien Stoïcisme.* Paris: Presses Universitaires de France, 1910.

Brunschwig, Jacques, ed. *Les Stoïciens et leur logique.* Paris: Vrin, 1978.

Frede, Michael. *Die stoische Logik.* Göttingen: Vandenhoeck & Ruprecht, 1974.

Goldschmidt, Victor. *Le système stoïcien et l'idée de temps.* Paris: Vrin, 1953.

Hadot, Pierre. *La citadelle intérieure: Introduction aux pensées de Marc Aurèle.* Paris: Fayard, 1992.

Inwood, Brad. *Ethics and Human Action in Early Stoicism.* Oxford: Clarendon Press, 1985.

Long, Anthony A. *Hellenistic Philosophy: Stoics, Epicureans, Sceptics.* Berkeley: University of California Press, 1971.

Long, Anthony A., ed. *Problems in Stoicism.* London: Athlone, 1971.

Mates, Benson. *Stoic Logic.* Berkeley: University of California Press, 1953.

Rist, John, ed. *The Stoics.* Berkeley: University of California Press, 1978.

Schofield, Malcolm, Myles Burnyeat, and Jonathan Barnes, eds. *Doubt and Dogmatism.* Oxford: Clarendon Press, 1980.

Schofield, Malcolm, and Gisela Striker, eds. *The Norms of Nature.* Cambridge: Cambridge University Press, 1986.

Sharples, R. W. *Stoics, Epicureans and Sceptics: An Introduction to Hellenistic Philosophy.* London: Routledge, 1996.

Spanneut, Michel. *Permanence du Stoïcisme.* Gembloux: Duculot, 1973.

Striker, Gisela. "Kritèrion tès aletheias." In *Nachrichten der Akademie der Wissenschaften in Göttingen*. Philologische-historische Klasse 1. Göttingen: Vandenhoeck & Ruprecht, 1974. Pp. 51–110.

Related Articles

The Philosopher; The Sage and Politics; Cosmology; Theology and Divination; Hellenism and Christianity; Ethics; Schools and Sites of Learning; Logic; Language; Skepticism

CHRONOLOGY

CONTRIBUTORS

ILLUSTRATION SOURCES

INDEX

CHRONOLOGY

History	Culture	Science
1270(?)B.C.E.: Trojan War		
~1200: First Greek colonization (Asia Minor)		
	Composition of Homeric poems (~850–750 B.C.E.)	
753: Founding of Rome		
750: Second Greek colonization (Western and Eastern)	Hesiod (~700?)	
593: Solon's reforms in Athens	"Milesians": Thales, Anaximander and Anaximenes (~600–550). Anaximander writes the first Greek treatise in prose ~546	~585 B.C.E.: Eclipse predicted by Thales
540: Founding of Elea	Pythagoras teaches (~532?)	
509: Founding of Roman Republic	Heraclitus (~545–480)	510–490: Voyages of Hecataeus of Miletus
508–507: Cleisthenes' reforms in Athens		
490: Battle of Marathon, defeat of the Persians		
481: Alliance between Athens and Sparta (second Persian War)		
480: Battle of Salamis, Greek naval victory	Parmenides of Elea teaches (~478)	
	Aeschylus, *The Persians* (472); *Oresteia* (458)	
	~454: Anaxagoras (500–428) tried for impiety in Athens	
	Empedocles (~492–432)	
	Protagoras (~492–421)	
	Zeno of Elea (~490–454)	
443: Pericles General of Athens. Alcibiades (450–404), Athenian political leader, student of Socrates	~450: Herodotus (~484–425), *Histories*. Sophocles, *Antigone* (443)	~440: Leucippus, first expression of the theory of atomism

History	Culture	Science
	~435: Socrates (469–399) teaches in Athens	Hippocrates of Chios (~470–400), *Elements of Geometry*
Peloponnesian War (431–404)	Democritus (~460–?) Thucydides (~455–400) 427: Gorgias (~480–376) teaches rhetoric in Athens ~423: In *The Clouds*, Aristophanes ridicules the teaching of Socrates Antisthenes (~445–360	
404: Rule of the Thirty Tyrants in Athens	~405: Euclid of Megara founds the Megarian school	Hippocrates (~460–380)
403: Restoration of democracy	399: Trial of Socrates; death penalty. Aristippus founds a school at Cyrene ~390: Isocrates opens a school at Athens and teaches "philosophy" to a large audience Xenophon (~428–354) 387: Plato (429–347) founds the Academy	Mathematical works of the Academy (Theaetetus, Eudoxus, Archytas, Leodamas) 388–315: Work of Heraclides Ponticus (rotation of the earth)
384–322: Demosthenes	Diogenes of Sinope (400–325)	381: Observations of Eudoxus of Cnidus (400–347) in Egypt; epicycloidal movement of the planets (370)
343: Aristotle tutors Alexander the Great	347: Death of Plato; Speusippus succeeds him as head of the Academy	
340: War between Philip of Macedon and Athens 338: Defeat of Athens at Chaeronea		

HISTORY	CULTURE	SCIENCE
336: Accession of Alexander the Great, King of Macedonia	335: Aristotle (385–322) founds the Lyceum in Athens. Pyrrhon (~365–275) accompanies Alexander to Asia	Aristoxenes' theory of harmonics
332: Founding of Alexandria		
323: Death of Alexander at Babylon; formation of separate Hellenistic monarchies	322: Death of Aristotle; Theophrastes succeeds him	
	306: Epicurus (~342–271) founds the Epicurean School	
	~301: Zeno of Citium founds the Stoic School	~300: Euclid's *Elements*
	~295: Ptolemy I founds the Library at Alexandria	
	283–239: Antigonus Gonatas, King of Macedonia, protects philosophers, especially the Stoics	~281: Aristarchus of Samos and heliocentrism
		~270: Herophilus (physician) practices in Alexandria
	268–264: Arcesilaus succeeds Crates as head of the Academy and gives the school a skeptical orientation	~260: Erasistratus practices medicine
	262: Cleanthes succeeds Zeno as head of the Stoic school	
	The Septuagint	250: Teaching of Diophantus (mathematician)
		~245: Eratosthenes (~275–194) librarian in Alexandria

HISTORY	CULTURE	SCIENCE
	~232: Chrysippus (~280–207) succeeds Cleanthes as head of the Stoic school	
218: Second Punic War 217: First War of Macedonia		Archimedes (~287–212) killed by a Roman soldier during the siege of Syracuse ~200: Work of Apollonius (theory of conics)
169: War between the Seleucids and the Jews of Palestine	Polybius (208–118) 167–166: Carneades, Scholarch of the Academy	161–126: Teaching of Hipparchus (origins of trigonometry, excentric and epicyclic systems theory)
	155: Carneades becomes Ambassador to Rome; accompanied by Diogenes of Babylon (Stoic) and Critolaos (Peripatetic)	
148: Macedonia becomes a Roman Province 146: Greece becomes a Roman Province. Destruction of Carthage by Rome		~150: Hipparchus's geographical map
	110–109: Philon of Larissa becomes Scholarch of the Academy; in 88, flees Athens and seeks refuge in Rome	
~88–86: War of Mithridates		
	~79: Antiochus of Ascalon, Scholarch of the Academy, opens his own school at Athens and moves away from the "skeptical" orientation that lasted from Arcesilas to Philon of Larissa	Posidonius (~135–51) works in geography and astronomy

HISTORY	CULTURE	SCIENCE
	Lucretius, *De Natura Rerum* (~54–53) Cicero, *De Republica* (54–52) Philodemus of Gadara founds a center of Epicurian studies in Naples 48: First fire in the Library of Alexandria ~40: Andronicos of Rhodes publishes the works of Aristotle	
30: Battle of Actium; Egypt becomes a Roman Province. End of the Hellenistic period 27 C.E.: End of the Republic; beginning of the Roman Empire	30(?): Epicurian inscription of Diogenes of Oenoanda (dated by some scholars to ~125 C.E.) 29(?)C.E.: Death of Jesus of Nazareth	10–25 C.E.: Strabo, *Geography*
54–68: Nero's reign; burning of Rome (64); persecution of Christians	37–41: Embassy of Philon of Alexandria to Caligula 48–65: The Stoic Seneca becomes tutor, then advisor to Nero, before being forced to commit suicide; *Letters to Lucilius*, 63–64	
70: Titus takes Jerusalem	60: Teaching of Ammonius, a Platonist in Athens 64(?): Death of Saint Paul 93–94: Expulsion of the philosophers from Rome by Domitian. Epictetus (55–135) founds a school at Nicopolis, on the Greek coast of the Adriatic ~110: Plutarch (~46–~120) advisor to Trajan, then Hadrian, for Greek affairs	~60: Heron of Alexandria, *Mechanica* ~100: Nicomachus of Gerasa (theory of numbers) and Menelaus (on spheres)

HISTORY	CULTURE	SCIENCE
	~120: Christian apologists begin to present Christianity as philosophy	~125: Theon of Smyrna (numbers theory)
135: Jewish Diaspora	~133: Earliest evidence of gnosticism (Basilides)	
	~150: *Didaskalikos* (summary of Platonism) of Alcinous	Teaching of Ptolemy at Alexandria: *Almagest* (150); *Geography* (155)
161–180: Reign of Marcus Aurelius in Rome	176: Marcus Aurelius founds chairs in the four principal schools of philosophy at Athens: Platonic, Aristotelian, Stoic, Epicurian	
	~177: Celsus, Platonist and anti-Christian polemicist	Galen (129–200)
	~180: *Stromates* by Clement of Alexandria	
	~190: *Outlines of Pyrrhonism* by Sextus Empiricus, source of information on the arguments of early Skeptics (Agrippa and Aenesidemus)	
	~198: Teaching of Alexander of Aphrodisias (Peripatetic) in Athens	
	200: *Lives and Doctrines of the Philosophers* by Diogenes Laertius	
	244: Plotinus (205–269) opens a school in Rome	Diophantus: *Arithmetica*
	~260: Founding of the School of Antioch	
	263: Porphyry becomes a student of Plotinus; publishes the *Enneads* ~301	
312: Conversion of Emperor Constantine		

History	Culture	Science
313: Edict of Milan allows Christianity in Roman Empire	~313: Iamblichus (250–325) founds a Neoplatonist school at Apamea	
314: First partition of Roman Empire		~320: Pappus of Alexandria writes a commentary on Ptolemy and Euclid
	Writings of Basil of Caesarea, Gregory of Nazianzus, Gregory of Nyssa	Theon of Alexandria succeeds Pappus as professor of mathematics
361–363: Reign of Julian the Apostate, Neoplatonist philosopher; reaction against the Christians		
380: Christianity becomes official religion of Roman Empire	386: Conversion of Augustine; writes *Confessions*, 400; *The City of God*, 413–426	
410: Sack of Rome by Alaric		415: Death of Hypatia, daughter of Theon, scholar and a key figure in Neoplatonist philosophy
	~438: Proclus succeeds Syrianus as head of the Neoplatonist school	
476: Fall of the Western Empire		
	520: Damascius succeeds Zenodotus as head of the Neoplatonist school	
	529: Justinian closes the school of Athens. Seven Neoplatonist philosophers flee to Persia (including Simplicius and Damascius)	

CONTRIBUTORS

Julia Annas, University of Arizona

Serge Bardet, Université de Versailles–Saint-Quentin

Annie Bélis, Centre National de Recherche Scientifique, Paris

Enrico Berti, Università di Padova

Henry Blumenthal, University of Liverpool

Richard Bodéüs, Université de Montréal

Luc Brisson, Centre National de Recherche Scientifique, Paris

Jacques Brunschwig, Université Paris I

Monique Canto-Sperber, Centre National de Recherche Scientifique, Paris

Paul Cartledge, Clare College, Cambridge

Barbara Cassin, Centre National de Recherche Scientifique, Paris

Maurice Caveing, Centre National de Recherche Scientifique, Paris

François De Gandt, Centre National de Recherche Scientifique, Paris

Armelle Debru, Université Paris V

Fernanda Decleva Caizzi, Università di Milano

John Dillon, Trinity College, Dublin

Françoise Frazier, Université Montpellier III

Michael Frede, Keble College, Oxford

David Furley, Princeton University

Marie-Odile Goulet-Cazé, Centre National de Recherche Scientifique, Paris

François Hartog, Ecole des Hautes Etudes en Sciences Sociales, Paris

Carl Huffman, De Pauw University

Edward Hussey, All Souls College, Oxford

Christian Jacob, Ecole des Hautes Etudes en Sciences Sociales, Paris

Jacques Joanna, Université Paris IV

José Kany-Turpin, Université de Reims

Wilbur Knorr, Stanford University

André Laks, Université Lille III

Alain Le Boulluec, Ecole Pratique des Hautes Etudes, Paris

Carlos Lévy, Université Paris XII

Geoffrey E. R. Lloyd, Darwin College, Cambridge

Anthony A. Long, University of California, Berkeley

Mario Mignucci, Kings College, London; Università di Padova, *emeritus*

Donald Morrison, Rice University

Claude Mossé, Université Paris VIII

Oswyn Murray, Balliol College, Oxford

Carlo Natali, Università di Venezia

John David North, University of Groningen

Denis O'Brien, Centre National de Recherche Scientifique, Paris

Martin Ostwald, Swarthmore College

Pierre Pellegrin, Centre National de Recherche Scientifique, Paris
Gilbert Romeyer Dherbey, Université Paris IV
Malcolm Schofield, St. John's College, Cambridge
R. W. Sharples, University College London
Pierre Somville, Université de Liège
G. J. Toomer, Harvard University
Robert Wardy, St. Catharine's College, Cambridge

ILLUSTRATION SOURCES

FIRST SECTION

Helios on his chariot. Munich, Antikensammlung. Photo Erich Lessing/Magnum.

Gigantomachy scene. Paris, Louvre. Photo Réunion des Musées Nationaux.

The four cosmic elements. Fresco from the crypt of the cathedral in Anagni (Latium), 1250. Photo Dagli Orti.

Gnomon. Egypt, 1st century C.E. Munich, Deutsches Museum. Photo Deutsches Museum.

Map by Eratosthenes. *Eratosthenus Systema Geographicum*, 1790. Paris, Bibliothèque Nationale. Photo Bibliothèque Nationale.

Eudoxius, *On Spheres*. Egyptian papyrus, 2nd century C.E. Paris, Louvre. Photo Réunion des Musées Nationaux.

Claudius Ptolemy in the Alexandrian Library. *Claudius Ptolemeus Geographicorum Libri.* 15th century. Venice, Biblioteca Marciana. Photo Dagli Orti.

Claudius Ptolemy, map. 15th century. Venice, Biblioteca Marciana. Photo Dagli Orti.

Nicole Oresme at his desk, with an armillary sphere. *Le livre du ciel et du monde*, commentary on Aristotle's *De caelo* by Nicole Oresme. Manscript F2565, fol. 1, 15th century. Paris: Bibliothèque Nationale. Photo Bibliothèque Nationale.

Claudius Ptolemy, *Almagest.* Hebrew manuscript, fol. 99v–100, 15th century. Paris, Bibliothèque Nationale. Photo Bibliothèque Nationale.

Bust of Pythagoras. Rome, Museo Capitolino. Photo Araldo de Luca/Ikona.

Euclid, *Elements.* Greek manuscript 2344, fol. 39v, 12th century. Paris, Bibliothèque Nationale. Photo Bibliothèque Nationale.

Archimedes, *On the Sphere and the Cylinder,* Book II. Copied in 1544 by Christophe Auer. Greek manuscript 2361, fol. 99. Paris, Bibliothèque Nationale. Photo Bibliothèque Nationale.

Pythagoras and music. Cassiodorus, *Institutions.* Latin manuscript 8500, fol. 39v, ca. 1340. Paris, Bibliothèque Nationale. Photo Bibliothèque Nationale.

Aristides Quintilianus, treatise. Marc Meibom, ed. 1652. Photo Flammarion.

Theon of Smyrna, treatise. Greek manuscript 1817, fol. 116v, 16th century. Paris, Bibliothèque Nationale. Photo Bibliothèque Nationale.

Apollo and his *kithara.* Detail from a vase attributed to the "Berlin Painter ," ca. 480 B.C.E. Basel, Antikenmuseum. Photo Claire Niggli/Antikenmuseum.

SECOND SECTION

The Tower of the Winds, Athens. Photo Zefa.

Illustration from Vitruvius, *De Architectura* X.3.2, 1572 ed. Photo Jean-Loup Charmet.

Catapult. Athenaeus, *De Machinis.* Greek manuscript 2442, fol. 62. Constantinople, 11th century. Paris, Bibliothèque Nationale. Photo Bibliothèque Nationale.

Hero of Alexandria, *Baroulkos.* Greek manuscript 2430, fol. 117v, 16th century. Paris, Bibliothèque Nationale. Photo Bibliothèque Nationale.

Machine for attacking a tower. Philon of Byzantium, treatise. Greek manuscript 2442, fol. 94. Constantinople, 11th century. Paris, Bibliothèque Nationale. Photo Bibliothèque Nationale.

Examining a patient. Relief, 1st century B.C.E. Rome, Museo della Civiltà Romana. Photo Dagli Orti.

Surgical instruments and cupping instruments. Relief from the Asclepieion, Athens. Rome, Museo della Civiltà Romana. Photo Dagli Orti.

Manfredo de Monte Imperiali, *Book of Herbs and Plants*. Latin manuscript 6823, fol. 1v. Italy, first half of the 14th century. Paris, Bibliothèque Nationale. Photo Bibliothèque Nationale.

Apollonius of Citium, commentary on Hippocrates, *Peri arthrōn*. Manuscript 74,7 fol. 1v, late 10th century. Florence, Biblioteca Medicea Laurenziana. Photo Alberto Scardigli.

The four temperaments. *Guild Book of the Barber-Surgeons of York*, ca. 1500. Photo British Library/E.T. Archive.

Dioscorides, *De Materia Medica*. Greek manuscript 2179, fol. 5. Italy, 9th century. Paris, Bibliothèque Nationale. Photo Bibliothèque Nationale.

Asclepius curing a patient. Athens, Archaeological Museum of Piraeus. Photo Nimatallah/Artephot.

Divination scene. Boulogne-sur-Mer, Château-Musée. Photo Erich Lessing/Magnum.

The Pythia at Delphi. Bowl by the Kodros painter, ca. 440 B.C.E. Berlin, Staatliche Museen. Photo Bildarchiv Preussischer Kulturbesitz.

Odysseus consulting Tiresias in Hades' dwelling. Southern Italy, vase, 5th century B.C.E. Paris, Bibliothèque Nationale. Photo Erich Lessing/Magnum.

Gold strip from a Greek tomb. Vibo Valentia, Museo Vito Capialbi de Vibo Valentia. Photo Dagli Orti.

THIRD SECTION

Athens: View of the Acropolis, the Odeon, and the Theater of Dionysus. Photo Alberto Rossi/Ikona.

View of the Agora. Photo Vloo.

The Pnyx. Photo Percheron/Artephot.

Theater of Dionysus, Athens. Photo Zefa.

Construction of the wall of the Acropolis. Skyphos attributed to the "Penelope painter," ca. 440 B.C.E. Paris, Louvre. Photo Réunion des Musées Nationaux.

Bust of Solon. Naples, Museo Archeologico, Farnese Collection. Photo Pedicini/Ikona.

Law code of the city of Gortyn. Photo Salou/Artephot.

Decree of Callias, 418 B.C.E. Paris, Louvre. Photo Réunion des Musées Nationaux.

Democracy crowning Demos. Athens, Agora Museum. Photo American School of Classical Studies, Athens.

Klerōterion. Athens, Agora Museum. Photo Dagli Orti.

Ostrakon (ostraka). Athens, Agora Museum. Photo Nimatallah/Artephot.

Tokens for drawing lots. Athens, Agora Museum. Photo American School of Classical Studies, Athens.

Ballots for voting by judges. Athens, Agora Museum. Photo American School of
   Classical Studies, Athens.
Bust of Pericles. Berlin, Pergamum Museum. Photo Erich Lessing/Magnum.
Bust of Herodotus. Photo Nimatallah/Artephot.
Volute-krater by the "Darius painter," 340–320 B.C.E. Photo Araldo de Luca/
   Artephot.
Gravestone of two young hoplites. Athens, Museum of Piraeus. Photo Nimatallah/
   Artephot.
Bust of Thucydides. Paris, Louvre. Photo Erich Lessing/Magnum.
Head of Alexander. Rome, Museo Nazionale Romano. Photo Dagli Orti.

FOURTH SECTION

Statue of Chrysippus. Paris, Louvre. Photo Erich Lessing/Magnum.
Mosaic of a group of philosophers. Pompeii, Villa of Siminius Stephanus. Naples,
   Museo Archeologico. Photo Dagli Orti.
Bust of Socrates with a passage from Plato's *Crito*. Naples, Museo Archeologico,
   Farnese Collection. Photo Pedicini/Artephot.
Bust, thought to be of Plato. Naples, Villa dei Papiri. Photo Pedicini/Ikona.
Plato and Aristotle. Detail from Raphael, *The School of Athens*. Vatican, Stanza della
   Segnatura. Photo Erich Lessing/Magnum.
Bust of Aristotle, attributed to Lysippus. Vienna, Kunsthistorisches Museum. Photo
   Meyer/Artephot.
Relief of Diogenes and Alexander the Great. Rome, Villa Albani. Photo Alinari/
   Ikona.
Crates and his wife Hipparchia. Fresco in the Villa Farnesina. Rome, Museo delle
   Terme. Photo Ikona.
Diogenes. Engraving after F. Mazzola, 1540. Paris, Bibliothèque Nationale. Photo
   Bibliothèque Nationale.
Bust of Epicurus. Naples, Museo Archeologico. Photo Pedicini/Ikona.
Antisthenes. Naples, Museo Archeologico. Photo Pedicini/Artephot.
Cup from the Boscoreale hoard. Paris, Louvre. Photo Réunion des Musées
   Nationaux.
Helios. Mosaic from the Synagogue of Hammath near Tiberiades. Photo Zev
   Radovan.
Christ represented as Sun God. Mosaic from the necropolis located under the Basil-
   ica of St. Peter in Rome. Photo Babey/Artephot.
David playing the *lyra*, portrayed as Orpheus. Synagogue of Gaza. Jerusalem, Mu-
   seum of Israel. Photo Zev Radovan.
Orpheus represented with a halo and playing the *lyra*. Gregory of Nazianzus, *Ora-
   tions*. Greek manuscript Coislin 239, fol. 122v. Constantinople, 12th century.
   Paris, Bibliothèque Nationale. Photo Bibliothèque Nationale.
Sarcophagus of Prometheus. Rome, Museo Capitolino. Photo Araldo de Luca/Ikona.
Biagio d'Antonio, *Allegory of the Liberal Arts*, 15th century. Chantilly, Musée
   Condé. Photo Giraudon.

INDEX